MACMILLAN

INFORMATION NOW ENCYCLOPEDIA

World Religions

M A C M I L L A N

INFORMATION NOW ENCYCLOPEDIA

World Religions

SELECTIONS FROM THE SIXTEEN-VOLUME

Macmillan *Encyclopedia of Religion*

MACMILLAN REFERENCE USA
Simon & Schuster Macmillan
New York

Prentice Hall International
London Mexico City New Delhi Singapore Sydney Toronto

Designed by Kevin Hanek. Composition by G&H Soho, Inc.

Macmillan Reference USA
Simon & Schuster Macmillan
1633 Broadway
New York, NY 10019

Manufactured in the United States of America.

printing number
1 2 3 4 5 6 7 8 9 10

ISBN: 0-02-864921-4
LC #: 97-25525

Library of Congress Cataloging-in-Publication Data

The Library of Congress has cataloged another edition of this work as follows:

World Religions.
p. cm. — (Macmillan compendium)
Includes index.
1. Religions—Handbooks, manuals, etc. 2. Religions—Dictionaries. I. Series.
BL82.W67 1997
291—dc21 97-25525
CIP

This paper meets the requirements of ANSI/NISO Z39.48–1992 (Permanence of Paper).

Table of Contents

Cover Image: This interior view of the Blue Mosque in Istanbul, Turkey illustrates the diverse religious traditions described in this volume. Adam Woolfitt/Corbis

Preface

ORIGINS

Today the study of religion, perhaps for the first time, recognizes not only the unity of human races but also the spiritual values and cultural significance of their religious creations. As we approach the millennium, interest in world religions has deepened considerably and so has our need for reliable reference sources.

Those seeking information about world religions have learned to rely on the distinguished sixteen-volume *Encyclopedia of Religion* published by Macmillan Publishing Company. Since its publication in 1987, scholars, students, and general readers have expressed an interest in a condensed version of this classic work. The *Information Now Encyclopedia of World Religions* is designed to meet that need.

CRITERIA FOR SELECTION AND ORGANIZATION

Broad in scope, *The Information Now Encyclopedia of the World Religions* is organized in an A-to-Z format. Fascinating articles reveal significant religious ideas and practices of religions throughout the word. Covered in this extraordinary volume are traditions great and small, including the religious systems of the East as well as those of the West. A network of historical and descriptive articles, synthetic discussion and interpretive essays that make available contemporary insight into the long and multifaced history of religion. In preparing this one-volume version of the *Encyclopedia of Religion,* it was agreed that article subsections would be excerpted in their entirety in order to retain historical accuracy. Relying on advice from a team of scholars, articles were chosen to represent the ideas, beliefs, rituals, myths, symbols, and persons that have played a role in the universal history of religions from Paleolithic times to the present day. Entries have been titled and organized in a manner we hope readers will be most likely to consult first. A comprehensive index appears at the end of the volume to provide additional aid for the reader.

FEATURES

To add visual appeal and enhance the usefulness of the volume, the page format was designed to include the following helpful features.

- **Cross-Reference Quotations:** These quotations, extracted from related articles in the volume, will lead to further exploration of the subject. Page numbers are provided for easy reference.
- **Notable Quotations:** Found throughout the text in the margin, these thought-provoking quotations will complement the topic under discussion.
- **Definitions and Glossary:** Brief definitions of important terms in the main text can also be found the margin and in the glossary at the end of the book
- **Sidebars:** Appearing in a gray box, these provocative asides relate to the text and amplify topics.
- **Index:** A thorough index provides thousands of additional points of entry into the work.
- **Appendix:** We have included in the appendix a list of festivals and religious holidays for traditions throughout the world.

ACKNOWLEDGMENTS

The *Information Now Encyclopedia of the World Religions* contains over one hundred illustrations. Acknowledgments of sources for illustrations can be found in captions.

We are grateful to our colleagues who publish the *Merriam Webster's Collegiate® Dictionary.* Definitions used in the margins and most of the glossary terms come from the distinguished *Webster's Collegiate® Dictionary,* Tenth Edition, 1996.

The articles herein were written for the *Encyclopedia of Religion* (the original source for this volume) by leading authorities at work in the field. Mircea Eliade served as Editor in Chief of the original set and Lawrence E. Sullivan was Associate Editor. Professor Eliade was Sewell L. Avery Distingushed Service Professor of History of Religions at the Divinity School of the University of Chicago where he spent thirty distinguished years until his death in 1986. He collaborated often with philospher Paul Ricoeur and theologian Paul Tillich. His numberous writings include systematic works; historical studies; monographs on yoga, shamanism, folk religion and alchemy; textbooks; autobiographies; dramas; stories of the occult; and novels. Professor Sullivan is Professor of the History of Religions and Director of the Center for the Study of World Religions at Harvard University. The scholars selected for the Editorial Board for the Encyclopedia of Religion were Charles J. Adams, Joseph M Kitagawa, Martin E. Marty, Richard P. McBrien, Jacob Needleman, Annemarie Schimmel, Robert M. Seltzer, and Victor Turner.

This book would not have been possible without the hard work and creativity of our staff. We offer our deepest thanks to all who helped create this marvelous work.

Macmillan Reference USA

Abbreviations and Symbols

abbr. abbreviated; abbreviation
abr. abridged; abridgment
AD *anno Domini,* in the year of the (our) Lord
Afrik. Afrikaans
ah *anno Hegirae,* in the year of the Hijrah
Akk. Akkadian
Ala. Alabama
Alb. Albanian
Am. Amos
AM *ante meridiem,* before noon
amend. amended; amendment
annot. annotated; annotation
Ap. *Apocalypse*
Apn. *Apocryphon*
app. appendix
Arab. Arabic
'Arakh. *'Arakhin*
Aram. Aramaic
Ariz. Arizona
Ark. Arkansas
Arm. Armenian
art. article (pl., arts.)
AS Anglo-Saxon
Asm. Mos. *Assumption of Moses*
Assyr. Assyrian
A.S.S.R. Autonomous Soviet Socialist Republic
Av. Avestan
'A.Z. *'Avodah zarah*
b. born
Bab. Babylonian
Ban. Bantu
1 Bar. *1 Baruch*
2 Bar. *2 Baruch*
3 Bar. *3 Baruch*
4 Bar. *4 Baruch*
B.B. Bava' batra'
BBC British Broadcasting Corporation
BC before Christ
BCE before the common era
B.D. Bachelor of Divinity
Beits. *Beitsah*
Bekh. *Bekhorot*
Beng. Bengali
Ber. *Berakhot*
Berb. Berber
Bik. *Bikkurim*
bk. book (pl., bks.)
B.M. *Bava' metsi'a'*
BP before the present
B.Q. *Bava' qamma'*
Brah. Brahmana
Bret. Breton
B.T. Babylonian Talmud
Bulg. Bulgarian
Burm. Burmese
c. *circa,* about, approximately
Calif. California
Can. Canaanite
Catal. Catalan
CE of the common era
Celt. Celtic
cf. *confer*, compare
Chald. Chaldean
chap. chapter (pl., chaps.)
Chin. Chinese
C.H.M. Community of the Holy Myrrhbearers
1 Chr. *1 Chronicles*
2 Chr. *2 Chronicles*
Ch. Slav. Church Slavic
cm centimeters
col. column (pl., cols.)
Col. *Colossians*
Colo. Colorado
comp. compiler (pl., comps.)
Conn. Connecticut
cont. continued
Copt. Coptic
1 Cor. *1 Corinthians*
2 Cor. *2 Corinthians*
corr. corrected
C.S.P. Congregatio Sancti Pauli, Congregation of Saint Paul (Paulists)
d. died
D Deuteronomic (source of the Pentateuch)
Dan. Danish
D.B. Divinitatis Baccalaureus, Bachelor of Divinity
D.C. District of Columbia
D.D. Divinitatis Doctor, Doctor of Divinity
Del. Delaware
Dem. Dema'i
dim. diminutive
diss. dissertation
Dn. *Daniel*
D.Phil. Doctor of Philosophy
Dt. *Deuteronomy*
Du. Dutch
E Elohist (source of the Pentateuch)
Eccl. *Ecclesiastes*
ed. editor (pl., eds.); edition; edited by
'Eduy. *'Eduyyot*
e.g. *exempli gratia*, for example
Egyp. Egyptian
1 En. *1 Enoch*
2 En. *2 Enoch*
3 En. *3 Enoch*
Eng. English
enl. enlarged
Eph. *Ephesians*
'Eruv. *'Eruvin*
1 Esd. *1 Esdras*
2 Esd. *2 Esdras*
3 Esd. *3 Esdras*
4 Esd. *4 Esdras*
esp. especially
Est. Estonian
Est. *Esther*
et al. *et alii*, and others
etc. *et cetera*, and so forth
Eth. Ethiopic
EV English version
Ex. *Exodus*
exp. expanded
Ez. *Ezekiel*
Ezr. *Ezra*
2 Ezr. *2 Ezra*
4 Ezr. *4 Ezra*
f. feminine; and following (pl., ff.)
fasc. fascicle (pl., fascs.)
fig. figure (pl., figs.)
Finn. Finnish
fl. *floruit,* flourished
Fla. Florida
Fr. French
frag. fragment
ft. feet
Ga. Georgia
Gal. *Galatians*
Gaul. Gaulish
Ger. German
Git. *Gittin*
Gn. *Genesis*
Gr. Greek
Hag. *Hagigah*

Hal.	*Hallah*
Hau.	Hausa
Hb.	*Habakkuk*
Heb.	Hebrew
Heb.	*Hebrews*
Hg.	*Haggai*
Hitt.	Hittite
Hor.	*Horayot*
Hos.	*Hosea*
Hul.	*Hullin*
Hung.	Hungarian
ibid.	*ibidem,* in the same place (as the one immediately preceding)
Icel.	Icelandic
i.e.	*id est,* that is
IE	Indo-European
Ill.	Illinois
Ind.	Indiana
intro.	introduction
Ir. Gael.	Irish Gaelic
Iran.	Iranian
Is.	*Isaiah*
Ital.	Italian
J	Yahvist (source of the Pentateuch)
Jas.	James
Jav.	Javanese
Jb.	*Job*
Jdt.	*Judith*
Jer.	*Jeremiah*
Jgs.	*Judges*
Jl.	*Joel*
Jn.	*John*
1 Jn.	*1 John*
2 Jn.	*2 John*
3 Jn.	*3 John*
Jon.	*Jonah*
Jos.	*Joshua*
Jpn.	Japanese
JPS	Jewish Publication Society translation (1985) of the Hebrew Bible
J.T.	Jerusalem Talmud
Jub.	*Jubilees*
Kans.	Kansas
Kel.	*Kelim*
Ker.	*Keritot*
Ket.	*Ketubbot*
1 Kgs.	*1 Kings*
2 Kgs.	*2 Kings*
Khois.	*Khoisan*
Kil.	*Kil'ayim*
km	kilometers
Kor.	Korean
Ky.	Kentucky
l.	line (pl., ll.)
La.	Louisiana
Lam.	*Lamentations*
Lat.	Latin
Latv.	Latvian
L. en Th.	Licencié en Théologie, Licentiate in Theology
L. ès L.	Licencié ès Lettres, Licentiate in Literature
Let. Jer.	*Letter of Jeremiah*
lit.	literally
Lith.	Lithuanian
Lk.	*Luke*
LL	Late Latin
LL.D.	Legum Doctor, Doctor of Laws
Lv.	*Leviticus*
m	meters
m.	masculine
M.A.	Master of Arts
Ma'as.	*Ma'aserot*
Ma'as. Sh.	*Ma'aser sheni*
Mak.	*Makkot*
Makh.	*Makhshirin*
Mal.	*Malachi*
Mar.	*Marathi*
Mass.	Massachusetts
1 Mc.	*1 Maccabees*
2 Mc.	*2 Maccabees*
3 Mc.	*3 Maccabees*
4 Mc.	*4 Maccabees*
Md.	Maryland
M.D.	Medicinae Doctor, Doctor of Medicine
ME	Middle English
Meg.	*Megillah*
Me'il.	*Me'ilah*
Men.	*Menahot*
MHG	Middle High German
mi.	miles
Mi.	*Micah*
Mich.	Michigan
Mid.	*Middot*
Minn.	Minnesota
Miq.	*Miqva'ot*
MIran.	Middle Iranian
Miss.	Mississippi
Mk.	*Mark*
Mo.	Missouri
Mo'ed Q.	*Mo'ed qatan*
Mont.	Montana
MPers.	Middle Persian
MS.	manuscriptum, manuscript (pl., MSS)
Mt.	*Matthew*
MT Masoretic text	
n.	note
Na.	*Nahum*
Nah.	Nahuatl
Naz.	*Nazir*
N.B.	*nota bene*, take careful note
N.C.	North Carolina
n.d.	no date
N.Dak.	North Dakota
NEB New English Bible	
Nebr.	Nebraska
Ned.	*Nedarim*
Neg.	*Nega'im*
Neh.	*Nehemiah*
Nev.	Nevada
N.H.	New Hampshire
Nid.	*Niddah*
N.J.	New Jersey
Nm.	Numbers
N.Mex.	New Mexico
no.	number (pl., nos.)
Nor.	Norwegian
n.p.	no place
n.s.	new series
N.Y.	New York
Ob.	*Obadiah*
O.Cist.	Ordo Cisterciencium, Order of Cîteaux (Cistercians)
OCS	Old Church Slavonic
OE	Old English
O.F.M.	Ordo Fratrum Minorum, Order of Friars Minor (Franciscans)
OFr.	Old French
Ohal.	*Ohalot*
OHG	Old High German
OIr.	Old Irish
OIran.	Old Iranian
Okla.	Oklahoma
ON	Old Norse
O.P.	Ordo Praedicatorum, Order of Preachers (Dominicans)
OPers.	Old Persian
op. cit.	*opere citato*, in the work cited
OPrus.	Old Prussian
Oreg.	Oregon
'Orl.	*'Orlah*
O.S.B.	Ordo Sancti Benedicti, Order of Saint Benedict (Benedictines)
p.	page (pl., pp.)
P	Priestly (source of the Pentateuch)
Pa.	Pennsylvania
Pahl.	Pahlavi
Par.	*Parah*

para.	paragraph (pl., paras.)
Pers.	Persian
Pes.	*Pesahim*
Ph.D.	Philosophiae Doctor, Doctor of Philosophy
Phil.	*Philippians*
Phlm.	*Philemon*
Phoen.	Phoenician
pl.	plural; plate (pl., pls.)
PM	post meridiem, after noon
Pol.	Polish
pop.	population
Port.	Portuguese
Prv.	*Proverbs*
Ps.	*Psalms*
Ps.	*151 Psalm 151*
Ps. Sol.	Psalms of Solomon
pt.	part (pl., pts.)
1 Pt.	*1 Peter*
2 Pt.	*2 Peter*
Pth.	Parthian
Q	hypothetical source of the synoptic Gospels
Qid.	*Qiddushin*
Qin.	*Qinnim*
r.	reigned; ruled
Rab.	*Rabbah*
rev.	revised
R. ha-Sh.	Ro'sh ha-shanah
R.I.	Rhode Island
Rom.	Romanian
Rom.	*Romans*
R.S.C.J.	Societas Sacratissimi Cordis Jesu, Religious of the Sacred Heart
RSV	Revised Standard Version of the Bible
Ru.	*Ruth*
Rus.	Russian
Rv.	*Revelation*
Rv. Ezr.	Revelation of Ezra
San.	Sanhedrin
S.C.	South Carolina
Scot. Gael.	Scottish Gaelic
S. Dak.	South Dakota
sec.	section (pl., secs.)
Sem.	Semitic
ser.	series
sg.	singular
Sg.	*Song of Songs*
Sg. of 3	*Prayer of Azariah and the Song of the Three Young Men*
Shab.	*Shabbat*
Shav.	*Shavu'ot*
Sheq.	*Sheqalim*
Sib. Or.	Sibylline Oracles
Sind.	Sindhi
Sinh.	Sinhala
Sir.	*Ben Sira*
S.J.	Societas Jesu, Society of Jesus (Jesuits)
Skt.	Sanskrit
1 Sm.	*1 Samuel*
2 Sm.	*2 Samuel*
Sogd.	*Sogdian*
Sot	*Sotah*
sp.	species (pl., spp.)
Span.	Spanish
sq.	square
S.S.R.	Soviet Socialist Republic
st.	stanza (pl., ss.)
S.T.M.	Sacrae Theologiae Magister, Master of Sacred Theology
Suk.	*Sukkah*
Sum.	Sumerian
supp.	supplement; supplementary
Sus.	*Susanna*
s.v.	*sub verbo*, under the word (pl., s.v.v.)
Swed.	Swedish
Syr.	Syriac
Syr. Men.	Syriac Menander
Ta'an.	*Ta'anit*
Tam.	Tamil
Tam.	*Tamid*
Tb.	*Tobit*
T.D.	*Taisho shinshu daizokyo,* edited by Takakusu Junjiro et al. (Tokyo, 1922–1934)
Tem.	*Temurah*
Tenn.	Tennessee
Ter.	*Terumot*
Tev. Y.	*Tevul yom*
Tex.	Texas
Th.D.	Theologicae Doctor, Doctor of Theology
1 Thes.	*1 Thessalonians*
2 Thes.	*2 Thessalonians*
Thrac.	Thracian
Ti.	Titus
Tib.	Tibetan
1 Tm.	*1 Timothy*
2 Tm.	*2 Timothy*
T. of 12	*Testaments of the Twelve Patriarchs*
Toh.	*Tohorot*
Tong.	Tongan
trans.	translator, translators; translated by; translation
Turk.	Turkish
Ukr.	Ukrainian
Upan.	*Upanisad*
U.S.	United States
U.S.S.R.	Union of Soviet Socialist Republics
Uqts.	*Uqtsin*
v.	verse (pl., vv.)
Va.	Virginia
var.	variant; variation
Viet.	Vietnamese
viz.	*videlicet,* namely
vol.	volume (pl., vols.)
Vt.	Vermont
Wash.	Washington
Wel.	Welsh
Wis.	Wisconsin
Wis.	Wisdom of Solomon
W.Va.	West Virginia
Wyo.	Wyoming
Yad.	*Yadayim*
Yev.	*Yevamot*
Yi.	Yiddish
Yor.	Yoruba
Zav.	*Zavim*
Zec.	*Zechariah*
Zep.	*Zephaniah*
Zev.	*Zevahim*
*	hypothetical
?	uncertain; possibly; perhaps
°	degrees
+	plus
–	minus
=	equals; is equivalent to
x	by; multiplied by
→	yields

World Religions

AFRICAN RELIGIONS

AN OVERVIEW

Prior to the coming of Christianity and Islam to Africa, the peoples south of the Sahara developed their own religious systems, and these formed the basis of much of their social and cultural life. Today, the indigenous religions, modified by colonial and postcolonial experience, continue to exist alongside Christianity and Islam and to play an important role in daily existence.

African traditional religions are closely tied to ethnic groups. Hence it may be said that there are as many different "religions" as there are ethnic language groups, which number over seven hundred south of the Sahara. There are, however, many similarities among the religious ideas and practices of major cultural and linguistic areas (e.g., Guinea Coast, central Bantu, Nilotes), and certain fundamental features are common to almost all African religions. Although these features are not unique to Africa, taken together they constitute a distinctively African pattern of religious thought and action.

HISTORICAL BACKGROUND. Except for the most recent colonial and precolonial past, there is little evidence concerning the early history of African religions. Because of the conditions of climate and habitation, archaeological remains have been discovered at only a few places in eastern, western, and southern Africa, and the cultural contexts of these finds are largely unknown. It was once supposed that the various contemporary hunting-gathering, agricultural, and pastoral societies in Africa developed from a few basic cultural systems, or civilizations, each with its own set of linguistic, racial, religious, economic, and material cultural characteristics. Thus the early cultural and religious history of African societies was seen in terms of the interaction and intermixture of these hypothetical cultural systems, producing the more complex cultural and religious patterns of today. But it is now recognized that elements of language, race, religion, economics, and material culture are not so closely related as was assumed and that the early cultural systems were too speculatively defined. Hence historical reconstruction on these grounds has been abandoned.

Nevertheless, research from the past decade has been able to bring to light important evidence concerning the early phases of religion in certain areas. The rock paintings of southern Africa, which date mostly from the nineteenth century but also from 2000 and 6000 and 26,000 BP, appear to represent a continuous tradition of shamanism practiced by the San hunters and their ancestors. The paintings depict the ritual acts and visionary experiences by which the shamans governed the relationships between human beings, animals, and the spirits of the dead. These relationships lay at the core of San society, and the rock paintings may well record practices that date from the earliest times in southern Africa.

When agriculture began to spread south of the Sahara around 1500 BCE, an important religious development accompanied the gradual change from hunting-gathering to agricultural economies. This was the emergence of territorial cults, organized around local shrines and priests related to the land, crop production, and rain. These autochthonous cults provided political and religious leadership at the local level and also at the clan and tribal level. In central Africa the oral tradition and known history of some territorial cults date back five or six centuries and have been the key to historical reconstruction of religion in this area.

When ironworking penetrated sub-Saharan Africa in 400-500 CE, it gave rise to a number of myths, rites, and symbolic forms. Throughout West Africa ironmaking, hunting, and sometimes warfare formed a sacred complex of rites and symbols under the tutelage of a culture hero or deity.

In northern Nigeria over 150 terra-cotta figures have been found dating from at least 500 BCE to 200 CE, the earliest known terra-cotta sculpture in sub-Saharan Africa. This sculpture, known as Nok sculpture after the site at which it was first found, consists of both human and animal figures. Although it is likely that these pieces had religious significance, either as grave goods or as ritual objects (or both), their meaning at present is entirely unknown.

The famous bronze heads of Ife, Nigeria, date from the twelfth to fifteenth centuries and may be distantly related to Nok sculpture. The sixteen naturalistic heads were found in the ground near the royal palace at Ife. The heads have holes to which beards and crowns were attached. Each head may have represented one of the founders of the sixteen city-states that owed allegiance to Ife, and each may have carried one of the sixteen crowns. Among the Yoruba, the "head" *(ori)* is the

Ancestors are believed to be capable of intervening in human affairs, but only in the defined area of their authority, that is, among their descendants.

PAGE 30

A

AFRICAN RELIGIONS

An Overview

bearer of a person's destiny, and the "head" or destiny of a king was to wear the crown. The crown was the symbol of the sacred *ase*, or power of the king, which the crown or the head itself may have contained.

Wherever kingship arose in Africa during the thirteenth to fifteenth centuries, it became a dominant part of the religious system. The rulers, whether sacred or secular, generally attained total or partial control of the preexisting territorial cults above the local level. Most kings were regarded as gods or as the descendants of gods and were spiritually related to the fertility of the land and to the welfare of the people. Even in Buganda in central Uganda, where they did not have such mystical powers, the kings were regarded as sacred personages. It is now recognized that the institution of sacred kingship, which was once thought to be derived from ancient Egypt because of some general similarities with sub-Saharan kingships, was independently invented in various places in the African continent, not only in Egypt.

"One religion is as true as another."

ROBERT BURTON
ANATOMY OF MELANCOLY

From the seventeenth to early nineteenth centuries, there is evidence of two types of development: an increase in spirit possession and healing cults, generally known as cults of affliction, and an emphasis upon the concept of the supreme being. The emergence of popular healing cults seems to have been linked to a breakdown in local political institutions and to contact with outside forces and new diseases.

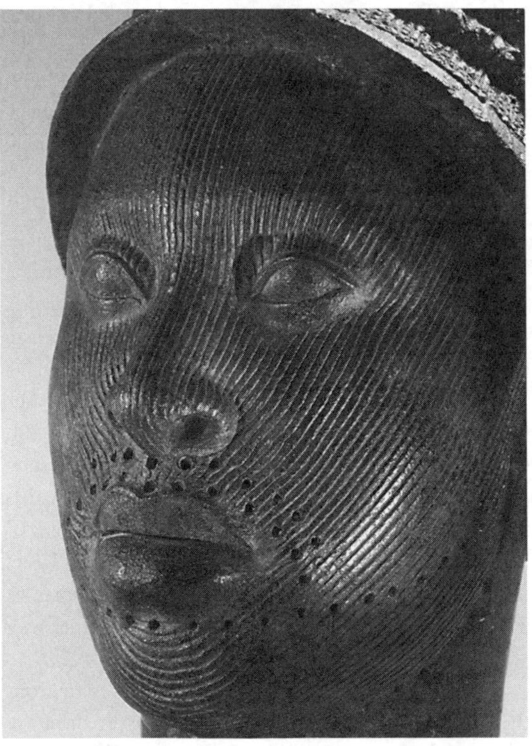

HEAD OF IFE

Among the Yoruba, the head is the bearer of destiny. This Nigerian head of Ife has holes for an attached crown; the destiny of a king was to wear the crown.

© WERNER FORMAN/CORBIS

GENERAL CHARACTERISTICS. Common to most African religions is the notion of the imperfect nature of the human condition. Almost every society has a creation myth that tells about the origins of human life and death. According to this myth, the first human beings were immortal; there was no suffering, sickness, or death. This situation came to an end because of an accident or act of disobedience. Whatever the cause, the myth explains why sickness, toil, suffering, and death are fundamental to human existence.

The counterpart to this idea is the notion that the problems of human life may be alleviated through ritual action. They do not promise personal salvation in the afterlife or the salvation of the world at some future time. Through ritual action misfortunes may be overcome, sicknesses removed, and death put off. The assumption is that human beings are largely responsible for their own misfortunes and that they also possess the ritual means to overcome them. The sources of suffering lie in people's misdeeds, or sins, which offend the gods and ancestors, and in the social tensions and conflicts that can cause illness. The remedy involves the consultation of a priest or priestess who discovers the sin or the social problem and prescribes the solution, for example, an offering to appease an offended deity or a ritual to settle social tensions.

At the theological level, African religions contain both monotheistic and polytheistic principles. The concept of a supreme God is widely known in tropical Africa and existed before the coming of Christianity and Islam. The idea of a supreme God expresses the element of ultimacy, fate, and destiny, which is part of most African religions. As the ultimate principle behind things, the supreme God usually has no cult, images, temples, or priesthood.

In contrast, the lesser gods and the ancestor spirits, which often serve as the supreme being's intermediaries, are constantly involved in daily affairs. People regularly attend their shrines to pray, receive advice, and make offerings, usually in the form of animal sacrifice. Thus African religions are both polytheistic and monotheistic, depending upon the context. In matters concerning the ultimate destiny and fate of individuals and groups, the supreme God may be directly involved. In matters concerning everyday affairs, the lesser gods and ancestors are more immediately involved.

From the point of view of African religion, a human being consists of social, moral, spiritual, and physical components joined together; the individual is viewed as a composite totality. That is why social conflicts can make people physically ill and why moral misdeeds can cause spiritual misfortunes. Rituals that are aimed at restoring social and spiritual relationships are therefore deemed to affect people's physical health and well-being. A person's life is also seen to pass through several stages. One of the important tasks of traditional religion is to move people successfully through the major stages of life: birth, puberty, marriage, elderhood, death, ancestorhood. Each phase has its duties, and rites of passage make sure that people know their responsibilities. Other rituals divide the year into seasons and give the annual cycle its form and rhythm.

Ritual authorities, such as diviners, prophets, priests, and sacred kings, serve a common religious purpose: the communication between the human world and the sacred world.

MYTHOLOGY: CREATION, HEROES, AND TRICKSTERS. African myths deal primarily with the origin of mankind and with the origin of social and ritual institutions. They explain both the structure of the world and the social and moral conditions of human life. Most creation myths posit an original state of cosmic order and unity, and they tell of a separation or division that arose between divinity and humanity, sky and earth, order and disorder, which resulted in human mortality. These myths explain why human beings are mortal by telling how they became mortal. Thus they presuppose that humanity was originally immortal and passed into a state of mortality. The myths usually say that mortality was the result of a deliberate or accidental misdeed committed by a human being—often a woman—or an animal.

Some myths explain the origins and significance of death by showing that it is essentially linked to the agents of human fertility and reproduction: women, food, sexuality, and marriage. The Nuer, who live near the Dinka, say that in the beginning a young girl descended from the sky with her companions to get food and that she fell in love with a young man whom she met on earth. When she told her companions that she wished to stay on earth, they ascended to the sky and spitefully cut the rope leading to the ground, thus severing the route to immortality. The myth reflects the choice that every Nuer woman must make in marriage when she leaves her childhood home and friends and goes to live with her husband.

Another widely known myth among Bantu-speaking peoples explains the origin of death in terms of a message that failed. In the beginning the creator god gave the message of life to a slow-moving animal (e.g., chameleon, sheep). Later, he grew impatient and gave the message of death to a faster animal (e.g., lizard, goat). The faster animal arrived first and delivered his message, and death became the lot of mankind. In this myth the natural slowness and quickness of the two animals determine the outcome, making death a natural and inevitable result. Other myths emphasize the similarity between death and sleep and the inability of human beings to avoid either. According to this myth, the creator god told the people to stay awake until he returned. When he came back they had fallen asleep and failed to hear his message of immortality. When they woke up he gave them the message of death.

Hero myths tell how important cultural discoveries, such as agriculture and ironmaking, originated and how major social and ritual institutions, such as marriage, village organization, kingship, priesthood, and cult groups, came into existence. Often the founding deeds of the hero are reenacted in ritual with creative and transforming effect. Many African deities are said to have been heroes who died and returned in spiritual form to serve as guardians and protectors of the people.

Another type of myth is the trickster story. Trickster stories range from fable-like satirical tales to accounts of world creation. The trickster may exist only as a character in stories or as an active deity. Whatever his particular form, the trickster image expresses the fundamental ambiguities of human life. He is both fooler and fooled, wily and stupid, maker and unmade. A seemingly misguided culture hero, the trickster introduces both order and disorder, confusion and wisdom into the world. His comic adventures convey a widely recognized African principle: life achieves its wholeness through the balance of opposites. The trickster's acts of disorder prepare the way for new order; death gives way to birth. In general, African trickster mythology expresses optimism about the paradoxes and anomalies of life, showing that cleverness and humor may prevail in a fundamentally imperfect world. [*See* Tricksters, *article on* African Tricksters.]

MONOTHEISM AND POLYTHEISM. African religions combine principles of unity and multiplicity, transcendence and immanence, into a single system; thus they generally contain both monotheistic and polytheistic aspects. Often there is also the concept of an impersonal power, such as the Yoruba concept of *ase* by which all things have their being. In different contexts each of these principles may come to the fore as the primary focus of religious thought and action, although each is part of the larger whole.

As ultimate principles, many supreme Gods are like African sacred kings: they reign but do not rule. They occupy the structural center of the system but are rarely seen or heard, and when they are it is only indirectly. For this reason the supreme Gods belong more to the dimension of myth than to that of ritual. However, the world would cease to exist without them, as would a kingdom without the king. Thus, in many instances the supreme God is the one, omniscient, omnipotent, transcendent creator, father, and judge. From the time of the first contact with Muslims and Christians, Africans recognized their supreme Gods to be the same as the God of Christianity and Islam.

DIVINITY AND EXPERIENCE. Unlike the supreme beings, which remain in the background of religious life, the lesser divinities and spirits are bound

African tricksters inject bawdiness, rebellion, and wild lying into the mythic history and the common experience of divine-human relations.

PAGE 675

A

AFRICAN RELIGIONS

An Overview

up with everyday experience. These powers are immanent, and their relation to human beings is reciprocal and interdependent. Hence they require many shrines, temples, priests, cult groups, images, rituals, and offerings to facilitate their constant interactions with people.

Often associated with elements of nature, such as lightning, rain, rivers, wild animals, and forests, they may be understood as images or symbols of collective psychological and social realities that resemble these natural phenomena in their powerful, dangerous, and beneficial aspects. The most common form of encounter between the human and the divine is spirit possession, the temporary presence of a deity or spirit in the consciousness of a person. Spirit possession is an integral part of religion and has a well-defined role within it. In some societies possession is regarded as an affliction, and the aim is to expel the intruding god or spirit so that the suffering person may resume a normal life. Usually the cause is some misdeed or sin that must be redressed through ritual action. In other societies possession is a more desirable phenomenon. People may regularly seek to come closer to their gods, even to identify personally with them, through possession-inducing dances that have beneficial psychological and social effects.

The term sacrifice, from the Latin sacrificium *carries the connotation of the religious act in the highest, or fullest sense.*

PAGE 587

MEDIUMS, DIVINERS, AND PROPHETS. Sometimes a divinity may wish to form a special relationship with an individual. The god usually makes his desire known through an illness. Indeed, sickness is sometimes seen as a sacred calling that is manifested in the form of a possession. The cure will take the form of apprenticeship and initiation into the service of the deity, and it will place the person in lasting debt to society. Henceforth, the chosen man or woman becomes professionally established at a shrine and becomes the god's medium, devoted to the healing of afflicted people. He or she treats illnesses and social problems through mediumship séances.

In Africa the distinction between mediums, diviners, priests, and prophets is a fluid one, and transition from one to the other is made easily. Generally, diviners and mediums are spiritual consultants, whereas prophets are leaders of men. Prophets may go directly to the people with programs for action and initiate religious and political movements. For this reason prophets are often sources of religious and political change. In circumstances of widespread political unrest, priestly mediums may develop prophetic powers and initiate socio-religious change. This occurred during colonial times in East Africa: traditional prophets became leaders of political resistance in parts of Sudan, Uganda, Tanzania, and Zimbabwe. In Kenya, the Mau Mau resistance movement was also significantly implemented and sustained by traditional ritual procedures.

A more indirect form of spiritual communication involves the use of divination equipment, such as cowrie shells, leather tablets, animal entrails, palm nuts, a winnowing basket, small animal bones, and animal tracks. After careful interrogation of the client, the diviner manipulates and interprets his material in order to reach a diagnosis. Such systems work according to a basic typology of human problems, aspirations, and causal factors. The diviner applies this framework to his client's case by manipulating his divination apparatus.

Diviners and mediums employ methods of treatment that usually involve a mixture of psychological, social, medical, and ritual means. Many illnesses are regarded as uniquely African in nature and hence as untreatable by Western methods. They include cases of infertility, stomach disorders, and a variety of ailments indicative of psychological stress and anxiety. The causes of such illnesses are generally attributed to social, spiritual, or physiological factors, either separately or in some combination.

RITUAL: SACRIFICE AND RITES OF PASSAGE. Ritual is the foundation of African religion. The ritual sphere is the sphere in which the everyday world and the spiritual world communicate with each other and blend into one reality. Almost every African ritual is therefore an occasion in which human experience is morally and spiritually transformed. The two most important forms of African ritual are animal sacrifice and rites of passage.

The sacrifice of animals and the offering of vegetable foods accomplish a two-way transaction between the realm of divinity and the realm of humanity. The vegetable offerings and animal victims are the mediating principles. They are given to the gods and spirits in return for their favors. Animal sacrifice is especially prominent because the life of the victim and its blood are potent spiritual forces. By killing the victim, its life is released and offered to the gods for their sustenence in exchange for their blessings, especially in the case of human life that is threatened. Through invocations, prayers, and songs, human desires are made known, sins are confessed, and spiritual powers attracted to the sacrificial scene.

Sacrifices are performed on a variety of occasions in seasonal, curative, life-crisis, divinatory, and other kinds of rituals, and always as isolable ritual sequences. Sacrifices that involve the sharing of the victim's flesh confirm the bond between the people and the spiritual power, to which a portion is given. At the social level, sacrifices and offerings bring together individuals and groups and reinforce common moral bonds. Fundamentally, blood sacrifice is a reciprocal act, bringing gods and people together in a circuit of moral, spiritual, and social unity. In this way sacrifice restores moral and spiritual balance—the healthy equilibrium between person and person, group and group, human beings and spiritual powers—which permits the positive flow of life on earth. As a sacred gift of life to the gods, sacrifice atones for human misdeeds and overcomes the human impediments to the flow of life; thus it is one of the keystones of African religions.

Rites of passage possess a threefold pattern consisting of rites of separation, transition, and reincorporation.The most fundamental rite of passage is that which initiates the young into adulthood. In this way a society not only moves its young into new social roles but also transforms them inwardly by molding their moral and mental disposition toward the world. A Nuer boy simply tells his father that he is ready to receive the marks of *gar*, six horizontal lines cut across the forehead. His socialization is already assumed. In many West African societies the rite is held in the confines of initiation groves where the initiates are given intensified moral and religious instruction. These rites may take place over a period of years and are organized into men's and women's initiation societies, such as the Poro society among the Senufo of the Ivory Coast, Mali, and Upper Volta. By means of stories, proverbs, songs, dances, games, masks, and sacred objects, the children and youths are taught the mysteries of life and the values of the adult world. The rites define the position of the intiates in relation to God, to society, to themselves, and to the world. Some form of bodily marking is usually done, and circumcision and clitoridectomy are widely practiced. Generally, the marks indicate that the transition to adulthood is permanent, personal, and often painful and that society has successfully imprinted itself upon the individual.

PERSONS, ANCESTORS, AND ETHICS. African concepts of the person, or self, share several characteristics. Generally, the self is regarded as composite and dynamic; it consists of several aspects, social, spiritual, and physical, and admits of degrees of vitality. The self is also open to possession by divinity, and its life history may be predestined before birth. After death, the self becomes a ghost, and in the course of several generations it becomes merged with the impersonal ancestors. Each of these aspects and potentialities of the person, sometimes misleadingly described as multiple souls, is important in different contexts and receives special ritual attention.

In West African societies, the success or failure of a person's life is explained by reference to a personal destiny that is given to the individual by the creator god before birth. To realize one's full potential, frequent recourse to divination is required to discover what destiny has in store and to ensure the best possible outcome.

At death, new problems of social and spiritual identity arise. When a family loses one of its members, especially a senior male or female, a significant moral and social gap occurs. The family, together with other kinsmen, must close this gap through funerary procedures. At the same time the deceased must undergo spiritual adjustment if he or she is to find a secure place in the afterlife and remain in contact with the family left behind. This is accomplished by the construction of an ancestor shrine and sometimes also by the making of an ancestor mask and costume.

The carved images of the ancestors are not intended to be representational or abstract but conceptual and evocative. By means of stylized form and symbolic details the image conveys the characteristics of the ancestor and also helps to make the spiritual reality of the ancestor present among the people. Thus the carved ancestral icon enables the world of the living and the world of the living dead to come together for the benefit of human life

Superior to living kings and elders, the ancestors define and regulate social and political relations. It is they who own the land and the livestock, and it is they who regulate the prosperity of the lineage groups, villages, and kingdoms. Typically, when misfortune strikes, the ancestors are consulted through divination to discover what misdeeds have aroused their anger. The ancestors are also regularly thanked at ceremonial feasts for their watchful care, upon which the welfare of the community depends.

Not everyone may become an ancestor. Only those who led families and communities in the past as founders, elders, chiefs, or kings may serve in the afterlife as the social and political guides of the future. By contrast, ordinary people become ghosts after death. Such spirits require ritual attention at their graves, but they are finally sent away to "rest in peace," while the more positive influence of the ancestors is invoked generation after generation.

The sufferings and misfortunes brought by the gods and ancestors are punishments aimed at correcting human behavior. By contrast, the sufferings and misfortunes caused by witches and sorcerers are undeserved and socially destructive; they are unequivocally evil. The African concept of evil is that of perverse humanity: the human witch and sorcerer. The African image of the witch and sorcerer is of humanity turned against itself.

For the most part witchcraft accusations in Africa flourished in contexts where social interaction was intense but loosely defined, as between members of the same extended family or lineage group. In such cases witchcraft was sometimes thought to be an inherited power of which the individual might be unaware until accused. In other instances it existed in the form of deliberately practiced sorcery procedures, so-called black magic, which was effective at long range and

"Death has a thousand doors to let out life: I shall find one."

PHILIP MASSINGER
A VERY WOMAN

Among the Egba, Egbado, and Ketu Yoruba it is the power of "our mothers" that is celebrated in the spectacle of the Efe/Gelede festival of masquerade, dance, and song at the time of the spring rains.

PAGE 298

across lineage groups. [*See* Witchcraft, *article on* African Witchcraft.]

SHRINES, TEMPLES, AND RELIGIOUS ART. Shrines and temples serve as channels of communication with the spiritual world, and they may also serve as dwelling places of gods and spirits. Shrines may exist in purely natural forms, such as forest groves, large rocks, rivers, and trees, where gods and spirits dwell. Every African landscape has places of this kind that are the focus of ritual activity. Man-made shrines vary in form. A simple tree branch stuck into the ground is a shrine for a family ghost among the Nuer. A large rectangular building serves as the ancestor stool chapel among the Ashanti. Whatever its form, an African shrine acts as a symbolic crossroads, a place where paths of communication between the human and spiritual worlds intersect. If the shrine serves as a temple, that is, as the dwelling place of a spiritual being, it is built in house-like fashion, like the "palaces" of the royal ancestors in Buganda. Such shrines usually have two parts: the front section, where the priest and the people gather, and the rear section, where the god or spirit dwells. An altar stands between the two and links them together.

African ritual art, including masks, headdresses, sacred staffs, and ceremonial implements, is fashioned according to definite stylistic forms in order to express religious ideas and major social values. The carved *chi wara* antelope headdress of the Bamana of Mali represents the mythic farming animal, called Chi Wara, that originally showed the people how to cultivate, and the antelope shape of the headdress expresses the qualities of the ideal farmer: strength, industriousness, and graceful form. Male and female headdresses are danced together, while women sing songs to encourage the young men's cultivation groups to compete with each other for high agricultural achievements. The Gelede masks of the Yoruba honor the spiritual power of women, collectively known as "our mothers." This power is both creative (birth) and destructive (witchcraft). The Gelede mask depicts the calm and serene face of a woman and expresses the feminine virtue of patience. The face is often surmounted by elaborately carved scenes of daily activity, for the spiritual power of "the mothers" is involved in every aspect of human life.

— BENJAMIN C. RAY

OUR MOTHERS

The Gelede Masks of the Yoruba honor the spiritual power of women, both creative (birth) and destructive (witchcraft).

SEATTLE ART MUSEUM/CORBIS

MODERN MOVEMENTS

Over seven thousand new religious movements exist in sub-Saharan Africa. Together they claim more than thirty-two million adherents. These movements have arisen primarily in areas where there has been intensive contact with Christian missionary efforts. However, the groups that are generally referred to as the new religious movements of sub-Saharan Africa are those that have emerged since the early 1930s. Some of these movements actually began earlier but did not gain momentum until that time. Many have persisted in largely the same form that they took fifty years ago. Others have gone underground and resurfaced, often retaining their initial doctrinal and membership requirements.

With reference to doctrinal base, organizational structure, and geographic distribution, three types of new religious movements may be designated:

1. indigenous or independent churches,
2. separatist churches, and
3. neotraditional movements. These groups have taken different forms in central, southern, West and East Africa. They blend elements of African traditional religion with those of the introduced religions, Christianity and Islam. Many of these groups arose in response to the loss of economic, political, and psychological control engendered by colonial domination.

The impetus for the growth of new African religious movements can be traced to five basic factors:

1. The disappointment of local converts with the premises and outcomes of Christianity led to the growth of prophetic, messianic, and millenarian groups.
2. The translation of the Bible into African vernaculars stimulated a reinterpretation of scripture and a spiritual renewal in Christian groups.
3. The perceived divisions in denominational Christianity and its failure to meet local

needs influenced the rise of separatist churches and community-based indigenous churches.

4. The weakness of Western medicine in the face of psychological disorders, epidemics, and natural disasters stimulated concern with spiritual healing among new African religious movements.

5. The failure of mission Christianity to break down social and cultural barriers and generate a sense of community led to the strengthening of social ties in small, sectarian groups. In general, the new African churches have tried to create a sense of community and continuity in the new, multiethnic urban environment and in the changing context of the rural village.

INDIGENOUS CHURCHES. Indigenous churches are groups that have been started under the initiative of African leaders outside the immediate context of missions or historic religions. Membership is estimated to comprise nearly 15 percent of the Christian population of sub-Saharan Africa. Also called independent churches, these groups have devised unique forms of social and political organization and have developed their own doctrines. These churches were initially a response to the political and religious situation of colonialism. Groups as diverse as the Harrist church in the Ivory Coast, the Aladura church in Nigeria, the Kimbanguist church in Zaire, and the Apostolic movements of Zimbabwe may be classified as indigenous churches. Nevertheless, each of these churches has a distinctive doctrinal thrust and response to government control. These groups also vary on the organizational level depending on the extent of their local appeal and the demographic and cultural composition of their membership. Indigenous churches may be divided into three specific subtypes: prophetic, messianic, and millenarian. All three subtypes evidence doctrinal innovation, efforts at spiritual renewal, and a reaction against the presence of mission churches.

Prophetic indigenous churches. Prophetic groups are tied to the influence of an individual prophet. They generally have a strong central organization and an emphasis on healing. One of the most important prophetic churches in central Africa is the Kimbanguist church, which has more than four million adherents in Zaire. Triggered by Simon Kimbangu's initial healing revival in 1921, this movement grew and increased in intensity after its founder's death in 1951. The group has transformed from a prophetic protest movement to an established church and is currently one of the four officially recognized religious bodies in Zaire. The Kimbanguist church was admitted to the World Council of Churches in 1969 and resembles many other prophetic movements that have acquired legitimacy in postindependence Africa.

Churches with similar origins and leadership structures that focus on a prophetic figure are found in other regions: for example, Alice Lenshina's Lumpa church in Zambia; the Harrist church in Liberia, the Ivory Coast, and Ghana; and the Zionist churches of South Africa. Common to all these movements is an emphasis on spiritual and physical health.

In 1954, the Lumpa church was begun by Alice Lenshina Mulenga in the Copperbelt of Northern Rhodesia (present-day Zambia). Lenshina claimed at the time that she had died and come back to life with a religious calling. She was viewed as a visionary prophetess and healer. Like Kimbangu, she attracted many former mission catechists and teachers to her movement. Naming her church Lumpa (the "highest" or the "supreme" in Bemba), Lenshina promised health and a new life to those who forsook traditional magic and witchcraft to follow her. Her followers resisted government taxation and political authority; as a result, the cohesiveness of the Lumpa movement was ultimately broken through political struggles and in 1970 its followers were expelled from the country.

Toward the end of 1913 William Wade Harris, a Liberian of Grebo origin, claimed that the Angel Gabriel had appeared to him in a vision and instructed him to spread the Christian message as God's prophet. Traveling to the Ivory Coast and the Gold Coast (now Ghana), Harris propagated his message of divine revelation, faith healing, and an improved life for Africans. Although he spent only a short time in the Ivory Coast, the number of his adherents grew rapidly. Within a few months of the movement's inception Harris had baptized an estimated 120,000 people. After Harris's death in 1929 the prophet John Ahui and the faith healer Albert Atcho continued to expand the Harrist church in the Ivory Coast. Between 1955 and 1961 especially it grew and attracted many former Roman Catholics. In 1973, the Harrist church celebrated its sixtieth anniversary in the Ivory Coast with governmental support and recognition. Like the Kimbanguists, the Harrists have proceeded successfully from a prophetic movement to an official church with national appeal.

The Aladura movement in Nigeria has often been compared with the Harrist church. It is one of several prophetic movements that developed in western Nigeria in the late 1920s in strong reaction against Anglican mission control. These groups emphasized spiritual healing, divine revelation, prophecy, and self-reliance. The term *aladura* ("people of prayer") refers to several related groups, drawn largely from the Yoruba-speaking population, who share certain spiritual characteristics.

Common characteristics of a new religion include founding by a charismatic figure whose career often recalls the shamanistic model.

PAGE 486

The Aladura movement continues to grow and has now established branches outside Africa.

Of the approximately three thousand indigenous churches in South Africa, three-quarters are churches that emphasize spiritual healing and the charismatic powers of their leaders. These churches are classified as Zionist because they trace their origins to John Alexander Dowie's Evangelical Christian Catholic Church, which was established in 1896 in Zion City, Illinois. The concept of Zion represents utopian spiritual liberation. Members of these churches place considerable emphasis on divine healing, spiritual revelations, and testimony. Concentrated heavily among the Zulu and Swazi peoples of South Africa, these Zionist churches have diverse doctrinal and ritual formats but are linked by their focus on the prophetic and healing powers of charismatic leaders. Colorful, almost theatrical, ceremonies are typical of these groups.

Miracles are caused to occur "naturally" by charismatic figures who have succeeded in controlling their consciousness through visions, dreams, or the practices of meditation.

PAGE 442

Messianic indigenous churches. Resembling the prophetic movements in their origins, messianic churches crystallize around a single figure who is regarded as a new messiah. Messianic groups occasionally experience a crisis and a decline in their appeal after the founder dies or disappears. The prophetic message remains closely tied to the leader and his or her charismatic attraction. Movements of this type include the Mai Chaza church and the Apostolic Church of John Masowe in Zimbabwe and the Isaiah Shembe movement in South Africa.

In October 1932 an African prophet calling himself John the Baptist, and otherwise known as Shoniwa or Johane Masowe, began to preach among the Shona people in the Hartley district of Southern Rhodesia. Like Mai Chaza, he claimed to have been resurrected from death and consequently endowed with healing and prophetic powers. Masowe moved from village to village baptizing those who accepted his message of healing and a better life.

"If a prophet arises among you, or a dreamer of dreams, you shall not listen."

DEUTERONOMY 13:1

Masowe's movement combined prophetic, messianic, and millenarian elements. He exhorted his followers to abstain from wage labor for the colonial authorities and to resist colonial religious structures and doctrine. Under political pressure the Apostolic Church of John Masowe, whose members are also known as *vahosanna* (the "hosannas") or as Basketmakers, moved to the Korsten suburb of Port Elizabeth, South Africa, in 1943. In 1960 his church was expelled from South Africa as a political threat. In the meantime many of his followers had already started to move northward, to Northern and Southern Rhodesia. Masowe actually died (according to news accounts) in Ndola, Zambia, in 1973, leaving behind messianic hopes and a millenarian promise of freedom. The group has not chosen a leader to replace him.

MAI CHAZA
Moses, Jesus, and Mai

Mai ("mother") Chaza was initially a member of the Methodist church in Southern Rhodesia (now Zimbabwe). She became seriously ill in 1954 and her followers believed her to have died. Upon recovery, Mai Chaza reported that while she was dead she had communicated with God and had received the gift of healing. She sought out the blind, the crippled, and those possessed by alien spirits. Mai Chaza believed that she was a messenger of God and compared herself to Moses and Jesus. To the members of her movement she was both a savior and a miracle worker.

Mai Chaza died in 1960 leaving no heirs. A Malawian adherent called Mapaulos began to perform extraordinary healings in her name. He assumed the title *vamutenga* ("he who is sent from heaven") and continued the mission of healing at Mai Chaza's center, Guta ra Jehovah, or the City of God. After Mai Chaza's death her followers referred to her as Mai Chaza Jesus, the black messiah and savior of Africa. Like Lenshina, Mai Chaza was seen as a chief and medium. The extent to which women have been leaders and founders of prophetic and messianic groups—including the Lumpa church, the Aladura movement, and the Mai Chaza group—is particularly noteworthy. The influence of women in these movements may be viewed as a reaction to the ecclesiastical authority of men in the mission churches.

— BENNETTA JULES-ROSETTE

Isaiah Shembe (c. 1870-1935) was a self-proclaimed Zulu prophet who founded the amaNazaretha church in South Africa. A man of compelling personality and significant influence, Shembe was widely known as a holy man and divine healer. He is said to have portrayed himself as a messianic figure, a liberator, and a messenger of God. He established a village, Ekuphakameni, to which his followers flocked for festivals, faith healing, and meditation. After his death, the prophet was succeeded by his son, Johannes Galilee Shembe, or Shembe II, who is believed to have inherited his father's charismatic gifts but not his full messianic status.

The messianic movements typified by these three groups center on the personalities and myths of leadership established by their founders. Their doctrinal innovations are rooted in the messages of hope, healing, and possibility offered by their founders. Even after the death of the founders, their messianic traits have been perpetuated as a means of bolstering the faith of the followers and providing a challenge to European missionary efforts.

Many new African religious movements have millenarian tendencies. One of the most widespread millenarian movements in sub-Saharan Africa is the Church of the Watchtower, or Kitawala. Linked to the American Jehovah's Witnesses, who began missionary activities in Africa at the beginning of the twentieth century, several Watchtower movements arose across central and southern Africa. Among the best known was the Watchtower group formed by Elliot Kamwana of Nyasaland (modern-day Malawi) in 1908. Since 1910 other groups have formed in eastern Zaire, in Zambia, and in South Africa. All these groups believe in the autonomy of religion apart from political control and hope for a coming spiritual golden age.

SEPARATIST CHURCHES. Separatist groups are those that have broken off from established Christian churches or Islamic congregations. In this sense, separatist churches are distinct from indigenous groups that have never been affiliated with a mission body. They may, nevertheless, also be examined in terms of the prophetic, messianic, and millenarian categories that have been used to classify the indigenous churches. Among separatist groups in the Roman Catholic tradition are the Jamaa, the Catholic Church of the Sacred Heart, and the Legio Maria.

The Jamaa movement was started by a Belgian Franciscan, Placide Tempels. Jamaa ("family" in Swahili) emphasizes the importance of the nuclear family, individuality, personhood, fecundity, and love. Officially, certain Jamaa affiliates have remained within the Roman Catholic church. By 1953, however, Jamaa had developed an independent organizational structure. As the group became more established, it was closely scrutinized by the Catholic authorities and was eventually discouraged and repressed in certain areas.

The Legio Maria, or Legion of Mary, began as an offshoot of the Irish Roman Catholic lay organization of the same name. Its origin in Kenya dates from 1963. By the early 1970s the group had over ninety thousand members, primarily drawn from the Luo ethnic group. Among the Bemba of Zambia, a similar group, the Catholic Church of the Sacred Heart, broke away from the established missions in 1955. Each of these separatist movements has emphasized brotherhood, community, and the use of an original form of worship in the local vernacular.

The East African Revival movement, or Balokole ("the Saved Ones"), stands as a primary example of a Protestant separatist church. It began as a charismatic renewal within the Protestant churches of Uganda, Kenya, Tanganyika, and Ruanda-Urundi. Initially part of the activities of the former Rwanda Mission, an evangelical branch of the Anglican Church Missionary Society, the revival had become by 1935 a separatist church with indigenous organizational characteristics and worship practices. It has emphasized conversion, testimony, and aggressive proselytizing.

NEOTRADITIONAL MOVEMENTS. Other religious movements have maintained the form of traditional cults. They include the secret societies of West Africa within the Poro-Sande complex; reformative cults, such as the Bwiti in Gabon; and newer groups, such as the Église de Dieu de Nos Ancêtres (Church of the God of Our Ancestors) in southwestern Zaire. In each case the neotraditional cults preserve aspects of traditional religion in a new social and cultural context.

Originally formed as a protective warriors' society, the Poro cult initiates young men into adulthood by instructing them in ritual and social obligations. It continues to be an important form of religious, social, and political organization among the Mande-speaking peoples of Sierra Leone, Liberia, and the Ivory Coast. The counterpart society, the Sande or Bundu, prepares

PORO MASK

The secret societies of Western Africa, including the Poro warrior cult, preserve aspects of traditional religion in a new context.

women for their social obligations and shares political authority with the Poro society. The societies themselves remain outside mission control and make no official attempt to incorporate Christian practices.

In contrast, the Bwiti cult, originating at the turn of

Millenarianism is the belief that the end of the world is at hand and that in its wake will appeal a new harmonious world.

PAGE 431

the century among the Fang of Gabon, attempted to revitalize a traditional ancestral cult by incorporating rituals and beliefs of neighboring people. At a later date elements of Christian theology and symbolism were added. By the 1950s Bwiti cult leaders had adopted the pattern of the messianic prophetic leadership characteristic of some of the indigenous churches. The group was also known as the Église des Banzie (Church of the Initiates) and had nearly ten thousand Fang members by 1965. In recent years the cult has drawn its membership from dissident Roman Catholic catechists and from Protestants, incorporating elements of their beliefs into its new doctrines and religious symbols.

The Église de Dieu de Nos Ancêtres, appearing in the 1950s in the Belgian Congo, has followed a similar pattern. This group combines belief in Luba ancestral spirits and traditional religion with elements of Christianity. Like the Bwiti cult, the Église de Dieu de Nos Ancêtres has moved away from a small cultic organization to the formal model of a church in response to the pressures of urban migration and cultural change experienced by its members.

"There is always something new out of Africa."

PLINY THE ELDER
NATURAL HISTORY, BOOK I

In all cases these groups have had to confront the increasing pressures of missionary presence and the influence of Christianity or Islam in their areas of operation.

THE FUTURE OF THE NEW AFRICAN RELIGIONS. A major debate in the field centers on the extent to which new movements may be considered stable over time. It has been argued that the new religions develop through a process of schism and renewal. They break away from the influence of both mission and newly established churches to develop bonds of family and community that are particularly strong at the local level. Utopian ideals and fundamentalist interpretations of scripture reinforce the initial break and the sense of spiritual renewal in these groups.

Although some of the new Christian groups of Africa originate in ethnically homogeneous areas, most emphasize the potential of, and even the necessity for, cultural exchange through overarching symbols and doctrine. These processes of cultural combination and reconstruction allow the members of new religious movements to acquire a reflective stance toward their immediate problems and to preserve past cultural ideas. The neotraditional, millenarian, and revitalistic responses resolve social and cultural clashes through blending old and new interpretations of the sacred.

At the same time a question of stable leadership and its institutionalization arises. As the discussion of prophetic and messianic churches emphasizes, the death or demise of a leader creates an important challenge to the viability of a group. Thus schism continues to threaten the new religious movements even after they have established autonomy from missions or historic churches. This problem has led some scholars to speculate that the new African religions are unstable and highly mutable and that their appearance merely marks one phase of social or religious protest in the emergence of Africa's new nation-states. Nevertheless, historical evidence suggests that these groups have considerable longevity in spite of their shifting leadership structures and new membership. The persistence of such groups as the Bwiti cult and the Kitawala movement—from the turn of the century—follows this trend.

Another important tendency contributing to the eventual stability of the new religious movements is the shift toward ecumenism. Between 1969 and 1981, several well-established indigenous churches affiliated themselves with the World Council of Churches in an attempt to become international in outlook through an association with worldwide ecumenical movements. They include the Church of the Lord Aladura in Nigeria, the Kimbanguist church in Zaire, the African Israel Nineveh Church in Kenya, and the African Church of the Holy Spirit in Kenya.

Local voluntary associations formed by these churches often attempt to retain the doctrinal autonomy of each group while developing joint fund-raising, educational, and cultural efforts. This type of cooperation is evident in the African Independent Churches' Association, formed in 1965 in South Africa, and in similar ecumenical councils and associations that have formed in central and East Africa. Although such associations do not solve the problem of internal group conflict and leadership succession, they do appear to reinforce cooperation and political stability within the independent church movement as a whole.

CULTURAL AND SOCIAL CONTRIBUTION OF AFRICA'S NEW RELIGIONS. Many of Africa's new religious movements, from the 1920s to the present, have started as religions of the oppressed and have become movements of protest. Several of these groups, including the early Watchtower movement inspired by Kamwana in Nyasaland, Kimbanguism in Zaire, and the Harrist church of the Ivory Coast, have also led to or supported movements of political liberation and national independence. The close relationship between political and religious symbols of freedom has contributed to this development.

The social influences of Africa's new religions are not limited to the political sphere. The new images and ideals of community promoted by these groups offer alternative modes of existence to their members and to others who come into contact with the new movements. Through tightly knit communities and internal support structures, Africa's new religions establish claims to loyalty. Culturally they promise a religion that is not alien to the masses. Nevertheless, some of the contemporary groups also emphasize the ultimate attainment of rewards promised in orthodox doctrines. This goal is accomplished through isolation and strict personal adherence to the Bible or the Qur'an. These literal interpretations of sacred writings serve to develop a new fabric of ideas through which individuals attempt to create alternative types of social relationships. In some instances this return to fundamentalist doctrines within the African context has also had the effect of triggering charismatic renewals and new forms of proselytizing within established mission churches.

By means of Africa's new religious movements, conventional cultural and symbolic forms are revived and reinterpreted. Taken from their original source, some of these religious beliefs have been applied to secular life. The ultimate viability of these new religions may, in fact, reside in the capacity of their beliefs and practices to become integrated into the mainstream of modern Africa's social and cultural life. Thus, the greatest impact of these groups may take place through cultural diffusion and sharing rather than through the spread and historical evolution of any particular movement.

— BENNETTA JULES-ROSETTE

HISTORY OF STUDY

The classical world had little knowledge of Africa and its peoples, let alone of its religions. With the obvious exceptions of Egypt and, to a limited extent, of the coastal strip facing the Mediterranean, Africa was alleged to be inhabited by fabulous, not wholly human creatures.

Though the Romans ruled the whole of northern Africa for centuries, their interest in the local religions seems to have been as slight as that of the Greeks. In the eleventh century, *al-Bakri* likewise mentions a mountain tribe in southern Morocco that allegedly adored a ram. However, neither he nor the other Arab travelers and geographers of the Middle Ages who visited the Maghrib and the Sudan and described their political organization, trade, and customs tell us much about their religion.

The Portuguese discovery of sub-Saharan Africa's coastal regions in the fifteenth century gave Europeans the first opportunity to observe a number of African societies; however, it took a surprisingly long time before any accurate report of their religions reached Europe.

Throughout the eighteenth and early nineteenth centuries, information on native African religions continued to stagnate at these poor levels. As a consequence of the slow pace of exploration into the African interior, reports focused on the peoples of the coastal western and central areas and on the eastern and northern countries that were permeated, or at least influenced, by Islam. The observers were mostly navigators, explorers, tradesmen, and naturalists who had no ethnological grounding and only a marginal interest in religious matters. Missionaries, who might have been better qualified to investigate the people's beliefs, were usually biased by a general attitude of contempt or pity for the "heathen" and by a deeply rooted ethnocentrism.

MISSIONARY REPORTS. In the second half of the nineteenth century, missionaries began to show more care and tolerance in the study of native beliefs. An example of this can be found in the works of the Italian abbot Giovanni Beltrame (*Il Sennaar e lo Sciangallah*, Verona and Padua, 1879; *Il fiume bianco e i Denka*, Verona, 1881), whose attempts to evangelize the tribes of the upper Nile dated back to 1854-1855. Beltrame published, both in the original language and in translation, the splendid chant with which the Dinka celebrate the creative actions of their supreme being known as Dendid, or Dengdit ("great rain"). He also noticed that the Dinka have two verbs, *ciòr* and *lam*, to express the act of praying to God and a separate verb, vtiég, used to indicate "to pray to a man." Moreover, he noted that verbs related to God are always used in the present tense. Hence the Christian expression "God has always been and always will be" is rendered "God is and always is"—a grammatical detail with significant theological implications. Of the neighboring Nuer, Beltrame wrote: "They believe in the existence of God, but pay no cult to him" (Beltrame, 1881, pp. 191, 275).

Another example of this new attitude can be found in *Among the Primitive Bakongo* (London, 1914) and other works by the English missionary John H. Weeks, who lived for thirty years among the riverine natives of the Kongo and provided a realistic picture of the local religion. He not only recognized the nature of Nzambi as a supreme being but equated this deity with the God of Christianity.

An even more authoritative and sophisticated contribution was given a few years later by another Protestant missionary, Henri A. Junod, who lived among the Thonga of coastal Mozambique from 1907 onward. Whereas Weeks had declared in his preface that he had "no particular leaning towards any school of anthropologists," Junod, by the time he collected his earlier materials for publication in 1927, was fully aware of the theoretical discussions in which anthropologists and historians of religion were engaged and was impressed by the fashionable tenets of evolutionism and the requirements of comparativism. Having found among the Thonga the coexistence of beliefs in a sky god and

Missionaries have gone so far in identifying with those they have come to serve as to renounce their own nation and to accept naturalization in the countries they have made their own.

PAGE 453

in ancestral spirits, he attempted to assess the respective antiquity of the two apparently conflicting creeds. To do so, he compared these beliefs with others found among southern Bantu-speaking societies. He followed the assertion of W. Challis and Henry Callaway that the sky was prayed to by the forebears of the Swazi and Zulu before the worship of ancestor spirits was introduced. Though Junod called this change "evolution," he realized that this succession was contrary to the schemes of orthodox evolutionism. In an appendix to the 1936 French edition of *The Life of a South African Tribe* (London, 1912), he states that the two sets of creeds could be parallel among the Bantu speakers. At the same time, however, he conjectures, on the basis of psychological considerations, a chronological sequence—naturism, animism, causalism, euhemerism—that partly accepts Nathan Sderblom's hypotheses as stated in his *Das Werden des Gottes-*

COLONIAL PERSPECTIVE
Prejudices and Misconceptions

The earliest writings that contain some mention of religious matters are by Duarte Pacheco Pereira (1505-1506) and Valentim Fernandes (1506-1507), which seem to refer to the coastal tribes of what are now the Republic of Guinea and Sierra Leone. Here is Yves Person in his essay "The Coastal Peoples," included in volume 4 of UNESCO's *General History of Africa*, edited by D. T. Niane (London, 1984):

> *The people paid honour to idols carved out of wood; the chief divinity was called Kru; they also practised worship of the dead, who were embalmed before burial. "It is usual to make a memento for all those who die: if he was a notable person, an idol is made resembling him; if he was merely a commoner or a slave, the figure is made of wood and is put in a thatched house. Every year, sacrifices of chickens or goats are made to them."(Person, in Niane, 1984, p. 307)*

In 1483, Portuguese navigator Diogo Cão reached the mouth of the Kongo; by 1491, missionaries had joined the explorers and mariners. These missionaries were devoted far more to converting the people than to understanding the traditional creeds. The most widely read report on central Africa was Filippo Pigafetta's *Relazione del Reame di Congo* (1591; reprint, Milan, 1978), which was based on the notes of Duarte Lopes, a Portuguese merchant who had lived there for many years before he was appointed an envoy to the pope by the converted Kongo king, Alvaro I. According to this report, the natives of Loango "adore whatever they like, holding the greatest god to be the Sun as male, and the Moon as female; for the rest, every person elects his own Idol, which he adores according to his fancy." Of the Kongo proper an even more improbable picture is drawn: "Everyone worshipped whatever he most fancied without rule or measure or reason at all," and when all the religious relics were collected to be destroyed at the summons of the now-baptized king, Afonso I, it is reported that "there was found a huge quantity of Devils of strange and frightful shape," including "Dragons with wings, Serpents of horrible appearance, Tigers and other most monstrous animals. . . both painted and carved in wood and stone and other material." This is an unlikely collection, judging from what we know of Kongo sculpture.

In 1586, the Portuguese author Santos wrote of another Bantu-speaking ethnic group, the Yao of Mozambique, in less derogatory terms: "They acknowledge a God who, both in this world and in the next, measures the retribution for the good or evil done in this" (cited by Andrew Lang, *The Making of Religion*, London, 1898). This view, however, again does not tally with what we know today of Yao traditional beliefs.

A century later, Giovanni Antonio Cavazzi's *Istorica descrizione de' tre' regni Congo, Matamba Angola* (Bologna, 1687) marks a slight improvement in accuracy, recording in almost correct form the name for the supreme being of certain central African peoples, Nzambia-mpungu. His reports, however, retain the derogatory view of his predecessors:

> *Before the light of the Holy Gospel dispelled superstition and idolatry from the minds of the Congolese, these unhappy people were subject to the Devil's tyranny.. . . [Apart from Nzambi] there are other gods, inferior to him, but nevertheless worthy of homage; to these too, therefore, cult and adoration are due.... The pagans expose a certain quantity of idols, mostly of wood, roughly sculpted, each one of which has its own name.*
>
> *(my trans.)*

An early account of Khoi religion was casually given by the Jesuit priest Gui Tachard in his *Il viaggio di Siam de' padri gesuiti mandati dal re di Francia all'Indie, e alla China* (Milan, 1693). He writes:

> *These people know nothing of the creation of the world, the redemption of mankind, and the mystery of the Holy Trinity. Nevertheless they adore a god, but the cognition they have of him is very confused. They kill in his honor cows and sheep, of which they offer him meat and milk in sign of gratitude toward this deity that grants them, as they believe, now rain and now fair weather, according to their needs.*

— VINIGI GROTTANELLI

glaubens (Leipzig, 1916). Junod's ambiguous conclusions reflect the case of an experienced researcher trying to combine personally observed realities with the theoretical speculations of others.

COMPARATIVE SYNTHESES: THE QUEST FOR ORIGINS. The decades during which missionaries collected most of our information on African religions coincided with the flourishing of a series of ambitious comparative works that attempted to establish the logical, if not chronological, succession of religious ideas in the world. An early prototype of such attempts was Charles de Brosses's *Du culte des dieux fétiches* (Paris, 1760), which compared black African beliefs and rites with those of ancient Egypt. Several of his data and theses were used in Auguste Comte's six-volume *Cours de philosophie positive* (Paris, 1830-1842). The rise of evolutionist theories in the second half of the nineteenth century—a period that saw the intensive exploration of central Africa—encouraged an increasing use of examples from peoples encountered for the first time in addition to those known through previous literature. These examples were often indiscriminately used to represent instances of the stages of "primitive" religion: fetishism, ancestor worship or euhemerism, animism, totemism, idolatry, polytheism, and so on.

These various evolutionary theories were based only in part on artfully selected African materials in order to support the different authors' theses, and their value has been polemical rather than interpretative. They have served to synthesize previously known facts in attractive combinations and to bring them jointly to the broad public's attention. Examples of such comparative syntheses are John Lubbock's *Origin of Civilisation* (London, 1870), Grant Allen's *The Evolution of the Idea of God* (London, 1897), R. R. Marett's *The Threshold of Religion* (London, 1909), and parts of James G. Frazer's immense work.

One of the earliest comprehensive ethnographic surveys is Theodor Waitz's *Anthropologie der Naturvölker* (Leipzig, 1859-1872). In the second of its six volumes, Waitz discusses African blacks and their kin. Drawing from the investigations of field observers, Waitz writes:

> *We reach the amazing conclusion that several Negro tribes . . . in the development of their religious conceptions are much further advanced than almost all other savages* [Naturvölker], *so far that, though we do not call them monotheists, we may still think of them as standing on the threshold of monotheism.*
>
> *(Waitz, 1860, p. 167)*

Other eminent evolutionists, such as Lubbock and Herbert Spencer, included some African tribes in the list of backward societies as surviving examples of primitive atheism or as having no religious ideas whatsoever. This categorization was promptly refuted in Gustav Roskoff's *Das Religionswesen der rohesten Naturvölker* (Leipzig, 1880) and in Albert Réville's *Les religions des peuples non-civilisés* (Paris, 1883). This latter work, which was widely read at the time, deals separately with the peoples of different continents. The author's position represents a compromise, as it were, between the derogatory judgments of the early evolutionists and the gradual rehabilitation of African religious ideas. Réville writes:

> *Naturism, the cult of personified natural features, sky, sun, moon, mountains, rivers, etc., is general of African soil. . . . Animism, the worship of spirits detached from nature and without a necessary link with natural phenomena, has taken a preponderant and so to speak absorbing role. Hence the Negro's fetishism, a fetishism that little by little rises to idolatry. . . . Nevertheless one should not omit, I shall not say a trait, but a certain tendency to monotheism, easily emerging from this confused mass of African religions. Undoubtedly, the African native is not insensitive to the idea of a single all-powerful God.*
>
> *(Réville, 1883, vol. 1, pp. 188-190)*

Such admissions, which clearly contradict the widespread evolutionary theories of the time, were largely ignored in academic circles of the English-speaking world until they were systematically assembled in Andrew Lang's *The Making of Religion* (London, 1898; 3d rev. ed., 1909). Just as Réville had spoken contemptuously of "the incoherence and undisciplined imagination of the Negro," so Lang referred to Africans as belonging to the "low races" and as the "lowest savages." This view did not prevent him, however, from expressing his final opinion of their traditional religion "as probably beginning in a kind of Theism, which is then superseded, in some degree, or even corrupted, by Animism in all its varieties" (Lang, 1909, p. 304).

Lang's assertion of the antiquity of African beliefs in a high god ran parallel to a similar conviction, within a different scientific milieu, in the emerging notion of *Kulturkreiselehre*, or "doctrine of culture circles."

Among the relevant works written by this generation of researchers on the general themes of African religion are those devoted to mythology. Alice Werner's *Myths and Legends of the Bantu* appeared in 1933 and was followed, in 1936, by Hermann Baumann's *Schöpfung und Urzeit des Menschen im Mythus der afrikanischen Völker*, a true masterpiece of erudition by a leading German ethnologist.

Raffaele Pettazzoni, a staunch adversary of

According to the Yoruba, there are 401 orisa (deities) who line the road to heaven.

PAGE 714

> *"Our ancestors have turned a savage wilderness into a glorious empire."*
>
> EDMUND BURKE
> THE THIRTEEN RESOLUTIONS

Schmidt's theory of primeval monotheism, also made a valid contribution to the study of African religious ideas with his four-volume *Miti e leggende* (Turin, 1948-1963). The first volume remains the fullest and most aptly annotated collection of myths from all parts of Africa. In the work that concluded his long career as a historian of religions, *L'onniscienza di Dio* (Turin, 1955), Pettazzoni devotes the first chapter to sub-Saharan Africa. The book closed the century-long controversy among specialists, documenting from a wholly nonconfessional viewpoint the worldwide distribution of beliefs in a supreme being.

TRIBAL MONOGRAPHS. With the development of colonialism an important new type of literature appeared and spread rapidly: the tribal monograph. Based on the image of the "closed society," this type of book often ignored both cross-cultural comparison and diachronic developments. It described all aspects of a single tribe or ethnic group, starting with geographical distribution, racial characteristics, and linguistic classification and analyzing all facts of its social structure and culture, including religion. The first decades of the twentieth century produced a particularly rich series of such books, which contributed greatly, though often at a superficial level, to the knowledge of countless African religions. The authors were mostly colonial administrators (or district commissioners) and missionaries but also included scientists, such as linguists and anthropologists.

The scientific merits of these books vary. On principle, and on the positive side, they respect the scientific requirements summarized in Edwin W. Smith's *African Ideas of God: A Symposium* (London, 1950): "Sociologically speaking, African religion is one aspect of African culture. No one element can be exhaustively studied and understood in isolation from the rest" (p. 14). On the other hand, even before that rule was stated, the progress of studies had clearly shown the religions of preliterate peoples to be far too complex to be adequately condensed in a mere chapter of a general monograph.

Before World War II, researchers had been almost exclusively European. The most significant American contribution was Melville J. Herskovits and Frances S. Herskovits's *An Outline of Dahomean Religious Belief* (Menasha, Wis., 1933). Generally, educated Africans had not yet written about or begun to vindicate their own traditional religions. However, in his well-known *Facing Mount Kenya* (London, 1938), with an appreciative but critical preface by Bronislaw Malinowski,

WILLIAM SCHMIDT

Pygmies As Monotheistic Prototype

One of the founders of the school of thought known as *Kulturkreiselehre* or "doctrine of culture circles" was Wilhelm Schmidt. He published an early introduction to his monumental work, *Der Ursprung der Gottesidee*, at the same time as the publication of the third edition of Lang's *The Making of Religion*; but almost half a century passed before the twelve-volume work appeared (Münster, 1912-1955). Three volumes are dedicated to the peoples of Africa. Schmidt's much debated thesis of a worldwide primeval monotheism that was corrupted by later trends in successive cultural "cycles" cannot be discussed here. It should be noted, however, that according to Schmidt, the remnants of the world's earliest religious ideas are to be found among African Pygmies, considered to be monotheistic and surviving representatives of the world's most archaic, or "primeval," culture.

Independently of the acceptance or rejection of this theory, Schmidt's presentation of the data marks a striking contrast to that of his predecessors. Rather than arbitrarily assembling data from all sources according to a specific topic, he systematically collected and grouped data in reference to specific ethnic groups. Whenever possible, a summary of information on the geographical and anthropological position of a given tribe is followed by data that are arranged in separate sections devoted to beliefs, myths, sacrifices, prayers, conceptions of the soul, eschatology, ancestor worship, and so on. The materials that were assembled by Schmidt remain to this day an invaluable quarry of carefully sifted and well-ordered information. The arduous field investigation of nomadic forest hunter-gatherers such as the Pygmies, in which Schmidt was particularly interested, also should be credited to his influence. He incessantly encouraged, advised, and sponsored fellow missionaries such as O. Henri Trilles, Peter Schumacher, and especially Paul Schebesta, keeping abreast of their ongoing investigations. The final results of this research were synthesized by Schmidt in 1933 (see Schmidt, 1912-1955, vol. 3) and eventually published in Schebesta's masterly *Die Bambuti Pygmäen vom Ituri* (Brussels, 1938-1950), the third volume of which is dedicated entirely to religion, and in Martin Gusinde's *Die Twiden* (Vienna and Stuttgart, 1956), a concise book remarkable for its scientific objectivity and exhaustive bibliography.

— VINIGI GROTTANELLI

WELL-KNOWN TRIBAL MONOGRAPHS

Author	Title
A.C. Hollis	*The Masai, The Nandi*
Deidrich Westermann	*The Shilluk People*
Gunter Tessmann	*Die Pangwe*
Alberto Pollera	*I Baria e I Cunama*
Gerhard Lindblom's	*The Akamba in British East Africa*
E. Smith and A. Dale	*The Ila-speaking Peoples of Northern Rhodesia*
Henrich Veder	*Die Bergdama*
John Roscoe	*The Baganda, The Bakitara or Banyoro*
Louis Tauxier	*Le noir du Souden, Religion, moers et coutumes des Agnis de la Côte d'Ivoire.*

Jomo Kenyatta devoted two chapters to the religion of his Kikuyu; but, here again, his analysis was only a minor part of an all-embracing monograph. The most significant exception was The *Akan Doctrine of God* (London, 1944) by J. B. Danquah, which is devoted entirely to the exposition of the religious creeds of the writer's own nation, Ashanti. A more appropriate title for the book would be *The Ashanti Doctrine* because Danquah, an Ashanti, was concerned with the creeds, epistemology, and ethics of his own powerful tribe and had little regard for the corresponding, but not identical, systems of other branches of the Akan linguistic family (e.g., Anyi, Baule, Brong, Nzema, etc.). Dense with original quotations, subtle though sometimes odd philological arguments and comparisons, and sophisticated speculation, the book struck a decidedly new note in the concert of previous literature on the subject. It left the reader, however, uncertain as to whether it was a true picture of widespread Ashanti beliefs or the outcome of the author's personal philosophical and theological reflections.

ANTHOLOGIES AND NEW OUTLOOKS. In the postwar years a few scholars devised anthologies that arranged side-by-side, condensed accounts of several religions. Well-known examples are *African Ideas of God: A Symposium* (London, 1950), edited by Edwin W. Smith in collaboration with a team of qualified Protestant missionaries, and *Textes sacrés d'Afrique noire* (Paris, 1965), edited by Germaine Dieterlen, which contains a preface by a leading African intellectual, Amadou Hampaté Ba, and a series of essays by lay ethnologists.

The topics examined in these anthologies include cosmology, epistemology, and a general view of the universe, as is the case in *African Worlds* (London, 1954), edited by Daryll Forde, then director of the International African Institute. Forde assembled a series of essays by anthropological authorities such as Mary Douglas on the Lele of Kasai, Günter Wagner on the Abaluyia of Kavirondo, Jacques J. Maquet on Rwanda, Kenneth Little on the Mende of Sierra Leone, and the Ghanaian scholar and politician K. A. Busia on the Ashanti.

Knowledge of African religions is also drawn from works devoted to myths, proverbs, oral literature, social and political structures, and most aspects of a people's culture. The work that most stimulated a reconsideration of African creeds in the postwar years was *La philosophie bantoue* (Elisabethville, Belgian Congo, 1945), written by a Belgian Franciscan friar, Placide Tempels. This book is not merely a synthesis of religious beliefs and rites; it also discusses criteriology, ontology, "wisdom," metaphysics, psychology, jurisprudence, and ethics. It stresses that in all these realms, the universe is seen as a system of "vital forces," originating in God and radiating to spirits, human beings, animals, plants, and even minerals. These forces can be benign or hostile, strengthened or weakened, as they incessantly influence one another. The idea of the cosmos as a hierarchy of forces was surely not new. What was new was that Tempels seems to have derived this system from his missionary experiences and from conversations with the Luba rather than from sociological or philosophical literature. He quotes no literature throughout the book, with the one exception of Diedrich Westermann's *Der Afrikaner heute und morgen* (Essen, 1934), in which he was surprised to find the fundamental principles of his own theory. Furthermore, Tempels felt sure that these concepts were shared by all Bantu-speaking peoples.

NEW DEVELOPMENTS. With the collapse of the colonial system tribal monographs have dwindled and have been replaced tendentially by anthropological monographs and articles that analyze religious beliefs and practices within the broader framework of whole sociocultural systems. In *Theories of Primitive Religion* (Oxford, 1965), Evans-Pritchard writes: "These recent researches in particular societies bring us nearer to the formulation of the problem of what is the part played by religion, and in general by what might be called non-scientific thought, in social life" (p. 113). In cases such as John Middleton's *Lugbara Religion* (London, 1960) and Godfrey Lienhardt's work on the Dinka, *Divinity and Experience* (Oxford, 1961), religion is the central topic; in others, such as Antonio Jorge Dias and

Origin myths, festival rituals, and oral traditions associate the indigenous peoples with Obatala, the deity (orisa) who fashions the human body.

PAGE 713

Margot Dias's four-volume *Os Macondes de Moçambique* (Lisbon, 1964-1970), it is dealt with only peripherally. In *Una societ guineana: Gli Nzema* (Turin, 1977-1978), a two-volume work, Vinigi Grottanelli discusses the Nzema of Ghana, the southernmost branch of the Akan group, who, in spite of nominal conversion to Christianity, have remained staunchly faithful to their traditional "fetishist" beliefs and cults, and I analyze through microbiographical accounts the impact of religion on everyday life.

As the general trend of scientific interests shifted from an abstract theological to a positive social and psychological context, attempts to make worldwide comparisons of religions and to ascertain the relative age of religious conceptions have gradually been abandoned, while detailed studies of specific traits, symbols, and rites are becoming more frequent. One subject, divination, has retained the attention of field anthropologists. Victor Turner's *Ndembu Divination: Its Symbolism and Techniques* (Manchester, 1961) and William R. Bascom's *Ifa Divination* (Bloomington, Ind., 1969), which examines the Yoruba of Nigeria, are the most valuable contributions in this area since Schilde's work. New knowledge has also been acquired concerning the notion of sacrifice, which is the subject of five consecutive issues of the series "Systèmes de pensée en Afrique noire" (1976-1983), published by the École Pratique des Hautes Études, Paris.

By far the most numerous and popular, though not scientifically faultless, sidelights illuminating African religions come from the domain of art history. A growing number of studies on the symbolic meaning and ceremonial use of masks, figurines, and other ritual accessories are shedding an indirect light on vital aspects of African mythology and religious rites, particularly those of West and central Africa. Dominique Zahan's *Antilopes du soleil* (Vienna, 1980), on antelope figures in the sculpture of western Sudanese peoples, is one of the finest among such books. More generally, the fifteen-volume Italian *Enciclopedia universale dell'arte* (Rome, 1958-1967; translated as *Encyclopedia of World Art*, New York, 1959-1983) devotes constant attention to the visual aspects of African religions. [*See* Iconography, *article on* Traditional African Iconography.]

Not only the traditional systems of creeds but also the syncretic, pseudo-Christian, and prophetic move-

MARCEL GRIAULE AND GERMAIN DIETERLEN
Two Insightful Investigations

Two of the contributors to Darryl Forde's *African Worlds*, the French ethnologists Marcel Griaule and Germaine Dieterlen, who jointly wrote the essay on the Dogon, deserve special mention on account of the novelty and sophistication of the cosmological and religious systems they were able to investigate and reveal. The team of Africanists led by Griaule, which included Solange de Ganay and Dieterlen, had been conducting intermittent field research for fifteen years among the Dogon of what is now Mali. One day in 1946, Griaule was unexpectedly summoned by a venerable blind sage called Ogotemmli and, in the course of a month's conversations, obtained from him the revelation of a whole mythological and cosmological system. The complexity of this system far exceeded knowledge of Dogon beliefs that had been previously acquired by the team. The ensuing book, *Dieu d'eau* (Paris, 1948), translated by Robert Redfield as *Conversations with Ogotemmêli* (London, 1965), was received in academic circles with mixed feelings of bewilderment, admiration, and perplexity. Some critics judged that it was inspired by the personal speculations of a single native thinker or, at best, that it was a summary of esoteric teachings that were restricted to a choice minority of the initiated. Griaule had foreseen such doubts and, in the preface to his book, had declared that Ogotemmêli's ontological and cosmological views were understood and shared by most adult Dogon, and that the rites connected with them were celebrated by the whole local population.

Although Dieterlen's *Essai sur la religion bambara* (Paris, 1951) revealed a comparable wealth of symbols, proclivity to abstractions, and original systematization of the universe among the Bambara, these are by no means identical to the Dogon conceptions. This distinction confirms the general fact that even neighboring tribes that share a similar cultural background and, occasionally, belong to the same ethnolinguistic family have developed and maintained independent, and often markedly different, religious systems. Dieterlen's book is also instructive as an example of a new methodology of investigation that resulted in a striking difference between her account and that published only a generation earlier in Louis Tauxier's *La religion bambara* (Paris, 1927), which was based on field data collected not merely by Tauxier but also by two other experienced Africanists, J. Henry and Charles Monteil. Aware that these discrepancies might cause either the objectivity of the various scholars or the general reliability of native informants to be questioned, Dieterlen benevolently commented on the conscientiousness of her predecessors, if not on the coherence of their reports.

— VINIGI GROTTANELLI

ments that continue to attract millions of Africans have been studied with growing attention by both missionaries and anthropologists. An impressive example of these studies is Valeer Neckebrouck's *Le peuple affligé* (Immensee, Switzerland, 1973), which includes a discussion of these movements in Kenya and neighboring countries.

The many books and articles devoted to the religions of single tribes, with their great wealth of details and depth of analysis, have made summaries of the subject a difficult task. The most popular syntheses remain Geoffrey Parrinder's *West African Religion* (London, 1949) and *African Traditional Religion* (London, 1954). In the postwar years, native Africans themselves have written similar surveys, such as E. Bolaji Idowu's *African Traditional Religion* (London, 1973) and John S. Mbiti's *African Religions and Philosophy* (New York, 1969) and *Introduction to African Religion* (London, 1975). These contributions are more valuable when restricted to the religion of the writer's own nation, such as The *Religion of the Yorubas* by J. Olumide Lucas (London, 1948). The African scholar Alexis Kagame has pursued the critical reexamination of what Tempels had termed "Bantu philosophy," displaying a wealth of references and a soundness of method that makes his work, *La philosophie bantu comparée* (Paris, 1976), not only far superior to that of his predecessor but also a stimulating encouragement to further studies in this inexhaustible field.

— VINIGI GROTTANELLI

AFRO-AMERICAN RELIGIONS

AN OVERVIEW

THE LEGACY FROM AFRICA. Separated from kin, culture, and nation, African slaves of diverse origin could not re-create their religions in North America, but they did retain the fundamental perspectives and worldviews symbolized in their religions, even as they adopted religious traditions from Europeans, Native Americans, and other Africans and combined them in new, "creole" religions. In certain countries (e.g., Haiti, Cuba, and Brazil) the African character of black religious life is still obvious.

In contrast, the influence of Africa upon black religions in North America is more subtle and more difficult to observe. Two major factors help account for this divergence in Afro-American cultures: the differences between Roman Catholic piety and Protestant piety and the differences between patterns of slave distribution in colonial America. In Roman Catholic colonies, like Haiti, Cuba, and Brazil, the cult of the saints provided slaves with a convenient structure to both cover and support their worship of the gods of Africa. In British North America this support was lacking, because Protestants condemned the veneration of saints as idolatry.

THE COLONIAL PERIOD TO THE CIVIL WAR. In British North America during the colonial period, efforts to convert the slaves to Christianity did not begin until the eighteenth century and did not prove effective until the 1740s. During that decade, a series of religious revivals led significant numbers of slaves to accept Christianity. Many more would convert during the revivals at the turn of the century.

Abolition and other social causes. The abolition of slavery was the second great issue with which the Northern black churches and clergy grappled. The most radical attacks against slavery, like those of David Walker (1785-1830) and Henry Highland Garnet (1815-1882), were couched in religious apocalyptic language. In these and other polemics, Afro-Americans began to articulate in print their theological reflections upon their history in North America. Many of the leading black abolitionists were ministers. Besides antislavery movements, they were usually involved in the major social causes of the antebellum period: temperance, moral reform, and women's rights.

Religion under slavery. In the South, Christianity gradually reached more and more slaves during the decades immediately preceding the Civil War. Some slaves attended church with whites, while others, mainly those in urban areas, belonged to separate black churches. Many held their own prayer meetings on the plantations and small farms of the South. Sometimes these prayer meetings were attended by whites; others were held in secret at risk of severe punishment.

EMANCIPATION AND RECONSTRUCTION. During the Civil War, Northern missionaries, both white and black, journeyed to the South to educate the former slaves and to make them church members. Along with material assistance, the missionaries brought schools, to which the former slaves flocked in large numbers.

TRANSITION: POST-RECONSTRUCTION TO WORLD WAR I. The period from the end of Reconstruction in 1877 to World War I was a period of tremendous transition for Afro-Americans. It was a period of the rise of white terrorism, Jim Crow laws, and the beginning of the "great migration" of rural blacks to cities in the South and North. The response of blacks to virulent racism, segregation, and urbanization was largely formulated through the churches, though increasingly voices other than those of the ministers were heard.

African religions combine principles of unity and multiplicity, transcendence and immanence, into a single system; thus they generally contain both monotheistic and polytheistic aspects.

PAGE 3

"Gods wills us free, man wills us slave, I will as God wills."

JAMES BOSWELL
JULY 26, 1763

Despite the difficulties of the period, few Afro-Americans immigrated to Africa. They did migrate on a large scale within the United States, however—northward, westward, and especially from the country to the city.

AFRO-AMERICANS IN AN URBAN SETTING. During the twentieth century, urbanization had a tremendous impact upon black culture and religion. From the familiar rural setting, with its social intimacy and traditional values, a basically peasant people was transplanted into the unfamiliar surroundings of anonymous, impersonal, urban America. Crowded into ghettos in a hostile and foreign environment, black migrants sought security in the church.

Under the guidance of socially concerned ministers, some of the larger city churches developed elaborate social programs to help the migrants and other residents of the growing ghettos. The migrants themselves attempted to re-create the closeness of the small rural church by establishing new churches, usually in homes or rented storefronts. The house church and storefront church became familiar sites in urban black communities. In these new church structures, a new religious movement, Holiness-Pentecostalism, took root, though it was in fact a return to the emotionalism and ecstasy of the old-time religion that had waned in many Baptist and Methodist churches.

Urbanization also brought more black people than ever before into contact with Roman Catholicism. Through the mechanism of the parochial school, American blacks came to convert to Roman Catholicism in large numbers for the first time.

The most popular movement, however, was that of Marcus Garvey (1887-1940), a West Indian black whose Universal Negro Improvement Association (founded in 1914) united interest in Africa as a black Zion with the assertion of black racial pride. The association was itself a quasi-religious organization, with its own hymns, sermons, catechism, and baptismal service. At the same time, it enlisted widespread support among black ministers of various denominations.

CIVIL RIGHTS AND BLACK POWER. As the movement for civil rights grew in the 1950s and 1960s, the black churches as the historic centers of social and political organization within the black community assumed leadership. But the involvement of particular congregations or individual ministers did not exhaust the participation of black religion in the movement. For many blacks, the movement itself was a religious movement, and they consciously drew upon the spiri-

MARTIN LUTHER KING, JR.

"I Have a Dream"

KING, MARTIN LUTHER, JR. (1929-1968), Baptist minister and civil rights leader. The son and grandson of Baptist preachers, Martin Luther King, Jr., was born into a middle-class black family in Atlanta, Georgia. As an adolescent, King grew concerned about racial and economic inequality in American society. Sociology classes at Morehouse College taught him to view racism and poverty as related aspects of social evil, and reading Henry David Thoreau's essay "Civil Disobedience" (1849) convinced him that resistance to an unjust system was a moral duty. At Morehouse, King decided to become a minister, and after graduation he enrolled at Crozier Theological Seminary to study divinity. There he acquired from Walter Rauschenbusch's *Christianity and the Social Crisis* (1907) the conviction that the Christian churches have an obligation to work for social justice. In Mohandas Gandhi's practice of nonviolent resistance he discovered a tactic for transforming Christian love from a merely personal to a social ethic.

King's interest in theology, philosophy, and social ethics led him to enter the graduate program at Boston University School of Theology, where he earned a Ph. D. degree and developed his own philosophical position based upon the tenet that "only personality—finite and infinite—is ultimately real." In Boston, he met and courted Coretta Scott, and in 1953 they were wed. A year later, King accepted a call to be pastor of Dexter Avenue Baptist Church in Montgomery, Alabama. Chosen by E. D. Nixon, president of the Montgomery National Association for the Advancement of Colored People, to lead a boycott of the city's segregated buses, he gained national recognition when the boycott resulted in a Supreme Court decision that declared laws requiring segregated seating on buses unconstitutional.

Following the Montgomery bus boycott, King founded the Southern Christian Leadership Conference (SCLC) to coordinate scattered civil rights activities and local organizations. Operating primarily through the black churches, the SCLC mounted successive attacks against segregation in the early 1960s. For his nonviolent activism, he received the Nobel Peace Prize in 1964.

While organizing a "poor people's campaign" to persuade Congress to take action on poverty, King accepted an invitation to participate in marches for striking sanitation workers in Memphis, Tennessee. There, on 4 April 1968, he was assassinated. Considered a modern prophet by many, King ranks with Gandhi as a major ethical leader of the twentieth century.

— ALBERT J. RABOTEAU

tual resonance of hymns, sermons, and biblical imagery to move the conscience of the nation. The classic example of the religious dimension of the civil rights struggle was the leadership of Baptist minister Martin Luther King, Jr. King's career and, in a different way, that of Malcolm X (Malcolm Little, 1925-1965), demonstrated the religious nature of the struggle for equality.

— ALBERT J. RABOTEAU

MUSLIM MOVEMENTS

MOORISH SCIENCE. In the late nineteenth century, black intellectuals became increasingly critical of white Christians for supporting racial segregation in America and colonialism in Africa. Europeans and Americans, they charged, were in danger of turning Christianity into a "white man's religion." After the turn of the century, Timothy Drew (1886-1929), a black delivery man from North Carolina, began teaching that Christianity was a religion for whites. The true religion of black people, he announced, was Islam. In 1913, the Noble Drew Ali, as his followers called him, founded the first

MARCUS GARVEY

The Universal Negro Improvement Association (founded by Garvey in 1914) was a great source of racial pride, proclaiming Africa as a black Zion.

UNDERWOOD & UNDERWOOD/ CORBIS-BETTMAN

MALCOLM X
Ex-smoker, Ex-drinker, Ex-Christian, Ex-slave

MALCOLM X (1925-1965), American Black Muslim leader, born Malcolm Little on 19 May 1925 in Omaha, Nebraska. His father, the Reverend Earl Little, a follower of Marcus Garvey and a Baptist minister, died when Malcolm was six years old, and his mother, the sole support of nine children, was later committed to an insane asylum. Malcolm attended school in East Lansing, Michigan, dropped out in the eighth grade, and then moved to live with an older sister in the Roxbury section of Boston. An unemployed street hustler, he was the leader of an interracial gang of thieves in Roxbury. During his prison years (1946-1952), he underwent the first of his two conversion experiences when he converted to the Nation of Islam led by Elijah Muhammad. Following the tradition of the Nation of Islam, he replaced his surname with an X, symbolizing what he had been and what he had become: "Ex-smoker. Ex-drinker. Ex-Christian. Ex-slave."

An articulate public speaker, charismatic personality, and indefatigable organizer, Malcolm X expressed the rage and anger of the black masses during the major phase of the civil rights movement from 1956 to 1965. He organized Muslim temples throughout the country and founded the newspaper *Muhammad Speaks* in the basement of his home. He articulated the Nation of Islam's beliefs in racial separation, rose rapidly through the ranks to become minister of Boston Temple No. 11. He was later rewarded with the post of minister of Temple No. 7 in Harlem, the largest and most prestigious temple of the Nation of Islam after the Chicago headquarters. Recognizing Malcolm's talents and abilities, Elijah Muhammad also named him "national representative" of the Nation of Islam, second in rank to Elijah Muhammad himself.

In 1963, after his public comments on President John F. Kennedy's assassination, Malcolm X was ordered by Elijah Muhammad to undergo a period of silence, an order that reflected the deep tensions and disputes among Black Muslim leaders. In March 1964, Malcolm left the Nation of Islam and founded his own Muslim Mosque, Inc. During his pilgrimage to Mecca that same year, he experienced a second conversion, embraced the orthodox universal brotherhood of Sunni Islam, and adopted the Muslim name el-Hajj Malik el-Shabazz. He then renounced the separatist beliefs of the Nation of Islam. In 1965, he founded the Organization for Afro-American Unity as a political vehicle to internationalize the plight of black Americans, to make common cause with Third World nations, and to move from civil rights to human rights. On 21 February 1965, Malcolm X was assassinated while delivering a lecture at the Audubon Ballroom in Harlem.

— LAWRENCE H. MAMIYA

There is also in the United States a significant phenomenon of conversion to Islam among local blacks, originating in the social protest movement against white ascendancy.

PAGE 340

Moorish Science Temple in Newark, New Jersey. Though heretical in the view of orthodox Muslims, the Moorish Science Temple was the first organization to spread awareness of Islam as an alternative to Christianity among black Americans.

NATION OF ISLAM. In 1930, a peddler named Wallace D. Fard (later known as Walli Farrad, Professor Ford, Farrad Mohammed, and numerous other aliases) appeared in the black community of Detroit. Fard claimed that he had come from Mecca to reveal to black Americans their true identity as Muslims of the "lost-found tribe of Shabbazz." Like the Noble Drew Ali, Fard taught that salvation for black people lay in self-knowledge. In 1934, Fard disappeared as mysteriously as he had come. The leadership of the Nation of Islam was taken up by Fard's chief minister, Elijah Poole (1897-1975), a black laborer from Georgia, whom Fard had renamed Elijah Muhammad.

Elijah Muhammad announced to the members of the Nation that Wallace D. Fard was actually the incarnation of Allah and that he, Elijah, was his messenger. For the next forty years, he was regarded as such by his followers, who came to be known as the Black Muslims. According to the teachings of Messenger Muhammad, as he was called, humankind was originally black, until an evil scientist created a race of white people through genetic engineering. The whites he created turned out to be devils.

In the 1950s, Malcolm Little (1925-1965), who had converted to the Nation of Islam in prison, rose to prominence as chief spokesman for Elijah Muhammad. As Malcolm X he became one of the most articulate critics of racial injustice in the country during the civil rights period. Rejecting the nonviolent approach of Martin Luther King, Jr., he argued that separatism and self-determination were necessary if blacks were to achieve full equality. Breaking with Elijah Muhammad, he founded his own organization, the Muslim Mosque, Inc., in New York City. Shortly thereafter, he was assassinated. The life and death of Malcolm X helped to increase interest in Islam among black Americans.

In 1975, Elijah Muhammad died, and his son Warithuddin (Wallace Deen) Muhammad succeeded to the leadership of the Nation of Islam. Under the leadership of Minister Louis Farrakhan, this faction has broken with the American Muslim Mission, returned to the original teachings and ideals of Elijah Muhammad, and readopted the old name, the Nation of Islam.

— ALBERT J. RABOTEAU

ALCHEMY

AN OVERVIEW

The vocable *alchemia* appears in the West from the twelfth century onward in reference to the medieval

MILLION MAN MARCH

In October 1995, The Nation of Islam co-sponsored this day of "atonement and reconciliation" which called for men to take responsibility for their own lives and families.

JACQUES M. CHENET/CORBIS

quest for a means of transmuting base metals into gold, for a universal cure, and for the "elixir of immortality." In Chinese, Indian, and Greek texts alchemy is referred to as "the Art," or by terms indicating radical and beneficial change, for example, *transmutation*. Until quite recently, historians of science have studied alchemy as a protochemistry, that is, an embryonic science. But the alchemist's quest was not scientific but spiritual.

ESOTERIC TRADITIONS AND THE IMPORTANCE OF SECRECY. In every culture where alchemy has flourished, it has always been intimately related to an esoteric or "mystical" tradition: in China to Taoism, in India to Yoga and Tantrism, in Hellenistic Egypt to *gnosis*, in Islamic countries to Hermetic and esoteric mystical schools, in the Western Middle Ages and Renaissance to Hermetism, Christian and sectarian mysticism, and Qabbalah.

For this reason, great emphasis is placed by the alchemist on secrecy, that is, the esoteric transmission of alchemical doctrines and techniques. The oldest Hellenistic text, *Physike kai mystike* (probably written around 200 BCE), relates how this book was discovered hidden in a column of an Egyptian temple.

It is significant that the injunction to secrecy and occultation is not abolished by the successful accomplishment of the alchemical work. According to Ko Hung, the adepts who obtain the elixir and become "immortals" *(hsien)* continue to wander on earth, but they conceal their condition, that is, their immortality, and are recognized as such only by a few fellow alchemists. Likewise, in India there is a vast literature, both in Sanskrit and in the vernaculars, in relation to certain famous *siddhis*, yogin-alchemists who live for centuries but who seldom disclose their identity. One encounters the same belief in central and western Europe.

ORIGINS OF ALCHEMY. The objects of the alchemical quest, namely, health and longevity, transmutation of base metals into gold, production of the elixir of immortality—have a long prehistory in the East as well as in the West. But the central aim of the alchemist was the transformation of ordinary metals into gold. This "noble" metal was imbued with sacrality.

MINING, METALLURGY, AND ALCHEMY. Even if the historical beginnings of alchemy are as yet obscure, parallels between certain alchemical beliefs and rituals and those of early miners and metallurgists are clear. Indeed, all these techniques reflect the idea that man can influence the temporal flux. Mineral substances, hidden in the womb of Mother Earth, shared in the sacredness attached to the goddess. Very early we are confronted with the idea that ores "grow" in the belly of the earth after the manner of embryos. Metallurgy thus takes on the character of obstetrics.

With the help of fire, metalworkers transform the ores (the "embryos") into metals (the "adults"). The underlying belief is that, given enough time, the ores would have become "pure" metals in the womb of Mother Earth. Further, the "pure" metals would have become gold if they had been allowed to "grow" undisturbed for a few more millennia.

THE ALCHEMIST COMPLETES THE WORK OF NATURE. The transmutation of base metals into gold is tantamount to a miraculously rapid maturation. As Simone da Colonia put it: "This Art teaches us to make a remedy called the Elixir, which, being poured on imperfect metals, perfects them completely, and it is for this reason that it was invented" (quoted in Eliade, 1978, p. 166).

Moreover, the elixir is said to be capable of accelerating the temporal rhythm of all organisms and thus of quickening their growth. It was said to cure all maladies, to restore youth to the old, and to prolong life by several centuries.

ALCHEMY AND MASTERY OF TIME. Thus it seems that the central secret of "the Art" is related to the alchemist's mastery of cosmic and human time. Their elixir was reputed to heal and to rejuvenate men as well, indefinitely prolonging their lives. In the alchemist's eyes, man is *creative:* he redeems nature, masters time; in sum, he perfects God's creation.

— MIRCEA ELIADE

As a religion of salvation, [Taoism] had to offer an afterlife: the human being was thought to have many souls, but only one body for them to live in.

PAGE 316

CHINESE ALCHEMY

Alchemy began in close alignment with popular religion, especially among educated groups in the Yangtze region. It was considered one of several disciplines that could lead to individual spiritual perfection and immortality. Some Taoist movements took up its practice after about 500 CE; it influenced both Buddhist and Taoist symbolism and liturgy.

AIMS AND MEANS. Chinese ideals of individual perfection combined three ideas that would have been incompatible in Egypt or Persia. The desire for immortality, which long preceded formal philosophy or religion, was the first of these ideas. [*See* Immortality.] In popular culture ideals of long life evolved into the notion that life need not end. This was not immortality of the soul in isolation, but immortality of the personality of all that selfhood implied within an imperishable physical body.

The potent personal force that may linger on after someone dies was undifferentiated in the thought of the uneducated, but in the conceptions of specialists it was separated into ten "souls" (three *yang hun* and seven *yin p'o*). Their normal postmortem dissipation could be prevented only if the body, their common site, could be made to survive with them. That, as Lu Gweidjen and Joseph Needham have suggested, is why Chinese immortality was bound to be material.

"Man is a witness unto his deeds."

QUR'AN 75:14

A second implication of immortality was perfection of the spirit. Because there was no dichotomy between the spiritual and the somatic, the refining of the body was not distinct from the activity of spiritual self-cultivation. Immortality was salvation from decrepitude and death. Piety, ritual, morality, and hygiene were equally essential to the prolongation of life.

A third implication of immortality, alongside spiritual and physical perfection, was assumption into a divine hierarchy. In popular thought this hierarchy was bureaucratic, a mirror of the temporal order. In fact, the bureaucratic ideal—of a symmetrical organization in which power and responsibility belonged to the post, and only temporarily to the individual who filled it—evolved more or less simultaneously in politics and religion.

The Han emperor Wu (140-87 BCE) devoted much effort to attaining immortality, as had his Ch'in predecessor.

PAGE 136

HISTORY. Whether alchemy originated earlier in Hellenistic Egypt or China remains uncertain. Cinnabar and similar blood-colored compounds have been connected with ideas of death and immortality since the Neolithic period; that is how most scholars interpret the archaic custom of sprinkling red powders on corpses to be buried. The splendidly preserved corpse of the Lady of Tai (or Dai; died shortly after 168 BCE, excavated 1972) contained high concentrations of mercury and lead. These elements were distributed in a way consistent with ingestion before death. Traces in the intestines include native cinnabar, frequently prescribed by physicians as an immortality drug, rather than an artificial elixir. An edict dated 144 BCE against falsifying gold is sometimes said to show the prevalence of alchemy, but it presents no evidence that anything more was involved than artisans' use of alloys. In 133 BCE the Martial Emperor was told by an occultist that eating from plates of artificial gold would lengthen his life so that he could seek out certain immortals and, with their help, become an immortal himself by performing certain rituals.

ALCHEMY, SCIENCE, AND RELIGION. Alchemy has been studied mainly by historians of chemistry, who have shown that the Chinese art exploited the properties of many chemical substances and even incorporated considerable knowledge of quantitative relations. Scholars of medical history have demonstrated close connections between alchemy and medicine, in the substances and processes on which both drew and in the use of artificial, mainly inorganic "elixirs" by physicians to treat disease and lengthen life. Historians have tended to see alchemy as a fledgling science, a precursor of modern inorganic chemistry and iatrochemistry.

This view overlooks the fact that the goals of alchemy were not cognitive. They were consistently focused on immortality and largely concerned with reenacting cosmic process for purposes of contemplation. It is impossible to say with certainty that alchemists discovered any new chemical interaction or process. Since alchemists were literate and craftsmen were not, it is only to be expected that innovations by the latter would be first recorded by the former (who were almost the only members of the elite greatly interested in the chemical arts).

The idea that alchemy is Taoist by nature, or was invented by Taoists, has not survived advances since about 1970 in historical studies of Taoism. In the Celestial Master sect and other early Taoist movements drugs (including artificial preparations) were forbidden; only religious exercises could procure health and divine status. Upper-class initiates gradually began to use fashionable immortality drugs in the north. As refugees after the fall of Lo-yang in 311 they encountered elixirs in the Yangtze region, where alchemy had long been established among popular immortality practices. The aristocratic southerners they displaced in positions of temporal power invented new religious structures to assert, by way of compensation, their spiritual superiority. Michel Strickmann (1979) has demonstrated that in doing so they adapted northern Taoist usages to local popular practices, in which immortality and alchemy were central, and in which the religious use of inorganic drugs was usual. T'ao Hung-ching, a man of noble southern antecedents, drew on revelations inherited from fourth-century predecessors when he founded the Supreme Purity (or Mao-shan) Taoist movement under imperial patronage in about 500. T'ao adapted not only old southern techniques but elaborate structures of alchemical and astral imagery. T'ao thus formed a movement that captured upper-class allegiance, supported state power, and was supported in return for more than five centuries. He united alchemy with Taoism—the particular Taoism that he created—for the first time.

— NATHAN SIVIN

INDIAN ALCHEMY

"Gold is immortality." This correspondence from the Brahmanas grounds the worldview of the Indian alchemist. Just as gold neither corrodes nor loses its brilliance with time, so too the human body may realize a perfect and immutable state. In Indian alchemy, this is accomplished through *rasayana*, "the way of *rasa*" (i. e., of essences), which is the Sanskrit term for the alchemist's craft.

There are early references to chemical and metallurgical alchemical processes in the *Arthasastra*, the *Susruta Samhita*, and the so-called Bower manuscript. But the Indian alchemical tradition proper did not begin until these processes were correlated with techniques and goals of perfecting the body. The

Indian alchemist's cosmology and metaphysics have their roots in the "emanationism" and microcosm-macrocosm analogues of Samkhya philosophy, of the yogic Upanisads, and of Vedanta. According to these philosophies, everything that exists is an emanation or emission (*vyapana* or *srsti*) from an original source or essence. It is destined for reabsorption (*laya* or *pralaya*) into the same. The emanated universe is hierarchical in structure. At the top of the hierarchy is the Absolute, which is variously conceived as Purusa, Prakrti, *brahman*, or a union of Siva and Sakti. Emanation proceeds down from the Absolute into the manifested world of the five sentient qualities, the senses, and the elements. Here the elements are conceived as stages rather than substances. The process of reintegration conceptually entails the stripping away of sheaths of ultimately illusory form in order to reveal a true and perfect essence.

Because it emphasizes the use of mercury and drugs in transmutation and in the realization of a perfect (*siddha*) and immortal body, Hindu alchemy is also known as mercurial (*dhatuvada*) alchemy, in contrast to Buddhist *rasayana*. The Buddhist yogic and Hindu chemical approaches often overlap, however, and one finds elements of both in the Nath, Siddha, Sahajiya, and Vajrayana Tantric traditions. The flowering of alchemical thought and practice was contemporaneous with that of Tantra, spanning roughly the sixth to the fifteenth centuries CE. Indian alchemists were often characterized as *siddhas* whose metaphysics and techniques at once embraced alchemy, yoga, and Tantra.

The Hindu mercurial alchemist's laboratory is portrayed as a microcosm of the universe. Just as the gross elements of the manifested world ultimately return to the Absolute according to Vedantic philosophy, here the alchemist attempts to effect an analogous reintegration by using physical substances. He makes use of plant, animal, and mineral substances to remount the hierarchy of metals: lead, tin, copper, silver, and gold. The most essential elements that he employs are mercury (*rasa* or *parada*) and sulphur (*gandhaka*). In Hindu alchemy these elements are conceived as the seed (*bija* or *bindu*) of the male Siva and the sexual essence or blood (*sonita* or *rajas*) of the female Sakti, respectively.

According to Indian alchemy, yoga, and Tantra, every substance and combination of elements in the universe has its sexual valence. In the Hindu Tantric worldview, the manifest world is the emanation of the eternal union of *Siva* and *Sakti*. Their sexual essences, of which mercury and sulphur are hierophanies, are the means for reintegrating and perfecting the world. The alchemical *samskaras* are described in highly evocative language: mercury pierces or penetrates (*vedhana*) sulphur in order that it may be killed (*mrta*) and be "reborn" into a purer, more stable state (*bandha*) where it has a greater capacity for transmuting other elements. In the transmutation process mercury penetrates base metals. They are "killed" and "reborn" into increasingly higher states in the hierarchy of metals until finally perfect alchemical gold emerges from the sloughed-off sheaths of its grosser stages. The language of these samskaras is simultaneously one of initiation (as *diksa*), sexuality, and rebirth. The alchemist's craft is conceived of as a spiritual exercise, a ritual, a sacrifice, an act of devotion, and a participation in the divine play of an expanding or contracting universe. It is in such a context that we may best understand immortality as the ultimate goal of mercurial alchemy. In the alchemical universe, mercury (i. e., *Siva's* seed or *bija*) is capable of purifying and perfecting the human body in the same way that it perfects metallic "bodies."

— DAVID WHITE

HELLENISTIC AND MEDIEVAL ALCHEMY

By the beginning of the Christian era, a change in secular and religious attitudes can be discerned. The rationalism that had guided the thinking of the elite in previous times waned, and the rise of skepticism and loss of direction led to a philosophical vacuum that stimulated a recourse to mystic intuition and divine mysteries. The area of the Roman empire in which this process became primarily manifest was Egypt, where, after the conquest by Alexander the Great (in 332 BCE), the culture of Hellenism with its fusion of Greek and Eastern features was centered. The fashionable mystery beliefs subsumed under the names of gnosticism and Hermetism exerted a strong attraction for practitioners of the occult sciences (astrology, magic, and medicine) as well as alchemy, the art of making gold: previously, men of science had by thought process and investigations obtained what they now expected to receive through divine revelation or supernatural inspiration. In short, science as revealed knowledge and, for the alchemist, as a means of creating gold, turned into religion.

Such a link between alchemy and gnosticism and Hermetism is most tangibly documented in the occult literature of Hellenistic Egypt from about the second to the fourth century. This emphasizes, first, the fact that alchemy, beyond being a craft devoted to changing matter, also has a place within the history of religions and, second, that in the alchemist's religious beliefs the general gnostic tenets blended with his specific alchemical approach to the world.

DOCTRINE. The soul is enchained in matter and is to be freed. Science as traditionally expounded in the schools was unable to liberate it. Only gnosis, the

"Gold is immortality."

BRAHMANAS

Alchemy flourished at Alexandria until the seventh century.

PAGE 533

Among the Taoist techniques of immortality, alchemy is perhaps the most significant.

PAGE 657

knowledge of God, could accomplish the task, and to convey gnosis, alchemy transformed itself into an esoteric religion. The doctrines of alchemy as a religion echoed the principles of alchemy as a science. These were essentially three: primal matter, sympathy, and transmutation.

Primal matter. The *opus alchimicum*, ("the alchemist's labor") centered on matter. Nobody knew, of course, what matter was, and it remained a secret of alchemy, although many chemical, mythological, and philosophical definitions were ventured in the course of time (Jung, 1953, p. 317). Thus, the *Tabula Smaragdina* (the revelation of secret alchemical teaching, of the ninth century but based on Hermetic sources) identified matter with God, because all created objects come from a single primal matter; and Comarius, an alchemist-philosopher (first century CE?) identified it with Hades, to whom the imperfect souls were chained (Jung, pp. 299, 319). Such perceptions of matter echo the alchemist's craft: his operation was, in mythical terms, a replica of divine creativity, aiming at the liberation of imprisoned matter.

Sympathy. The anthropomorphic perception of matter that assigned to the metal a human soul correlated with an occult system according to which the supposed affinity between substances expressed itself in a mutual attraction or rejection, that is, either "sympathy" or "antipathy." Such a bond linked, in particular, our world "below" to the world "above," the microcosm of man to the macrocosm of plantetary divinities. The system of correspondences elaborated, for example, by the second-century astrologer Antiochus of Athens (Sheppard, *Ambix 7,* p. 46) embraced, in addition to "above" and "below," also elements, metals, and colors:

COLOR	ELEMENT	METAL	MACROCOSM	MICROCOSM
black	earth	lead	Saturn	body
white	water	silver	Moon	spirit
yellow	fire	gold	Sun	soul

Already Maria Prophetissa (fl. early third century), also known as the "founding mother of alchemy," heralded the principle of parellelism: "Just as man results [from the association] of liquids, of solids, and of spirit, so does copper." Zosimos of Panopolis in Egypt (fl. c. 300), recognizing the identity between the behavior of matter and the events in his own (unconscious) psyche, condensed this complex insight into the formula "What is within is also without."

Transmutation. The third facet of alchemical religiosity was also linked to the alchemist's practice. A basic alchemical tenet stated that all substances could be derived through transmutation from primal matter. The technique of change consisted essentially in "coloring": the Egyptian alchemists did not intend to "make" gold but to color (*baptein*) metals and textiles through tinctures and elixirs so that they would "appear" like gold (or silver or some other metal). A "changed" metal, then, was a "new" metal. The technique of coloring evolved, in the end, into a powerful symbol of alchemical doctrine; for just as the alchemist transformed lead into silver, and silver into gold, so too he posited for matter, in his anthropomorphic view of it, a similar change, from body to spirit to soul. And in the frame of his doctrine, he identified this escalation with the renewal of man, to which he assigned the same chain of transmutations to reach the goal of redemption.

The mystagogues. The myth of transmission added the religious component to alchemical mysticism. The spokesmen invoked the authority of the supreme being, or its prophets, or the sages of old: "Behold [says Isis to her son as alchemist], the mystery has been revealed to you!" (Festugière, 1950, p. 260). Maria Prophetissa claimed that alchemical secrets were revealed to her by God. The Byzantine monk Marianus quoted alchemists saying to Maria: "The divine, hidden, and always splendid, secret is revealed to you."

With Egypt providing the setting of the cult, Egyptian mythical figures and divinities were the prime well-spring of inspiration: chiefly Thoth (hellenized as Hermes Trismegistos), the legendary author of the Hermetica, and Isis, turned into the creators and teachers of alchemy to whom alchemical sayings and doctrines were attributed. Various Greek writings on alchemy that contained traces of Jewish monotheism were ascribed to Moses, probably in a homonymic transfer from the alchemist Moses of Alexandria. Later on, Jewish alchemical tradition evoked Enoch, the Jewish counterpart to Hermes.

Symbols. The alchemist, in the formulation of Wayne Shuhmaker, "did not analyze but analogized," and his own universe, metallurgy, provided the mythical imagery and stimulated new meanings. The alchemical *opus* centered on the change of matter, and transmutation of matter became the recurrent theme of the alchemist's cult. To him, the soul imprisoned in matter symbolized the spirit striving to purify itself from the roughage of the flesh. Matter was represented above all by metal and symbolized life and man, its growth comparable to the growth of the fetus.

Many lexical items were drawn into the process: thus, in the Valentinian system of gnosticism (deriving from the second-century Egyptian Valentinus), metallurgical terms such as the following symbolized spiritual concepts. Pneuma signified, first, the product of natural sublimation, then, "divine spirit"; ebullient ("boiling up"), referring to the alchemical process of "separating the pure from the impure," was applied to wisdom; sperma (the "embryonic germ") yielded the "seed" of gnosis; in a similar way, such terms as *refine*, *filter*, and *purify* acquired spiritualized meanings. The transfer, through alchemy, from the literal to the symbolic realm contributed richly to the language of religion and, generally, abstraction. It indicates a conscious effort of the alchemist to frame his views in the terms of his craft.

Antonyms. Hellenistic alchemy tended to emphasize the varied contraries inherent in the craft: hot/cold, moist/dry, earth/air, fire/water. Antonymic structure was symbolically superimposed on matter: Maria Prophetissa distinguished metals as male and female as if they were human, and Zosimos distinguished between the metals' souls and bodies. The same antonymy, but with the focus on man himself, characterizes gnostic dualism with its model of spiritual versus carnal man.

Classical philosophy. The great cognitions of the classical tradition, from the pre-Socratics to Plato, Aristotle, and the Stoics, resurfaced in eclectic Hellenistic philosophy. Numerous doctrines prefigured crucial phases of the alchemical worldview: the concept of a primal matter; the unity of matter (seen in, say, water or fire); cosmic correspondences; the affinity of the similar; the microcosm reflecting the macrocosm; the notion of sympathy; transformation through *pneuma*, the all pervading spirit; genesis, that is, the origin of one element from another, proceding by way of opposites.

Mystery creeds. Hermetism and the alchemical cult overlap in various features. The tie between them is substantiated in the writings of Zosimos, the "divine," the "highly learned," and the outstanding representative of both creeds. The common ground consisted of "mystic reveries" (Festugière): observation and inquiry were rejected, and intuition replaced science; the "sacred craft" was revealed through divine grace; the chosen were few, bound to secrecy; and the goal was the liberation of the soul from the body.

Convergence. These four components of spiritual alchemy can be traced in Hellenistic Egypt. The craft of the goldsmith was flourishing, and metallurgy yielded the imagery while boosting, by its very nature, the identification, ever present in the human mind, of self and matter; Greek philosophy, in a stage of revival then and there, provided the basic concepts of the doctrine; and Hermetism supplied the vital climate of mystery.

Alchemy is described here as a facet of the ancient mystery religions, and this description centers on its style and manifestations in the Hellenistic period. But other cultures, tending in a similar direction, produced other varieties of spiritual alchemy. The relationship (involving the question of polygenesis or monogenesis) between the Chinese, Indian, and Hellenic forms of spiritual alchemy is not very clear. Islamic culture, on the other hand, played a vital role in the transmission of alchemical knowledge; many of the Greek texts were translated into Arabic and through this link, reached the West during the late Middle Ages. Thus, the transmutation of matter continued, with its occult framework, into the Renaissance and beyond.

[*See also* Gnosticism.]

— HENRY AND RENÉE KAHANE

ISLAMIC ALCHEMY

The Arabic term for alchemy is *al-kimiya'*. The word *kimiya'* is alternately derived from the Greek *chumeia* (or *chemeia*), denoting the "art of transmutation," or from *kimiya*, a South Chinese term meaning "gold-making juice."

In the Islamic context, *al-kimiya'* refers to the "art" of transmuting substances, both material and spiritual, to their highest form of perfection. The word *kimiya'* also refers to the agent or catalyst that effects the transmutation and hence is used as a synonym for *al-iksir* ("elixir") and *hajar al-falasifah* ("philosopher's stone"). The search for the ideal elixir has been an ancient quest in many cultures of the world; it was supposed to transform metals to their most perfect form (gold) and minerals to their best potency and, if the correct elixir were to be found, to achieve immortality. All matter of a particular type, metals for example, were supposed to consist of the same elements. The correct *kimiya'* or *iksir* would enable the transposition of the elements into ideal proportions and cause the metal concerned to be changed from a base form to a perfected form, for instance, copper to gold.

> *"The Divine, hidden, and always splendid, secret is revealed to you."*
>
> MARIANUS

HISTORICAL BACKGROUND. In Muslim tradition, alchemy enjoys ancient roots. The cultivation of alchemy is traced back to Adam, followed by most of the major prophets and sages. This chain of transmission is then connected to the "masters" from the ancient world, including Aristotle, Galen, Socrates, Plato, and others. Muslims are considered to have received the art from these masters. In Islamic times, the prophet Muhammad (d. 632 CE), is said to have endorsed the art, lending it grace and power.

The Jabirian corpus. Modern scholarship places the development of Islamic alchemy in the ninth century. Jabir ibn Hayyan is indeed recorded as the first major alchemist, but the writings attributed to him are mainly pseudepigraphical, and many appeared as late as the tenth century. *The Book of Mercy, the Book of the Balances*, the *Book of One Hundred and Twelve*, the *Seventy Books*, and the *Five Hundred Books* are some of the important works in the collection. Movements such as the Ikhwan al-Safa' (Brethren of Purity) probably influenced or even contributed to some of the treatises in the Jabirian corpus, which forms an important source of information on alchemic techniques, equipment, materials, and attitudes.

According to the sulfur-mercury theory of metals introduced in the corpus, all metals were considered to possess these two elements, or the two principles they represent, in varying proportions, the combination of which lends each metal its peculiarities. Sulfur was responsible for the hot/dry features and mercury, the cold/moist ones. (Aristotle considered these four features to be represented by fire, earth, air, and water respectively.) Sulfur and mercury embody the positive and negative aspects of matter, also referred to as male and female properties.

OPPOSITION TO THE ART. Although widespread, alchemy did not have the approval of all Muslim scholars. Thus Ibn Sina (d. 1035) censured it as a futile activity and contested the assertion that man is able to imitate nature. The great North African historian Ibn Khaldun (d. 1406) also made a critical assessment of Arab-Islamic alchemical activities. He characterized alchemy as the study of the properties, virtues, and temperatures of the elements used for the preparation of and search for an elixir that could transform lesser metals into gold. Ibn Khaldun rejected the alchemists' claims that their transmutations were intended to perfect the work of nature by mechanical and technical procedures.

— HABIBEH RAHIM

Alchemy flourished at Alexandria until the seventh century.

PAGE 533

AL-RAZI
The Secret of Secrets

The physician and philosopher Muhammad ibn Zakariya' al-Razi (d. 925) followed Jabiribn Hayyan and made a major impact on the art. To the sulfur-mercury theory of the constitution of metals he added the attribute of salinity. The popular conception of alchemy with three elements—sulfur, mercury, and salt—reappeared in Europe and played an important role in Western alchemy. According to al-Razi, bodies were composed of invisible elements (atoms) and of empty space that lay between them. These atoms were eternal and possessed a certain size. This conception seems close to the explanation of the structure of matter in modern physics. Al-Razi's books, *Sirr al asrar* (The Secret of Secrets) and *Madkhal al-ta'limi* (Instructive [or Practical] Introduction), are important sources for understanding the principles and techniques of alchemy as practiced in the tenth-century Muslim world, specifically Iran. In them, he provides a systematic classification of carefully observed and verified facts regarding chemical substances, reactions, and apparatus, described in language that is free of mysticism and ambiguity.

— HABIBEH RAHIM

RENAISSANCE ALCHEMY

The Renaissance and post-Renaissance period marked both the high point and the turning point of alchemy in the West. During the same years in which Kepler, Galileo, Descartes, Boyle, and Newton wrote their revolutionary scientific works, more alchemical texts were published than ever before. But under the impact first of the Reformation and later of the seventeenth-century scientific revolution, alchemy was profoundly changed and ultimately discredited. The organic, qualitative theories of the alchemists were replaced by an atomistic, mechanical model of change, which eventually undermined the alchemical theory of transmutation. The balance between the spiritual and the physical, which had characterized alchemical thought throughout its long history, was shattered, and alchemy was split into two halves, theosophy and the practical laboratory science of chemistry.

THE PRACTICE OF ALCHEMY. For the most part Renaissance alchemists accepted the theories and practices of their ancient and medieval predecessors. By the time the study of alchemy came to Europe, it was already an established discipline with a respected past. The theories upon which it was based were an integral part of ancient philosophy. Western scientists accepted these theories precisely because they provided plausible explanations for the way events were observed to occur in nature and the laboratory.

ALCHEMY AS A SPIRITUAL DISCIPLINE. Mystery and religion, which were a part of alchemy from its beginnings, gained in importance from the Renaissance onward. In many cases alchemy moved out of the laboratory altogether and into the monk's cell or philosopher's study. The popularity of alchemy as a spiritual discipline coincided with the breakdown of religious orthodoxy and social organization during the Renaissance and the Reformation.

The interpretation of alchemy as a spiritual discipline offended many churchmen, who viewed the combination of alchemical concepts and Christian dogma in the writings of spiritual alchemists as dangerous heresy. One of the most daring appropriations of Christian symbolism was made by Nicholas Melchior of Hermanstadt, who expounded the alchemical work in the form of a mass.

Alchemists of the sixteenth and seventeenth centuries drew many of their ideas from Renaissance Neoplatonism and Hermetism. In all three systems, the world was seen as a single organism penetrated by spiritual forces that worked at all levels, the vegetable, animal, human, and spiritual. Frances Yates has brillantly described the "magus" mentality that evolved from these ideas and encouraged men to believe they could understand and control their environment. This state of mind is illustrated in the writings of Paracelsus (1493-1541). For Paracelsus, God was the divine alchemist, who created the world by calcinating, congealing, distilling, and sublimating the elements of chaos. Chemistry was the key to the universe, which would disclose the secrets of theology, physics, and medicine. The alchemist had only to read the reactions in his laboratory on a grand scale to fathom the mysteries of creation.

RENAISSANCE ALCHEMY AND MODERN SCIENCE. No one knows who wrote the Rosicrucian manifestos. They have been attributed to Johann Valentin Andrea (1586-1654), whose acknowledged writings contain a similar blend of utopianism and spiritual alchemy. In his most famous work, *Christianopolis*, Andrea describes an ideal society organized to promote the health, education, and welfare of its citizens. One of the institutions in this society is a "laboratory" dedicated to the investigation of nature and to the application of useful discoveries for the public good.

Francis Bacon (1561-1626) was one of the many philosophers influenced by the Rosicrucian manifestos. Bacon looked forward to what he called a "Great Instauration" of learning that would herald the return of the Golden Age. He described this in his own utopia, *The New Atlantis*.

Neither Andrea nor Bacon said much that was new or significant in terms of science. What was novel in their visions was the idea of a scientific institution whose members worked by a common method toward a common goal. The secrecy and mystery that had been such a basic part of alchemy played no role in the scientific societies each describes, although their visions had been sparked by the utopian schemes of spiritual alchemists. This was one of the most important innovations to emerge in all the utopian literature of the seventeenth century and the one that had the greatest impact on the decline of alchemy. Once alchemists openly communicated their discoveries, the stage was set for the tremendous advances we have come to expect from the natural sciences.

— ALLISON COUDERT

ALTAR

The English word *altar*, meaning "a raised structure on which sacrifices are offered to a deity," derives from the Latin *altare* ("altar") and may be related to *altus* ("high"). This ancient meaning has been further verified by the corresponding Classical Greek term *bomos* (raised platform, stand, base, altar with a base," i. e., the foundation of the sacrifice). The Latin *altaria* is, in all likelihood, related to the verb adolere ("to worship"; originally, "to burn, to cause to go up in smoke or odor"), so that the word has come to signify a "place of fire" or "sacrificial hearth."

THE CLASSICAL WORLD AND ANCIENT NEAR EAST. Greeks and Romans made careful distinctions between different altar forms: the raised altar site where sacrifices to the heavenly gods were performed; the pit (Gr., *bothros*; Lat., *mundus*) that was dug to receive the offerings to the deities of the underworld; and the level ground where gifts to the earth gods were deposited. The altar was a symbol of the unseen presence of the gods and was therefore considered a sacred spot.

Egyptian ritual worship included both portable and stationary altars. Most of the extant stationary altars were used in the sun temples and were surrounded by a low wall indicating the special sacred nature of their place during sun rites that were devoid of imagery.

HINDUISM. The nomadic Indo-Aryans who invaded India around 1500 BCE carried with them a portable fire altar drawn on a chariot (*ratha*) and protected by a canopy that marked the holiness of the

Thomas Aquinas himself believed in alchemy and attributed its efficacy to the occult forces of the heavenly bodies.

PAGE 658

HINDU ALTAR

The Sanskrit word vedi *refers to "an elevated place of ground serving as a sacrificial altar." It is synonymous with* pitha *(seat, throne), on which an idol or idols is placed.*

TED STRESHINSKY/CORBIS

shrine. This eternally burning fire on a rolling base was eventually replaced by fires kindled for the occasion by rubbing sticks together. In the case of domestic sacrifices, the head of the family made the fire in the home hearth (*ayatana*). For communal offerings, a fire was made on a specially consecrated spot (*sthandila*).

There were no temples during the Vedic period, but a sacrificial hall (*yagasala*) could be erected on holy ground that had first been thoroughly leveled. It consisted of a framework of poles covered with thatching. The sacred area, which like the domestic hearth was called *ayatana*, included subsidiary enclosures and a sacrificial stake (*yupa*) to which the victim was tied. This stake, which represented the cosmic tree, constituted an intermediate station between the divine world and life on earth.

We hear about the patriarchs building altars in various places in the land of Canaan and we also find that during the time of the judges altars were built in the fields and on rocks

PAGE 373

ISRAELITE RELIGION AND EARLY JUDAISM. The Hebrew term for altar is *mizbeah* ("a place of sacrificial slaughter"), which is derived from *zabah* ("to slaughter as a sacrifice"). In time, the animal slaughter came to be performed beside, not on, the altar. Other kinds of oblations offered on the altar were grain, wine, and incense. The altar sometimes served a nonsacrificial function as witness (*Jos.* 22:26ff.) or refuge (1 *Kgs.* 1:50f.) for most crimes except murder.

The altars, if not made from natural or rough-hewn rocks, were constructed from unhewn stone, earth, or metal. The tabernacle, or portable desert sanctuary of the Israelites, had a bronze-plated altar for burnt offerings in the court and a gold-plated incense altar used within the tent. Both of these altars were constructed of wood, and each was fitted with four rings and two poles for carrying.

The function of the Israelite altar was essentially the same as in other sanctuaries of the ancient Near East but with some important differences. While sacrifices were still referred to as "the bread of your God" (*Lv.* 22:25) and "a pleasing odor to the Lord" (*Lv.* 1:17), the notion of actually feeding Yahveh was not implied.

Abraham's binding of Isaac on the altar in the land of Moriah is considered the supreme example of self-sacrifice in obedience to God's will, and the symbol of Jewish martyrdom throughout the ages. Abraham himself was, from this point of view, the first person to prepare for martyrdom, and his offering was the last of the ten trials to which he was exposed.

CHRISTIANITY. Paul contrasted the Christian service with the pagan sacrificial meal by stating that we cannot partake of the Lord's table and the devil's table at the same time (*1 Cor.* 10:21). He thus distinguished between pagan sacrificial altars and the table at which Christ celebrated the Last Supper with his disciples. The New Testament constitutes the dividing point between Judaism and Christianity: Christ has, once and for all, made the full and sufficient sacrifice of himself (*Heb.* 8-10). The terminology of the sacrifice is used figuratively in reference to the dedication of Christian life (*Rom.* 12:1) and to the mission of Paul himself (*Phil.* 2:17).

The Western church eventually settled on the Latin term *altare* ("a raised place") since it corresponded not only to the sacrificial altars of the Temple-centered Israelite religion but also to the various non-Christian cults of the Roman world. The Christians differentiated their altars from pagan ones by using the terms *altare* and *mensa* instead of *ara*, and by referring to their altar in the singular, reserving the plural *altaria* for pagan places of sacrifice.

Following the adoption of the altar by the early Christian churches, its sacred nature became increasingly emphasized. It was the foundation of the elements of the Eucharist, and the special presence of Christ was expressed in the epiclesis of the eucharistic liturgy. A rich symbolism could therefore develop. The altar could be seen as a symbol of the heavenly throne or of Christ himself: the altar is made of stone, just as Christ is the cornerstone (*Mt.* 21:42). It also could be his cross or his grave.

After the Reformation, with its opposition to relic worship and to the conception of the Mass as a sacrifice, it was primarily the Eucharist of the early church that came to be associated with the altar table. The reformers emphasized the importance of the true and pure preaching of the word of God, with the result that the pulpit gained a more prominent position, sometimes at the expense of the altar.

— CARL-MARTIN EDSMAN

TRANSLATED FROM SWEDISH BY KJERSTI BOARD

ANCESTOR WORSHIP

GENERAL CHARACTERISTICS AND RESEARCH PROBLEMS

Ancestor worship has attracted the enduring interest of scholars in many areas of the study of religion. In the late nineteenth century, it was identified as the most basic form of all religion, and subsequent studies of the subject in specific areas have provided a stimulating point of access to related problems of religion, society, and culture.

The worship of ancestors is closely linked to cosmology and worldview, to ideas of the soul and the afterlife, and to a society's regulation of inheritance and succession. In East Asia ancestor worship is found combined with the practice of Buddhism, and ancestral rites compose a major part of the practice of Confucianism. It is generally acknowledged that ancestor worship functions to uphold the authority of elders, to support social control, and to foster conservative and traditionalist attitudes. In addition, ancestor worship is clearly linked to an ethic of filial piety and obedience to elders.

The institution of ancestor worship is properly regarded as a religious practice, not as a religion in itself. It is generally carried out by kinship groups and seldom has a priesthood separable from them. It is limited to the practice of the ethnic group; there is no attempt to proselytize outsiders. Its ethical dimension primarily refers to the proper conduct of family or kinship relations. It does not have formal doctrine as such; where texts exist, these are mainly liturgical manuals. In most cases ancestor worship is not the only religious practice of a society; rather, it exists as part of a more comprehensive religious system.

The meaning of *worship* in *ancestor worship* is problematic. Ancestor worship takes a variety of forms in different areas, and its attitudinal characteristics vary accordingly. The ancestors may be regarded as possessing power equivalent to that of a deity and hence may be accorded cult status and considered able to influence society to the same extent as its deities. Typically, the conception of ancestors is strongly influenced by ideas of other supernaturals in the society's religious system. Ancestors may be prayed to as having the power to grant boons or allay misfortune, but their effectiveness is regarded as naturally limited by the bonds of kinship. Thus, a member of a certain lineage prays only to the ancestors of that lineage; it would be regarded as nonsensical to pray to ancestors of any other lineage.

The rites of death, including funerary and mortuary rituals, are regarded as falling within the purview of ancestor worship only when memorial rites beyond the period of death and disposition of the corpse are carried out as a regular function of a kinship group. Thus, the funerary rites and occasional memorials common in Europe and the United States are not regarded as evidence of ancestor worship.

ANCESTOR WORSHIP IN THE HISTORY OF THE STUDY OF RELIGION

In *Principles of Sociology* (1877) Herbert Spencer wrote that "ancestor worship is the root of every religion." According to his view, the cult of heroes originated in the deification of an ancestor, and in fact all deities originate by an analogous process. Spencer's euhemerist theory rested on the idea, familiar in the scholarship of his day, that religion as a whole has a common origin from which its many forms derive. Knowledge of this original form would provide the key to understanding all subsequent developments.

In *Totem and Taboo* (1913), Sigmund Freud postulated that the belief that the living can be harmed by the dead serves to reduce guilt experienced toward the dead. That is, in kinship relations characterized by conscious affection there is inevitably a measure of hostility; however, this hostility conflicts with the conscious ideal of affectionate relations and hence must be repressed. Repressed hostility is then projected onto the dead and takes the form of the belief that the dead are malevolent and can harm the living.

Meyer Fortes considerably refined Freud's hypothesis on the basis of African material. In *Oedipus and Job in West African Religion* (1959), Fortes found that among the Tallensi belief in the continued authority of ancestors, rather than fear of them, is the principle means of alleviating guilt arising from repressed hostility.

Among the Tallensi relations between fathers and sons are affectionate, but, because a son cannot attain full jural authority until his father's death, sons bear a latent resentment of their fathers. However, this resentment does not manifest itself as belief in the malevolence of the dead. Instead, the Tallensi believe that the authority of the father is granted to him by his ancestors, who demand from the son continued subordination. Thus the function of ancestor worship is to reinforce the general, positive valuation of the authority of elders, quite apart from the individual personality of any specific ancestor. A related function is to place a positive value upon subordination of the desires of the individual to the collective authority of tribal elders. This value is useful in ensuring the continued solidarity of the group.

In *Death, Property, and the Ancestors* (1966), Jack Goody studied ancestor worship among the LoDagaa of West Africa. Property to be inherited by descendants is not distributed until the death of the father. Prevented from commanding the full possession of this property, a son experiences a subconscious wish for the father's death. Repression of this guilt takes the form of the belief that the dead have eternal rights to the property they formerly held. In order to enjoy those rights, the dead must receive sacrifices from the living. If sacrifices are not forthcoming, the ancestors will afflict their descendants with sickness and misfortune. Thus beliefs concerning ancestral affliction are inextricably linked to social issues of inheritance and succession.

ANCESTOR WORSHIP IN PRACTICE

This section describes the practice of ancestor worship in various cultural areas and in relation to several religious traditions.

AFRICA. A person without descendants cannot become an ancestor, and in order to achieve ancestorhood, proper burial, with rites appropriate to the person's status, is necessary. After an interval following death, a deceased person who becomes an ancestor is no longer perceived as an individual. Personal charac-

Superior to living kings and elders, the ancestors define and regulate social and political relations.

PAGE 5

"Ancestor worship is the root of every religion."

HERBERT SPENCER
PRINCIPLES OF SOCIOLOGY

A

teristics disappear from the awareness of the living, and only the value of the ancestor as a moral exemplar remains. Ancestors are believed to be capable of intervening in human affairs, but only in the defined area of their authority, that is, among their descendants.

In an important study of African ancestor worship, Max Gluckman (1937) established the distinction between ancestor worship and the cult of the dead. Ancestors represent positive moral forces who can cause or prevent misfortune and who require that their descendants observe a moral code. The cult of the dead, on the other hand, is not exclusively directed to deceased kinsmen, but to the spirits of the dead in general. Here spirits are prayed to for the achievement of amoral or antisocial ends, whereas ancestors can be petitioned only for ends that are in accord with basic social principles.

A man's most important ancestors are his father, mother, father's father, and father's mother, as well as the father's brothers who act with and share sacrifices offered to deceased parents and grandparents.

PAGE 723

Among the Edo the deceased is believed to progress through the spirit world on a course that parallels the progress of his son and other successors. Events in this world are punctuated by rites and are believed to have a counterpart in the spirit world. Thus it may be twenty years before a spirit is finally merged into the collective dead and descendants can receive their full complement of authority. In this sense the ancestors continue to exert authority over their descendants long after death. Until that authority ceases, the son must perform rites as prescribed and behave in approved ways.

Among the Ewe of Ghana, ancestor worship is the basis of the entire religious system and a point of reference for the conceptualization of all social relations. The Ewe believe that the human being has two souls. Before birth the being resides in the spirit world; it comes into this world when it finds a mother, and it returns to the spirit world at death. This cycle of movement through the realms is perpetual. The ancestors are invoked with libations on all ceremonial occasions. Rites range from simple, personal libations to complicated rituals involving an entire lineage. During a ritual, the soul of the ancestor returns to be fed through the ceremonial stool that serves as its shrine.

MELANESIA. Ancestors are one of many types of spirits recognized by Melanesian tribal peoples. Regarding the role of ancestor worship in tribal life, Roy A. Rappaport's study *Pigs for the Ancestors* (1977) presents an innovative approach not seen in the study of ancestor worship in other areas. Among the highland Tsembaga, ancestral ritual is part of a complex ecological system in which a balanced cycle of abundance and scarcity is regulated. Yam gardens are threatened by the unhindered growth of the pig population, and human beings must supplement their starch-based diet with protein. Propelling this cycle is a belief that pigs must be sacrificed to the ancestors in great numbers. These sacrifices provide the Tsembaga with protein in great quantity. Pigs sacrificed when someone dies or in connection with intertribal warfare supplement the regular diet of yams, which is adequate for regular activity but not for periods of stress. Thus ancestor worship plays a vital role in the ecological balance of the tribe in its environment.

INDIA. Ancestor worship in India takes a variety of forms, depending upon the area and the ethnic group concerned; however, providing food for the dead is a basic and widespread practice. Orthodox Hindu practice centers on an annual rite between August and September that includes offering sacred rice balls (*pinda*) to the ancestors. *The Laws of Manu* includes specific instructions for ancestral offerings. Descendants provide a feast for the brahmans, and the merit of this act is transferred to the ancestors. The feast itself is called the Sraddha. The form of this rite varies depending on whether it is observed during a funeral or in subsequent, annual observances.

SHAMANISM. Shamanism in East Asia today

BUDDHISM
Aid for Ailing Ancestors

Based on a canonical story, the All Souls Festival, or Avalambana, is observed throughout Southeast and East Asia. The story concerns one of the Buddha's disciples, Maudgalyayana, known for skill in meditation and supranormal powers. The mother of Maudgalyayana appeared to her son in a dream and revealed to him that she was suffering innumerable tortures in the blackest hell because of her *karman*. Through magic Maudgalyayana visited his mother in hell, but his power was of no avail in securing her release. Eventually the Buddha instructed him to convene an assembly of the priesthood which then would recite *sutras* and transfer the merit of those rites to ancestors. In other words, descendants must utilize the mediation of the priesthood in order to benefit ancestors. The result is an annual festival, traditionally observed on the day of the full moon of the eighth lunar month. At this festival special *sutra* recitations and offering rites for the ancestors are held in Buddhist temples, and domestic rites differing in each country are performed. In addition to rites for ancestors, observances for the "hungry ghosts" and for spirits who have died leaving no descendants are performed.

— HELEN HARDACRE

consists in large part of mediumistic communications in which the shaman enters a trance and divines the present condition of a client's ancestors. These practices are based on the folk notion that if a person suffers from an unusual or seemingly unwarranted affliction, the ancestors may be the cause. If the ancestors are suffering, if they are displeased with their descendants' conduct, or if they are offered inappropriate or insufficient ritual, they may cause some harm to come to their descendants. However, it is only rarely that this belief is straightforwardly expressed as the proposition that ancestors willfully, malevolently afflict their descendants.

CHINA. An important component at work in the metaphysics of Chinese ancestor cults is indigenous theories of the soul. First of all, since Chou times (c. 1123-221 BCE) the idea of the soul as the pale, ghostly shadow of a man has been a perduring notion found in popular stories. These apparitions are called *kuei*, meaning demons, devils, and ghosts, as opposed to *shen*, the benevolent spirits of ancestors (a word used also to refer to all deities).

Together with this idea of the ghostly soul there developed a conception of the soul in terms of *yin* and *yang*. According to this theory, the *yin* portion of the soul, called *p'o*, may turn into a *kuei* and cause misfortune if descendants do not perform proper ancestral rites. If the *p'o* is satisfactorily placated, however, it will rest peacefully. Meanwhile, the *yang* portion of the soul, called *hun*, associated with *shen*, will bless and protect descendants and their families. Thus Chinese ancestral rites have been motivated simultaneously by the fear of the vengeful dead and by the hope for ancestral blessings.

Chinese ancestor worship is closely linked to property inheritance; every deceased individual must receive offerings from at least one descendant who will provide him with sustenance in the next life. However, a specific person is only required to worship those ancestors from whom he has received property.

KOREA. In Korea women and men hold quite different images of ancestors. A woman marries away from her natal village and enters her husband's household under the authority of his mother and father. The wife's relations with her husband's kin are expected to be characterized by strife and competition. Her membership in the husband's lineage is tenuous and is never fully acknowledged in ritual until her death. Because women's relation to the lineage is strained in these ways, they hold more negative views of the ancestors than do men. Women's negative conceptions are expressed in the idea that ancestors maliciously harm their descendants by afflicting them with disease and misfortune. Men worship ancestors in Confucian rites from which women are excluded, while women perform rites for ancestors in a shamanic mode, utilizing widespread networks of shamans, most of whom are women. This gender-based bifurcation in ancestor worship is a special characteristic of Korean tradition.

JAPAN. Since the Tokugawa period (1600-1868) Japanese ancestor worship has mainly been carried out in a Buddhist mode, though Shinto rites also exist. As in China, ancestral ritual reflects relations of authority and inheritance, but instead of lineage rites, rites are performed by main and branch households of the traditional family system, the *ie*. Branch families (*bunke*) accept the ritual centrality of the main household (*honke*) by participating in its rites in a subordinate status. The *honke* does not reciprocate. In addition to *honke-bunke* rites, domestic rites performed before a Buddhist altar are a prominent feature of Japanese ancestral worship.

The "new religions" of Japan are a group of several hundred associations that have appeared in the nineteenth and twentieth centuries. Most reserve a special place for ancestor worship in some form. Reiyukai Kyodan (Association of Friends of the Spirits) represents a rare example of a religious group in which wor-

CONFUCIANISM
Filial Piety or Else

Confucianism lays heavy emphasis upon the correct practice of ancestral ritual. Special attention is given to minute details concerning the content and arrangement of offerings, proper dress, gesture and posture, and the order of precedence in appearing before ancestral altars. According to the *Book of Family Ritual* of the Neo-Confucian scholar Chu Hsi, the *Chu-tzu chia-li*, commemoration of ancestors became primarily a responsibility of eldest sons, and women were excluded from officiating roles in the celebration of rites.

The highest virtue in Confucian doctrine is filial piety, quintessentially expressed in the worship of ancestors. When Buddhism was first introduced to China, one of Confucianism's strongest arguments against it was the assertion that Buddhism was in essence opposed to filial piety and was likely to disrupt the practice of ancestor worship. If sons took the tonsure and failed to perform ancestral rites, then not only would spirits in the other world suffer from lack of ritual attention but social relations in society would also be undermined.

— HELEN HARDACRE

The religious activities of the early Chou aristocracy were focused on their ancestors, who were believed to reside in a celestial court presided over by T'ien, "Heaven," the Chou high god.

PAGE 132

"Everyman hath a good and a bad angel attending on him, all his life long."

ROBERT BURTON
ANATOMY OF MELANCOLY

ship of ancestors is the main focus of individual and collective rites. Reverence for ancestors in the new religions and in Japanese society in general is closely linked to social and political conservatism and to a traditionalist preference for the social mores of the past.

— HELEN HARDACRE

ANCIENT NEAR EASTERN RELIGIONS

[*See articles* Canaanite Religion, Egyptian Religion, Israelite Religion, Philistine Religion.]

ANGELS

Angels belong to the enormous variety of spiritual beings who mediate between the transcendental realm of the sacred and the profane world of man. The term *angel* is specifically used in Western religions to distinguish benevolent from malevolent demons. In most other religions, however, the distinction between good and evil demons is less clear; their behavior depends on the situation and on the conduct of individuals and communities.

It is not easy to understand the Zoroastrian concept of the beneficent immortals who form the retinue of the Wise Lord Ahura Mazda.

PAGE 721

ORIGIN AND FUNCTION. The word *angel* is derived from the Greek *aggelos*, translated from the Hebrew *mal'akh*, meaning "messenger." The literal meaning of the word indicates the primary function of angels as divine messengers. They are sent by God to inform men of their ultimate being, purpose, and destiny.

The role of angels is most fully elaborated in religions based on revelation, such as Zoroastrianism, Judaism, Christianity, and Islam. These religions emphasize the distance between man and God and, consequently, have the greatest need for intermediaries between the two. In polytheistic religions the gap between man and the gods is less pronounced; angelic functions are often performed by the gods themselves in their human incarnations. In monistic religions, angelic intermediaries play a minor part since the gap between man and God is nonexistent. Nevertheless, in both polytheistic and monistic religions, spiritual beings similar to angels do exist to help individuals achieve a proper rapport with the gods and spirits.

JUDAISM AND ZOROASTRIANISM. Angels experienced a similar moral metamorphosis through the centuries. In early biblical stories (e.g., *Ps.* 78:49, 1 *Sm.* 18:10), they can be malevolent and murderous. Later writers stress their benevolence, or at least their righteousness, in contrast to other, malevolent, spirits. The origin of the evil demons and their leader, Satan, was a subject of intense speculation in later Judaism, Christianity, and Islam. The general view was that Satan and his followers were fallen angels, expelled from heaven for envy, pride, or lust.

The development of an elaborate angelology in Judaism was a consequence of the Babylonian exile (sixth century BCE) and the influence of Zoroastrianism. The Zoroastrian myth of the cosmic battle between Ahura Mazda ("benevolent deity") and Angra Mainyu ("hostile deity"), with their attendant armies of angels and devils, profoundly influenced the angelology and demonology of the Hebrew scriptures and the Apocrypha, which, in turn, influenced later Jewish, Christian, and Islamic thought. Like Ahura Mazda, the Old Testament God, Yahveh, is surrounded by an angelic army. He is the "Lord of Hosts," and his warrior angels fight against the forces of evil led by Satan, who gradually assumes the characteristics of the archfiend, Angra Mainyu.

Judaism adopted the Zoroastrian division of the universe into three realms: heaven, earth, and hell. Heaven is the celestial region inhabited by God and his angels; earth, the terrestrial world of man, limited by time, space, cause and effect; hell, the subterranean world of chaos, darkness, and death, the abode of Satan and his demon followers. This tripartite scheme provided the foundation for the religious, metaphysical, and scientific ideas of Jews, Christians, and Muslims until it was undermined by the Copernican revolution in the sixteenth century. In this tripartite cosmos, the earth is an imperfect halfway house inhabited by man, a hybrid creature with conflicting impulses, ignorant of his origin, nature, and destiny. The primary function of the angels is to bridge the cosmic gap separating God and man. In Zoroastrianism, this gap was the result of the primordial battle between the gods that left man stranded in an alien world. In Judaism, Christianity, and Islam, the rift was the result of man's sin and consequent fall. Whatever the reason, humans have become alienated and no longer understand their relationship to their creator or the purpose of their creation. Because angels are able to assume human form, they can bridge the gulf between heaven and earth and reveal the divine plan, will, and law. In emphasizing the revelatory role of angels, Judaism followed Zoroastrianism. Vohu Manah ("good mind"), one of the Amesha Spentas ("holy immortals") in Zoroastrianism, appeared to Zarathushtra (Zoroaster) and revealed the true nature of God and his covenant with man.

In the Hebrew scriptures, angels perform the same functions as in Zoroastrianism: they praise and serve God, reveal divine truth, and act as extensions of the divine will, rewarding the good and punishing the wicked. They help humans understand God and achieve a proper rapport with him, and they conduct the souls of the righteous to heaven.

Angels can be merciless when they enforce the divine law and punish the wicked (*Ez.* 9). In their dealings with the righteous, however, they are models of care and concern. In the apocryphal *Book of Tobit* (second century BCE) the archangel Raphael guides the young hero Tobias on a dangerous journey and reveals the magic formulas that protect him from the demon Asmodeus and restore his father's sight. In his solicitude for Tobias, Raphael behaves like the guardian angels who became so important in the popular piety of later Judaism and Catholicism. These guardian angels were modeled after Zoroastrian spirits known as *fravashis*, a cross between ancestral spirits, guardian spirits, and the immortal components of individuals.

Two archangels are mentioned in the Hebrew scriptures: Michael ("like God"), the warrior leader of the heavenly hosts, and Gabriel ("man of God"), the heavenly messenger (*Dn.* 8:16). Two other archangels are named in the Apocrypha: Raphael ("God has healed"), who appears in *Tobit*, and Uriel ("God is my light"), who appears in *2 Esdras*. Seven archangels, unnamed, are also mentioned in Tobit. In addition to these archangels, two angelic orders appear in the Hebrew scriptures: the six-winged Seraphim, who surround the divine throne and praise God (*Is.* 6:2ff.), and the Cherubim, described by Ezekiel (1:5ff.)

ARCHANGEL GABRIEL

The archangel Gabriel foretells the birth of Christ.

FRANCIS G. MAYER/CORBIS

ANGELS IN CHRISTIANITY. New Testament angels perform the same functions as their Old Testament counterparts. Christian angelology, however, is more elaborate and reflects the influence of gnostic and popular beliefs. The gnostics, who flourished during the first four centuries of the common era, were a heterogeneous group with Christian, Jewish, and pagan offshoots, but they shared a dualistic view of the universe as a battleground for good and evil. They believed man to be a prisoner within a cosmos created by an evil demiurge. Man's mission lay in returning to the heavens from which he had come. To do this, a soul had to pass through the seven spheres, each of which was controlled by an angel. The angels allowed to pass through only those souls who addressed them with the proper names and recited the appropriate formulas. The knowledge of these names and formulas provided the gnostics with their name, which literally means "the knowing ones."

Many Christians as well as Jews accepted the gnostic belief that angels participated in creation and contributed to the continuance of the cosmos. Clement of Alexandria (AD 150?-215?) believed that angels controlled the movement of the stars and the four elements. The identification of angels with stars explains their enormous number, beauty, and radiance. Some early Christians, probably recruited from among the gnostics, worshiped angels and considered them more powerful mediators than Christ, which explains the polemic against angel worship in the New Testament (*Col.* 2:18, *Heb.* 1:4ff.). The gnostic invocations to angels contributed to the angelic magic that developed in popular Judaism, Christianity, and Islam.

Like the angels in the Hebrew scriptures, Christian angels are God's messengers and ministers. They announced the birth of Christ and authenticated his mission on earth, as well as the mission of the apostles, saints, and martyrs. Angels are actively involved in the daily lives of Christians. They preside over the sacraments and are therefore present at the most significant moments in a Christian's life. They will announce the Last Judgment and separate the just from the unjust. The archangel Michael weighs the souls of the dead. Angels help Christians achieve salvation in countless ways; no service is beneath them. They carry the prayers of the faithful to God. They strengthen the weak and comfort the oppressed, particularly martyrs. Legend has it that the guardian angels of children occupy a privileged place in heaven, close to God (*Mt.* 18:10).

Thereupon the lower angels created the body of Adam after the image that they had seen, an imitation of the Man, who clearly serves as an ideal archetype for the human body.

PAGE 236

ANGELS IN ISLAM. Islamic angelology closely follows Judaic and Christian patterns. According to Islamic tradition, angels revealed the Qur'an to Muhammad. But, mistrusting the source of his revelation and fearing he was possessed by *jinn* or devils, Muhammad was about to throw himself off a mountain when Jibril (Gabriel) appeared and confirmed him as God's prophet. As the angel of revelation, Jibril took Muhammad (mounted on the winged steed Buraq) on a tour of the seven heavens. Other angels are mentioned in the Qur'an. Mikal (Michael) provides men with food and knowledge; 'Izra'il is the angel of death; Isafal places souls in bodies and sounds the trumpet signaling the Last Judgment.

According to popular belief, a group of female angelic beings, the *huris*, inhabit the Muslim paradise and have the specific function of providing male Muslims with erotic delight. The *huris* are similar to the enchanting and sexually skilled *apsaras* in the Hindu heavens. The sexuality of both groups is in marked contrast to the asexuality of Christian angels.

ANGELS IN THE MODERN WORLD. The Copernican revolution undermined the Western tradition of belief in angels. The tripartite division of the universe no longer made sense in a cosmological scheme in which the earth was one planet among others revolving around the sun in a possibly infinite universe. Since there was no longer an up or a down, or a perfect, unchanging heaven, the physical existence of heaven and hell was also questioned.

But whereas the physical sciences undermined belief in the concrete reality of heaven, hell, angels, and devils, the psychological discoveries of the last two centuries have given these entities new plausibility as psychic phenomena. Sigmund Freud located the tripartite cosmos in the structure of the personality itself, with its division into superego, ego, and id. C. G. Jung postulated the existence of a collective unconscious and discussed mythology and religion in terms of the "primordial images," or "archetypes," in the collective unconscious, which every human being inherits. With the insights into psychic conflict provided by modern psychology, the image of angels and devils fighting over individual souls assumes new meaning and relevance.

— ALLISON COUDERT

ANGELIC HIERARCHIES
Ranking the Angels

Angels are usually grouped in four or seven orders. Four orders are described in the *Sibylline Oracles*, Roman sacred books with Jewish and Christian interpolations. The number four represents the four cardinal points and signifies perfection. As the number of known "planets" (five visible planets plus the sun and the moon), seven played an important part in Babylonian astronomy. The influence of Babylonian science on Zoroastrianism is suggested by the significance that the number seven assumed in Zoroastrian cosmology. The seven Holy Immortals are identified with the seven planets and the seven spheres in which the planets were believed to move. Opposed to the Holy Immortals were seven evil spirits, ancestors of the Christian seven deadly sins. Gnostics recognized seven orders of angels and identified them with the seven spheres. Seven angelic orders are enumerated in the New Testament: Thrones, Dominions, Virtues, Powers, Principalities, Archangels, and Angels. Clement of Alexandria, along with other early Christian theologians, accepted these seven orders.

In the writings of Dionysius the Areopagite (late fifth century), the various strands of Jewish and Christian angelology were united in a systematic whole. To the seven angelic orders mentioned in the New Testament, Dionysius added the two orders mentioned in the Old Testament, the Cherubim and the Seraphim, arranging the total of nine orders into three distinct hierarchies with three choirs apiece. (Thus three, the number of the Trinity, is repeated three times.) The highest of these three new orders, comprising Seraphim, Cherubim, and Thrones, was dedicated to the contemplation of God. The second order, comprising Dominions, Virtues, and Powers, governed the universe, while the third order, comprising Principalities, Archangels, and Angels, executed the orders of their superiors.

— ALLISON COUDERT

In the traditional account the call came as the vision of the angel Gabriel, who said, "O, Muhammad, thou art the Messenger of God," and commanded Muhammad, "Recite."

PAGE 564

ANGLICANISM

ANGLICANISM, also called the Anglican communion, is a federation of autonomous national and regional churches in full intercommunion through the archbishop of Canterbury of the Church of England. The Anglican churches share a tradition of doctrine, polity, and liturgy stemming from the English Reformation in the sixteenth century. Often classified as "Protestant," they also claim a "Catholic" heritage of faith and order from the ancient, undivided church.

Characteristic of Anglicanism is the endeavor to hold together in a comprehensive middle way (*via media*) the tensions of its Protestant and Catholic elements. This endeavor is a legacy of the English Reformation, which was essentially an act of state and not a popular movement. Without the coercive power of the state, Anglicanism might have died aborning. The long reign of Queen Elizabeth I (r. 1558-1603) ensured its survival. Elizabeth had no intention of submitting England to any papal authority, which her sister, Mary I (r. 1553-1558), had restored. She was equally adamant against agitation for a presbyterian form of church government that would dispense with the royal supremacy, episcopacy, and the liturgy.

Many episcopal sees, including Canterbury, were vacant at Elizabeth's accession. Most of Mary's bishops were deprived of their offices for refusal to accept the new settlement. Careful to maintain the episcopal succession, Elizabeth chose Matthew Parker, a moderate reformer, for her archbishop of Canterbury. He was consecrated on 17 December 1559. Vacant sees were then filled with the queen's supporters.

In 1571, Parliament approved the Thirty-nine Articles, the only official confessional statement of Anglicanism, still printed in most editions of the prayer book. They are not a complete system of doctrine, but point out differences from Roman Catholicism and Anabaptism and indicate nuanced agreement with Lutheran and Reformed positions. The queen added in Article 20 the statement: "The Church hath power to decree Rites and Ceremonies."

Elizabeth's settlement remains the foundation of Anglicanism. It affirms the canonical scriptures to be the final arbiter in all matters of doctrine and to contain all things necessary to salvation.

Today most Anglicans accept as reasonable modern methods of literary and historical criticism of the scriptures and other religious documents. Anglicanism has never had a dominant theologian such as Thomas Aquinas, Luther, or Calvin. The apologetic work of Richard Hooker (1554-1600), *Of the Laws of Ecclesiastical Polity*, is still influential, with its appeal to scripture, church tradition, reason, and experience. Anglican theology tends to be biblical, pastoral, and apologetic rather than dogmatic or confessional.

Anglican polity is episcopal and preserves the ordained orders of bishops, presbyter-priests, and deacons that go back to apostolic times. There is no official doctrine of episcopacy. In all negotiations for unity or intercommunion with other churches, Anglicans insist that an unbroken succession of bishops, together with the other two orders, be maintained.

All Anglican churches are constitutionally governed, each church having its own appropriate canons for executive and legislative authorities. Bishops, clergy, and laity participate in all synodical decision making, but a consensus of these orders, voting separately, is necessary for decisions about major doctrinal, liturgical, or canonical matters. Outside England, bishops are generally elected by a synod of the diocese in which they will serve, subject to confirmation by other bishops and representative clergy and laity from each diocese.

ELIZABETH I

The long reign of Queen Elizabeth I solidified the foundation of Anglicanism.

CORBIS-BETTMANN

The Church of England is today the only Anglican church that is state-established. The archbishop of Canterbury has a primacy of honor among all Anglican bishops, but he has no jurisdiction outside of his own diocese and province. The Crown, after appropriate consultations, nominates the English bishops, who are then elected by their respective cathedral chapters. Parliament retains final control over doctrine and liturgy, but the Synodical Government Measure of 1969 gave the English church large freedom to order its internal life through a General Synod of bishops, clergy, and laity.

"I die a Christian according to the Profession of the Church of England."

KING CHARLES I

For almost three centuries the expansion of Anglicanism was hindered by the Church of England's lack of any overall missionary strategy and its concept of a church that must be established by the state and sufficiently endowed. Within the British Isles, the Church in Wales, whose roots go back to the ancient church in Roman Britain, was part of the province of Canterbury from the Norman Conquest until its disestablishment and disendowment in 1920. The English Reformation in Ireland was rejected by 90 percent of the people. Yet not until 1870 was the (Anglican) Church of Ireland disestablished and largely disendowed. Four Anglican dioceses now straddle the border between Northern Ireland and the Republic of Ireland. The Reformation in Scotland was predominantly presbyterian.

A national church was formed at a general convention in 1789, which adopted a constitution, canons, and a revised prayer book. By the General Convention in 1835, the Episcopal church was strong enough to begin concerted missionary strategy and it organized the Domestic and Foreign Missionary Society, which to this day includes all its baptized members. A bishop

Roman Catholicism is distinguished from other Christian traditions and churches in its understanding of, commitment to, and exercise of the principles of sacramentality, mediation, and communion.

PAGE 577

THE PRAYER BOOK

Common Prayers and Rites

In addition to the episcopate, Anglicanism is bonded by a common liturgy, contained in various recensions of *The Book of Common Prayer,* based either upon the Elizabethan version of 1559 or that of 1549. Use of the prayer book is prescribed in all Anglican churches. With the Bible and a hymnal, it provides everything needed for the churches' rites and ceremonies. The prayer book has been in continuous use since the sixteenth century, except for the years of the English Commonwealth (1645-1660), when it was proscribed in public and private use. It is the only vernacular liturgy of the Reformation period still in use.

The prayer-book formularies, many of them derived from the ancient church, are a principal source of doctrine and a primary basis of the spirituality of both clergy and laity. The daily and Sunday liturgies are set within the framework of the traditional seasons of the Christian year and fixed feasts of Christ and the saints. The sacraments of baptism and the Lord's Supper (also called Holy Communion or Eucharist) are considered generally necessary to salvation.

— MASSEY H. SHEPHERD, JR.

was chosen to organize dioceses on the western frontier; and a bishop was resident in China in 1844 and in Japan in 1874. Liberia received its first bishop in 1851.

The Church of England was slow, however, in providing bishops for its burgeoning missions overseas, and voluntary societies could not legally do so. Canada received its first bishop in 1787, followed by India in 1814, the West Indies in 1824, Australia in 1836, New Zealand in 1841, and South Africa in 1847.

In 1960 the first Anglican executive officer, serving under the archbishop of Canterbury, was chosen. His duties were to visit and assess the problems of the various Anglican churches and to promote communication and common strategy for mission among them. In 1971 the Anglican Consultative Council came into being, and the Anglican executive officer became its secretary general. The council meets every two or three years in various parts of the Anglican world. The archbishop of Canterbury is its president, but the council elects its own chairman. Members consist of representative bishops, clergy, and laity of the several Anglican churches.

Anglicanism is much involved in endeavors for Christian unity. The Episcopal church, under the leadership of Bishop Charles Henry Brent (1862-1929), planned the first World Conference on Faith and Order at Lausanne in 1927, over which Brent presided. Delegates from more than one hundred Protestant and Eastern Orthodox churches attended. This movement became part of the World Council of Churches, constituted in 1948.

At Bonn in 1931 the Anglican communion entered into an agreement with the Old Catholic churches of the Union of Utrecht (1889) for full intercommunion, which stated that this does "not require from either Communion the acceptance of all doctrinal opinion, sacramental devotion, or liturgical practice characteristic of the other, but implies that each believes the other to hold all the essentials of the Christian Faith."

Serious efforts to achieve the future reunion of Anglicanism with the Roman Catholic church began in an official visit of Archbishop Ramsey of Canterbury with Pope Paul VI in March 1966. A joint preparatory commission in 1967-1968 sorted major

BRANCHING OUT

The Church in America

Beginning in Virginia in 1607, the English church came to be established in the American colonies. Except in Virginia, Anglicans were outnumbered.

After a brief visit to Maryland, the Reverend Thomas Bray (1658-1730) founded in 1701 the voluntary Society for the Propagation of the Gospel in Foreign Parts, but the American Revolution decimated these accomplishments. With independence, all SPG support was withdrawn. A large proportion of clergy and laity had left for England or Canada. There were no more establishments, and in Virginia disendowment also followed. The remnant of clergy and laity, both patriots and loyalists, began to organize in state conventions. The consecration of Bishop Seabury for Connecticut by Scottish bishops, who were considered schismatic by the Church of England, spurred the English bishops to obtain an act of Parliament in June 1786 enabling them to consecrate American bishops without the customary oaths of obedience to the royal supremacy and the archbishop of Canterbury. Three Americans were so consecrated: for Pennsylvania and New York in 1787 and for Virginia in 1790.

— MASSEY H. SHEPHERD, JR.

theological issues for dialogue and made recommendations for areas of cooperation. Between 1970 and 1981 the Anglican-Roman Catholic International Commission published substantial agreements on eucharistic doctrine, ministry, and ordination and two agreements on authority in the church. These were gathered, with some elucidations, in the commission's *Final Report* (1982). When Pope John Paul II visited Britain in 1982, he and Archbishop Runcie signed the "Common Declaration" at Canterbury Cathedral on 29 June for a new commission to study further theological issues, pastoral problems, and practical steps for "the next stage" toward unity.

— MASSEY H. SHEPHERD, JR.

ANTI-SEMITISM

The term *anti-Semitism* was coined in 1879 by the German agitator Wilhelm Marr, author of the anti-Jewish *Der Sieg des Judenthums über das Germanthum*, a work with a gloomy view of the Germanic future. Marr himself was antireligious as well as anti-Jewish, and his term arose out of the pseudoscience of the modern era that regarded race rather than religion as the decisive factor separating Jews from Germans. For this reason, racist anti-Semitism is usually distinguished from medieval Christian anti-Semitism and its antecedents in the patristic and New Testament periods, in which the religious element was paramount.

While anti-Jewish hostility existed in pre-Christian times, notably in ancient Alexandria where local tensions led to the propagation of many anti-Jewish slanders, anti-Judaism was never part of pagan religion as such. It was, rather, a concomitant of ancient ethnocentrism with its proud conviction of Greek (and later Roman) superiority. Judaism was seen as tribalistic, and Jews who resisted the benefits of enlightenment were considered to be filled with enmity toward the human race.

ANTI-JUDAISM IN THE NEW TESTAMENT. Today, even Christian scholars generally concede that the Gospels and other sections of the New Testament are colored in some measure by hostility toward the Jewish antagonists of the apostolic church in the troubled milieu of the first and second centuries, although the exact nature of this hostility is still under investigation. The *Gospel of Mark*, a work addressed to a Roman gentile audience, reveals an apparent apologetic shift from Roman to Jewish responsibility for the execution of Jesus, possibly because the redactor did not wish to present Jesus as a Jewish insurrectionist at a time when Jews were highly unpopular in Rome as a result of the Judean War (66-70 CE). Thus, a reluctant Pilate allows a Jewish council and a Jewish rabble to force his hand. The *Gospel of Matthew* embroiders this theme, portraying the death of Jesus as largely a Jewish deed for which the instigators acknowledge their guilt with a self-inflicted curse: "His blood be on us, and on our children!" (*Mt.* 27:25).

As a postwar composition, the *Gospel of Matthew* seems to reflect the harsh atmosphere of judgment and recrimination characteristic of such eras. Given the redactor's hostile stance, it is not surprising that the Matthaean Jesus is made to hurl angry denunciations at his Pharisaic opponents. From this diatribe (*Mt.* 23) emerges the composite image, so deeply encased in the Christian imagination, of the hypocritical, legalistic, impious, blind, fanatical, and murderous Pharisee, an image that has played havoc with Jewish-Christian relations ever since. It is, of course, a caricature, but even in milder form, the image remains a problem.

Luke and *Acts*, two works of gentile authorship, reinforce the view that the Jewish populace was responsible for the death of Jesus and that the later destruction of Jerusalem was a consequence of God's wrath. However, although these anti-Jewish themes are present in *Luke* and *Acts*, their impact is softened by other passages, perhaps because Luke hoped for missionary success among Diaspora Jews (Hare, in Davies, 1979).

The *Gospel of John*, a complex and highly stylized composition, casts the Jews in a profoundly hostile light as symbols of a "fallen universe of darkness" who oppose Jesus at every turn in the great drama of the Messiah's "hour" when the Messiah manifests his glory. So negative and intense is the Johannine image that John has sometimes been regarded as the "father of anti-Semitism." Because of its deceptively simple character and the great religious power of its language, this gospel has long been the favorite text of Christian piety, conditioning Christians to think almost instinctively in anti-Jewish terms.

The religious roots of anti-Semitism can also be traced to Paul, sometimes seen as a fanatical convert whose polemic against the Law (*Gal., Rom.*), coupled with his charge that a veil has descended over Jewish minds (*2 Cor.*), has made him seem an archenemy of Judaism. Ruether (1974) argues that Paul, under gnostic influence, conceived of the Torah as a means of demonic rulership over the fleshly man of the dying age, whereas freedom from the Torah signifies freedom from the evil powers for the spiritual man of the coming age. Thus Judaism, or the Israel of flesh, is superseded by Christianity, the Israel of spirit. Although Paul speaks warmly of the Jews, whose covenant remains intact, and of the Torah as "holy, just and good" (*Rom.* 7:12), he nevertheless focuses, in chapters 9-11, on the fact of Jewish disbelief.

Together with the written deposit of their memories of Jesus in the Gospels, the writings of Paul and several other documents were circulated widely in Christian communities throughout the Mediterranean world.

PAGE 152

A

ANTI-SEMITISM

Developments during the Middle Ages and the Reformation

"Of all the bigotries that savage the human temper there are none so stupid as the anti-Semitic."

DAVID LLOYD GEORGE

DEVELOPMENTS DURING THE MIDDLE AGES AND THE REFORMATION. Frequent attention has been drawn to the gradual demonization of the Jews in art and folklore, notably in the late Middle Ages. The myths of Jewish crimes such as ritual murder, desecration of the Host, and conspiracy against Christendom intensified the imagined association of Jews with the Prince of Darkness. This process became pronounced in northern Europe as it sank into a state of social crisis colored by religious anxiety after the thirteenth century, when preoccupation with the supernatural was strong. As Norman Cohn reminds us in *The Pursuit of the Millennium: Europe's Inner Demons* (New York, 1970), Catholics and heretics demonized not only each other but also the real or fictional secret societies (e.g., Templars, witches, and Jews) on whom the ills of the time might be blamed. To many Christian sectarians, anticipating a violent climax to history, the Antichrist would prove to be a Jew. Not only sectarians, however, but—if Jeremy Cohen (1982) is correct—also the great religious orders founded in the thirteenth century, the Dominicans and the Franciscans, contributed to the demonization of the Jews by attacking the Talmud as a blasphemous and evil writing that stood between the Jews and their conversion. In addition, the peculiar economic roles forced on the Jewish community by feudal society placed its members under a new stigma. As hucksters and usurers, the latter were not only Cain, who murdered Abel (Christ), but also Judas, who sold Christ for thirty pieces of silver. From this fusion of economic and religious symbols arose the deadly image of the ruthless and rapacious Jew, still an intrinsic part of *antisemitica* today.

SHYLOCK

The anti-Semitic stereotype of Jewish hucksters and moneylenders endures to this day in literature and legend.

HULTON-DEUTSCH COLLECTION/CORBIS

MODERN ANTI-SEMITISM. Although Christian belief was slowly eroded by the rise of secularism and modernity, negative images of Jews were too deeply embedded in the cultural substratum to disappear easily from the European consciousness. Rather, they persisted even among the Enlightenment critics of religion, as the case of Voltaire clearly shows. Within the churches, moreover, neither post-Tridentine Catholicism nor post-Reformation Protestantism was disposed to reconsider traditional ideas about Jews and Judaism until the ravages of modern totalitarianism made this morally urgent. A new liberal mood in Protestant thought at the end of the eighteenth century softened orthodox doctrine: Friedrich Schleiermacher, for example, in *The Christian Faith* (1821), recognized Judaism as an authentic religion, even if inferior to Christianity because of its "lingering affinity" with fetishism. But classical prejudice remained. As early as J. G. Fichte (1762-1814), a refusal to believe that Jesus was a Jew because of the supposedly materialistic character of Talmudic Judaism was becoming evident. Even the ex-Catholic Ernest Renan in his *Life of Jesus* (Paris, 1863) could only make sense of his hero by describing him as too great to be possessed by an inferior Semitic spirit. In this fashion, the old malevolence survived in new forms, finally with infamous results.

ANTI-JUDAISM IN ISLAM. Anti-Semitism in the Muslim world appears in considerable measure to have stemmed from the infiltration of Christian and Western influences, since the religious basis for anti-Judaism in Islam is smaller than in Christianity, which has the deicide motif. Even the hostile Qur'anic passages echo Christian opinions. Earlier, in pre-Islamic Arabia, such doctrines as Israel's rejection and punishment by God had been propagated by local Christian communities (Poliakov, 1955-1961); not surprisingly, similar sentiments found their way into the Qur'an: "Because of their iniquity, we forbade the Jews good things which were formerly allowed them . . . because they practice usury . . . and cheat others of their possessions" (Surah 4:160-161). Abraham is not regarded as a Jew but as the first Muslim: "Surely the men who are nearest to Abraham are those who follow him, this Prophet, and the true believers. . . . Some of the People of the Book wish to mislead you; but they mislead none but themselves, though they may not perceive it" (Surah 3:67-68). Furthermore, the Jews on occasion

MARTIN LUTHER'S VIEWS
A Precursor to Hitler?

The religious and folkloric anti-Judaism of the late Middle Ages came to a boil in the intemperate writings of the old Martin Luther, especially his 1543 tract *On the Jews and Their Lies.* His belief that Christ had been insulted, together with his conviction that Judaism was an evil religion, and further his abhorrence of religious legalism and his disappointment at the Jewish failure to convert to the reformed faith, drove Luther into an anti-Jewish fury so unrestrained that he has since been compared to Hitler. However, unlike Hitler, Luther was no racist, and his anger at the Jews, as Heiko Oberman (1984) has emphasized, was intimately connected with his anger at both the Roman papacy and the Turks, whom the reformer also saw as the devil's storm troops in a final assault on the church during the end time. Moreover, Luther's savage recommendations—the burning of synagogues and the suppression of Jewish worship and teaching—seem to have been motivated by his belief that Jewish "blasphemy" was an active menace in Christian society. The rediscovery of his anti-Jewish works during the renaissance of Luther studies in 1918 coincided with a rebirth of German nationalism, and this fact assisted his transformation into a Germanic hero and greatly distorted his true character. Significantly, Luther's Protestant contemporaries held a poor opinion of his tract; Bucer commented that it sounded like the composition of a swineherd rather than that of a "renowned shepherd of the soul." Yet it cannot be denied that such abuse of the Jews cast a dark shadow over European Christianity, making matters easy for the anti-Semites of the twentieth century.

— ALAN DAVIES

are portrayed in Christian fashion as blind and deaf to the truth, and even murderous toward its messengers (including Muhammad himself): "We made a covenant with the Israelites and sent forth apostles among them. But whenever an apostle came to them with a message that did not suit their fancies they either rejected him or slew him. They thought no harm would come to them: they were blind and deaf. God turned to them in mercy, but many of them again became blind and deaf" (Surah 5:70-71). Because of these evil deeds and their disbelief, the Jews have suffered and continue to suffer chastisement on earth as the objects of God's anger: "Ignominy shall attend them wherever they are found, unless they make a covenant with God or with man."

Only in recent times, when the shadow of Western anti-Semitism has descended on a Middle East unsettled by the Arab-Israeli conflict, has a fundamentalist tendency to demonize Jews and Judaism crept into Islam. The contemporary crisis of modernity in Muslim society has not been salutary for Western-Muslim relations, and Western (Christian?) support for the presence of a Jewish state on what is regarded as Islamic territory has greatly exacerbated this crisis. In this context, some Muslim theologians have exploited the hostile side of their tradition in order to vilify Jews in the most unqualified terms.

— ALAN DAVIES

ARCTIC RELIGIONS

AN OVERVIEW

Arctic religions may be treated together, as constituting a more or less unified entity, for two reasons. First, these religions are practiced by peoples situated in the polar North, who mostly live on the tundra (permanently frozen ground) and partly in the taiga (the northern coniferous forest belt that stretches around the world); like their cultures in general, the religions of these peoples reflect to no little extent the impact of the severe natural environment. Second, the whole Arctic zone constitutes a marginal area and an archaic residue of the old hunting culture and hunting religion. Whereas in the south the waves of Neolithic agriculture and animal husbandry inundated the originally Paleolithic hunting culture, the latter was preserved in the high north, where no cultivation of the ground was possible.

ETHNIC AND CULTURAL SURVEY. The tribes and peoples of the Arctic culture area belong to several linguistic families. All of them, with the exceptions of some Paleosiberian peoples and the Inuit, are also represented in cultures south of the high Arctic zone. In the following survey, names of peoples will be given as they are authorized today by their respective governments and by the peoples themselves.

1. *The Uralic language family.* In Scandinavia, in Finland, and on the Kola Peninsula, the Arctic tundra and coast and the northern interior woodland are inhabited by the Saami (Lapps). Most of them are fishing people, but

Luther's final years were overshadowed by his growing antagonism toward the papal church. He died on 16 February, 1546.

PAGE 426

The shaman's important and essential characteristics are attained through dreams.

PAGE 489

in the mountain regions and in parts of the woodland areas reindeer breeding is a common way of life. East of Lake Onega live the Komi (Zyrians), who are divided into two main groups: the Nentsy (Yuraks), from the Northern Dvina River to the Ural Mountains, and the Nganasani (Tavgi), from the Ob River to Cape Chelyuskin. Along the lower parts of the Ob and Irtysh rivers live two Ugric peoples (related to the Hungarians), the Khanty (Ostiaks) and the Mansi (Voguls), mostly fishermen and hunters.

2. *The Tunguz language family.* The wide areas from west of the Yenisei River to the Anadyr River in the east and from the tundra in the north to the Sayan Mountains in the south are the country of the dispersed Tunguz tribes: the Evenki, west of the Lena River, and the Eveny, east of it. Their typical habitat is the taiga, where they subsist as reindeer breeders on a limited scale.
3. *The Turkic language family.* The numerous Yakuts on the Lena River and farther east combine reindeer breeding with horse breeding. Their language is also spoken by the Dolgans in the Taimyr Peninsula area, a group of earlier Tunguz tribes.
4. *The Yukagir.* Now almost extinct, the Yukagir, a group that may be related to the Finno-Ugric peoples, once covered a large area east of the Lena. They were hunters and fishermen until the seventeenth century, when they turned into reindeer-breeding nomads.
5. *The Paleosiberian language family.* The Chukchi, on the Chukchi Peninsula, and the Koriak and the Itelmen (Kamchadal), on the Kamchatka Peninsula, make up the Paleosiberian language family. The inland Chukchi are reindeer breeders; the coastal Chukchi, the Koriak, and the Itelmen are ocean fishermen.
6. *The Inuit.* The Inuit (Eskimo) ultimately may be related to the Paleosiberian peoples. Their territory stretches from the easternmost tip of Asia over the coasts and tundras of Alaska and Canada to Greenland. The Aleut, inhabitants of the Aleutian Islands who are closely related to the Inuit, should also be mentioned here. The Inuit are sea hunters and fishermen and, in northern Alaska and on the barren plains west of the Hudson Bay, caribou hunters.

COMMON RELIGIOUS ELEMENTS. It is not surprising that a wide range of religious phenomena are spread out over most of the region, usually as a combined result of ecological and historical factors. The available data bear out Robert H. Lowie's observation that the whole Arctic area constitutes one gigantic entirety from the angle of religious belief. I would here make a certain reservation for the New World Arctic area, however, because both archaeologically and ethnologically the Inuit lack several common circumpolar features, and the same holds for their religion.

The main characteristics of Arctic religions are the special relationships of people to animals and the elaboration of shamanism. It is possible that the strain of the Arctic climate has stimulated strong religious forms of reaction, just as it has provoked the psychic reactions known as Arctic hysteria. No such explanation can be given for the hypertrophic extension of animal ceremonialism. It has its roots, of course, in ancient Eurasian hunting rituals, but its prolific occurrence in the Arctic probably has to do with the necessary dependence on an animal diet in these barren regions.

The spiritual universe. According to the religious beliefs of the Arctic peoples, the whole world is filled with spirits: mountains, trees, and other landmarks have their spirits, and animals have their spirit masters. It is among all these spirits that the shaman finds his supernatural helpers and guardians. However, such man-spirit relationships could also occur among common people, as the evidence shows among the Saami and North American Indians, and there are obvious tendencies in the same direction among the Chukchi, as their "general shamanizing" testifies. The multifarious world of spirits may have something to do with the fact that the figure of a supreme being is so often diffuse. There is, it seems, a pattern of spiritualism here.

Supreme power. The inclination to conceive the highest supernatural being or beings more as nonpersonal power than personal figure or figures is generally part of Arctic religions and particularly characteristic of the Samoyeds, the Paleosiberian tribes, and the Inuit. The Saami constitute a great exception, but their high-god beliefs have been heavily influenced by Scandinavian and Finnish as well as Christian religious concepts.

Other spirits and divinities. Next to the supreme being, the most important spirits of the upper world are the Sun, the Moon, and the thunder spirits. The Sun is often related to the high god (as among the Tunguz), and the Moon can represent the mistress of the dead or, among some Inuit, the mistress of the sea animals (who is herself, secondarily, a mistress of the dead).

The surface of the earth is the habitat of a large crowd of spirits—some rule the animal species, some are spirits of the woods, lakes, and mountains (among

Eurasian Arctic groups), and some are dangerous ogres, giants, and dwarfs.

Throughout the Eurasian Arctic, the mother goddesses have connections with the doors of dwellings and are supposed to live under the ground. The Inuit have no particular birth goddess, but Sedna, the mistress of the sea animals, is in her unclean states a prototype of the woman who is ritually unclean, particularly when pregnant or giving birth. The birth goddess is primarily the protectress of women, and in some tribes female spirits are inherited from mother to daughter.

Cultic practices. Characteristic of the cultic complexes among Arctic peoples is the simple development of ritual forms and the use of cultic objects—such as crude sculptures in wood and peculiarly formed stones—as symbolic receivers of offerings. The relationships between the sacrificers and these objects varies from veneration to coercive magic.

Cultic images. The stone cult is prominent everywhere. Among the Saami, strangely formed stones, called *seite*, are connected with spirits that control the animals in the vicinity or the fish in water where the stone stands. The Samoyeds make offerings to similar stone gods, as do the Khanty, the Mansi, the Tunguz, and the Inuit. In some reports the stones seem, at least momentarily, identical with the spirits, but otherwise the general idea is that the stone represents the spirit or serves as its abode.

The most common custom, however, was to make crude wooden sculptures of the spirits. Such spirit figures occur all the way from Lapland to Alaska. Throughout northern Eurasia they are surprisingly similar—pointed at the top, usually without limbs, and occasionally decorated with cross marks on the body. The Khanty and the Samoyeds dress up these spirit images.

Wooden figures also occur in Siberian shamanism among the Tunguz and the Dolgans. For these peoples, the figures symbolize the shaman's helping spirits and the world pole or world tree. A line of seven or nine pillars represents the lower sky worlds, where the shaman's soul or guardian spirit rests on the way to heaven.

Animal ceremonialism. Much of the cultic life centers on animal ceremonialism, that is, the rituals accorded the slain game. Several animal species are shown a ceremonial courtesy after hunting; for example, their bones are buried in anatomical order. All over the area, a special complex of rites surrounds the treatment of the dead bear.

Paleosiberian peoples and Alaska Inuit paid similar attention to the whale. The Inuit celebrated the dead whale ritually for five days, a period corresponding to the mourning period for a dead person. The Alaska Inuit also had a bladder festival in December, at which the bladders of the seals that had been slain during the year were restored to the sea.

Shamanism and soul beliefs. It seems that the extreme development of shamanistic ritual farther to the south in Siberia is somewhat attenuated in the northern Arctic. On the other hand, in the Arctic the intensity of the shaman's ecstatic trance is certainly not weaker, but is in fact stronger, than it is in Siberia. North and south are also remarkably different in regard to the conception of the soul basic to shamanism. As always where true shamanism operates, there is a dualism between the free soul that acts during dream and trance and that represents man in an extracorporeal form and the one or several body souls that keep man alive and conscious during his waking hours. It is typically the shaman's free soul that, in a trance, tries to rescue a sick man's soul (of either type), which has left its body and gone to the land of the dead and possibly reached this place. This is indeed the conception of the soul and disease among the Arctic peoples.

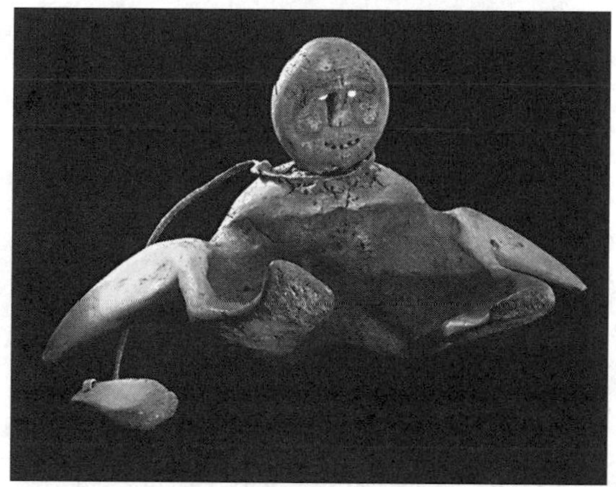

INUIT SHAMAN

In the Arctic, many believe that the shaman's trance-released soul can rescue the soul of a sick man, thus delivering it from the land of the dead.

Afterlife. Unlike most other hunting peoples, the peoples in the North generally believe that the realm of the dead is situated in the underworld. The Khanty think that the world of shades extends close to the mouth of the Ob River; it is characterized by cold, eternal darkness, hunger, and silence. The Tunguz view of the underworld is more optimistic. The people there live in birchbark tents, hunt, fish, and tend to their reindeer in the woods. The Central and Eastern Inuit realm of the dead is identical with Sedna's place at the bottom of the sea. It is not bright, but endurable. The rule in most places is that only those who have suffered a violent death go to heaven; among the Chukchi and Inuit these fortunate beings make their appearance in the aurora borealis. Often, the underworld is conceived to be contrary to our world in every respect; for instance, while it is night in the underworld it is day on earth.

[*For discussion of specific Arctic traditions, see* Inuit Religion.]

— ÅKE HULTKRANTZ

"Where it is a duty to worship the sun it is sure to be a crime to examine the laws of heat."

VOLTAIRE

According to eastern Inuit religious tradition, each animal had its own inua *(its "man," "owner," or "spirit") and also its own "soul."*

PAGE 334

HISTORY OF STUDY

THE DEVELOPMENT OF CIRCUMPOLAR STUDIES. The exploration of Siberian and Canadian Arctic cultures at the turn of the century made scholars aware of their great similarities. Since this was the time when geographic environmentalism swayed high—and the Arctic is known for its extreme climate—Arctic cultures were readily given an environmentalist interpretation.

Most ethnologists and anthropologists have favored a cultural-historical analysis in which all the Arctic cultures belong together, either as a common field of diffusion or as an archaic residue. This approach originated with the American anthropologist Franz Boas, who compared Paleosiberian and Northwest American Indian mythologies. His speculations resulted in the assumption of a direct communication between North America and North Asia. This perspective was expanded by Austrian and Danish diffusionists.

PARTICULAR AREAL STUDIES. Most authors have concentrated their efforts on the study of subfields or tribes within the Arctic area. It is possible to distinguish three main Arctic regions of exploration, usually (but not always) treated as separate from each other:

- ***The Saami field.*** The scientific analyses of Saami religion on the basis of older sources (there were few vestiges left in the nineteenth century besides folkloric materials) began late in the nineteenth century.
- ***The northern Eurasian field.*** The first accounts of the "primitive" peoples of the Russian empire and their religious customs date from the seventeenth and eighteenth centuries.

  During the postrevolutionary era, Soviet scholars have made several tribal ethnographic investigations of considerable importance, although one-sidedly Marxist and evolutionist in outlook.
- ***The Inuit field.*** The Danes had already secured important information on the Greenland Inuit in the eighteenth century. Danish scholarship in the field started in the nineteenth century when Gustav Holm and H. Rink described, in particular, the East Greenland Inuit religion.

  The twentieth century has seen a rich scholarship on Inuit religion, most of it directed from Copenhagen. Knud Rasmussen covered the whole Inuit area with his insightful analyses of Inuit religious thinking, but especially the Greenland, Central, and Polar Inuit.

— ÅKE HULTKRANTZ

AUSTRALIAN RELIGIONS

AN OVERVIEW

A LIVING TRADITIONAL RELIGION. Throughout Aboriginal Australia, we could speak of one religion with many differing sociocultural manifestations: basic religious concepts are the same, but there is also considerable variation. Several factors contributed to this seeming diversity. There were regional differences not only in language and in social organization but also in terrain and in climatic conditions. Religious responses to environmental factors are probably just as significant as the ways in which different people structure their relations within and between social groups, categorizing persons they regard as kin and defining those who are responsible for arranging and performing religious rites. Within the range of possible religious content, local aesthetic styles emphasize or select some elements rather than others, so that distinctive patterns emerge.

Aboriginal religion was closely and sensitively linked with local group territories and with the particular physiographic features within them. Nevertheless some religious cults, in terms of their ritual and mythic sponsorship, are spatially widespread and mobile. The Kunapipi (Gunabibi), for example, covers some thousands of kilometers, from Arnhem Land to the Western Desert and beyond, assuming different guises but retaining key symbolic representations. More generally, many mythic beings (or deities) in the creative era of the Dreaming traveled over large stretches of country, through several language or dialectal groups. The mythic fact that they were travelers does not negate or diminish their local relevance to particular areas and sites. However, the high level of mythic and ritual mobility may have had a bearing on the development of key religious similarities.

Source of the sacred. Throughout the continent, Aborigines generally believed that the natural world was originally, and essentially, formless. It was there, as a "given," waiting to be activated. Human time began with the emergence and appearance of mythic beings or gods, in human or other forms. They moved across the country, meeting other characters, changing the contours and shapes of the land and imbuing it with specific meanings. Everywhere they went, whatever they left behind them contained something of their own mythic or sacred essence. Some of them were responsible for creating the first people, the far-distant forebears of contemporary Aborigines. They put such people at places that were to be their "estates," or local group territories, noting the customs they were to follow, the languages they were to speak, and the rites they would have to perform. When those deities "died" physically, or disappeared beyond the sociocultural confines of a particular social unit, or were transformed into something else, they left evidence of their presence on earth in the shape of hills, rocks, paintings, and so on.

The deities are also responsible for the maintenance of all natural growth, the coming and the going of the seasons, the renewal of the land's fertility, and the replenishment of the species within it. The sites at which the mythic beings reside are reservoirs of this precious force, considered to be an indestructible power that remains unimpaired and active from the beginning of time. However, the power is accessible only in particular circumstances and can be released only by persons who are specifically linked spiritually to the deity concerned. Every region contains a large number of resource centers, each associated with one or more deities or mythic beings. Each of these beings is responsible for a particular species—in some cases, for several species. In order to generate seasonal renewal, a fairly wide patterning of ritual cooperation is necessary. This usually involves persons variously associated with differing mythic beings and their representations. The whole country is a living thing: the sites of the deities are latent repositories of life, of particular forms of life, awaiting activation through the intervention of human beings.

While the spiritual animation of a child's fetus might appear to be fortuitous, from an Aboriginal viewpoint it is an essentially predictable occurrence. Two factors need to be taken into account. In the first place, any woman in the appropriate condition is vulnerable when passing near a site where a particular life essence is located. The expectation is that, provided the deity in question is also relevant to her potential child, some event is likely to take place which triggers off the act of animation—or can be interpreted as doing so. The second factor is the actual event itself, an event (that is, consisting of some sign) that must occur before the life essence can be transferred. Thus the life force controlled by a deity is not released automatically: human intervention is necessary, and ritual is the key to that.

Social structuring of religion. Most traditional Aboriginal societies have words that can be translated

TIME EVERLASTING
The Dreaming

The Aboriginal deities and all that is associated with them, belong to the Dreaming—a time everlasting, eternal. Their spiritual essence lives on at particular sites, within the concept of the Dreaming *and* within the mundane world. However, the idea of a world everlasting depended on them and on the ability of human beings to gain access to the power, the concentrated spiritual quality, that they were believed to possess. This power is, partly, the major concern of the dimension of the sacred: partly, because everything that is either directly or indirectly related to the Dreaming is sacred. And the most sacred of all are the deities themselves. At their sites they remain enshrined in their aura of sacredness, their special power, an ever-present spiritual resource and inspiration for all living things, including human beings.

To understand the idea of the sacred in Aboriginal religion, it is necessary to identify the nature of the power inherent in the deities. Two points are especially relevant to this. First, deities in a spiritual sense are represented in the tangible world by particular creatures or elements. Many of them, not all, were shape-changing, which, in the Dreaming, exemplifies their affinity with nature. They may be simultaneously both human and in the form of an animal or other natural phenomenon. This means that such creatures share the same life force as the deity with which they are associated. Second, in a different sense, human beings also have a direct spiritual relationship with particular deities. Traditional Aborigines believe that no child can be conceived or born without its fetus being first animated through some action relating to a particular mythic character that also involves the child's parents and/or other consanguineous relatives.

For instance, in the central desert area, an unusual event, or one that is interpreted in those terms, must be experienced in order for animation or conception to occur. A man may spear a kangaroo which behaves in a "strange" manner. Later he gives some of the meat to his wife, who vomits after eating it. She may know immediately, or after he has identified the cause in a dream, that a mythic being has either transferred part of his or her sacred essence, via the medium of an intermediary, to the fetus within her or has stimulated or activated the conception. In northeastern Arnhem Land, spirit-landings fulfill this function. Spirit children (or child spirits) are associated with particular water holes or sites and with the relevant mythic beings connected with them. They take the shape of some creature that, when caught, escapes from the hunter or otherwise behaves unusually. Then the spirit child appears to him (or to one of his close sisters or father's sisters) in a dream asking where its mother is. In all such cases, the particular area in which such an incident takes place is of significance in the social and ritual life of the child who is eventually born, and the area concerned is preferably related to the father's country.

— RONALD M. BERNDT

Such forms are referred to collectively by a word that can be translated as "sacred law," and it is as "sacred law" that art mediates between the ancestral past and the world of living human beings.

PAGE 299

as "sacred" or "set apart." These imply a special quality which may prove dangerous to persons who do not have the appropriate knowledge and skill and right to handle it. Such words as *mareiin, daal,* or *duyu* (in northeastern Arnhem Land), *daragu* or *maia* (in the southeastern Kimberley), *djugurba* or *dumar* (in the Western Desert) or *tjurunga* (in central Australia), and so on refer to particular rituals, emblems, locations or places, songs, objects, or persons who are separated in some way from ordinary everyday affairs. The deities are sacred, as are all things associated with them. The condition of being "set apart" involves particular rules of access and exclusion on the basis of age, sex, and ritual status. However, while such Aboriginal vernacular terms do imply some measure of secrecy, Aborigines do not suggest that their religion is confined solely to that dimension. Religion has a much wider connotation, as does the idea of sacredness. In relation to any one Aboriginal society, all adult members, men and women, have a reasonably good grasp of the main tenets of their religion and what it is intended to achieve. Moreover, although much of the early literature has emphasized men's secret-sacred rituals, there is now recognition of a similar sphere having the same connotation of secrecy in relation to the ritual activities of women (Kaberry, 1939; C. H. Berndt, 1965). What is involved here is a division of labor between the sexes, with each sex being concerned with different but complementary aspects of the same religious system of belief. Each division involves the gradual movement of novices and participants from one level of understanding to the next, and each provides processes that ensure that religious information (*their* information: both general and specific) is handed on from one generation to the next.

With a very few exceptions, the structure of religion in most Aboriginal areas makes it obligatory for men and women to separate on particular occasions as far as their own secret-sacred matters are concerned. Since religion constitutes a celebration in community terms, most large mythic and ritual sequences provide opportunities, and indeed stipulate necessary occasions, for men and women to come together in the performance of ritual and song. Such collective manifestations may take place in a general camping area where a cleared space has been prepared, and they are an integral part of the proceedings. Virtually all of the most important ritual cycles have "inside" and "outside" sections. The efficacy of dramatic performances associated with a ritual sequence would be impaired if, for some reason, they did not incorporate both inside and outside sections.

It is useful to think of Aboriginal religion as including both secret-sacred and open-sacred components. Within the context of the open-sacred dimension, all members of a community participate—men and women, the uninitiated, and children. It is generally agreed, however, that the most spectacular rituals, with the use of a wide range of emblems, are carried out on a corporate basis by fully initiated men on their own secret-sacred ground, which is usually situated away from the main domestic camping areas. Less obtrusive, but no less significant religiously, are the rituals that women in certain regions organize and perform on their own secret-sacred ground. Both concern the same religious mythology, but in partly differing interpretative frames. Each draws on the life-giving properties inherent in such ritual sequences and pays special attention to relationships with particular land.

Two further, mutually exclusive, points should be noted about the secret-sacred grounds of men and women. First, it would be unthinkable in a traditional context for a man to enter or even go near the ground that is set aside for women-only affairs or for a woman to encroach on a men-only domain. Should that occur, even inadvertently, insofar as a woman is concerned it would have once meant her death by spearing or through sorcery. In any case, the sacred grounds of men and women are mostly regarded as being dangerous to members of the opposite sex. Not all adults of the relevant sex can freely enter the men's or women's secret-sacred ground; entry rests on invitation from those persons who are authorized to give it. The right to enter is dependent, for instance, on a person's position in the religious hierarchy or on the degree of familiarity he or she has with the ritual and songs. Only religious leaders and fully initiated men (or women, in their sphere) could go freely to their own ground.

The second point is that most of the large ritual sequences, which traditionally continued over a period of several weeks, usually contained both secret- and open-sacred components. This called for a great deal of preparation. Emblems had to be made or refurbished, the secret-sacred ground had to be attended to, and invitations had to be sent to people in surrounding areas. Not least, food had to be collected and prepared, usually by women. However, specified men would be sent out fairly regularly in order to supplement the diet with meat. Men of ritual importance—who by reason of their spiritual linkage with a particular mythic being are "owners" of the appropriate territorial and myth and ritual combination—act in a directive role. Chronological age is not crucial in this respect. Other things being equal, religious authority devolves upon a man who has considerable religious experience and knowledge as well as influence in his community. Such men are usually middle-aged or a little older. The efficacy of a ritual depends on them. They are the directors, supervising the actual performances that are carried out by the so-called workers, but in a different ritual sequence, controlled by other owners, their roles will be reversed. Any large ritual enterprise is a cooperative undertaking by members of the home camp as well as by visitors from adjacent areas.

Formal exposure to religion. An initiation sequence would normally attract quite a large number of visitors who are specially invited to attend and to participate. A person's initiation really commences with the events surrounding his or her conception. Those events are ritualized to the extent that they constitute a personal experience with minimal social involvement. Nevertheless, this represents an essential stage in the progression of life because it transfers to the potential social being a sacred quality that is also a hallmark of humanity. Where physical birth is concerned, no such ritual dramatization takes place: it is simply regarded as a natural ritual in itself. In other words, in this respect the importance of the physical act of birth has been transferred to a "man-made" ritual context and is consequently generalized to serve as a basic model that can relate to life renewal. Around that basic concept has been woven a symbolic patterning that is relevant to all initiation rituals and to many of the great ritual epics.

Thus the crises in the life of all males are clustered around prebirth, the onset and completion of formal initiation, subsequent ritual involvement, and eventual physical (not spiritual) death. The process is somewhat different and less formalized for females. Whatever importance may be placed socially and personally on betrothal and marriage, these features have little part to play in religion—except that in a number of examples a man who is responsible for initiating a boy or youth (for example, in relation to circumcision) is usually one of his potential affines and obliged to arrange that he receive a wife. There is, however, no direct religious underpinning in regard to marital arrangements.

Initiation flows, as it were, from and into something else of a religious nature. For example, in northeastern Arnhem Land there are two forms of initiation. One is relevant to novices of the Dua moiety; the other to novices of the complementary moiety, Yiridja. (In that society patrilineal moieties are important social indicators in religious mythology and ritual.) Each is associated with distinctive initiatory ritual. Dua novices between the ages of about six to nine years are introduced to the Djunggawon, the first of three ritual sequences that concern differing aspects of the great Wawalag mythology.

There is, or was, agreement among Aborigines that particular rituals are most appropriate for novices to be exposed to for preliminary religious purposes. Such events are usually marked by a physical operation (or its equivalent) that symbolizes the passing of boys or youths through one stage and indicates their preparedness to go further; the pressures to continue are just as strong as they are for the first initiation rites. The important aspect, however, is that any initation rite, although focused on particular novices, is also a teaching and learning experience that concerns older youths and men as well. Learning is correlated with active participation and occurs in a gradual progression through a series of mythic and ritual revelations. Whatever religious ritual is being carried out, there are always present some persons who are being taught. Thus a major task of religious leaders and fully initiated men is to

RITUAL ACTIVATION
Summoning a Mythic Diety

Myth and ritual are interdependent and mutually supporting. From the viewpoint of Aborigines, myths portray real events that belong to the realm of the Dreaming. It is true that they are said to have happened in the past. But the mythic characters who participated in them remain in the land, metamorphosed but spiritually alive, still possessing their life-giving power. In many parts of Aboriginal Australia, special words are used to express the idea of this power. In order to gain access to it and to activate it, ritual must be carried out in a particular way and under particular conditions. First, it must be planned and organized by religious leaders and others who are directly related to the mythic being or beings concerned. Second, it must re-create symbolically the original mythological events and circumstances associated with the deity or deities in the same way as they first experienced them. Third, a symbol or image of the deity (or deities), or an emblemic representation, must be present on the ritual ground. The deity (deities) must be attracted to it (them) and temporarily occupy the appropriate vehicle(s). A wide variety of such vehicles is used: for example, the Aranda tjurunga; the rangga (ritually charged) posts of northeastern Arnhem Land and various other pole and brush structures decorated in ocher designs and hung with feathered pendants; and ground paintings, carved and ornamented posts, bull-roarers, and so on. Fourth, there must be ritual performances in which the actors portray the deities in either their human or other forms. Such performances must replicate in all essential details the events in the myth associated with the deities; they are accompanied by stipulated songs that also recount the mythic deeds

— RONALD M. BERNDT

The substance of Aboriginal ceremonies and rituals consists of enactments of events from the Dreaming.

PAGE 299

According to Australian Aboriginal religious beliefs, a deceased ancestor, after a sojourn of an unspecified length of time in the land of the dead, returns to the world of the living by entering the body of a mother at the moment of conception.

PAGE 575

pass on their knowledge selectively, to those persons who are entitled or have been prepared to receive it. This is a process that traditionally continues throughout life. Associated with it is the application or utilization of sacred knowledge in order to achieve the aims that are stipulated in regard to specific rites.

Where female initiation is concerned, the focus is on puberty and the time is usually the onset of first mentruation. Generally speaking, female initiation rites are not as spectacular, nor do they extend over such long periods, as those of boys. Moreover, they need not involve the whole community or visitors from other areas.

Women are more heavily involved than men in the domestic round of activities, particularly in regard to nurturing children. Additionally, in the traditional Aboriginal scene, women were usually the main "breadwinners," responsible for supplying the greater part of the food supply for themselves, their menfolk, and their children. On the whole, the men's contribution to the food supply mainly concerned meat or large sea creatures, the supply of which was much less predictable.

There is an additional issue that has a bearing on this division of labor between the sexes. Much of men's ritual, especially when it concerns access to the life force controlled by either male or female deities or both, has to do with species and seasonal renewal. In such circumstances, the physiological attributes of females are emphasized, either directly or in symbolic terms. Where this point was specifically articulated by men, they asserted that women possessed such things naturally, while men needed to simulate them in order to accomplish what was required. There is another factor here. In many areas of Aboriginal Australia, mythic statements claim that women originally had complete control of the realm of the sacred and of all its ritual, verbal, spatial, and material components.

The final life crisis is physical death. The rites associated with death have much in common with the initiation of boys and girls. Initiation is usually treated as symbolic death, followed by ritual and social rebirth—more conspicuously so for boys. In actual physical death, the ritual is designed to ensure the spiritual survival of the deceased and his or her potential rebirth. In both cases, people have claimed that the life power derived from the deities makes such a transition possible. Mortuary rites vary considerably throughout the continent. In all cases they are concerned with re-creating or rechanneling life out of death, releasing the spiritual component of a human being from its physical receptacle and preparing it for its journey to a land of the dead—which in some instances is synonymous with the home of the immortals—there to await reincarnation. The cycle of life, therefore, continues after death, from the physical to the wholly spiritual, returning in due course to the physical dimension. That cycle is also relevant to all natural species. This view recognizes the equal importance of the physical and the spiritual and emphasizes that human beings are spiritually indestructible because they possess that germ of life that was theirs at conception and that came from the mythic beings of the Dreaming.

REGIONAL RELIGIOUS SYSTEMS. Some specific ritual examples, drawn from a cross section of regional religious systems, provide a range of apparently different interpretions.

Mobile adaptive systems. The great Kunapipi (Gunabibi), under different names, has spread across the continent from Arnhem Land to the central-western Northern Territory and as far as the southeastern Kimberley. In all these areas, local people regard it as a "cult in movement," that is, as having been brought from one place to another. It has reached, indirectly, a number of other areas as well. It does not submerge or replace what was already present in terms of local religious ritual. The outcome is rather a matter of coexistence, although in some areas it is also a matter of coordination and adaptation. In Arnhem Land, the culturally defined indigenous systems remained more or less intact. The Kunapipi brought with it both circumcision and subincision. In northeastern Arnhem Land, for instance, there is no subincision, although novices are circumcized; subincision was not accepted there, although that proved no handicap to the incorporation of basic tenets of that cult. On the other hand, in western Arnhem Land neither circumcision nor subincision was traditionally practiced, but the Kunapipi was accepted.

Northeastern Arnhem Land, as noted, recognizes two patrilineal moiety divisions, and the great mythic and ritual cycle for the Dua moiety is the Djanggawul (Djanggau), sponsored by the mythical two sisters and brother of that name. They shaped the land, gave birth to the first people, and introduced the appropriate Dua moiety *nara* ("nest" or "womb") sacred rituals. Essentially, the myth and songs makes clear the primary intentions in the ritual, which reenacts all the major incidents that took place during the original travels of the Djanggawul, including the natural species they saw.

On the sacred ground, a special hut representing a uterus is erected. Within it are stored secret-sacred *rangga* poles, representing those used by the Djanggawul as well as the unborn children (that is, the first people) within the wombs of the two sisters. In ritual dancing, *rangga* are removed from the hut by one postulant after another, and their actions in manipulating these refer to the revitalization of particular aspects of nature. In the main camp, women and uninitiated youths are covered with *ngainmara* (conical mats) that, again, represent the wombs of the sisters. These are later cast aside and the people emerge, thus reenacting the first mythic scene of birth. Additionally, in the present sense of the ritual, participants reaffirm the continuity of the birth process. Among the ritual sequences is the sacramental eating of cycad palm nut "bread" that has been specially prepared by women. Sacred invocations are called and songs sung over the bread, which is said to be transformed from being ordinarily sacred to achieve the status of a *rangga* emblem possessed of the power inherent in the Djanggawul. On the one hand this bread symbolizes all possible food resources available in the places invoked. On the other, when eaten by Djanggawul ritual participants it is said to enhance their sacred quality and strengthen the bonds between them.

Complementing the Djanggawul cycle is the Laindjung, of the opposite moiety. Laindjung is a mythic being represented as Banaidja, a barramundi fish, who emerged from the sea on the eastern coast of Arnhem Land. A range of mythic characters are associated with him; one, Fire, destroyed a ritual shelter where men were assembled for performances; Crocodile, who was among them, was seriously burned.

Whereas the Djanggawul myth sequences reveal a land resonant with growth and security, the Laindjung-Banaidja provides a view of a potentially dangerous world—where heavy rain and inevitable flooding of the countryside make travel difficult, and where later, when the floodwaters dry up and the grass grows and eventually dries too, fires spread across the land. The supreme danger is expressed in the mythic destruction by fire of the ritual shelter, with the loss of *rangga* and of life.

In the great Wawalag cycle, also a significant mythic and ritual cycle in this region, two sisters in conjunction with Yulunggul, the Great Python, are responsible for the coming of the monsoonal rains. The sisters, however, are not creators; they are only indirectly instrumental in activating a natural phenomenon that, in turn, fertilizes the land. The Djunggawon is an example of a Wawalag ritual which focuses on circumcision. Carved and painted *wangidja* poles, representing the Wawalag, are set up in the main camp. On the secret-sacred ground a triangular cleared space symbolizes the body of Yulunggul. At one end is a hole that is his home and water hole, and there is a special shelter containing a long, decorated drone pipe (*didjeridu*). Novices are painted with ocher designs in the same way as were the mythic Wawalag women, and they are said to represent them. Finally they are taken to the main camp where, screened by a group of men, they are circumcised.

In spite of major sociocultural differences between western and northeastern Arnhem Land, the basic religious themes are similar or complementary. Whereas the Djanggawul came from the east, from the mythical island of Bralgu, their western Arnhem Land counterpart came from the west (from, it is said, the Indonesian islands). Paul Foelsche, prior to 1881, was probably the first person to refer directly to a fertility

"Knowledge by suffering entereth, And life is perfected by death."

ELIZABETH BARRETT BROWNING,
A VISION OF POETS
1844

Aboriginal Ritual
The dance has always been an important element of Aboriginal worship.
PENNY TWEEDIE/CORBIS

WANGIDJA POLE

Carved and painted wangidja poles, shown here in Northeast Arnhem Land, represent deities or demons and play a central role in Aboriginal Rituals.

PENNY TWEEDIE/CORBIS

mother, whom he called Warahmoorungee. Baldwin Spencer (1914, pp. 275-279) called her Imberombera, and since he refers to her in association with the mythic man Wuraka, there is no doubt that he (like Foelsche) was referring to the mother, Waramurungundji, whose husband, Wuragag, was eventually metamorphosed as Tor Rock on the Murganella Plain.

In the Ubar rituals an elongated, triangular secret-sacred ground represents the body of Ngalyod; within it is a shade or hut and the headstone of Ngalyod. The narrow end of the ground is her tail, and at one side is an extension of the dancing ground—her arm(s). Postulants entering the ground are said to be going into the Mother's womb; novices taken for initiation are "swallowed" by her. During the ritual a hollow log (gong, or drum, which is itself the *ubar*) is beaten; this is the Mother, and the sound is her voice informing people that she is spiritually present at the ground. During the final scenes, in the main camp, men and women dance; in pairs, selected women and men climb a *Pandanus* palm or forked stick to call the sacred invocations (see Berndt and Berndt, 1970, pp. 117-120, pp. 128-132).

Such ritual sequences, while focusing on a bountiful mother goddess, are usually associated with a male mythic counterpart. Although conceptually they differ from the Kunapipi, they certainly have much in common with it, both structurally and ideologically. For example, the eastern Arnhem Land manifestation, while utilizing a basic ritual pattern, provides an interpretative system that relates to local Wawalag mythology. The intrusion of the Kunapipi into western Arnhem Land also draws upon local mythology, in this case a father-son pair named Nagugur. They are mythically responsible for performing, as well as introducing, this ritual to different groups as they traveled across the countryside.

A number of examples of the Kunapipi myth (with considerable variations) and associated rites have been recorded. W. E. H. Stanner (1959-1961), for example, discussing his Port Keats (southwest of Darwin) material, writes of "the Mother of All." In that case her name is Mutjingga (an everyday Murinbata word for "old woman"). The relevant ritual concerns the Kalwadi "bull-roarer ceremony" (as Stanner called it; ibid., p. 110). He also discusses the myth of Kunmanggur (the Rainbow Snake; ibid., pp. 234ff.), which has no ritual sequence. This mythic creature is seen as a counterpart of Mutjingga, although mythic interaction between them is minimal. Several parallels can be drawn with Ngalyod in western Arnhem Land.

Segmentary systems. A kind of transitional area demarcates the northern fertility mother cults from those that are more distinctively of the "central" variety. These may be called segmentary because they embrace varying mythic traditions of similar ritual status that are sometimes mythically related but need not be. For example, M. J. Meggitt (1966), in discussing the religious system of the Walbiri, refers to a particular ritual constellation as being the Gadjeri ("old woman," an alternative name for the Kunapipi mother). In the area of which he writes, south of Wave Hill (in the Northern Territory), the Gadjeri rituals are called Big Sunday in English. While they utilize some of the major symbols that are highlighted in the northern versions of the cult, their supporting mythology concerns the two mythic male characters, Mamandabari (either two brothers or a father-son pair). They travel over a large part of Walbiri country, so that no one person would know the whole of the myth. Meggitt points out (ibid., p. 23) a characteristic Western Desert mythology—namely, that by following one myth, one is led to others, which *in toto* form an interconnected pattern. There is separation between myths in terms of content, but multiple ownership of such a constellation is based on the different territories through which the principal characters travel. Meggitt (1966, p. 25) considers that the Gadjeri is an importation, with the Mamandabari providing a rationale that differs considerably from the northern versions.

At Balgo, in southeastern Kimberley, an area contiguous on the southeast and east with the Walbiri and Woneiga, or northern Walbiri, the sociocultural perspective of the Gugadja and Ngadi is typically that of the Western Desert—except that it too has been influenced by the Gadjeri. The religious system is supported by a number of mythic and ritual traditions called Dingari. These are secret-sacred and are associated with various mythic characters, the main ones being the Ganabuda (often equated with the Gadjeri). In these versions, the Ganabuda are a group of women who follow a Dingari ritual group of men who, accompanied by novices, move from one site to another across the country. In their travels they initiate youths and meet other mythic characters who have their own separate traditions.

As preliminaries to the main Dingari ritual, novices, accompanied by their guardians, make a pilgrimage to the main Dingari sites within their own and adjacent territories. While this takes place, cult leaders prepare their secret-sacred *daragu* boards and other emblems. These are incised with designs relating to small sections of the territories over which the Dingari traveled, and they also represent vehicles for the mythic beings to enter during the actual ritual. When the novices return, they are separated from their parents and close kin and sleep in a special camp not too far from the men's secret-sacred ground. This ground contains a *nanggaru* pit (the womb) and a *ganala (kanala)* crescent trench (both similar to those in the northern Gadjeri). Within these a number of dramatic reenactments of the mythology take place. Novices are brought to the ground with their heads covered; the covering is removed only briefly for them to witness a performance. In some of these sequences, when only fully initiated men are present, arm blood is used as an adhesive for feather down decoration on the bodies of participants or on emblems, and it is sipped to provide strength and oneness among those men present. In the final rites, novices are placed within the *nanggaru* while firebrands are thrown over them, some of the coals falling on them and burning them. (This is equivalent to Mamandabari rituals mentioned by Meggitt, 1966, p. 71.) Later, parents of the novices present gifts to the men who have initiated them, and a feast precedes the showing of sacred objects.

Clearly, preliminary initiation rites cannot be separated from rituals that are also intended to achieve other things beside ensuring that youths are prepared for their adult religious commitments. While novices are experiencing their own initial exposure to ritual, other men are participating in varying ways, depending on their knowledge and ritual status. Moreover, whenever large rituals are held, participants fall within one of two groups: active workers; and the executives or owners whose right it is to direct proceedings. In the case of circumcision ritual, women and children usually enter or come close to the sacred place, where they may dance. At that time novices are regarded as being ritually dead. On leaving the ground, women and children return to the main camp and the actual circumcision takes place. Afterward, novices are given their first bull-roarers *(daragu)* and are anointed with arm blood. Until a youth's subincision, he is traditionally obliged to attend all the rituals (or those sections which are relevant to him at this level). He must learn the songs and the meaning of the ritual performances.

Although the Dingari is known farther south in the Western Desert, its association with the Ganabuda or Gadjeri gradually disappears, and the desert system becomes dominant. While it is useful to separate the western from the eastern side of the desert for particular purposes, mainly because of the complexities of Aranda religion, here both may be regarded as being of desert inspiration.

Given mythological variation, the structure of Western Desert initiation ritual remains reasonably constant. While women wail, youths are taken from their domestic camps to a seclusion area: the removal signifies their ritual death. Arm blood from initiated men is collected in a wooden receptacle, which is then passed around for all, including the novices, to sip from; the residue is smeared over the novices' bodies. This symbolically refers not only to their ritual death but also to their spiritual life. At this time, a novice would have his nasal septum pierced, the middle tooth of the top row loosened and knocked out, and a pattern of scars cut on his back. These three operations probably came into the desert areas through early contact with eastern groups. After a lengthy seclusion period, a novice is tossed into the air and then given a waistband and a pearl-shell necklet. An important part of this sequence is the throwing of firebrands. This occurs near the circumcision ground as women perform a special shuffling dance which repeats the mythic actions of the Minmarara or Gunggaranggara women in the Nyirana-Yulana cycle. As the women, making deep grooves in the earth, reach a row of fires that have been placed near the ground, men throw firebrands at and over them and they retreat to the main camp.

A range of postcircumcisional rites takes place over the next couple of years. They include sacred mythic reenactments in which particular emblems are revealed, together with subincision. This rite is regarded as having major religious significance; only after it is performed can a man participate fully in the secret-sacred life. The initial act of subincision is relatively informal, and the main focus is on subsequent rites. During the period of seclusion, blood from the incision is sprinkled over the newly subincised youth or man, and this is accompanied by dance and songs from the Wadi Gudjara and the Nyirana-Yulana mythology (see also Tonkinson, 1978, pp. 76-77). Beyond the explana-

In Australia, the voices of the bull-roarers, symbols of the Great Spirit's presence, are heard throughout every initiation ceremony.

PAGE 87

tion that it was originally carried out by a particular mythic character and must, therefore, be followed by human beings, subincision has been said to be primarily therapeutic. In areas farther north, men explicitly state that its purpose is to simulate female menstruation, and the periodic ritual opening and enlarging of the incision seems to support this explanation.

Except for the Aranda and affiliated groups, initiatory themes on the eastern side of the desert do not differ markedly from those in the west. Aranda initiation rites include much variation in detail. Spencer and Gillen (1938, pp. 212-270) reported five basic divisions: tossing of the novice, circumcision, head biting, subincision, and fire ritual. These agree for the most part with information from Strehlow (1947, pp. 96-100). Events commence on the *pulla* secret-sacred ground, where both circumcision and subincision take place. On this ground a novice is introduced to some of the ritual of his group and, after circumcision, receives a bull-roarer. During his subsequent seclusion, he must swing this to warn noninitiated persons of his presence. Generally, during this period he is instructed in the appropriate myths and witnesses relevant rites. In one part of the sequence, men bite the initiand's head so that blood flows, although (as Strehlow points out: ibid., p. 99) the scalp is first opened with a sharp stick. The aim is allegedly to ensure a strong growth of hair. Subincision follows and is accompanied by mythic reenactments. Just prior to the actual subincision, men embrace decorated *tnatantja* poles that represent the mythic Bandicoot. When a youth is seized for the operation, certain women cicatrize themselves in the main camp; the marks are said to represent the incised designs on a *tjurunga*. Women dance as the men return to the main camp, and the undecorated, newly subincised youth is presented to them, then disappears rapidly into the bush. The next morning he is led to a group of dancing women who hold wooden dishes. He holds a shield before his face and the women throw their dishes at this. Then they press their hands on his shoulders and rub their faces on his back, taking the opportunity to cut off locks of his hair, which they later incorporate in the hair-string ornaments they wear.

In the oldest myths of many nations, the creation of the world itself is the result of miraculous divine actions.

PAGE 265

Despite the issue of segmentation, two aspects draw people together into a religious bond, even though that bond may be a distant one. The first is cooperation within the ritual sphere, where owners of a myth cycle receive direct aid from other persons in the performance of the associated rites. This is a constantly sustaining feature. The other is that secret-sacred boards and relics that are symbolic representations of mythic beings are moved about the desert from one group to another, substantiating the concept of a community of common interests and faith.

DESERT TRACKS

One Myth, Many Approaches

In the desert, Aboriginal peoples place particular emphasis on dreaming tracks made by the deities during their extensive travels across the land. Members of local descent groups associated with sections of such tracks are in a position to perform the relevant rituals and pass on their knowledge to others. Mythic knowledge is consequently fragmented ritually. In the past, it was not possible or practical to bring together all local sections of one particular myth cycle for a total dramatic performance. This state of affairs has several important implications. It emphasizes the localization of religion in the desert, where within any one region an overview or a total religious perspective could not be achieved through observation—as, broadly speaking, it could be in the big ritual constellations of the northern areas. In the desert, one particular myth is likely to be known, or known about, at the level of intellectual understanding over a very wide region; a large number of persons may recognize its significance even though they may never meet for the actual performances. The wide range of spatially extensive myths, dispersed among culturally similar people, reveals differing approaches to basic themes—for example, in regard to initiation and species-renewal ritual. One further feature concerns people's mythic and ritual (and personal) identification with specifically noted stretches of country. The deities, although shape-changing, are also virtually manifestations and expressions of local areas. They may be defined partly in relation to those areas.

— RONALD M. BERNDT

Aranda religion is more formalized but still segmented. It too was heavily oriented in terms of particular local groups, each represented by a mythic father-son pair (Strehlow, 1947, pp. 7-8, in relation to the Bandicoot named Karora). Strehlow (1947, p. 25) notes that the northern Aranda, particularly, were a "strongly patrilineal society" in which the people prided themselves on the belief that they and their forefathers had all "come into being from the primal *tnatantja*" (a ritual pole with life-containing properties).

Over and above the large ritual sequences held in particular territories, concentrating on the recreation of the original mythic scenes, special "increase" rites were intended to ensure a plentiful supply of the appropriate species represented by the local guardian deity: for instance, the well-known Witchetty Grub center at Emily Gap (near Alice Springs). The ritual associated with this site is secret-sacred. Such localized rites for species-renewal purposes are common throughout the desert and Aranda areas. Some include the making of elaborate ground designs which represent topographically, in a conventionalized form, the country associated with a particular mythic being; they are obliterated at the conclusion of the ritual.

Mythic sites are, everywhere, a salient focus in Aboriginal religion. In the Western Desert they loom more obviously, and because sections of a particular myth are in the hands of small local groups, they tend, to a greater degree perhaps than in the north, to be more significant ritually. At the same time, such sites are visible manifestations of the "reality" of what took place in the Dreaming, a reality that is transformed into ritual and, in turn, directed toward everyday living and needs.

Focus on deity. Information on eastern and southeastern Australia includes two significant key points. One is the reference to dominant deities of the All-Father type or the equivalent to a high god. Their categorization in those terms ignores associated descriptions, but there is no doubt that using such labels for an outstanding mythic being has its own appeal.

Typical of what are usually called Bora rituals was the Guringal (Kuringal) of the Yuin (south of Sydney). The Guringal took place on a specially prepared ground where a number of objects had been assembled: for instance, a spiny anteater made of earth with protruding sticks as quills, a molded brown snake of clay, and a figure of Daramulun (the mythic deity) made of earth and surrounded by implements and weapons. With these were exhibited magical substances. This is the second key point. Aboriginal "doctors" or "clever men" played a major part in the rituals; during the initiation rites, where tooth evulsion was the primary operation, novices witnessed some of their activities. These included disgorging quartz crystals and other substances symbolizing their power. Novices were also taken to see a large figure of Daramulun incised on a tree trunk. Before this image, decorated men danced toward the novices who, one by one, had a couple of teeth loosened with a succession of blows and finally removed by a doctor. Novices were then taken to stand before the figure of Daramulun and told of his power and that he lived beyond the sky and watched what people did. A number of ritual dances followed, among them some related to the mother (or two mothers) of this deity, and there were others that reproduced the behavior of certain natural species. During the final part of the Guringal, a grave was prepared. Within it a Yuin man, said to represent Daramulun, lay covered with branches and leaves and with a small tree, the roots resting on his chest. The novices were then placed alongside the grave. To the accompaniment of songs and the actions of the doctors, the supposedly dead person would rise and perform a magical dance within the grave, holding his magical substances in his mouth. Finally, the grave was covered up.

The contrast between southeastern Bora and rituals of other areas lies mainly in the emphasis on one deity, represented by an image of earth, clay, or as an incised figure on a tree. These were evidently comparable or equivalent to the emblematic poles, posts, wooden boards, and stone *tjurungas* of desert and northern groups and intended as vehicles for the deity to inhabit temporarily. A close inspection of Bora material suggests that other mythic beings were also present (as among the Wuradjeri of western New South Wales), as well as in the Guringal, where performances related to differing natural species. However, the aspect of species renewal is not directly mentioned. A further contrast lies in the presence of clever men and in the magical component of many of these rituals. Wuradjeri evidence suggests that such performances extended over several years, that clever men received their power from Daramulun, and that the "mother of Daramulun" (mentioned in the Guringal) was Emu (categorized as his wife, among the Wuradjeri). In my *Australian Aboriginal Religion* (1974, fasc. 1, p. 29), I note that much of southeastern ritual was preoccupied with the hereafter and with achieving identification with the deity Daramulun (or Baiame). Moreover, spirits of the dead played an important part. For instance, the grave scene in the Guringal (although it could certainly be interpreted in other terms) was possibly intended to symbolize the common initiation theme of death with subsequent rebirth.

The southeastern sector of Queensland is characterized by rituals that in some respects resemble the Bora, although there are marked differences. For instance, the training of novices in fishing, hunting, and fighting proficiency and the bestowal on novices of power-endowed names were emphasized. It would seem that fighting was a cultural focus (Howitt, 1904, pp. 595-599); fighting is included as part of an initiation sequence. Of course, fighting per se is not excluded from Aboriginal religious mythology, where it appears as a normal aspect of social living.

Transformation of ancestors. The religion of Cape York Peninsula focused on patrilineal clan territories containing auwa sites, or water holes. Near them live particular creatures in spirit form (which have been called "totemic" or, in this case, *pulwaiya*), and it is to these auwa that the spirits of the dead are said to go. As McConnel (1957, p. 171) puts it, the landowners approach the *auwa* of their *pulwaiya* with respect and

The concept of the cycling of spiritual power down the generations from the ancestral past characterizes Aboriginal religious thought.

PAGE 299

affection. The rites performed there to ensure the spiritual renewal of the representative species differ from one *auwa* to the next; however, it is to spirits of the dead (of the past), identified with the pulwaiya, that invocations are addressed. Also, the *pulwaiya* are associated with a wide range of myths. There are male and female *auwa* with spirit children awaiting rebirth through the performance of the appropriate ritual by a woman who has conceived.

In contrast to ritual connected with *auwa* are the initiation rites discussed by Thomson (1933, pp. 461-489). These concern a culture hero (that is, a mythic being). A secret-sacred area is protected by screens, behind which sacred objects are prepared and stored in readiness for dancing sequences. There are a large number of dances, and in some, actors use masks. Many of the myths associated with these dances are connected with the Torres Strait Islands and the mainland of Papua New Guinea. However, some of the *auwa* dances suggest possible linkages with Arnhem Land.

The Australians believe that death is the final rite of passage that leads one from the profane world to the sacred universe. At death, the true soul leaves the body and goes back to live forever in the eternal Dreaming, where it was before the individual's birth.

PAGE 315

Variations on a common theme. The Lake Eyre basin (in northeastern South Australia) is best represented by the Dieri, with information derived largely from the early work of Samuel Gason (1874) and Howitt (1904). In many respects the Dieri were culturally close to Western Desert people, especially in their variety of mythic beings, which were referred to as *muramura*. Each deity was associated with a particular ritual sequence. Like their counterparts in other areas, they were metamorphosed into stones or other natural features at specific sites where their spirits remain. Some were regarded as creative. For example, one Dieri myth tells how the *mardu* (a natural species spirit, regarded as a person's own flesh from his or her mother) came into being. They emerged from the earth as natural species (crow, parakeet, emu, etc.), but at that stage they were physically incomplete. They became whole by remaining in the sun, when they stood up as human beings and then scattered over the country. In another myth the Mandra-mankana, a mythic man, swallowed a large number of people. However, some escaped. Helped by the *muramura* Kanta-yulkana ("grass swallower"), they ran off in various directions in the form of natural species (becoming mardu).

The actual localities of these beings were traditionally indicated by wooden guide posts called *toa*. The designs carved or printed on these showed topographic features relevant to particular *muramura* or to their mythic adventures, and in this respect they were similar in intent to the incised tjurunga of the desert.

By far the most important of the postinitiatory rites was the Mindari, which normally followed the Wilyaru. Sponsored by the *muramura* Emu, this was probably the most sacred of all Dieri rituals. A large flattened mound was made and decorated with feathers and red ocher, representing Emu's body. Two women would walk across it to the accompaniment of singing, and as the mound was broken up, invocations were called to persuade emus to breed. Women were also sent as messengers to invite members of neighboring groups to attend the Mindari.

Dieri influences extended farther south, but not along the lower Murray River and the Lakes district, or on the Adelaide plains. There seems to have been more or less equal participation of women and men in ritual life, with a minimal division of labor between them in social activities. Song and dance sequences covered a wide range of subjects: natural species, food collecting and hunting, sickness prevention, and so on, and some songs provided sketches of current events. The major mythic being (deity) was Ngurunderi, who appears only in human form. In a bark canoe, he chased the great Murray Cod down the Murray River, and as it swished its tail from side to side it formed the river's bends and swamps. He was also responsible for setting in train all religious rites; wherever he traveled and camped or wherever some important event took place, part of his sacred essence remained. While these were sacred sites, they were not the subject of ritual or regarded as species-renewal places. However, there are indications that special rites took place, with Ngurunderi as the main focus—especially his going into the sky to enter the spirit world. The fact that Ngurunderi came from the upper reaches of the Murray suggests that he is associated with the Baiame/Daramulun tradition. In contrast to other areas, Yaraldi (as one language group within the Narrinyeri grouping) men and women possessed spirit familiars or protectors who indirectly referred to mythic beings.

One clue to the religious life of the lower Murray River lies in the concept of *narumba*, a term meaning "sacred" or "taboo." Initiation rites involved depilation of facial hair and observation of a wide range of food taboos; during his period of segregation, a novice was himself *narumba*.

In many respects, the cultures of southwestern Western Australia (now referred to as Nyungar) roughly paralleled those of the lower Murray River in South Australia. Many Nyungar myths told of beings associated with sacred sites. One of the most important was Waugal (a Rainbow Snake), who was responsible for shaping parts of the land and the rivers. Another, Motogen, was said to be a male creative being. There were a number of dance and song sequences, many of which dramatized birds, animals, reptiles, and so on, along with hunting scenes and the feats of clever men.

On the northern side of the continent, Bathurst and Melville islanders culturally resemble, in some respects, the people who lived on the lower Murray River. There

THE KULAMA RITUAL
Dancing for the Community's Welfare

The Kulama ritual, first described by Spencer (1914, pp. 91-115), and later by Charles W. M. Hart and Arnold R. Pilling (1960, pp. 93-95), among others, is particularly important. Its mythology involves several beings, among them the White-headed Sea Eagle and the Owl, and its rites are organized by initiated men who enter a state of *pukamani* (which signifies sacredness and taboo). The *kulama* is a dangerous but sacred plant, which produces yams that need to be processed before being eaten. At the appropriate season, the yams are collected and cooked in ovens. Then they are cut up and rubbed on the bodies of men, women, and children; some are mashed up with red ocher and the resultant substance rubbed into men's hair. This is believed to prevent sickness. The yam symbolizes a range of natural phenomena, some of which are explicitly mentioned in the songs and accompanying dances. The power inherent in the Kulama triggers off the monsoonal period and stimulates all growth, but it is also said to control the rain and prevent flooding. In other words, the Kulama, through the special ritual approach to it, safeguards the welfare of the community

— RONALD M. BERNDT

is, for instance, no physical operation at initiation except depilation, and they make no major distinctions on the basis of sex in religious matters.

There is some evidence that this particular culture was not restricted to Bathurst and Melville islands but extended on to the mainland, especially into parts of western Arnhem Land where the traditional Mangindjeg ritual (also focusing on an edible root) paralleled the Kulama in certain respects. As we have seen, one important feature which links northern Australian religion is the fertility mother concept. On Bathurst and Melville islands, traditionally, earth mothers were identified as being responsible for creating human and other natural species. Four of the five phratries that are recognized as social categories there are named after earth mothers who introduced that form of social organization. Among the Laragia (Larrakia) of Darwin, and the Daly River people to the southwest, circular stone structures were built to represent the wombs of their creative mothers.

In contrast to Bathurst and Melville islands and the lower Murray River, where religious life is, or was, relatively open insofar as men and women are concerned, Groote Eylandt culture (on the eastern side of Arnhem Land) traditionally offered a somewhat extreme case of sexual dichotomy in religious affairs. However, that area has been heavily influenced by mainland (northeastern Arnhem Land) religion and emphasizes mortuary ritual designed to transfer a dead person's spirit to the appropriate land of the dead. Subsequently, a lock of the deceased person's hair was ritually put into a small spirit bag and kept for a number of years until it was finally returned to that person's own territory, where it was buried. There were also additional mortuary rites for important persons, which resembled the nara rituals of northeastern Arnhem Land and in which most of the dramatic enactments were secret-sacred and included the use of sacred objects.

Among other localized religious types, the Wandjina are probably the best known. Widely spread in the northwest Kimberley of Western Australia, their graphic representations appear in cave and rock-shelter paintings. The basic rite connected with such paintings, intended to renew species and their environment, calls for retouching the designs and singing. This region has been influenced by the spread of cults from the Northern Territory which have been expanding for a consid-

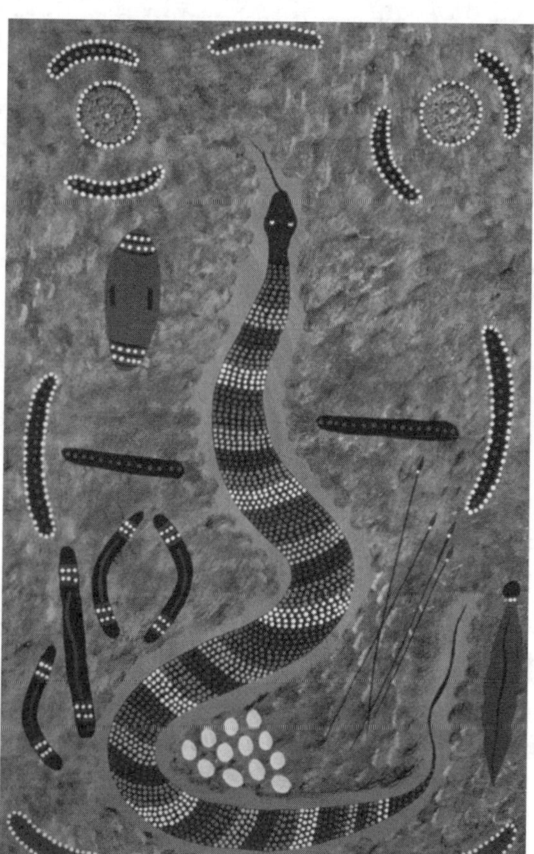

ROCK-SHELTER PAINTINGS

The Wandjina Rock Paintings in Western Australia portray the natural environment and symbolize species renewal.

MICHAEL FOGDEN & PATRICIA FOGDEN/CORBIS

A belief in reincarnation in some form or another is to be found in non-literate cultures all over the world.

PAGE 574

erable period of time, probably long before the first European settlement. For instance, Gurangara (Kurangara) ritual (a segment of the Kunapipi) is known and performed over much of the northern Kimberley.

DIVERSIFIED PATTERNS, COMMON AIMS. One of the problems facing students of Aboriginal religion has been the very real issue of differing cultural patterning, which has often obscured what is considered to be an essential commonality of religious purpose in relation to basic belief and what is intended to be achieved. When comparisons are drawn between regional manifestations, much depends on what criteria are distinguished and how differences and similarities are correlated, as well as delineated.

The patterns that have been presented here are by no means complete; there are others. However, their selection has been made mainly on the basis of contrasts between them, as well as what they have to offer in explanatory terms. For example, what have been called "adaptive mobile systems" have not only a wide spatial relevance; they are also easily distinguishable in relation to a bountiful (but sometimes dangerous) mother figure who—usually but not always operating with a male counterpart—dominates the ritual scene. The movement of such cults over wide stretches of country is far from unique in Aboriginal Australia. What distinguishes these constellations (for example, the Kunapipi, Gadjeri, and so on) is the ease with which they adapt to localized systems as well as the way they clarify such aspects as the power of a deity and how the life essence is released to ensure the continuance of the status quo for nature as for human beings and for the deities themselves.

The segmentary systems, on the other hand, refer to compartmentalization of extensive mythic and ritual cycles, the details of which are held by members of a number of local descent groups who may or may not live near each other. Each group is traditionally responsible for sustaining part of the total corpus of knowledge relevant to a particular mythic being and his or her travels in the Dreaming. There are major differences in structure between these and the adaptive mobile systems (as they are described here). The Western Desert examples are, of course, mobile but require (except in the Walbiri case) no adaptation. Each segment is a reflection or microcosm of the whole but is not complete in itself. The adaptive mobile systems, on the other hand, always appear to be complete in themselves, no matter what adjustments are made to accommodate local manifestations.

The Bora is distinctive, though not so much because of the attention that has been placed on a lone deity (since in other areas outstanding characters are given prominence). Rather, its uniqueness lies in two directions. One is the pervasive influence of magic in a way which does not occur in other Aboriginal religions. The other feature is the removal of the deity (in spite of the creation of his image and the images of those associated with him in the ritual context) from intimate contact with ritual postulants.

Spirits of the dead had a role to play in the Bora; but turning to the Cape York Peninsula area, we find that role is elaborated in respect of the auwa sites. In both cases, the intention is to transform postulants or newly dead persons into becoming representatives of, or identified with, particular mythic beings, or to merge them into the Dreaming. In comparing the ideologies of these groups with those of others discussed here, we can see that while processes differ, the aims are similar. In a sense, the auwa bring us back to the Dieri system, at least in part. Its religious system has been influenced by external cultures, but it apparently had no difficulty in retaining its distinctive patterning—even though it suggests close similarities to Western Desert religion.

Territorially peripheral, but no less significant, are the systems of the Murray River (South Australia) and Melville and Bathurst islands (with area extensions). While these two cultures are almost as far apart spatially as they could be, there are striking parallels between them in their initiations and highly structured taboo systems. At the same time, they differ radically in regard to the dominance of male or female deities. These two areas also provide examples of equality between males and females in ritual affairs, with virtually no secret-sacred dimension for either sex. At the other extreme, on Groote Eylandt, it would appear that women traditionally had no place in male-dominated religious activities.

CONTINUING SIGNIFICANCE OF ABORIGINAL RELIGION. Main-stream Aboriginal religion today takes two basic forms. Although modified through non-Aboriginal contact, Aboriginal religion still displays its own traditional orientations. Not all of the religious systems discussed in this contribution are now living realities. The religions of people who originally occupied the southwest of Western Australia, the Lake Eyre basin, the lower Murray River, New South Wales, Victoria, and southwest Queensland have all but disappeared. Two dominant mainstream religions remain, in general terms, in the northern coastal and the central desert regions. In the northern example, the fertility cults have traveled far across the Northern Territory to the edges of the Western Desert and proved sufficiently attractive, at least in border areas, to influence the distinctive desert form. The creative mother, usually present in conjunction with a male deity, is a major focus of mythic and ritual activity, either as a pivotal personage or seen in relation to other characters. Moreover, such cults have been sufficiently resilient to maintain their key identifying symbols through the vicissitudes of cultural differences. They are essentially flexible, adaptive, and responsive to changing circumstances.

In the case of the desert, there is no single coordinating theme; instead, the theme is manifested in a number of similar forms relating to differing mythic occurrences. In the desert, too, male deities predominate, although there is no lack of female mythic representation. Also, an additional contrast can be drawn. In the northern area, the physical aspect of procreation is emphasized, even though the spiritual component is present; in the desert, the spiritual aspects receive more attention. In both examples, the secret-sacred domain of men is similarly stressed. In the northern coastal region women do not usually have their own secret-sacred domain; in the desert, women usually have their own rituals. In both regions men and women come together for the performances of some sections of the major ritual cycles.

Non-Aboriginal influences, including missionary activities, have made some drastic inroads, but where traditional Aboriginal culture has survived it remains defined in terms of its members' commitment to the indigenous religious form. This was the case in the past, and is so today, particularly insofar as the two mainstream religious constellations are concerned.

The 1970s and 1980s saw a religious renaissance, which has taken a number of forms. It is one consequence of an upsurge of interest on the part of Aborigines in their unique identity vis-à-vis the wider Australian society. A contributing factor has been the attempt by governments (both federal and state) to implement more enlightened policies in regard to Aborigines. Not least, there has been a growing interest in the Aboriginal land-rights platform, which basically depends on the linkage of Aboriginal persons and groups to specific land defined in religious terms.

These developments emphasize the resilience of traditional religion, not only in more conspicuous survival zones, but also in many peripheral areas where some of the traditional background has continued to be a part of the background of social life. This is because the traditional religion continues to meet, in some measure, emotional and practical needs *and* political aspirations. Within the two main surviving regional spreads, some innovative religious movements have emerged. These have incorporated alien elements within a traditonal setting and in the presence of continuing traditional religious forms.

This traditional resilience is of particular significance. It is not due solely to the persistence of factors reinforcing or enhancing personal and social identity or to the use of religious knowledge to justify land claims. More particularly, it rests on two features which seem to have characterized all Aboriginal religions. One is their seeming conservatism. The other is their ability to allow room for varying interpretations, provided certain basic values are not impaired. There is a degree of flexibility in Aboriginal religion that permits coordination with changing circumstances.

— RONALD M. BERNDT

MODERN MOVEMENTS

In the history of conquest and dispossession of Australian Aborigines, well-defined and well-organized religious movements have not been characteristic. Melanesian-type cargo cults have been conspicuous by their absence, although a cargo cult element has been reported in a few instances. Nor has Aboriginal Australia produced any notable prophetic figures or millenarian movements. Initially, Aborigines generally responded to invasion and dispossession of their land with violence, but this resistance eventually proved futile and was followed by a period of quiet adaptation. Only in recent decades has an active political struggle to remedy the injustices of the past arisen. In a theoretical framework of linear evolution, one would have expected an interim period of religious movements whose purpose was to rid the land of intruding aliens or to arrive at a more satisfactory relationship. With a few exceptions, which are described below, such was not the case.

Aboriginal deities and all that is associated with them, belong to the Dreaming–a time everlasting, eternal.

PAGE 43

It is true—if not a truism—that the culture of the foraging and seminomadic Aborigines throughout Australia was so vastly different from that of the invaders, and so devastated by superior force, that an effective response to the invasion, aside from short-lived physical resistance in each locale, was unthinkable until a long period of cognitive adjustment had elapsed. Fortunately, sparsely settled areas of the island continent provided circumstances enabling the continuance of Aboriginal traditions during this long period—a continuance which has become the basis of a cultural regeneration adapted to present circumstances. The cataclysmic effect of the invasion on Aboriginal culture does not by itself, however, explain the dearth of well-defined religious movements. It is to the characteristics of Australian Aboriginal religion that attention must be drawn to explain the seeming anomaly.

TRADITIONAL ABORIGINAL RELIGION. Because of its relative homogeneity throughout the continent, traditional Aboriginal religion can be viewed as a single entity. From place to place and region to region, the complex of mythological figures, specific ritual forms, and ritual emphases vary, but the general outlines of religious ideology and practice remain constant. The Dreaming—a world inhabited by the spiritual ancestors of human and nonhuman life forms alike—is the basis of all Aboriginal religion. It laid down the patterns of the Aboriginal universe for all time. A conservative concept, it is not conducive to rapid adaptation; nevertheless, it is hospitable to changes that fit the elaborate but involuted complex of symbols used by each religious community. The religious duty of all initiated members of the community is to perform faithfully the ceremonies which activate the life-sustaining power of the ancestors. The concept of the Dreaming is decidedly nonmillenarian, nonutopian, and indeed nonhistorical.

Much has been written of the egalitarian nature of Australian Aboriginal society, though some allowances must be made for differences of age and sex. Although Aboriginal women have a religious life of their own in most parts of Australia, in general men maintain a marked attitude of superiority about their secret rites and exclude women from the inner core of their religious life. Over a number of years male novices pass through several ritual grades, or rites of passage, often marked by painful physical ordeals. Ceremonies are controlled by elders who have acquired ritual experience and knowledge after decades of participation.

As a population is missionized, new patterns of educational, familial, cultural, and political-economic conditions are routinized into a transformed "tradition" on new foundations.

PAGE 444

Aboriginal ceremonies have been categorized as local totemic rites and transcendental rites (Maddock, 1972, pp. 117ff.). Performances of local rites are the prerogative of local clan members and are oriented to the interests of the clan and its territories. Transcendental rites embrace several clans and sometimes several language communities; they are concerned more with rites of passage and with interclan and intertribal interests. Thus transcendental rites often occurred across a whole region and sometimes "traveled" hundreds of miles; these "traveling cults" have been traced and documented in historical times.

THE CONTEXT OF CHANGE. Aboriginal religious structures—developed over millennia on an island continent with little alien contact except along the north coast—were initially incapable of absorbing the onslaught of European culture. Traditions, which were adapted to slow change and in which continuity was valued above all else, either disappeared quickly in regions of intense colonization or persisted, although increasingly dissociated from social realities. Aboriginal cosmology encoded in the concept of the Dreaming was unable to account for cataclysmic changes. Seduced by the material rewards and relative freedom of European employment, young men became estranged from the authority of religious elders. The religious status of men was undermined by their observable inferiority in situations of paternalism at best and outright racism at worst. Parochial concerns of local traditions were of little relevance to the mixture of clans and language communities gathered on reserve lands set aside by governments. In many areas of Australia, Aboriginal religion failed to cope with the changed situation: the young rebelled, others were disillusioned, leaders were demoralized.

In areas of Australia more remote from the gathering momentum of colonization, persisting religious traditions were granted the opportunity to adapt by the historical and geographical circumstances. The bearers of these traditions were subject to similar pressures as their less fortunate coreligionists elsewhere, but the pressures were more extended over time. What appear at this time to be viable adaptations, have been contingent on several factors: non-Aboriginal Australians' improved tolerance of the continuation of Aboriginal culture, a developing Aboriginal consciousness of common identity and interests, and enhanced Aboriginal mobility and communication through the adoption of modern technology.

SYNCRETIC MOVEMENTS. Christian missionaries followed hard on the heels of settlers and in some cases ventured beyond the frontiers of pastoral settlement. The results were mixed and sometimes unexpected. At the remote Aboriginal community of Jigalong in the Western Desert (Western Australia), rejection of Christianity, at least in the early stages of missionary expansion, was almost complete (Tonkinson, 1974). At Aurukun on Cape York Peninsula in the far northeast, a mixture of local Aboriginal religion and nearby Torres Strait Islands traditions coexist with Christianity in the same ceremonies (as documented in Judith McDougal's film *The House Opening*, 1980). In more densely settled regions, orthodox Christianity filled the vacuum left by the Aboriginal traditions that were totally unable to adapt. In at least two places in Australia, however, creative attempts at syncretism occurred.

Bandjalang-speakers in northeastern New South Wales were missionized by the interdenominational United Aboriginal Mission (UAM). Preaching a fundamentalist version of Christianity, the UAM believed and taught that traditional spirits and mythic figures were not illusory but were evil manifestations of the devil. Traditional beliefs lingered on, despite their incompatibility with social realities: the breakdown of clan organization, the "liberation" of youths, the undermining of the status of male elders, and general anomie. An Aboriginal non-Bandjalang Pentecostal preacher found fertile ground in this demoralized community. Spirit possession, characteristic of Pentecostalism, was individualized in conformity with Aboriginal custom; elements of local Aboriginal myths were incorporated into the Pentecostal belief system and Christian mythology reinterpreted; degrees of initiation (beginning with baptism) were emphasized and elaborated; and various taboos were adopted. The Bandjalang version of Pentecostalism was decidedly anti-European: Europeans were equated with Romans who killed Christ (who was humble and poor like the Bandjalang, who would be rewarded when Christ returned in glory). There was little or no contact with European Pentecostal groups. Bandjalang Pentecostalism provided an outlet for grievances against the Aborigines' oppressors and a means of restoring self-respect as well as satisfying religious experience and belief in keeping with both Aboriginal and Christian pasts (Calley, 1964).

The fundamentalist movement has spread rapidly across eastern and central Arnhem Land. The features of the movement are not clear at present, but it appears to be another offer of compromise. The religious belief system is more purely Christian, but ritual forms are more akin to Aboriginal than to European traditions. In the context of renewed threats to the inviolability of the Arnhem Land Reserve from government and mining companies, the adherents preach the equality of Aborigines and Europeans, which may convey an appeal—consciously or unconsciously—for Aboriginal control over land and society. Although the movement has had considerable success, adherence to it is by no means universal. A more direct threat to traditional religion than the earlier movement, it has set father against son and traditionalists against Christians.

A UNIFICATION ATTEMPT
Sharing Secrets

On Elcho Island, off the central-north coast of Australia (northeast Arnhem Land), a syncretic movement developed in the late 1950s (Berndt, 1962). Sacred-secret objects *(rangga)* were publicly displayed, and spiritual ancestors were equated with prophets within the Christian belief system. The Methodist mission on Elcho Island had refrained from denigrating Aboriginal religion, and the leadership of the movement had strong links with both the church and traditional religion. Occupying a remote corner of a large reserve, the Elcho islanders were sheltered from the worst effects of colonization, and the movement, although it was an attempt to stem the drift toward assimilation by offering a compromise, was not overtly anti-European. Its aims were pragmatic: to retain control over Aboriginal affairs, to obtain better educational and employment opportunities, and to unite hitherto parochially oriented Aboriginal groups of eastern Arnhem Land, and perhaps beyond, by publicly sharing religious secrets. The means, however, were based on the false assumption that what eastern Arnhem Landers valued most highly among their possessions, the *rangga*, were also valued highly by Europeans. The movement failed on several counts. Although, as a sign of the new order, women were shown the *rangga* for the first time, they were not told the meanings, which every male novice has revealed to him. Other eastern Arnhem Landers did not follow suit. Worst of all, European government administrators and missionaries were unimpressed.

— STEPHEN A. WILD

WESTERN DESERT MOVEMENTS. The cultural block traditionally occupying the huge desert region of eastern Western Australia and western areas of the Northern Territory and South Australia was the area most isolated from Western encroachment. Mainly since the 1930s and particularly since World War II, Aborigines of the Western Desert have moved into government settlements and into the pastoral regions of the southern Kimberley Plateau of northwestern Australia. Here Aborigines have been most successful at adapting their traditional religion to the exigencies of European domination.

On the southern Kimberley Plateau cults here are exchanged across hundreds of miles. An important impetus seems to have been the Pastoral Award in 1969, which granted Aboriginal employees equal pay on cattle properties in the region but was followed by mass expulsion of Aborigines from land on which they had come to feel secure. The expulsion coincided with a rise in Aboriginal political consciousness and a growing sense of common interests. The cultic movement is intimately linked with demands for Aboriginal title to land.

In the southern Kimberley and in many other places in the Western Desert, a conflict exists between Christians and cultists on the issues of symbolic identity and appropriate role in the wider Australian community. The cultists have adapted traditional religion to meet the demands of youth and women's emancipation, pan-Aboriginal identity, and economic development: initiation ordeals have been considerably reduced, women are admitted into cults on a more equal footing, religious parochialism has been transcended by incorporating ritual elements from various locales, political and religious leadership have separated but remain collaborative, and the ritual calendar is adjusted to the requirements of economic enterprise. Some or all of these elements are accepted in various Western Desert Aboriginal communities, as their members participate in the cult exchanges emanating mainly from the southern Kimberley.

Organized militancy is the feature that most clearly distinguishes fundamentalists from other evangelicals.

PAGE 217

HISTORY OF STUDY

The study of Australian Aboriginal religions has been the study of religions without a written record provided by their adherents. We depend on what outsiders to Aboriginal religion have thought worthwhile to commit to writing. Moreover the history of contact in Australia has been a sorry one in the main—Aborigines were dispossessed of land, regarded with contempt, and made socially and politically inferior. The amateur anthropologist A. W. Howitt could observe in 1880 that the frontier was often marked by a line of blood. Indeed, between the late eighteenth century, when European settlement began, and the 1920s, Aboriginal numbers fell so sharply that prophecies of race extinction were neither alarmist by some nor wishful thinking by others. After World War II, in keeping with a new policy of assimilating Aborigines to an ill-defined general Australian standard, there was a great expansion of administrative interference with them. But a more sympathetic attitude toward tradition became prevalent during the 1970s; "self-management" and "self-determination" entered common usage as policy slogans; and a few Aborigines even began to call for sovereignty. In what is now a highly politicized atmosphere, with laws passed or proposed for the grant of land rights, the protection of sacred sites, and the recognition of customary law, it can be an advantage for Aborigines to be—or to appear to be—traditional in outlook and values. It is amid such aftermaths and in such contexts that scholars (mostly anthropologists) have studied Aboriginal religion.

In the course of this strained and unhappy history a remarkable change has occurred in the appreciation of Aboriginal religion. It can best be illustrated by juxtaposing two pairs of quotations. In 1828 Roger Oldfield (pseudonym of the Reverend Ralph Mansfield) wrote that "the religion of the Aborigines, or rather their superstition, is very absurd," and in 1841 another clergyman, Lancelot Edward Threlkeld, described Aborigines as "deluded men" who, "like most ignorant savage tribes, are remarkably superstitious." But by the

A COMMUNITY CASE STUDY
Replacing the Old with the New

Established as a government Aboriginal settlement in about 1950, Lajamanu, formerly Hooker Creek, is a predominantly Walbiri (Warlpiri) community in the central northwest of the Northern Territory. Traditional clan territories of most Lajamanu residents are located to the south in the Tanami Desert, but many clan members have never seen their territory, and few have ever lived there. After the establishment of the settlement, local totemic ceremonies declined in importance. The local Baptist mission gradually acquired converts, and by the mid-1970s, as traditional religion became increasingly anachronistic, the Christian future at Lajamanu looked bright. Local Christians experimented with adaptations of Walbiri ritual forms to Christian content and earned themselves mission-sponsored trips to southern cities to display their minimally syncretic creations.

From about 1976 onward, a new cult from the southern Kimberley was enthusiastically embraced at Lajamanu. The adoption was managed by relatively youthful Aboriginal administrators who were articulate in English, skilled in negotiations with Europeans, politically aware, and in control of the community's telecommunications and motorized transportation facilities. Exchange visits of large contingents were arranged with Aboriginal communities far to the west across the Western Australian border. Far more dramatic and less stylized than Walbiri ritual forms, the ritual forms of the newly arrived cult were well-suited to performance by younger people. Women were admitted to the cult in a seemingly more equal role than in traditional rites, and ritual experience of male elders was set at nought.

The aim of cult leaders at Lajamanu—to replace the old ceremonies with the new—was met with some resistance. To avoid initiation into the new cult, Walbiri Christians gathered in the mission yard, and other people fled to distant places. The European missionary bemoaned the passing of traditional rites. Old men insisted on their sons being initiated traditionally. Youths were more interested in participating in the universal youth culture of rock and roll and in the country-and-western traditions of rural Australia. Whether the new cult succeeds, however, will depend on the extent to which the Lajamanu Walbiri choose to adopt a religious movement which currently seems to offer the best chance of maintaining an Aboriginal identity which is in harmony with the aims of an emerging national Aboriginal polity.

Located directly west of the southern Kimberley corridor of the movement, Lajamanu represents an extension of the movement's axis. If the new cult does take hold and the community enters more fully into cult exchanges with their new allies, these traditional elements may be modified or disappear. Since there are historical precedents for cult exchanges to the north and northeast of Walbiri country, Lajamanu may become a pivot for a more widespread Aboriginal religious movement.

— STEPHEN A. WILD

mid-twentieth century, a number of writers had discussed the status of Aboriginal religion more sympathetically. In 1965, the anthropologist W. E. H. Stanner referred to "the facts that have convinced modern anthropologists that the Aborigines are a deeply religious people."

Such a rise in estimation reflects growing knowledge of and deepening sympathy with Aborigines, but another important cause is the loss of confidence in the validity or usefulness of earlier criteria for distinguishing true religion from false, or religion from superstition and magic. Assertions of Aboriginal religiosity (or spirituality, as it is often called) and studies of aspects of Aboriginal religion have proliferated since the 1950s—coinciding, ironically, with a growing inclusion of Aborigines in the Australian polity and an increasing erosion of the more tangible features of traditional culture. No longer as objectively "other" as they once were, the Aborigines have become subjectively "other" through being credited with a religious dimension largely absent from the secularized society which engulfs them. It would be wrong, however, to imagine that an unbridgeable gulf has opened between earlier and later bodies of opinion. A degree of continuity can be seen even in the writings of Stanner, who worked passionately and to great effect to dispel misperceptions of Aboriginal life and thought.

The Aborigines, he wrote in 1953, have no gods, their afterlife is only a shadowy replica of worldly existence, their ethical insights are dim and coarsely textured, their concept of goodness lacks true scruple, and their many stories about the Dreaming (the far-off creative period when nature and culture were formed) are plainly preposterous, lacking logic, system, and completeness. Does this differ much from Howitt, half a century earlier, who could not see that the Aborigines had any form of religion, and who thought that the supernatural beings in whom they believed showed no trace of a divine nature (being, at most, ideal headmen living in the sky instead of on earth)? Does it differ from Howitt's contemporaries, Baldwin Spencer and F. J. Gillen, in whose monumental works such words as *god*, *religion*, and *divinity* are conspicuous by their absence, though they saw a religious aspect in the Intichiuma, or totemic increase ceremonies, of central Australia? Yet Stanner insisted not only that Aborigines had made the longest and most difficult move toward the formation of a truly religious outlook, but that they had gone far beyond that first step.

RELIGION'S LUXURIANT GROWTH. Stanner suggested in 1965 that one of the best avenues of study of Aboriginal religion was through the surviving regional cults. In fact, anthropological attention has long tended to focus on them, as can be seen by the studies that Howitt and Robert Hamilton Mathews (1841-1918) made of the Bora, or initiation, ceremonies in southeast Australia and that Spencer and Gillen made of the increase and initiation ceremonies of central Australia. This tradition, as it can justly be regarded, has continued until the most recent times. Some of the more notable examples are Ronald M. Berndt's monographs on the Kunapipi and Djanggawul of northern Australia, A. P. Elkin's papers on the Maraian and Yabuduruwa, also of the north, and M. J. Meggitt's monograph on the Gadjari of central Australia, though there has also been valuable work of a more general nature, such as Catherine H. Berndt's and Diane Bell's studies of women's religious beliefs and observances.

The popularity of the cult for study stems from the fact that it is in many ways a natural whole—it seems to be self-bounding. Commonly it has a name (Kunapipi or Kuringal, for example), includes a sequence of ritual episodes—the performance of which may stretch over several weeks—and usually one or more cycles of songs, and has attached to it a body of myths and tangible symbols, such as a musical instrument which may stand for a mythical founder of the cult and be known by the same name as the cult. An outsider who attends a performance may well be reminded of European plays, operas, or ballets, though it would be wrong to think of a cult as necessarily an enactment of a straightforward story. Some episodes do have a narrative quality, but others can be quite cryptic. The performers are not self-chosen or selected at random but occupy roles prescribed according to such criteria as sex, degree of initiatory advancement, moiety (where, as is usual, a dual organization exists), totemic identity, or localized group. All of these criteria, and perhaps others as well, can be relevant in the course of a single cult performance. Another typical aspect of a cult is its anchorage in the landscape: myths and songs refer to numerous places, rites are symbolically or actually performed at such places, and the groups and categories of the social order in terms of which the performers are chosen stand in a variety of jurisprudential relations to those places. A cult, then, is virtually a microcosm of Aboriginal culture.

Throughout much of central and western Australia the maintenance or promotion of fertility in plant and animal nature was aimed at in cult performances. Disposal of the remains of the dead can be an important purpose, as can transformation of spirits of the dead into a state in which they can return to ancestral waters (or other places) and from which they can (in some regions) be reincarnated. Several such purposes can be achieved in a single cult performance. We should not, that is to say, think of there necessarily being a one-to-one correlation of cult and institutionalized purpose. Nor should we think of express purposes as the motives for cult performances. As musical, dramatic, and aes-

"Facts have convinced modern anthropologists that the Aborigines are a deeply religious people."

W.E.H. STANNER

"Know then thyself, presume not God to scan; The proper study of mankind is man"

ALEXANDER POPE
AN ESSAY ON MAN

thetic occasions, as mappings-out of landscape and social organization, they can be deeply satisfying for their own sake. This has been brought out especially in the writings of Stanner on the Murinbata of northern Australia, and of T. G. H. Strehlow (1908-1978), the linguist-anthropologist son of Carl Strehlow, on the Aranda.

In spite of seeming to be the natural unit of study, no cult has yet been the subject of a truly comprehensive published work. Howitt and Mathews, for example, concentrated on the sequence of ritual episodes, with the latter also providing detailed descriptions of the shape and dimensions of ceremonial grounds, of the paths between them, and of the objects of art by which they were surrounded. Berndt's Kunapipi monograph runs to 223 pages and his Djanggawul monograph to 320, but both are stronger on myth and song than on ritual description. Elkin on the Maraian, like Meggitt on the Gadjari and Stanner on the cults performed by the Murinbata, neglects the songs (the Yabuduruwa lacks singing). None of these scholars shows, in a really detailed way, how the cults are anchored in landscape and social organization. In short, even at a purely descriptive level, each of our accounts suffers pronounced weaknesses as well as showing characteristic strengths. It is as though the student of a cult is defeated by the sheer abundance of what it offers to eye, ear, and mind. But even if we had a truly comprehensive account of, say, the Kunapipi or Yabuduruwa, we would still be far removed from an adequate grasp of the religious life of the area concerned, for usually several cults coexist.

In southern Arnhem Land, for example, where religious studies have been made by myself, following on earlier work by Elkin, five cults were extant in the 1960s and 1970s, with others still remembered by some older people. The five, in order of degree of secrecy or importance, were Bugabud, Lorgon, Kunapipi and Yabuduruwa (this pair being ranked about equally), and Maraian. All men and women could expect to take part in each of them—they were not the concern, then, of specialized and mutually exclusive groups of votaries. The dual organization, divided into patrilineal moieties named Dua and Yiridja, imposed its pattern on the set of cults: Bugabud, Lorgon, and Maraian existed in two versions, one for each moiety; Kunapipi was classified as Dua and Yabuduruwa as Yiridja. But in each case performers would necessarily be drawn from both moieties by virtue of a prescribed division of labor and responsibilities.

To write an adequate description of such a set of cults would be a mammoth undertaking. But to think of portraying the religious life of southern Arnhem Land by describing discrete cults would be to remain in the condition of theoretical backwardness remarked upon by Kenelm Burridge in 1973. What marks recent advances in the study of religion, he argued, is the transformation of functionalism into some kind of structuralism, by which he meant the abandonment of the concrete institution in favor of the search for the elements of a total semantic field. Institutions would be seen as particular constellations of these elements, and the value of an element would be determined by its position in a constellation. Something like this view is now fairly widely held, and two anthropologists have published substantial approximations of it. Stanner is one, with his perceptive and influential analyses of Murinbata religion. The other is William Lloyd Warner, whose classic study, *A Black Civilization* (New York, 1937), includes a valiant attempt to demonstrate pervasive and recurring themes and symbols in the myths and rites of the Murngin of northern Arnhem Land.

It is clear from the literature that important work can be done in tracing chains of connection between the religious complexes of different areas. Some of the early writers were aware of this possibility—Howitt, for example, in distinguishing eastern and western types of initiation, was recognizing far-flung patterns of similarity and difference—and it has been explored by later writers, including Elkin, Berndt, and Meggitt. The most ambitious effort has come from Worms, who made continent-wide studies of religious vocabulary and also sought to enumerate the "essentials" of Aboriginal religion and to distinguish them from "accidental accretions."

MAIN PHASES OF STUDY. It may seem artificial to distinguish periods in the study of Aboriginal religion, as distinct from recognizing certain enduring problems posed by the material, yet all but a few of the scholars likely to be taken seriously today belong to one of three main groupings. To a great extent the ways in which they have worked their data have been conditioned, if not determined, by fashions and theories of overseas origin—Stanner, Worms, and the younger Strehlow would be notable exceptions.

A first phase, spanning the late nineteenth and early twentieth centuries, is dominated by the names of Howitt, Spencer and Gillen, Mathews, and the elder Strehlow. Except for Strehlow, who concentrated his researches on the Aranda and their Loritja neighbors, these scholars amassed information over very great areas indeed, although Howitt's work mainly concerned the southeast of the continent and Spencer and Gillen's the Northern Territory. Some of the descriptions of ritual dating from this period, which of course preceded the rise of professional anthropology, are as thorough and detailed as any that have been written since, if not a good deal more so. (It should be noted that the elder Strehlow felt constrained as a missionary not to attend cult performances, so his knowledge of ritual was hearsay, but in studying myths and songs he reaped the benefits of long acquaintance with his informants and of a thorough grasp of their language.) An indication of the quantity of data collected by the workers of this phase is given by Spencer and Gillen's first book, *The Native Tribes of Central Australia* (London, 1899). It has eight chapters, totaling 338 pages, on totems, ceremonies, and the like, with some material in other chapters also being relevant to what we would call religion.

A second phase, beginning in the mid-1920s and flowering especially during the 1930s, the first decade of the journal *Oceania*, owed much to the initial impetus given by A. R. Radcliffe-Brown, Australia's first professor of anthropology. Those years saw the advent of professional anthropology, inspired by functionalist ideas and committed to intensive fieldwork in relatively small areas. Yet the harvest of religious data was meager in comparison with what had been collected in the preceding phase. Before World War II the most substantial portrayal of religious life to emerge from the new wave of scholars was Warner's study of the Murngin, but the chapters of *A Black Civilization* devoted to the subject run to barely two hundred pages (including a good deal of interpretation)—fewer than Berndt would later devote to the Kunapipi alone. The strong point of the writers of this period was their sense of the interconnectedness of the institutions that go to make up a culture, and besides Warner a number of them made useful, albeit somewhat limited, contributions to our religious knowledge. Donald F. Thomson, Ralph Piddington, Ursula H. McConnel, and Phyllis M. Kaberry may particularly be mentioned. Except for Warner they have since been greatly overshadowed by Elkin, Stanner, and the younger Strehlow—scholars who were active in research before World War II, but published their best work on religion long after it, thus overlapping the third phase, which indeed they did much to stimulate.

The third phase really got under way with the expansion of anthropology departments in the universities and the foundation of the Australian Institute of Aboriginal Studies in the 1960s. Intellectually it owes a special debt to papers published by Stanner between 1959 and 1967. Stanner's writings, the product of intensive ratiocination and prolonged reflection, best fit his own prescription for study of, and not merely about, religion. But much that he has to say is difficult, if not positively cryptic, and is best tackled by readers who already enjoy a familiarity with Aboriginal thought and ritual. The store of personally gathered field data on which he relies is far less plentiful than that amassed by Ronald M. Berndt and Catherine H. Berndt or by the younger Strehlow, writers whose work has exerted less influence on their fellows.

The third phase is less clearly distinguishable from the second than the second from the first. The greater degree of continuity is partly due to the shared emphasis on intensive fieldwork by professional anthropologists, as well as to the survival into the 1970s of scholars who had already begun to make their mark forty years earlier and to the appearance of a few students of religion (notably the two Berndts and Meggitt, all trained by Elkin) during the intervening period. Apart from a vast increase in the number of persons doing research, the main differences between the two phases consist in an abandonment of old-style functionalism, a rise of approaches influenced in varying degree by forms of structural or symbolic anthropology, and an intense interest in the significance of the landscape in which Aboriginal lives are set. There is still little sign of philosophers or students of comparative religion challenging the ascendancy of anthropologists.

— KENNETH MADDOCK

AZTEC RELIGION

Aztec religion developed in the capital city of Tenochtitlán in the Valley of Mexico between the fourteenth and sixteenth centuries CE. The Aztec religious tradition combined and transformed a number of ritual, mythic, and cosmic elements from the heterogeneous cultural groups who inhabited the central plateau of Mesoamerica.

Mexico's central highlands had been the dominant cultural region of central Mesoamerica since the beginning of the common era, when the great imperial capital of Teotihuacán ("abode of the gods") had been established thirty miles north of where Tenochtitlán would later rise. Like Tenochtitlán, Teotihuacán was organized into four great quarters around a massive ceremonial center. Scholars and archaeologists have theorized that the four-quartered city was a massive spatial symbol for the major cosmological conceptions of Aztec religion. In many respects, the cultural and religious patterns of Teotihuacán laid the groundwork for all later developments in and around the Valley of Mexico. The mythologies of successive cultures—the Toltec and the Aztec most prominent among them—looked back to Teotihuacán as their symbolic place of origin and as the source for the legitimacy of their political authority.

Between 1300 and 1521 all roads of central Mesoamerica led into the lake region of the valley from which the magnificent capital of the Aztec arose. When the Aztec's precursors, the Chichimec ("dog lineage"; lit., "dog rope") migrated into the region in the thirteenth century, the valley was held by warring city-states constantly competing for land and tribute. This

The Aztec sytlistic and iconographic tradition differs principally in displaying an even greater naturalism in human and animal imagery.

PAGE 304

A

AZTEC RELIGION

Cosmogony and Cosmology

> *"The more we realize our minuteness and our impotence in the face of cosmic forces, the more astonishing becomes what human beings have achieved."*
>
> BERTRAND RUSSELL
> NEW HOPES FOR A CHANGING WORLD

fragmented world was partly the result of the twelfth-century collapse of the northern Toltec empire centered at the illustrious capital of Tollan ("place of reeds"). The Toltec collapse brought waves of Chichimec and Toltec remnants into the Valley of Mexico, where they interacted with different city-states and religious traditions.

The basic settlement of central Mexico from Teotihuacán times was the *tlatocayotl*, or city-state, which consisted of a capital city surrounded by dependent communities that worked the agricultural lands, paid tribute, and performed services for the elite classes in the capital according to various ritual calendars and cosmological patterns. Around 1325, a Chichimec group who called themselves *Méxica* settled Tenochtitlán and within a hundred years had organized a political unit with the power to dominate an expanding number of cities and towns in the central valley.

One of the major problems in the study of Aztec religion is the fragmentary nature of the pictorial, written, and archaeological sources associated with Tenochtitlán. The Spanish military conquest of Mexico was accompanied by a sustained campaign to eliminate Aztec symbols, images, screenfolds, and ceremonial buildings, as well as members of the military and priestly elites. Surprisingly, a counter attitude developed among certain Spanish officials and priests, who collected indigenous documents and organized their reproduction in order to enhance missionary work and inform Spanish officials about native religion and life. The result is a spectrum of sources including art and architecture; pre-Columbian screenfolds depicting the ritual, divinitory, historical, and genealogical traditions of different cities; post-Conquest codices sometimes accompanied by Spanish commentary; prose sources dependent on indigenous pictorial and oral traditions; histories written by descendants of Aztec royalty; Spanish eyewitness accounts; and large histories and ritual descriptions by Spanish priests who vigorously researched Aztec religion. It is only through a skillful combination of these sources that the complex character of Aztec religion can be discerned.

COSMOGONY AND COSMOLOGY. The image of the capital city as the foundation of heaven, which the Aztec conceived of as a vertical column of thirteen layers extending above the earth, points to the cosmological conviction underpinning Aztec religion that there existed a profound correspondence between the sacred forces in the universe and the social world of the Aztec empire. This correspondence between the cosmic structure and the political state was anchored in the capital of Tenochtitlán.

In his important summary of religion in pre-Hispanic central Mexico, H. B. Nicholson (1971) outlines the "basic cosmological sequential pattern" of the Aztec cosmogony found in the myths and historical accounts associated with the Méxica. A summary view reveals that Aztec life unfolded in a cosmic setting that was dynamic, unstable, and finally destructive. Even though the cosmic order fluctuated between periods of stability and periods of chaos, the emphasis in many myths and historical accounts is on the destructive forces.

This dynamic universe appears in the sixteenth-century prose accounts *Historia de los Mexicanos por sus pinturas* and the *Leyenda de los soles*. In the former, the universe is arranged in a rapid, orderly fashion after the dual creative divinity, Ometeotl, dwelling in Omeyocan ("place of duality") at the thirteenth level of heaven, generates four children, the Red Tezcatlipoca ("smoking mirror"), the Black Tezcatlipoca, Quetzalcoatl ("plumed serpent"), and Huitzilopochtli ("hummingbird on the left"). They all exist without movement for six hundred years, whereupon the four children assemble "to arrange what was to be done and to establish the law to be followed." Quetzalcoatl and Huitzilopochtli arrange the universe and create fire, half of the sun ("not fully lighted but a little"), the human race, and the calendar. Then, the four brothers create water and its divine beings.

Following this rapid and full arrangement, the sources focus on a series of mythic events that constitute a sacred history. Throughout this sacred history, the dynamic instability of the Aztec universe is revealed. The universe passes through four eras, called "Suns." Each age was presided over by one of the great gods, and each was named for the day (day number and day name) within the calendrical cycle on which the age began (which is also the name of the force that destroys that Sun). The fifth (and last) cosmic age, augured the earthquakes that would inevitably destroy the world.

The creation of this final age, the one in which the Aztec lived, took place around a divine fire in the darkness on the mythical plain of Teotihuacán (to be distinguished from the actual city of that same name). According to the version of this story reported in Fray Bernardino de Sahagún's *Historia general de las cosas de la Nueva España* (compiled 1569-1582; also known as the Florentine Codex), an assembly of gods chose two of their group, Nanahuatzin and Tecuciztecatl, to cast themselves into the fire in order to create the new cosmic age. Following their self-sacrifice, dawn appears in all directions, but the Sun does not rise above the horizon. In confusion, different deities face in various directions in expectation of the sunrise. Quetzalcoatl faces east and from there the Sun blazes forth but sways from side to side without climbing in the sky. In this cosmic crisis, it is decided that all the gods must die at the sacrificial hand of Ecatl, who dispatches them by cutting their throats. Even this massive sacrifice does not move the Sun until the wind god literally blows it into motion. These combined cosmogonic episodes demonstrate the fundamental Aztec conviction that the world is unstable and that it draws its energy from massive sacrifices by the gods. Large-scale sacrifice became a basic pattern in Aztec religion, a ritual means of imposing or maintaining social and cosmological order.

With the creation of the Fifth Sun, the focus of the sacred history shifts from heaven to earth, where agriculture is discovered and human sacrifice is established as the proper ritual response to the requirements of the gods. In one account, Quetzalcoatl, as a black ant, travels to Sustenance Mountain with a red ant where they acquire maize for human beings. Other accounts reveal the divine origins of cotton, sweet potatoes, different types of corn, and the intoxicating drink called pulque. In still others, we learn that warfare was established so that human beings could be captured and sacrificed to nourish the Sun on its heavenly and nocturnal journey. Typically, a god like Mixcoatl creates four hundred human beings to fight among themselves in order for captives to be sacrificed in ceremonial centers to provide the divine food, blood, for the gods who ensure cosmic life.

Finally, a number of accounts of the cosmic history culminate with the establishment of the magnificent kingdom of Tollan where Quetzalcoatl the god and Topiltzin Quetzalcoatl the priest-king organize a ceremonial capital divided into five parts with four pyramids and four sacred mountains surrounding the central temple. This city, Tollan, serves as the heart of an empire.

The spatial paradigm of the Aztec cosmos was embodied in the term *cemanahuac*, meaning the "land surrounded by water." At the center of this terrestrial space, called *tlalxico* ("navel of the earth"), stood Tenochtitlán, from which extended the four quadrants called *nauchampa*, meaning "the four directions of the wind." The waters surrounding the inhabited land were called *ilhuicatl*, the celestial water that extended upward to merge with the lowest levels of the thirteen heavens. Below the earth were nine levels of the underworld, conceived of as "hazard stations" for the souls of the dead, who, aided by magical charms buried with the bodies, were assisted in their quests for eternal peace at the lowest level, called Mictlan, the land of the dead.

THE PANTHEON. One of the most striking characteristics of the surviving screenfolds, which present ritual and divinatory information, is the incredible array of deities who animated the ancient Mesoamerican world. Likewise, the remaining sculpture and the sixteenth-century prose accounts of Aztec Mexico present us with a pantheon so crowded that H. B. Nicholson's authoritative study of Aztec religion includes a list of more than sixty distinct and interrelated names. Scholarly analysis of these many deities suggests that virtually all aspects of existence were considered inherently sacred and that these deities were expressions of a numinous quality that permeated the "real" world. While it does not appear that the Aztec pantheon or pattern of hierophanies was organized as a whole, it is possible to identify clusters of deities organized around the major cult themes of cosmogonic creativity, fertility and regeneration, and war and sacrificial nourishment of the Sun.

Aztec deities dwelt in the different levels of the thirteen-layered celestial sphere or the nine-layered underworld. The general structuring principle for the pantheon, derived from the cosmic pattern of a center and four quarters, resulted in the quadruple or quintuple ordering of gods. For instance in the Codex Borgia's representation of the Tlaloques (rain gods), the rain god, Tlaloc, inhabits the central region of heaven while four other Tlaloques inhabit the four regions of the sky, each dispensing a different kind of rain. While

AZTEC DEITIES

Aztec Deities were invisible to the human eye but elaborately decorated "deity impersonators" were often created in stone, wood, dough, or costume.

GIANNI DAGLI ORTI/CORBIS

deities were invisible to the human eye, the Aztec saw them in dreams, visions, and in the "deity impersonators" (*teixiptla*) who appeared at the major ceremonies. These costumed impersonators, sometimes human, sometimes effigies of stone, wood, or dough, were elaborately decorated with identifying insignia such as conch shells, masks, weapons, jewelry, mantas, feathers, and a myriad of other items.

As we have seen, Aztec religion was formed by migrating Chichimec who entered the Valley of Mexico and established important political and cultural centers there. This process of migration and urbanization informed and was informed by their concept of deity.

After death, Warriors slain on the battlefield and all those who have been sacrificed on an altar, as well as traders who have died on their journeys, become companions of the Sun.

PAGE 316

A

AZTEC RELIGION

Creator Gods

The Aztec divinity, Tezcatlipoca ("smoking mirror"), uses an obsidian mirror to distort images.

PAGE 676

A familiar pattern in the sacred histories of Mesoamerican tribal groups is the erection of a shrine to the patron deity as the first act of settlement in a new region. This act of founding a settlement around the tribal shrine represented the intimate tie between the deity, the *hombre-dios*, and the integrity of the people. In reverse fashion, conquest of a community was achieved when the patron deity's shrine was burned and the *tlaquimilolli* was carried off as a captive.

This pattern of migration, foundation, and conquest associated with the power of a patron diety is clearly exemplified by the case of Huitzilopochtli, patron of the wandering Méxica. According to Aztec tradition, Huitzilopochtli inspired the Méxica *teomama* to guide the tribe into the Valley of Mexico, where he appeared to them as an eagle on a cactus in the lake. There they constructed a shrine to Huitzilopochtli and built their city around the shrine. This shrine became the Aztec Great Temple, the supreme political and symbolic center of the Aztec empire. It was destroyed in 1521 by the Spanish, who blew up the temple with cannons and carried the great image of Huitzilopochtli away.

CREATOR GODS. There are multiple versions of the Aztec creations story and, depending on the version, different names for the same entities are used and different aspects of the deity are emphasized.

The Aztec high god, Ometeotl ("lord of duality") was the celestial, androgynous, primordial creator of the universe, the omnipotent, omniscient, omnipresent foundation of all things. In some sources he/she appears to merge with a number of his/her offspring, a sign of his/her pervasive power. Ometeotl's male aspects (Ometecuhtli and Tonacatecuhtli) and female aspects (Omecihuatl and Tonacacihuatl) in turn merged with a series of lesser deities associated with generative and destructive male and female qualities. The male aspect was associated with fire and the solar and maize gods. The female aspect merged with earth fertility goddesses and especially corn goddesses. Ometeotl inhabited the thirteenth and highest heaven in the cosmos, which was the place from which the souls of infants descended to be born on earth. Ometeotl was more "being" than "action." Most of the creative effort to organize the universe was acomplished by the divine couple's four offspring: Tezcatlipoca, Quetzalcoatl, Xiuhtecuhtli, and Tlaloc.

Tezcatlipoca ("smoking mirror") was the supreme active creative force of the pantheon. He was the archsorcerer whose smoking obsidian mirror revealed the powers of ultimate transformation associated with darkness, night, jaguars, and shamanic magic.

Another tremendous creative power was Xiuhtecuhtli, the ancient fire god, who influenced every level of society and cosmology. Xiuhtecuhtli was the generative force at the New Fire ceremony, also called the Binding of the Years, held every fifty-two years on the Hill of the Star outside of Tenochtitlán. At midnight on the day that a fifty-two-year calendar cycle was exhausted, at the moment when the star cluster we call the Pleiades passed through the zenith, a heart sacrifice of a war captive took place.

FERTILITY AND REGENERATION. A pervasive

GREAT TEMPLE

The Aztec Great Temple, built as a shrine to Huitzilopochtli, was destroyed by the Spanish in 1521.

CHARLES & JOSETTE LENARS/CORBIS

theme in Aztec religion was fertility and the regeneration of agriculture. Aztec society depended on a massive agricultural system of *chinampas* ("floating gardens") that constituted large sections of the city's geographical space. Also, surrounding city-states were required to pay sizable amounts of agricultural goods in tribute to the capital. While many female deities inspired the ritual regeneration of agriculture, the most ancient and widespread fertility-rain god was Tlaloc, who dwelt on the prominent mountain peaks, where rain clouds were thought to emerge from caves to fertilize the land through rain, rivers, pools, and storms. The Aztec held Mount Tlaloc to be the original source of waters and vegetation. Tlaloc's supreme importance is reflected in the location of his shrine by that of Huitzilopochtli in the Templo Mayor. Surprisingly, the great majority of buried offerings excavated at the temple were dedicated to Tlaloc rather than Huitzilopochtli.

Two other major gods intimately associated with Tlaloc were Chalchiuhtlicue, the goddess of water, and Ehécatl, the wind god, an aspect of Quetzalcoatl.

The most powerful group of female fertility deities were the *teteoinnan*, a rich array of earth-mother goddesses, who were representatives of the usually distinct but sometimes combined qualities of terror and beauty, regeneration and destruction. These deities were worshiped in cults concerned with the abundant powers of the earth, women, and fertility. Among the most prominent were Tlazolteotl, Xochiquetzal, and Coatlicue. Tlazolteotl was concerned with sexual powers and passions and the pardoning of sexual transgressions. Xochiquetzal was the goddess of love and sexual desire and was pictured as a nubile maiden associated with flowers, feasting, and pleasure. A ferocious goddess, Coatlicue ("serpent skirt") represented the cosmic mountain that conceived all stellar beings and devoured all beings into her repulsive, lethal, and fascinating form. Her statue is studded with sacrificed hearts, skulls, hands, ferocious claws, and giant snake heads.

A prominent deity who linked agricultural renewal with warfare was Xipe Totec, whose gladiatorial sacrifice renewed vegetation in the spring and celebrated success on the battlefield. Part of his ceremony, called the Feast of the Flaying of Men, included the flaying of the sacrificial victim and the ceremonial wearing of the skin by the sacred specialist.

Aztec religion, as we have seen, was formed during the rise to empire of a minority population who inherited urban traditions and sociopolitical conflicts of great prestige and intensity. This remarkable tradition came to an abrupt end during the military conquest of Tenochtitlán by the Spanish and the subsequent destruction of ceremonial life. But it is important to note that one of the last images we have of the Templo Mayor of Tenochtitlán before it was blown apart by Spanish cannon is the image of Aztec warriors sacrificing captive Spanish soldiers in front of the shrine to Huitzilopochtli.

— DAVID CARRASCO

The themes of order and disorder play a role in Aztec sacrifice as does the theme of sacrificial exchange.

PAGE 588

CEREMONY AND SACRIFICE
Nourishing the Gods

An important facet of Aztec religious practice was human sacrifice, usually carried out for the purpose of nourishing or renewing the Sun or other deity (or to otherwise appease it), thus ensuring the stability of the universe. The mythic model for mass human sacrifice was the story of the creation of the fifth age, in which the gods themselves were sacrificed in order to empower the Sun. Tonatiuh, the personification of that Sun (whose visage appears in the center of the Calendar Stone), depended on continued nourishment from human hearts.

Cosmology, pantheon, and ritual sacrifice were united and came alive in the exuberant and well-ordered ceremonies carried out in the more than eighty buildings situated in the sacred precinct of the capital and in the hundreds of ceremonial centers throughout the Aztec world. Guided by detailed ritual calendars, Aztec ceremonies varied from town to town but typically involved days of ritual preparation included fasting; offerings of food, flowers, and paper; use of incense and purification techniques; embowering; songs; and processions of deity-impersonators to various temples in ceremonial precincts.

Following these elaborate preparations, blood sacrifices were carried out by priestly orders specially trained to dispatch the victims swiftly. The victims were usually captive warriors or purchased slaves. The typical ritual involved the dramatic heart sacrifice and the placing of the heart in a ceremonial vessel *(cuauhxicalli)* in order to nourish the gods.

All of these ceremonies were carried out in relation to two ritual calendars, the 365-day calendar or *tonalpohualli* ("count of day") consisting of eighteen twenty-day months plus a five-day intercalary period and the 260-day calendar consisting of thirteen twenty-day months. More than one-third of these ceremonies were dedicated to Tlaloc and earth fertility goddesses. Beside ceremonies relating to the two calendars, a third type of ceremony related to the many life cycle stages of the individual. In some cases, the entire community was involved in bloodletting.

— DAVID CARRASCO

B

BAPTISM

The word *baptism* comes from the Greek *baptein*, which means to plunge, to immerse, or to wash; it also signifies, from the Homeric period onward, any rite of immersion in water. The baptismal rite is similar to many other ablution rituals found in a number of religions, but it is the symbolic value of baptism and the psychological intent underlying it that provide the true definition of the rite, a rite usually found associated with a religious initiation.

PRE-CHRISTIAN RELIGIONS. The purifying properties of water have been ritually attested to ever since the rise of civilization in the ancient Near East. In Babylonia, according to the *Tablets of Maklu*, water was important in the cult of Enki, lord of Eridu. In Egypt, the *Book of Going Forth by Day* (17) contains a treatise on the baptism of newborn children, which is performed to purify them of blemishes acquired in the womb.

The property of immortality is also associated with baptism in the Greek world: according to Cretan funeral tablets, it was associated especially with the spring of Mnemosyne (memory). A bath in the sanctuary of Trophonios procured for the initiate a blessed immortality even while in this world (Pausanias, *Description of Greece* 9.39.5).

In Hellenistic philosophy, as in Egyptian speculation, divine water possessed a real power of transformation. Hermetism offered to man the possibility of being transformed into a spiritual being after immersion in the baptismal crater of the *nous*; this baptism conferred knowledge on man and permitted him to participate in the gnosis and, hence, to know the origins of the soul.

In the cult of Cybele, a baptism of blood was practiced in the rite of the *taurobolium*: the initiate went down into a pit and was completely covered with the blood of a bull, whose throat was cut above him. A well-known inscription attests that he who has received baptism of blood is *renatus in aeternum*, that he has received a new birth in eternity (*Corpus inscriptionum Latinarum* 6.510).

The liturgical use of water was common in the Jewish world. Under Persian influence, rites of immersion multiplied after the exile. Some prophets saw in the requirement of physical purity a sign of the necessity of inner and spiritual purification (*Ez.* 36:25-28). The Essenes linked the pouring forth of the divine life in man to purification by baptism in flowing water.

Toward the beginning of the Christian era, the Jews adopted the custom of baptizing proselytes seven days after their circumcision, the rabbis having added the impurity of converted gentiles to the chief impurities enumerated in the Torah. After their baptism, new converts were allowed access to the sacrifices in the Temple.

The ministry of John the Baptist in the Jordanian desert was connected with this baptist movement, which symbolically linked immersion in a river of flowing water to the passage from death to a new and supernatural life. The Mandaeans take their baptismal practice directly from the example of John, whom they consider the perfect gnostic; they administer baptism in the flowing water of a symbolic Jordan.

CHRISTIAN BAPTISM. John baptized Jesus, like others who came to him, in the waters of the Jordan. Jesus' baptism inaugurated his public ministry, and he

"I will sprinkle clean water upon you to cleanse you from all impurities."

EZEKIEL, 36:26

JOHN THE BAPTIST

By baptizing Jesus in the waters of the river Jordan, John broke from official practice and drew the wrath of Jewish authorities.

ARTE VIDEO IMMAGINE ITALIA SRL/CORBIS

later gave his disciples the mission of baptizing in the name of the trinitarian faith—a mission that they carried out even before their master's death (*Mt.* 28:19, *Jn.* 4:1-2). The apostles continued to practice the baptism of water of the type administered by John; but they emphasized the necessity of an inner conversion preceding the profession of the trinitarian faith, the focus of the new belief.

Every detail of the Christian ritual is intended to symbolize birth to a new life in Jesus Christ. Christian baptismal practice is founded on the commandment of Jesus himself to his disciples (*Mt.* 28:19). Its administration during the first centuries of the church took place at Easter night and Pentecost and was limited to bishops, the heads of the Christian communities. Reception of baptism seems often to have been put off until the moment of death by neophytes who were reluctant to accept the full consequences of inner conversion; and infant baptism, though possible, was probably not practiced in the early period of the church (cf. *Mt.* 19:14, *Acts* 16:33, 1 *Tm.* 2:4).

The other action of the community of Christian worship on whose "sacramental" character all Christians would agree is baptism.

PAGE 167

Because it was the sacrament that indicated entrance into the life of faith and the community of the church, baptism was also considered a means to inner enlightenment. In the Eastern church, those who were initiated into the Christian mysteries by baptism were called the "enlightened," for, as Gregory of Nazianzus explains, the baptismal rite opens the catechumen's eyes to the light that indicates God's symbolic birth in man (Discourse 40: *On Baptism*).

But because it was also the fundamental rite of entry into the church community, baptism was quickly claimed as a prerogative by several rival churches, each of which called itself orthodox and accused the others of heresy and schism. Modifications of baptismal rites by the various sects were inevitable.

From the sixth century on at the latest, the Catholic church permitted the baptism of children, the engagement to follow the faith being taken in their name by adult Christians. The custom of baptizing infants soon after birth became popular in the tenth or eleventh century and was generally accepted by the thirteenth (Thomas Aquinas, *Summa theologiae* 3.68.3). In the fourteenth century, baptismal ritual was simplified, and a rite of spiritual infusion, in which water is poured on the head of a child held above the baptismal font, replaced baptism by immersion. After 1517, the questions posed by the practice of the baptism of small children served as a major foundation for dissident Christian movements stemming from the Reformation.

In 1633, a group of English Baptists immigrated to North America, beginning the development in the New World of a number of Baptist sects and churches, whose members founded their belief on the theological baptism of Paul (cf. *Rom.* 6:4, *Col.* 2:12) and insisted upon a return to strict apostolic practice. These sects and churches have in common the practice of baptism by immersion administered in the name of the Trinity only to adults who believe and confess their faith in Jesus Christ.

—MICHEL MESLIN
TRANSLATED FROM FRENCH BY
JEFFREY C. HAIGHT AND ANNIE S. MAHLER

BAPTIST CHURCHES

As with most denominational names, the name *Baptist* began as a pejorative nickname. It first appeared as *Anabaptist*, or "rebaptizer," since in the sixteenth century, when this group arose in Western Christendom, virtually all persons had already been baptized as infants. These rebaptizers were scandalously denying the validity of that first baptism, setting themselves up as a truer church if not, indeed, the true church. Gradually, as infant baptism became less prevalent and as alternative modes of worship grew more widespread, this still young denomination adopted the shortened form of "Baptist" both as a convenient distinction and a point of honor.

Sharing many of the Puritan concerns about a Church of England still too "papist," still too engrossed with civil enforcement and ecclesiastical preferment, these separating Puritans early distinguished themselves by insisting that the church be a voluntary society. That voluntarism had two critical components: (1) the insistence that members choose their church rather than be born into it; and (2) the conviction that the covenant of believers to work and worship together was a private agreement with which the state had nothing to do, for conscience must be left free. As Thomas Helwys, one of that first generation of English Baptists, wrote, "the King is a mortal man and not God, therefore hath no power over the immortal souls of his subjects, to make laws and ordinances for them, and to set spiritual lords over them."

The leadership of Helwys and two others, John Smyth and John Murton, proved decisive in the first two decades of the seventeenth century as the English "General Baptists" (that is, non-Calvinist, affirming an unrestricted or general atonement for mankind) grew from a scarcely visible knot of believers in 1609 to around twenty thousand members by 1660. Despite this impressive showing, however, the major strength of the modern Baptist churches was to come from a somewhat later development. Under the leadership of John Spilsbury, in the decade following 1633, a single church became mother to six more. By the time seven such churches existed in and around London, these Calvinist Baptists had also reintroduced the ancient Christian practice of baptism by immersion, this mode being preferred as a more suitable symbol of one's burial with Christ followed by one's new birth or resurrection.

The great growth of Baptists in North America (and by extension in the world) followed the eighteenth century's Great Awakening, that Calvinist explosion of evangelical zeal and intense religious experience. Even though Baptists were not prime leaders in the movement, they were the prime beneficiaries of it. Moreover, the Awakening, even if it did not make an itinerant ministry respectable, did make such traveling evangelism both popular and pervasive.

After the American Revolution, Baptists also made phenomenal advances among the nation's blacks. Using a persuasive preaching style, an accessible theology, an appealing baptismal ritual, and an ecclesiology that granted freedom from white rule, the Baptist message found ready hearers among both enslaved and free blacks. By the end of the nineteenth century, black Baptists had formed their own national organizations, publishing boards, and mission societies. By the mid-twentieth century, approximately two-thirds of America's black Christians were Baptists.

In the bitter conflict over slavery, white Baptists split along geographical lines in 1845, and the Southern Baptist Convention was organized in Augusta, Georgia. (A national organization of Baptists dating back to 1814 enjoyed but a brief life.) The Southern Baptist Convention, with its base initially in the states of the southern Confederacy, moved aggressively to the West, to the North, and to "foreign fields" to become the largest single Baptist entity in the world. By the mid-twentieth century it had also become the largest Protestant denomination in the United States.

In the early 1980s, the northern and southern "halves" had an aggregate membership of around fifteen million, the two oldest black denominations a combined membership of eight to ten million. This leaves uncounted some four or five million Baptists in America who are scattered among a wide variety of other organizations.

Outside the United States, the Baptist churches are unevenly and often sparsely scattered. One may speak most conveniently in terms of continents rather than individual nations in offering estimates of membership: in Africa and Europe, about one million in each area; in Asia, about 1.5 million; and in Central and South America, something less than one million. In Canada, to which New England Baptists began to migrate in the late eighteenth century, there are between one and two hundred thousand Baptists.

— EDWIN S. GAUSTAD

BIBLICAL LITERATURE

HEBREW SCRIPTURES

The terms *Hebrew scriptures* and *Hebrew Bible* are synonyms here restricted to that received, definitive corpus of ancient literature, written in Hebrew except for some sections in Aramaic (*Genesis* 31:47, *Jeremiah* 10:11, and parts of *Daniel* and *Ezra*), that has been traditionally accepted by Jews and Christians alike as having been divinely inspired and, as such, authoritative in shaping their respective faiths and practices.

The word *Bible* is ultimately of Greek derivation and passed into many languages of the world through the medium of Latin. It meant simply "the Books."

Among Christians, the Hebrew Bible has traditionally been referred to as the Old Testament (i. e., Covenant), in contradistinction to the New Testament—theological appellations based upon a christological interpretation of *Jeremiah* 31:30-34. In recognition of the partisan nature of this title, and under the impact of the ecumenical movement of recent times, many scholars have increasingly preferred instead to refer to the Hebrew Bible or Hebrew scriptures.

CANON. As generally used in scholarly parlance, the term *canon* relates particularly to the received and definitively closed nature of the sacred corpus.

The completed canon of the Hebrew Bible exerted a profound influence, first upon the Jewish people that produced it, and then upon a large section of the rest of humanity. It was the major factor in the preservation of the unity of the Jews at a time of desperate national crisis after the destruction of their state in the year 70 (or 68) CE and their subsequent wide dispersion.

Contents. The tripartite division of the Hebrew Bible roughly describes its variegated contents, although, admittedly, some of the books of the third part would not be out of place in the second.

The Torah. More fully called the Torah of Moses, the Torah comprises the first five books of the biblical canon, usually known in English as the Pentateuch: *Genesis*, *Exodus*, *Leviticus*, *Numbers*, and *Deuteronomy*.

The Hebrew term *torah* means "instruction, teaching." In the present context, the Pentateuch comprises a continuous narrative from the creation of the world to the death of Moses in which is embedded a considerable amount of legal and ritual prescription. *Genesis's* first eleven chapters deal with universal history up to the birth of Abraham, and the rest of the book is devoted to the ancestors of the people of Israel. *Deuteronomy*, largely summarizes discourses of Moses and is marked by its own characteristic style and theological tendency. The intervening three books deal with two generations of the people of Israel from the period of the Egyptian oppression and the Exodus.

The quintessential "book religions" are those that trace their lineage in some fashion to the Hebrews, the prototypical "people of the book."

PAGE 592

It is not certain how this corpus was materially preserved in early times. For convenience of study, the material was written on five separate scrolls, but it was also written on a single scroll. It is solely in this form that it has played a role in the Jewish synagogal liturgy.

The Nevi'im. The prophetic corpus naturally divides into two parts. The Former Prophets continues the historical narrative of the Torah, closing with the destruction of the First Temple in Jerusalem, the end of the monarchy, and the Babylonian exile of the Judeans up to the year 560 BCE. This material is contained in the books of *Joshua*, *Judges*, *Samuel*, and *Kings*.

BOOKS OF THE HEBREW SCRIPTURES

Genesis	2 Chronicles	Daniel
Exodus	Ezra	Hosea
Leviticus	Nehemiah	Joel
Numbers	Esther	Amos
Deuteronomy	Job	Obadiah
Joshua	Psalms	Jonah
Judges	Proverbs	Micah
Ruth	Ecclesiastes	Nahum
1 Samuel	Song of Songs	Habakkuk
2 Samuel	Isaiah	Zephaniah
1 Kings	Jeremiah	Haggai
2 Kings	Lamentations	Zechariah
1 Chronicles	Ezekial	Malachi

"You shall read this law aloud in the presence of all Israel."

DEUTERONOMY, 31:1

The second part of the Nevi'im, the Latter Prophets, comprises the works of the literary prophets in Israel and Judah from the eighth to the fifth centuries BCE. These are *Isaiah*, *Jeremiah*, and *Ezekiel*, and "the Book of the Twelve," known in English as the Minor Prophets: *Hosea, Joel, Amos, Obadiah, Jonah, Micah, Nahum, Habakkuk, Zephaniah, Haggai, Zechariah,* and *Malachi*.

The Ketuvim. The Writings, often also called Hagiographa in English, are actually a miscellany of sacred writings of several genres of literature, as the nonspecific nature of the name indicates. There is religious poetry *(Psalms* and *Lamentations)*; love poetry (the *Song of Songs)*; wisdom or reflective compositions *(Proverbs, Job,* and *Ecclesiastes)*; historical works *(Ruth, Esther, Ezra-Nehemiah,* and *Chronicles)*; and apocalypse *(Daniel)*.

Tripartite canon. It is widely held that the tripartite nature of the canon represents three successive stages of canonization of the separate corpora. Repeated reference to this threefold division comes from the literature of the period of the Second Temple. *Ben Sira* 39:1, probably written around 180 BCE, mentions the "law of the Most High, the wisdom of all the ancients . . . , and . . . prophecies." About fifty years later, Ben Sira's grandson, who translated the work into Greek, writes in his prologue about "the law and the prophets and the others that came after them," which last are also called "the other books of our fathers" and "the rest of the books," while *2 Maccabees* (2:2-3, 2:13) has reference to "the law, the kings and prophets and the writings of David." In Alexandria, Egypt, the Jewish philosopher Philo Judaeus (d. 45-50 CE) mentions, besides "the law," also "the prophets and the psalms and other writings" (*De vita contemplativa* 3.25). The Jewish historian Josephus Flavius (37-c. 100 CE) tells of the Pentateuch of Moses, the "prophets" and "the remaining books" (*Against Apion* 1.39-41). Similarly, in the New Testament, the *Gospel of Luke* speaks of "the law of Moses and the prophets and the psalms" (24:4). This persistent allusion to the threefold division of the Hebrew scriptures, and the lack of any uniform title for the third collection of writings, in addition to the heterogeneous nature of that corpus, all argue in favor of two closed collections—the Torah and the Prophets—with a third being somewhat amorphous and having no uniform name, undoubtedly a sign of its late corporate canonicity.

Of course, the closing of a corpus tells nothing about the canonical history of the individual books within it. Some parts of the Ketuvim, such as the *Psalms,* for instance, would most likely have achieved canonical status before some of those included within the Nevi'im.

Samaritan canon. The religious community centered on Nablus (ancient Shechem) that calls itself Benei Yisra'el ("children of Israel") or Shomrim ("keepers," i. e., of the truth), and that is known by outsiders as Samaritans, claims to be directly descended from the Israelites of the Northern Kingdom who escaped deportation at the hands of the Assyrian kings who destroyed it in 722/1 BCE (*2 Kgs.* 17:5-6, 17:24-34, 17:41). Their canon consists solely of the Pentateuch, excluding the Prophets and the Writings. This fact has not been satisfactorily explained. The older view, that the final breach between the Samaritans and the Jews occurred in the time of Ezra and Nehemiah (fifth century BCE), before the canonization of the rest of the Hebrew Bible, is no longer tenable because both documentary and archaeological evidence leads to the conclusion that the schism was the culmination of a gradual process of increasing estrangement. A major step was the construction of a Samaritan shrine on Mount Gerizim early in the Hellenistic period; the destruction of the temple on that site by John Hyrcanus in 128 BCE completed the rupture.

Canon at Qumran. The discovery of a hoard of more than five hundred manuscripts in the region of the sectarian settlement at Khirbat Qumran, northwest of the Dead Sea, has raised the question of the nature of the biblical canon recognized by that community, which came to an end about 70 CE. The question is legitimate both in light of the variant canon preserved by the Greek Septuagint, as discussed below, and because copies of extrabiblical books, apocryphal and pseudepigraphical works such as *Tobit*, *Ben Sira*, the *Letter of Jeremiah*, *1 Enoch*, and *Jubilees*, not to mention the sect's own productions, were included among the finds.

A variety of factors combine to render a decisive conclusion all but impossible in the absence of a list that would determine contents and sequence. This lack is aggravated by the practice at that time of writing each biblical book on a separate scroll, and by the very fragmentary form of the overwhelming majority of extant scrolls. Furthermore, since the manuscripts had generally been hidden in the caves in great disorder, we cannot be sure whether we are dealing with a living library or a *genizah*, a storeroom of discarded works.

The following items of evidence are pertinent to the discussion: (1) With the exception of *Esther*, fragments of all the books of the Hebrew Bible have turned up; hence the Qumran canon would have included at least almost every book of the Hebrew Bible. (2) The category of Qumran literature known as the *pesharim*, or contemporizing interpretations of prophetic texts, is, so far, exclusively restricted to the books of the standard Hebrew canon. (3) The Manual of Discipline (*Serekh ha-yahad*, 1QS IX:11) expresses the hope for the renewal of prophecy, the same as is found in *1 Maccabees* 4:46. This suggests that the Qumran community recognized a closed corpus of prophetic literature. (4) The great psalms scroll (11QPs[a]), on the other hand, exhibits not only a deviant order of the standard psalms, but also contains other compositions, largely deriving from Hellenistic times. This scroll circulated in more than one copy, and several other Qumran manuscripts of psalms also vary in sequence and contents. At first glance it would seem that this phenomenon proves that the Qumran community could not have had a concept of a closed canon. However, it may be pointed out that the compiler of 11QPs[a] certainly was dependent on a Hebrew book of psalms much the same as that of the Hebrew Bible, and he may simply have been putting together a liturgical collection, not creating or copying a canonical work. Moreover, the caves of Qumran have yielded numerous psalters that contain only known canonical psalms, apparently without any deviation from the standard sequence. (5) As to the presence of noncanonical works, we have no means of knowing whether these had authority for the community equal with that of the standard Hebrew canonical books. (6) In sum, the evidence so far at hand does not justify the assumption that Qumran sectarians had a concept of canon different from that of their Palestinian Jewish brethren, although the opposite too cannot be proven.

Alexandrian canon (Septuagint). To meet the needs of worship and study, the populous hellenized Jewish community of Alexandria produced a Greek translation of the Hebrew Bible known as the Septuagint, begun in the third century BCE and completed before about 132 BCE. As it has come down to us, it differs from the traditional Hebrew Bible both in content and form, and often textually. It includes works that rabbinic Judaism rejected as noncanonical, and in it the books of the Prophets and Writings are not maintained as separate corpora but are distributed and arranged according to subject matter: historical books, poetry and wisdom, and prophetic literature. This situation has given rise to a widely held hypothesis of an Alexandrian or Hellenistic canon; that is to say, the Septuagint is said to represent a variant, independent concept of canon held by Diaspora Jewry. Alternatively, it is suggested that it derives from a rival canon that circulated in Jewish Palestine itself.

The Qumran sect saw itself as the sole possessor of the correct interpretation of the Bible.

PAGE 194

Christian canon. The Christian canon of the Jewish scriptures differs in three ways from the Bible of the Jews. First, its text is not that of the received Hebrew, usually called the Masoretic text, but is based on the Greek and Latin versions. Second, although all the books officially recognized as canonical by the Jews were also accepted by the Christian church, many segments of the latter also included within its canon additional Jewish works that date from the days of the Second Temple. These, generally termed "deuterocanonical" by theologians of the Roman Catholic church, are books of historical and didactic content, composed in Hebrew or Aramaic. They were not sectarian in origin, and they circulated widely in both Palestine and the Greek-speaking Jewish Diaspora in their original language and in Greek translation long after the close of the Hebrew canon. The third way in which the Christian canon diverges from the Jewish canon relates to the order of the books. The Hebrew tripartite division, clearly attested in *Luke* 28:44, was disregarded, and the contents were regrouped, as in the manuscripts of the Septuagint, according to literary categories—legal, historical, poetic-didactic, and prophetic. The variant sequence was best suited to express the claim of the church that the New Testament is the fulfillment of the Hebrew scriptures of the Jews.

CANONIZING PROCESS. The available sources are silent about the nature and identity of the validat-

Torah contains God's fullest truth for humankind, making it the arbiter of all wisdom.

PAGE 403

BIBLICAL BOOKKEEPING
Twenty-two or Twenty-four?

Until the sixth century CE, it was customary among Jews for the scribes to copy each biblical work onto a separate scroll. The number of books in the biblical canon therefore relates to the number of scrolls onto which the completed Hebrew Bible was transcribed, and which were physically kept together as a unit. Josephus (*Against Apion* 1. 39-41, ed. Loeb, p. 179) is emphatic that there were no more than twenty-two such. What is not clear is whether this figure was arrived at by conjoining books, such as *Judges* and *Ruth*, and *Jeremiah* and *Lamentations*, or whether two books were not yet included in his canon, perhaps the *Song of Songs* and *Ecclesiastes*.

A variant tradition counting twenty-four books eventually prevailed among Jews. This is first found in *2 Esdras* 14:45, written circa 100 BCE. The books are listed by name in a text that antedates 200 BCE cited in the Babylonian Talmud (B. B. 14b). Thereafter, this figure is explicitly given, and it becomes standard in rabbinic literature (cf. B. T., *Ta'an.* 5a). Whether the number has any significance is uncertain. It is of interest that the Old Babylonian bilingual lexical series known as Har-ra-Hubullu is inscribed on twenty-four tablets, the Mesopotamian *Epic of Gilgamesh* on twelve tablets, the Greek *Theogony* of Hesiod comes in twelve parts, and the old Roman law code was eventually codified as the Twelve Tablets (of wood). At any rate, in Jewish tradition, the biblical books become twenty-four by treating all the twelve Minor Prophets as one.

— NAHUM M. SARNA

ing authorities, about the criteria of selectivity adopted in respect of the books included and excluded, and about the individual crucial stages in the history of the growth of the Hebrew biblical canon. This deficiency is aggravated by the fact that the literature that has survived represents at least six hundred years of literary creativity, in the course of which Israelite society underwent far-reaching, indeed metamorphic, change, much of it convulsive. Such a state of affairs militates against the likelihood of uniformity in the processes involved or of unbroken consistency in the considerations that swayed decision-making about individual works and collections of works. For these reasons, any reconstruction of the history of the phenomenon of the canonization of biblical literature must of necessity remain hypothetical.

Nonetheless, it should be noted that well before the year 1000 BCE, the libraries of the temples and palaces of Mesopotamia had organized the classical literature into a standardized corpus in some kind of uniform order and with a more or less official text. In similar manner, by order of Peisistratus, tyrant of Athens, the Homeric epics were codified in the sixth century and endowed with canonical authority. The idea of a canon was thus well based in the ancient world. There is every reason to assume that in Israel, too, temples served as the repositories of sacred texts from early times, and that the priests and scribes played an important role in the preservation and organization of literature. Hence, the formation of the biblical canon should not be viewed as a late development in Israel but as an ongoing process that is coextensive with the biblical period itself.

The definition of *canon* should, furthermore, be extended beyond the purely historical, external, formal aspects relating just to the end result of a process, to which it is usually restricted. In Israel, the conviction that the texts record the word of God or were divinely inspired, however these concepts were understood, would have been a decisive factor in their preservation. For the same reason, they would have been periodically read or recited, and the very force of repetition would inevitably and powerfully have informed the collective mind and self-consciousness of the community. This, in turn, would have subtly shaped and reshaped both the existing literature and new compositions in a continual process of interaction between the community and its traditions. A text that appears to be directed to a specific situation in time and space acquires a contemporizing validity and relevance that is independent of such restrictive dimensions and develops a life of its own.

The earliest testimony to the canonizing process of the Torah literature comes from *Exodus* 24:1-11, which describes how Moses mediated the divine commands to the entire people assembled, how the people orally bound themselves to obedience, how Moses then put the stipulations into writing, and how a cultic ceremony was held at which the written record of the covenant just made was given a public reading. This was followed by a collective pledge of loyalty to its stipulations.

Another important text is *Deuteronomy*, chapter 31 (verses 9-13, 24-26). Here, too, Moses writes down the Teaching (Torah), this time entrusting the document to the ecclesiastical authorities for safekeeping, with provision for its septennial national public reading in the future. What is then called "this book of the Torah" is placed beside the Ark of the Covenant. In this case, the sanctity of the book is taken for granted, as is its permanent validity and authority, independent of the person of Moses.

The only other record of a preexilic public reading of Torah literature comes from near the end of the period of the monarchy. *2 Kings* 22-23 (cf. *2 Chr.* 34) recounts the chance discovery of "the book of the Torah" in 622 BCE in the course of the renovations being carried out at the Temple in Jerusalem at the initiative of Josiah, then king. The scope of this work cannot be determined from the narrative, but the royal measures taken as a consequence of the find prove beyond cavil that it at least contained *Deuteronomy*. What is of particular significance is that it had long been stored in the Temple, that its antiquity, authenticity, and authority were recognized at once, and that its binding nature was confirmed at a national assembly. The ceremony centered upon a document that had already achieved normative status, but the impact of the event—the thoroughgoing religious reformation that it generated and sustained ideologically—left an indelible imprint on the subsequent literature and religion of Israel and constituted a powerful stimulus to the elevation of the Torah literature as the organizing principle in the life of the people. In this sense, the developments of 622 are an important milestone in the history of canonization. Between this year and 444 the process gathered apace. It is reasonable to assume that it was consummated in the Babylonian exile after 587/6, for it is impossible to explain the extraordinary survival of the small, defeated, fragmented community of Israelites, bereft of the organs of statecraft, deprived of its national territory, living on alien soil amid a victorious, prestigious civilization, other than through the vehicle of the book of the Torah, which preserved the national identity.

In the period of the return to Zion (the Land of Israel) and beyond, after 538 BCE, the convention of attributing the entire Torah to Moses is frequently attested—in *Malachi*, *Ezra-Nehemiah*, *Daniel*, and *Chronicles*. It also appears in *Joshua* (8:32, 23:6) and in *1 Kings* (2:3) and *2 Kings* (14:6, 23:25), but many scholars maintain that these references result from a later revision of these works. At any rate, by the year 444 the "Torah of Moses" had received popular acceptance. *Nehemiah* 8-10 records that in that year a public, national assembly took place in Jerusalem at which the people requested that "the scroll of the Torah of Moses with which the Lord had charged Israel" be read to them. This was done by Ezra, who is himself described as "a scribe, expert in the Torah of Moses," "a scholar in matters concerning the commandments of the Lord and his laws to Israel . . . a scholar in the law of the God of heaven" (*Ezr.* 7:6, 7:11-12, 7:21). It is quite evident that the stress is on the teaching, dissemination, interpretation, and reaffirmation of the Torah, long popularly recognized and accepted, not on its promulgation anew. Ezra had been commissioned by the Persian king Artaxerxes I "to regulate Judah and Jerusalem according to the law of God," which was in his care (*Ezr.* 7:14). True, the texts do not define the scope of this literature, but it can be safely assumed that it was little different from the Pentateuch that has come down to us, for the author of *Chronicles* who composed his history about 400 repeatedly refers to the "Torah of Moses," and it can be shown that this phrase in context applies comprehensively to the entire Pentateuch.

THE BIBLE AND THE ANCIENT NEAR EAST. It is not surprising that there exist numerous, close affinities in subject matter and form between the biblical writings and the literatures of the ancient Near East. This phenomenon is not necessarily to be explained in terms of dependency or borrowing, but more likely as a result of the sharing of a common cultural heritage. Furthermore, correspondences and parallels are not the same as identity. Contrast is as important a dimension as similarity, and it is the former that accords the Israelite productions their claim to singularity. It is apparent that what was drawn upon from the common Near Eastern stock was thoroughly refined and reshaped to bring it into conformity with the national religious ideology.

The primeval history in *Genesis*, chapters 1-11, well exemplifies this situation. The genealogies, for instance, belong to the same type of document as the Sumerian king-list, but they are used both as connectives to bridge the gap between narrative blocks and for theological purposes. Thus, ten generations are delineated to span the period between Adam and Noah, and another ten between Noah and Abraham, the symmetry being intended to convey the idea that history is the unfolding of God's predetermined plan for humankind. The biblical version has a singularly didactic function and is uniquely placed within a spiritual and moral framework.

The law collection in the Pentateuch is another case in point. No less than six law codes have survived from the ancient Near East, the earliest probably deriving from about seven hundred years before Moses. All these, plus innumerable documents of law-court proceedings, leave no doubt of the existence of a common legal culture in the area that found expression in a similarity of content, legal phraseology, and literary form that Israel shared.

The genre that was truly an international phenomenon is that of biblical wisdom literature. It deals with observations on human behavior and the world order, drawn from experience. One such category has the individual as its focus of interest and is essentially pragmatic and utilitarian, containing precepts for success in

The two covenants presented in the Pentateuch were patterned after the type of covenant prevalent in the ancient Near East between suzerains and vassals.

PAGE 373

TORAH OF MOSES *Hebrew Scriptures often attribute the entire Torah to Moses "with which the Lord had charged Israel."*

CHRIS HELLIER/CORBIS

living. Its artistic forms are mainly the maxim, the proverb, the pithy question, and the riddle. The other is reflective in nature and is more concerned with the human condition, and with the wider issues of divine-human relationships. Here the literary unit is much longer. Both Egypt and Mesopotamia produced an extensive body of literature of this type, and the analogues with *Proverbs*, *Job*, and *Ecclesiastes* are striking. Yet here, again, although these latter are mostly devoid of national or special Israelite content, they are distinctive in their uncompromising monotheism, in the absence of dream interpretation as an attribute of the sage, and in their insistence on the fear of the Lord as being the quintessence of wisdom.

HISTORICAL COMPLEXITY OF THE TEXT. The model for printed editions of the Hebrew Bible was the second "Great Rabbinic Bible" published at Venice by Daniel Bomberg, 1524-1525, and edited by Ya'aqov ben Hayyim ibn Adoniyyah. All printed editions, as well as all extant medieval Hebrew manuscripts of the Bible—the earliest deriving from the ninth century CE—represent a single textual tradition, known as the Masoretic ("received") text (MT). This standard text comprises three distinct elements: the Hebrew consonants, vocalization signs, and accentuation marks.

THE HEBREW SCRIPTURES AS POETRY

From Psalm 84

How lovely is thy dwelling place
O Lord of hosts!
My soul longs, yea, faints
for the courts of the Lord:
my heart and flesh sing for joy
to the loving God.

Even the sparrow finds a home,
and the swallow a nest for herself,
where she may lay her young,
at thy altars, O Lord of hosts,
my king and my God.
Blessed are those who dwell in thy house,
ever singing thy praise! Selah

Blessed are the men whose strength is in thee
in whose heart are the highways to Zion.
As they go through the valley of Baca
they make it a place of springs;
the early rain also covers it with pools.
They go from strength to strength;
the God of gods will be seen in Zion.

GREEK TRANSLATIONS. The history of the Jewish community in Egypt can be traced back at least to the beginning of the sixth century BCE. There Jews spoke Aramaic and knew Hebrew, but the influx of Greek-speaking settlers had far-reaching effects on their cultural life. With the conquest of Egypt by Alexander the Great, the local Jewish population was swelled by a great wave of immigration attracted there by the opportunities afforded by the Ptolemies. The Jews concentrated mainly in Alexandria, where they formed an autonomous community with its own synagogues and sociocultural institutions, and where they came to form a significant segment of the population. They soon adopted Greek as their everyday language.

By the third century BCE, both liturgical and educational considerations dictated the need for a Greek translation of the scriptures, at least of the Pentateuch. The version known as the Septuagint was revolutionary in its conception, its execution, and its impact. No lengthy Eastern religious text had previously been translated into Greek, nor had a written translation of the Jewish scriptures been made hitherto. The Septuagint was one of the great literary enterprises of the ancient world, and it served to fashion and shape a distinctively Jewish-Hellenistic culture, which attempted to synthesize Hebraic and Greek thought and values. Eventually, it became a powerful literary medium for the spread of early Christianity throughout the far-flung Greek-speaking world, thereby transforming the culture and religion of a goodly segment of humanity.

The Septuagint ("seventy") received its Latin name from a legend current among the Jews of Alexandria that it was executed by seventy-two scholars in seventy-two days. Originally applicable only to the translation of the Pentateuch, this abbreviated title was gradually extended to the complete Greek rendering of the entire Jewish scriptures. In the course of time, the origins of the Septuagint came to be embroidered in legend and enveloped in an aura of the miraculous. The *Letter of Aristeas*, Philo's Moses (II, v-vii, 25-40) and rabbinic writings (e.g., B. T., *Meg. 9a*; *Avot de Rabbi Natan*, ms. b, 37) are the principal witnesses to this development, whereby the initiative for the translation was said to have come from Ptolemy II Philadelphus (r. 285-246 BCE).

The fullest and most popular version of the legend is that found in the first of the above-mentioned sources. That the *Letter* is a fiction is apparent from internal evidence, and it has been shown to have been composed by a hellenized Jew writing in the second half of the second century BCE, about a hundred years after the publication of the original Septuagint. It is certain that it was the needs of the Alexandrian Jewish community that called forth the translation in the course of the third century BCE. It is not impossible,

"Your name shall be Abraham; for I have made you the father of a multitude of nations."

GENESIS 17:5

On the eve of the battle, they insisted, Constantine had experienced the vision (or visions) that inspired his conversion to Christianity.

PAGE 154

however, that the project did receive royal approval, given the known interest and activities of the Ptolemies as patrons of culture. Furthermore, it is quite likely that the translators did come from Palestine and worked in Egypt.

The Greek of the Septuagint is essentially the Koine, that form of the language commonly spoken and written from the fourth century BCE until the middle of the sixth century CE by the Greek-speaking populations of the eastern Mediterranean. Hence, the Septuagint stands as a monument of Hellenistic Greek. The Septuagint was generally competently rendered. If its style is not consistent throughout, this is partly due to the multiplicity of translators and partly to the revolutionary nature of the undertaking in that the translators had neither experience nor real precedent to fall back on.

The turning point in the production of Greek Bibles comes in the fourth century CE attendant upon the conversion to Christianity of Constantine (c. 280-337) and the conferring upon that religion of a privileged position in the Roman empire. An order from Constantine in 332 for fifty vellum Bibles for use in the new churches he was erecting in Constantinople afforded an immense stimulus to the creation of the great and handsome Greek Bibles known technically as majuscules or uncials ("inch high") because of the practice of the scribes to employ capital-size letters without ligatures. The three most important codices of this type that have come down to us in a reasonably complete state are the Codex Sinaiticus (usually designated for scholarly purposes by *S* or by the Hebrew letter alef), the Codex Alexandrinus (given the siglum *A*), and the Codex Vaticanus (indicated by the initial *B*). The Sinaiticus, executed in the fourth century CE, is not complete and in places has been seriously damaged by the action of the metallic ink eating through the parchment. Despite the often careless orthography, the manuscript is witness to a very early text tradition. The Vaticanus, also produced in the fourth century, is nearly perfect and constitutes the oldest and most excellent extant copy of the Greek Bible, even though it is not of uniform quality throughout. It was used as the basis of the Roman edition of 1587, the commonly printed Septuagint. The Alexandrinus, containing practically the entire Bible, was probably copied in the early fifth century.

CONSTANTINE'S CONVERSION

After Constantine's conversion to Christianity, the Septuagint (Greek Bible) became the official Bible.

CORBIS-BETTMANN

The adoption of the Septuagint instead of the Hebrew as the Bible of the church was itself a source of discomfort to Greek-speaking Jews. That the Greek rendering frequently departed from the by then universally recognized Hebrew text constituted additional and decisive cause for its rejection by the synagogue. Doubtless, the conviction on the part of the Jews that christological changes had been introduced into the original Septuagint also played a role.

On the Christian side, the lack of uniformity and consistency within the Greek manuscripts themselves were to be an embarrassing disadvantage to Christian missionaries in their theological polemics with Jews. This situation would be exacerbated by the discrepancies between the translation used by Christian disputants and the Hebrew text, which was the only authoritative form of the scriptures recognized by Palestinian Jews. Exegetical debate could proceed only on the basis of a mutually acknowledged text, which in this case had to be the only Hebrew text tradition accepted by the Jews.

TRANSLATIONS BASED ON THE SEPTUAGINT. The great prestige that the Septuagint acquired as the official, authoritative Bible of the church generated a number of secondary translations as Christianity spread to non-Greek-speaking lands and the churches had to accommodate themselves to the native language. Whereas the early translations had been the work of scholars who knew Hebrew, this was now no longer a requirement. The Greek itself served as the base for subsequent translations. Such was the case in respect to the Coptic, Ethiopic, Armenian, Georgian, Gothic, and Old Latin versions, all of which have little bearing on the history of the Hebrew text but are of lesser or greater importance for the study of the Septuagint itself.

The most important of all the secondary renderings

of the Bible is the Latin. This language advanced with the expansion of Roman power, first throughout Italy, then into southern Gaul and throughout the Mediterranean coastal regions of Africa. In Rome itself, Greek remained the cultural language of the church until the third century, but in the African communities Latin was very popular, and it is most probable that the earliest translations thereinto emanated from these circles. The needs of the liturgy and the lectionary dictated renditions into the vernacular, which at first remained oral and by way of interlinear glosses. It is not impossible but cannot be proven that the earliest such efforts were made by Jews directly from the Hebrew. At any rate, by the middle of the second century CE, an Old Latin version, in the colloquial form of the language, based on the Septuagint, was current. Whether we are speaking here of a single text or a plurality of translations is a matter of dispute because of the great variety of readings to be found in extant manuscripts and citations. These divide roughly into African and European types, but it must be remembered that the two interacted with each other.

Despite the fact that the Old Latin is a translation of a translation, and for that reason must be used with extreme caution for text-critical studies, it is nevertheless important since it was made from a pre-Hexaplaric Greek text. For example, it has much in common with the Lucianic recension and with the Vatican and Sinaitic codices. In the case of *Job* and *Daniel*, it has renderings that presuppose a Greek reading that has not otherwise been preserved and that, in turn, indicates an original Hebrew text not identical with that received. The psalms, in particular, are significant for the numerous texts available as a consequence of their having been used in the liturgy, although they were frequently reworked.

— NAHUM M. SARNA

APOCRYPHA AND PSEUDEPIGRAPHA

The Apocrypha and the Pseudepigrapha, written by Jews during the Hellenistic and Roman periods, closely relate to the thirty-nine Old Testament books canonized by Jews and Christians and sometimes relate to the twenty-seven New Testament books canonized by Christians. These documents were very influential and were frequently considered inspired by many Jewish and Christian communities. However, they are usually preserved only in late manuscripts that are translations of lost originals.

The Apocrypha

The Apocrypha has been variously defined, for there is, of course, no set canon of either the Apocrypha or the Pseudepigrapha. The word *apokrypha* is a transliteration of a Greek neuter plural that means "hidden." Jerome (c. 342-420), however, used the term to denote extracanonical documents. This position is the one adopted by Protestants today; Roman Catholics, since the Council of Trent (during session 4 on 8 April 1546), consider these works "deuterocanonical" and inspired, as do most Eastern Christians.

The Apocrypha contains thirteen writings. They have been dated by experts over a wide period, from the fourth century BCE to the late first century CE; most scholars today correctly date all of them from circa 300 BCE to 70 CE, when the Temple was burned by the Romans. Almost all were written in a Semitic language, except the *Wisdom of Solomon* and *2 Maccabees*, which were probably written in Greek.

BOOKS OF THE APOCRYPHA

2 Ezra	The Wisdom of Solomon	Susanna
Tobit	The Song of the Three Young Men	Bel and the Dragon
Judith	The Prayer of Azariah	1 Baruch
The Letter of Jeremiah		1 Maccabees
The Rest of Esther		2 Maccabees

"But the Lord Almighty has foiled them by the hand of a woman."

JUDITH 16:5

LEGENDS, ROMANTIC STORIES, AND EXPANSIONS OF THE HEBREW SCRIPTURES. Nine documents of the Apocrypha can be regarded as forming a group of legends, romantic stories, and expansions of the Hebrew scriptures: the *Letter of Jeremiah*, *Tobit*, *Judith*, *2 Ezra*, the additions to *Esther*, the *Prayer of Azariah* and the *Song of the Three Young Men*, *Susanna*, *Bel and the Dragon*, and *1 Baruch*.

Letter of Jeremiah. The *Letter of Jeremiah* is the oldest writing in the Apocrypha according to a Greek fragment dating from around 100 BCE, found in Qumran Cave VII (around 300 is most likely). The document is "a letter" *(epistole)* pseudonymously attributed to Jeremiah, which presents a passionate sermon or plea to fellow Jews not to fear or worship idols.

Tobit. Written in a Semitic language, probably Aramaic, around 180 BCE, it attempts to edify the reader and to illustrate that God is efficacious and helps the righteous.

Judith. The dramatic and didactic story of Judith was written in Hebrew around 150 BCE in Palestine, relating the attack upon the Jews by Holofernes, the general of the Assyrian king Nebuchadrezzar (chaps. 1-7).

2 Ezra (1 Esdras in the Septuagint, 3 Esdras in the Vulgate). Probably written in Hebrew or Aramaic, this work is a reproduction and rewriting of parts of the Hebrew scriptures, especially *2 Chronicles* 35:1-36:23, all of *Ezra*, and *Nehemiah* 7:38-8:12. Although very difficult to date, it may derive from the late second century, or around 150-100 BCE. Although this document is, of all the apocryphal writings, the one most closely connected to the Hebrew scriptures, its purpose is unclear. Some characteristics are notable. The author emphasizes the Temple and its cult.

1 Baruch. Modern scholars have concluded that at least parts of this document were composed in Hebrew, others in Hebrew or perhaps Greek from the second or first centuries BCE. W. O. E. Oesterley (*An Introduction to the Books of the Apocrypha*, New York, 1935, p. 260) and Whitehouse (in Charles, 1913, p. 575) were certainly wrong to have dated *1 Baruch* after 70 CE. The provenience may be Palestinian.

The document contains a confession of sins and a plea for God's compassion after the destruction of Jerusalem.

WISDOM AND PHILOSOPHICAL LITERATURE. Two books in the Apocrypha are from the wisdom school of Hellenistic Judaism, but while each is written by a single author, they are very different. *Ben Sira*, written in Hebrew, is by a conservative traditionalist from Palestine, perhaps even Jerusalem. The *Wisdom of Solomon*, written in Greek, is by a liberal thinker, thoroughly open to and influenced by non-Jewish ideas and philosophy—reminiscent to a certain extent of Philo Judaeus of Alexandria and *4 Maccabees*; it comes from Egypt, probably Alexandria.

The Pseudepigrapha

The Pseudepigrapha has been inadvertently defined incorrectly by the selections from this corpus published in German under the editorship of Emil Kautzsch in *Die Apokryphen und Pseudepigraphen des Alten Testaments*, 2 vols. (Tübingen, 1900), and in English under the editorship of R. H. Charles in *The Apocrypha and Pseudepigrapha of the Old Testament*, 2 vols. (Oxford, 1913). Charles's edition of the Pseudepigrapha contains all the documents in Kautzsch's collection plus four additional writings: *2 Enoch*, *Ahiqar*, a Zadokite work, and *Pirke Aboth (Pirqei avot)*. The last two works belong, respectively, among the Dead Sea Scrolls and the rabbinic writings. All the others and many more, to a total of fifty-two writings plus a supplement that contains thirteen lost Jewish works quoted by the ancients,

FROM THE DANIEL CYCLE
A Prayer and Two Colorful Tales

Three additions to *Daniel* are collected into the Apocrypha. Two of these, the story of Susanna and the story of Bel and the dragon, are separate, self-contained works in the *Daniel* cycle; the third, the *Prayer of Azariah*, like the additions to Esther, should be read as an insertion of sixty-eight verses into the *Book of Daniel*; in the Septuagint these verses are numbered from 3:24 to 3:90 (hence, the addition begins after 3:23).

All three additions were probably written originally in Hebrew; the date of the additions is difficult to discern; in their present form all, of course, must post-date 164/5, the date of the *Book of Daniel*. The three additions are probably from different times. It is possible that all three, or portions of them, originally reflected a setting different from their present place in the Septuagint.

The *Prayer of Azariah*, clearly composed in Hebrew (see Otto Plöger, *Züsatze zu Daniel*, Gütersloh, 1973, p. 68), emphasizes that there is only one God and that he is always just. This addition to *Daniel* shifts the focus from the evil king and his golden idol to three potential martyrs and their faithfulness in prayer.

The colorful tale of Susanna, told in only sixty-four verses, may originally have been independent of the Danielic cycle and is perhaps considerably earlier than the *Book of Daniel*. It describes how a beautiful woman, Susanna, is brought to court because she refuses to submit to two aroused influential men (elders, *presbuteroi*, and judges, *kritai*), who approached her while she was bathing. There her fate is sealed; the people and judges condemn her without hearing her. As she is being led to be stoned, the Lord hears her cry (verse 44) and arouses a youth, Daniel, who asks the judge to cross-examine the accusors. The story illustrates how God hears and helps the faithful and virtuous woman, and it demonstrates the wisdom of God in Daniel.

The forty-two-verse Bel and the Dragon contains two separate tales. The first, describes how Daniel, by pointing out footprints in the ashes he had strewn on the floor of a temple, reveals to the king that the priests, their wives, and children had been eating the food offered to Bel, the Babylonian idol. The king becomes enraged and orders their deaths. Daniel is told to destroy the idol and its temple. The second story tells how Daniel destroys an idol, a great dragon (*drakon*, v. 23), and is subsequently thrown into a lions' den. He survives. The king releases Daniel and casts his enemies into the pit.

— JAMES H. CHARLESWORTH

especially Alexander Polyhistor (c. 112-30s BCE), are included in *The Old Testament Pseudepigrapha*, 2 vols., edited by James H. Charlesworth (Garden City, N. Y., 1983-1984).

The fifty-two main documents in *The Old Testament Pseudepigrapha (OTP)*—which is not a canon of sacred writings but a modern collection of Jewish and Christian writings from circa 200 BCE to 200 CE—can be organized in five categories: (1) apocalyptic literature and related works; (2) testaments, which often include apocalyptic sections; (3) expansions of biblical stories and other legends; (4) wisdom and philosophical literature; and (5) prayers, psalms, and odes. To represent the corpus of the Pseudepigrapha within the confines of this relatively short article demands that comments on each category of writings be brief and sharply focused.

APOCALYPTIC LITERATURE AND RELATED WORKS. Nineteen pseudepigrapha can be grouped in the category of apocalyptic literature and related works. These nineteen works cover three overlapping chronological periods.

1. Antedating the burning of Jerusalem by the Romans in 70 ce, the great watershed in the history of Early Judaism (250 BCE-200 CE), are *1 Enoch*, some of the *Sibylline Oracles*, the *Apocrypha of Ezekiel*, and perhaps the *Treatise of Shem*.
2. After 70, the great varieties of religious thought in Judaism waned markedly as religious Jews, with great anxiety, lamented the loss of the Temple and pondered the cause of their defeat. *4 Ezra*, *2 Baruch*, *3 Baruch*, and the *Apocalypse of Abraham* are characterized by an intense interest in theodicy. *4 Ezra* is very pessimistic; its author finds it difficult to see any hope in his remorse. 2 Baruch is much more optimistic than *4 Ezra*; the Temple was destroyed by God's angels because of Israel's unfaithfulness (7:1-8:5), not by a superior culture or the might of the enemy.
3. Later works are documents 3, some of 4, 9, 10, 11, 12, 13, 18, and 19, ranging in date from the lost purported Jewish base of (or traditions in) the *Apocalypse of Adam* in the first or second century CE to the *Apocalypse of Daniel* in the ninth. These works are important for an understanding of Early Judaism only because they apparently preserve some edited works and record some early Jewish traditions.

The most important pseudepigraphon in this group is the composite book known as *1 Enoch*. It is preserved in its entire, final form only in Ethiopic, although versions of early portions of it are preserved in other languages. Of these the most important are the Greek and Aramaic. The Qumran Aramaic fragments, because of their paleographic age, prove that portions of *1 Enoch* date from the third, second, and first centuries BCE.

1 Enoch consists of five works that were composed over three centuries. In chronological order they are *Enoch's Astronomical Book* (*1 Enoch* 72-82), from the third century BCE; *Enoch's Journeys* (*1 Enoch* 1-36), from pre-160 BCE; *Enoch's Dream Visions* (*1 Enoch* 83-90), from pre-160 BCE), *Enoch's Epistle* (*1 Enoch* 91-105), from the second or first century BCE; and *Enoch's Parables* (*1 Enoch* 37-71), from pre-70 CE. Addenda (*1 Enoch* 106-108) are of uncertain date.

Some of the chapters that begin and end the divisions in *1 Enoch* were added or edited as the separate works were brought together into one document; this composite work circulated in Palestine before 70. While the precise dates for these sections of *1 Enoch*, or *Books of Enoch*, are debated, it is clear that the ideas they contain, such as the advocation of a solar calendar, were characteristic of some Jews from the third century BCE to the first century CE. *1 Enoch* is one of our major sources for Hellenistic Jewish ideas on cosmology, angelology, astronomy, God, sin, and mankind.

TESTAMENTS. Eight testaments, some of which include apocalyptic sections, make up a second group of pseudepigrapha. Of these, only the *Testament of Job* and the *Testament of Moses* clearly predate 70 CE. *The Testament of Adam*, in its present form, may be as late as the fifth century CE. *The Testament of Solomon* is earlier, perhaps from the third century CE. *The Testament of Isaac* and the *Testament of Jacob* were possibly added in the second or third century to the *Testament of Abraham*, which in its earliest form probably dates from the end of the first century or the beginning of the second century CE.

The most important—and most controversial—document in this group is the *Testaments of the Twelve Patriarchs*. This documents consists of twelve testaments, each attributed to a son of Jacob and containing ethical instruction often with apocalyptic visions.

— JAMES H. CHARLESWORTH

NEW TESTAMENT

"New Testament" is the name commonly given to a collection of twenty-seven different writings that function as normative scripture within the Christian churches, namely, the gospel according to Matthew, the gospel according to Mark, the gospel according to Luke, the gospel according to John, the *Acts of the Apostles*, the letter of Paul to the Romans, the first and second letters of

"Teach them to carry out everything I have commanded to you."

MATTHEW, 28:20

B

BIBLICAL LITERATURE

New Testament

The Bible of the Christians consisted of two "testaments": the books they had inherited from Judaism, and the combination into a "New Testament" of four gospels about the life and teachings of Jesus.

PAGE 153

Paul to the Corinthians, the letter of Paul to the Galatians, the letter of Paul to the Ephesians, the letter of Paul to the Philippians, the letter of Paul to the Colossians, the first and second letters of Paul to the Thessalonians, the first and second letters of Paul to Timothy, the letter of Paul to Titus, the letter of Paul to Philemon, the *Letter to the Hebrews*, the *Letter of James*, the first and second letters of Peter, the first, second, and third letters of John, the *Letter of Jude*, and the *Revelation to John*. These writings were composed by various Christian authors over approximately one century (c. AD 50-150). They represent a significant portion of early Christian literature, but they do not in every instance represent the oldest extant Christian writings.

The collection and identification of this particular group of writings as a distinct and normative entity was the result of a complex development within the Christian churches. The process, known as canonization, took approximately four centuries. The oldest indisputable witness to the New Testament canon is Athanasius, a fourth-century bishop of Alexandria. Paraphrasing the prologue of the gospel according to Luke in an Easter letter addressed to his congregation in the year 367, Athanasius summarily cited the circumstances that led to the development of the canon. He wrote: "Forasmuch as some have taken in hand, to reduce into order for themselves the books termed apocryphal, and to mix them up with the divinely inspired Scriptures . . . it seemed good to me also . . . to set before you the books included in the Canon, and handed down, and accredited as Divine" (Philip Schaff and Henry Wace, eds., *The Nicene and Post-Nicene Fathers*, vol. 4, Grand Rapids, Mich., 1978, pp. 551-552).

PARTS OF THE NEW TESTAMENT

The Gospel of Matthew	1 Thessalonians
The Gospel of Mark	2 Thessalonians
The Gospel of Luke	1 Timothy
The Gospel of John	2 Timothy
Acts of the Apostles	Titus
1 Corinthians	Philemon
2 Corinthians	Hebrews
Galatians	James
Ephesians	1 Peter
Philippians	2 Peter
Colossians	1 John
	2 John
	3 John
	Jude
	Revelation

Early Formation

There is no evidence in the New Testament that the Christians of the first two or three generations were a literary group. The only indication that Jesus himself wrote anything is in *John* 8:6-8, a dubious reference in light of scholars' common estimation that *John* 7:53-8:11 did not originally belong to the text of John's gospel. According to the gospel evidence, Jesus' command to his disciples was that they should preach (e.g., *Mk*. 3:14, *Mt*. 28:20); nothing is said about a command or exhortation to write. The Lucan overview of early Christianity contained in the *Acts of Apostles* focuses on the preaching of the apostles. It specifically states that at least Peter and John were unlearned (*agrammatoi*, lit. "illiterate," in *Acts* 4:13). Moreover, even though the greater portion of *Acts* is devoted to Paul's activity, *Acts* presents Paul as a preacher and does not once mention his letter-writing. Paul did write letters, of course, and on occasion he referred to letters he has written (*1 Cor*. 5:9, *2 Cor*. 2:3-9; see also *2 Thes*. 2:3). The only New Testament indication of an authoritative command to write concerns the letters to the seven churches in the Book of Revelation (*Rv*. 1:11; see also *Rv*. 2:1, 2:8, 2:12, 2:18, 3:1, 3:7, 3:14). Thus there is no evidence in the New Testament itself that the earliest Christian communities experienced a need to have what later Christian generations would call a New Testament.

APOCALYPTIC CONTEXT. Not only were the first generations of Jesus' disciples largely unlearned, but the message that Jesus preached was couched in apocalyptic terms. He proclaimed, "The time is fulfilled, and the kingdom of God is at hand" (*Mk*. 1:15). This message, like that of John the Baptizer before Jesus, focused on the imminent coming of the reign of God. The apocalyptic proclamation of the coming of the kingdom of God was derived from the prophetic proclamation of the Day of the Lord.

Within a generation after the death of Jesus, the expectation of the coming of God's kingdom was associated with the expectation that Jesus himself would return as Son of man and Lord. This was the expectation of the Parousia ("presence" or "arrival," frequently identified in later Christian writings as the Second Coming). Although Paul was a Hellenistic Jew, he too expected that Jesus would come as eschatological Lord during Paul's own lifetime (see *1 Thes*. 4:17). This expectation of an imminent Parousia was characteristic of the hope for the future that first-generation Christians held.

The New Testament is consistent in its affirmation that God raised Jesus from the dead. The Christians' belief in the resurrection of Jesus was the basis of their hope for the future. Jesus' resurrection was understood as an act of God and as the initial event in the eschatological drama. More than a half-century after the death of Jesus, the gospel according to Matthew uses apocalyptic imagery (*Mt.* 27:51-54, 28:2-4) to attest that the death and resurrection of Jesus had been understood within Matthew's Jewish-Christian circles as an eschatological event.

The belief of the earliest Christians that God's kingdom was imminent not only gave a sense of urgency to the proclamation of Jesus' message by his disciples but also impeded production of a specifically Christian literature among the first generation of Jesus' disciples. For the most part they were incapable of literary activity; their expectation of an imminent Parousia rendered such activity redundant.

BELIEF IN THE HOLY SPIRIT. Another factor tended to forestall the production of literature among the first generation of Christians: the role attributed to the Holy Spirit. This was the Spirit of the end time, that is, the age to come. This eschatological Spirit empowered and impelled Jesus to proclaim the coming of the Kingdom and to effect exorcisms. As the fragment of a traditional creedal formula cited by Paul in Romans 1:4 explicitly attests, that same Holy Spirit continued to be operative in the resurrection of Jesus.

The conviction that the echatological and prophetic Spirit of God was operative in their midst led the first generations of Christians to revere the voice of Spirit-inspired prophets, among whom Jesus was the paradigm. Even Paul, who avowed that he also had the Spirit of God (*1 Cor.* 7:40), boasted that he was a preacher (see *1 Cor.* 1:17, 2:1-5). He had recourse to writing only because the circumstances of his later preaching prevented him from being personally present to those whom he had previously evangelized and with whom he wished to be in additional communication (see, e.g., *1 Thes.* 2:17-3:10, *1 Cor.* 4:14-21). Paul appears to have valued personal presence and the spoken word over the written word.

Both Papias (AD 60-130) and Justin Martyr (c. 100-163/165) bear witness to the high regard in which oral tradition, as distinct from written documents, was held as late as the middle of the second century. In fact, Eusebius, the fourth-century church historian, writing at a time when there was considerable discussion among the Christian churches about which writings were traditional, and noting that some writings were commonly accepted by the churches and others were not, recalls that Papias had said: "I did not suppose that information from books would help me so much as the word of a living and surviving voice" (*Church History* 3.39.4). Thus, even when the process of canonization was reaching its climax, the foremost church historian of the time continued to recall that earlier generations of Christians had higher regard for the Spirit-inspired oral message than they did for written words.

The general illiteracy of the first Christians, the expectation of an imminent Parousia, and the high regard for Spirit-inspired prophetic utterance together ensured that the first generations of Christians would be itinerant, charismatic-type prophetic figures rather than scholarly authors of written works. Their social circumstances and their activity mutually served to prevent their producing written records.

HEBREW SCRIPTURES. The early Christians were even less disposed to produce a specifically religious literature. Jesus and the twelve disciples already had their scriptures: the New Testament portrays Jesus and the disciples as being present in the Temple of Jerusalem and in synagogues, where the scriptures were expounded. All four evangelists describe Jesus interpreting the scriptures, both in rabbinic-type disputation and by way of expository comment. While many of these descriptions owe as much to the creativity and theological purposes of the evangelists as they do to historical reminiscence and the conservative force of tradition, there is little doubt that Jesus accepted the scriptures of his people and his own religious tradition. For Jesus the Hebrew scriptures (*hai graphai* in Greek, the language in which the gospels were written) were a normative expression of the word of God

Letters

Because the Hebrew scriptures were the scriptures *par excellence*, and because the first generation(s) of Christians were essentially Jews who acknowledged the risen Jesus as Christ or Lord, it was unlikely that these early Christians would have produced a sacred literature to compete with that of their Jewish tradition. Even so, the high regard accorded the Hebrew scriptures within both Palestinian and Diaspora Judaism, and the apocalyptic perspective evidenced by the preaching of Jesus and the early writings of Paul, did not preclude the writing of letters. Nonetheless the oldest extant Christian literature consists of the letters of Paul. These letters have always been found in the manuscript and printed editions of the New Testament following the four Gospels and the *Acts of the Apostles;* they are the oldest part of the New Testament.

THE HELLENISTIC MODEL. Although A. J. Malherbe pleaded that *1 Thessalonians* be understood within the category of the paraenetic letter, it is more generally acknowledged that Paul employed the Hellenistic personal letter as a model for his own correspondence. Paul's first letter to the Thessalonians is substantially longer than the average personal letter of Hellenistic correspondents, but it has the essential form of such a letter.

Hellenistic letters typically followed a tripartite schema: the protocol (introduction), the body of the letter (the *homilia*, or basic message), and the eschato-

Paul was responsible for the transformation of Christianity from a Jewish sect to a gentile movement by the end of the first century of the common era.

PAGE 152

B

BIBLICAL LITERATURE

New Testament

"The time is fulfilled, and the Kingdom of God is at hand."

MARK, 1:15

col (conclusion). The protocol normally followed the format of "A to B, greetings and a health wish." Opening with "Paul, Silvanus, and Timothy, to the church of the Thessalonians in God the Father and the Lord Jesus Christ: Grace to you and peace," Paul's first letter to the Thessalonians followed the traditional format, with the exception of the health wish. The health wish is omitted from all the New Testament epistolary literature, with the exception of *3 John* (v. 2). As with all the Pauline letters deemed authentic by critical scholarship (*Romans*, *1-2 Corinthians*, *Galatians*, *Philippians*, *1 Thessalonians*, *Philemon*), other Christian evangelizers are associated with Paul in the sending of the greetings. The recipients of *1 Thessalonians* are an assembly (*ekklesia*, "church") of believers, rather than a single individual. This too sets a precedent, since Paul's later letters were similarly addressed to churches. The greeting of *1 Thessalonians* clearly represents a modification of the typical Hellenistic greeting, a simple "greetings" (sg., *chaire*; pl., *chairete*). The greeting of *1 Thessalonians* is a literary neologism (*charis*, "grace"), somewhat homonymous with the Hellenistic greeting, expanded by the typical Semitic greeting (*eirene*, "peace," the Greek equivalent of the Hebrew *shalom*, used as a greeting in personal encounters as well as in letters). Paul may well have taken the two-part greeting from the liturgical usage of the bicultural Christians at Antioch in Syria. Although the greeting of *1 Thessalonians* is the relatively simple "grace and peace," the formula was expanded in his later correspondence to become "grace to you and peace from God the Father and the Lord Jesus Christ." In short, Paul seems to have employed the typical Hellenistic introduction but adapted it to his own purposes.

SAINT PAUL

Paul's first letter to the Thessalonians is generally regarded to be the oldest section of the New Testament.

ARTE VIDEO IMMAGINE ITALIA SRL/CORBIS

THE FIRST LETTER TO THE THESSALONIANS. From the standpoint of Paul's appropriation of the personal-letter form, some specific features of *1 Thessalonians* are particularly noteworthy. Paul's use of the "recall motif," his constant allusions to being among the Thessalonians, shows that the letter is an occasional writing. Yet the body of the letter focuses upon God's activity among the Thessalonians. Paul gives thanks that the proclamation of the gospel has been effective among them. He represents his presence to the Thessalonians as that of an "apostle of Christ" (*1 Thes.* 2:7) so that there results a significant modification of the *parousia* function of the letter. Since Paul's presence is an apostolic presence, the section of the letter in which Paul specifically writes of his desire to be with the Thessalonians (*1 Thes.* 2:17-3:13) has been styled "the apostolic parousia" (Robert W. Funk). Paul's later letters have a similar feature.

But Paul's apostolic presence is overshadowed by a still greater presence, that of Jesus Christ the Lord. In *1 Thessalonians* Paul uses the technical term *parousia*, a term used elsewhere in the New Testament in this technical sense only in *2 Thessalonians* and *Matthew*, to express the object of Christian hope. Paul's second thanksgiving period concludes with a wish-prayer (*1 Thes.* 3:11-13) that focuses on the Parousia. Questions about the relationship between the Parousia of the Lord Jesus and the resurrection of the dead seem to have been singularly important among the specific concerns that prompted the writing of the first letter to the Thessalonians. However, Paul's concluding the second thanksgiving period (see also *1 Thes.* 2:12) with reference to the awaited and desired Parousia inaugurated a pattern of eschatological climax to the thanksgiving period that would characterize his later writings.

The eschatocol of the typical Hellenistic letter consisted of a series of greetings, prayers, and wishes. These elements are in the concluding verses of *1 Thessalonians* (5:23-27). Noteworthy is Paul's exhortation that the letter "be read to all the brethren" (v. 27), which shows that Paul intended that the letter be read to the entire assembly of the Thessalonian Christians. This is the first indication that Christian writings were to be read during the (liturgical) assemblies of Christians. The ensuing practice would be of major significance in the development of the New Testament canon in the following decades.

The Gospels

While reliance upon the voice of Christian prophets, the expectation of an imminent Parousia, and traditional respect for the scriptures impeded production of a specifically religious literature among early generations of Christians, these same factors imparted a sense of urgency to the oral proclamation of the gospel. The message that Jesus had preached was not only the simple, prophetic-like dictum "The time is fulfilled, and the kingdom of God is at hand; repent, and believe in the gospel" (*Mk.* 1:15). It also made use of proverbs, beatitudes, and especially parables. Proverbs and parables alike were types of *mashalim*, figures of comparative speech. Many of the sayings attributed to Jesus in the New Testament are similar to sayings attributed to rabbis and other sages in nonbiblical literature. These similarities allow these sayings to be typed and located in certain social settings.

Jesus himself was an apocalyptic preacher. His story was not written down until about forty years after his death, but in the intervening years his disciples believed that the reign of God Jesus had proclaimed had begun with his own death and resurrection. This conviction was a key element in the process whereby the gospel of Jesus came to be the gospel about Jesus. In the classic words of Rudolf Bultmann, the proclaimer became the proclaimed. What was written down in the form of gospel during the last third of the first century was not only what Jesus said but also what he did.

In the more than two generations that intervened between Jesus' death and the writing of the first gospel, the tradition about Jesus was handed down in oral fashion. The oral tradition was essentially the living memory of Jesus' immediate disciples and the first generations of Christians. Because it was memory, the oral tradition was essentially conservative, as a number of Scandinavian exegetes have pointed out; and because it was living, the oral tradition was essentially creative, as the early form-critics (especially Bultmann) have shown. An appreciation of the oral tradition about Jesus can only be had through an examination of the Gospels. The Gospels are the record of the church's proclamation of Jesus (Willi Marxsen). They are more than that, but they are the only available documentary evidence of that proclamation. [*See also* Gospel.]

THE SYNOPTICS. Since the late eighteenth century, it has been customary to identify *Matthew*, *Mark*, and *Luke* as the synoptic Gospels in distinction from the *Gospel of John*. Although John's gospel also provides an account of Jesus' activity from the time of his encounter with John the Baptist until the time of Jesus' death and resurrection, it differs in so many respects from the other three gospels that is should be treated apart from the others. The synoptic ("look-alike") Gospels are remarkably similar to one another, not only in structure but also in the choice of the events narrated and in details of the narration. This similarity of content, form, and structure gives rise to the so-called synoptic problem, namely, how to determine the literary relationship among these three remarkably similar documents.

Mark's gospel, written around AD 70, was the first written New Testament gospel. Just after World War I, Karl Ludwig Schmidt clearly demonstrated that the gospel genre was a Marcan literary creation. Mark was the originator of the genre insofar as he created a quasi-biographical framework into which he incorporated independent units of traditional material. Available to him were independent sayings and stories—some of which may have been previously joined together in small collections—handed down by means of the church's missionary, catechetical, and liturgical activity. These three types of activity were the typical settings in which the traditional material about Jesus was both handed down and shaped by the church. The church's activity thus served to stylize the tradition about Jesus, especially as it adapted the tradition to its own needs. In any event, the Gospels do not constitute a bland historical witness to Jesus of Nazareth. They are a witness in faith to the Jesus who has been acknowledged as Lord. The traditions about Jesus were transmitted by the church into its kerygmatic, didactic, and worship activity because of the belief that the Jesus who died on the cross was the Jesus who had been raised from the dead. Faith in Jesus as the Risen One colors the gospel narrative. This is true in all instances, but in some cases postresurrectional accounts have been retrojected into the gospel narrative. Mark's gospel has been described as a "passion narrative with an extended introduction" (Martin Kähler). The passion narrative concludes with a brief resurrection account that features the kerygmatic statement "He has risen; he is not here" (*Mk.* 16:1-8). As such the Marcan text demonstrates that the individual traditions about Jesus were to be understood in the light of Jesus' death and resurrection. The literary format suited to conveying that conviction was the product of Mark's religious and literary genius. Nonetheless, a few scholars (notably Charles H. Talbert) maintain that, as a literary form, the written gospel is dependent upon the Hellenistic form of the biographical sketch.

The specific circumstances of Mark's composition were not those of the Syrian Christian churches to which Matthew and Luke belonged in the eighties.

The earliest parchment codices of the New Testament, entitle the Gospels "according to Matthew," "according to Mark," and so on.

PAGE 252

"As it is written, 'I have made you the father of many nations.'"

ROMANS 4:17

THE NEW TESTAMENT AS POETRY
From Christ's Sermon on the Mount

Blessed are the poor in spirit, for theirs is the kingdom of heaven.
Blessed are those who mourn, for they shall be comforted.
Blessed are the meek, for they shall inherit the earth.
Blessed are those who hunger and thirst for righteousness, for they shall be satisfied.
Blessed are the merciful, for they shall obtain mercy.
Blessed are the pure in heart, for they shall see God.
Blessed are the peacemakers, for they shall be called sons of God.
Blessed are those who are persecuted for righteousness' sake, for theirs is the kingdom of heaven."

— MATTHEW 5:1-10

Matthew's Hellenistic Jewish-Christian community had its own needs, as did Luke's largely gentile-Christian community. Accordingly both Matthew and Luke rewrote the Marcan narrative with the help of traditional material taken from other sources. Their compositions attest to the early church's need for a witness to Jesus that was pertinent to specific situations.

JOHN. The gospel according to John was written in the last decade of the first century for the benefit of a Christian church that can be cryptically described as "the community of the Beloved Disciple" (Raymond E. Brown). That community had its origins in the circle of the disciples of John the Baptist. It had contacts with various forms of esoteric Judaism (many Johannine idioms and thought patterns are remarkably similar to both Qumranite and gnostic expressions and thoughts), and it had received an influx of Samaritan believers. Somehow this community had maintained a Christian existence in relative independence from other Christian communities, even to the point that some scholars believe it best to conceive of the Johannine community as a Christian sect. Only a relatively small number of scholars hold that the gospel produced within this community was literarily dependent upon one or another of the synoptic Gospels. Nonetheless, the literary form created by Mark had sufficient authority among the Christian churches of the late first century to ensure that the Johannine community's faith narrative about Jesus took the form of a gospel.

Foundations of the Canon

While the literary form of the apostolic letter had its origins in the middle of the first century, and the written gospel came into being about a quarter of a century later, forces at work within the Christian churches, forces that continued to be operative after a distinctively Christian literature had been produced, would eventually give rise to a discernible New Testament canon.

AUTHORITY. In a fashion similar to that of other first-century Jewish groups, the early Christians interpreted their experience in the light of the scriptures. The Second Isaian servant canticles, Psalms 2 and 100, were the key elements in the "scriptural apologetic" (Barnabas Lindars) of first-century Christianity. They served to place the Jesus experience in a meaningful context. It was especially the death and resurrection of Jesus that were interpreted "according to the scriptures" (*see 1 Cor.* 15:3-4). In the exposition of this message, Paul argued from the Torah (e.g., *Gn.* 17:5 in *Rom.* 4:17), the prophets (*Hb.* 2:4 in *Rom.* 1:17), and the psalms (*Ps.* 51:4 in *Rom.* 3:4). Citations from and allusions to the Hebrew scriptures served to interpret Paul's own experience. There could be no doubt that the scriptures were authority for Jesus and the first generations of his disciples.

The word of the Lord. A real concern was with other Spirit-endowed authorities. Preeminent among these authorities was the word of the Lord Jesus. Barely a generation after Jesus' death, Paul appealed to the word of the Lord (*1 Thes.* 4:15) in an attempt to assuage the grief over the unexpected death of some Christians at Thessalonica. In *1 Corinthians* 7, Paul carefully distinguished the authority of the word of the Lord from his own. Contemporary with Paul's earliest letters was the collection of a number of Jesus' sayings in a florilegium, no longer extant, known to contemporary scholars as the Q source. Application of the criteria of multiple attestation (sayings contained in different texts and/or different literary forms) and dual exclusion (neither attested in contemporary Jewish sources nor serving specific ecclesiastical needs) allows scholars to judge that many of the gospel sayings derive from Jesus' own words. A history-of-tradition study of the *logia* (sayings of Jesus), as well as a comparative, redaction-critical study of a single saying contained in more than one of the Gospels, indicates that the sayings of Jesus were transmitted by the early Christians in such a way as to be applicable to later situations. Thus the sayings of Jesus enjoyed significant and relevant authority in the churches of the first generations. They were remembered from the past, but they were also applied to contemporary circumstances.

The apostles. As witnesses, the apostles possessed considerable authority among the churches. *Acts* offers a stylized account of the authority enjoyed by Peter. Even more indicative is the biographical section of the letter to the Galatians, where Paul vehemently argues for his own authority on the basis that he had received a revelation of Jesus Christ (*Gal.* 1:12) but acknowledges the contacts he had with the Jerusalem apostles (1:18-19, 2:1).

Within the New Testament, the name "apostle" was not restricted to the twelve disciples, named apostles (*Lk.* 6:12-16, *Mk.* 3:13-19, *Mt.* 10:1-4). Paul himself was an apostle in his own right (*Gal.* 1:1), as even Luke acknowledges in *Acts* (14:4, 14:14). Not only did Paul preach in the power of the Holy Spirit, but he also used his Spirit-endowed authority to render authoritative decisions (*see 1 Cor.* 7:10-11, 7:40). Those whom Paul had evangelized appealed to him to resolve disputes and uncertain matters (*see 1 Cor.* 1:11, 7:1). He served as an authority for the churches he had founded, that is, those he had served as an apostle. The authority of the apostles is also attested to in the phenomenon of apostolic pseudepigraphy: works written by authors unknown to us were attributed to apostles so that they would have apostolic authority *(Ephesians, Colossians, 2 Thessalonians, 1-2 Timothy, Titus, James, 1-2 Peter, Jude)*.

TRADITION. In the first century the tradition about Jesus became stylized and stereotyped in a variety of oral and literary forms. The New Testament evidence shows how important maintaining the tradition about Jesus was. One of the earliest indications of this was the emergence of creedal formulas that articulated the core content of the kerygma. In AD 50 three different creedal formulas were incorporated into the first letter to the Thessalonians (1:10, 4:14, 5:9-10). Paul used the technical language of the rabbinic schools, "receive" (Gr., *paralambanein*; Heb., *qibbel*) and "deliver" *(paradidomi, masar)*, to attest that he was handing along the tradition faithfully (*1 Cor.* 15:3-5). The creedal formulas principally articulated faith in the death and resurrection of Jesus, but the scope of tradition was broader. For example, it included the "liturgical" tradition of the Lord's Supper (*see 1 Cor.* 11:23-32).

The later writings of the New Testament offer evidence of the importance placed on transmitting the tradition faithfully. Luke offers an exhortation on the faithful transmission of the gospel within the context of Paul's farewell discourse at Miletus (*Acts* 20:28-31). The Pastoral letters to Timothy and Titus portray the two as having been carefully taught by Paul (e.g., *1 Tm.* 1:2a) and charged with responsibility for conveying that teaching to others (e.g., *1 Tm.* 4:11). "The saying is sure" functions as a refrain, setting a seal of approval on authoritative pieces of tradition (e.g., 1 Tm. 1:15).

Within early Christianity, Spirit-authority-tradition formed a constellation that can be perceived as constitutive of Christianity itself. The individual writings of the New Testament incorporated and bore witness to these elements in specific and concretized fashions. Each New Testament document was composed within a specific church situation and addressed to a specific situation.

Text of the New Testament

The New Testament was written entirely in Greek. Approximately five thousand ancient Greek New Testament manuscripts exist. These are categorized according to the material on which the texts are transcribed, the type of calligraphy, and the use made of the manuscripts. The oldest complete manuscript of the New Testament is the fourth-century Codex Sinaiticus, which originally contained both the Old and the New Testaments. Written on parchment, the New Testament portion of the codex is the only complete extant copy of the Greek New Testament written in uncial script. The codex was discovered by Konstantin von Tischendorf in the Monastery of Saint Catherine on Mount Sinai in 1844. To symbolize its antiquity, it has been designated in scholarship with the Hebrew letter alef.

PAPYRI. The oldest available manuscripts of the New Testament are papyrus fragments, none of which offers a complete text of any New Testament book. In the technical literature these fragments are indicated by a Gothic P with an Arabic numeral in exponent position indicating the specific papyrus. Eighty-eight New Testament papyri have been identified and cataloged thus far. The most ancient is P^{52}, a second-century fragment containing some letters from *John* 18:31-33 on the recto side and some letters from *John* 18:37-48 on the verso side. These letters are in an uncial script and written with no space between the words. The discovery of the fragment was particularly important because it led scholars almost unanimously to place the time of composition of the gospel according to John in the late first century, when the dominant tendency of critical scholarship was to identify that gospel as a second-century work.

The most important papyri that serve as witnesses to the text of the New Testament are those that belong to the Chester Beatty and Bodmer collections. Three third-century papyri were acquired by A. Chester Beatty in 1930-1931. P^{45} designates 30 leaves (of a 220-leaf codex) with parts of *Matthew, Mark, Luke, John*, and *Acts*; P^{46}, the oldest of the three papyri, consists of 86 leaves (of 104) with parts of *Romans, 1 Corinthians, 2 Corinthians, Ephesians, Galatians, Philippians, Colossians*, and *1 Thessalonians*. P^{47} has 10 leaves (of 32) with *Revelation* 9:10-17:2.

PARCHMENT. Most New Testament manuscripts

The nearly contemporary writings of the Qumran community, the people of the Dead Sea Scrolls, and the New Testament reveal contrasting uses of covenant ideas.

PAGE 193

B

BLESSING

Phenomenology of Blessing

"The Lord bless thee and keep thee."

THE FOURTH BOOK OF MOSES, NUMBERS, 6:24-26

are written on parchment. For purposes of editing the text of the New Testament, the most important manuscripts are the parchment manuscripts written in uncial script, of which 274 are known to exist. These manuscripts are identified by a system of sigla devised by Johann Jakob Wettstein (1693-1754), who used the letters of the Latin and Greek alphabets to designate the ancient Greek manuscripts. The discovery of additional manuscripts and the recognition that some manuscripts that Wettstein had designated by a single letter were in fact parts of two manuscripts have rendered his system scientifically inadequate, but it is classic and remains in common use. A more exact system of classification was devised by Caspar René Gregory (1846-1917), who used Arabic numerals preceded by a zero (01, 02, 03, etc.) to designate the manuscripts. Thus the Codex Sinaiticus is designated by the Hebrew letter alef or 01. In addition to the Codex Sinaiticus, for purposes of editing the text of the New Testament, the more important uncial manuscripts are the Codex Alexandrinus, the Codex Vaticanus, the Codex Ephraemi Rescriptus, the Codex Bezae Cantabrigensis, the Codex Claromontanus, the Codex Regius, the Codex Washingtoniensis, and the Codex Koridethi.

THE MINUSCULES. The uncial style of transcribing New Testament manuscripts predominated for about five centuries. In the ninth century a minuscule or cursive style of writing was introduced. Most of the New Testament manuscripts written in the second millennium of Christianity are written in this minuscule style. Almost three thousand extant minuscule manuscripts of the New Testament exist, dating from the tenth century to the sixteenth century. As a group they are generally considered to bear witness to the Byzantine or ecclesiastical type of text, but a more recent trend identifies them simply as "the majority." In the technical literature they are simply identified by Arabic numerals. Some of the miniscules share such textural particularities with other manuscripts that they can be recognized as having some sort of dependence on one another. Among the groups so identified are the Lake (MSS 1, 18, 131, etc.) and Ferrar (MSS 13, 69, 124, 346, etc.) families, respectively named after Kirsopp Lake and William Hugh Ferrar, who first identified (Lake in 1902, Ferrar in 1868) the textural relationships among the manuscripts of the groups that today bear their names.

THE LECTIONARIES. A final category of Greek manuscripts is the lectionaries. More than two thousand lectionaries have been classified thus far. The oldest fragmentary lectionary dates from the sixth century; the oldest complete lectionary dates from the eighth. The lectionaries contain New Testament texts arranged for liturgical reading. The text of the lectionaries is characterized by the insertion of appropriate introductory phrases and the additional use of proper nouns for clarity.

— RAYMOND F. COLLINS

BLESSING

The term *blessing* has two fundamental meanings. In its first meaning, it is a form of prayer; it is man's adoration and praise of God. In its second meaning, blessing is a divine gift that descends upon man, nature, or things; it is a material or spiritual benefit that results from divine favor. In this second meaning, blessing is the transfer of a sacred and beneficent power, a power that emanates from the supernatural world and confers a new quality on the object of the blessing.

PHENOMENOLOGY OF BLESSING. Man as *homo religiosus* "believes that there is an absolute reality, the *sacred*, that transcends this world but manifests itself in this world, thereby sanctifying it and making it real" (Mircea Eliade, *The Sacred and the Profane*, New York, 1959, p. 202). A blessing is thus a type of hierophany. It is one of those mysterious acts through which a transcendent power becomes immanent in this world. In every blessing, therefore, a power intervenes to bestow benefits of divine origin upon a being or object.

Considered as an action, every blessing includes three elements: first, the establishment of a relationship with the realm of the Wholly Other, which is the source of the desired beneficial effect; second, the transfer, to a being or object, of an efficacious quality emanating from that realm, through some form of mediation; finally, the enhancement of the existence of the being or object that receives this quality.

Power. At different times and places, man has given names to the transcendent power or reality that is the source of all blessings. One of the best known of these is *mana*. Of Melanesian origin, *mana* denotes a supernatural reality attached to beings or things—a reality full of the power, authority, and strength inherent in life and truth. Indeed, the idea of a real and effective power is found again and again in nonliterate traditions throughout the world, receiving such names as *orenda* (Iroquois), *manitou* (Algonquian), *wakan* (Lakota), and *uxbe* (Pueblo). In the high civilizations of antiquity, it appears as *brahman* (India), *tao* (China), *kami* (Japan), *khvarenah* (ancient Iran), *me* (Sumer), and *melammu* (Mesopotamia).

Transfer. However conceived, this transcendent power is transferred to the human realm through the blessing. The divine will can carry out this transfer *motu proprio*, without the aid of an intermediary. Nevertheless, a blessing commonly makes use of some form of mediation. The intermediary, who uses both ritual and symbols, may be a king or a priest, a saint, a prophet, or the head of a family. By ritual means he animates the mysterious forces that make communication with the transcendent power possible and thereby creates a special relationship with the divinity.

The spoken word occupies a special place in the symbolism of mediation. The mystical power of words is particularly prominent among archaic peoples. In Australia, the voices of the bull-roarers, symbols of the Great Spirit's presence, are heard throughout every initiation ceremony. In Vedism, *vac* is the celestial word, an aspect of the *brahman*; and the syllable *om* is believed to encompass the universe, the *brahman*, the sound that gives fullness to the sacrifice. The word is also the instrument of divine power, which may be invoked by the civilizing word, the prophetic word, or in the evocation of holy names. The presence of theophoric names and all manner of incantations in all ancient civilizations demonstrates man's belief in the power of the word. Indeed, the Akkadian *amatu* and the Hebrew *davar* refer to the word understood as coincidental with reality itself.

Gifts and favors. The third element of a blessing is the actual benefit that a being or object receives through contact with the transcendent power. This power is dynamic. The Sanskrit *ojas*, the Avestan *aojo*, and the Latin *augustus* all have the sense of an enabling power, one that literally empowers its possessor to fulfill the religious function allotted to him. In *Genesis* 9:1, God blesses Noah and his sons directly, saying to them, "Be fruitful and multiply." In *Numbers* 6:22-27, the sacerdotal blessing is intended to assure divine protection, benevolence, and peace to the faithful. Blessings may also produce less spiritual results: fertility, health, and long life in men or animals, bountiful harvests, material prosperity. Whatever the nature of the gifts or favors he receives, man is always conscious of their divine origin, acknowledging the transcendent power that lies behind the effectiveness of blessing.

TYPOLOGY OF BLESSING. This section presents a selective survey of the great variety of forms of blessing practiced by *homo religiosus* at different times and places. It will classify types of blessing according to the methods of transfer that they employ, the methods that actually set the blessing in motion. In particular, it will focus on three essential aspects of such methods: language, gesture, and ritual.

Religions of peoples with oral traditions. Among peoples without writing, blessing is intimately linked to myth. Indeed, in the life of these peoples, myth constitutes a sacred history that puts man in contact with the supernatural world, joining present and primordial time and linking present action to the initial acts of creation. This sacred history furnishes archaic man with models for his life. In addition, he grasps the meaning of the celestial archetype through the symbolic language of myth; blessing constitutes one of the archaic ritual forms that he uses in his various efforts to orient himself in reference to that archetype. Within the vast magico-religious context of archaic ritual, word and gesture are inseparably linked.

In a great many religious traditions, the sacred word, the word spoken by God, appears at the first moment of creation. Among the Dogon, for example, the Nommo spoke three times, pronouncing words of light, of dampness, and of music. In archaic belief, man's spoken word, addressed to the Wholly Other, allows him to participate in divine power or, at least, to benefit from it. Such a belief, admirably documented in the stone prayer carvings of Valcamonica, underlies the beginnings of prayer and is expressed in the incantations that are part of every people's patrimony—incantations that seek to constrain divine power through the repetition of spoken words. In sub-Saharan Africa, the word approaches its fullest power to the extent that it is joined with rhythm and image, its most effective mediators. The hand also carries meaning, and among the Dogon, the Bambara, and the Fali, the thumb is the symbol of power. Word, rhythm, and gesture are fully integrated in the rituals associated with myths of fertility and initiation; indeed, when used in celebrations of myth, they reestablish, through the reactualization of the archetypal event, the complete harmony believed to have existed at the beginning. Africans have created from myth, word, and ritual an effective symbolic unity used to reestablish the original harmony. Ancestors are also important in these rituals, for they exist in primordial time and have a major role in the transfer of favors to the living. Likewise, the human intermediary has an important role in the ritual of blessing.

African myths deal primarily with the origin of mankind and with the origin of social and ritual institutions.

PAGE 3

Among the ethnically related groups in Burundi and Rwanda in central Africa, all religious life revolves around belief in Imana, the supreme being, omnipotent creator, good and omniscient protector of man and nature. A child is placed under Imana's blessing at birth, and on the eighth day his father gives him a name associated with the god. In fact, theophoric names signify Imana's permanent blessing and guidance of those who bear them. Human intermediaries, especially heads of families, play an important role in obtaining the effects of blessing. During Kurya Umwaka, the New Year festival celebrated in Burundi in May, the father presides over a meal that consists of "eating the old year"; acting as both intermediary of the god and head of the family, he distributes food from Imana and pronounces wishes for happiness in the new year.

Dexiosis and blessing in Mithraism and Manichaeism. The *dexiosis* played a major role in the myth and ritual that are intertwined in Mithraic liturgy. A number of illustrated documents from Rome, Dura-Europos (present-day Salahiyeh, Syria), and the Danubian area represent the *dexiosis* of Mithra and Helios,

> **SYMBOLS OF THE RIGHT HAND**
> **Mysterious Bonds of Union**
>
> A number of Mediterranean and Eastern religions have particularly emphasized the symbolic role of the right hand. In the Syrian cults of Jupiter Dolichenus, Atargatis, and Hadad, as in the Phrygian cult of the god Satazius, votive hands indicate the divine presence and symbolize God's power. Statuaries from both the East and—especially—the West furnish many examples of gods extending their hand in a gesture of blessing and protection; indeed, Zeus is sometimes called Hyperdexios, the protector with the extended hand. This gesture is also represented on effigies of Asklepios, the god of healing. In all these artifacts invoking the vast symbolic system surrounding blessing, the right hand is both a sign of power and the expression of a benevolent divine will, of the gods' transfer of part of their strength and power.
>
> The symbolism of the hand appears in another form in the *dexiosis*, the handshake—always of right hands—that creates mysterious bonds of union. A number of documents concerning the dexiosis come from the Roman world, where the gesture was associated with the fides, an agreement of alliance and voluntary, reciprocal obligation. Representations of the *dexiosis* sometimes show clasped hands together with ears of wheat, symbols of the prosperity that comes from concord, itself the result of the divine blessing of the goddess Fides; here, the *dexiosis* shifts notions of concord and obligation into the religious domain of the blessing. The *dexiosis* is found in the liturgy of the cults of Dionysos, Sabazios, and Isis; in all these cults, the ritual signifies both the celestial apotheosis of the god and the entrance of the devout into the elite group of initiates who have received divine gifts. The *dextrarum iunctio* is a gesture binding the initiate to his god's power; as ancient Latin authors wrote, "Felix dextra, salutis humanae pignus."
>
> — JULIEN RIES
>
> TRANSLATED FROM THE FRENCH BY JEFFREY C. HAIGHT AND ANNIE S. MAHLER

"Blessed be Abram by God Most High."

GENESIS, 14:19

seated together in the celestial chariot; the scene evokes the apotheosis of the young Mithra, conqueror of evil and darkness, and at the same time presents the mythical archetype to which the ritual dexiosis alludes in the Mithraic initiation. At the conclusion of the initiation ceremony, the *pater*, the *magister sacrorum* ("chief priest") of the Mithraic community, welcomes the initiate by extending his right hand to him; by this gesture, the initiate becomes one of the participants in the rite, who then join in the same gesture and are thereby introduced to the cult's salvation mysteries. This dexiosis seals the agreement between Mithra and the initiate and creates a bond that insures the initiate's salvation. By joining their right hands, the initiates take part in the mystic *dexiosis* of Mithra and Helios and at the same time ensure, through this authentic ritual of blessing, the transfer of the benefits of salvation promised by Mithra to those inducted into his mysteries.

The ritual of the *dexiosis* in Mithraic mysteries of the Roman empire has been clarified by evidence recently discovered at Nimrud-Dagh and at Arsameia Nymphaios in the ancient province of Commagene, where Mithraism was a royal cult during the centuries immediately preceding the Christian era. Several representations show the gods Mithra, Herakles, Zeus, and Apollo extending their right hands to King Antiochus I, son of the cult's founder, Mithradates I Kallinikos.

The pattern uniting myth, ritual, and *dexiosis* is found again in Manichaeism in Mani's great myth of the struggle between Light and Darkness. The Living Spirit, second messenger of the Father of Greatness, walks toward the boundary of the Realm of Darkness to save Primordial Man, prisoner of Darkness; he lets out a great cry, "Tochme," heard by Primordial Man, who replies, "Sotme." The Living Spirit then extends his right hand; grasping it, Primordial Man, the savior saved, regains the Paradise of Light. Used similarly in the Manichaean community, the saving gesture of the *dexiosis* became the gnostic gesture *par excellence* since it both symbolized and realized the communication of the dualistic mysteries, the sources of salvation.

Power of the word. The energy of the word is central to Indian religious thought; indeed, the word is considered a power in itself. Sanskrit includes a number of words that are close in meaning to "blessing" or "to bless" or that suggest the result of a blessing: *asis* ("wish, blessing"), *asirvada* ("benediction"), *kusala* ("prosperous"), *dhanya* ("that which brings good fortune"), *kalyana* ("excellent"). The word *brahman* means "sacred word"; originally, it signified "the word that causes growth."

Brahmanaspati, or Brhaspati, is chaplain of the gods, charged with reciting the sacred formulas. As *purohita*, or chief priest of the gods, he is charged with reciting the sacred formulas; they become beneficent in

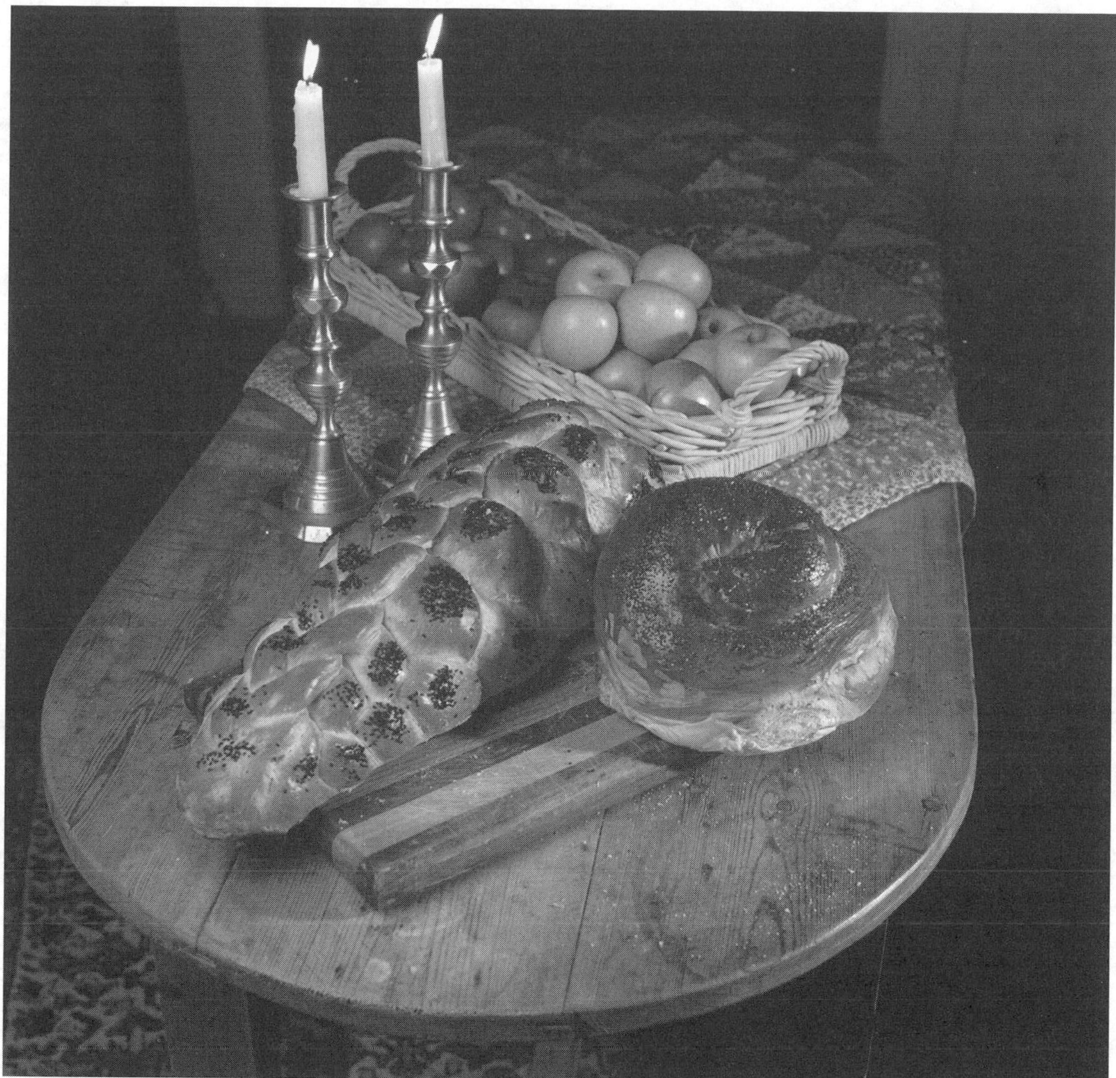

SABBATH TABLE

In Judaism, God's blessing is applied to the sabbath table, a ritual that assists in the execution of the divine plan.

RICHARD T. NOWITZ/CORBIS

his mouth. Indeed, to be effective, the formulas must be pronounced, but once pronounced they are real, beneficent, and effective by themselves, not through the chaplain's mediation. The Vedic priest, the *brahmana*, sometimes asks for the help of Brahmanaspati, who can suggest effective words to him. "I put a splendid word in your mouth," the *purohita* says to the *brahmana* (Rgveda 10.98.2). Words of blessing are also spoken by the father at the birth of a son: "Be imperishable gold. Truly you are the One called son. Live a hundred autumns."

Blessing in the Hebrew scriptures. The Semitic root *brk*, "bless," was the common property of all peoples of the ancient Near East. In its plural form, *brk* is used to indicate the act of blessing, which may be carried out by God, angels, or men.

In the typology of blessing found in the Hebrew scriptures a first major tendency is exemplified by God's dispensation of benefits among people or among created things generally. After the creation, he blesses the beings he has just made (*Gn.* 1:22-28); after the Flood, he blesses Noah and his children (*Gn.* 9:1). Likewise, he blesses the patriarchs Abraham, Isaac, and Jacob, and finally, all the children of Israel (*Gn.* 12:2-3, 27:16, 35:9; *Dt.* 1:11), all of whom become *barukh*, beneficiaries of divine blessing. This blessing can also apply to nonliving things that assist in the execution of the divine plan: the Sabbath (*Gn.* 2:3), bread and water (*Ex.* 23:25), the home of the righteous (*Prv.* 3:33). Faith in the value of God's blessing underlies the many wishes for good fortune found in the Hebrew scriptures: "Blessed be Abram by God Most High" (*Gn.* 14:19).

In addition, blessing appears in the Old Testament in a truly original way, one that goes well beyond the conventional Semitic meaning of *brk*. To the ancient Hebrews, blessing was also the expression of the divine favor stemming from God's choice of a particular people whom he surrounds with his solicitude. This spiritual and universal idea of divine blessing finds its fullest development in the Covenant and the teachings of the

"Jesus Himself stood among them and said to them "Peace be with you."

LUKE 24:36

B

BLESSING

Typology of Blessing

prophets, where the blessing conferred on Abraham becomes a program of salvation upon which God insists (*Gn.* 18:18-19, 22:16-18, 26:4-5, 28:13-15). Israel's mission, which is the Covenant, and the prophetic movement are rooted in God's blessing of Abraham; hence, this blessing is part of the history of salvation.

The second important tendency in the Old Testament typology of blessing involves the blessing conferred by God through an intermediary—family head, king, or priest—charged with a mission. Among the Phoenicians and the Arameans, the father of the family was the intermediary, addressing the gods on behalf of his wife and children; among the nomadic clans of Syria and Canaan, the ancestral cult and the chiefs' hereditary authority strongly influenced life in the clan and were, in fact, as important in malediction as in blessing. Nevertheless, while this Semitic heritage is present in certain customs of the chosen people, the Hebrew scriptures are marked chiefly by the presence of God in the midst of the people whom he has chosen for himself and whom he leads through selected intermediaries. Words of blessing pronounced by the king, or in his favor, are rooted in God's choice of David and of his dynasty (*2 Sm.* 7:29, *1 Chr.* 17:27). The father of the family gives his blessing by both the spoken word and the laying on of hands, a practice that seems to be a specific mark of the chosen people. An archetypal rite that goes back to the patriarchal period, the laying on of hands is described at length in Genesis 48:1-20 and appears throughout both the Old and the New Testaments.

Muslim faith creates an attitude of total and confident surrender (islam) to God who is reliable, omnipotent, and benevolent.

PAGE 249

Barakah among the Arabs and in Islam. In the pre-Islamic Arab world, *baraka* came to mean "having many descendants"; it also suggested the transfer of strength and fertility from father to children. Additionally, *baraka* meant "to prosper, to enjoy large herds, abundant grasses, and rich harvests"; it denoted a quality in beings and things that brought them prosperity and success. In the Arab mind, the idea seems to have developed of transferring this quality; *barakah* (noun; pl., *barakat*) could be transferred to such acts as kissing a hand or touching a holy object. In popular Islam, traces of this nomadic notion of *barakah* remain in attitudes toward localities, historical personalities, and sacred objects.

In the uncompromising monotheism of Islam, the omnipotence and omnipresence of God stand at the center of the life of the faithful and the community. God is the source of all that is sacred; the sacred refers only to the will of Allah, the holy God, Al-Quddus, a term that implies the power, strength, and mastery that God alone can possess. In the Qur'an, *barakat* are sent to people by God; *barakah* is God's blessing, the gift that he makes to mortals of the power to dispense his benefits, all of which proceed from him. Linked to the holiness of God, barakah is an influence that proceeds from all that touches God closely: the Qur'an, the Prophet, the Five Pillars of Islam, the mosques, and the saints. Yet because Islam has neither clergy nor ministry, *barakah* finds no human intermediary: all blessing comes from God.

Christian blessing. The Septuagint translates *berekh* with the word *eulogein*, which in the Vulgate is *benedicere. Berakhah* is rendered by eulogia, a word that can denote either the praise creatures lift up to God or the gifts God makes to his creatures. *Eulogia* results from an act of blessing; it is the blessing itself, the gift given to a being. Eulogesis denotes the act through which the blessing is conferred, the action of the church's minister, who gives the blessing.

The Gospels report a number of Jesus' blessings of persons and things. He blesses little children (*Mk.* 10:16) and the bread that he will multiply (*Mt.* 14:19); immediately before his ascension, he blesses his disciples (*Lk.* 24:50). The editors of *Luke* and *Mark* also recorded Jesus' gestures. He blessed the children by laying his hands on them, while to the disciples he raised his hands in blessing. Such gestures of blessing were already familiar to the Jews. According to the Talmud, the priests gave the blessing in the temple daily, during the morning sacrifice; they remained standing, their arms upraised, during the ceremony.

The expression "Pax vobis," used by Jesus when speaking with his disciples, is an authentic formula of blessing (*Lk.* 24:36, *Jn.* 20:19, 20:21). Christ charges those whom he sends forth to pronounce this blessing in their apostolic work (*Mt.* 10:12, *Lk.* 10:5, *Jn.* 20:21); Paul uses it repeatedly in his letters (*Rom.* 1:7, *Phil.* 4:7, *Col.* 3:15); John of Patmos places it at the beginning of the *Revelation* (Rv. 1:4). As the epistles of Ignatius of Antioch attest, the church quickly took up this formula, thus establishing what will become a long ecclesiastical tradition. The "Pax vobis" is by no means intended merely as a polite greeting. It is, rather, a blessing that brings to its recipients the messianic peace, with all that that implies. The apostles' use of the words *charis* ("grace") and *eirene* ("peace") should be understood in the context of this blessing (*Rom.* 1:7, 1 *Cor.* 1:7, 1 *Pt.* 1:2).

Jesus' words and gestures of blessing passed into the various Christian communities. From the *Clementine Homilies* and the *Acts of Thomas*, it is clear that the ritual of blessing was customary in Christian circles. At a very early date, blessing appears in liturgical regulations such as the *Apostolic Tradition*. In the eyes of the church, the sacerdotal blessing is effective because it comes from God through his priests, who are also his ministers. Hence, the Council of Laodicea (c. 363) prohibited receiving blessings from the hands of heretics, and theologians later defined blessing as a sacred ritual through which the church brings divine favors—primarily spiritual favors—upon people and things.

Ancient documents dealing with rites of blessing are plentiful. Catacomb paintings and references in literature show that in the second century the usual gesture of Christian blessing was the laying on of hands; during the third century, this gesture was gradually replaced by the *sphragis tou Christou* ("the sign of the cross"). Indeed, it is evident from the *Sibylline Oracles*, from writings of Tertullian and Cyril of Jerusalem, and from mural paintings and the first Christian sarcophagi that the sign of the cross pervaded Christian customs from the third century onward. The shift from the laying on of hands to the sign of the cross as the characteristic gesture of blessing, combined with the increased use of prayer formulas, shows that Christians were aware of the transcendence of the ritual of blessing and hence were indifferent about actual physical contact with the hand or hands, and about the hands' position, in the ritual itself. Over the centuries, blessings multiplied and took different forms in different countries; until the Middle Ages, they were grouped with other rites of the church under the general name of sacraments. In the twelfth century, however, from the influence of Hugh of Saint-Victor (d. 1142), Abelard (d. 1142), and Alger of Liège (d. 1131), the denomination of sacred rite was given to blessing, and emphasis in the rite was placed more upon its formula than upon gestures. This emphasis was accentuated by Luther's Reformation. To the reformers, God's presence and action are known and carried out through the word; in the word, therefore, is found the whole effectiveness of blessing.

— JULIEN RIES

TRANSLATED FROM FRENCH BY
JEFFREY C. HAIGHT AND ANNIE S. MAHLER

BUDDHISM

AN OVERVIEW

Buddhism began around the fifth or fourth century BCE as a small community that developed at a certain distance, both self-perceived and real, from other contemporary religious communities, as well as from the society, civilization, and culture with which it coexisted.

Despite the importance of this early phase of Buddhist history our knowledge about it remains sketchy and uncertain. Three topics can suggest what we do know: the source of authority that the new Buddhist community recognized, the pattern of development in its teaching and ecclesiastical structures, and the attitude it took toward matters of political and social order.

One primary factor that both accounts for and expresses Buddhism's emergence as a new sectarian religion rather than simply a new Hindu movement is the community's recognition of the ascetic Gautama as the Buddha ("enlightened one") and of the words that he had reportedly uttered as a new and ultimate source of sacred authority.

Some scholars have maintained that early Buddhism was a movement of philosophically oriented renouncers practicing a discipline of salvation that subsequently degenerated into a popular religion. A second group has contended that Buddhism was originally a popular religious movement that took form around the Buddha and his religiously inspiring message, a movement that was subsequently co-opted by a monastic elite that transformed it into a rather lifeless clerical scholasticism. A third group has argued that as far back as there is evidence, early Buddhist teaching combined philosophical and popular elements, and that during the earliest period that we can penetrate, the Buddhist community included both a significant monastic and a significant lay component. This argument, which is most convincing, has included the suggestion that the philosophical/popular and monastic/lay dichotomies should actually be seen as complements rather than oppositions, even though the understandings of the relative importance of these elements and their interrelationships have varied from the beginning of the Buddhist movement.

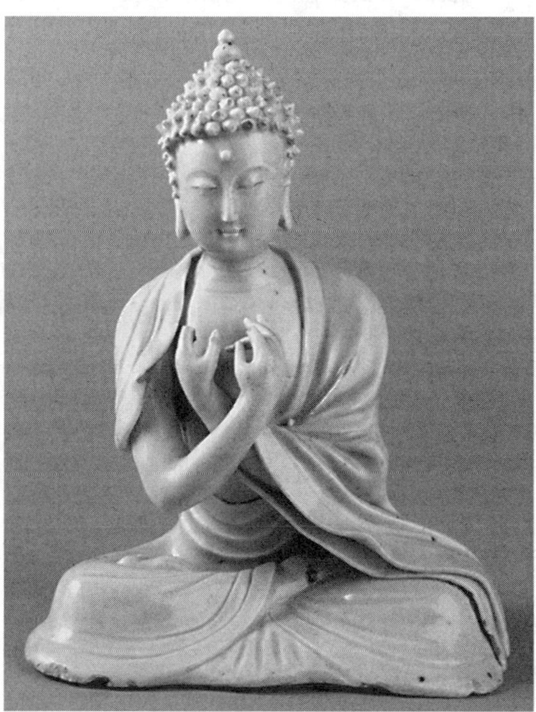

ENLIGHTENED ONE

Most Buddhists honor Sudhartha Guatama the Buddha, founder of Buddhism.

ROYAL ONTARIO MUSEUM/ CORBIS

"For hatred does not cease by hatred: hatred ceases by love."

THE PALI CANON, SUTTAPITAKA DHAMMAPADA 1.5

Dharma was and still is employed by all the religious denominations that have originated in India to indicate their religious beliefs and practices.

PAGE 206

Buddhism as Civilizational Religion

Buddhism has never lost the imprint of the sectarian pattern that characterized its earliest history, largely because the sectarian pattern has been reasserted at various points. But Buddhism did not remain a purely sectarian religion. With the reign of King Asoka, Buddhism entered a new phase of its history in which it became what we have chosen to call a "civilizational religion," that is, a religion that was associated with a sophisticated high culture and that transcended the boundaries of local regions and politics.

HISTORY AND LEGEND OF THE ASOKAN IMPACT. Asoka (r. circa 270-232 BCE) was the third ruler in a line of Maur-yan emperors who established the first pan-Indian empire through military conquest. In one of the many inscriptions that provide the best evidence regarding his attitudes and actual policies, Asoka renounced further violent conquest and made a commitment to the practice and propagation of Dharma. He also sent special representatives to ensure that the Dharma was appropriately practiced and taught by the various religious communities within his realm.

It would seem from Asoka's inscriptions that the Dharma that he officially affirmed and propagated was not identical to the Buddhist Dharma, although it was associated with it, especially insofar as Buddhist teaching impinged on the behavior of the laity. However, the inscriptions give clear evidence that if Asoka was not personally a Buddhist when he made his first commitment to the Dharma, he became so soon thereafter.

During the Asokan and immediately post-Asokan era there are at least three specific developments that sustained the transformation of Buddhism into a civilizational religion. The first, a realignment in the structure of the religious community, involved an innovation in the relationship and balance between the monastic order and its lay supporters. In addition, this realignment in the structure of the Buddhist community fostered the emergence of an important crosscutting distinction between monks and laypersons who were participants in the imperial-civilizational elite on the one hand, and ordinary monks and laypersons on the other.

The transformation of Buddhism into a civilizational religion also involved doctrinal and scholastic factors. During the Asokan and post-Asokan periods, factions within the monastic community began to formulate aspects of the teachings more precisely, and to develop those teachings into philosophies that attempted to explain all of reality in a coherent and logically defensible manner.

Developments in the areas of symbolism, architecture, and ritual were also significant components in the transformation of Buddhism into a civilizational religion. Some changes were related to the support Buddhism received from its royal and elite supporters. Royal and elite patronage seems to have been crucial to the emergence of large monastic establishments throughout India.

IMPERIAL BUDDHISM REASSERTED AND TRANSCENDED. Despite the importance of Asoka to the history of Buddhism, the imperial order that he established persisted only a short time after his death. Within fifty years of his death (i. e., by the year 186 BCE), the Buddhist-oriented Mauryan dynasty collapsed and was replaced by the Sunga dynasty, more supportive of Brahmanic Hindu traditions. Buddhism emerged as a dominant religion in areas outside northeastern India where the Sungas were unable to maintain the authority and prestige that their Mauryan predecessors had enjoyed.

From the second century BCE through the first century CE Buddhism became a powerful religious force in virtually all of India. A major aspect of the transformation of Buddhism into a fully civilizational religion was the differentiation that occurred between Buddhism as a civilizational religion and Buddhism as an imperial religion. During late Mauryan times the civilizational and imperial dimensions had not been clearly differentiated. However, by the beginning of the common era Buddhism had become a civilizational religion that transcended the various expressions of imperial Buddhism in particular geographical areas. As a direct correlate of this development, an important distinction was generated within the elite of the Buddhist community. By this period this elite had come to include both a truly civilizational component that maintained close international contacts and traveled freely from one Buddhist empire to another and beyond, as well as overlapping but distinguishable imperial components that operated within the framework of each particular empire.

Closely associated developments were taking place at the level of cosmology and its application to religious practice. In the Hinayana context the most important development was probably the rich portrayal of a set of six cosmological *gatis*, or "destinies" (of gods, humans, animals, *asuras* or titans, hungry ghosts, and beings who are consigned to hell), which depicted, in vivid fashion, the workings of *karman* (moral action and its effects). These texts, which were probably used as the basis for sermons, strongly encouraged Buddhist morality and Buddhist merit-making activities.

BUDDHISM AS PAN-ASIAN CIVILIZATION. The geographical expansion of Buddhism was both a cause and an effect of its civilizational character. But Buddhism's role as a pan-Asian civilization involved much more than a pan-Asian presence. Buddhist monasteries, often state supported and located near capitals of the various Buddhist kingdoms, functioned in ways analogous to modern universities. There was a constant circulation of Buddhist monks, texts, and artistic forms across increasingly vast geographical areas. Indian and Central Asian missionaries traveled to China and with the help of Chinese Buddhists translated whole libraries of books into Chinese, which became a third major Buddhist sacred language alongside Pali and Sanskrit. In the fifth century Buddhist nuns carried their ordination lineage from Sri Lanka to China. Between 400 and 700 a stream of Chinese pilgrims traveled to India via Central Asia and Southeast Asia in order to visit sacred sites and monasteries and to collect additional scriptures and commentaries. In the sixth century Buddhism was formally introduced into Japan; in the following century Buddhists from Central Asia, India, and China made their way into Tibet. Beginning in the eighth and ninth centuries monks from Japan visited China in order to receive Buddhist training and acquire Buddhist texts. These are only a few illustrations of the kind of travel and interaction that characterized this period.

Within the Mahayana tradition this period of Buddhist efflorescence as a civilizational religion was characterized by a high level of creativity and by a variety of efforts toward systematization. In the earlier centuries the Mahayanists produced a rich and extensive collection of new *sutras*, including the *Saddharmapundarika Sutra* (Lotus of the True Law), the *Mahaparinirvana Sutra*, the *Lankavatara Sutra*, and the *Avatamsaka Sutra*. With the passage of time, voluminous commentaries were written on many of these *sutras* in India, Central Asia, and China.

By the second half of the first millennium CE a new strand of Buddhist tradition, the Vajrayana, or Esoteric Vehicle, began to come into the foreground in India. This new vehicle accepted the basic orientation of the Mahayana, but supplemented Mahayana insights with new and dramatic forms of practice, many of them esoteric in character. The appearance of this new Buddhist vehicle was closely associated with the composition of new texts, including new *sutras* (e.g., the *Mahavairocana Sutra*), and the new ritual manuals known as tantras. By the eighth and ninth centuries this new vehicle had spread through virtually the entire Buddhist world and was preserved especially in Japan and in Tibet.

During the period of its hegenomy as a pan-Asian civilization, Buddhism retained a considerable degree of unity across both the regional and text-oriented boundaries that delimited particular Buddhist traditions.

Buddhism as Cultural Religion

For more than a thousand years, from the time of King Asoka to about the ninth century, Buddhism exhibited a civilizational form that began as pan-Indian and ultimately became pan-Asian in character. Like the sectarian pattern that preceded it, this civilizational pattern left an indelible mark on all subsequent Buddhist developments.

THE PERIOD OF TRANSITION. The increasing importance of Tantra in late Indian Buddhism and the success of the Pure Land (Ching-t'u) and Ch'an (Zen) schools in China during the Sui and T'ang period (598-907) are further indications that the Buddhist tradition was becoming more local in self-definition. Chinese Buddhism had a new independent spirit in contrast to the earlier India-centered Buddhism. Moreover, the new movements that emerged at that time seem to be the result of a long development that took place apart from the major cosmopolitan centers. Far more than in the past, expressions of Buddhism were being made at all levels of particular societies, and there was a new concern for the interrelation of those levels within each society.

During the last centuries of the first millennium CE, Buddhist civilization developed a new, somewhat independent center in China that reached its peak during the Sui and T'ang dynasties. Thus, when Buddhist texts and images were introduced into Japan during the sixth century they were presented and appropriated as part and parcel of Chinese culture.

The processes of acculturation that had first become evident in the sixth century in India and China repeated themselves beginning in the tenth century in Japan, Korea, Tibet, Sri Lanka, and Southeast Asia. In each of these areas distinct cultural forms of Buddhism evolved. There was a reorganization of the Buddhist community with an increased emphasis on the bonds between elite and ordinary Buddhists in each particular area. There was a renewed interest in efficacious forms of Buddhist practice and the Buddhist schools that preserved and encouraged such practice. Within each area there was a development of Buddhist symbols and rituals that became representative of distinct Buddhist cultures, particularly at the popular level.

Buddhism had some limited success in India during the last centuries of the first millennium. It benefited from extensive royal and popular support in northeastern India under the Pala dynasty from the eighth to the twelfth century, but Hindu philosophy and theistic *(bhakti)* movements were aggressive critics of Buddhism. Hardly any distinct Buddhist presence continued in India after the last of the great monasteries were destroyed by the Muslims. In China there was more success, although the Confucian and Taoist traditions were powerful rivals. As a result of persecutions in the ninth century, Buddhism lost its distinctively civilizational role, but it continued as a major component of Chinese religion, becoming increasingly synthesized with other native traditions.

After about 500 CE, Indian Buddhism began to decline.

PAGE 324

From 843 to 845 Emperor Wu-tsung, an ardent Taoist, issued decrees that led to the destruction of 4,600 monasteries and 40,000 temples and shrines.

PAGE 142

MONASTIC ORDER, ROYAL ORDER, AND POPULAR BUDDHISM. The transformation of Buddhism from a civilizational religion to a cultural religion depended on a fundamental realignment in the structure of the Buddhist community. As a civilizational religion, Buddhist community life had come to include a largely monastic elite that traveled extensively, was multilingual, and operated at the civilizational level; an imperial elite made up of monks and laypersons associated more closely with royal courts and related aristocracies; and a less exalted company of ordinary monks and laypersons living not only in urban areas but in the countryside as well. At Buddhism's zenith as a civilizational religion the central organizing relationship was that between the largely monastic civilizational elite and the imperial elites. With the transformation of Buddhism into a cultural religion, however, this situation was drastically altered.

One aspect of this transformation was major changes that took place at three different levels: monastic, imperial, and popular. The demise of the monastic network through which the civilizational aspect of Buddhism had been supported and maintained was decisive. To be sure, there were elements of the monastic community that never lost their international vision, and travel and exchanges between specific cultural areas was never totally absent, but it would be difficult to speak of a pan-Asian Buddhist elite after the ninth or tenth century.

The pattern at the imperial level was altered by the loss of monastic power and influence coupled with increased state control in monastic affairs. In China and Japan, and to a lesser extent in Korea and Vietnam, state control became thoroughly bureaucratized. In Sri Lanka and the Theravada areas of Southeast Asia, state control was implemented more indirectly and with considerably less efficiency by royal "purifications" of the *sangha*.

The demise of the international Buddhist elite and the weakening of the large and powerful establishments were counterbalanced by a strengthening of Buddhist life at the grass-roots level. Smaller, local institutions that for a long time had coexisted with the great monasteries took on new importance as focal points in Buddhist community life.

THE PREEMINENCE OF PRACTICE. The era of comprehensive Buddhist philosophizing and the formulation of original systems of thought came to an end, for the most part, with the demise of Buddhism as a civilizational religion. There continued to be philosophical innovations, and some of the great systems that were already formulated were adjusted to meet new circumstances. However, the real creativity of Buddhism as a cultural religion came to the fore in schools and movements that emphasized efficacious modes of Buddhist practice.

A major component in the development of various Buddhist cultures is the ascendancy of schools or

ARHAT
The Enlightened

History and Development of the Term. In Vedic and non-Vedic contexts, the noun *arhat* and the verb *arhati* applied generally to persons or gods whose particular status earned for them the characterization of "worthy" or "deserving of merit." The terms also denoted "being able to do," or "being capable of doing."

In the Jain *sutras* the term is often used in a sense closer to that found in Buddhist writings. Here the *arhat* is described as one who is free from desire, hatred, and delusion, who knows everything, and who is endowed with miraculous powers. While these characterizations are consistent with the Buddhist use of the term, it should be noted that the Jains applied the word exclusively to the *tirthamkaras* or revealers of religion, whereas in Buddhism arhatship is an ideal to be attained by all serious religious strivers. In its most typical usage in *Theravada* Buddhism, however, the term *arahant* signifies persons who have reached the goal of enlightenment or *nibbana* (Skt., *nirvana*).

The Arhat as Cult Figure. In popular Buddhism the arhat has become a figure endowed with magical and apotropaic powers. In Burma, the arahant Shin Thiwali (Pali, Sivali), declared by the Buddha to be the foremost recipient of gifts among his disciples, is believed to bring prosperity and good fortune to those who petition him. The arahant Upagupta, who tamed Mara and converted him to Buddhism, is thought to have the power to prevent storms and floods as well as other kinds of physical violence and unwanted chaos.

The *arhat*, as one who has realized the *summum bonum* of the spiritual path, is worshiped on the popular level as a field of merit *(puny aksetra)* and source of magical, protective power. Claims of arhatship are continuously being made on behalf of holy monks in countries like Sri Lanka, Burma, and Thailand.

In short, the *arhat* embodies one of the fundamental tensions in the Buddhist tradition between the ideal of enlightenment and equanimity and the extraordinary magical power concomitant with this attainment.

— DONALD K. SWEARER

movements that combined a strong emphasis on the importance of discipline (particularly although not exclusively the monastic discipline) with an accompanying emphasis on meditation. In China and Japan, Ch'an and Zen, with their emphasis on firm discipline and meditative practices, are representative of this kind of Buddhist tradition. [*See* Zen.]

Esoteric or Tantric modes of religion also were a significant part of cultural Buddhism in East Asia. In China the Esoteric elements were closely related to influences from the Vajrayana tradition in Tibet as well as interactions with forms of indigenous Taoism. In Japan more sophisticated Esoteric elements persisted in the Tendai (Chin., T'ien-t'ai) and Shingon schools, while more rustic and indigenous elements were prominent in groups that were integrated into these schools, for example, the Shugendo community that was made up of mountain ascetics known as *yamabushi*.

In Sri Lanka in the twelfth and thirteenth centuries devotional religion also seems to have been influential in the Buddhist community, generating new genres of Buddhist literature that were written primarily in Sinhala rather than Pali. Although no specifically devotional "schools" were formed, a whole new devotional component was incorporated into the Theravada tradition and subsequently diffused to the Theravada cultures in Southeast Asia. Similarly, there were, as far as we know, no "schools" that were specifically Esoteric or Tantric in character. However, there is some evidence that indicates that Esoteric elements played a very significant role in each of the premodern Theravada cultures. This kind of influence seems to have been particularly strong in northern Burma, northern Thailand, Laos, and Cambodia.

Another important component of Buddhism as a cultural religion was the mitigation, in some circles at least, of traditional distinctions between monks and laity. This trend was least evident in the more discipline-oriented contexts, but even here there was some movement in this direction. For example, in the Ch'an and Zen monasteries, monks, rather than being prohibited from engaging in productive work as the Vinaya had stipulated, were actually required to work. In the Pure Land schools in Japan, and in some of the Esoteric schools in Japan and Tibet, it became permissible and common for clergy to marry and have families.

THE PERVASIVENESS OF RITUAL. Alongside the particular schools and movements that characterized Buddhism as a cultural religion there were also modes of Buddhist practice that, although influenced by those schools and movements, were more pervasively involved in Buddhist cultures as such. Pilgrimage was in the forefront of these practices.

Virtually every instance of Buddhism as a cultural religion had its own particular patterns of Buddhist pilgrimage. In many cases these pilgrimage patterns were a major factor in maintaining the specificity of particular, often overlapping, religious and cultural complexes. Many of the sites that were the goals of major Buddhist pilgrimages were mountain peaks or other places that had been sacred from before the introduction of Buddhism and continued to have sacred associations in other traditions that coexisted with Buddhism.

Wherever Buddhism developed as a cultural religion it penetrated not only the sacred topography of the area but also the cycle of calendric rites. In China, for example, the annual cycle of Buddhist ritual activities included festivals honoring various Buddhas and *bodhisattvas*, festivals dedicated to significant figures from Chinese Buddhist history, a great vegetarian feast, and a very important "All Soul's" festival in which the Chinese virtue of filial piety was expressed through offerings intended to aid one's ancestors. While these rituals themselves involved much that was distinctively Chinese, they were interspersed with other festivals, both Confucian and Taoist, and were supplemented by other, lesser rituals associated with daily life that involved an even greater integration with non-Buddhist elements.

Buddhism in its various cultural expressions also became associated with life cycle rites, especially those of the male initiation into adulthood and those associated with death. The Buddhist involvement in male initiation rites was limited primarily to Southeast Asia. In many Buddhist countries children and young men were educated in the monasteries, but only in Southeast Asia did temporary initiation into the order, either as a novice (as in Burma) or at a later age as a full-fledged monk (as in central Thailand), become a culturally accepted necessity for the attainment of male adulthood. Buddhist involvement in funerary rituals was, on the other hand, a phenomenon that appeared again and again all across Asia. Once Buddhism became established as a cultural religion, it was these rituals that enabled it to maintain its position and influence, and to do so century after century on into the modern era.

Buddhism in the Modern World

The modern encounter of cultures and civilizations has not been monolithic. Three stages can be identified in Buddhist Asia. The first was the arrival of missionaries with traders in various parts of Asia. This onslaught was sometimes physically violent, as in the Portuguese destruction of Buddhist temples and relics in Sri Lanka, but for the most part it was an ideological assault. A second stage was more strictly colonial, as some European powers gained control over many different areas of the Buddhist world. Some Buddhist countries, such as Sri Lanka, Burma, and the Indochinese states, were

Based on a canonical story, the All Souls Festival, or Avalambana, is observed throughout Southeast and East Asia.

PAGE 30

"The law that I have preached will be your master after my disappearance."

THE PALI CANON, DIGHA NIKAYA II

fully colonized while others, such as Thailand, China, and Japan, were subjected to strong colonial influences. In virtually every situation (Tibet was a notable exception), the symbiotic relationship between the political order and the monastic order was disrupted, with adverse effects for Buddhist institutions.

The twentieth-century acceptance of Western political and economic ideologies, whether democratic capitalism or communism, represents a third stage. Buddhists in China, Mongolia, Tibet, and parts of Korea and Southeast Asia now live in communist societies, and the future of Buddhist communities in these areas looks bleak. Capitalism has been dominant in Japan, South Korea, Sri Lanka, and parts of Southeast Asia (Thailand being the prime example), and greater possibilities for the Buddhist tradition are presumed to exist in these areas.

Conclusion

Buddhism as a whole has not yet developed a distinctive character in the modern period. On the contrary, there is a great deal of continuity between the historical development of Buddhism and the current responses and innovations. Thus the sectarian, civilizational, and cultural patterns continue to exert a predominant influence in the evolution of Buddhist tradition.

At the same time, we can see that Buddhism, like other world religions, participates in a modern religious situation that is, in many respects, radically new. Buddhism has thus come to share certain modern elements with other contemporary religions. We can see such elements in the search for new modes of religious symbolism, as is found in the writings of the Thai monk Buddhadasa and the Japanese Kyoto school of Buddhist philosophy. We can also see these common elements in the preoccupation with the human world and this-worldly soteriology that is emerging in many Buddhist contexts.

[*Various regional surveys treat Buddhism as a component of local and regional cultures. See in particular* Indian Religions, Southeast Asian Religions, Tibetan Religion, Chinese Religion, Korean Religions, *and* Japanese Religion.]

— FRANK E. REYNOLDS AND CHARLES HALLISEY

BUDDHISM IN INDIA

BUDDHA. Scholars generally tend to accept the years 563 to 483 BCE as the most plausible dating for the life of Gautama Buddha. Assuming, moreover, that the legend is reliable in some of its details, we can say that the history of the religion begins when he was thirty-five (therefore, in about 528), with his first sermon at Sarnath (northeast of the city of Varanasi).

His first sermon was followed by forty-five years of wandering through the Ganges River valley, spreading his teachings. Although tradition preserves many narratives of isolated episodes of this half century of teaching, no one has been able to piece together a convincing account of this period.

At the age of eighty (c. 483), Siddhartha Gautama, the Buddha Sakyamuni, died near the city of Kusinagara. To his immediate disciples perhaps this fading away of the Master confirmed his teachings on impermanence, but the Buddha's death would soon come to be regarded as a symbol of his perfect peace and renunciation: with death he had reached his *parinirvana*, that point in his career after which he would be reborn no more.

BUDDHIST POPULATIONS PER WORLD REGION

	Buddhists	Population
Africa	38,000	748,130,000
Asia	321,985,000	3,513,218,000
Europe*	1,563,000	72,767,800
Latin America	569,000	490,444,000
Northern America	920,000	295,677,000
Oceania	200,000	28,973,000
Total	325,275,000	5,804,120,000

*Includes former Soviet Union.
**United Nations Medium Variant Figures, mid 1996
Source: *The 1997 Britannica Book of the Year*

DHARMA. His first preaching, known as the "First Turning of the Wheel of Dharma" symbolizes the appearance in history of the Buddhist teaching, whereas Sakyamuni's enlightenment experience, or "Great Awakening" *(mahabodhi)*, which occurred in the same year, represents the human experience around which the religion would develop its practices and ideals. This was the experience whereby Sakyamuni became an "Awakened One" *(buddha)*. His disciples came to believe that all aspects of Buddhist doctrine and practice flow from this experience of awakening *(bodhi)* and from the resultant state of freedom from passion, suffering, and rebirth called *nirvana*. The teachings found in the Buddha's sermons can be interpreted as definitions of these two experiences, the spiritual practices that lead to or flow from them, and the institutions that arose inspired by the experience and the human beings who laid claim to it.

It is difficult to determine to what extent early Buddhism had an accompanying metaphysics. Some of the earliest strata of Buddhist literature suggest that the early community may have emphasized the joys of renunciation and the peace of abstention from conflict—political, social, and religious—more than a philosophical doctrine of liberation. Such are the ascetic ideals of one of the earliest texts of the tradition, the *Atthakavagga (Suttanipata)*. There is in this text a rejection of doctrine, rule, and rite that is a critique of the exaggerated claims of those who believed they could become pure and free through ritual, knowledge, or religious status.

If such statements represent some of the earliest moments in the development of the doctrine, then the next stage must have brought a growing awareness of the need for ritual and creed if the community was to survive. This awareness would have been followed in a short time by the formation of a metaphysic, a theory of liberation, and a conscious system of meditation. In the next strata of early Buddhist literature these themes are only surpassed in importance by discussions of ascetic morality. The ascetic ideals of the early community were then expanded and defined by doctrine—as confession of faith, as ideology, and as a plan for religious and moral practice. The earliest formulations of this type are perhaps those of the Eightfold Path, with its triple division into wisdom, moral practice, and mental concentration. The theoretical or metaphysical underpinnings are contained in the Four Noble Truths and in the Three Marks (impermanence, sorrow, and no-self), both traditionally regarded as the subject matter of the Buddha's first sermons.

Buddhist Remnants and Revivals

After the last days of the great monastic institutions (twelfth and thirteenth centuries) Indian Buddhism lingered on in isolated pockets in the subcontinent. During the period of Muslim and British conquest (thirteenth to nineteenth century) it was almost completely absorbed by Hinduism and Islam, and gave no sign of creative life until modern attempts at restoration (nineteenth and twentieth centuries).

ATTEMPTED REVIVAL: THE MAHABODHI SOCIETY. Attempts to revive Buddhism in the land of its origin began with the Theosophical Society, popularized in Sri Lanka in the early 1880s by the American Henry S. Olcott. Although the society eventually became the vehicle for broader and less defined speculative goals, it inspired new pride in Buddhists after years of colonial oppression. The Sinhala monk Anagarika Dharmapala (1864-1933; born David Hewavitarane) set out to modernize Buddhist education. He also worked untiringly to restore the main pilgrimage sites of India. To this end he founded in 1891 the Mahabodhi Society, still a major presence in Indian Buddhism.

AMBEDKAR AND "NEO-BUDDHISM." The most significant Buddhist mass revival of the new age was led by Dr. Bhimrao Ramji Ambedkar (1891-1956). He saw Buddhism as the gospel for India's oppressed and read in the Buddhist scriptures ideals of equality and justice. After many years of spiritual search, he became convinced that Buddhism was the only ideology that could effect the eventual liberation of Indian outcastes. On 14 October 1956 he performed a mass "consecration" of Buddhists in Nagpur, Maharashtra.

OTHER ASPECTS OF MODERN BUDDHISM. The most fruitful and persistent effort in the rediscovery of Indian Buddhism has been in the West, primarily among Western scholars. The combined effort of Indian, North American, and European historians, archaeologists, and art historians has placed Indian Buddhism in a historical and social context, which, though still only understood in its rough outlines, allows us to see Buddhism in its historical evolution.

Another interesting phenomenon of the contemporary world is the appearance of "neo-Buddhists" in Europe and North America. Although most of these groups have adopted extra-Indian forms of Buddhism, their interest in the scriptural traditions of India has created an audience and a demand for research into India's Buddhist past. The Buddhist Society, founded in London in 1926, and the Amis du Bouddhisme, founded in Paris in 1928, both supported scholarship and encouraged the Buddhist revival in India.

In spite of the revived interest in India of the last century, the prospects of an effective Buddhist revival in the land of Sakyamuni seem remote. It is difficult to imagine a successful living Buddhism in India today or in the near future. The possibility of the religion coming back to life may depend on the reimportation of the Dharma into India from another land. It remains to be seen if Ambedkar and Anagarika Dharmapala had good reasons for hope in a Buddhist revival.

[*See also* Indian Religions.]

— LUIZ O. GÓMEZ

BUDDHISM IN SOUTHEAST ASIA

The classical Southeast Asian religio-cultural synthesis, of which Theravada Buddhism has been a major component, has given the cultures of Burma, Thailand, Cambodia, Laos, and Vietnam a unique sense of identity and has sustained them to the present. Faced with Western imperialistic expansion from the seventeenth century onward and the challenge of modernity, the classical religious worldview, institutional structures, and cultural ethos have been changed, modified, and reasserted in a variety of ways.

MODERNIZATION AND REFORM. The eve of

Most dictionaries record two related senses of the term doctrine: according to the first, it is the affirmation of a truth; according to the second, it is a teaching.

PAGE 208

Orthodox Buddhism made sense to Southeast Asians because of the pre-Buddhist idea that religious virtue is not a product solely of descent from particular ancestors but also a consequence of one's own religiously effective actions.

PAGE 628

the assertion of colonial power in the Buddhist countries of Southeast Asia found them in differing states and conditions. The Burmese destruction of Ayutthaya in 1767 provided the Thai (the designation applied to Tai living in the modern nation-state) the opportunity to establish a new capital on the lower Chaophraya River at present-day Bangkok. Because of its accessibility to international commerce the new site was much better situated for the new era about to dawn; the new dynastic line was better able to cope with the increasing impact of Western influence and was also committed to building a new sense of national unity.

The classical Thai Buddhist worldview had been set forth in the *Traibhumikatha* of King Lü Thai of Sukhothai. In one sense this text must be seen as part of Lü Thai's program to reconstruct an administrative and political framework and to salvage the alliance structure that had collapsed under the policies of his predecessor. In laying out the traditional Buddhist stages of the deterioration of history, Lü Thai meant to affirm the meaningfulness of a karmically calculated human life within a given multitiered universe. As a Buddhist sermon it urges its listeners to lead a moral life and by so doing to reap the appropriate heavenly rewards.

Modernization of the Thai Buddhist worldview was accompanied by a reform of the Buddhist *sangha*. Before his coronation in 1851 King Mongkut had been a monk for twenty-five years. During that time his study of the Pali scriptures and his association with Mon monks of a stricter discipline convinced him that Thai Buddhism had departed from the authentic Buddhist tradition. He advocated a more serious study of Pali and Buddhist scripture as well as the attainment of proficiency in meditation. His efforts at religious reform resulted in an upgrading of monastic discipline in an effort to make it more orthodox. The group of monks who gathered around Mongkut at Wat Bovornives called themselves the Thammayut ("those adhering to the doctrine") and formed the nucleus of a new, stricter sect of Thai Buddhism.

The development of a reformist Buddhist tradition that embodied Mongkut's ideals brought about further changes in the monastic order, especially as the *sangha* became part of the policies and programs of Mongkut's son Chulalongkorn. At the same time that he implemented reforms designed to politically integrate outlying areas into the emergent nation-state of Thailand, Chulalongkorn also initiated policies aimed at the incorporation of all Buddhists within the kingdom into a single national organization. As a consequence, monastic discipline, as well as the quality of monastic education, improved throughout the country. A standard monastic curriculum, which included three levels of study in Buddhist history, doctrine, and liturgy, and nine levels of Pali study, was established throughout the country. In addition, two Buddhist academies for higher studies were established in Bangkok.

Buddhism and the Modern Nation-State. Buddhism proved to be a crucial factor during the end of the colonial and the postcolonial periods, as Burma, Thailand, Cambodia, Laos, and Vietnam became modern nation-states. On the one hand, Buddhism contributed decisively to the development of the new nationhood; on the other, it resisted in various ways changes forced upon traditional Buddhist thought and practice.

Historically, Buddhism played an important role in the definition of the classical Southeast Asian states. It was inevitable, therefore, that it would be a crucial factor in the redefinition of these states. In those cases, for example, in which a country was dominated by a colonial power, nationalist movements grew out of, or were identified with, a religious base or context. Take Burma as a case in point. Buddhism provided the impetus for the independence movement that arose there during the first decades of the twentieth century. The YMBAs (Young Men's Buddhist Association) of Rangoon and elsewhere in Burma quickly assumed a political role.

When U Nu became prime minister in January 1948, following Aung San's assassination, he put Buddhism at the heart of his political program. He created a Buddhist Sasana Council in 1950 to propagate Buddhism and to supervise monks, appointed a minister of religious affairs, and ordered government departments to dismiss civil servants thirty minutes early if they wished to meditate. In 1960 U Nu committed himself and his party to making Buddhism the state religion of Burma, an unpopular move with such minorities as the Christian Karens. This attempt was one of the reasons given for General Ne Win's coup in March 1962, which deposed U Nu as prime minister.

Buddhism figured prominently in other Southeast Asian countries, both as a basis of protest against ruling regimes and as an important symbolic component of political leadership. In the 1960s politically active Vietnamese monks contributed to the downfall of the Diem regime, and afterward the United Buddhist Association, under the leadership of Thich Tri Quang and Thich Thien Minh, remained politically active. In Cambodia, Prince Sihanouk espoused a political philosophy based on Buddhist socialism and was the last Cambodian ruler to represent, although in an attenuated way, the tradition of classical Southeast Asian Buddhist rule.

In Thailand the centralization of the Thai *sangha* under King Chulalongkorn and his able *sangharaja*, Vaji-rañana, not only improved monastic discipline and education but also integrated the monastic order more fully into the nation-state. Chulalongkorn's successor, Vajiravudh (1910-1925), made loyalty to the nation synonymous with loyalty to Buddhism; in effect, he utilized Buddhism as an instrument to promote a spirit of nationalism.

Buddhism has continued to be an important tool in the government's policy to promote national unity. In 1962 the Buddhist Sangha Act further centralized the organization of the monastic order under the power of the secular state. In the same year the government organized the Dhammadhuta program, and in 1965 the Dhammacarika program. The former supported Buddhist monks abroad and those working in sensitive border areas, especially the northeastern region of the country, while the latter has focused on Buddhist missions among northern hill tribes.

Other, more radical Buddhist responses to the emerging nation-state developed in various parts of Southeast Asia and usually centered on a charismatic leader who was sometimes identified as an incarnation of the *bodhisattva* Maitreya. In Burma several rebellions in the early twentieth century aimed to overthrow British rule and to restore the fortunes of both Burmese kingship and Burmese Buddhism. One of these was led by Saya San, who had been a monk in the Tharrawaddy district in lower Burma but disrobed to

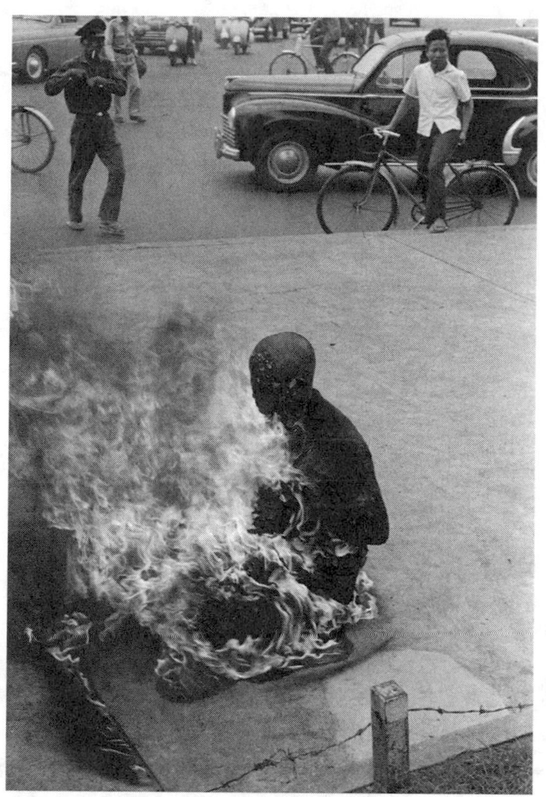

EXTREME SACRIFICE

As a protest against the Ngo Din Diem government's anti-Buddhist policies, a young Vietnamese monk performs ritual suicide (October 1963).

UPI/CORBIS-BETTMANN

FOUR NOBLE TRUTHS
A Path Toward Salvation

All strands of the Buddhist tradition recognize in the Four Noble Truths (Skt., *catvary aryasatyani;* Pali, *cattari ariyasaccani*) one of the earliest formulations of the salvific insight gained by the Buddha on the occasion of his enlightenment. For the Theravada tradition, the discourse on the Four Truths constitutes part of the first sermon of the Buddha, the *Dhammacakkappavattana Sutta,* delivered in the Deer Park near Banaras to his five original disciples. The standard formulaic enumeration of the Four Truths as found in this discourse is as follows:

> This, monks, is the noble truth of dukkha ["suffering"]: birth is dukkha, old age is dukkha, disease is dukkha, dying is dukkha, association with what is not dear is dukkha, separation from what is dear is dukkha, not getting that which is wished for is dukkha; in brief, the five groups of grasping [i. e., the five khandhas; Skt., skandhas] are dukkha.
>
> And this, monks, is the noble truth of the uprising [samudaya] of dukkha: this craving, which is characterized by repeated existence, accompanied by passion for joys, delighting in this and that; that is to say, craving for sensual desires, craving for existence, craving for cessation of existence.
>
> And this, monks, is the noble truth of the cessation [nirodha] of dukkha: complete dispassion and cessation of craving, abandonment, rejection, release of it, without attachment to it.
>
> And this, monks, is the noble truth of the path [magga] leading to the cessation of dukkha; just this Noble Eightfold Way; that is to say, proper view, proper intention, proper speech, proper action, proper livelihood, proper effort, proper mindfulness, proper concentration.
>
> (Samyutta Nikaya 5.420ff.)

These Four Noble Truths (formulaically, *dukkha,* samudaya, *nirodha, magga*) constitute a "middle way" between rigorous asceticism and sensual indulgence. The twin foci of truths are craving (Skt., *trsna;* Pali, *tanha*) and ignorance *(avidya),* craving to hold that which is impermanent, grasping for substantiality where there is no abiding substance, and not knowing that this orientation inevitably yields unsatisfactoriness (Pali, *dukkha;* Skt., *duhkha*). Hence the twin foci draw attention to the fundamental cause *(samudaya)* of dukkha, and meditation on *dukkha* leads to a discernment that craving and ignorance are its matrix.

The Eightfold Path, the fourth of the Four Noble Truths, provides a means especially adapted to lead one into salvific insight, a way conforming completely to the Buddha's own salvific realization. In this sense, the Eightfold Path is the proper mode of religious living, one that subsumes ethics into soteriology.

— JOHN ROSS CARTER

work in a more directly political way to overthrow the British. Saya San's movement had a strongly traditional religious and royal aura, and much of his support came from political monks associated with nationalistic associations *(wunthanu athins)* that had formed in the 1920s. Saya San was "crowned" as "king" in a thoroughly traditional Burmese manner in a jungle capital on 28 October 1930. An armed group was trained and the rebellion launched toward the end of December. As the conflict spread throughout lower Burma and into the Shan States, the British army was called in to help the police forces repress the rebellion. Only after eight months of fighting did the warfare end.

All Tibetan religious orders have accepted unquestioningly the monastic rule of one particular Indian Buddhist order, namely that of the Mulasarvastivadins.

PAGE 112

RECENT TRENDS. The modern period has seen increased lay leadership at various levels of religious life. The YMBAs of Burma and the Buddhist "Sunday schools" that have arisen in Thailand have obviously been influenced by Western Christian models. Lay associations have developed for various purposes. For example, prior to the revolution Cambodia had the Buddhist Association of the Republic of Cambodia (1952), the Association of Friends of the Buddhist Lycée (1949), the Association of Friends of Religious Welfare Aid Centers, the Association of Religious Students of the Republic of Cambodia (1970), the Association of the Buddhist Youth of Cambodia (1971), and so on. Buddhist laity have also been actively involved in the worldwide Buddhist movement. Most notable of the laity groups are the World Fellowship of Buddhists, which has headquarters in Bangkok, and the World Council of Churches, which holds interreligious dialogue consultations.

While meditation has become a lay as well as monastic practice in contemporary Southeast Asian Buddhism, this development has not precluded a movement to formulate a strong, activist social ethic. The Vietnamese Zen monk Thich Nhat Hahn attempted to work out a Buddhist solution to the military conflict in his country during the 1960s, and there has been a widespread interest in formulating a Buddhist theory of economic development that is critical of Western capitalism but not necessarily indebted to Marxism. Buddhists have also acted to solve particular social problems, such as drug addiction, and have spoken out strongly against the proliferation of nuclear arms. Southeast Asian Buddhists have also joined with members of other religious groups, both within their own countries as well as in international organizations, to work for such causes as world peace and basic civil rights for all peoples. Buddhist interpreters, such as the Thai monk Bhikkhu Buddhadasa, have referred to Buddhism as a practical system of personal and social morality.

[*An examination of the relationship between the samgha and the larger societies of which it is a part can be found in* Southeast Asian Religions. *See also* Vietnamese Religion.]

— DONALD K. SWEARER

BUDDHISM IN TIBET

THE MODERN ERA. Among the intellectual giants of the eighteenth century, Ka'-thog Rig-'dzin Tshe-dban-nor-bu (1698-1755) must be mentioned. He was not content with merely repeating what secondary sources claimed to be authoritative, but attempted to go back to the original sources, often reaching startling conclusions. His main interests were history and geography. No less important is 'Jigs-med-glin-pa (1730-1798) whose major contributions are the *Klon chen sñin thig* practices, which he developed after having had a vision of Klonchen Rab-'byams-pa. Despite his wide interests, profoundness of thought, and remarkable scholarship, 'Jigs-med-glin-pa never attained the brilliant organization and beauty of style that mark the writings of his model, Klonchen Rab-'byams-pa. Another important figure of this period was Gzan-phan-mtha'-yas (b. 1740), who stressed the importance of monastic rules (which he considered indispensable for education) and held that monks had an obligation to society. In this sense he was the first social reformer in Tibet.

The Ris-med movement in the nineteenth century counted among its members such illustrious persons as 'Jam-mgon Kon-sprul Blo-gros-mtha'-yas (1813-1899), a competent physician and the author of the encyclopedia *Ses bya kun khyab* and a unique nonsectarian collection of texts pertaining to spiritual training, the *Gdams nag mdzod*; 'Jam-dbyans Mkhyen-brtse'i-dban-po (1820-1892), a master of Buddhist poetry; and, last but not least, 'Ju Mi-pham 'Jam-dbyans-rnam-rgyal-rgya-mtsho (1841-1912), who wrote on every imaginable topic. There were, and still are, other figures of significance.

When the Chinese occupied Tibet in 1959, a move that probably was a preemptive strike against other aspirants, the initial policy was one of destruction. This policy has changed from time to time, however, and reports coming from Tibet are conflicting. What may be stated with assurance is that the political power that the monasteries once wielded is a matter of the past. In those monasteries where the lamas are permitted to continue to perform religious ceremonies, no other activities are allowed, which means that no intellectual support is forthcoming.

— HERBERT GUENTHER

BUDDHISM IN CHINA

The late nineteenth century witnessed the first attempts, undertaken by some cultured laymen, to

DALAI LAMA *In 1959 the Chinese abolished the traditional Tibetan government, ending three hundred years of hierocratic rule by the Dalai Lama.* CRAIG LOVELL/CORBIS

revive Buddhism. It was part of a general effort to overcome China's backwardness in the face of Western and Japanese dominance, and also, more specifically, a reaction to the impact of the Christian missions in China. After the revolution and the establishment of the republic (1912), various attempts were made to organize the Buddhist clergy on a national scale, to raise its cultural level through the founding of Buddhist seminars, and to establish contacts with Japan, India, and the Buddhist countries in South and Southeast Asia.

Following the establishment in 1949 of the People's Republic, official Chinese policy toward the Buddhist clergy oscillated between political supervision (exercised through a completely politicized Buddhist Association) and violent suppression, notably during mass campaigns such as the Cultural Revolution (1966-1969). Where Buddhism is tolerated, it is clearly a truncated Buddhism, limited to devotional activities and divested of all the social and economic functions that the monasteries once had. The clergy itself, on which no reliable quantitative data are available, has no doubt been decimated by laicization and the lack of new ordinations. In general, prospects for Buddhism on the Chinese mainland are gloomy.

[*See also* Chinese Religion.]

— ERIK ZURCHER

BUDDHISM IN KOREA

After the annexation of Korea in 1910, some Korean monks felt that the fortunes of the religion were dependent upon arranging a merger with a major Japanese sect. Yi Hoe-gwang went so far as to negotiate a combination of the Korean church with the Japanese Soto sect, but most Korean Son monks regarded the gradualistic teachings of the Soto sect as anathema to the subitist orientation of their own tradition, and managed to block the merger. Another movement threatened to further divide the Buddhist church. As early as 1913, Han Yong-un (1879-1944), the only Buddhist signatory to the 1919 Korean independence

DALAI LAMA
Ruler in Exile

DALAI LAMA, title of the spiritual and formerly political leader of the Tibetan people, is a combination of the Mongolian dalai ("ocean"), signifying profound knowledge, and the Tibetan blama ("religious teacher"). The title dates from 1578 CE, when it was conferred by Altan Khan of the Mongols upon Bsod-nams-rgya-mtsho (1543-1588), third hierarch of the Dge-lugs-pa school of Tibetan Buddhism, commonly called the Yellow Hat sect. After 1578 the title was given to each of the successive reincarnations of the Dalai Lama. The present Dalai Lama is fourteenth in the lineage.

Incarnation (Tib., *sprul sku*), the manifestation of some aspect of the absolute Buddhahood in human form, is an ancient doctrine and one common to various schools of Mahayana Buddhism, but the concept of the reincarnation *(yan srid)* of a lama is unique to Tibetan Buddhism.

From the inception of the institution, traditional procedures for discovering the rebirth of a Dalai Lama, similar to those used for other reincarnate lamas, were followed. Indicative statements made by the previous Dalai Lama during his lifetime, significant auguries surrounding his death and afterward, and meditative visions by special lamas were recorded and interpreted as guides to finding his rebirth. In time, but no sooner than nine months after the death of the previous Dalai Lama, the people began to expect reports of an exceptional male child born in accordance with various omens. Such a child, usually two or three years old when discovered, was subjected to tests to determine physical fitness, intelligence, and the ability to remember events and objects from his previous existence.

The fifth Dalai Lama was a learned scholar and the author of many texts, including a history of Tibet. During the forty years he was head of state, the Mongols helped to protect his newly established government and to expand its territorial control. In recognition of the important role he played in religio-political history, he is referred to in Tibetan literature as the Great Fifth.

During his long reign as head of state, the thirteenth Dalai Lama was forced to flee to Mongolia to escape invading British troops (1904) and again invading Chinese forces (1910). The Chinese revolution of 1911 that overthrew the Manchu dynasty and established the Republic of China also marked the end of Manchu domination of Tibetan affairs. From 1913 until his death in 1933, the thirteenth Dalai Lama was the head of an independent government. Living in exile in British India motivated the thirteenth Dalai Lama to implement various reforms in Tibet to improve the welfare of his people.

The fourteenth and present Dalai Lama, Bstan-'dzin-rgya-mtsho, was born in 1935 of Tibetan parentage in the Chinghai province of China. During the next decade, half of which was taken up by World War II in Asia, the young Dalai Lama was educated and prepared for the time he would assume his role as religio-political ruler of Tibet.

— TURRELL V. WYLIE

declaration and a major literary figure, had shocked his contemporaries by advocating that monks be allowed to marry, a move he felt was necessary if Buddhism were to maintain any viable role in modern secular society. While this position was diametrically opposed to the traditional celibate orientation of the Korean ecclesia, the Japanese colonial government ultimately sustained it in 1926 with its promulgation of new monastic regulations that legalized matrimony for monks. Within a decade, virtually all temple abbots were married, thereby producing a dramatic change in the traditional moral discipline of the Korean church.

After independence in 1945, Korean Buddhism was badly split between two irreconcilable sects. The T'aego-chong, a liberal sect of married monks, had flourished under Japanese patronage and was based principally in the cities where it catered to the lay Buddhist population. The Chogye-chong was a smaller, religiously conservative faction of monks who had managed to maintain their celibacy during the long years of Japanese occupation; their concern was to restore the meditative, scholastic, and disciplinary orientations of traditional Korean Buddhism. Only after years of intense conflict did the Chogye-chong finally win government support for its position in 1954.

— ROBERT EVANS BUSWELL, JR.

BUDDHISM IN JAPAN

The modern period in Japanese history began with the Meiji restoration in 1868 and brought a series of radical changes in all spheres of life, including religion. Buddhism was deeply affected both in a positive and negative sense by the rapid process of modernization. One of the most pronounced changes took place on the institutional level, particularly in the relation of Buddhism to the state. In its attempt to mobilize the nation under the authority of the emperor, the Meiji government gave a definite priority to Shinto and thereby put an end to the age-old Shinto-Buddhist syncretism. Certainly, in the beliefs and practices of the common people the two traditions are still regarded as harmoniously united. Even today, many Japanese pay homage to Shinto shrines at the same time that they are associated with Buddhist temples.

These changes in the social milieu, combined with the influences from the Christian West that began to enter the country beginning in the latter half of the nineteenth century, elicited a number of responses from traditional Buddhist organizations on different levels and in various forms. One was a new and active engagement in educational and social work projects. Parallel to this trend, one can also observe a renewal of missionary efforts, which in some cases even led to the establishment of overseas missions.

Side by side with these reforms, many Buddhist leaders felt the need to cope with the challenge of modernity. Thus, new academic studies of Buddhism, both philosophical and philological in nature, were initiated.

Finally, a number of new movements appeared on the fringes of or outside the established groups. Insofar as they do not conform to the traditional clerical framework, they may be loosely characterized as lay Buddhist movements. Some of them remain rather small, consisting of only a handful of people dedicated to spiritual quest and the study of Buddhist ideas.

[*For an overview of the role of Buddhism in Japanese culture, see* Japanese Religion.]

— TAMARU NORIYOSHI

BUDDHISM, SCHOOLS OF

AN OVERVIEW

Like all world religions, Buddhism presents a picture of bewildering variety: doctrinal, liturgical, linguistic, and organizational. This diversity was largely the combined result of geographical diffusion and cultural adaptation. Wherever it was introduced, over an area ranging from Afghanistan to Indonesia and Japan, Buddhism became an integral part of different cultures, partly coexisting with local beliefs and cults, and partly absorbing them into its own system. But diversity was also stimulated by certain features within Buddhism itself: the absence of a central doctrinal authority; social stratification within the clergy; the relation of the Buddhist order with the temporal powers; royal patronage; the influence of the laity; and, in some cases, competition between large monastic centers. However, in spite of all this diversity we must not lose sight of the basic and always recognizable identity of Buddhism: a doctrine of salvation, aimed at the acquisition of liberating insight and at the complete extinction of attachment, and, consequently, of continued rebirth in the world of suffering. In most cases, the way to achieve that goal is indissolubly connected with the monastic life (with a few exceptions, such as the Japanese Jodo Shinshu with its married preachers, or Chinese lay Buddhism in Indonesia); the Buddhist order of monks, or *samgha*, has remained the very heart of religious life and the most important unifying element throughout the Buddhist world.

A clarification of terms is needed, for much confusion has been created by the indiscriminative use of these words.

MOVEMENTS. In the course of its long history, Buddhism has seen the development of three huge

Buddist leaders, determined to meet the challenge of Western thought and scholarship, sent able young monks to Western universities.

PAGE 385

The monastic person is identified as one whose self-perception and public role include membership in a special religious category of persons, a status which is deliberate and extraordinary.

PAGE 456

complexes of religious doctrine and practice, each of which represents a well-defined "way leading to release"; these are characteristically called *yana* ("vehicles"). We shall refer to them as "movements." They represent three basic orientations within Buddhism, each with its own doctrinal ideas, cultic practices, sacred scriptures, and iconographic traditions.

The first movement comprises the whole complex of ancient Buddhism, of which one type is still alive in Sri Lanka and most of continental Southeast Asia. Since the name *Hinayana*, the "Lesser Vehicle," sounds pejorative, its adherents now prefer their type of Buddhism to be called Theravada, "the Doctrine of the Elders" (originally the name of one school). Theravada Buddhism has, among other things, always been characterized by an extreme emphasis on monastic life; by the ideal of becoming an *arhat*, who has reached individual saintliness and is assured of his total extinction at the end of his life, and a conception of the Buddha as a sublime yet mortal teacher who, after having reached his final *nirvana*, has ceased to be at any level of existence whatsoever.

Since the beginning of the common era, Hinayana was challenged by a new movement that called itself the "Great Vehicle" (Mahayana). It claimed to be a more comprehensive and universal way toward liberation, with a more ambitious religious ideal (Buddhahood instead of arhatship); the belief in *bodhisattvas* as superhuman guides and saviors; the idea of a transcendental, all-pervading and eternal Buddha or "Buddha nature"; a philosophical reinterpretation (in many variations) of the most basic ontological concepts of ancient Buddhism, and a much higher estimate of the status of lay believers as potential "candidates for release."

In the sixth century, possibly even somewhat earlier, a third orientation emerged, the movement called the "Diamond Vehicle" (Vajrayana), commonly referred to as Tantric or Esoteric Buddhism in the West. It was characterized by its use of spells, symbols, and very complicated rituals, and the acquisition of magic powers as a way toward enlightenment; by the development of psychophysical "techniques" (partly of a sexual nature); and by a system of esoteric transmission from master to disciple.

It is clear that in these three cases we cannot speak of "schools," let alone "sects." They were by no means localized: both Mahayana and Vajrayana spread like waves throughout the Buddhist world. Above all, they were not mutually exclusive. In the Mahayana vision, the whole complex of Theravada teachings is not rejected but incorporated as a kind of "simple revelation," intended by the Buddha to raise the minds of his "hearers" *(sravaka)* to a certain level of preliminary insight. In the same way, Tantric Buddhism claims to incorporate (and, of course, to transcend) the two previous Vehicles, without denying their limited applicability. In fact, Mahayana doctrinal literature freely

MONASTIC TRADITIONS

Spreading the Word without Doctrinal Control

What we call monastic traditions are basically different from the large and many-sided movements. Their origin is closely related to the paramount role of the disciplinary code (Vinaya), and notably of the detailed set of rules governing the monk's daily life that had to be recited at every fortnightly Pratimoksa confessional by all monks resident in a single self-governing "parish" or begging circuit *(sima)*. The early dissemination of Buddhism over the Indian subcontinent was a continuous process of expansion of contact: since any local center of population could only support a certain number of mendicants, the clerical surplus had to move out to establish new parishes elsewhere. The process was further stimulated by the itinerant life led by many monks outside the rainy season, and by the missionary ideal that has been characteristic of Buddhism from the very beginning. Thus, Buddhism spread in ever-widening circles, but without any central authority that could impose doctrinal and ritual uniformity. The only binding element was the Vinaya, and the frequent Pratimoksa recitation in fact functioned as the only instrument to preserve the homogeneity of the Buddhist order.

However, as the territory covered by Buddhism widened, local variations in the disciplinary code started to develop, partly owing to lack of communication and probably also caused by the necessity to adapt the rules to local circumstances. If the Buddhist tradition speaks of the emergence of eighteen of such monastic traditions in the first two centuries after the Buddha's decease, we must realize that the difference that divided them mainly concerned details of discipline rather than doctrinal matters. No less than five different Vinayas of various early schools have been preserved in the Chinese Buddhist canon: extensive works that differ among themselves as to number of rules, prescriptions governing minute details of daily behavior, and the degree of elaboration of stories justifying each particular rule, but that as far as doctrine is concerned show very little variation.

— ERIK ZURCHER

quotes from Theravada scriptures as teachings of the Buddha that are, at that level, both authentic and authoritative.

SCHOOLS. Of quite another nature are the schools found in Theravada and (to a much larger extent) in Mahayana Buddhism. Here the accent is on the interpretation of certain basic elements of the doctrine of release, issues such as the nature of the *arhat*, the nonexistence of a permanent self, the process of causation, and so forth. In Mahayana Buddhism we find a proliferation of such schools, ranging from the earliest propagation of the doctrine of universal "emptiness" *(sunyavada)* in India to Chinese and Japanese Ch'an (Zen) Buddhism, with its iconoclastic message of "no words" and "no mind."

In spite of their endless variety, such schools share some common features. In the first place, their field of activity is not discipline but scholastics: the various Abhidharma of Theravada Buddhism and the many systematizing treatises of Mahayana scholars. A second feature shared by most schools is the prominent role of famous "masters of the Law," both as founding fathers and as transmitters of the teachings of a particular school: Katyayaniputra, Vasumitra, and other "patriarchs" of the Sarvastivada tradition that flourished in northwestern India and Kashmir; Nagarjuna and Aryadeva, who systematized the doctrines of the School of Emptiness; Asanga and Vasubandhu, who, probably in the fifth century CE, founded the Yogacara school, and, in East Asia, the great masters who founded and developed the major schools of Chinese Buddhism: the vast and complicated system of the T'ien-t'ai school founded by Chih-i (538-597), the Hua-yen doctrine of all-pervading totality of Fa-tsang (643-712); the Pure Land (Ching-t'u) devotionalism of T'an-luan (476-542) and Tao-ch'o (562-645), and the many "patriarchs" and branch founders of Ch'an (Zen) in China, Korea, and Japan.

Third, although such schools recognize the validity of all Buddhist scriptures (even if in some schools texts favored by other schools are considered "provisional teachings," as we have seen), many of them tend to be focused on one particular scripture or group of scriptures that are supposed to contain the final and supreme revelation of truth. Thus, the School of Emptiness largely relied on the class of Mahayana scriptures known as the Prajñaparamita ("perfection of wisdom") literature, just as the Yogacara school appealed to the authority of the *Lankavatara Sutra*. For the founder of the T'ien-t'ai school, the highest revelation was to be found in the message of universal salvation as expounded in the *Saddharmapundarika Sutra* (Scripture of the Lotus of the Good Law), whereas Fa-tsang found the expression of ultimate truth in the vast *Avatamsaka Sutra* (Chin., *Hua-yen*; Flower Garland Scripture). And even Ch'an, in spite of its rejection of written texts, in its first stage largely relied on the *Lankavatara Sutra*. The scholastic and "learned" nature of all such schools also appears from the fact that they essentially remained a clerical phenomenon: the creation and exclusive domain of an elite of scholar-monks, in which the laity took no part. Their bastions were the large and richly endowed monasteries that all over the Buddhist world

BUDDHIST MONK

Buddhist monks would travel from one monastery to another, studying several different scriptural interpretations.

ASIAN ART & ARCHAEOLOGY, INC./CORBIS

functioned as centers of Buddhist learning and doctrinal disputes. However, one of their most remarkable features is that they were by no means exclusive communities with a well-defined "membership." Monks would travel from one monastery to another irrespective of the school that dominated in each center; in many cases several scholastic interpretations could be studied successively or even simultaneously, and both eclecticism and syncretism flourished without any stigma of "unorthodoxy."

SECTS. This, then, may be the dividing line between schools and sects, the latter being characterized by a high degree of exclusivity, a clear concept of "membership," and, in general, a very important role played by the laity. As a rule, sectarian movements are centered around a charismatic leader who in his own person exemplifies the religious message of the sect: in many cases he claims to be the incarnation or the manifestation of a Buddha (notably the future Buddha Maitreya) or a powerful *bodhisattva*. In contrast to the schools that are not confined to one area (the Repre-

The written scriptural text symbolizes or embodies religious authority in many traditions

PAGE 593

sentation-Only doctrine reached from India to Japan, and Ch'an/Zen was found all over East Asia), most sects are localized, and deeply rooted in local circumstances. As I shall show, sects generally belong to strata lower, both socially and intellectually, than the schools mentioned above; the latter may be said to represent the "great tradition" of Buddhism at its highest level of expression.

PARAMETERS OF DIVERSIFICATION. In the diffusion of Buddhism we can recognize a number of factors that contributed to the process of ongoing diversification. Only the most important ones can be treated within the limits of this article.

Distance from the center. As noted above, the spread of Buddhism over the Indian subcontinent mainly took the form of gradual expansion of contact, a process that offers the best chances for maintaining a fairly high degree of homogeneity. However, once outside its country of origin, the propagation of Buddhism assumed the character of long-distance diffusion in various directions: from northwestern India through the empty heart of the continent to China; along the sea routes from the east coast of India to continental Southeast Asia, Sumatra, and Java; from the Ganges Basin crossing the Himalayas into Tibet. In all those outlying regions, far from the center of expansion, Buddhism developed independently. As a result, both China and Tibet eventually became secondary centers of diffusion: Korean and Japanese Buddhists were inspired by Chinese examples and had hardly any contact with India; in all of East Asia, classical Chinese became the Buddhist scriptural language. In the same way, Tibetan Buddhism, especially in its lamaist form, developed into a unique system far removed from any Indian prototype. In the sixteenth century Tibet also became a secondary center of expansion, from which Lamaism was spread to Mongolia.

The movement of Buddhism to China, one of the great cultural interactions of history, was slow and fortuitous, carried out almost entirely at a private level.

PAGE 137

In Southeast Asia, Buddhism at first was introduced not independently but as one element in a general process of cultural borrowing; from the second to the fifth centuries, the spread of Indian culture in the whole area from Burma to Sumatra led to the formation of a whole series of more or less indianized states in which Buddhism (mainly in its Mahayana and Tantric forms) coexisted with Hinduism. This independent development of Buddhism in peripheral areas was naturally reinforced by its disappearance in India itself after the twelfth century. It may not be fortuitous that around that time Sri Lanka, where the Theravada *sangha* had been restored and reorganized under the powerful king Parakkamabahu II (1236-1271), became a strong center of diffusion. It was owing to Sinhala missionary efforts that Theravada Buddhism became the state religion in Burma, Thailand, Laos, and Cambodia between the twelfth and fourteenth centuries.

Confrontation with local cultures. Wherever it arrived, Buddhism was in varying degrees influenced by local beliefs and practices, the incorporation of which led to further differentiation. In some areas, like the oasis kingdoms along the Silk Road and Southeast Asia, the cultural resistance against Buddhism appears to have been slight; there the Indian religion was taken over as an instrument of higher civilization, often together with other elements of Indian culture like statecraft, astronomy, representational arts, and the script. Elsewhere, notably in China, Buddhism had to compete with strong preexisting philosophical and social traditions that on many points were opposed to Buddhist ideals and practices. In China, it had to grow up in the shadow of the dominant Confucian ideology, and much that is characteristic in Chinese Buddhism is the result of "adaptation under pressure." However, everywhere, and especially at a popular level, Buddhism merged with and incorporated non-Buddhist traditions: Taoist eubiotics and Confucian morality in China; Shinto in Japan; elements borrowed from the indigenous Bon religion in Tibet; and from shamanism in Mongolia.

Social stratification. Since the earliest times, monastic Buddhism was for its very existence dependent on the patronage of the ruling elite; the close ties between the *samgha* and the temporal powers form a constant feature in the history of all countries where Buddhism penetrated. This cooperation (and in some areas, such as Sri Lanka, even complete interdependence) has produced both positive and negative results: on the one hand, corruption and abuse of power; on the other hand, the formation of a clerical elite within the *samgha*, associated with the largest monastic centers, to whom we owe the most sophisticated products of Buddhist thought, literature, and art. This articulate group only constituted a tiny minority—the thin top layer of the Buddhist establishment. In all Buddhist countries, we find a vertical differentiation between the cultured clerical elite residing in the major monasteries and the vast majority of "priests among the people," who perform their humble services in countless small temples and local shrines, at the grass-roots level, where they often are the only people who can boast of a modicum of literary training. If the world of court priests, learned doctors, and scholastic philosophy constitutes the "great tradition" of Buddhism, it is everywhere counterbalanced by an endless variety of popular Buddhist beliefs and cults that represent its "little traditions." It is at that level that we mostly find the traces of (generally not well documented) sectarian movements of the type mentioned above. In general, their message is extremely simple, centering around one or two basic ideas derived from the Buddhist scriptural tradition: the theme of the dark "final age" in which the doctrine will disappear and the world will be steeped in chaos and corruption, and the belief in the imminent appearance of the Buddha Maitreya, who will come to create a world of piety and justice.

Movements espousing such ideas have often been persecuted as "subversive," both by the temporal powers and by the representatives of the clerical establishment. These movements sometimes assumed a violent character. Examples of such sectarian activities can be found in many parts of the Buddhist world: the millenarian movements that have time and again appeared in continental Southeast Asia in times of crisis; the militant and protonationalist sect founded by the Japanese reformer Nichiren (1222-1282), who combined socio-religious activism and opposition against the established clergy with an extremely simple way to salvation, and, in China, the equally militant activities of the complex of Buddhist-inspired secret societies collectively known as the White Lotus, which harassed Chinese political authorities from the fourteenth century until modern times. But such violent activism and social protest have always been the exception rather than the rule—the vast majority of Buddhist religious life at the grass roots level presents the familiar and peaceful picture of local societies, fraternities, and associations devoted to mutual help, charitable activities, and collective ceremonies. [*See also* Millenarianism.]

Linguistic differentiation. Unlike the Brahmanic tradition, which is based on Sanskrit as a scriptural medium, Buddhism never has known the concept of a "sacred language." Buddhist scriptures have for many centuries been translated in a great variety of regional languages, and even Pali, the written medium of Theravada Buddhism, certainly does not represent the language of the original Buddhist sermons. However, in the course of time the diffusion of Buddhism from secondary centers led to the use of some languages, in petrified forms, as what we may call "clerical literary idioms": classical Chinese in Japan and Korea; Pali in continental Southeast Asia; and literary Tibetan. But here again, social stratification was at work, for in all these areas, popular tracts and other types of simplified religious literature (both written and oral) generally made use of the living language—in fact, Chinese vernacular literature owes its origin to simple Buddhist stories written in the metropolitan dialect and destined to be recited to a largely illiterate public of lay devotees. Thus, the linguistic aspect combines the two main features that we have observed in the spread of Buddhism as a whole: geographic diffusion coupled with ongoing regional differentiation, and internal stratification producing a great diversity of expression at various social levels, both within the Buddhist clergy and among the lay population.

[*For a review of the geographic dispersion of the tradition, see* Missions, *article on* Buddhist Missions.]

— ERIK ZURCHER

B

BUDDHISM, SCHOOLS OF

Hinayana Buddhism

HINAYANA BUDDHISM

The term *Hinayana* refers to the group of Buddhist schools or sects that appeared before the beginning of the common era and those directly derived from them. The word *Hinayana*, which means "small vehicle," was applied disdainfully to these early forms of Buddhism by the followers of the great reformist movement that arose just at the beginning of the common era. The Mahayana charged those of the Hinayana with selfishly pursuing only their own personal salvation, whereas they themselves claimed an interest in the liberation of all beings and vowed to postpone their own deliverance until the end of time.

According to an ancient tradition, the Buddha himself sent out the first group of disciples to spread the new faith: "Go, monks, preach the noble Doctrine, . . . let not two of you go into the same direction!"

PAGE 448

Although it is directly descended from the earliest Buddhism—that originally preached by the Buddha himself—this early Buddhism is distinguished from it by the continual additions and reformulations of its adherents and teachers in their desire to deepen and perfect the interpretation of the ancient teaching.

The Indic word, both Sanskrit and Pali, that we translate here as "school" or "sect" is *nikaya*, meaning, properly, "group." In our context, it refers to a group of initiates, most likely monks *(bhiksus)* rather than laymen, who sincerely profess to be faithful disciples of the Buddha but are distinguishable from other similar groups in that they base their beliefs on a body of canonic texts that differs from others to a greater or lesser extent. These differences between canonic texts involve not only their wording or written form but also a certain number of doctrinal elements and rules of monastic discipline. Schisms did occur within many of them, leading to the formation of new schools, but to judge from the documents we have—though these are unfortunately very scarce—it seems that relations among these various groups were generally good. Their disputes remained at the level of more or less lively discussion.

Several factors account for these divisions and for the formation of these sects or schools. First of all, the Buddhist monastic community *(samgha)* never knew a supreme authority.

For at least five centuries, the Buddha's teaching was actually preserved by oral transmission alone, very probably in different, though related, dialects. This, and the absence of an authoritative ecclesiastical hierarchy in the *samgha*, constitute two obvious sources of progressive distortion and alteration of the message left by the Blessed One to his immediate disciples. Furthermore, this message was not entirely clear or convincing to everyone it addressed. Thus, monks and lay disciples, as well as people outside Buddhism but curious and interested in its doctrine—brahman opponents, Jains, and others—easily found numerous flaws, errors, and contradictions in the teaching. Although the Buddhist preachers who improvised answers to these varied questions and objections were guided by what they knew and understood of the Buddha's teaching, their attempts expanded upon the original teaching and at the same time inevitably created new causes for differences and disputes within the heart of the community itself.

The arhat embodies one of the fundamental tensions in the Buddhist tradition between the ideal of enlightenment and equanimity and the extraordinary magical power concomitant with this attainment.

PAGE 94

All the documents from which we can draw information about the origin of the early Buddhist groups were written after the beginning of the common era and are therefore unreliable. Nevertheless, since the oldest of these texts generally agree on the main points, we can attempt to restore with a certain amount of confidence the common tradition from which they derive.

The first division of the community probably occurred toward the middle of the fourth century BCE. The schism was probably caused by a number of disagreements on the nature of the *arhats*, who, according to some authorities, retained imperfections even though they had attained *nirvana* in this world. Because they were more numerous, the supporters of these ideas formed a group called the Mahasamghikas, "those of the larger community." Their opponents, who claimed to remain faithful to the teaching of the Buddha's first disciples and denied that the *arhat* could retain any imperfections, took the name Sthaviravadins, "those who speak as the elders."

Each of these two groups were then, in turn, divided progressively into several sects or schools.

Among the groups that developed from the Mahasamghika were the Ekavyavaharika, then the Gokulika, and finally the Caitika schools. The Ekavyavaharikas probably gave rise, in turn, to the Lokottaravadins, but it may be that the Lokottaravadins were simply a form taken by the Ekavyavaharikas at a particular time because of the evolution of their doctrine. From the Gokulikas came the Bahusrutiyas and the Prajñaptivadins. At least a part of the Caitika school settled in southern India, on the lower Krishna River, shortly before the beginning of the common era. From them two important sects soon arose: the Purvasailas and the Aparasailas, then a little later the Rajagirikas and the Siddharthikas. Together, the four sects formed Andhraka group, which took its name from the area (Andhra) where they thrived during the first few centuries CE.

The Sthaviravada group seems to have remained united until about the beginning of the third century BCE, when the Vatsiputriyas, who maintained the existence of a quasi-autonomous "person" *(pudgala)*, split off. A half century later, probably during the reign of Asoka (consecrated c. 268 BCE), the Sarvastivadins also separated from the non-Vatsiputriya Sthaviravadins and settled in northwest India. This time the dispute was over the Sarvastivadin notion that "everything exists" *(sarvam asti)*. In the beginning of the second century, the remaining Sthaviravadins, who appear to have taken at this time the name Vibhajyavadins, "those who teach discrimination," to distinguish themselves from the Sarvastivadins, found themselves divided once again. Out of this dispute were born the Mahisasakas and the Dharmaguptakas, who opposed each other over whether the Buddha, properly speaking, belonged to the monastic community and over the relative value of offerings made to the Blessed One and those made to the community. At an unknown date about the beginning of the common era four new groups sprang from the Vatsiputriyas: the Dharmottariyas, the Bhadrayaniyas, the Sannagarikas, and the Sammatiyas. The Sammatiyas, who were very important in Indian Buddhism, later gave rise to the Avantaka and the Kurukulla schools. One group broke from the Sarvastivadins: the Sautrantikas, who can be identified with the Darstantikas and the Samkrantivadins.

Some of the Vibhajyavadins settled in southern India and Sri Lanka in the mid-third century BCE and seem to have maintained fairly close relations for some time with the Mahisasakas, whose presence is attested in the same area. Adopting Pali as a canonical language and energetically claiming their teaching to be the strict orthodoxy, they took the name Theravadins, a Pali form of the Sanskrit Sthaviravadins. Like the Sthaviravadins, they suffered from internal squabbles and divisions: some years before the common era, the Abhayagirivasins split from the Mahaviharas, founded at the time of the arrival of Buddhism in Sri Lanka; later, in the fourth century, the Jetavaniyas appeared.

Except for a few of the more important of these sects and schools—such as the Theravadins, who left us the treasure of their celebrated Sinhala chronicles—we know nothing of the history of these different groups. Their existence is nevertheless assured, thanks to the testimony of a fair number of inscriptions and other substantial documents.

— ANDRÉ BAREAU

TRANSLATED FROM FRENCH BY DAVID M. WEEKS

MAHAYANA BUDDHISM

The Sanskrit term *mahayana* literally means "the great vehicle [to enlightenment]." It refers to a form of Buddhism that developed in northern India and Central Asia from about the first century before the advent of the common era, and that is prevalent today in Nepal, Sikkhim, Tibet, China, Mongolia, Vietnam, Korea, and Japan. Mahayana Buddhism was also transmitted to Sri Lanka and the Indo-Chinese peninsula, but it eventually vanished from South Asia.

Mahayana Buddhism is characterized by a variety of doctrines, practices, and orientations that at once distinguish it from the Hinayana tradition.

WORSHIP OF MULTIPLE BUDDHAS AND BODHISATTVAS. In early Buddhism the term *bodhisattva* referred to the Buddha (or, later, to *a* Buddha) prior to the time of his enlightenment, including all previous existences during which he had aspired to become a Buddha. In keeping with the soteriology and cosmology of these early teachings, it was assumed that there was only one *bodhisattva* in any one world cycle. Later, this idea was elaborated and integrated into the Jataka stories, tales of Sakyamuni Buddha's previous lives. A few Conservative Buddhists embraced the belief that there were many Buddhas at any one time, but this belief was most highly developed in Mahayana, where myriads of Buddhas are said to inhabit myriads of world systems simultaneously.

Some Mahayana *sutras* enjoin adoration of all Buddhas in an equal manner (e.g., *The Sutra Enumerating Buddha's Names*) and some twenty-one sutras extol recitation of the names of many Buddhas. Repeated utterance of the names of Buddhas and *bodhisattvas* is also encouraged in the *Namasamgiti*.

But it is not simply in their profusion that the Buddhas of the Mahayana differ from their Hinayana counterparts. Mahayana Buddhas enjoy many more superhuman and divine traits than does the single Buddha of the Conservative tradition. Nonetheless, they retain many of the same physical and spiritual characteristics. Glorification of and speculation on the nature of Buddhas led Mahayana practitioners to develop the theory of the "triple body" *(trikaya)* of the Buddha, in which the Buddha is conceived as having three aspects or "bodies": a cosmic body *(dharmakaya)*, the ineffable Absolute itself; an "enjoyment" body *(sambhogakaya)*, a body of magical transformation that the Buddha "enjoys" as the fruit of the merit generated through aeons of religious practice (often conceived as surrounded by a supernal region, a Pure Land, similarly generated); and the body that appears in living form to save people from suffering (nirmanakaya). Sakyamuni, of course, is such a Buddha (i. e., nirmanakaya) for our age.

The *bodhisattva* Mañjusri plays an important role in many sutras. One sutra (T. D. no. 463) describes the efficacy of worship of Mañjusri at the moment of death. In another (T. D. no. 464), Mañjusri explains enlightenment; and elsewhere (T. D. no. 843) he demonstrates animitta ("formlessness") through magical power.

As in Hinayana Buddhism, the *bodhisattva* Maitreya was worshiped as a Buddha of the future, one who, at some time to come, will leave his present abode in the Tusita Heaven and be born on earth for the benefit of sentient beings. Devotees of Maitreya thus focused their aspirations on rebirth in Tusita and eventual descent to earth in his company.

But the *bodhisattva* most adored throughout Asia is Avalokitesvara, the "Lord Who Looks Down [with infinite pity on all beings]." The best-known scripture concerning his virtues is the twenty-fourth chapter of the *Saddharmapundarika* (Lotus Sutra), which emphasizes the rewards in this world that he grants to believers and the virtue of helpfulness to others that he represents. In the *Gandavyuha*, his homeland is called Potalaka. In Pure Land Buddhism, he is Amitabha's companion and attendant.

But if there is one feature of the Mahayana *bodhisattva* doctrine that truly separates it from that of other forms of Buddhism, it is the Mahayana insistence that the goal of all religious practice is Buddhahood itself, making all those whose conceive of the aspiration to be liberated *bodhisattvas*, or future Buddhas. The Mahayana *bodhisattva* is committed to work ceaselessly for the benefit of other beings and to transmit to them the merit generated by his or her own religious practice.

DISCIPLINES. There is no unanimously agreed upon code of discipline in Mahayana, reflecting the fact that it is institutionally less coherent than is Conservative Buddhism. But Mahayana distinguishes two ways of practice: the *sravakamarga* ("way of the disciples") for those who follow the Hinayana practices and the *bodhisattvamarga* ("way of *bodhisattvas*") for those who adhere to Mahayana values, particularly the intention to save other suffering beings. Those who practice the latter way are deemed worthy of worship and are relied upon because they have refrained from entering Buddhahood, preferring instead to dwell among the living in order to save them from their sufferings.

Mahayana ethics were most explicitly set forth in the "Discipline Sutras," the essence of which is altruism. Among the sutras that provided the theoretical basis for the Mahayana orders is the *Sarvadharmapravrttinirdesa*, which was highly esteemed by the Japanese monk Saicho (767-822). Others that explicated Mahayana discipline are the "Buddha Treasure Sutra" (T. D. no. 653), the "Enlightenment-mind Sutra" (T. D. no. 837), and the *Dharmavinayasamadhi Sutra*. Some texts reflect the Mahayana idea that discipline is to be practiced by both clergy and laity; one, the *Bodhisattvapratimoksa Sutra*, sets forth the "Vinaya" of *bodhisattvas*, here referring to both clerics and lay practitioners. The precepts in the *Srimaladevi Sutra* were well known in China and Japan.

"All that is comes from the mind."

THE PALI CANON, SUTTAPITAKA DHAMMAPADA, CH I.

Both Hindu and Buddhist Tantrism can be described as reinterpretations, in a new spirit, of their respective traditions.

PAGE 644

The most famous and controversial of these texts is the *Brahmajala Sutra*. Greatly esteemed in China, it became the fundamental discipline text for Japanese monks. Scholars now believe that this text was produced in China, where there is evidence that it was in use in some form as early as the year 350.

Repentance is the theme and object of several Mahayana *sutras*. One of these *sutras* (T. D. no. 1493) shows that repentance leads to delight in the deeds of others, moral admonition, and transference of merit. Another text teaches that a reaffirmation of the insight that all things are originally pure can dissolve the obstacles created by *karman* (T. D. no. 1491). Bondage in *karman (karmavarana)* can be destroyed by repentance, meditation, or by repeated application of magical formulas.

LAY BUDDHISM. The position of the layman was recognized and exalted by most Mahayana texts, although a few display a tendency to place the ascetic life of the monk above the lay life. However, the notion of emptiness *(sunyata)* that is the foundation of most Mahayana thought provides for the identity of liberation and mundane existence, *nirvana* and *samsara*, thus providing a rationale for the sanctity of lay life.

To be sure, many Mahayana practitioners were *bhiksus*, and some were termed *bodhisattva bhiksus* (in the *Mahayanasutralamkara*, the *Siksasamuccaya*, etc.). But the tendency toward lay Buddhism remained conspicuous. The *Ugradattapariprccha*, an early Discipline Sutra composed before Nagarjuna (fl. 150-250), prescribes five conditions for the lay practice of the Mahayana. Later, codes of discipline intended specifically for laymen were composed. Among the disciplines required of laymen was observance of the regulations for *uposadha* days (when the fortnightly confessions were made).

The presence of the notion of filial piety, another lay ideal, in Buddhism represents an accommodation and syncretization of values that occurred under the stimulus of Chinese culture. Filial piety was the most important virtue in Confucian ethics, which required one-sided obedience from children toward their parents. A Buddhist concept of filial piety also took shape in the Ullambana Sutra, which extols a rite that centers on offerings to one's dead parents.

— NAKAMURA HAJIME

ESOTERIC BUDDHISM

Buddhist esotericism is an Indian movement obscure in its beginnings. Combining yoga and ritual, it calls itself the Diamond Vehicle (Vajrayana)—where *diamond* means "the unsplittable"—or the Mantra Vehicle (Mantrayana)—where *mantra* means "magical speech." The revealed texts of the tradition are called *tantra*, in contrast to *sutra* (the generic name of the non-Tantric Buddhist scriptures), but both these words have the implication "thread" or "continuous line." In the case of the Tantras, the "continuous line" can be understood in various ways: the lineage of master-disciple, the continuity of vows and pledges in the practitioner's stream of consciousness, or the continuity of practice leading to a religious goal.

Much of Tantric literature is ritualistic in nature, manifesting Brahmanic influence by the use of incantations *(mantra)* and the burnt offering *(homa)*, both of which were employed for magical purposes. Many of the hand gestures and foot stances of Buddhist Tantric practice are also found in Indian dance. However, as specifically Buddhist Tantras, such texts are colored both by Buddhist theories and practices and by the typical terminology of Mahayana Buddhism. These texts regularly employ such ancient Buddhist formulations as the triad body, speech, and mind, and draw upon such common Mahayana notions as the pair "means" *(upaya)* and "insight" *(prajña)*. The Tantras accept the old Buddhist ontology of three worlds filled with deities and demons, and contribute the premise that one can relate to these forces by ritualistic manipulation of one's nature (body, speech, and mind), thereby attaining "success" *(siddhi)* in such mundane forms as appeasing the deities, or the supermundane success of winning complete enlightenment (Buddhahood), possibly in a single lifetime. The old Buddhist terminology "son or daughter of the family," here the Buddhist family, was extended to refer to Buddha families. Initially, the texts propose a triad of three Buddhas or Tathagatas: Vairocana, Amitabha, and Aksobhya. Later, Ratnasambhava and Amoghasiddhi are added to make up a family of five, and Vajrasattva to make a family of six. A supreme Buddha, referred to variously as Maha-Vajradhara, Heruka, or Adibuddha ("Primordial Buddha"), is also mentioned. But the texts do not use the term "Dhyani Buddhas" that is sometimes found in Western books on the subject.

— ALEX WAYMAN

CHINESE BUDDHISM

In any discussion of the schools of Chinese Buddhism it is important to bear in mind that the widely used English term *school* is simply the conventional translation of the Chinese word *tsung*. The practice of equating school and tsung has resulted in some persistent misconceptions about what actually constitutes a school in Chinese Buddhism. In Buddhist texts, it is used primarily in three different senses: (1) it may indicate a specific doctrine or thesis, or a particular interpretation of a doctrine; (2) it may refer to the underlying theme, message, or teaching of a text; and (3) it may signify a religious or philosophical school.

JAPANESE BUDDHISM

Prior to its official introduction into the court in 552 CE, Buddhism had been brought to Japan by Chinese and Korean immigrants and was presumably practiced widely among their descendants.

Although Japanese understanding of Buddhism was superficial and fragmented in the early stages of assimilation, it gained religious depth through the course of history. The rise of Japanese Buddhism and the growth of schools or sects were closely related to and influenced by the structure of the state bureaucra-

BODHIDHARMA
The Founder of Zen Buddhism

BODHIDHARMA (fl. c. 480-520), known in China as Ta-mo and in Japan as Daruma; traditionally considered the twenty-eighth patriarch of Indian Buddhism and the founder of the Ch'an (Jpn., Zen) school of Chinese Buddhism.

According to the Ch'uan fa-pao chi, Bodhidharma practiced wall-gazing at Sung-shan monastery for several years. He thus became known as the "wall-gazing brahman," the monk who remained without moving for nine years in meditation in a cave on Sung-shan (eventually losing his legs, as the popular iconography depicts him). There he also met Hui-k'o, who, to show his earnestness in searching for the Way, cut off his own arm. (The Ch'uan fa-pao chi severely criticizes Tao-hsüan for claiming that Hui-k'o had his arm cut off by bandits.) This tradition, fusing with the martial tradition that developed at Sung-shan, resulted in Bodhidharma becoming the "founder" of the martial art known as Shao-lin boxing (Jpn., Shorinji kempo).

Bodhidharma's legend continued to develop with the Li-tai fa-pao chi (c. 774), the Pao-lin chuan (801), and the Tsu-t'ang chi (Kor., Chodangjip, 952), and reached its classical stage in 1004 with the Ching te chuan teng lu. In the process, it borrowed features from other popular Buddhist or Taoist figures such as Pao-chih or Fu Hsi (alias Fu Ta-shih, "Fu the Mahasattva," 497-569, considered an incarnation of Maitreya). But its main aspects were already fixed at the beginning of the eighth century.

It is also noteworthy that many early Ch'an works formerly attributed to Bodhidharma have recently been proved to have been written by later Ch'an masters such as Niu-t'ou Fa-jung (594-657) or Shen-hsiu (606-706). That so many works were erroneously attributed to Bodhidharma may be due simply to the fact that the Ch'an school was at the time known as the Bodhidharma school, and that all works of the school could thus be considered expressive of Bodhidharma's thought. Whatever the case, these works have greatly contributed to the development of Bodhidharma's image, especially in the Japanese Zen tradition. Further confusing the issue is the "discovery," throughout the eighth century, of epitaphs supposedly written shortly after his death. In fact, these epitaphs were products of the struggle for hegemony among various factions of Ch'an.

Bodhidharma in Popular Religion. The *Genkoshakusho,* a well-known account of Japanese Buddhism written by a Zen monk named Kokan Shiren (1278-1346), opens with the story of Bodhidharma crossing over to Japan to spread his teachings (a development of the iconographic tradition representing him crossing the Yangtze River). In Japan, Bodhidharma's legend seems to have developed first within the Tendai (Chin., T'ien-t'ai) tradition brought from China at the beginning of the Heian period (794-1191). Kojo (779-858), a Japanese monk, was instrumental in linking the Bodhidharma legend to the Tendai tradition and to the legend of the regent Shotoku (Shotoku Taishi, 574-622), who was considered a reincarnation of Nan-yüeh Hui-ssu (515-577), one of the founders of the T'ien-t'ai school. In his *Denjutsu isshin kaimon,* a work presented to the emperor, Kojo mentions the encounter that took place near Kataoka Hill (Nara Prefecture) between Shotoku and a strange, starving beggar—considered a Taoist immortal in the version of the story given by the Kojiki. Kojo, arguing from a former legendary encounter between Hui-ssu and Bodhidharma on Mount T'ien-t'ai in China, and from Bodhidharma's prediction that both would be reborn in Japan, has no difficulty establishing that the beggar was none other than Bodhidharma himself.

This amalgam proved very successful and reached far beyond the Tendai school. Toward the end of the Heian period a Zen school emerged from the Tendai tradition, and its leader, Dainichi Nonin (dates unknown), labeled it the "Japanese school of Bodhidharma" (Nihon Darumashu). This movement was a forerunner of the Japanese Zen sect.

But it is in popular religion that Bodhidharma's figure developed most flamboyantly. Early in China, Bodhidharma not only borrowed features from Taoist immortals but became completely assimilated by the Taoist tradition; there are several Taoist works extant concerning Bodhidharma. In Japan, Bodhidharma's legend developed in tandem with that of Shotoku Taishi; a temple dedicated to Daruma is still to be found on the top of Kataoka Hill.

— BERNARD FAURE

But the concept of the reincarnation (yan srid) of a lama is unique to Tibetan Buddhism.

PAGE 102

TSUNG AS DOCTRINE

Buddhism's Theses

Tsung in the sense of doctrine or thesis is frequently encountered in fifth-century texts in such phrases as *k'ai-tsung*, "to explain the [basic] thesis," or *hsü-tsung*, "the doctrine of emptiness." Especially common was the use of the term *tsung* to categorize doctrinal interpretations of theses enumerated in a series.

The term *tsung* was also used to designate the major categories of Buddhist doctrines. Although there were classifications that reduced the Buddhist teachings to two, three, four, five, six, and ten types of doctrine *(tsung)*, the most influential were the four-doctrine classification devised by Hui-kuang (468-537) and the ten-doctrine classification established by Fa-tsang (643-712). Hui-kuang divided the Buddhist teachings into four essential doctrines *(tsung)*, none of which refers to an institutionalized Buddhist school: (1) the doctrine that phenomena arise in accordance with preexisting causes and conditions *(yin-yüan tsung)*, the basic teaching of the Abhidharma, advanced in refutation of the non-Buddhist view of spontaneous production; (2) the doctrine of the *Ch'eng-shih lun* that phenomena were no more than empirical names *(chia-ming tsung)* insofar as they could not exist independently of the causes and conditions that produced them; (3) the doctrine proclaimed in the *Po-jo ching* and the *San-lun* (Three Treatises) that even empirical names are deceptive *(k'uang-hsiang tsung)* insofar as there are no real or substantial phenomena underlying them; and (4) the doctrine taught in the *Nieh-p'an ching (Mahaparinirvana Sutra), Hua-yen ching* (*Avatamsaka Sutra*; Flower Garland Sutra), and other such *sutras* that the Buddha nature is ever abiding *(ch'ang tsung)* and constitutes the ultimate reality.

— STANLEY WEINSTEIN

cy, which was itself in the initial stages of development. Yomei (r. 585-587) was the first emperor officially to accept Buddhism, but it was his son, the prince regent Shotoku (574-622), who was responsible for creating Japan's first great age of Buddhism. In addition to building many Buddhist temples and sending students and monks to study in China, he wrote commentaries on three texts—the *Saddharmapundarika* (Lotus) *Sutra*, the *Vimalakirti Sutra*, and the Srimala *Sutra*—and is supposed to have promulgated the famous "Seventeen-Article Constitution" based on Buddhist and Confucian ideas. Later, Shotoku was worshiped as the incarnation of the *bodhisattva* Avalokitesvara. His promotion of Buddhism fell strictly within the bounds of the existing religio-political framework of Japanese sacral kingship: he upheld the imperial throne as the central authority and envisioned a "multireligious system" in which Shinto, Confucianism, and Buddhism would maintain a proper balance under the divine authority of the emperor as the "son of Heaven." Shotoku's religious policies, his indifference to the doctrinal and ecclesiastical divisions of Buddhism, his dependence on the universalistic soteriology of the *Lotus Sutra*, and his emphasis on the path of the lay devotee significantly influenced the later development of Japanese Buddhism.

— ARAKI MICHIO

TIBETAN BUDDHISM

The various sects or schools of Buddhism in Tibet are probably best referred to as "religious orders" in that most of them are in many ways analogous to Christian monastic orders in the West, namely Benedictines, Dominicans, and so forth. Thus, not only do they accept as fundamental the same Tibetan Buddhist canon, but many of them were founded by outstanding men of religion, just as the various Christian orders were established. So far as doctrine and religious practice is concerned there are no considerable differences between them. Conversely, the various sects or schools of Indian Buddhism were clearly distinguishable at two levels: first, they began to separate according to their various diverging versions of the traditional "monastic rule" (Vinaya), attributed by all of them to Sakyamuni Buddha himself; second, ever greater divergences developed from the early centuries CE onward as some communities adopted philosophical views and religious cults typical of the Mahayana, while other communities held to the earlier traditions.

Distinctions of these kinds do not exist in Tibetan Buddhism, since all Tibetan religious orders have accepted unquestioningly the monastic rule of one particular Indian Buddhist order, namely that of the Mulasarvastivadins, who happened to be particularly strong in Central Asia and in northern India, and it was in these circles that the Tibetans found their first Indian teachers. Moreover, the form of Buddhism which became established in Tibet represents Indian Buddhism in its late Mahayana and Vajrayana form, with the result that the earlier sects, known collectively as Hinayana, have left no impression on Tibetan Buddhism and are known in Tibet only in a historical and doctrinal context. These considerations inevitably lent an overall unity to Tibetan Buddhism that was lacking in India.

The idea of a religious lineage, that is to say, of a particular religious tradition, usually involving special kinds of religious practice, which is passed in succession from master to pupil, is absolutely fundamental in Tibetan thought, and it is precisely this idea which gives coherence to their various religious orders and explains the many links which may exist between them. As distinct from a "lineage," which is bound up with the personal relationships of those involved in the various lines of transmission, who may often belong to different religious orders, we may define a "religious order" (or sect) as one which is to outward appearances a separate corporate body distinguished by its own hierarchy and administrative machinery, by the existence of its various monastic houses, and by its recognized membership. It is precisely in these respects, as well as in the manner of its foundation, that some Tibetan orders may be said to resemble Christian ones. However, religious lineage remains so important in Tibetan Buddhism that some supposed religious orders exist rather as a group of lineages than as an order in any understandable Western sense.

— DAVID L. SNELLGROVE

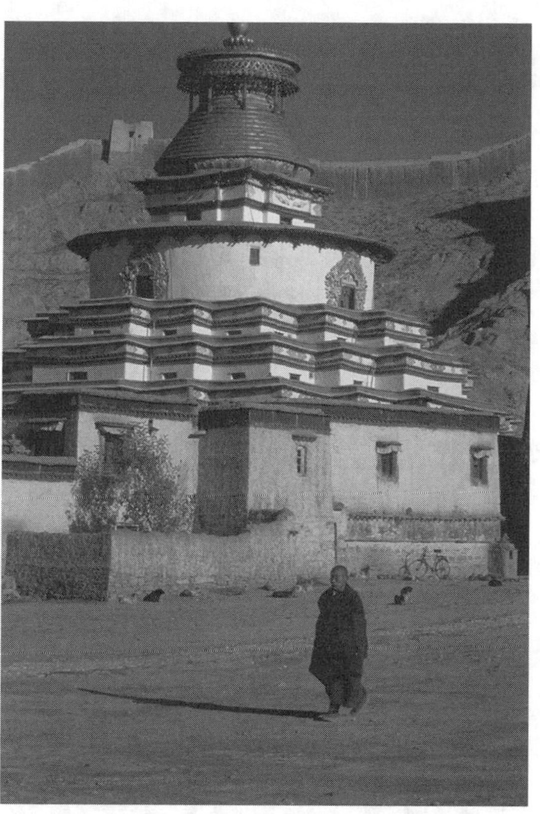

BUDDHIST TEMPLE

All Tibetan religious orders have accepted the monastic rule of the Mulasarvastivadins, who were strong in Central Asian and northern India.

BRIAN VIKANDER/CORBIS

C

CANAANITE RELIGION

AN OVERVIEW

Before the late nineteenth century, there were only two sources for the study of the Canaanite religion. The first, the Hebrew scriptures, contains numerous references to the Canaanites and their practices, which are generally condemned as abominable (e.g., *Lv.* 18:3, 27-28). It is generally agreed that the biblical witness to Canaanite religion is highly polemical and, therefore, unreliable; biblical evidence must at the least be used with extreme caution, and in conjunction with extrabiblical sources.

The second source for knowledge of Canaanite religion was those classical texts that preserve descriptions of aspects of it. The best known of these are the *Phoenician History of Philo Byblius,* of which portions are preserved in Eusebius's *Praeparatio evangelica,* and *The Syrian Goddess,* attributed (perhaps falsely) to Lucian of Samothrace. At best, Philo's information probably sheds light on the religion of late hellenized Phoenicians, and offers no direct evidence for second-millennium Canaanite religion. The same generalization applies to (Pseudo-) Lucian.

Firsthand evidence for Canaanite culture in the second millennium BCE (or, in archaeological terms, the Middle Bronze and Late Bronze periods) comes from artifactual evidence found at many archaeological sites (more than sixty for the first part of the Middle Bronze period alone—mostly tombs) and from textual evidence stemming mainly from three great discoveries: (1) the eighteenth-century royal archives of "Amorite" Mari; (2) the diplomatic correspondence between several Levantine vassal princes and the pharoahs Amenophis III and IV (first half of the fourteenth century), found at Tell al-'Amarna; and (3) the mainly fourteenth- and thirteenth-century texts found at Ras Shamra (ancient Ugarit) and nearby Ras Ibn Hani, both within the present-day administrative district of Latakia, on the Mediterranean coast of Syria. The artifactual evidence is crucial for understanding material culture, socioeconomic developments, population movements, and the like, and provides considerable data about funerary practices. Most significant for the study of religion are the figurines, thought to represent gods and goddesses, that have been recovered in virtually every archaeological context.

The ancient city of Mari was peripheral to both the Mesopotamian and the Levantine spheres of influence. Culturally and linguistically, it was clearly West Semitic, but to label it "Canaanite" goes beyond the evidence (the designation "Amorite" represents, to some extent, a scholarly compromise). The Mari texts are virtually all concerned with economic, juridical, and administrative matters. One text in particular testifies to the eclecticism and heterogeneity of Mari's religious cult in the eighteenth century, listing the sacrificial sheep distributed among the various gods and temples of Mari. The most striking group of Mari texts is the small collection of so-called prophetic texts. These twenty-odd letters attest to a type of oracular speaking that shows significant affinities with biblical prophecies of a millennium later. Some of this oracular speaking seems to have been done by cultic personnel, and some apparently consisted of messages transmitted by the gods through ordinary people. It may be suggested, on the basis of these Mari texts and related evidence, that the phenomenon broadly termed *"prophecy"* represented a peculiar and peripheral kind of divine intermediation among the West Semites generally.

"For the famine had reached the land of Canaan."

GENESIS 42:5

Most of the Amarna letters report on Levantine military, economic, and political matters to the Egyptian court. The letters were written in Babylonian, the diplomatic language of the period, but they regularly reveal the Canaanite character of their authors.

By far the most significant evidence for Canaanite religion in the second millennium is found at Ugarit. From the beginning of the millennium until the city's destruction at the hands of the Sea Peoples (c. 1180-1175 BCE), Ugarit was a thriving cosmopolitan trading center. In the Middle Bronze period, Ugarit underwent considerable expansion. During this period, two large temples (dedicated to the gods Baal and Dagan respectively) were erected on top of older ruins, forming, in effect, an acropolis in the city. The pottery of the period is predominantly Canaanite, and other material evidence demonstrates that Ugarit was in contact with Egypt, the Aegean, and Mesopotamia. At the same time, Ugarit's population was augmented by an influx of Indo-European-speaking Hurrians from the northeast.

The best-attested period at Ugarit is the last two

C

CANAANITE RELIGION

An Overview

The members of the Philistine pantheon were all dieties worshipped for centuries by the pre-Philistine occupants of Canaan

PAGE 550

centuries of its existence (Late Bronze III, c. 1365-1180). The Ugaritic texts date from this period, although some of the religious texts are undoubtedly older, and were merely written down at this time.

In addition to the mythological texts from the high priest's library, the excavations of this and several other archives of Ugarit and Ras Ibn Hani have turned up related mythological material, descriptive ritual texts, lists of sacrificial offerings, god-lists, prayers and liturgies, incantations, divinatory texts, and dedicatory inscriptions.

DEITIES. The essential information about Ugarit's deities comes from what appears to be a canonical god-list. Two reasons are generally given for the order of the gods in the list: either it reflects their relative importance, or else it gives the order in which their symbols were paraded in a cultic procession. The list begins with two or three Ils (El)—the sources are evenly split on the number. *Il* is the common Semitic word for "god"; it is the proper name of the head of the Ugaritic pantheon in the mythological texts. The first Il in the god-list is associated with Mount Sapan (Tsafon), the Canaanite Olympus, which was traditionally identified with Jebel al-Aqra, about fifty kilometers north of Ugarit at the mouth of the Orontes River. (The mountain was itself deified, and appears in the god-list.)

The second Il is called *Ilib.* The Akkadian and Hurrian parallels show that this name is a portmanteau composed of the elements *il* ("god") and *ab* ("father"), but the precise significance of the combination is uncertain. Most likely the name denotes an ancestral spirit, the numen manifest in the Ugaritic cult of the dead.

The third Il is presumably to be identified with the head of the pantheon in the mythological texts. His epithets and activities in those, and in the cultic texts, provide a fair picture of his character. He is the father of the gods, who are called his "family" or "sons," and he is styled "father of humankind" and "builder of built ones." He may have been regarded as the creator of the world, but the Ugaritic evidence is inconclusive on this point. He bears the epithet "bull," a symbol of virility and power (although one mythological text casts some doubt on his sexual prowess).

The next deity on the list is Dagan. The Mari texts attest to his great importance in the Middle Euphrates region (especially Terqa). One of the two temples on the acropolis of Ugarit was evidently consecrated to Dagan. During excavations carried out in 1934, two inscribed stone slabs were found just outside the temple. The inscriptions, the only known examples of Ugaritic carved in stone, commemorate *pgr* sacrifices of a sheep and an ox offered to Dagan.

Following Dagan come seven Baals. The first is the Baal of Mount Sapan, who dwells in the same place as the Baal in the mythological texts (the "heights" or "recesses" of Sapan); the term *sapan* surely refers to the Baal temple of Ugarit as well. The Akkadian rendition of *Baal* is *Adad,* which is the name of the most promi-

UGARIT RUINS

The most significant archeological evidence for Canaanite Religion is found at Ugarit, a thriving metropolis during the second century.

CHARLES & JOSETTE LENARS/CORBIS

nent West Semitic mountain and weather god. The significance of the other six Baals (none qualified by epithets and all identified with Adad) is uncertain, although sevenfold lists of all sorts, including divine heptads, are common throughout the ancient Near East: the number seven evidently denotes completeness or perfection.

The name *Baal* is derived from the common Semitic noun meaning "lord, master, husband." In contrast to the numinous Il, Baal represents the divine power that is immanent in the world, activating and effectuating things or phenomena. Given the paucity of rainfall in most of the Levant, it is not surprising that the lord of the storm is the most prominent god of this type.

Following the seven Baals, the god-list continues with Ars wa-Shamem ("earth and heaven"). Binomial deities are common in Ugaritic; they represent either a hendiadys (as in this case) or a composite of two related gods who have been assimilated to one another. This god's function is unknown; perhaps the domain over which Baal holds sway is deified. There are also two other geographical deities: Sapan (discussed above) and "Mountain and Valley" (significance unknown, unless it defines the domain of Athtar, the god occupying the preceding place on the god-list).

The remaining divine names on the list may be grouped in four categories: individual goddesses and gods who are known or at least mentioned in the mythological texts; collective terms that designate groups of lesser deities; Hurrian deities; and otherwise unknown or poorly attested gods.

The two most prominent goddesses in the mythological texts are Athirat (Asherah) and Anat. Athirat is the consort of Il, and as such she is the highest-ranking goddess in the pantheon. In contrast, Anat is a violent goddess of sexual love and war, "sister" (perhaps consort) of Baal and vanquisher of Baal's enemy Mot. Her principal epithet is "maiden," a tribute to her youth, beauty, and desirability, but pugnacity is her primary trait.

There are three other Canaanite goddesses on the god-list. Shapash is the all-seeing sun (male in Mesopotamia, but female at Ugarit), "luminary of the gods." Pid-ray ("fat"?) and Arsay ("earth," perhaps, on the basis of the Akkadian parallel, having some connection with the netherworld) are two of the daughters of Baal; the third, Talay ("dew"), does not appear on the god-list. Two other non-Canaanite goddesses are on the list, undoubtedly via the Hurrians, although the deities themselves are not necessarily Hurrian in origin: Ushharay (Ishhara), the scorpion goddess, who appears in several cultic texts but never in the myths, and Dadmish, probably a warrior goddess but very poorly attested. The one remaining goddess on the list is Uthht (pronunciation uncertain; the sex of the deity is, in fact, only surmised from the feminine ending); possibly Mesopotamian in origin, and most likely signifying a deified incense burner.

Seven male deities remain on the god-list, all but one of whom are at least mentioned in the mythological texts. Yarikh is the moon god, and he figures prominently in a poem that describes his marriage to the moon goddess, Nikkal. This text is undoubtedly a Hurrian myth in Ugaritic guise. The other clearly astral god is Shalim (the divine element in the name of the city Jeru*salem* and of King *Solom*on), who represents the evening twilight or Venus as evening star.

BAAL

The Akkadian rendition of Baal is Adad, which is the name of the most prominent West Semitic mountain and weather god.

GIANNI DAGLI ORTI/CORBIS

The god Kothar ("skilled one"; also known as Kothar wa-Hasis, "skilled and wise one") is the divine craftsman. In various sources he is a master builder, weapon maker, seaman, and magician. It has been suggested that he is the genius of technology.

The god Rashap (the biblical *Reshef,* which means both "pestilence" and "flame") is blamed in the epic of

"Burnt offerings and sacrifice for sin, hast thou not required."

PRAYER BOOK, 8, 1662

Kirta for the demise of part of the title character's family. But Rashap's real importance at Ugarit and Ras Ibn Hani emerges from the cultic texts, where he is the recipient of numerous offerings.

The remaining god on the list is Kinar, who is perhaps the deified lyre. Nothing is known about him, but he has been identified with the Cypriot hero Kinyras, father of Adonis.

RITUALS AND CULTIC PERSONNEL. Assuming that the biblical and related data are reliable, they evidently refer to local manifestations of first-millennium Phoenician cults (such as that of northern Israel). The simple assumption of continuity between second-millennium Canaan and first-millennium Phoenicia is unjustified—as is, more generally, the facile identification of "Canaanites" with "Phoenicians."

Theologians usually distinguish four intentions of sacrifice: praise (acknowledgment, homage), thanksgiving, supplication, and expiation.

PAGE 588

As for the myth-and-ritual claim, the seasonal interpretation of the Baal texts is by no means certain. There is no evidence that the Baal texts were ever used in conjunction with cultic activity. In fact, there is only one Ugaritic mythological text containing rubrics for ritual performance; it apparently entails some sort of fertility rite, but one not necessarily connected with the seasonal cycle. Knowledge of the Ugaritic calendar and its fixed festivals is too scanty to permit the claim that Ugaritic religion was organized with respect to the agricultural year.

The Ugaritic ritual texts describe a highly organized sacrificial cult under the patronage of the king. The sacrifices seem to be of the gift or tribute type; that is, they were performed to curry favor with the gods, to secure their aid and protection. It is undeniable that offerings might have been made to deities (particularly chthonic ones) to promote the fertility of the land and the fecundity of the flocks. But the one mass public ritual that has survived, and the one attested prayer to Baal as well, both seem more concerned with protection from Ugarit's potential military opponents. In view of the shifting alliances and political instability that marked Ugarit's last two centuries, this concern seems only natural.

Most of the known Ugaritic rituals were performed by or on behalf of the king. The best-attested type of ritual is found in seven different texts. In it the king of Ugarit performs, at specified times, a ritual lustration to purify himself, and then offers a series of sacrifices to various deities. At sundown, the king "desacralizes" himself in a way that is not clear. The most interesting of these texts is evidently a prescriptive ritual to which is appended a prayer to Baal, perhaps recited by the queen, that seems to specify the occasion on which the rites were to be performed.

A second type of ritual is preserved in three texts that describe the transfer of cult statues from one place to another. The remainder of the text describes essentially the same rituals as those performed for a different collection of gods (on a different occasion?), the poorly attested *gthrm.*

One substantial ritual text is unique in the corpus, and has been the subject of many studies. It is unique in its poetic/hymnic quality and in the acts it describes. It seems to depict a great public assembly in which the entire population of Ugarit, male and female, king and commoner alike, participated. The ritual appears to have been a mass expiation or purgation of sins, or some sort of mass purification rite, designed to protect Ugarit against its threatening neighbors. A parallel has been drawn between it and the Jewish Yom Kippur, the "day of purgation [of sin]." In the Ugaritic text, the men and women of the community are alternately summoned to offer sacrifices, which they do. While the sacrifices are performed the people sing, praying that their offerings will ascend to "the father of the sons of Il" (that is, to Il himself), to the "family of the sons of Il," to the "assembly of the sons of Il," and to *Thkmn wa-Shnm,* Il's son and attendant (the one who cares for him when he is drunk; in one of his epithets, Il is called "father of *Shnm*").

Only one mythological text, the poem about the birth of Shahr and Shalim (the *ilima naimima,* "gracious gods"), includes rubrics for ritual performance. These rubrics, interspersed throughout the poem, describe the activities of the king and queen, and of cultic functionaries called *aribuma* (some kind of priests?) and *tha-nanuma* (members of the king's guard?). They offer sacrifices, participate in a banquet, and sing responsively to musical accompaniment. It seems almost certain that the poem itself was acted out as a type of ritual drama. It describes the subjugation of Death by some sort of pruning rite, followed by Il's sexual relations with Athirat and Rahmay ("womb" = Anat?). The poem concludes with the birth of Shahr and Shalim, and their youthful activities. The text and its accompanying ritual may commemorate (or attempt to foster) the birth of a royal heir to the reigning king and queen of Ugarit; they bear some relation to Mesopotamian sacred marriage rites and to Hittite rituals designed to protect the life and vigor of the king and queen.

POPULAR RELIGION. As is generally the case in the ancient Near East, little can be said with any certainty about popular religion at Ugarit, since only kings, priests, and members of the elite are represented in the texts. The Ugaritic texts were apparently only a part of the larger cosmopolitan scribal tradition of Ugarit, which was modeled on the Babylonian scribal schools. The same scribes who produced the *Baal* texts were also trained to write in Babylonian cuneiform, and they copied Sumerian and Akkadian texts in almost every genre. Surviving evidence demonstrates that Ugarit's

THE UGARITIC CULT OF THE DEAD
Kings and Healers

Most difficult to reconstruct, but obviously of great importance, was the Ugaritic cult of the dead. The dead were summoned, by a liturgy accompanied by offerings, to participate in a banquet. The banquet, which was apparently a drunken orgy, was intended to propitiate the dead and to solicit the aid and protection provided by their numinous power. The most important group of the deified dead was comprised of Ugarit's kings *(malikum).* The larger assemblage, variously called "healers" *(rpim),* "healers of the netherworld" *(rpi ars),* "ancient healers" *(rpim qdmyn),* "divine spirits" *(ilnym),* and "assembly of Ditan/Didan" *(qbs dtn/ddn),* included two men who are prominent in the epic texts, Danil and Kirta, as well as several other spirits who are identified by name in a liturgical invocation of the dead.

Another important text invokes the god Rapiu, "king of eternity" (that is, of the netherworld). Rapiu is clearly the patron of the deified dead; at first he is invited to drink, and at the end of the text he is asked to exert his "strength, power, might, rule, and goodness" for the benefit of Ugarit. If Rapiu is indeed to be identified with Il, this text comports well with the mythological fragment that depicts Il getting drunk at a *marzih.*

Alongside the cult of the dead must be placed the texts that apparently describe the ritual offerings to the gods of the netherworld *(ilm ars).* The clearest of these begins with an offering to Rashap and mentions several other chthonic deities. There is also a strange god-list that appears to include a collection of netherworld demons. Finally, an inscribed clay model of a liver may record a sacrifice offered to a person (or deity?) who is "in the tomb."

— ALAN M. COOPER

educated elite was conversant with the Mesopotamian Gilgamesh traditions, wisdom and proverbial literature, and legal formulas, although little of this material is reflected in texts in the Ugaritic language.

It is not at all certain, then, how much of the literary tradition might have filtered down to the commoners of Ugarit. Still, speculation about popular religion may be made in four areas: conceptions of gods reflected in personal names; the evidence of votive figurines; evidence for magic and divination; and possible religious, ethical, or "wisdom" teachings derived from the texts.

Popular conceptions of the gods may emerge from a consideration of personal names, since a great number of names are composites of divine names (or surrogates) and nominal or verbal elements. The standard collection of Ugaritic personal names, Frauke Gröndahl's *Die Personennamen der Texte aus Ugarit* (Rome, 1967), lists over fifty divine elements that appear in them. The most popular are Il, Baal, Ammu ("uncle," a surrogate for a divine name), Anat and her "masculine" equivalent Anu, Athtar, Yamm, Kothar, Malik, Pidr (masculine equivalent of Pidray?), Rapiu, Rashap, and Shapash. In some names, a god is described as father, mother, brother, sister, or uncle (e.g., *Rashapabi*). In others, the bearer of the name is the god's son, daughter, servant, or devotee (e.g., *Abdi-Rashap,* "servant of Rashap"). A large class of names describes characteristics of the gods.

The second class of evidence for popular religion comes from metal figurines that are generally thought to represent gods and goddesses. A comprehensive catalog of these figurines, compiled by Ora Negbi (1976), describes over seventeen hundred of them. They are considered to have been miniature copies of now-lost wooden cult statues, and were probably used as votive idols. The fact that so many have been found at cultic sites suggests that they had some ceremonial function. Negbi notes that these idols "may have been used as amulets for magic purposes in domestic and funerary cults as well" (p. 2).

Some textual evidence has been recovered for magic and divination at Ugarit. There are two versions of a long and impressive incantation against the bite of a venomous serpent; several important deities are summoned from their mythical abodes during the course of the incantations.

Finally, one very difficult text reports a divine oracle. It begins: "When the lord of the great/many gods [Il?] approached Ditan, the latter sought an oracle concerning the child." Some individual presumably wishes to inquire of Il about his (sick?) child. (A comparable episode occurs in the Kirta epic.) Il can be reached through an intermediary, Ditan, the eponymous patron of those deified dead known as the "assembly of Ditan." The text continues with a series of instructions (broken and unclear) that will enable the inquirer to obtain the desired oracular response. The text seems to conclude with several instructions, "and afterward there will be no suffering [?]".

Taken together, these texts indicate a lively interest in the mantic arts at Ugarit. There is practically no evidence, however, about the specialists who practiced

The worship of ancestors is closely linked to cosmology and worldview, to ideas of the soul and the afterlife, and to a society's regulation of inheritance and succession.

PAGE 28

Members of the Philistine pantheon—Dagon, Baalzebub and Ashtoret—were all deities worshiped by pre-Philistine occupants of Canaan.

PAGE 550

those arts; perhaps that is because they operated on the periphery of the official cultic institutions.

The most problematic aspect of popular religion is the interpretation of the Ugaritic religious texts. Assuming that they were in some way normative and that they were diffused orally, they would embody the religious "teachings" of Ugarit. There are, however, no surviving interpretations of the texts or expositions of religious doctrine that explain what those teachings might have been or what impact they had on the life of a community of believers. The Ugaritic mythic and epic texts (as opposed to the descriptive ritual texts) can be read as homilies on the nature of the world in which people live. Ancient readers or hearers of these texts would have sought their own place in the "cosmos" they describe. Ugaritic believers, like modern believers, would presumably have formulated a special application of sacred texts to their own lives.

The *Baal* texts punctualize eternal truths in a symbolic realm that is only superficially remote from human experience. The gods experience joy and mourning, battle and tranquillity, life and death, power and impotence. The mightiest of the gods confronts the world's challenges and surmounts them all, until he encounters Death, the one enemy to whom gods and humans alike succumb. Baal's triumphs and trials, furthermore, illustrate the contiguity and interrelationship of everything in the world: the gods, nature, the political order, and human life are all part of the same order. When Baal is vanquished, political order collapses and the earth turns infertile—not because Baal "symbolizes" order and fertility in some simplistic way, but because the intricate balance of the world has been subverted. The same upset of the natural order occurs when Kirta, a human king, becomes mortally ill.

Overarching the flux of the world, and apparently not subject to it, is the wise and beneficent Il. At critical moments in the *Baal* texts, the gods journey (or send emissaries) to him in order to obtain his favor and advice. After Kirta's family is annihilated by malevolent forces, Il comforts the king in a dream; later on, Il provides the cure for Kirta's terrible illness. And in the Aqhat epic, Baal implores Il to grant a son to the childless Danil. Il consents, and appears to Danil in a dream with the good news. In every case, Il manifests transcendent power that is wielded justly, in response to urgent pleas.

The epic texts (perhaps "historico-mythic" would be a better designation for them) Aqhat and Kirta parallel and supplement the mythic texts. They narrate the existential encounter of humans with the gods. Historical (or pseudohistorical) figures become exemplary or admonitory paradigms of human behavior.

The crises that move the plot of the Aqhat text demonstrate the conjunction and contiguity of the human and divine realms. Danil, who is, like Kirta, a man become god (one of the deified rapium—from the point of view of the reader, that is), is an embodiment of that contiguity. Danil is clearly an ideal type, pious and just; he brings his plea for a son before the gods in humble obeisance, and he is rewarded. The incubation rite performed by Danil at the beginning of the story seems to be a model of personal piety.

The Kirta epic, like that of Aqhat, begins with its hero childless, this time because of catastrophe instead of impotence. Dramatic tension arises from the situation of a king without an heir, which could result in disruption of both the political and the natural order. The story conveys the fragility of power and the delicate relationship between humans and deities.

The texts are all firmly on the side of reward for virtue and piety, and punishment for wickedness, blasphemy, and folly. Yet even someone who is justly suffering the wrath of the gods may appeal to the gracious Il and be heard.

SURVIVALS. Survivals of Canaanite religion are observable in two first-millennium cultural spheres, the Levant and the Aegean. Phoenician religion, both in the Levant and in its wider Mediterranean sphere of influence, represents, to some extent, a continuation of Canaanite traditions. Northern Israel's official cult was among the Levantine successors of Canaanite religion. It has often been noted that biblical polemics against that cult (for example, in the *Book of Hosea*) are directed against a characteristically Canaanite feature—the idea that the god (in this case Yahveh = Baal) was immanent in nature and subject to its flux. The Israelite god was, on the other hand, comfortably assimilated to the transcendent Il.

In the Aegean area, the nature of Canaanite influence is more controversial. But there is compelling evidence for the existence of direct West Semitic contact with Mycenaean Greece, creating a legacy of Semitic names, literary motifs, and religious practices that became part of the Hellenic cultural heritage.

— ALAN M. COOPER

CARIBBEAN RELIGIONS

PRE-COLUMBIAN RELIGIONS

European explorers noted three major aboriginal groups in the Caribbean at the time of contact (1492 and the years immediately following): Island Arawak, Island Carib, and Ciboney. There is an abundance of information concerning the religious practices of the Island Arawak and Island Carib, but very little is known of Ciboney religion.

This essay will focus on the Island Arawak and the Island Carib. The Island Arawak were concentrated in the Greater Antilles, a group of large, mainly sedimentary islands near Puerto Rico. The Island Carib inhabited the small, mainly volcanic islands of the Lesser Antilles.

Both the Island Arawak and the Island Carib originally migrated from the South American mainland (Rouse, 1964). The Island Arawak settled in the Greater Antilles at about the beginning of the common era and were followed several hundred years later by the Carib, who claimed to have begun their migrations into the Lesser Antilles only a few generations before the arrival of Columbus.

DEITIES. Both the Island Arawak and the Island Carib possessed a notion of a high god, though, as the chroniclers' reports make clear, their high god differed conceptually from the God of Christianity. We know, too, that aboriginal high gods were thought to exert very little direct influence on the workings of the universe. Many of the early chroniclers, including Fray Ramón Pané, Gonzalo F. de Oviedo, and Raymond Breton, refer to Arawak and Carib high gods as kinds of *deus otiosus;* that is, they are inactive gods far removed from human affairs and concerns. Neither the Island Arawak nor the Island Carib conceived of their high god as creator of the universe, and it is unclear how powerful the high god was thought to be. Chroniclers differ somewhat on this. Pané suggests that the high god was a powerful deity who chooses to be inactive. Other chroniclers stress the inactivity of the high god and the lack of attention accorded him. The bulk of the evidence, including what we know of other American Indian religions (Hultkrantz, 1979), supports the latter interpretation.

Island Arawak. The identification of Island Arawak deities is often a problem. Their high god was known by two names: Iocauna and Guamaonocon (spellings differ from chronicler to chronicler). Peter Martyr reports that the Arawak supreme being was not self-created but was himself brought forth by a mother who has five names or identities. He also reports other appellations for the high god, including Jocakuvaque, Yocahu, Vaque, Maorocon, and Macrocoti. Pané provides an equally complex list of male and female deities, and it is apparent that most deities in the Arawak pantheon were recognized by a number of appellations.

Other prominent Island Arawak deities include: Guabancex, goddess of wind and water, who had two subordinates: Guatauva, her messenger, and Coatrischio, the tempest-raiser; Yobanua-Borna, a rain deity; Baidrama (or Vaybruma), a twinned deity associated with strength and healing; Opigielguoviran, a doglike being said to have plunged into the morass with the coming of the Spanish; and Faraguvaol, a tree trunk able to wander at will.

One of the most important differences between Arawak and Carib religions is that among the Island Arawak nature worship seems to have been closely associated with ancestor worship. The bones of the Island Arawak dead, especially the bones of their leaders and great men, were thought to have power in and of themselves. This notion also existed among the Island Carib, but their ceremonies and representations were not so elaborate.

ARAWAK GRAVESTONE

The bones of the Island Arawak dead were thought to have intrinsic power.

PAUL ALMASY/© CORBIS

Island Carib. Like the Island Arawak, the island Carib recognized a multitude of spirit beings as well as a high god whose name varies according to text.

Of the spirits directly involved in human affairs, Icheiri and Mabouia are the most frequently mentioned. Icheiri, whose name comes from the verb *ichéem,* meaning "what I like" (Breton, 1665, p. 287), has been interpreted as a spirit of good, while Mabouia, from the same root as the word *boyé,* or "sorcerer," has been interpreted as a spirit of evil. The Carib informed Breton that it was Mabouia who brought about eclipses of the sun and caused the stars to disappear suddenly.

Another major category in the Island Carib spirit world was that of the *zemiis. Zemi,* too, appears to have been a very general term; the word is of Arawak origin and indicates the strong influence of Island Arawak lan-

The extensive Arawak family of languages includes the Chané of Argentina.

PAGE 622

C

CARIBBEAN RELIGIONS

Pre-Columbian Religions

guage and culture on the Island Carib. Among the Carib, to get drunk, *chemerocae,* literally meant "to see *zemiis.*" *Zemiis* were thought to live in a paradise far removed from the world of the living, but every so often, according to La Borde (1704), Coualina, chief of the *zemiis,* would become angry about the wickedness of some *zemiis* and drive them from paradise to earth, where they became animals. This is but one example of the constant transformations from deity to animal in Island Carib mythology.

AFTERLIFE. Both the Island Arawak and the Island Carib had a notion of the afterlife. The Island Arawak conceived of spirits of the dead, called *opias* or *hubias,* who were said to wander about the bush after dark. Occasionally *opias* joined the company of the living and were said to be indistinguishable from the living, except for the spirits' lack of navels. In both Arawak and Carib religions, the activities of the dead were thought to resemble the activities of the living.

"The ancients dreaded death: the Christian can only fear dying."

JULIUS HARE AND AUGUSTUS HARE
GUESSES AT TRUTH, 1827

Pané reports that the Arawak of Haiti believed in a kingdom of death, Coaibai, which was situated on their own island. Every leader of importance had his own kingdom of death, usually located within his own dominion. In addition, there were uninhabited places where the spirits of evil people were said to roam.

The Island Carib, on the other hand, had a much more diffuse notion of the afterlife. All spirits of the body, *omicou,* went to the seashore or became *mabouias* in the forest. There was no concept of an underworld.

Elaborate burial ceremonies were noted among both the Island Arawak and the Island Carib. Archaeological evidence indicates that the Island Arawak performed several types of burials: (1) direct interment; (2) interment within a raised mound; (3) interment within a grave covered with an arch of branches; and (4) burial in caves.

Burial customs among the Island Carib were not so varied. Breton (1665) noted that the Island Carib dreaded death, and that it was forbidden to utter the name of the deceased. The Island Carib referred to the dead indirectly (e.g., "the husband of so-and-so") because to do otherwise would cause the deceased to come back to earth.

RITES AND CEREMONIES. The most important ceremonies among the Island Arawak pertained to rain and the growth of crops, but there were also important ceremonies for success in war, burial of the dead, curing of the sick, canoe building, cutting hair, the births of children, marriage, and initiation. In most instances these rites took the form of elaborate dances known as *areitos.* Fewkes (1907) notes that dramatization played a part in all ceremonies. For example, in their war dances the entire war sequence was portrayed: the departure of the warriors, surprise of the enemy, combat, celebration of victory, and return of the war party.

The island Carib conducted ceremonies on many of the same occasions as did the Island Arawak. According to La Borde, the Island Carib held rites whenever a council was held concerning their wars, when they returned from their expeditions, when a first male child was born, when they cut their children's hair, when their boys became old enough to go to war, when they cut down trees, and when they launched a vessel.

Island Carib rites met individual as well as societal needs. Each individual had his own personal deity or *zemi.* These personal deities were thought to reveal things to the individual, and it is reported that individuals customarily withdrew from society for six or seven days, without taking any sustenance save tobacco and the juice of herbs. During this period, the individual experienced visions of whatever he or she desired (victory over enemies, wealth, and so on).

DRUGS. Tobacco, narcotics, and stimulants played an important part in both Island Arawak and Island Carib rites. Tobacco, called *cohiba,* was used in a number of different forms in all ceremonies. Among the Island Arawak, tobacco smoke was used as an incense to summon the gods. Tobacco was sprinkled on the heads of idols as an offering. Religious leaders among the Island Arawak and Island Carib "stupefied" themselves with tobacco when they consulted their oracles; they also used tobacco in curing rituals.

Throwing *aji* (pepper) onto live coals was part of Island Arawak and Island Carib preparations for warfare. Ricardo E. Alegría (1979) contends that the pepper caused irritation of the mucous membrane, a racking cough, and other discomforts that were thought to induce the proper psychological state for war.

Island Arawak. Major duties of the Arawak *piaie* were to divine the future by consulting their personal *zemiis* and to direct offering to *zemiis* during public ceremonies. In both of these duties, they served as intermediaries between the Island Arawak and their gods (Deive, 1978).

Accounts of Arawak shamanism provide very little detail concerning the *piaie's* role in public ceremonies, and it is unclear whether or not all *piaies* were able to conduct public ritual. It is possible that some *piaies* functioned solely as curers or diviners and could not perform other rites.

Island Carib. The Carib never went to war without first consulting the spirit world to find out if conditions were favorable for victory. Since chiefs were unable to make direct contact with spirits, they required the services of a *boyé* whose predictions had tremendous impact on public opinion. *Boyés* also needed to develop working relationships with chiefs to defray the high costs of apprenticeship. We have no clear notion of the actual length of apprenticeship for shamans among the Island Carib, though in some tribes of the Guianas apprenticeship is said to have lasted from ten to twenty years (Métraux, 1949). This period of training was probably considerably shorter among the Carib.

Boyés were a professional class in Island Carib society. They charged for all services, and I contend that they did not train new shamans without demanding something in return. War chiefs and their families, as wealthier members of their society, were in the best position to take on obligations to senior *boyés* (Glazier, 1980). They were perhaps the wealthiest members of their society. While war chiefs and families had considerable control over the distribution of some resources and war booty, *boyés* had control over the distribution of goods outside kinship obligations.

The *boyés* had great potential for wealth, for there was always demand for their services. In times of trouble, they were called upon to dispel evil spirits; in times of prosperity, they were called upon to insure its continuance; and when there was doubt, they gave assurances for the future.

— STEPHEN D. GLAZIER

AFRO-CARIBBEAN RELIGIONS

This essay concentrates on syncretic religious cults found in the Caribbean region. The experience of Caribbean blacks under the political, economic, and domestic conditions of slavery modified character in a stressful direction, and those who were most sensitive to the stress advanced innovative religious and secular systems to deal with their anxiety. The new religious institutions consisted of elements of African and European beliefs and practices, and, in some cases, parts of American Indian and South Asian religious traditions. A number of new religions arose from the interaction of three major variables: socioeconomic, psychological, and cultural.

HAITIAN VOODOO. The African dances that were performed in the seventeenth century by slaves in the western part of the island of Hispaniola and the religious beliefs of the Fon, Siniga, Lemba, Yoruba, and other African peoples who had been brought to Hispaniola were combined with certain beliefs of European folk origin about Roman Catholic saints, and, as a result, the neo-African religion of Voodoo developed.

The supernatural phenomena of greatest importance in Voodoo are the *lwa.* Erica Bourguignon (1980) suggests that variety and inconsistency in Haitian Voodoo have developed, and continue to develop, in part through the mechanism of altered states of consciousness, particularly in the forms of possession-trance and dreams. In Haiti, possession-trance is not highly stereotyped and prescribed. During possession-trance, cult leaders and members speak and act in the names of the spirits, behaving in ways that may modify the future performance of the ritual or the adherents' perception of the spirits.

The grand *lwa* comprise both nature spirits and functional spirits that are of African origin. Prominent among the nature spirits are Dambala, the serpent spirit identified with the rainbow and associated with floods; Bade, spirit of the winds; Sogbo, a Fon spirit of thunder; Shango (Yor., *Sango*), the Yoruba spirit of thunder and lightning; and Agwé, spirit of the sea.

The *lwa* are also identified with Catholic saints. For instance, Dambala is identified with Saint Patrick, on whose image serpents are depicted. The *marassa,* spirits of dead twins, are believed to be the twin saints Cosmas and Damian (Price-Mars, 1928; Herskovits, 1937a).

The relationship between Voodoo adherents and the *lwa* is thought to be a contractual one; if one is punctilious about offerings and ceremonies, the *lwa* will be generous with their aid. The lwa must be paid once or twice a year with an impressive ceremony, and small gifts must be presented frequently.

In West Africa, concepts of the "soul" are highly elaborated. In traditional Fon belief, all persons have at least three souls, and adult males have four (Herskovits, 1938). In Haitian Voodoo, every man has two souls.

Adherents fear the power of the dead and observe funerary and postfunerary rites meticulously. A wake is held on the night of death; the funeral itself follows and, if possible, is held in accordance with the rites of the Catholic church. On the ninth night after death is the "last prayer," and on the tenth night a ritual is held in which sacrifices are offered to all the family dead (Métraux, 1959; Herskovits, 1937b).

François Duvalier, the dictatorial president of Haiti

Voodoo, or Vodou (according to official Haitian Creole orthography), is a misleading but common term for the religious practices of 80 to 90 percent of the people of Haiti.

PAGE 702

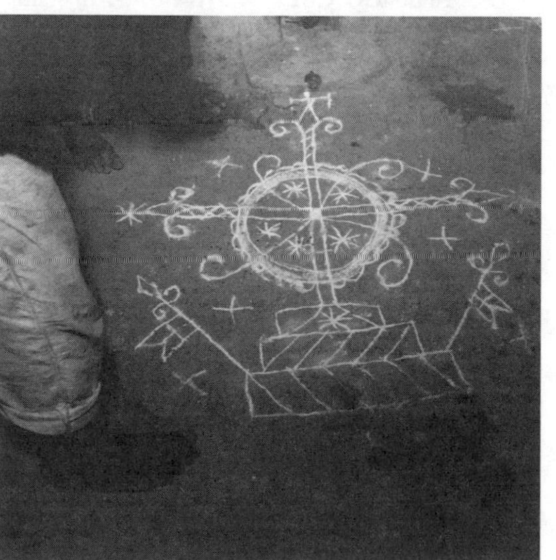

VOODOO ICON

Haitian Voodoo is derived from a combination of traditional African religious rituals and European folk beliefs.

BRADLEY SMITH/CORBIS

from 1957 to 1971, successfully exploited Voodoo for political purposes (Rotberg, 1976). Nevertheless, most observers agree that the cult has been weakened in recent years. An important factor in its decline has been the decay of the large extended family in the rural areas. Many of the large cult centers have split up into minor sects under priests whose training has been inadequate.

CUBAN SANTERÍA. Most of the non-European elements in the Afro-Cuban syncretic religion known as Santería are derived from Yoruba beliefs and rituals. Animals are sacrificed to Yoruba deities, Yoruba music is played on African-type drums, songs with Yoruba words and music are sung, and dancers are possessed by the *orisha* (Yor., *orisa,* "spirit"). Yoruba foods are cooked for the gods and for devotees, beads of the proper color are worn, and leaves with Yoruba names are used in preparing medicines and in washing the stones of the *orisha* and the heads of cult members. In Santería, Elegba (Yor., Esu or Elegba) is identified with Saint Peter, and Shango (Yor., Sango), god of thunder, is identified with Saint Barbara. Shakpana (also Babaluaiye; Yor., Sopona) is equated with Saint Lazarus. Oya (Yor., Oya), one of Shango's wives, is the equivalent of Saint Teresita. Obatala (Yor., Obatala) is Our Lady of Mercy, and Yemaja (Yor., Yemoja) is identified with the Virgin of Regla (a suburb of Havana).

Reincarnation implies that the returning ancestor is recognized and present in the memory of the living, and it can only occur in a child of the same lineage and sex.

PAGE 315

During a Santería ceremony, the blood of animals sacrificed to the gods is allowed to flow onto the sacred stones of the *santero* (Santería priest). The blood is the food of the deities, and the stones are the objects through which they are fed and in which their power resides (Bascom, 1950). The *lucumis* (Afro-Cubans of Yoruba extraction) honor each of the gods with choral dances and pantomime in accordance with authentic Yoruba tradition (see Ortiz, 1951, for a detailed and vivid account of *lucumi* dances; and Simpson, 1978).

THE SHANGO CULT IN TRINIDAD. In southwestern Nigeria, each Yoruba deity, including Sango, god of thunder and lightning, has his or her own priests, followers, and cult centers. In the Shango cult in Trinidad, Shango is only one of several dozen "powers," which include twenty or more Yoruba deities (Lewis, 1978). Several non-Yoruba powers—especially Gabriel and Mama Latay—are popular in Trinidad. Ancient African gods are identified with certain Catholic saints. Each god has his or her favorite colors, foods, and drinks; each is thought to have certain physical traits and to possess certain powers. In Shango, as in Voodoo and Santería, participants can recognize the major spirits who are well known throughout the country, or the principal spirits known in a given locality, by the stylized behavior of devotees possessed by them (Bourguignon, 1980).

Each Shango cult center holds an annual ceremony in honor of the *orisha* known to its worshipers. The four-day ritual begins with the recitation of original prayers, followed by several repetitions of the Lord's Prayer, Hail Mary, and the Apostle's Creed. The leader then recites in succession prayers such as Saint Francis's prayer, Saint George's prayer, and Blessed Martin's prayer; he recites each prayer line-by-line, and the worshipers repeat each line after him. Next, in an act of dismissal, food for the deity Eshu is placed outside the ceremonial area. Drumming, dancing, singing, and spirit possession continue through the night; the climax comes at dawn with the sacrificing of pigeons, doves, chickens, agoutis, land turtles, goats, and sheep. Similar rites are performed on the following three nights, and often a bull is sacrificed. Aspects of Trinidadian cult life that are closely related to African religious behavior include divination, conjuring, and folk medicine, which are often strikingly similar to West African procedures (Simpson, 1978).

ANCESTRAL CULTS. This type of hybrid religious cult has fewer African and more European components than does the neo-African-type religion.

Kumina. According to Monica Schuler (1980), Kumina was brought to Jamaica by post-emancipation immigrants from central Africa who chiefly settled in the eastern parish of Saint Thomas. Kumina is primarily a family religion, and each group honors a number of family spirits in addition to other divinities. The three ranks of Kumina spirits (known as zombies) are the sky gods, the earthbound gods, and ancestral zombies. Most Kumina dances are memorial services held to pay respects to the dead ancestors of the participants, but ceremonies are performed on other occasions, such as betrothal, marriage, burial, the naming of a baby, the anniversary of emancipation, and Independence Day (Moore, 1953; Schuler, 1980).

Convince. The Convince ritual practiced in the Jamaican parishes of Saint Thomas and Portland has a number of Christian elements, but its principal powers are the spirits of persons who belonged to the cult during their lifetime. The most powerful *bongo* ghosts come from Africa, but the spirits of ancient Jamaican slaves and the Maroons (descendants of runaway slaves), who perpetuated the cult until recent times, are also of importance

Each *bongo* man holds a sacrificial ceremony annually and conducts Convince rites as the need for them arises. Christian prayers, the reading of Bible passages, and hymn singing precede the main ceremony. Special *bongo* songs, hand clapping, and dances performed by *bongo* men call the spirits to the ceremony. Later, the spirits of the ancestors (that is, devotees possessed by the ghosts) dance.

The Kele cult in Saint Lucia. The Kele ceremony in Saint Lucia resembles, in attenuated form, the

Shango ritual in Trinidad. The ritual is performed to ask the ancestors of devotees for health, protection against misfortune in agriculture, and success in important undertakings, as well as to thank the forebears for past favors. The paraphernalia essential for the Kele rite consists mainly of Amerindian polished stone axes (which are called *pièrres tonnerres,* "thunderstones," by devotees, who believe them to have fallen from the sky), drums, and agricultural implements such as machetes, axes, hoes, and forks. Several of the stone axes are placed on the ground to form a cross, with additional axes arranged around the central grouping (Simpson, 1973; Simmons, 1963). A ram is then sacrificed to the ancestors.

Ancestral cult of the Black Carib of Belize. The Black Carib of Belize are descendants of African slaves who escaped from other parts of the West Indies and settled first among the Island Carib in Saint Vincent. At the end of the eighteenth century, they were deported by the English to Roatan, near Honduras, then they spread out along the coast of the mainland. The Black Carib of Belize speak a South American Indian language.

The supernatural beliefs, rites, and practices of the Black Carib are a mixture of African and non-African elements. Singing, drumming, and dancing are intended to placate the ancestors of the family giving the ceremony, and some participants become possessed by the spirits of their deceased ancestors.

REVIVALIST CULTS. This type of cult descends from the Afro-Protestant cults of the late eighteenth century and, in the case of Jamaica, from the Great Revival of 1861-1862.

Revival Zion. A religious movement known as Myalism emerged in the 1760s to protect slaves against European sorcery. This "native" Baptist movement was without serious competition during the forty-year period (1780-1820) when a reinterpretation of Christianity spread across Jamaica. Eventually, a hybrid religion of the Myalists, or Black Baptists, resurfaced. And its vitality has been seen in the multiplication and flourishing of black revivalist cults (Curtin, 1955; Schuler, 1979).

The Holy Spirit possesses followers during revivalist ceremonies, as do the spirits of Old Testament figures such as Jeremiah, Isaiah, Joshua, Moses, Shadrach,

RASTAFARIANISM

Uniting for Racial Redemption

An important factor underlying the rise of Rastafarianism is that, since at least the beginning of the twentieth century, Jamaican blacks have identified with Ethiopia on account of its biblical symbolism. The early 1930s saw the founding of a number of associations for black people and the emergence of the Rastafarian movement, named after Ras ("prince") Tafari, who was crowned emperor Haile Selassie of Ethiopia (Abyssinia). Marcus Garvey had formed the Universal Negro Improvement Association in Jamaica in 1914, and his doctrine of racial redemption, together with the coronation of Haile Selassie, furthered interest in the Ethiopian tradition (Hill, 1980).

Since emancipation, persons on the lower rungs of Jamaican society have struggled continuously against exploitation. In the early 1930s, the basic issues for rural Jamaicans were land, rent, and taxation, and their struggles over these questions gave rise to the millenarian visions of the Rastafarian movement, in the face of prejudices.

According to Rastafarian doctrines in 1953, (1) black people were exiled to the West Indies because of their transgressions; (2) the white man is inferior to the black man; (3) the Jamaican situation is hopeless; (4) Ethiopia is heaven; (5) Haile Selassie is the living God; (6) the emperor of Abyssinia will arrange for expatriated persons of African descent to return to the homeland; and (7) black men will soon get their revenge by compelling white men to serve them (Simpson, 1955). These remain the basic beliefs of the movement, but not all adherents subscribe to all of them, nor do they give them equal emphasis. Rastafarians reinterpret the Old Testament in claiming that they are true present-day prophets, the "reincarnated Moseses, Joshuas, Isaiahs, and Jeremiahs." They also believe that they are "destined to free the scattered Ethiopians who are black men" (Nettleford, 1970, pp. 108-109).

Between 1953 and 1960, the Rastafarian movement grew rapidly and became more complex doctrinally. This growth continued through the 1970s and the early 1980s. Membership came to be drawn from all levels of the society. The militancy of present-day Rastafarianism is seen clearly in its concept of a modern Babylon that includes Britain, the former colonial power; the United States, the present major industrial power; the bourgeois state of Jamaica; and the church. Babylon is said to be the source of Jamaica's misfortunes (Chevannes, 1977). A recent theme of the movement has to do with its concept of nature. In Rastafarian thought nature is nonindustrial society; and this underlies certain aspects of Rastafarian lifestyle—for example, dietary rules, uncombed locks and beards, and the importance of ganja (Chevannes, 1977).

— GEORGE EATON SIMPSON

Meshach, and Abednego; New Testament apostles and evangelists such as Matthew, Mark, Luke, John, Peter, and James; the archangels Michael, Gabriel, and Raphael; Satan and his chief assistant, Rutibel; beings from Hebrew magical tradition, such as Uriel, Ariel, Seraph, Nathaniel, and Tharsis; Constantine, Melshezdek, and the Royal Angel; and the dead, especially prominent revivalist leaders of the past (Moore and Simpson, 1957; Simpson, 1978).

Weekly services include "spiritual" dancing, stamping feet, hyperventilating, and groaning rhythmically.

Spiritual Baptists (Shouters) of Trinidad. In many ways, the Spiritual Baptist cult (Shouters) in Trinidad is similar to Revival Zion in Jamaica, but there are several noteworthy differences. Among the Shouters, no drums or rattles accompany hymn singing. Spiritual Baptists do not become possessed by the wide variety of spirits that possess Revivalists in Jamaica; as a rule, devotees are possessed only by the Holy Spirit. Certain groups among the Shouters do, however, make ritual offerings to the spirits "of the sea, the land, and the river," and occasionally a Shango "power" may enter a person who is taking part in a ritual.

The nickname Shaking Quaker, or Shaker, was applied to the movement because of its unstructured and highly emotional services, during which members sang, shouted, danced, spoke in tongues, and literally shook with emotion.

PAGE 595

Spiritual Baptists are often men and women of the lower classes, most of African descent.

The Shakers of Saint Vincent. English rule of the island of Saint Vincent began in 1783, and the first direct religious influence intended for the slave population was brought to the island by a Methodist missionary in 1787. The Shaker cult, which goes back to at least the early part of the twentieth century, has a Methodist base, with an admixture of elements of other Christian denominational traditions. An important feature of this religion is the mild state of dissociation, attributed to possession by the Holy Ghost, that some of its adherents experience.

CELTIC RELIGION

By about 500 BCE the Celts were already widely dispersed over central and western Europe, including perhaps Gaul and the Iberian Peninsula, and evidence from the fifth century testifies to further territorial expansion. About 400 BCE this process quickened as tribal bands invaded northern Italy and there established settlements which in due course were to become the Roman province of Gallia Cisalpina. Some Celtic bands raided farther south, as far as Rome and Apulia and even Sicily, and about 387 they captured and sacked the city of Rome. To the east, other Celtic tribes penetrated into the Carpathians and the Balkans during the fourth century BCE. In 279 some of them entered Greece and plundered the shrine at Delphi, and in the following year three Celtic tribes, known collectively to the Greeks as Galatae, crossed into Asia Minor and eventually settled in the region which still bears the name Galatia.

MANUSCRIPTS. Written literature in Irish dates from the second half of the sixth century CE, when monastic scholars adapted the Latin alphabet, and it gradually increases in volume during the following centuries. In addition to a good deal of typically monastic learning, both religious and secular, the literature comprises a vast amount of varied material recorded or adapted from oral tradition. However, only fragments of this literature survive in contemporary manuscripts, mostly in the form of annals or of notes and glosses accompanying Latin texts; all the vernacular manuscripts written before the end of the eleventh century have perished. Then, around 1100, came *Lebhor na hUidhre* (The Book of the Dun Cow), probably written in the monastery of Clonmacnois and the first of a series of great vellum manuscript compilations which are part of a conscious endeavor, in the face of ominous political and social change, to conserve the monuments of native tradition. It was followed around 1130 by an untitled collection now at the Bodleian Library, Oxford (MS Rawlinson B 502), and around 1150-1200 by *Lebhor na Nuachongbhála* (The Book of Leinster). Over the next couple of centuries appeared a number of major manuscripts of which the most important are the Great Book of Lecan, the Yellow Book of Lecan, the Book of Ballymote, the Book of Lismore, and the Book of Fermoy. These are capacious *bibliothecae* which embrace all the various genres of traditional literature: hero and king tales, mythological tales, origin legends, genealogies, and so on. It is important to remember that, though the surviving manuscripts date from a relatively late period, the matter they contain has generally been copied more or less faithfully from earlier manuscripts. Thus the texts are often demonstrably centuries older than the manuscripts.

As well as these manuscript collections there are several specialized compilations, including *Leabhar Ga-bhála Éireann* (The Book of the Taking of Ireland), commonly known as the *Book of Invasions*, an amalgam of myth and pseudohistory which purports to recount the coming of the Gaels to Ireland and the several immigrations which preceded it; the *Cóir Anmann* (Fitness of Names), a catalog of names of "historical" personages with many imaginative etymologies and references to traditional legends; and the *Dinnshenchas* (Lore of Famous Places), which does in a much fuller and more elaborate fashion for place-names what the *Cóir Anmann* seeks to do for personal names.

Evidence indicates that the early oral literature of Wales was comparable in volume and variety with that of Ireland. Unfortunately, because of a weaker scribal tradition, the Welsh literature is poorly documented for the pre-Norman period.. However, from the ninth or tenth century onward the Taliesin became the focus of poems and stories (extant only in much later versions) which represent him as a wonder child, seer, and prophet; some of these motifs clearly derive from native mythological tradition. Another important source is the *Trioedd Ynys Prydein* (Triads of the Island of Britain), which contains numerous references to mythological as well as historical characters and events; it may have been compiled in the twelfth century.

ARTIFACTS. The plastic art of the Celto-Roman period is so evidently based on that of Rome that it might appear at first glance to have been borrowed whole and unchanged, but on closer scrutiny it reveals many elements which derive from the Celtic rather than from the Roman tradition. There are forms quite foreign to classical art, such as the tricephalous god, the god with stag's antlers, and the god depicted in the Buddha-like cross-legged position. Animal horns are commonly regarded as signs of fertility, and the antlers which the Celtic deity wears on the Gundestrup Caldron and elsewhere are taken to symbolize his power and fecundity. Another frequent emblem of divinity is the ornamented torque, which, according to Pierre Lambrechts, denotes the "powerful god who affords protection against maleficent spirits."

Probably the most important element in the religious symbolism of the Celts is the number three; the mystic significance of the concept of threeness is attested in most parts of the world, but among the Celts there seems to have been a particularly strong and continuous awareness of it. There are three-headed deities (and even a triphallic Mercury) and triads of mother goddesses; the latter has an endless variety of ternary groups in which the triad is an expressive restatement of an underlying unity: goddesses like the three Brighids and inseparable brothers like the three companions of the tragic heroine Deirdre.

CONTINENTAL DEITIES AND INSULAR EQUIVALENTS. Given that the bulk of the relevant evidence belongs to the Roman period, it follows that our view of Gaulish religion is for the most part through Roman eyes, which means that it is perceived and presented in terms of Roman religion.

In Gallo-Roman dedications, deities may be assigned a Roman name, a native Gaulish name, or a Roman name accompanied by a native epithet. In the last two cases we clearly have to do with indigenous gods, and even with the first group this may be so. For example, the numerous statues and reliefs of Mercury in the guise of the Greco-Roman god might have been intended to honor that god, but equally they might have been intended to honor a native god by borrowing the classical form together with the classical name. A large proportion of the Gaulish forms attested in dedications are mere epithets or bynames, and even of those which may be taken to be proper names it would be quite erroneous to suppose that each indicates a separate deity.

Although the functional roles of the several deities are not clearly defined and delimited and frequently overlap with one another, this does not imply that they may be reduced to a single, all-purpose divine overlord.

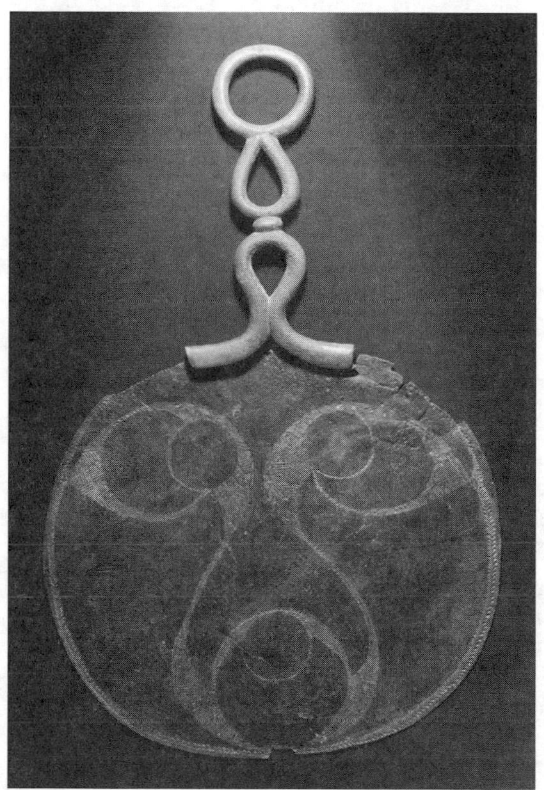

CELTIC CARVING

The number three is one of the most important Celtic symbols and it occurs frequently in Celto-Roman iconography.

It has often been remarked that in polytheistic systems each god tends to move beyond his normal functional field toward a kind of universalism. Yet, despite this tendency toward the assimilation of roles, the insular Celtic gods are far removed from functional indifferentism, and there are some, like Goibhniu, the smith, and Dian Cécht, the leech, whose central responsibilities are defined very precisely.

Mercury or Lugh. Caesar's observation that "Mercury" was the deity with the greatest number of images in Gaul is confirmed by the surviving evidence of inscriptions, stone statues and reliefs, bronze statuettes, and terracotta figures. His image often appears in the mode of the classical Mercury: youthful, naked, and beardless; equipped with caduceus, petasos, and purse; and accompanied by cock, ram, or tortoise. But his image is also found in Gallo-Roman guise: mature, bearded, and dressed in a heavy cloak. Sometimes, as in the east and the north of Gaul, he is tricephalous.

"The immortal Gods alone have neither age nor death."

SOPHOCLES
OEDIPUS AT COLONUS

C

CELTIC RELIGION

Continental Deities and Insular Equivalents

Unlike his Roman counterpart, he has a frequent consort named Maia or Rosmerta, the Provider, and includes the art of war in his range of competence.

One cannot assume that Caesar's "Mercury" coincides with a single native deity throughout the Celtic areas, but there is cogent evidence for identifying him substantially with the Irish god Lugh. In Ireland Lugh was the youthful victor over malevolent demonic figures, and his great achievement was to kill the cyclopean Balar with a slingshot. Lughnasadh, his feast, was a harvest festival, and at least two of its principal sites, Carmun and Tailtiu, were the burial places of eponymous goddesses associated with the fertility of the earth (as was, apparently, the Gaulish Mercury's consort Rosmerta). Lugh was the divine exemplar of sacred kingship, and in the tale *Baile in Scáil* (The God's Prophecy) he appears seated in state as king of the otherworld and attended by a woman identified as the sovereign of Ireland, reminiscent of Rosmerta. His usual epithet, *lámhfhada* ("of the long arm"), relates to his divine kingship. In the Christian period Lugh survived in the guise of several saints known by variants of his name—Lughaidh, Molua, and others—and the motif of the arm is reflected in these Christian traditions as well.

Gaulish Apollo. The classical form of Apollo in Romano-Celtic monuments only partly conceals the several native deities who have been assimilated to him. The use of the plural is probably justifiable, since several of the fifteen or more epithets attached to Apollo's name have a wide distribution, which suggests that they were independent gods. Yet some of these epithets may have referred to a single deity. Belenus was especially honored in the old Celtic kingdom of Noricum in the eastern Alps, as well as in northern Italy, southern Gaul, and Britain. He is sometimes accompanied by a goddess named Sirona. Borvo or Bormo, whose name denotes boiling or seething water, is associated with thermal springs, as at Bourbonne-

DRUIDS

The King Rendered Justice but the Druid Made the Law

In his brief description of Gaulish society of the first century BCE, Caesar divides his text into three unequal parts dedicated to the druids, the knights, or equites, and the plebs (Gallic Wars 6.13). His account of the druids is concise and clear:

> In all of Gaul there are two classes of men who count and are honored. Of these two classes, one is the druids and the other the knights. The former watch over divine matters, administer public and private sacrifices, and rule all matters of religion. It is they, in fact, who settle disputes, both public and private, and if any crime has been committed, if there has been a murder, or if any dispute arises in regard to an inheritance or boundaries, it is they who decide and assess the damages and fines; if some person or persons do not agree with their decision, that person or those persons are forbidden to participate in the sacrifices. A single leader commands all these druids, and he exercises supreme authority over them. Upon his death, he is succeeded by the preeminent druid; if there are several of equal status, they decide the title by a vote of the druids and sometimes by force of arms. At a certain time of the year, they assemble in a sacred place in the land of the Carnutes, which is thought to be the center of Gaul. To that place come all those with disputes, and they submit to the druids' judgments and decisions. Their doctrine was developed in Britain, and from there, it is thought, it came to Gaul; even today, most of those who wish to learn more about this doctrine go there to learn it. Above all they try to instill the conviction that souls do not perish, but pass after death from one body to another; this strikes them as being a particularly suitable way to inspire courage by suppressing the fear of death.

Holders of Spiritual Authority. As the holder of spiritual authority, the druid took precedence over temporal power, represented by the king, with whom he formed a couple; the druid was the intermediary between the gods and the king, and the king played the same role between the druid and society. Thus, it was the king who rendered justice, but the druid who made law. The druid was not bound by any obligation, either fiscal or military, but he had the right to bear arms and to make war whenever he wished. The warrior druid is a common personage in Irish epic. Again it was the druid who pronounced the geasa ("injunctions, interdicts") that bound all individuals—especially the king—to a closed network of interdicts and obligations of all kinds. One of the most famous interdicts of Ulster was that the Ulates were not to speak before the king and that the king was not to speak before the druid. But the druid—who never courted royalty, save for aberrant and extremely rare cases—was in the service of the king, to whom he owed counsel, information, or prediction that would allow the king to rule his kingdom well.

The alliance between the king and the druid explains why the druid disappeared in Gaul after the Roman conquest: the Gauls' adoption of the Roman political system based on the municipium removed the druid's entire raison d'être, and it is likely that druidism, despite its initial vitality, declined slowly and became almost clandestine.

— FRANCOISE LE ROUX AND CHRISTIAN J. GUYONVARC'H
TRANSLATED FROM FRENCH BY ERICA MELTZER

les-Bains and other sites named after him. His consort is Damona ("divine cow") or Bormana.

His Irish equivalent was Mac ind Óg ("young lad or son"), otherwise known as Oenghus, who was believed to dwell in Bruigh na Bóinne, the great Neolithic, and therefore pre-Celtic, passage grave of Newgrange. He was the son of Daghdha, chief god of the Irish, and of Boann, eponym of the sacred river of Irish tradition. As his name and relationship suggest, he is a youthful god, and, perhaps in keeping with this, he is often treated with a certain affection in the literature, particularly in his familiar roles of trickster and lover.

Gaulish Minerva or Irish Brighid. The goddesses of insular Celtic tradition are involved in a wide range of activities, only one of which Caesar ascribes to "Minerva," namely arts and crafts. Dedications to Minerva are found throughout the Celtic areas of the continent and in Britain. At Bath she was identified with the goddess Sulis, who was worshiped there in connection with the thermal springs.

The nearest equivalent to Minerva in insular tradition is the goddess known in Ireland as Brighid, daughter of the father god, Daghdha. Like Minerva she was concerned with healing and craftsmanship, particularly metalwork, but she was also patron of *filidhecht,* that is, poetry and traditional learning in general. A remarkable continuity stretches from the pagan goddess to her Christian namesake of the early sixth century, the saint Brighid of Kildare, whose monastery of Cell Dara, the "church of the [sacred] oak," was doubtless on the site of a pagan sanctuary.

Celtic Vulcan. Since he functioned as a very specialized deity, there is a strong probability that his native name among the continental Celts made reference to his craft, as it did in Ireland and Wales, where he was known as Goibhniu and Gofannon, both names derived from the word for "smith." He was known for his healing powers and is invoked in an Old Irish charm for the removal of a thorn. Until the nineteenth century, and in some areas even into the twentieth century, the country smith was still believed to retain something of his ancient preternatural faculty, and he was constantly called on for the healing effects of his charms and spells.

Gaulish Hercules or Irish Oghma. Hercules is well represented in Celto-Roman iconography and has a number of regional epithets assigned to him. Doubtless his popularity derives largely from his identification with native Celtic gods who correspond approximately to his classical character. One of these is mentioned in a curious passage by the Greek writer Lucian in the second century CE describing a Gaulish picture of Hercules "whom the Celts call Ogmios." It showed him armed with his familiar club and bow but pictured him uncharacteristically as an old man, bald and gray, with his skin darkened and wrinkled by the sun. He pulled behind him a willing band of men attached by slender chains which linked their ears to the tip of his tongue.

Gaulish Dis Pater or Irish Donn. All the Gauls believed with their druids that they were descended from Dis Pater. The reference is brief but is sufficient to indicate at least an analogy between the Gaulish god of the dead and his Irish counterpart Donn ("brown or dark one"), whose dwelling place was a small rocky island off the southwest coast of Ireland known as Tech nDuinn ("house of Donn"). Its English name, the Bull, echoes its other name in early Irish, Inis Tarbhnai ("island of Tarbnae"). *Tarbhnae* derives from *tarbh* ("bull"), and thus there are strong grounds for identifying the god Donn with the great bull of Cuailnge which provides the central motivation for the saga *Táin Bó Cuailnge* and which is also called Donn.

Nature associations. Underlying the tradition of *dinnshenchas* is the belief that prominent places and geological features throughout Ireland were the scene of mythic events or the abode, or even the embodiment, of mythic personages. Many of the numerous women who populate this world of onomastic legend are clear reflexes of the multifaceted goddess whose origins are bound up with the physical landscape—figures like Tailtiu and Carmun, whose burial places, named after them, were the sites of great royal assemblies.

Apart from the general cult of the earth goddess there exists an extensive repertory of deity names attached to individual places or topographical features. There was a god of the clearing or cultivated field (Ialonus), of the rock (Alisanos), of the confluence (Condatis), of the ford (Ritena), and of the fortified place (Dunatis). Water, particularly the moving water of rivers and springs, had its special deities, generally female in the case of the rivers. One can perhaps glimpse the lost mythology of such rivers as the Seine (Sequana), the Marne (Matrona), and the Saône (Souconna) through the legends of insular equivalents like the Boyne (Boann). The names of many rivers throughout the Celtic lands, for example, the French Dives or the Welsh Dyfrdwy, are derived from the stem *dev-* and mean simply "the divine one." Sacred springs are deified, as for example Aventia (Avenches), Vesunna (Périgeux), and Divona (Cahors).

In many instances the holy wells of the Christian period stand close to a specific tree which shares their supernatural aura. Obviously, this is one aspect of the widespread cult of sacred trees. In the Pyrenees there are dedications to the beech (Deo Fago) and to the Six Trees (Sexarbori deo, Sexarboribus) and at Angoulême to the oak (Deo Robori). The Romano-Celtic name of the town of Embrun, *Eburodunum,* contains the name of the deified yew tree.

Zoomorphic gods. Celto-Roman iconography

A tree symbolizes the cross in many cultures: the oak of the Celts and Gauls, the ash of the Greeks in Hesiod, the cedar of Lebanon.

PAGE 195

contains a rich abundance of animal imagery, frequently presenting the deities in combinations of zoomorphic and anthropomorphic forms. The animal connections of the Celtic gods are extensive and varied. The iconography shows Cernunnos ("the horned one") associated with the stag, the ram-headed serpent, the bull, and, by implication, with the whole animal world. The iconography also includes boars, horses, dogs, and bears, as well as fish and various kinds of birds, all connected more or less closely with certain deities.

The horse, index and instrument of the great Indo-European expansion, has always had a special place in the affections of the Celtic peoples. Sometimes in insular tradition, particularly in folk tales, he is the bearer of the dead to the otherworld, a role probably reflected in some monuments in southern Gaul, such as the frieze of horses' heads on a lintel from the Celto-Ligurian sanctuary of Roquepertuse, Bouches-du-Rhône. Epona (from **epos,* "horse") was an important Celtic deity and was particularly favored as patron of the cavalry of the Roman army. She has insular analogues in the Welsh Rhiannon and in the Irish Édaín Echraidhe (echraidhe, "horse riding") and Macha, who outran the fastest steeds. There was also a Dea Artio (as well as a Mercurius Artaios), whose name connects her with the bear (Ir., *art,* "bear"); a little bronze group from Bern shows her seated before a large bear with a basket of fruit by her side. Dea Arduinna, who appears seated on a wild boar, may be compared with the Irish goddess Flidhais, who ruled over the beasts of the forest and whose cattle were the wild deer.

A firm belief in an afterlife is attested by the funerary practices of the Celts.

PAGE 318

CELTIC CARVING

Celtic deities are often portrayed in zoomorphic and anthropomorphic forms which can shift shape and appearance.

ROBERT ESTALL/CORBIS

GODS OF BRITAIN. Early Welsh literary tradition, like the medieval Welsh language, seems further evolved from its archaic roots than its Irish counterpart. This is probably due partly to the cultural effects of the Roman colonization of Britain from the first to the fifth century and partly to the late redaction of the extant material, particularly the prose. But whatever the causes, the result is that Welsh mythological narrative, while preserving some remarkably archaic elements, nevertheless lacks the extensive context found in Irish narrative.

Family of Dôn. The main source for Welsh mythological tradition is the collection of tales known as the *Mabinogi* or *Mabinogion,* especially the group known as the Four Branches. These four tales, which were probably redacted toward the end of the eleventh century, take the gods of Britain as their *dramatis personae.* The last of the four, *Math Son of Mathonwy,* deals in particular with the group of gods sometimes referred to as the family of Dôn. The Math of the title is lord of Gwynedd in north Wales. His peculiarity is that he must keep his feet in a virgin's lap except in time of war. When his virginal footholder is violated by his sister's son, Gilfaethwy son of Dôn, with the connivance of his brother Gwydion son of Dôn, Math turns the two brothers into male and female animals—stags, boars, and wolves—for three years, during which time they give birth to three sons.

Subsequently, Math seeks a new footholder, and Gwydion suggests his sister, Aranrhod daughter of Dôn. Math asks her to step over his magic wand as a test of her virginity, and as she does so, she drops a yellow-haired boy and something else which Gwydion promptly conceals in a chest. The boy is baptized Dylan and immediately makes for the sea and takes on its nature, for which reason he is henceforth called Dylan Eil Don ("Dylan son of wave"). The object concealed by Gwydion turns out to be another male child, who in due course is given the name Lleu Llaw Gyffes ("Lleu of the skillful hand"). The rest of the tale is taken up with Lleu's relations with his mother, Aranrhod, and with his beautiful but treacherous wife, Blodeuwedd ("flower-aspect"), who had been created for him by Gwydion from the flowers of the oak, the broom, and the meadowsweet.

Family of Llyr. The three members of the family of Llyr—Branwen, Bendigeidvran ("Brân the blessed"), and Manawydan—appear in the Second Branch of the Mabinogi, though it is only in the Third Branch that Manawydan assumes an independent role. The tale is dominated by the enormous figure of Bendigeidvran. When his sister Branwen is ill treated in Ireland, where she has gone as the wife of Matholwch, king of Ireland, he goes with an army to exact vengeance. The British gain victory in a fierce battle with the Irish, but only seven of them survive beside Bendigeidvran, who is wounded in the foot by a poisonous spear. He commands his companions to cut off his head and to bury it at the White Mount in London as a safeguard against invasions. They set out for London and on the way enjoy two periods of otherworldly peace and joy in the presence of his uncorrupted head, at Harlech and on the isle of Gwales.

Pwyll, Rhiannon, and Pryderi. In the First Branch of the *Mabinogi,* Pwyll, lord of Dyfed in southwest Wales, comes to the aid of Arawn, king of Annwn, by slaying his otherworld enemy Hafgan in a single combat which is in fact an ordeal by battle of the kind known in early Irish as *fír fer* ("truth of men or heroes"). As a result he is henceforth known as Pwyll the Head of Annwn. The *Mabinogi* represents him here as a mortal, but since his name literally means "wisdom" and since he is designated lord of Annwn, the otherworld, it is probable that he was originally a deity. The latter part of the tale is concerned with the death of the hero Pryderi. Pwyll marries the lady Rhiannon, who first appears to him riding a white horse, and from their union Pryderi is born. But the newborn child is mysteriously abducted, to be discovered later by Teyrnon, lord of Gwent Is-coed, and reared by him and his wife for several years until they realize the child's true origins and restore him to Pwyll and Rhiannon. After Pwyll's death Pryderi succeeds to the lordship of Dyfed. Later, in the Third Branch, Rhiannon becomes the wife of Manawydan.

KINGS AND HEROES. Virtually all early Irish narrative literature is to some degree heroic, but there are differences of emphasis that distinguish the king tales from the more specifically heroic narratives. Though the king tales involve heroic values, these are not their main preoccupation. Rather, they are concerned with the affirmation of political and social realities: the status and functions of the king, the ritual of inauguration and relations with the goddess of sovereignty, the origins of tribes and dynasties, battles of historical moment, the deeds and judgments of famous rulers, and so on. The sacral kingship was both the pivot and the foundation of the social order, and the king was its personification; if his conduct or even his person were blemished in any way, this blemish would be visited on his kingdom, diminishing its integrity and prosperity. As the instrument of justice, the king must be fair and flawless in his decisions. Thus the great Cormac mac Airt is pictured as a paragon of kingship and

GODDESSES OF THE INSULAR CELTS
Sex for Fertility's Sake

GODDESSES OF THE INSULAR CELTS. J. M. Synge in his *The Aran Islands* (1907) says of the Aran Islanders of the beginning of the twentieth century that they were interested in fertility rather than eroticism, and on the evidence of the extant monuments and literature, his observation could apply to those people who created the mythology of the Celtic goddesses. The Celts had no goddess of love, and so far as one can judge from insular tradition, the numerous sexual liaisons of the goddesses generally were motivated by ritual or social causes, not by erotic ones. Their sexuality was merely the instrument of their fertility, whether in terms of progeny or of the fruitfulness of the land with which they were so often identified.

As leader of the Connacht armies Medhbh is associated with war as well as with sovereignty, but in general the warlike aspect of the goddess is manifested indirectly: she influences the fortunes of war rather than actually participating. Other goddesses teach the art of fighting; examples include Buanann ("the lasting one"); Scáthach ("the shadowy one"), from whom Cú Chulainn acquired his heroic skills; and the formidable trio of Morríghan ("phantom queen"), Bodhbh ("scald-crow"), and Nemhain ("frenzy") or Macha, who haunt the battlefield to incite the fighters or to hinder them by their magic. These had their equivalents throughout the Celtic world: the name *Bodhbh Chatha* ("crow/raven of battle") is the exact cognate of *Cathubodua*, attested in Haute Savoie, and the trio of war goddesses recurs in Britain in the Benwell inscription "Lamiis tribus" ("to the three Lamiae").

In direct contrast to these ruthless furies are those charming women who inhabit the happy otherworld in such numbers that it came to be called Tír inna mBan, "the land of women." Sometimes they come as emissaries from the land of primeval innocence where the pleasures of love are untainted by guilt and where sickness and disease are unknown. Conla son of Conn is induced to go there by "a young and beautiful woman of noble race whom neither death awaits nor old age," and Bran son of Febhal is similarly persuaded by a woman bearing a silvery branch from the wondrous apple tree which is a characteristic feature of the Celtic otherworld. But the multiforms of the insular Celtic goddesses are endless, and sometimes the named figure changes her role from one context to another.

— PROINSIAS MAC CANA

Since Chou times the idea of the soul as the pale, ghostly shadow of a man has been a perduring notion found in popular stories.

PAGE 31

as an Irish Solomon: his accession came about when he proposed a just judgment after his predecessor Lughaidh mac Con had been deposed for delivering an unjust one. Conaire Mór is likewise an exemplary king whose reign brings peace and well-being to the land until he tempers justice with excessive mercy in the case of his three marauding foster brothers. Immediately a train of events is set in motion which leads inexorably to his death in a welter of violence.

Every kingdom, however small, had its sacred king and its inauguration site, but the focus of sacral kingship was at Tara, the goal of ambitious kings throughout the early Middle Ages. Situated in the central province, Midhe (lit., "middle"), and surrounded by the other four provinces, Tara is itself the heart of the Irish cosmographic system, and the traditional accounts of the disposition of the court of Tara show that it was conceived as a microcosmic replica of this cosmographic schema. Feis Temhra ("the feast of Tara") was the great festival held in pagan times to confirm a new king and to celebrate his ritual marriage to his kingdom. At Tara stood the Lia Fáil ("stone of Fál"), the "stone penis" which cried out when it came in contact with the man destined to be king.

— PROINSIAS MAC CANA

CHINESE RELIGION

EARLY HISTORICAL PERIOD

THE SHANG DYNASTY. The formation of the Shang kingdom was due to technological innovation such as bronze casting, and to the development of new forms of social and administrative control. Extant evidence provides information about the religion of the Shang aristocracy, characterized by elaborate graves and ceremonial objects for the dead.

From inscriptions on oracle bones and in bronze sacrificial vessels, we learn that the most common objects of petition and inquiry were the ancestors of aristocratic clans. These deified ancestors were believed to have powers of healing and fertility in their own right, but also could serve as intermediaries between their living descendants and more powerful gods of natural forces and Shang-ti. Ancestors were ranked by title and seniority.

To contact these sacred powers the Shang practiced divination and sacrificial rituals. The subjects of divination include weather, warfare, illness, administrative decisions, harvests, and other practical issues. Sacrificial animals included cattle, dogs, sheep, and human beings.

There is an emphasis on precision in sacrifice; the correct objects offered in the right way were believed to obligate the spirits to respond. Thus, in Shang sacrifice we already see the principle of reciprocity, which has remained a fundamental patten of interaction throughout the history of Chinese religions.

THE CHOU DYNASTY. The Chou, who were considered to be an important tributary state, were at first culturally and technologically inferior to the Shang, but learned rapidly and by the eleventh century BCE challenged the Shang for political supremacy. The final Chou conquest took place in about 1050 BCE. Remnants of the Shang royal line were allowed to continue their ancestral practices in the small state of Sung.

The religious activities of the early Chou aristocracy were focused on their ancestors, who were believed to reside in a celestial court presided over by T'ien, "Heaven," the Chou high god. These ancestors had power to influence the prosperity of their descendants, their fertility, health, and longevity. In addition, royal ancestors served as intermediaries between their descendants and T'ien.

Ancestral rituals took the form of great feasts in which the deceased was represented by an impersonator, usually a grandson or nephew. In these feasts the sharing of food and drink confirmed vows of mutual fidelity and aid. The most important ancestor worshiped was Hou Chi, who was both legendary founder of the ruling house and the patron of agriculture. As was true for the Shang, Chou rituals were also directed toward symbols of natural power such as mountains and rivers; most significant natural phenomena were deified and reverenced.

Chou-dynasty diviners eventually produced a text to support and codify their work, the *I ching* (Classic of Change), which classifies human situations by means of sixty-four sets of six horizontal lines (hexagrams), broken and unbroken. The broken line sets represent *k'un,* the female force that completes, while those with solid lines represent *ch'ien,* the male force that initiates. The *I ching* is essentially a book of wisdom for personal and administrative guidance, used since at least the seventh century BCE. However, from the sixth century BCE on commentaries were written to amplify the earliest level of the text and by the first century CE there were ten such levels of exposition, some quite philosophical in tone. The *Classic of Change* was believed to reflect the structure of cosmic movement, and hence became an object of reverent contemplation in itself.

A third focus of Chou worship, in addition to ancestors and nature gods, was the *she,* a sacred earth mound located in the capital of each state and in at least some villages. The state *she* represented the sacred powers of the earth available to a particular domain, and so was offered libations upon such important occasions in the life of the state as the birth of a prince, ascension to rule, and military campaigns. Beside the earth mound stood a sacred tree, a symbol of its connection to the powers of the sky.

The early Chou aristocracy carried out sacrificial rituals to mark the seasons of the year and promote the success of farming. These sacrifices, performed in ancestral temples, were offered both to the high god T'ien and to ancestors.

The most distinctive early Chou contribution to the history of Chinese religions was the theory of *t'ien-ming,* the "mandate of Heaven," first employed to justify the Chou conquest of the Shang. According to this theory, Heaven as a high god wills order and peace for human society. This divine order is to be administered by pious kings who care for their subjects on Heaven's behalf. These kings, called *t'ien-tzu,* "son of Heaven," are granted divine authority to rule, but only so long as they rule well. If they become indolent, corrupt, and cruel, the "mandate of Heaven" can be transferred to another line.

The idea of the mandate of Heaven has gripped the Chinese political imagination ever since. It became the basis for the legitimacy of dynasties, the judgment of autocracy, and the moral right of rebellion. This status it owed in part to its support by Confucius and his school, who saw the mandate of Heaven as the foundation of political morality. In sum, early Chou religion was robust and positive in spirit, a spirit that foreshadowed the confident reciprocity of Chinese rituals in later periods, as well as the positive view of human moral potential characteristic of the tradition as a whole.

The early Chou political and social synthesis began to deteriorate in the eighth century as competing local states moved toward political, military, and ritual independence. Rulers from clans lost their power, which reverted to competing local families. This breakdown of hereditary authority led to new social mobility. Changes in religion accompanied those in economy and society. Although many older rituals were continued, they became more elaborate and were focused on the ancestors of the rulers of the states rather than on those of the Chou kings.

Confucius. It was in this context that Chinese philosophy was born, in the teachings of Confucius (c. 551-479 BCE). Confucius (the latinate form of K'ung Fu-tzu, or Master K'ung) was the son of an obscure family in the small state of Lu, a state in which the old Chou cultural traditions were buffeted by repeated invasions and by local power struggles. Confucius's goal was the restoration of the ethical standards, just rule, and legitimate government of the early Chou period as he understood them. To this end he sought public office himself and exhorted the rulers of his day. He also gathered a small group of disciples whom he taught to become *chün-tzu* ("superior men"), men of ethical sensitivity and historical wisdom who could administer benevolent government. In the process he initiated a new level of ethical awareness in Chinese culture and a new form of education, education in what he believed were universal principles for mature humanity and civilization. He assumed that the criteria for holding office were intelligence and high moral principles, not hereditary status, and so further undermined the Chou feudal system that was crumbling around him.

Confucius began a long Chinese tradition of ethical reform in the name of apparently reactionary principles. Statements recorded by his disciples show that in crisis situations the master emphasized that he had a mission from Heaven to restore social harmony. His models for such restoration were the founding kings of the Chou dynasty as described in the ancient *Book of Poetry,* kings who ruled with reverence toward their ancestors and kindness toward their people, ever fearful of losing Heaven's approval. These models had mythic force for Confucius, who saw himself as their embodiment in his own age.

RITUAL VESSEL

This ritual vessel was used by aristocracy from the early Chou dynasty. Sacrificial rituals would mark the seasons of the year and promote the success of farming.

All of Confucius's ethical teachings were intended to describe the "way" *(tao)* of the superior man, a way originating in the will of Heaven for its people. At its best, the inner character of such persons was to be formed by *jen* ("perfect co-humanity"), an ultimately transcendental quality that Confucius believed he had never attained. The actions of an ethically aware person were to be carried out in a balanced way in accord with refined social custom *(li).* Confucius's teachings reveal

Confucius had a clear sense of his mission: he considered himself a transmitter of the wisdom of the ancients (Analects 7.1).

PAGE 177

For Meng-tzu, all people possess innate knowledge of the good and an innate ability to do good. Evil is due merely to circumstance and self-neglect.

PAGE 178

"Hold faithfulness and sincerity as first principles."

CONFUCIUS, THE CONFUCIAN ANALECTS, 1:8, II

a religious consciousness that was restrained, philosophical, and prophetic; it is thus not surprising to learn that he did not participate in the exorcism and divination common in his day, nor speculate on the nature of lesser deities and spirits, although he did support veneration of ancestors.

By the fourth and third centuries BCE the end result of Confucius's gentle skepticism was a psychological interpretation of religion in his own school and the absence of any theological discussion by the formative thinkers of other traditions such as the individualists and the theorists of administrative laws and methods (Legalists).

Mo-tzu. Mo-tzu was a thorough-going utilitarian who taught that the fundamental criterion of value was practical benefit to all. He was from Confucius's home state of Lu, and educated in the emerging Confucian tradition, but turned against what he perceived to be its elitism and wasteful concern with elaborate rituals. In his ethical teaching Mo-tzu reinterpreted along utilitarian lines earlier principles such as righteousness and filial reverence, centered on the theme of universal love without familial and social distinctions. He also attracted a group of disciples whom he sent out to serve in various states in an attempt to implement his teachings.

The most significant aspect of Mo-tzu's thought is his concern to provide theological sanctions for his views. For Mo-tzu, T'ien, or Heaven, is an active creator god whose will or mandate extends to everyone; what Heaven wills is love, prosperity, and peace for all. Heaven is the ultimate ruler of the whole world; T'ien sees all, rewards the good, and punishes the evil. In this task it is aided by a multitude of lesser spirits who are also intelligent and vital and who serve as messengers between T'ien and human beings. Mo-tzu advocates that since this is the nature of divine reality, religious reverence should be encouraged by the state as a sanction for moral order.

Meng-tzu. Meng-tzu (or Meng K'e) was a teacher and would-be administrator from the small state of Tsou who amplified Confucius's teachings and placed them on a much firmer philosophical and literary base. Meng-tzu was concerned to prepare his disciples for enlightened and compassionate public service, beginning with provision for the physical needs of the people. He believed that only when their material livelihood is secure can the people be guided to higher moral awareness. This hope for moral transformation is grounded in Meng-tzu's conviction that human nature is potentially good. What is needed are rulers who nourish this potential as "fathers and mothers of the people." These teachings Meng-tzu expounded courageously before despotic kings whose inclinations were otherwise.

Hsün-tzu. Hsün-tzu (Hsün Ch'ing, d. 215 BCE), was a scholar from the state of Chao who held offices for a time in the larger states of Ch'i and Ch'u. Hsün-tzu's chief contribution was his reinterpretation of *t'ien* as the order of nature, an order that has no consciousness and is not directly related to human concerns. This interpretation is parallel to the views of the *Lao-tzu (Tao-te ching)* and *Chuang-tzu* texts concerning the cosmic "Way" (Tao). Hsün-tzu was concerned to separate the roles of heaven, earth, and man, with human attention directed toward ethics, administration, and culture.

Early Taoist thought. The earliest writings concerned to direct attention toward the mysterious cosmic "Way" that underlies all things are the first seven chapters of the extant *Chuang-tzu,* a text attributed to a philosopher-poet named Chuang Chou of the fourth century BCE. Chuang Chou was convinced that the world in its natural state is peaceful and harmonious, a state exemplified by the growth of plants and the activities of animals. Disorder is due to human aggression and manipulation. The answer to this problem is to understand and affirm the relativity of views, and thus harmonize them all. This the sage does by perceiving the constant rhythms of change within all life and identifying with them. In his view all dichotomies are unified; hence there is no need for struggle and competition. The sage intuits the Tao within and behind all things, and takes its all-embracing perspective as his own.

The other major early book devoted to discussing the Tao behind all things is the early third-century BCE *Tao-te ching* (The Way and Its Inner Power), also known as the *Lao-tzu,* after its eponymous "author," Lao Tan. The *Tao-te ching* discusses the Way in more direct, metaphysical terms than does the *Chuang-tzu,* all the while protesting that such discussion is ultimately futile. Here we are told that the Tao is the source of all things, "the mother of the universe," the ineffable cosmic womb out of which all emerges. The Tao also "works in the world," guiding all things in harmonious development and interaction. As both source and order of the world the Tao serves as a model for enlightened rulers who gain power by staying in the background and letting their people live spontaneously in response to their own needs.

There are several passages in these books that describe the enlightened person as living peacefully and long because he does not waste his vital powers on needless contention and aggression.

THE BEGINNINGS OF EMPIRE

In the fifth century BCE the disintegration of the Chou feudal and social order quickened under the pressure of incessant civil wars. The larger states formed alliances and maneuvered for power, seeking hegemony over the others, aiming to reunify the area of Chou culture by force alone. In 256 BCE the state of Ch'in, under the influence of a ruthlessly applied ideology of laws and punishments suggested in the fourth century BCE by Shang Yang, one of the founders of the Authoritarian school, eliminated the last Chou king and then finished off its remaining rivals. Finally, in 221 the state of Ch'in became the empire of Ch'in (221-207 BCE), and its ruler took a new title, "First Emperor of Ch'in" (Ch'in Shih-huang-ti). With this step China as a semicontinental state was born. There were many periods of division and strife later, but the new level of unification achieved by the Ch'in was never forgotten, and became the goal of all later dynasties.

THE CH'IN DYNASTY. The Ch'in was noteworthy both for its suppression of philosophy and its encouragement of religion. For the Authoritarian (Legalist) tradition, dominant in the state of Ch'in, the only proper standard of conduct was the law, applied by officials concerned with nothing else, whose personal views were irrelevant as long as they performed their task. The only sanctions the state needed were power and effective organization. Not long after Ch'in became an empire it attempted to silence all criticism based on the assumption of inner standards of righteousness that were deemed to transcend political power and circumstance. In 213 BCE the court made it a capital offence to discuss Confucian books and principles and ordered that all books in private collections be burned, save those dealing with medicine, divination, and agriculture, as well as texts of the Authoritarian school. In this campaign, several scores of scholars were executed, and a number of philosophical schools were eliminated as coherent traditions.

By contrast, Ch'in policy toward religion, encouraged a variety of practices to support the state. To pay homage to the sacred powers of the realm and to consolidate his control, the First Emperor included worship at local shrines in his extensive tours. Representatives of regional cults, many of them spirit mediums, were brought to the court, there to perform rituals at altars set up for their respective deities. The Ch'in expanded the late Chou tendency to exalt deities of natural forces; over one hundred temples to such nature deities were established in the capital alone. Elaborate sacrifices of horses, rams, bulls, and a variety of foodstuffs were regularly offered at the major sites, presided over by officials with titles such as Grand Sacrificer and Grand Diviner.

THE HAN DYNASTY. The defeat of Ch'in forces in the civil wars leading up to the founding of the Han dynasty deposed Authoritarian political thought along

The Latin altaria *is, in all likelihood, related to the verb* adolere *("to worship"; originally, "to burn, to cause to go up in smoke or odor"), so that the word has come to signify a "place of fire" or "sacrificial hearth".*

PAGE 27

CHINESE DYNASTIES AND RELIGIOUS ACTIVITY

Dynasty	Dates	Religious activity
Hsia	c. 1994 – c. 1523 BCE	First use of written symbols.
Shang or Yin	c. 1523 – c. 1027 BCE	Well-developed writing; first calendar.
Chou	c. 1027 – c. 256 BCE	Teachings of Confucius, Mo-tzu, Meng-tzu, and Hsün-tzu; Lao-tzu and Chuang-tzu texts.
Ch'in	c. 221 – 207 BCE	Written language standardized.
Han	202 BCE – 220 CE	Confucianism made basis of bureaucratic state. Buddhism introduced. Huai-nan-tzu.
Three Kingdoms	220 – 265 CE	Importance of Confucianism is eclipsed by Buddhism and Taoism.
Tsin or Chin	265 – 420	Continued growth of Buddism.
Sui	581 – 618	Buddhism and Taoism favored.
T'ang	618 – 907	Buddhism temporarily suppressed. Civil ser vice examinations are based on Confucianism.
Five Dynasties and Ten Kingdoms	907 – 960	Period of warfare and general hardship.
Sung	960 – 1279	Neo-Confucianism attains supremacy over Taoism and Buddhism.
Yüan	1271 – 1368	Confucian ideals discouraged.
Ming	1368 – 1644	Confucianism reinstated bureaucratically.
Ch'ing or Manchus	1644 – 1912	Foreign powers divide China into spheres of influence.

with the second and last Ch'in emperor. It took several decades for the new Han dynasty to consolidate its power. Since the Authoritarians had developed the most detailed policies for administering an empire, many of these policies were followed in practice in modified form.

Some early Han scholars and emperors attempted to ameliorate royal power with a revival of Confucian concern for the people and Taoist principles of noninterference *(wu-wei)*. A palace counselor named Chia I (200-168 BCE) echoed Meng-tzu in his emphasis that the people are the basis of the state, the purpose of which should be to make them prosperous and happy, so as to gain their approval. A similar point of view is presented in more Taoist form in the *Huai-nan-tzu*, a book presented to the throne in 139 BCE by a prince of the Liu clan who had convened a variety of scholars in his court. This book discusses the world as a fundamentally harmonious system of resonating roles and influences. The ruler's job is to guide it, as an experienced charioteer guides his team.

For Meng-tzu, all people possess innate knowledge of the good and an innate ability to do good. Evil is due merely to circumstance and self-neglect.

PAGE 178

However, the oldest and most widely established of the early Han philosophical schools was the Confucian, and the Confucians survived the Ch'in suppression rather well. Numbers of their books escaped the flames of 213 BCE, and those that did not were reconstructed or written anew, with little but the old titles intact. In the third century BCE scholars such as Hsün-tzu had already incorporated the best thought of their day into fundamentally Confucian expositions that advocated a strong centralized state and an ethical teaching enforced by law. This expanded interpretation of Confucius's teachings served his followers well in the early Han. By the second century BCE Confucian scholars such as Tung Chung-shu (c. 179-104 BCE) incorporated into their teaching the theories of Tsou Yen and the "Naturalists," who in the fourth century BCE had taught that the world is an interrelated organic whole that operates according to such cosmic principles as *yin* and *yang*. The *Huai-nan-tzu* had already given this material a Taoist interpretation, stressing the natural resonance between all aspects of the universe. In the hands of Tung Chung-shu this understanding became an elaborate statement of the relationship of society and nature, with an emphasis on natural justification for hierarchical social roles, focused on that of the ruler.

Tung Chung-shu provided a more detailed cosmological basis for Confucian ethical and social teachings and made it clear that only a unified state could serve as a channel for cosmic forces and sanctions. Tung was recognized as the leading scholar of the realm, and became spokesman for the official class. At his urging, in 136 BCE the Confucian classics were made the prescribed texts studied at the imperial academy. As the generations passed, the tablets of the most influential scholars of the age came to be placed in these temples as well, by imperial decree, and so the cult of Confucius became the ritual focus of the scholar-official class.

Han state rituals were based upon those of Ch'in, but were greatly expanded and more elaborate. The first emperor, Kao-tsu, instituted the worship of a star god believed to be associated with Hou Chi, the legendary founder of the Chou royal line. Temples for this deity were built in administrative centers around the realm, where officials were also instructed to worship gods of local mountains and rivers. Kao-tsu brought shamans to the palace and set up shrines for sacrifices to their regional deities.

It should be noted, that the old Chou concept of the "mandate of Heaven" continued to influence Han political thought in a form elaborated and attenuated at the same time. The "mandate of Heaven" in its earlier and starker form was evoked chiefly as justification for rebellion in periods of dynastic decay. Nonetheless, portent theory in the hands of a conscientious official could be used in attempts to check or ameliorate royal despotism, and hence was an aspect of the state religious system that could challenge political power as well as support it.

The Han emperor Wu (140-87 BCE) devoted much effort to attaining immortality, as had his Ch'in predecessor. As before, shamans and specialists in immortality potions were brought to court, and expeditions were sent off to look for the dwelling places of those who had defeated death.

A common expression of hope for some sort of continuity after death may be seen in tombs of Han aristocrats and officials, many of which were built as sturdy brick replicas of houses or offices, complete with wooden and ceramic utensils, attendants, and animals, as well as food, drugs, clothing, jade, bamboo books, and other precious objects.

What came to be called the Former Han dynasty ended in 8 CE when the throne was occupied by a prime minister named Wang Mang (r. 9-23 CE), who established a Hsin ("new") dynasty that was to last for fourteen years. Wang's chief contribution to the history of Chinese religions was his active promotion of prognostication as a way of understanding the intimate relationship between Heaven and the court. In 25 CE Liu Hsiu (r. 25-57), a member of the Han royal line, led a successful attack on Wang Mang and reestablished the (Latter) Han dynasty. Like Wang Mang, he actively supported prognostication at court, despite the criticism of rationalist scholars such as Huan T'an (43 BCE-28 CE), who argued that strange phenomena were a matter of coincidence and natural causes rather than messages from Heaven.

A related development was controversy between two movements within Confucian scholarly circles, the so-called New Text school of the Former Han, and a later rationalistic reaction against it, the Old Text school. The New Text school developed out of Tung Chung-shu's concern with portents. Its followers wrote new commentaries on the classics that praised Confucius as a supernormal being who predicted the future hundreds of years beyond his time. By the end of the first century BCE this interpretation of the sage in mythological terms was vigorously resisted by an Old Text school that advocated a more restrained and historical approach. These two traditions coexisted throughout the remainder of the Han dynasty, with the New Text scholars receiving the most imperial support through the first century CE.

THE PERIOD OF DISUNION

By the time the first Buddhist monks and texts appeared in China around the first century CE, the Han dynasty was already in decline. At court, rival factions competed for imperial favor, and in the provinces restless governors moved toward independence. Political and military fragmentation was hastened by the campaigns against the Yellow Turban uprising, after which a whole series of adventurers arose to attack each other and take over territory. In the first decade of the third century three major power centers emerged in the north, southeast, and southwest, with that in the north controlling the last Han emperor and ruling in his name. By 222 these three centers each had declared themselves states, and China entered a period of political division that was to last until late in the sixth century.

THE BEGINNINGS OF BUDDHISM IN CHINA. From about 100 BCE on it would have been relatively easy for Buddhist ideas and practices to come to China with foreign merchants, but the first reliable notice of it in Chinese sources is dated 65 CE. In a royal edict of that year we are told that a prince administering a city in what is now northern Kiangsu Province "recites the subtle words of Huang-Lao, and respectfully performs the gentle sacrifices to the Buddha." He was encouraged to "entertain *upasakas* and *sramanas,*" Buddhist lay devotees and initiates. In 148 CE the first of several foreign monks, An Shih-kao, settled in Lo-yang, the capital of the Latter Han. Over the next forty years he and other scholars translated about thirty Buddhist scriptures into Chinese, most of them from pre-Mahayana traditions, emphasizing meditation and moral principles. However, by about 185 three Mahayana Prajñaparamita (Perfect Wisdom) texts were translated as well.

A memorial dated 166, approving Buddhist "purity," "emptiness," nonviolence, and control of sensual desires, further informs us that in that year the emperor performed a joint sacrifice to Lao-tzu and the Buddha. In 193/194 a local warlord in what is now Kiangsu erected a Buddhist temple that could hold more than three thousand people. It contained a bronze Buddha image before which offerings were made and scriptures were read.

The movement of Buddhism to China, one of the great cultural interactions of history, was slow and fortuitous, carried out almost entirely at a private level. The basic reason for its eventual acceptance throughout Chinese society was that it offered several religious and social advantages unavailable to the same extent in China before. These included a full-time religious vocation for both men and women in an organization largely independent of family and state, a clear promise of life after death at various levels, and developed conceptions of paradise and purgatory, connected to life through the results of intentional actions *(karman).*

In the early fourth century North China was invaded by the Hsiung-nu, who sacked Lo-yang in 311 and Ch'ang-an in 316. Thousands of elite families fled south below the Yangtze River, where a series of short-lived Chinese dynasties held off further invasions. In the North a succession of kingdoms of Inner Asian background rose and fell, most of which supported Buddhism because of its religious appeal and its non-Chinese origins.

It was in the South that Buddhism first became a part of Chinese intellectual history. Buddhist thought was already well developed and complexly differentiated before it reached China. The Chinese knew of it only through scriptures haphazardly collected, in translations of varying accuracy, for very few Chinese learned Sanskrit. Since all the *sutras* claimed to be preached by the Buddha himself, they were accepted as such, with discrepancies among them explained as deriving from the different situations and capacities of listeners prevailing when a particular text was preached. In practice, this meant that the Chinese had to select from a vast range of data those themes that made the most sense in their pre-existing worldview. For example, as the tradition develops we find emphases on simplicity and directness, the universal potential for enlightenment, and the Buddha mind as source of the cosmos, all of them prepared for in indigenous thought and practice. The most important early Chinese Buddhist philosophers, organizers, and translators contributed to the growth of the young church.

The first important school of Buddhist thought developed in China was the T'ien-t'ai, noted for its synthesis of earlier Buddhist traditions into one system, divided into five periods of development according to stages in the Buddha's teaching.

Buddhism had to compete with strong preexisting philosophical and social traditions that on many points were opposed to Buddhist ideals and practices.

PAGE 106

In 581 China was reunified by the Sui dynasty (581-618) after three and a half centuries of political fragmentation. The Sui founder supported Buddhism, particularly the T'ien-t'ai school, as a unifying ideology shared by many of his subjects in both North and South. After four decades of rule the Sui was overthrown in a series of rebellions, to be replaced by the T'ang (618-907). Although the new dynasty tended to give more official support to Confucianism and Taoism, Buddhism continued to grow at every level of society, and reached the high point of its development in China during the next two centuries.

THE RISE OF TAOIST RELIGION. Taoism is China's own indigenous higher religion, characterized by the fourth century by a literate and self-perpetuating priesthood, a pantheon of celestial deities, complex rituals, and revealed scriptures in classical Chinese. Taoism is fundamentally a religion of *ch'i,* the vital breath out of which nature, gods, and humans evolve. The source and order of this vital substance is the Tao, the ultimate power of life in the universe. The gods are personified manifestations of *ch'i,* symbolizing astral powers of the cosmos and organs of the human body with which they are correlated. Under the conditions of existence *ch'i* becomes stale and worn out, so it must be renewed through ritual processes that restore its primal vitality.

All branches of Taoism eventually traced their origin to a new revelation from the Most High Lord Lao to Chang Tao-ling, the grandfather of Chang Lu, in 142 CE, establishing him as "Celestial Master." He was empowered to perform rituals and write talismans that distributed this new manifestation of the Tao for the salvation of humankind. Salvation was available to those who repented of their sins, believed in the Tao, and pledged allegiance to their Taoist master. The master in turn established an alliance between the gods and the devotee, who then wore at the waist a list (register)

TAOIST TEMPLE

Taoism is a religion of ch'i, the vital breath from which nature, gods, and humans evolve. In Taoist temples, ch'i is renewed through ritual processes to restore its primary vitality.

EYE UBIQUITOUS/CORBIS

of the names of the gods to be called on for protection. The register also served as a passport to heaven at death. Taoist ritual consists essentially of the periodic renewal of these alliances by confession, visualization, petition, and the offering of incense and sacred documents. Taoist texts are concerned throughout for moral discipline and orderly ritual and organization.

When the Celestial Master sect was officially recognized by the state of Wei (220-266) in the early third century its leadership was established in the capital, Lo-yang, north and east of the old sect base area in modern Szechwan. In the North remnants of the Yellow Turbans still survived, and before long the teachings and rituals of these two similar traditions blended together. A tension remained, however, between those who saw secular authority as a manifestation of the Way and those determined to bring in a new era of peace and prosperity by militant activity. Uprisings led by charismatic figures who claimed long life and healing powers occurred in different areas throughout the fourth century and later.

When the northern state of Chin was conquered by the Hsiung-nu in 316, thousands of Chin gentry and officials moved south, bringing the Celestial Master sect with them. The eventual result was a blending of Celestial Master concern for priestly adminstration and collective rituals with a more individualistic and esoteric alchemical traditions growing in the southeast.

Taoism continued to be active in the North as well, in the Northern Wei kingdom (386-534), which established Taoist offices at court in 400. In 415 and 423 a scholar named K'ou Ch'ien-chih (d. 448) claimed to have received direct revelations from Lord Lao while he was living on a sacred mountain. The resulting scriptures directed K'ou to reform the Celestial Master tradition; renounce popular cults, messianic uprisings, and sexual rituals; and support the court as a Taoist kingdom on earth. K'ou was introduced to the Wei ruler and was promptly appointed to the office of "Erudite of Transcendent Beings." The next year he was proclaimed Celestial Master, and his teachings "promulgated throughout the realm." For the next two decades K'ou and Ts'ui cooperated to promote Taoism at the court. As a result, in 440 the king accepted the title Perfect Ruler of Great Peace, and during the period 444 to 446 proscribed Buddhism and local "excessive cults." Although Ts'ui Hao was eventually discredited and Buddhism established as the state religion by a new ruler in 452, the years of official support for Taoism clarified its legitimacy and political potential as an alternative to Confucianism and Buddhism. Although it continued to develop new schools and scriptural traditions, the basic shape of Taoism for the rest of Chinese history was thus established by the fifth century.

THE CONSOLIDATION OF EMPIRE: SEVENTH TO FOURTEENTH CENTURY

The Chinese religious traditions that were to continue throughout the rest of imperial history all reached maturity during the T'ang (618-907) and Sung (960-1279) periods. These traditions included Buddhism, Taoism, Neo-Confucianism, Islam, and popular religion in both its village and sectarian forms.

MANICHAEISM AND ISLAM. The area of the T'ang dynasty rivaled that of the Han, with western boundaries extending far into Central Asia. This expansion encouraged a revival of foreign trade and cultural contacts. Among the new foreign influences were not only Buddhist monks and scriptures but also the representatives of other religions. There is evidence for Zoroastrianism in China by the early sixth century, a result of contacts between China and Persia that originated in the second century BCE and were renewed in an exchange of envoys with the Northern Wei court in 455 and around 470. [*See* Zoroastrianism.]

A foreign tradition with more important influence on the history of Chinese religions was Manichaeism, a dynamic missionary religion teaching ultimate cosmic dualism founded by a Persian named Mani (216-277?). In 755 a Chinese military commander named An Lu-shan led a powerful rebellion that the T'ang court was able to put down only with the help of foreign support. One of these allies was the Uighur, from a kingdom based in what is now northern Mongolia. In 762 a Uighur army liberated Lo-yang from rebel forces, and there a Uighur kaghan was converted to Manichaeism. The result was new prestige and more temples for the religion in China.

However, in 840 the Uighurs were defeated by the Kirghiz, with the result that the Chinese turned on the religion of their former allies, destroyed its temples, and expelled or executed its priests. Nonetheless, at least one Manichaean leader managed to escape to Ch'üan-chou in Fukien Province on the southeast coast. In Fukien the Manichaeans flourished as a popular sect until the fourteenth century, characterized by their distinctive teachings, communal living, vegetarian diet, and nonviolence. They were called the Ming-chiao ("religion of light"). They disappeared as a coherent tradition as a result of renewed persecutions during the early Ming dynasty (1368-1644). Several Manichaean texts were incorporated into the Taoist and Buddhist canons, and it is likely that Manichaean lay sects provided models for similar organizations that evolved out of Buddhism later. Manichaean dualism and demon exorcism may have reinforced similar themes in Taoism and Buddhism as they were understood at the popular level.

"Avoid what is evil, do what is good; purify the mind."

THE PALI CANON, SUTTAPITAKA DHAMMAPADA, 14:183

It was Khubilai (r. 1260-1294), the last great Mongol khan, who brought China under Mongol rule.

PAGE 333

The major influx of Muslim peoples occurred during the Yüan dynasty (1271-1368) and the Mongols brought in large numbers of their non-Chinese subjects to help administer China. It was in this period that Islam spread all over China and established major population bases in the western provinces of Yunnan and Kansu. Here their numbers increased through marriage with Chinese women and adoption of non-Muslim children, all converted to Islam. Although the result was a dilution of Arab physical characteristics, the use of the Chinese language, and the adoption of some Chinese social customs, for most the Islamic core remained.

Muslims in China have always been predominantly Sunni, but in the sixteenth century Sufism reached China through Central Asia. By the late seventeenth century Sufi brotherhoods began a reform movement that advocated increased use of Arabic and a rejection of certain Chinese practices that had infiltrated Islam, such as burning incense at funerals. Sufism also emphasized ecstatic personal experience of Allah, the veneration of saints, and the imminent return of the Mahdi, who would bring a new age, this last theme due to Shi'i influence as well.

These reformist beliefs, coupled with increased Chinese pressure on Islam as a whole, led eventually to a powerful uprising in Yunnan between 1855-1873, an uprising allowed to develop momentum because of old ethnic tensions in the area and the distraction of the Chinese court with the contemporary Taiping Rebellion (1851-1864). The Yunnan rebellion was eventually put down by a combination of Chinese and loyalist Muslim forces, and the Muslims resumed their role as a powerful minority in China, called the Hui people.

T'ANG DYNASTY BUDDHISM. The first T'ang emperor, Kao-tsu (r. 618-626) approved of a plan to limit both Taoist and Buddhist temples. His son T'ai-tsung (r. 626-649) agreed with the Taoist contention that the imperial family was descended from Lao-tzu, whose legendary surname was also Li; however, T'ai-tsung also erected Buddhist shrines on battlefields and ordered monks to recite scriptures for the stability of the empire. Buddhist philosophical schools in this period were matters of both belief and imperial adornment, so, to replace the T'ien-t'ai school, now discredited on account of its association with the Sui dynasty, the T'ang court turned first to the Fa-hsiang, or Idealist school, the Indian teaching of "consciousness-only." Some texts of this tradition had been translated earlier by Paramartha (499-569), but it came to be thoroughly understood in China only after the return of the pilgrim Hsüan-tsang in 645. Hsüan-tsang was welcomed at court and provided with twenty-three scholar-monks from all over China to assist in translating the books he had brought back from India. The emperor wrote a preface for the translation of one major Vijñanavada text, and his policy of imperial support was continued by his son Kao-tsung.(r. 649-683).

However, the complex psychological analysis of the Vijñanavada school, coupled with its emphasis that some beings are doomed by their nature to eternal rebirth, were not in harmony with the Chinese worldview, which had been better represented by T'ien-t'ai. Hence, when imperial support declined at Kao-tsung's death in 683, the fortunes of the Fa-hsiang school declined as well. At the intellectual level it was replaced in popularity by the Hua-yen ("flower garland") school as formulated by the monk Fa-tsang (643-712). This school taught the emptiness and interpenetration of all phenomena in a way consonant with old Chinese assumptions.

It is no accident that the Hua-yen school was first actively supported by Empress Wu Chao (Wu Tse-t'ien, r. 690-705) who took over the throne from her sons to set up her own dynasty, the Chou. Since Confucianism did not allow for female rulers, Empress Wu, being a devout Buddhist, sought for supporting ideologies in that tradition, including not only Hua-yen but also predictions in obscure texts that the Buddha had prophesied that several hundred years after his death a woman would rule over a world empire. Monks in Wu-Tse asserted that she was a manifestation of the future Buddha Maitreya.

When Empress Wu abdicated in 705 her son continued to support the Hua-yen school, continuing the tradition of close relationship between the court and Buddhist philosophical schools. However, during this period Buddhism continued to grow in popularity among all classes of people. Thousands of monasteries and shrines were built, supported by donations of land, grain, cloth, and precious metals, and by convict workers, the poor, and serfs bound to donated lands. Tens of thousands of persons became monks or nuns, elaborate rituals were performed, feasts provided, and sermons preached in both monastery and marketplace.

By the third century CE texts describing various "pure realms" or "Buddha lands" had been translated into Chinese, and some monks began to meditate on the best known of these "lands," the Western Paradise of the Buddha Amitabha. In the fourth century Chih Tun (314-366) made an image of Amitabha and vowed to be reborn in his paradise, as did Hui-yüan in 402. These early efforts concentrated on visualization of Buddha realms in states of meditative trance.

Philosophers of the fifth and sixth centuries such as Seng-chao and Chih-i discussed the Pure Land concept as part of larger systems of thought, but the first monk to devote his life to proclaiming devotion to Amitabha as the chief means of salvation for the whole of society was T'an-luan (476-542), a monk from

North China where there had long been an emphasis on the practical implementation of Buddhism. T'an-luan organized devotional associations whose members both contemplated the Buddha and orally recited his name. It was in the fifth and sixth centuries as well that many Chinese Buddhist thinkers became convinced that the final period of Buddhist teaching for this world cycle was about to begin, a period (called in Chinese mo-fa, the Latter Days of the Law) in which the capacity for understanding Buddhism had so declined that only simple and direct means of communication would suffice.

The next important preacher to base his teachings solely on Amitabha and his Pure Land was Tao-ch'o (562-645). It was he and his disciple Shan-tao (613-681) who firmly established the Pure Land movement and came to be looked upon as founding patriarchs of the tradition. Owing to their efforts, Pure Land devotion became the most popular form of Buddhism in China, from whence it was taken to Japan in the ninth century. Pure Land teachings supported the validity of lay piety as no Buddhist school had before, and hence both made possible the spread of Buddhism throughout the population and furthered the development of independent societies and sects outside the monasteries.

The last movement within orthodox Buddhism in China to emerge as an independent tradition was Ch'an (Jpn., Zen), characterized by its concentration on direct means of individual enlightenment, chiefly meditation. Such enlightenment has always been the primary goal of Buddhism, so in a sense Ch'an began as a reform movement seeking to recover the experiential origins of its tradition. Such a reform appeared all the more necessary in the face of the material success of T'ang Buddhism, with its ornate rituals, complex philosophies, and close relationships with the state.

The first references to a "Ch'an school" appeared in the late eighth century. By that time several branches of this emerging tradition were constructing genealogies going back to Sakyamuni himself; these were intended to establish the priority and authority of their teachings. The genealogy that came to be accepted later claimed a lineage of twenty-eight Indian and seven Chinese patriarchs, the latter beginning with Bodhidharma (c. 461-534), a Central Asian meditation master active in the Northern Wei kingdom. Legends concerning these patriarchs were increasingly elaborated as time passed, but the details of most cannot be verified. The first Chinese monk involved whose teachings have survived is Tao-hsin (580-651), who was later claimed to be the fourth patriarch. Tao-hsin specialized in meditation and monastic discipline, and studied for ten years with a disciple of the T'ien-t'ai founder, Chih-i. He is also noted for his concern with image worship and reciting the Buddha's name to calm the mind.

The Ch'an tradition as a whole has always been characterized by disciplined communal living in monasteries, centered on group meditation. Characteristics of early Ch'an monasteries were their independent establishment in remote areas, their rejection of a central hall containing images in favor of "Dharma

EMPRESS WU BURIAL GROUND

Empress Wu Chao, founder of the Chou dynasty, promoted the Hua-yen school of Buddhism.

LOWELL GEORGIA/CORBIS

The demise of the monastic network through which the civilizational aspect of Buddhism had been supported and maintained was decisive.

PAGE 94

halls" with meditation platforms along the sides, private consultations with abbots, and frequent group discussions. Frugality and shared responsibility for work were also emphasized in order to reduce dependence on outside donations with the reciprocal obligations they involved.

By the ninth century Ch'an was widely supported in Chinese society; during the Northern Sung dynasty (960-1127) it was the major form of monastic Buddhism and hence a focal point of institutionalization. In this context Ch'an produced a new type of literature, the "recorded discussions" *(yü-lu)* of patriarchs and abbots with their disciples as they struggled to attain enlightenment. It is these records, codified as "cases" (Chin., *kung-an;* Jpn., *koan*), that were meditated upon by novices as they sought to experience reality directly.

Although Buddhism flourished at all levels of Chinese society in the T'ang period, an undercurrent of resentment and hostility toward it by Confucians, Taoists, and the state always remained. This hostility came to a head in the mid-ninth century, strongly reinforced by the fact that Buddhist monasteries had accumulated large amounts of precious metals and tax exempt land. From 843 to 845 Emperor Wu-tsung (r. 840-846), an ardent Taoist, issued decrees that led to the destruction of 4,600 monasteries and 40,000 temples and shrines, and the return of 260,500 monks and nuns to lay life. Although this suppression was ended in 846 by Wu-tsung's successor, monastic Buddhism never fully regained its momentum.

T'ANG DYNASTY TAOISM. Taoism continued to develop during the T'ang period, in part because it received more support from some emperors than it had under the Sui. The most important Taoist order during the T'ang was that based on Mao-shan in Kiangsu, where temples were built and reconstructed, disciples trained, and scriptures edited. Devotees on Mao-shan studied Shang-ch'ing scriptures, meditated, practiced alchemy, and carried out complex rituals of purgation and cosmic renewal, calling down astral spirits and preparing for immortality among the stars. These activities were presided over by a hierarchical priesthood, led by *fa-shih,* "masters of doctrine," the most prominent of whom came to be considered patriarchs of the school.

TAOISM IN THE SUNG AND YÜAN DYNASTY. The destruction of the old T'ang aristocracy in the turmoil of the ninth and tenth centuries helped prepare the way for a more centralized state in the Sung, administered by bureaucrats who were selected through civil service examinations. This in turn contributed to increased social mobility, enhanced by economic growth and diversification, the spread of printing, and a larger number of schools. These factors, combined with innovations in literature, art, philosophy, and religion, have led historians to describe the Sung period as the beginning of early modern China. It was in this period that the basic patterns of life and thought were established for the remainder of imperial history.

During the tenth through thirteenth centuries Taoism developed new schools and texts and became more closely allied with the state. A century later, during the reign of Emperor Hui-tsung (r. 1101-1126), the most famous imperial patron of Taoism, three new Taoist orders appeared, one with a popular base in southeastern Kiangsi, another a revival of Mao-shan teachings, and the third the Shen-hsiao Fa (Rites of the Divine Empyrean).

In 1126 the Sung capital Kaifeng was captured by the Jurchen, a people from northeastern Manchuria who, with other northern peoples, had long threatened the Sung. As a result the Chinese court moved south across the Yangtze River to establish a new capital in Hang-chou, thus initiating the Southern Sung period (1127-1279). During this period China was once again divided north and south, with the Jurchen ruling the Chin kingdom (1115-1234). It was here in the north that three new Taoist sects appeared, the T'ai-i (Grand Unity), the Ta-tao (Great Way), and the Ch'üan-chen (Total Perfection). The T'ai-i sect gained favor for a time at the Chin court because of its promise of divine healing. Ta-tao disciples worked in the fields, prayed for healing rather than using charms, and did not practice techniques of immortality. Both included Confucian and Buddhist elements in a Taoist framework.

The Ch'üan-chen sect was founded in similar circumstances by a scholar named Wang Che (1113-1170), but continued to exist into the twentieth century. Wang claimed to have received revelations from two superhuman beings, whereupon he gathered disciples and founded five congregations in northern Shantung. After his death seven of his leading disciples continued to proclaim his teachings across North China. One of them was received at the Chin court in 1187, thus beginning a period of imperial support for the sect that continued into the time of Mongol rule, particularly after another of the founding disciples visited Chinggis Khan at his Central Asian court in 1222.

In its early development the Taoist quest for personal immortality employed a combination of positive ritual techniques: visualization of astral gods and ingestion of their essence, internal circulation and refinement of *ch'i,* massage, eating elixirs of cinnebar and mica, and so forth, all accompanied by taboos and ethical injunctions. By the eleventh century this quest was further internalized, and alchemical potions were reinterpreted as forces within the body, a tendency well expressed in the writings of Chang Po-tuan (983-1082). Under Confucian and Ch'an influence the Ch'üan-chen school "spiritualized" the terminology of these older practices, turning its physiological referents into abstract polarities within the mind, to be unified through meditation. Perhaps in part because of this withdrawal into the mind, Ch'üan-chen was the first Taoist school to base itself in monasteries, although celibacy to maintain and purify one's powers had been practiced by some adepts earlier, and some Taoist monasteries had been established in the sixth century under pressure from the state and the Buddhist example.

THE REVIVAL OF CONFUCIAN PHILOSOPHY. Confucianism had remained a powerful tradition of morality, social custom, and hierarchical status since the fall of the Han, but after the third century it no longer generated fresh philosophical perspectives. From the fourth through the tenth century the best philosophical minds in China were devoted to Buddhism. However, in the eleventh century there appeared a series of thinkers determined to revive Confucianism as a philosophical system. In this task they were inevitably influenced by Buddhist theories of mind, enlightenment, and ethics; indeed, most of these men went through Buddhist and Taoist phases in their early years and were converted to Confucianism later. Nonetheless, at a conscious level they rejected Buddhist "emptiness," asceticism, and monastic life in favor of a positive metaphysics, ordered family life, and concern for social reform. With a few exceptions the leaders of this movement, known in the West as Neo-Confucianism, went through the civil service examination system and held civil or military offices.

In retrospect we can see that Neo-Confucianism split into two general tendencies, the rationalistic and the idealistic, the first more concerned with the ordering principles *(li)* of life and society, the second with awakening the moral consciousness of the mind *(hsin)*.

In the history of Chinese religions, the impact of Neo-Confucianism is evident at different levels. The intellectual and institutional success of this movement among the Chinese elite led many of them away from Buddhism and Taoism, away from any form of sectarian religion, toward a reaffirmation of the values of family, clan, and state. Another long term impact was the confucianization of popular values, supported by schools, examinations, distribution of tracts, and lectures in villages. This meant that from the Sung dynasty on the operative ethical principles in society were a combination of Confucian virtues with Buddhist *karman* and compassion, a tendency that became more widespread as the centuries passed.

These developments were rooted in the religious dimensions of the Neo-Confucian tradition, which from the beginning was most concerned with the moral transformation of self and society. [*See* Confucian Thought.]

SUNG DYNASTY BUDDHISM. Sung Buddhist activities were based on the twin foundations of Ch'an and Pure Land, with an increasing emphasis on the compatability of the two. Although the joint practice of meditation and invocation of the Buddha's name had been taught by Chih-i and the Ch'an patriarch Tao-hsin in the sixth and seventh centuries, the first Ch'an master to openly advocate it after Ch'an was well established was Yen-shou (904-975). This emphasis was continued in the Yüan (1271-1368) and Ming (1368-1644) dynasties, so that by the late traditional period meditation and recitation were commonly employed together in monasteries as two means to the same end of emptying the mind of self-centered thought.

During the Sung dynasty Buddhism physically recovered from the suppression of the ninth century, with tens of thousands of monasteries, large amounts of land, and active support throughout society. By the tenth century the Ch'an school was divided into two main branches, both of which had first appeared earlier, the Lin-chi (Jpn., Rinzai), emphasizing dramatic and unexpected breakthroughs to enlightenment in the midst of everyday activities, and the Ts'ao-tung (Jpn., Soto), known for a more gradual approach through seated meditation. There was some recovery of philosophical studies in Ch'an monasteries, but it did not recapture the intellectual vitality of the T'ang period. However, for the larger history of Chinese religions the most important development in Sung Buddhism was the spread of lay societies devoted to good works and recitation of the Buddha's name.

THE PERIOD OF MONGOL RULE. The Mongols under Chinggis Khan (1167-1227) captured the Chin capital of Yen-ching (modern Peking) in 1215 and established the Yüan dynasty (1271-1368). From China they ruled their vast domain, which extended all the way to central Europe. For the next several decades the "Middle Kingdom" was the eastern end of a world empire.

The Mongols were attracted by the exorcistic and healing rituals of Tantric Buddhism in Tibet, the borders of which they also controlled. In 1260 a Tibetan monk, 'Phags-pa (1235-1280), was named chief of Buddhist affairs and Tibetan monks were appointed as leaders of the *saṃgha* all over China,

By the early fourteenth century another form of popular religion appeared, the voluntary association or sect that could be joined by individuals from different families and villages. The sects were characterized by predominantly lay membership and leadership, hierarachical organization, active proselytism, congregational rituals, possession of their own scriptures in the vernacular, and mutual economic support. Their best known antecedent was the White Lotus school, an

Chu Hsi taught that in order for man not to be engulfed by selfishness and evil he must cultivate himself in a manner that rectifies the human mind and develops the mind of Heaven.

PAGE 182

"When you have faults, do not fear to abandon them."

CONFUCIUS,
THE ANALECTS, I:8, IV

independent sect founded by a monk named Mao Tzu-yüan (1086-1166). Mao combined simplified T'ien-t'ai teaching with Pure Land practice, invoking Amitabha's saving power with just five recitations of his name.

MING AND CH'ING RELIGION

Mongol rule began to deteriorate in the early fourteenth century. After twenty years of civil war Chu Yüan-chang, from a poor peasant family, defeated all his rivals and reestablished a Chinese imperial house, the Ming dynasty (1368-1644). Chu (Ming T'ai-tsu, r. 1368-1398) was an energetic ruler of strong personal religious beliefs who revised imperial rituals, promulgated strict laws against a variety of popular practices and sects, and recruited Taoist priests to direct court ceremonies. For him the mandate of Heaven was a living force that had established him in a long line of sacred emperors.

MING DYNASTY. Under the Ming, such factors as the diversification of the agricultural base and the monetization of the economy had an impact on religious life. Sectarian scriptures appeared as part of the same movement that produced new vernacular literature of all types, morality books to inculcate Neo-Confucian values, and new forms and audiences for popular operas. More than ever before the late Ming was a time of economic and cultural initiatives from the population at large, as one might expect in a period of increasing competition for resources by small entrepreneurs. These tendencies continued to gain momentum in the Ch'ing period.

Ming Buddhism showed the impact of these economic and cultural factors, particularly in eastern China where during the sixteenth century reforming monks such as Yün-ch'i Chu-hung (1535-1615) organized lay societies, wrote morality books that quantified the merit points for good deeds, and affirmed Confucian values within a Buddhist framework. Chu-hung combined Pure Land and Ch'an practice and preached spiritual progress through sparing animals from slaughter and captivity. The integration of Buddhism into Chinese society was furthered as well by government approval of a class of teaching monks, ordained with official certificates, whose role was to perform rituals for the people.

Taoism was supported by emperors throughout the Ming, with Taoist priests appointed as officials in charge of rituals and composing hymns and messages to the gods. The Ch'üan-chen sect continued to do well, with its monastic base and emphasis on attaining immortality through developing "internal elixirs." Its meditation methods also influenced those of some of Wang Yang-ming's followers, such as Wang Chi (1497-1582). However, it was the Cheng-i sect led by hereditary Celestial Masters that had the most official support during the Ming and hence was able to consolidate its position as the standard of orthodox Taoism. Cheng-i influence is evident in scriptures composed during this period, many of which trace their lineage back to the first Celestial Master and bear imprimaturs from his successors. The forty-third-generation master was given charge of compiling a new Taoist canon in 1406, a task completed between 1444 and 1445. It is this edition that is still in use today.

By the seventeenth century, Confucian philosophy entered a more nationalistic and materialist phase, but the scholar-official class as a whole remained involved in a variety of private religious practices beyond their official ritual responsibilities. These included not only the study of Taoism and Buddhism but the use of spirit-writing, séances, and prayers to Wen-ch'ang, the god of scholars and literature, for help in passing examinations. Ming T'ai-tsu had proclaimed that each of the "three teachings" of Confucianism, Buddhism, and Taoism had an important role to play, which encouraged synthetic tendencies present since the beginnings of Buddhism in China. In the sixteenth century a Confucian scholar named Lin Chao-en (1517-1598) from Fukien took these tendencies a step further by building a middle-class religious sect in which Confucian teachings were explicitly supported by those of Buddhism and Taoism. Lin was known as "Master of the Three Teachings," the patron saint of what became a popular movement with temples still extant in Singapore and Malaysia in the mid-twentieth century. This tendency to incorporate Confucianism into a sectarian religion was echoed by Chang Chi-tsung (d. 1866) who established a fortified community in Shantung, and by K'ang Yu-wei (1858-1927) at the end of imperial history. Confucian oriented spirit-writing cults also flourished in the late nineteenth and early twentieth centuries, supported by middle level military and civil officials. These cults produced tracts and scriptures of their own.

CH'ING DYNASTY. The Manchus, a tribal confederation related to the Jurchen, had established their own state in the northeast in 1616 and named it Ch'ing in 1636. As their power grew, they sporadically attacked North China and absorbed much Chinese political and cultural influence. In 1644 a Ch'ing army was invited into China by the Ming court to save Peking from Chinese rebels. The Manchus not only conquered Peking but stayed to rule for the next 268 years. In public policy the Manchus were strong supporters of Confucianism, and relied heavily on the support of Chinese officials. Most religious developments during the Ch'ing were continuations of Ming traditions, with the exception of Protestant Christianity and the Taiping movement it helped stimulate.

Early Ch'ing emperors were interested in Ch'an Buddhism. The Yung-cheng emperor (r. 1723-1735) published a book on Ch'an in 1732 and ordered the reprinting of the Buddhist canon, a task completed in 1738. He also supported the printing of a Tibetan edition of the canon, and his successor, Ch'ien-lung (r. 1736-1795) sponsored the translation of this voluminous body of texts into Manchu. The Pure Land tradition continued to be the form of Buddhism most supported by the people.

The most significant innovation in Ch'ing religion was the teachings of the T'ai-p'ing T'ien-kuo (Celestial Kingdom of Great Peace and Prosperity), which combined motifs from Christianity, shamanism, and popular sectarian beliefs. The Taiping movement was begun by Hung Hsiu-ch'üan (1814-1864), a would-be Confucian scholar who first was given Christian tracts in 1836. After failing civil service examinations several times, Hung claimed to have had a vision in which it was revealed that Hung was the younger brother of Jesus Christ, commissioned to be a new messiah. Hung proclaimed a new kingdom upon earth, to be characterized by theocratic rule, enforcement of the ten commandments, the brotherhood of all, equality of the sexes, and redistribution of land. Hung and other Taiping leaders were effective preachers who wrote books, edicts, and tracts proclaiming their teachings and regulations and providing prayers and hymns for congregational worship.

They forbade ancestor veneration and the worship of Buddhas and Taoist and popular deities. Wherever the Taipings went they destroyed images and temples. They rejected geomancy and divination and established a new calendar free of the old festivals and concerns for inauspicious days. But, in the end, Taiping teachings and practices had no positive effect on the history of Chinese religions after this time, while all the indigenous traditions resumed and rebuilt.

THE END OF EMPIRE AND POSTIMPERIAL CHINA

The Ch'ing government, in 1911, collapsed from internal decay, foreign pressure, and military uprisings. Some Chinese intellectuals, free to invest their energies in new ideas and political forms, avidly studied and translated Western writings, including those of Marxism. One result of this westernization and secularization was attacks on Confucianism and other Chinese traditions, a situation exacerbated by recurrent civil wars that led to the destruction or occupation of thousands of temples. However, these new ideas were most influential in the larger cities; the majority of Chinese continued popular religious practices as before. Many temples and monasteries survived, and there were attempts to revive Buddhist thought and monastic discipline.

Since 1949 Chinese religions have increasingly prospered in Taiwan, particularly at the popular level. The same can be said for Chinese popular religion in Hong Kong and Singapore. The Taoist priesthood is active in Taiwan, supported by the presence of hereditary Celestial Masters from the mainland who provide ordinations and legitimacy. Buddhist monasteries and publishing houses are also doing well in Taiwan and Hong Kong.

The constitution of the People's Republic establishes the freedom both to support and oppose religion, although in practice religious activities of all types declined there after 1949, particularly during the Cultural Revolution of 1966 to 1969. In general religion has been depicted along Marxist lines as "feudal superstition" that must be rejected by those seeking to build a new China. Nonetheless, many religious activities continued until the Cultural Revolution, even those of the long proscribed popular sects. The Cultural Revolution was a massive attack on old traditions, including not only religion, but education, art, and established bureaucracies. At the same time a new national cult arose, that of Chairman Mao and his thought, involving ecstatic processions, group recitation from Mao's writings, and a variety of quasi-religious ceremonials. These included confessions of sins against the revolution, vows of obedience before portraits of the Chairman, and meals of wild vegetables to recall the bitter days before liberation. Although the frenzy abated, the impetus of the Cultural Revolution continued until Mao's death in 1976, led by a small group, later called "the Gang of Four," centered around his wife. This group was soon deposed.

Since 1980 many churches, monasteries, and mosques have reopened, and religious leaders reinstated, in part to establish better relationships with Buddhist, Christian, and Muslim communities in other countries.

[*For further discussion of the various traditions treated in this article, see* Buddhism, Taoism, and Confucian Thought. *For a discussion of the influence of the major monotheistic religions on Chinese religion, see* Islam, Christianity, *and* Judaism. *For the influence of Inner Asian civilizations on Chinese thought, see* Inner Asian Religions, *and* Buddhism.]

— DANIEL L. OVERMYER

CHRISTIAN ETHICS

The three primary manifestations of Christianity—Eastern Orthodoxy, Roman Catholicism, and Protestantism—have recognized that Christian faith involves a particular way of life. The good news of salvation in

The official party position, is that Neo-Confucianism played a major role in Chinese history, albeit one that served a feudal society, and thus is worthy of continued study.

PAGE 184

When relaxation of government control occurred in 1980, it was revealed that several million Chinese had remained faithful to the Christian church.

PAGE 454

C

CHRISTIAN ETHICS

Christian Ethics in General

"Whatever makes men good Christians, makes them good citizens."

DANIEL WEBSTER, SPEECH AT PLYMOUTH, MASSACHUSETTS DECEMBER 22, 1820

Jesus Christ calls for a life of discipleship. The scriptures point out that Christian believers are to live and act in certain ways. Conversion to Jesus Christ and membership in the Christian community involve moral exigencies.

CHRISTIAN ETHICS IN GENERAL. The Bible is the book of Christianity, but it does not contain Christian ethics as such. The Bible does include moral teachings and descriptions of the moral life of believers in Yahveh and in Jesus. The distinction between morality and ethics is most significant. Morality refers to the actions, dispositions, attitudes, virtues, and ways of life that should characterize the moral person and society, in this case the Christian person and the Christian community. Christian ethics operates on the level of the theoretical and the scientific and tries to explain the Christian moral life in a thematic, systematic, coherent, and consistent manner. It is possible for one to attempt a biblical ethic that makes such an explanation of biblical morality, but that ethic would be based on the moral teaching found in scripture. Biblical ethics and Christian ethics are not coextensive. The subject matter of Christian ethics is the Christian moral life and teaching, which is much broader than biblical moral life and teaching.

The relationship between Christian ethics and philosophical ethics is most important. The significant differences between the two result from the different sources of ethical wisdom and knowledge employed. Philosophical ethics is based on human reason and human experience and does not accept the role of faith and revelation that is central to Christian ethics. However, Christian ethics poses the same basic questions and has the same formal structure as philosophical ethics. All ethics attempt to respond to the same questions: what is the good? what values and goals should be pursued? what attitudes and dispositions should characterize the person? what acts are right? what acts are wrong? how do the individual and society go about making ethical decisions?

Contemporary ethicists speak about three generally accepted formal approaches to ethics. The classical forms are teleology and deontology. The teleological approach determines what is the end or the good at which one should aim and then determines the morality of means in relationship to the end. The deontological model understands morality primarily in terms of duty, law, or obligation. Such an approach is primarily interested in what is right. Some contemporary ethicists (e.g., H. Richard Niebuhr) have proposed a third model: the responsibility model, which is primarily interested in what is "fitting." Within Christian ethics all these different models have been employed.

SOURCES. What distinguishes Christian ethics from philosophical ethics and other religious ethics are the sources of wisdom and knowledge that contribute to Christian ethics. All Christian ethics recognizes the Christian scriptures, tradition, and church teaching as the revelatory sources of moral wisdom and knowledge. However, there is much discussion as to how these sources relate to one another and to the nonrevelatory sources of Christian ethics. The three major expressions of Christianity—Eastern Orthodoxy, Roman Catholicism, and Protestantism—and their corresponding ethical traditions emphasize different sources of Christian ethics. At least in theory, all these traditions give primary emphasis to sacred scripture, but there is no general agreement about how the scriptures should be used in Christian ethics.

Christian ethics has always grappled with the question of whether human nature, human reason, and human experience can be sources of ethical wisdom and knowledge. The Roman Catholic tradition has emphasized natural law based on the ability of human reason to arrive at ethical wisdom and knowledge. This emphasis has often been more primary than the influence of revelatory sources. Eastern Orthodox and Protestant ethics have been more suspicious of human reason and experience, although today many ethicists in these traditions give reason an important though still subordinate role.

THE EASTERN ORTHODOX TRADITION. Eastern Orthodox theology, in both its Greek and Russian approaches, is distinguished from other Christian ethics by its emphasis on tradition, especially the teachings of the church fathers, as important sources of moral wisdom and knowledge. The most distinctive characteristic of Orthodox ethics is its relationship to spirituality. Pastoral practice has emphasized the role of monks and confessors as spiritual directors who help guide the spiritual life of the faithful. The goal or end of the moral life is to become like God.

Within the Orthodox tradition there is doubt that natural law is a source of ethical wisdom and knowledge. Many affirm such knowledge on the basis of creation and the image of God embodied in human moral capacity, but others strongly deny this knowledge. At times the polemical nature of discussions between the Orthodox and Roman Catholic traditions seems to have influenced the Orthodox denial of natural law.

Orthodox ethics has been accused of lacking a world-transforming aspect and failing to develop an adequate social ethic, but many defenders of the Orthodox tradition deny this charge. In the past, social ethics was colored by recognition of a "symphony" between the church and the state in the single organism of the Christian empire. Today the diverse settings in which the Orthodox church functions have forced it to try to work out a social ethic and the church's relationship to the state.

HISTORICAL DEVELOPMENT OF EASTERN ORTHODOX ETHICS. Christian ethics as a separate discipline emerged comparatively late in the Orthodox tradition. After the Great Schism of the ninth century the penitentials continued to be an important genre of moral teaching in the East. Despite some legalistic and ritualistic tendencies, Orthodoxy's emphasis on spirituality and striving for perfection served as a safeguard against a minimalistic legalism.

In Russian Orthodoxy the seventeenth-century Kiev school attempted to refute Roman Catholicism and its ethics by developing a theology strongly influenced by scholasticism. *The Orthodox Confession* of Petr Moghila (d. 1646), which was approved with slight modifications by the Greek patriarch at the Synod of Jerusalem (1672), explains Christian moral teaching on the basis of the nine precepts of the church, the seven sacraments, the Beatitudes, and the Ten Commandments. However, even the Kiev school stressed more distinctly Russian and patristic theology in its ascetical and spiritual works.

The eighteenth and nineteenth centuries in Russian Orthodox ethics again saw both dialogue and polemics with Roman Catholic and Protestant ethics in the West. Feofan Prokopovich (d. 1736) ignored the Orthodox tradition, rejected Catholic scholasticism, and turned to Protestant authors for his ethical principles.

In the twentieth century, Nikolai Berdiaev and Sergei Bulgakov appealed to the Russian Orthodox tradition in developing what can be called a communitarian personalism with emphasis on subjectivity, freedom, love, and the need to transform the objective world.

According to Stanley S. Harakas, Christian ethics as a separate theological discipline in Greek Orthodoxy developed in the modern period and emerged as a separate, distinct, scientific discipline only in the nineteenth century. Three different schools or approaches characterize Greek Orthodox moral theology from that time. The Athenian school, strongly influenced by philosophical idealism, sees no vital differences between Christian ethics and philosophical ethics. The Constantinopolitan school is Christocentric and depends heavily on scripture and the church fathers. The Thessalonian school is apophatic in character, stresses a personalist perspective, and is heavily dependent on the monastic tradition. In his *Toward Transfigured Life,* Harakas tries to bring these three schools together.

THE ROMAN CATHOLIC TRADITION. The characteristics of Roman Catholic "moral theology," as Christian ethics has come to be called in the Catholic tradition, are insistence on mediation, acceptance of natural law, and the role of the church. Mediation is perhaps the most characteristic aspect of Roman Catholic theology in general. There is a distinctive Catholic emphasis on conjunctions—of scripture and tradition, faith and reason, faith and works, grace and nature, the divine and human, Jesus and the church and Mary and the saints, love as well as the virtues and the commandments. This approach is an attempt to be universal and to embrace all elements, but it may fall into dichotomy. For example, rather than seeing tradition as a mediation of revelation whose privileged witness is in sacred scripture, scripture and tradition were seen as two separate fonts of revelation. Further, faith and works, properly understood, mean that the gift of salvation is mediated in and through the human response; a perennial danger is to absolutize works. Likewise, mediation insists on the importance of love, but love mediated through all the other virtues and commandments, which, however, must not be emphasized only in themselves.

In the Roman Catholic tradition, natural law can best be understood as human reason directing human beings to their end in accord with their nature. In the classic tradition based on Thomas Aquinas (d. 1274), human nature has a threefold structure: that which is shared with all substances, that which is common to humans and all the animals, and that which is proper to human beings as such.

The third characteristic of Roman Catholic moral theology is its insistence on relationship to the church. Catholic ecclesiology recognizes a special teaching

C

CHRISTIAN ETHICS

The Roman Catholic Tradition

Roman Catholicism is distinguished from other Christian traditions in its understanding of, commitment to, and exercise of the principles of sacramentality, mediation, and communion.

PAGE 577

THOMAS AQUINAS

The Roman Catholic tradition of natural law, based on St. Thomas Aquinas, teaches that human nature is divided into thirds: that shared with all substances, that common to animals, and that which is exclusively human.

THE NATIONAL GALLERY, LONDON/CORBIS

office in matters of faith and morals that is given to, specifically, the pope and the bishops. Catholic ecclesiology in accord with the teaching of Vatican I (1870) recognizes an infallible teaching function that is exercised through ecumenical councils and the *ex cathedra* teaching of the pope as well as definitive teachings by the pope and the bishops. A noninfallible, authoritative teaching office is also exercised by the councils and especially by the pope through encyclicals, allocutions, and the various offices of the Curia Romana. The vast majority of Catholic moral theologians agree that there has never been an infallible papal teaching on a specific moral matter.

Church rites and practice have also influenced Catholic moral theology. Ever since the seventeenth century the primary purpose of moral theology textbooks has been to train confessors for the sacrament of penance, with emphasis on their role as judges. This narrow orientation resulted in an act-centered approach that was casuistic, based primarily on law, and aimed at determining the existence and gravity of sins.

John designed the council to foster reform and reunion, believing that a contemporary reformulation of the Christian tradition would revitalize the Catholic church and ultimately benefit all humankind.

PAGE 549

HISTORICAL DEVELOPMENT OF ROMAN CATHOLIC ETHICS. Roman Catholic moral theology or Christian ethics developed into a scientific discipline earlier than in Eastern Orthodoxy. In the thirteenth century, systematic and scientific theology appeared with the work of the great Scholastic theologians, especially Thomas Aquinas. Moral theology in Thomas's thought is an integrated part of his systematic theology, not a separate discipline. The basic structure of Thomas's moral theology is teleological. The ultimate end of human beings is a happiness attained when the intellect knows perfect truth and the will loves the perfect good. For the Christian, the beatific vision fulfills and perfects human nature. The Franciscan school, represented by Alexander of Hales (d. 1245), Bonaventure (d. 1274), and John Duns Scotus (d. 1308), affirmed the primacy of the will and of charity and emphasized moral theology as wisdom.

The fourteenth century saw a criticism of Thomas from a nominalist perspective that grounded the good not in ontological reality but solely in the will of God and employed a more deontological approach to ethics. After the thirteenth century there appeared the penitentials, very practical handbooks without any philosophical basis or analysis, which often arranged in alphabetical order the problems that the confessor would face in practice.

The three-volume *Institutiones theologiae* moralis appeared in the seventeenth century. These manuals, which became the standard textbooks of Catholic moral theology until the Second Vatican Council, began with a brief description of the ultimate end, which was followed by treatises on human acts, law as the objective norm of morality, and conscience as the subjective norm of morality. The virtues are mentioned, but sin remains the central concern. The sacraments are discussed, but almost exclusively from the viewpoint of moral and legal obligations. In the seventeenth and eighteenth centuries a controversy that arose between rigorists and laxists was finally resolved after papal intervention through the moderate approach of Alfonso Liguori (1696–1787), who was later named the patron of Catholic moral theology and of confessors.

Beginning with Leo XIII's encyclical *Rerum novarum* in 1891, a series of official teachings on the social question appeared. Leo and his immediate successors used a natural-law methodology, understood the state as a natural human society, proposed an anthropology that insisted on both the personal and communitarian aspects of human existence (thus avoiding the extremes of capitalism and socialism), recognized the right of workers to organize, and called for the state to intervene when necessary to protect the rights of workers or any particular class that was suffering. The tradition of official social teaching still exists, but now it stresses some of the newer methodological emphases in Catholic theology and deals with contemporary political and economic problems, especially in a global perspective.

Bernhard Häring's *The Law of Christ* (1954) was the most significant single work in the renewal of Catholic moral theology in the pre-Vatican II period. Häring proposed a biblically inspired, Christocentric approach to moral theology based on the divine call to be perfect even as the gracious God is perfect.

The Second Vatican Council greatly influenced the renewal of moral theology. Now there was greater dialogue with other Christians, non-Christians, and the modern world in general. Contemporary Catholic moral theology, while upholding the goodness of the natural and of the human, has tried to overcome the dichotomy or dualism between the supernatural and the natural. The gospel, grace, Jesus Christ, and the Holy Spirit are related to what happens in daily life in the world. Contemporary moral theology recognizes the need to consider more than acts and lays more emphasis on the person and the virtues and attitudes of the person. No longer is there a monolithic Catholic moral theology based on a Thomistic natural law; instead, many different philosophical approaches are used. In general there has been a shift from classicism to historical consciousness, from the objective to the subjective, from nature to person, from order to freedom. In addition to developments in methodology, there are also widespread debates in contemporary Catholic moral theology about the existence of intrinsically evil actions, absolute norms, and the possibility of dissent from noninfallible church teaching. As a result of these differences, some contemporary

Catholic moral theologians are calling into question some official Catholic teachings in such areas as sexual and medical ethics, but the official teaching office has not changed on these issues.

THE PROTESTANT TRADITION. Protestant Christian ethics has as its distinctive characteristics an emphasis on freedom, an anticasuistic approach, the primacy of scripture, and an emphasis on the theological nature of the discipline. Martin Luther (d. 1546) and the reformers in general stressed the freedom of the Christian, and freedom has characterized much of Protestant life and ethics. In Protestantism there is no central church teaching authority to propose authoritative teaching on specific issues or to insist upon a particular approach, as in Roman Catholicism. Consequently, in Protestant ethics there is a great pluralism and a diversity of approaches.

The emphasis on freedom colors the Protestant understanding of God and how God acts in human history. God is free to act and to intervene in history. Generally Protestant ethics opposes any attempt to claim that God must always act in a particular way. The stress on God's freedom has also influenced a general Protestant unwillingness to base absolute norms on human reason and nature. The freedom of the believer as well as God is safeguarded in Protestant ethics.

The early reformers objected to the Roman Catholic emphasis on merit. They held that salvation comes from faith, not from human works. Protestantism ultimately rejected the Catholic sacrament of penance and thus never developed the casuistry involved in carrying out the role of the confessor as judge. Protestant ethics has been described as an ethics of inspiration, primarily because it does not usually get into a minute philosophical discussion of the morality of particular acts.

The Reformation insistence on the importance of the scripture characterizes much of Protestant ethics, but scripture has been used in different ways. When God's immanence is stressed, there is a tendency to find in scripture a moral message that can be lived by Christians in this world. When the transcendence of God is stressed, scripture tends to be used more dialectically to include a judging and critical role with regard to every human enterprise. Perhaps the greatest change in Protestantism came to the fore in the nineteenth-century dispute over a critical approach to scripture. Whereas liberal Protestantism and soon most of mainstream Protestantism employed literary and historical criticism to understand the Bible, fundamentalist Protestantism has continued to see the Bible primarily in terms of propositional truths or ethical norms and rules that God has revealed for all time and that Christians are called to obey. Such a deontological approach based on God's absolute laws given in scripture cannot be accepted by Protestants who approach scripture with the hermeneutical tools of biblical scholarship. Many contemporary Protestants see in scripture the description of the mighty acts of God in history to which followers of Jesus must respond, and they consequently adopt a responsibility model of Christian ethics rather than a deontological approach.

Protestantism in general gives more significance to the theological aspects of Christian ethics than did traditional Roman Catholic ethics. Catholic ethics tended to see the moral life of all in this world in the light of natural law, whereas Protestantism has generally understood life in this world in relationship to the Bible and to theological concerns.

For some Protestants the primacy of grace and of Christ rules out any significant role for the human and the natural in Christian ethics. For others the effects of sin are so strong that human reason and human nature cannot be valid sources of ethical wisdom and knowledge. Even those Protestant ethicists who would be more open to the human on theological grounds shy away from the ontology and metaphysics that undergird Roman Catholic natural-law thinking. Protestants have also tended to give more significance to history than to nature, because history is more compatible with biblical categories and with the insistence on the freedom of God and of human beings.

HISTORICAL DEVELOPMENT OF PROTESTANT ETHICS. The first systematic, scientific, and independent treatment of Protestant ethics separated from dogmatic theology was produced by Georg Calixtus (d. 1656). Although the early reformers did not write scientific Christian ethics as such, they dealt with significant methodological and substantive issues affecting Christian ethics.

Justification by faith active in love stands at the heart of Lutheran theology and is opposed to merit, justification by works, and legalism. The emphasis on scripture, even to the point of accepting the axiom "scripture alone," is another characteristic of the Reformation. Luther stressed freedom above all, but the dialectical aspect of his thought is seen in his famous saying "A Christian is a perfectly free lord of all, subject to none. A Christian is a perfectly dutiful servant of all, subject to all."

Lutheran social ethics is based on the two-realm theory, referring to the realm of creation and the realm of redemption. In the realm of creation, which involves the social life of human beings, there are true vocations for Christians, but the content of these vocations and what one does are not affected by Jesus, faith, or grace. Redemption affects only one's motivations. For this reason Lutheran social ethics has often been accused of passivism and acceptance of the status quo.

"Whatever your heart clings to and confides in that is really your God."

MARTIN LUTHER

JOHN CALVIN

Reformer, Scholar, Theologian

CALVIN, JOHN (1509-1564), primary Protestant reformer, biblical scholar, church organizer, and theologian. Also a humanist and linguist, Calvin helped to shape and standardize French language and literary style.

Calvin was reclusive and reticent; hence the only Calvin we know is the public figure. He spent his first thirteen years in Noyon, benefiting from the rich traditions of this historic episcopal city where his father served as attorney for the cathedral and secretary to the bishop, Charles de Hangest.

Intimately associated as a youth with the de Hangest household, Calvin developed aristocratic tastes and demeanor. Church benefices permitted him to further his education at the University of Paris; he spent nearly eleven years in Paris, participating in the intellectual life both of the university and the large circle of humanist scholars at the court of the king, Francis I.

At the university, preparing for a career in theology, Calvin had completed the master of arts degree when his father had a falling-out with the bishop. The father ordered his son to change to a career in law. Obediently Calvin moved to Orléans, where the best law faculty in France, under the leadership of Pierre de l'Étoile, was located. Though more interested in humanist studies, he completely immersed himself in the law (at Orléans, Bourges, and Paris) and took his doctorate and his licentiate in three years.

In 1532 Calvin published his first book, a commentary on Seneca's *On Clemency*. Though distinguished for its learning, the book did not win him any acclaim. His days of humanist study in Paris were cut short when, in 1533, his close friend Nicholas Cop, rector of the University of Paris, delivered an address that incorporated ideas of the Lutheran Reformation. Reaction by the theologians at the Sorbonne was strong, and because Calvin had a hand in the composition of the address, he, along with Cop, was forced to flee for his life. Although scholarly opinion differs, it appears that shortly thereafter he underwent the "sudden conversion" he speaks about later. A marked man in France, Calvin spent the rest of his life in exile.

Having turned his considerable talents to the support of the Reformation, in early 1536 Calvin published at Basel the first edition of his epochal *Institutes of the Christian Religion*. Intended as a defense of the French Protestants to the king of France, it marked Calvin as the foremost mind of Protestantism. The desired life of solitude and study that permitted its composition could never again be Calvin's. In late July of 1536, he happened to stop in the small city of Geneva; there God "thrust him into the fray," as he was to say. Geneva had recently declared for the Protestant faith under the urging of the fiery evangelist Guillaume Farel, one of Calvin's colleagues from his Paris days. Farel, learning of Calvin's presence in the city, sought him out and urged him to join in the work of reform at Geneva. When Calvin refused, Farel thundered that God would punish him for turning his back on that work. The shaken Calvin agreed to stay. He was henceforth associated with the city and republic of Geneva in a stormy ministry designed to bring the city into conformity with the biblical model as he understood it.

Calvin's ideal for Geneva was that church and state work hand in hand to create and govern a utopian society in which the biblical worldview was enforced. But the Genevan state was determined to keep the church under its control. A man of courage and indomitable will, Calvin took up the battle. Armed only with the power of the pulpit and of the church institutions, through persistence, adherence to biblical principles, organizational talents, and moral conviction, he managed to overcome massive resistance and to see most of his ideals realized. Geneva was transformed from a city of ill repute to one in which a strict moral code regulated the lives of all.

Unquestionably, Calvin was first and foremost a man of ideas, although he effectively blended thought and action. True to his Renaissance humanist orientation, he was interested only in what was useful. As a theologian he intended only to set forth scriptural teaching.

For Calvin, the word of God in scripture is generated by the Holy Spirit and, therefore, properly interpreted only by the Holy Spirit. It is, thus, a spiritual message. Hence Calvin should not be viewed as an academic theologian, or as a theologian writing for intellectual purposes. He wrote for the church, for believers; his purpose was to edify, to form the pious mind that would emerge in reverential, grateful worship and adoration of God. He constantly warned his readers not to indulge in idle speculation, not to seek to know anything except what is revealed in the scripture, not to forget that theology is more of the heart than of the head.

The principal source for Calvin's thought is, of course, the *Institutes*. This book is best understood as a manual on spirituality. And, although the corpus of his writings is great, Calvin's ideas, whether found in sermons, biblical commentaries, or polemical literature, are consistent with what is presented in the *Institutes*.

In general Calvin had fully accepted Luther's idea that salvation is by grace alone through faith. The often-discussed doctrines of providence and predestination, for example, are presented by Calvin as the response or affirmation of a man of faith, affirming the control of God in his life, not as an epistemological program. To approach his theology from specific topics such as these has not been fruitful.

— BRIAN G. ARMSTRONG

John Calvin (d. 1564) shared much of Luther's theological presuppositions but gave greater emphasis to the will both in God and in human beings. God is primarily sovereign will. Justification does not involve a pietistic response in trust; it means that the will of God becomes active in believers. Calvin comes closer to a Roman Catholic understanding, and Calvinists (like Catholics) have tended to become legalists. Like Luther, Calvin stresses the secular vocation of Christians but interprets Christian work in the world in a more active and transforming way. Some later Calvinists see in worldly success a sign of God's predestining will for the individual. In the twentieth century, Max Weber proposed the controversial theory that the spirit of capitalism was compatible with and abetted by Calvinist ethics.

The Anabaptist-Mennonite tradition, or the left wing of the Reformation, from its sixteenth-century origins has stressed the radical call of discipleship, believer's baptism, and a committed, inflexible following of the radical ethical demands of the gospel. The believers form a sect that stands in opposition to the existing culture and society and bears witness to the gospel, especially the call to peace and nonviolence.

There has been no dominant figure in Anglican ethics and thus no established pattern of doing Anglican ethics. However, in the Anglican community there have been important ethical thinkers who have served as a bridge between Roman Catholic ethics and Protestant ethics. Methodism developed a moral theory calling for spiritual growth and moral renewal.

The Enlightenment had a great influence on Protestant theology and ethics. Nineteenth-century Protestantism saw the emergence of liberal theology. Friedrich Schleiermacher (d. 1834), the most outstanding theologian in the nineteenth century, stressed experience and has been called the founder and most famous proponent of Protestant liberalism. Schleiermacher proposed an ethical theory dealing with goods, duties, and virtues, and he saw moral concerns as present and influencing all other areas of life, especially political, intellectual, aesthetic, and religious. Late nineteenth- and early twentieth-century liberal theology stressed the immanence of God working in human experience and history, the possibility of Christians living out the ethics of Jesus, and evolutionary human progress, and downplayed divine transcendence and the power of sin. Within the context of liberal Protestant theology, the Social Gospel movement came to the fore in the first two decades of the twentieth century in the United States, especially under the leadership of Walter Rauschenbusch (d. 1918). In response to the problems created by the industrial revolution and in response to the privatism and individualism of past Christian ethics, the Social Gospel stressed that the kingdom of God should be made more present on earth and that the social order can and should be christianized. In England and in Germany many Christian thinkers embraced a moderate Christian socialism.

The harsh realities of World War I and the Depression occasioned the rise of the neoorthodoxy of Karl Barth in Europe and the Christian realism of Reinhold Niebuhr in the United States. The reaction stressed the transcendence of God, the dialectical relationship between the existing world and the kingdom of God, the power of sin, and the fact that the fullness of God's kingdom lies outside history. In respect to the contemporary international scene, the World Council of Churches has addressed many contemporary social issues with strong support for liberation movements and has called for just, participative, and sustainable societies.

— CHARLES E. CURRAN

JOHN CALVIN

John Calvin (d. 1564) preached that the will of God becomes active in believers, transforming the world.

CORBIS-BETTMANN

Karl Barth, described by Pope Pius XII as the greatest theologian since Thomas Aquinas, was certainly the most influential of the twentieth century.

PAGE 159

CHRISTIANITY

Christianity is defined by one of its leading modern interpreters, Friedrich Schleiermacher (1768-1834), as "a monotheistic faith . . . essentially distinguished from other such faiths by the fact that in it everything is related to the redemption accomplished by Jesus of Nazareth." While many interpreters of the meaning of Christianity would dispute the content that Schleier-

> *"I am the God of Abraham, Isaac, and Jacob."*
>
> EXODUS, 3:6

macher gave to each of the crucial terms in that definition, the definition as such would probably stand. It is beyond the scope of this article, or even of this encyclopedia, to present an exhaustive summary of all that Christianity is and has ever been: entire encyclopedias several times the size of this one (some of them listed in the bibliography, below) have been devoted to such a summary, and even they have been far from exhaustive. What this article can do, supported by other articles throughout this work, is to sketch some of the main points in the history of Christianity and then to identify some of the features of Christianity that most students of the movement, whether professing personal allegiance to it or not, would probably recognize as belonging to its "essence." Although both the "history" and the "essence" are, unavoidably, controversial in that not everyone would agree with this (or with any) account of them, such an account as this can claim to represent a majority consensus.

THE HISTORY OF CHRISTIANITY

Christianity is a historical religion. It locates within the events of human history both the redemption it promises and the revelation to which it lays claim: Jesus was born under Caesar Augustus and "suffered under Pontius Pilate," at particular dates in the chronology of the history of Rome (even though the specific dates of those two events may be impossible to determine with absolute precision). In this respect Christianity shows its continuing affinities with the Judaism out of which it came, for there too the historical process becomes the peculiar arena of divine activity. The primal revelation for Judaism—and for Christianity—is the divine declaration to Moses (*Ex.* 3:6): "I am the God of Abraham, Isaac, and Jacob." To this primal revelation Christianity adds the assertion (*Heb.* 1:1-2) that the God who in past times had spoken through the prophets and acted through the Exodus from Egypt has now spoken definitively and acted decisively in the life, death, and resurrection of Jesus, seen as the "Christ," the anointed and chosen one of God.

THE CALLING OF THE APOSTLES

Almost everything we know of Jesus of Nazareth, shown here, comes from those who followed him.

ARALDO DE LUCA/CORBIS

EARLY CHRISTIANITY. It is, then, with Jesus of Nazareth that the history of Christianity takes its start. [See Jesus.] Almost everything we know of him, however, comes from those who responded, in loyalty and obedience, to the events of his life and the content of his teaching. Therefore the history of the earliest Christian communities, to the extent that we are in a position to reconstruct it, is at the same time the history of Jesus as they remembered him. His own immediate followers were all Jews, and it is within that framework that they interpreted the significance of what they had received and perceived: he was the Christ, or Messiah, who had been promised to the patriarchs of Israel. As the record of those promises, the Hebrew scriptures were sacred for early Christians no less than for Jews, enabling them to claim a continuity with the history of the people of God since the creation of the world. The apostle Paul both summarized and reinterpreted the message of the first generation of believers. Together with the written deposit of their memories of Jesus in the Gospels, the writings of Paul and several other documents were circulated widely in Christian communities throughout the Mediterranean world, eventually becoming the Christian addendum (or "New Testament") to the Hebrew scriptures (or "Old Testament"). [*See* Biblical Literature; *and* Gospel.]

Paul was also responsible for the transformation of Christianity from a Jewish sect to a gentile movement by the end of the first century of the common era. The importance of this change for Christian history is impossible to exaggerate. Jesus had been born in an obscure corner of the Roman empire, but now his followers took upon themselves the assignment of challenging that empire and eventually of conquering it in his name. The opposition between empire and church during the second and third centuries sometimes took the form of persecution and martyrdom, but all that was replaced in the fourth century by the creation of a Christian Roman empire, when the emperor Constantine (306-337) first made the new faith legal, then made it his own, then made it the official religion of the realm. As part of their political and philosophical defense against their adversaries, the apologists for Christianity in the second and third centuries had also sought to clarify its relation to Greek and Roman thought, but with its official adoption their successors in the fourth and fifth centuries undertook to interpret Christian theology as the perennial philosophy in which the aspirations of all religions were now corrected and fulfilled. Among these later apologists, Augustine of Hippo (354-430) in his *City of God* articulated the Christian case against those who charged that by undermining the traditional values of Roman religion the church had been responsible for the decline and fall of the Roman empire. On the contrary, he said, Christianity was the support of just rulers and legitimate governments, and by its faith in the God of history, as well as by its moral teachings about work and the family, it promoted the welfare of society; the City of Earth would function best if it acknowledged the transcendent reality of the City of God, which was beyond history but which had made its presence known within this particular history.

The century that began with Constantine and ended with Augustine also saw the stabilization of the internal life and structure of the Christian movement. One by one, alternative ways of thought and belief that were adjudged to be aberrations were sloughed off or excluded as "heresies" or "schisms." Some of these (particularly the various species of apocalyptic or millenarian expectation) were efforts to perpetuate ways of being Christian that no longer suited the needs of the life of the church when the long-expected second coming of Jesus Christ failed to materialize, while others (notably the several gnostic systems) involved the adaptation to the Christian message of schemes of revelation and salvation that were also manifesting themselves in other religions. [*See* Gnosticism.] In opposition to these alternative ways of thought and belief, Christianity, since before the days during which the books of the New Testament were being written, identified the content of orthodox belief and fixed its form in a succession of creedal statements. The earliest of these, including that eventually formulated as the Apostles' Creed, are put into the mouth of one or another or all twelve of the apostles of Jesus, and the most important creedal statement was adopted (under Constantine's patronage) at the Council of Nicaea in 325 (see "The Pattern of Christian Belief," below).

During those same early centuries, Christianity was also identifying the structures of authority that were thought to guarantee the preservation of "apostolic" faith and order: the Bible and the bishops. As already noted, the Bible of the Christians consisted of two parts (or "testaments"): the books they had inherited from Judaism, and the combination into a "New Testament" of four gospels about the life and teachings of Jesus, epistles attributed to Paul and other apostolic figures, the *Acts of the Apostles*, and (from among the many extant apocalyptic writings) the *Revelation to John*. The bishops through their uninterrupted succession were believed to certify the continuity of the church with its apostolic foundations. As the church that could claim to have been shepherded by all twelve apostles, Jerusalem held a unique place; but as the church that Peter had governed and to which Paul had written (and where both Peter and Paul had been martyred), and as the congregation at the capital of the civilized world, Rome early acquired a special position as "*the* apostolic see," which it would consolidate by the leadership in faith and life that it exercised during the crises of the fourth and fifth centuries. Actually, the criterion of "apostolicity" was a circular one: apostolic foundation of episcopal sees, apostolic authorship of biblical books, and apostolic orthodoxy of creedal belief supported one another, and no one of them was ever sufficient of itself—even in the case of the see of Rome—to serve as such a criterion in isolation from the others.

OFFICIAL ESTABLISHMENT OF CHRISTIANITY. Constantine's acceptance of Christianity and the eventual establishment of it as the official faith of the Roman empire is rightly seen as the most portentous event—for good or ill or some combination of the two—in all of Christian history; conversely, "the end of the Constantinian era," which is how many thoughtful observers have characterized the twentieth century, has brought about the reshaping and rethinking of all the structures of faith and life that Christianity evolved in the aftermath of its new status from the fourth century on. Both in the Roman West, where Constantine prevailed in 312 "by the power of the cross," as he believed, and in the Byzantine East, where Constantine established the new capital of the Christian Roman empire two decades later, Christianity undertook to create a new civilization that would be a continuation of ancient Greece and Rome and yet would be a transformation of those cultures through the infusion of the spiritual power of Christ as Lord.

The Christian culture of Byzantium. That pattern of continuation with transformation took a special form in the Christian culture of the Byzantine empire, whose history persisted for more than a thousand years from the creation of Constantinople as "New Rome" in 330 CE to its fall to the armies of the Turkish sultan Mehmed II (and its change of name to Istanbul) in 1453. Constantine and his successors—and, above all, the emperor Justinian (r. 527-565)—saw themselves in their Roman capacity as the legitimate heirs of the ancient pagan caesars, but at the same time in their Christian capacity as "equal to the apostles" *(isapostolos)*. In the exercise of this special authority, they frequently became involved in the administrative, liturgical, and doctrinal affairs of the church, and often

Augustine of Hippo understood the essence of God to be truth itself, which is at once goodness itself.

PAGE 247

without opposition and with great success. Contemporary historians tell us that it was the emperor Constantine who came up with the formula "one in being [*homoousios*] with the Father," which resolved, at the Council of Nicaea in 325, the dispute over the metaphysical relation between Christ and God. Later historians have coined for this special status of the Byzantine emperor the term *Caesaropapism*, implying that what the pope was in the West, the caesar was in the East. While the reign of Constantine, and even more that of Justinian, may have merited such a designation, the patriarch of Constantinople repeatedly asserted the authority of the church to determine its own destiny, above all in the areas of belief and worship. Most notably, in the iconoclastic controversies of the eighth and ninth centuries, which were brought on by the campaign of a series of emperors to remove images from the worship of the church, the defenders of the church's autonomy, who included especially monks and empresses, eventually carried the day, and the authority of the emperor to legislate unilaterally for the church was significantly curtailed.

One reason for this success in the iconoclastic disputes was the special place of icons in Byzantine (and later in Slavic) Orthodoxy, which one scholar has called its "distinctive identity." As interpreted by its defenders, the cult of the icons was anything but the relapse into idolatrous paganism of which it was accused by the

CONSTANTINE
Changing the Course of Christian History

CONSTANTINE (272/273-337), known as Constantine the Great, Roman emperor and agent of the christianization of the Roman empire. Born at Naissus, the only son of Helena and Flavius Constantius, Constantine was assured a prominent role in Roman politics when Diocletian, the senior emperor in the Tetrarchy, appointed his father Caesar in 293. He doubtless expected to succeed to his father's position when Diocletian and Maximian abdicated in 305. But Galerius, who may have contrived the abdication and as the new eastern emperor controlled the succession, ignored Constantine and instead nominated as Caesar his own nephew, Severus. Constantine could not challenge this decision immediately, but when his father died at York in July 306, he reasserted the claim, this time backed by the British and Gallic armies, and requested confirmation from the eastern emperor. Galerius resisted, but to avoid a confrontation offered Constantine the lesser rank of Caesar. For the next seven years civil war disrupted the western half of the empire.

In the end it was Constantine who triumphed. Christian observers who produced accounts of the event a few years later proclaimed this was more than a political triumph. On the eve of the battle, they insisted, Constantine had experienced the vision (or visions) that inspired his conversion to Christianity. Constantine's motives are beyond reconstruction, but it is clear that he believed the victory had been won with divine assistance, Constantine's legislation and activities after 312 attest the evolution of his Christian sympathies.

Whether the "conversion" represented a dramatic break with the pagan past is more problematic. Unlike Galerius, who had vigorously persecuted Christians in the East, Constantine was a tolerant pagan, content with the accumulation of heavenly patrons (Sol Invictus, Apollo). In 312 he may well have considered the God of the Christians simply another heavenly patron, demonstrably more powerful than others but not necessarily incompatible. Though he refused to participate after 312 in distinctly pagan ceremonies, Constantine retained the title *pontifex maximus* and evidently did not find the demands of government and religion irreconcilable. Exclusive commitment and a sense of mission, however, would develop over time. After 324 he did not hesitate to use his office to condemn pagan beliefs and practices and to promote the christianization of the empire.

Politics accounts in large measure for Constantine's transformation from benefactor to advocate. The conversion did not alienate pagans, for religion had not been an issue in the civil war, and nothing indicates that Licinius, whom Galerius had chosen as co-emperor in 308, objected to Constantine's evident Christian sympathies in 312. As political rivalry developed over the next few years, however, the religious policies of the emperors diverged, especially after the inconclusive civil war of 316/7. Politics and religion became so entangled that Constantine, using attacks on Christians in the East as pretext, could declare his campaign against Licinius in 324 a crusade against paganism. His victory at Chrysopolis (18 September) simultaneously removed the last challenge to his authority and legitimized his emerging sense of mission.

Denunciations of pagan practices followed immediately, coupled with lavish grants for the construction of churches and preferential treatment of Christian candidates for administrative posts. Constantine also took the lead in efforts to restore order in an increasingly divided church. The bishops assembled in Nicaea (Bithynia), responding to the counterarguments of Alexander (bishop of Alexandria) and others who did not believe in the divinity of Christ, condemned Arianism and adopted the Nicene Creed that declared the Father and Son to be of the same essence.

— JOHN W. EADIE

iconoclasts; instead it represented the commitment of Orthodoxy to the reality of the full incarnation of the Son of God in the human figure of Jesus: worship of the image of Jesus Christ was in fact addressed to one who was in his single person completely God and completely man. Thus, to a degree unknown in the West even in the high Middle Ages, Greek Christianity defined itself by its liturgy and devotion, not only (perhaps not primarily) by its dogma and life. The very term *orthodoxia* in Greek, and its Slavic counterpart *pravoslavie*, meant in the first instance "correct worship," which also included "correct doctrine." Embodied as it was in the curriculum of Byzantine educational institutions at all levels, the continuing hold that a christianized Neoplatonism exercised over its expositors enabled them to make use of its metaphysics and epistemology in the service of the church's message. The Byzantine icons were only one part of a total Christian culture, in which architecture, poetry, and music also contributed their special part. One feature of this culture was a commitment to preserving the indigenous culture of each people to which the Christian message came: while the Western missionaries, in introducing the Mass, taught each nation Latin when they taught it the gospel (and thus, even without intending to do so, gave it at least some access to pre-Christian Roman culture), Eastern missionaries translated not only the Bible but also the liturgy into the language of the people. [*See* Missions, *article on* Christian Missions.] It was, above all, in the Byzantine missions to the Slavs (where the two philosophies about the proper language of the liturgy clashed) that this peculiarity of the Eastern church served to create an integrally Slavic Orthodoxy, through which the Ukraine, Bulgaria, Russia, and Serbia came of age as nations. [*For further discussion, see* Eastern Christianity.]

Christianity in the Middle Ages. In the Latin West, by contrast, the outcome of the Constantinian settlement took a radically divergent form, in which it was not principally the Christian emperor and the Christian empire, but the bishop of Rome and the papacy, that was to set the tone of the historical development of Christianity. [*See* Roman Catholicism *and* Papacy.] With the transfer of the capital to Constantinople, the pope came to symbolize and to embody the continuity with ancient Rome. Within less than a century after that transfer, the bishop of Rome was calling himself "supreme pontiff" *(pontifex maximus),* a title that had belonged to the pagan caesars. When the various Germanic tribes arrived in western Europe, they found the papacy already present as a political and cultural force. Those tribes that chose to ignore that force

"In this sign shalt thou conquer."

EMPEROR CONSTANTINE, 312

BYZANTINE ICON

Icons held a distinctive place within the Byzantine Orthodoxy.

GIANNI DAGLI ORTI/CORBIS

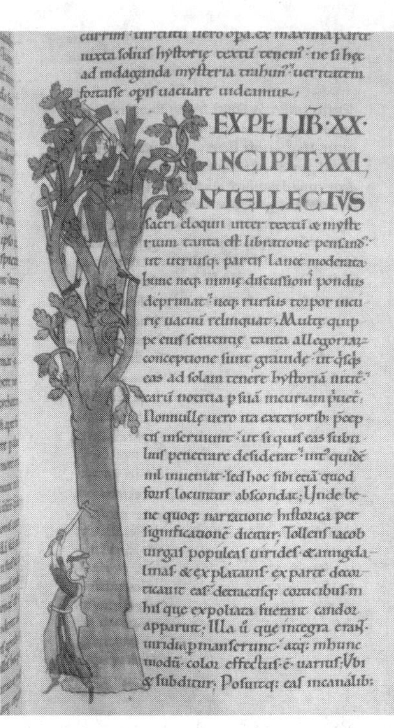

MEDIEVAL MANUSCRIPT

Monks were often scribes, copying and preserving religious texts like this for the ages.

GIANNI DAGLI ORTI/CORBIS

by clinging too long to Germanic paganism or to forms of Christianity that had been outlawed as heretical also lost the opportunity to shape the future of European history, but the Franks, by allying themselves with the bishop of Rome, were to determine its subsequent course through much of the Middle Ages. The symbolic high point of the alliance came on Christmas Day in the year 800 with the crowning of the Frankish king Charles, known to history as Charlemagne (c. 742-814), as "emperor" at the hands of Pope Leo III in Rome, even though there was still an emperor in Constantinople. With its own emperor—and, above all, its own bishop and supreme pontiff—the West was free to pursue its own destiny. And although the schism between West and East, in a technical and canonical sense, did not take place until several centuries later, and in a spiritual sense may be said to have happened in 1204, the historical intuition that located it as having originated in the ninth century was in many ways sound.

Confrontation with Islam. Each in its own way, both Eastern and Western Christendom were compelled, from the seventh century onward, to come to terms with the reality of Islam. During the one hundred years after the death of the prophet Muhammad in 632 CE, the geographical spread of Islam was both more rapid and more effective than that of Christianity had been during its first several centuries. Several of the major centers of the Eastern churches—Antioch, Alexandria, Jerusalem itself—became Muslim in gov-

THE MONKS AND THE CLOISTER

Defenders of the Faith

Because its administrative structure and intellectual tradition were so different from those of the Byzantine East, the medieval Christianity of the West expressed its relation to society and culture in a distinctive fashion as well. In even greater measure than in the East, the bearers of its civilizing force were monks. [*See* Monasticism.] The missionaries who brought the gospel to the barbarians—for example, Boniface (680-754), the "apostle of Germany" sent from Rome, and Cyril (c. 826-869) and Methodius (c. 815-c. 884), the "apostles to the Slavs" sent from Constantinople—were monks. So were the scribes who then brought Classical civilization to the same barbarians; thus the Benedictine monk the Venerable Bede (c. 673-735) laid many of the foundations of scholarship in England. Most of the reformers who throughout the Middle Ages recalled the church to its primitive faith and its ancient loyalties came from monasticism, as was evident above all in the work of Bernard of Clairvaux (1090-1153), "the unmitered pope" of the twelfth century, and then in the program of Francis of Assisi (1181/2-1226). The cloisters likewise supplied most of the theologians who systematized and defended the faith: Anselm of Canterbury (c. 1033-1109) was a Benedictine abbot, Thomas Aquinas (c. 1225-1274) was a Dominican friar, and Bonaventure (c. 1217-1274) and Duns Scotus (c. 1266-1308) were both Franciscans.

Repeatedly, of course, the monastic communities themselves needed to be reformed, and in virtually every century of the Middle Ages there arose movements of renewal dedicated to the purification of the monastic ideal and, through it, renewal of the life of the total church. When the leaders of such movements managed to establish themselves as leaders of the total church, the result was often a great conflict. Thus in the eleventh century the reformer Hildebrand became Pope Gregory VII (in 1073) and set about renewing the administration, the morals, and the faith and life of the church. He sought to enforce the law of clerical celibacy, to root out financial and political corruption, to free bishops and prelates from the dominance of secular princes, and to purge the church of heresy and schism. This brought him into collision both with his own ecclesiastical subordinates and with the empire, but it also gave him the opportunity to formulate for all time the special prerogatives of the church and the bishop of Rome (see "The Community of Christian Worship," below).

— JAROSLAV PELIKAN

ernment, although a large Christian population was able to practice its faith under varying degrees of pressure. Eventually, in 1453, Constantinople also became a Muslim city. The Muslim conquest of Palestine was likewise responsible for the most historic confrontation ever between Christianity and another faith, in the Crusades, as successive armies of Western Christians sought to reconquer the "holy places" associated with the life of Jesus—an enterprise that eventually failed. [*See* Crusades.]

Reformation Christianity. Reform movements, it seemed, could always be counted on to rescue the church in times of crisis—until, through Martin Luther (1483-1546) and the Reformation, a crisis arose in which the primary impetus for reform was to express itself not *through* monasticism or the papacy, but *against* both monasticism and the papacy (although it must be remembered that Luther, too, was originally a monk). Already in various late medieval reformations, such as those of the "Spiritual" Franciscans and the Hussites, there was the sense that (to cite the four standard "marks" of the church enumerated in the Nicene Creed) Christendom could be neither one nor holy nor catholic nor apostolic until it had replaced the secularized and corrupt authority of the bishop of Rome with the authenticity of the word of God, for which some looked to a church council while others put their confidence in the recovery of the message of the Bible. That sense finally found its voice in the program of the Protestant reformers. Beginning with the belief that they were merely the loyal children of Mother Church recalling her to her genuine self, they soon found themselves so alienated from the structures and teachings of the church of their time that they were obliged to look for, and if need be to invent, alternative structures and teachings of their own.

The structures and teachings of the several Protestant groups covered an extremely wide spectrum, such that those at one end of the spectrum (Lutherans and Anglicans) were in many ways closer to Roman Catholicism and even to Eastern Orthodoxy, despite the schisms both of the Middle Ages and of the Reformation, than they were to Socinianism or even to Anabaptism or even perhaps to Calvinism. In their ecclesiastical structures, the churches that came out of the Reformation ranged from a retention of the historic episcopate (e.g., in England and Sweden) to a presbyterian form of church government (e.g., in Scotland and in many, though by no means all, of the Calvinist churches on the European continent) to an insistence on the primacy and autonomy of the local congregation (e.g., in various of the dissenters from Anglicanism in the seventeenth and eighteenth centuries, including the Congregationalists and Baptists, especially in the New World). While the mainstream of Protestantism has in its doctrine maintained a loyalty to the doctrines of the Trinity, of the person of Christ, of original sin, and of salvation through the death of Christ, as these had been developed in the early and medieval church, it has diverged from earlier development (and thus from Roman Catholicism and Eastern Orthodoxy) above all in its understanding of the nature of the church and of the meaning (and hence the number) of the sacraments, with only baptism and the Lord's Supper being regarded as authentic sacraments by most Protestants. (See "The Pattern of Christian Belief," below.) The principal difference, at least as seen both by the Protestant reformers and by their Roman Catholic adversaries, lay in the area of religious authority: not the church or its tradition, not the papacy or a church council, but the Bible alone, was to be the norm that determined what Christians were to believe and how they were to live. [*See* Reformation.]

The Roman Catholic response to the Protestant Reformation is sometimes called the "Counter-Reformation," although that term has come to be regarded by many scholars as excessively negative in its connotations because it seems to ignore the positive reforms that were not merely a reaction to Protestantism. "The Roman Catholic Reformation" is in many ways a preferable designation. First through a series of responses to the theology and program of the reformers, then above all through the canons and decrees of the Council of Trent (1545-1563), the Catholic Reformation took up the issues addressed by Luther and by his most eminent successor, John Calvin (1509-1564), both in the area of church life and morals and in the area of church teaching and authority. Many of the corruptions that had acted as tinder for the Reformation received the careful attention of the council fathers, with the result that Roman Catholicism and the papacy emerged from the crisis of the Reformation diminished in size but chastened and strengthened in spirit. The creation of the Society of Jesus by Ignatius Loyola (c. 1491-1556) in 1534 provided the church with a powerful instrument for carrying out the program of reform and renewal, and many of the tools employed by the reformers (e.g., the printing press and the catechism) lent themselves to that program just as effectively. A deepening mystical devotion gave new life to medieval spirituality, particularly in sixteenth-century Spain, and the theology of Thomas Aquinas acquired new authority as the defenders of the faith closed ranks against Protestant thought. The historical coincidence of the discovery of the New World and the Protestant Reformation, which both Protestants and Roman Catholics interpreted as providential, enabled Roman Catholic missionaries to recoup in North and South America the losses in prestige and membership caused by the

The Crusades continued the old tradition of pilgrimage to the Holy Land that was often undertaken in fulfillment of a vow or as a penance.

PAGE 198

Reformation. It was above all in Latin America that this recovery became a decisive religious and cultural force. Although divided (by the papal Line of Demarcation of 1493) between Spain and Portugal, Latin America was "united" in the sense that it was colonized and converted by Roman Catholic Christianity; the process of the christianization of native populations was a gradual one, and many beliefs and practices of their pre-Christian history were carried over into their new faith. The effect of these and other missionary campaigns in the sixteenth and seventeenth centuries was to make the term *catholic* in *Roman Catholic* begin to mean in fact what it had always meant in principle: present throughout the known world.

COUNTER REFORMATION

Ignatius Loyal created the Society of Jesus which carried out a program of reform and renewal within the Roman Catholic Church in response to the Protestant Reformation.

MICHAEL NICHOLSON/CORBIS

THE CHRISTIAN EAST. Throughout the Middle Ages and the Reformation there were sporadic efforts in the West to establish (or reestablish) contact with the East; these ranged from the dispatch of various legations, to the translation of various classic works in one direction or the other, to marriages between Western monarchs and Byzantine or Russian princesses. The Crusades, which the East sometimes invited and sometimes dreaded, did at least reacquaint many members of the two traditions with one another, although the most unforgettable instance of such reacquaintance was the catastrophe of the sack of Christian Constantinople by the armies of the Fourth Crusade in 1204. Followed as it was two and a half centuries later by the Muslim capture of Constantinople and the end of the Byzantine empire, the tragedy of 1204 is probably better entitled than any other event to the dubious distinction of being the point at which the Eastern and Western churches came into schism—a schism that, except for repeated but short-lived attempts at reunion (the most notable of which was probably the Union of Florence in 1439), has persisted ever since. Although the loss of Constantinople to the Turks drastically reduced its sphere of influence, the ecumenical patriarchate of Constantinople continued to enjoy a preeminence of honor within Eastern Orthodoxy, as it does to this day. Numerically as well as politically, however, it was Slavic Orthodoxy, above all in Russia, that became the "heir apparent," uniting itself with Russian culture as it had with medieval Greek culture. Plagued though it was by internal schisms, and caught in the political and cultural upheavals of the tsarist empire, the church in Russia went on producing saints and scholars, and through the icons and the liturgy it suffused the faith and life of the common people with the meaning of the Christian faith: the icon painter Andrei Rublev (c. 1360-c. 1430) and, in more modern times, the novelist and spiritual thinker Fedor Dostoevskii (1821-1881) were among the products of this tradition best known in the West. The nineteenth and twentieth centuries witnessed an upsurge of interest in Eastern Orthodoxy throughout Western Christianity, as a consequence partly of the ecumenical movement and partly of the Russian Revolution, as both Protestants and Roman Catholics looked to Orthodoxy for the correction of what had come to be seen as Western deficiencies and overemphases in the aftermath of the Reformation.

POST-REFORMATION CHRISTIANITY. The ecclesiastical map of the West after the Reformation shows a Europe divided between an almost solidly Roman Catholic south and a predominantly Protestant north, with the latter in turn divided between Anglican, Lutheran, and Reformed or Calvinist forms of Christianity. [*See* Protestantism.] The same competition was exported into Christian missions in Africa and Asia and into the Americas. Among the most influential developments of the centuries following the Reformation was the effort, which took a distinct form in each denomination but nevertheless manifested a similarity of spirit, to encourage a deeper seriousness about the claims of the Christian gospel upon personal faith and life: Jansenism within French (and then North American) Roman Catholicism, Puritanism (and later on Methodism) within English Protestantism, and Pietism within the Lutheran and Reformed churches of the continent and of the New World. Especially during the eighteenth century, these movements had it as one of their primary goals to combat and counteract the influence, both in the church and in public life, of the rationalism, freethinking, and "infidelity" associated with the Enlightenment. Combining as it did the application to Christian history and biblical literature of the methods of historical criticism (particularly in German theological scholarship) with the reexamination or even the rejection of the special claims of Christianity to a privileged place in Western society (particularly in the legislation of the French Revolution), the Enlightenment came to represent the campaign for the secularization of culture. An important feature of that combination of emphases in Enlightenment thought was a fundamental reconsideration of the traditional Christian assertions of finality and uniqueness. As the philosophical and historical basis for such assertions was coming under increasing attack from within such traditionally Christian institutions as the theological faculties of universities, the discovery of other religions both in the historical past and in the distant parts of the present world was bringing such concepts as the uniqueness of the Christian message into serious question. The special privileges that Christianity had enjoyed since the Constantinian era were gradually withdrawn. Separation of church and state, as developed especially in the United States, and the growth of religious toleration and religious liberty were the social and political expressions of the new sit-

KARL BARTH
The Message of the Cross

BARTH, KARL (1886-1968), Swiss Reformed theologian, described by Pope Pius XII as the greatest theologian since Thomas Aquinas, and certainly the most influential of the twentieth century.

Throughout his life Barth endeavored to interpret the gospel and examine the church's message in the context of society, the state, war, revolution, totalitarianism, and democracy, over against the pretensions of man to solve the problems of his own destiny, without the judgment of the message of the cross and the resurrection of Jesus Christ.

Barth used Paul's letter to the Romans for a critique of philosophical idealism, romanticism, and religious socialism. If his concern was that the church should listen to the divine word of judgment on our political and intellectual towers of Babel, his concern throughout his life was also to assert "that there is joy with God . . . and that the Kingdom on earth begins with joy." Together with his lifelong friend Eduard Thurneysen (1888-1974), he discovered in the Bible "a strange new world, the world of God," which is the kingdom of God, established by God and not man.

There were distinctive stages in Barth's theological development, in each of which he wrestled with the polarities of God and man. At first, like Herrmann, he identified conscience with the voice of God, but increasingly he argued that the voice of God is heard only in scripture, in encounter with Christ, the living Word.

The chasm between God and man can be bridged by God alone, and not by man. The Word of the cross means that God says no to our human sin and pride and pretensions, while in grace God says yes to his own good creatures in a word of forgiveness. Barth saw that there are elements of negation and affirmation in all human knowledge of God, leading him to see an analogy of "relation," but not of "being," between God and man grounded in grace.

In 1927 Barth began writing *Christian Dogmatics*, intending to expound all the main Christian doctrines, by grounding all he had to say on God's self-revelation in Jesus Christ. The first volume was entitled *Christian Doctrine in Outline, Volume I: The Doctrine of the Word of God, Prolegomena to Christian Dogmatics*. In it he argues that possibility of Christian knowledge of God is grounded on the actuality of the revelation in Jesus, as he makes himself known to faith by the Holy Spirit.

Within this self-revelation of the triune God we can distinguish three forms of the one Word of God: the eternal Word incarnate in Jesus Christ, the written Word in the witness of the Bible to that primary Word, and the Word of God as proclaimed in the church.

The reviewers of this first volume criticized Barth for so casting the gospel into the language of an immediate timeless encounter with God that he was in danger of dehistoricizing the gospel and transposing theology into a new philosophical mold. Barth took this criticism seriously. In 1931 he published *Fide quaerens intellectum* (Faith Seeking Understanding). From Anselm he had learned that the Word of God has its own rational content in God. The polarity of God and man must be interpreted, not so much in the language of an existential encounter between God and man in the crisis of faith, but primarily in terms of the given unity of God and man in Jesus Christ, the incarnate Lord, in whom God has come—not simply *in* a man, but *as* a man—in a once and for all reconciling act in which we are called to participate through the Holy Spirit.

Barth was concerned to unpack the implications of this Christ-centered perspective in every area of life. It proved highly significant in his outspoken opposition to Hitler, to the persecution of the Jews, and to the so-called German Christians who sought to justify National Socialism and its racist policies. Barth felt that this was a betrayal of the Christian understanding of grace by its appeal to sources of revelation other than that given to us in Jesus Christ.

— JAMES B. TORRANCE

"Man still bears in his bodily frame the indelible stamp of his lowly origin."

CHARLES DARWIN
DESCENT OF MAN
1871

uation that was beginning to become evident at the end of the eighteenth century.

The nineteenth century. Despite the losses in both influence and numbers that it suffered in the period of the Enlightenment, Christianity entered the nineteenth century with a strong sense of its continuing relevance and special mission. The critical reexamination of the Christian toleration of slavery—long overdue, in the opinion of observers inside and outside the church—came to full realization in the nineteenth century, even though a civil war in the United States was necessary to bring this about. It was likewise in the nineteenth century, surnamed "the great century" in the leading history of Christian missions, that most of the major Christian denominations of the West, Protestant as well as Roman Catholic, set out to evangelize the globe. Although the Christian missionary and the colonialist conqueror often marched arm in arm across that globe, the results for native cultures were quite ambiguous: sometimes a loss of national identity and cultural deracination, but on the other hand no less often a deepening sense of historical particularity and the acquisition of scholarly instruments for understanding it and thus of overcoming both the colonialism and the missions. Significantly, it was from the mission schools founded in the nineteenth century that a disproportionately high number of the revolutionary leaders of the twentieth century in developing nations were to emerge. On the home front, the confrontation between traditional Christian beliefs and the discoveries of modern science engaged the attention of the churches. The most violent such confrontation was brought on by the work of Charles Darwin, whose books *The Origin of Species* (1859) and *The Descent of Man* (1871) called into question the traditional Christian belief in a special creation of the human species in the image of God as based on the biblical accounts of creation in the *Book of Genesis*. [*For broader discussion, see* Evolution.] Yet as the nineteenth century ended, there was a widespread expectation that the next would truly be "the Christian century." *Christianizing the Social Order* by Walter Rauschenbusch (1861-1918), first published in 1912, was a representative statement of that expectation.

The twentieth century. As things turned out, the twentieth century proved to be the age of two world wars, of the coming to power of Marxist regimes throughout most of historic Eastern Christendom, and of moral and intellectual crises (including the Nazi Holocaust and the issues raised by modern technology) that would shake the traditional beliefs and historical confidence of Christians with unprecedented force. The reaction was, if not an overt loss of faith, then a growing indifference in many traditionally Christian groups. The most influential Christian theologian of the twentieth century, Karl Barth (1886-1968), protested the synthesis of the gospel with human culture and called for a reassertion of that gospel in its native power and uniqueness. At the same time, however, the most influential Christian event of the twentieth century, the Second Vatican Council of 1962-1965, undertook a reform of Christian faith and life that reached out to other Christians and to other religious traditions with a new openness. The council was the manifestation within Roman Catholicism of a new ecumenical consciousness that had its origins in Protestantism; the divisions that had followed in the wake of the Reformation now came under question in the light of the recognition that what separated Christians from one another was less significant than all the things that still held them together. That ecumenical consciousness throughout the Christian movement found expression in the recovery of historic Christian beliefs, in the creation of contemporary forms of worship, and in the reexamination of patterns of Christian life both individual and corporate. [*For further discussion, see* Vatican Councils, *article on* Vatican II.] It remains to consider these three areas of belief, worship, and life, which, taken together, may be said to constitute the essence of Christianity.

THE ESSENCE OF CHRISTIANITY

In these nearly two thousand years of its history, Christianity has manifested an almost infinite variety of expressions as it has spread its presence and influence into all the major cultures of the Western world and into most of those of the East as well. With a billion or more adherents throughout the human race at the end of the twentieth century, it continues to be heterogeneous and pluralistic in its forms of organization and worship, belief, and life—so much so that it appears difficult or foolhardy or impossible to attempt to identify any characteristics as the distinctive genius or continuing essence of Christianity. A well-known criterion was the one proposed by Vincent of Lérins in the fifth century—what has been accepted "everywhere, always, by all" *(ubique, semper, ab omnibus)*—but the welter of detail about the history of Christianity scattered across the hundreds of articles dealing with the subject in the volumes of this encyclopedia should convince even the most casual reader that if there is an "essence of Christianity" it cannot possibly be everything that Christianity has ever been to everyone in every time and every place. Therefore, to quote again from Schleiermacher, "the only pertinent way of discovering the peculiar essence of any particular faith and reducing it as far as possible to a formula is by showing the element which remains constant throughout the most diverse religious affections within this same communion, while it is absent from analogous affections within other communions."

The search for an essence of Christianity is as old as

the primary deposits of Christianity themselves. Already in the Hebrew scriptures, which Christianity took over as its Old Testament, the prophet Micah had declared: "God has told you what is good; and what is it that the Lord asks of you? Only to act justly, to love loyalty, to walk wisely before your God" (NEB *Mi.* 6:8). And an unknown first-century Christian writer, author of what came to be called the letter to the Hebrews in the New Testament, stated that "anyone who comes to God must believe that he exists and that he rewards those who search for him" (*Heb.* 11:6). The most successful formula for the essence of Christianity, however, was that of the apostle Paul: "In a word, there are three things that last for ever: faith, hope, and love; but the greatest of them all is love" (*1 Cor.* 13:13). Already in the second century, Irenaeus (c. 130-c. 200), bishop of Lyons, was invoking this formula as a summary of what "endures unchangeably," and in the fifth century it became the basis and the outline for Augustine's *Enchiridion*, to which Augustine himself usually referred as *On Faith, Hope, and Love*. From Augustine, in turn, the formula went on to provide the table of contents for the early catechisms in the age of Charlemagne and then for the rapid expansion in the number and use of catechisms by all parties in the age of the Reformation. Hence it may serve as a device for organizing this description of the essence of Christianity in its historical sweep, its geographical expansion, and its genius. Considered both in its history and in its contemporary expressions, Christianity has been, and is, a system of faith, of hope, and of love, a pattern of belief (and thought), a community of worship (and culture), and a way of life (and society). Paul's triad of faith, hope, and love may thus be used to correspond to the even more universal schema of the true, the beautiful, and the good. [*For further discussion in broad religious perspective, see* Faith.]

THE PATTERN OF CHRISTIAN BELIEF. As a system of faith, Christianity manifests "faith" in all the various meanings that this term has acquired in the history of religion: as loyalty to the divine, based on the prior loyalty of the divine to the world and to humanity; as the confidence that God is trustworthy in truth and love; as dependence on the Father of Jesus Christ, who is the source of all good in this life and in the life to come; as the commitment to direct thought and action in accordance with the divine word and will; and as the affirmation that certain events and

ENCHIRIDION

Augustine's Enchiridion is based on 1 Corinthians 13:13, which many call the "essence" of Christianity.

NORTH CAROLINA MUSEUM OF ART/CORBIS

"In a word , there are three things that last forever, faith, hope, and love: but the greatest of them all is love."

CORINTHIANS 13:13

declarations, as given by divine revelation, are a reliable index to that will and word. It is the last of those meanings that provides a basis for describing in an

CHRISTIAN POPULATIONS PER WORLD REGION

	Africa	Asia	Europe*	Latin America	Northern America	Oceania	Total
Roman Catholics	125,376.000	94,250,000	269,021,000	408,968,000	75,398,000	8,452,000	981,465,000
Protestants	114,726,000	45,326,000	79,534,000	34,816,000	121,361,000	8,257,000	404,020,000
Orthodox	25,215,000	13,970,000	171,665,000	460,,000	6,390,000	650,000	218,350,000
Anglicans	27,200,000	650,000	28,357,000	1,089,000	6,300,000	5,540,000	69,136,000
Total Christians	360,874,000	303, 127,000	555,614,000	555,614,000	255,542,000	24,253,000	1,955,229,000

*Includes former Soviet Union.
**United Nations Medium Variant Figures, mid 1996
Source: *The 1997Britannica Book of the Year*

C

CHRISTIANITY

The Essence of Christianity

epitome what it is that Christianity believes, teaches, and confesses.

"Whoever wishes to be saved must, above all, hold to the catholic faith." These opening words of the so-called Athanasian Creed (not in fact written by Athanasius, but a Latin and Western creed, compiled perhaps in the fifth century) would not, as they stand, automatically elicit the assent and support of all Christians; nor, for that matter, would all Christians who do accept such a statement be agreed on the precise content and extent of that "catholic faith." Differ though they do on these questions, however, Christians throughout history have affirmed the importance of the act of believing, as well as of the content of what is believed, as a mark of identification by which believers would be known.

The person of Jesus Christ. Christian belief began with the need to specify the significance of the person of Jesus, seen as the "Christ." The initial stages of that process are visible already in the pages of the New Testament. Its titles for him—in addition to Christ, such titles as Son of man, Son of God, Word of God (Logos), and Savior—were an effort to account for that significance, for within the events of Jesus' human life the God of Israel and the creator of the world had been disclosed. Before the theologians had invented ways of defining the content of these titles in any satisfying detail, the devotion and worship of the church were already identifying Jesus with God. This is evident, for example, from the earliest non-Christian account of the church that we possess, the letter of Pliny the Younger (62-113), governor of Bithynia, to the Roman emperor Trajan (r. c. 98-117), which describes Christians as gathering for worship and "addressing a song to Christ as to God" *(Christo ut deo)*. But this devotional practice had yet to be squared both with the monotheism that the church inherited from and shared with Israel and with the concrete events of the life of Jesus as these were described in the Gospels. During the second and third centuries the reality of his human life needed to be defended; during the fourth century the divine dimension of his being demanded attention; during the fifth and sixth centuries the relation between the divine and the human in him required clarification. What emerged from the process of debate and definition—especially in the creeds formulated at the councils of Nicaea in 325, Constantinople in 381, and Chalcedon in 451—was a picture of Jesus Christ as having two "natures," divine and human: he was simultaneously "one in being" with God and "one in being" with humanity, and therefore able to mediate between them. The full content of the two natures and of the relation between them has continued to engage the speculative talents of Christian theologians ever since. [*See* God, *articles on* God in the New Testament *and* God in Postbiblical Christianity.]

The Trinity. The final creedal statement of the relation between Christ and God was part of a more complete statement of belief, the Christian doctrine of the Trinity, which many theological exponents of Christianity would regard as the central teaching of the Christian faith. Its fundamental outline is already given in the "great commission"—which, according to the Gospels, Jesus entrusted to his disciples before withdrawing his visible presence from them (*Mt.* 28:19)—to baptize "in the name of the Father and of the Son and of the Holy Spirit." Threefold though that single "name" was, it was the relation of the Son to the Father that carried the principal weight in the clarification of the formula. Thus the original creed adopted at Nicaea, after enumerating the various "titles of majesty" belonging to Jesus Christ as the Son of God, simply added "And [we believe] in the Holy Spirit," with no similar elaboration of how and why the Third Person was entitled to stand alongside the Father and the Son. But before the fourth century was over, the status of the Holy Spirit, and thus the complete dogma of God as Trinity, had achieved the form it has held in Christian orthodoxy throughout the history of the church. The dogma presents itself as strictly monotheistic. The opening words of the Nicene Creed are "We believe in one God," and everything that follows about Father, Son, and Holy Spirit is set into that framework. The technical philosophical term for the oneness of God was *ousia* in Greek, *substantia* or *essentia* in Latin. But this single divine *ousia* had its being in three *hupostaseis*, or "persons."

The doctrine of the Trinity has from the beginning been one of the most productive–and one of the most problematic–points of contact between Christian theology and speculative philosophy.

PAGE 162

The doctrine of the Trinity has from the beginning been one of the most productive—and one of the most problematic—points of contact between Christian theology and speculative philosophy. Both the Greek Neoplatonist Plotinus (c. 205-270) and the German idealist G. W. F. Hegel (1770-1831), with many others between them, taught a philosophical version of the Trinity with which many theologians felt obliged somehow to come to terms. The metaphysical ingenuity of philosophers and theologians—from the first of Latin theologians, Tertullian (160?-225?), and the boldest of Greek theologians, his contemporary Origen (c. 185-c. 254), to philosophical theologians of the twentieth century, such as the Protestant Paul Tillich (1886-1965) and the Roman Catholic Karl Rahner (1904-1984)—has therefore continually experimented with new ways of accounting for (if not of "explaining") the relation between the One and the Three. Perhaps the most creative of such speculations was that of Augustine's *On the Trinity*, which constructed a series of trinitarian analogies in the universe and in the human mind as "images [or footprints] of the divine Trinity." [*For further discussion, see* Trinity.]

Sin and grace. All the councils that formulated

these basic doctrines of the Trinity and of the person of Christ were held in the Greek-speaking eastern part of the Christian Roman empire under the patronage of the Christian emperor, who was from the year 330 onward resident at Constantinople, and the creeds, which are in Greek, bear the marks of that origin. Still it is a mistake to ignore the role of the Latin West in the determination of normative Christian teaching: both at Nicaea and at Chalcedon there were decisive interventions from Western theologians and bishops. Nevertheless, the most distinctive and original Western contributions during the first five centuries came not in the doctrines of God and Christ but in the doctrines of sin and grace. With significant anticipations in various Western thinkers, it was once again Augustine who formulated these latter doctrines in the concepts and terms that were to dominate most of subsequent Christian teaching in the West, that of Roman Catholicism but no less the theology of Protestantism. Many early interpreters of Christian belief—for example, Gregory of Nyssa (c. 335-c. 395) in his treatise *On the Creation of Man*—had articulated the biblical teaching (*Gn.* 1:26-27) that, among all creatures on earth, humans alone possessed the special prerogative of having been created "in the image of God," with the promise of immortal life and of a "participation in the divine nature" (*2 Pt.* 1:4). But in so doing they had often spoken more explicitly about human free will than about human sinfulness. Yet this did not imply, Augustine insisted, that every human being faced the same choice between good and evil that Adam and Eve had faced. On the contrary, humanity had since Adam and Eve been under a curse of what Augustine called "the sin of origin" *(peccatum originis)*, which infected every human being except Jesus Christ (and perhaps his mother, the Virgin Mary). Even without committing acts of sin, therefore, each member of the human race was corrupted from birth; the tradi-

MARY
The Virgin Mother of Jesus

MARY, the mother of Jesus. The New Testament description of Maria, or Mariam, includes her virginal conception of Jesus. [*See* Jesus.] Preeminent among the saints, the Virgin Mary later became the object of piety and cult and, especially in the Roman Catholic church, of dogmas such as the Immaculate Conception and the Assumption. Protestant treatment of her as a biblical saint varies. She is honored in the Qur'an (surahs 3 and 19).

Mary in the New Testament. The *Gospel of Mark* (written about AD 70) describes Jesus' mother and brothers on the edge of a crowd listening to him teach (*Mk.* 3:31-35). "His own" (3:20), likely "his family" (RSV), have come to take him away because Jesus was, they thought, "beside himself"; they are like the hostile scribes who claim that he is "possessed by Beelzebub" (3:22). The passage in *Mark* 6:1-6a, about the rejection of Jesus in his home synagogue, does nothing to change this picture of Mary and Jesus' brothers as sharing the unbelief of those of the surrounding countryside. Hence the overall picture of Mary in *Mark* is a negative one. (For details, see Brown et al., 1978, pp. 51-72, 286-287.)

In the *Gospel of Matthew* (perhaps before AD 90), a more positive view of Mary results, especially from the first two chapters about the birth and infancy of Jesus, the fruit of meditation upon the Hebrew scriptures within the Matthean community.

Matthew's portrait of Mary during the ministry of Jesus is also ameliorated by other details. In the scene of Jesus' eschatological family (*Mt.* 12:46-50) no reference is made to Jesus' natural family coming to take custody of him. In the synagogue scene at Nazareth (*Mt.* 13:53-58), Matthew drops out the Marcan reference to "his own relatives" in what Jesus says (12:57; cf. *Mk.* 6:4).

The most positive synoptic portrayal of Mary comes in the *Gospel of Luke* plus *Acts* (perhaps after AD 90). In *Acts* 1:14, Mary is a member of the Jerusalem church. In *Luke* 1-2, Mary is described as Joseph's "betrothed" (*Luke* 2:1-20). Accounts show Mary's faith in God (*Lk.* 1:38, 1:45); tell of the virginal conception (*Lk.* 1:31-34, cf. 3:23) and of Mary's status as a "favored one" (*Lk.* 1:28; Vulgate, *gratia plena*), employing the term hail (*ave*); and relate Simeon's prophecy to Mary: "A sword will pierce through your own soul also" (*Luke* 2:35, probably meaning that Mary, too, must transcend the natural bonds of family and come to faith in Jesus).

The *Gospel of John* (c. 90) contains no reference to the virgin birth, in part because the preexistence and incarnation of the Word are emphasized (*Jn.* 1:1-18). The scenes involving "the mother of Jesus" (never "Mary") during Jesus' ministry are totally different from those in the synoptic Gospels. In the story about a wedding feast at Cana (*Jn.* 2:1-11), his mother does not yet seem to have grasped that his "hour" does not parallel the wishes of his natural family. Although she accompanied Jesus to Capernaum (*Jn.* 2:12), perhaps this was because she was seeking to bring him home (cf. *Mk.* 3:20-35). The mother of Jesus appears in one other Johannine scene (*Jn.* 19:25-27), standing at the foot of the cross with the Beloved Disciple. This *stabat mater* reference occurs only in *John*, among all the Gospels.

— JOHN REUMANN

"Jesus Christ came into the world to save sinners."

FIRST EPISTLE OF PAUL THE APOSTLE TO TIMOTHY, 1:15

tional practice of infant baptism (see "The Community of Christian Worship," below) was for Augustine evidence of the universality of this sinful condition.

Redemption. Neither the belief in God as Trinity nor the dogma of Christ as divine and human in nature nor the doctrine of humanity as created in the image of God but fallen into sin is, however, an end in itself for Christian faith. As a religion of redemption, Christianity presents itself as the message of how, through Christ, reconciliation has been achieved between the holiness of God and the sin of a fallen humanity. But while the Trinity, the person of Christ, and (though less universally or explicitly) the doctrine of original sin all have been subjects of a public and ecumenical confession of the church, the manner of this reconciliation has not received such attention. It has been left more to hymnody and preaching than to dogma and metaphysics to supply the metaphors for describing it. One of the most widely distributed such metaphors in early Christian writers, beginning with the sayings of Jesus himself (*Mt.* 20:28), is the description of *redemption* as "ransom" (which is, of course, what redemption means): the death of Christ was paid (to God or to the devil) as the price for setting humanity free. The difficulties that such a notion entailed for the Christian picture of God made a modification of the ransom theory seem imperative: the death of Christ took place in the course of a battle between God-in-Christ and the devil with his allies, a battle in which death triumphed initially by the nailing of Christ to the cross but in which Christ was victorious in the end through his resurrection. It remained once again for the medieval West to provide the most inventive of these theories. According to Anselm (c. 1033-1109) in his *Why God Became Man*, the reconciliation of the human race with God was fundamentally the reconciliation between the justice of God, which was committed to upholding "the moral order of the universe" *(rectitudo)* and therefore could not ignore human sin or forgive it by a simple fiat, and the mercy of God, which was bent on restoring humanity to the condition for which God had intended it by its creation. God became man in Christ, because as man he would be able, by his death, to produce the satisfaction demanded by divine justice, but as God he would render a satisfaction of infinite worth that could thus be applied to the entire human race. With some modifications and refinements, Anselm's theory has established itself both within Roman Catholicism and within most of classical Protestantism.

Justification. Classical Protestantism differs from Roman Catholicism in the interpretation of redemption not on the way redemption was achieved by God in Christ, but on the way it is appropriated by the Christian. Luther's doctrine of justification by faith—or, more fully and more precisely, justification by grace through faith—directed itself against what he perceived to be the widespread tendency of medieval Christianity to give human works part of the credit for restoring the right relation between God and man. This he attacked as a denial of the purely gratuitous character of salvation. The role of the human will in salvation was purely passive, accepting the forgiveness of sins as a sheer gift and contributing nothing of its own goodness to the transaction with God. Faith, accordingly, was not (or, at any rate, not primarily) an act of the intellect accepting as true what God has revealed but an act of the will entrusting itself unconditionally to the favor of God as conferred in Christ. Such unconditional trust led to the transformation of human life from the self-centered quest for gratification to the God-centered service of others (see "The Christian Way of Life," below). Partly in response to Luther's doctrine, the Council of Trent at its sixth session affirmed that "faith is the beginning of human salvation, the foundation and the root of all justification," but it condemned anyone who "says that the sinner is justified by faith alone, as though nothing else were required to cooperate."

THE COMMUNITY OF CHRISTIAN WORSHIP. As a system of hope, Christianity holds forth the promise of eternal life through Jesus Christ. In the words of what has been called "the gospel in a nutshell" (*Jn.* 3:16), "God loved the world so much that he gave his only Son, that everyone who has faith in him may not die but have eternal life." But that promise and hope of life for those who have faith does not stand in isolation from the full range of Christian hope, the expectation of all the gifts of God for time and for eternity, and the acceptance of those gifts in thankfulness and praise. Hope, consequently, expresses itself chiefly in prayer and worship, both the personal prayer of the individual Christian believer and the corporate worship of the Christian community.

The Holy Catholic church. One integral component of Christianity both as " a pattern of belief" and as "a community of worship" is expressed in the words of the Apostles' Creed: "I believe in the holy catholic church, the communion of saints." According to the accounts of the New Testament, it was the intention of Jesus to found a church (*Mt.* 16:18): "I will build my church." Whether one accepts the literal historicity of those accounts or not, Jesus did, in fact, gather a community of disciples and establish a table fellowship. The earliest Christianity we are able to uncover is already a churchly Christianity, to which in fact we owe the Gospels and all the other books of the New Testament. For Christians of every persuasion and denomination, the church is at the same time the primary context of worship.

There is, however, far less unanimity about the nature of the church or about its organization and its authority. The tripartite complex of authority that emerged from the conflicts of early Christianity (see "The History of Christianity," above) vested in the office of the monarchical bishop the visible governance of the church and defined the church accordingly. Two formulas of Cyprian (d. 258), bishop of Carthage, summarize this definition: "Where the bishop is, there the church is" *(Ubi episcopus, ibi ecclesia)* and "There is no salvation apart from the church" *(Extra ecclesiam nulla salus)*. For Cyprian himself, as became evident in his disputes with Stephen I (bishop of Rome from 254 to 257), each bishop carried the authority of the office on his own and was answerable to the authority of Christ and of his brother bishops, but not to any one bishop as monarch of the entire church. But there were already signs of a developing pyramidal structure of authority, with certain centers having clear jurisdiction over others. Among these, the see of Rome had, and has, preeminence. As noted earlier, this understanding of authority led in the Middle Ages to a definition of the church as a visible monarchy, analogous in some ways to other monarchies, of which the pope was the absolute ruler—"judging all, but being judged by none," as the *Dictatus papae* of Gregory VII said. Orthodoxy, by contrast, has resisted the pyramidal model of church authority, preferring to see the entire company of the church's bishops, particularly when they are in council assembled, as a corporate and collegial entity, with the bishop of Rome as "first among equals" *(primus inter pares)* but not as monarch. One of the major accents of the Second Vatican Council was a new emphasis on episcopal colle-

JOHN THE BAPTIST
The Beginning of the Gospel

Born of a poor priestly family in the hill country of Judea, John renounced the priesthood and entered upon an ascetic existence in the wilderness surrounding the Jordan River. There he inaugurated a baptism rite so unprecedented that he was named for it. His contemporary Jesus unhesitatingly ascribed the impetus for John's baptism to divine revelation (*Mk.* 11:30), and even though priestly lustrations in the Temple, the daily baths at Qumran, or even proselyte baptism (first attested in the second century CE) may provide certain parallels, they are wholly inadequate to account for John's demand that Jews submit to a once-only immersion in anticipation of an imminent divine judgment by fire. Rejecting all claims to salvation by virtue of Jewish blood or the "merits of Abraham," John demanded of each person works that would reflect a personal act of repentance. The examples preserved in *Luke* 3:10-14 indicate that John stood squarely in the line of the prophets, siding with the poor ("He who has two coats, let him share with him who has none; and he who has food, let him do likewise"). He demanded that toll collectors and soldiers desist from extorting unjust exactions from travelers and pilgrims. His dress was the homespun of the nomad, his diet the subsistence rations of the poorest of the poor (locusts and wild honey, *Mk.* 1:6). He even described the eschatological judge, whose near advent he proclaimed, in terms of a peasant or a man of the soil (chopping down trees, separating wheat from chaff).

Through baptism, John provided a means by which common people and other "sinners" (tax collectors and harlots, *Mt.* 21:32) could be regenerated apart from meticulous observance of the Jewish law. His influence on Jesus in this and other respects was profound. Jesus and his disciples were baptized by John. But whereas John demanded that people come out to him in the wilderness, Jesus went to the people in their towns and villages, rejecting an ascetic life (*Mt.* 11:18-19), and began to regard the future kingdom as an already dawning reality (*Mt.* 11:2-6). Despite these differences, Jesus continued to speak of John in terms of highest respect (*Mt.* 11:7-9, 11a).

John's execution by Herod Antipas was provoked by John's criticism of Herod for divorcing the daughter of the Nabatean king Aretas IV and entering upon an incestuous remarriage with Herodias, his half-brother's wife. John's attacks on Herod took place in Perea, a region controlled by Herod but bordered by Nabatean territory, an area inhabited by Arabs and infiltrated in winter by nomads. Herod's divorce provoked guerrilla warfare, and ultimately Aretas avenged his daughter's shame by a shattering defeat of Herod's army—a defeat that Josephus directly ascribes to divine punishment for Herod's execution of John (*Jewish Antiquities* 18.116-119). John's preaching must also have contributed substantially to popular disaffection from Herod.

All four evangelists treat John as "the beginning of the gospel." This reflects both the historical fact and the theological conviction that through John, Jesus perceived the nearness of the kingdom of God and his own relation to its coming. The church continued to treat John as the perpetual preparer for the coming of Christ, calling out for people to repent and let the shift of the aeons take place in their own lives, to "make ready the way of the Lord" (*Mk.* 1:2).

— WALTER WINK

giality but not at the expense of the primacy of the bishop of Rome within the college. That accent was closely joined in the decrees of the council to a recovery of the definition of the church as principally the community of Christian worship.

Protestant views of the church. The Protestant rejection of the authority of the pope is closely joined to a redefinition of the nature of the church. There had always been the recognition in the medieval doctrine of the church, particularly as this had come down from Augustine, that the organizational, empirical church was not coextensive with the church as it exists in the eyes of God: some who participate in, or even preside over, the church as an institution today will ultimately perish, while others who now persecute the church are destined to become members of the body of Christ. That definition of the true church as "the company of the elect," and hence as invisible in its membership and in its essence, appears in one form or another in the thought of most of the Protestant reformers. It did not imply, except in the polemics of a radical few, that there was no visible church. With differing forms of ecclesiastical administration (see "Reformation Christianity," above), the reformers took over or adapted patterns of organization that would suit the church for its function as the community of Christian worship and the center of Christian instruction. A favorite Protestant term for the church, therefore, is the phrase in the Apostles' Creed, "the communion of saints."

In fulfillment of the words and promise of Jesus, "This is my body" and "This is my blood," the bread and wine presented for the sacrament become the very body and blood of Christ.

PAGE 166

The preaching of the word of God. Although they would agree that the church is the community of Christian worship, the several denominations disagree about the structure of that community—and about the content of that worship. It is characteristic of most Protestant groups that in their liturgies and forms of worship they assign centrality to communication of the Christian message through preaching: "Where the word of God is, there the church is" *(Ubi verbum Dei, ibi ecclesia)* is how they have recast Cyprian's formula. As the leader of the worshiping community, the minister is principally (though never exclusively) the proclaimer of the word of God, a word of God that is found in, or identified and even equated with, the Bible. The emphasis on biblical preaching has sometimes led to a didactic understanding of worship, but this has been counterbalanced in Protestantism by the literally tens of thousands of "psalms and hymns and spiritual songs" (Col. 3:16) that the Protestant churches have developed because of their equally great stress on the participation of the congregation and of each individual worshiper in the service. The traditional concern of Protestant Christianity with the authentic faith and experience of the individual—expressed in Luther's axiom "You must do your own believing as you must do your own dying"— is likewise audible in these hymns, many of which, typically, are cast in the language of the first person singular.

The sacraments. It would, however, be a grave distortion (albeit a distortion to which even sympathetic interpreters of Protestant Christianity have sometimes been subject) to interpret Protestantism as a thoroughgoing individualism in its understanding of worship, for the definition of the church as "the community of Christian worship," in Protestantism as well as in Orthodoxy and in Roman Catholicism, is embodied above all in the celebration of the sacraments. Except for certain details (e.g., whether it is the recitation of the words of institution or the invocation of the Holy Spirit in the epiclesis that effects the transformation of bread and wine into the body and blood of Christ in the Eucharist), Eastern Orthodoxy and Roman Catholicism stand in basic agreement on the nature of sacramental worship and the meaning of the seven sacraments. Among the many definitions of *sacrament* that have appeared in the Christian tradition, two (one from the East and one from the West) may suffice here: "the mystery of faith," since in Christian Greek *musterion* means both "mystery" and "sacrament"; and, in a formula based on Augustine, "sacred sign," which by a visible means represents (or re-presents) an invisible divine grace.

The Eucharist. The primary sacrament and the center of Christian worship is, for both the Eastern and the Western tradition, the Eucharist or Lord's Supper, which is, in one form or another, celebrated by all Christian groups. Although the celebration is also a memorial and an expression of community, what sets the Roman Catholic and Orthodox understanding of the Eucharist apart from that of most other groups is their definition of this sacrament as real presence and as sacrifice. In fulfillment of the words and promise of Jesus, "This is my body" and "This is my blood," the bread and wine presented for the sacrament become the very body and blood of Christ, identical in their substance with the body born of Mary, even though the taste, color, and other attributes or "accidents" of bread and wine remain. The Fourth Lateran Council in 1215 defined this doctrine as "transubstantiation," and it was reaffirmed by the Council of Trent in 1551. As the real presence of the body and blood of the one whose death on the cross and resurrection effected the redemption of the world, the Eucharist is as well a sacrifice—not as though the first sacrifice were inadequate and Christ needed to be sacrificed over and over, but "in union with the sacrifice" of Calvary. The daily offering of that sacrifice for the living and the dead is at the center of Roman Catholic worship, devotion, and doctrine; and although Orthodoxy is, characteristically, less explicit in some of its detailed formulations about the metaphysics of the presence and more content to speak of it as a "mystery," its representatives, when pressed, will come up with language not far removed from that of the West—especially of the West as in the twentieth century it has, thanks to a repossession of the tradition of the Greek fathers, come to speak about the mystery of the Eucharist.

Whatever differences of emphasis there may be between Roman Catholicism and Eastern Orthodoxy about the Eucharist, they are much smaller than the differences among the several Protestant groups. Luther objected to transubstantiation as an excessively philosophical formula, and above all to the sacrificial understanding of the Eucharist as a diminution of the redemptive work of Christ, but he vigorously defended the real presence against his fellow Protestants. They in turn laid stress on the "true presence" of Christ in his spirit and power rather than on the "real presence" of the actual body and blood. Within Protestantism, consequently, the memorial aspects of the celebration of the Lord's Supper, which Christ according to the Gospels instituted to be eaten in his remembrance, have been prominent and sometimes even central. The other historic accent of Christian eucharistic worship that has found a new emphasis in Protestant practice and devotion is the understanding of the Lord's Supper as a corporate expression of the "communion" of Christian believers with one another. "Body of Christ" in the New Testament refers sometimes to the Eucharist, sometimes to the church, and sometimes (notably in *1 Corinthians*) to both at the same time. Compared with those two themes of memorial and communion, the specification of just how the body and blood of Christ can be present in the sacrament is of lesser significance. [*For further discussion, see* Eucharist.]

Baptism. The other action of the community of Christian worship on whose "sacramental" character all Christians would agree is baptism. Throughout the *Acts of the Apostles*, baptism functions as the means of initiation into the Christian movement and into the reality of Christ himself, and in the epistles of Paul baptism is the way of appropriating the benefits of the death and resurrection of Christ. Although all the explicit references in the New Testament to the practice of baptism mention only adults as its recipients, and that generally only after a profession of their faith, the custom of administering it also to children began quite early; just how early is a matter of controversy, but by the end of the second century infant baptism was sufficiently widespread to have called forth objections from Tertullian. Except for that difference from subsequent tradition, Tertullian formulated in his treatise *On Baptism* what can be regarded as an all but universal consensus about

The purifying properties of water have been ritually attested to ever since the rise of civilization in the ancient Near East.

PAGE 67

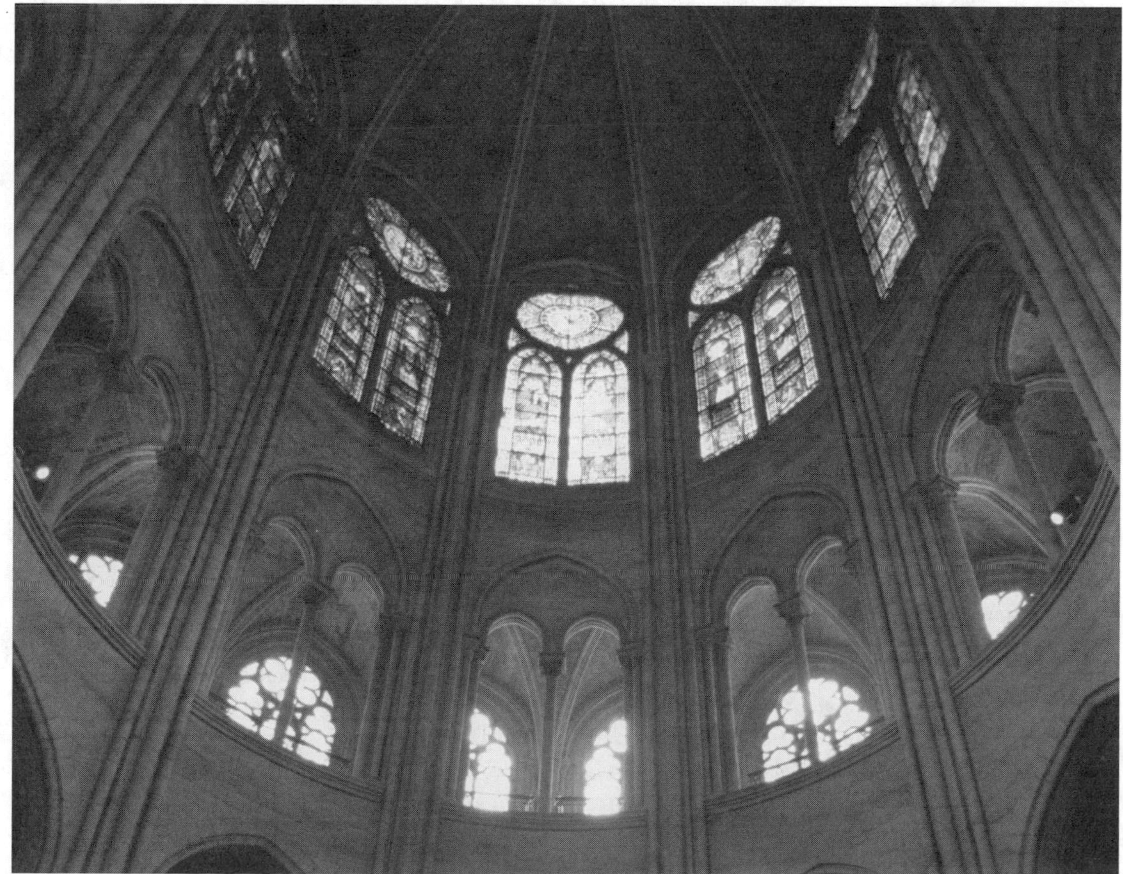

ALTAR

The Eucharist, performed at altars in churches like the Cathedral de Notre Dame, is a sacrament shared by all Christians.

ROBERT HOLMES/© CORBIS

the effects of baptism: remission of sins, deliverance from death, regeneration, and bestowal of the Holy Spirit. Eastern and Western church fathers, all the medieval scholastics, and many of the Protestant reformers would be able to subscribe to that formulation. Because of their misgivings about any view of any of the sacraments that might appear magical, Protestants have tended to avoid describing the conferral of these effects as something automatic. The Anabaptists of the sixteenth century on the continent, and the several bodies of Baptists in England and especially in the United States since the seventeenth century, have carried that position to the conclusion of repudiating the practice of infant baptism and insisting on "believers' baptism" as the only form of administering the sacrament that is consistent both with the original intention of Jesus and with the true nature of the Christian community. [*For further discussion, see* Baptism.]

"*Draw near faith, and take this Holy Sacrament to your comfort.*"

PRAYER BOOK, THE INVITATION, 1662

Other sacraments. Although baptism and the Lord's Supper are for most Protestants the only two ordinances that qualify as sacraments, the medieval development in the West led to a system of seven sacraments, which Eastern Christianity, when obliged to become specific, has likewise affirmed. The sacrament of penance (together with the reception of absolution) developed as a way of coping with sins committed after the reception of forgiveness in baptism. As the contrition of the heart, the confession of the mouth, and the satisfaction of a work restoring what had been taken away by the sin, penance became, in the Latin Middle Ages, one of the principal means by which the imperatives and the promises of the Christian gospel were applied to individuals and communities. With the universal acceptance of infant baptism, the individual's assumption of the responsibilities of Christian discipleship, originally associated with adult baptism, came to be the central content of the sacrament of confirmation. As infant baptism attended the beginning of life with sacramental grace, so at death, or in a crisis or illness that might portend death, the anointing of the sick (or the sacrament of "extreme unction") brought that grace to the end of life as well. The only one of the seven "sacraments" to which the name was applied in the New Testament (*musterion* in Greek, *sacramentum* in Latin) was marriage (*Eph.* 5:32); on that authority, it became part of the sacramental system. And as the ordinance by which all the other sacraments were usually made possible, the ordination of priests itself was defined to be a sacrament. Each of the seven, therefore, combines in a special way what is also the special emphasis of Christian hope and of Christian worship: the sacredness of each person, but in the context of the sacred community.

[*For further discussion of Christian worship, see* Priesthood *and* Ministry. *Related issues are discussed in broad religious perspective in* Confession of Sins; Prayer; *and* Ordination. *For discussion of Christian expression in the arts, see* Iconography.]

THE CHRISTIAN WAY OF LIFE. As a system of love—and love is, in the formula of Paul, the "greatest" of the three (*1 Cor.* 13:13)—Christianity presented itself to its hearers as a way of life; especially in *Acts*, "the way" became a standard designation for Christianity itself. In its symbiosis with the societies and cultures in which it has taken root, the Christian way of life has been characterized by even greater heterogeneity than Christian belief or Christian worship. That heterogeneity makes generalizations about it in such a summary as this even more hazardous, and the specifics of the forms of Christian ethics in society must be left for treatment elsewhere in this encyclopedia. It is nevertheless possible to single out briefly certain leitmotifs that run across the varieties of Christian morality, both individual and social.

The imitation of Christ. Ever since the New Testament, the human life of Jesus Christ has served as an example set forth for imitation; it has usually been more than an example, but never less. "Bend your necks to my yoke, and learn from me, for I am gentle and humble-hearted; and your souls will find relief" the New Testament (*Mt.* 11:29) represents him as commanding. Just what that imitation implies concretely for the Christian in the world has been, however, a continuing issue and problem, for the Christ whom the believer is invited to imitate was not married, did not hold public office, and was not supported chiefly from a trade or profession. The imitation of his example has come to mean, therefore, the application to one's own situation of the love and faithfulness that Christ brought to his. Repeatedly, when the demands of society or, for that matter, the requirements of the church have proved to be too complex or abstract, "the imitation of Christ" has become a way of reducing them to their essence. Thus, in what has probably been, except for the Bible itself, the most widely circulated book in Christian history, *Imitation of Christ* by Thomas à Kempis (1379/80-1471), the summons of the figure in the Gospels rises above the intervening voices with a clarity and directness that has spoken to followers in every century; and in the twentieth century, *The Cost of Discipleship*, by the young Lutheran theologian and martyr under the Nazis, Dietrich Bonhoeffer (1906-1945), has applied that New Testament summons of "Follow me" to a new generation of disciples.

Obedience. The imitation of Christ has also implied obedience to his will, as this was expressed both in his own teachings and in the Mosaic law. In its treatment of that law, the New Testament manifests an ambivalence: Christ is seen as "the end of the law" (*Rom.* 10:4), and yet he himself is represented as warning in the Sermon on the Mount (*Mt.* 5:17), "Do not suppose that I have come to abolish the law and the prophets." The ambivalence manifests itself likewise in the descriptions of the Christian way of life as obedience. The Christian catechisms that have proliferated especially since the sixteenth century (see "Reformation Christianity," above) have usually incorporated an exposition and application of the Mosaic Decalogue as their description of what it means in practical terms to be a Christian. That has been perhaps even more true of Protestant than of Roman Catholic catechisms, despite the polemic of Protestants against "moralism" and "legalism" in Roman Catholic theology and ethics. But both Roman Catholic and Protestant ethicists and teachers have also repeatedly defined Christian obedience as not the strict observance of a legal code, not even of the legal code in the Ten Commandments, but as the spontaneity of the Spirit. "Love God, and do what you will" was Augustine's characteristically epigrammatic way of describing that spontaneity; but that same Augustine is at the same time one of our earliest authorities for the use of the Ten Commandments in Christian pedagogy. Augustine is as well an early source for the adaptation to Christian purposes of the philosophical consideration of the nature and the number of the "virtues": to the classical (or, as they came to be called in Christian parlance, "cardinal") virtues of prudence, temperance, fortitude, and justice, Christian ethical thought added the three "theological" virtues of faith, hope, and love. Obedience to the will of God and the cultivation of these seven virtues were seen as the content of the Christian way of life. [*See* Israelite Religion, *sidebar* Ten Commandments, *and* Christian Ethics.]

The transformation of the social order. Each of the "cardinal" and "theological" virtues makes sense only in a social context, and obedience to the will of God has traditionally been seen as pertaining to society as well as to the individual. The petitions of the Lord's Prayer, "Thy kingdom come, thy will be done, on earth as it is in heaven," have been taken to mean that the reign of God and the will of God have as their object here on earth the creation of a social order that conforms as closely as possible to the reign of God in heaven. That is indeed how both the East (see "The Christian Culture of Byzantium," above) and the West (see "Christianity in the Middle Ages," above) have interpreted their mission through most of Christian history, and that was how they carried out their mission within those societies. Calvinism and Puritanism were especially committed to the creation of social and political institutions that lived up to the will of God, and the pacifism of Anabaptist and Quaker groups during the sixteenth and seventeenth centuries was inspired by a similar commitment. During the nineteenth and twentieth centuries, however, such an interpretation of the Christian mission has taken on new urgency—and has occasioned new controversy—in a society where the institutions of Christianity no longer command attention or widespread obedience. The Social Gospel associated with the name of Walter Rauschenbusch (see "The Nineteenth Century," above) was the most ambitious of modern efforts to rethink the fundamentals of the Christian way of life in relation to the situation of an industrial society and to define the very meaning of salvation (as well as of other themes of Christian teaching and devotion) in social terms. Although the Social Gospel has in greater or lesser measure affected the ethical thought of most Protestant groups, Roman Catholicism has, during most of the twentieth century, been the major center for the development of new social and political theory. In a series of "social encyclicals" beginning with the *Rerum novarum* of Pope Leo XIII (1810-1903) of 15 May 1891, the papacy itself has often taken the lead in stimulating such development. But the application of the theory to twentieth-century society—the phenomenon of "worker priests" in France, and especially the creation of "liberation theology" by Roman Catholic theologians in Latin America—has often produced confusion and provoked controversy. Even those whose political or theological conservatism finds such trends dangerous, however, usually speak in the name of a particular definition of the social order that they regard as conforming, at least in some measure, to the same ideals.

Christian universalism. The Christian way of life as love is conventionally seen as finding its ultimate fulfillment in the church as the loving community of believers set apart from the world. But alongside that strain in the Christian tradition there has always stood a concern and a love for the entire world, a Christian universalism no less pronounced than is Christian particularism. It has sometimes expressed itself in a sense of urgency about Christian missions, to "bring the world to Christ." But a less prominent, yet no less persistent, expression of Christian universalism has sought to probe the implications of the unavoidable statements of the New Testament about the entire world as the object of the love of a God "whose will it is that all men should find salvation and come to know the truth" (*1 Tm.* 2:4). Origen in the third century, Gregory of Nyssa in the fourth century, Nicholas of Cusa in the fifteenth century—these and other theologians, committed though they were to the church and to its orthodoxy, have taken up the exposition of a universal vision in which the love of God revealed in Christ cannot be completely fulfilled until all God's creation has been reconciled.

FAITH, HOPE, AND LOVE. The complex, sometimes labyrinthine, interactions of faith, hope, and love with one another throughout Christian history and

Paul, believing that he had received a commission as apostle of the gentiles, worked out a master plan for establishing Christian groups in all the main centers of the Greco-Roman world.

PAGE 450

throughout Christianity as a system suggest the absence of a set of universal principles that could, in the fashion of Euclid's geometry, yield *the* Christian worldview. Christianity is, rather, the product of a continuing and organic history. Its principal institutional expression has been the church in its various organizational forms, but Christianity is more than the church. Although its chief intellectual product has been a theological development that spans twenty centuries, the Christian message is not coextensive with its theology. Its most telling effect on history has been in the faith and life of its celebrated saints and seers, but Christianity has consistently declared that its power and spirit can be found as well among the silent in the land, the meek who shall inherit the earth.

— JAROSLAV PELIKAN

"The spirit is an invisible force made visible in all life."

MAYA ANGELOU

CHRISTIAN SCIENCE

Christian science is a religious movement emphasizing Christian healing as proof of the supremacy of spiritual over physical power. Founded by Mary Baker Eddy, a New Englander of predominantly Calvinistic background, Christian Science emerged as a distinct phenomenon in American religious life during a period of both social and religious crisis.

Mary Baker Eddy from her earliest years showed a deep-seated longing for the divine that was broadly characteristic of the Christian tradition and especially prominent in Puritanism. She found it impossible, however, to reconcile her deepest religious feelings with the theology of a then decadent Calvinism. Yet while other revolts against Calvinism, such as those of Unitarianism and Transcendentalism, led to an attenuation or even an abandonment of Christian convictions, Eddy's Christianity was so deeply ingrained that she found it impossible to think of any ultimate answer to what she called the "problem of being" outside of a theistic, biblical context.

Running parallel to this search, and contributing heuristically to it, was Eddy's own long quest for health. She had exhausted the healing methods of the time, including homeopathy, and although she found useful hints concerning the mental causes of disease, she never found the permanent health for which she was looking. Her growing disenchantment with all curative methods returned her to her spiritual quest, which led to a radically different perception of God and creation. Namely, that reality is, in truth, wholly spiritual.

Eddy identified the advent of this conviction with her "instantaneous" recovery in 1866 from the effects of a severe accident while reading an account of one of Jesus' healings. She described the event as follows: "That short experience included a glimpse of the great fact that I have since tried to make plain to others, namely, Life in and of Spirit; this Life being the sole reality of existence."

There can be no doubt that this moment of recovery marked an important turning point in Eddy's life, impelling the development of the theology and metaphysics to which she gave expression in her major book, *Science and Health with Key to the Scriptures,* first published in 1875. The primary purpose of the book was not to set forth a new systematic theology, but rather to serve as a textbook for religious practice. The focus throughout was on awakening the capacity of its readers to experience the presence of God directly; the "honest seekers for Truth".

A key point of Christian Science is that the understanding of God must include a changed view of reality itself. In effect, *Science and Health* challenged the traditional Christian view of God as the creator of a material world—not on philosophic grounds, even though Eddy's conclusions are partially articulated in philosophic terms—but on the grounds of a radical reinterpretation of the meaning of the gospel. Christian Science takes the works of Jesus, culminating in his resurrection and final ascension above all things material, as pointing to the essential spiritual nature of being. Accordingly, his life exemplifies the possibility of action outside of and contrary to the limits of a finite, material sense of existence. From the standpoint of traditional Christianity, Jesus' works constituted supernatural interruptions of natural process and law; from the standpoint of Christian Science, they resulted from the operation of divine power comprehended as spiritual law.

Christian Science does not deify Jesus, a point that its severest critics have sometimes said separates it conclusively from traditional Christianity. Jesus' actual role in the achievement of humanity's salvation is as important to its theology as for traditional Christianity. His life of obedience and sacrifice is understood as the means through which the reality of being for humankind has broken through in the midst of ordinary human experience. This true spiritual selfhood is identified as the eternal Christ, as distinct from Jesus, although uniquely and fully incarnated in him. His mission is viewed as opening up the possibility for all men and women to make actual their own spiritual union with God. He did this by proving practically that neither sin nor suffering is part of authentic spiritual selfhood, or Christ.

While Christian Science holds that evil has no God-derived existence and therefore can be regarded ontologically as not real, it strongly emphasizes the need for healing rather than ignoring the manifold manifestations of the carnal mind, and as operating with hypnotic intensity in human experience. Such

MARY BAKER EDDY *Founded by Mary Baker Eddy, the Church of Christ, Scientist, is a religious movement emphasizing Christian healing as proof of the supremacy of spiritual over physical power.* LIBRARY OF CONGRESS/CORBIS

healing is to be accomplished through yielding to the action of the divine Mind. Salvation, while seen as the effect of divine grace, requires prayer, self-renunciation, and radical, unremitting warfare against the evils of the mortal condition.

Salvation includes obedience to Jesus' command to heal the sick. Sickness is one expression of the fundamental error of the mortal mind that accepts existence as something separate from God. Healing, therefore, must be predicated on the action of the divine Mind or power outside of human thought. Healing is regarded not merely as a bodily change, but as a phase of full salvation from the flesh as well. It is the normalization of bodily function and formation through the divine government of the human mentality and of the bodily system that that mentality governs.

"Healing is a matter of time, but it is sometimes also a matter of opportunity."

HIPPOCRATES
PRECEPTS

The emphasis in Christian Science upon healing—primarily of sin, secondarily disease—is based on the concrete issues of everyday lived experience. The healing emphasis differentiates Christian Science from philosophies of idealism with which it is often carelessly identified, including the Emersonian transcendentalism that was part of its immediate cultural background. Indeed, departures from Eddy's teaching within the Christian Science movement itself have tended generally toward metaphysical abstraction, wherein her statements almost completely lose their bearings on daily experience.

In the context of Eddy's writings, however, such statements almost always point to the demand and possibility of demonstrating in actual experience what she understood as spiritual fact. Her abstract statement that "God is All," for instance, taken by itself could imply a pantheistic identification of humankind and the universe with God. Taken in the full context of her teachings, it indicates that God's infinitude and omnipotence rule out the legitimacy, permanence, and substantiality of anything contrary to God's nature as Principle, Mind, Spirit, Soul, Life, Truth, and Love, an assertion that is taken to be demonstrably practical in concrete situations, to some degree at least.

MOTHER CHURCH

The First Church of Christ, Scientist, in Boston is considered the Mother Church.

LEE SNIDER/CORBIS

Although Christian Science is explicitly committed to universal salvation, it focuses initially and primarily on the potential for transformation and healing within the individual. This focus, deviant as it has often seemed to conservative Christians, tends to associate it with the traditional Protestant concern over individual salvation, giving it a conservative cast in the eyes of more liberal Christians who wish to transform the social order. The identification of Christian Science with a conservative, well-to-do, middle-class ideology may be as misleading in a sociological sense as it is theologically. In fact, a greater segment of the movement comes from rural or lower-middle-class backgrounds than most outside accounts would suggest.

On the whole, the church does not share the social activism of many mainstream denominations, but its purpose in publishing *The Christian Science Monitor* indicates a substantial commitment to an interest in the public good. Eddy founded the *Monitor* in 1908 as the most appropriate vehicle for the political and social expression of the practical idealism of her teaching. The character of the *Monitor,* to a degree, reflects the educational purpose of the church that publishes it.

It was not part of her original purpose to found a separate denomination; rather, she and a group of her students founded the Church of Christ, Scientist, in 1879, when it became clear that other Christian churches were not disposed to accept her teaching. The overall structure of the church was laid out in a document of skeletal simplicity, the *Manual of The Mother Church,* which Eddy first published in 1895 and continued to develop until her death.

The central administrative functions of this "mother" church, the First Church of Christ, Scientist, in Boston, are presided over by a five-member, self-perpetuating board of directors. The Mother Church, with its branches, including some 3,000 congregations in fifty countries, constitute the Church of Christ, Scientist; the congregations are self-governing within the framework provided by the *Manual.*

The absence of an ordained clergy, ritualistically observed sacraments, and all but the most spare symbols point to the almost Quaker-like simplicity of the Christian Science concept of worship, in which silent prayer has an important role and the sacraments are conceived of as a process of continuing purification and quiet communion with God.

Christian Science practitioners, listed monthly in *The Christian Science Journal,* are members who devote themselves full time to the ministry of spiritual healing, and a significant body of testimonies of healing—amounting to some 50,000 published accounts—has been amassed in Christian Science periodicals over the years. There is good evidence that this sustained commitment of an entire denomination over more than a century to the practice of spiritual healing has been a significant factor in the reawakening of interest in Christian healing among many denominations in the 1960s and 1970s.

By the 1979 centennial of the founding of the church, the Christian Science movement found itself experiencing greater challenges from the currents of secular materialism than it had encountered since the early days of its founding.

— STEPHEN GOTTSCHALK

CONFESSION OF SINS

The word *confession* has a twofold meaning that can be partially explained by etymology. The Latin *confiteor,* from which *confession* derives, means specifically "to confess a sin or fault," but also, in a more general sense, "to acknowledge or avow." Thus one may speak both of the sinner who confesses his sins and of the martyr who confesses his faith. Since the confession or witness of a martyr normally took place before a tribunal, it did in fact bear a formal resemblance to the confession of sins.

CONFESSION OF SINS IN NONLITERATE CULTURES. An interpretation of the confession of sins among nonliterate peoples must consider that there is indeed a tension between theistic conceptions of confession, where the goal is divine forgiveness, and nontheistic conceptions, where the efficacy of confession is intrinsic to the act itself.

One of the most typical, perhaps the most typical subject of confession, is a woman's confession of adultery, particularly when the confession is occasioned by the act of childbirth. The recipient of the confession may be a priest, a sorcerer, the husband, or perhaps another woman. The woman making the confession must either enumerate her partners or identify them by name. This requirement may be intended to allow the offending partner to redress his wrong by offering a sacrifice or paying a fine (as among the Luo of Dyur and the Nuer of East Sudan respectively). Unconfessed adultery possesses an inherently obstructive power that must be removed by means of ritual confession. The Luo, the Nuer, and also the Atcholi of Uganda believe that the destructive power of unconfessed adultery may become manifest through the death of the delivered child.

Another typical occasion for making a confession in nonliterate societies is the activity of hunting or fishing. Women must observe particular taboos while their husbands are away hunting in order not to compromise the success of the expedition. The husbands, during the days preceding departure, must abstain from various activities, in particular from cohabitation with their wives. Individual members of the hunting or fishing party must confess their sins prior to departure, since the unacknowledged breaking of a taboo or a persistent condition of impurity and culpability would endanger the success of the entire expedition.

Among the Lotuko of East Sudan, there is a public confession by the warriors at the beginning of the great hunting season. Their confessions are made individually with lowered voice and then repeated by the priest serving the rain god. Probably, the custom is meant symbolically to preserve, to the extent that it is possible, the originally individual character of confession. Other instances of confession on the occasion of annual ceremonies of renewal are found among the Bechuana, the Algonquin, and the Ojibwa.

Confession is also found in association with other rituals. Among the Nandi, a solemn form of confession is associated with circumcision. Among the Sulka (New Britain) and the Maya (Yucatán), confession is associated with initiation, and in Chiapas (Mexico) with marriage. In other words, confession may be an element in rites of passage, both individual and seasonal. Confession is sometimes associated with such ritual and ascetic procedures as fasting, abstinence, and chastity, evidently because of their importance in achieving ritual and/or ethical purity.

Finally, we must note the connection of confession of sins with the ordeal that may be used to test the sincerity of the confessing person. Here two different ritual procedures are intermingled. Evil is not the consequence of a sin that goes unconfessed; it is rather the consequence of a confession that was not sincere. The ethical side of confession becomes paramount; a reference to the elimination of occult sin would be out of place here. This instance makes clear the inadequacy of reducing confession strictly to a material utterance having magic, autonomous effects.

CONFESSION OF SINS IN TRADITIONAL HIGH CULTURES AND WORLD RELIGIONS. We pass now to the significance of confession of sins in traditional high cultures (both past and present), which are mostly polytheistic, and to the world religions.

Mexico and Peru. Confession was practiced in old Mexico in connection with Tlacolteótl, the goddess of impurities. She symbolized the sexual offenses (particularly adultery) that were the main object of confession. The priests of the goddess acted as the recipients of confession, and the confession itself was understood as taking place before the great, omniscient god Tezcatlipoca. The confession was secret and was followed by the imposition of a rather complicated penance, to be performed on the festival day of the goddess.

In modern Mexico, confession is practiced by the Huichol at the time of the annual expedition to collect the hikuli, a sacred plant. This expedition requires a condition of purity in the participants, achieved

Many cultures believe that fasting purifies or prepares the person (or group) for greater receptivity in communion with the spiritual.

PAGE 225

through confession of sexual offenses. For mnemonic purposes, knots corresponding to sins are tied in a rope that is then burned at the end, a typical symbolic form of elimination.

Confession was also practiced in Peru, associated with the bath *(upacuna)* and with other eliminatory or symbolic acts, such as blowing away powders. The recipient of confession was the *ichuri,* who was not a priest but belonged, rather, to a low class of diviners. The typical occasion for confession was sickness, whether of oneself or of one's relatives, and the integrity of the confession could be tested by ordeal. Other occasions included bad weather and times of preparation for festivals. The emperor (the *inca*) and the high priest ordinarily confessed their sins directly to the Sun and to the great god Viracocha, respectively.

The site of confession in Peru was the peninsula that provided access to the shrine of the Sun, located on a sacred island in Lake Titicaca. A long and detailed list of sins was employed, and some had to be confessed before the high priest.

Right religious conduct is minutely defined, giving rules for habitation and wandering, begging, study, confession, and penances.

PAGE 376

Japan and China. The biannual Shinto ceremony of Oho-harahi resembles a rite of confession, but it is only a recitation of a complete list of possible sins or impurities by the *nakatomi,* a high dignitary, or by other priests. In China, eliminatory rituals were related to the grand conception of the Tao, the universal, heavenly order. A disturbance of this order, whether caused by the emperor or by his people, had serious consequences. It was the emperor's duty to redress the wrong, often through the vicarious performance of penance and a written confession of sins. Individual confession was also practiced in China, particularly in the context of the Taoist tradition, especially in the case of sickness.

India. In the Vedas there is an insistence on the purifying properties of fire and water together with faith in Varuna, a heavenly and omniscient god. Varuna punishes sinners by entangling and binding them in his net. He can also liberate the sinner from these bonds. He is connected with ethical laws, especially with the eternal order of *rta,* yet his *modus operandi* is clearly magical, and his jurisdiction extends to involuntary offenses. Nevertheless, the Vedas know nothing of confession proper; they know only of generic declarations of fault.

Jainism. Confession in Jainism (*alocana* and, more generally, *pratikramana*) is mainly a monastic institution, performed twice daily. The laity make confession before their respective gurus. Jainism combines the elimination of sin with the doctrine of the annihilation of *karman,* conceived of as something substantial. Confession before death is considered important, and an insincere confession can perpetuate the cycle of rebirths.

Buddhism. The Patimokkha of the Buddhist monks is a gradated list of possible sins or transgressions, recited bimonthly at the night services called Uposatha. The participant monks must be in a state of purity; sins must be confessed in an individual and reciprocal form. Similar occasion for confession was the pavarana ("invitation"), which occurred during the rainy season, when the monks led a sedentary life. Monks would invite from their fellows statements concerning their (i. e., the inviter's) individual conduct.

With Buddhism, the objective conception of sin and purification, found in both Jain and Brahmanic conceptions of *karman,* was abolished. *Karman* was now understood to be produced through the subjective element of volition.

Western Asia and Greece. It is difficult to assimilate the practices described in some of the epigraphic and literary texts of the religions of antiquity to the category of confession of sins. These texts mention the mere acknowledgment and subsequent public declaration of a sin or other offense by an individual. It is scarcely possible to speak of the confession of sins when the regent of Byblos writes to Amenophis IV that he has confessed his fault to the gods, or when the Hittite king Mursilis confesses a sin before the god of heaven. The same applies to the repeated confessional utterances *(homologein, exomologeisthai)* of the "superstitious man" described by Plutarch, a man continually and scrupulously resorting to purificatory rituals in the sanctuary. Nor can the term "confession" be applied to certain texts of Roman poets concerning personal experiences in the context of the cult of Egyptian deities or describing the vicissitudes of mythic or legendary characters.

None of these records mentions the recipient of an oral confession, a necessary element of any penitential structure or institution.

Southern Arabia, Babylon, Egypt. Some confessional inscriptions have been discovered in southern Arabia, although their chronology is uncertain. They seem similar to the confessional inscriptions of Phrygia, but with a peculiar emphasis on sexual sins.

Babylonian religion recognized several theistic and magical means for eliminating ethical and ritual offenses. For instance, lists of sins were written on tablets and were then destroyed. Nevertheless, a ritual of confession properly so called is far from clearly attested. The same holds for the Babylonian penitential psalms, despite their ritual background. Herodotus attributed to the people of Babylon the custom of placing the sick in the public square so that they might confess their sins publicly.

More akin to present typology is the negative confession of the king at the beginning of the New Year festival in Babylon, the Akitu festival. True, a negative confession in which the king declares his innocence of a series of offenses against the city and the people is in a sense the opposite of a confession of sins. Yet both establish an immediate connection between the evocation of sin and the annihilation of it and its consequences. The most famous example of a negative confession is found in the Egyptian *Book of Going Forth by Day* (no. 125) where two complete lists of possible sins are used for the examination and weighing of the soul in the afterlife.

Israelite religion. Strong objections can be raised against the interpretation of many Old Testament texts, including the penitential psalms, as evidence for an institutionalized ritual of the confession of sins within the vast scope of the purification rituals. The same applies to the so-called collective confessions, where the general wording "we have sinned" (corresponding to the "I have sinned" of the former texts) does not properly fit into our typology Although the procedure has an oral, declaratory element, it cannot be assigned to the typology of confession.

Christianity. In the first centuries, the Christian church practiced a canonical penance for sins considered "mortal" or "capital." The penitential act started with the sinner entering the order of the penitents through a confession rendered before the bishop, or at least with the acceptance of the assigned penance. With the gradual introduction of the private form of confession, from the seventh century onward, a new form of the celebration of reconciliation came into practice. The private form of confession necessarily emphasized the "accusation" made by the penitent. The spiritual personality of the priest recipient of private confession was particularly stressed in the tradition of Eastern Christianity.

Zoroastrianism, Mandaean religion, and Manichaeism. From Sasanid times on, Zoroastrianism recognizes a form of the confession of sins, the *patet* ("expiation"), made before a priest or, in his absence, before the sun, the moon, and the divine fire. An annual confession is encouraged, in the month of Mihr (after Mihr, the god Mithra).

There are three main Manichaean texts used in confession. (1) The *Xastvanift,* consists of a list of sins and is intended for the laity (the "hearers"). Also employed were (2) a prayer composed in Chinese and used for communal confession and (3) a form of confession composed in Sogdian and intended for the elite, bearing the title *Manichaean Book of Prayer and Confession.*

The Mandaeans, adherents of a gnostic, ethnic religion that survives still in Iraq, recognize a confession for sins that can be repeated no more than two times before the sinner is excommunicated.

— UGO BIANCHI

CONFUCIAN THOUGHT

[This entry consists of four articles: Foundations of the Tradition, Neo-Confucianism, *and overviews of two specific cultures, namely* Confucianism in Japan *and* Confucianism in Korea.]

FOUNDATIONS OF THE TRADITION

CONFUCIUS AND CONFUCIAN THOUGHT. Confucius (the latinized form of the Chinese K'ung Fu-tzu, "Master K'ung") could trace his family heritage to nobility, but by the time of his birth the K'ung family was poor. Without benefit of a regular teacher, Confucius nonetheless managed to become a highly learned man, perhaps the most learned of his age, and had by his twenties begun to attract students. According to legend, in his thirties or forties he journeyed to the capital of Chou to consult the Taoist philosopher Lao-tzu (then the custodian of archives) on ceremonies. Upon returning to Lu several months later he encountered a steadily worsening political situation. In order to avoid the outbreak of civil hostilities, he fled to the neighboring state of Ch'i, where he was cordially consulted on government. Later, he returned to Lu and attracted more students. In 501 BCE, when he was fifty-one, he was made a magistrate in Lu. In that same year he also became minister of public works. Subsequently, he served Lu as a minister of justice, whose duties included foreign relations. As a magistrate, Confucius was said to have brought great peace.

Tradition holds that Confucius wrote the *Spring and Autumn Annals (Ch'un-ch'iu)* on the basis of records of his native state from the years 722 to 481 BCE (hence the name of the period), as well as the ten commentaries ("ten wings") of the *Book of Changes (I ching).* He is also credited with having edited the rest of the Six Classics, namely, the *Book of Odes (Shih ching),* the *Book of History (Shu ching),* the *Book of Rites (Li chi),* and the *Book of Music (Yüeh ching).* Modern scholarship has rejected much of this tradition, though recognizing that he was surely familiar with many poems and documents that later entered into these classics. On the other hand, it is likely that he wrote the *Spring and Autumn Annals* and at least one of the "ten wings." He died at the age of seventy-three, disappointed perhaps in public life but regarded by posterity as surely the greatest sage in Chinese history.

For over two thousand years he exercised a tremendous influence on Chinese life and thought. Korea, Japan, and Vietnam, too, periodically benefited from his teachings. Generally speaking, Confucius taught literature, ways of behavior, loyalty, and faithfulness. He often talked about history, poetry, and the performance of ceremonies. In this he started a tradition of liberal and moral education in China that was to

"The superior man acts before he speaks, and afterwards speaks according to his actions."

CONFUCIUS
THE ANALECTS, 2:13

eclipse the utilitarian and professionally oriented tradition that had hitherto dominated Chinese education. What is more important, while education had traditionally been reserved for the nobility, for Confucius education was open to all, without any class distinction. Following tradition, he glorified Heaven *(t'ien)* as great and august. He taught his pupils to know Heaven and to stand in awe of it. Significantly, however, Confucius did not regard Heaven as Ti, the Lord or the divine ruler, but as a supreme spiritual presence, the greatest moral power, and the source of everything.

It is clear that the superior man is possessed of many virtues. The greatest virtue that Confucius taught is *jen,* which specifically means benevolence but in a more general sense refers to humanity or what makes man a moral being. This is another new concept advanced by Confucius. Before his time, words like *shan,* meaning "goodness," or *te,* meaning "virtue," were widely employed, but these are terms for specific virtues, not terms for the universal virtue out of which all specific virtues grow. Forty-eight chapters out of 499 in the *Analects* (a record of Confucious's conversations with his disciples) were devoted to reflections on this concept. Confucius never defined it, perhaps because he felt the concept of a universal virtue was incapable of definition. In answer to his pupils' many questions, however, he did say that the man of *jen* loves man. He is a man of earnestness, liberality, truthfulness, diligence, and generosity. He is respectful in private life, serious in handling affairs, and loyal in dealing with others.

Confucius began a long Chinese tradition of ethical reform in the name of apparently reactionary principles.

PAGE 133

CONFUCIUS

The greatest sage in Chinese history, Confucius's teachings continue to influence Chinese life and thought.

JACK FIELDS/CORBIS

Confucius said that there is "one thread" running through his teachings. As his outstanding pupil, Tseng-tzu (505?-436? BCE), understood it, this one thread refers to loyalty in one's moral nature *(chung)* and treating others like oneself *(shu).* Commentators on the *Analects* are unanimous that *chung* and *shu* are the two sides of *jen,* for they cover the total moral life, that is, both the individual and society. In a word, the man of *jen* is a man of total virtue.

To rule a state and restrain human behavior by insisting on fixed ethical norms, liturgically expressed, was unusual advice to give rulers in an age in which men were accustomed to ruling by force alone. Confucius said, "If a ruler is to govern his kingdom with the compliance proper to the rule of propriety (rites), what difficulty will he have?" When a duke asked Confucius how the ruler should employ his ministers and how the ministers should serve the ruler, he said, "A ruler should employ his ministers according to the rules of propriety, and ministers should serve their ruler with loyalty."

On the surface Confucius's political doctrines seem to center on the ruler, and, to be sure, this perceived emphasis in Confucius's teachings often led to autocracy in later times. However, Confucius gave equal importance to the plight of the ruler's subjects. He said a ruler must be economical in expenditure, love the people, and employ them at the proper seasons; he must enrich the people and educate them. When a pupil asked about government, he replied that there must be sufficiency of food, sufficiency of military equipment, and the confidence of the people; if one or two must be dispensed with, food and military equipment must go first. The ideal state, he declared, is one in which people living inside it are happy and people outside want to come in.

Another ethical doctrine that later became formalized as a philosophical notion is that of the "mean" *(chung).* When commenting on two pupils, he said one went too far and the other not far enough, and that to go too far is the same as not to go far enough. For Confucius this doctrine means nothing more than moderation, but in the *Doctrine of the Mean* it has become a universal principal of harmony and equilibrium. Confucius himself led a life of moderation. He had no fixed limit for the amount of wine he would drink, but he never became confused or disorderly. In his ideas, he was both a conservative and a radical. To him, "Perfect is the virtue that is according to the Mean."

THE SECOND AND THIRD GENERATIONS AFTER CONFUCIUS. Very little attention has been paid to Confucius's followers from 500 to 350 BCE, but it is impossible to understand how and why Confucianism came to dominate Chinese history and why it

CONFUCIUS

Interpreter of Ancient Wisdom

CONFUCIUS (552?–479 BCE), known in Chinese as K'ung Ch'iu (also styled Chung-ni); preeminent Chinese philosopher and teacher. The name *Confucius* is the Latin rendering of *K'ung Fu-tzu* ("Master K'ung"). Confucius was born in the small feudal state of Lu, near modern Ch'ü-fu (Shantung Province). Little can be established about his life, forebears, or family, although legends, some of very early origin, are abundant and colorful. The biography in Ssu-ma Ch'ien's *Shih chi* (Historical Annals, second century BCE) is unreliable. The *Lun-yü* (Analects), a record of Confucius's conversations with his disciples, likely compiled in the third century BCE, is probably the best source, although here, too, apocryphal materials have crept in. The *Analects* may be supplemented by the *Tso chuan*, a commentary to the *Ch'un-ch'iu* (Spring and Autumn Annals; also third century BCE), and by the *Meng-tzu* (Mencius; second century BCE).

In the *Analects*, Confucius says that he was of humble status. Perhaps he came from the minor aristocracy, as he received an education—although not from a famous teacher—and also trained in archery and music. He probably belonged to an obscure and impoverished clan. He would say of himself that by age fifteen he had fixed his mind on studying (*Analects* 2.4). As a young man, he held minor offices, first overseeing stores with the task of keeping accounts, and later taking charge of sheep and cattle (*Meng-tzu* 5B.5). Confucius probably served in a junior post at the Lu court, if the *Tso chuan* is correct about his encounter in 525 with the viscount of T'an, a visitor in Lu, of whom he asked instructions regarding the ancient practice of naming offices after birds. At this point Confucius would have been twenty-seven years old.

Confucius lived in an age of great political disorder. The Chou royal house had lost its authority and the many feudal lords were competing for hegemony. He himself was concerned with the problems of restoring order and harmony to society and of keeping alive the ancient virtues of personal integrity and social justice. For him, a good ruler is one who governs by moral persuasion and who loves the people as a father loves his children. Confucius was especially learned in rites and music, finding in them both the inspiration and the means for the achievement of moral rectitude in society. He reflected deeply on the human situation about him in the light of the wisdom of the ancients. By about the age of thirty he felt himself "standing firm" (*Analects* 2.4) on his insights and convictions.

Confucius's place in history derives from his activities as a teacher and from the teachings that he crystallized and transmitted. In an age when only aristocrats had access to formal education he was the first to accept disciples without regard to status. He instructed them—according to each disciple's ability—not only in the rituals, knowledge of which was expected of all gentlemen, but also in the more difficult art of becoming one who is perfectly humane *(jen)*. Although none of his disciples attained high political office, Confucius the teacher wrought a real social change. Because of his teaching, the word *gentlemen* (*chün-tzu*, literally, "ruler's son") came to refer not to social status but to moral character. A new class gradually emerged, that of the *shih* (originally, "officers" or "government counselors"), a class of educated gentry. Those among the shih especially distinguished for scholarship and character were known as the *ju* (originally meaning "weaklings"?). Hence the Confucian school is known in Chinese as "the Ju school."

Confucius had a clear sense of his mission: he considered himself a transmitter of the wisdom of the ancients (*Analects* 7.1), to which he nonetheless gave new meaning. His focus was on the human, not just the human as given, but as endowed with the potential to become "perfect." His central doctrine concerns the virtue *jen*, translated variously as goodness, benevolence, humanity, and human-heartedness. Originally, *jen* denoted a particular virtue, the kindness that distinguished the gentleman in his behavior toward his inferiors. Confucius transformed it into a universal virtue, that which makes the perfect human being, the sage. He defined it as loving others, as personal integrity, and as altruism.

Confucius's teachings give primary emphasis to the ethical meaning of human relationships, finding and grounding what is moral in human nature and revealing its openness to the divine. Although he was largely silent on God and the afterlife, his silence did not bespeak disbelief (*Analects* 11.11). His philosophy was clearly grounded in religion, the inherited religions of Shang-ti ("lord on high") or T'ien ("heaven"), the supreme and personal deities of the Shang and Chou periods, respectively. He made it clear that it was Heaven that protected and inspired him: "Heaven is the author of the virtue that is in me" (*Analects* 7.23). Confucius believed that human beings are accountable to a supreme being, "He who sins against Heaven has no place left where he may pray" (*Analects* 3.13); nevertheless, he showed a certain scepticism regarding ghosts and spirits (*Analects* 6.20).

Confucius's philosophy might appear unstructured to those who cast only a cursory glance at the *Analects*, perhaps because the book was compiled several generations after Confucius's death. But the teachings found in the *Analects*, with all their inner dynamism, assume full coherency only when put into practice. Confucius did not attempt to leave behind a purely rationalistic system of thought. He wanted to help others to live, and by so doing, to improve the quality of their society.

—JULIA CHING

unfolded in the directions it did without understanding how Confucius's teachings were developed by his pupils and his pupils' pupils.

MENG-TZU AND HSÜN-TZU. The two most prominent followers of Confucius, Meng-tzu (372?-289? BCE) and Hsün-tzu (fl. 298-238 BCE), were contemporaries, but although both traveled extensively they never met. They shared an adoration of Confucius, and both believed that all men are capable of becoming the *chün-tzu.* Both held in high regard the Confucian moral values of humanity and righteousness. Both strongly advocated education, the rectification of names, kingly government (in which taxes are light, punishments are slight, and war is avoided), and the necessity of social distinctions such as that between senior and junior.

Hsün-tzu was concerned to separate the roles of heaven, earth, and man, with human attention directed toward ethics, administration, and culture.

PAGE 134

In their own doctrines, however, they proceeded in opposite directions. Confucius had said merely that people were born alike but that practice made them different. His thesis that all men could become superior men, however, argued by implication for the innate goodness of human nature. Meng-tzu's thought begins at this point by categorically affirming the original goodness of our nature. He maintains that man is born with what he termed the "four beginnings," that is, compassion, which is the beginning of humanity, shame and dislike, which is the beginning of righteousness, the feeling of respect and reverence, which is the beginning of propriety, and the feeling of right and wrong, which is the beginning of wisdom. For Meng-tzu, all people possess innate knowledge of the good and an innate ability to do good. Evil is due merely to circumstance and self-neglect. If one should fully develop his nature and recover his "lost mind," he will become a sage. Hsün-tzu attacked Meng-tzu severely, claiming that man's nature is originally evil. Man is born with desires that cannot be fully satisfied. If followed, these desires, together with envy, which is also inborn, inevitably lead to conflict. Virtue is acquired through man's activities, most notably, education, discipline, and rites.

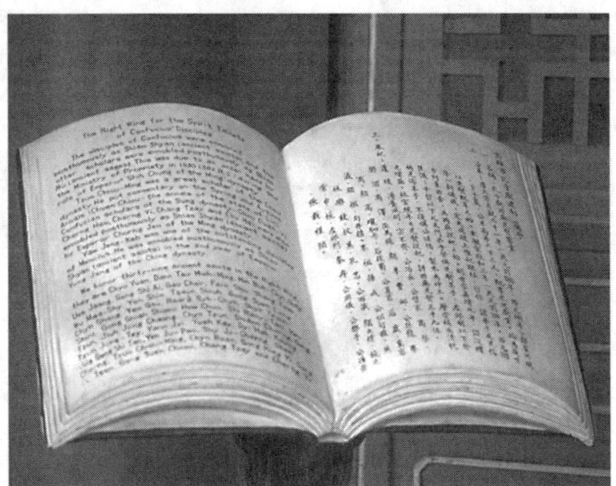

HOLY BOOK

The Lun-yu (Analects) are a record of Confucius's conversations with his disciples from the third century BCE.

KEVIN R. MORRIS/CORBIS

For Hsün-tzu, however, Heaven is simply nature, devoid of ethical principles, impartial to all men, regular and almost mechanical in its operation.

Both Meng-tzu and Hsün-tzu promoted kingly government, but for Meng-tzu a kingly government must be humane. In fact, Meng-tzu was the first to use the term "humane government" *(jen-cheng).* To Hsün-tzu, a kingly government was one ruled by the most worthy, powerful, and discriminating. The ideal ruler, a sage-king, keeps order through an organized system of laws, regulations, and taxation. Both subscribed to the Confucian doctrine of love for all, but Meng-tzu insisted that the special relationship between son and father must be the foundation of love. Because of this conviction, he bitterly attacked Mo-tzu (fl. 479-438 BCE), who taught universal (i. e. undifferentiated) love, and Yang Chu (440?-360? BCE), who was primarily concerned with self-preservation and hedonism.

THE SUPREMACY OF CONFUCIANISM AND TUNG CHUNG-SHU. Under the leadership of the Legalists, the Ch'in empire replaced the feudal domains with a system of provinces that is still in existence today. The Ch'in also united and somewhat simplified the Chinese written language, finished the Great Wall, and expanded military power beyond existing Chinese boundaries. To forestall critical opinion, books of the ritual schools were burned in 213 BCE, although those in official archives were retained. Confucians were ousted from office. But in fourteen short years rebellions broke out. The successful rebel, Liu Pang, defeated his rivals, overthrew the Ch'in, and founded the Han dynasty in 206 BCE. In spite of the burning of books, many Confucian works had been hidden in walls or committed to memory. Now the Confucian classics once more came into circulation. Since they required glosses and explanations, Confucian scholars gradually acquired importance and began to replace the Legalists in the government.

However, those in control of the government were Taoists, chiefly because both the emperors and empresses were devout followers of the new Taoist religion. As a result of the application of the Taoist philosophy of simple government, the reigns of Wen-ti (r. 179-157 BCE) and Ching-ti (156-141 BCE) were times of peace and adequate supply. Emperor Wu-ti (r. 140-87 BCE) ordered scholars to appear for personal interviews. Among the hundred-odd scholars summoned to court was Tung Chung-shu (176-104 BCE), who convinced the emperor to practice the teachings of Confucius and eliminate whatever trace there was of the harsh rule of Ch'in. The emperor immediately appointed Tung to be chief minister of a princely state. In 136 BCE, at the recommendation of Tung, Emperor Wu officially promoted the classics and established doctoral chairs for them, thus establishing Confucianism as the state ideology. Later, in 125 BCE, again at Tung's advice, he founded a national university to which fifty of the most talented students in the classics were selected. This institution lasted until the twentieth century.

T'ANG CONFUCIANISM: HAN YÜ AND LI AO. The central Confucian theme of human nature was strongly reasserted in the T'ang period (618-907) by Han Yü (768-829) and Li Ao (fl. 798). In his famous *Yüan-hsing* (An Inquiry on Human Nature), Han Yü offered his own theory of three grades of human nature, the superior, the medium, and the inferior. This theory was meant to refine Meng-tzu's doctrine of original goodness, but inasmuch as the idea of three grades can be found in the classics and was advanced by several thinkers before Han Yü's time, it represents no real advance in Confucian thought. The theory does reaffirm the fundamental Confucian interest in human nature.

Han Yü's friend and possibly his pupil, Li Ao, advocated a principle that he referred to as "recovering one's nature" *(fu-hsing)*, which is highly suggestive of Meng-tzu's injunction to recover one's lost mind. Li Ao's method of having no deliberation or thought may sound Buddhistic, and his recommendation of the fasting of mind *(hsin-chai)* may be derived from Chuang-tzu (369?-286? BCE), but the phrase "having no deliberation or thought" *(wu-ssu wu-lü)* comes from the *Book of Changes* and his "fasting of mind" is essentially the doctrine of "tranquility before the feelings are aroused" as taught in the *Doctrine of the Mean.*

In quoting from the *Doctrine of the Mean* and also the *Great Learning,* Han Yü and Li Ao contributed to the prominence of these two chapters in the *Book of Rites* so that eventually they, along with the *Book of Changes,* became basic texts in Neo-Confucianism. Both Han and Li singled out Meng-tzu as the one who transmitted the true doctrine of Confucius to later generations. All in all, they saved Confucianism from possible eclipse by Buddhism and Taoism, determined the direction of future development of Confucianism in Chinese history, and fixed the line of orthodox transmission from Confucius and Meng-tzu. In these respects, Han and Li were truly precursors of Neo-Confucianism.

— WING-TSIT CHAN

NEO-CONFUCIANISM

THE COSMOLOGY OF CHOU TUN-I. Chou Tun-i (given name, Chou Mou-shu; literary name, Chou Lien-hsi) laid the foundation for the Sung dynasty's metaphysical and ethical systems and is generally considered the true founder of Neo-Confucian philosophy. His works include the *T'ung-shu* (Penetrating the *Book of Changes*) in forty "chapters," or short passages, and the *T'ai-chi t'u shuo* (An Explanation of the Diagram of the Great Ultimate). The latter, a short essay of 263 words, has become the most important work in Neo-Confucian literature and invariably heads every Neo-Confucian anthology.

In his explanation of the diagram Chou develops a theory of creation, maintaining that the *wu-chi* ("ultimate of nonbeing"), that is, reality beyond space and time, is also the *t'ai-chi* ("great ultimate"), reality in its totality. Through its movement, the Great Ultimate generates *yang,* the active cosmic force; through tranquility, it generates *yin,* the passive cosmic force. *Yin* and *yang* alternate, each becoming the "root" of the other. This alternation and transformation gives rise to the *wu-hsing* ("five agents"): metal, wood, water, fire, and earth, which in turn produce the myriad things. Of these, man is the most intelligent. When the five moral principles of man's nature (humanity, righteousness, propriety, wisdom, and faithfulness) become active this activity begets good and evil and the various human affairs. The sage, who is in accord with his nature, settles these affairs through the principles of the "mean" *(chung),* correctness, humanity, and righteousness. Chou adds that while the two material forces and the Five Agents operate to produce the myriad things, the many are ultimately one and the one is actually differentiated in the many. This chapter is entitled "Hsing-li-ming," or "Nature, Principle, and Destiny," three terms that became key words in the Neo-Confucian vocabulary.

THE NUMERICAL COSMOLOGY OF SHAO YUNG. Shao Yung, like Chou Tun-i, based much of his thought on the concept of cosmic generation found in the *Book of Changes.* He was most influenced by the passage in the *I ching* that states that the Great Ultimate produces two forces (*yin* and *yang*), which produce four forms (*yin* and *yang* in both major and minor forms), which in turn generate the eight trigrams. These latter ultimately give rise to the myriad things. Reinterpreting this passage, Shao coupled its cosmology to a system of numerology. Underlying universal operations is what he termed "spirit" *(shen),* from which number arises. Number then produces form and form produces concrete objects. Shao's system takes the number four as the basis for the classification of all phenomena. Thus, there are four heavenly bodies (sun, moon, stars, and zodiacal space), four earthly substances (water, fire, earth, and stone), four kinds of creatures (animals, birds, grass, and plants), four sense organs (eye, ear, nose, and mouth), four ways of transforming the world (by truth, virtue, work, and effort), four kinds of rulers, four kinds of the mandate of Heaven, and so forth. To support his theory of numer-

In the eleventh century there appeared a series of thinkers determined to revive Confucianism as a philosophical system.

PAGE 143

ical evolution and production Shao expanded this systematic, yet arbitrary, scheme of classification to include a mathematical progression from the number 4 to the number 64 (the number of hexagrams in the *Book of Changes*).

UNITY AND MATERIAL FORCE IN CHANG TSAI. Chang Tsai's most important works are the *Cheng-meng* (Correcting Youthful Ignorance), in seventeen chapters, and his short essay, *Hsi-ming* (The Western Inscription). Central to these texts is the concept of material force *(ch'i)*. Chang was considered an expert on the *Book of Changes* and was renowned for his public lectures on it. However, unlike Chou Tun-i and Shao Yung, he departed from the normative interpretation of the passage in the *I ching* that speaks of the Great Ultimate generating the two modes, *yin* and *yang*. To Chang, *yin* and *yang* are but two aspects of the Great Ultimate, which is itself identified with material force. In its original reality or substance, material force is formless and as yet unconsolidated. He called this aspect of material force *t'ai-hsü* ("great vacuity"). In its operation or function, it is called *t'ai-ho* ("great harmony"). As *t'ai-ho,* it functions through *yin* and *yang* in their interaction, rise and fall, integration and disintegration, and tranquility and activity, as is borne out by the way in which day and night, life and death, advance and decline in history, and so forth all proceed in natural harmony.

From the Sung dynasty forward, ethical principles in society were a combination of Confucian virtues with Buddhist karman and compassion.

PAGE 143

Equally influential is Chang's short essay *The Western Inscription,* which he inscribed on a panel in the western window of his study. He begins by claiming that Heaven and Earth are our parents and all things are our brothers, and that we must therefore devote ourselves to filial piety, education of the young, and care for the elderly in order to complete our lives in peace. Here again, we find evidence of Chang's insistence that man forms one body with the universe.

THE CH'ENG BROTHERS' THEORY OF PRINCIPLE. The Ch'eng brothers neither spoke of the Great Ultimate nor made material force the focal point of their doctrine. Instead, they were the first in the history of Chinese philosophy to base their thought entirely on the concept of principle *(li)*. They conceived of principle as self-evident, self-sufficient, extending everywhere, and governing all things. Principle cannot be augmented or diminished. It is possessed by everyone and everything and is that by which all things exist and can be understood. By claiming that all specific principles are but one universal principle, they bound man and all things into a unity. Most significant is the fact that they were the first to identify the principle inherent in things with *t'ien-li* (the "principle of Heaven"). This is especially true of Ch'eng Hao, for whom, as for all other Neo-Confucians, the principle of Heaven represents natural law; the principle of Heaven is the universal process of production and reproduction. The Ch'engs further equated principle with the mind and with (human) nature *(hsing)*. Indeed, their declaration that "the nature is principle" has come to characterize the entire Neo-Confucian movement.

The Ch'engs followed Meng-tzu's teaching that human nature is originally good. When Ch'eng Hao said that our nature possesses both good and evil, he meant merely that because our endowment of material force is imbalanced and deviates from the Mean there is bound to be both good and evil. He was quick to stipulate that the imbalance is not due to our original nature. While Ch'eng Hao equated principle with the principle of Heaven and stressed the dynamic and creative aspects of the universe, his younger brother, Ch'eng I, strongly emphasized the unity or universality of principle and the diversity of its manifestations. His dictum "Principle is one but its manifestations are many," reminiscent of Chou Tun-i's idea of the relationship between the one and the many, became a standard formula in Neo-Confucianism.

METAPHYSICS, THE GREAT ULTIMATE, AND PRINCIPLE. It was Chou Tun-i's *Explanation of the Diagram of the Great Ultimate* that provided the metaphysical basis for Chu Hsi's theory of principle. Chu Hsi interpreted the *chi* of *t'ai-chi* as the "ultimate," that point beyond which one can go no further. He defined *t'ai-chi,* or Great Ultimate, as both the sum total of the principles of all discrete phenomena and the highest principle within each of them. He thus extended Ch'eng I's concept of principle beyond the realm of human affairs to include all affairs within the universe. He posited a theory in which principle transcends time and space: there was principle before the existence of the universe and there will be principle after the collapse of the universe. In Chu Hsi's scheme the whole universe is but one principle, the Great Ultimate, one universal whole with which all individual things are endowed. At the same time, however, he emphasized that each phenomenon is endowed with its own defining principle. Thus, it is by their respective principles that a boat travels on the water and a vehicle travels on the road. The Great Ultimate is also the repository for all actualized and potential principles: as new things appear, their principles also appear. In this way, Chu Hsi was able to explain Ch'eng I's formulaic expression, "Principle is one but its manifestations are many."

Chu Hsi attributed the generative or creative ability to the Great Ultimate rather than to principle or material force. He reaffirmed Chou Tun-i's theory that creation begins with the Great Ultimate, but held that the Great Ultimate transcends such limitations of function and thus cannot be subject to either activity or tranquillity. Rather, the Great Ultimate embodies the principles of activity and tranquility. It is out of these principles that the material forces of *yin* and *yang* naturally ensue. The process of creation is dynamic and ever changing. New principles are always forthcoming and the universe is daily renewed.

THE RELATIONSHIP BETWEEN PRINCIPLE AND MATERIAL FORCE. Chu Hsi's greatest contribution to Neo-Confucian thought was his clarification of the relationship between principle and material force and his concomitant explanation of the actualiza-

T'AI-CHI
The Great Ultimate

In the *I-ching* (Book of Changes; a wisdom book in ancient China that is widely believed to have been a major source of inspiration for Confucianism and Taoism), the term *t'ai-chi* ("great ultimate") signifies the origin and ground of Heaven and earth and of all beings. It is the Great Ultimate that is said to engender or produce *yin* and *yang,* the twin cosmic forces, which in turn give rise to the symbols, patterns, and ideas that are, indeed, forms of *yin* and *yang.* The interaction of the two modalities of these cosmic forces bring about the eight trigrams that constitute the basis of the *Book of Changes.* Combining any two of the eight trigrams, each of which contains three broken *(yin)* and three unbroken *(yang)* lines, forms one of the sixty-four hexagrams. These are taken as codes for all possible forms of change, transformation, existence, life, situations, and institutions both in nature and in culture. The Great Ultimate, then, is the highest and the most fundamental reality, and is said to generate and underlie all phenomena.

However, it is misleading to conceive of the Great Ultimate as the functional equivalent of either the Judeo-Christian concept of God or the Greek idea of Logos. The Great Ultimate is neither the willful creator nor pristine reason, but an integral part of an organic cosmic process. The inherent assumption of this interpretation is that the universe is in a dynamic process of transformation and, at the same time, has an organic unity and an underlying harmony. The universe, in Joseph Needham's understanding, is well-coordinated and well-ordered but lacks an ordainer. The Great Ultimate, so conceived, is a source or root, and is thus inseparable from what issues from it.

It was the Sung-dynasty Neo-Confucian master Chou Tun-i (Chou Lien-hsi, 1017-1073) who significantly contributed to the philosophical elaboration of the notion. In his *T'ai-chi t'u-shou* (Explanation of the Diagram of the Great Ultimate), strongly influenced by the cosmology of the *Book of Changes,* Chou specifies the cosmic process as follows: the Great Ultimate through movement and tranquility generates the two primordial cosmic forces, which in turn transform and unite to give rise to the Five Agents or Five Phases (*wu-hsing,* water, fire, wood, metal, and earth). When the five vital forces *(ch'i),* corresponding to each of the five "elements" (agents or phases), interact among themselves and reach a harmonious order, the four seasons run their orderly course. This provides the proper environment for the Five Agents to come into "mysterious union." Such a union embraces the two primordial cosmic forces, the female and the male, which interact with each other to engender and transform all things. The continuous production and reproduction of the myriad things make the universe an unending process of transformation. It is in this sense, Chou Tun-i states, that "the Five Agents constitute a manifestation of *yin* and *yang,* and *yin* and *yang* constitute a manifestation of the Great Ultimate." This is the basis for the commonly accepted Neo-Confucian assertion that the Great Ultimate is embodied both singly by each thing and collectively by all things.

It has been documented that Chou's *Diagram of the Great Ultimate* grew out of a long Taoist tradition. Indeed, it is believed that Chou received the diagram itself from a Taoist master: Taoist influences are evident even in his explanatory notes. His introduction of the term "the Non-Ultimate" or "the Ultimate of Non-being" *(wu-chi)* generated much controversy among Sung and Ming dynasty Confucian thinkers because the notion "non-ultimate" or "non-being" seems closer to the Taoist idea of nothingness than the Confucian concept that the human world is real. However, by defining human spirituality in terms of the notion that it is "man alone who receives the cosmic forces and the Five Agents in their most refined essence, and who is therefore most sensitive," Chou clearly presents a philosophical anthropology in the tradition of Confucian humanism.

In the folk tradition, the symbol of the Great Ultimate carries a connotation of mysterious creativity. The spiritual and physical exercise known as *t'ai-chi ch'üan* (a form of traditional Chinese shadow boxing) is still widely practiced. This slow, firm, and rhythmic exercise disciplines the body and purifies the mind through coordinated movements and regulated breathing. It is a remarkable demonstration that cosmological thought can be translated into physical and mental instruction for practical living without losing its intellectual sophistication. After all, in the Chinese order of things, to know the highest truth is not simply to know about something but to know how to do it properly through personal knowledge.

— TU WEI-MING

"He who sins against heaven has no place where he may pray."

CONFUCIUS
THE ANALECTS, 3:13

tion of phenomena. Despite the fact that principle and material force are merged in each phenomenon and cannot be separated, they are definitely two different things. Principle is incorporeal, one, eternal, unchanging, and indestructible. It constitutes the essence of things, is the reason for creation, and is always good. Principle represents the metaphysical world. By contrast, material force is necessary to explain physical form and the production and transformation of things. In Ch'eng I's terms, material force constitutes "what exists within form." It is corporeal, many, transitory, individual, changeable, unequal, and destructible. Material force is the vehicle and material for creation and involves both good and evil.

CHU HSI'S ETHICS AND THEORY OF MIND. Chu Hsi's metaphysical speculations on the Great Ultimate, principle, and material force provided the basis for his understanding of man's mind and nature and for his development of a system of ethics and a method for moral self-cultivation. He welcomed Ch'eng I's notion that *jen* is the seed from which all other virtues will grow. Reinterpreting the passage in the *Book of Changes* that claims "the great virtue of Heaven and Earth is to give life," Ch'eng I had declared that "the mind *(hsin)* of Heaven [the mind of the Tao] and Earth is to produce things." In his treatise on humanity, Chu Hsi brings this interpretation to bear on the nature of man's mind, defining *jen* as the "character of the mind and the principle of love." Thus, he conceives of *jen* as being derived from Heaven:

"Man and things have received this mind of Heaven and Earth as their [own] mind." This aspect of the mind, which Chu calls the "mind of the Tao" *(tao-hsin),* embodies principle in its transcendent form and is associated with man's original nature *(pen-hsing).* It is characterized by humanity and is free from self-interest and selfish desires. The other aspect of the mind, which he called the "human mind" *(jen-hsin),* is determined by man's imbalanced endowment of material force. Because it is the part of the mind that is bound to material force, the human mind is often characterized by selfish desires and causes man to act out of pure self-interest. Chu Hsi taught that in order for man not to be engulfed by selfishness and evil he must cultivate himself in a manner that rectifies the human mind and develops the mind of Heaven.

THE SCHOOL OF MIND. Chu Hsi's strongest opponent was Lu Hsiang-shan, who conceived of the mind as morally self-sufficient, endowed with the innate knowledge of good and the innate ability to do good. Going beyond Meng-tzu's statement that all things are complete within the self, Lu proclaimed that "the mind is principle." The universe is one's mind, he held, and one's mind is the universe. Consequently, he advocated complete reliance on the mind, self-sufficiency, self-accomplishment, and self-perfection. Lu criticized Chu's theory of human nature, in which the principle of Heaven, which is always good, is contrasted with human desires, which may or may not be good. Lu also refused to accept Chu Hsi's claim that while there is only one mind, a distinction can be made between the human mind and the mind of the Tao.

THE CHEKIANG SCHOOL. Early in 1175 Lü Tsu-ch'ien and his friend Chu Hsi collaborated in the compilation of the first Chinese philosophical anthology, the *Chin-ssu lu* (Reflections on Things at Hand). On many issues, however, they differed radically. While Chu Hsi viewed the classics as sacred texts, Lü looked to the dynastic and comprehensive histories for moral and philosophical lessons. He held that history does not simply gather disjointed facts but is a record of growth and transformation.

THE HUNAN SCHOOL. In his work *Chih-yen* (Knowing Words) Hu Hung, the founder of the Hunan school, maintained that the mind is the master of all things and that depending on the way the mind uses nature, nature may become good or evil. He challenged the distinction between the principle of Heaven and human desires, claiming instead that in substance they were the same but in function they differed. Chu Hsi was too young to have met Hu Hung, but he strongly criticized *Knowing Words* for philosophically contradicting the traditional Neo-Confucian doctrine of the original goodness of human nature and for equating evil human desires with the principle of Heaven.

NEO-CONFUCIANISM IN THE YÜAN DYNASTY. With the fall of the Sung dynasty in 1179 and the rise of Mongol hegemony over China the spread of the various Neo-Confucian schools virtually came to an end. The only school to survive was that of Chu Hsi. Its survival was due both to its established domination and to a chance set of circumstances. A Confucian scholar, Chao Fu (c. 1206-1299), was captured by the Mongols in Hupei Province, an area of China under the control of the Chin (1115-1234) and hence little influenced by the Neo-Confucian trend in the south. When Chao was sent to the Mongol capital at Yen-ching (modern-day Peking) he took with him several Neo-Confucian texts, most notably, Chu Hsi's commentaries to the Four Books. In Yen-ching, Chao attracted a large following, including the Chinese scholar Hsü Heng (1209-1281). Later, in his capacity as director of the T'ai-hsüeh (the national university), Hsü was able to influence and in effect dominate the intellectual current of China under the Mongols. Hsü Heng vigorously championed the *Hsiao-hsüeh* (Elementary Education), compiled by Chu Hsi in 1189 for the moral edification of the young in their daily conduct. Hsü also advocated use of the Four Books, which he regarded as sacred, and Chu Hsi's commentaries, which he personally copied. There is no doubt that Hsü Heng's adoration of Chu Hsi and his commentaries on the Four Books contributed to the imperial edict of 1313 making the Four Books and the Five Classics the basic required texts for the civil service examinations.

NEO-CONFUCIANISM IN THE MING DYNASTY. By the beginning of the Ming dynasty (1368-1644) the philosophy of the Ch'eng-Chu school was the established orthodoxy. Outstanding philosophers of the period—Ts'ao Tuan (1376-1434), Wu Yü-pi (1391-1469), Hsüeh Hsüan (1392-1464), Hu Chu-jen (1434-1484), and others—were all faithful followers of Chu Hsi. However, these thinkers tended to disregard metaphysical speculation on the Great Ultimate, *yin* and *yang,* and the relation of principle to material force and instead turned their attention toward understanding the mind, nature, self-cultivation, and seriousness *(ching).*

NEO-CONFUCIANISM IN THE CH'ING DYNASTY. Although Wang Yang-ming's doctrine of innate knowledge dominated the philosophy of the fifteenth and sixteenth centuries, it never entirely eclipsed the teachings of the Ch'eng-Chu school. The Manchu rulers, who conquered China in 1644, reaffirmed the philosophy of the Ch'eng-Chu school as the

WANG YANG-MING
The School of the Mind

WANG YANG-MING AND THE SCHOOL OF MIND. The central thesis of Wang Yang-ming's thought is that principle and mind are one. Outside the mind there is no principle and, conversely, all principles are contained within the mind. Related to this is his concept that the mind is master of the body. These concepts brought Wang into direct opposition to the thought of Chu Hsi. Wang took great exception to Chu's redaction of the *Great Learning,* in which he had emended a chapter so as to expound his theory of the investigation of things and had rearranged the order of the text so as to place the chapter on the extension of knowledge before the chapter on the sincerity of the will. In his own *Ta-hsüeh wen* (Inquiry on the *Great Learning*) Wang also criticizes Chu Hsi for establishing a dualism between "making one's virtue clear" *(ming-te)* and "loving the people" *(ch'in-min).* The essential point of this work is that, for Wang, all things form a unity *(i-t'i).*

In general, Wang claimed that Chu Hsi divided principle and mind in advocating that one should direct the mind outside to seek principles in external things. Rather than follow Chu's interpretation of *ko-wu* as an investigation *(ko)* of things, Wang revived the interpretation found in the *Meng-tzu,* where *ko* means "rectification." Thus to Wang, *ko-wu* involved rectifying the mind by eliminating incorrectness and removing evil. Wang also asserted that since it is the will of the mind to realize principle, sincerity of the will must precede the investigation of things. To redress these wrongs, in 1518 Wang published the old text of the *Great Learning* as it is found in the *Li chi* (Book of Rites).

Wang's answer to many of the difficulties raised by Chu's thought was a theory of self-cultivation that combined the concept of innate knowledge *(liang-chih),* derived from the *Meng-tzu,* with the notion of the extension of knowledge *(chih-chih),* derived from the *Great Learning.* Wang equated nature, knowledge, and the original substance of the mind, which is always good and manifests an innate knowledge of the good. It is man's innate knowledge that gives him his moral sense of right and wrong. Thus, man's mind, in its original substance, understands all principles. To cultivate oneself one need not investigate the principles of things external to the mind; rather, one has only to follow the impulses of one's innate knowledge.

To clarify these points, Wang advanced what is regarded as his most original and significant contribution to Neo-Confucianism: a doctrine of the unity of knowledge and action. Knowledge, which in Wang's thought is limited to moral knowledge, must have its logical expression in action and action must be firmly based in knowledge. "Knowledge in its genuine and earnest aspect is action and action in its intelligent and discriminating aspect is knowledge." To illustrate this, Wang refers to the experience of pain, which one cannot know unless one suffers. (This illustration demonstrates the essentially subjective nature of knowledge in Wang's system.) With respect to moral behavior, Wang said that a man who knows the duties of filial piety will fulfill them, but at the same time, can truly understand those duties only through their fulfillment. This doctrine gave Ming Neo-Confucianism a new dynamic, for it suggests that the extension of innate knowledge is a natural and even irresistible impulse that is true to man's nature. The extension of innate knowlege leads not only to the fulfillment of filial obligations but to love for all beings and the identification of oneself with all things in the universe. This notion is highly reminiscent of Ch'eng Hao's concept that man forms one body with Heaven, earth, and the myriad things.

— WING-TSIT CHAN

The constitution of the People's Republic establishes the freedom both to support and oppose religion, although in practice religious activities of all types declined there after 1949.

PAGE 145

orthodox teaching. The Four Books and Chu Hsi's commentaries on them were upheld as the required school texts and the basis for the civil service examinations. The general tendency of scholars in the late seventeenth century was either to follow the teachings of Chu Hsi or to attempt a compromise between the perceived rationalism of Chu Hsi and the idealism of Wang Yang-ming. There were, however, outstanding Neo-Confucian scholars like Ku Yen-wu (1613-1682) who began to reevaluate their intellectual heritage. Although Ku was strongly influenced by and inclined toward the philosophy of the Ch'eng-Chu school, he attacked the abstract thinking associated with their theories of the Great Ultimate, the mind, and human nature. In their stead he called for practical and objective learning, the pursuit of empirical knowledge, and involvement in practical affairs. Among the thinkers who followed Ku Yen-wu, Yen Yüan (1635-1704) and Tai Chen (1723-1777) took the tendency toward practical learning and objective truth even farther.

Yen Yüan rejected the philosophy of both Chu Hsi and Wang Yang-ming. He believed that all the subjects of Sung and Ming speculation—principle, nature, destiny, and the sincerity of the will—could only be found in such practical arts as music, ceremony, agriculture, and military craft. Yen maintained that there is no principle apart from material force; he insisted that the physical nature endowed with material force is no different from the original nature endowed by Heaven. Because the physical nature is not evil, there is no need to transform it or to repress physical desires. He believed that the investigation of things involved neither the study of principle nor the rectification of the mind, but rather the application of practical experience to the solution of practical problems.

Tai Chen, another critic of Chu Hsi, is generally recognized as the greatest thinker of the Ch'ing dynasty. He was a proponent of the new intellectual movement known as "investigations based on evidence" *(k'ao-cheng)*. He was a specialist in mathematics, astronomy, water-works, and phonetics and was widely respected as an expert in literary criticism. He complained that philosophers like Chu Hsi and Wang Yang-ming looked upon principle "as though it were a thing." Tai Chen advocated the Han dynasty understanding of principle as an order that is found only in things, by which he meant the daily affairs of men. Principle, he believed, could not be investigated by intellectual speculation, but rather through the objective, critical, and analytical observation of things. He did not follow the Sung Confucians in contrasting the principle of Heaven and human desires as good and evil, respectively. Instead, he held that principle prevails only when feelings are satisfied and that feelings are good as long as they "do not err." In conjunction with this, he postulated the existence of "necessary moral principles," that is, objective and standard principles, that are definite and inherent in concrete things.

THE NINETEENTH AND EARLY TWENTIETH CENTURIES. As China was progressively weakened by both the disintegration of Manchu rule and the onslaught of Western imperialism, Confucianism lost favor as the official state ideology.

During these turbulent times groups of intellectuals continued the effort to reinterpret and reestablish their Confucian heritage. K'ang Yu-wei (1858-1927), an outstanding scholar of the Confucian classics, justified his attempts at institutional reform by recourse to Confucian ideology. Believing that the strength and prosperity of Western nations derived from their having a state religion, K'ang petitioned the emperor to establish Confucianism as the national cult. At the same time, however, other groups of intellectuals called for the final defeat of Confucianism. The intellectual renaissance of 1917 declared Confucianism unsuited to modern life.

For a time it seemed as though Confucianism was doomed. As the revolutionary fervor cooled, however, Chinese intellectuals began to reconsider the role of the tradition in the future of China. Liang Shu-ming (1893-) published a study comparing Chinese and Western civilizations. He championed Confucian moral values and condemned the wholesale adoption of Western institutions as unsuited to the Chinese spirit. During the following twenty years, Fung Yu-lan (1895-) and Hsiung Shih-li (1895-1968) emerged as prominent spokesmen for Confucianism. Fung's *Hsin-li hsüeh* (New Learning of Principle), published in 1939, is a reconstruction of the Ch'eng-Chu school of Neo-Confucianism.

THE STATUS OF CONFUCIANISM IN THE LATE TWENTIETH CENTURY. The Communist victory in 1949 and the Cultural Revolution in the 1960s brought a decided end to the attempts to make Confucianism the state ideology and religion. However, scholars never suspended their study of Confucianism; along with members of China's political hierarchy, they have continued to discuss the historical significance and relevancy of Confucianism.

In 1980 a conference was held to study the philosophy of Chu Hsi and Wang Yang-ming. The participants' appraisal of Neo-Confucianism was objective and fair, and their remarks about Chu and Wang at once favorable and unfavorable. The official party position, affirmed at this session, is that Neo-Confucianism played a major role in Chinese history, albeit one that served a feudal society, and thus is worthy of continued study.

— WING-TSIT CHAN

THE WISDOM OF CONFUCIUS
From "To Live among the Excellent"

No. 5. "Wealth and honors are what men desire; but if they come undeserved, don't keep them. Poverty and low estate are what men dislike; but if they come undeserved, don't flee them. If the perfect gentleman avoids manhood at its best, how can we call him such? The perfect gentleman does not flee manhood at its best even for the duration of a meal. Even in haste he must abide by it; even in the direst straits he must abide by it."

No. 18. "As you serve your parents you should remonstrate with them only slightly. If on doing so you find that they are set in having their own way, be even more respectful and do not contrary them. Even though this overwhelms you with toil, do not become angry with them."

— *The Best of Confucius* By James R. Ware
Garden City, N.Y.: Halcyon House, 1950.

CONFUCIANISM IN JAPAN

The earliest Japanese chronicles tell us that Confucianism was introduced to Japan near the end of the third century CE, when Wani of Paekche (Korea) brought the Confucian *Analects* (Chin., *Lunyü;* Jpn., *Rongo*) to the court of Emperor Ojin. It is also likely that continental emigrants familiar with Confucian teachings arrived in Japan prior to the formal introduction of Confucianism.

JAPANESE CONFUCIANISM TO 1600. Both supporting and being supported by the political forces of centralization in the nascent Japanese state, Confucian teachings first achieved prominence in Japan during the time of Shotoku Taishi (573-621), who served as regent to his aunt, the empress Suiko (592-628). In 604, Shotoku Taishi wrote and promulgated the Seventeen-Article Constitution, which was intended to centralize further the administration of Japan by emphasizing administrative efficiency and harmony among contending factions. The constitution reflected the Confucian cosmology that regarded the universe as a triad composed of heaven, earth, and man, with each element having specific and mutual responsibilities. Again under Confucian influence, the cause of centralization and unification was furthered by the Taika Reforms of 645 and 646, which asserted the Confucian imperial principle of unified rule, and by the introduction of a complex legal and administrative system patterned after the codes of the Chinese T'ang dynasty during the eighth century.

The influence of Confucian principles in government administration declined during the ninth and tenth centuries along with the political power of the imperial court. Perhaps disillusioned by this trend, Japanese Confucians of the eleventh and twelfth centuries engaged more in textual analysis and criticism than in original thought or interpretation.

The Neo-Confucian doctrines of Chu Hsi (Jpn., Shuki, more commonly, Shushi; 1130-1200) were introduced to Japan, if the sources are to be believed, soon after Chu Hsi's death. Institutionally, the doctrines were taught in Zen monasteries where such Neo-Confucian practices as "maintaining reverence and sitting quietly" (*jikei seiza)* were regarded as intellectually stimulating variations of what Zen practitioners already knew as "sitting in meditation" *(zazen).* Though Neo-Confucian doctrines were from time to time favorably received at the imperial and shogunal courts, Neo-Confucianism would remain largely in the shadow of its Zen patrons through the sixteenth century.

TOKUGAWA CONFUCIANISM (1600-1868). Perhaps the only positive result of the abortive Japanese invasions of Korea in the 1590s was the consequent introduction of new texts from the Confucian tradition into Japan. Fujiwara Seika (1561-1619) was made aware of this new tradition during his study in a Zen monastery. He had his first interview with Tokugawa Ieyasu (1542-1616), the future empire builder, in 1593, a decade before Ieyasu would be granted the title of *shogun.* Regarding Neo-Confucianism as a possible basis for stable international relations, Ieyasu invited the philosophically eclectic Fujiwara Seika to join his government, but Seika declined and recommended in his stead a young student of his, Hayashi Razan (1583-1657).

Like his teacher, Hayashi Razan had studied Zen but was soon drawn to the orthodox teachings of Chu Hsi. With his appointment to Ieyasu's government, a degree of official attention was conferred on these teachings, and his descendants would serve as official Confucian advisers to the Tokugawa government throughout the period.

The final important champion of fidelity to the teachings of Chu Hsi in Japan was Yamazaki Ansai (1618-1682). His school, the Kimon, had as its goal the popularization of the ethics of Chu Hsi. Like other Neo-Confucians, this school generally took a dim view of human emotions and feelings, regarding them as potentially disruptive to the delicate balance that must lie at the heart of both man and the cosmos.

During the second half of the seventeenth century, Neo-Confucian assumptions and vocabulary penetrat-

Throughout the Tokugawa period, Confucian scholars, particularly those of the Shushigaku, Oyomeigaku, and Kogaku schools, exerted lasting influence on the warriors-turned-administrators.

PAGE 384

ed the new popular culture of Japan, but what has been called the "emotionalism" of the Japanese at this time made the puritanical Neo-Confucian stance on emotions and feelings incompatible with the mainstream of Japanese culture.

In China, the most compelling Confucian alternative to the orthodox teachings of Chu Hsi were the teachings of the fifteenth-century figure Wang Yangming (Jap., Oyomei). His teachings, known in Japan as Yomeigaku, were first propagated by Nakae Toju (1608-1648), who emphasized the Wang school's teachings on intuition and action. Kumazawa Banzan (1619-1691), a pupil of Toju, interpreted these activist teachings in terms of their relevance to the samurai class. These teachings would have their greatest impact in Japan during the nineteenth century when such leaders as Sakuma Shozan (1811-1864) and his disciple Yoshida Shoin (1830-1859) became ideological leaders of the Meiji restoration.

"Nonreligious" Confucian ethics supported "super-religious" State Shinto until the end of World War II.

PAGE 385

In Japan, however, the most intellectually compelling alternative to Neo-Confucian teachings was presented by a succession of schools known collectively as Ancient Learning (Kogaku). Yamaga Soko (1622-1685), the first proponent of Ancient Learning, argued that if the goal of Confucian exegesis was to find the true message of the sages, then that end might better be served by reading the works of Confucius and Mencius (Meng-tzu) directly rather than by reading the commentary on those works by Chu Hsi or others. Yamaga was drawn to the relevance of Confucian teachings in a military age, and he is regarded as the modern founder of the teachings of Bushido, the Way of the Warrior.

The most important Ancient Learning figure, however, was Ogyu Sorai (1666-1728), who located his school, known as the Kobunjigaku (School of Ancient Words and Phrases), in Edo. An ardent Sinophile, Sorai regarded ancient Chinese writings as the repository of intellectual resources for establishing the organization of social institutions, the performance of ancient rituals, and principles of governmental administration. He revolutionized Confucian teachings in East Asia by insisting that the principles of the Confucian way were not a priori principles but were, rather, the products of the sages' own inventive wisdom. Sorai thus insisted that aspiration to sagehood was at the least irrelevant to, and at worst destructive of, the polity.

With the decline of the school of Ogyu Sorai during the mid-eighteenth century, Confucianism as a whole began to decline.

CONFUCIANISM IN MODERN JAPAN. Confucianism played a relatively passive role through the end of World War I. By this time the originally Confucian notions of loyalty and filial piety had come to be regarded as native Japanese virtues, and in 1937 these virtues were propounded in a work entitled *Kokutai no hongi* (Essentials of the National Polity) as the cardinal principles of Japanese national morality. Confucianism served Japanese imperialist aims in Korea after its annexation in 1910, in Manchuria after 1932, and in the Japanese-controlled portions of North China after 1937. After World War II, Confucian teachings were removed from the Japanese curriculum by the occupation authorities, and Confucianism has not yet recovered from this blow.

— PETER NOSCO

CONFUCIANISM IN KOREA

In the seventh century, the Silla government, at first a tribal federation, turned to Confucianism as a tool of centralization. In 651, the Royal Academy was established, in which officials, drawn from the aristocracy, were exposed to the Confucian classics. Furthermore, Confucian precepts found their way into aristocratic codes of behavior, even becoming incorporated into the rules of conduct for the *hwarang,* a knightly class instrumental in the Silla unification of the Korean Peninsula in 668.

From the inception of the Koryo dynasty (918-1392) an expanded role for Confucian doctrine was envisioned. In the celebrated "Ten Injunctions" addressed to his descendants by the dynastic founder, Wang Kon (r. 918-943), Buddhism was chosen to govern spiritual matters, geomancy was to be used for prophecy and prognostication, and Confucianism was chosen as the guiding principle in the sociopolitical sphere.

In the late tenth century the government was reorganized into a centralized bureaucratic structure. Local officials were appointed by the central government. The Koryo polity transformed into an aristocratic-bureaucratic state in which the power of the ruling elite derived from government position rather than an ancestral seat. This change reflected the Confucian rhetoric of government.

Under this Confucian system, civil officials served in the capital, where the mode of life included the pursuit of scholarly and literary activities.

The military coup of 1170 disrupted this Confucian social order. The Mongols, who invaded Korea in 1231, were instrumental in bringing about the end of military rule in 1259. Koryo kings, married to Mongol princesses and devoid of power, spent a great deal of time prior to their accession and after their retirement in the cosmopolitan Yüan capital. Establishments such as that of the scholar-king Ch'ungson (r. 1289, 1308-1313) served as meeting places for Chinese and Korean scholars, and Korean scholars for the first time had first-hand exposure to Sung dynasty (960-1279) Neo-

Confucian scholarship, particularly that of the Ch'eng-Chu school. The result was an impressive array of scholars beginning with An Hyang (1243-1306) and Paek Ijong (fl. 1300), commonly regarded as having introduced Neo-Confucianism to Korea. They succeeded in including the Neo-Confucian texts—the Four Books and Five Classics—in the civil service examination and in the curriculum at the Royal College and in reinstituting the royal lecture, complete with Neo-Confucian texts and teacher-officials who lectured to the king-student.

FOUNDING OF THE YI NEO-CONFUCIAN POLITY. The founding of the Yi dynasty (1392-1910) was, in its sense, not merely a change in political power. Its founders were all confirmed Neo-Confucians and they sought to create a new sociopolitical order based on their moral vision. Chong Tojon (1342-1398), the leader of this group, campaigned to discredit Buddhism. Motivated by the Neo-Confucian belief in the centrality of man, Chong challenged the Buddhist view that this world, the phenomenal world, was illusion, terming such a view invalid and harmful.

Beginning with changes in the political structure, the Yi government launched a massive transformation of Korean society that was not fully realized for several centuries. The most conspicuous changes were the adoption of a new system of education, a restructuring of social organization along patrilineal groups, the adoption of Confucian ritual, and the propagation of Confucian ethics through local associations. In order to disseminate Confucian values more widely to the educated class, the Yi government sought to establish a nationwide public school system. Four schools in the capital and one school in each county supposedly would make primary education widely available, while the Royal College in the capital would provide advanced education for qualified students.

THE DEVELOPMENT OF CONFUCIAN SCHOLARSHIP. By the sixteenth century, Korean scholars turned to the more purely intellectual and speculative aspects of Confucian learning, looking directly to the Ch'eng-Chu school. Despite close ties with Ming dynasty (1368-1644) scholarship, Korean Neo-Confucianism developed independently of contemporary scholarship there. While Korean scholars accepted the authority of the Ch'eng-Chu school, they defined issues in their own way, adding insights and interpretations. The scholars Pak Yong (1471-1540), So Kyongdok (1489-1546), and Yi Onjok (1491-1553) reflect the diversity and independence of the Korean school.

But it was Yi Hwang (1501-1570), better known as T'oegye, who brought Korean Neo-Confucianism to maturity. Working at a time when Wang Yang-ming's thought seemed to be gaining influence in the Korean scholarly community, he devoted himself to defining orthodoxy, to distinguishing "right learning" from deviant thought. The definition of a Korean orthodoxy within the tradition of the Ch'eng-Chu school, one that excluded the ideas of the Wang Yang-ming school, is often attributed to his efforts. T'oegye accepted Chu Hsi's dual theory of principle and material force and the relationship between them. While Chu Hsi acknowledged that principle and material force cannot exist in isolation, he held that principle is prior and material force posterior. The superiority of principle was a defining feature of his philosophy: principle was identified with the Way *(tao)* and the nature *(hsing)*, which are permanent and unchanging, while material force was identified with physical entities, which constantly change. But Chu Hsi's position proved somewhat ambiguous. One could ask whether the priority of principle was existential or evaluative, that is, did it exist first or did it just have a superior moral value? Further, in what sense did principle exist prior to material force if it could not manifest itself without material force? Much of T'oegye's work was devoted to this question. He concluded that the priority of principle applied in the realm of ethical values, and that principle exerted a positive ethical influence.

Like the Sung Neo-Confucians, Korean scholars including T'oegye were deeply concerned with the problem of human evil. If man's original nature was good, then how can one explain evil? T'oegye again accepted Chu Hsi's concept of human nature based on his dual theory of principle and material force. Principle is immanent in everything in the universe. What individuates one thing from another is material force. Since principle is good, what determines the moral quality of an entity is its material force. Man has an original nature and a physical nature and only when he returns to original nature does he act in accordance with moral principle. What determines the morality of human action is mind. The mind possesses innate knowledge of moral principle and has the cognitive capacity to discern it. Yet, this capacity of mind can be prevented from functioning when it becomes clouded by selfish desire.

Meanwhile, Yi I (1536-1584), known by his pen name, Yulgok, took the formula "obtain truth through one's own effort" as his credo; he regarded adhering too rigidly to previous masters' positions as contrary to the spirit of Neo-Confucian learning.

The intellectual scene in the eighteenth century was somewhat freer and more diverse. This period witnessed the flowering of the Sirhak ("practical learning") school. Centuries of factional struggle and growing competition for office had left many scholars outside the mainstream of political power. Practical

Confucianism, Taoism, and Buddhism, often said to be Korea's major religions, all came to Korea from or through China.

PAGE 419

Learning scholars were disaffected intellectuals who wrote treatises on social and economic reform. They fall largely into two groups. Yu Hyong-won (1622-1673) and Yi Ik (1681-1763) accepted the Confucian vision of an agrarian society presided over by the rule of virtue and urged social improvement through land reform and moral rule. Pak Chi-won (1737-1805), Hong Taeyong (1731-1783), and Pak Che-ga (b. 1750), on the other hand, searched for alternatives. They addressed themselves to such issues as commerce, trade, and technology. Pak Chi-won's biting satire of the class system, Hong Taeyong's interest in science as it was expressed in his notion of the moving earth, and Pak Che-ga's belief in technology founded on a startling theory of a consumer economy clearly departed from the conventional mode of thinking. Chong Yagyong (1762-1836), often considered the greatest Practical Learning scholar, encompassed both trends in his reform ideas. His attention to the improvement of local government is well known. While these scholars worked within the Confucian political and value system, they are regarded as precursors of modernization for their critique of contemporary society and their innovative proposals for reform.

In the late nineteenth century as Korea came under increasing pressure from the major powers and the Confucian value system itself came under attack, Confucian thinking turned defensive. Confucian scholars committed to preserving the orthodox tradition became conservatives who opposed treaties and modernizing measures. Seeing themselves as the defenders of the only true civilization, they put up real resistance.

JONATHAN EDWARDS

Edwards, a great American theologian from Northampton, Massachusetts, was prominent in the early Congregational church.

LIBRARY OF CONGRESS/CORBIS

The role of Confucianism in the twentieth century, which began with anti-Confusianistic movements, needs yet to be examined in depth.

[*See also* Buddhism, *and* Korean Religion.]

— JAHYUN KIM HABOUSH

CONGREGATIONALISM

HISTORICAL SURVEY

The roots of the "Congregational way" lay in Elizabethan Separatism, which produced Congregationalism's first three martyrs, Henry Barrow, John Greenwood, and John Penry. Some of the Separatists settled in Holland (and it was from among these that the *Mayflower* group set out for New England in 1620). The Restoration of Charles II was a disaster for their cause, and the Act of Uniformity of 1662 was the first of many efforts to suppress them.

The accession of William and Mary in 1688 made life more tolerable for Congregationalists, and, after a threatened setback in the reign of Queen Anne, they played a significant minor part in eighteenth-century England, where they were particularly active in education.

English Congregationalism shared fully in nineteenth-century ecclesiastical prosperity. As members of the emerging lower middle classes crowded into the churches, they became more politically minded. Voluntarism, opposing state support of denominational education, and the Liberation Society, advocating the disestablishment of the Church of England, were influential.

Congregationalists have also been strong in Wales, where the Welsh-speaking churches, known as the Union of Welsh Independents, retain their identity.

It is in the United States that Congregationalism achieved its greatest public influence and numerical strength. The Separatists of the Plymouth Colony were more radical than the Puritans of Massachusetts Bay, but they had enough in common to form a unified community. Their statement of faith, the Cambridge Platform of 1648, accepted the theology of the English Presbyterian Westminster Confession of 1646 but laid down a Congregational rather than a Presbyterian polity. In this it was followed by the English Savoy Declaration of 1658.

The original New Englanders were not sectarian; they worked out an intellectually powerful and consistent system of theology and church and civil government that they strove, with considerable success, to exemplify. The very success of the New England settlement made it difficult for succeeding generations to retain the original commitment, and the Half-Way

Covenant was devised to find a place for those who were baptized but could not make a strong enough confession of faith. Education was seen as vital from the outset. Harvard College was founded in 1637 to maintain the succession of learned ministers. Yale and others followed, precursors of a long succession of distinguished colleges founded under Congregational auspices across the country.

New life came with the Great Awakening, the revival movement begun in 1734, in which Jonathan Edwards, a minister at Northampton, Massachusetts, and one of the greatest American theologians, was prominent. Differences emerged at the turn of the century between the two wings of Congregationalism, those who continued to accept the modified Calvinism represented by Edwards and those who were moving toward Unitarianism.

Despite the loss to the Unitarians, who took with them many of the most handsome colonial churches, Congregationalism flourished in the nineteenth century and was active in the westward expansion of the nation. In 1847, Horace Bushnell, a representative theologian, challenged the traditional substitutionary view of the atonement; his book *Christian Nurture* questioned the need for the classic conversion experience. The so-called Kansas City Creed of 1913 summed up this liberalism, which represented a break with the Calvinist past. This liberalism continues to prevail, although substantially modified after World War II by the influence of neoorthodoxy.

BELIEFS AND PRACTICES

The beliefs and practices of most Congregationalists have been broadly similar to those of other mainline evangelical Protestant churches of the more liberal kind. The English historian Bernard Manning described them as "decentralized Calvinists," but this fails to allow for their emphasis on the free movement of the Holy Spirit, which gives them some affinity with the Quakers as well as with Presbyterians.

Preaching is important in Congregationalism because the word in scripture is thought of as constitutive of the church. Baptism and the Lord's Supper are the only recognized sacraments, and infant baptism is customary. Traditionally, public prayer has been *ex tempore,* but in this century set forms have been widely used. Hymns are important.

One of the most distinctive Congregational institutions is that of the church meeting, a regular gathering at which all church members have the right and responsibility to participate in all decisions.

Congregational churches have existed chiefly in English-speaking countries and in communities related to them, and although they have not been among the larger Christian groups, their tradition continues to exercise influence as one element in the life of larger reunited churches in many lands.

— DANIEL JENKINS

CONSERVATIVE JUDAISM

BACKGROUND AND INSTITUTIONAL HISTORY

Conservative Judaism originated in the conviction that the earlier Reform Jewish movement had simply gone too far in its efforts to accommodate modern Judaism to the visible models of Christian church society. In 1845, at the (Reform) Rabbinical Conference in Frankfurt am Main, Zacharias Frankel grew concerned about the increasingly radical tenor of the discussions and finally decided that he could not agree with his Reform colleagues' decision that the Hebrew language was only an "advisable," not a "necessary," feature of Jewish worship. He withdrew from the meeting and issued a widely circularized public denunciation of the extremist departures from tradition that had been countenanced by the participants.

While Frankel did not see fit to launch a new movement, he did insist on periodically expounding his new theological approach to modern Judaism, which he named positive-historical Judaism.

ORIGINS IN THE UNITED STATES. In the United States, Conservative Judaism was formally launched in 1886 with the founding of the Jewish Theological Seminary of America. The new seminary was organized in direct reaction to the issuance of the Pittsburgh Platform by a representative group of Reform rabbis in 1885, which set forth their ideological commitment to a Judaism of morality and ethics, but one that was devoid of its national and ritual dimensions and that entertained only a God "idea," not a deep-rooted conviction in a "personal" God. A broad coalition of moderate Reform rabbis, together with several traditionalist rabbis, joined together to establish the new seminary.

The Jewish Theological Seminary began its classes in 1886 in rooms provided by the Shearith Israel congregation in New York. It was largely staffed and funded by its founding volunteers during its early years and was led by its president, Sabato Morais of Philadelphia. Its initial broad constituency, however, did not long endure; American Jewry was polarized between the German Jews, who inclined toward Reform, and the recent immigrants from eastern Europe, inclined toward Orthodoxy. By the time Sabato Morais died, in 1897, the prospects for the Conservative seminary's survival seemed increasingly dim.

Calvin's fourfold ordering of ministry was taken over by the Reformed church and the Puritans in the British Isles and colonial America in the Presbyterian and Congregational churches.

PAGE 441

C

CONSERVATIVE JUDAISM

Background and Institutional History

REORGANIZATION OF THE JEWISH THEOLOGICAL SEMINARY. At that low point, a new and powerful coalition appeared on the seminary's horizon, possessing both the intellectual energy and the material resources necessary to reverse its decline. Organized by Cyrus Adler, librarian of the Smithsonian Institution, this strong cadre of cultured philanthropists included the renowned attorney Louis Marshall, the eminent banker Jacob Schiff, the judge Mayer Sulzberger, and industrialists like Adolph Lewisohn and Daniel and Simon Guggenheim. Adler successfully persuaded them that the Jewish Theological Seminary of America could become a powerful americanizing force for the thousands of Jews who were beginning to arrive from eastern Europe. Through respect for their traditions, it could provide a healthful synthesis of learning and observance, while drawing them into the modernist world of new ideas and open horizons. Above all, it could produce rabbis who would combine the wisdom of the Old World with the disciplines and skills of the New World and facilitate the generational transition from Yiddish-speaking immigrant to upstanding American citizen.

The key to the successful reorganization of the seminary in the minds of these philanthropists and community leaders was the appointment of a world-renowned Jewish scholar and personality to oversee the new institution. The person they sought was Solomon Schechter (1850-1915).

After considerable negotiation, Schechter agreed to undertake the new challenge, and Adler, Schiff, and Marshall proceeded with the reorganization of the Jewish Theological Seminary, appropriating the main administrative positions. Schechter arrived in 1902 to implement the type of academic standards for the seminary to which he had become accustomed..

GROWTH OF THE MOVEMENT. Adler's successor in 1940 as titular head of the Conservative movement (begun in 1913 with the advent of the United Synagogue of America) was Louis Finkelstein, a seminary alumnus who had studied under Schechter and had become a mainstay of the seminary faculty and administration during the Adler era. Finkelstein almost immediately launched a broad-based expansion of the seminary's programs during the wartime and postwar periods, an expansion that was carried forward with vision, energy, effectiveness, and a large measure of success.

The Finkelstein era (1940-1972) was characterized by enormous growth in the number of congregations affiliated with Conservative Judaism, a sharp escalation in the number of programs offered by the institutions of the movement, and greater recognition of the responsibilities that devolved upon the movement in view of its newfound preeminence in American and world Jewish affairs. Having grown from about 200 affiliated congregations in 1940 to some 830 congregations by 1965, the movement had become the largest federation of synagogues in the Diaspora.

The phenomenal growth of Conservative Judaism

JEWISH THEOLOGICAL SEMINARY

Traditional seder services were held on the eve of Passover, 1944 at the Jewish Theological Seminary, an institution at the forefront of Conservative Judaism tapered off in the mid-1960s. By then the movement had established a full network of professional and lay organizations designed to enhance its local, national, and international functioning. Its California branch, the University of Judaism, had become a major force in the growth of West Coast Jewry. The Mesorati ("traditional," i. e., Conservative) movement was launched to establish Conservative congregations in Israel. The Cantors Institute, the Teachers Institute, and the seminary's various graduate schools were seeking to meet the perennial shortage of qualified Jewish professionals. The burgeoning Association for Jewish Studies, serving the academic community, was heavily populated by scholars trained in the Conservative Jewish institutions. Prayer books for the Sabbath, festivals, High Holy Days, and weekday services had been published by the United Synagogue and the Rabbinical Assembly.

In 1972 Finkelstein announced his retirement. His successor, Gerson D. Cohen, also a seminary alumnus, had served with distinction as a professor of Jewish history at Columbia University and at the seminary. He became chancellor of an institution that was now in the forefront of American Jewish institutional life and titular head of the largest of the Jewish religious movements. The agenda for the new administration included resolving some of the lingering ideological issues that had been brushed aside during the rapid expansion period of Conservative Judaism, consolidating the many activities of the movement, and addressing the capital improvement projects that had become increasingly imperative as the movement had grown.

MAJOR ORGANIZATIONS

Over the course of the century, the Conservative movement spread from the Jewish Theological Seminary of America into a web of religious and social institutions which are herewith described.

THE UNITED SYNAGOGUE OF AMERICA. Founded by Solomon Schechter in 1913, the United Synagogue is the national association of Conservative congregations, responsible for the coordination of activities and services of the Conservative movement on behalf of its constituent congregations. Divisions of the United Synagogue created for this purpose include some of the most important bodies of the movement. Among these are: The Commission on Jewish Education; The Department of Youth Activities; The National Academy for Adult Jewish Studies; and The Israel Affairs Committee.

THE RABBINICAL ASSEMBLY. The Rabbinical Assembly (RA) is the organization of Conservative rabbis and has a membership of over eleven hundred rabbis. The Rabbinical Assembly has historically served as the religious policy-making body in the Conservative movement; its Committee on Jewish Law and Standards (CJLS) has been recognized as the authoritative forum for the development of Jewish legal precedents for the movement.

THE WOMEN'S LEAGUE FOR CONSERVATIVE JUDAISM. More than eight hundred synagogue sisterhoods are affiliated with the Conservative movement through the coordinating body of the Women's League. Founded by Mathilde Schechter in 1918, the Women's League has historically proven to be one of the pioneering organizations in Conservative Judaism in the development of social, educational, and philanthropic programs for the entire movement.

THE NATIONAL FEDERATION OF JEWISH MEN'S CLUBS. The four hundred men's clubs affiliated with the Conservative movement plan joint ventures for the advancement of Conservative Judaism. The National Federation of Jewish Men's Clubs is particularly active in the areas of social action, youth activities, and Israeli affairs.

THE WORLD COUNCIL OF SYNAGOGUES. The international arm of the Conservative movement, the World Council of Synagogues was established in 1959 to assist in bringing the message of Conservative Judaism to the attention of world Jewry outside the borders of North America. It maintains offices in Jerusalem, Buenos Aires, and New York and meets in convention every two years in Jerusalem.

— HERBERT ROSENBLUM

COPTIC CHURCH

The Coptic church is the ancient church of Egypt; the name Copt derives from the Greek *Aiguptioi* ("Egyptians"). According to tradition within the church, its founder and first patriarch was Mark the Evangelist, who preached Christianity in the first century AD. For several centuries the new faith engendered by Mark's preaching and the old pagan culture mingled with the teachings of both Neoplatonism and gnosticism, amid waves of Roman persecutions.

Biblical papyri and parchment codices found in Egypt are testimonies of the penetration of the new faith into Egypt long before the end of the age of persecutions. Such papyri attest to the antiquity of Christianity in Egypt. With the Edict of Milan (313), whereby Constantine made Christianity the official religion of the empire, Alexandria became the seat of Christian theological studies. There, the doctrines of what was an amorphous faith were formulated into a systematic theology.

THE CATECHETICAL SCHOOL OF ALEXANDRIA. The catechetical school of Alexandria, which began in about 190, was to become a center of Christian scholarship under the leadership of some of the

Mark's gospel has been described as a "passion narrative with an extended introduction."

PAGE 83

"If you seek perfection, go, sell your possessions, and give to the poor."

MATTHEW 19:21

greatest church fathers. It came of age under Origen, perhaps the most prolific author of all time. One of Origen's works, the *Hexapla,* is the first collation of the texts of the Bible in six columns of Greek and Hebrew originals. Origen's exegetical, philosophical, and theological writings had broad influence on the early church. His pupils included the patriarch Heraclas (230-246), who was the first in the annals of Christianity to bear the title of pope, Athanasius, Cyril of Alexandria, and others.

ECUMENICAL MOVEMENT. An ecumenical movement intended to combat heresy was inaugurated by Constantine with the Council of Nicaea (325). At this and subsequent councils, orthodoxy was defined for theological questions concerning divine essence and the divinity and humanity of Christ. At the time of the Second Council of Ephesus (449), a change of emperors drew together Rome and Constantinople, greatly affecting the Alexandrian ecclesiastical hegemony. Cyril's nephew, Dioscorus I, who had dominated that council, was summoned to Chalcedon in 451 by the eastern emperor Marcian and forced to defend his views on Christology (the essence of Christ's divinity and humanity). The council condemned Dioscorus, who was consequently deposed and exiled.

Henceforth, the place of the Coptic church in the Christian world was curtailed. A wave of persecution was begun against the Copts to curb their separatism, with disastrous consequences on the eve of the Arab conquest of Egypt.

MONASTIC RULE. Though severe social and economic factors must have played a role in accelerating the flight of Copts to the desert, it remains true that monasticism as an institution was initiated principally by Coptic piety. The first or founding stage is associated with Antony (c. 251-356), who fled to the solitude of the eastern desert from his native village of Coma after hearing *Matthew* 19:21. Others followed his example, and a monastic colony arose around his cave in the Red Sea mountains. All practiced a life of austerity and the torture of the flesh to save the soul. Although committed to complete solitude, these men of religion found it spiritually profitable to be within sight of their great mentor for guidance, and physically protective to be within reach of other brothers. These circumstances led to the development of the second stage in monastic evolution, a stage that may be called collective eremiticism.

The third and final stage in the development of cenobitic life must be ascribed to Pachomius (d. 346). Originally a pagan legionary, he was inspired by the goodness of Christian villagers who ministered to the needs of the soldiers and was baptized a Christian. After spiritual training by a hermit, Pachomius developed a community and subsequently an original rule. The rule prescribed communal life in a cenobium and repudiated self-mortification. According to the rule, monks should develop their potential in useful pursuits, both manual and intellectual, while preserving the monastic vow of chastity, poverty, and obedience.

MISSIONARY ENDEAVOR. Those who lived in Pachomian monasteries and later took Pachomian monasticism to their homelands may be regarded as unchartered ambassadors of Coptic Christianity, but, further, the Copts themselves were active in extensive missionary enterprise. In North Africa, the Copts concentrated on the easternmost part of Libya, called the Pentapolis. They also penetrated Nubia in the upper reaches of the Nile. The conversion of the kingdom of Ethiopia took place in the fourth century. Coptic activities in Asia lack written evidence, but isolated cases provide instances of missionary work on that continent as well. In Europe, Coptic monks followed in the steps of Roman legionaries to preach the gospel in Gaul, Switzerland, and Britain.

The Swiss mission may be traced to a group of Christian legionaries from Egypt led by Mauritius about the year 285.

The Copts appear to have introduced Christianity to the British Isles. In England, Egyptian monastic rule prevailed until the coming of Augustine of Canterbury in 597, and the powerful Irish Christianity that shaped the civilization of northern Europe may be regarded as the direct descendant of the Coptic church.

FROM DOCTRINAL CONFLICT TO ECUMENISM. The Council of Chalcedon in 451, with its condemnation of the Coptic patriarch Dioscorus I, and its interpretation of Cyril's formula of the nature and person of Christ contrary to the Coptic profession, led to the cleavage of Christendom into two divergent camps. To this day, Chalcedon is bitterly remembered by the Coptic natives of Egypt, as well as by others (Syrians, Ethiopians, and Armenians). The outcome of Chalcedon was immediately felt in Egypt: the Byzantine emperors who aimed at unity within the church as the sole bearer of cohesion in the empire forcibly imposed that unity on the Egyptian people. Persecution was inaugurated to obliterate all vestiges of separatism. Excessive taxation and horrible torture and humiliation were inflicted upon Egyptians throughout the period from 451 to 641, until the Arab conquest.

The Arabs promised religious freedom to all the "people of the book," that is, to Christians and the Jews. In fact, after the downfall of Alexandria, the conquerors offered the fugitive Coptic patriarch Benjamin I honorable safe-conduct and possession of the vacated Melchite churches. At the time of the conquest, the Arabs referred to Egypt as Dar al-Qibt (Home of the Copts).

Muslim rule created a new barrier between the

Christians of the East and those of the West. Internally, the growing Muslim majority generally accorded the Copts a certain status as good neighbors and honest civil servants. In modern times, the Copts were on occasion offered integration with other Christian powers. Peter the Great (1689-1725) offered a merger with the Copts on the condition that they become a Russian protectorate. The Copts, however, systematically chose a life of harmony with their Muslim compatriots.

When the French expedition of 1798-1802 entered Egypt, the Copts began to establish a measure of communication with Western Christendom. Soon after, with the emergence of democracy and the enfranchisement of the Egyptians, the Copts emerged from their closed communities.

Perhaps the most significant demonstration of the rebirth of interaction between East and West is Coptic participation in the World Council of Churches meeting that convened in 1954 in Illinois. Since then, the Copts have been active in the council.

— A. S. ATIYA

COVENANT

A central idea in the Hebrew scriptures (Old Testament) is that a covenant, a formal sworn agreement, exists between God and certain individuals or the whole chosen people, Israel. Not content with thinking of God as revealed in nature, or under metaphors from family life (as father or mother), Israel sought to capture and express the stability of the deity's relation to men under this figure from political or legal experience. Aspects of ancient Israel's covenant notions were revived by the Essene covenanters, the people of the Dead Sea Scrolls, and, in much revised form, in early Christianity. The idea of a covenant was not, however, prominent in subsequent Christian theology until after the Reformation of the sixteenth century, when Old Testament ideas were deliberately exploited in some varieties of Protestant theology, and eventually had even wider influence.

THE COVENANT OF GRANT IN THE OLD TESTAMENT. One type of Old Testament covenant is an unconditional divine gift to some man or men. The divine promise to Noah (Gn. 9:8-17) after the Flood is called a covenant, and the rainbow is the "sign of the covenant." Examination of the story shows that the deity alone undertakes obligations; Noah and his descendants are not bound in any way. The significant word *remember* is used of God; God will remember what he has promised.

THE COVENANT OF OBLIGATION IN THE OLD TESTAMENT. The other main conception of a covenant pointed in the opposite direction: the deity undertook no specific obligation, but the human partners swore to abide by certain stipulations, the penalty for disobedience being calamitous curses on the community and ultimately its exile. This conception of the religious covenant, which was at times a social and political reality, not just an idea, called for allegiance to a single God and observance of important mutual obligations in the society (respect for life, property, justice, etc.) and thus was a powerful force for national union, an operative principle rather than a theological abstraction.

This and a rich body of other materials have been vigorously exploited in recent scholarly attempts to elucidate the complex of ideas that makes up the Israelite conception of a covenant of obligation, Mendenhall's study of 1954 being the earliest. In his view, the Israelite covenant is similar to these early Near Eastern treaties in major emphases and intent: God gives the covenant—as at Sinai (*Ex.* 20) or Shechem (*Jos.* 24)—based on his past gracious actions, but without himself swearing to any performance. The human partners are bound to specific obligations toward him and one another (the Decalogue), transgression of which will bring awful retribution.

BLENDING OF OLD TESTAMENT COVENANT IDEAS IN THE PRIESTLY WRITER. Although two separate and nearly opposite conceptions of the covenant prevailed in ancient Israel, they did not remain apart. The late (sixth-century BCE?) priestly writer provides the most impressive and influential example of an arrangement of contrasting covenants and use of them to structure history. Human history from creation through the time of Moses is divided into eras by the covenants (of grant) with Noah, and then Abraham; finally comes the Sinai covenant (of obligation), for which a separate Hebrew term (*'edut*) is used. This discrimination underlies that of Paul (*Gal.* 3) and ultimately much dispensationalism.

COVENANT AT QUMRAN AND IN THE NEW TESTAMENT. The nearly contemporary writings of the Qumran community, the people of the Dead Sea Scrolls, and the New Testament reveal contrasting uses of covenant ideas: the former amounts to a repristination of Old Testament practices, with a basic change in orientation, while the latter displays some theological and polemical use of the term but in effect abandons the idea and associated social forms in favor of others.

The Essenes styled themselves "those who entered the new covenant in the land of Damascus" (C D [Damascus Document] VI 19), and the community bound themselves to the Law of Moses by a formal ceremony of oaths involving blessing and cursing, much in the old style. But while the Israelite covenant of obligation was thought of as given by God, at his

The human partners swore to abide by certain stipulations, the penalty for disobedience being calamitous curses on the community and ultimately its exile.

PAGE 193

"I am now establishing my covenant with you and your descendants after you."

GENESIS 9:9

initiative, the Essene covenant is the result of human determination. Blessing and curse now lie respectively on those within and those outside of the community; they are no longer possibilities confronting those bound to the covenant.

The writer of the letter to the Hebrews uses the term *covenant* rather often, and views Jesus as the "mediator of a new covenant" *(diatheke),* but the covenant concept is not fundamental to his view of the new faith. The reverse is closer to the truth: "covenant" is one Old Testament idea, along with the concepts of priesthood, sanctuary, and so on, whose sense is illumined by Christ.

Paul's employment of *covenant* is rather similar, with a sharp polemical point. The covenant of grace (grant) is older than the Sinai covenant and thus superior in force (*Gal.* 3); the superiority of the new covenant in Christ, which continues the Abrahamic covenant, is argued in *2 Corinthians* 3. Paul uses the Greek *diatheke* for "covenant," following the usage of the ancient Greek

DEAD SEA SCROLLS
A Sacred Covenant

Discovery. In Qumran, in 1947, a young bedouin entered what is now designated Cave I and found a group of pottery jars containing leather scrolls wrapped in linen cloths. Scientific exploration of the cave in 1949 by G. Lankester Harding and Roland de Vaux uncovered additional fragments and many broken jars. From 1951 on, a steady stream of manuscripts has been provided by bedouin and archaeologists.

From the beginning, the dating of the scrolls was a matter of controversy. Some saw the new texts as documents of the medieval Jewish sect of the Karaites. Others believed they dated from the Roman period, and some even thought they were of Christian origin.

Of primary importance for dating the scrolls was the excavation of the building complex immediately below the caves on the plateau. Numismatic evidence has shown that the complex flourished from circa 135 BCE to 68 CE, interrupted only by the earthquake of 31 BCE. Similar conclusions resulted from carbon dating of the cloth wrappings. It is certain, then, that the scrolls once constituted the library of a sect that occupied the Qumran area from after the Maccabean Revolt of 166-164 BCE until the great revolt against Rome of 66-74 CE.

The Scrolls. The scrolls can be divided into three main categories: biblical manuscripts, apocryphal compositions, and sectarian documents.

Fragments of every book of the Hebrew scriptures have been unearthed at Qumran, with the sole exception of the *Book of Esther.* Among the more important biblical scrolls are the two *Isaiah* scrolls (one is complete) and the fragments of *Leviticus* and *Samuel* (dated to the third century BCE). William Albright and Frank Moore Cross have detected three recensional traditions among the scrolls at Qumran: Palestinian; Alexandrian; and Babylonian.

By far the most interesting materials are the writings of the sect that inhabited Qumran. Numerous smaller texts throw light on mysticism, prayer, and sectarian law. As of 1986, many of these texts have not yet been published or are still awaiting thorough study.

The Sect and Its Beliefs. The Qumran sect saw itself as the sole possessor of the correct interpretation of the Bible. The sect believed that the messianic era was about to dawn and lived a life of purity and holiness on the shore of the Dead Sea.

The sect was organized along rigid lines. There was an elaborate initiation procedure, lasting several years, during which members were progressively received at the ritually pure banquets of the sect. All legal decisions of the sect were made by the sectarian assembly, and its own system of courts dealt with violations and punishments of the sectarian interpretation of Jewish law. New laws were derived by ongoing inspired biblical exegesis.

Dominant scholarly opinion has identified the Dead Sea sect as the Essenes described in the writings of Philo Judaeus and Josephus Flavius of the first century CE. Indeed, there are many similarities between this group and the sect described by the scrolls.

In many details, however, the Dead Sea Scrolls do not agree with these accounts of the Essenes. If, indeed, the Dead Sea community was an Essene sect, perhaps it represented an offshoot of the Essenes who themselves differ in many ways from those described by Philo and Josephus. A further difficulty stems from the fact that the word essene never appears in the scrolls and that it is of unknown meaning and etymology.

The contribution of the biblical scrolls to our understanding of the history of the biblical text and versions is profound. We now know of the fluid state of the Hebrew scriptures in the last years of the Second Temple. With the help of the biblical scrolls from Masada and the Bar Kokhba caves, we can now understand the role of local texts, the sources of the different ancient translations of the Bible, and the process of standardization of the scriptures that resulted in the Masoretic text.

In the years spanned by the Dead Sea Scrolls, the text of the Hebrew scriptures was coming into its final form, the background of the New Testament was in evidence, and the great traditions that would constitute rabbinic Judaism were taking shape.

— LAWRENCE H. SCHIFFMAN

translation of the Old Testament (Septuagint). In secular Greek usage, *diatheke* mostly meant "last will" or "testament," a sense never borne by the Hebrew *berit.* Paul exploits the Greek sense to make the point that a covenant (testament), such as that with Abraham, is unchangeable. In so doing he illustrates the extent to which *covenant* has become a word remote from the way the community defines its identity.

COVENANT IN CHRISTIAN THEOLOGY AND CHURCH HISTORY. Although the Christian church ultimately retained the Old Testament as sacred scripture and thus assured continued acquaintance with covenant ideas, the interests of its theologians and the forms of its polity led away from any profound concern with the ancient Israelite covenant. This state of affairs endured until the Reformation of the sixteenth century opened the door to a search for new forms of common life and a renewed interest in the Old Testament, especially on the part of Calvin and his followers. The best known, though not the earliest, of the "covenant theologians" was John Koch (Cocceius; 1603-1669), whose teaching of a sequence of divine covenants was especially appealing within Calvinism as grounding human salvation in an arbitrary divine act. The Scottish national covenants of the seventeenth century were an early expression of biblical covenant ideas in the political as well as religious sphere, and influenced the development of English Protestantism. The Puritan movement in England and America drew liberally on biblical covenant ideas.

[*For further discussion of God's covenant with the people of Israel, see* Israelite Religion *and* Judaism.]

— DELBERT R. HILLERS

CROSS

The cross is a sign formed by the meeting of two lines intersecting at a center from which four directions depart. The cruciform sign is used in artistic and scientific expression—in mathematics, architecture, geography, and cosmology. It also occupies an important position in culture in a more general sense and, especially, in religion. Sources from remotest antiquity in Egypt, Crete, Mesopotamia, India, and China show that this sign is an important symbol in the life of *homo religiosus.* What are the symbolisms of the cross in Christian and Non-Christian cultures?

NON-CHRISTIAN CROSSES

On statues of Assyrian kings preserved in the British Museum, the cross can be seen hanging from a necklace, whether as jewelry or as a religious sign. In Mesopotamia the cross with four equal arms is the sign for heaven and the god Anu. A cross of four equal branches found in a chapel at Knossos has been considered a symbol of the sovereign divinity of heaven. The cross appears as a decoration on the walls of many Cretan sanctuaries. Thus the cross is present in the ancient cultures of Asia, Europe, North Africa, and America. In sub-Saharan African art, cruciform motifs are numerous in diverse cultures.

The extraordinary dissemination of the cross throughout many different parts of the world prior to Christianity and outside its influence is explained by the multivalence and density of its symbolic signification. In the symbolism of the cross, we will limit ourselves to four essential elements: the tree, the number four, weaving, and navigation.

In the eyes of primordial man, the tree represents a power. It evokes verticality. It achieves communication between the three levels of the cosmos: subterranean space, earth, and sky. It provides one with an access to the invisible, as exemplified by the shaman's stake, Jacob's ladder, the central column of a house or temple, the pole of a Voodoo sanctuary, and the tree symbolizing Mount Meru in India. In many cultures a particular species or a single tree is designated: the oak of the Celts and the Gauls; the oak of Zeus at Dodona, of the Capitoline Jupiter, of Abraham at Sichem and at Hebron; the ash of the Greeks in Hesiod; the date palm of the Mesopotamians; the fig tree in India; the Siberian birch; the Chinese *chien-mu* tree; and the cedar of Lebanon.

CELTIC CROSS

The cross is an important historical symbol for Christian and non-Christian cultures.

MICHAEL NICHOLSON/CORBIS

Mircea Eliade has classified the principal meanings of the tree into seven groups: (1) the rock-tree-altar microcosm present in the most archaic stages of religious life (Australia, China, India, Phoenicia, the Aegean); (2) the tree as image of the cosmos (Mesopotamia, India, Scandinavia); (3) the tree as cosmic theophany (Mesopotamia, India, the Aegean); (4) the tree as symbol of life in relation to the mother goddess and water (India, the Near East); (5) the tree as center of the world (Altaic peoples, Scandinavians, American Indians); (6) the mystical tree in human life, like the sacrificial stake in India and Jacob's ladder; and (7) the tree as symbol of the renewal of life. Such a wealth of meanings shows a symbolic system encompassing the essential functions of *homo religiosus:* life, ascension toward the invisible, meditation, enlightenment, fertility. The symbolism of the cross draws widely on this multivalence.

"When I survey the wondrous cross/On which the Prince of Glory died"

ISAAC WATTS
1807

In its association with water and the altar, the tree is linked to center symbolism, as in the Australian totemic centers, in India, at Mohenjo-Daro, in Greece, in the Minoan world, and among the Canaanites and the Hebrews. Tree, water, and altar make up a microcosm, a sacred space around the tree representing the *axis mundi.* Associated with water as a sign of life, and with rock, which represents duration, the tree manifests the sacred strength of the cosmos and of life.

Aryan thought in particular has emphasized the symbol of the cosmic tree. India readily represents the cosmos as a giant tree. The *Katha Upanisad* (6.1) shows it as an eternal fig tree with its roots in the air and its branches turned downward to the earth. The same figure of the tree is found in the *Maitri Upanisad* (6.4): brahman is a fig tree with its three roots pointed to the sky and its branches extending toward earth. The *Bhagavadgita* (15.1-3) compares the cosmos to a giant tree, an imperishable *asvattha,* roots skyward and branches turned toward the earth, its leaves being the hymns of the Veda. For the ancient Scandinavians, Yggdrasill, an *askr* (ash, yew, or oak), is the world's axis or support. Its three roots plunge into the realms of gods, giants, and men respectively. It is the beam of Mímir, Odin's adviser. It is also Larad, the tree protecting the family, a sign of fertility. Inhabited by the weaving Norns, it is the tree of destiny. The three springs at its roots make it the tree of all life, knowledge, and destiny. It binds the universe in a coherent whole.

Orientation is a basic need in the life of *homo religiosus.* This need explains the importance of center symbolism. The cosmic tree is a symbol of absolute reality: the tree of earthly paradise, the shaman's tree, the tree against which the Aryan temple is built, the tree of gnosis (knowledge). It is where the divinity lives. The tree Kiskanu of Babylonian cosmology extends toward the ocean, sustaining the world. It is the dwelling place of the fertility goddess Ea. In Vedic India the *yupa*—the sacrificial stake fashioned by the priest after the ritual cutting down of the tree—becomes the road permitting access from the earth to the sky, linking the three cosmic regions. It is by way of the tree, the *axis mundi,* that heaven descends toward man. It is at the foot of a fig tree that the Buddha received enlightenment. Sun and moon descend in the shape of birds, by means of the Siberian larch. In China the chien-mu tree is placed in the center of the world with nine branches and nine roots that touch the nine springs and the nine heavens; by means of it the sovereigns, mediators between heaven and earth, ascend and descend. In Egypt the djed column, representing a tree stripped of branches, plays an essential role in the cult of Osiris and in religious life.

The number four is the number symbolizing the totality of space and time. It is linked to the symbolism of the center that marks the meeting of four directions and the transcendence of them. Four is also linked to the symbol of the cosmic tree. The tree and the notion of quaternity are the essential elements in a symbolism of completeness that plays a primordial role in the life of *homo religiosus.*

The number four has various cosmological aspects: four cardinal points, four winds, four lunar phases, four seasons, and the four rivers at the beginning of the world. According to Hartley B. Alexander (1953), the number four is basic to the mind of North American Indians. There are four parts of the terrestrial world and four divisions of time (day, night, moon, year). There are four parts of a plant: root, stem, flower, fruit. To the four celestial beings—sky, sun, moon, stars—correspond four kinds of animals: those that crawl, those that fly, quadrupeds, and bipeds. Among the Dakota, the four masculine virtues of courage, endurance, generosity, and honor correspond to the four feminine virtues of ability, hospitality, fidelity, and fertility. The Indian mystery Wakantanka is fourfold: God the chief, God the spirit, God the creator, God the doer. Alexander observes that the religious philosophy of the Dakota and of all the peoples of the Plains is reminiscent of the Pythagorean tetrad, a numerical symbol of the world order.

Jacques Soustelle has shown that for the ancient Mexicans the cardinal points merged with space and the four directions. There are four quarters of the universe, linked to four time periods *(L'univers des Azteques,* Paris, 1979, pp. 136-140). The fifth direction in space is the center, where the other directions cross and where up meets down. The Codex Borgia designates the center by a multi-colored tree crowned by a quetzal. The Mexicans distinguish four winds. Four colors characterize the directions of space. The center is the synthesis and meeting place of the four colors, as among the Pueblo. The four primary gods are each designated by one of these colors. (These concepts relating to the cardinal points and colors are identical in China.)

C

CROSS

The Christian Cross

"The Message of the Cross (to us who are experiencing salvation) is the power of God."

I CORINTHIANS 1:18

The world is built on a cross, on crossroads that lead from east to west and from north to south. In manuscripts, the center and the four cardinal points are shown by stylized trees. Space and time are linked; to be precise, each time connects with a predetermined space. In this cosmological outlook, natural phenomena and human deeds are all immersed in space-time. For the Dogon of Mali, four is the symbol of creation. The Luba of the Kasai River region imagine the world divided into four planes on the branches of a vertical cross oriented from west to east.

The Vedas are divided into four parts. The *Chandogya Upanisad* (4.5) distributes the Brahmanic teachings into quarters, making them correspond to the four realms of the universe: spaces, worlds, lights, senses. In India there are four classes: the three Aryan classes *(brahmana, ksatriya, vaisya)* and the *sudra* class. The three Aryan classes are invited to pass through four *asramas,* stages of life: *brahmacarya* (student), *grhastha* (householder), *vanaprastha* (forest dweller), *samnyasa* (ascetic renunciant).

This idea of wholeness and universality symbolized by the number four is also found in the biblical texts. Out of the Garden of Eden ran a river that divided into four branches (*Gn.* 2:10-15). The twelve tribes of Israel form four camps around the meeting tent. In Ezekiel's vision, there are four animals in the center, each having four faces and four wings (*Ez.* 1:5-6). *Revelation* appropriates this number as characterizing the universe in its totality: four angels, four corners of the earth, and four winds (*Rv.* 7:1). It also speaks of four living beings (*Rv.* 4:6-8).

THE CHRISTIAN CROSS

For Christians, the cross is a sign evoking a historical event basic to the history of salvation: the crucifixion and death of Jesus at Calvary.

Against the mysteries of pagan religions, the church fathers set the Christian mystery. In their eyes, the salvation decree proclaimed by God was revealed in the crucifixion of Christ. For Christians, Christ's death on the cross marked the end of Judaism as well as radical separation from pagan cults. They later vigorously opposed the various gnostic theories that refused to see history unfolding within the context of salvation through Christ and his achievement in the world. The Fathers quoted Paul (*Eph.* 1:10) to emphasize that in the crucifixion of Jesus creation was completed and a new world begun. They stressed the reality of the events related by the evangelists: agony, blood, human death, the heart wounded, the cross made of two pieces joined in the center. From the shocking to simplicity of the elements, the Christian fathers developed an understanding of the great mystery of the cross (see *1 Cor.* 1:24-25, 2:8).

Greek thought was familiar to the church fathers in the first centuries. They saw in the cross the cosmic symbolism described by Pythagorean wisdom and developed in the works of Plato (*Timaeus* 36b-c). The two great circles of the world that intersect, forming a prone Greek *chi* around which turns the celestial arch, became for the Christians the cross of heaven. Hanging from the cross, the Logos—creator of the world—contains the cosmos. Thus, in the eyes of Justin Martyr (*1 Apology* 60.1) the celestial chi of Plato symbolizes the cross. For Irenaeus (*Against Heresies* 5.18.3), the sign of the cross is the totality and the visible manifestation of the cosmic future: the four dimensions of the cosmos are reproduced by the cross.

The Latin Christians soon moved in the same direction. At the end of the second century, precisely when pagan mysticism and the solar cults were reaching their apogee, Hippolytus of Rome celebrated the cross by reviving the entire range of ancient symbolic associations (*Paschal Homily* 6). For him, the cross was a tree rising from the earth to the sky, a point of support and repose, a cosmic pole. The mystery of the cross marks all creation: the human body, the flight of birds, agriculture, and the Christian in prayer with arms outstretched.

Christian symbolism of the cross is linked to the mystery of creation as well as to the mystery of redemption. As the church fathers reinterpreted ancient cosmic symbolism, they also reinterpreted images from the Hebrew scriptures (Old Testament). On the day of Christ's crucifixion, the curtain of the Temple was torn revealing in all its fullness the mystery of God hidden within the Ark of the Covenant.

In the writings of the Fathers, each reference to wood in the Old Testament becomes a symbol of the cross. One tree in particular, however, symbolizes the mystery of Golgotha: the Tree of Life planted near the four rivers in the midst of Paradise (*Gn.* 2:9), which is mentioned in *Revelation* (22:14). This tree prefigures the mystery of the cross, for in its place, and in the place of the first Adam, we now have the new Adam whose tree of salvation is erected toward the sky, embracing the cosmos and making the baptismal spring of life flow at its feet. This symbolism of tree and water, taken from *Genesis* and applied to the event at Golgotha, has had extraordinary repercussions. It has inspired the baptismal theology of both the Eastern and Western church fathers.

From the second century on, this symbol system is taken up and developed by Christian thinkers. Justin Martyr devotes all of the fifty-fifth chapter of his first Apology to this symbolism. To show the pagans that the cross is the sign of Christ's strength and power, he asks them to consider a series of objects that come before their eyes: "Could one cut through the sea if that

Once the crucifixion came to be widely depicted, the preferred type in both East and West through the ninth century was a robed, open-eyed victorious Christ hanging on the cross.

PAGE 311

trophy was not raised intact on the ship in the shape of a sail? Is work possible without the cross? Can pioneers or manual laborers work without instruments bearing that shape?" (55.2). He then enumerates several signs that suggest the power of the cross: the human body, its arms outstretched; the banners and trophies that go before armies, and statues of emperors (55.6-7). Justin emphasizes the figure of the trophy shaped by the mast and by the yard on which the sail is hung, because it permits him to elaborate his argument. Just as the mast and the sail are indispensable to the security of sailors and passengers, so only the cross of Christ that they symbolize is capable of granting salvation. Justin similarly perceives the vexilla and tropaia that led the troops into battle in the same way.

— JULIEN RIES
TRANSLATED FROM FRENCH BY
KRISTINE ANDERSON

CRUSADES

CHRISTIAN PERSPECTIVE

Crusades were military expeditions against various enemies of the church; the term refers particularly to the medieval campaigns aimed at liberating the Holy Land from the Muslims. The word *crusade* (Span., *cruzada;* Fr., *croisade*) derives from the Latin *crux* (cross); the Latin term *cruciata* does not occur before the thirteenth century. It recalls the ceremony of "taking the cross" (*Mt.* 10:38), the public act of committing oneself to participate in a crusade. Crusaders wore a red cloth cross sewn to their cloaks as a sign of their status.

ROOTS AND CAUSES. While the roots of the movement were complex, a major religious impulse came with the fusion of pilgrimage and holy war. The Crusades continued the old tradition of pilgrimage to the Holy Land that was often undertaken in fulfillment of a vow or as a penance. Attractive for pilgrims were not only the holy places themselves but their relics, above all the Holy Sepulcher, to which the emperor Heraclius had restored the True Cross in AD 627.

During the twelfth century armed pilgrimages began to be regarded as just wars fought in defense of the Holy Land against its illegitimate occupation by the Muslim infidel. The notion of a just war as revenge for an injury done to Christ had been invoked in the fight against Muslims in Spain and Sicily and in expeditions against pagans and Saracens. In 878, Pope John VIII offered spiritual incentives to those who would arm themselves against his foes in Italy. Gregory VII (1073-1085) envisaged a militia Christi for the fight against all enemies of God and thought already of sending an army to the East. An additional factor was the expectation of religious benefits. In the popular perception, the Crusade indulgence offered nothing less than full remission of sins and a sure promise of heaven.

Among the political causes of the Crusades, the appeals for help from the Byzantine emperors were prominent. The year 1071 saw the defeat of the Byzantine army at Manzikert in Asia Minor. Jerusalem fell to the Seljuk Turks in 1077. These events caused great alarm and spurred papal offers of assistance. Moreover, in dealing with the fighting spirit of the aristocracy, reform movements such as the Cluniac and the Gregorian were promoting the "Peace of God" (protection of unarmed persons) and the "Truce of God" (*treuga Dei,* suspension of all fighting during specified times). In this situation, participation in holy warfare provided an outlet for the martial vigor of Christian knights.

CAMPAIGNS. Any attempt at systematizing the Crusades remains arbitrary. Nevertheless, for clarity's sake, we shall follow the customary numbering of the main expeditions.

First Crusade (1096–1099). Urban II's call for participation in an expedition to the East at the Council of Clermont on 27 November 1095 met with an enthusiastic response. Thousands took the cross, especially French, Norman, and Flemish knights. Several bands of badly armed pilgrims from France and Germany, most of them poor and inexperienced, set out for Constantinople even before the army gathered. Some started by massacring Jews on their way through Germany. Many died in Hungary, and the remnants perished in Anatolia. The main force, under the papal legate Bishop Adhémar of Le Puy and an illustrious baronial leadership (including Godfrey of Bouillon, Baldwin II of Flanders, Raymond IV of Toulouse, Robert II of Normandy, and Bohemond I of Taranto), assembled at Constantinople (December 1096 to May 1097) and set out on a long, arduous march through Asia Minor. After costly victories at Nicaea and Dorylaeum (June-July 1097) and enormous hardships, the Crusaders captured Antioch (3 June 1098) and finally Jerusalem (15 July 1099), consolidating their victory by the defeat of a Fatimid army at Ascalon (12 August 1099). A side expedition under Baldwin had already taken Edessa to the north (6 February 1098). Only Nicaea was returned to the Byzantine emperor, and four Crusader states were organized along the Syro-Palestinian coast. Measured against the original goal, the First Crusade was the only successful one. Its territorial gains, protected by inland ridges and a system of fortresses along the coast, formed the basis that future Crusades sought to defend against mounting Muslim pressure. Constant quarrels among the leaders and rival

THE CRUSADES

1090 Council of Clermont; Pope Urban II calls for war to rescue the Holy Land from Moslem infidels.

1096 First Crusade; about 500,000 peasants led by Peter the Hermit prove so troublesome that the Byzantine Emperor Alexius ships them to Asia Minor; only 25,000 return after massacre by Seljuk Turks.

1097 Organized army, led by members of the European nobility, reaches Constantinople.

1099 European army conquers Jerusalem.

1100 European army establishes Latin Kingdom protected by the Knights of St. John the Hospitaller.

1104 European army conquers Acre.

1123 European army establishes Latin Kingdom protected by the Knights Templar.

1144 Seljuk Turks start series of counterattacks.

1146 Second Crusade led by King Louis VIII of France and Emperor Conrad III.

1147 Crusaders perish in Asia Minor.

1171 Saladin controls Egypt, unites Islam in holy war (jihad) against Christians.

1187 Saladin and his army recapture Jerusalem.

1189 Third Crusade under kings of France, England, and Germany fails to reduce Saladin's power.

1200–1204 Fourth Crusade: French kings sack Greek Christian Constantinople and establish Latin empire in Byzantium.

1212 Children's Crusade: only 1 of 30,000 French children and about 200 of 20,000 German children survive to return home.

1217 Crusade against Egypt.

1228 Sixth Crusade.

1248 Seventh Crusade.

1270 Eighth Crusade.

1262 Greeks reestablish Orthodox faith in Byzantium.

1291 The Crusades end as Mamelukes conquer Acre.

The Muslim conquest of Palestine was likewise responsible for the most historic confrontation ever between Christianity and another faith, in the Crusades.

PAGE 157

interests of the major European powers, however, prevented any effective cooperation and success.

Second Crusade (1147–1149). The preaching of the Second Crusade had its immediate cause in the loss of Edessa to the Muslims of Syria (1144). Moved by the preaching of Bernard of Clairvaux, Louis VII of France and Conrad III of Germany led separate armies through Asia Minor. The losses suffered by the troops were disheartening. Furthermore, rather than aiming at Edessa, the remnant joined the Palestinian knights in an unsuccessful siege of Damascus (July 1148), which had been at peace with the kingdom of Jerusalem. This diversion worsened the plight of Edessa, Antioch, and Tripoli. The crusade was soon recognized as a disaster.

Third Crusade (1189–1192). At the initiative of the archbishop of Tyre, the Third Crusade responded to the defeat of the Palestinian knights at Hittin in Galilee (4 July 1187) and the resulting loss of Jerusalem to the sultan, Saladin. The leadership included Frederick I Barbarossa, Philip II Augustus of France, and Richard I ("the Lionhearted") of England. But Frederick accidentally drowned during the march, and the crusading effort disintegrated through attrition, quarreling, and lack of cooperation.

Fourth Crusade (1202–1204). Pope Innocent III (1198-1216) made the reorganization of the crusade under papal auspices one of the priorities of his pontificate. At the request of the Venetians, the Crusaders first attacked the Christian city of Zara in Dalmatia (November 1202) and then sailed on to Constantinople, where they hoped to enthrone Alexios, an exiled Byzantine pretender to the crown, and to receive the material assistance they needed. When these plans failed, the Crusaders laid siege to the city and finally stormed it (12 April 1204). Byzantium was looted for its treasure of relics, art, and gold, and was made the residence of a Latin emperor, with Baldwin IX of Flanders as the first incumbent. A Byzantine army recaptured the city almost casually in 1261.

Fifth Crusade (1217–1221). In the Levant, Acre had become the center of Christian activity. From there an expedition under baronial and clerical leadership attempted to strike at the heart of Ayyubid power in Egypt (May 1218). The harbor city of Damietta was forced to surrender (5 November 1219), but further hopes were dashed by the defeat on the way to Cairo (24 July 1221). A stunning novelty was the expedition of Emperor Frederick II of Hohenstaufen (the so-called Sixth Crusade, 1228-1229). Frederick sailed to Cyprus and Acre (June 1228), secretly negotiated a ten-year truce that included the return of Jerusalem, Bethlehem, and Lydda to the Christians, and crowned himself king of Jerusalem (18 March 1229), although he had been excommunicated by Gregory IX for his failure to act on a Crusade vow earlier. The Holy City was retaken by Muslim allies in 1244.

Seventh and Eighth Crusades. Two crusades of the thirteenth century are connected with the name of Louis IX (Saint Louis) of France. In fulfillment of a vow, Louis sailed to Cyprus with a splendid host of fifteen thousand men and attacked Egypt (Seventh Crusade, 1248-1254). Damietta was occupied again (June 1249) but had to be returned together with a huge ransom when the king and his army were routed and taken captive on their slow march south (6 April 1250). Louis took up residence in Acre for four years, attempting to strengthen the Crusader states by, for example, working toward an alliance with the Mongol khan. Another expedition against the sultan of Tunis (Eighth Crusade, 1270-1272) also ended in failure. The king died in North Africa (25 August 1270), and the Muslims succeeded in buying off the Crusaders. In the meantime, all of Palestine as well as Antioch was lost to the Baybars. The last Christian bastion on the Syrian coast, Acre, was stormed by the sultan in 1291.

The fourteenth and fifteenth centuries saw several papal attempts to revive the crusade or support expeditions to the East. In 1365, King Peter I of Cyprus captured Alexandria; this victory was inconsequential. Soon the fight against the Ottoman Turks turned into a defense of Christian lands, especially after Muslim victories over the Serbs, the Hungarians (Nicopolis, 1396), and a last Crusader army under John Hunyadi and Julian Cardinal Cesarini (Varna, 1444). The fall of Constantinople in May 1453 led to a serious initiative on the part of Pius II, who wished to go on the crusade in person. He died on the way to joining the fleet at Ancona (July 1464).

"He who will not take up his cross and come after me is not worthy of me."

MATTHEW 10:38

OUTCOME. The results of the Crusades are difficult to assess. In terms of religion, the failures nourished doubts about God's will, church authority, and the role of the papacy. Religious fervor yielded to apathy, cynicism, and legalism. On the other hand, the Crusades stimulated religious enthusiasm on a large scale and gave Christendom a unifying cause that lasted for centuries. They inspired a great literature of tracts, chronicles, letters, heroic tales, and poetry, not only in Latin but in the vernaculars. Ignorance of Islam was replaced by a measure of knowledge, respect, and occasionally tolerance.

Politically, the Crusades brought few lasting changes. The Crusader states and the Latin empire remained episodes. Their precarious status forced new diplomatic contacts with Eastern powers but also strengthened the Muslim conviction that holy war *(jihad)* could be carried farther west. In this sense the Crusades led directly to the Turkish wars of later centuries, during which Ottoman expansion threatened even central Europe.

The effect of the Crusades on relations with Byzantium was primarily negative. The Crusades needed Byzantine support as much as Byzantium needed Western armies. But what started as an effort to help Eastern Christians ended in mutual mistrust and enmity.

The Crusades imposed huge burdens on clergy and laity; at times the papacy was unable to support any other cause. Yet they also furthered the growth of a money economy, banking, and new methods of taxation. The widening of the geographic horizon prepared Europe for the age of discovery.

— KARLFRIED FROEHLICH

MUSLIM PERSPECTIVE

The Muslims of Syria, who were the first to receive the assault of the Crusaders, thought the invaders were Rum, the Byzantines. Accordingly, they regarded the invasion as still another Byzantine incursion into Islamic territory, and, in fact, one inspired by previous Muslim victories in Byzantine domains. It was only when the Muslims realized that the invaders did not originate in Byzantium that they began referring to them as Franks, never as Crusaders, a term for which there was no Arabic equivalent until modern times. The establishment of Frankish kingdoms in Islamic territory, the periodic reinforcement of troops from Europe, and the recurrence of invasion all contributed to a growing Muslim consciousness of the nature of the Frankish threat in Syria and Palestine.

This consciousness was reflected in the development of propaganda in Arabic designed to support the mobilization of Muslim forces against the infidel troops. The second half of the twelfth century saw the emergence of both a major Muslim leader and a literature to abet his efforts. The leader was Nur al-Din (1118-1174), who succeeded in forging the political unity of the Muslims of northern Syria and upper Mesopotamia, thereby providing the basis of a military force strong enough to confront the Franks. Fatimid Egypt was brought under the control of Nur al-Din's lieutenant, Salah al-Din, known to the West as Saladin (1138-1193). After the death of Nur al-Din, Salah al-Din was able to build on the former's political and military accomplishments and exploit the fervor engendered for a Muslim hero as a means of achieving spectacular success against the Crusaders. Although no single Muslim leader of equal stature emerged under the Ayyubid or Mamluk dynasties that followed, literary support for prosecution of war against the Franks flourished until the very end.

It should be emphasized, however, that with few exceptions active support for a concerted Muslim campaign against the Franks was limited to the areas threatened with occupation, namely Syria, Palestine, and Egypt. Various attempts to enlist the help of the Abbasid caliph of Baghdad were futile, partly, no doubt, because the institution of the caliphate was by this time virtually defunct. Even Salah al-Din, who was assiduous in seeking caliphal sanction for his activities, never received more than symbolic recognition from a reluctant caliph.

It should also be pointed out that war against the Franks was never total, that Muslim rulers often felt no compunctions about allying themselves with Crusader princes in order to gain their own ends. Salah al-Din himself did not hesitate to strengthen Egyptian ties with the Italian commercial cities in order to obtain the materials he needed from Europe for his campaigns.

With the exception of their fortresses and churches, the Franks left few traces in Muslim territory or consciousness. Although the Muslims looted columns and at least one portal from Crusader structures and incorporated them into their mosques as trophies of victory, Islamic architecture developed independently. Nor is there any evidence of significant influence of Crusader minor arts on Islamic counterparts or, for that matter, of substantial Crusader influence on any aspect of Islamic cultural and intellectual life. There are indications, certainly, in the memoirs of the Syrian knight Usamah ibn Munqidh (1095-1188) and the Spanish traveler Ibn Jubayr (1145-1217) that Muslims observed their Frankish neighbors with interest, interacted with them on occasion, and even approved of some aspects of their behavior—their treatment of peasants, for example. But the Muslims apparently made no effort to imitate the Franks.

— DONALD P. LITTLE

D

DEMONS

Demons are spirits or spiritual beings, numinous powers both benevolent and malevolent in nature. In Classical Greek culture, *daimon* may refer to a lesser divinity, a deified hero, a tutelary or protective spirit, an attendant, ministering, or indwelling spirit, or in some cases the genius of a place (e.g., the portal, the hearth, the cattle pen). In Greek mythology, *daimones* are superhuman in that their natures are superior to that of humans, but they are not supernatural because, like humans, their natures are created by God (both evil and good spirits, demons and devils as well as angels).

TRIBAL CULTURES. Among tribal peoples in various geographic locales, it is commonly held that evil spirits or demons are nothing more than the spirits of deceased ancestors who are hostile and malevolent to living humans. In order to neutralize, if not destroy, the vicious powers of such creatures, elaborate rites of ancestor worship and exorcism have been developed in cultures ranging from the simplest primal societies in Australia and Tierra del Fuego at the southernmost tip of South America to the most advanced, including Hinduism, Buddhism, Christianity, and Islam.

Another category of demons in nonliterate cultures assumes a nonanthropomorphic guise—usually that of animals, birds, or sea creatures.

HINDUISM. In the Vedas, the most ancient scriptures of Hinduism, the class of demonic beings is divided between the lower deities who, though not fully divine, are largely benevolent to humanity and are localized in the sky (the highest heaven or the high regions of the sky) and the demonic and fiendish hosts who inhabit the earth, caves, and subterranean caverns; these latter demons strike human beings and animals with diseases, poverty, and death and haunt the spirits of mortals even after death.

The pages of the Hindu epics (*Mahabharata* and *Ramayana*) are littered with images of semidivine, angelic, and demonic creatures of a dizzying variety. There are, first of all, the *locii spiritii*, sprites of rivers, mountains, trees, groves, and numerous species of vegetation. Then, there is a diverse array of animal divinities who embody demonic powers (both beneficial and detrimental to humans). In addition, the canvas of Hindu mythology is populated with an impressive variety of other superhuman creatures, among which are *pretas*, ghosts or spirits of deceased ancestors; *pitrs*, the spirits of the fathers; *bhutas*, spirits per se that are generally associated with ghosts, ghouls, and goblins in cremation grounds, with a predominant tendency toward evil; and *raksasas*, *yatudhanas*, and *pisacas*, a triad of spirits, not precisely evil but not sufficiently divine to be regarded as gods.

BUDDHISM. At the level of popular religion, Buddhism inherited many of the formulaic features as well as the *dramatis personae* of the demonology of Hinduism. In Buddhism, sentient beings are divided into six types: gods, humans, *asuras*, animals, hungry ghosts *(pretas)*, and denizens of hell. In both traditions, beings are subject to rebirth in all of these forms as they undergo the vicissitudes of karmically determined existence.

In Buddhism, the archfiend is Mara, conceived to be either an antigod *(asura)* or a member of the lower order of gods *(deva)*. Mara confronts Gautama on the night preceding his enlightenment with a series of temptations (hedonistic pleasure, power, and wealth, as well as threats of physical destruction) to prevent him from gaining the power of omniscience.

Whereas the worship of evil spirits and demonic forces occupies a minor status in the teachings of the Buddha and the earliest strata of the Buddhist tradition, the fact remains that the masses continued the ancient customs of spirit worship as a necessary and integral part of their religious lives. References to demons in the earliest texts are few in number and quite unsystematic in their treatment. Citations of belief in spirits of all kinds are more numerous in the birth stories (Jatakas) of the Buddha; however the term *yaksa* (Pali, *yakkha*) is used more frequently than *bhuta*, the more customary term in the later literature.

In its simplest form, the Buddha's message is composed of the doctrines of the Four Noble Truths and the Eightfold Path along with a wealth of psychological and ethical instructions for the disciple seeking salvation. Although the Buddha did not deny the existence of good and evil spirits, he viewed them as he did the *devas*—as existent and active throughout the universe but as impotent to affect a person's search for liberation, whether for good or ill. Indeed, it might be argued that the primary objective of the Buddha *dharma* is to free the person from moral and psychological servitude to the kinds of mental states in which

> *"Decay is inherent in all things! Work out your salvation with diligence."*
>
> THE PALI CANON, MAHAPARINIBBANA-SUTTA, 6:10

D

DEMONS

Judaism

"They offered sacrifice to demons."

DEUTERONOMY, 32:17

one feels either threatened or blessed by invisible beings.

JUDAISM. In its demonology as in other areas of its theology, Judaism inherited a number of concepts and names of individual demons (e.g., Bel and Leviathan) from its Mesopotamian and Canaanite predecessors. In the earlier books of the Hebrew scriptures, before the Babylonian exile in 587/6 BCE, the belief in demons and evil spirits plays a marginal role in the life of Israel. While these books do not deny the existence of demonic powers, such beings are placed under the suzerainty of the absolute will of Yahveh (*Dt.* 4:35). It was only after the biblical writers came under the influence of foreign ideas, especially the Persian dualistic systems of Zoroastrianism and Zurvanism, that we find a clear separation of powers and personages into good and evil sectors and the solidification of the concept of evil spirits into a distinct company of malicious beings. In rabbinic Judaism, the demons appear prominently only in the *aggadah* (folkloristic rabbinic thought), rarely, if at all, in the *halakhah* (learned tradition).

In the Hebrew scriptures, all spiritual beings, both benign and malevolent, are controlled by the power of God (*2 Sm.* 24:16-17). Even Satan himself is conceived of as a servant or messenger of God, commissioned to test men's loyalty to God (*Jb.* 1:6-12, 2:1-7) or to prosecute them for transgressions before the divine tribunal (*Zec.* 3:1-2). However, the imprint of popular Israelite religion upon the biblical literature is attested to by the occurrence of such entities as *shedim* (evil spirits, *Dt.* 32:17), which orthodox writers related to the pagan gods *se'irim* (*Lv.* 17:7) or *lilit* (*Is.* 34:14). These pagan gods traditionally have been depicted as satyrs, as were the *sa'ir* ("hairy ones," *Is.* 13:21).

SATAN

Hebrew scriptures present Satan as a servant of God, sent to test man's loyalty.

CORBIS-BETTMANN

CHRISTIANITY. Demonology in the New Testament is a complex amalgamation of historical patterns from other, earlier neighboring traditions, enriched by the emergence of novel concepts unique to Palestine during the first decades of the Christian era.

The general framework for the growth of the Christian concepts of demons was largely inherited from Jewish apocalyptic literature of the second and first centuries BCE. According to *1 Enoch* 6, the angels or offspring of heaven cohabited with the irresistible daughters of men (cf. *Gn.* 6:1-4) and produced a race of giants who in turn gave birth to a bevy of evil spirits. Because the primary motive for this illicit congress was the satisfaction of sexual desire, lawlessness and warfare spread throughout the world. At this stage, mention is made of numerous devils, but it was left to the New Testament writers to synthesize this company of evil spirits into a single satanic figure who served as the leader of the demonic troops or fallen angels.

It was also at this same time that Satan came to be identified with the serpent in the Garden of Eden who provoked the fall of mankind through the sins of the first couple and, as a result, was himself expelled from heaven.

Jesus, the gospel writers, and the apostle Paul seem to have adopted wholesale the Jewish understanding of the nature and activities of evil spirits. In keeping with his general theological orientation, Paul represents Satan and the evil powers as operating within a cosmic theater—in the air (*Eph.* 2:2), on the earth, and in the underworld. He also pictures Satan as the personified ruler over the kingdom of evil as well as the force to be embodied in the Antichrist who is expected to precede the second coming of Christ at the end of the world.

The *Book of Revelation* contains a rich and complicated demonology informed by Jewish apocalyptic, Babylonian, and Persian sources. The book dwells primarily upon the final struggle between the forces of good and evil in the Battle of Armageddon and the ultimate triumph of the forces of God.

ISLAM. From the time of the Qur'an onward, the universe was populated with a diverse array of good and evil spirits exercising direct and formative influence upon the affairs of humanity. One group of such beings, known as *jinn*, possess ethereal or luminescent bodies and are intelligent and invisible. Proud, rebellious creatures in both the human and animal kingdoms, the *jinn* were created from unsmoking fire. They are related in a rather amorphous manner to both the *shaitans* and to the personage Shaiyan (Satan) as well as to a figure addressed as Iblis (a personal name of the devil).

While the *jinn* appear in a majority of orthodox Muslim writings as shadowy, ephemeral creatures who, at most, make life difficult for humans, the shaitans actively assist Iblis in maintaining his position of rebellion against God. They are aggressively involved in leading from God's law those persons who are already inclined to go astray. Orthodox Muslim writers debated questions pertaining to the existence, the nature, and the status of the jinn and formulated an elaborate system for the grading of the various angelic orders. Other writers, such as Ibn Khaldun, flatly denied their existence.

A MODERN ASSESSMENT. With the spread of scientific and technological values and the propagation throughout the world of the idea of universal education based largely upon modern Western values, belief in heaven and hell and a postmortem existence in a realm apart from this one has receded progressively from the central core of beliefs of many religions throughout the world. On the other hand, belief in the existence of evil forces has far from disappeared altogether. Images of evil powers and the demonic have played a pervasive role in the contemporary arts, though largely in demythologized and depersonalized forms.

C. G. Jung, founder of the school of analytical psychology, offered an unsettling judgment concerning the presence of evil forces that he believed are, even now, at work within the human psyche:

> *The daemonism of nature, which man had apparently triumphed over, he has unwittingly swallowed into himself and so become the devil's marionette. . . . When these products [demonic factors in the psyche] were dubbed unreal and illusory, their sources were in no way blocked up or rendered inoperative. On the contrary, after it became impossible for the daemons to inhabit the rocks, woods, mountains, and rivers, they used human beings as much more dangerous dwelling places.*
>
> *(Collected Works, Princeton, 1955, vol. 18, pp. 593-594)*

— J. BRUCE LONG

DHARMA

HINDU DHARMA

It is somewhat difficult to find a suitable South Asian word to represent what in English is known as "religion." Perhaps the most suitable would be the Sanskrit *dharma*, which can be translated in a variety of ways, all of which are pertinent to traditional Indian religious ideas and practices.

TYPES OF DHARMA. South Asian religious and legal systems have presented a variety of definitions of *dharma* and have seen different modes of its expression in the world and in society. Despite those variations, however, certain notions have remained consistent throughout South Asian history.

Dharma and rta in the Vedic period. The oldest sense of the word—which appears as early as the *Rgveda* (c. 1200 BCE), usually as *dharman*—signifies cosmic ordinance, often in connection with the sense of natural or divine law. As such, it is closely related conceptually to the Vedic notion of *rta*, the universal harmony in which all things in the world have a proper place and function.

In *Rgveda* 5.63.7, for example, the terms *rta* and *dharman* appear together in association with *vrata* ("vow, religious rite"): "You, Mitra and Varuna, through the creative powers of the gods, protect the ceremonial vows [*vrata*] with actions which uphold the world [*dharma*]. Through cosmic order [*rta*] you rule over the whole universe. You placed the sun in the heavens, like a shining chariot."

Varnasramadharma and svadharma. *Varnasramadharma* reflects a temporal dimension in orthodox Hindu normative thought. That is, just as a person gains rights and responsibilities while moving in this life from one *asrama* (stage of life) to the next, he claims certain privileges and accepts specific obligations according to his present *varna* (social class), which is determined by his actions in a previous life. Here we see a close ideological assumption connecting *dharma* and *karman*.

The term *svadharma* (particular responsibilities) in this last passage is not to be understood as referring to one's individual or chosen personal obligations. Rather, *svadharma* describes an impersonal generic ethical category which encapsulates one's duties determined by one's place in society. All farmers therefore have the same *svadharma*, but no farmer has the same *svadharma* as, say, a military officer.

Apaddharma. Some texts note that at times such as severe economic or natural calamity the norms determined by *varna* and *asrama* may be suspended so that society can survive the stress. For example, a priest may assume in those times the duties of a soldier, or a king may take up the responsibilities of a merchant, but they may do so only for the shortest possible time. Such a "duty determined by emergency" is known as *apaddharma*.

Sadharanadharma, samanyadharma, and sanatana-dharma. Most authoritative texts further assert that all people, regardless of their age and occupation, should observe some common moral obligations. Such rules are known as *sadharana* ("pertaining to everybody"), *samanya* ("common"), or *sanatana* ("eternal") in scope.

Sometimes, however, the obligations derived from *svadharma* directly contradict those imperatives of *sad-*

The "law of karma" (karman) or "law of causality" represents a strict and universal cause-effect continuum that affects any action that is motivated by desire (kama), whether it be desire for good or for ill.

PAGE 275

"This is the noble truth which leads to the stopping of sorrow, the noble eightfold path."

THE PALI CANON

haranadharma, and a person trying to make an ethical decision must choose between opposing demands. What happens, for instance, when a priest must offer a blood sacrifice or a soldier must fight and kill the enemy? *Sadharanadharma* admonishes them to practice noninjury to all living beings, yet their respective *svadharmas* command them to kill.

Different religious traditions offered various responses to such a quandary. In general, those based most thoroughly in Brahmanic ideology maintained that in order to support cosmic and social harmony one must follow one's *svadharma* at all times. On the other hand, traditions influenced by the Vedanta, Buddhism, and Jainism taught that the demands of *sadharanadharma* always overrule those of *svadharma*.

AUTHORITATIVE SOURCES OF DHARMA. Metaethical quandaries ("how does one know what is right?") appear in legal as well as in theological circles, and therefore questions of authority arose even in systems revolving around the structures of *varnasramadharma*.

Sruti. According to orthodox thought the primary source for all knowledge, legal and otherwise, lies in the Vedic canon comprised of the Mantra Samhitas (liturgical hymns of the *Rgveda*, *Yajurveda*, *Samaveda*, and *Atharvaveda*), ceremonial instructions (Brahmanas), and philosophical treatises (Aranyakas and Upanisads). Together these texts constitute *sruti*, revealed eternal truths (literally, "that which is heard"). In all orthodox traditions *sruti* was the primary source of normative guidance.

Smrti. Not all questions of *dharma* could be resolved through reference to the timeless *sruti*. Thus, orthodox philosophers and legalists looked also to those more temporal literatures that were passed through the generations. These texts were known as *smrti*, "remembered" truths and injunctions. *Smrti* comprises the six Vedangas ("ancillary texts," collections of aphoristic treatises [*sutras*] that interpret the Veda), the epics *Mahabharata* (including the *Bhagavadgita*) and *Ramayana*, and the Puranas ("stories of old; sacred myths").

Sadacaradharma and sistacaradharma. Most classical texts admit that the example given by the honored members of society serves as a third means by which *dharma* may be discerned. If *sruti* and *smrti* both fail to elucidate a problem, then the community may look for guidance in the actions of people who "practice what is right" *(sadacara)*, or who generally "act according to [Vedic] instruction" *(sistacara)*.

"Conscience." The *Laws of Manu* and other Dharmasastras teach, finally, that when these three sources of *dharma* fail to enlighten an ethically perplexed person, then he or she has recourse to what is described as "that which satisfies the self" (*atmanas tustir; Laws of Manu* 2.6) or "that which pleases the self" (*priyam atmanah; Laws of Manu* 2.12). The vagaries of this category, however, are such that in legal terms personal feelings carry relatively little weight and are always superseded by *sruti*, *smrti*, and *sadacara*.

WILLIAM K. MAHONY

BUDDHIST DHARMA AND DHARMAS

The pan-Indian term *dharma* (from the Sanskrit root *dhr*, "to sustain, to hold"; Pali, *dhamma*; Tib., *chos*) has acquired a variety of meanings and interpretations in the course of many centuries of Indian religious thought. *Dharma* can imply many different meanings in various contexts and with reference to different things.

GENERAL USAGES. *Dharma* was and still is employed by all the religious denominations that have originated in India to indicate their religious beliefs and practices. In this sense, *dharma* refers broadly to what we would term "religion." *Dharma* also designates the universal order, the natural law or the uniform norm according to which the whole world *(samsara)* runs its course. Within the Buddhist context this universal order is coordinated in the doctrine of dependent origination *(pratitya-samutpada)*. This rigorous natural law, which controls the sequence of events and the behavior and acts of beings, has no cause or originator. It is beginningless and functions of its own nature.

The shortest and yet the clearest exposition of *dharma* as the Buddha's word *(buddhavacana)* is epitomized in Sakyamuni's first sermon, when he "set in motion" (i. e., proclaimed) the wheel (lore) of *dharma*: the Four Noble Truths and Eightfold Noble Path. There is suffering and it has a cause that can be eliminated through the knowledge and practice of the path of *dharma* as summarized by the Eightfold Noble Path: right views, right conduct, and so forth. Another presentation of the same path is articulated within the basic trilogy of monastic practice of cultivating wisdom *(prajña)*, morality *(sila)*, and meditation *(dhyana)*. Through wisdom one acquires a full vision of *dharma*, through morality one purifies all that obscures the vision of *dharma*, and through meditation one matures *dharma* within oneself and indeed transforms oneself into an epitome of *dharma*.

TECHNICAL USAGES. Buddhism makes an emphatic and "dogmatic" statement that a "soul" *(atman)* as interpreted by non-Buddhist schools in India does not exist. By denying the existence of a soul as a permanent and unifying factor of a human entity it has removed all grounds for asserting the permanency of the human entity or the existence of any indestructible element therein. Having removed the notion of substance Buddhism has construed an explanation as to how this world functions. According to this explanation, the universe is seen as a flux of *dharmas*, the smallest elements or principles of which it consists, but this flux is not merely a flux of incoherent motion or change. On the contrary, the world evolves according to the strict law of dependent origination *(pratitya-samutpada)*.

Dharmas are divided into conditioned *(samskrta)* and unconditioned *(asamskrta)*. The conditioned *dharmas* (seventy-two in all) comprise all the elements of phenomenal existence *(samsara)*. They are called conditioned because by their nature and in their flow they cooperate in and are subject to the law of causality; they conglomerate or cooperate in the production of life *(prthagjana)*. The unconditioned elements (three in all) are those that are not subject to the law that governs phenomenal existence. *Dharmas* are also divided into those that are influenced or permeated by negative tendencies or depravities (*asrava*; in a moral sense, bad *karmas*) and those that are not under the influence of depravities (*anasrava*; morally, good *karmas*). By their nature the unconditioned *dharmas* must be classed among the *dharmas* that are not under the influence of depravities. We should recall here that the chief characteristic of *samsara* is motion or unrest, *duhkha*, and that of *nirvana* is tranquillity, *nirodha*. The *dharmas* can be also divided in relationship to the Four Truths. Here again we have a twofold division. The first two truths (unrest, *duhkha*, and its cause, *samudaya*) refer to the seventy-two *dharmas* that are permeated by depravities or that are conditioned. The two other truths (rest, *nirodha*, and the means to it, *marga*) refer to the three unconditioned *dharmas* that are always at rest *(nirodha)* and to the *dharmas* that are on the way *(marga)* to become extinguished *(nirodha)*.

Having described the general divisions I shall now proceed to list a set of three standard classifications within which individual *dharmas* are distributed. The first classification, which includes the conditioned *dharmas* alone, refers to their grouping as perceived in a sentient life. This classification divides *dharmas* into five aggregates or *skandhas*. Here we have (1) matter or body *(rupaskandha)*: eleven *dharmas*; (2) feelings, sensations, or emotions *(vedanaskandha)*: one *dharma*; (3) perceptions *(samjñaskandha)*: one *dharma*; (4) impulses or will-forces *(samskaraskandha)*: fifty-eight *dharmas*; (5) consciousness or mind *(vijñanaskandha)*: one *dharma*.

The second classification divides *dharmas* with reference to the process of cognition. Here we have the six sense organs *(indriya)* and the six sense objects *(visaya)* jointy called the "bases" or "foundations" *(ayatana)* of cognition. The six sense organs or internal bases are (1) sense of vision *(caksur-indriyayatana)*; (2) sense of hearing *(srotra-)*; (3) sense of smell *(ghrana-)*; (4) sense of taste *(jihva-)*; (5) sense of touch *(kaya-)*; and (6) consciousness or intellectual faculty *(mana-)*. The six sense objects or external bases are (7) color and form *(rupa-ayatana)*; (8) sound *(sabda-)*; (9) smell *(gandha-)*; (10) taste *(rasa-)*; (11) contact *(sprastavya-)*; and (12) nonsensuous or immaterial objects *(dharma-)*. The first eleven *ayatanas* have one *dharma* each; the immaterial objects comprise sixty-four *dharmas*.

The third classification groups *dharmas* in relationship to the flow *(santana)* of life that evolves within the threefold world (*kama-*, *rupa-*, and *arupya-dhatu*) as described by Buddhist cosmology. This group is divided into eighteen *dhatus*, or elements. It incorporates the previous division into the twelve bases, to which is added a corresponding set of six kinds of consciousness to the intellectual faculty. Thus we have (13) visual consciousness *(caksur-vijñanadhatu)*; (14) auditory consciousness *(srotra-)*; (15) olfactory consciousness *(ghrana-)*; (16) gustatory consciousness *(jihva-)*; (17) tactile consciousness *(kaya-)*; and (18) nonsensuous consciousness *(mano-)*. Within this group the five sense organs and their five objects contain one *dharma* each (ten *dharmas* in all).

The sixty dharmas that are included in all three classifications (skandha, ayatana, and dhatu) are divided into two main groups. One group comprises forty-six associated dharmas or mental dharmas (caitta-dharma) that arise from or in association with pure consciousness or mind (citta-samprayuk-tasamskara); these include ten mental dharams that are present in a sentient life (citta-mahabhu-mika). The other group comprises fourteen unassociated dharmas; that is, dharmas that can be associated with neither matter nor mind (rupa-citta-viprayukta-samskara).

THE SIXTY DHARMAS

Mental Dharmas Present in a Sentient Life

1. feeling
2. perception
3. will
4. contact
5. desire
6. comprehension
7. memory
8. attention
9. aspiration
10. concentration

His first preaching, known as the "First Turning of the Wheel of Dharma" symbolizes the appearance in history of the Buddhist teaching.

PAGE 96

His disciples came to believe that all aspects of Buddhist doctrine and practice flow from this experience of awakening (bodhi).

PAGE 96

Morally Good Dharmas Present in Favorable Conditions

11. faith
12. courage
13. equanimity
14. modesty
15. aversion to evil
16. detachment from love
17. detachment from hatred
18. nonviolence
19. dexterity
20. perseverance in good

Obscuring Dharmas That Enter a Sentient Life at Unfavorable Moments

21. confusion (ignorance)
22. remissness
23. mental dullness
24. lack of faith
25. indolence
26. addiction to pleasure

Additional Obscuring Dharmas That May Occur at Different Times

27. anger
28. hypocrisy
29. maliciousness
30. envy
31. ill-motivated rivalry
32. violence
33. malice
34. deceit
35. treachery
36. self-gratification

Universally Inauspicious Dharmas

37. irreverence
38. willful tolerance of offences

Undetermined/Undifferentiated Dharmas (Which Can Have Different Moral Implications)

39. remorse
40. deliberation
41. investigation
42. determination
43. passion
44. hatred
45. pride
46. doubt

The Unassociated Dharmas

47. acquisition, or the controlling force of an individual flux of life
48. force that suspends some elements
49. force of homogeneity of existence
50. force that leads to trance
51. force produced by effort to enter trance
52. force that stops consciousness, thus effecting the highest trance
53. force that projects life's duration
54. origination
55. duration
56. decay
57. extinction
58. force that imparts meaning to words
59. force that imparts meaning to sentences
60. force that imparts meaning to sounds

The first forty-six dharmas cannot be associated with (or cofunction with) consciousness at the same time on the general principle that their inner inclinations are variously geared toward either good or evil.

— TADEUSZ SKORUPSKI

DOCTRINE

Most dictionaries record two related senses of the term *doctrine*: according to the first, it is the affirmation of a truth; according to the second, it is a teaching. The two are not mutually exclusive: to affirm something as true is a way of teaching it, and that which is taught is usually held to be true.

The denotation of the term is thus reasonably clear. However, the connotations (i. e., the feelings and attitudes associated with it), differ according to where the emphasis is placed in a given instance. As the statement of a truth, doctrine has a philosophical cast; as a teaching, it suggests something more practical. The first connotation prevails among the secular sciences.

The doctrine of evolution, for example, comprises a body of knowledge that is appropriately characterized as a theory, but not a teaching.

Religious doctrines tend to be characterized by their practical intent. For example, the orientation of Judaism is toward practical obedience to the law of God, not speculative knowledge of his being. [*See* Torah.] The doctrinal element in Judaism thus reveals an intimate connection with the notion of teaching. The most important figure is the rabbi ("teacher"); the most important word is torah ("instruction"), which refers to God's revelation in the Hebrew scriptures and, more specifically, to his law as presented in the five books of the Pentateuch. In a broader sense, *torah* encompasses the oral as well as the written law, together with the continuing tradition of rabbinical interpretations. The Talmud ("study") is an authoritative compilation of expositions of the law and applications of it to particular circumstances. It has been observed that the phrase "to read the Talmud," while grammatically correct, is a violation of the text's religious character, since the only appropriate response to the Talmud is to study it.

A CATEGORY OF COMPARATIVE RELIGION. Doctrine is not restricted to Christianity. It is significant that each religion makes use of words that, though not exact synonyms for the terms *doctrine* or *teaching*, are very close to them in meaning: *torah* ("instruction") in Judaism and *kalam* ("doctrine, theology") in Islam; *darsana* ("school, viewpoint") in Hinduism; Dharma ("teaching") in Buddhism; *chiao* ("teaching") in Confucianism and Taoism; *Butsudo* ("way of the Buddha") in Japanese Buddhism; kami no michi ("way of the Japanese divinities") in Shinto.

The prevalence of a doctrinal factor in all of the world's major religions suggests that it ought to be treated as a general category in the academic study of religion. This has, at times, not been recognized with sufficient clarity because of a romantic bias that exalts feeling over thought and deems "doctrine" an alien intrusion into a religious form of existence that is essentially nonrational in character.

However, the notion of a dichotomy between thought and feeling in the religious life is not tenable. Feelings, perceptions, and emotions require form and structure to become the content of human experience. By the same token, mysticism and rationalism reveal an intimate affinity, since most mystics become known to us through the discursive accounts of their ineffable experiences that they produce. Even the symbol systems of nonliterate societies have a doctrinal or rational aspect that gives religious shape to communal life.

Doctrine, then, is a category in the comparative study of religion that belongs with ritual, sacrament, mystical experience, and other factors whose importance has been recognized for some time. Like them, doctrine is designed to focus the mind, emotions, and will on the religious goal that the community has accepted as its ultimate concern.

THEOLOGY AND DOCTRINAL FORM. At the present time, doctrine is frequently associated with systematic theology. For over a thousand years of church history, theology had diverse meanings, some of which were remote from those of Christian doctrine. Plato used the word *theology* to describe the stories about the gods told by poets; Aristotle used it to describe his doctrine of immutable substance. Augustine distinguished three senses: the theology of the poets, a civic theology based on public ceremonies, and a theology of nature. Sometimes the term was used in a narrow sense by Christian thinkers, who restricted it to the doctrine of God.

Muslim theologians such as al-Ghazali (1058-1111 CE) participated in a golden age of theology devoted to the task of reconciling Greek philosophy with the faith of Islam. During the same period, Maimonides (Mosheh ben Maimon, 1135/8-1204) worked on the reconciliation of Greek thought with Judaism; Thomas Aquinas (1225-1274) undertook a similar task in respect to the Roman Catholic faith. Even more important is the fact that during the twelfth and thirteenth centuries revisions in medieval education were made that, among other things, introduced the notion of doctrinal theology as an academic discipline with a status similar to that of the secular subjects taught in the university curriculum.

Hugh of Saint-Victor (c. 1096-1141) developed an approach to theology that subsumed the two senses of the term *theory* (i. e., both intellectual endeavor and contemplation of God) under the complex notion of "speculation," which had previously been applied, for the most part, to religious meditation. Hugh characterized the method of theology as a kind of thought that is theoretical, both in the rational sense of submission to the norms of logic and in the contemplative sense of religious aspiration and vision. However, the delicate balance that he proposed is the prescription of an ideal and not what most works of systematic theology are, in fact, like.

The fourth book of Augustine's *Christian Doctrine* offers comments about doctrine that are still relevant to the contemporary scene. Augustine suggests that rhetoric is as important as logic in the communication of doctrine. He makes use of the rhetorical tradition derived from Aristotle to explore the capacity of Christian doctrine to teach, delight, and persuade.

— W. RICHARD COMSTOCK

In Proverbs the word torah *is used as a parallel for the terms* musar *("instruction," Prv. 1:8),* mitsvah *("commandment," Prv. 3:1, 6:20), and* leqah tov *("a good doctrine," Prv. 4:2).*

PAGE 670

EASTERN CHRISTIANITY

Eastern Christendom is subdivided at present into three main bodies: the Eastern Orthodox church, the "separated" Eastern churches, and the Uniate churches.

EASTERN ORTHODOX CHURCH

The Eastern Orthodox church is the second largest church in the contemporary Christian world, next to—but much smaller than—the Roman Catholic church. It developed from the Greek-speaking church of the eastern Roman or Byzantine empire, but numerically its main strength now lies in the Slavic countries (Russia, Yugoslavia, Bulgaria) and in Romania. It is a fellowship of some fifteen sister churches, all of them agreed in faith, using the same forms of worship, and joined with the others in sacramental communion, but each administratively independent. All acknowledge the honorary primacy of the ecumenical patriarch at Constantinople (Istanbul). The patriarch does not lay claim to a supremacy of universal jurisdiction such as is ascribed to the pope in Roman Catholicism. His position is more similar to that of the archbishop of Canterbury within the worldwide Anglican communion.

The Eastern Orthodox church today comprises various jurisdictions, named here according to the traditional order of precedence. Of first importance are the four ancient patriarchates: Constantinople, Alexandria, Antioch, and Jerusalem. The heads of these four jurisdictions are called patriarchs. The patriarchate of Constantinople consists mainly of Greeks living in Crete and Greeks who emigrated to the United States, Australia, and Western Europe. In the patriarchate of Alexandria, embracing the whole African continent, the episcopate is predominantly Greek, but about half the faithful are Africans in Kenya, Uganda, and Tanzania. The head of this church bears the formal title "Pope and Patriarch." The episcopate and faithful of the patriarchate of Antioch, which has its main centers in Syria and Lebanon, are Arabic-speaking. At Jerusalem the episcopate is Greek, but the flock is almost entirely Arab. The patriarchate of Jerusalem includes within its sphere of influence the semi-independent Church of Sinai.

Second in order of precedence are other patriarchates and the autocephalous (i. e., self-governing) churches of the Eastern Orthodox church: Russia, Serbia, Romania, Bulgaria, Cyprus, Greece, Poland, Albania, Georgia, Czechoslovakia, and America. The heads of the churches of Russia, Serbia, Romania, and Bulgaria bear the title Patriarch. The head of the Georgian church (the position of which in the order of precedence has not been agreed on) is styled Catholicos-Patriarch. The heads of the other churches are known either as Archbishop (Cyprus, Greece, Albania) or as Metropolitan (Poland, Czechoslovakia,

BAPTIZED MEMBERS OF THE EASTERN ORTHODOX CHURCH

Ancient Patriarchates	
Constantinople	5,000,000
Alexandria	350,000
Antioch	600,000
Jerusalem	80,000
Autocephalus Churches	
Russia	50,000,000
Serbia*	8,000,000
Romanian	15,000,000
Bulgaria	8,000,000
Cyprus	440,000
Greece	8,000,000
Poland	450,000
Albania	250,000**
Georgia	500,000
Czechoslovakia	100,000
America	1,000,000
Autonomous Churches	
Finland	66,000
Japan	25,000

* In the former Yugoslavia.

** In 1945.

The ecumenical patriarchate of Constantinople continued to enjoy a preeminence of honor within Eastern Orthodoxy, as it does to this day.

PAGE 158

Within the art of the Eastern Orthodox church, the image (as icon) relates to the liturgy in a manner distinguished from that of its Western counterparts.

PAGE 312

America). The autocephalous status of the last three churches—Georgia, Czechoslovakia, and, more particularly, the Orthodox Church in America—is called into question by some of the other Orthodox churches. Two of the above churches, Cyprus and Greece, are Greek in language and culture; five of them—Russia, Serbia, Bulgaria, Poland, and Czechoslovakia—are Slav, while Romania is predominantly Latin in culture. Georgia (within the Soviet Union) and Albania stand apart, each with its own linguistic and cultural tradition, but many of the Albanian Orthodox are Greek-speaking.

Third in order of precedence are two churches, not as yet fully self-governing, that are termed "autonomous" rather than autocephalous. These are the churches of Finland and Japan.

"SEPARATED" EASTERN CHURCHES

One of the "separated" Eastern churches, the East Syrian church (the Nestorian church), developed historically from the bishops and dioceses that refused to accept the Council of Ephesus (431), regarded by other Christians as the third ecumenical council. Theologically the East Syrian church has been influenced above all by the school of Antioch, and especially by Theodore of Mopsuestia (c. 350-428). It does not use the title *theotokos* ("God-bearer" or "Mother of God"), assigned to the Blessed Virgin Mary by the Council of Ephesus, and it rejects the condemnation passed on Nestorius, patriarch of Constantinople, by that council. With its main centers from the fifth century onward inside the Persian empire, the Nestorian church was largely cut off from Christians under Byzantine rule, and still more from Christians in the West. Nestorian missionaries traveled widely, founding communities in Arabia, India, and across eastern Asia as far as China. Now greatly reduced, the Nestorian church numbers no more than 200,000, living in Iraq, Iran, India, and above all the United States. Its head is known as "Catholicos-Patriarch of the East."

Also among the "separated" Eastern churches are the non-Chalcedonian Orthodox churches, which like the Eastern (Chalcedonian) Orthodox church represent a communion of sister churches, although in the case of the non-Chalcedonians there is a wider variety in the forms of liturgical worship. The non-Chalcedonians, also known as the Oriental Orthodox, are so called because they reject the Council of Chalcedon (451), accepted by Eastern Orthodox and Western Christians as the fourth ecumenical council. Thus, whereas Eastern Orthodoxy recognizes seven ecumenical councils, the most recent of them Nicaea II (787), and Roman Catholicism recognizes twenty-one, the most recent Vatican II (1962-1965), the non-Chalcedonians recognize only three: Nicaea I (325), Constantinople I (381), and Ephesus (431). Often called "monophysites" because they ascribe to Christ only one nature *(phusis)* and not two, the non-Chalcedonian churches have been chiefly influenced in their theology by Cyril of Alexandria (375-444). There are five independent non-Chalcedonian churches: the Syrian Orthodox Church of Antioch, also known as the West Syrian or Jacobite church, headed by a patriarch resident in Damascus, and with members mainly in Syria and Lebanon; the Syrian Orthodox Church of India closely connected with the Syrian Orthodox Church of Antioch, under the leadership of a patriarch resident in Kottayam, Kerala, South India; the Coptic Orthodox church in Egypt, headed by a patriarch; the Armenian Orthodox church, with a catholicos resident in Echmiadzin, Soviet Armenia, a second catholicos resident in Antelias, Lebanon, and two patriarchs, at Jerusalem and Constantinople (in the Armenian tradition a patriarch ranks lower than a catholicos); and the Ethiopian Orthodox church, which until 1950 was partially dependent on the Coptic church but since then has been fully self-governing, and whose head is known as the patriarch.

BAPTIZED MEMBERS OF SEPARATED EASTERN CHURCHES

Syrian Orthodox Church of Antioch*	200,000
Syrian Orthodox Church of India	1,800,000
Coptic Orthodox church in Egypt	4,000,000
Armenian Orthodox church	2,500,000
Ethiopian Orthodox church	16,000,000

*Also known as the West Syrian or Jacobite church.

UNIATE CHURCHES

While accepting the primacy of the pope and the other doctrines of the Roman Catholic church, the Uniate churches (Eastern Catholics) have retained their own ritual and distinctive practices, such as allowing the clergy to marry. There are Uniate churches parallel to the great majority of the Orthodox churches mentioned above, whether Eastern Orthodox or Oriental. The largest groups among the Uniate churches are the Ruthenians (including the Ukrainians and the Byelorussians); the Malabar Church in India; the Melchites, mainly in Syria and Lebanon; and the Maronites, also in Lebanon, who alone among the Uniate churches have no parallel within the Eastern Orthodox or Oriental Orthodox churches.

BAPTIZED MEMBERS OF UNIATE CHURCHES	
Ruthenians*	2,000,000
Malabar Church in India	2,000,000
Melchites	500,000
Maronites	1,400,00

*Includes Ukrainians and Byelorussians

THE MODERN PERIOD

At the end of the twentieth century Orthodox Christianity exists in three different circumstances. (1) As a state church it enjoys official government support; this is the position in Cyprus and to a diminishing extent in Greece. (2) It exists as a minority in predominantly Islamic environments, which is the situation of the ancient patriarchates of Alexandria, Antioch, and Jerusalem. (3) Finally, it exists as a minority in the Western world, settled in lands traditionally associated with Roman Catholicism or Protestantism.

The great majority of the Orthodox churches, both Eastern and Oriental, participate in the ecumenical movement and are full members of the World Council of Churches. In addition, most are involved in bilateral dialogues with other Christians. The Eastern Orthodox began official doctrinal discussions, on a worldwide level, with Roman Catholics in 1980, with Old Catholics in 1975, with Anglicans in 1973, and with Lutherans in 1981. During 1964-1971 there were four positive meetings between the Eastern and the non-Chalcedonian Orthodox, at which both parties were able to agree that, despite differences in terminology, there was no essential discrepancy in christological faith, and a promising solution was proposed for the old dispute concerning the number of the natures and wills in Christ. Even though no formal act of union has as yet been effected, there appears to be no fundamental obstacle on the doctrinal level.

— KALLISTOS WARE

EGYPTIAN RELIGION

AN OVERVIEW

At the very beginnings of Egyptian history the slate palette of Narmer (c. 3110-3056 BCE) shows this king of Upper Egypt, who is wearing the white crown of the south, smiting a northerner, while on the reverse side of the palette Narmer is shown wearing the red crown of Lower Egypt. Whether Narmer or his son, Aha, was actually the first king (later known as Menes) of the first dynasty is still debatable, but some of the emblematic representations on the palette may have mythological significance. The divinity of the pharaoh and the notion of divine or sacred kingship have recently been challenged because of specific later references indicating that there were clear distinctions between the respect accorded the kings and the worship accorded the greatest gods.

For the first half of the Old Kingdom—the third and fourth dynasties—the great pyramids themselves remain, unfortunately, the principal monuments to then current beliefs. The attention given to these elaborate tombs clearly surpassed any other contemporaneous projects and would seem to show that the power of the king was reflected in the cult of his divine kingship.

Much more significant for our understanding of the religion of this period and of much that had been developing and evolving before it are the Pyramid Texts, first recorded in the interior burial rooms of the pyramid of Unas, the last king of the fifth dynasty. These texts in vertical columns, lacking the illustrations and rubrics of later such mortuary or funerary literature, provided a combination of rituals, hymns, prayers, incantations, and offering lists, all designed to ensure that the king would reach his goal in the afterlife and have the information and provisions that he would need there.

PYRAMID OF UNAS

The Pyramid Texts, recorded in the burial rooms of the Pyramid of Unas, enrich our understanding of early Egyptian religion.

ROGER WOOD/© CORBIS

Apart from the central theme of this collection, we learn much more about the religion of Egypt from these texts through the king's relationship to various deities and also through citations or mythological allusions from the texts of the other religions of the Egyp-

EGYPTIAN RELIGION

An Overview

From the time of the Old Kingdom, the Egyptians envisaged a complex spiritual pattern, modeled on the divine life and made up of three elements necessary for life to exist.

PAGE 316

E

EGYPTIAN RELIGION

An Overview

"Hail to you gods, on that day of the great reckoning."

THE BOOK OF THE DEAD

tians. Here the king's genealogy is presented clearly by making him the product of the Heliopolitan Ennead. This family of nine gods represents a cosmological or cosmogonical explanation of creation by Atum (the complete one), who by himself created Shu (air) and Tefnut (moisture). From this pair, Geb (earth) and Nut (watery sky) came forth, and in the next generation they produced the two brothers Osiris and Seth and their sisters, Isis and Nephthys. Osiris, the eldest, ruled on earth in place of his father, but he was slain by his stronger brother, Seth. It fell to Osiris' son, Horus, born after his death, to avenge the slaying and assume the rule of this world.

In the fifth dynasty society in general became more open, and many of the highest offices in the land could be attained by people not related to the royal family. At least a few utterances from the Pyramid Texts indicate that they were not written originally for a king, so that the goal of a blessed hereafter was not exclusively a royal prerogative. Further decentralization of power occurs in the sixth dynasty, and local nomarchs are provided with quite respectable tombs. These tombs may have been equipped with religious texts on coffins or papyri that have not survived, but certainly in the First Intermediate Period, with the breakdown of central authority, several claimants to kingship, and actual civil war, the claimants to earthly power also made claim to divinity.

On the inside surface of the bottom of most of the El Bersha coffins was painted an elaborate illustrated plan or map with descriptive texts known today as the Book of Two Ways. (The Book of Two Ways is a collection within the Coffin Texts.) This cosmological plan provided the earliest illustrated guidebook to the beyond and attempted to locate various uncommon demons as well as some commonly known terms for places in the afterlife.

Beginning with Senusret I (1971-1928 BCE) important new claims to kingly divinity surface. In the *Story of Sinuhe* Senusret I is called a god without peer, "no other came to be before him." In order to consolidate his power, Senusret III deposed a number of powerful nomarchs and divided the country into departments that were to be administered from the capital by his appointees. At the same time, in a cycle of songs in his honor and in a loyalist instruction he is called the "unique divine being" and is identified as Re (the sun god) himself. Remarkably, the propaganda literature of this dynasty remained popular for at least 900 years, and the tradition of Senusret's special position among the kings of Egypt also survived through Greek sources to the present.

The Second Intermediate Period was marked both by internal weakness eventually giving way to division and by foreign occupation of at least the major part of the delta. These Hyksos rulers were eventually driven out of their capital at Avaris by a new Theban family, which reunited the land and began the period of greatest imperialistic expansion, the New Kingdom. The new family was devoted to the cult of Amun-Re at Karnak, and also had a special interest in the moon god in several earlier forms, including Iah (the moon itself), Thoth, and Khonsu, who was now the son of Amun-Re and Mut (the mother).

The religious texts with which people were buried in the New Kingdom and later are now known as the *Book of Going Forth by Day* but they actually constituted at least two different collections, again emphasizing in introductions or conclusions either an Osirian or a solar afterlife, often with some elements of both in between. These papyri, illustrated with vignettes, vary greatly in length and include many interesting chapters, such as that with the servant statue or Shawabti spell (chap. 6), the heart spell (chap. 30), a spell to enable the deceased to have all requisite knowledge in one chapter (chap. 162), and the famous negative confession and judgment scene (chap. 125). The negative confession is not confession at all but rather a protestation of innocence between forty-two judges of the underworld. Following the psychostasia, or weighing of the deceased's heart, in relation to the feather of Maat, or Truth, the deceased inevitably escapes the devourer and is presented to Osiris, but most often goes forth past the gatekeepers and joins Re as well. The New Kingdom copies of the *Book of Going Forth by Day* are commonly called the Theban recension because so many copies come from Theban tombs.

From the beginning of the eighteenth dynasty the principal religious text selected to decorate the walls of the royal burial chambers was the so-called book of Amduat, or *That Which Is in the Netherworld.* This book, which resembles a large-scale papyrus unrolled on the walls, treats of the voyage of the solar bark through the hours of the night sky, but it involves Sokar, the god of the Memphite necropolis (Rosetau), as chief god of the underworld. The nineteenth-dynasty kings, different as they may have been from their eighteenth-dynasty counterparts, were also buried in tombs in the Theban Valley of the Kings, but their tombs were more elaborately decorated, with relief carving and paintings of the Book of Gates and the journey of the sun through the body of the goddess Nut.

Ramses III of the twentieth dynasty was the last great pharaonic ruler of Egypt. His building efforts included a separate small temple at Karnak, as well as a very large mortuary temple for himself at medinet Habu. This latter, which survives in very good condition, contains descriptions of the complete festivals of Min and Sokar in addition to the usual battle scenes, and it also has an elaborate calendar of feasts and offerings.

Throughout the Ramessid period there are indications that all was not what it was supposed to be in this period of religious fervor. Banquet songs stress a *carpe diem* attitude; a workman in the royal necropolis shows no respect for his deceased king, and eventually almost all of the Theban tombs were systematically looted. Some of the robbers were accused and tried, but evidently those chiefly responsible got away with their crimes. The priests reburied the royal mummies, but with none of their original trappings or treasure. The priests apparently did not approve of the reinstatement of Seth by the Ramessid kings, and the god's name was attacked at their capital in the north.

With the Persian conquest of Egypt by Cambyses in 525 BCE, there are indications that the conquering kings had good intentions with regard to maintaining the cultural, legal, and religious traditions of the Egyptians, but with several native rebellions and one last gasp of independence in the thirtieth dynasty, Egypt fell again to the Persians, and in turn welcomed Alexander the Great in 332 BCE as a savior from the Persian oppressors.

Alexander was probably convinced of his own divinity on visiting the oracle of Amun at the Siwa oasis, but this was not enough to guarantee a long life. Under his successor, Philip Arrhidaeus, the sanctuary of the Karnak temple was rebuilt. When Alexander's general, Ptolemy, became king of Egypt, much new construction was begun. Alexandria, with its library, museum, and new government offices, was founded, while other Greek cities in Egypt were enlarged or planned. Under the Ptolemys truly great temples were erected at some ancient cult sites, and countless smaller temples, gates, appendages, and inscriptions were added to other places. All the main structures at the temple of Horus at Edfu are Ptolemaic. The vast main temple and its surrounding walls are covered from top to bottom with scenes and texts dealing with Horus, his myths and rituals. The texts have undergone a complicated encoding with a sixfold increase in the number of hieroglyphic signs used, and a wide range of possible substitutions for many standard signs is also encoun-

OSIRIS
God of the Dead

OSIRIS was the ancient Egyptian god of the dead, whose myth was one of the best known and whose cult was one of the most widespread in pharaonic Egypt. The mythology of Osiris is not preserved completely from an early date, but allusions to it from the earliest extant religious texts indicate that the essentials of the story are as related by Plutarch in *On Isis and Osiris.*

As the oldest son of Geb ("earth"), Osiris became ruler of the land, but he was tricked and slain by his jealous brother, Seth. According to the Greek version of the story, Typhon (Seth) had a beautiful coffin made to Osiris' exact measurements and, with seventy-two conspirators at a banquet, promised it to the one who would fit it. Each guest tried it for size, and of course Osiris was the one to fit exactly. Immediately Seth and the conspirators nailed the lid shut, sealed the coffin in lead, and threw it into the Nile. The coffin was eventually borne across the sea to Byblos, where Isis, who had been continually searching for her husband, finally located it. After some adventures of her own, she returned the body to Egypt, where Seth discovered it, cut it into pieces, and scattered them throughout the country. Isis, however, found all the pieces (except the penis, which she replicated), reconstituted the body, and, before embalming it to give Osiris eternal life, revivified it, coupled with it, and thus conceived Horus. According to the principal version of the story cited by Plutarch, Isis had already given birth to her son, but according to the Egyptian *Hymn to Osiris,* she conceived him by the revivified corpse of her husband. Although Seth challenged the legitimacy of Isis' son, the gods decided in favor of Horus. *The Contendings of Horus and Seth* is preserved on a late New Kingdom papyrus, which indicates that Re, the chief god, favored Seth, but all the other great gods supported the cause of Horus. In the actual contest, Horus proved himself the more clever god. Horus avenged and succeeded his father without completely destroying Seth, toward whom Isis showed pity.

The popularity of the cult of Osiris is explained in part by the recurring cycle of kingship, with each dead king becoming Osiris and being succeeded by his son, Horus. The cult was also important because of its emphasis on the resurrection of the god and a blessed afterlife.

There were numerous cult centers of Osiris; this is explained mythically either by the burial places of the fourteen (or sixteen) parts of his body or by Isis' attempt to conceal the real burial place from Seth. Busiris was the town of his birth, and Abydos was the necropolis generally believed to have been the place of his burial. It was at Abydos that the greatest number of shrines and stelae were set up in honor of the god and to seek blessings from him. A common scene in the funeral rites depicted on nobles' tombs in the New Kingdom commemorated a pilgrimage with the mummy by boat to Abydos.

— LEONARD H. LESKO

In fulfillment of the words and promise of Jesus, "This is my body" and "This is my blood," the bread and wine presented for the sacrament become the very body and blood of Christ.

PAGE 166

tered. The language is classical Middle Egyptian, and presumably the texts were from earlier material chosen by Egyptian priests from their own libraries, or perhaps from several sites in Egypt. The inscriptions are quite distinctive but often difficult to translate. They seem intentionally obscure despite their accessibility, and the encoding must have been used to make these texts more esoteric or arcane to their own followers and perhaps to the Greeks as well.

MYTHOLOGY. Mythology is encountered in almost everything that survives from ancient Egypt. Texts, whether religious, historical, literary, medical, or legal, or merely personal correspondence, all contain mythological allusions. Art of all kinds and on all scales, and artifacts of all types, made use of easily recognizable mythological symbols.

It is not surprising to find that the Egyptians' mythology was not detailed and collected in any one place, but surely the various traditions were handed down by word of mouth and were generally well known. Temple libraries, known in the Late Period as "houses of life," certainly contained medico-magical texts, and also would have had many ritual, historical, and theological texts and treatises. There may have been individual texts relating to the individual cults or sites, such as Papyrus Jumilac. The cosmogonical myths that were excerpted for use in the mortuary literature and that have been briefly summarized above were included in the Pyramid Texts to indicate the power of the king, his genealogy, or his goal, rather than to explain or justify the other gods. The temple texts of individual gods are remarkable for the little mythological information they contain and the vast amount of knowledge they presume.

Some texts, such as the *Story of the Two Brothers* and the *Blinding of Truth by Falsehood,* are in large part mythological without being mythic in purpose. The *Contendings of Horus and Seth* has a totally mythological setting, but it is a burlesque of the real myth, and perhaps a sophisticated attack on the entire pantheon as well. The *Myth of the Destruction of Mankind* is slightly more serious in intent, showing men to be totally at the mercy of the gods if they cross them.

— LEONARD H. LESKO

EUCHARIST

The Eucharist, also known as the Mass, Communion service, Lord's Supper, and Divine Liturgy, among other names, is the central act of Christian worship, practiced by almost all denominations of Christians. Though varying in form from the very austere to the very elaborate, the Eucharist has as its essential elements the breaking and sharing of bread and the pouring and sharing of wine (in some Protestant churches, unfermented grape juice) among the worshipers in commemoration of the actions of Jesus Christ on the eve of his death.

The word *eucharist* is taken from the Greek *eucharistia,* which means "thanksgiving" or "gratitude" and which was used by the early Christians for the Hebrew *berakhah,* meaning "a blessing" such as a table grace. When Christians adopted the word from the Greek into other languages, the meaning was narrowed to the specific designation of the ritual of the bread and wine.

Eucharist is understood by all Christians to commemorate the saving death and resurrection of Jesus, and to mediate communion with God and community among the worshipers. Beyond this basic concept, the theology of the Eucharist varies very widely among the Christian denominations and has often been a cause of bitter dispute between them.

Both Orthodox and Roman Catholic Christians understand the presence of Christ very concretely, taking seriously the so-called words of institution, "This is my body . . . this is my blood." However, the Orthodox insist that while there is an actual change in the bread and wine that justifies these words, the manner of the change is a mystery not to be analyzed or explained rationally.

The meaning and effect of the Eucharist have also been discussed in Catholic theology under the term *real presence.* This emphasizes that the presence of Christ mediated by the bread and wine is prior to the faith of the congregation. Protestant theology has generally rejected the term *real presence* as one liable to superstitious interpretation.

Orthodox and Catholic Christians also agree on an interpretation of the Eucharist in terms of sacrifice; that is, a renewed offering by Christ himself of his immolation in death. Again, there have been determined efforts in the Catholic theological tradition to give intellectually satisfying explanations of this, while Orthodox theology tends to tolerate a variety of explanations at the same time as it insists on fidelity to the words of the liturgy itself.

— MONIKA K. HELLWIG

EVANGELICAL AND FUNDAMENTAL CHRISTIANITY

The term *evangelicalism* usually refers to a largely Protestant movement that emphasizes (1) the Bible as authoritative and reliable; (2) eternal salvation as possible only by regeneration (being "born again"), involving personal trust in Christ and in his atoning work; and (3) a spiritually transformed life marked by moral conduct, personal devotion such as Bible reading and prayer, and zeal for evangelism and missions.

"Fundamentalism" is a subspecies of evangelicalism. The term originated in America in 1920 and refers to evangelicals who consider it a chief Christian duty to combat uncompromisingly "modernist" theology and certain secularizing cultural trends. Organized militancy is the feature that most clearly distinguishes fundamentalists from other evangelicals. Fundamentalism is primarily an American phenomenon, although it has British and British empire counterparts, is paralleled by some militant groups in other traditions, and has been exported worldwide through missions.

Both evangelicalism and fundamentalism are complex coalitions reflecting the convergences of a number of traditions.

Although evangelicalism is largely an Anglo-American phenomenon, its origins give it ties with European Protestantism.

In America, evangelicalism was extremely influential. Evangelical religion had fewer well-established competitors than in the Old World. The rise of the United States as a new nation and the rise of evangelicalism coincided, so that the religion often assumed a quasi-official status. Evangelical emphasis on voluntary acceptance of Christianity also was well matched to American ideas of individual freedom.

The character of American evangelicalism began to take shape during the Great Awakening of the eighteenth century. This movement, really a series of revivals throughout the middle decades of the century, brought together several movements. These included New England Puritanism, continental pietism, revivalist Presbyterianism, Baptist antiestablishment democratic impulses, the Calvinist revivalism of the Englishman George Whitefield (1714-1770), and Methodism (which surpassed all the others after the Revolutionary era).

In the latter half of the nineteenth century, the vigorous evangelicalism that had grown so successfully in the early industrial era found itself in a new world. The concentrated new industrialism and the massively crowded cities tended to overwhelm the individualistic and voluntaristic evangelical programs. Conceptions of dominating the culture became more difficult to maintain. Evangelicals, accordingly, increasingly stressed those aspects of their message that involved personal commitment to Christ and personal holiness rather than social programs, although aspirations to be a major moral influence on the culture never entirely disappeared.

Some holiness groups, most notably the Salvation Army, founded in England in 1865, combined their evangelism with extensive charitable work among the needy. Others among an emerging number of holiness denominations emphasized more the personal experience of being filled by the Holy Spirit. Such emphases in heightened forms were apparent in the rise in America after 1900 of Pentecostalism, which also brought separate denominations and almost exclusive emphasis on intense personal spiritual experience. By the early twentieth century, evangelicalism was thus subdivided into a variety of camps on questions of personal holiness and the nature of spiritual experience.

Equally important during this same era, from the latter decades of the nineteenth century to World War I, was that evangelicals were finding themselves in a new world intellectually. Darwinism became the focal symbol of a many-faceted revolution in assumptions dominating the culture. A deeper issue, however, was a broader revolution in conceptions of reality and truth. Rather than seeing truth as fixed and absolute, Western people were more and more viewing it as a changing function of human cultural evolution. Religion in such a view was not absolute truth revealed by the deity, but the record of developing human conceptions about God and morality. Such conceptions were devastating when applied to the Bible, which in the higher criticism of the late nineteenth century often was regarded as simply the record of Hebrew religious experience. The widespread evangelical consensus was shaken to its foundations. The absolute authority of the Bible as the source of the doctrine of salvation was widely questioned, even within the churches.

Fundamentalism arose in this context. It combined an organized militant defense of most traditional evangelical doctrines with some of the revivalist evangelical innovations of the nineteenth century. Most important of these innovations, eventually accepted by most fundamentalists, was the elaborate system of biblical interpretation known as dispensationalism. Dispensationalism was a version of the premillennialism popularized among revivalists in the later nineteenth century. Originated in England especially by the Plymouth Brethren leader John Nelson Darby (1800-1882), dispensationalism was developed and promoted in America principally by Bible teacher associates of Dwight L. Moody, such as Reuben A. Torrey (1856-1928), James M. Gray (1851-1935), and C. I. Scofield (1843-1921), editor of the famous dispensationalist *Scofield Reference Bible,* published in 1909. Dispensationalism is a systematic scheme for interpreting all of history on the basis of the Bible, following the principle of "literal where possible"; biblical prophecies, especially, are taken to refer to real historical events. This approach yields a rather detailed account of all human

"God looks upon you as worthy of nothing, but to be cast into the fire."

JONATHAN EDWARDS
1741

Some holiness groups, most notably the Salvation Army, founded in England in 1865, combined their evangelism with extensive charitable work among the needy.

PAGE 217

history, which is divided into seven dispensations, or eras of differing relationships between God and humanity.

In America, fundamentalism was only the prominent fighting edge of the larger evangelical movement. During the decades from 1925 to 1945 the public press paid less attention to fundamentalist complaints, but the movement itself was regrouping rather than retreating. During this time fundamentalism developed a firmer institutional base, especially in independent local churches and in some smaller denominations, although considerable numbers of fundamentalists remained in major denominations. The revivalist heritage of the movement was especially apparent in this era, as it turned its strongest efforts toward winning America through evangelization.

It should be emphasized that Darwin (even science as a whole) was only a secondary and indirect target of the fundamentalists.

PAGE 219

Fundamentalist-evangelicals were also founding new sorts of ministries, such as Youth for Christ, begun in 1942, which soon had hundreds of chapters across the country. Bible institutes, such as Moody Bible Institute in Chicago, the Bible Institute of Los Angeles, and many others, remained important centers for the movement, training and sending out evangelists and missionaries, conducting Bible conferences, establishing effective radio ministries, and publishing many books and periodicals.

Following World War II some younger leaders, notably Harold John Ockenga, Carl F. H. Henry, and Edward J. Carnell, organized a "neoevangelical" movement with the explicit purpose of moderating and broadening fundamentalist-evangelicalism.

BILLY GRAHAM

America's leading evangelist during the second half of the twentieth century, Billy Graham calls his ministry evangelical rather than fundamentalist.

LIBRARY OF CONGRESS/CORBIS

Joined by Charles E. Fuller, they organized the Fuller Theological Seminary in Pasadena, California, in 1947. Their efforts were vastly aided by the emergence of Billy Graham as America's leading evangelist after 1949. This group in 1956 also founded *Christianity Today* to provide a solid periodical base for the movement.

The final break in the fundamentalist-evangelical movement came with Billy Graham's New York crusade in 1957. Graham accepted the cooperation of some prominent liberal church leaders. Separatist fundamentalists such as Bob Jones, Sr. (1883-1968), founder of Bob Jones University; John R. Rice (1895-1980), editor of the influential *Sword of the Lord;* and Carl McIntire anathematized Graham and the neoevangelicals as traitors from within. Neoevangelicals in turn soon ceased altogether to call themselves fundamentalists, preferring the designation "evangelical."

— GEORGE M. MARSDEN

EVIL

If there is one human experience ruled by myth, it is certainly that of evil. One can understand why: the two major forms of this experience—moral evil and physical evil—both contain an enigmatic element in whose shadows the difference between them tends to vanish.

On the one hand, it is only at the conclusion of a thoroughgoing critique of mythical representations that moral evil could be conceived of as the product of a free act involving human responsibility alone. Social blame, interiorized as guilt, is in fact a response to an existential quality that was initially represented as a stain infecting the human heart as if from outside. And even when this quasi-magical representation of a contamination by an external or superior power is replaced by the feeling of a sin of which we are the authors, we can feel that we have been seduced by overwhelming powers. Moreover, each of us finds evil already present in the world; no one initiates evil but everyone has the feeling of belonging to a history of evil more ancient than any individual evil act. This strange experience of passivity, which is at the very heart of evildoing, makes us feel ourselves to be the victims in the very act that makes us guilty.

On the other hand, it is also only at the conclusion of a comparable critique of mythical representations that physical evil is recognized as the effect of natural causes of a physical, biological, and even social nature: sickness, which often takes the form of great epidemics ravaging entire populations, simultaneously attacks each person in the very depths of his existence by making him suffer and is spontaneously experienced as an aggression, at once external and internal, coming from maleficent powers that are easily confused with those that seduce the human heart and persuade it to do evil. Moreover, the sort of fate that seems to lead the sick and aging to the threshold of death tends to make mortality the very emblem of the human condition. From this, it is easy to take the next step and consider suffering and death as punishments. Do not guilt and mortality constitute the same enigma?

The persistence of mythical representations of evil can be explained by a third phenomenon, namely the extraordinary way in which guilt and suffering remain intertwined with a stage of development in which the human mind believes it has freed itself from the realm of mythical representations. To declare someone guilty is to declare that person deserving of punishment. And punishment is, in its turn, a suffering, both physical and moral, inflicted by someone other than the guilty party. Punishment, as suffering, therefore bridges the gap between the evil committed and the evil suffered. This same boundary is crossed in the other direction by the fact that a major cause of suffering lies in the violence that human beings exercise on one another. In fact, to do evil is always, directly or indirectly, to make someone else suffer. This mutual overlapping of evil done and evil suffered prevents the two major forms of evil from ever being entirely separate and, in particular, from ever being entirely stripped of their enigmatic character. An essential opaqueness in the human condition is therefore bound up with the experience of evil, which is continually carried back to its darkness, its obscurity, by the exercise of violence, always unjust, and of punishment, even when it is held to be just.

This invincible connection of moral evil and physical evil is expressed on the level of language in the specific "language game" designated by the general term *lamentation.* Lamentation, indeed, is not confined to the moanings rising up from the abyss of suffering, announcing the coming of death. It encompasses the guilty and the victims, for the guilty suffer twice over, first by blame, which states their unworthiness, and then by punishment, which holds them under the reign of violence. With lamentation, the experience of evil becomes heard. The cry becomes a voice, the voice of the undivided enigma of evil. Lamentation forms a bridge between the evil committed or suffered and the myth. And indeed it connects suffering to language only by joining a question to its moaning. "Why evil?" "Why do children die?" "Why me?" In turning itself into a question, lamentation itself appeals to myth.

— PAUL RICOEUR

EVOLUTION

Fundamentalism versus Darwinism

EVOLUTION

EARLY RELIGIOUS RESPONSES TO DARWIN. Even the famous first review of *The Origin of Species,* written by the Anglican bishop of Oxford Samuel Wilberforce for *The Quarterly Review* in 1860, has far more to do with pure science than with matters of faith. Though Wilberforce is remembered as the most notorious of Darwin's clerical foes and as the main antagonist of "Darwin's bulldog" Thomas Huxley, his review is a model of competence and courtesy. It poses only a few modest theological objections toward the end; the bulk of the piece is devoted to studied scientific criticism.

From the viewpoint of well-informed religious thinkers, Darwin's theory was but one more aspect of a challenge that had been under discussion throughout the nineteenth century and with which many had long since made their peace. Together with ancient and biblical archaeology, these critical philological studies had been steadily replacing a naive scriptural literalism with a richer, more rational approach to the Bible. Well before the *Origin* was published, James Hutton's *Theory of the Earth* (1795) and Charles Lyell's *Principles of Geology* (1830-1833) had already made the case that the earth was far older than a literal reading of the Bible would suggest. For those liberal clergy who had come to terms with the new geology and with the findings of scriptural scholarship, it was hardly difficult to accommodate what Darwin had to say about the prehistory of life on the planet. Among the more prominent of these was the Christian Darwinist St. George Jackson Mivart, a biologist who had been born an evangelical and later converted to Catholicism. In his book *On the Genesis of Species* (1871), Mivart sought to demonstrate that the theory of evolution was harmonious with "ancient and most venerable authorities" reaching as far back as Augustine.

Darwinism became the focal symbol of a many-faceted revolution in assumptions dominating the culture.

PAGE 217

FUNDAMENTALISM VERSUS DARWINISM. It should be emphasized that Darwin (even science as a whole) was only a secondary and indirect target of the fundamentalists. Their primary grievance was moral, and it was addressed to the dominant liberals or "modernists" of the major congregations, whose intellectual pluralism and more compliant ethical standards were viewed as a compromise of traditional Christian teachings. In effect, fundamentalism may be seen as a backlash within the Christian community on the part of those in all the Protestant churches—but mostly the rural, the economically insecure, and meagerly educated—who felt most threatened by the increasing pressures of the surrounding secular civilization. But until well after World War II, the fundamentalists were no more than a beleaguered fringe even within the religious community. In America, fundamentalism, in the

This universalized sense of covenant responsibility accounts for the astonishing record of modern Jewish contributions to the improvement of human welfare.

PAGE 410

form of well-organized and well-financed groups like the Moral Majority, was to find its most potent expression only much later, during the 1970s and 1980s.

LIBERAL AND LEFT-WING RESPONSES. The response of the religious center to evolution has been part of a general adaptation by liberal Christians and Jews to the intellectual standards of a scientific and humanistic culture. In making that adaptation, liberal religious thought has tried to draw a significant line of demarcation between itself and science. Its main concession to science has been to withdraw the authority of the scriptures from the areas of history, anthropology, and the physical sciences. As Raymond J. Nogar puts it in *The Wisdom of Evolution,* "The Bible is not a scientific textbook but a book that sets forth religious truths designed to manifest to man the path to eternal salvation" (p. 296). If this represents a retreat by religion, the withdrawal may be viewed as an honorable and orderly one that relinquishes ground improperly occupied or held only by default during the prescientific era. It has also worked to strengthen appreciation of the ethical and existential aspects of the Bible and of theological thought generally. It is surely significant that in the post-Darwinian period, when liberal Christian leaders were busily stripping scripture of its scientific authority, their commitment to the Social Gospel was rapidly expanding. What the Bible was losing as a biological treatise and a historical text, it was gaining as a work of moral wisdom and spiritual counsel.

RELIGIOUS CONTRIBUTIONS TO EVOLUTIONARY THEORY. It is important to emphasize that the various religious responses to evolution dealt with here do not stand on the same footing with respect to science. It continues to insist that the *Book of Genesis* contains a valid account of how the physical universe and life began. It cannot accept the age of the universe as this is now known from numerous empirical sources ranging from astronomical observations to radioactive dating methods; it cannot accept fossil evidence for the history of life on earth.

On the other hand, both religious liberals and metaphysical evolutionists have sought to remain on speaking terms with science and may even have something of value to offer theoretical biology. While scientists may not be able to endorse the more speculative flights of the metaphysical evolutionists, there are at least a few important issues that have emerged from the center-left religious response to Darwin. Two points in particular deserve attention.

1. *Increasing complexity.* Insofar as evolution describes a steady, overall increase in the complexity of living forms (including the complexity of human sentience and human culture), might this not reasonably be identified as the direction in which nature is moving? To that degree, the process is not formless or haphazard but may be said to have a favored tendency. This is not quite the same as teleology; no specific goal need be named, only a net gain in intricacy over time. But this may be enough to serve as a way of finding human meaning in the universe.

2. *Human transcendence.* Insofar as no obvious selective advantage can be adduced for such cultural creations as art, music, higher mathematics, philosophy, or religion, might the human mind not be reasonably regarded as a special element in nature that escapes, perhaps transcends, the forces that determine physical evolution?

— THEODORE ROSZAK

EXORCISM

The Greek root of *exorcism, exorkosis* ("out-oath"), implies the driving out of evil powers or spirits by solemn adjuration or the performance of rituals. Such practices are worldwide, present in archaic as well as modern societies.

ANCIENT AND MODERN JAPAN. Some of the most striking descriptions of exorcisms in past and present times have come from Japan. The thirty-fifth and thirty-sixth chapters of the famous *Tale of Genji,* written by the court lady Murasaki Shikibu in the eleventh century CE, give lengthy accounts of possessions and exorcisms. The *Pillow Book* of Sei Shonagon, written during the same period, presents other vivid pictures of exorcism.

Linking such classical examples to modern times, Carmen Blacker (1975) has given accounts of present-day exorcisms, as revealed by her own research among Nichiren Buddhist priests in Japan. Four kinds of possession are distinguished. The first kind, when only the body is affected by mysterious pains, frequently is attributed to an angry spirit. The second kind consists of hallucinations; the third, of an altered personality which could be blamed on possession by an animal such as a fox. The fourth kind consists of more rare cases when different voices and personalities appear and indicate possession. Blacker notes that the Roman Catholic church now recognizes only cases in the fourth category as true possession.

Any of these afflictions may be treated in Nichiren Buddhist temples. There, exorcisms are based on the teachings of the *Lotus Sutra.* Methods of prayer spells with the help of a medium are used in some temples, but in others, mediums have been generally abandoned "in favour of a direct confrontation between exorcist and patient" (Blacker, 1975, p. 302).

CHINA AND NORTH ASIA. In China down to modern times exorcisms are held more frequently on behalf of the sick than for any other purpose. J. J. M. De Groot describes a typical healing exorcism. After reciting spells, burning papers of incantations, and offering incense, the shaman began his or her "communication with the medium" (de Groot, 1892-1910, vol. 6, p. 1274). The medium shivered and yawned, but as incantations became louder to the accompaniment of drums and as "eye-opening papers" were burnt in quick succession, he or she began to jump about. Assistants forced the medium to a seat, his limbs shaking, his head and shoulders jerking from side to side, and his eyes staring as if into the invisible world. The consultant (the sufferer or the shaman) put questions to the medium, who replied with incoherent sounds which were interpreted as a divine language and were written down on paper. When the spirit announced its intention to depart, drums were beaten, water and ashes were spurted over the medium, and gold paper money was burned for the spirit. The medium swooned, and when he revived he declared that he had no recollection of the event.

Exorcism was practiced both by Taoist priests and by esoteric Buddhist sects. They performed before altars, surrounded by candles, incense, long scrolls with painted figures, and the accompaniment of drums. Reciting texts from the *Shih ching* (Book of Odes) and later writings, they expelled demons by making noise, striking out at the demons with clubs, and spitting water from the mouth in the four cardinal directions.

The shamanistic tradition of the ancient Bon religion of Tibet was preserved almost in its entirety in Buddhist Lamaism. The most famous Tibetan Buddhist monks were said to have performed miracles and exorcisms like other shamans. In one Tibetan legend a notable lama expelled the spirit of sickness in the form of a black pin from a queen, and his fellow worker flew through the air and danced on the roof of a house. However, not a great deal has been done to investigate the shamanistic elements in Bon and Lamaism.

INDIA AND SOUTH ASIA. Parallels to shamanistic techniques and exorcisms are found in Indian classical texts. The *Atharvaveda* (5.15-16) gives spells for exorcising, "speaking away" *(apa-vaktri),* warding off or averting pests and their leaders, as well as rites against demons.

In Indian village religion the activities of professional exorcisers ranged from warding off hailstorms to expelling evil spirits from those possessed by them. L. S. S. O'Malley (1935) describes an exorcism during an epidemic in the sub-Himalayan districts of Uttar Pradesh. The exorcist was simply carried outside the village tied upside down on a bedstead. Driving a wooden peg into the ground, he assured the villagers that the evil spirit had been tied up.

In South India and in Sri Lanka professional exorcisers paint their faces, put on hideous masks, dress in gaudy costumes, arm themselves with symbolic weapons, and take to dancing in order to impersonate particular demons. In this way they induce evil spirits to leave the persons they have possessed. Sinhala exorcism has been described in detail by Paul Wirz (1954).

When a person is ill in Sri Lanka, he sends first for the general medical practitioner, but if the practitioner's remedies do not help the invalid, a soothsayer is called in to determine the cause of the sickness. The soothsayer may suggest an astrologer, who is cheaper, or an exorcist. The exorcist makes his diagnosis by asking where the patient has stayed, whether he has come into contact with harmful spirits, eaten food that attracted them, or lived in a haunted house. He ties a charm on the patient to prevent the sickness from getting worse and to show the demons that a fuller ritual offering will be made.

> *"It is by the finger of God that I cast out devils."*
>
> LUKE 11:20

Other sufferers from evil spirits go to popular shrines, such as the famous center of Kataragama in southeastern Sri Lanka, named after a god who is the second son of the Hindu god Siva. Although primarily a Hindu center for the Tamils, this shrine attracts members of other religions. Enthusiastic devotees have become notorious for walking on fire or hanging in the air by means of skewers through their back muscles. At Kataragama are claimed cures of physical, mental, and spiritual possession. More simply, Buddhists may claim that evil spirits can be exorcised by recitation of the Three Refuges, which causes spirits and ghosts to flee.

In Burma and other countries of Southeast Asia, Buddhist sects practice exorcism for diseases believed to be caused by witchcraft or demonic possession. Combining ancient indigenous beliefs in spirits with faith in the Buddha and his attendants, some monks exorcise evil spirits by enlisting both traditional esoteric skills and the powers of benign Buddhist gods.

AFRICA AND ISLAMIC LANDS. In Africa, belief in possession by good or evil spirits flourished in ancient indigenous religions and has survived in modern Islamic and Christian contexts.

In Somalia a victim is said to have been entered or seized by spirits. When this happens, both the spirits and the resulting illness are called *sar* (*zar* in Ethiopia). Somalians believe that these evil spirits are consumed with greed and lust after luxurious food, clothing, jewelry, and perfume. Women, especially married women, are particularly vulnerable to such possession. I. M. Lewis (1971) suggests that this results from women's depressed social status, for divorce and absent husbands are common. Speaking through the lips of the possessed woman, the spirits demand fine clothes, perfumes, and dainties with an authority that the women rarely achieve in ordinary life.

In Tanzania a similar "devil's disease" reveals its

presence by hysterical symptoms of craving for food and presents. The exorcism includes not only cathartic dances but also the continuing presence of the exorcist in the house of the possessed woman.

The Islamic world tolerates the belief in witchcraft and possession. Although such beliefs at times are condemned, their prevalence is not questioned. *Sihr* ("glamour, magic") is based upon belief in a world of spirits. Magicians claim that they can control the spirits by obeying Allah and using his name in exorcisms. Illicit magicians are believed to enslave spirits for evil purposes and do so by performing deeds displeasing to God.

— GEOFFREY PARRINDER

FAITH

Faith, in probably the best-known definition of it, is "the assurance of things hoped for, the conviction of things not seen." Although this definition itself comes from the Christian scriptures, specifically from the anonymous epistle to the Hebrews in the New Testament, it can, *mutatis mutandis,* be applied across a broad spectrum of religions and religious traditions. More importantly, however, *faith* is used, even in Judaism and Christianity (where it has been the most successfully domesticated), to cover an entire cluster of concepts that are related to one another but are by no means identical.

FAITH-AS-FAITHFULNESS. In its most fundamental meaning, faith has been defined as faithfulness, and as such, it has been taken as an attribute both of the divine and of believers in the divine. The Latin adjective *pius*, for example, was used in Vergil's *Aeneid* in such a phrase as *pia numina* to characterize the reciprocal fidelity that the gods manifested in their dealings with human beings; something of both senses, presumably, attached to the word when it became a standard part of the official title of the Roman emperor, most familiarly in the case of Antoninus Pius (r. 138-161 CE). The reciprocity implied in the concept of faith when predicated of human social relations, where (as in the notion of "keeping faith" with someone) "faith" has become almost synonymous with "loyalty," has carried over likewise into its use for the divine-human relation. Wherever the gods were said to promise something in that relation, *faith* would seem to be an appropriate term for their keeping or fulfilling the promise.

FAITH-AS-OBEDIENCE. The precise content of such obedience has varied enormously with the content of what was perceived to have been the divine will or law. Obedience, therefore, carried both liturgical and moral connotations. An imperative to reenact, periodically or once in a lifetime, the acts of the divine model required the obedient and meticulous observance of the demands that those acts had placed upon the believer. Initiation into the faith involved learning the specific methods of such ritual observance, with rites of passage frequently serving as the occasion for such learning. Where the divine will was conceived of as having laid down rules not only for ritual actions but for ethics, the obedience of faith meant moral behavior in conformity with divine commands; thus in Hinduism, *dharma* as moral law required righteous conduct.

FAITH AND WORKS. The definition of faith as obedience, and yet as somehow not reducible to obedience, points to the perennial and unavoidable problem of the relation between faith and works. On the one hand, even the most theocentric versions of faith have found themselves obliged to assert, often in self-defense against the charge that they were severing the moral nerve, that they were in fact reinforcing ethics precisely by their emphasis on its vertical dimension: it has been a universal conviction of believers, across religious boundaries, that "faith without works is dead." On the other hand, those religious systems that have appeared to outsiders, whether critical or friendly, to equate faith and works and to be indifferent to any considerations except the "purely" moral ones prove, upon closer examination, to have been no less sensitive to the dialectic between works and faith. Confucius repeatedly professed ignorance about the mysteries of "Heaven" and avoided discussing the miraculous phenomena in which conventional faith had sought manifestations of supernatural power; even the question of personal immortality did not admit of a clear and definite answer. Rather, he concentrated his attention on works of piety and of service to others, preferring generosity to greed and virtue to success.

Luther's doctrine of "justification through grace by faith alone, apart from works of law," forms the core of Lutheranism.

PAGE 425

FAITH-AS-TRUST. Such a confidence in the providential care of "Heaven" underlies the definition of faith-as-trust. In the classic formulation of Martin Luther, "to 'have a god' is nothing else than to trust and believe him with our whole heart," since "it is the trust and faith of the heart alone that makes both God and an idol" *(Large Catechism).* Many of the conventional metaphors for the divine in various traditions, from "rock" and "mountain" to "mother" or "father," have served as representations of the conviction that "the trust and faith of the heart" could appropriately be vested in such an object, and that the divine object would prove worthy of human trust..

FAITH-AS-DEPENDENCE. If obedience to the divine will was the completion of the circle of faith in the moral realm, dependence on the divine will was the way faith-as-trust affirmed the relation of human weakness to divine power. In those traditions in which the divine has been seen as creator and/or preserver, faith-as-dependence has been, in the first instance, an affirmation of the origin and derivation of humanity and of its world; in those traditions that have tended not to distinguish as sharply between "being" as applied to the divine and as applied to human beings, dependence has been the basis for identifying the locations of both the divine and the human within the "great chain of Being".

FAITH-AS-EXPERIENCE. In one way or another, each of these definitions of faith has been derived from faith-as-experience. For even the most transcendent notions of the mystery of the divine will have, by their very act of affirming the mysteriousness of that mystery, laid claim to an experience in which the individual believer or the community tradition has caught a glimpse of just how mysterious the divine could be. Inseparability of faith-as-experience from all the other experiences of life has persuaded some observers of the phenomenon to see it as in fact the sublimation and "supernatural" reinterpretation of an essentially "natural" event.

Almost every African ritual is an occasion in which human experience is morally and spiritually transformed.

PAGE 4

THE COMMUNITY OF FAITH. In the sacred literatures of religious faith, faith-as-experience has often been described in highly individualistic terms: how the poet or prophet has come to know the holy in personal experience has dominated how he or she has described that experience for others, so that they in turn, one at a time, might also come to share in such an experience and duplicate it for themselves. Except for passing moments of intense mystical rapture, however, such individualism has been shown to be illusory. And except for occasional glossolalia, the very language in which the individual has spoken about faith-as-experience has been derived from the history of the community, even when that language has been aimed against the present corruption of the community or when it has been directed toward the founding of a new and purer community.

FAITH AND WORSHIP. The community of faith has always been a community of worship. One of the most important scholarly sources for the new and deeper recognition of faith-as-worship has been the investigation of the interrelation between myth and ritual: myth came to be read as the validation, in the deeds of the ancients or of the gods, of what the ritual now enjoined upon believers; and ritual acquired a new dimension by being understood as not merely outward ceremonial performed *ex opere operato* but as the repetition in the believers' actions of what the myth recited in words about the divine actions that had made the world and founded the community.

FAITH-AS-CREDO. One of the definitions of "faith" is "credo" (which is the Latin for "I believe"). In medieval usage, for example, the Latin word *fides* must commonly be translated as "*the* faith" rather than simply as "faith,". To "have faith," then, meant first of all to "hold *the* faith" as this had been laid down in the apostolic "deposit of faith" and legislated by church fathers, councils, and popes.

FAITH AND TRADITION. "Traditionary religion" has defined itself and its faith on the basis of received tradition. The myth of how holy things have happened; the ritual of how holy acts were to be performed; the rules of conduct by which the faithful were expected to guide their lives; the structure through which the holy community was founded and governed; the doctrine by which the community gave an account of the myth and ritual—all these expressions of faith have been the subject and the content of the holy tradition.

FAITH AND KNOWLEDGE. Faith has been taken to be a species of knowledge, differing from ordinary knowledge by its superior claims: an arcane character, a transcendent content, privileged channels of communication, or divine certainty (or all of the above). So long as such claims remained publicly uncontested, faith could stand as objectively sure, even when subjectively the individual believer might question or doubt it.

— JAROSLAV PELIKAN

FASTING

Although the origins of fasting as a moral or religious discipline are obscure, the custom or practice of fasting is attested in many ancient cultures.

Within certain Greco-Roman philosophical schools and religious fellowships (e.g., the Pythagorean), fasting, as one aspect of asceticism, was closely aligned to the belief that humanity had originally experienced a primordial state of perfection that was forfeited by a transgression. Through various ascetic practices such as fasting, poverty, and so forth, the individual could be restored to a state where communication and union with the divine was again made possible. In some religious groups (for example, Judaism, Christianity, and Islam) fasting gradually became a standard way of expressing devotion and worship to a specific divine being.

Although it is difficult to pinpoint a specific rationale or motivation for an individual's or a group's fasting, in most cultures that ascribe to it at least three motivations are easily discernible: (1) preliminary to or preparatory for an important event or time in an individual's or a people's life; (2) as an act of penitence or purification; or (3) as an act of supplication.

PREPARATORY FASTING. In addition to the basic underlying assumption that fasting is an essen-

tial preparation for divine revelation or for some type of communing with the spiritual, many cultures believe that fasting is a prelude to important times in a person's life. It purifies or prepares the person (or group) for greater receptivity in communion with the spiritual. In the Greco-Roman mystery religions, for example, fasting was deemed an aid to enlightenment by a deity, and an initiate into most of these religions had to abstain from all or certain specified foods and drink in order to receive knowledge of the mysteries of the specific religion.

Within some of the mystery cults, fasting was incorporated as part of the ritual preparation for the incubation sleep that, by means of dreams, was to provide answers to specific questions and needs of the person. Dreams and visions were viewed as media through which spiritual or divine revelations were made manifest. Both Greek philosophers (e.g., Pythagoreans and Neoplatonists) and Hebrew prophets believed that fasting could produce trancelike states through which revelations would occur. Plutarch narrates how the priests of ancient Egypt abstained from meat and wine in order to receive and interpret divine revelations *(Isis and Osiris* 5-6), and Iamblichus tells how the prophetess fasted three days prior to giving an oracle (*Egyptian Mysteries* 3.7).

Among the Eastern traditions Hindu and Jain ascetics fasted while on pilgrimage and in preparation for certain festivals. Within classical Chinese religious practice, *chai*, or ritual fasting, preceded the time of sacrifices. By contrast, later Chinese religious thought, particularly Taoism, taught that "fasting of the heart" *(hsin-chai)*, rather than bodily fasting, was more beneficial to arriving at "the Way" *(tao)*. Confucianism followed the practice of Confucius in approving fasting as preparation for those times set aside for worship of ancestral spirits. Although the Buddha taught moderation rather than excessive fasting, many Buddhist monks and nuns adhered to the custom of eating only one meal per day, in the forenoon, and they were obliged to fast on days of new and full moon.

Within the Judaic tradition only one day of fasting was imposed by Mosaic law, Yom Kippur, the Day of Atonement (*Lv.* 16:29-34), but four additional days were added after the Babylonian exile (*Zec.* 8:19) to commemorate days on which disasters had occurred.

Although formalized fasting was spoken against in the New Testament (*Mt.* 6:16-6:18), it eventually became the favorite ascetic practice of the desert dwellers and monastic men and women who saw it as a necessary measure to free the soul from worldly attachments and desires. Within the Christian tradition there gradually developed seasonal fasts such as the Lenten one of forty days preparatory to Easter; Rogation Days in spring in supplication for good crops; and Ember Days, days of prayer and fasting during each of the four seasons of the year. There were also weekly fasts on Wednesdays and Fridays and fasts prior to solemn occasions celebrating important moments in people's lives (e.g., baptism, ordination to priesthood, admission to knighthood, and reception of the Eucharist).

For the fast day of Tish'ah be-Av, commemorating the destruction of the Temple, the rabbis enjoined a reading of the Book of Lamentations.

PAGE 398

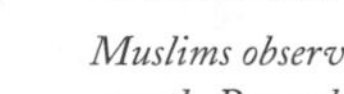

RAMADAN

Muslims observe the ninth month, Ramadan, as one of rigorous fasting. No food or liquid is allowed between dawn and sunset.

RICHARD T. NOWITZ/CORBIS

F

FASTING

Fasting as Penance or Purification

In the Islamic tradition Muslims continue to observe the ninth month, Ramadan, as one of rigorous fasting *(sawm)*, during which days no liquid or food is allowed between dawn and sunset, as stipulated in the Qur'an (2:180ff.). Some of the stricter Muslim groups fast each Monday and Thursday, and the Qur'an recommends fasting as a penance during a pilgrimage, three days going and seven returning (2:193).

Basic to the beliefs of many Native American tribes was the view that fasting was efficacious for receiving guidance from the Great Spirit. In New South Wales, Australia, boys had to fast for two days at their *bora* ceremonies. In the Aztec culture the ritual training required of one who aspired to become a sacrificing priest included fasting as one form of abstinence. While fasting was often viewed as a disciplinary measure that would strengthen the body and character of the individual, prolonged fasting and other austerities were also undergone so that the individual might see or hear the guardian spirit who would remain with him or her for life.

"A fast to placate the Lord was proclaimed for all the people of Jerusalem."

JEREMIAH 36:9

FASTING AS PENANCE OR PURIFICATION. Ancient Egyptian and Babylonian customs included ritualized fasting as a form of penance that accompanied other expressions of sorrow for wrongdoing. Like people of later times, these nations viewed fasting as meritorious in atoning for faults and sins and thus turning away the wrath of the gods. In the *Book of Jonah,* for example, the Assyrians are depicted as covered with sackcloth, weeping, fasting, and praying to God for forgiveness (*Jon.* 3:5ff.).

For the Jews, fasting was an outward expression of inner penitence, and on various occasions a general fast was proclaimed as a public recognition of the sin of the people (*1 Sm.* 14:24, *1 Kgs.* 21:9, *Jer.* 36:9). Yom Kippur, the Day of Atonement, is such a day of fasting and praying for forgiveness of sins. But fasting is also viewed as a means of orienting the human spirit to something or someone greater. According to Philo Judaeus (25 BCE-50 CE), the Therapeutae, a group of Jewish contemplatives living in community, fasted as a means of purifying the spirit so that it could turn itself to more spiritual activities such as reading and study *(On the Contemplative Life)*. The Essenes, a Jewish group who followed their "righteous teacher" into the wilderness at Qumran (c. 135 BCE-70 CE), in their *Manual of Discipline* prescribed fasting as one of the ways of purification, of preparing for the coming of the "end of days."

Although fasting as a means of atonement and purification is evident in other traditions, it was among the Christians that fasting became a predominant feature. With the rapid growth of ascetic movements that incorporated Greek dualism into their thought patterns, fasting became an important means of ridding the body of its attachment to material possessions and pleasures, thus freeing the person for attaining the higher good, the love for and imitation of Christ. The prevailing notion was that whereas food in moderation was a necessary good for maintaining health, abstention from food was particularly effective in controlling the balance between body and spirit.

Modern-day Christian denominations display a considerable diversity of opinion and practice in regard to fasting. For most Protestant denominations, except for some of the more evangelically oriented groups, fasting is left to the discretion of the individual. Although within the Roman Catholic and Greek Orthodox churches prescriptions still govern both individual and corporate practices, rigid fasting practices have been abolished. Roman Catholics still practice partial fasting and abstinence from meat on Ash Wednesday and Good Friday. Within the Greek Orthodox church fasting is usually one of the acts of purification preparing one for participation in the liturgical mysteries.

Although Buddhists generally favor restraint in taking food, and many consider fasting a non-Buddhist practice, it is listed as one of the thirteen Buddhist practices that can serve as an aid to leading a happy life, a means of purification *(dhutanga)*. Therefore, many Buddhist monks have the custom of eating only one meal a day, often eating only from the alms bowl and declining a second helping. For other Buddhists enlightenment was considered more easily attainable by renunciation of wrong ideas and views rather than by fasting. Within Jainism there is the belief that certain ascetic practices, like fasting, are purificatory in that they can remove the accumulation of *karman* that weighs down the life-monad.

Within some of the Native American tribes, the practice of fasting was considered conducive to purifying the body prior to some great feat or challenge. The Cherokee Indians believed that prior to slaying an eagle the individual had to undergo a long period of prayer and fasting that purified the body, strengthening it for the necessary combat. Siouan-speaking Indians believed that before both hunting and war the body had to be purified through fasting for these noble tasks. Among the Incas, fasting from salt, chili peppers, meat, or *chicha* (beer made from maize) was one of the ways of preparing the body for an important event and also for a public form of penance.

FASTING AS SUPPLICATION. Although it is difficult in many instances to distinguish clearly between fasting as a means of penitence and fasting as a means of supplication, within certain traditions the latter has widespread usage. Within Judaism, for example, fasting was one way of "bending the ear of Yahveh," of asking God to turn to the Jews in mercy and grant them the favor requested. Ahab, for example, fasted to avert the disaster predicted by Elijah (*1 Kgs.* 21:27-29, cf. *Nm.* 1:4, 2 *Chr.* 20:3, *Jer.* 36:9). Since penitence and supplication were often dual motivational forces for fasting within Judaism, fasting emerged as both conciliatory and supplicatory. As in the Christian and Islamic traditions, the Jewish notion of fasting reflected an attitude of interior sorrow and conversion of heart. Within the Christian ascetic circles, fasting was viewed as one of the more meritorious acts, which exorcised demons and demonic temptation from the individual's consciousness.

Within other groups fasting was also viewed as meritorious in obtaining rewards from higher powers. In the Intichiuma ceremonies of the tribes in central Australia fasting was practiced to assure an increase in the totem food supply. Young Jain girls fasted as one means of requesting the higher power to give them a good husband and a happy married life. Fasting frequently accompanied or preceded the dance rituals of certain tribes who prayed for a renewal of fertility and a productive harvest from the earth (e.g., the Dakota Sun Dance; the Cheyenne New Life Lodge; the Ponca Sacred Dance, or Mystery Dance).

— ROSEMARY RADER

FREEMASONS

A system of moral teachings and a set of fraternal organizations that practice these teachings, Freemasonry cannot properly be called a "secret society," though secrecy is both practiced as a device for instruction during initiation into its rites and used as a symbol. In some instances, the names of members and the existence of the society itself have been withheld from political authorities because of Freemasonry's historical association with political movements in Italy, Spain, and Latin America. As modern fraternal orders, however, Masonic lodges and related organizations have been more open to public scrutiny, and membership is in almost all cases publicly displayed.

HISTORY. The history of Freemasonry is shrouded in legend and ambiguity. This historical obscurity stems from the institution's use of legendary history in its rituals and ceremonies, and from the fragmentariness of the records of the early Masonic organizations. Few historians have undertaken a comprehensive study of Freemasonry's history and cultural significance. However, in recent years, both social historians and historians of ideas have sought to understand the significance of Masonic development as an institution and a set of philosophical symbols.

The origin of Freemasonry can be traced to periodic gatherings of operative stonemasons engaged in the building of churches and cathedrals in England. The earliest manuscripts associated with the work and moral symbolism of these stonemasons date from the late fourteenth century. The most noted of these manuscripts is the so-called *Regius Manuscript* (c. 1390). This and similar documents make up the "Gothic Constitutions" that trace the legendary history of the craft of masonry back to the Flood or to the building of the Egyptian pyramids or Solomon's Temple. This collection also contains specific moral responsibilities that are enjoined upon members as apprentices, fellowcraftsmen (or journeymen), and master masons. It is probable that secrecy as a device for teaching and as a symbol dates from this period, when knowledge of the building techniques of individual master masons was restricted to guild members.

The historian of ideas Frances A. Yates claims that during the seventeenth century Freemasonry merged with Elizabethan courtly philosophy and continental, particularly German, Rosicrucianism *(Giordano Bruno and the Hermetic Tradition,* 1964). Elizabethan philosophy was associated with such figures as John Dee, Robert Fludd, Thomas Vaughan, and Giordano Bruno. It was Neoplatonic in character, and evoked the memory of the legendary Hermes Trismegistos, understood in the seventeenth century to be a pre-Christian prophet of Christianity. Rosicrucianism was, according to Yates, a self-conscious reform movement that bore the imprint of classical and Renaissance humanism. The impact of these two movements upon the stonemasons' tradition was twofold: (1) it transformed the working tools of the operatives into a system of symbols for personal morality and transformation through initiation, and (2) it projected the Masonic motif, and subsequently the Masonic institutional organization, into the nonoperative arena of eighteenth-century world affairs. The Masonic initiation in 1646 of the antiquarian Elias Ashmole recommends Yates's interpretation of this period.

Freemasonry as an institution can be dated from the formation of the first national Masonic organization, the "Grand Lodge" of England, which resulted from the combining of four small lodges of nonoperative masons at the Goose and Gridiron alehouse, London, on 24 June 1717. From this time, a general narrative history of Freemasonry can be pieced together from journals, minutes, and newspaper accounts. The order attracted royal patronage, and several members of the Royal Society became members of the Masonic fraternity. Notable among these members was John Theophilus Desaguliers, an Anglican priest of Huguenot ancestry who became the order's third elected Grand Master.

The introduction of the order into France in the

Anglican polity is episcopal and preserves the ordained orders of bishops, presbyter-priests, and deacons that go back to apostolic times.

PAGE 35

As a religion of redemption, Christianity presents itself as the message of how, through Christ, reconciliation has been achieved between the holiness of God and the sin of a fallen humanity.

PAGE 164

early eighteenth century signified the transition of the institution from a largely nonpolitical organization into a body that was closely identified with the Enlightenment concepts of deism and equality. The ritual and symbolism of the craft tradition were soon embellished into a system of *hautes grades,* or high degrees, which altered noticeably the character of the fraternity. The higher degrees were later grouped into two main rites, or systems: the Scottish, which was derived from the French *hautes grades,* and the York, which was the result of a commingling of English and American ceremonials. Several rites of numerous degrees were erected and a new knightly or chivalric motif was added to the earlier craft or stonemason tradition. The rites of the Freemasons in continental Europe incorporated the legends of the Knights Templar, the Teutonic Knights, and Knights Hospitaler of Saint John (or Knights of Malta). These Masonic bodies became avidly anticlerical and advocates of political and social reform.

British Freemasonry, organized into separate Irish, Scottish, and English grand lodges, remained nonpartisan during the political-religious disputes of the eighteenth century, but removed any requirement that its initiates be Christians with the adoption of the *Constitutions of 1723,* revised in 1738 by Scots Presbyterian minister James Anderson. Largely as a result of British imperial expansion, lodges of Freemasons were established in North America, India, and the West Indies.

During the late eighteenth century a schism occurred within English-speaking Freemasonry that signaled the development of a general class distinction among Masons between the "Antients" and the "Moderns." Further, this division led to the addition of the Holy Royal Arch to the basic three-degree system of English Freemasonry, which comprises Entered Apprentices, Fellow Craftsmen, and Master Masons. While not of the highly imaginative character of continental *hautes grades,* the Royal Arch provided Freemasons with a degree that proposed to impart the ineffable name of deity to the degree's recipient. This degree was incorporated into the British Masonic system when the two rival "Antient" and "Modern" grand lodges merged under the grand mastership of Augustus Frederick, Duke of Sussex, son of George III. The Royal Arch, essentially an "Antient" invention, won wide acceptance throughout the Masonic fraternity in the nineteenth century.

Freemasonry in the nineteenth and twentieth centuries continued to develop along the lines established by the differing English and French models. English, Irish, and Scottish Freemasonry shaped the fraternity and its teachings in Canada, the United States, the West Indies, India, and much of Africa. The impact of the French tradition, with its anticlerical, rationalistic,

FREEMASONRY'S DETRACTORS

Does It Jibe with Christianity?

Because Freemasonry has transposed a system of moral and noetic teaching upon a graded institutional structure, it has frequently been deemed both a threat to confessional and orthodox religion and a religion itself. The basis for such assumptions is the fraternity's use of symbols that describe the change of personal moral character and human awareness by stages, or degrees. These degrees have been interpreted as a plan for spiritual redemption. A study of the basic ceremonials and teachings, however, suggests that the goal of Masonic initiation is not redemption but rather a shift in the initiate's perception toward the betterment of his personal moral character. The lack of central authority and the multitude of Masonic degrees and ceremonials make it impossible to state unequivocally that Freemasonry is religious in any final or conclusive sense. Since Clement XII's encyclical *In eminenti* in 1738, the Roman Catholic church has proscribed Masonic affiliation. The identification of many major southern European and Latin American revolutionary leaders—such as Benso, Garibaldi, Bolívar, O'Higgins, and Martí y Pérez—with Masonic lodges evoked further condemnation by the nineteenth-century Roman Catholic church. More recently, the Lutheran Church-Missouri Synod, U. S. A., and the General Conference of the Methodist Church in England and Wales have legislated claims that Freemasonry is a system of faith and morals outside of the magisterium of the church.

Protestant opposition to Freemasonry stems from the elements of deism and Hermetic Rosicrucianism in Masonic rituals and is thus more theological in tone. Confessional churches and churches with strong traditions of scholastic orthodoxy, such as Lutheranism, have deemed the humanistic and Neoplatonic elements in Masonic philosophy to be inconsistent with Christian teaching. Churches that have maintained a less exclusive understanding of revelation have been more tolerant of Freemasonry's belief in a universal brotherhood of man under the fatherhood of God.

— WILLIAM H. STEMPER, JR.

and politicized emphasis, was more deeply felt in Austro-Hungary, Spain, Portugal, Italy, and Latin America. By 1877, communication between these two groups had virtually ceased. This separation was formalized when the Grand Orient of France removed the requirement that its initiates declare a belief in the existence of God as the "Great Architect of the Universe." In English-speaking areas, Freemasonry has in general prospered as a support to constituted government and organized religion. One notable exception is the anti-Masonic episode in the United States. The alleged abduction and murder of William Morgan of Batavia, New York, in 1829 caused a widespread reaction against Freemasonry throughout the country. Other secret societies, including Phi Beta Kappa, were affected, largely as a reaction against the perceived influence of political and social elites. An interesting result of this movement was its precipitating the first American political party convention, that of the Anti-Masonic party in 1832.

MASONIC TEACHINGS. Since the origin of Freemasonry as a speculative system, Masonic teachings have remained remarkably consistent. Despite there being no demonstrable, historical tie between Freemasonry in the seventeenth century and the medieval operative stonemasons, the teachings of Freemasonry have been linked to medieval and even to biblical sagas, notably the accounts in *1 Kings and 2 Chronicles* of the building of the Solomonic Temple. Two other strata—the Hermetic-Rosicrucian and the Enlightenment rationalistic-deistic—are superimposed upon the biblical and medieval traditions within the superstructure of Masonic degrees. All Masonic degrees are related to the transformation of the human personality from a state of primitive darkness to a higher level of human consciousness. Mozart's opera *Die Zauberflöte* is in many ways a prototype of Masonic ceremonial.

Freemasonry has a worldwide membership of approximately six million people. It is governed by independent national grand lodges, except in the United States, Canada, and Australia, where grand lodges are organized by state or province. While Freemasonry is racially mixed, there are independent, largely black, grand lodges. The largest of these black lodges is traced to Prince Hall, a freed slave in eighteenth-century Massachusetts. Numerous appendant and collateral bodies, such as the Ancient Arabic Order, Nobles of the Mystic Shrine, and the Order of the Eastern Star are associated with the grand lodges.

— WILLIAM H. STEMPER, JR.

G

GERMANIC RELIGION

GERMANIC CULTURE. The earliest Germanic culture that archaeologists identify as such is the so-called Jastorf culture, a cultural province of northern Europe in the early Iron Age (c. 600 BCE), covering present-day Holstein, Jutland, northeast Saxony, and western Mecklenburg. From the linguistic point of view, however, the Germanic people constitute an archaic branch of the Indo-European family. At the time they entered into history, their closest neighbors were the Celts in Gaul, as Germanic tribes had spread south toward the Rhine and the wooded hills of southern Germany. To the east their neighbors were the Balts and the Scythians and Sarmatians, Iranian tribes that roamed the plains of Russia. To the north, they were in contact with Lapps and with Finns. Most of the information we have about them from early times comes from classical authors such as Caesar and Tacitus. Although they were primarily pastoralists, they also practiced agriculture. Their cattle were rather puny and could not entirely be depended upon for a livelihood; hunting provided an additional supply of meat. Their social organization was originally geared toward egalitarian communalism, but as contact with the Roman empire changed economic conditions, a more diversified society developed in which wealth and rank tended to prevail, although, nominally, power still rested in the hands of the Þing (Thing), the popular assembly, of all free men able to carry arms.

THE IMAGE OF THE GERMANIC MYTHICAL WORLD. Man lives in the center of the universe; the major Germanic traditions concur in calling his dwelling place Midgard ("the central abode"; Goth., Midjungards; OHG, Mittilgart; OE, Middangeard; ON, Midgardr). But the center is also the place where the gods built their residence, Ásgardr. It is described as spacious, with numerous dwellings, surrounded by a beautiful green pasture, Idavollr, and by a palisade built by a giant. Outside is Útgardr, the dangerous world of demons, giants (in Jotunheimr), and other frightening creatures.

Germanic myth evinces a real fear of this no-man's-land outside the settlement, and the idea of the frontier is there all the time, with the gods serving to ward off dangers from the wild. The islanders and the people along the shore believe that a universal ocean surrounds the earth, with an unfathomable abyss at the horizon and a huge snake curling at the edge to hold the world together.

For the Germanic people in Norway Útgardr must have been represented by the high mountains and the arctic territories to the north. The road is over land; Skírnir rides to Útgardr on Freyr's horse *(Skírnismál* 10), and Þórr's adventures always take him eastward. There are the realms of Hymir, who lives at the "end of the world"; of Þrymr and Hrymr (*Voluspá* 49); and the "iron forest" *(iarnvir)*, where the brood of demons is born (*Voluspá* 39).

The sky is the abode of the gods in the later conception of the Germanic people, which transfers Ásgardr to heaven. There, the gods' residences bear names like *Himinbjorg* ("protection of heaven"), for the hall of Heimdallr, the watchman of the gods, located at the rim of the sky (where the celestial outlook Hlidskjálf is also located). Valholl is a typical example of the shift. Originally, it was a subterraneous hall for warriors killed in combat; later connected with Ódinn, it becomes the heavenly residence of his heroic retinue, the *einherjar.* Like the netherworld, the sky is linked with the world by a bridge, this one guarded by Heimdallr; it is called Bilrost ("wavering road," i. e., the rainbow) or Bifrost ("shivering road"). In *Grímnismál* 29, the "bridge of the gods" *(ásbrú)* is "ablaze with flames." Here , the concept may represent a different cosmological view, symbolizing the Milky Way, which the forces of evil from Múspell will walk at the twilight of the world, and which, in many religious systems, is described as the "path of the souls."

"All men have need of the gods."
HOMER
THE ODYSSEY

THE WAR OF THE ÆSIR AND THE VANIR. The Germanic gods are divided into two groups, the Æsir and the Vanir. The Æsir, appear as ruling gods, while the Vanir appear as gods of fertility.

Though the Vanir live in peace with the Æsir, this was not always the case. At the dawn of time, a bitter war was fought between the two groups, which Snorri Sturluson reports (with varying details) in two distinct works, the *Ynglingasaga* and the *Skáldskaparmál.* According to Snorri, Ódinn leads his army against the Vanir, but they resist vigorously. The two sides are alternately victorious, and they loot each other's territory until they grow tired of fighting and conclude a peace that puts them on equal footing. They exchange hostages: the Vanir Ñordr and his son Freyr are trans-

ODINN *The Germanic God Odinn wields magical powers of sovereignty. He intervenes in battle to give victory to whomever he chooses.* CHRISTEL GERSTENBERG/CORBIS

ferred to the world of the Æsir, who, in turn, deliver Mímir and Hœnir to the Vanir. As Mímir is very wise, the Vanir reciprocate by sending "the cleverest among them"—Kvasir—to the Æsir. In the *Skáldskaparmál,* however, Snorri claims that Kvasir was created from the saliva of the Vanir and the Æsir when they spat into the communal caldron at the conclusion of the peace. Other evidence linking Kvasir's blood to the "mead of poetry" suggests that this second version is closer to the original.

The *Poetic Edda* describes the war between the Æsir and the Vanir in rather allusive terms (*Voluspá* 21-24), but since the theme was well known to any Scandinavian, the poem did not need to be explicit. The object of the poet is not to teach but to enliven the tale for his listeners.

THE PANTHEON. The main god is Mercury, whose Latin name, *Mercurius,* is a Roman interpretation of the Germanic name **Wodn*[*az*], as also appears from the loan translation of Latin *Mercurii dies* into the Germanic **Wodniz-dag*[*az*] (Eng., Wednesday; Du., *woensdag*). As Mercury/*Wodan[az] is the only Germanic god credited by Tacitus with receiving human sacrifice, many scholars assume that the *regnator omnium deus* ("god reigning over all") venerated by the Suevian tribe of the Semnones in their sacred grove and honored as their ethnic ancestor with regular human sacrifices must be the same deity, though perhaps Allan Lund is right in claiming that he must have been worshiped as an eponymous founder under the name **Semno.*

Tacitus also refers to other locally worshiped Germanic deities such as Nerthus, Mother Earth, for whom the Inguaeonic people hold a yearly pageant during which they celebrate the powers of fertility that she incarnates, or the divine twins whom he calls Alcis (Germanic, *Alhiz) and equates with the Roman twins Castor and Pollux. In both cases he supplies a few details about cult and ritual, specifying, for example, that Nerthus shrouds herself in mystery: she remains hidden in a curtained chariot during her peregrinations among her worshipers; only her priest can approach her, and after the completion of her ceremonial journey she is bathed in a secret lake, but all those who officiate in this lustration rite are drowned afterward to maintain the "sacred ignorance" about her.

In the *Annals,* Tacitus refers to other Germanic deities, such as Tamfana, whose sanctuary was an important center of cultural activities in the territory of the Marsi (between the Lippe and the Ruhr rivers). Her "temple" was allegedly leveled by the Romans during the celebration of an autumnal festival in 4 CE. Its very existence contradicts Tacitus's statement in the *Germania* that the Germanic people "refuse to confine their gods within walls" and the contention that worship generally took place alfresco and in the woods, as with the Frisian goddess, Baduhenna, near whose sacred grove a Roman detachment was massacred.

In the Roman period, inscriptional material provides further data on the deities venerated by the Germanic people (within the boundaries of the empire), such as Nehalennia, whose sanctuary near Domburg

THE MYTH OF BALDR
Beware the Mistletoe

The story of Baldr's fate is probably the most moving and most controversial of all the Germanic myths. In this story, best known in Snorri Sturluson's rendition in the *Gylfaginning,* Ódinn's resplendent son Baldr is plagued by evil dreams of impending death. To protect against any danger his mother, Frigg, exacts an oath from everything in the world not to harm him, but neglects the puny mistletoe. Jealous of the attention Baldr receives in the games of the gods, Loki, in the disguise of a woman, wheedles the secret of Baldr's invulnerability out of his mother. He then persuades Baldr's blind brother, Hodr, who has been prevented by his infirmity from any participation in the sportive tossing of objects at Baldr, to throw a dart of mistletoe. Under Loki's guidance the missile hits Baldr and kills him. The gods are dumbfounded, and while preparations for Baldr's ship burial are in progress, they send out Hermódr on Ódinn's horse to the kingdom of Hel to entreat the goddess of the netherworld for the release of the unfortunate god. Meanwhile, Baldr's wife, Nanna, dies of grief and her body is carried onto the ship Hringhorni ("curved prow"), where she joins her husband on the funeral pyre. As for Hermódr, he returns with the message that Baldr will be released only on the condition that "everything in the world, both dead and alive, weeps for him." Immediately the Æsir dispatch messengers all over the universe to request everyone and everything to weep Baldr out of Hel's clutches. Even the stones and the metals participate in the universal grief, but a giantess called Pokk says she has no use for Baldr; as far as she is concerned, Hel can keep him! This is again Loki in disguise, and thus he succeeds in preventing the return of Baldr, who will only come back after Ragnarok.

— EDGAR C. POLOMÉ

Human sacrifice is a gift that binds deities to people in an exchange or that serves to propitiate the gods.

PAGE 588

in Sjæland has yielded an abundance of altars and statues. She was worshiped mainly by seamen and traders, mostly natives of the northwestern provinces of the empire, who dedicated the monuments to the goddess in return for the help received from her. Her attributes (cornucopias, specific fruits, dog, etc.) characterize her as a fertility goddess with strong chthonic overtones, but she apparently also shares the patronage of navigation with Isis, whose presence Tacitus mentions "among part of the Suevians" (presumably the Hermunduri, who were in close contact with the Roman province of Noricum where the cult of Isis had been integrated with that of the national goddess Noreia).

The Romans also turned certain gods of Greek origin into gods of victory.

PAGE 580

NORSE GODS AND GODDESSES

- Aesir — chief gods of Asgard
- Asynjur — goddesses of Asgard
- Baldr — god of light, spring, peace
- Brage — god of poetry
- Freyr — god of fertility and crops
- Freyja — goddess of love and beauty
- Frigga — goddess of the sky
- Hel — goddess of the dead
- Hoth — blind god of night and darkness
- Loki — god of evil and mischief
- Skuld — demigoddess of fate (future)
- Thor — god of thunder
- Tyr — god of war
- Urdur — demigoddess of fate (past)
- Verdandi — demigoddess of fate (present)

Important also are the *matres,* or *matronae,* documented by votive stones with dedicatory inscriptions found mainly in the territory of the Ubii on the left side of the Rhine in the second and third centuries CE. Their worshipers belonged essentially to the lower classes but also included some high officeholders in the Roman administration and army. They were invoked for protection against danger and catastrophes or for the prosperity of the family, and were described as bestowing their blessings generously, as such epithets as *Gabiae* ("givers"), *Friagabis* ("generous donors"), and *Arvagastiae* ("hospitable ones") indicate. As they often appear in groups of three and seem to be associated with the fate and welfare of man, they have been compared with the Nornir, especially since one stone carries the inscription "Matrib[us] Parc[is]," referring directly to the *interpretatio Romana* of the three deities of fate.

The blossoming of Scandinavian literature provides ample information about the pagan gods and the myths and cults of the Germanic North. Moreover, in their peregrinations, the Vikings carried with them their religious practices and beliefs, and reports from various sources attest to the prevalence of the worship of Þórr among them.

The pantheon, then, can be sketched as follows in keeping with the Dumézilian trifunctional pattern:

1. Sovereignty is represented in its magical aspect by Ódinn, in its juridical aspect by Tyr.
2. War and physical force are represented by Þórr.
3. Fertility and wealth are presented by Freyr, Freyja, and Ñordr.

Such a presentation, however, oversimplifies the picture of the Scandinavian system, and not only fails to show the characteristic slant toward the second (war) function, as Dumézil himself acknowledges, but ignores such complex figures as Heimdallr and Loki, who hardly fit into this neat matrix. Moreover, some very important functions of the major deities are not covered by the labels in the Dumézilian tripartite ideology. For example, Ódinn is essentially the god of "inspired cerebral activity" and therefore the patron of the poets. Further, though he manifests his sovereign power through potent magical interventions, he is definitely not the only one to wield magical powers.

As for the involvement with war, there is a basic difference between Ódinn's intervention in battles to give victory to whomever he chooses to favor and the direct participation in combat of the divine champion Þórr: the only time Ódinn personally takes to the battlefield is in his deadly encounter with the Fenriswolf at Ragnarok. On the other hand, it seems that the transfer of the Vanic gods as hostages to the realm of the Æsir made them partake of some of the latter's combative spirit, as when the peaceful Freyr, who having readily given up his sword to obtain the favors of a giant maiden he eagerly desired, faces the giant Beli without a weapon and kills him with a hart's horn. And while Ódinn collects half of the heroes who die on the battlefield to serve as his *einherjar* in Valholl, it is certainly striking that Freyja gets the other half.

As for fertility, it is well known that, as thunder god, Þórr was the protector of the peasant class, which depends on the weather for its crops, but he shares control of the atmosphere with Ñordr, who controls the path of the wind and, as sea god, counteracts the effects of the thunderstorms, quieting the sea and smothering the fire.

Heimdallr occupies a marginal position in the pantheon; it is not even clear to which group of gods he should be assigned. Heimdallr was gifted with extraordinary aural perception: "He can hear the grass grow on the earth and the wool on sheep." Therefore, it has been assumed that the Old Norse term *hljóð*—generally translated "horn" in this context (*Voluspá* 27), but usually meaning "silence; listening, hearing," also "music, noise"—must designate one of Heimdallr's ears. On the other hand, as guardian of the gods and watchman of Ásgardr, Heimdallr assumes a military function, which would make him a second-function god in the Dumézilian system.

Similarly, Loki is extremely difficult to classify. Originally a giant, he nevertheless played an important part in the decisions and activities of the gods. Although primarily a mischievous trickster, Loki cannot be described as an "evil demon." He is restless and inventive, but also deceptive and unreliable. Although he frequently got the gods in trouble, he usually redeemed himself by ultimately solving the problem he created.

The minor deities are also problematic: some of them can in some way be integrated into the tripartite functional scheme, for example, Ullr, an archer god living in Ydalir ("yew dales") in Ásgardr, whose importance is made clear by Ódinn's statement in the *Grímnismál* (st. 42) that Ullr especially, among all the gods, will grant his blessing to he who "first quenches the fire." Bragi is another lesser god about whom little is known. His name seems to be related to the Old Norse word bragr, which designates "poetic form," and he is described as the "foremost of poets," being in this way in competition with Ódinn as patron of poetry.

Very little information is usually given about the goddesses. Frigg, Ódinn's wife, is the devoted mother of Baldr; she lives in Fensalir ("marshy halls"), attended by her confidant Fulla. Loki claims that she shared her sexual favors with her husband's brothers, Vili and Vé (*Lokasenna* 26).

Jord ("earth"), the mother of Þórr, is also known under the name of *Fjorgyn,* which may mean "goddess of the furrow" (cf. Frisian, *furge;* Germanic, **furho;* Old High German *fur[u]h,* German *Furche,* Old English *furh,* and English *furrow*). Her male counterpart is Fjorgynn, who is either the father or the lover of Frigg, called *Fjorgyns mær* in the *Lokasenna,* (st. 26). The goddess Gefjun is said to have torn away from Sweden a sizable chunk of land, which was dragged to the Danish island of Sjælland; to perform this deed she turned the four sons she had begotton in Jotunheimr into oxen and yoked them to the plow. Though she is mentioned as a separate deity in the *Lokasenna* (st. 20), she seems to be an alter ego of Freyja, who is also known as Gefn ("giver"), a name befitting a fertility goddess.

In many cases it is questionable whether some names of deities quoted by Snorri Sturluson are more than local variants of the names of major gods, used largely to enhance the poetic expressions of the skalds. Thus we have no myths relating to such goddesses as Eir ("the best of physicians," according to the *Gylfaginning*) or to those specializing in bringing people to love, like Siofn, or who, like Lofn ("permission"), bring together those for whom marriage is apparently excluded.

[*For discussion of Germanic religion in a broader context, see* Indo-European Religions.]

— EDGAR C. POLOMÉ

GNOSTICISM

"Upon it was seated, up above, one who had the appearance of a man."

EZEKIEL: 1:26

Gnosis ("knowledge") is a Greek word of Indo-European origin, related to the English *know* and the Sanskrit *jñana.* The term has long been used in comparative religion to indicate a current of antiquity that stressed awareness of the divine mysteries. This was held to be obtained either by direct experience of a revelation or by initiation into the secret, esoteric tradition of such revelations.

Ever since the congress on the origins of gnosticism held at Messina, Italy, in 1966, scholars have made a distinction between gnosis and gnosticism. *Gnosticism* is a modern term, not attested in antiquity. Even the substantive *gnostic* (Gr., *gnostikos,* "knower"), found in patristic writings, was never used to indicate a general spiritual movement but was applied only to a single, particular sect. Today gnosticism is defined as a religion in its own right, whose myths state that the Unknown God is not the creator (demiurge, YHVH); that the world is an error, the consequence of a fall and split within the deity; and that man, spiritual man, is alien to the natural world and related to the deity and becomes conscious of his deepest Self when he hears the word of revelation. Not sin or guilt, but unconsciousness, is the cause of evil.

Until recent times the gnostic religion was almost exclusively known by reports of its opponents, ecclesiastical heresiologists such as Irenaeus (c. 180 CE), Hippolytus (c. 200), and Epiphanius (c. 350). Not until the eighteenth century were two primary sources, the Codex Askewianus (named for the physician A. Askew) and the Codex Brucianus (named after the Scottish explorer James Bruce), discovered in Egypt. These contained several Coptic gnostic writings: (1) *Two Books of Jeû* from the beginning of the third century; (2) book 4 of *Pistis Sophia* from about 225; and (3) *Pistis Sophia,* books 1, 2, and 3, from the second half of the third century. To these can now be

Ancestors are one of many types of spirits recognized by Melanesian tribal peoples.

PAGE 33

added the writings found near Nag Hammadi in Upper Egypt in 1945. The stories told about the discovery are untrustworthy. The only certain fact is that, to date, about thirteen of the codices (books, not scrolls) comprising some fifty-two texts are preserved at the Coptic Museum in Old Cairo.

ORIGINS

The hypothesis once supported by Richard Reitzenstein, Geo Widengren, and Rudolf Bultmann that gnosticism is of Iranian origin has been abandoned; the alleged Iranian mystery of the "saved saviour" has been disproved. At present, many scholars are inclined to believe that gnosticism is built upon Hellenistic-Jewish foundations and can be traced to centers like Alexandria, which had a large Jewish population, much as the city of New York does today. Polemics in the writings of the Jewish philosopher Philo, who himself was an opponent of local heresies, make it clear that he knew Jewish groups that had already formulated certain basic elements of gnosticism, although a consistent system did not yet exist in pre-Christian times.

JEWISH GNOSTICISM. The church father Irenaeus indicates not all those whom modern scholars call "gnostics" but only the adherents of a specific sect. It is misleading to call them Sethians (descendants of Seth, the son of Adam), as some scholars do nowadays. Notwithstanding its name, the *Apocryphon of John* (a disciple of Jesus) contains no Christian elements apart from the foreword and some minor interpolations. It can be summarized as follows: from the Unknown God (who exists beyond thought and name) and his spouse (who is his counterpart and mirror) issued the spiritual world. The last of the spiritual entities, Sophia, became wanton and brought forth a monster, the demiurge. He organized the zodiac and the seven planets. He proclaimed: "I am a jealous god, apart from me there is no other." Then a voice was heard, teaching him that above him existed the Unknown God and his spouse. Next, the "first Man in the form of a man" manifested himself to the lower angels. He is the Glory of *Ezekiel* 1:26. His reflection appears in the waters of chaos (cf. the mirror of the Anthropos in *Poimandres*). Thereupon the lower angels created the body of Adam after the image that they had seen, an imitation of the Man, who clearly serves as an ideal archetype for the human body. For a long time the body of Adam lay unable to move, for the seven planetary angels were unable to raise it up. Then Sophia caused the demiurge to breathe the *pneuma* he had inherited from her into the face of his creature. So begins a long struggle between the redeeming Sophia and the malicious demiurge, the struggle for and against the awakening of human spiritual consciousness.

Written in Alexandria about the beginning of the Christian era, the myth of the *Apocryphon of John*, a pivotal and seminal writing, combines the Anthropos model and the Sophia model. It is very complicated and confusing but had enormous influence in the Near East, where so many remnants of great religions survive today. Their religion features ablutions in streaming water and a funerary mass. When a Mandaean has died, a priest performs a complicated rite in order to return the soul to its heavenly abode, where it will receive a spiritual body. In this way, it is believed, the deceased is integrated into the so-called Secret Adam, the Glory, the divine body of God. This name confirms that, along with the Anthropos of *Poimandres* and the Adam Qadmon of later Jewish mysticism, this divine and heavenly figure is ultimately derived from the vision of the prophet Ezekiel. In Mandaean lore Sophia appears in degraded form as a mean and lewd creature called the Holy Spirit. The creation of the world is attributed to a lower demiurge.

The apostle Paul (or one of his pupils) maintains that Christ, who is for him the second Adam, is "the head of his Church, which is his body" (*Eph.* 1:22-23). The Christian is integrated into this body through baptism. Mandaean speculations about the Secret Adam may elucidate what Paul meant. In defining his view of the church as the mystical body of Christ, the apostle may be reflecting a familiarity with comparable Jewish and Hellenistic speculations about the *kavod* as the body of God. As a matter of fact, it has become clear from the verses of Ezekiel Tragicus that such ideas circulated in Alexandria long before the beginning of our era. They surfaced in Palestine toward the end of the first century CE in strictly Pharisaic circles that transmitted secret, esoteric traditions about the mystical journey of the sage through the seven heavenly places to behold the god Man on the throne of God. The author of the writing *Shi'ur Qoma*, the "measurement of the Body" of God, reports the enormous dimensions of the members of the Glory. The Orphics had taught that the cosmos was actually a divine body. Already early in Hellenistic Egypt similar speculations arose; these were the origin of the remarkable speculations of Palestinian rabbis concerning the mystical body of God. (These speculations ultimately led to the *Zohar.*)

In the ninth century several groups of Islamic gnostics arose in southern Iraq, where several other gnostic sects had found refuge during late antiquity and where the Mandaeans (the Aramaic term for gnostics) continue to live today. The best-known Islamic gnostics are the Isma-'iliyah, of which the Aga Khan is the religious leader. Mythological themes central to their religion are (1) the cycles of the seven prophets; (2) the throne and the letters; (3) Kuni, the creative principle, who is feminine (a typical remythologizing of a monotheistic Father religion); (4) the higher Pentad;

GNOSTICISM

Origins

(5) the infatuation of the lower demiurge; (6) the seven planets and the twelve signs of the zodiac; (7) the divine Adam; and (8) the fall and ascent of the soul.

Since the discovery of the Nag Hammadi codices it has been established that these themes are best explained as transpositions into an Islamic terminology of the gnostic mythemes that are found in the *Apocryphon of John* and kindred documents of Jewish gnosticism.

CHRISTIAN GNOSIS. According to a reliable tradition, Barnabas, a missionary of the Jerusalem congregation, was the first to bring the gospel to Alexandria, a relatively easy journey. Egyptian Christianity is Judaic in origin, not gentile, and the great Egyptian gnostics seem all to have been of Jewish birth. The adherents of Basilides claimed: "We are no longer Jews and not yet Christians." The followers of Valentinus reported: "When we were Hebrews, we were orphans." Basilides and Valentinus both proclaimed a God beyond the Old Testament God, and both were familiar with the myth of the *Apocryphon of John,* which they christianized. The case of Marcion is similar: he was so well-informed about the Hebrew Bible and its flaws that his father, a bishop, may well be presumed to have been Jewish. Through a certain Cerdo, Marcion came to know an already existing gnostic system. Those who reject the god of the Old Testament obviously no longer hold to the Jewish faith, but nevertheless still belong ethnically to the Jewish people. Both Valentinus and Marcion went to Rome and were excommunicated there between 140 and 150. Basilides, who stayed in Alexandria, remained a respected schoolmaster there until his death. The Christians in Alexandria were divided among several synagogues and could afford to be tolerant, for a monarchic bishop did not yet exist and their faith was pluriform anyhow. Basilides, Valentinus, and Marcion were Christocentric and let themselves be influenced by the *Gospel of John* and the letters of Paul.

MODERN GNOSIS. The gnosis of modern times, launched by the shoemaker Jakob Boehme (c. 1600), was generated spontaneously as a result of direct experience. It differs from ancient gnosticism in that it derives not only the light but also the darkness (not only good but also evil) from the ground of being. Inspired by Boehme is the influential gnosis of the English poet and artist William Blake (1757-1827), the only authentic gnostic of the entire Anglo-Saxon world. It is in the school of Boehme that the scholarly study of gnosticism has its roots, beginning with the *Impartial History of the Churches and Heresies* (1699) by Gottfried Arnold. In this extremely learned work all heretics, including all gnostics, are represented as the true Christians—innocent and slandered lambs.

Ever since, the study of gnosticism has been an accepted academic subject in Germany, but in Germany alone. In his youth Goethe read Arnold's book and conceived his own gnostic system, as reported in his autobiography. Toward the end of his life Goethe recalled the love of his youth when he wrote the finale to *Faust,* the hierophany of "the Eternally Feminine," a version of the gnostic Sophia, the exclusive manifestation of the deity. Johann Lorenz von Mosheim and other great historians also took gnosis quite seriously. The brilliant August Neander, who belonged to the conservative reaction to the Enlightenment called the Great Awakening Revivalism *(Erweckungsbewegung),* wrote his *Genetic Evolution of the Most Important Gnostic Systems* in 1818. Ferdinand Christian Baur, a prominent Hegelian, published his monumental *Christian Gnosis* in 1835, in which he defends the thesis that gnosis was a religious philosophy whose modern counterpart is the idealism of Schelling, Schleiermacher, and Hegel, all based upon the vision of Boehme. According to Baur, even German idealism was a form of gnosis. Yet when "the people of poets and thinkers" became, under Bismarck, a people of merchants and industrial workers, this wonderful empathy, this fantastic feel of gnosis, was almost completely lost.

Adolf von Harnack (1851-1930), the ideologue of

"Upon it was seated, up above, one who had the appearance of a man."

EZEKIEL 1:26

DEATH'S DOOR

This etching by William Blake, the only authentic gnostic of the Anglo-Saxon world, depicts the end of earthly existence and reconnection with the divine, spiritual self.

HISTORICAL PICTURE ARCHIVE/CORBIS

Wilhelm's empire, defined gnosticism as the acute, and orthodoxy as the chronic, hellenization (i. e., rationalization) and hence alienation of Christianity. At the time it was difficult to appreciate the experience behind the gnostic symbols. Wilhelm Bousset, in his *Main Problems of Gnosis* (1907), described this religion as a museum of hoary and lifeless Oriental (Indian, Iranian, Babylonian) fossils. The same unimaginative approach led Richard Reitzenstein, Geo Widengren, and Rudolf Bultmann to postulate an Iranian mystery of salvation that never existed but was supposed to explain gnosticism, Manichaeism, and Christianity.

Existentialism and depth psychology were needed to rediscover the abysmal feelings that inspired the movement of gnosis. Hans Jonas (*The Gnostic Religion,* 1958) has depicted these feelings as dread, alienation, and an aversion to all worldly existence, as if the gnostics were followers of Heidegger. In the same vein are the writings of Kurt Rudolph, the expert on Mandaeism.

The gnostics viewed man as a combination of matter and spirit and saw the body as the prison which holds the soul after its fall.

PAGE 319

Under the influence of Carl Gustav Jung, I and other scholars (e.g., Henri-Charles Puech and Károly Kerén-yi) have interpreted the gnostic symbols as a mythical expression (i. e., projection) of self-experience. As a lone wolf, the Roman Catholic convert Erik Peterson suggested that the origins of gnosticism were not Iranian or Greek but Jewish. The gnostic writings from Nag Hammadi have shown Jung and Peterson to be in the right. At last the origins, development, and goal of this perennial philosophy have come to light.

— GILLES QUISPEL

GNOSTICISM AS A CHRISTIAN HERESY

The pluralism of early Christianity in regional faith and praxis, as well as the shifting lines of authority within the first and second centuries, make it difficult to draw the sharp boundaries required to exclude a particular opinion or group as heretical. In *Against Heresies,* Irenaeus says that his predecessors were unable to refute the gnostics because they had inadequate knowledge of gnostic systems and because the gnostics appeared to say the same things as other Christians. Christian gnostics of the second century claimed to have the esoteric, spiritual interpretation of Christian scriptures, beliefs, and sacraments. Their orthodox opponents sought to prove that such persons were not Christians on the grounds that gnostic rites were occasions of immoral behavior, that their myths and doctrines were absurd, and that their intentions were destructive to true worship of God. In short, it appears that gnostics were defined as heretics by their opponents well before they stopped considering themselves to be spiritual members of the larger Christian community.

Three periods characterize the interaction of gnosticism and Christianity: (1) the late first century and early second century, in which the foundations of gnostic traditions were laid at the same time that the New Testament was being written; (2) the mid-second century to the early third century, the period of the great gnostic teachers and systems; and (3) the end of the second century into the fourth century, the period of the heresiological reaction against gnosticism.

The fluid boundaries of Christianity in the first period make it difficult to speak of gnosticism at that time as a heresy. Four types of tradition used in the second-century gnostic systems were developed in this period. First, there was a reinterpretation of *Genesis* that depicts the Jewish God as jealous and enslaving: freedom means escaping from bondage to that God. Second, there arose a tradition of Jesus' sayings as esoteric wisdom. Third, a soteriology of the soul's ascent to union with the divine from the popular forms of Platonism was adopted. And fourth, possibly, there was a mythical story of the descent of a divine being from the heavenly world to reveal that world as the true home of the soul. Each of the last three types of tradition lies behind conflicts or images in the New Testament writings.

Some scholars have argued that the incorporation of the sayings of Jesus into the gospel narrative of his life served to check the proliferation of sayings of the risen Lord uttered by Christian prophets. The soteriology of the soul's divinization through identification with wisdom has been seen behind the conflicts in *1 Corinthians.* Second-century gnostic writings use the same traditions from Philo that scholars invoke as parallel to *1 Corinthians.* The question of a first-century redeemer myth is debated in connection with the Johannine material. While the image of Jesus in the *Gospel of John* could have been developed out of existing metaphorical traditions and the structure of a gospel life of Jesus, the Johannine letters show that Johannine Christians were split over interpretation of the gospel. Both *1 John* and *2 John* condemn other Christians as heretics. Heretics deny the death of Jesus and may have held a docetic Christology.

The second century brought fully developed gnostic systems from teachers who claimed that their systems represented the inner truth revealed by Jesus. During this period, the Greek originals of the Coptic treatises were collected at Nag Hammadi. From the orthodox side, Irenaeus's five books refuting the gnostics marked a decisive turn in Christian self-consciousness. These were followed by the antignostic writings of Hippolytus, Clement of Alexandria, Origen, Tertullian, and Epiphanius. Though Irenaeus may have drawn upon earlier antignostic writings, such as Justin's lost *Suntagma,* his work suggests a turn toward the systematic refutation of gnosticism. Rather than catalog sects and errors, Irenaeus turned to the refutation of gnostic systems using the rhetorical skills and *topoi* of philosophical debate. At the same time, he sought to provide a theoretical explication of orthodox Christian belief that would answer arguments advanced by gnostic teachers.

Irenaeus provided two guidelines for drawing the boundary that would exclude gnostic teachers from the Christian community. The first is reflected in the *regula fidei* of his *Against Heresies* (1.10.3), which gives topics about which legitimate theological speculation is possible and consequently rules out much of the cosmological speculation of the gnostic teachers. The second guideline is Irenaeus's rejection of gnostic allegorization of scripture. He insists that biblical passages must mean what they appear to mean and that they must be interpreted within their contexts. In book five, Irenaeus argues that the gnostics failed to support their claims for a spiritual resurrection in *1 Corinthians* 1:50 because they ignored the eschatological dimensions of the verses that follow.

The heresiologist's concern to draw boundaries between orthodox Christianity and gnostic teachings ran counter to the practice of second-century gnostics. Several of the Nag Hammadi treatises were apparently composed with the opposite aim. Writings such as the *Gospel of Truth* and the *Tripartite Tractate* drew explicit connections between gnostic teaching and both the teaching practice and the sacramental practice of the larger Christian community. Other gnostic writings fell within the developing patterns of ascetic Christianity in Syria and Egypt (e.g., *Gospel of Thomas, Book of Thomas the Contender, Dialogue of the Savior*). The ascetic tradition tended to reject the common Christian assumption that baptism provides a quality of sinlessness adequate to salvation and to insist that only rigorous separation from the body and its passions will lead to salvation.

Other gnostic writings show that the efforts of heresiologists to draw boundaries against gnostics resulted in repressive measures from the orthodox side and increasing separation by gnostics (cf. *Apocalypse of Peter, Second Treatise of the Great Seth*). The *Testimony of Truth*, apparently written in third-century Alexandria, not only contains explicit attacks on the beliefs of orthodox Christians but also attacks other gnostic sects and teachers like Valentinus, Isidore, and Basilides. The author of this gnostic work considers other, nonascetic gnostics as heretics. However, the author still holds to something of the nonpolemical stance that had characterized earlier gnostic teachers, saying that the true teacher avoids disputes and makes himself equal to everyone. Another example of the effectiveness of the orthodox polemic in defining gnostics as heretics is found in what appears to be a gnostic community rule that calls for charity and love among the gnostic brethren as a sign of the truth of their claims over against the disunity of the orthodox in *Interpretation of Knowledge*. This call reverses one of Irenaeus's polemical points that the multiplicity and disunity of gnostic sects condemn their teaching when contrasted with the worldwide unity of the church.

Some scholars think that this third period, in which the gnostics were effectively isolated as "heretic" by orthodox polemic, led to a significant shift within gnostic circles. Gnosticism began to become dechristianized, to identify more with the non-Christian, esoteric, and hermetic elements within its traditions. Gnostics became members of an independent esoteric sect, moved toward the more congenial Mandaean or Manichaean circles, existed on the fringes of Alexandrian Neoplatonism in groups that emphasized thaumaturgy, or joined the monks in the Egyptian desert, where they found a kindred spirit in the combination of asceticism and Origenist mysticism. Those associated with Manichaeism or Origenism would continue to find themselves among the ranks of heretical Christians. The rest were no longer within the Christian sphere of influence.

— PHEME PERKINS

GOD

GOD IN THE NEW TESTAMENT

The New Testament enunciates no new God and no new doctrine of God. It proclaims that the God and Father of Jesus Christ is the God of Abraham, Isaac, and Jacob, the God of earlier covenants. What the New Testament announces is that this God has acted anew in inaugurating God's final reign and covenant through the career and fate of Jesus of Nazareth. [*For discussion of Jesus' life and of Christology, see* Jesus.]

THE PRE-EASTER JESUS. Jesus inherited the Old Testament Jewish faith in Yahveh, which held that God was the creator of the world (*Mk.* 10:6 and parallel) and the one God who elected Israel as his people and gave them his law (*Mk.* 12:29 and parallels). Moreover, God promised the Israelites final salvation (*Is.* 35, 61). At the same time, the sense in the New Testament that God is now realizing ancient promises and is acting anew (cf. *Mt.* 11:4-5, an indubitably authentic saying of Jesus) gives Jesus' image of God a sense of immediacy. God was not merely creator some thousands (or billions) of years ago; he is creator now, feeding the birds and clothing the flowers (*Mt.* 6:26-30, *Lk.* 12:24, and Q, the purported common source of

The name of God, Yahveh (preserved only unvocalized in the texts, i. e., YHVH) is not known before Moses.

PAGE 370

Matthew and *Luke*). Not only did God give the law through Moses, but God now demands radical obedience in each concrete situation (cf. the antitheses of the Sermon on the Mount in *Mt.* 5:27-48). Above all, God is now offering in the proclamation and activity of Jesus a foretaste of final salvation. Jesus' announcement of the inbreaking of God's reign (*Mk.* 1:15, *Mt.* 10:7, *Lk.* 9:2, Q) is not an abstract concept detached from Jesus' own word and work. Jesus' word and work are the occasions through which God acts definitively and savingly. The same is true of Jesus' exorcisms: "If I by the Spirit [finger, *Lk.* 11:20] of God cast out demons, then the kingdom [i. e., reign] of God has come upon you" (*Mt.* 12:28, *Lk.* 11:20, Q).

"The Son of man will be delivered into the hand of men who will put him to death."

MARK 9:31

Jesus issues a call, "Follow me" (*Mk.* 1:17, 2:14; cf. *Mt.* 8:22, *Lk.* 9:59, Q?), not because he advances any claim for himself as such, but only because in that call, as in his word and work in the world, God is issuing the call to end-time salvation. To confess Jesus (*Mt.* 10:32, *Lk.* 12:8, Q, *Mk.* 8:38) or to deny him before others is to determine one's ultimate fate on the last day—whether it be judgment or salvation. The verdict of the Son of man on that day will be determined by whether men and women confess Jesus now. Thus, in Jesus' call God is proleptically active as judge and savior. The Fourth Gospel puts it more thematically: God's salvation and judgment are already meted out here and now in the word of Jesus and people's response to it (*Jn.* 3:18, 5:22-27).

Jesus' conduct. Jesus eats with outcasts, and he defends his conduct by telling the parables of the lost (*Lk.* 15). These parables interpret Jesus' action as God's action in seeking and saving the lost and celebrating with them here and now the joy of the reign of God. Ernst Fuchs points out in *Studies of the Historical Jesus* (Naperville, Ill., 1964) that "Jesus . . . dares to affirm the will of God as though he himself stood in God's place" (p. 21).

God as Abba. Jesus' word and work are God's word and work because Jesus has responded to God's call in complete faith and obedience. This is brought out in the baptism, temptation, transfiguration, and Gethsemane narratives of the synoptists (*Mk.* 1:9-11 and parallels, *Mt.* 4:1-11, *Lk.* 4:1-13, Q, *Mk.* 9:2-8 and parallels, *Mk.* 14:32-42 and parallels), and once again it is thematically treated in the discourses of the Fourth Gospel (e.g., *Jn.* 8:28-29). This relation of call and obedience is summarized in Jesus' intimate address to God as Abba ("father"). This is no new doctrine, for the Old Testament and Judaism knew God as Father (e.g., *Is.* 63:16), nor does it imply a claim to metaphysical identity with the being of God or with an aspect of that being, as in later New Testament traditions. Again, Jesus does not pass the Abba appellation on to others to make the same response, they too may call God "Abba" (cf. the Lukan version of the Lord's Prayer, *Lk.* 11:2).

Jesus' death. The saving activity in word and deed which fills the whole career of Jesus culminates in his journey to Jerusalem in order to make the last offer of salvation or judgment to his people at the very center of their national life. As a prophet, Jesus is convinced that he will be rejected and put to death and that this death will be the culmination of Israel's constant rejection of God's word as known through the prophets: "It cannot be that a prophet should perish away from Jerusalem" (*Lk.* 13:33; cf. the parable of the vineyard, *Mk.* 12:1-9 and parallels). Since it is the culmination of his obedience, his death, like all his other activity, is seen by Jesus as the saving act of God. The most primitive form of the suffering-Son-of-man sayings, namely, "The Son of man will be delivered into the hands of men" (cf. *Mk.* 9:31), if authentic, expresses this by using the divine passive: God will deliver the Son of man to death. It is God's prerogative to inaugurate covenants. Therefore, at the Last Supper, Jesus speaks of his impending death as a supreme act of service (*Lk.* 22:27; cf. the foot washing in *Jn.* 13:2-15), which inaugurates the final covenant and reign of God (*Lk.* 22:29; cf. *Mk.* 14:24, 25 and parallels). In the references to service, covenant, and kingdom (reign) at the Last Supper lies the historical basis for the post-Easter message of atonement.

EASTER. The Easter experiences created in the disciples the faith that, despite the apparent debacle of the crucifixion, God had vindicated Jesus and taken him into his own eternal presence. The early community expressed this conviction chiefly through testimony about Jesus' resurrection: "God raised Jesus from the dead" (*Rom.* 4:24, 10:9; *1 Thes.* 1:10) or "Christ was raised" (*Rom.* 4:25, 6:9; *1 Cor.* 15:4—a divine passive). After Easter, for the believing community, God is preeminently the God who raised Jesus from the dead. Insofar as there is any specific New Testament definition of God, this is it (e.g., again, *Rom.* 10:9). This results in the ascription of titles of majesty to Jesus. At the resurrection, God made him Lord and Christ (Messiah) (*Acts* 2:36) and even Son of God, originally a royal title (*Rom.* 1:4). Jesus is exalted to a position as close as possible to God, to God's "right hand." That means God continues to act savingly, even after Easter, toward the community and toward the world through the proclamation of Jesus as the Christ. In saving activity, God and Christ become interchangeable subjects: what God does, Christ does at the same time. However, Christ does not replace God. All the titles of majesty declare that Christ is God's agent, not God's surrogate.

THE MESSAGE OF THE POST-EASTER CHURCH. Like Jesus in his pre-Easter life, the early church did not approach Israel with a new doctrine of God. Its message was that God had decisively inaugurated the fulfillment of his promises in the career and fate of Jesus of Nazareth, and above all in his resurrection. This is the burden of the sermons in the early chapters of the *Acts of the Apostles*: "Jesus of Nazareth, a man attested to you by God with mighty works and signs which God did through him . . . this Jesus, delivered up according to the definite plan and foreknowledge of God . . . God raised him" (*Acts* 2:22-24).

The Hellenistic-Jewish mission. Members of the Greek-speaking Jewish community, initially led by Stephen (*Acts* 6, 7), first found themselves preaching the Christian message to Greek-speaking non-Jews (*Acts* 11:20). In approaching them, it was found necessary to change tactics. Instead of launching straight in with the Christ event as God's act of salvation, they had to start further back, with belief in God. Because these non-Jewish Greeks came from a pagan and often polytheistic environment, it was necessary first to establish belief in the one God before speaking about what this God had done in Christ and was now doing salvifically. In other words, the Hellenistic-Jewish Christians needed an apologetic for monotheism, arguments for the existence of the one God, in their mission to non-Jews. They were able to draw upon the apologetic which had earlier been worked out by Greek-speaking Jews in their approach to the pagan world. One of the earliest references to such an apologetic for monotheism is attested to by Paul when he reminds the Thessalonians of his original preaching to them before their conversion to Christianity: "You turned from idols to serve a living and true God" (*1 Thes.* 1:9). Note how this precedes the second part of the message: "and to wait for this Son from heaven, whom he raised from the dead" (*1 Thes.* 1:10). A further example of Pauline apologetic for monotheism, and a claim that creation contains a natural revelation of God and his moral demands, occurs in *Romans* 1:18-32 and 2:14-15. Humanity has, however, frequently rejected this revelation and disobeyed God's moral demands, and Paul seeks to recall pagans to such knowledge and obedience. He sees a close connection between idolatry and immorality: "They . . . exchanged the glory of the immortal God for images resembling mortal man or birds or animals or reptiles. . . . Therefore God gave them up in the lust of their hearts to impurity" (*Rom.* 1:23-24). Later examples of an apologetic for monotheism are to be found in *Acts* 14:15-17, addressed to an unsophisticated audience, and in *Acts* 17:24-29, addressed to a cultured one.

Pauline theology. Paul's theology is entirely occasional, that is, it was worked out in response to concrete problems in the Christian communities he knew. The focus of his theology is the death and resurrection of

Jesus Christ and its saving consequences. He inherited from the liturgical tradition an understanding of Christ's death as a sacrifice. It was the blood that inaugurated the new covenant (*1 Cor.* 11:25). Christ was the paschal lamb (*1 Cor.* 5:7). But Paul did not develop these sacrificial images in his reflection on Christ's death, perhaps because such language tended to drive a wedge between Jesus and the Father, as though the sacrifice was offered in order to propitiate or appease an angry deity. The language of the (probably pre-Pauline) hymn in *Romans* 3:25-26, especially the word translated in the King James Version as "propitiation" (Gr., *hilasterion*), might be taken in that way. But God is the initiator in the atoning death of Christ ("whom God set forth"), and the word is better translated "expiation," as in the Revised Standard Version. This means that the crucifixion was an act of God dealing with and removing sin, the barrier between God and humanity, rather than an act of Christ directed toward God. It is an act of God's reconciling love, directed toward sinful humanity (*Rom.* 5:8). Through it God justifies the ungodly (*Rom.* 4:5). *Reconciliation*, like *expiation*, is a word denoting God's activity toward us, rather than Christ's activity toward God. Christ does not reconcile the Father to humanity, as traditional theology has often asserted (see, e.g., article 2 of the 1563 Thirty-nine Articles), rather, "God in Christ was [or, was in Christ] reconciling the world to himself" (*2 Cor.* 5:19). Justification and reconciliation (two slightly different images for the same reality) are expressions of the righteousness of God, a central concept in Paul's thinking

IS JESUS GOD?

In the New Testament, the Johanine writings directly predict the deity of Christ.

ARALDO DE LUCA/CORBIS

Paul's apostolic presence is overshadowed by a still greater presence, that of Jesus Christ the Lord.

PAGE 82

about God. Righteousness is both an attribute and an activity of God; it is God's action of judging and saving.

A writing on the fringe of the Pauline corpus, not by Paul himself, is the *Letter to the Hebrews*, which interprets the saving act of God in Christ in terms of Christ as the high priest. Once again, this author is careful not to drive a wedge between God and Christ. As high priest, Christ does not offer a sacrifice to God for the purpose of propitiation. Rather, the Son offers his life in perfect obedience to the Father (*Heb.* 10:5-10) in order to make purification for sin. As in Paul, the object of Christ's deed is not God, but sin.

Within the events of Jesus' human life the God of Israel and the creator of the world had been disclosed.

PAGE 162

THE INCARNATION AND THE BEING OF CHRIST. All levels of tradition in the New Testament examined thus far speak of Christ's relation to God in functional terms. He is commissioned, called, and sent as divine agent. God is present with and in him and active through him. These biblical traditions do not raise the question about Jesus' personal identity in relation to God. There is no discussion of Jesus' "divinity" or of his "divine nature" in the earliest sources; these are Greek rather than Hebrew concepts. But given the exalted status of Jesus, which the Christian community believed him to have received at Easter, it was inevitable that the question of Jesus' identity would eventually be raised, especially by the Greek-speaking world. Such reflection initially employed the concept of the divine wisdom to elucidate the revelatory work of Jesus. Historically, Jesus had appeared as a spokesman for the divine wisdom, using the speech forms of the wisdom tradition as these are seen, for example, in *Proverbs*. The content of Jesus' wisdom utterances contained an implicit claim that he was wisdom's last and definitive spokesman; this view is drawn out explicitly in the Q material (*Mt.* 11:25-27 and Q parallel). Matthew himself even identifies Jesus with wisdom, although in a functional rather than ontological sense (*Mt.* 11:28-30; cf. *Sir.* 24:25, 51:23-24).

In first-century Judaism, however, the concept of God's wisdom was advancing beyond the stage of poetical personification of an aspect of God's activity, toward a hypostatization (i. e., an attribution of distinct, concrete existence) of an aspect of the being of God. As such, the wisdom of God was an outflow of his being, through which he created the world, became self-revelatory to humanity, called Israel, gave the law, and came to dwell with Israel's notables, such as Abraham, Moses, and the prophets, but this wisdom was constantly rejected by most of the people. In certain hymns in the New Testament (*Phil.* 2:6-11, *1 Cor.* 8:6, *Col.* 1:15-20, *Heb.* 1:1-3) the career and fate of Jesus are linked to this earlier activity of *wisdom* (though the term wisdom itself is not used); a single, continuous subject covers the preincarnate activity of wisdom and the earthly career of Jesus. The result is that Jesus becomes personally identified with the hypostatized wisdom of God. The agent of creation, revelation, and saving activity finally becomes incarnate in Jesus. But this development occurs only in

JESUS ACCORDING TO JOHN
The Incarnation of Divine Wisdom

The final step toward an incarnation Christology is taken in the Johannine literature, especially in the Fourth Gospel. This gospel is prefaced by the Logos hymn (*Jn.* 1:1-18). *Logos* ("word") was used as a synonym for the divine wisdom in the later wisdom literature. In this hymn *logos* is equated with, yet distinguishable from, the being of God: "In the beginning was the word [*logos*] and the word was with God and the word was God" (*Jn.* 1:1), which we may paraphrase as "God is essentially a self-communicating God. This self-communication was a distinct aspect within God's being, related to him, and partaking in his divine being."

The hymn goes on to speak of the activity of the Logos as the agent of creation, revelation, and redemption and finally states that the Logos became flesh, that is, incarnate (*Jn.* 1:14). There could be no clearer statement of the identity of Jesus of Nazareth with an aspect of the very being of God. In the rest of this gospel, the evangelist sets forth the life of Jesus as the incarnation of the divine wisdom, or Logos. (After *John* 1:14 neither *wisdom* nor *logos* is used in the Fourth Gospel, but imagery from the wisdom/Logos tradition is appropriated, especially in the "I am" sayings.) Jesus speaks as one fully conscious of personal preincarnate existence within the being of God. It is significant, however, that this new "high" christological language does not replace the "lower" Christology, which speaks in terms of call, commission, and the response of obedience. Apparently John understands his "higher" Christology to be an interpretation of the "lower," refraining from abandoning the terms in which the pre-Easter Jesus spoke and acted. Much of later traditional church Christology has ignored the presence of these two levels in *John* and has rewritten the earthly life of Jesus exclusively in terms of the "higher" Christology.

—REGINALD H. FULLER

hymnic materials and at this stage is hardly the subject of theological reflection.

IS JESUS GOD? Only very cautiously and gradually does the New Testament use the predicate God for Jesus. First, there are possible examples in some Pauline doxologies (e.g., *Rom.* 9:5), although there are problems of text, punctuation, and grammar that make it difficult to decide whether in such passages Paul actually does equate Jesus with God. Then the *Letter to the Hebrews* transfers Old Testament passages which speak of Yahveh-Kurios (Lord) to Christos-Kurios (e.g., *Heb.* 1:10). Only the Johannine writings directly and unquestionably predicate the deity of Christ. First, he is the incarnation of the Logos which was God. Then, according to the now generally accepted reading, he is the "only-begotten God" during his incarnate life (*Jn.* 1:18). Finally, Thomas greets the risen Christ as "my Lord and my God" (*Jn.* 20:28). Then *1 John* sums it up by predicating God as the preexistent, incarnate, and exalted one in a summary formula: ". . . in his Son Jesus Christ. This is the true God and eternal life" (*1 Jn.* 5:20). Thus the New Testament can occasionally speak of Jesus as God, but always in a carefully nuanced way: he is not God-as-God-is-in-himself, but the incarnation of that aspect of the being of God which is God-going-out-of-himself-in-self-communication.

The Trinity. There is a triadic structure in the Christian experience of God. Through the power of the Holy Spirit, believers know Jesus Christ as the revelation of God the Father. This experience becomes crystallized in triadic formulas (*2 Cor.* 13:14, *Mt.* 28:19) or in unreflected theological statements (*1 Cor.* 12:4-6). But there is no attempt to work out a doctrine of the Trinity, or to integrate the Old Testament Jewish faith in the oneness of God with the Christian threefold experience. Like the doctrine of the incarnation, this was left to the post-New Testament church. [*For discussion of the development of Christian doctrines concerning God, see* Trinity.]

— REGINALD H. FULLER

GOD IN POSTBIBLICAL JUDAISM

THE RABBINIC APPROACH. Rabbinic thought as contained in the Talmud and the Midrash is unsystematic in presentation. While there is an abundance of references in these sources to the nature of God and his relationship to man and the world, the statements are general responses to particular stimuli, not precise, theological formulations. It is consequently imprecise to speak of the rabbinic doctrine of God, even though the expression is used by some scholars. The Talmud and Midrash are the record of the teachings of many hundreds of individuals, each with his own temperament and disposition, as these individuals reflected on God's dealings with the Jewish people. Nevertheless, on the basic ideas about God there is total agreement. All of the rabbis are committed to the propositions that God is One, creator of heaven and earth; that he wishes all men to pursue justice and righteousness; that he rewards those who obey his will and punishes those who disobey; and that he has chosen the Jewish people from all the nations to give them his most precious gift, the Torah.

"Hear O Israel, the Lord our God, the Lord is One."

DEUTERONOMY 6:4

From an early period, the tetragrammaton, *YHVH*, was never pronounced by Jews as it is written because it is God's own, special name, too holy to be uttered by human mouth. The name *Adonai* ("my lord") was substituted as a euphemism with regard to which a degree of familiarity was allowed.

The two most frequently found names for God in the Talmud are *Ribbono shel 'olam* ("Lord of the universe"), used when addressing God in the second person, and *ha-Qadosh barukh hu'* ("the Holy One, blessed be he"), used when speaking of God in the third person (B. T., *Ber.* 4a, 7a, and very frequently).

It is incorrect, however, to think of these names as implying the transcendence and immanence of God. Abstract terms of this nature are entirely foreign to rabbinic thinking. The description of God as king is ubiquitous in the rabbinic literature with antecedents in the Bible. This metaphor is also founded on the rabbis' experiences of earthly rulers. God is the divine king whose laws must be obeyed. When he is stern to punish evildoers, he is said to be seated on his throne of judgment. When he is gracious to pardon, he is said to be seated on his throne of mercy (B. T., *'A. Z.* 3b).

Especially after the dispersal of many Jews from the Holy Land and the destruction of the Temple in 70 CE, the idea, found only sporadically in the Bible, that God shares human suffering, grieving with the victims of oppression, was deepened by the rabbis. Whenever Israel is in exile, they taught, the Shekhinah is in exile with them (B. T., *Meg.* 29a). The idea that God is affected by human degradation is applied even to a criminal executed for his crimes. The Shekhinah is said to be distressed at such a person's downfall (*San.* 6.5).

Both idolatry and dualism were strongly condemned by the rabbis. The twice-daily reading of the Shema' ("Hear O Israel, the Lord our God, the Lord is One," *Dt.* 6:4), Israel's declaration of faith in God's unity, was introduced at least as early as the first century BCE, probably in order to constantly reject the dualistic ideas prevalent in the Near East. The third-century Palestinian teacher Abbahu, in a polemic evidently directed against both Christian beliefs and dualism, expounded the verse: "I am the first, and I am the last, and beside Me there is no God" (*Is.* 44:6). His interpretation is 'I am the first,' for I have no father;

'and I am the last,' for I have no son; 'and beside me there is no God,' for I have no brother" (*Ex. Rab.* 29.5).

In rabbinic Judaism there is little denial that the legitimate pleasures of the world are God's gift to man, who must give thanks to God when they are enjoyed. In one passage it is even said that a man will have to give an account to God for his rejection of what he is allowed to enjoy (J. T., *Qid.* 4.12, 66d). Yet the emphasis is on spiritual bliss in the hereafter, when man, as a reward for his efforts in this life, will enjoy the nearness of God forever.

THE PHILOSOPHICAL APPROACH. Unlike the Talmudic rabbis, the medieval thinkers presented their ideas on God in a systematic way. Pascal's distinction between the God of Abraham, Isaac, and Jacob and the God of the philosophers generally holds true for the distinction between the rabbinic mode of thinking and that of the medieval theologians. For these theologians, the doctrine that God is One means not only that there is no multiplicity of gods but that God is unique, utterly beyond all human comprehension, and totally different from his creatures, not only in degree but in kind. Moses Maimonides (Mosheh ben Maimon, 1135/8-1204), the most distinguished of the medieval thinkers and the most influential in subsequent Jewish thought, adapts for his purpose the rabbinic saying (B. T., *Ber.* 33b) that to overpraise God is akin to praising a human king for possessing myriads of silver pieces when, in reality, he possesses myriads of gold pieces.

Moses Maimonides faced an intellectual crisis: the resolution of the Torah's teachings with the views of Aristotle

PAGE 408

In addition to their discussions regarding God's nature, the medieval thinkers examined God's activity in the finite world, that is, his role as creator and the scope of his providence. That God is the creator of the universe is accepted as axiomatic by all the medieval thinkers, although Gersonides (*Milhamot ha-Shem* 6) is radical here, too, in accepting the Platonic view of a hylic substance, coeternal with God, upon which God imposes form but does not create. Maimonides *(Guide of the Perplexed* 2.13-15), while at first toying with the Aristotelian idea of the material universe as having the same relation to God as the shadow of a tree to the tree, eventually accepts the traditional Jewish view that God created the world out of nothing. Maimonides' motivation is not only to preserve tradition but to emphasize the otherness of God, whose existence is necessary, whereas that of all created things is contingent.

Like the God of the biblical authors and the rabbis, the God of the medieval thinkers is a caring God whose providence extends over all of his creatures. Both Maimonides *(Guide of the Perplexed* 3.17-18) and Gersonides *(Milhamot ha-Shem* 4) limit, however, God's special providence to humans. For animals there is only a general providence that guarantees the continued existence of animal species, but whether, for instance, this spider catches that fly is not ordained by God but is by pure chance. Yehudah ha-Levi (1075-1141) in his *Kuzari* (3.11) refuses to allow chance to play any role in creation: God's special providence extends to animals as well as to humans.

Sa'adyah Gaon (882-942) anticipated Thomas Aquinas's statement that "nothing that implies a contradiction falls under the scope of God's omnipotence" (*Summa theologiae* 1.25.4). Sa'adyah (*Book of Beliefs and Opinions* 2.13) observes that the soul will not praise God for being able to cause five to be more than ten without adding anything to the former, nor for being able to bring back the day gone by to its original condition.

THE QABBALISTIC APPROACH. The qabbalists accepted the arguments of the philosophers in favor of extreme negation of divine attributes. Yet they felt the need, as mystics, to have a relationship with the God of living religion, not with a cold abstraction. In the theosophical scheme worked out by the qabbalists, a distinction is drawn between God as he is in himself and God in manifestation. God as he is in himself is Ein Sof ("no end, i. e., the limitless"), the impersonal ground of being who emerges from concealment in order to become manifest in the universe. From Ein Sof there is an emanation of ten *sefirot* ("spheres"; sg., *sefirah*), the powers of potencies of the godhead in manifestation, conceived of as a dynamic organism. Of Ein Sof nothing whatsoever can be said. More extreme than the philosophers in this respect, the qabbalists refuse to allow even negative attributes to be used of Ein Sof, but God in his aspect of manifestation in the *sefirot* can be thought of in terms of positive attributes. The living God of the Bible and of religion is the godhead as manifested in the sefirot. Ein Sof, on the other hand, is only hinted at in the Bible since complete silence alone is permissible of this aspect of deity. A later qabbalist went further to hold that, strictly speaking, even to use such a negative term as Ein Sof is improper (see I. S. Ratner, *Le-or ha-Qabbalah*, Tel Aviv, 1961, p. 39, n. 40).

The *sefirot* represent various aspects in the life of the godhead, for instance, wisdom, justice, and mercy. These are combined in a very complex order, and through them the worlds beneath, including the finite, material universe, are controlled, the whole order conceived as a great chain of being from the highest to the lowest reaching back to Ein Sof. There is a male principle in the realm of *sefirot* and a female principle, a highly charged mythological concept that opponents of Qabbalah, medieval and modern, considered to be a foreign, verging on the idolatrous, importation into Judaism (see *responsa* of Yitshaq ben Sheshet Perfet, *Rivash*, edited by I. H. Daiches, New York, 1964, no. 157, and S. Rubin, *Heidenthum und Kabbala,* Vienna, 1893).The sacred marriage between these two means that there is complete harmony on high, and the divine grace can flow through all creation. But the flow of the divine grace depends upon the deeds of man, since he is marvelously fashioned in God's image. Thus in the qabbalistic scheme God has made his purposes depend for their fulfillment on human conduct; in this sense it is not only man who needs God but God who needs man.

The eighteenth-century mystical movement of Hasidism, particularly the more speculative branch of the movement known as Habad, tended toward a panentheistic understanding of the idea of *tsimtsum. Tsimtsum* does not really take place, since the Infinite is incapable of suffering limitation, but *tsimtsum* represents no more than a screening of the divine light so that finite creatures might appear to enjoy separate existence. The only true reality is God. There is a basic difference between this panentheistic ("all is in God") or acosmic view and that of pantheism ("all is God"). In the pantheistic thought of Barukh Spinoza (1632-1676), God is the name given to the totality of things. God is the universe and the universe is God. In Habad thought, without God there could be no universe, but without the universe God would still be the unchanging same; in fact, God is the unchanging same even after the creation of the universe, since from God's point of view there is no universe. The traditionalist rabbis and communal leaders, the *mitnaggedim* ("opponents"), saw the Hasidic view as rank heresy. For them the verse that states that the whole earth is filled with God's glory (*Is.* 6:3) means only that God's providence extends over all and that his glory can be discerned through its manifestation in the world. Speculative Hasidism understands the verse to mean that there is only God's glory as an ultimate.

MODERN APPROACHES. Modern Jewish thinkers have been obliged to face the challenges to traditional theism provided by modern thought. The rise of modern science tended to favor mechanistic philosophies of existence and, in more recent years, both linguistic philosophy and existentialism, in their different ways, cast suspicion on all metaphysics. Although the Jew did not begin to participate fully in Western society and to assimilate Western patterns of thought until the end of the eighteenth century, modern Jewish thinkers have been influenced by all of these trends in Western thought, compelling them to rethink the traditional views concerning God. The result has been an espousal of differing attitudes toward theism, from a reaffirmation of the traditional to a radical transformation in naturalistic terms. In any event, the vocabulary used since, by both the traditionalists and the nonconformists, is that of modern thought, even when it is used to interpret the tradition.

Among twentieth-century Jewish thinkers, Mordecai Kaplan (1881-1983) is the most determined of the naturalists. For Kaplan and his disciples God is not a supernatural, personal being but the power in the universe that makes for righteousness. Kaplan maintains that people really were referring to this power when they spoke of God, even though, in the prescientific age, they expressed their belief in terms of a supreme being, the creator of the world who exercises care over it.

Martin Buber (1878-1965), the best-known of Jewish religious existentialists, stresses, on the contrary, the personal aspect of deity. In Buber's thought, when man has an I-Thou relationship to his fellows and to the world in general, he meets in dialogue the Thou of God. While the medieval thinkers devoted a significant part of their thought to reasoning about God's nature, Buber rejects such speculations as futile, cosmic talk, irrelevant to the life of faith. God cannot be spoken about, but he can be met as a person by persons.

Avraham Yitshaq Kook (1865-1935), the first chief rabbi of Palestine, is completely traditional in his concept of God but accepts the theory of evolution, which, as a qabbalist, he believed to be in full accord with the qabbalistic view. The whole of the universe is on the move, and man is rising to ever greater heights ultimately to meet God.

More than any other event, the Holocaust, in which six million Jews perished, compelled Jewish religious thinkers to examine again the doctrine that God is at work in human history. Efforts of medieval thinkers like Yehudah ha-Levi and Maimonides to account for evil in God's creation were, for many, totally inadequate to explain away the enormity of the catastrophe. Some contemporary thinkers invoke the idea found in the ancient sources that there are times when the face of God is hidden, when God surrenders his universe to chance if not to chaos and conceals himself because mankind has abandoned him. There is a reluctance, however, to explore such ideas, since they appear to condemn those who were destroyed, laying the blame, to some extent, at the door of the victims. The free-will defense has also been invoked by contemporary thinkers, both Jewish (e.g., Avraham Yitshaq Kook, Milton Steinberg) and non-Jewish (e.g., John Hick). For man to be free and exercise his choice in freedom to meet his God, the world must be a place in which naked evil is possible, even though the price might seem too high.

— LOUIS JACOBS

GOD IN POSTBIBLICAL CHRISTIANITY

There was during the early centuries of the Christian era a great divide. On one side were those classical religious thinkers who continued to reflect on God in strictly philosophical ways, trusting their reason to suffice. This tradition reached its apex in Neoplatonism. On the other side were those who accepted the authority of Jewish (supplemented later by Christian or Islamic) scriptures, correlating the ideas found there with the fruits of reason.

Like all significant personal involvements, an I-Thou relationship with God (the "Eternal Thou") evokes responsive action—it "commands."

PAGE 415

Justin Martyr provides an early picture of how Christians understood the relation of their doctrine of God to the wider culture. He reports that he sought knowledge of God from philosophy with little success. A Christian then persuaded him that the human mind lacks the power to grasp the truth of God and that one must begin with what God has revealed. Accordingly, Justin turned to the Hebrew scriptures, read now through Christian eyes, and found there what he wanted.

The matter primarily in dispute was the content of divine activity in relation to humankind, what God had done, was doing, and would do. To be a Christian was to affirm that the God of whom the Hebrew scriptures speak had acted in Jesus for the redemption of the world. This conviction expressed itself in the doctrine of incarnation, and it was this doctrine that most distinguished Christian thought from Jewish and philosophical ideas. While the church insisted that what was incarnate was truly God, it did not simply identify what was incarnate with the one whom Jesus called "Father." Instead, following the prologue in the *Gospel of John,* the Word (or Son) who was with God and who was God was the incarnated one. This required a distinction within the one God. Even so, the church lacked a conceptuality that could show how the Word could both be one with God and become incarnate in Jesus without diminution of Jesus' humanity; and so the assertion, unsupported by intelligible conceptuality, became a "mystery."

The fourteenth century saw a criticism of Thomas from a nominalist perspective that grounded the good not in ontological reality but solely in the will of God.

PAGE 148

Although there was broad consensus that all things derive from God, there were alternative images of the relationship between God and the world. One image emphasized creation as an external act of will. The world is envisaged as coming into being by divine fiat out of nothing. Another image, which envisioned the world as the outworking of the dynamism of the divine life, found its clearest expression in Plotinus's doctrine of emanation. Insofar as this image implied that the world was made of divine substance, it was rejected by the church, but some of its language remained influential. A third image was that of participation, wherein God is seen as perfect being, and creatures are thought to exist as they participate in this being in a creaturely way. A fourth image was that of inclusion, according to which God is the "uncontained, who contains all things" *(Preaching of Peter).*

The Platonic influence on developing Christian beliefs encouraged a correlation between the human intellect and God. A related concept held that the human soul or mind possessed a kinship with God that was lacking to the body. Such ideas encouraged intellectualistic mysticism and bodily asceticism. The Christian struggle to overcome this dualism can be traced from the fourth-century Cappadocians through the fourteenth-century Greek-speaking church. It required both the denial that God is of the order of thought or idea and the rejection of a further development in the thought of Plotinus, which located God as the One beyond thought who could be reached only through thought. At the same time it required the clarification of how human beings could have real communion with God by grace.

The impact of Platonic philosophy in Western thought of God took a different turn chiefly because of

THOMAS AQUINAS

God Wills What Is Good

The Augustinian tradition argues that knowledge of God's existence is already implicitly given in thought. Thomas Aquinas, on the other hand, seeks to lead the mind by inference from what is known through the senses to the affirmation of God as the supreme cause of the world. The emphasis in Thomas's idea of God shifts, accordingly, from that of the illuminator of the mind to the cause of the existence and motion of all creaturely things.

Thomas subordinated the divine will to the divine wisdom. That is, God wills what is good. In this doctrine, his thought followed that of the church fathers, including Augustine. God remains for Thomas, as for them, the One, the True, and the Good. But there were others for whom this Platonic way of thinking ceased to be convincing, for whom there were no truth and goodness existing in themselves and attracting the human mind and will; they asserted that God is much more the efficient cause of natural motion, that God is free agent, bound to nothing, and, in short, that God is almighty will, determining thereby what is true and good. This voluntaristic emphasis is associated with the rise of medieval nominalism, influenced especially by William of Ockham. Nominalism is the doctrine that universals are names given to certain things. These universals have no existence in themselves. Furthermore, since there is an element of arbitrariness in how we name things, human choice and decision are accented instead of discernment of what is objectively there for the mind to discover. This doctrine entails the theory that God alone chooses what to require of human beings and what to do for them. What God has chosen cannot be learned by human reason; it can only be revealed by God.

— JOHN B. COBB, JR.

Augustine of Hippo. He understood the essence of God to be all that which is common to the persons of the Trinity. God is truth itself, which is at once goodness itself. As the sun is the source of light by which our eyes see the visible world, so God is the source of illumination of the mind by which it sees eternal truths.

During the Renaissance a new wave of Platonic influence gave rise to the Hermetic tradition, which emphasized the mathematical character of the world, the power of movement immanent in things, and the interrelatedness of human thought with these things. The divine was perceived as indwelling power rather than as transcendent will. The voluntaristic tradition had earlier separated revelation from the support of reason and encouraged an authoritarian spirit; the Hermetic tradition, too, separated reason from revelation, but encouraged instead a critique of hierarchical structures in church and society. Together they paved the way for modern philosophy in the seventeenth century, whereupon there ended definitively the unity of theology and philosophy that had dominated Western thought for more than a thousand years.

In the eighteenth century the chief issue was whether God, having established natural laws, ever acted contrary to them. All agreed that God was supernatural. The issue was whether God caused supernatural events in the created world, that is, whether miracles occurred. Orthodox Christians held that the biblical accounts of miracles were true, whereas the Deists held that natural law was perfect and that therefore God did not violate it.

Reflection about God on the European continent in the nineteenth and early twentieth centuries was shaped by the critical philosophy of Immanuel Kant. Kant points out that in addition to the sphere of theoretical reason there is another sphere of practical reason, which deals with how people should act. In this sphere, too, the fundamental moral principle is independent of theology. People should act always according to maxims that they can will to be universal principles. For example, if one cannot will that people in general lie, cheat, or steal whenever it is to their personal advantage to do so, then one ought not to lie, cheat, or steal for one's own advantage. This principle—the "categorical imperative"—holds whether or not God exists.

Although few have followed the exact way in which Kant correlated God with ethics, many have agreed that belief in God belongs with ethics rather than with science. Later in the nineteenth century Albrecht Ritschl was to found a neo-Kantian school, which interpreted theology as statements about values rather than about facts. God is that which is supremely valuable, not a being about whose existence it is suitable to argue.

The most influential theologian of the twentieth century was Karl Barth. He denied, more radically than the Protestant reformers, that God can be known by human reason. We are entirely dependent, Barth maintained, on God's self-revelation, who is Jesus Christ. This revelation is known only in the scriptural witness to him. Central to what is revealed of God is radical, sovereign, dynamic freedom. We can lay no claims on God and make no judgments about how God will act except as we take hold of the divine promises and the divine self-disclosure.

The appearance soon after World War II of the writings of Dietrich Bonhoeffer from a Nazi jail struck a responsive chord in those already uncomfortable with Barth's theology. The ideas sketched in these writings indicate a quite different way of thinking of God. "Only a powerless God," Bonhoeffer wrote, "can help." It is the Crucified One rather than the all-determining Lord who can speak to suffering humanity

Although few have followed Bonhoeffer's rhetoric of divine powerlessness, there has been considerable new reflection on the nature of God's power. Alfred North Whitehead held that God's power is persuasive rather than coercive. That this was true with respect to human beings had long been taught—for example, by Augustine. But in Whitehead's view, to exist at all is to have some measure of self-determination. Hence God's relation to all creatures is persuasive. Wolfhart Pannenberg argues that God is to be thought of as the Power of the Future. God is not now extant as one being alongside others making up the given reality, but rather that which will be all in all. Pannenberg argues that all creative realization in the present comes into being from this divine future. Hence God remains all-determinative, but the mode of this determination is quite different from that against which people have protested for the sake of human freedom. Instead it is God's determination of the present that makes us free.

The association of God with the future, building on the eschatological language of the New Testament, has had other supporters. Whereas for Pannenberg it has ontological meaning, for J. B. Metz and Jürgen Moltmann it is associated with a "political theology," which locates salvation primarily in the public historical realm. It is also central to the "liberation theology" of Rubem Alves, Gustavo Gutierrez, Juan Segundo, and other Latin Americans. These German and Latin American theologians argue that God's will is not expressed in the present structures of society or in some romanticized past, but rather in the promise of something quite different. Hence, the overwhelming tendency of religion to justify and even sanctify existing patterns, or to encourage nostalgia for a lost paradise, is opposed by the prophetic challenge in view of the hoped-for future.

"So act, that the moral of thy doing shall, at thy will, become universal law."

IMMANUEL KANT
THE CATEGORICAL IMPERATIVE

Among these theologians, the image of God has been more important than the concept. Indeed, recognition of the difference between image and concept and of the great importance of image has played a large role in recent thought about God. Blacks then need to image God as black to claim their human and religious identity.

Similarly, although theologians have insisted that God is beyond gender, feminists have had no difficulty showing that the Christian image of God is overwhelmingly male: whereas God's whiteness is clearly not biblical and is rightly rejected in the name of the Bible, God's maleness is biblical. Hence the denial of maleness to God requires a radical approach to scripture. Furthermore, the characteristics attributed to God by even those theologians who have rejected anthropomorphism have usually been stereotypically masculine ideals: omnipotence, impassibility, self-sufficiency. Feminists challenge this whole theological tradition. They divide between those, such as Mary Daly, who believe that the Christian God is inherently and necessarily patriarchal, and hence incompatible with women's liberation, and those, such as Rosemary Ruether and Letty Russell, who believe that the Christian deity is a liberator who can free us also from patriarchalism.

The God of the Qur'an is a transcendent, powerful, and merciful being.

PAGE 340

The diversity of interests that lead to reflection on God witnesses to the continuing importance of the topic. It also produces great confusion. It is not clear that different statements using the word *God* have, any longer, a common topic. In the Christian context, however, one can almost always understand that, despite all the diversity of concepts and imagery, *God* refers to what Christians worship and trust. Further—with a few exceptions, such as Edgar S. Brightman and William James—God is associated with perfection. Part of the confusion lies in the changing ideal. Whereas for many centuries it seemed self-evident to most Christians that the perfect must be all-determining, affected by nothing external to itself, timeless, and completely self-sufficient, that supposition is no longer so evident today. Much of the debate about God is a debate about what we most admire and most desire to emulate.

— JOHN B. COBB, JR.

GOD IN TRADITIONAL MUSLIM RELIGIOUS THOUGHT

From a sociophenomenological viewpoint, in every revealed religion the message written down in the book (or books) held to be sacred has a normative value for the religious thought it generates. Faith, by answering man's religious aspirations, cannot avoid the demands for rationality inherent in the human spirit. Indeed, faith provokes and activates this demand and in so doing positions itself in relation to reason. But in this effort of reflection, the first generations of believers always hesitate, if not refuse, to free themselves from the explicit terms (notions and/or terminology) of the message accepted as revealed. Their work nevertheless retains a preferential and normative value for later generations of believers who would periodically attempt a "return to the source."

HISTORICAL OUTLINE OF THE PROBLEM. The God of the Qur'an is al-'Azim, the Inaccessible (e.g., 2:255, 42:4), well beyond the bounds of human understanding, which cannot limit him in any way or compare him to anything. In his knowledge and by his knowledge alone man cannot reach him "whom one does not question" (21:23; see also 21:110). Consequently, it is not surprising that all the schools devoted long preliminary discussions to what human reason can know of God on its own or on the basis of Qur'anic texts.

The Muslim tradition, always active among the community of believers (the *ummah*), has never ceased to confirm, even to protect, the inaccessibility of God, sometimes to the point of jealousy. The doctors of *kalam (mutakallimun),* or Muslim "theologians," were always obliged to contend with the reticence shown by the "pious elders" or their successors, the traditionists, toward any attempt to justify dogma by purely rational means, and the tension was alternately a source of inspiration and controversy. This reticence, transmitted from one generation to the next within the *ummah,* would manifest itself with particular vigor in Hanbali thought, developed by the great and rigid traditionist Ibn Hanbal (ninth century), whose profession of faith was "The Qur'an and the *sunnah* [Muslim tradition]: that is religion." This tendency would continue to oppose the rationalist or modernist trends that were never totally excluded from Islam any more than from Christianity.

The fundamental reaction of the Muslim faith to the inaccessibility of God and the corresponding intellectual attitude is nonetheless not one of narrowmindedness or intellectual laziness. On the contrary, it rejects a passive and meaningless acceptance of the revealed message and the facile recourse to *taqlid* (acquiescence to accepted opinions), even though the majority of the Hanabilah make *taqlid* the conscious imitation of the Prophet and his companions, who believed without looking for "proofs." It calls instead for a personal effort of enquiry, but one that is always based on the intangible letter of the Qur'an and on the *sunnah.* The ultimate aim of this quest is always to better align the behavior of the believer to the "correct path" that God wishes him to take (e.g., 1:6-7, 37:118). A remarkable example of this attitude is found in the person of the famous Hanbali Ibn Taymiyah (fourteenth century), whose successors the contemporary "orthodox reformers" claim to be.

The concept of divine inaccessibility, uncompromising and absolute as it may be, does not isolate God in an abstract heaven. It is the expression of a separate and separating transcendence in the sense that the intimate life of God remains a guarded mystery. This does not mean, however, that God is distinct from and indifferent to humans. In studying the Qur'anic preaching on God, have we not seen that every affirmation concerning his existence, his perfections, or his means of action toward his creatures was merely a repetition of the unformulated mystery of divine unity-unicity presented in ever renewed expression through the style and rhythm of Qur'anic Arabic? At the same time, each affirmation communicated to man what he needed to know to glorify God on earth and to be worthy of paradise in the hereafter. Thus Muslim faith creates in the souls of true believers an attitude of total and confident surrender *(islam)* to God, whom they know, on his word, to be a reliable, omnipotent, and benevolent guide (as in surah 93).

In Islam the Qur'an is presented and received as the Word revealed by a God who reveals nothing of himself. God imparts no confidence about his mystery. He "stood in majesty on the highest horizon" when the Prophet "approached him to within two bow-lengths"—woe to him who attempts to go further, to receive from on high the Qur'anic revelation in its literal form (see 53:1-10). The problems of exegesis *(tafsir)* would consequently take on a singular importance for two basic reasons. On the one hand there was a lack of any doctrinal authority to give the guaranteed meaning of what had been supernaturally "dictated." On the other the problems of exegesis exist in their own right. How can one understand and interpret the revealed words to grasp the thought of "he who spoke"?

THE EXISTENCE OF THE UNIQUE GOD. According to Qur'anic teaching, man has no excuse for not knowing how to affirm the existence of God. On one hand he carries from birth the mark of the *mithaq* like a seal affixed to his heart. This innate predisposition to Islam, traditionally called *fitrah,* appears as a kind of primordial natural religion that finds its fulfillment only in *shahadah.* On the other, "in creation . . . there are truly signs for those who have intelligence" (3:190-191). This does not mean that faith is merely the outcome of a process of metaphysical reasoning using the principle of causality and the analogousness of being to arrive at an Aristotelian "prime mover." Man must learn to recognize the "signs of God" in the "signs of the universe." Faith appears then as a flash of recognition, revitalizing the *mithaq* in the heart of man attracted by the beauties of creation and tempted to go no further in spite of the signs that God has given through them. Man sees the impermanence of the transient world both in and through this dazzling revelation. Muslim thought would always affirm that human reason can and must decipher the "signs of the universe." It would take Abraham's faith as a starting point for a "proof" of God's existence. This was a proof by allusion that, under the influence of Greek thought and logic, would become demonstrative through an argument combining the concept of a beginning in

"In the name of God, the All-merciful, the Compassionate Master of the Day of Judgment You alone do we worship."

PAGE 567

LEARNING QUR'AN

These Muslim children are learning the Qur'an which teaches that they must recognize the signs of God in the signs of the universe.

EARL KOWALL/CORBIS

time and that of the contingency of the world (proof *a novitate/a contingentia mundi).*

The Mu'tazili schools taught that, starting from creation, human intelligence can and must rise to the affirmation of God even without the help of a new explicit revelation (the Qur'anic preaching) to make this obligatory. This was to be done by inference, by a dialectic grasp of opposition—an intellectual process that parallels the gift of faith to Abraham but comes about by means of the two-stage reasoning so characteristic of Arab-Muslim thought. The responsibility, or the honor, of giving form to this demonstration of the

THE DIVINE ATTRIBUTES

The Essence of God

The appellations and actions ascribed to God by the Qur'anic teaching incited the intelligence of believers to attribute perfections to him. The list of divine attributes was formed even before the birth of the schools of *kalam.* This list would remain effectively unchanged since the *sifat* have, and can have, only one source, the Qur'an. No attribute can be affirmed that is not taught in the Qur'an, either directly or by way of immediate consequence *(tafwid).*

Scholastic disputes would begin with the efforts of the doctors of *kalam* to systematize to some degree the data provided by the Qur'an. These debates would center principally on the meaning of the attributes of God. At the same time they would deal with the reality of the *sifat* and, by extension, the relationship of the latter to the divine essence and/or whether these *sifat* were eternal or not. With time these debates would become increasingly technical and sterile (logic, philology, and so forth) and would lose their appeal even within the Islamic world; consequently I shall allude to them here only in very brief fashion.

1. *Attribute of the essence.* Existence, the attribute consubstantial with the essence, was the positive term expressing the essence without adding any other significance. This was *dhat Allah,* the "self" of God bearing neither comparison with nor analogy to the essence of perishable things. This was his existence *(wujud).*
2. *"Essential" attributes.* These were subdivided into two groups. First came the negative attributes (eternity, everlastingness, dissimilarity from the created, subsistence through himself) that underline divine transcendence and consequently manifest that God has neither equal nor opposite of any sort. Second were the *ma'ani* attributes that "add a concept to the essence." They are not identical to the essence but are not other than it (in a separated or separating way). Some are *'aqliyat,* "rational" (power, will, knowledge, life); the others are *sam'iyat,* "traditional." These latter cannot be grasped by human reason and can only be known by the Qur'anic teaching. Among this group we can mention seeing, hearing, speech, visibility, and perception; their exact meaning has been keenly disputed by the Mu'tazilah and Ash'ariyah.
3. *Attributes of "qualification."* These are the divine names or the *ma'ani* attributes in the verbal form (present participle), such as possessing power, willing, and so forth.
4. *Attributes of action.* These do not intrinsically qualify the essence, but designate what God can do or does not do (creation, command, predetermination, and so on). The schools differed in their view of the relationship of these attributes with knowledge and will; the Ash'ariyah were usually more "voluntarist," the Maturidiyah more "intellectualist."

The "pious elders" had already affirmed several attributes without providing any reasoning, just as they had affirmed the existence of God, both by punctiliously respecting the letter of the Qur'an and by accepting that the divine names were synonyms. However, their fundamentalist attitude with regard to the text of the Qur'an came into conflict with the ambiguities and anthropomorphisms of the *mutashabih* verses. This led them into contradiction, even to the point of being open to the accusation of comparing God to his creatures. Particularly aware of the purity of any affirmation concerning God, the Mu'tazilah, who saw themselves as "the people of justice and *tawhid,"* submitted the divine attributes to a severe critique. They rejected by the practice of *tanzih* "distancing" all that evoked the created, supporting themselves by those passages in the Qur'an that invite such an interpretation (e.g., 6:103, 42:9). Finally, this "stripping away" of the attributes *(ta'til)* by a rigorous *via remotionis* tends to weaken the notion of them and to compromise their reality in God. Purified in this way, the attributes exist in God but are identical with the essence. This double affirmation rests on a distinction that can hardly be anything but nominal.

— LOUIS GARDET

TRANSLATED FROM FRENCH BY RICHARD SCOTT

existence of God *a contingentia mundi* and of giving it a more easily transmitted probative value would fall to the great *falasifah* who had adopted Aristotelian formal logic, such as al-Farabi and Ibn Sina.

The Ash'ari school on the contrary, and al-Ghazali after them, took the position that the (real) capacity of reason can be exercised only if revelation makes this an obligation without which man could not escape the trivialities of the world. For the followers of al-Maturidi reason can in principle exercise this power, but in reality it also requires the authentic signs that the Qur'anic verses constitute: by divine benevolence these correspond to the "signs of the universe" (the same word, *ayat,* designates both "signs"). We can see how such positions, each in its own way, maintain or restore the primacy of Qur'anic teaching over reason (in its approach and its arguments).

These scholastic disputes can appear tedious, and indeed, they sometimes are. I shall conclude by quoting Louis Massignon's remark at the end of his study on salvation in Islam: "God is not within the reach of man. Man should not be allowed to try to reach God. An abyss separates us from him. Thus emerge the strictness and intransigence of a monotheistic faith among a people to whom prophets have come to remind men that God is separate from them and inaccessible to them. Indeed faith, pure faith, is without doubt the only gift worthy of being offered to him." This is truly what is shown by those pious believers whose submission *(islam)* to the commands of the Law is the basis of a total surrender to God through an act of trust that does not question.

— LOUIS GARDET

TRANSLATED FROM FRENCH BY RICHARD SCOTT

GOSPEL

THE SEPTUAGINT. In the Septuagint (a Greek translation of the Hebrew scriptures), the verb *euaggelizein,* cognate with *euaggelion,* is commonly used in the profane sense with the meaning "to announce."

The notion of the bearer of the good news of salvation persisted in both Hellenistic and Palestinian Judaism (see the Targum on *Isaiah* 40:9 as well as 1QM 18:14 from among the Dead Sea Scrolls). The mid-first-century *Psalms of Solomon* (11:1-2) uses *euaggelizein* in the eschatological sense, while in post-biblical Judaism *bsr* and its cognate verb refer not only to concrete historical news but also to prophetic messages of weal and woe, angelic messages, and divine announcements of consolation and blessing.

NEW TESTAMENT. Within the New Testament, *euaggelion* is used far more frequently by Paul than by any other author. His writings are the first literary attestation to the Christian usage of the term. To some authors this suggests that Paul first gave a Christian connotation to the term *euaggelion,* while to others it implies that Paul had taken over an earlier Christian usage. In any event, there is little doubt that the term acquired its Christian significance in a Hellenistic environment.

Paul. In the Pauline letters two passages confirm the thesis that Paul has taken over the absolute use of *euaggelion* from early Christian usage. The passages in question are *1 Corinthians* 15:1-4 and *Romans* 1:1-4. In his first letter to the Corinthians, Paul uses classic language to describe the handing on of traditional teaching and employs *euaggelion* to identify the content of that teaching. Paul explicates the content of the *euaggelion* by citing a creedal formula, probably derived from Palestinian Christian circles, that focuses on the death and resurrection of Jesus. In the opening verses of the letter to the Romans, the content of the gospel is the disclosure of Jesus as the Son of God and our Lord by his resurrection from the dead. Thus, for Paul, the basic content of the gospel is the resurrection by means of which Jesus is constituted as Lord.

Mark. Both in understanding of the term *euaggelion* and in frequency of its usage (seven times), Mark is similar to Paul. Mark, however, uses only *euaggelion,* the noun, and not the related verb. For Mark, *euaggelion* is a technical expression used to denote the kerygmatic announcement of salvation. Jesus is the subject of the gospel insofar as he proclaimed the coming of the kingdom of God (*Mk.* 1:15). When proclamation occurs, that which is proclaimed becomes a reality. Accordingly, the activity of Jesus became the object of the gospel. Mark editorializes on the tradition he has incorporated into his work in order to affirm that the gospel relates to that which has been done in and through Jesus.

Matthew and Luke. Neither Matthew nor Luke employs *euaggelion* so frequently as does Mark, and the Johannine literature does not use the term at all. Matthew uses the term four times but never without further qualification. He writes of "the gospel of the kingdom" (*Mt.* 4:23, 9:35), of "this gospel" (*Mt.* 26:13), and of "this gospel of the kingdom" (*Mt.* 24:14). In all four instances Matthew uses *euaggelion* in relation to a speech complex. For him Jesus is no longer the content of the gospel; instead, he is the communicator of the gospel. The speeches of Jesus are "gospels." Matthew's emphasis is on Jesus' preaching and teaching as providing a paradigm for the Christian way of life.

Luke does not use *euaggelion* at all in the first part of his written work, but it appears twice in *Acts* (15:7, 20:24). Nonetheless, Luke employs the verb *euaggelizomai* ("I bring the good news") frequently both in his

To meet the needs of worship and study, the populous hellenized Jewish community of Alexandria produced a Greek translation of the Hebrew Bible known as the Septuagint.

PAGE 71

"This good news of the Kingdom will be proclaimed throughout the world."

MATTHEW 24:14

gospel (ten times) and in Acts (fifteen times). By doing so, Luke emphasizes the act of preaching, which is then explained by the direct object that accompanies the verb.

THE WRITTEN GOSPEL. Even when *euaggelion* came to be applied to a written text, the word continued to be employed in the singular, and this use of the singular was still widespread in the third century. The usage bespeaks the conviction that the gospel was identical with the teaching of the Lord. This usage is reflected in the formulaic expression "the Lord says in the gospel" (e.g., *2 Clem.* 8:5), but it is also reflected in the titles of the Gospels. The earliest parchment codices of the New Testament, namely, the fourth-century Sinaiticus and Vaticanus codices, entitle the Gospels "according to Matthew," "according to Mark," and so on. This manner of providing each of the written gospels with a title suggests that *euaggelion* applied to the whole collection of the four canonical gospels. Nonetheless, three of the early New Testament papyri have made use of more complete titles: *Gospel According to Matthew* (P^4) and *Gospel According to John* (P^{66}, P^{75}). Even this is a strange turn of phrase if the sole intention is to designate authorship. These titles seem to suggest that the single gospel was narrated according to the vision of a specific evangelist. There was only one message of final, eschatological salvation, namely, salvation accomplished through the death and resurrection of Jesus, but the message could be conveyed in different ways.

The transference of *euaggelion* from the designation of an oral proclamation to a written text—a usage that most probably derives from the first verse of Mark—attests that these texts had the same content and purpose as the oral proclamation. Both the oral proclamation of the gospel and the written gospel speak of eschatological salvation accomplished in the life and death of Jesus of Nazareth.

— RAYMOND F. COLLINS

GREEK ORTHODOX CHURCH

In the modern and ethnic sense, Greek Orthodoxy is understood to include those churches whose language, liturgy, and spirit keep Orthodoxy and the Greek ethnic cultural tradition united.

THE CHURCH OF GREECE. Prior to the Greek War of Independence, which began in 1821, Christianity in what is now known as Greece was, for most of its history, part of the ecumenical patriarchate of Constantinople. Even though the church was self-declared autocephalous in 1833, it understands itself to be in direct continuity with the founding of Christianity in Thessalonica, Phillipi, Corinth, Athens, Nicopolis, and other Greek cities by the apostle Paul. Following the early period, when metropolitan sees had been established in the major cities, Greece came under Constantinople, where it stayed—with a few interruptions—until the nineteenth century. Originally, the autocephalous Church of Greece included only the southern part of the modern nation of Greece, since only that area was liberated in 1830. Over the years, as the Greek nation expanded, the church also grew in territorial size and numbers. But this equation of the boundaries of the state and the jurisdiction of the Church of Greece is not absolute. Several areas of the nation of Greece are ecclesiastically under the control of the ecumenical patriarchate: the Dodecanese, Crete, and Mount Athos.

THE PATRIARCHATE OF CONSTANTINOPLE. In 1955, after years of general harassment, government-inspired riots wrought havoc on the Greek community of Istanbul, including churches. Economic and administrative pressures forced a large part of the Greek Orthodox population to leave the last remaining enclave of Greek Orthodoxy in Turkey. Only a few thousand now remain, as the patriarchate clings to its legal rights to remain in its historic city. The patriarchate's numerical strength resides in the numerous Greek Orthodox dioceses, or "eparchies," within its jurisdiction in the diaspora. In addition to four eparchies in Turkey, the Patriarchate of Constantinople exercises jurisdiction over local and national members.

THE PATRIARCHATE OF ALEXANDRIA. Egypt was one of the first areas to come under the influence of Islam in the eighth century. Nevertheless, the Greek Orthodox patriarchate of Alexandria continued to exist in Egypt throughout the centuries. Even though the numerical strength of the Greek Orthodox patriarchate in Egypt was broken with the rise of Gamal Abdel Nasser in 1954, the patriarchate continued to serve about 350,000 (1980s figures) Orthodox Christians.

THE PATRIARCHATE OF JERUSALEM. In 1517 the area came under the control of the sultan in Constantinople while the church continued to struggle to maintain its rights to the holy places of Jerusalem. Changing political circumstances in the area have required the negotiation of agreements regarding the status of the patriarchate with the British, Jordanians, and Israelis. At the beginning of the 1980s, the patriarchate counted eighty thousand members with sixteen bishops.

THE CHURCH OF CYPRUS. The Church of Cyprus, consisting exclusively of Greek Cypriots, received its independence as an autocephalous church through the eighth canon of the Council of Ephesus (431), but its history goes back to New Testament times (*Acts* 11:19). The Orthodox church is very close to the people of Cyprus, especially since the 1974 Turkish invasion of the island nation when almost half of its members were made refugees in their own land. In 1985, the Church of Cyprus counted more than 440,000 members with six dioceses, seven bishops, and twelve hundred priests.

THE GREEK ORTHODOX DIASPORA. The Greek Orthodox Christians found throughout the world today in traditionally non-Orthodox lands are primarily under the jurisdiction of the Patriarchate of Constantinople.

— STANLEY SAMUEL HARAKAS

GREEK RELIGION

MYTHOLOGY AND RELIGION

As adults, the Greeks learned about the world of the gods through the voices of the poets. The rise of a written narrative tradition modified and preserved the very ancient tradition of oral poetry and came to occupy a central place in the social and spiritual life of Greece. Had it not been for all the works of the epic, lyrical, and dramatic poetry, we could speak of Greek cults in the plural instead of a unified Greek religion.

The scholars of the Renaissance, as for the great majority of the scholars of the nineteenth century, agreed that Greek religion was, above all, an abundant treasure of legendary tales transmitted to us by the Greek authors (assisted by the Romans) in which the spirit of paganism remained alive long enough to offer the modern reader in a Christian world the surest path to a clear view of ancient polytheism.

In the fifth century, work was begun that would be systematically pursued in essentially two directions. First, chroniclers undertook the collection and inventory of all the legendary oral traditions peculiar to a city or a sanctuary. Like the atthidographs of Athens, these scholars attempted to set down in writing the history of a city and its people from its earliest beginnings, going back to the fabulous time when the gods mingled with men. Parallel to this effort, which aimed at a systematic summary of the legends common to all Greeks, there became apparent a certain hesitation and uneasiness—already perceptible among the poets—about how much credit should be accorded to the scandalous episodes that seemed incompatible with the eminent dignity of the divine. But it was with the development of history and philosophy that interrogation reached full scale; from then on criticism assailed myth in general. Subjected to the investigations of the historian and the reasonings of the philosopher, the fable, as fable, was deemed incompetent to speak of the divine in a valid and authentic fashion. Yet, from one point of view, no matter if the ancients were carefully collecting myths, if they interpreted or criticized them or even rejected them in the name of another, truer kind of knowledge—it all came down to recognizing the role generally assigned to myths in the Greek city-state, namely, to function as instruments of information about the otherworld.

During the first half of the twentieth century, however, historians of Greek religion took a new direction. Many refused to consider the legendary traditions as strictly religious documents that could be useful as evidence of the real state of the beliefs and feelings of the faithful. For these scholars, religion lay in the organization of the cult, the calendar of sacred festivals, the liturgies celebrated for each god in his sanctuaries.

Today, the rejection of mythology is based on an anti-intellectualist presumption in religious matters. Scholars of this standpoint believe that behind the diversity of religions—just as beyond the plurality of the gods of polytheism—lies a common element that forms the primitive and universal core of all religious experience. This common element is placed, therefore, outside of intelligence, in the sacred terror that man feels each time he is compelled to recognize, in its irrecusable strangeness, the presence of the supernatural. Such awe would be the basis of the earliest cults, the diverse forms taken by the rites answering, from the same origin, to the multiplicity of circumstances and human needs.

Similarly, it is supposed that behind the variety of names, figures, and functions proper to each divinity, a ritual brought into play the same general experience of the divine, considered a suprahuman power *(kreitton).* This indeterminate divine being (Gr., *theion*, or *daimonion*), underlying the specific manifestations of particular gods, took diverse forms according to the desires and fears to which the cult had to respond. From this common fabric of the divine, the poets, in turn, cut singular characters; they brought them to life, imagining for each a series of dramatic adventures in what Festugière does not hesitate to call a "divine novel." On the other hand, for every act of the cult, there is no other god but the one invoked. From the moment he is addressed, "in him is concentrated all divine force; he alone is considered. Most certainly, in theory he is not the only god since there are others and one knows it. But in practice, in the actual state of mind of the worshiper, the god invoked supplants at that moment all the others" (Festugière, 1944, p. 50).

THE WORLD OF THE GODS

Greek religion presents an organization so complex that it excludes recourse to a single reading code for the

Germanic myth evinces a real fear of this no-man's-land outside the settlement. with the god serving to ward off dangers from the wild.

PAGE 231

entire system. To be sure, a Greek god is defined by the set of relationships that unite him with or put him in opposition to other divinities of the pantheon, but the theological structures thus brought to light are too numerous and, especially, too diverse to be integrated into the same pattern. According to the city, the sanctuary, or the moment, each god enters into a varied network of combinations with the others. Groups of gods do not conform to a single model that is more important than others; they are organized into a plurality of configurations that do not correspond exactly but compose a table with several entries and many axes, the reading of which varies according to the starting point and the perspective adopted.

Take the example of Zeus. His name clearly reveals his origin, based on the same Indo-European root (meaning "to shine") as Latin *dies/deus* and the Vedic *dyeus*. Like the Indian Dyaus Pitr or the Roman Jupiter (Iovpater), Father Zeus (Zeus Pater) is the direct descendant of the great Indo-European sky god. However, the gap between the status of the Zeus of Greece and that of his corresponding manifestations in India and in Rome is so evident, so marked, that even when comparing the most assuredly similar gods one is compelled to recognize that the Indo-European tradition has completely disappeared from the Greek religious system.

ZEUS ON THE THRONE

In the Greek religious system, Zeus is the celestial and judicious supreme power, the founder of order, guarantor of justice, governor of marriage, father, ancestor, and patron of the city.

CHRISTEL GERSTENBERG/CORBIS

Celestial and judicious wielder of supreme power, founder of order, guarantor of justice, governor of marriage, father and ancestor, and patron of the city, the tableau of the sovereignty of Zeus includes still other dimensions. His authority is domestic as well as political. In close connivance with Hestia, Zeus has supreme control not only over each private hearth—that fixed center where the family has its roots—but also over the common household of the state in the heart of the city, the Hestia Koine, where the ruling magistrates keep watch. Zeus Herkeios, the god of the courtyard and the household, circumscribes the domain within which the head of the house has the right to exercise his power; Zeus Klarios, the divider of estates, delineates and sets boundaries, leaving Apollo and Hermes in charge of protecting the gates and controlling the entries.

The different epithets of Zeus, wide as their range may be, are not incompatible. They all belong to one field and emphasize its multiple dimensions. Taken together, they define the contours of divine sovereignty as conceived by the Greeks; they mark its boundaries and delimit its constituent domains; they indicate the various aspects that the power of the king-god may assume and exercise in more or less close alliance (according to circumstances) with the other divinities.

THE CIVIC RELIGION

Between the eleventh and eighth centuries, technical, economic, and demographic changes led to what the English archaeologist Anthony Snodgrass called the "structural revolution," which gave rise to the city-state *(polis)*. The Greek religious system was profoundly reorganized during this time in response to the new forms of social life introduced by the *polis*. Within the context of a religion that from then on was essentially civic, remodeled beliefs and rites satisfied a dual and complementary obligation. First of all, they fulfilled the specific needs of each group of people, who constituted a city bound to a specific territory. The city was placed under the patronage of its own special gods, who endowed it with a unique religious physiognomy. Every city had its own divinity or divinities, whose functions were to cement the body of citizens into a true community; to unite into one whole all the civic space, including the urban center and the *chora*, or rural area; and to look after the integrity of the state—the people and the land—in the presence of other cities. Second, the development of an epic literature cut off from any local roots, the construction of great common sanctuaries, and the institution of pan-Hellenic games and panegyrics established and reinforced, on a religious level, legendary traditions, cycles of festivals, and a pantheon that would be recognized equally throughout all of Hellas.

Without assessing all the religious innovations brought about during the Archaic period, the most important should be mentioned. The first was the emergence of the temple as a construction independent of the human habitat, whether houses or royal palaces. With its walls delimiting a sacred enclosure *(temenos)* and its exterior altar, the temple became an edifice separated from profane ground. The god came to reside there permanently through the intermediacy of his great anthropomorphic cult statue. Unlike domestic altars and private sanctuaries, this house of the god was the common property of all citizens.

Another innovation with partly comparable significance left its mark on the religious system. During the eighth century, it became customary to put into service Mycenaean buildings, usually funerary, that had been abandoned for centuries. Once they were fitted out, they served as cult places where funeral honors were rendered to legendary figures who, although they usually had no relationship to these edifices, were claimed as ancestors by their "progeny," noble families or groups of phratries. Like the epic heroes whose names they carried, these mythical ancestors belonged to a distant past, to a time different from the present, and constituted a category of supernatural powers distinct from both the *theoi,* or gods proper, and the ordinary dead. Even more than the cult of the gods (even the civic gods), the cult of heroes had both civic and territorial value. It was associated with a specific place, a tomb with the subterranean presence of the dead person, whose remains were often brought home from a distant land.

The spread of the cult of the hero did not just comply with the new social needs that arose with the city; the adoration of the heroes had a properly religious significance. Different from the divine cult, which was obligatory for everyone and permanent in character, and also from the funerary rites, which were limited in time as well as to a narrow circle of relatives, the heroic institution affected the general stability of the cult system.

For the Greeks, there was a radical opposition between the gods, who were the beneficiaries of the cult, and men, who were its servants. Strangers to the transience that defines the existence of men, the gods were the *athanatoi* ("the immortals"). Men, on the other hand, were the *brotoi* ("the mortals"), doomed to sickness, old age, and death.

The heroes were quite another matter. To be sure, they belonged to the race of men and thus knew suffering and death. But a whole series of traits distinguished them, even in death, from the throng of ordinary dead. The heroes had lived during the period that constituted the "old days" for the Greeks, a bygone era when men were taller, stronger, more beautiful. Thus the bones of a hero could be recognized by their gigantic size. It was this race of men, later extinct, whose exploits were sung in epic poetry. Celebrated by the bards, the names of the heroes—unlike the names of ordinary men, which faded into the indistinct and forgotten mass of the nameless—remained alive forever, in radiant glory, in the memory of all the Greeks. The race of heroes formed the legendary past of the Greece of the city-states and the roots of the families, groups, and communities of the Hellenes.

Although it did not bridge the immeasurable gulf that separates men from the gods, heroic status seemed to open the prospect of the promotion of a mortal to a rank that, if not divine, was at least close to divinity. However, during the entire Classical period, this possibility remained strictly confined to a narrow sector. It was thwarted, not to say repressed, by the religious system itself. Indeed, piety, like wisdom, enjoined man not to pretend to be the equal of a god; the precepts of Delphi—"know who you are, know thyself"—have no other meaning than that. Man must accept his limits. Therefore, apart from the great legendary figures, such as Achilles, Theseus, Orestes, and Herakles, the status of the hero was restricted to the first founders of the colonies or to persons, such as Lysander of Samos and Timoleon of Syracuse, who had acquired exemplary symbolic worth in the eyes of a city.

The appearance of the hero cult, however, was not without consequences. By its newness it led to an effort to define and categorize more strictly the various supernatural powers. Plutarch noted that Hesiod was the first, in the seventh century, to make a clear distinction between the different classes of divine beings, which he divided into four groups: gods, daemons, heroes, and the dead. Taken up again by the Pythagoreans and by Plato, this nomenclature of the divinities to whom men owed veneration was common enough in the fourth century to appear in the requests that the consultants addressed to the oracle of Dodona. On one of the inscriptions that have been found, a certain Euandros and his wife question the oracle about which "of the gods, or heroes, or daemons" they must sacrifice to and address their prayers to.

"From Zeus, let us begin whom we mortals never leave unnamed."

ARATUS
PHAENOMENA

THE SACRIFICIAL PRACTICES

To find his bearings in the practice of the cult, the believer, therefore, had to take into account the hierarchical order that presided in the society of the beyond. At the top of the hierarchy were the theoi, both great and small, who made up the race of the blessed immortals. These were the Olympians, grouped under the authority of Zeus. As a rule they were celestial divinities, although some of them, such as Poseidon and Demeter, bore chthonic aspects. There was indeed a god of the underworld (Hades), but he was in fact the only one who had neither temple nor cult. The gods

Greek temples were not congregational buildings. The congregation (which at the chief festivals of major cults was very large, to be counted in tens of thousands) gathered round the altar.

PAGE 662

were made present in this world in the spaces that belonged to them: first of all, in the temples where they resided but also in the places and the objects that were consecrated to them and that, specified as *hiera* ("sacred"), could be subject to interdiction. These include the sacred groves, springs, and mountain peaks; an area surrounded by walls or boundary markers *(temenos);* crossroads, trees, stones, and obelisks. The temple, the building reserved as the dwelling of the god, did not serve as a place of worship. The faithful assembled to celebrate the rites at the exterior alter *(bomos)*, a square block of masonry. Around it and upon it was performed the central rite of the Greek religion, the burnt offering *(thusia)*, the analysis of which is essential.

This was normally a blood sacrifice implying the eating of the victim: a domestic animal, crowned and decked with ribbons, was led in procession to the altar to the sound of flutes. If accepted, the victim was immediately carved. The long bones, entirely stripped of flesh, were laid on the altar. Covered with fat, they were consumed with herbs and spices by the flames and, in the form of sweet-smelling smoke, rose toward heaven and the gods.

In the Olympian sacrifice, the orientation toward the heavenly divinities was marked not only by the light of day, the presence of an altar, and the blood gushing upward when the throat of the victim was cut. A fundamental feature of the ritual was that it was inseparably an offering to the gods and a festive meal for the human participants. Although the climax of the event was undoubtedly the moment that, punctuated by the ritual cry *(ololugmos)*, life abandoned the animal and passed into the world of the gods, all the parts of the animal, carefully gathered and treated, were meant for the people, who ate them together. The immolation itself took place in an atmosphere of sumptuous and joyful ceremony. The entire staging of the ritual—from the procession in which the untied animal was led freely and in great pomp, to the concealment of the knife in the basket, to the shudder by which the sprayed animal, sprinkled with an ablution, was supposed to give its assent to the immolation—was designed to efface any traces of violence and murder and to bring to the fore aspects of peaceful solemnity and happy festivity.

As the central moment of the cult, the sacrifice was an indispensable part of communal life (whether family or state) and illustrated the tight interdependence of the religious and the social orders in the Greece of the city-states. The function of the sacrifice was not to wrest the sacrificer or the participants away from their families and civic groups or from their ordinary activities in the human world but, on the contrary, to install them in the requisite positions and patterns, to integrate them into the city and mundane existence in conformity with an order of the world presided over by the gods (i. e., "intraworld" religion, in the sense given by Max Weber, or "political" religion, in the Greek understanding of the term). Without any special preparation, every head of a family was qualified to assume religious functions in his home. Each head of a household was pure as long as he had not committed any misdeed that defiled him. In this sense, purity did not have to be acquired or obtained; it constituted the normal state of the citizen.

Sacrifice established man in his proper state, midway between the savagery of animals that devour one another's raw flesh and the perpetual bliss of the gods, who never know hunger, weariness, or death because they find nourishment in sweet smells and ambrosia. This concern for precise delimitations, for exact apportionment, closely unites the sacrifice, both in ritual and in myth, to cereal agriculture and to marriage, both of which likewise define the particular position of civilized man. Just as, to survive, he must eat the cooked meat of a domestic animal sacrificed according to the rules, so man must feed on *sitos,* the cooked flour of regularly cultivated domestic plants. In order to survive as a race, man must father a son by union with a woman, whom marriage has drawn out of savagery and domesticated by setting her in the conjugal home. By reason of this same exigency of equilibrium in the Greek sacrifice, the sacrificer, the victim, and the god—although associated in the rite—were never confused.

GREEK MYSTICISM

Blood sacrifice and public cult were not the only expressions of Greek piety. Various movements and groups, more or less deviant and marginal, more or less closed and secret, expressed different religious aspirations. Some were entirely or partly integrated into the civic cult; others remained foreign to it. All of them contributed in various ways to paving the way toward a Greek "mysticism" marked by the search for a more direct, more intimate, and more personal contact with the gods. This mysticism was sometimes associated with the quest for immortality, which was either granted after death through the special favor of a divinity or obtained by the observance of the discipline of a pure life reserved for the initiated and giving them the privilege of liberating, even during their earthly existence, the particle of the divine present in each.

In this context, a clear distinction must be made between three kinds of religious phenomena during the Classical period. Certain terms, such as *telete, orgia, mustai,* and *bakchoi*, are used in reference to all three, yet the phenomena they designate cannot in any way be considered identical. Despite some points of contact, they were not religious realities of the same order; nor did they have the same status or the same goals.

First, there were the mysteries. Those of Eleusis, exemplary in their prestige and their widespread influence, constituted in Attica a well-defined group of cults. Officially recognized by the city, they were organized under its control and supervision. They remained, however, on the fringe of the state because of their initiatory and secret nature and their mode of recruiting (they were open to all Greeks and based not on social status but on the personal choice of the individual).

Next there was the Dionysian religion. The cults associated with Dionysos were an integral part of the civic religion, and the festivals in honor of the god had their place like any other in the sacred calendar. But as god of *mania,* or divine madness—because of his way of taking possession of his followers through the collective trance ritually practiced in the *thiasoi* and because of his sudden intrusion here below in epiphanic revelation—Dionysos introduced into the very heart of the religion of which he was a part an experience of the supernatural that was foreign and, in many ways, contrary to the spirit of the official cult.

Finally, there was what is called Orphism. Orphism involved neither a specific cult, nor devotion to an individual deity, nor a community of believers organized into a sect as in Pythagoreanism, whatever links might have existed between the two movements. Orphism was a nebulous phenomenon that included, on the one hand, a tradition of sacred books attributed to Orpheus and Musaios (comprising theogonies, cosmogonies, and heterodox anthropogonies) and, on the other, the appearance of itinerant priests who advocated a style of existence that was contrary to the norm, a vegetarian diet, and who had at their disposal healing techniques and formulas for purification in this life and salvation in the next. In these circles, the central preoccupation and discussion focused on the destiny of the soul after death, a subject to which the Greeks were not accustomed.

What was the relationship of each of these three great religious phenomena to a cult system based on the respect of *nomoi,* the socially recognized rules of the city? Neither in beliefs nor in practices did the mysteries contradict the civic religion. Instead, they completed it by adding a new dimension suited to satisfying needs that the civic religion could not fulfill.

— JEAN-PIERRE VERNANT

TRANSLATED FROM FRENCH BY ANNE MARZIN

H

HALAKHAH

STRUCTURE OF HALAKHAH

Halakhah, in the general sense of the word, is the entire body of Jewish law, from scripture to the latest rabbinical rulings. It is a complete system of law governing every aspect of human life. It has been traditionally viewed as wholly rooted in God's revealed will (B. T., *Hag.* 3b) but subject to the ongoing interpretation of the Jewish jurists (B. T., *B. M.* 59b).

In its more specific sense *halakhah* (pl., *halakhot*) refers to those laws that were traditionally observed by the Jewish people as if they were scriptural commandments *(mitsvot)* even though they were nowhere explicitly found in scripture. The term itself, according to Saul Lieberman in *Hellenism in Jewish Palestine* (New York, 1962), seems to refer to the statement of a juristic norm as opposed to actual case law. The task of much rabbinic exegesis, especially during the tannaitic period (c. 70-200 CE), was to show that through the use of proper hermeneutics the *halakhot* could be derived from the text of scripture, especially the Pentateuch.

ORIGINS. Concerning the origins of *halakhah* there are three main theories.

The first, the traditional, rabbinic approach, is founded on the literal meaning of "a law of Moses from Sinai," namely, that Moses received two sets of teachings at Mount Sinai, one written (the Pentateuch) and the other oral *(torah she-be'al peh),* and that the oral Torah is the authoritative explanation of the written Torah (B. T., *Ber.* 5a).

The second theory is that of Moses Maimonides (Mosheh ben Maimon, 1135/8-1204). Although he too reiterated the literal meaning of the totally Mosaic origin of *halakhah,* in his specific treatment of the constitution of halakhic authority he states that *halakhah* is based on scripture and, equally, on the rulings of the Great Court in Jerusalem (*Mishneh Torah,* Rebels 1.1ff.)

The third theory is that of Zacharias Frankel (1801-1875). Expanding certain medieval comments into a more general theory, Frankel, in *Darkhei ha-Mishnah* (Leipzig, 1859), saw the term "a law of Moses from Sinai" as primarily referring to ancient laws that had become widespread in Jewish practice and whose origins were obscure.

SCRIPTURAL EXEGESIS. Because of the Pharisaic and rabbinic emphasis on the essential unity of the written Torah and the *halakhah,* in contradistinction to the Sadducean, which accepted only the former as authoritative (B. T., *Hor.* 4a), an elaborate hermeneutical system was worked out to derive as many of the halakhot as possible from the words of scripture, which was considered normatively unintelligible without the process of specifically relating it to the *halakhah* (B. T., Shab. 31a). This entire process was called *midrash,* literally meaning "inquiry" into scripture.

RABBINIC LAW. In the amoraic period (c. 220-c. 500) there emerged a more clear-cut distinction between laws considered scriptural *(de-oraita')* and laws considered rabbinic *(de-rabbanan).* The difference between scriptural law and rabbinic law by this time was that the latter was considered to be evidently rational. As for scriptural law, despite attempts to discover "reasons for the commandments" *(ta'amei ha-mitsvot),* God's will was considered sufficient reason for it.

Rabbinic law, although occasionally justified by indirect scriptural exegesis *(asmakhta'),* was then usually justified as being for the fulfillment of some religious or social need (B. T., *Ber.* 23b). This developed to such an extent that it was claimed that there were only three rabbinic laws for which no reason could be immediately discerned (B. T., *Git.* 14a). Furthermore, the lines between direct and indirect exegesis were considerably blurred (B. T., *Pes.* 39b). Finally, Rava', a fourth-century Babylonian sage who became the most prominent advocate of rational jurisprudence, indicated that the rabbis actually had more legislative power than even scripture (B. T., *Mak.* 22b).

The question of the extent of scriptural law versus rabbinic law was deeply debated among the medieval Jewish jurists. Maimonides, following the Talmudic opinion that scriptural law is limited to 613 Pentateuchal commandments (B. T., *Mak.* 23b), considered any other laws, whether traditional or formulated through exegesis or rabbinical legislation, as having the status of rabbinic laws *(Sefer ha-mitsvot,* intro., sec. 2). Moses Nahmanides (Mosheh ben Nahman, c. 1194-1270), on the other hand, was of the opinion that anything designated by the rabbis as scriptural law, especially those laws derived hermeneutically in rabbinic literature, has the status of scriptural law. Only those laws specifically designated by the rabbis as rabbinic are to be considered as such. This difference of

"Fear God and keep his commandments: this is the whole duty of man."

SONG OF SOLOMON 12:11

The major tenets of Orthodoxy include the dogma that Jews are obligated to live in accordance with the halakhah as interpreted by rabbinic authority.

PAGE 539

opinion concerning the very character of *halakhah* is philosophical. Maimonides' prime concern seems to have been with the process of legislation, that is, with the ability of the duly constituted authorities to make new laws and repeal old ones. Nahmanides' prime concern seems to have been with a revival of the whole process of rabbinical exegesis. This distinction can be seen in the fact that Maimonides' chief halakhic contribution was that of a highly innovative codifier, whereas Nahmanides' was that of an exegete. This difference of approach can be seen in the Talmud and throughout the history of the *halakhah,* namely, the apodictic approach (B. T., *Nid.* 73a) as contrasted with the expository approach (B. T., *B. M.* 33a).

SYSTEM OF LAW

Halakhah is the entire body of Jewish law, from scripture to the latest rabbinical rulings. This Rabbi is studying the Talmud

CORBIS-BETTMANN

CURRENT ROLE OF HALAKHAH. Although *halakhah* is a system of law governing every aspect of personal and communal life, there is no Jewish community in the world today where *halakhah* is the sole basis of governance. This inherent paradox—namely, a total system of law forced by historical reality to share legal authority with another system of law, if not to be actually subordinate to it—has led to a number of tensions both in the state of Israel and in the Diaspora.

The bulk of rabbinic literature concentrates on how the ordinary Jewish man ought to conduct himself so as to sanctify his life.

PAGE 396

Halakhah in the State of Israel. In the state of Israel, *halakhah,* as adjudicated by the rabbinical courts, is recognized as the law governing all aspects of public Jewish religious ritual and all areas of marriage and divorce. (The same privilege is extended to the respective systems of law of the various non-Jewish religious communities there.) This political arrangement has led to a number of areas of tension. Thus many secularist Israeli Jews object to having to submit in questions of personal and familial status to the authority of religious courts, whose very religious justification they do not accept. This conflict has manifested itself in the demand by many secularist Israelis for civil marriage and divorce in the state of Israel, something that *halakhah* rejects as unacceptable for Jews. Even more profound is the fact that there is a conflict between *halakhah* and Israeli law on the most basic question of

CUSTOM AND THE LAW
The Universally Jewish

Minhag ("custom") basically has three functions.

It is invoked when rabbinic law itself is ambiguous. If there are two reputable opinions as to what a law is, then there are two ways of deciding what is to be done. Either the majority view of the sages is followed (B. T., *Hul.* 11a), or the popular practice of the people is consulted and followed (J. T., *Pe'ah* 8.2, 20c). In the latter situation custom does not establish law but distinguishes between law that is considered normative *(halakhah le-ma'aseh)* and law that is considered only theoretical (*ein morin ken,* J. T., *Yev.* 12.1, 12c).

Custom is considered a valid form of law, supplementing scriptural commandments and formal rabbinical legislation. Certain customs are considered universally Jewish. For example, the Orthodox object to the modern practice of men and women sitting together in non-Orthodox synagogues. Although some have attempted to find formal halakhic objections to it, is actually based on the fact that theretofore the separation of the sexes in the synagogue was undoubtedly universal Jewish custom.

Custom sometimes takes precedence over established Jewish practice even when it has no foundation in *halakhah.* Usually this power of custom was used to rescind privileges the *halakhah* had earlier granted (Elon, 1978, pp. 732ff.). However, sometimes custom even had the power to abrogate, *de facto,* scriptural law. For example, the law that certain portions of slaughtered animals be given to descendants of Aaronic priests irrespective of time and place was not considered binding because of customary neglect.

— DAVID NOVAK

Jewish identity, that is, who is a Jew. According to *halakhah,* anyone born of a Jewish mother or himself or herself converted to Judaism is considered a Jew. According to the Israeli Law of Return (Hoq ha-Shevut), any Jew (with the exception of one convicted of a crime in another country) has the right of Israeli domicile and Israeli citizenship. However, in 1962 in a famous decision the Israeli Supreme Court ruled that Oswald Rufeisen, a Jewish convert to Christianity and a Roman Catholic monk, was not entitled to Israeli citizenship as a Jew because in the popular sense of the term he was not a Jew even though he was one in the technical, halakhic sense. On the other hand, in 1968, in another famous decision, the Israeli Supreme Court ruled that the wife and children of an Israeli Jew, Binyamin Shalit, were not to be considered Jews for purposes of Israeli citizenship because they had not been converted to Judaism, even though they identified themselves as Israeli Jews in the secular sense of the term. In this case, unlike the earlier one, the court accepted a halakhic definition of who is a Jew.

At the present time, furthermore, there is considerable debate in the state of Israel and the Diaspora about what actually constitutes valid conversion to Judaism.

Halakhah in the Diaspora. In the Diaspora, where adherence to *halakhah* is a matter of individual choice in practically every country that Judaism may be freely practiced, there is little ability to enforce the communal authority inherent in the halakhic system itself. This has led to a number of vexing problems. For example, the Talmud empowers a rabbinical court to force a man to divorce his wife for a variety of objective reasons that make normal married life impossible. When Jewish communities enjoyed relative internal autonomy, such enforcement could be carried out regularly. However, today, because of the loss of such communal autonomy, such enforcement is impossible, and many Jewish women, although already civilly divorced and no longer living with their former husbands, are still considered married according to *halakhah* and are unable to remarry because of the refusal of their former husbands to comply with the order of a rabbinical court.

This growing problem in societies where mobility and anonymity are facts of life has led to basically three different approaches. Many in the Orthodox community have attempted to resort to legal measures in the civil courts to force compliance with *halakhah.* In addition to a lack of success heretofore, this has raised, especially in the United States, the constitutional issue of governmental interference in private religious matters. On the other hand, the Conservative movement since 1968 has revived the ancient rabbinical privilege of retroactive annulment (B. T., *Git.* 33a) in cases where it is impossible to obtain a Jewish divorce from the husband. The Reform movement, not being bound by the authority of *halakhah,* accepts a civil divorce as sufficient termination of a Jewish marriage. These three widely divergent approaches to a major halakhic problem are further evidence of the growing divisiveness in the Jewish religious community in both the state of Israel and the Diaspora.

Reconstitution of the Sanhedrin. The only chance for effecting any halakhic unanimity among the Jewish people would be the reconstitution of the Sanhedrin in Jerusalem as the universal Jewish legislature and supreme court. This proposal was actually made by the first minister of religious affairs in the state of Israel, Judah Leib Maimon (1875-1962). However, considering the fact that this reconstitution itself presupposes much of the very unanimity it is to effect, it would seem that it is rather utopian, something the Talmud euphemistically called "messianic *halakhah*" (B. T., *Zev.* 45a).

— DAVID NOVAK

HASIDISM

Hasidism is the common appellation of a Jewish pietistic movement that developed in eastern Europe in the second half of the eighteenth century, became, before the end of that century, a major force in modern Judaism, and has remained as such into the twentieth century.

HISTORY

The history of the early Hasidic movement can be divided into four main periods, each a major step in its development.

1. *The circle of the Besht (c. 1740-1760).* The Besht (Yisra'el ben Eli'ezer) seems to have been in contact with a group of wandering preachers, like himself, who in their homiletics preached a new kind of worship and presented a new conception of the role of the elect in Jewish religion. They were qabbalists, following the main mystical symbols of the Lurianic school but emphasizing the achievements of the individual and his ability to assist his brethren in religious matters. *Devequt* (communion with God) was one of the main subjects they preached, stressing man's ability to attain constant communion with God. It is possible that parallel to the Besht's circle of adherents there were other pietistic groups in some of the major centers of Jewish culture in eastern Europe.

2. *The first Hasidic center in Mezhirich (1760-1772).* After the Besht's death, the leadership of the Hasidic movement was assumed by his disciple, Dov

Orthodox Judaism is the branch of Judaism that adheres most strictly to the tenets of the religious law.

PAGE 538

To the Hasidim, God's nearness implied that life should be lived with joy and enthusiasm.

PAGE 406

Ber of Mezhirich (now Miedzyrzecz, Poland). He held "court" in his home, where many young Jewish intellectuals as well as common people gathered to listen to his sermons. These were transcribed by his disciples and later published in several versions. In this period begins the history of Hasidism as an organized movement, led by an accepted authority.

3. *The disciples of Dov Ber (1773–1812).* This is the most important period, in which Hasidism became a major force within Judaism. Several of Dov Ber's disciples created "courts" like that of their teacher, and led *'edot* ("communities"), around which thousands, and then tens of thousands, of adherents gathered, accepting the leadership of that disciple and making their community an alternative social and religious organization of Jews, distinct from the hegemony of the traditional rabbinate. In this period the Hasidic theory of the tsaddiq was developed and began to shape both Hasidic thought and social organization. At this same time the Hasidim became a distinct group, not only because of the internal development of Hasidism, but also because of the growing opposition to it from the school of Eliyyahu ben Shelomoh Zalman, the "Gaon of Vilna," which published several pamphlets against Hasidic ideology and practice, denouncing them as heretics and excommunicating them, even trying to enlist the help of the Russian government against their leaders. This fierce opposition was motivated both by fears that the Hasidim were going to undermine the traditional Jewish social structure.

It was in this period that Hasidic literature was initially published. The first works were those of Ya'aqov Yosef of Polonnoye, the Besht's greatest disciple, whose voluminous collections of sermons include most of the material we have concerning the teachings of the Besht and Dov Ber. By the beginning of the nineteenth century the Hasidic movement had an organized leadership, prolific literature, well-defined communities and areas of influence, and an established standing in the general framework of Jewish life.

4. *The development of Hasidic "houses" or "lines of succession" (shoshalot).* To a very large extent this process has continued to the present. Many of Dov Ber's disciples served as founders of several Hasidic communities. When their disciples scattered, each established his own "house" and community. The custom of passing Hasidic leadership from father to son or, in some cases, son-in-law, became more and more frequent, until it was universally accepted that the new leader had to be from the family of the previous leader. These "houses" usually bore the names of the towns in which they were established, even after the center was moved to another country—Poland, for instance, where many centers were located in Warsaw before the Second World War—or to another continent such as to the United States or Israel, where many of the centers are today. The history of Hasidism has since fragmented into the separate histories of various houses or schools. Only two of the communities have preserved their specific ideological and organizational profile, remaining distinct from all others, throughout this period—Habad Hasidism, founded by Shne'ur Zalman of Lyady, and Bratslav Hasidism, the followers of Nahman of Brat-slav, the Besht's great-grandson. The rift between Hasidim and their opponents has obtained until this day; most Jews of east European descent belong to family lines of either Hasidim or *mitnaggedim* ("opponents").

SPREAD OF THE MOVEMENT

The persecution by their opponents did not halt the spread of the movement, which gathered momentum and gained new communities and adherents in the end of the eighteenth century and the first half of the nineteenth century. The disciples of Dov Ber and their disciples established the great Hasidic houses. Levi Yitshaq established an important Hasidic community in Berdichev, while Menahem Nahum built the house of Chernobyl, which was continued by his son, Mordechai Twersky, and went on for many generations. Yisra'el of Rizhyn (now Ruzhin, Ukraine), a descendant of Dov Ber, built the Rizhyn-Sadigora house; his four sons who followed him made it into one of the most important and eminent Hasidic communities in Russia. In Poland and Lithuania Hasidism became a major force through the work of Shelomoh ben Me'ir of Karlin and Hayyim Haiqel of Amdur (Indura). Hasidic communities in the Land of Israel were established in Safad and Tiberias by Menahem Mendel of Vitebsk and Avraham ben Aleksander Kats of Kalisz who migrated to the Land of Israel in 1777. In the beginning of the nineteenth century a group of great leaders gave renewed impetus to the spread of Hasidism, among them Ya'aqov Yitshaq ("the Seer of Lublin"), Ya'aqov Yitshaq ben Asher of Pshischa (now Przysucha, Poland), and Avraham Yehoshu'a Heschel of Apt in Moldavia (now Opatow, Poland). Menahem Morgenstern established the great house of Pshischa-Kozk, and Shalom Rokeah the Belz Hasidim. Mosheh Teitelbaum, a disciple of Ya'aqov Yitshaq of Lublin, created the powerful and influential Satmar Hasidism in Hungary. By the middle of the nineteenth century Hasidism was the dominant force in most Jewish communities in eastern Europe, and most Hasidic houses continued their existence and development until the Holocaust.

THEOLOGY AND ETHICS

It is nearly impossible to describe Hasidic theology and ethics as being distinct from previous Jewish ideologies because Hasidic teachers preached their ideas in the form of sermons, which included all layers of earlier

Jewish thought. Almost all the main ideas and trends found in early-eighteenth-century Hebrew homiletical literature also appear in Hasidic thought, and attempts to define specifically Hasidic ideas, or even emphases, usually fail because similar examples can easily be produced from earlier homiletical literature. A second difficulty is that every Hasidic teacher developed his own theology and ethics and his own list of priorities which may distinguish him or his group but could never characterize all the hundreds of teachers and writers who created Hasidic literature. It is unfeasible to generalize from one or a group of Hasidic teachers to the movement as a whole. Every definition is therefore a necessarily subjective one. Thus only a few general outlines, qualified by the preceding statements, can be presented concerning Hasidic theology.

RELATIONSHIP TO LURIANIC QABBALAH. Hasidic theology, like other qabbalistic schools of the eighteenth century, downplayed the most dramatic mythical symbols of Lurianic mysticism, especially that of *shevirat ha-kelim* ("the breaking of the divine vessels"), the description of the catastrophe within the divine world which is the origin of evil, according to Luria. The idea of *tsimtsum* (divine self-contraction) was elaborated by the Hasidim (especially by Dov Ber), but in a completely different manner than in Luria's original thought. Instead of the original Lurianic idea of a mythological catastrophe, the Hasidim presented a theology in which this process was the result of divine benevolence toward the faithful.

The Hasidim also deemphasized the Lurianic concept of *tiqqun* (restoration), the process by which messianic redemption is enhanced by the collective efforts of the Jewish people as a whole; they preferred instead the concept of *devequt* (communion with God), a process of individual redemption by which a person uplifts his own soul into contact with the divine powers.

EXTENT OF MESSIANISM IN HASIDISM. There is an emphasis in Hasidic literature on personal religious achievement rather than on the general, national, and cosmic impact of religious life. The redemptive element, while still strong in Hasidism, often emphasizes the redemption of the individual's soul rather than that of the nation or of the cosmos as a whole. This is a slight departure from Lurianic Qabbalah.

HASIDIC APPROACH TO GOD. In early Hasidic literature there is an emphasis on direct, emotional worship of God and a deemphasis on contact with God through constant study of the Torah and Talmud and diligent observance of the particulars concerning the performance of the *mitsvot.* This does not mean that the Hasidim did not study the Torah or that they disregarded the *mitsvot,* as their opponents often claimed; rather, the Hasidim stressed the importance of mystical contact with God through *devequt,* usually attained while praying but also achieved when a person is working for his livelihood or engaged in any other physical activity.

GOOD AND EVIL. Hasidic teachers, more than non-Ha-sidim, contributed to the development of a conception of the way to fight evil within one's soul. Unlike Lurian theology, Dov Ber of Mezhirich and other Hasidic teachers insisted that evil can and should be overcome by absorbing it, uplifting and making it again a part of goodness, believing that the spiritual stature of the "corrected" or "repentant" evil is higher than that of the elements that were always good.

HASIDISM AS REVIVAL OF TRADITIONAL SPIRITUALITY. The spiritual side of religious life holds a central place in Hasidic teachings, following the traditions of medieval Hebrew ethical and homiletical literature. Great emphasis is placed on the correct qabbalistic intentions in prayers *(kavvanot),* on spiritual repentance, on the love and fear of God, and on social justice and love for fellow men. While very few new ideas on these subjects are to be found in the vast Hasidic literature, the movement undoubtedly represents a revival of these spiritual values within the framework of everyday religious life. In this respect, then, there is no basis to the frequent descriptions of Hasidism as an original phenomenon that changed the face of traditional Judaism; but it can be claimed that the Hasidim collected many spiritualistic ideas and practices from previous Jewish sources and brought them to the foreground of their teachings.

— JOSEPH DAN

HAWAIIAN RELIGION

PRIESTHOODS AND WORSHIP PLACES

The priests, or *kahunas,* who mediated between gods and people, were professional specialists trained, commonly by older kin, in the material techniques and rituals essential for success in their calling. Of the several organized priesthoods, the higher-ranking and stricter order for priests in service to the Ku gods of war and sorcery and the lower and milder order for priests in service to the Lono gods of peace and abundance were given support by the Hawaiian king Kamehameha I (called Kamehameha the Great, 1758?-1819). Each order's high priest, the kahuna-nui, was considered to be its founder's direct descendant and an expert in every branch of religion. The high priest wielded political power by advising the ruler on how to win divine support.

"Depart from evil and do good; seek peace and pursue it."

PSALMS 34:14

In the Hawaiian Islands, sacrifice stands for transformation, communion, and the capacity to reorder what has been disordered.

PAGE 588

Public worship took place at *heiaus,* or open-air religious centers. Only a king or paramount chief could build the most sacred type of *heiau,* where burned human sacrifices were offered to the highest Ku gods. A chief had a religious duty to build these heiaus in which to pray for divine aid for his chiefdom or to give thanks. Each deity had specific requirements as to size, amount, and color of offerings.

MAJOR DEITIES

KANALOA. Called Tangaroa or one of many other cognate names (e.g., Tangaloa, Ta'aroa) elsewhere in Polynesia, Kanaloa was Kane's younger brother. For Hawaiians he was the god of squid and, because of a play on words, also a god of healing (the Hawaiian word *he'e* means both "squid" and "to put to flight").

KANE. Called Tane in southeastern Polynesia, Kane, whose name means "male" or "man," was the most approachable, forgiving, and revered of the four major gods. One worshiper in his prayer would chant, "You and I warm to each other, Kane," and other worshipers would often say, "Life is sacred to Kane." According to more than one myth, Kane, while dwelling on earth with Kanaloa, had plunged his digging stick into the ground to release springs of fresh water to mix with his and Kanaloa's kava (a narcotic drink made from the pounded root of the shrub *Piper methysticum*). The release of fresh water by Kane-of-the-water-of-life, as he was frequently called, was a symbolic sexual act, for the gesture served to fructify the earth.

LONO. The god of two related sources of abundance—peace and seasonal winter storms—Lono (called Rongo or Ro'o in southeastern Polynesia) was also a god of healing. He had numerous *heiaus,* called "houses of Lono," devoted to rainmaking and medical purposes. The Makahiki, the longest ceremonial period, involved everyone in celebrating Lono's annual *(makahiki)* return for four months of the rainy season to preside over rituals for health and ample rain, and over the ritualized collection of taxes, recreation, and release from work. When Captain Cook arrived in 1778, he was greeted as Lono-i-ka-makahiki because he arrived during this period and anchored at the bay called Kealakekua ("the path of the god," i. e., Lono) and because his masted sails resembled the Lono symbol that led the procession of tax collectors and Lono priests on their coastal circuit of the island.

KU AND HINA. There were many gods in the class called Ku (Tu was the southern Polynesian cognate of the name). Hawaiians regarded the Ku gods either as independent gods or as aspects of a single Ku. Usually an epithet attached to the name suggested the special function or distinctive trait of each particular Ku god. The same principle applies to the class of goddesses called Hina (cognates of the name elsewhere in Polynesia are Hine, Sina, and 'Ina). Some Hinas had more than one name. Hina-of-the-moon is also known as Maimed Lono because, according to myth, her husband tore off her leg as she fled to the moon. Pele's sacred name is Hina-of-the-fire, and Lea's other name is Hina-of-the-ohia-growth. (The ohia is a kind of tree.) Ku and Hina, as well as their varied aspects, function as man and wife in daily rites performed by the populace. With his sister-wife Hina (whose name means "prostrate"), Ku ("upright") united the people into a single stock, for Ku and Hina represented the male and female reproductive principles.

THE STATE RELIGION AND ITS DEMISE

At his death in 1819, Kamehameha the Great, who believed his many gods had made him head of a unified feudal kingdom, left a state religion based on the taboo system that protected the *mana* and authority of the gods and their chiefly descendants from spiritual contamination and consequent weakness. That same year, however, Kamehameha's son Liholiho (1797-1824) took power, adopted the title Kamehameha II, and abolished the official religion without replacing it with another. The Ku priests began destroying heiaus and images, and the excited populace followed suit. Some hid their images and worshiped in secret. Not all customs and beliefs vanished: even today, faith in the aumakuas, for example, lingers on.

— KATHARINE LUOMALA

HELLENISTIC RELIGIONS

Whereas religion is never a mere reflex of political, economic, and social conditions, there are periods in history when these factors exert a palpably strong influence on religious thinking. The Hellenistic age was certainly such a period. Its early phase, which began with the conquests of Alexander the Great in 334 BCE and continued with the rule of his successors, brought military and political upheaval to many peoples. When Roman imperialism later became the dominating power, there was greater apparent political stability, and the consciousness of a unified world, which Alexander's victories had furthered, was enhanced.

Culturally this was a world that gave primacy to the Greek language, and Alexander himself, although a Macedonian, was a fervent disseminator of Greek culture. Alexandria largely replaced Athens as the world's cultural capital and gave a Greek form to its glittering artistic and intellectual achievement. Even before this the Greek world was no narrow enclave, for Greek colonies had long since spread to Asia Minor and the Black Sea area, to Egypt and North Africa, and to southern Italy, Sicily, Spain, and Gaul. In the wake of the military thrust, Greek settlements and cities were established in many non-Greek areas.

It was not the brute power of military aggression that brought about the change in outlook. Alexander had a dream of unity.

NEW TRENDS IN STATE-SUPPORTED RELIGION

In spite of the great change in worldview thus effected, the old order was not swept away quickly. The Athenians continued to honor their patron goddess Athena.

A popular feature of the religious life of this age was the great vitality of the associations or clubs formed by adherents of the various cults, with or without the sanction of the state. While these associations were often allowed the use of sacred premises, their main activities were usually convivial and charitable. Naturally the religious element was not ignored, and the name of the patron deity normally appears in records of their proceedings.

A new development that imparted fresh vitality, albeit of dubious sincerity, to the official state worship was the gradual establishment of the cult of the ruler, whether king or emperor. The first clear instance of it in this period was the worship of Alexander the Great as a divine person. In his case it was conspicuously an upshot of religious practices long prevalent in the Eastern countries that he had conquered. In the nations of Mesopotamia the king had regularly been associated with the gods. He had not been defined theologically as a god, but there was an aura of divinity about him.

An aspect of the ruler cult that affected the minds of men was the whole question of divine incarnation. Was it possible to conceive of the divine taking human form? In early Greek thought it is sometimes suggested that the gulf between man and god is not wide and that an affinity exists between them. In the early fifth century BCE Pindar expresses it thus: "Of one stock are men and gods, and from one mother do we draw our breath" *(Nemean Odes* 6.1). Some of the heroes of Greek mythology were deemed to be offspring of mixed unions, the father being divine and the mother moral. Herakles is in this category, for his father was said to be Zeus and his mother the mortal Alkmene, daughter of a king of Mycenae. Zeus was not able to achieve union with her until he disguised himself as a victorious warrior.

Rather different is the process by which historical heroes came to be worshiped after death. Their historicity cannot always be demonstrated, but the likely evolution followed from a lively memory of their deeds. One might rephrase Shakespeare to explain the distinctions enacted: "Some men are born divine, some achieve divinity, and some have divinity thrust upon them." The hero worship that developed among the Greeks outside mythology is akin to the second category; it involved outstanding individuals who by their own merit and fame came to be especially honored after death. The triumphant commander who "liberated" or "saved" a city naturally qualified for special honors akin to those paid to divinity. An early and successful candidate was the Spartan commander Lysander, whose deeds secured for him this type of apotheosis even during his lifetime. But Alexander decisively outshone heroes of such caliber since his deeds encompassed not only the Greek world but much else as well. When his cult was established in Egypt, followed by that of the Ptolemies, several of the new royal divinities were inevitably ill qualified to attract real worship. They might be said to have had divinity thrust upon them automatically.

MAGIC, MYTH, AND MIRACLE

In considering ancient magic, one must avoid any notion of conjuring tricks made possible by sleight of hand or by various illusionary processes. Some charlatans did resort to such stratagems, but the true medium of divine power did not approach his task thus. In the oldest myths of many nations, the creation of the world itself is the result of miraculous divine actions, and the teasing thought of what lay beyond the beginning of things often produced the image of one creator god, who was unbegotten and who had to initiate a process of creation without the help of a spouse.

Removed from the category of gods and heroes was the human purveyor of magic and miracle. At his best he had to be a knowledgeable person. Astrology was often within his professed prowess, and the secrets of astrology were not available to any ignoramus. His attitude to the gods seems to have varied. Respect and devout loyalty characterized him in the role of their chosen instrument. Yet sometimes the magician was expected to compel the gods to act in a certain way, and a number of magical spells are extant in which the gods are fiercely threatened unless they comply. But it was important to use the correct formula and to know the functions and mythology of the deity concerned. In the Hellenistic era magic was especially used for treating disease.

Here the doctrine of demons was often basic. This view regarded all disease as the creation of evil demons. To conquer the disease therefore demanded the defeat

In Greek mythology, diamones (demons) are both evil and good spirits, demons and devils as well as people.

PAGE 203

and expulsion of the baleful spirit that had taken possession of the victim. The magician was expected to announce the name of the hostile power and to order its expulsion in the name of a superior and beneficent power.

This was not, however, the only technique practiced by magicians and priests. Instead of a frontal attack on the demon, a mollifying approach was sometimes adopted, as when insanity was treated by the playing of soft music. A multitude of medical charms have come down to us, and they combine popular medicine with magical rites.

Magic is customarily divided into the categories of "black" and "white," a division that can certainly be applied to the practice of it by the Greeks. In early prototypes, such as Circe and Medea, the two aspects appear. The Homeric Circe, semidivine in origin, is a powerful magician who uses potions and salves and also teaches Odysseus to summon the spirits of the dead. Medea was the outstanding enchantress of the myths used in Greek tragedy. She enabled the Argonauts to get the golden fleece by putting the dragon of Colchis to sleep; moreover, she possessed the evil eye and could make warriors invulnerable. Orpheus was another master of magic. Son of the muse Calliope, he rendered wild beasts spellbound with his music.

GREEK GODS AND GODDESSES

Aglaia	beautiful goddess (one of the three Graces)
Amphitrite	sea goddess
Anteros	god who avenges unrequited love
Aphrodite	goddess of love and beauty
Apollo	god of beauty, poetry, and music
Ares	god of war
Artemis	goddess of the moon
Astraes	goddess of justice
Athena	goddess of wisdom
Atropos	goddess of destiny (one of the three Fates)
Calliope	goddess of epic poetry (one of the Muses)
Clio	goddess of history (one of the Muses)
Clotho	goddess of destiny (one of the three Fates)
Cronus	god of harvests
Cybele	nature goddess
Demeter	goddess of agriculture
Dione	Titan goddess
Dionysus	god of wine
Eos	goddess of dawn
Erato	goddess of lyric and love poetry (one of the Muses)
Eris	goddess of discord
Eros	god of love
Euphrosyne	beautiful goddess (one of the three Graces)
Euterpe	goddess of music (one of the Muses)
Gaea	goddess of the earth
Hebe	goddess of youth
Hecate	goddess of sorcery and witchcraft
Helios	god of the sun
Hephaestus	god of fire
Hermes	god of physicians and thieves; messenger of the gods
Hestia	goddess of the hearth
Hymen	god of marriage
Hyperion	sun god
Hypnos	god of sleep
Iris	goddess of the rainbow
Lachesis	goddess of destiny (one of the three Fates)
Melpomene	goddess of tragedy (one of the Muses)
Mnemosyne	goddess of memory
Momus	god of ridicule
Morpheus	god of dreams
Nemesis	goddess of retribution
Nike	goddess of victory
Nyx	goddess of night
Oceanus	god of waters
Pan	god of woods and fields
Polyhymnia	goddess of sacred poetry (one of the Muses)
Pluto	god of Hades
Plutus	god of wealth
Pontus	sea god
Poseidon	god of the sea
Priapus	god of regeneration
Proteus	sea god
Selene	moon goddess
Terpsichore	goddess of choral dance and song (one of the Muses)
Thalia	beautiful goddess (one of the three Graces); also goddess of comedy and bucolic poetry (one of the Muses)
Thanatos	god of death
Themis	Titan goddess of laws of physical phenomena
Titans	early gods from whom Olympian gods were derived
Triton	demigod of the sea
Urania	goddess of astronomy (one of the Muses)
Zeus	chief of the Olympian gods

In the context of magic and miracle the most remarkable person in the second sophistic movement was undoubtedly Apollonius of Tyana, who lived in the first century CE and came from Cappadocia in Asia Minor. An account of his life, written about 217 CE by another Sophist, Philostratus, presents him as a wandering scholar whose travels embraced Babylon, India, Egypt, and Ethiopia. In spite of his fame, his life was ascetic and disciplined and modeled on Pythagorean ideals. In addition, however, he frequently performed miracles that included acts of healing, magical disappearances, and even raising the dead, deeds that recall the claims made for Jesus of Nazareth.

Another important divinatory method was by oracle. In the Greek tradition the personal mouthpiece of the god of the oracle was the *prophetes,* who might be a man or a woman. He or she was thought to be possessed by a divine power, a process that Plato compared to poetic inspiration. The medium became *entheos* ("full of the god") and was in a state of *ekstasis* ("standing out of oneself"). In the oracles the power of prophecy was linked to special sites and to particular gods. Here a paradox emerges: the Greeks are famed for their rationalism and are regarded as the pioneers of intellectual enquiry and scientific thinking, yet their belief in oracles belies this approach. To some extent, the inconsistency can be explained through social division: the credulous majority trusted oracles while the educated elite evinced skepticism, the latter trend becoming more pronounced in the Hellenistic era, as Plutarch showed in the first and second centuries CE.

The paradox reveals itself to some degree in the figure of Apollo himself. He is the god of light and reason, yet he is the dominant god at Delphi, seat of the most celebrated oracle. In his *Birth of Tragedy,* the philosopher Nietzsche contrasts Apollo and Dionysos, the one representing the cool temper of rationalism, the other the passionate surrender to ecstasy. Certainly this antithesis is at the heart of Greek thinking.

Oracles in other countries were also much frequented, such as that of Zeus Amun in Libyan Siwa, where Alexander had a significant personal experience. Sometimes the questions raised were those of individuals, reflecting the private problems of simple people: a man is anxious to know whether his wife will give him a child, a woman wants to be cured of a disease, someone asks a commercial question about the best use of property, or a man wonders whether the child his wife is carrying is his own.

UNIVERSALISM AND SYNCRETISM

Although Alexander the Great did not establish a world state in the world as then known, his empire transcended the national states and induced a sense of cohesion and interdependence. It was in this era that the word *kosmopolites* ("citizen of the world") came into vogue. It was the Stoics, however, who succeeded in giving to this approach a positive and meaningful basis. Initially they were intellectually indebted to the Cynics, but Zeno of Citium in Cyprus (335-263 BCE) went far beyond them and included a religious interpretation in his cosmopolitanism. According to Zeno the whole universe is governed by divine reason, and men should therefore live in conformity with it and with the order of nature established by it.

It was indeed an age when several "utopias" were written. Plato had set an example with his *Republic.* There were a few practical ventures, too, in utopianism. Alexarchus, brother of King Cassander of Macedonia, after being given some land on the Athos peninsula, built a big city that he called Ouranopolis ("city of heaven"), where the citizens were called Ouranidai ("children of heaven"), and the coinage was adorned with figures of the sun, moon, and stars.

In the context of Stoic philosophy the doctrine of world citizenship was elaborated somewhat by Chrysippus (c. 280-207 BCE), who noted that the word *polis* was given two senses: the city in which one lived; the citizens and the state machinery. Similarly, he argued, the universe is a *polis* that embraces gods and men, the former wielding sovereignty while the latter obey; yet gods and men, for all their difference in status, have a means of contact and converse since they both use reason, which is "law by nature." In the last phrase he is overturning a contrast present in previous political thought. A later Stoic, Panaetius (c. 185-109 BCE), was more pragmatic in his approach. A world state seemed no longer within practical reach, but he continued to believe in the general unity of all mankind. At the same time he restored to the city-state a certain secondary role, admitting its usefulness in a realistic sense while denying its claim to decide in any final sense, matters of right and wrong; such decisions were to remain in the domain of reason and nature.

It thus appears that the idea of being a citizen of the world, vague and ill defined as it often was, came to include, under Stoic inspiration, the religious concept of a ruling divine reason. Although the reality of a world state was missing, the idea of mankind as one community had a powerful spiritual effect.

Whatever the variety of the traditions so freely transmitted in the Hellenistic age, in religious matters there was usually a readiness to acknowledge and respect diverging ways of belief, worship, and ritual. A process that went even beyond this was that of syncretism, a term often hailed as the hallmark of the age. In English and other modern languages the noun denotes the attempted union or reconciliation of diverse or opposite tenets or practices, especially in the philosophy of religion. The usage is also often extend-

"The direction in which education starts a man will determine his future life."

PLATO
THE REPUBLIC

Apollonius reportedly performed even the miracle of raising the dead while he was in Rome.

PAGE 442

Osiris was the ancient Egyptian god of the dead, whose myth was one of the best known and whose cult was one of the most widespread in pharaonic Egypt.

PAGE 215

ed to include the equation or identification of diverse deities and the combination or fusion of their cults, the latter practice being a specifically Hellenistic development. Earlier experience was indeed fully conversant with the equation of deities.

In ancient religions the most thorough process of syncretism in this sense is found in the developed phase of Roman religion, when Roman deities were identified with Greek counterparts—Jupiter with Zeus, Juno with Hera, Venus with Aphrodite, Ceres with Demeter, Mars with Ares, and so on. A simple act of comparison could lead to syncretism of this kind: one community compares its own gods with those of another; when similar powers or functions are recognized, the comparison may lead to identification. Of course, this process is valid only with polytheistic communities since monotheism rejects comparisons. Nor does the process arise when there is no contact between communities and therefore no need to make comparisons, except in instances where a plurality of deities within communities of the same culture invites an equation of functions. This may lead to assimilation and the use of one divine name instead of several. Thus it appears that among the Greek communities there were several forms of the corn mother, but eventually the name of Demeter, best known, was applied to most of them.

In the fifth century BCE the Greek historian Herodotus indulged freely in the kind of syncretism that meant identifying the gods of different nations. In his second book, which deals with Egypt, he consistently identifies the Egyptian Osiris with the Greek Dionysos and the Egyptian Isis with the Greek Demeter. Probably this was prompted only by recognition of their similar functions, although he does refer to festivals. Later, however, in Hellenistic times, the cults of these deities influenced one another. Isis, for example, was often depicted with ears of wheat on her headdress in a manner traditionally associated with Demeter, while ivy, the plant of Dionysos, figured in the rites of Osiris.

Increasingly in Hellenistic times, the cults of Oriental deities were introduced to the cities of the Greek world and Italy. Such a procedure had been very difficult, and indeed dangerous, in previous ages, for the orgiastic nature of some of these cults was much feared, and all public cults were rigidly controlled by the state. But a radical change of attitude came in Hellenistic times. State control remained, but often it now actively supported foreign cults, as for instance the cult of Dionysos in Ptolemaic Egypt.

Usually the Greeks raised a temple in honor of one particular deity, as Athena was honored in the Parthenon at Athens, Zeus in the great temple at Olympia, and Apollo in his temples at Delphi and Delos. Yet it was very natural that associated deities, especially those connected in myth, legend, and cult, should be represented and worshiped in the same temple. Thus Artemis was honored with Apollo as his twin sister, just as Hadad was honored with the Syrian goddess Atargatis as her consort.

Popular religious practice and belief are undoubtedly best reflected in inscriptions, whether in temples, on tombstones, or on amulets, and in magical incantations. Often the gods of different countries are named together in dedications and formulaic expressions of thanksgiving. This is also true of inscriptions that are official and public in character. Thus, in an inscription dated between 50 and 35 BCE, Antiochus I of Commagene, a small kingdom north of Syria, presents an exposition of his religion. He begins by calling himself "the God, the righteous God" and "friend of Romans and Greeks," and then declares that he has made his kingdom "the common dwelling place of all the gods." He alludes to the ancient doctrine of Persians and Greeks and refers with reverence to Zeus-Oromasdes, to Apollo-Mithra-Helios-Hermes, and to Artagnes-Herakles-Ares. This showpiece of syncretism contains an element of political expediency: the king is eager to pander to both Romans and Greeks (the Seleucid rulers); his religion is basically Iranian but with Greek embellishments.

One of the results of syncretism in religion was a sense of tolerance and sympathy. People who are ready to borrow from other religions are clearly not about to condemn them. Judaism and Christianity are again the exceptions, and their fervid intolerance was a source of strength in the struggle for survival. Only very rarely does a sense of conflict and hostility appear among the adherents of the pagan religions. Plutarch sometimes inveighs against the primitive cruelties unveiled in facets of mythology; his method is fairly radical in that he is prepared to reject such elements as unworthy of the gods.

In his novel about the ass-man rescued by Isis, Apuleius is appreciative and respectful in his allusions to most other religions. Here there was almost a logical imperative operating since Isis, as he often stresses, combined the attributes of all other goddesses. Yet there are two glaring exceptions to his tolerant attitude. One is the portrait of the baker's wife (9.14), who is described as a retailer of all the vices and as one who "scorned and spurned divine beings and instead of accepting a definite faith . . . falsely and blasphemously professed belief in a god whom she regarded as the one and only god."

In general, syncretism tended to induce a belief in pantheism. The free mingling of many varying divinities suggested to some minds that the world was full of God in some form or another.

— J. GWYN GRIFFITHS

HINDUISM

[*This entry deals exclusively with the Hindu tradition. For a more general survey of the religions of India and their interaction with each other, see* Indian Religions.]

Hinduism is the religion followed by about 70 percent of the roughly seven hundred million people of India. Elsewhere, with the exception of the Indonesian island of Bali, Hindus represent only minority populations. The geographical boundaries of today's India are not, however, adequate to contour a full account of this religion. Over different periods in the last four or five millennia, Hinduism and its antecedents have predominated in the adjacent areas of Pakistan and Bangladesh and have been influential in such other regions as Afghanistan, Sri Lanka, Southeast Asia, and Indonesia. But in these areas Hindu influences have been superseded or overshadowed by the influences of other religions, principally Buddhism and Islam. This account will treat only of Hinduism as it has taken shape historically in the "greater India" of the Indian subcontinent. [*For discussion of Hinduism outside the Indian subcontinent, see* Southeast Asian Religions.]

INDUS VALLEY RELIGION

There are good reasons to suspect that a largely unknown quantity, the religion of the peoples of the Indus Valley, is an important source for determining the roots of Hinduism.

The Indus Valley civilization arose from Neolithic and Chalcolithic village foundations at about the middle of the third millennium BCE as a late contemporary of Egyptian and Mesopotamian riverine civilizations. It engaged in trade with both, though mostly with Mesopotamia. Reaching its apogee around 2000 BCE, it then suffered a long period of intermittent and multifactored decline culminating in its eclipse around 1600 BCE, apparently *before* the coming of the Aryan peoples and their introduction of the Vedic religious current. At its peak, the Indus Valley civilization extended over most of present-day Pakistan, into India as far eastward as near Delhi, and southward as far as the estuaries of the Narmada River. It was apparently dominated by the two cities of Mohenjo-Daro, on the Indus River in Sind, and Harappa, about 350 miles to the northwest on a former course of the Ravi River, one of the tributaries to the Indus. Despite their distance from each other, the two cities show remarkable uniformity in material and design, and it has been supposed that they formed a pair of religious and administrative centers.

The determination of the nature of Indus Valley religion and of its residual impact upon Hinduism are, however, most problematic. Although archaeological sites have yielded many suggestive material remains, the interpretation of such finds is conjectural and has been thwarted especially by the continued resistance of the Indus Valley script, found on numerous steatite seals, to convincing decipherment. Until it is deciphered, little can be said with assurance. The content of the inscriptions may prove to be minimal, but if the language (most likely Dravidian) can be identified, much can be resolved.

At both Harappa and Mohenjo-Daro, the cities were dominated on the western side by an artificially elevated mound that housed a citadel-type complex of buildings. Though no temples or shrines can be identified, the complex probably served both sacred and administrative functions. A "great bath" within the Mohenjo-Daro citadel, plus elaborate bathing and drainage facilities in residences throughout the cities, suggests a strong concern for personal cleanliness, cultic bathing, and ritual purity such as resurface in later Hinduism. Indeed, the "great bath," a bitumen-lined tank with steps leading into and out of it from either end, suggests not only the temple tanks of later Hinduism but the notion of "crossing" associated with them through their Sanskrit name, *tirtha* ("crossing place, ford").

A granary attached to the citadel may also have involved high officials in ceremonial supervision of harvests and other agricultural rituals. Terracotta female figurines with pedestal waists, found especially at village sites, reveal at least a popular cultic interest in fertility. They are probably linked with worship of a goddess under various aspects, for while some portray the figure in benign nurturing poses, others present pinched and grim features that have been likened to grinning skulls: these are likely foreshadowings of the Hindu Goddess in her benign and destructive aspects.

But most controversial are the depictions on the seals, whose inscriptions remain undeciphered. Most prominently figured are powerful male animals. They are often shown in cultic scenes, as before a sort of "sacred manger," or being led by a priestly ministrant before a figure (probably a deity and possibly a goddess) in a peepul tree, one of the most venerated trees in Hinduism. Male animals also frequently figure in combination with human males in composite animal-human forms. With female figures seemingly linked to the Goddess and males associated with animal power, it has been suggested that the two represent complementary aspects of a fertility cult with attendant sacrificial scenarios such as are found in the animal sacrifice to the Goddess in post-Vedic Hinduism. In such sacrifices the Goddess requires male offerings, and the animal represents the human male sacrificer. Most interesting and controversial in this connection is a figure in a yogic posture who is depicted on three seals and a faience sealing. Though features differ in the four

From the archaeological evidence, however, which includes frescoes, seals, and figurines, one may conclude that the representation of the divine was both anthropomorphic and theriomorphic.

PAGE 305

portrayals, the most fully defined one shows him seated on a dais with an erect phallus. He has buffalo horns that enclose a treelike miter headdress, possibly a caricatured buffalo face, wears bangles and necklaces or torques, and is surrounded by four wild animals. Some of these associations (yoga, ithyphallicism, lordship of animals) have suggested an identification with the later Hindu god Siva. Other traits (the buffalo-man composite form, association with wild animals, possible intimations of sacrifice) have suggested a foreshadowing of the buffalo demon Mahisasura, mythic antagonist and sacrificial victim of the later Hindu goddess Durga. Possibly the image crystallizes traits that are later associated with both of these figures.

Vedic thought was based on the belief in an inextricable coordination of nature, human society, ritual, and the sphere of myth and the divine.

PAGE 322

The notion that features of Indus Valley religion form a stream with later non-Aryan religious currents that percolated into Hinduism has somewhat dismissively been called the substratum theory by opponents who argue in favor of treating the development of Hinduism as derivable from within its own sacred literature. Though this "substratum" cannot be known except in the ways that it has been structured within Hinduism (and no doubt also within Jainism and Buddhism), it is clear that a two-way process was initiated as early as the Vedic period and has continued to the present.

VEDISM

The early sacred literature of Hinduism has the retrospective title of Veda ("knowledge") and is also known as *sruti* ("that which is heard"). Altogether it is a prodigious body of literature, originally oral in character (thus "heard"), that evolved into its present form over nine or ten centuries between about 1400 and 400 BCE. In all, four types of texts fall under the Veda-*sruti* heading: Samhitas, Brahmanas, Aranyakas, and Upanisads. At the fount of all later elaborations are the four Samhitas ("collections"): the *Rgveda Samhita* (Veda of Chants, the oldest), the *Samaveda* and *Yajurveda Samhitas* (Vedas of Melodies and Sacrificial Formulas, together known as the "liturgical" Samhitas), and the *Atharvaveda Samhita* (the youngest, named after the sage Atharvan). These constitute the four Vedas, with some early sources referring to the "three Vedas" exclusive of the last. The material of the four was probably complete by 1000 BCE, with younger parts of the older works overlapping older parts of the younger ones chronologically. The Samhitas, or portions of them, were preserved by different priestly schools or "branches" *(sakhas)* through elaborate means of memorization. Many of these schools died out and their branches became lost, but others survived to preserve material for literary compilation and redaction. The subsequent works in the categories of Brahmana, Aran-yaka, and Upanisad are all linked with one or another of the Vedic schools, and thus with a particular Vedic Samhita, so that they represent the further literary output of the Vedic schools and also the interests of the four types of priests who came to be associated differentially with the ritual uses of the four Samhitas. It is from the *Rgveda* that Vedic religion in its earliest sense must be reconstructed.

SIVA

Siva, whose ancient name is Rudra, the Wild God, is also known as Lord of Animals.

JANEZ SKOK/CORBIS

Although the urban civilization of the Indus Valley had run its course by the time of the arrival of the Aryans in about 1500 BCE, the newcomers met heirs of this civilization in settled agricultural communities. The contrast between cultures was striking to the Aryans, who described the indigenous population as having darker skin, defending themselves from forts, having no gods or religious rituals but nonetheless worshiping the phallus. As small stone phallic objects have been found at Indus Valley sites, this is probably an accurate description of a cult continued from pre-Vedic Indus Valley religion that prefigures the later veneration of the *linga* (phallus) in the worship of Siva. In contrast to this predominantly agricultural population, the invading Aryans were a mobile, warlike people, unattached to cities or specific locations, entering Northwest India in tribal waves probably over a period of several centuries. Moreover, their society inherited an organizing principle from its Indo-European past that was to have great impact on later Indian civilization in the formation of the caste system. The ideal arrangement, which myths and ritual formulas propounded and society was to reflect, called for three social "functions": the priests, the warriors, and the

agriculturalist-stockbreeders. Early Vedic hymns already speak of three such interacting social groups, plus a fourth—the indigenous population of *dasa*, or *dasyu* (literally, "slaves," first mythologized as demon foes of the Aryans and their gods). By the time of the late *Rgveda*, these peoples were recognized as a fourth "class" or "caste" in the total society and were known as *sudras*.

Most crucial to the inspiration of the early Vedic religion, however, was the interaction between the first two groups: the priesthood, organized around sacerdotal schools maintained through family and clan lines, and a warrior component, originally led by chieftains of the mobile tribal communities but from the beginning concerned with an ideal of kingship that soon took on more local forms. Whereas the priests served as repositories of sacred lore, poetry, ritual technique, and mystical speculation, the warriors served as patrons of the rites and ceremonies of the priests and as sponsors of their poetry. These two groups, ideally complementary but often having rival interests, crystallized by late Vedic and Brahmanic times into distinct "classes": the *brahmanas* (priests) and the *ksatriyas* (warriors).

Although the *Rgveda* alludes to numerous details of ritual that soon came to be systematized in the religion of the Brahmanas, it brings ritual into relief only secondarily. The primary focus of the 1,028 hymns of the *Rgveda* is on praising the gods and the cosmic order *(rta)*, which they protect. But insofar as the hymns invoke the gods to attend the sacrifice, there is abundant interest in two deities of essentially ritual character: Agni and Soma. Agni (Fire) is more specifically the god of the sacrificial fire who receives offerings to the gods and conveys them heavenward through the smoke. And Soma is the divinized plant of "nondeath" *(amrta)*, or immortality, whose juices are ritually extracted in the *soma* sacrifice, a central feature of many Vedic and Brahmanic rituals. These two gods, significantly close to mankind, are mediators between men and other gods. But they are especially praised for their capacity to inspire in the poets the special "vision" *(dhi)* that stimulates the composition of the Vedic hymns. Agni, who as a god of fire and light is present in the three Vedic worlds (as fire on earth, lightning in the atmosphere, and the sun in heaven), bestows vision through "illumination" into the analogical connections and equivalences that compose the *rta* (which is itself said to have a luminous nature). *Soma*, the extracted and purified juice of the "plant of immortality," possibly the hallucinogenic fly agaric mushroom, yields a "purified" vision that is described as "enthused" or "intoxicated," tremulous or vibrant, again stimulating the inspiration for poetry. The Vedic poet (*kavi*, *rsi*, or *vipra*) was thus a "see-er," or seer, who translated his vision into speech, thus producing the sacred *mantras*, or verse-prayers, that comprise the Vedic hymns. Vedic utterance, itself hypostatized as the goddess Vac (Speech), is thus the crystallization of this vision.

Vedic religion is decidedly polytheistic, there being far more than the so-called thirty-three gods, the number to which they are sometimes reduced. Though the point is controversial, for the sake of simplification we can say that at the core or "axis" of the pantheon there are certain deities with clear Indo-European or

SIVA
Rudra, the Wild God

The ancient name of Siva is *Rudra*, the Wild God. His seminal myth is told in the most sacred, most ancient Indian text, the *Rgveda* (c. 1200-1000 BCE; hymns 10.61 and 1.71). When time was about to begin he appeared as a wild hunter, aflame, his arrow directed against the Creator making love with his virgin daughter, the Dawn. They had the shape of two antelopes. Some of the Creator's seed fell on the earth. Rudra himself as Fire (Agni) had prepared the seed, from which mankind was to be born. From a rupture of the undifferentiated plenum of the Absolute some of the seed fell on the earth. Rudra's shot failed to prevent its fall; time, which was about to begin, came into being between, in the shape of the flight of his arrow. The Creator, Prajapati, terribly frightened, made Rudra Lord of Animals (Pasupati) for sparing his life (*Maitrayani Samhita* 4.2.12; after 1000 BCE). The gods, as they witnessed the primordial scene, made it into a mantra, or incantation, and out of this mantra they fashioned Vastos-pati, "lord of the residue *(vastu)*," "lord of the site *(vastu)*," or "lord of what is left over on the sacrificial site." However, Pasupati—"lord of animals," "lord of creatures," "lord of the soul of man"—is Rudra-Siva's most significant name.

Fundamental pairs of antitheses inhere in the primordial Rgvedic myth of Rudra Pasupati and Rudra Vastospati. As Fire he incites Prajapati toward creation; as the formidable hunter he aims at the act of creation, meaning to prevent the "incontinence" of the Creator, the shedding of the seed. Rudra acts as hunter and yogin in one. The scene has for its background the plenum of the uncreated or the Absolute that was and is before the mythical moment of the inception of the life.

— STELLA KRAMRISCH

The oldest sense of the word–which appears as early as the Rgveda (c. 1200 BCE), usually as dharman–signifies cosmic ordinance, often in connection with the sense of natural or divine law.

PAGE 205

"The immortal gods alone have neither age or death."

SOPHOCLES
OEDIPUS AT COLONUS 607

at least Indo-Iranian backgrounds: the liturgical gods Agni and Soma (cf. the Avestan deity Haoma) and the deities who oversee the three "functions" on the cosmic scale: the cosmic sovereign gods Varuna and Mitra, the warrior god Indra, and the Asvins, twin horsemen concerned with pastoralism, among other things. Intersecting this structure is an opposition of Indo-Iranian background between *devas* and *asuras*. In the Rgveda both terms may refer to ranks among the gods, with asura being higher and more primal. But asura also has the Vedic meaning of "demon," which it retains in later Hinduism, so that the deva-asura opposition also takes on dualistic overtones. Varuna is the *asura par excellence*, whereas Indra is the leader of the *devas*. These two deities are thus sometimes in opposition and sometimes in complementary roles: Varuna being the remote overseer of the cosmic order *(rta)* and punisher of individual human sins that violate it; Indra being the dynamic creator and upholder of that order, leader of the perennial fight against the collective demonic forces, both human and divine, that oppose it. It is particularly his conquest of the *asura* Vrtra ("encloser")—whose name suggests ambiguous etymological connections with Varuna—that creates order or being (*sat*, analogous to *rta*) out of chaos or nonbeing *(asat)* and opens cosmic and earthly space for "freedom of movement" *(varivas)* by gods and men. Considerable attention is also devoted to three solar deities whose freedom of movement, thus secured, is a manifestation of the *rta*, a prominent analogy for which is the solar wheel: Surya and Savitr (the Sun under different aspects) and Usas (charming goddess of the dawn). Other highly significant deities are Yama, god of the dead, and Vayu, god of wind and breath. It is often pointed out that the gods who become most important in later Hinduism—Visnu, Siva (Vedic Rudra), and the Goddess—are statistically rather insignificant in the Veda, for few hymns are devoted to them. But the content rather than the quantity of the references hints at their significance. Visnu's centrality and cosmological ultimacy, Rudra's destructive power and outsiderhood, and the this-worldly dynamic aspects of several goddesses are traits that assume great proportions in later characterizations of these deities.

Although it is thus possible to outline certain structural and historical features that go into the makeup of the Vedic pantheon, it is important to recognize that these are obscured by certain features of the hymns that arise from the type of religious "vision" that inspired them, and that provide the basis for speculative and philosophical trends that emerge in the late Veda and continue into the early Brahmanic tradition. The hymns glorify the god they address in terms generally applicable to other gods (brilliance, power, beneficence, wisdom) and often endow him or her with mythical traits and actions particular to other gods (supporting heaven, preparing the sun's path, slaying Vrtra, and so on). Thus, while homologies and "connections" between the gods are envisioned, essential distinctions between them are implicitly denied. Speculation on what is essential—not only as concerns the gods, but the ritual and the *mantras* that invoke them—is thus initiated in the poetic process of the early hymns and gains in urgency and refinement in late portions of the *Rgveda* and the subsequent "Vedic" speculative-philosophical literature that culminates in the Upanisads. Most important of these speculations historically were those concerning the cosmogonic sacrifices of Purusa in *Rgveda* 10.90 (the *Purusasukta*, accounting for, among other things, the origin of the four castes) and of Prajapati in the Brahmanas. Each must be discussed further. In addition, speculations on *brahman* as the power inherent in holy speech and on the *atman* ("self") as the irreducible element of personal experience are both traceable to Vedic writings (the latter to the *Atharvaveda* only). We shall observe the convergence of all these lines of speculation in the Upanisads and classical Hinduism.

RELIGION OF THE BRAHMANAS

The elaboration of Vedic religion into the sacrificial religion of the Brahmanas is largely a result of systematization. The first indication of this trend is the compilation of the liturgical Samhitas and the development of the distinctive priestly schools and interests that produced these compendiums. Thus, while the *Rgveda* became the province of the *hotr* priest, the pourer of oblations and invoker of gods through the *mantras* (the term *hotr*, "pourer," figures often in the *Rgveda* and has Indo-Iranian origins), the newer collections developed around the concerns of specialist priests barely alluded to in the *Rgveda* and serving originally in subordinate ritual roles. The *Samaveda* was a collection of verses taken mostly from the *Rgveda*, set to various melodies *(samans)* for use mainly in the *soma* sacrifice, and sung primarily by the *udgatr* priest, who thus came to surpass the *hotr* as a specialist in the sound and articulation of the *mantras*. And the *Yajurveda* was a collection of *yajus*, selected sacrificial *mantras*, again mostly from the *Rgveda*, plus certain complete sentences, to be murmured by the *adhvaryu* priest, who concerned himself not so much with their sound as with their appropriateness in the ritual, in which he became effectively the master of ceremonies, responsible for carrying out all the basic manual operations, even replacing the *hotr* priest as pourer of oblations. A fourth group of priests, the *brahmanas*, then claimed affiliation with the *Atharvaveda* and assumed the responsibility for overseeing the entire ritual performance of the other priests and counteracting any of their mistakes (they were supposed to know the other three Vedas as well as their own) by silent recitation of *mantras* from the *Atharvaveda.* As specialization increased, each priest of these four main classes took on three main assistants.

The Brahmanas—expositions of *brahman,* the sacred power inherent in *mantra* and more specifically now in the ritual—are the outgrowth of the concerns of these distinctive priestly schools and the first articulation of their religion. Each class of priests developed its own Brahmanas, the most important and comprehensive being the *Satapatha Brahmana* of one of the *Yajurveda* schools. The ritual system was also further refined in additional manuals: the Srautasutras, concerned with "solemn" rites, first described in the Brahmanas and thus called *srauta* because of their provenance in these sruti texts, and the Grhyasutras, concerned with domestic rites (from *grha,* "home"), justified by "tradition" *(smrti)* but still having much of Vedic origins. The Srautasutras were compiled over the period, roughly, from the Brahmanas to the Upanisads, and the Grhyasutras were probably compiled during Upanisadic times.

The domestic rites take place at a single offering fire and usually involve offerings of only grain or ghee (clarified butter). Along with the maintenance of the household fire and the performance of the so-called Five Great Sacrifices—to *brahman* (in the form of Vedic recitation), to ancestors, to gods, to other "beings," and to humans (hospitality rites)—the most prominent *grhya* ceremonies are the sacraments or life-cycle rites *(samskaras).* Of these, the most important are the rites of conception and birth of a male child; the Upanayana, or "introduction," of boys to a *brahmana* preceptor or *guru* for initiation; marriage; and death by cremation (Antyesti, "final offering"). The Upanayana, involving the investiture of boys of the upper three social classes *(varnas)* with a sacred thread, conferred on them the status of "twice-born" (*dvija,* a term first

THE SRAUTA RITES

It All Begins with Faith

The *srauta* rites are elaborate and representative of the Brahmanas sacrificial system in its full complexity, involving ceremonies that lasted up to two years and enlisted as many as seventeen priests. Through the continued performance of daily, bimonthly, and seasonal *srauta* rites one gains the year, which is itself identified with the sacrificial life-death-regeneration round and its divine personification, Prajapati. In surpassing the year by the Agnicayana, the "piling of the fire altar," one gains immortality and needs no more nourishment in the otherworld (see *Satapatha Brahmana* 10.1.5.4).

Srauta rites required a sacrificial terrain near the home of the sacrificer *(yajamana),* with three sacred fires (representing, among other things, the three worlds) and an upraised altar, or *vedi.* Nonanimal sacrifices required by domestic rites involved offerings of milk and vegetable substances or even of *mantras.* Animal sacrifices *(pasubandhu)*—which required a more elaborate sacrificial area with a supplemental altar and a sacrificial stake *(yupa)*—entailed primarily the sacrifice of a goat. Five male animals—man, horse, bull, ram, and goat—are declared suitable for sacrifice. It is likely, however, that human sacrifice existed only on the "ideal" plane, where it was personified in the cosmic sacrifices of Purusa and Prajapati. The animal *(pasu)* was to be immolated by strangulation, and its omentum, rich in fat, offered into the fire. *Soma* sacrifices, which would normally incorporate animal sacrifices within them plus a vast number of other subrites, involved the pressing and offering of *soma.* The most basic of these was the annual Agnistoma, "in praise of Agni," a four-day rite culminating in morning, afternoon, and evening *soma* pressings on the final day and including two goat sacrifices. Three of the most ambitious *soma* sacrifices were royal rites: the Asvamedha, the horse sacrifice; the Rajasuya, royal consecration; and the Vajapeya, a *soma* sacrifice of the "drink of strength." But the most complex of all was the aforementioned Agnicayana.

A thread that runs through most *srauta* rituals, however, is that they must begin with the "faith" or "confidence" *(sraddha)* of the sacrificer in the efficacy of the rite and the capacity of the officiating priests to perform it correctly. This prepares the sacrificer for the consecration *(diksa)* in which, through acts of asceticism *(tapas),* he takes on the aspect of an embryo to be reborn through the rite. As *diksita* (one undergoing the *diksa*), he makes an offering of himself (his *atman*). This then prepares him to make the sacrificial offering proper (the *yajña,* "sacrifice") as a means to redeem or ransom this self by the substance (animal or otherwise) offered. Then, reversing the concentration of power that he has amassed in the *diksa,* he disperses wealth in the form of *daksinas* (honoraria) to the priests. Finally, the rite is disassembled (the ritual analogue to the repeated death of Prajapati before his reconstitution in another rite), and the sacrificer and his wife bathe to disengage themselves from the sacrifice and reenter the profane world.

— ALF HILTEBEITEL

used in the *Atharvaveda*), and their "second birth" permitted them to hear the Veda and thereby participate in the *srauta* rites that, according to the emerging Brahmanic orthodoxy, would make it possible to obtain immortality.

In the elaboration of such ceremonies and the speculative explanation of them in the Brahmanas, the earlier Vedic religion seems to have been much altered. In the religion of the Brahmanas, the priests, as "those who know thus" *(evamvids)*, view themselves as more powerful than the gods. Meanwhile, the gods and the demons *(asuras)* are reduced to representing in their endless conflicts the recurrent interplay between agonistic forces in the sacrifice. It is their father, Prajapati, who crystallizes the concerns of Brahmanic thought by representing the sacrifice in all its aspects and processes. Most notable of these is the notion of the assembly or fabrication of an immortal self *(atman)* through ritual action *(karman)*, a self constructed for the sacrificer by which he identifies with the immortal essence of Prajapati as the sacrifice personified. And by the same token, the recurrent death (*punarmrtyu*, "redeath") of Prajapati's transitory nature (the elements of the sacrifice that are assembled and disassembled) figures in the Brahmanas as the object to be avoided for the sacrificer by the correct ritual performance. This Brahmanic concept of Prajapati's redeath, along with speculation on the ancestral *grhya* rites *(sraddhas)* focused on feeding deceased relatives to sustain them in the afterlife, must have been factors in the thinking that gave rise to the Upanisadic concept of reincarnation (*punarjanman*, "rebirth"). The emphasis on the morbid and transitory aspects of Prajapati and the sacrifice, and the insistence that asceticism within the sacrifice is the main means to overcome them, are most vigorously propounded in connection with the Agnicayana.

In the Brahmanas' recasting of the primal once-and for-all sacrifice of Purusa into the recurrent life-death-regeneration mythology of Prajapati, a different theology was introduced. Though sometimes Purusa was identified with Prajapati, the latter, bound to the round of creation and destruction, became the prototype for the classical god Brahma, personification of the Absolute *(brahman)* as it is oriented toward the world. The concept of a transcendent Purusa, however, was not forgotten in the Brahmanas. *Satapatha Brahmana* 13.6 mentions Purusa-Narayana, a being who seeks to surpass all others through sacrifice and thereby become the universe. In classical Hinduism, *Narayana* and *Purusa* are both names for Visnu as the supreme divinity. This Brahmana passage neither authorizes nor disallows an identification with Visnu, but other Brahmana passages leave no doubt that sacrificial formulations have given Visnu and Rudra-Siva a new status. Whereas the Brahmanas repeatedly assert that "Visnu is the sacrifice"— principally in terms of the organization of sacrificial space that is brought about through Visnu's three steps through the cosmos, and his promotion of the order and prosperity that thus accrue—they portray Rudra as the essential outsider to this sacrificial order, the one who neutralizes the impure forces that threaten it from outside as well as the violence that is inherent within. Biardeau (1976) has been able to show that the later elevation of Visnu and Siva through yoga and *bhakti* is rooted in oppositional complementarities first formulated in the context of the Brahmanic sacrifice.

Religious traditions most thoroughly in Brahmanic ideology maintained that in order to support cosmic and social harmony one must follow one's svadharma at all times.

PAGE 206

THE UPANISADS

Several trends contributed to the emergence of the Upanisadic outlook. Earlier speculations on the irreducible essence of the cosmos, the sacrifice, and individual experience have been mentioned. Pre-Upanisadic texts also refer to various forms of asceticism as performed by types of people who in one way or another rejected or inverted conventional social norms: the Vedic *muni*, *vratya*, and *brahmacarin*, to each of whom is ascribed ecstatic capacities, and, at the very heart of the Brahmanic sacrifice, the *diksita* (the sacrificer who performs *tapas* while undergoing the *diksa*, or consecration). These speculative and ascetic trends all make contributions to a class of texts generally regarded as intermediary between the Brahmanas and Upanisads: the Aranyakas, or "Forest Books." The Aranyakas do not differ markedly from the works that precede and succeed them (the *Brhadaranyaka Upanisad* is both an Aranyaka and an Upanisad), but their transitional character is marked by a shift in the sacrificial setting from domestic surroundings to the forest and a focus not so much on the details of ritual as on its interiorization and universalization. Sacrifice, for instance, is likened to the alternation that takes place between breathing and speaking. Thus correspondences are established between aspects of sacrifice and the life continuum of the meditator.

An *upanisad* is literally a mystical—often "secret"—"connection," interpreted as the teaching of mystical homologies. Or, in a more conventional etymology, it is the "sitting down" of a disciple "near to" (*upa*, "near"; *ni*, "down"; *sad*, "sit") his spiritual master, or *guru*. Each Upanisad reflects the Vedic orientation of its priestly school. There are also regional orientations, for Upanisadic geography registers the further eastern settlement of the Vedic tradition into areas of the Ganges Basin. But the Upanisads do share certain fundamental points of outlook that are more basic than their differences. Vedic polytheism is demythologized, for all gods are reducible to one. Brahmanic ritualism is reassessed and its understanding of ritual action *(karman)* thoroughly reinterpreted. *Karman*

can no longer be regarded as a positive means to the constitution of a permanent self. Rather, it is ultimately negative: "the world that is won by work *(karman)*" and "the world that is won by merit *(punya)*" only perish (*Chandogya Upanisad* 8.1.6). The "law of karma" *(karman)* or "law of causality" represents a strict and universal cause-effect continuum that affects any action that is motivated by desire *(kama)*, whether it be desire for good or for ill. Thus even meritorious actions that lead to the Vedic heaven "perish," leaving a momentum that carries the individual to additional births or reincarnations. The result is perpetual bondage to the universal flow-continuum of all *karman*, or *samsara* (from *sam*, "together" and *sr*, "flow"), a term that the Upanisads introduce into the Vedic tradition but that is shared with Jainism and Buddhism. As with these religions, the Upanisads and Hinduism henceforth conceive their soteriological goal as liberation from this cycle of *samsara*: that is, *moksa* or *mukti* ("release").

Moksa cannot be achieved by action alone, since action only leads to further action. Thus, though ritual action is not generally rejected and is often still encouraged in the Upanisads, it can only be subordinated to pursuit of the higher *moksa* ideal. Rather, the new emphasis is on knowledge *(vidya, jñana)* and the overcoming of ignorance *(avidya)*. The knowledge sought, however, is not that of ritual technique or even of ritual-based homologies, but a graspable, revelatory, and experiential knowledge of the self as one with ultimate reality. In the early Upanisads this experience is formulated as the realization of the ultimate "connection," the oneness of *atman-brahman*, a connection knowable only in the context of communication from *guru* to disciple. (Herein can be seen the basis of the parable context and vivid, immediate imagery of many Upanisadic teachings.) The experience thus achieved is variously described as one of unified consciousness, fearlessness, bliss, and tranquillity.

Beyond these common themes, however, and despite the fact that Upanisadic thought is resistant to systematization, certain different strains can be identified. Of the thirteen Upanisads usually counted as *sruti*, the earliest (c. 700-500 BCE) are those in prose, headed by the *Brhadaranyaka* and the *Chandogya*. Generally, it may be said that these Upanisads introduce the formulations that later Hinduism will develop into the *samnyasa* ideal of renunciation (not yet defined in the Upanisads as a fourth stage of life) and the knowledge-path outlook of nondualistic *(advaita)* Vedanta. Even within these early Upanisads, two approaches to realization can be distinguished. One refers to an all-excluding Absolute; the self that is identified with *brahman*, characterized as *neti neti* ("not this, not this") and is reached through a paring away of the psychomental continuum and its links with *karman*. Such an approach dominates the *Brhadaranyaka Upanisad*. *Avidya* here results from regarding the name and form of things as real and forming attachment to them. The other approach involves an all-comprehensive Absolute, *brahman-atman*, which penetrates the world so that all forms are modifications of the one; ignorance results from the failure to experience this immediacy. In the *Chandogya Upanisad* this second approach is epitomized in the persistent formula "Tat tvam asi" ("That thou art").

The later Vedic Upanisads (c. 600-400 BCE) register the first impact of theistic devotional formulations, and of early Samkhya and Yoga. Most important of these historically are two "yogic" Upanisads, the *Svetasvatara* and the *Katha*, the first focused on Rudra-Siva and the second on Visnu. Each incorporates into its terminology for the absolute deity the earlier term *purusa*. As Biardeau has shown in *L'hindouisme* (1981), they thus draw on an alternate term for the Absolute from that is made current in the *brahman-atman* equation. The Purusa of *Rgveda* 10.90 (the *Purusasukta*) is sacrificed to create the ordered and integrated sociocosmic world of Vedic man. But only one quarter of this Purusa is "all beings"; three quarters are "the immortal in heaven" (RV 10.90.3). This transcendent aspect of Purusa, and also a certain "personal" dimension, are traits that were retained in the characterization of Purusa-Narayana in the *Satapatha Brahmana* and reinforced in the yogic characterizations of Rudra-Siva and Visnu in the previously mentioned Upanisads. The Upanisadic texts do not restrict the

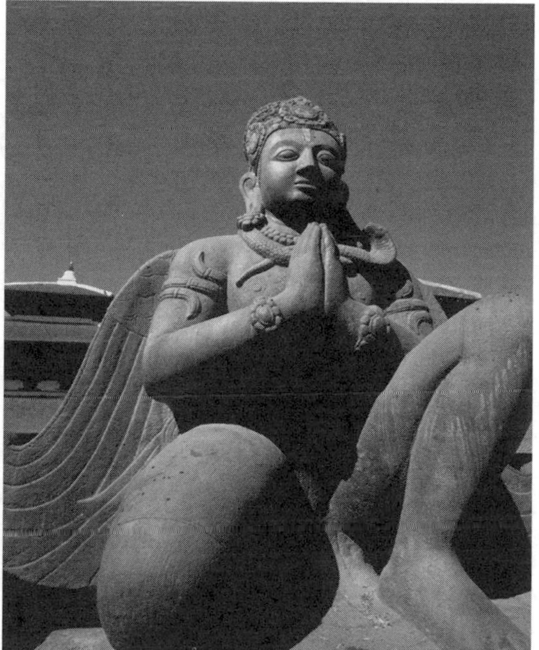

VISNU

A late Vedic Upanisad, called the Katha, focuses on the supreme deity Visnu.

DAVID PATERSON/CORBIS

The divine word is also commonly held to be eternal, as in the Hindu concept of the eternal Veda.

PAGE 594

usage of the term *purusa* to mean "soul," as classical Samkhya later does; rather, it is used to refer to both the soul and the supreme divinity. The relation between the soul and the Absolute is thus doubly defined: on the one hand as *atman-brahman*, on the other as *purusa*-Purusa. In the latter case, the *Katha Upanisad* describes a spiritual itinerary of the soul's ascent through yogic states to the supreme Purusa, Visnu. This synthesis of yoga and *bhakti* will be carried forward into the devotional formulations of the epics and the Puranas. But one must note that the two vocabularies are used concurrently and interrelatedly in the Upanisads, as they will be in the later *bhakti* formulations.

THE CONSOLIDATION OF CLASSICAL HINDUISM

A period of consolidation, sometimes identified as one of "Hindu synthesis," "Brahmanic synthesis," or "orthodox synthesis," takes place between the time of the late Vedic Upanisads (c. 500 BCE) and the period of Gupta imperial ascendancy (c. 320-467 CE). Discussion of this consolidation, however, is initially complicated by a lack of historiographical categories adequate to the task of integrating the diverse textual, inscriptional, and archaeological data of this long formative period. The attempt to cover as much of this span as possible with the name "epic period," because it coincides with the dates that are usually assigned to the formation and completion of the Hindu epics (particularly the *Mahabharata*), is misleading, since so much of what transpires can hardly be labeled "epic." On the other hand, attempts to define the period in terms of heterogeneous forces operating upon Hinduism from within (assimilation of local deities and cults, geographical spread) and without (heterodox and foreign challenges) either have failed to register or have misrepresented the implications of the apparent fact that the epics were "works in progress" during the whole period. The view one takes of the epics is, in fact, crucial for the interpretation of Hinduism during this period. Here, assuming that the epics already incorporated a *bhakti* cosmology and theology from an early point in this formative period, I shall try to place them in relation to other works and formulations that contributed to the consolidation of classical Hinduism.

The overall history can be broken down into four periods characterized by an oscillation from disunity (rival regional kingdoms and tribal confederacies on the Ganges Plain) to unity (Mauryan ascendancy, c. 324-184 BCE, including the imperial patronage of Buddhism by Asoka) to disunity (rival foreign kingdoms in Northwest India and regional kingdoms elsewhere) back to unity (Gupta ascendancy, c. 320-467 CE). The emerging self-definitions of Hinduism were forged in the context of continued interaction with heterodox religions (Buddhists, Jains, Ajivikas) throughout this whole period, and with foreign peoples (Yavanas, or Greeks; Sakas, or Scythians; Pahlavas, or Parthians; and Kusanas, or Kushans) from the third phase on. In this climate the *ideal* of centralized Hindu rule attained no practical realization until the rise of the Guptas. That this ideal preceded its realization is evident in the rituals of royal paramountcy (Asvamedha and Rajasuya) that were set out in the Brahmanas and the Srautasutras, and actually performed by post-Mauryan regional Hindu kings.

When we look to the component facets of the overall consolidation, these four periods must be kept in mind, but with the proviso that datings continue to be problematic: not only datings of texts, but especially of religious movements and processes reflected in them, and in surviving inscriptions. Most scholars ordinarily assume that when a process is referred to in a text or other document, it has gone on for some time.

SRUTI AND SMRTI. Fundamental to the self-definition of Hinduism during this period of its consolidation is the distinction it makes between two classes of its literature: *sruti* and *smrti*. Sruti is "what is heard," and refers to the whole corpus of Vedic literature (also called Veda) from the four Vedas to the Upanisads. *Smrti*, "what is remembered" or "tradition," includes all that falls outside this literature. Exactly when this distinction was made is not certain, but it is noteworthy that the six Vedangas or "limbs of the Veda" (writings on phonetics, metrics, grammar, etymology, astronomy, and ritual) are *smrti* texts that were composed at least in part during the latter half of the Vedic or *sruti* period. The ritual texts (Kalpasutras) are subdivided into three categories: Srautasutras, Grhyasutras, and Dharmasutras. Whereas the first two (discussed above under Brahmanic ritual) pertain to concerns developed in the Vedic period, the Dharmasutras focus on issues of law *(dharma)* that become characteristic of the period now under discussion. [*See* Dharma, *article on* Hindu Dharma.] Dates given for the composition of these texts run from 600 to 300 BCE for the earliest (*Gautama Dharmasutra*) to 400 CE for the more recent works. Both Grhyasutras and Dharmasutras were sometimes called Smartasutras (i. e., *sutras* based on *smrti*), so it seems that their authors regarded them as representative of the prolongation of Vedic orthodoxy (and orthopraxy) that the *smrti* category was designed to achieve. As the term *smrti* was extended in its use, however, it also came to cover numerous other texts composed in the post-Upanisadic period.

This *sruti/smrti* distinction thus marks off the earlier literature as a unique corpus that, once the distinction was made, was retrospectively sanctified. By the time of the *Manava Dharmasastra*, or *Laws of Manu*

(c. 200 BCE-100 CE; see Manu 1.23), and probably before this, *sruti* had come to be regarded as "eternal." Its components were thus not works of history. The Vedic *rsis* had "heard" truths that are eternal, and not only in content—the words of the Vedas are stated to have eternal connection with their meanings—but also in form. The works thus bear no stamp of the *rsis'* individuality. Such thinking crystallized in the further doctrine that the Vedas (i. e., *sruti*) are *apauruseya*, not of personal authorship (literally, "not by a *purusa*"). They thus have no human imperfection. Further, it was argued that they are even beyond the authorship of a divine "person" *(Purusa)*. Though myths of the period assert that the Vedas spring from Brahma at the beginning of each creation (as the three Vedas spring from Purusa in the *Purusasukta*), the deity is not their author. Merely reborn with him, they are a self-revelation of the impersonal *brahman*. In contrast to *sruti*, *smrti* texts were seen as historical or "traditional," passed on by "memory" *(smrti)*, and as works of individual authors *(pauruseya)*, even though mythical authors—both human and divine—often had to be invented for them.

Smrti texts of this period thus proclaim the authority of the Veda in many ways, and nonrejection of the Veda comes to be one of the most important touchstones for defining Hinduism over and against the heterodoxies, which rejected the Veda. In fact, it is quite likely that the doctrines of the eternality and impersonality of the Veda were in part designed to assert the superiority of the Veda over the "authored" and "historical" works of the heterodoxies, whose teachings would thus be on a par with *smrti* rather than *sruti*. But it is also likely that the *apauruseya* doctrine is designed to relativize the "personal" god of *bhakti*. In any case, these doctrines served to place a considerable ideological distance between *sruti* and *smrti*, and to allow *smrti* authors great latitude in interpreting *sruti* and extending Hindu teachings into new areas. *Smrti* thus supposedly functioned to clarify the obscurities of the Veda. But the claim that *smrti* texts need only not contradict the Veda left their authors great freedom in pursuing new formulations.

VARNASRAMADHARMA ("CASTE AND LIFE-STAGE LAW"). The most representative corpus of *smrti* literature, and the most closely tied to the continued unfolding orthodox interests of the Vedic priestly schools, is that concerned with *dharma* ("law" or "duty"). As a literary corpus, it consists of two kinds of texts: the Dharmasutras (600/300 BCE-400 CE), already mentioned in connection with the *sruti/smrti* distinction, and the Dharmasastras. The most important and earliest of the latter are the *Manava Dharmasastra*, or *Laws of Manu* (c. 200 BCE-100 CE), and the Yajñavalkya Smrti (c. 100-300 CE). But other Dharmasastras were composed late into the first millennium, to be followed by important commentaries on all such texts. The main focus of these two classes of texts is fundamentally identical: the articulation of norms for all forms of social interaction, thus including but going far beyond the earlier Sutras' concern for ritual. Four differences, however, are noteworthy: (1) Whereas the Dharmasutras are in prose, the Dharmasastras are in the same poetic meter as the epics, *Manu* in particular having much material in common with the *Mahabharata*; (2) whereas the Sutras are still linked with the Vedic schools, the Sastras are not, showing that study and teaching of *dharma* had come to be an independent discipline of its own; (3) the Sastra legislation is more extended and comprehensive; (4) the Sastras are more integrated into a mythic and cosmological vision akin to that in *bhakti* texts, but usually ignoring *bhakti* as such, with references to duties appropriate to different *yugas* (ages), and the identification of north central India as the "middle region" *(madhyadesa)* where the *dharma* is (and is to be kept) the purest.

Orthodox philosophers and legalists looked also to those more temporal literatures that were passed through the generations. These texts were known as smrti, *"remembered" truths and injunctions.*

PAGE 206

The theory of *varnasramadharma*, the law of castes and life stages, was worked out in these texts as a model for the whole of Hindu society. There is little doubt that it was stimulated by the alternate lay/monastic social models of the heterodoxies, and no doubt that it was spurred on by the incursions of barbarian peoples—frequently named in these texts as *mlecchas* (those who "jabber")—into the Northwest. The model involves the working out of the correlations between two ideals: first, that society conform to four hierarchical castes, and second, that a person should pass through four life stages *(asramas)*: student *(brahmacarin)*, householder *(grhasthin)*, forest dweller *(vanaprasthin)*, and renunciant *(samnyasin)*. The first ideal is rooted in the *Purusasukta*. The second presupposes the *sruti* corpus, since the four life stages are correlated with the four classes of *sruti* texts. Thus the student learns one of the Vedas, the householder performs domestic and optimally also *srauta* rituals of the Brahmanas, the forest dweller follows the teachings of the Aranyakas, and the *samnyasin* follows a path of renunciation toward the Upanisadic goal of *moksa*. But although all the life stages are either mentioned (as are the first two) or implied in the *sruti* corpus, the theory that they should govern the ideal course of individual life is new to the Dharmasutras. Together, the *varna* and *asrama* ideals take on tremendous complexity, since a person's duties vary according to caste and stage of life, not to mention other factors like sex, family, region, and the quality of the times. Also, whereas a person's development through one life ideally is regulated by the *asrama* ideal, the passage through many reincarnations would involve birth into different

"Having regard for thine own caste duty, Thou shouldst not tremble"

BHAGAVADGITA 2:30

castes, the caste of one's birth being the result of previous *karman*. A further implication is that the life stages can be properly pursued only by male members of the three twice-born *varnas*, as they alone can undergo the Upanayana ritual that begins the student stage and allows the performance of the rites pertinent to succeeding stages.

Each of these formulations has persisted more on the ideal plane than the real. In the case of the four *asramas*, most people never went beyond the householder stage, which the Sutras and Sastras actually exalt as the most important of the four, since it is the support of the other three and, in more general terms, the mainstay of the society. The forest-dweller stage may soon have become more legendary than real: in epic stories it was projected onto the Vedic *rsis*. The main tension, however, that persists in orthodox Hinduism is that between the householder and the renunciant, the challenge being for anyone to integrate into one lifetime these two ideals, which the heterodoxies set out for separate lay and monastic communities.

As to the four *varnas*, the ideal represents society as working to the reciprocal advantage of all the castes, each one having duties necessary to the proper functioning of the whole and the perpetuation of the hierarchical principle that defines the whole. Thus *brahmanas* are at the top, distinguished by three duties that they share with no other caste: teaching the Veda, assisting in sacrifice, and accepting gifts. They are said to have no king but Soma, god of the sacrifice. In actual fact the traditional *srauta* sacrifice counted for less and less in the *brahmana* householder life, and increasing attention was given to the maintenance of *brahmana* purity for the purpose of domestic and eventually temple rituals which, in effect, universalized sacrifice as the *brahmana's dharma*, but a sacrifice that required only the minimum of impure violence. This quest for purity was reinforced by *brahmanas'* adoption into their householder life of aspects of the *samnyasa* ideal of renunciation. This was focused especially on increasing espousal of the doctrine of *ahimsa* (nonviolence, or, more literally, "not desiring to kill") and was applied practically to vegetarianism, which becomes during this period the *brahmana* norm. *Brahmanas* thus retain higher rank than *ksatriyas*, even though the latter wield temporal power *(ksatra)* and have the specific and potentially impure duties of bearing weapons and protecting and punishing with the royal staff *(danda)*. The subordination of king to *brahmana* involves a subordination of power to hierarchy that is duplicated in contemporary rural and regional terms in the practice of ranking *brahmanas* above locally dominant castes whose power lies in their landed wealth and numbers. *Vaisyas* have the duties of stock breeding, agriculture, and commerce (including money lending). Certain duties then distinguished the three twice-born castes as a group from the *sudras*. All three upper *varnas* thus study the Veda, perform sacrifices, and make gifts, whereas *sudras* are permitted only lesser sacrifices *(pakayajñas)* and simplified domestic rituals that do not require Vedic recitation.

Actual conditions, however, were (and still are) much more complex. The four-*varna* model provided the authors of the *dharma* texts with Vedic "categories" within which to assign a basically unlimited variety of heterogeneous social entities including indigenous tribes, barbarian invaders, artisan communities and guilds *(srenis)*, and specialists in various services. Susceptible to further refinement in ranking and regional nomenclature, all such groups were called *jatis*, a term meaning "birth" and in functional terms the proper word to be translated "caste." Thus, although they are frequently called subcastes, the *jatis* are the castes proper that the law books classified into the "categories" of *varna*.

To account for this proliferation of *jatis*, the authors asserted that they arose from cross-breeding of the *varnas*. Two possibilities were thus presented: *anuloma* ("with the grain") unions, in which the husband's *varna* was the same as his wife's or higher (in anthropological terms, hypergamous, in which women are "married up"), and *pratiloma* ("against the grain") unions, in which the wife's *varna* would be higher than the husband's (hypogamous, in which women are "married down"). Endogamous marriage (marriage within one's own *varna*) set the highest standard and was according to some authorities the only true marriage. But of the other two, whereas *anuloma* marriages were permitted, *pratiloma* unions brought disgrace. Thus the *jatis* supposedly born from *anuloma* unions were less disgraced than those born from *pratiloma* unions. Significantly, two of the most problematic *jatis* were said to have been born from the most debased *pratiloma* connections: the Yavanas (Greeks) from *sudra* males and *ksatriya* females (similar origins were ascribed to other "barbarians") and the *candalas* (lowest of the low, mentioned already in the Upanisads, and early Buddhist literature, as a "fifth caste" of untouchables) from the polluting contact of *sudra* males and *brahmana* females. It should be noted that a major implication of the prohibition of *pratiloma* marriage is the limitation for *brahmana* women to marriages with only *brahmana* men. This established at the highest rank an association of caste purity with caste endogamy (and the purity of a caste's women) and thus initiated an endogamous standard that was adopted by all castes—not just *varnas* but jatis—by the end of the first millennium.

This accounting of the emergence of *jatis* was integrated with further explanations of how society had departed from its ideal. One is that "mixing of caste"—the great abomination of the *dharma* texts and also of the *Bhagavadgita*—increases with the decline of *dharma* from *yuga* to *yuga*, and is especially pernicious in this Kali age. Another is the doctrine of *apad dharma*, "duties for times of distress" such as permit inversion of caste roles when life is threatened. A third doctrine developed in the Dharmasastras identifies certain duties *(kalivarjyas)* as once allowed but now prohibited in the *kaliyuga* because people are no longer capable of performing them purely. Through all this, however, the ideal persists as one that embraces a whole society despite variations over time and space.

PHILOSOPHICAL "VIEWPOINTS" (DARSANAS) AND PATHS TO SALVATION. As an expression of Hinduism's increasing concern to systematize its teachings, the fourth goal of life *(moksa)* was made the subject of efforts to develop distinctly Hindu philosophical "viewpoints" (*darsanas*, from the root *drs*, "see") on the nature of reality and to recommend paths to its apprehension and the release from bondage to *karman*. Six Hindu *darsanas* were defined, and during the period in question each produced fundamental texts—in most cases *sutras*—that served as the bases for later commentaries.

In terms of mainstream developments within Hinduism, only two schools have ongoing continuity into the present: the Mimamsa and the Vedanta. And of these, only the latter has unfolded in important ways in the postsynthesis period. Nonetheless, all six have made important contributions to later Hinduism. It must thus suffice to discuss them all briefly at this point in terms of their basic features and major impact, and reserve fuller discussion of the Vedanta alone for the period of its later unfolding.

Of the six schools, two—Mimamsa and Vedanta—are rooted primarily in the Vedic *sruti* tradition and are thus sometimes called *smarta* schools in the sense that they develop *smarta* orthodox currents of thought that are based, like smrti, directly on sruti. The other four—Nyaya, Vaisesika, Samkhya, and Yoga—claim loyalty to the Veda, yet are quite independent of it, their focus instead being on rational or causal explanation. They are thus sometimes called *haituka* schools (from *hetu*, "cause, reason").

Of the *smarta* schools, the Mimamsa is most concerned with ritual traditions rooted in the Vedas and the Brahmanas, whereas the Vedanta is focused on the Upanisads. It is notable that both sustain Vedic orientations that reject (Mimamsa) or subordinate (Vedanta) *bhakti* until the Vedanta is devotionalized in its post-Sankara forms. Beginning with Jaimini's *Mimamsa Sutra* (c. 300-100 BCE), Mimamsa ("reflection, interpretation") provides exegesis of Vedic injunctive speech, in particular as it concerns the relationship between intentions and rewards of sacrifice. Great refinement is brought to bear on issues relating to the authority and eternalness of the Veda and the relationship between its sounds, words, and meanings. Vedic injunctions are taken literally, the many Vedic gods are

THE GOALS OF MAN

Shed Desire and Be Free

The theory that the integrated life involves the pursuit of four goals *(arthas)* is first presented in the Dharmasastras and the epics, in the latter cases through repeated narrative illustrations. The development of distinctive technical interpretations of each *artha*, or facets thereof, can also be followed during the period in separate manuals: the *Arthasastra*, a manual on statecraft attributed to Candragupta Maurya's minister Kautilya but probably dating from several centuries later, on *artha* (in the sense now of "material pursuits"); the Kamasutras, most notably that of Vatsyayana (c. 400 CE), on *kama* ("love, desire"); the already discussed Dharmasutras and Dharmasastras on *dharma*; and the Sutras of the "philosophical schools" *(darsanas)* insofar as they are concerned with the fourth goal, *moksa*. Early sources often refer to the first three goals as the *trivarga*, the "three categories," but this need not imply that the fourth goal is added later. The Dharmasastra and epic texts that mention the trivarga are focused on the concerns of the householder—and, in the epics, particularly of the royal householder—these being the context for the pursuit of the *trivarga*. The fourth goal, *moksa*, is to be pursued throughout life—indeed, throughout all lives—but is especially the goal of those who have entered the fourth life stage of the *samnyasin*. The *trivarga-moksa* opposition thus replicates the householder-renunciant opposition. But the overall purpose of the *purusartha* formulation is integrative and complementary to the *varnasramadharma* theory. From the angle of the householder, it is *dharma* that integrates the *trivarga* as a basis for *moksa*. But from the angle of the *samnyasin*, it is *kama* that lies at the root of the *trivarga*, representing attachment in all forms, even to *dharma*. Paths to liberation will thus focus on detachment from desire, or its transformation into love of God.

— ALF HILTEBEITEL

Metaphorically, Vedanta is also understood to represent the consummation or culmination (anta) of the entire Vedic speculation, or indeed of all knowledge (veda).

PAGE 697

The Yoga and Samkhya darsanas are so much alike that most of the assertions made by the one are valid for the other.

PAGE 709

seen as real although superfluous to salvation (there is an anti-*bhakti* stance here), and it is maintained that the proper use of injunctions is alone enough to secure the attainment of heaven (not a higher release, or *moksa*, as propounded by all the other systems, including *bhakti*). Mimamsa persists in two subschools, but only in small numbers among brahman ritualists.

As to the Vedanta ("end of the Veda," a term also used for the Upanisads), the foundational work is Badara-yana's *Vedanta Sutra*, or *Brahma Sutra* (c. 300-100 BCE), an exegesis of various Upanisadic passages in aphoristic style easily susceptible to divergent interpretations. These it received in the hands of later Vedantic thinkers.

The *haituka* schools are notable for their development, for the first time within Hinduism, of what may be called maps and paths: that is, maps of the constituent features of the cosmos, and paths to deliverance from bondage. Emerging within Hindusim at this period, and particularly in the schools least affiliated with the Vedic tradition, such concerns no doubt represent an effort to counter the proliferation of maps and paths set forth by the heterodoxies (not only Buddhism and Jainism, but the Ajivikas). They allow for a somewhat more open recognition of the deity of *bhakti* (Samkhya excepted) than do the *smarta* schools, though none of the *haituka* schools makes it truly central.

Nyaya and Vaisesika, systems first propounded in Gautama's *Nyaya Sutra* (c. 200 BCE-150 CE) and Kanada's *Vaisesika Sutra* (c. 200 BCE-100 CE), were quickly recognized as a hyphenated pair: Nyaya-Vaisesika. Nyaya ("rule, logic, analysis"), emphasizing logic and methods of argumentation as means to liberation, was viewed as complementary to Vaisesika ("school of distinct characteristics"), which advanced a theory of atomism and posited seven categories to explain such things as atomic aggregation and dualistic distinction between soul and matter. At least by about the fifth century, when the two schools had conjoined, Nyaya logic and Vaisesika cosmology served to provide influential arguments from design for the existence of God as the efficient cause of the creation and destruction of the universe and liberator of the soul from *karman*.

Far more influential, however, were the pair Samkhya ("enumeration") and Yoga. The foundational texts of these schools may be later than those of the others, but they are clearly distillations of long-continuing traditions, datable at least to the middle Upanisads, that had already undergone considerable systematization. Thus Patañjali's *Yoga Sutra* is from either about 200 BCE or 300-500 CE, depending on whether or not one identifies the author with the grammarian who lived at the earlier date. And Isvarakrsna's *Samkhyakarikas* probably date from the fourth century CE. Even though Samkhya's "atheism" and its soteriology of the isolation *(kaivalya)* of the soul *(purusa)* from matter *(prakrti)* have been modified or rejected in other forms of Hinduism (both doctrines may link Samkhya with Jainism), Samkhya's cosmology and basic terminology have become definitive for Hinduism at many levels: not only in the Vedanta, but in *bhakti* and Tantric formulations as well. In fact, given the preclassical forms of theistic Samkhya founded in the Upanisads and the *Mahabharata* and their use in *bhakti* cosmologies, it may well be that the atheism of the classical Samkhya results from a rejection of *bhakti* elements from a fundamentally theistic system. Samkhya thus posits *purusa* without a transcendent, divine Purusa, and its *prakrti* is also abstract and impersonal.

In any case, a number of Samkhya concepts became basic to the Hindu vocabulary, only to be integrated and reinterpreted from different theological and soteriological perspectives by other schools. These include the concepts of the evolution and devolution of *prakrti*, the sexual polarity of *purusa* as male and *prakrti* as female, the enumeration of twenty-three substances that evolve from and devolve back into the *prakrti* "matrix," the concept of matter as a continuum from subtle psychomental "substances" to gross physical ones (in particular the five elements), and the notion of the three "strands" or "qualities" called *gunas* (*sattva*, goodness, lucidity; *rajas*, dynamism; *tamas*, entropy), which are "braided" together through all matter from the subtle to the gross.

Meanwhile, whereas Samkhya provides the map to be "known," Yoga defines the path by which *purusa* can extricate itself from *prakrti*. The "eight limbs" of Yoga (an answer to the Eightfold Path of Buddhism?) represent the most important Hindu formulation of a step-by-step (though also cumulative) path to liberation. The first two "limbs" involve forms of restraint *(yama)* and observance *(niyama)*. The next three involve integration of the body and senses: posture *(asana)*, breath control *(pranayama)*, and withdrawal of the senses from the dominance of sense objects *(pratyahara)*. The last three achieve the integration of the mind or the "cessation of the mental turmoil" that is rooted in the effects of *karman*: "holding" *(dharana)* to a meditative support, meditative fluency *(dhyana)*, and integrative concentration *(samadhi)* through which the freedom of *purusa* can be experienced.

The classical Yoga of Patañjali, known as *rajayoga* ("royal yoga"), diverges from the Samkhya in acknowledging the existence of God (Isvara). But Isvara is a focus of meditation, not an agent in the process of liberation. The use of the term *rajayoga*, however, suggests that by Patañjali's time the term *yoga* had already been used to describe other disciplines or paths, resulting in a situation where the terms *yoga* ("yoke") and *marga*

("path") had become interchangeable. One will thus find *rajayoga* mentioned later along with the more generalized "yogas", or "paths," that become definitive for Hinduism through their exposition in the *Bhagavadgita* (c. 200 BCE): the paths (or yogas) of *karman* ("action"), *jñana* ("knowledge"), and *bhakti* ("devotion").

CLASSICAL BHAKTI HINDUISM. The consolidation of Hinduism takes place under the sign of *bhakti*. And though Mimamsa ritualism and Vedantic and other "knowledge" trends continue to affiliate with an "orthodox" strain that resists this synthesis, or attempts to improve upon it, classical *bhakti* emerges as constitutive henceforth of mainstream Hinduism, including forms of devotional sectarianism.

Intimations of *bhakti* developments are registered as early as the late Vedic Upanisads, and in inscriptions and other records of syncretistic worship of Hindu deities (Visnu and Siva) alongside foreign and heterodox figures in the early centuries of the common era. However, the heterogeneity and scattered nature of the nontextual information available on the emergence of *bhakti* during this period have allowed for conflicting interpretations of the salient features of the process. But rather than reweave a fragile developmental web from supposedly separate sectarian and popular strands, it is better to look at the texts themselves to see what they attempted and achieved. We should note, however, that to the best of our knowledge it was achieved relatively early in the period of consolidation, for the *Bhagavadgita*—the text that seals the achievement—seems to be from no later than the first or second century BCE (it is cited by Badarayana in the *Vedanta Sutra*), and possibly earlier. Of course, continued unfolding occurred after that.

The achievement itself is a universal Hinduism that, following Biardeau's discussion of *bhakti* in "Études de mythologie hindoue" (1976), we may designate as *smarta*. It inherits from the Brahmanic sacrificial tradition a conception wherein Visnu and Siva are recognized as complementary in their functions but ontologically identical. The fundamental texts of this devotional *smarta* vision are the two epics—the *Mahabharata* (c. 500 BCE-400 CE) and the *Ramayana* (c. 400-200 BCE)—and the *Harivamsa* (c. 300-400 CE?). These works integrate much Puranic mythic and cosmological material, which later is spun out at greater length in the classical Puranas ("ancient lore"), of which there are said to be eighteen major and eighteen minor texts. The epics and Puranas are thus necessarily discussed together. But it should be recognized that whereas the *smarta* vision of the epics and the *Harivamsa* is fundamentally integrative and universal in intent, the Puranas are frequently dominated by regional and particularistic interests, including in some cases the strong advocacy of the worship of one deity (Siva, Visnu, or the Goddess) over all others. It is thus tempting to think of the period of Purana composition (c. 400-1200 CE?) as one that extends the integrative vision of the fundamental texts but develops it in varied directions. Still, as it is not clear that instances of Puranic theological favoritism are motivated by distinct sects, it is misleading to speak of "sectarian" Puranas.

Taken together, then, the *Harivamsa* and the *Mahabharata* (which includes the *Bhagavadgita*) present the full biography of Krsna, and the *Ramayana* that of Rama. The *Harivamsa* (Genealogy of Hari—i. e., Krsna), the more recent of the texts concerning Krsna, presents the stories of his birth and youth, in which he and his brother Balarama take on the "disguise" *(vesa)* of cowherds. Thus they engage in divine "sport" *(lila)* with the cowherd women *(gopis)*, until finally they are drawn away to avenge themselves against their demonic uncle Kamsa, who had caused their exile. The *Mahabharata* (Story of the Great Bharata Dynasty) focuses on Krsna's assistance to the five Pandava brothers in their conflicts with their cousins, the hundred Kauravas, over the "central kingdom" of the lunar dynasty (the Bharata dynasty) at Hastinapura and Indraprastha near modern Delhi. Both texts incorporate telling allusions to the other "cycle," and since both stories must have circulated orally together before reaching their present literary forms, any notions of their separate origins are purely conjectural. The *Ramayana* (Exploits of Rama) tells the story of Rama, scion of the solar dynasty and embodiment of *dharma*, who must rescue his wife Sita from the demon *(raksasa)* Ravana. Though each of these texts has its special flavor and distinctive background, they become in their completed forms effectively a complementary triad. Indeed, in the "conservative" South, popular performances of Hindu mythology in dramas and temple recitations are still dominated by three corresponding specializations: *Mahabharata*, *Ramayana*, and *Bhagavata Purana*, the latter (c. 800-900 CE?) enriching the devotional themes of the *Harivamsa* in its tenth and eleventh books and in effect replacing it as representing the early life of Krsna.

The *smarta* universe in these texts is structured around Visnu, and more particularly around his two heroic incarnations, Rama and Krsna. Thus other deities are frequently represented as subordinated to or subsumed by these figures. But there is also recognition of Visnu's complementarity with Siva: some passages that stress mutual acknowledgment of their ontological unity, others that work out the interplay between them through stories about heroic characters who incarnate them, and scenes in which Visnu's incarnations do homage to Siva. It should be clear that efforts to find

The Bhagavadgita *is perhaps the most widely read and beloved scripture in all Indian religious literature.*

PAGE 323

"tendencies toward monotheism" in such texts involve the reduction of a very complex theology to distinctly Western terms. The same applies to those Puranas that are structured around Siva or the Goddess rather than Visnu but are still framed within the same cosmology and the same principles of theological complementarity and subordination.

This *smarta* vision is not, however, limited to one theological conundrum, for it extends to encompass Siva and Visnu's interaction with other major figures: the god Brahma, masculine form of the impersonal Absolute *(brahman)*, now subordinated to the higher "personal" deities; the Goddess in her many forms; Indra and other *devas* (now "demigods"); their still perennial foes, the demons *(asuras)*; and of course humans, animals, and so on. It also presents an overarching *bhakti* cosmology in which the yogic supreme divinity (Siva or Visnu) encompasses the religious values of *samnyasa*, *tapas*, knowledge, and sacrifice, and introduces the view that taken by themselves, without *bhakti*, these values may be incomplete or even extreme "paths." Further, it incorporates the *smarta* social theory of the Dharmasutras and the Dharmasastras, and works out its implications within the cosmology.

Siva's many-sided character, to which accreted features of great gods as well as demoniac powers, is split up into many partial manifestations representing aspects of his ambivalent nature.

PAGE 324

HINDU CHRONOMETRIC THEORY

Counting in Divine Years

Time is structured according to three main rhythms, hierarchically defined, the longer encompassing the lesser. Most down-to-earth is the series of four *yugas* named after four dice throws, which define a theory of the "decline of the *dharma*": first a *krtayuga* ("perfect age"), then a *tretayuga* and a *dvaparayuga*, and finally a degenerate *kaliyuga* ("age of discord"). A *krtayuga* lasts 4,000 years, a *tretayuga* 3,000, a *dvaparayuga* 2,000, and a *kaliyuga* 1,000, each supplemented by a dawn and twilight of one-tenth its total. A full four-*yuga* cycle thus lasts 12,000 years and is called a *mahayuga* ("great yuga"). These are not human years, however, but divine years, which are 360 times as long as human years. Thus a *mahayuga* equals 360 times 12,000, or 4,320,000 human years, and a *kaliyuga* is one-tenth of that total. A thousand *mahayugas* (4,320 million human years) is a *kalpa*, the second major time unit, which is also called a "day of Brahma." Brahma's days are followed by nights of equal duration. Brahma lives a hundred years of 360 such days and nights, or 311,040 billion human years, all of which are sometimes said to pass in a wink of the eye of Visnu. The period of a life of Brahma, called a *mahakalpa*, is the third major temporal rhythm.

— ALF HILTEBEITEL

Working backward, we may observe the *modus operandi* of Visnu and Siva (and of course others) as it is envisioned in the *smarta* Hinduism of our texts.

First, at the highest level, Visnu and Siva are great yogins, interacting with the rhythms of the universe in terms of their own oscillations between activity and yogic concentration *(samadhi)*. At the *mahapralaya* ("great dissolution"), the deity (usually Visnu in these early texts, but just as often Siva or the Goddess in later Puranic ones) oversees the dissolution of the universe into the primal *prakrti* in accord with the cosmological theory of Samkhya-Yoga. This ends the life of Brahma, but it is also to be noted that it marks the restoration to its primordial unity of *prakrti*, which—as feminine—is regarded mythologically as the ultimate form of the Goddess. From a Saiva standpoint, the male (the deity as Purusa) and the female (the Goddess as Prakrti) are reunited at the great dissolution of the universe, a theme that is depicted in representations of the deity as Ardhanarisvara, "the Lord who is half female." Their union is nonprocreative and represents the unitive experience of the bliss of *brahman*. Creation then occurs when the deity (whether Siva or Visnu) emerges from this *samadhi* and instigates the renewed active unfolding of *prakrti*.

The coincidence of the death of Brahma with not only the dissolution of the universe but the reintegration of the Goddess and her reunion with Siva is highly significant. The Goddess is an eternal being, worthy of worship because—like Visnu and Siva—she outlasts the universe and can bestow *moksa*. Brahma, ultimately mortal and bound to temporality, is worshiped not for *moksa* but rather—and mostly by demons—for earthly power and lordship. Stories that portray Siva's severing of Brahma's fifth head and refer to the "head of Brahma" *(brahmasiras)* as the weapon of doomsday, are perhaps mythic echoes of this ultimate cosmological situation wherein the coming together of Purusa and Prakrti coincide with his death.

The primary creation has as its result the constitution of a "cosmic egg," the *brahmanda* ("egg of Brahma"). Further creation, and periodic recreations, will be carried out by Brahma, the personalized form of the Absolute *(brahman)*. Insofar as the *brahman* is personalized and oriented toward the world, it is thus subordinated to the yogin Purusa, the ultimate as defined through *bhakti*. Moreover, the activity of Brahma—heir in his cosmogenic role of the earlier Prajapati—is conceived in terms of sacrificial themes that are further encompassed by *bhakti*.

It is at this level that the three male gods cooperate as the *trimurti*, the "three forms" of the Absolute: Brahma the creator, Siva the destroyer, and Visnu the preserver. Within the *brahmanda*, Brahma thus creates the Vedic triple world of earth, atmosphere, and heaven (or alternatively heaven, earth, and underworld). These three samsaric worlds are surrounded by four ulterior worlds, still within the *brahmanda*, for beings who achieve release from *samsara* but still must await their ultimate liberation. These ulterior worlds are not henceforth created or destroyed in the occasional creations or destructions. As to the triple world, Brahma creates it by becoming the sacrificial boar *(yajñavaraha)* who retrieves the Vedas and the earth from the cosmic ocean. The destruction of the triple world is achieved by Siva. As the "fire of the end of time," he reduces it to ashes, thus effecting a cosmic funerary sacrifice. And Visnu, the god whom the Brahmanas identify as "the sacrifice," maintains the triple world while it is sustained by sacrifices, and also preserves what is left of it after the dissolution when he lies on the serpent Sesa ("remainder") whose name indicates that he is formed of the remnant of the previous cosmos, or more exactly of the "remainder" of the cosmic sacrifice. This form of Visnu, sleeping on Sesa, is called Narayana, a name that the *Satapatha Brahmana* already connects with the Vedic Purusa, the "male" source of all beings. When Visnu-Narayana awakens, Brahma—who in some fashion awakens with him—recreates the universe. Through all these myths the earth is a form of the Goddess, indeed the most concretized form she takes as a result of the evolution of *prakrti* (earth being the last of the evolutes emitted and the first to dissolve).

Thus the greater universe whose rhythms are integrated within the divine yoga of Visnu and Siva encompasses an egg of Brahma, which encloses a triple world whose rhythms form a round sustained by the divine sacrificial acts of the *trimurti*. This pattern is transposed onto the third temporal rhythm, that of the *yugas*. Thus the characteristic religious virtues of the *yugas* are as follows: *dhyana* ("meditation") or *tapas* ("asceticism") in the *krtayuga*; *jñana* ("knowledge") in the *tretayuga*; *yajña* ("sacrifice") in the *dvaparayuga*; and *dana* ("the gift") in the *kaliyuga*. Thus the two *sruti*-based ideals of knowledge and sacrifice are enclosed within a frame-work that begins with yogic meditation as a divine *krtayuga* activity and ends in the *kaliyuga* with the devotional gift. *Bhakti* thus encompasses knowledge and sacrifice.

The distinctive feature of the rhythm of the *yuga* cycle is that it is calibrated by the rise and fall of *dharma* in the triple world. Beings who have achieved release from the triple world oscillate between the four higher worlds, enduring periodic destructions of the triple world and awaiting the great dissolution of the universe that will dissolve the egg of Brahma (coincident with his death) and result in a vast collective ultimate liberation of reabsorption into the supreme Purusa. Needless to say, this is to occur only after an almost incalculable wait. But beings who have attained these ulterior worlds are no more affected by *dharma* than the yogic deity beyond them. The maintenance of *dharma* within the triple world thus engages the deities in their third level of activity, that of "descent." In classical terms this is the theory of the *avatara*. Though the term is not used in the epics or the *Harivamsa* in its later, specialized sense, these texts are suffused by the concept and its *bhakti* implications, which include narrative situations wherein the divinity looks to all concerned, and sometimes even to himself, as a mere human. The programmatic statement of the *avatara* concept (without mention of the term itself) is thus stated by Krsna in the *Bhagavadgita*: "For whenever the Law [*dharma*] languishes, Bharata, and lawlessness flourishes I create myself. I take on existence from eon to eon [*yuga* to *yuga*], for the rescue of the good and the destruction of evil, in order to establish the Law" (4.7-8; van Buitenen, trans.).

The classical theory of the ten *avataras*—most of whom are mentioned in the epics and the *Harivamsa*, but not in a single list—is worked out in relation to Visnu. One thus has the following "descents" of Visnu in order of appearance: Fish (Matsya), Tortoise (Kurma), Boar (Varaha), Man-Lion (Narasimha), Dwarf (Vamana), Rama with the Ax (Parasurama), Rama of the *Ramayana*, Krsna, the Buddha, and the future *avatara* Kalki, who will rid the earth of barbarian kings and reestablish the *dharma* at the end of the *kaliyuga*. There are various attempts to correlate appearances of the *avataras* with distinct *yugas* and even *kalpas*, but the one feature that is consistently mentioned in these formative texts is that Krsna appeared at the interval between the last *dvaparayuga* and *kaliyuga*, and thus at the beginning of our present age. It is likely that the theory was first formulated around Krsna and Rama along with the Dwarf (the only form to be associated with Visnu in the *sruti* literature) and the apocalyptic Kalki. But in actuality, the *avatara* theory is more complex. In the epics and in living Hinduism, Visnu does not descend alone. In the literature, his incarnations take place alongside those of other deities, including most centrally Vayu, Indra, Surya, the Goddess, and—at least in the *Mahabharata*—Siva. And in localized temple mythologies throughout India, one hears of *avataras* of Siva and the Goddess as well as of Visnu. In devotional terms, the *avatara* is thus a form taken on earth (or, better, in the three worlds) by any one of the three

"For whenever the Law languishes, and lawlessness flourishes I create myself."

KRSNA
BHAGAVADGITA

deities we find at the ultimate level of cosmic absorption, where all that remains beside the liberated beings who join them are the eternal yogic deities Visnu and Siva and the primal Goddess.

The classical concept of the *avatara*, structured around Visnu, remains, however, the chief Hindu use of the term. Its formulation in the epics and the *Harivamsa* is thus constitutive for succeeding eras of Hinduism, in which it will only be enriched but not essentially changed by later *bhakti* theologies. Looking at these texts comprehensively, then, with the *Gita* as our main guide, we can outline its main contours. Against the background of the vast, all-embracing *bhakti* cosmology, the involvement of the yogic divinity on earth takes place completely freely, as "sport" or "play" *(lila)*. Still, the god takes birth to uphold the *dharma* and to keep the earth from being unseasonably inundated in the waters of dissolution under the weight of adharmic kings. The *avatara* thus intercedes to uphold the system of *varnasramadharma* and to promote the proper pursuit of the four *purusarthas*. Since he appears in times of crisis, a central concern in the texts is with the resolution of the conflicts between ideals: renunciation versus householdership, *brahmana* versus *ksatriya*, killing versus "not desiring to kill" *(ahimsa)*, *dharma* versus *moksa*, *dharma* versus *kama* and *artha*, and conflicts between different *dharmas* (duties) such as royal duty and filial duty. But though the texts focus primarily on the two upper castes, the full society is represented by singular depictions of figures who evoke the lowest castes and tribal groups. It is also filled in with figures of real and reputed mixed caste.

Low castes worship the pure gods in their temples. And high castes acknowledge the power of the impure deities.

PAGE 293

Confusion of caste is a particularly prominent issue in the *Mahabharata*, where it is raised by Krsna in the *Gita* as the worst of ills. Most significantly, the *Mahabharata* and the *Harivamsa* identify a particularly pernicious form of caste confusion among the barbarian *(mleccha)* peoples of the Northwest (the Punjab), mentioning Yavanas, Sakas, and Pahlavas among others as enemies of the *dharma* and causes for such "mixing." The fact that events of the period from 300 BCE to 300 CE are projected into the distant past indicates that part of the *bhakti* synthesis was the articulation of a mythical theory of historical events. One may thus look at these *smrti* texts as posing a model for the revival of Hinduism in accord with "eternal" Vedic models, with the descent of the *avatara*—and indeed of much of the Vedic pantheon along with him—guaranteeing the periodic adjustment of the sociocosmic world to these eternal norms. Furthermore, the tracing of all Hindu dynastic lines back to the defunct if not mythical "lunar" and "solar" dynasties provided the model for the spatial extension of this ideal beyond the central lands of Aryavarta where the *dharma*, according to both *Manu* and the *Mahabharata*, was the purest.

But the focus of the *avatara* is not solely on the renovation of the *dharma*. He also brings to the triple world the divine grace that makes possible the presence, imagery, and teachings that confer *moksa*. The epics and the *Harivamsa* are full of *bhakti* tableaux: moments that crystallize the realization by one character or another of the liberating vision *(darsana)* of the divine. Most central, however, is the *Bhagavadgita*, which is both a *darsana* and a teaching.

The *Bhagavadgita* (Song of the Lord) takes place as a dialogue between Krsna and Arjuna just before the outbreak of the *Mahabharata* war. Although he is the third oldest of the five Pandavas, Arjuna is their greatest warrior, and Krsna's task in the *Gita* is to persuade him to overcome his reluctance to fight in the battle. Fundamental to the argument is Arjuna's requirement to fulfill his *dharma* as a *ksatriya* rather than adopt the ideal—unsuitable for him in his present life stage—of the renouncer. Thus the *Gita* champions the theory of *varnasramadharma* as upholding the sociocosmic order.

Krsna presents his teaching to Arjuna by revealing a sequence of "royal" and "divine" mysteries that culminate in his granting a vision of his "All-Form" *(Visvarupa-darsana)* as God, creator and destroyer of the universe. In this grand cosmic perspective, Arjuna is told that he will be but the "mere instrument" of the deaths of his foes, their destruction having now come to ripeness through Visnu's own agency in his form as cosmic time, or *kala* (*Bhagavadgita* 11.32-33). Arjuna thus recognizes this omniform deity as Visnu in this climactic scene.

On the way to this revelation, however, Krsna acknowledges the three paths *(yogas)* to salvation: action, knowledge, and devotion. These are presented as instructions by which Arjuna can gain the resolute clarity of insight *(buddhi)* and yogic discipline by which to recognize the distinctions between soul and body, action and inaction, and thus perform actions—including killing—that are unaffected by desire. Ritual action and knowledge are set forth as legitimate and mutually reinforcing paths, but incomplete unless integrated within and subordinated to *bhakti*. Krsna thus presents himself as the ultimate *karmayogin*, acting to benefit the worlds out of no personal desire. He thus bids his devotees *(bhaktas)* to surrender all actions to him as in a sacrifice, but a sacrifice *(karman)* no longer defined in Vedic-Mimamsa terms as a means to fulfill some personal desire. Krsna also presents himself as the object of all religious knowledge, the highest purusa *(uttamapurusa)* and supreme self *(paramatman)*, beyond the perishable and the imperishable, yet pervading and supporting all worlds (15.16-17).

One other facet of the *bhakti* synthesis to which the

Gita alludes is the transition from traditional Vedic sacrifice *(yajña)* to new forms of offering to the deity (*puja*, literally, "honoring"). This corresponds to the theory that the "gift" is the particularly appropriate religious practice for the *kaliyuga*. Thus Krsna says: "If one disciplined soul proffers to me with love [*bhakti*] a leaf, a flower, fruit, or water, I accept this offering of love from him. Whatever you do, or eat, or offer, or give, or mortify, make it an offering to me, and I shall undo the bonds of *karman*" (9.26-27; van Buitenen, trans.). The passage probably refers to domestic worship of the "deity of one's choice" *(istadevata)*. But it is also likely to allude to temple worship, for it is known from inscriptions and literary sources from the third to first century BCE that sanctuaries existed for Vasudeva and Kesava (presumably as names for Krsna and Visnu), as well as for other deities. By the beginning of the Gupta period, around 320 CE, temple building was in full swing, with inscriptions showing construction of temples for Visnu, Siva, and the Goddess. Temples were built at sites within cities, as well as at remote holy places, and sanctuaries at both such locations became objectives along pilgrimage routes that are first mentioned in the *Mahabharata*. From very early if not from the beginning of such temple worship, the deities were represented by symbols and/or iconic images.

Certain aspects of temple construction and worship draw inspiration from the Vedic sacrifice. The plan of the edifice is designed on the ground as the Vastupurusamandala, a geometric figure of the "Purusa of the Site" *(vastu)*, from whom the universe takes form. The donor, ideally a king, is the *yajamana*. The *sanctum sanctorum*, called the *garbhagrha* ("womb house"), continues the symbolism of the Vedic *diksa* hut: here again the *yajamana* becomes an embryo so as to achieve a new birth, now taking into his own being the higher self of the deity that he installs there in the form of an image. The temple as a whole is thus a Vedic altar comprising the triple world, but also an expanded image of the cosmos through which the deity manifests himself from within, radiating energy to the outer walls where his (or her) activities and interactions with the world are represented. [*See* Temple, *article on* Hindu Temples.]

But the use of the temple for ordinary daily worship involves radically non-Vedic objectives. The Vedic sacrifice is a means for gods and men—basically equals—to fulfill reciprocal desires. *Puja* rites are means for God and man to interact on a level beyond desire: for man to give without expectation of reward, or, more exactly, to get back nothing tangible other than what he has offered but with the paradoxical conviction that the deity "shares" (from the root meaning of *bhakti*) what is given and returns it as an embodiment of his or her grace *(prasada)*. God is thus fully superior, served as a royal guest with rites of hospitality. Basically four moments are involved: offerings, taking sight *(darsana)* of the deity, receiving this *prasada*, and leave-taking by circumambulation of the *garbhagrha* and the image within. The offerings are the *puja* proper and comprise a great variety of devotional acts designed to please the deity, some of which may be worked into a daily round by the temple priests, who offer on behalf of others.

Finally, one last element of the consolidation of Hinduism achieved by early Gupta times is the emergence of the Goddess as a figure whose worship is recognized alongside that of Visnu and Siva and is performed with the same basic rites. Indeed, it is possible that aspects of *puja* ceremonialism are derived from non-Vedic *sudra* and village rites in which female deities no doubt figured highly, as they do in such cults today. The two epics, the *Mahabharata* and the *Ramayana*, reflect themes associated with the Goddess in the portrayals of their chief heroines, Draupadi and Sita, but the *Harivamsa* is probably the first text to acknowledge the Goddess as such. There she takes birth as Krsna and Balarama's "sister" (actually she and Krsna exchange mothers). Some of her future demon enemies are mentioned, and there is also reference to her having numerous places of worship and a cult that apparently included animal sacrifice. Thus the Goddess is integrated even within the texts of the early *smarta* Hinduism that are centered on Visnu. But the text that registers her full emergence is the *Devimahatmyam* (Glorification of the Goddess). Probably from about 400-600 CE, it was included in the *Markandeya Purana*. Here the Goddess is recognized under all her major aspects, as primal matter embodied in the universe yet beyond it, incarnate in many forms, cause of the joys and miseries of this world and of liberation from it, the power *(sakti)* enabling the roles of the *trimurti*, yet higher than the gods and their last resort in the face of certain demons, most notably the buffalo demon Mahisasura, her most dedicated and persistent foe through cults and myths both ancient and current. This emergence of the Goddess is registered more fully in the development of Tantric Hinduism.

TANTRIC HINDUISM

Tantra is literally "what extends." In its Hindu form it may be taken, according to its name, as a movement that sought to extend the Veda (whose pedigree it loosely claimed) and more particularly to extend the universalistic implications of *bhakti* Hinduism. However, although it was quick to integrate *bhakti* elements and to influence *bhakti* in nearly all its forms (late Puranic, popular, and sectarian), its earliest and most enduring forms "extend" Hinduism in ways that were directly opposed to the epic-Puranic *bhakti* synthesis. Nonetheless, it is still formulated within the same cosmology.

In the Hindu temple, the axis of cosmic creation and the ritual path for release of the aspirant/worshiper/sacrificer (yajamana) meet.

PAGE 659

Early Tantrism developed most vigorously, from the fourth to sixth centuries CE, in areas where Brahmanic penetration had been weakest: in the Northwest, in Bengal and Assam in the East, and in the Andhra area of the South. These are areas where one must assume non-Aryan influences in general, and more particularly probably also tribal and folk practices involving shamanism, witchcraft, and sorcery, and, at least in the East and South, a cult of the Goddess. As Tantrism gained currency in succeeding centuries throughout India, the shamanistic and magical features were assimilated to yogic disciplines, while the elevation of the Goddess gave full projection on a pan-Indian scale to roles and images of the Goddess that had been incorporated, but allowed only minimal scope, in the early orthodox *bhakti* and even earlier Vedic sacrificial traditions. The earliest extant Tantric texts are Buddhist, from about the fourth to sixth centuries. [*See* Buddhism, Schools of, *article on* Esoteric Buddhism.] Hindu Tantric texts include Vaisnava Samhitas, Saivagamas from a slightly later period, and Sakta Tantras (exalting the Goddess as Sakti, or Power) from perhaps the eleventh century on. But from its start Tantrism represented a style and outlook that placed the Goddess at the center of its "extensions" and to a certain extent cut across sectarian and religious distinctions, whether Hindu, Buddhist, or even Jain.

THE GODDESS

Tantrism places The Goddess at the center of its "extensions."

THE PURCELL TEAM/CORBIS

Tantric practice (sadhana) addresses itself to experiencing the unity of purusa and prakrti (purusa being both "soul" and deity, prakrti being both "matter" and Goddess).

PAGE 307

Though Hindu Tantra thus asserts its Vedic legitimacy, its stance is intentionally anti-Brahmanic. It was especially critical of Brahmanic concepts of hierarchy, purity, and sexual status, all of which had been reinforced by the orthodox *bhakti* synthesis and which were in particular bound up with a theology that viewed the supreme divinity as a male (a Purusa, whether Siva or Visnu) whose ultimate form was accessible only beyond the rhythms of the cosmos and its hierarchy of impure and pure, gross and subtle worlds. For Tantrics, dualities were artificial and their experience was the result of delusion. On the analogy of the union between Siva and Sakti, which in Puranic devotional terms is conceivable only at the end of the *mahapralaya*, or great dissolution of the universe, Tantric practice *(sadhana)* addresses itself to experiencing the unity of *purusa* and *prakrti* (purusa being both "soul" and deity, *prakrti* being both "matter" and Goddess), male and female, pure and impure, knowledge and action, and so on. Most important, all this takes place here and now, not only in this world, where *prakrti* and *purusa* on the macrocosmic scale are one, but in the human body, where their microcosmic embodiments can be experienced. The body thus becomes the ultimate vehicle for liberation, the dissolution of opposites taking place within the psychophysical continuum of the experience of the living adept, who realizes beyond duality the oneness of *brahman*.

Beyond these practices, "left-handed" Tantrics pursue in literal fashion the ceremonial of the "five *m*'s" *(pañca-makarapuja)*. That is, they incorporate into their cultic practice five "sacraments" beginning with the syllable *ma*: fish *(matsya)*, meat *(mamsa)*, parched grain (*mudra*, regarded as an aphrodisiac), wine *(madya)*, and finally sexual intercourse *(maithuna)*. It is likely that most if not all of these practices involve the incorporation of elements of the cult and mythology of the Goddess, who already in the *Devimahatmyam* delights in meat and wine and is approached by lustful demons for sexual intercourse. Tantric texts stress that these practices are to be carried out within a circle of adepts and supervised by a male and female pair of "lords of the circle" who insist on strict ritual conventions that guard against an orgiastic interpretation. Classically, the male is to retain his semen at the point of orgasm, this being a sign not only of profound dispassion but an actualization of the nonprocreative union of Siva and Sakti at the dissolution of the universe of dualities.

It is interesting to note that, although their historical validity is debated by scholars, there are strong Indian traditions suggesting that Sankara's philosophical nondualism had practical Tantric repercussions. [*See also* Tantrism.]

TANTRIC PRACTICE
Right and Left Hands

Two types of Tantra are mentioned in Hindu texts: "left-hand" and "right-hand." The Tantric rejection and indeed inversion of orthopraxy is most pronounced in the former, as the right-hand Tantra interprets the most anti-Brahmanic practices of the left metaphorically, and also includes under its heading a wide variety of ceremonial rituals assimilated into *bhakti* Hinduism that are simply non-Vedic. These include the use of non-Vedic *mantras* as well as *yantras* and *mandalas*, aniconic and non-Vedic geometric devices used for visualization and integration of divine-cosmic forces. Adepts come from all castes, but low-caste and even tribal practitioners and teachers are especially revered. The goal of liberation within the body takes the specific form of seeking magical powers *(siddhis)*, which in orthodox forms of Hinduism are regarded as hindrances to spiritual achievement. Under the tutelage of a guru, who embodies the fulfillment sought and its transmission and who is thus all-important, the *siddhis* are sought through yoga disciplines that show the impact of Tantra through their anatomical analysis of the "subtle body" *(linga sarira)*. First practiced is hathayoga, the "yoga of exertion or violence," that is, rigorous physical discipline geared to coordinating the body's "ducts" or "channels" *(nadis)* and "energy centers" *(cakras)*. This is followed by *kundaliniyoga*, which awakens the dormant *sakti*, conceived as a coiled-up "serpent power" in the lowest *cakra* between the genitals and the anus, so that it (or she) can pierce and transform all the *cakras* (usually six) and unite with Siva in the "thousand-petaled *cakra*" in the region of the brain.

— ALF HILTEBEITEL

SANKARA'S ADVAITA VEDANTA AND SMARTA ORTHODOXY

The Advaita (nondualist) interpretation of the Vedanta can be traced back at least to Gaudapada (c. 600 ce), but it is Sankara (c. 788-820) who established this viewpoint as the touchstone of a revived smarta orthodoxy. Born in a small Kerala village, Sankara spent his alleged thirty-two years as a vigorous champion of the unity of Hinduism over and against intra-Hindu divisions and the inroads of Buddhism and Jainism. He toured India, setting up monasteries (mathas) near famous temples or holy places at each of the four compass directions, and appointed a disciple at each center to begin a line of renunciant "pontiffs." And he wrote works of great subtlety and persuasiveness, including commentaries on the Upanisads, the Brahma Sutra, and the Bhagavadgita that inspired contemporaries, disciples, and authors of later generations to write additional important works from the perspective that he developed.

An essential feature of Sankara's argumentation is that lower views of reality must be rejected as they are contradicted or "sublated" by higher experiences of the real. Finally, all dichotomous formulations must be abandoned upon the nondual experience of the self *(atman)* as *brahman*. The world of appearance is sustained by ignorance *(avidya)*, which "superimposes" limitations on reality. *Maya* ("illusion" or "fabrication"), itself neither real nor unreal, is indescribable in terms of being or nonbeing. It appears real only so long as *brahman* is not experienced. But it is empirically real relative to things that can be shown false from the standpoint of empirical observation. Maya is thus said to be more mysterious and unknowable than brahman, which is experienced as being, consciousness, and bliss *(sat-cit-ananda)*.

As philosophy, Advaita is thus a guide to *moksa*, which is experienced when the ignorance that results from superimposing *maya* on *brahman* is overcome. Liberation arises with knowledge *(jñana)*, but from a perspective that recognizes relative truth in the paths of both action and *bhakti*. Practically, Sankara fostered a rapprochement between Advaita and *smarta* orthodoxy, which by his time had not only continued to defend the *varnasramadharma* theory as defining the path of *karman*, but had developed the practice of *pañcayatana-puja* ("five-shrine worship") as a solution to varied and conflicting devotional practices. Thus one could worship any one of five deities (Visnu, Siva, Durga, Surya, Ganesa) as one's *istadevata* ("deity of choice"). As far as *varnasramadharma* was concerned, Sankara left householder issues largely aside and focused instead on founding ten orders of *samnyasis* (the *dasanami*, "ten names"), each affiliated with one of the four principle *mathas* he founded. But traditional orthodox views of caste were maintained. According to Sankara, as *sudras* are not entitled to hear the Veda, they cannot pursue knowledge of *brahman* as *samnyasis*; rather they may seek *moksa* through hearing the *Mahabharata* and the Puranas. Four of the ten *samnyasi* orders were thus restricted to *brahmanas*, and it does not seem that any accepted *sudras* until long after Sankara's death. *Bhakti* sectarian reformers were generally more liberal on this point. As to the god (or gods) of *bhakti*, Sankara views the deity (Isvara) as

Mantrasastra, the teaching of mantras, is often taken as meaning tantrasastra, the teaching of the Tantras.

PAGE 648

essentially identical with *brahman* and real relative to empirical experience. But by being identified "with qualities" *(saguna)*, God can be no more than an approach to the experience of *brahman* "without qualities" *(nirguna)*. Viewed from the experience of the self as *nirguna brahman*, which "sublates" all other experiences, the deity is but the highest form of *maya*. Clearly, *bhakti* traditions could not rest with this solution. But it should be noted that in opposing Sankara and abandoning the universalist vision of the epic-Puranic devotional synthesis, the sects turned their backs on the main impulses that had attempted to sustain the unity of Hinduism.

SECTARIAN HINDUISM

The elaboration of *bhakti* Hinduism continued to unfold in the later Puranas, linking up with the temple and pilgrimage cultus and with local and regional forms of worship. It thus established itself until the time of Sankara as the main expression of Brahmanic orthodoxy and the main shaping force of popular Hinduism. But though it proclaimed a universal Hinduism, it gave little weight to the problem of the immediate accessibility of salvation. While caste hierarchy was to remain in effect on earth to assure, among other things, the pure temple worship of the gods by the *brahmanas*, the ultimate release that the Puranas promised was almost infinitely postponed. It is possible that their postponement of a collective liberation was a kind of purification process for liberated souls and thus a prolongation of the concern for *brahmana* purity on earth. In any case, the remoteness of salvation and the defense of caste purity and hierarchy in the Puranic devotionalism of Brahmanic orthodoxy were probably incentives for the development of alternate forms of *bhakti*. These emerged in sectarian traditions, in movements led by saint-singers who inspired vernacular forms of *bhakti* revivalism, and more generally in local and regional forms of Hinduism.

"This embodied [soul] is eternally unslayable."

BHAGAVADGITA, 2:30

SECTARIAN TRADITIONS. Sectarianism and *bhakti* revivalism are movements of separate origins that converge for the first time in the eleventh and twelfth centuries in the Tamil-speaking area of South India. There the fusion was accomplished in the traditions of the Sri Vaisnavas and the Saiva Siddhanta, sects whose names indicate their distinctive theological preferences for Visnu and Siva. Henceforth, sectarianism and *bhakti* revivalism continued to interact and produce hybrid forms as they spread over all of India.

Generally speaking, sects followed a reformist impulse, and in most of them one can identify the emergence of the *guru* as a new type of figure: not the transmitter of an "impersonal" Vedic teaching, but one who takes inspiration from the personal deity of the sect, with whom he may even be identified. Traditional hierarchy was generally respected, but with the proviso that within the sect divine grace was not limited by caste boundaries. Nonetheless, as groups formed around masters and their teachings, they took on many of the characteristics and functions of castes (endogamy, interior ranking), and certain sects formulated their stands with particularly positive attitudes (the northern school of Sri Vaisnavas) or negative attitudes (Lingayats and Virasaivas) toward *brahmanas*. Sects distinguish themselves over and against each other by many means, and often quite passionately: by bodily markings, forms of yoga discipline, worship, theology, and in particular by their choice of supreme deity, whether Siva, Visnu, Sakti, or, in the North, Krsna or Rama. Nonetheless, they generally participate in wider Hindu activities such as pilgrimage, festival, and temple worship (the Lingayats are an exception) and draw upon fundamental Hindu belief structures. Thus most sects acknowledge other deities as subordinate to the supreme deity of the sect. In particular, most have worked out ways of encompassing the relation of the God and the Goddess at some fundamental theological level. Persistently the supreme deity is identified both as the ultimate brahman and also as in some way personal. The sects also frequently define various stages of divine descent or interaction with the world, various stages of the soul's ascent, and various types of relation between the soul and God. Thus the sects elaborate upon the epic-Puranic cosmology while modifying and refining the theological and soteriological terms. It is only against this background that their formulations are intelligible.

From the historical vantage point, one may note that the consolidation of the separate strands of sectarianism and *bhakti* revivalism occurs after, and is no doubt in part a response to, the growing success of Sankara's Advaita Vedanta. Prior to Sankara, sectarian groups had centered primarily around distinctive ritual traditions that were increasingly influenced by Tantrism: not only in forms of worship and theological formulation, but also, in some Saiva sects, in actual practice. Thus the Vaisnava Pañcaratras and Vaikhanasas and the Saiva Pasupatas (all mentioned first in the late *Mahabharata*) between the fifth and tenth centuries produced their Samhitas and Agamas to regularize the construction of temples, iconography, and *puja* ceremonialism. Some Pasupatas and Kapalikas (a Tantric Saiva sect) also incorporated forms of abrupt anticonventional behavior modeled on Siva's character as the great yogin ascetic. With the exception of the Pañcaratras, who elaborated an influential doctrine of the emanations *(vyuhas)* of Visnu that paralleled the cosmogonic theory of evolution in the Samkhya system, the theological formulations of these movements were apparently among their secondary concerns.

SAINT-SINGER TRADITION. Whereas the early sectarian movements were able to spread their impact from north to south using Sanskrit as their medium, the *bhakti* revivalist movement began in the South, drawing on Tamil. Like the sectarian movements, the saint-singers developed their traditions along Vaisnava and Saiva lines. The sixty-three Nayanmar (or Nayanars) promoted the worship of Siva, while the twelve Alvars similarly honored Visnu. Part of the revivalist motivation was provided by the earlier spread of Buddhism and Jainism in the South, both of which lost considerable following as a result of the efforts of the Nayanmar and Alvars, as well as those of their contemporary Sankara.

Some of the most renowned among these two companies of saint-singers have left songs that they composed at the temples of Visnu and Siva, praising the form and presence of the deity therein, the place itself as his manifestation, and the communal attitude of worship generated there through pilgrimage and festival. Though they honor the deities in terms familiar from Puranic myths, the stories are set in the local terrain. The emotional side of *bhakti* thus draws from deep Tamil traditions, including a revival of classical Tamil poetic conventions involving the correlations between different types of landscape, different divinities, and different types of male-female love. In the hands of the saint-singers, erotic love in particular was drawn on as a metaphor for devotional feelings that stressed the feminine character of the soul in relation to the deity and idealized a softening of the mind or heart that could take the forms of "melting" into the divine, ecstatic rapture, divine madness, and possession.

Following the advent of Sankara, most of the sectarian and revivalist movements found common cause in their devotionalist stance against Advaita nondualism and continued to develop for the most part interdependently. Thus, most formatively, the songs of the Alvars were collected in the ninth century for eventual use by the Sri Vaisnavas. And the poems of the Nayanmar—supplemented by the songs of Manikkavacakar, who apparently lived just after the list of sixty-three Nayanmar had been set (ninth century)—were collected to form parts of the canon of the Saiva Siddhanta. However, the revivalist and sectarian strains could also at times follow somewhat independent courses. The saint-singer tradition continued to take Saiva and Vaisnava forms among the Lingayats and the Haridasas of Karnataka, and also to be associated there with sects (the Lingayats themselves and the Brahma Sampradaya or Dvaita Vedanta tradition of Madhva, respectively). But its spread through Maharashtra, the Hindi-speaking areas of North India, and through Bengal was most focused on Visnu, or more accurately on his forms as Rama and Krsna, who in turn, in the Hindi and Bengali areas, became the deities of different sects. In the case of Krsna, erotic devotional poetry opened new dimensions on the theme of Krsna's loveplay with his "new" consort, Radha (her name does not appear before the twelfth-century Sanskrit *Gitagovinda* by the Bengali court poet Jayadeva). In Hindi and Bengali poems, not only are the emotions of motherly love for the baby Krsna and erotic love for the youthful Krsna explored, but they are tied in with a classical theory of aesthetic appreciation *(rasa)*.

As to the sects, the impact of Sankara's Advaita is evident at many points. Although Saiva monasticism may predate Sankara by about a century, his establishment of *mathas* around India was highly influential. Certain post-Sankara sects thus adopted institutionalized forms of "monastic" renunciation, either like Sankara setting their *mathas* alongside the temples (Sri Vaisnavas, Dvaita Vedantins, Saiva Siddhantins) or in opposition to the whole temple cultus (Lingayats). Vaisnava sects also assume henceforth the mantle of new "Vedantas" in order to seek Vedic authority for their advocacy of *bhakti* theologies over and against Sankara's nondualism and in their efforts to subordinate the path of knowledge to that of *bhakti*.

Sankara established a monastic order and monasteries (mathas), which, like the many hermitages (asramas) and the great shrines, became centers of religious activity and contributed to the realization of his ideal of Hindu unity.

PAGE 325

Most distinctive and most important theologically among the Vaisnava schools are those of Ramanuja (c. 1017-1137) and Madhva (1238-1317), both of whom attempted to refute Sankara's interpretations of the Upanisads, the *Brahma Sutra*, and the *Bhagavadgita* with their own commentaries on those texts. The more prolific Madhva also wrote commentaries on the *Rgveda* and the epics. Ramanuja, drawing on the ceremonialism and theological formulations of the Pañcaratra sect as well as on the revivalist poetry of the Alvars, developed for the Sri Vaisnavas the first *bhakti* sectarian repudiation of the Advaita. In his "qualified nondualistic Vedanta" *(visistadvaita vedanta)*, he argued that Visnu-Narayana is the ultimate *brahman*, his relation to the world and souls being "qualified" as substance to attribute. World and souls are thus real, as of course is God—all in opposition to Sankara's view that there is no reality other than *brahman*. For Ramanuja the three paths not only culminate in *bhakti* but are crowned by *prapatti*, "surrender" to God or "falling forward" at his feet. Criticizing both Sankara and Ramanuja, Madhva's "dualistic Vedanta" *(dvaita vedanta)* stressed the absolute sovereignty of God and the fivefold set of absolute distinctions between God and souls, God and the world, souls and souls, souls and the world, and matter in its different aspects—all of which are real and not illusory.

On the Saiva side, the most distinctive sect is the Kashmir Saiva, or Trika, school, established in the ninth century, with possibly earlier roots. It is nondualist, but from the standpoint that all is essentially Siva.

MOHANDAS GANDHI *Gandhi is venerated by many who seek an intercultural and socially conscious religion and see him as representative of a universal faith.* CORBIS-BETTMANN

MOHANDAS GANDHI

Hindu Leader, Reformer, Champion of Non-Violence

GANDHI, MOHANDAS (1869-1948), political leader, social reformer, and religious visionary of modern India. Although Gandhi initially achieved public notice as a leader of India's nationalist movement and as a champion of nonviolent techniques for resolving conflicts, he was also a religious innovator who did much to encourage the growth of a reformed, liberal Hinduism in India. In the West, Gandhi is venerated by many who seek an intercultural and socially conscious religion and see him as the representative of a universal faith.

Gandhi's Religious Thought. Although the influences on Gandhi's religious thought are varied—from the Sermon on the Mount to the *Bhagavad-gita*—his ideas are surprisingly consistent. Gandhi considered them to be Hindu, and in fact, they are all firmly rooted in the Indian religious tradition. His main ideas include the following.

1. *Satya* ("truth"). Gandhi equated truth with God, implying that morality and spirituality are ultimately the same. This concept is the bedrock of Gandhi's approach to conflict, *satyagraha,* which requires a fighter to "hold firmly to truth." While Gandhi did not further define the term, he regarded the rule of *ahimsa* as the litmus test that would determine where truth could be found.

2. *Ahimsa* ("nonviolence"). This ancient Indian concept prohibiting physical violence was broadened by Gandhi to include any form of coercion or denigration. For Gandhi, *ahimsa* was a moral stance involving love for and the affirmation of all life.

3. *Tapasya* ("renunciation"). Gandhi's asceticism was, in Max Weber's terms, "worldly" and not removed from social and political involvements. To Gandhi, *tapasya* meant not only the traditional requirements of simplicity and purity in personal habits but also the willingness of a fighter to shoulder the burden of suffering in a conflict.

4. *Swaraj* ("self-rule"). This term was often used during India's struggle for independence to signify freedom from the British, but Gandhi used it more broadly to refer to an ideal of personal integrity. He regarded *swaraj* as a worthy goal for the moral strivings of individuals and nations alike, linking it to the notion of finding one's inner self.

In addition to these concepts, Gandhi affirmed the traditional Hindu notions of *karman* and *dharma.* What is distinctive about Gandhi's Hinduism is his emphasis on social ethics as an integral part of the faith, a shift of emphasis that carries with it many conceptual changes as well. Gandhi's innovations include the use of the concept of truth as a basis for moral and political action, the equation of nonviolence with the Christian notion of selfless love, the broadening of the concept of *karmayoga* to include social service and political action, the redefinition of untouchability and the elevation of untouchables' tasks, and the hope for a more perfect world even in this present age of darkness *(kaliyuga).*

After Gandhi retired from politics in 1933, he took as his central theme the campaign for the uplift of untouchables, whom he called *harijans* ("people of God"). Other concerns included the protection of cows, moral education, and the reconciliation of Hindus and Muslims. The latter was especially important to Gandhi during the turmoil precipitated by India's independence, when the subcontinent was divided along religious lines. It was opposition to Gandhi's cries for religious tolerance that led to his assassination, on 30 January 1948, by a fanatical member of the Hindu right wing.

Gandhi's Legacy. Since Gandhi's death, neither Indian society nor Hindu belief has been restructured along Gandhian lines, but the Gandhian approach has been kept alive in India through the Sarvodaya movement, for which Vinoba Bhave has provided the spiritual leadership, and Jaya Prakash Narayan the political. Gandhi has provided the inspiration for religious and social activists in other parts of the world as well. These include Martin Luther King, Jr., and Joan Baez in the United States, E. M. Schumacher in England, Danilo Dolci in Sicily, Albert Luthuli in South Africa, Lanza del Vasto in France, and A. T. Ariyaratna in Sri Lanka.

Over the years, the image of Gandhi has loomed larger than life, and he is popularly portrayed as an international saint. This canonization of Gandhi began in the West with the writings of an American Unitarian pastor, John Haynes Holmes, who in 1921 proclaimed Gandhi "the greatest man in the world today." It continues in an unabated flow of homiletic writings and films, including David Attenborough's *Gandhi,* one of the most widely seen motion pictures in history. At the core of this Gandhian hagiography lies the enduring and appealing image of a man who was able to achieve a significant religious goal: the ability to live simultaneously a life of moral action and spiritual fulfillment. For that reason Gandhi continues to serve as an inspiration for a humane and socially engaged form of religion in India and throughout the world.

— MARK JUERGENSMEYER

Visnu, Siva, and Devi are the basic visual images of Hinduism. Each of these deities is worshiped in a concrete image (murti) that can be seen and touched.

PAGE 307

As pure being and consciousness, Siva is aware of himself through his reflection in the universe, which he pervades as the *atman* and in which he is manifest through his *sakti* (power, or female energy, personified as the Goddess). The universe is thus an expression of Siva's aesthetic experience of his creative awareness as self and his delight in unity with his Sakti. "Recognition" of Siva as the *atman*, and experience of the self through *spanda* ("vibration")—an attunement to the blissful throbbing waves of divine consciousness in the heart—are among the means to liberation. One of the foremost systematizers of this school was Abhinavagupta (c. 1000 CE), who developed the view that states of aesthetic appreciation (*rasas*, "tastes") are modes of experiencing the divine Self. Though favoring *santarasa* (the *rasa* of peacefulness), Abhinavagupta's theories influenced the North Indian medieval devotional poetry that explored *bhakti* itself as a state of *rasa*, with such powerfully evocative modes as love of Krsna in the relationships of servant-master, parent-child, and lover-beloved. This type of devotional intensity reached its peak in the person of the Bengali saint Caitanya (1486-1533), founder of the Gaudiya Vaisnava sect, whose ecstatic dancing and singing enabled him to experience the love of Radha and Krsna. Popular tradition regards him as an *avatara* of Krsna, a form assumed by Krsna to experience in one body his union with his Sakti.

POPULAR HINDUISM

The main current of living Hinduism is popular Hinduism. It has been affected by every change the tradition has gone through and may fairly be assumed to have ancient roots, in some aspects traceable to Indus Valley religion, in others to *sudra*, village, and tribal forms of religion that were never more than alluded to—and then negatively—in the ancient and classical sources. *Bhakti* and Tantra are two movements within Hinduism that draw inspiration from this broad current, and popular Hinduism today remains dominated by *bhakti* and Tantric expressions.

It is, however, perilous to look at popular Hinduism from the perspective of what it might have once been: that is, to attempt to isolate or reconstruct its Dravidian, pre-Aryan, or non-Brahmanic components. Although hypotheses about pre-Aryan and non-Aryan forms of popular Hinduism are certainly worth pursuing, they must be informed and restrained by a sound understanding of the comprehensive structures through which both popular and Brahmanic forms of Hinduism are integrated at the popular level. Aspects of popular religion that might look non-Aryan turn out on closer examination to involve Vedic prolongations. Nor are recent constructs like sanskritization, brahmanization, or ksatriyazation—all useful up to a point, but stressing only the adoption by low-caste groups of high-caste models—adequate to account for the multivectored process that must have occurred for a long time as it continues to occur today.

Amid the bewildering variety of popular Hindu rites, customs, and beliefs, two broad structures can be identified that clarify this overall integration. One involves the working out of the implications of *bhakti* in relation to temple worship; the other involves the working out of the implications of the caste system in relation to local forms of worship more generally. As they function, the two structures are intimately related.

Generally speaking, whether one defines a locality in large terms (a region, a former kingdom) or small terms (a city, town, or village), one will find two types of divinities: pure and impure. The pure divinities are forms taken locally—*avataras*—of the great gods Visnu and Siva. Sometimes the Goddess is also purified to this rank, often with a myth explaining her change from violent to peaceful habits (as with the alleged conversion of the goddess Kamaksi at Kanchipuram, Tamil Nadu, by Sankara). And in certain regions Siva's sons Murukan/Skanda (in Tamil Nadu) and Ganesa (in Maharashtra) also assume this role. In their temples, these gods are offered pure vegetarian food by brahmans. Today, all castes can worship in such temples, thanks to temple entry legislation by the postindependence government; formerly, low castes were excluded. These castes still maintain their own temples where impure gods are served with nonvegetarian offerings, that is, sacrifices of male animals, usually cocks and goats but occasionally water buffalo. Legislation prohibiting buffalo sacrifices has so far had mixed results.

Whereas worship of pure gods—especially at remote pilgrimage sites—is focused ultimately on renunciation and liberation, that of impure gods is dominated by down-to-earth concerns. One thus finds among the general category of impure gods lineage deities *(kuladevatas)*, caste deities, and village deities *(gramadevatas)*. The first are usually but not always male, and some are deities for brahman as well as low-caste lineages. Caste deities and village deities are usually female, and the category may overlap where the deity of a locally dominant caste becomes also the village deity. Where the village deity (usually a goddess) is the deity of a vegetarian caste or has had her cult purified to bring it into accord with high-caste standards, she frequently has one or more male assistants—impure demons converted to her cause and frequently lineage gods themselves—who handle the animal sacrifice (real or symbolic) for her, often out of her line of sight.

Nonetheless, though opposing principles are each given their play, it is their overlap and interrelation that is most striking. Low castes worship the pure gods in their temples. And high castes acknowledge the power of the impure deities, not only as *kuladevatas*, but through selective (pure) means of participation in festivals sponsored by lower castes. Through the universalization of *bhakti*, the impure gods are sometimes also the prototypes for the demons whose deaths at the hands of the pure deities transform them into their devotees. These local myths have their roots in Puranic mythologies, and the sacrificial practices they evoke involve at least in part prolongations and reinterpretations of the Vedic animal sacrifice.

HINDU POPULATIONS PER WORLD REGION

	Hindu	Total Population
Africa	1,986,000	748,130,000
Asia	786,991,000	3,513,218,000
Europe*	1,650,000	727,678,000
Latin America	760,000	490,444,000
Northern America	1,365,000	295,677,000
Oceania	323,000	28,973,000
Total	793,075,000	5,804,120,000

*Includes former Soviet Union.
**United Nations Medium Variant Figures, mid 1996
Source: *The 1997 Britannica Book of the Year*

The second issue—working out of the implications of the caste system in relation to local forms of worship—has thus already been touched upon, but with the focus of issues of purity and impurity as defined by brahman and low-caste involvements. There remains the issue of the role of the *ksatriya*, or more particularly the king, as the ruler of the land. The caste system has traditionally functioned in locally defined territories, "little kingdoms," where the local ruler had certain roles to perform. No matter what his actual caste, whether high or low, pure or impure, he had to function as a *ksatriya*. In his ceremonial status, he performed the role of *jajman*, engaging him at the core of a system of prestations and counterprestations with other castes as a sort of patron for those who perform services for him. Most significantly, this title derives from the Vedic *yajamana*, "sacrificer," and prolongs not only the yajamana's function as patron of other castes (particularly brahmans, who offer sacrifices for him), but that of "sacrificer" itself. The model of the king as jajman on the regional territorial level has its counterpart in the village in the person(s) of the leader(s) of the locally dominant caste, who assumes the role of *yajamana* at village festivals. When, as was until recently widely the case, the village festival involves the sacrifice of a buffalo, it thus occurs within a continuum that includes the royal buffalo sacrifice traditionally performed in connection with the pan-Hindu festival of Dussera, and the mythology of the goddess Durga and the buffalo demon Mahisasura that is traceable to the *Devimahatmyam* in the *Markandeya Purana*. There are many local and regional transformations of this pattern, but a basic theme is that the Goddess, who personifies victory, acts for the *yajamana* and the kingdom or village in her conquest over demonic forces (impure barbarians, drought, diseases) that threaten the welfare of the local terrain over which she, as goddess, presides.

HINDU RESPONSES TO ISLAM AND WESTERNIZATION

Self-conscious Hindu responses to influences from the West were first worked out in the classical period in the epics, the Dharmasastras, and the Puranas. It seems that military dominance by "barbarian" peoples in that period provided one of the incentives for the articulation of Hindu orthodoxy. Islamic rule and Western rule in India have provided similar incentives, but this often goes unmentioned as historians place their emphasis on what is supposedly new. A full accounting of the impact of almost ten centuries of Islam and five centuries of Western presence in India would have to deal not only with their distinctive new influences but also with the ways in which traditional Hindu models have been revived and applied in new and adaptive ways, often on the folk and popular level. That, however, can only be alluded to here.

Islamic influence on Hinduism has many dimensions, all difficult to assess. From the time of the raids of Mahmud of Ghazni into Northwest India (977-1030) into the period of Mughal dominance, Hindus had to deal periodically with outbreaks of violence and iconoclastic zeal. Regional defense of Hindu traditions against Islam—first by the Rajputs in Rajasthan, then by the Vijayanagar rulers and their successors in South India (1333 eighteenth century), and finally by the Marathas in Maharashtra and the South (late sixteenth century-1761)—clearly fostered the Hindu ideal of the territorial kingdom, big or "little," as a model for the protection of ongoing Hindu values. Under the Muslim rulers, in fact, many Hindu chiefs and petty rajas were left in control of their local realms so long as they paid tribute and supplied military support. In these circumstances, conservative and puritanical tendencies seem to have gained momentum in orthodox Hinduism, particularly in regard to caste and the purity of

"There is no higher god than truth."

MAHATMA GANDHI
TRUE PATRIOTISM
1939

women. Nonetheless, one finds numerous cases where Muslim themes and figures have been integrated into popular Hindu myth and ritual, but usually in ways that indicate Muslim subordination to a local or regional Hindu deity.

While orthodox, popular, and domestic forms of Hinduism thus drew in on themselves, however, Hindu sectarian traditions multiplied, particularly in the period of the breakup of the Delhi sultanate (1206-1526). Notable at this time were Caitanya in Bengal, and two exemplars of the North Indian *sant* (holy man) tradition: Kabir (c. 1440-1518, from Banaras) and Nanak (1469-1539, from the Punjab). These two latter figures both preached a path of loving devotion to one God that combined aspects of Islamic Sufism and Hindu *bhakti*. They thus formulated probably for the first time in terms partly Hindu an exclusivist monotheism like that found in the Abrahamic traditions of Islam, Christianity, and Judaism. Over and against the direct experience of this one God, all else was mediate and external, whether the practices were Muslim or Hindu. Thus not only caste but idol worship was rejected by these teachers. But though their syncretistic poetry remained highly popular, it did little to change the Hindu practices it criticized. Nanak's work in particular provided the foundation for the Sikh tradition, an increasingly non-Hindu and non-Muslim movement on its own. Nor did the syncretistic interests of the great Mughal emperor Akbar (ruled 1555-1605) do much to encourage theological synthesis, despite the popularity of his, for the most part, religiously tolerant rule. Akbar's successors on the Mughal throne abandoned his policies and pursued expansionist goals that aroused resistance from the heirs of the Vijayanagar and the Rajput kingdoms, and especially from the Sikhs and the new power of the Marathas. The seeds of a nationalist vision of Hinduism may be traced through these movements and back to the imperial ideal of the epics.

Other converts, oppressed by the burden of sin, are drawn by the promise of forgiveness in Christ, so different from the inexorable law of karman in Hinduism.

PAGE 453

Under the British, certain reform tendencies initiated under Muslim rule were carried forward, freshly influenced by Christian missionary activity and Western education. Most notable were the reform movements of the nineteenth century. The Brahmo Samaj was founded in 1828 by Raja Ram Mohan Roy (1772-1833, from Calcutta). In an early treatise Roy wrote an attack on idolatry that showed Muslim influence, but by the time he founded the Samaj he had been more affected by Christianity, and particularly by the Unitarians. Roy thus introduced a kind of deistic monotheism and a form of congregational worship to go along with a rejection of idolatry, caste, sacrifice, transmigration, and *karman*. The Arya Samaj, founded in 1875 by Swami Dayananda Sarasvati (1824-1883, from Kathiawar), denied authenticity to Puranic Hinduism and attempted a return to the Vedas. Showing that the Vedas lent no support to image worship and various social practices, he went further to assert that they were monotheistic. As regards caste, he championed the *varna* theory as an ancient social institution but denied that it was religious. Both movements split into rival camps.

The Ramakrishna Mission, established on the death of its founder Ramakrishna (1834-1886) and carried forward by his disciples, most notably Vivekananda (1863-1902), is more representative of traditional Hindu values. Strong *bhakti* and Tantric strains converged in the mystical experiences of Ramakrishna and were held in conjunction with an initiation into Advaita Vedanta and experiences of the oneness of all religions through visions not only of Hindu deities but of Jesus and Allah. For many followers, this humble priest of Kali has thus come to be regarded as an *avatara*, in the tradition of Caitanya. Vivekananda, Western-educated and keenly intellectual, attended the World's Parliament of Religions in Chicago in 1893, lectured widely, and established the Vedanta Society of New York. When he returned to India as a recognized champion of Hindu self-pride, he helped to organize the disciples of Ramakrishna into the pan-Indian Ramakrishna Mission.

The first such teacher to gain prominence in India by popularity gained abroad, Vivekananda thus inadvertently set up a pattern that has been followed by many prominent gurus and swamis in the twentieth century. Notable among them are Swami A. C. Bhaktivedanta (1896-1977), founder of the Hare Krishna movement (ISKCON) as an outgrowth of the Bengal Caitanya tradition and Swami Muktananda (1908-1982), exponent of *siddhayoga* teachings that draw on Kashmir Saivism.

An earlier figure, one who attracted a large Western following without ever leaving India, was Sri Aurobindo (1872-1950), whose career spanned nationalist political activism in Bengal (up to 1908), followed by the establishment of an ashram (hermitage) in Pondicherry for the teaching of a type of integral yoga that stressed the "evolutionary" progress of the soul toward the divine. One must also mention Mohandas K. Gandhi (1869-1948), whose reputation upon returning to India in 1915 after twenty-one years in England and Africa was not that of a guru but a champion of Indian causes against social and economic discrimination. As he took on more and more ascetic and saintly aspirations, however, Gandhi sought to combine an ideal of dispassioned and nonviolent service to humanity, modeled on the *Bhagavadgita's* doctrine of *karmayoga*, with work for Indian *svaraj* ("self-rule").

Although sometimes referred to as a Hindu renaissance, the effect of the various reformers since the nineteenth century has been to a certain extent more ideological than religious. Where they founded religious movements, these attracted only small followings. But their religious views—that Hinduism is essentially monotheistic, that caste is not essentially Hindu, that Hindu tolerance does not deny the truths of other religions, that Hinduism is in accord with modern science, and so on—have had major influence on a Western-educated, largely urban elite that, at least for now, controls the media and the educational processes of contemporary India. It remains to be seen how this new vision of unity will square with the traditionally diverse Hinduism of the vast population of the countryside.

— ALF HILTEBEITEL

I

ICONOGRAPHY

TRADITIONAL AFRICAN ICONOGRAPHY

Only by examining the religious iconography of a variety of cultures can one fully understand how visual images represent distinctive ways of experiencing the world for the peoples of sub-Saharan Africa.

ANCESTORS AND KINGS. On the granary doors of the Dogon people of Mali, rows of paired ancestor figures called Nommo stand watch over the precious millet stored within. Similar figures, at times androgynous, are placed next to the funeral pottery on ancestral shrines of families and on the shrine in the house of the *hogon,* the religious and temporal leader of a clan. Their elongated, ascetic bodies and proud, dispassionate faces provide images of the Dogon's myths of origin, as well as their perception of themselves when life is filled with spiritual vitality, *nyama.*

Dogon myth, ritual, and iconography express a view of life in which, through a process of differentiation and pairing of related beings, called Nommo, an ordered, fruitful world is to be created. Creation involves human participation through ritual actions that restore life and maintain an ordered world. Among the materials of the ritual process are village shrines representing a set of twins; shrine sculpture, as well as granary doors with their bas-relief of paired figures, snakes and lizards, zigzag patterns, and female breasts, all symbolically associated with the creation myth; geometric patterns or "signs" on shrine walls, which refer to the basic ontological properties of the world; funerary masquerades and dances through which the deceased is transformed into a venerated ancestor; and secret languages through which the incantations and texts describing the creation of the world and the appearance of death are conveyed from one generation to another.

Among the Edo people along the coastal forest of southeast Nigeria, the iconography of the Benin kingdom reflects a culture with a very different spirituality, one shaped by a monarchical tradition. The magnificently carved ivory tusks projecting from the top of the bronze memorial heads on the royal ancestral shrines (until the British punitive expedition of 1897) symbolized the powers of the king—his political authority and his supernatural gifts. While his authority depended upon statecraft and military conquest, it was by virtue of his descent from *obas* who had become gods and his possession of the coral beads, said to have been taken from the kingdom of Olokun, god of the sea, that the *oba* had *ase,* "the power to bring to pass," the power over life and death.

Over the centuries the royal guild of blacksmiths created more than 146 memorial bronze heads of deceased *obas,* queen mothers, and conquered kings and chiefs; and the royal guild of carvers portrayed on 133 ivory tusks the king, his wives, chiefs, and retainers, as well as leopards and mudfish, emblems of his

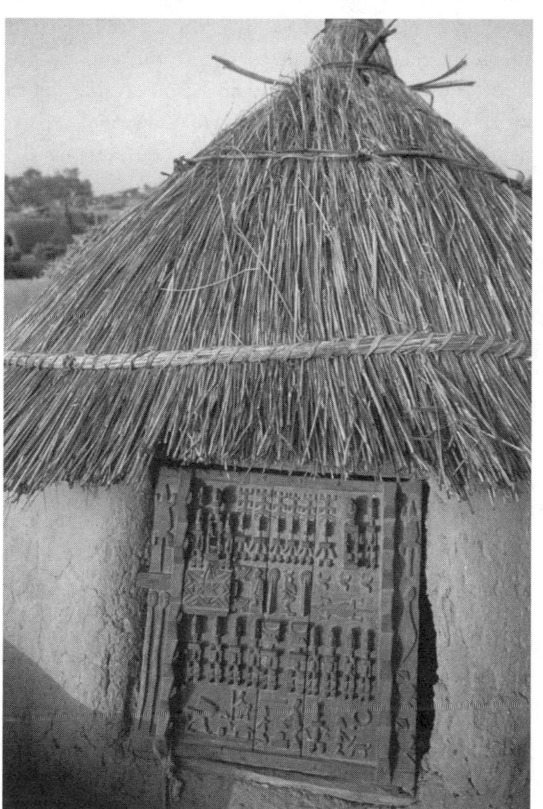

ANCESTRAL SPIRITS

The Dogon people of Mali, carved pairs of ancestor figures on granary doors. These icons, shown here, represented their perception of themselves when filled with spirituality.

NIK WHEELER/CORBIS

power over forest and water and of his ability to move across boundaries distinguishing disparate realms.

The Cult of the Hand, *ikegobo,* also known as *ikega,* provides a means for celebrating the ability of the individual to accomplish things and, within limits, to achieve new status. Containers for offerings to the

Ancestors are believed to be capable of intervening in human affairs, but only in the defined area of their authority, that is, among their descendants.

PAGE 30

The Elefon and Epa festivals are masquerades performed in honor of persons and families whose lives embodied the social values by which Yoruba culture has been defined in the northeastern area.

PAGE 713

Hand, crafted in bronze for kings and in wood for titled persons, bear images of power such as an *oba* sacrificing leopards, a warrior holding the severed head of an enemy, Portuguese soldiers with guns, or the tools and emblems of office for the blacksmith, carver, or trader. All shrines for the Hand bear the image of the clenched fist, showing the ventral side, with the thumb pointing upward and outward.

FORM AND MEANING. Notwithstanding the particularity of traditional African iconography, the general observation may be made that it is, in general, essentially conceptual and evocative. It is not representational and illustrative, and it is not abstract.

Presence of power. Among the Igbomina Yoruba of southwestern Nigeria the costumes of the masquerades for the patrilineal ancestors, *egungun paaka,* combine materials of the forest with those of human manufacture, such as layers of richly colored cloths, bits of mirror, and beaded panels. The carved headdress portion will often meld animal and human features. Packets of magical substances will be secreted within the costume. It is the peculiar state of being of the living dead, who cross boundaries and move between two realms, who dwell in heaven yet profoundly affect the well-being of the living, that is materialized, for masquerades are created to reveal a reality not otherwise observable and to evoke an appropriate response, such as awe and dependency, on the part of the observer. Thus, among the Pende of Zaire the concept of *mahamba* signifies an object, such as a mask, or a ritual given by the ancestors to the living for the common good and through which the ancestors periodically manifest themselves and communicate with their descendants.

A similar observation may be made about the reliquary figures of the Kota people of Gabon. Referred to as *mbulu-ngulu,* "image of the dead," the two-dimensional figures consist of a large ovoid head above a simple, diamond-shaped wooden base. On a shrine the sculptured form is seated in a bark container holding the bones of several generations of ancestors. The ovoid face and coiffure are created by applying thin sheets or strips of brass and copper to a wooden form in a variety of interrelated geometric patterns. In every case, it is the power of the eyes that holds and penetrates the beholder, expressing the bond between the living and the deceased and the protective power of the ancestors in and for the life of the extended family.

It is not only the reality of the ancestral presence that Africa's religious art presents. Among the Egba, Egbado, and Ketu Yoruba it is the power of "our mothers" that is celebrated in the spectacle of the Efe/Gelede festival of masquerade, dance, and song at the time of the spring rains. "Our mothers," *awon iya wa,* is a collective term for female power. The total sculpted image is perceived as a visual metaphor, often understood as having multiple levels of significance.

Models of response. Ritual sculpture provides not only images of the powers on which the living depend but models for appropriate response to gods and spirits. The naked male or female, arms at their sides or touching their abdomens, on Lobi shrines in Burkina Faso as well as the figure of a kneeling woman with a thunder ax balanced upon her head and holding a dance wand for the Yoruba god Sango are images of man and woman as devotees, as inspirited and powerful. They are images through which persons see their spirituality and by which their spirituality is deepened.

Perhaps the most extraordinary images of self and of personal power are carvings that incorporate magical substances (in or on images) to the extent that they alter the human form of the image. They are found for the most part among the Songye and Kongo peoples of the lower Kongo (Zaire) Basin. Some figures have an antelope horn filled with "medicines" projecting from the head, others have nails and small knives pounded into the body or a magic-holding resin box imbedded in the belly. They are visualizations in the extreme of ritual action as manipulative power.

RITUAL ACTIVITY. There are essentially two types of rituals—those in which a person or group undergoes a change in status, usually referred to as rites of passage, and rituals of world maintenance through which a person or group affirms and seeks to secure in the words and actions of sacrifice a worldview.

Rites of passage. Among many African peoples the masquerade is associated with rites of passage. Among the Mende people of Sierra Leone, Nowo, a female spirit, appears in dance and masquerade to girls being initiated into the Sande (also known as Bundu) ceremonial society. As far as is known, it is the only female mask danced by a woman in Africa. While associated with the Sande society and thought of as the Sande spirit, Nowo appears in other ritual contexts. Her image is carved on the finial of the rhythm pounders used in the boys' initiation rites, on the staff carried by the leader of the men's Poro society, on the carved mace of the Mende king, as well as on divination implements, women's ritual spoon handles, and on weaving-loom pulleys. But it is only to the female initiates into Sande that Nowo appears in the fullness of the masquerade and the movements of the dance.

In the rituals, Nowo is a spiritual presence and images the beauty and power, the nobility, of woman. The head is crowned with an elaborate coiffure into which are woven cowrie shells and seed pods, symbols of wealth and fertility. Black is said to be woman's color, the color of civilized life. The glistening black surface suggests the lustrous, well-oiled skin with which the initiates will reenter the world. Nowo thus provides an image of the physical beauty and the spiritual power of woman.

World maintenance rituals. The role of iconography in Africa's rituals of world maintenance is no less important than in rites of passage. Among the Yoruba, to cite only one example, paired bronze castings of male and female figures joined at the top by a chain, *edan,* are presented to an initiate into the higher ranks of the Osugbo secret society, who worship Onile, "the owner of the house." The house is the cult house, which is a microcosm of the universe. The secret, visualized in the linking of male and female, appears to refer to a vision of life in terms of its completion and transcendence of time.

The seated male and female figures present to the viewer the signs of their power and authority, *ase.* The female holds a pair of *edan,* as she would twin children. The male figure, with clenched fists, makes the sign of greeting to Onile. Four chains with tiny bells are suspended from the sides of each figure's head. The number four, as well as multiples of four, are important in Ifa divination; Orunmila (also called Ifa), the divination god, knows the secret of creation and the sacrifices that will make one's way propitious. Above the spare, ascetic bodies, the heads of the paired figures radiate with their *ase.* Twelve chains are suspended from the plate below each figure. Twelve is a multiple of three and four, also numbers associated with Osugbo and Ifa ritual symbolism.

— JOHN PEMBERTON III

AUSTRALIAN ABORIGINAL ICONOGRAPHY

Art has a central place in Australian Aboriginal religion. The substance of Aboriginal ceremonies and rituals consists of enactments of events from the Dreaming, or ancestral past, events that are conserved in the form of the songs, dances, designs, and sacred objects that belong to a particular clan or totemic cult group. Such forms are referred to collectively by a word that can be translated as "sacred law," and it is as "sacred law" that art mediates between the ancestral past and the world of living human beings.

Designs can be referred to then as "Dreaming," and they are manifestations of the ancestral past in a number of senses. Each originated as a motif painted on an ancestral being's body, as an impression left in the ground by that being, or as a form associated in some other way with ancestral creativity. The meaning of the designs on the objects often refers to the acts of ancestral creativity that gave rise to the shape of the landscape; in this respect, the designs can be said to encode Dreaming events. And finally, the designs can be a source of ancestral power. Paintings on the bodies of initiates are thought to bring the individuals closer to the spiritual domain; sacred objects rubbed against the bodies can have similar effect. In eastern Arnhem Land, upon a person's death, designs painted on his or her chest or on the coffin or bone disposal receptacle help to transfer the soul back to the ancestral world to be reincorporated within the reservoirs of spiritual power associated with a particular place. Art is linked in with the concept of the cycling of spiritual power down the generations from the ancestral past to the present that characterizes Aboriginal religious thought.

ABORIGINAL ICON

Aboriginal art mediates between the ancestral past and the world of living human beings.

PENNY TWEEDIE/CORBIS

Designs in Aboriginal art exist independent of particular media. The same design in Arnhem Land may occur as a body painting, a sand sculpture, an emblem on a hollow log coffin, or an engraving on a sacred object *(rangga).* In central Australia the same design may be incised on a stone disc (tjurunga), painted on the body of a dancer in blood and down, or made into a sand sculpture. Further, it is the design that gives the object its particular ancestral connection: the designs are extensions of ancestral beings and are sometimes referred to as their "shadows." Thus, they can be used in different contexts for different purposes.

SYSTEMS OF REPRESENTATION. Meaning in Aboriginal art is encoded in two distinct systems of

"Great art is the work of the whole living creature, body and soul."

JOHN RUSKIN
THE STONES OF VENICE
1851–53

representation, one iconic and figurative, the other aniconic and geometric. The iconography of Aboriginal religious art arises out of the interplay between these two complementary systems. This distinction extends outside the area of the visual arts to dance and ceremonial action, which involve some components and actions that are essentially mimetic and represent the behavior and characteristics of natural species as well as other components that are abstract and have a conventional and nonrepresentational meaning. The balance between the figurative and the geometric varies from one region to another. The art of central Australia, of groups such as the Walbiri, the Aranda, the Pintubi, and the Pitjantjatjara, is characterized by geometric motifs, whereas western Arnhem Land in contrast is associated with a highly developed figurative tradition.

The forms of Aboriginal art are linked to its various functions in a systematic way. The figurative art presents images of the Dreaming that at one level can be readily interpreted as representations of totemic species and the forms of ancestral beings. The X-ray art of western Arnhem Land, for example, is a figurative tradition that creates images of totemic ancestors associated with particular places, thus linking them directly to the natural world. The figures are in part accurate representations of kangaroos, fish, snakes, and so on. But they are more than that. The X-ray component, representing the heart, lungs, and other internal organs of the animal, adds an element of mystery to the figures and differentiates the representations from those of ordinary animals.

Much of the ceremonial art and most of the secret art of Australia is, however, geometric in form. This property of geometric art enables it to encode the relationship between different phenomena or orders of reality. On one level, a circle in a design may represent a water hole, and the line joining it may represent a creek flowing into the water hole. On another level, the circle may be said to represent a hole dug in the ground and the line, a digging stick. On yet another level, the circle may be interpreted as the vagina of a female ancestral being and the line, the penis of a male ancestor. All three interpretations are related, for digging in the sand is an analogue for sexual intercourse, and the water hole was created through sexual intercourse between two ancestral beings in the Dreaming.

SYSTEMS OF INTERPRETATION. As people go through life they learn the meanings of designs such as the Wild Honey pattern; they associate it with places created by the ancestral being and with ceremonies that celebrate that being's creative power. For the individual the design is no longer an abstract sign but a manifestation of the ancestral being concerned. Aesthetic aspects of the design reinforce this understanding. In northeastern Arnhem Land, body paintings convey a sense of light and movement through the layering of finely cross-hatched lines across the skin surface. Similar effects are created in central Australian painting through the use of white down and the glistening effect of blood, fat, and red ocher.

Throughout much of Australia, rights to designs and other components of "sacred law" are vested in social groups that exercise some control over their use and have the responsibility to ensure that they continue to be passed down through the generations.

— HOWARD MORPHY

NATIVE AMERICAN ICONOGRAPHY

Iconography is a living force in North American Indian religious life, past and present. Rooted in mythical imagery, it informs the content of individual dreams and nourishes the themes of contemporary Indian art. A study of the iconography of a people provides a unique opportunity to gain insight into what Werner Müller calls the "pictorial world of the soul" (*Die Religionen der Waldlandindianer Nordamerikas,* Berlin, 1956, p. 57).

Concerning the wide variety of media used, the following general distribution can be observed: in the Far North—ivory, bone, and stone; the Northeast and Southeast Woodlands—wood, bark, skin, quillwork, and beadwork; the Plains—skin, beadwork, pipestone, quillwork, and painting of bodies and horses; the Northwest Coast—cedar, ivory, argillite, blankets, and copper; California—baskets and some stone; the Southwest—sand painting, wood, stone, baskets, pottery, jewelry, and dolls.

THE COSMOS. Cosmologies vary from tribe to tribe in both content and imagery. But whereas the mythical image of the universe (its cosmography) may be highly detailed, the iconographical rendering is necessarily restricted. The cosmos is most often graphically limited to those elements that characterize its basic nature and structure, including its nonvisual aspects.

The most widespread symbol of the whole cosmos is the ceremonial lodge, house, or tent. The fundamental idea of the ceremonial lodge, such as the Delaware xingwikáon ("big house"), is that all of its parts symbolize, and in ritual contexts actually are, the cosmos. Usually the realms of this cosmos are interconnected with a central post, which is conceived of as extending itself like a world tree up to the heavens. Renewing such a house constitutes the actual renewal of the cosmos.

Representations of the cosmos can refer to the more subtle manifestations of the world, as in the sand paintings of the Luiseño of California, but they can also approach the reality of topographical maps, as in the sand paintings of the neighboring Diegueño. In a completely different approach to the visualization of the cosmos, the well-known Navajo sand painting of Father Sky and Mother Earth illustrates the anthropomorphic representation of the cosmos.

SUPREME BEINGS. Among the myriad images found in North American Indian iconography are certain divine beings whose representations cut across taxonomic groups; these include supreme beings, tricksters/culture heroes, guardian beings, and other mythical beings. Since the majestic, all-encompassing supreme being is difficult to visualize, its morphology is relatively simple. When not visualized as some object or animal intimately associated with the supreme being, its form tends to be anthropomorphic. For example, the Ojibwa song charts visualize the supreme being, Kitsi Manitu, with a pictograph of a human head, belonging to an initiate in the Mide secret society.

On the other hand, the all-pervasiveness of the supreme being among the Plains Indians can result in the use of symbols of lesser deities to represent it.

TRICKSTERS/CULTURE HEROES. The most widespread iconographic trickster type is theriomorphic: Raven, Coyote, or Rabbit. The most well-known image is that of Raven among the Northwest Coast tribes, a character who encompasses all of the classical features of the trickster. He is pictured in raven-form on virtually every object throughout the Northwest, usually in the context of a mythical event that somehow affected the ancestor of the house in which the object is found. Even though the trickster is an animal, in mythical thought he can change to human form, and this process is often reflected iconographically, as with the Navajo Coyote and the Delaware and Ojibwa Rabbit.

GUARDIAN BEINGS. Guardian beings associate themselves most often on a personal level with single individuals, and they function as guardians who bring blessings to their human partners. These guardians can appear in just about any form taken from the natural or the mythological world. Among the Oglala it may be necessary to paint a version of one's vision on the tipi in order to secure its validity, although generally images of the guardian are painted on shields.

In the cultures of the Far North and Arctic areas, the shaman and his guardians are a constant iconographic theme. His guardians are portrayed in several general ways: as diminutive human beings clustered near the shaman or as human faces clustered together, as a human visage under an animal visage such as seen in Alaskan masks, as an animal form reduced in size and resting on the head or shoulders of the shaman, as birdlike shamans or shamans in transformation, as flying spirits being ridden by shamans, as an animal or human being with skeletal markings, or as flying bears or other usually flightless beasts. These images are portrayed in contemporary drawings, ivory sculpture, masks, stone sculpture, bone sculpture, drumsticks, shaman staff, and so on.

ASTRONOMICAL BEINGS. The sun, the moon, and the stars are pictured as beings throughout North America. The sun is portrayed most intensely where it is strongest, in southeastern and southwestern North America. The Hopi portray the Sun, Taawa, anthropomorphically but, in keeping with Hopi iconography, he wears a mask that consists of a circular disc fringed with radiating feathers and horsehair. This radial representation of the sun is the most common image known. The moon is usually represented in its quarter phase, although images of the full moon are sometimes found. The stars most often pictured are the Morning Star (Venus), the Pleiades, Orion, Altair, the constellation Ursa Major (which is invariably pictured as a heavenly bear), and the Milky Way.

METEOROLOGICAL BEINGS. This group consists of Thunder, Wind, Rain, and Lightning. Thunder is often pictured as the Thunderbird, but other birds can also be used. Wind, on the other hand, is generally associated with the cardinal regions and therefore not visualized directly. Cultures with anthropocentric morphology, however, such as the Navajo and the Ojibwa, picture even this being in human shape.

Rain is usually illustrated as lines falling from cloud symbols or as a being from which rain is falling. Lightning is always shown as zigzag lines regardless of the tribe in question. The lines usually end in arrowheads.

ANIMAL BEINGS. There are a number of animals which are known and visualized throughout North America, such as the bear, the deer, and the buffalo. However, other animals peculiar to a particular region are the more common iconographical subjects, such as the whales and seals of the northern coasts, or the lizards and snakes of the desert regions. The general rule is that the animal is depicted in its natural form.

The Northwest Coast Indians are the most conspicuous users of totem symbols. These symbols are represented in literally every conceivable medium: poles, house fronts, hats, aprons, spoons, bowls, settees, boat prows, spearheads, fishhooks, dagger handles, facial painting, masks, speaker staffs, paddles, drums, rattles, floats, bracelets, leggings, pipes, and gambling sticks. The question of religious significance may be resolved by the fact that the totem animal is considered either a direct ancestor of the clan or somehow associated with an ancient human ancestor. Thus the symbol at least, if not its use, has religious meaning.

VEGETATION BEINGS. Corn is the plant most commonly visualized. The representation can simply refer to the plant itself, but frequently a maize deity is being invoked. The latter is the case throughout the Southwest, whether among the Pueblo or the Athapascan peoples. The maize deity is usually clearly anthro-

Many animal spirits, including tricksters, remained in the world as sources of specialized powers for human beings.

PAGE 509

pomorphized. Hallucinogenic plants such as peyote, jimsonweed, or the strong wild tobaccos are more or less realistically pictured; such images refer to the deities of these potent plants.

HUMAN BEINGS. This category concerns not only human ancestors but also a miscellaneous collection of beings that have human form. The first type are effigies of once-living human beings. These are most commonly figured on Northwest Coast mortuary poles.

Human images can also be material expressions of the ineffable. Human images, such as dolls, can symbolize or are actually considered to be small spritelike creatures who can have an array of functions and duties and who play a part in ceremonial contexts as well. Human representations can also signify the heroes or founders of cults; such is the case with many images on Pueblo altars and other representations on Northwest Coast poles.

Ancestor worship and the apotheosis of deceased rulers were essential aspects of Classic Maya religion.

PAGE 428

GEOLOGICAL BEINGS. This category of images is based on a type of religious geomorphology. The most prominent geological being envisioned is Mother Earth, although it is seldom that direct representations of it occur. In such anthropocentric iconographies as that of the Navajo, it is no problem to illustrate Mother Earth as a somewhat enlarged female human being. Usually, however, Mother Earth is symbolized by some fertility image, such as an ear of corn, or by a circle. Among the Delaware, the earth is symbolized by the giant tortoise who saved humankind from the flood and upon whose back the new earth was created by Nanabush. Sods of earth can also be used to represent Mother Earth, as in the Cheyenne buffalo-skull altar in the medicine lodge.

Another group of geological beings consists of images of mountains. Except for isolated pockets of flatlands and desert basins, most of North America is covered with mountains, and these are usually believed to be alive or at least filled with life, that is, they are the abodes of the gods. This feature of mountains is highly important and is also recognized iconographically.

[*See also* North American Indians.]

— ARMIN W. GEERTZ

MESOAMERICAN ICONOGRAPHY

Each major Mesoamerican culture developed its religious imagery in a distinctive fashion, although all were historically interlinked and drew from the common pool of Mesoamerican stylistic-iconographic tradition.

OLMEC. Most archaeologists agree that the earliest sophisticated religious iconographic system in Mesoamerica was that of the Olmec, which flourished between about 1200 and 400 BCE (Middle Preclassic), and was centered in the Gulf Coast region of eastern Veracruz and western Tabasco. [*See also* Olmec Religion.] Olmec style, which conveyed religious concepts imaginatively and effectively, was one of the most striking and original esthetic expressions ever achieved in pre-Hispanic Mesoamerica. Unfortunately, accurately ascertaining the connotations of the intricate Olmec symbol system presents formidable difficulties, and interpretations of prominent students often differ radically.

A major characteristic of Olmec iconography is the blending of anthropomorphic and zoomorphic features. Much of the controversy surrounding the interpretation of Olmec iconography has focused on these fused images, which often exhibit additional overtones of infantilism and dwarfism. The most popular interpretation has been that they merge feline with human characteristics, and the term *were-jaguar* has become fashionable to refer to them.

Other Olmec composite beings are recognized, but opinions differ concerning the precise zoological identification of their constituent elements. A considerable case has been presented for the importance of a polymorphic, essentially saurian creature with various aspects. Called the Olmec Dragon, it has been postulated as the ancestor of a variegated family of celestial and terrestrial monsters prominent in later Mesoamerican iconography.

IZAPA. A series of closely interrelated stylistic and iconographic traditions known as "Izapan," after the major site of Izapa, Chiapas, Mexico, flourished between about 500 BCE and 250 CE. Izapan iconography bears a close relationship to Olmec, from which it partly derives, but its formats are generally somewhat more complex. The style is most typically expressed by low-relief carving, commonly on the perpendicular stone monuments known as stelae, which are sometimes fronted by plain or effigy "altars."

Izapan iconography frequently displays a narrative quality in its compositions, depicting a variety of ritual-mythic scenes, some of considerable complexity. These scenes are often framed by highly stylized celestial and terrestrial registers, interpreted as monster masks. Also prominent on Izapan monuments are downward-flying, winged, anthropomorphic beings, downward-peering celestial faces, combat scenes (humanoid figures versus double-headed serpentine creatures), polymorphic bird monsters, cosmic trees with "dragon-head roots," and diminutive human ritual celebrants accompanied by various ritual paraphernalia.

CLASSIC LOWLAND MAYA. The Izapan tradition led directly into the most sophisticated of all Mesoamerican iconographic and stylistic traditions, that of the Classic Lowland Maya (c. 25-900 CE) [*See also* Maya Religion.] Nearly all of the most common

Izapan iconographic themes were retained and often further elaborated. These included the bi- and tricephalous polymorphic celestial-terrestrial creature now frequently conceived as the "ceremonial bar" held by the rulers, the long-lipped dragon in numerous manifestations that eventually evolved into the long-nosed god of rain (Chac), celestial and terrestrial enclosing frames, cosmic trees, and avian composite creatures (serpent birds). Some deities that were clearly prototypical to those represented in the iconography of Postclassic Yucatán can be discerned in Maya religious art of the Classic period. Classic Maya stelae—accurately dated, erected at fixed intervals, and containing long hieroglyphic texts—display profile and frontal portraits of the great Maya dynasts. Their elaborate costumes are replete with religious symbols that invested them with the aura of divinity.

MONTE ALBÁN. Another major Mesoamerican cultural tradition, connected in its origins with Olmec and having some Izapan ties, was that of Monte Albán, so named from the huge site near the modern city of Oaxaca. There is general agreement that a numerous pantheon of individualized deities was portrayed, especially in the famous funerary urns, theomorphic ceramic vessels placed in tombs. Many deities are identified by their "calendric names," the day in the 260-day divinatory cycle on which they were believed to have been born. Some can be tentatively connected with deities known to have been propitiated by the Zapotec-speakers who occupied most of the area around Monte Albán at the time of the Conquest, including the basic rain-and-fertility god, Cocijo. The walls of a few tombs at Monte Albán display painted images of deities or deity impersonators, some of them identical to those depicted on the ceramic urns.

TEOTIHUACÁN. Dominating the Classic period (c. 100-750 CE) in central Mexico—and spreading its influence throughout Mesoamerica—was the dynamic civilization of Teotihuacán. Symmetry and repetitiveness were hallmarks of Teotihuacán formats, which, particularly in the murals, include processions of ritual celebrants, frontal anthropomorphic and zoomorphic images flanked by profile figures, and complex scenes involving numerous personages engaged in a variety of activities. The dominant theme was clearly the promotion of fertility, featuring what appear to have been at least two major aspects of the preeminent rain-and-fertility deity that was prototypical to the Aztec Tlaloc. Aquatic and vegetational motifs are ubiquitous.

Certain images have also been identified as discrete deities of the Aztec type, and they have often been labeled with Nahuatl names. They include Tlaloc, the rain-and-earth god; a female fertility deity who may be the prototype of various Aztec goddesses (Chalchiuhtlicue, Xochiquetzal, Teteoinnan, and others); an old fire god (Aztec Huehueteotl or Xiuhtecuhtli); the flayed god (Xipe Totec); and Tecciztecatl, the male lunar deity.

CLASSIC VERACRUZ. During the Early Classic period (c. 100-600 CE), after the fade-out of the Olmec tradition in the Gulf Coast region, a distinct regional stylistic and iconographic tradition emerged, climaxing during the Late Classic and Epiclassic periods (c. 600-900 CE). It was best expressed at the major site of El Tajín, in northwest Veracruz, where a sophisticated style of relief carving, featuring double-outlined, interlocking scroll motifs, decorates a number of structures; these include the famous Pyramid of the Niches, two ball courts with friezes portraying complex sacrificial rituals connected with the ball game, and even more complicated ceremonial scenes on a series of column drums in the Building of the Columns.

The most famous exemplars of Classic Veracruz iconography are the handsomely carved stone objects worn by the ball players or replicas thereof: yokes (ball game belts); *hachas*, thin stone heads; and *palmas*, paddle-shaped stones, the latter two objects attached to the yokes worn by the players. Sculptured on these pieces are various anthropomorphic and zoomorphic beings, especially a monstrous creature probably symbolizing the earth. A major tradition of ceramic sculpture also flouished in this region during the Classic period. Some examples appear to represent deities that were prototypical to those of Postclassic times.

XOCHICALCO. With its apparent *floruit* during the Epiclassic period (c. 750-900 CE), the extensive hilltop site of Xochicalco flourished in what is now the state of Morelos, Mexico, and gave rise to another distinctive stylistic and iconographic tradition, mainly expressed in relief sculpture. The greatest amount of sculpture decorated one remarkable structure, the Pyramid of the Feathered Serpent. Aside from huge, undulating representations of the feathered serpent, various cross-legged seated personages, reflecting Lowland Maya stylistic influence, are depicted, many identified with their name signs and in some cases, seemingly, place signs as well. Calendric inscriptions are also present, and some scholars have suggested that the carvings may commemorate a major gathering of priests to discuss calendric reform and other ritual-religious matters.

TOLTEC. At the outset of the Postclassic period a new political and cultural power arose north of the Basin of Mexico, at Tollan, modern Tula, in the state of Hidalgo. Flourishing between about 900 and 1200, Tollan was a major metropolis, capital of an extensive empire. Its stylistic and iconographic tradition was quite eclectic and represented an amalgam of various earlier traditions (Teotihuacán, Xochicalco, El Tajín, and others).

"I would rather have men ask why I have not a statue, than why I have one."

CATO THE ELDER
QUOTED BY
PLUTARCH

Toltec iconography is known primarily from relief sculpture, decorated ceramics, figurines, and some remarkable cliff paintings at Ixtapantongo, southwest of Tula in the Toluca Basin. The militaristic flavor of Toltec imagery was also expressed by alternating representations of predatory animals and birds: jaguars, pumas, coyotes, eagles, and vultures.

MIXTECA-PUEBLA AND AZTEC. During the Toltec period a new stylistic and iconographic tradition was apparently emerging to the southeast, centered in southern Puebla, Veracruz, and western Oaxaca (the Mixteca), which has been labeled "Mixteca-Puebla." During the Postclassic period its pervasive influence was felt throughout Mesoamerica, as a kind of final iconographic synthesis of the earlier traditions already described. In contrast to its predecessors, it was characterized by a greater depictive literalness, plus a particular emphasis on symbolic polychromy.

"The Pyramids first, which in Egypt were laid."

ANONYMOUS
SEVEN WONDERS OF THE ANCIENT WORLD

The Aztec sytlistic and iconographic tradition, which flourished in central Mexico during the last century or so before the Conquest, can be considered, from one aspect, a regional variant of Mixteca-Puebla. [*See also* Aztec Religion.] It differs principally in displaying an even greater naturalism in human and animal imagery. It also was expressed much more frequently in monumental three-dimensional stone sculpture, particularly deity images. Virtually all of its principal symbols have been correctly identified as well as the great majority of the numerous deity depictions, which include almost every member of the crowded pantheon mentioned in the primary sources.

— H. B. NICHOLSON

EGYPTIAN ICONOGRAPHY

The principal iconographic sources for ancient Egyptian religion are the representations of scenes, both ritual and mythological, carved in relief or painted on the walls of Egyptian temples and tombs, as well as the numerous images and statues of gods and pharaohs. Additionally, there are many objects of ritual or practical function decorated with carved or painted religious motifs, and finally, numerous hieroglyphic signs belonging to the Egyptian writing system are representations of gods, religious symbols, and ritual objects. These types of sources remain constant throughout the more than three thousand years of ancient Egyptian history from the Old Kingdom to the Roman period (c. 3000 BCE-395 CE).

Scenes carved on the walls of tombs and temples as well as on furniture and ritual objects most frequently show the gods in the company of a king making offerings or performing other ritual acts (such as censing, purifying with water, or embracing the god). All representations of the king facing a divinity illustrate the ongoing relationship of reciprocity between them. In return for the precious object that he presents to the god, the pharaoh receives symbols of life, strength, stability, many years of kingship, and the like.

STATUARY. Numerous Egyptian statues made of all possible materials, such as stone, wood, gold, bronze, and faience, represent one, two, or three gods often accompanied by a king. Both gods and king wear crowns and hold characteristic insignia, among which the most frequent are the sign of life *(ankh)* and various types of scepters. Many elements of the king's dress are identical with those of the gods, thus visualizing the divine aspects of the monarch's nature.

The size of the statues varies according to their function. Small bronze statuettes of votive character were common, especially in the first millennium BCE. Many represent animals sacred to Egyptian gods; sometimes these figures are set on boxes containing mummies of the animals represented. The mummified bodies of larger animals, such as bulls, ibis, crocodiles, and cats, have been found buried within special necropolises near places connected with the cults of various gods.

Large stone statues served as cult objects in Egyptian temples. Pairs of colossal effigies of the seated king usually stood in front of the temple pylons. The sphinx, with its body of a lion and head of the king, was often placed in the front of the temple to symbolize the monarch's identity as solar god. Rows of sphinxes lined both sides of processional ways leading to the principal temple entrances.

FUNERARY ART. Another important part of our knowledge about ancient Egyptian iconography comes from the decoration of Egyptian tombs and coffins that comprises the great Egyptian religious "books"—literary compositions that combine spells of magical, mythological, and ritual character with pictures illustrating Egyptian visions of the netherworld. The most ancient of these "books" are the Pyramid Texts carved on the walls of some of the rooms inside the royal pyramids (Old Kingdom, c. 3000-2200 BCE).

GRECO-ROMAN ICONOGRAPHY

The religious structures of both Greeks and Romans conform to the typical patterns of divinity and belief found among the Indo-European peoples. Most notable of these is an organized pantheon of deities related by birth or marriage and presided over by a god of the sky who is both ruler and father (e.g., Zeus Pater and Jupiter). Nevertheless, although it is clear that such gods accompanied the movement of the Indo-Europeans into Greece and Italy, it is impossible to state with certainty what iconographic representation, if any, was used to worship them during this earliest period.

MINOAN-MYCENAEAN ICONOGRAPHY (2000-1200 BCE). The study of Cretan (Minoan) religion may be compared to a picture book without a text. The two symbols of Minoan civilization, the double ax and the horns of consecration, clearly had religious significance, perhaps as tools of worship, but their function is not understood. From the archaeological evidence, however, which includes frescoes, seals, and figurines, one may conclude that the representation of the divine was both anthropomorphic and the-

EGYPTIAN TEMPLES

Lives in Pictures and the Cult of the Dead

As the abode of the gods, Egyptian temples were accessible only to the kings and priests. The king, considered the mediator between the gods and the people, is usually shown in front of the gods in the ritual scenes that decorate the temple walls.

The sanctuary, usually situated at the far end of the temple along its axis, contained the sacred image of the god to whom the temple was dedicated. The statue of Amun-Re, the chief divinity of Thebes and the state divinity since the time of the New Kingdom, stood inside a shrine on a portable bark placed upon a sled.

Many temple scenes form standardized sequences of pictures showing summarily, sometimes almost symbolically, successive episodes of mythicized rituals that often refer to important historical events, such as the miraculous birth of the king, his coronation, his victories over enemies, his jubilee, and the founding of the temple. These representations appear in the inner parts of the temple, together with tableaux depicting the daily ritual performed before the statue of the temple's principal deity and scenes showing various offerings being made.

The interior of the walls enclosing the courts are often decorated with episodes of the most important feasts, while the grandiose tableaux found on the exterior of the walls and on the gates (frequently in the form of pylons) commonly illustrate the king's military achievements.

In addition to these scenes referring to particular events, the temple walls are also decorated with numerous motifs of a more symbolic nature, which give visual form to religious, political, or geographical ideas. The so-called geographical processions, for instance, symbolize the provinces of Egypt in the form of hefty divinities personifying the Nile, each bearing offerings in their hands.

Various iconographic patterns invented by the Egyptians give shape to the idea of the unification of Lower and Upper Egypt. The central motif of a great number of them is the heraldic symbol called *sma-tawy,* which is composed of two plants, papyrus (for Lower Egypt) and a kind of bulrush (for Upper Egypt), bound together around the spinal cord and the lungs of an animal. Two divine personifications of the Nile—the motive power of this unification—are often shown holding and binding together the two plants.

The Egyptian realm of the dead lay in the west. The best illustration of ancient Egyptian visual concepts of the netherworld appears in the decoration of New Kingdom royal and noble tombs situated in west Thebes; these iconographic patterns remained a favorite and repeated subject right up to the Roman period. Of the two principal groups of scenes depicted there, the first, usually found in the first room of the tomb, refers to various episodes in the earthly life of the deceased, including such religious ceremonies or feasts as the Beautiful Feast of the Valley, the royal jubilee, the New Year festival, or the harvest feast. Included in all these scenes are processions, offerings (including burnt offerings), incense burning, and performances with playing, singing, and dancing. Of special importance among Egyptian musicians was the harpist, who came to be represented by the squatting figure of a blind man shown in profile.

The other group of scenes, found in the inner room, illustrates various episodes of the funeral rites.

Of particular importance in every tomb were the places intended for the cult of the deceased. These featured niches with statues of the dead person (and sometimes of members of his family), stelae often depicting the deceased adoring and making offerings to various gods or royal personages, and lastly, false-door stelae constituting a symbolic passage between the realm of the dead and the world of the living.

Most important in each tomb, however, was the burial chamber, commonly situated underneath the accessible rooms at the bottom of a deep vertical shaft. Here were contained the sarcophagus with the mummy of the deceased and all the funerary offerings, including the four Canopic jars for the viscera of the deceased, the mummiform figures known as *shawabtis (ushabtis),* a copy of the *Book of Going Forth by Day* written on papyrus, and various ritual objects. The sarcophagi and coffins, made of wood or stone, took the form of cubical or body-shaped cases decorated with painted or carved religious motifs. The four Canopic jars were associated with the four sons of the royal deity Horus, with the four cardinal directions, and with the four protective goddesses; they each had distinctive stoppers, often representing the heads of the four sons of Horus or simply anthropomorphic heads.

— KAROL MYSLIWIEC

Celestial and judicious wielder of supreme power, founder of order, guarantor of justice, governor of marriage, father and ancestor, and patron of the city, the tableau of the sovereignty of Zeus includes still other dimensions.

PAGE 254

riomorphic. Found are depictions of female deities encoiled by snakes or with birds perched upon their heads; these figures may explain the prominence of snakes in later Greek religion as well as the association of Greek deities with specific birds. In addition, animal-headed figures reminiscent of contemporaneous Egyptian material have been uncovered. One such type, a bull-headed male, may be the source for the Greek myth of the Minotaur. Also found are representations of demonlike creatures who appear to be performing various ritual acts; these have been cited as evidence of Mesopotamian influence. A number of seals portray the figures both of a huntress, who is called "mistress of the beasts" and whom the Greeks associated with Artemis, and of a male deity, who stands grasping an animal by the throat in each hand. Finally, the seals present strong evidence for the existence of tree cults and pillar cults, the survival of which perhaps may be seen in the Greek myths about dryads, the woodland spirits of nature who inhabit trees.

ARCHAIC AND CLASSICAL ICONOGRAPHY. There is a great deal of evidence to indicate that, in the conservative ritual of Greek religion, the older forms of representation of the divine persisted. Aniconic images of the divine, such as the *omphalos* at Delphi, provide proof of its survival. This stone, which in Greek myth was described as the one that Rhea gave to Kronos to swallow when he wished to devour his infant son Zeus, and that the ruler of the Olympians then placed at the center of the world, is clearly a baetyl, a sacred stone that contains the power of the divine. Similarly, the widespread appearance of the herm, a pillar on which was carved an erect phallus and that acted as an agent of fertility and apotropaic magic, points to the survival of earlier conceptions of the divine. Myth also provides a clear illumination of the remnants of a theriomorphic iconography.

The amalgamation of a number of functional deities during the Archaic and Classical periods can be seen in the great variety of epithets by which each god was addressed. Many of the epithets of the Olympians can be considered as proof of older iconographic substrata that reveal functions closely linked to the world of nature: horselike Poseidon, owl-eyed Athena, cow-eyed Hera, cloud-gathering Zeus.

The evolution of the form and content of Greek iconography as a means of expressing spiritual ideals generally parallels that of Greek art, especially in sculpture. The earliest religious sculpture and architecture were executed in wood and have vanished; but in the the seventh century BCE we see the development of monumental stone architecture and sculpture. The most representative forms of sculpture are the *kouros* (male) and the *koure* (female) figures that stand rigidly with stylized features and dress. Perhaps votive offerings, they have been variously identified as divine or human but may represent something in between: an idealized existence shared by gods and mortals alike.

As the institutions of the state evolved, the original gods of nature were made citizens of the polis and given civic functions as protectors and benefactors of the city. Thus, the gold and ivory statue of Athena in the Parthenon portrayed the armed goddess in full regalia as the protector and patron of Athenian civilization, the goddess who had led her people to victory against the Persians. The Parthenon itself is a symbol of the bond between Athena and her city, for the temple frieze depicts the procession of the Panathenaea, a festival held in honor of both the goddess and the powerful city that worshiped her.

HELLENISTIC AND ROMAN ICONOGRAPHY. The declining political fortunes of the Greek states after the Peloponnesian War paved the way for the rise of Macedon and the magnificent career of Alexander the Great. Religious iconography in the Hellenistic period presents a curious admixture of Eastern and Western values that expressed themselves in the formal magnificence of the tomb of Mausolus at Halicarnassus as well as in the representations of Aphrodite that emphasize her naked human beauty, in sleeping satyrs and playful cupids as well as in the struggling Laocoön doomed by the gods. The Great Altar of Zeus at Pergamum, with its wide monumental stairway, was encompassed by a frieze that, in depicting the ancient Greek myth of the war between the Olympians and the Giants, displays a remarkable range and intensity of human emotions.

Roman religion seems to have remained rooted in nature to a much greater extent than civic Greek religion had; the early anthropomorphic representations of Mars and Jupiter are exceptions, perhaps occasioned by their clear identification with the political rather than the agricultural life of the Roman people. The conservative values of Roman religion not only inhibited the development of a distinctive iconography but at the same time led to the adoption of those elements in Hellenistic art that seemed best to reflect those values. Although Augustus's attempt to recreate the old Roman religious values through the resurrection of archaic rituals and priesthoods and the rebuilding of ancient temples and shrines was ultimately unsuccessful, his Altar of Augustan Peace (Ara Pacis) illustrates the Roman understanding of the connection between traditional expressions of piety and political success. One of its panels depicts Augustus offering solemn sacrifice; another reveals Mother Earth holding on her lap her fruitful gifts. The peace and prosperity of mortals and gods are attributed to Augustus's piety and devotion.

— TAMARA M. GREEN

HINDU ICONOGRAPHY

Visnu, Siva, and Devi are the basic visual images of Hinduism. Each of these deities is worshiped in a concrete image *(murti)* that can be seen and touched. The image is conceived in anthropomorphic terms but at the same time transcends human appearance. With certain exceptions, Hindu images have more than two arms. Their hands, posed in definite gestures, hold the attributes that connote the deity's power and establish its identity. While the images are concrete in their substantiality, they are but a means of conjuring up the presence of deity: this is their essential function. The image serves as a *yantra,* an "instrument" that allows the beholder to catch a reflection of the deity whose effulgence transcends what the physical eye can see. Visnu, Siva, and Devi (the Goddess) are represented in many types of images, for each of these main deities has multiple forms or aspects.

SIVA. The main object of Siva worship is the *linga.* The word *linga* means "sign," here a sign in the shape of a cylinder with a rounded top. The word *linga* also means "phallus" however; some of the earliest Siva *lingas* are explicitly phallus shaped. However, this sign is not worshiped in its mere anthropomorphic reference. It stands for creativity on every level—biological, psychological, and cosmic—as a symbol of the creative seed that will flow into creation or be restrained, transmuted, and absorbed within the body of the yogin and of Siva, the lord of yogins.

The images of Siva visualize the god's two complementary natures: his grace and his terror. Like all Hindu divine images, that of Siva has multiple arms; their basic number, four, implies the four cosmic directions over which extends the power of deity in manifestation. Siva's image of peace and serenity in one of its forms, Daksinamurti, is that of the teacher. Seated at ease under the cosmic tree, he teaches the sages yoga, gnosis, music, and all the sciences. In another image, standing as Pasupati, "lord of animals," Siva protects all the "animals," including the human soul.

The *linga* as both abstract symbol and partly anthropomorphic shape is the main Saiva cult object. In some of the sculptures, a human head adheres to the cylinder of the *linga,* or four heads are positioned in the cardinal directions, implying a fifth head (rarely represented) on top. Five is Siva's sacred number, and the entire Saiva ontology—the five senses, five elements, five directions of space, and further hierarchic pentads—is visualized in the iconic-aniconic, five-faced *linga.*

The facial physiognomy of the image reflects the nature of the particular aspect or manifestation of the god. His calm, inscrutable mien as well as Bhairava's distorted countenance are shown with many nuances of expression that convey the significance of each particular manifestation, defined as it is by specific attributes and cognizances. Siva's crown is his own hair. He is the ascetic god, and his crown shows the long strands of the ascetic's uncut hair piled high on his head in an infinite variety of patterns, adorned by serpents, the crescent moon, and the miniature figure of the celestial river Ganga (Ganges) personified.

An essential cognizance particular to Siva among gods—though not present in every Siva image—is the god's third eye (which also graces deities derived from the Siva concept, such as Devi and Ganesa). Vertically set in the middle of Siva's forehead above sun and moon, his two other eyes, the third eye connotes the fire of the ascetic god.

VISNU. The pervader and maintainer of the universe is represented by his anthropomorphic image in the innermost sanctuary. Invariably the image stands straight like a pillar, and its four arms symmetrically hold the god's main attributes: conch, wheel, mace, and lotus. In addition to the standing image, Visnu may assume two other positions, seated and recumbent. Indeed, no other Hindu god—except a Visnu-derived allegory, Yoganidra—is shown recumbent, and together, these three positions render the mode of the god's pervasive presence in the cosmos.

Visnu is also conceived in his five-fold aspect: as ultimate, transcendental reality *(para);* in his emanation *(vyuha);* in his incarnation *(vibhava);* as innermost within man *(antaryamin),* the inner controller; and as *arca* or consecrated image, this fifth instance being an *avatara,* a "descent" into matter.

DEVI. The Great Goddess, Devi, represents the creative principle worshiped as female. She is Sakti, the all-pervading energy, the power to be, the power of causation, cognition, will, and experience. She is the power of all the gods; she wields all their weapons in her main manifestations or images.

In certain traditions the buffalo demon while still in human shape adored the goddess. In some of the sculptures of the goddess as slayer of the demon—his body that of a man, his head that of a buffalo—he ecstatically surrenders to her as she slays him. When not depicted in action but standing straight in hieratic stance, the goddess is supported by a lotus or a buffalo head.

The Great Goddess has many forms. Like Siva she has three eyes; like Visnu, in her form as Yoganidra, "yoga slumber," she is represented lying, an embodiment of Visnu's slumber. Yoganidra is most beautiful and has only two arms, whereas the Goddess displays from four to sixteen arms in her other images. Like Siva, the Goddess is seen in divine beauty or in a shape of horror as Kali or Camunda.

Devi is not only represented in her own right as supreme goddess or as the consort of one of the main gods, she is also embodied as a group, particularly that

The pure divinities are forms taken locally—avataras—of the great gods Visnu and Siva.

PAGE 292

of the "Seven Mothers" *(saptamatrkas)* where, as Mother Goddess, she is shown as the sakti of seven gods, including Brahma, Visnu, and Siva.

Today most of the preserved images are made of stone or metal. The few paintings that have survived over the last four centuries are in watercolor on paper, as a rule small in size, and narrative rather than iconic.

— STELLA KRAMRISCH

BUDDHIST ICONOGRAPHY

In the course of its development and diffusion, Buddhism has expressed itself through an abundance of visual forms.

SAKYAMUNI BUDDHA. Because the Buddha as a personality was deemed to have passed outside of history altogether at his *parinirvana,* or death, his presence was instead symbolized by such motifs as the rich turban of the prince Siddhartha, the throne of the Blessed One, his footprints marked with the Wheel of the Law, the begging bowl *(patra),* or the Bodhi Tree (the Enlightenment). Similarly, the First Sermon among the monks in Banaras is evoked by the *triratna* ("three jewels," a three-pointed motif representing the Buddha, his Law, and his Community) surmounted by the Wheel (symbolizing by its movement the transmission of the dogma) and surrounded by deer. Most important of all, the *parinirvana* of the Buddha is recalled by the stupa, the domical shrine believed to have contained the precious relics of the Master. Together with the image of the Buddha, the stupa, as an actual monument or an iconic representation (and through such transformations as the *dagoba,* or step-pagoda, and the Tibetan *chorchen)* remains at the center of the cult and its visual imagery.

Esoteric or Tantric modes of religion also were a significant part of cultural Buddhism in East Asia.

PAGE 95

The representation of the Buddha that rapidly became universal probably originated in Gandhara or Mathura between the first century BCE and the first century CE; it shows the monk wearing the robe and mantle of the *bhiksu* (mendicant), with his head encircled by a nimbus, probably the result of Hellenistic influences. Among the thirty-two auspicious marks *(laksanas)* that designate a Buddha, the most characteristic ones are the *urna,* the circular tuft of hair on his forehead; the *usnisa,* the bump in his skull that looks like a bun of hair; the distended earlobes; the wrinkles on his neck; his webbed fingers; and his gold skin coloring. His posture, the serenity of his features, and his half-closed eyes suggest the depth of his meditation and detachment from the exterior world.

By the fifth century CE, representations of the Blessed One standing, seated, or reclining attained colossal dimensions in a variety of media: chiseled in cliffs or modeled in clay, cut into stone or cast in bronze.

THE TRANSCENDENT BUDDHA. With the Mahayana, the supernatural vision heralded in the Great Miracle of Sravasti culminates in the myriad Buddhas of the universe, which began to appear in the third and fourth centuries CE and were subsequently painted over and over on sanctuary walls and sculpted or modeled on temples and stupas. This concept of the Buddha's omnipresence is often combined with that of the lotus as cosmic image: each lotus petal constitutes a world, and each torus is occupied by one of the myriad Buddhas, evoking the universe past, present, and future.

These transcendent Buddhas, their bodies covered with images of Mount Meru, the stupa, the sun and moon, aquatic subjects and the lotus, the vajra (thunderbolt), wheel, triratna, and other signs and symbols, are encountered very early along the path of penetration of the Great Vehicle into China.

— SIMONE GAULIER AND ROBERT JERA-BEZARD
TRANSLATED FROM FRENCH BY INA BAGHDIANTZ

TAOIST ICONOGRAPHY

Taoist iconography symbolically expresses ideas concerning (1) the basic Chinese cosmology and mythology, (2) the Founders of the religion, (3) techniques of salvation, (4) those who have attained the goal, (5) immortality as a universal hope, and (6) Taoist concepts of, and relationships with, the numinous dimension and numinous beings.

ICONOGRAPHY AND WORLDVIEW. The most familiar symbol of the functioning of the Tao by means of its Vital Breaths is the ingenious design of the circle divided into two equal parts by a curving central line, one side of the circle representing the light of *yang* and the other side the darkness of *yin,* but with a bit of *yin* in the *yang* part and a bit of *yang* in the *yin* part. This expressive symbol is found on the liturgical robes of Taoists (a word we use to indicate professional clergy). The most sophisticated summary of the basic cosmology is the Diagram of the Ultimate *(t'ai-chi t'u)* devised by the eleventh-century philosopher Chou Tun-i, but it is not used iconographically.

The Eight Trigrams, each of which is formed from a combination of unbroken *(yang)* and broken *(yin)* lines, constitute another abstract symbol of common occurrence. These were in archaic times already invested with great significance as marks of the combinations and permutations of those forces that produced the world and all beings in it. The classical exposition of the Trigrams appears in the ancient *Chou i* or *I ching* (Scripture of Change), a seminal source for Taoism as for all traditional thought. The Eight Trigrams are also embroidered on Taoist sacerdotal robes.

Mythological figures in human form include the

traditionally accepted heroes of creation, cultural inventions such as cooking, housing, writing, and the calendar, and founders of the earliest polities, but while often encountered in Taoist iconography, they have little specifically Taoist meaning.

FOUNDERS. One of these mythological figures has definitely retained his persona as a Taoist, along with his broader identification as a Chinese hero: Huang-ti, the Yellow Emperor. Two millennia later he was followed by the second Founder, Lao-tzu, supposedly a historical person somewhat senior to Master K'ung (Confucius) in the mid-sixth century BCE. The third Founder is again only semihistorical: Chang Ling, or Chang Tao-ling, is presumed to have flourished around the end of the second century CE. All three of the Founders are represented in visual arts. Huang-ti, as an emperor, is depicted wearing a crown topped with a "mortar board" from the front and back of which hang the rows of jade tassels marking his exalted rank. Lao-tzu is most commonly shown as a snowy-bearded old gentleman riding an ox and holding a book, this memorializing the moment he rode off to the West after composing the *Tao-te ching* for the Chinese garrison commander at the frontier pass. Chang Tao-ling rides a tiger, or sits on a tiger throne, symbolizing the great spiritual powers attained during a lifetime of Taoist self-cultivation.

TECHNIQUES OF SALVATION. Salvation in Taoism is attained through various techniques—alchemical, yogic, dietary, sexual—and these are alluded to directly or indirectly in visual imagery. The caldron or mortar in which the elixir of immortality is prepared is a motif evoking the "alchemy of substances" *(wai-tan)*, or preparation and ingestion of the elixir; the Chinese see a rabbit pounding the elixir in a mortar rather than a man in the moon. The most common dietary symbol is the *ling-chih* or "efficacious mushroom," a plant whose consumption produces longevity or even immortality.

THOSE WHO HAVE ATTAINED. As a religion that has kept alive real hopes of immortality—or at least longevity—Taoism naturally has voluminous records of those who have attained the goal. The most common term for such adepts is *hsien*, a word whose graph suggests a person who has retired to the mountains—which was indeed the eremitic life recommended for the alchemist.

Out of the countless immortal transcendents in China's long past a few have naturally captured popular imagination. Outstanding among these is the group called the Eight Immortals, who are constantly depicted in all the arts as well as in literature. Among the eight, Lü Tung-pin, supposedly a historical figure of the eighth century, is foremost, as indicated by the fact that only he has his own temples in modern Taiwan.

Hsien may often be indicated simply by representation of their attributes. Thus, the Eight are denoted by sword, fan, flower basket, lotus, flute, gourd, castanets, and tube drum. The *ru-i* magic wand, the crooked cane, and the fly-whisk (a mark of spiritual attainment and authority taken over from Buddhism) are other common attributes of *hsien*. Perhaps the richest symbol is the gourd, which represents the alchemical caldron or its equivalent, the microcosm of the adept's own

TAOISM AND THE NUMINOUS DIMENSION
The Universe and the Body

The numinous realm of Taoism includes both macrocosm (the universe) and microcosm (the human body). Moreover, these two are essentially identical: the interior space corresponds with the exterior and is occupied by the same numinous beings.

Most iconographic representations of spiritual beings fall under the category of popular religion rather than Taoism. It is perhaps the occasion of the rituals of the Chiao, the major liturgical performance of Taoists on behalf of the community, that most commonly shows Taoist concepts in anthropomorphic form. The Chiao serves nicely to set off Taoist icons from popular ones, insofar as during that great service the icons of the popular gods are relegated to a subsidiary, "guest" position within the sacred arena, while the Taoist officiants focus upon the "altar of the Three Pure Ones" (San Ch'ing), who represent different aspects of the Tao. Represented in iconic scrolls as venerable sages, they are the Heaven-Honored One of the Tao and Its Virtues (Tao-te T'ien-tsun), the Heaven-Honored One of the Primal Beginnings (Yüan-shih T'ien-tsun), and the Heaven-Honored One of the Spiritually Efficacious Treasure (Ling-pao T'ien-tsun). As hypostases of the Tao they may also be characterized as the "dharma-bodies" of Lao-tzu. Hung at the same altar, in slightly subordinate positions to "stage left" and "stage right," are two other iconic portraits. On the left is that of the Supreme Emperor of Jadelike Augustness (Yü-huang Shang-ti), head of both the popular and the Taoist pantheons. The portrait on the right is that of the Lord of the Northern Bushel Constellation (Pei-tou-hsing Chün).

— LAURENCE G. THOMPSON

The divinization of the I ching is founded on a series of symbols or diagrams formed by the combination of unbroken lines (representing yang) and broken lines (representing yin).

PAGE 652

body, the universe, ancient notions of cosmogony, the dream of paradisiacal lands, and still other concepts. The paradisiacal lands, or abodes of *hsien,* are depicted very frequently.

IMMORTALITY AS A UNIVERSAL HOPE. Of course the goal of the Taoists is not their hope alone. Longevity, or even immortality, is one of the most conspicuously prayed-for desires of the Chinese. These desires are given visual form on the roofs of popular temples, where the ridge is lined with images of three star-gods, representing longevity, wealth and elite status, and many sons to carry on the family property and ancestral cult. The star-god of longevity, Shou Hsing, is of course shown as a *hsien.* His happy smile and rosy cheeks bespeak his healthy old age; his stout belly and bulging forehead indicate that he is an adept in cultivating his ch'i, and as he leans on his rough-hewn staff he holds a peach in his hand. The graph of longevity, *shou,* written in a hundred different ways, is a symbol in itself, omnipresent as a decoration on the products of art and craft. *Shou* is also the common euphemism for death, which, it is hoped, leads to immortality.

It has long been the custom for each member of the household to kindle the Hanukkah lights in an eight-branched candelabrum frequently called a menorah.

PAGE 311

JEWISH ICONOGRAPHY

Jewish iconography, whether actually represented in works of art or existing only as traditional imagery (and occasionally referred to in literature), was determined from the first by the biblical "prohibition of images." This prohibition, transmitted in the Bible in several versions, could be understood (1) as forbidding, in a religious context, all images, regardless of their subject matter (*Ex.* 20:4, *Dt.* 4:15-18), or (2) specifically forbidding the depiction of God and the ritual use of such a depiction as an idol (*Dt.* 27:15). While the first interpretation of the prohibition did not prevail (the Bible itself provides evidence of this in *1 Kgs.* 6:23-29, *Ez.* 8:5-12), the other was consistently implemented. Possibly the most striking feature of Jewish iconography throughout the ages is the systematic avoidance of any depiction of the figure of God.

HELLENISM. The meeting between Judaism and the Greek world—a process that lasted from early Hellenism to late antiquity (roughly, second century BCE to fifth century CE)—resulted in a body of religious images. While the Mishnah and Talmud were being compiled (roughly second to sixth centuries CE) Jewish communities produced a large number of representations, which have been uncovered in Jewish remains (mainly synagogues and burial places) from Tunisia to Italy and eastward to the Euphrates; sites in Israel are particularly rich. Occasionally this imagery includes human figures, either in biblical scenes or in pagan myths (frequently the image of Helios, the Greek sun god).

More often, however, these survivals show objects with definite ritual connotations. Most prominent are the seven-branched *menorah* (candelabrum), Aron ha-Qodesh (the Ark of the Covenant), *lulav* and *etrog* (palm branch and citron), and shofar (ceremonial animal horn). These objects (which reflect the crystallization of Jewish ritual) have no strict hierarchy, but the *menorah,* and the Ark of the Covenant, representing

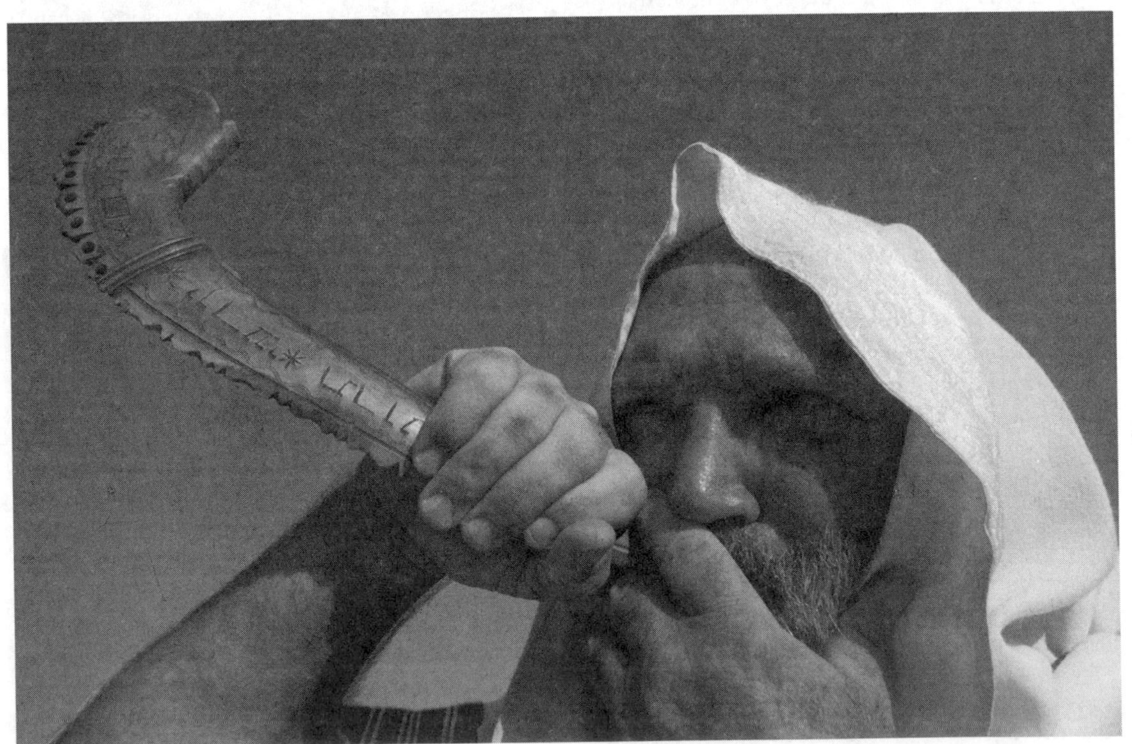

SACRED RITUAL

Ancient Jewish icons tend to be ritualistic in nature. This man is blowing an elaborately carved ceremonial animal horn, called a shofar

TED SPIEGEL/ CORBIS

the law itself, are more important than the others. When both are shown together, they always occupy the central place. Besides such explicitly ritual objects, Jewish remains abound in artistic motifs, taken over from Hellenistic art, whose symbolic character is obscure.

MIDDLE AGES. In the European Middle Ages, especially between the thirteenth and fifteenth centuries, Jewish religious imagery developed further. The illumination of manuscripts is the central aesthetic medium of the period; of particular significance are the manuscripts produced in Spain, Italy, and Germany. All these manuscripts are of a ritual nature, the most important groups being the Haggadah for Passover and prayer books for the holidays, the *mahzor.* The illuminations (and later, printed illustrations) represent many ritual utensils, but they also include, more often than in Jewish art of other periods and media, human figures, especially in biblical scenes. The iconographic repertoire is enlarged by mythical motifs, attesting to messianic beliefs. Among these motifs are the legendary beasts (such as the *shor habar,* a kind of wild ox), on which the just will feast on the day of redemption; these are particularly prominent in manuscripts produced in Germany. The future Temple that, according to common belief, is to be built after the redemption, is another frequent mythical motif.

QABBALISTIC SYMBOLISM. The qabbalistic tradition is a special field of iconographic creation. Qabbalistic literature abounds in visual metaphors, since the authors often tend to express (or to hide) their thoughts and mysteries in visual images and descriptions of supposed optical experiences. The central image of qabbalistic symbolism is the Tree of Sefirot. The godhead is imagined as structured in ten spheres, each of them representing a "divine quality" (Heb., *sefirah*). The shape and place of the spheres, and the spatial relationships between them, are firmly established in the qabbalistic imagination. The overall pattern vaguely resembles a tree (hence the name), but the basic character of the image is abstract rather than figurative.

Qabbalistic literature produced other visual symbols, among them the images of broken vessels, scattered sparks, Adam Qadmon (primordial man) as a figure of God, and so forth.

— MOSHE BARASCH

CHRISTIAN ICONOGRAPHY

For the greater part of Christian history, the church's images have been drawn from its liturgical texts, scriptures, and pedagogy and rendered in the styles of the particular age and place the images served. In modern times, the sources for Christian iconography have expanded to include psychological sociopolitical, and nontraditional elements.

EARLY CHRISTIANITY. Early Christian art surviving from the first half of the third century reflects the diversity of the Greco-Roman context from which it emerged. The earliest iconographic figures, borrowed directly from late antique conventions, were placed in new compositional and environmental settings on jewelry and other minor arts.

The earliest images of Christ were concerned with his person and role on earth and were borrowed from classical types of teaching figures, miracle workers, and heroes. Conventions for depicting divine attributes were missing, and there was no attempt at historical accuracy. Jesus did not look like an early first-century Jewish man from Palestine, but rather, like a Roman teacher-philosopher or like an Apollo-type mythic hero, such as the Christos-Helios figure in the necropolis of Saint Peter's Basilica in Rome.

IMPERIAL CHRISTIANITY. Following the adoption of Christianity as the state religion by the Roman emperor Constantine in the early fourth century, the figure of Christ as the imperial reigning Lord emerged. Jesus enthroned as the leader of the church, or in the heavens as an imperial judge, reflected the power the church had gained in that era. Within a hierarchically structured society, Jesus was depicted as a reigning philosopher-emperor who dispensed grace and judgment above all earthly power (see for instance the enthroned Christ in the apse mosaic of Santa Pudenziana in Rome). From the fourth through the sixth century the figure of Jesus, elevated to a ruler over all, came to represent the power of the church over state and society. Christ seated in majesty above the heavens in the apse mosaic of the mausoleum of Santa Constanza in Rome (c. 350) or in the apse mosaic of the Church of San Vitale in Ravenna, Italy (c. 550), reflects christological formulations. Mary appears as an enthroned queen in the mosaics of Santa Maria Maggiore, Rome, after the Council of Ephesus in 431, which declared her *theotokos,* Mother of God. Two types of Christ figures occupy the twenty-six mosaic panels of the Christ cycle in San Apollinare Nuovo in Ravenna (c. 520).

Explicit representation of the crucifixion of Jesus is conspicuously absent from early Christian iconography. Once the crucifixion came to be widely depicted, the preferred type in both East and West through the ninth century was a robed, open-eyed victorious Christ hanging on the cross, such as the ones in the illuminations of the Rabula Gospels from Mesopotamia (dated 586) or on the wall decorations of the Church of Santa Maria Antiqua in Rome.

"Cursed be the man who makes a carved or molten idol."

DEUTERONOMY 27:15

I

ICONOGRAPHY

Christian Iconography

For Christians, the cross is a sign evoking a historical event basic to the history of salvation: the crucifixion and death of Jesus at Calvary.

PAGE 197

BYZANTINE ART. Within the art of the Eastern Orthodox church, the image (as icon) relates to the liturgy in a manner distinguished from that of its Western counterparts. An icon can appear in a variety of media: painting, mosaic, sculpture, or illuminated manuscript. Its subject matter includes biblical figures, lives of the saints, scenes and narrative cycles that relate specifically to the liturgical calendar. To the present day, Byzantine tradition relies heavily on iconography in its worship.

Over the centuries, rules for iconographers in the East were formalized, and copy books determined the style and subject matter of iconography. Paintings of the crucifixion in the Byzantine tradition, for example, often include the figures of Mary and Saint John at the foot of the cross in attitudes of grief, and the corpus traditionally hangs in a limp curve against the rigidity of the cross. This form then became popular in the West, especially in medieval Italy, and influenced painters such as Cimabue (d. 1302?).

MIDDLE AGES. Christian iconography produced in the eighth and ninth centuries became regionally acculturated as its Roman origins disappeared from the face of indigenous expression. Elaborate decorated surfaces enclosed Christian symbols and figures, where, in the service of beautiful patterns, iconography became abstract and emblematic. During the ninth and tenth centuries a shift in emphasis from Christ the victor to Christ the victim took place in the thinking of the church; accordingly, images of the crucifixion with the victorious reigning Lord on the cross were replaced by those of the suffering human victim. The Gero Crucifix in the Cathedral of Cologne, Germany (c. 960), is one of the earliest representations of Christ as a suffering, dying figure.

By the twelfth century the decorative, narrative, and didactic role of the arts gave way to an explicitly sacramental function, one in which the imagery appeared in a context believed to be a model of the Kingdom of Heaven, the church building. Iconography in the church was believed capable of building a bridge that reached from the mundane world to the threshold of the divine spirit. Described in twelfth-century Christian literature as anagogical art, iconography served as an extension of the meaning of the mass.

In the Gothic era a proliferation of Old Testament imagery reflected renewed theological and political interests in manifestations of God working within and through royal hierarchies. During this period the suffering Christ of the Romanesque style became a more benign Savior.

In the late Gothic period, approximately the fourteenth and fifteenth centuries across northern Europe, the iconography of Christianity was populated with aesthetically appealing, elegant figures and decorative surfaces known in modern scholarship as the International Style. Attitudes, dress, and colors emphasized soft, flowing lines, gentle expressions, and rich textures.

RENAISSANCE AND REFORMATION. Christian iconography of the Renaissance in Italy acquired classically human characteristics as interest in Greco-Roman literature and art was revived. Jesus and his followers appeared in a human guise heretofore unknown. Scenes of biblical episodes and historically religious significance were given the illusion of three-dimensional settings that emphasized their reality in the natural world. Fifteenth-century Renaissance art reflected renewed interest in pagan mythology and Christian subject matter alike; therefore pagan iconography competed with traditional Christian iconography. Proportion, perspective, and human experience were new ingredients in the iconography of the Renaissance. For example, between 1495 and 1498 Leonardo da Vinci completed the Last Supper on the wall of the refectory of Santa Maria della Grazie in Milan, Italy.

In northern Europe in the fifteenth and sixteenth centuries exaggerated realism in the treatment of subject matter and pre-Reformation currents of thought shaped Christian iconography. Matthias Grünewald's famous crucifixion panel in the Isenheim Altarpiece (1510-1512) presents Christ as a victim whose physical appearance betrays mutilation and disease and emphasizes divine participation on behalf of human suffering.

The Council of Trent, held in the middle of the sixteenth century, formulated instructions on the uses of iconography on behalf of the church. If the Reformation in some areas limited or forbade the use of images in the church, the Counter-Reformation encouraged a proliferation of them, thereby stimulating the expansion of the Baroque style of art. Eventually the church's use of Baroque forms extended beyond traditional sculptural programs and painted panels to wall surface decor, ceiling plaster, frescoes, elaboration of vestments and liturgical vessels, and extensive programmatic designs for altars and chapels.

SEVENTEENTH AND EIGHTEENTH CENTURIES. Protestant iconography in the seventeenth century emphasized individual experience, and images of Jesus stressed his humanity and participation in the human condition. Rembrandt's portraits of Jesus, for example, show a thirty-year-old Jewish man. Roman Catholic iconography, by contrast, stressed the sacramental presence of a heroic Christ in programmatic sequences such as Peter Paul Rubens's early altarpieces and Nicolas Poussin's two series of paintings entitled *The Seven Sacraments* from the 1640s.

NINETEENTH CENTURY. In the nineteenth century, Christian iconography served more private and artistically formal purposes. The recovery of historical styles in nineteenth-century art and architecture carried with it renewed interest in Christian iconographic themes.

Vincent van Gogh (d. 1890), who in his early life had been a Christian missionary, created a personal iconography that eschewed for the most part any specifically Christian subject. Paul Gauguin's paintings of Old Testament subjects, the crucifixion, or religious imagery from life in Tahiti created a recognizable but private iconography that reflected individual interests and goals. The institutional church for the most part disengaged itself from major artists and movements. Under these circumstances, by the late nineteenth century a great part of Christian iconography had become copy work, sentimental and remote from the society at large.

TWENTIETH CENTURY. A highly individualized Christian iconography has been shaped in the twentieth century by the religious consciousness of individual artists. The German Expressionists, for example, insisted upon interpreting and revealing their individuality. When Wassily Kandinsky (d. 1944) wrote *Concerning the Spiritual in Art,* what was revealed in the art included the feelings of the artist and the expressive properties of color. Emil Nolde's nine-part *Life of Christ* altarpiece (1911-1912) combined Nolde's interest in the impact of color with a traditional Christian format. George Rouault more than any other recognized twentieth-century artist sought to create compelling Christian imagery. His 1926 *Miserere* series compared Christ's suffering with twentieth-century experiences of human sufferings in war. Max Beckmann (d. 1950) equated Adam and Eve in the Fall with the grotesque dimensions of the human condition under fascism. In contrast, the most popular and most often reproduced image of Jesus in the United States in the first half of the twentieth century was W. H. Sallmon's *Head of Christ,* a sentimental figure with widespread influence.

Fantasy painters like Salvador Dali and Marc Chagall used Christian subject matter in a unique manner in order to suggest visions of the mind or vistas of a dream world fashioned out of the subconscious. Paintings such as Dali's *Sacrament of the Last Supper* (1955) and Chagall's *White Crucifixion* (1938) identify a private vision in which traditional Christian iconography is reinterpreted.

The twentieth century has also seen the emergence of Christian iconography in new media, notably film and electronic communications. Biblical stories presented in films with titles like *The Bible, The Ten Commandments, The King of Kings,* and *The Gospel According to St. Matthew* have engaged a public separate from the church. The mass media, which now include home video, have offered traditional Christian subject matter in extended narrative form as dramatic entertainment.

— JOHN W. COOK

ISLAMIC ICONOGRAPHY

Islam is generally considered an iconoclastic religion in which the representation of living things has been prohibited from its very beginning. However, the Qur'an nowhere deals with this problem or explicitly speaks against representation.

EMERGING IMAGERY. The feeling that representation was alien to the original spirit of Islam resulted in the development of abstract ornamental design, both geometric and vegetal, notably the arabesque as the endless continuation of leaves, palmettes, and sometimes animal-like motifs growing out of each other; it also gave calligraphy its central place in Islamic art. However, it would be wrong to claim that early Islam was without any pictures. In secular buildings such as palaces, there was no lack of representations of kings, musicians, dancers, and the like. Decorative painting on ceramics includes not only more or less stylized animal or human figures as individual motifs but also scenes from (often unidentified) tales and romances.

New stylistic features came with the growing Chinese influence during the Mongol occupation of Iran in the late thirteenth century. (Persian literature speaks of China as the "picture house," where Mani, the founder of Manichaeism, acts as the master painter.) Henceforward, illustrative painting developed predominantly in Iran, where the great epic poems (an art form unknown to the Arabs) inspired miniaturists through the centuries to the extent that the iconography of Firdawsi's *Shah-namah* (Book of Kings) and Nizami's *Khamsah* (Quintet) became almost standardized. Early historical works, such as the world history of Rashid al-Din (d. 1317), were rather realistically illustrated.

Islamic painting reached its zenith in Iran and India in the sixteenth and seventeenth centuries, when, partly under the influence of European prints, naturalistic portraiture was developed to perfection. The Mughal emperor Jahangir (r. 1605-1627) inspired the court painters to express his dreams of spiritual world-rule in his portraits by using the motif of the lion and the lamb lying together, or by showing him in the company of Sufis.

THE SHAPE OF SPIRITUALITY. Portraits of Sufis and dervishes are frequent in the later Middle Ages: many drawings capture the spiritual power or the refinement of a solitary Muslim holy man or illustrate the "sessions of the mystical lovers" *(majalis al-'ushshaq).* Sufis are also shown as teachers or in their whirling dance.

While naturalistic representation of the Prophet and his family was increasingly objected to, other ways of presenting him developed. One might put a *hadith*

Depending on the Sufi group, the dance can be a marvel of esthetic movement or the frenetic writhings of the seemingly possessed.

PAGE 632

Domes, portals, and mihrabs are lavishly embellished with Qur'anic passages in stylized calligraphy.

PAGE 469

in superb calligraphy on a single page or write his *hilyah,* an elaboration of the classical Arabic description of his outward and inward beauty, in a special calligraphic style, as was done in Turkey from about 1600. The Prophet's footprints on stone, or representations of them, along with more or less elaborate drawings of his sandals, still belong to the generally accepted items in the religious tradition. One could also produce "pictures" of saintly persons such as 'Ali ibn Abi Talib from pious sentences written in minute script (although in Iran quite realistic battle scenes showing the bravery and suffering of Husayn and other members of the Prophet's family are also found in more recent times).

Calligraphic images have become more and more popular: the letters of the word *bismillah* ("in the name of God") can be shaped into birds and beasts; Qur'anic passages of particular protective importance, such as the "throne verse" (surah 2:256), appear in animal shape; and whenever a calligraphic lion is found, it usually consists of a formula connected with 'Ali, who is called the "Lion of God" (Asad Allah, Haydar, Shir, and so forth).

Indeed, the most typical and certainly the most widely used means of conveying the Islamic message was and still is calligraphy. The walls of Persian mosques are covered with radiant tiles on which the names of God, Muhammad, and 'Ali in the square Kufic script give witness to the Shi'i form of faith; Turkish mosques are decorated with Qur'anic quotations or with an enormous *Allah.*

Under European influence, a very colorful popular iconography has developed in some parts of the Muslim world. On posters, religious motifs from various traditions are strung together in highly surprising form: Raphael's little angels appear along with the Lourdes Madonna around a deceased Muslim leader in a lush Paradise, or an apotheosis of Ayatollah Khomeini is coupled with the earthbound figure from Andrew Wyeth's *Christina's World.* Such syncretistic pictures are certainly not acceptable to the large majority of pious Muslims. On the other hand, the calligraphic traditions are gaining new importance from Morocco to Indonesia, and some attempts at producing a kind of Qur'anic scriptorial picture (thus Sadiqain and Aslam Kamal in Pakistan) are remarkably successful and deserve the attention of the historian of religion and the art lover.

— ANNEMARIE SCHIMMEL

IMMORTALITY

The concept of immortality can be understood and expanded upon on three levels. In its first sense, immortality is the quality attributed to divine beings, mythical or angelic, who by their very nature are not subject to death. The second sense concerns those heroes who have attained a divine status that they share with the gods. In its third sense, the concept of immortality has to do with the human being who enters upon a new form of eternal and incorruptible existence after death. The present article will deal only with immortality in this third sense, treating the permanence of the human being beyond the phenomenon of death.

NONLITERATE PEOPLES. The study of nonliterate cultures affords insight into a number of the living values of these peoples, their relations with their ancestors, their initiation rites, their sense of time, and their eschatological myths, and in this way we arrive at a better comprehension of the basic patterns of the activity of *homo religiosus.*

Sub-Saharan Africa. For the African there are two kinds of time: mythical time, the time of the eternally valid group and its continuity, and real time, in which the life of the individual and the discontinuity of death take place. Between these two times lies the symbolic mediation of funeral rites, through which the deceased leaves contingent time and passes into mythical time, the time of the pyramid of beings. The funeral rites are the collective response to the death of an individual; they allow the group to endure.

Alongside this vision of the undying ethnos exists the belief in the deathlessness of the personal being, indispensable for the continuity of the group. Among the Bobo of Burkina Faso, real time lies under the sign of Dwo, an unchanging divinity who rules over spirits and genies, the life force *(nyama),* and the ancestors. Also in Burkina Faso, in the eschatology of the Dagai, a cyclic conception of time is accompanied by the notion of the reincarnation of the deceased—all new births arise from the transformation of the ancestors. After death, the deceased passes first to the land of the spirits, either to become an ancestor or to be reincarnated in the body of a totemic animal.

There are two classes of ancestors, those who are mythical and primordial and those who have entered this state after their life on earth. Ancestor worship holds a most important place in African belief and ritual. The conception of the ancestor is made up of two components: on the one hand, the purity of the social and religious ideal, and on the other, a concern with the continuity and identity of the community. Together the two components form the concept of individual and collective immortality. The ancestor represents the symbolic transposition of the human condition to a numinous plane while continuing to be a part of the world of the living. It is in the role of ancestor that the most important stage of one's destiny after death is realized.

Another aspect of ancestral immortality is found in African beliefs in reincarnation. Reincarnation brings about a reactualization of the deceased that partially interrupts his postmortem fate. Reincarnation implies that the returning ancestor is recognized and present in the memory of the living, and it can only occur in a child of the same lineage and sex.

In all cultures, funeral rituals serve as primary expressions of belief in immortality while at the same time serving as instruments that help to make it real by symbolically absorbing the shock caused by a death. Like the rites of birth and initiation, they effect a passage that is at once a separation and a coming together. In all African communities, funeral rites mark out the successive stages traversed by the deceased.

Australia. The appearance of man in his present form is placed in the Dreaming, a primordial era called *alchera* or *alcheringa* by the Aranda, a central Australian people. The creation myths revolve around the great gods and the civilizing heroes, so that primordiality is fundamental. The cosmogonic and primordial myths play a pivotal role because all the rites of initiation, reproduction, and fertility are reenactments of these myths.

Death is a shock to the tribe and is felt as a disruption of the collective life, hence the cries and wailing, the mourning rituals, the rhythmic chanting, and the search to discover the evil spirit who caused this death. But the Australians believe that death is the final rite of passage that leads one from the profane world to the sacred universe. Man has two souls. The true self, the primordial and preexistent spirit, comes from heaven, the totemic center. At death, the true soul leaves the body and goes back to live forever in the eternal Dreaming, where it was before the individual's birth, while the other soul remains on earth, taking up residence in another person and moving about among the living.

The funeral rites take various forms. Through the rites, the preexisting spirit regains its spiritual domain, sometimes thought of as the primordial totemic center. A whole ritual symbolism punctuates this journey, for example the occasional placing of bones within a totemic coffin. Beliefs in reincarnation, however, are rare and confused. For human beings the life cycle is simple: from the preexisting spirit, birth into a body and entry into the profane world, to the first stage of reintegration into the Dreaming via initiation, and finally the return to the original state through funeral rites.

The Americas. We come now to American Indian beliefs in immortality, as they are found outside the more advanced American civilizations. These are forms of religion that have survived through the post-Columbian era and still exist in some areas of North and South America. The belief in a life beyond the grave seems to have been firmly established in Indian thought in early times, to judge from their conception of the world and of life, from ancestral traditions, and from the testimonies of seers.

Among the American Indian peoples we find a conception of the soul that forms the basis of their beliefs in immortality. In North America the idea of a double soul is extremely widespread. The corporeal soul gives life, consciousness, and the faculty of movement to the body, whereas the dream soul is separate from the body and can move about in space and go to distant places. Death occurs when the separate soul becomes trapped in the realm of the dead. Then the corporeal soul is also detached from the body. The Indians believe that the soul goes to the region of the dead, which is known through myths and tales to be patterned after the world of the living. Thus in North America it is sometimes called the "happy hunting ground."

There are various methods of entombment: inhumation in South America, and in Canada placement of the body on a platform, in a tree, or on the ground. There is also incineration. Among the Iroquois, the Algonquians to the south of the Great Lakes, there are second funerals, involving the burial of the disinterred bones in a common grave or funeral urn. The provision of grave goods—food, drink, weapons, clothing, and jewelry—is widespread in the Andean region.

Inner Asia and the Finno-Ugric peoples. A great similarity in beliefs concerning the soul can be noted on both sides of the Urals. The Khanty (Ostiaks) and Mansi (Voguls), Ugrians from the Ob River region, believe in the existence of a double soul comprising the breath or bodily soul and the shadow or dream soul, which is free and quite incorporeal but is tied to the dead person after death. Thus, after the person's death, the soul that was free and immaterial in life takes on a bodily form because of its ties to the corpse. Corpse and soul together stand for the complete, personal identity of the deceased person. Thus while the body is in the grave, it is also somewhere else thanks to its soul. The Khanty and Mansi believe that the free soul enters a subterranean realm where it represents the deceased and his personality.

Finnic pneumatology is identical to that of the northern Eurasian world. The free soul (image soul, shadow soul) is the extracorporeal manifestation of the person, which can become separated from the body even during life, in dreams, ecstasy, or trance. The corporeal soul, bound to the body, animates physical and psychic life. This dualism has faded under the influence of Christianity, but has left numerous traces in religious practices.

MESOAMERICAN RELIGIONS. The Mesoamerican cultural and religious complex includes three major periods: the Preclassic concludes in the third

"The only secret people keep is immortality."

EMILY DICKINSON

century CE, and the Classic era extends from that time to the year 1000, followed by the Postclassic era. I shall consider here only the last period, for which we have relatively abundant archaeological and historical records.

The Aztec. The religion of the Aztec—the dominant people in Mexico at the time of the conquest—is a syncretic one in which three principal gods are found: the sun god Huitzilopochtli, the rain god Tlaloc, originally from Teotihuacán, and Quetzalcoatl, the feathered serpent of the Toltec.

After death, people are subject to different fates, according to the choice of the gods. Stillborn children go to the thirteenth heaven, where the "tree of milk" is found that provides them with nourishment for an eternal infancy. Warriors slain on the battlefield and all those who have been sacrificed on an altar, as well as traders who have died on their journeys, become companions of the Sun, who has chosen them to take part in the cosmic salvation.

This cosmological plan provided the earliest illustrated guidebook to the beyond.

PAGE 214

The second category of the deceased is made up of men and women chosen by Tlaloc, those killed by drowning, lightning, and marsh fevers. These are buried, and go to the eastern abode, to the gardens of the god. All other dying people go to the northern realm, the land of night, until they reach the underworld of the god Mictlan, who will annihilate them.

The Maya. Maya religion is known through the discovery of great cities such as Tikal, Copan, Palenque, and Uxmal. The period of its highest attainment extends from the third to the tenth centuries. In its funeral practices we find again three categories of the dead. The privileged groups are warriors who fall in battle, women dying in childbirth, priests, and suicides by hanging. These are immortal and enjoy eternal gladness in the Maya paradise beneath the sacred ceiba, the tree that crosses all the celestial spheres. This is the "tree of the beginning," Yache, which creates the junction between heaven and earth.

INCA RELIGION. At a time when various civilizations shared the Andean region (Peru, Bolivia, and Ecuador), new populations came on the scene. Chief among these were the Inca. Various witnesses of the Spanish conquest left accounts of Inca religion, all of which agree that the Inca believed in immortality and imagined the afterlife as a continuation of the present life. The evidence found in Peru attests to funeral customs such as the preservation of the corpse, the giving of a deceased ancestor's name to a newborn child, and the placing of the body in a fetal position in the grave or funeral jar.

DYNASTIC CHINA. China did not produce a hierarchical classification of its beliefs about the fate of the dead. Most of them were destined for the kingdom of the Yellow Springs, while the kings and princes ascended to be near the Lord on High. The lords lived out their afterlives in the temples of the family ancestors, near their graves. This ancient agrarian religion dissolved along with the early social structure once the Han dynasty came to power, beginning in 206 BCE. Taoism then developed spectacularly, reaching its peak under the Six Dynasties, from the fourth to the sixth centuries of our era. As a religion of salvation, it had to offer an afterlife, and as the human being was thought to have many souls, but only one body for them to live in, it was along these lines that thinkers sought immortality. Some envisioned a melting pot of souls, out of which the deceased would receive an undying body, provided that the living were assiduous in practicing the funeral rites. But most tended to the view that the living body was preserved and became an immortal one. To this end they felt one should develop certain organs to be substituted for the corporeal ones. This gave rise to various practices to which the adepts, *tao-shih,* applied themselves in the desire to ensure the immortality of the living (body)—dietary practices to kill demons and maintain bodily vigor, embryonic circular breathing to induce ecstatic experiences, and sexual practices involving a mixing of the semen with the breath in order to stimulate the brain (Henri Maspero, *Taoism and Chinese Religion,* Amherst, 1981). Spiritual techniques such as insight, meditation, and mystical union came to be added to these physical ones. Between the second and sixth centuries, these techniques were supplemented by ceremonies for the dead, rites intended to melt the souls in a fire that would transform them into immortals *(hsien).*

ANCIENT EGYPT. From the time of the Old Kingdom, the Egyptians envisaged a complex spiritual pattern, modeled on the divine life and made up of three elements necessary for life to exist. *Akh* is divine energy. *Ba* is the faculty of movement, human consciousness, and the ability to take various shapes. The divine breath and support of all created beings, *ka,* is the collection of qualities of divine origin that give eternal life; it is the life force connected with Ptah and Re, and it is the divine, living part of man. When the *ka* becomes separated from the body, it disintegrates, and the person must then be recreated through mummification and funeral rites if an afterlife is to be possible.

The *Book of Going Forth by Day* represents a confluence of various doctrines concerning immortality—mummification, psychostasia, or weighing of the *ba,* the judgment of the dead, the kingdom of the dead, the freedom of the *ba,* and the happy fate of those who have led their lives in accord with Maat. These seemingly contradictory features can be reconciled in terms of the trial of the soul before Osiris and his court. Mummification was intended to bind the *ba* to the body of the deceased and to this world. After vindicating himself before Osiris, the blessed one, *maa kheru,* was free to move about among the gods and spirits of the *tuat.* Meanwhile he also maintained ties with the world of the living, a world of joy in Egyptian eyes. Although Egyptians observed the Osirian funeral, the dependence of immortality on the preservation of the mummy need not be overemphasized. Even if the disintegration of the mummy broke the connection between the *ba* and the world, the deceased who had been consigned to the *tuat* continued to live happily in the Field of Reeds. The happy lot of the just person living in the boat of the Sun was reserved for those who were too poor to secure an Osirian funeral. The vast world of the immortals in the Middle and New Kingdoms was composed of Osirian immortals tied to their preserved mummies, and thus free to move about in the beyond and in this world of the living, Osirian immortals whose mummies had been destroyed but who were still happy in the *tuat* kingdom, where they were constrained to stay, and solarized, blessed immortals in the boat of the Sun. Their happy everlasting life had been prepared for by an ethical life in conformity with Maat ("justice"), by the arrangement of the tomb and mummification, and by all that went into the construction of the eternal home.

EGYPTIAN MUMMY

To ancient Egyptians, mummification was intended to bind the ba *(human consciousness) to the body of the deceased.*

CORBIS-BETTMANN

INDIA. In all three of the great directions in Indian religious thought—Vedic, Brahmanic, and *bhakti*—the belief in immortality is clear and constant.

Vedic India. In the Vedic texts, particularly in sacrificial contexts, *amrta* appears together with *soma. Amrta* is the heavenly elixir of immortality, as *soma* is a sacrificial libation offered to the gods by the priests. *Amrta* is the drink of immortality of gods and men; *soma* is the elixir of life that has come from heaven to bestow immortality *(amrtam).* Both words contain the idea of the winning of immortality, conceived as a perpetual renewal of youth and life.

In the *Rgveda* a distinction is made between the body and the invisible principle of the human being, designated by the words *asu,* the life force or breath, and *manas,* the spirit, the seat of intellect and internal feelings, located in the heart. The nature of the soul can be seen in the Vedic attitude toward death, for the dead are simply the shadows of the living. What survives is the individuality, the essence of the human person, which becomes immortal by being indefinitely prolonged in time, as part of a perfectly ordered cosmos. Immortality is a perpetual remaking in accord with universal law, and consists in being born everlastingly. The Rgvedic hymn 10.129.1-3 speaks of "the One that was before being and nonbeing, before death and non-death." Nondeath is understood in relation to both the birth of organized time and the womb that is synonymous with death and renewal.

Brahmanic India. The symbolism of immortality in the Brahmanas goes beyond the Vedic symbolism. The sacrifice confers long life and immortality, symbolized by the cosmic year; the days and nights are symbols of human lives, of mortal, transient time. The seasons make up the year in its real sense, a limitless rebirth; the year is the symbol of divine life and immortality, and Prajapati is the year. The sacrificial altar is constructed in the course of a year using 10,800 bricks, each one representing an hour. The *garhapatya* fire represents a womb, into which a special *mantra* inspires the breath of life. Through the *ahavaniya* fire the sacrificer rises to heaven, to be born a second time and attain immortality. Thus the sacrifice constitutes the transcendence of death by means of ritual.

The Vedic language possesses several words that have been thought to denote the "soul" as an immortal spiritual substance in man.

PAGE 575

Bhakti. *Bhakti* is a loving devotion that gives the believer a greater knowledge of the Lord (Krsna or Isvara) than any meditation or reflection, and it is a divine gift given only to those who have prepared themselves by a loving attitude. Within the wider context of the transmigration of souls, the *bhakti* movement affirms a monotheistic tendency and an emphasis on salvation. *Bhakti* takes the place of the elixir of life, conferring eternal life with Krsna. A number of texts emphasize the destiny of the *bhakta,* who is *siddha* ("perfect"), *amrta* ("immortal"), and *trpta* ("happy").

BUDDHISM. The Upanisads taught that there exists within every person an *I*, the *atman,* an enduring and eternal entity, an immutable substance underlying the ephemeral world of phenomena. Hence the way to

He who goes down to the nether world shall come up no more.

JOB 7:9

immortality was easily found. The *atman,* they said, becomes immortal not through sacrifice or ritual or ascetic discipline, but by taking possession of the immortal, the *brahman.* For the Upanisads, it is the identification of *atman* and *brahman* that bestows immortality.

The belief in an afterlife and immortality is not ignored by the Buddha. Like the brahman, the yogin, and the mendicant, he seeks "that which endures," "deliverance," and "what is undying."

CELTS, GERMANS, SCANDINAVIANS, THRACIANS, AND GETAE. A firm belief in an afterlife is attested by the funerary practices of the Celts, Germans, and Scandinavians. Archaeological evidence is abundant, including megalithic tombs, dolmens, and individual burials in coffins marked with solar symbols, and cremation is known from the urnfields as early as 1500 BCE.

The belief in the soul's immortality among the Celts and the Gauls is attested by numerous early witnesses. Caesar (*Gallic Wars* 6.14) says that the druids asserted that souls are immortal, that after death they pass into another body, and that this belief explains the reckless fearlessness of their warriors. For the Germans, the soul is reborn within the *Sippe* (the clan). Celtic traditions give accounts of an *aes sídh,* or "paradise of the dead," an open world connected by a bridge to the land of the living, sometimes also appearing as an island in the ocean.

The cult of Zalmoxis among the Thracians and the Getae (Herodotus, 4.94-95) also entails the belief in the deathlessness of the soul, obtained through an initiation ritual that belongs among the mystery cults of the Mediterranean world, particularly those having to do with the preparation for a happy existence in the other world.

THE HEBREW SCRIPTURES. From remotest times the Hebrews practiced inhumation, placing various objects, weapons, and provisions in the grave for the use of the dead, gestures which seem to constitute at least one facet of a *votum immortalitatis.* The Hebrew Bible sees the human being as a composite of flesh *(basar),* the breath of life, or soul *(nefesh),* and spirit *(ruah).*

After death, people go to She'ol—an immense, underground place, deep, dark, and bolted shut, the abode of shadows—to lead lives that are shadows of their lives on earth, and according to *Job* 7:9-10, this life is one of no return. This idea contrasts with the archaic concept of the "afterlife" of a corpse that makes use of objects and food, and is undoubtedly later. She'ol is not to be confused with the grave, the habitat of the corpse. The shade in She'ol is not the remnant of the mortal being in the grave, it is a "double"; She'ol is an extension of the grave.

The doctrine of She'ol was of popular origin and remained quite vague, but it demonstrates a spiritualistic tendency in the belief in an afterlife found in the Hebrew scriptures. References to an afterlife are found in the Bible. The human being is not destroyed after death, but is reunited with his ancestors. The miracles performed by Elijah and Elisha (*1 Kgs.* 17:17-24, *2 Kgs.* 4:31-37) show that life can be restored to the body. Moreover, the evocation of the dead, characteristic of popular beliefs in an afterlife, shows that the living attempted to get in touch with the deceased.

The *refa'im* of She'ol are the biblical forerunners of immortal souls. Several passages in *Job* and *Psalms* allude to a union with God that death will not destroy. During the persecutions of Antiochus Epiphanes, the fate of the dead is foremost among Israel's preoccupations; the vision of dry bones in *Ezekiel* 37:1-14 serves as the basis of a meditation on resurrection and God's power to bring his believers out of She'ol. In the *Book of Daniel* 7:9, the motif of the "book of life" marks a gradual shift toward individual judgment, and the faith in individual eschatological resurrection is clearly attested in both *Daniel,* which dates from 165 BCE (*Dn.* 11:40-12:13), and in *2 Maccabees* (chaps. 7, 9, 11), written in Greek sometime after 124 BCE.

In the *Wisdom of Solomon,* written in Greek around 50 BCE, the concept of the afterlife is rendered for the first time by *aphtharsia,* "immortality" (1:11-15, 2:23-25), and the immortality of the souls of the righteous is clearly affirmed. They are in the hand of God (3:1-4), and their souls enjoy a never-ending life with God in peace, rest, love, grace, and mercy (3:9, 4:7, 5:15). After the destruction of the Temple in the year 70 CE, a doctrine of resurrection for everyone—not only the righteous but also for nonbelievers—appears within the circle of the tannaim.

THE QUMRAN TEXTS. The Essenes, as described by Josephus Flavius, believed in the immortality of the soul and its future life freed from bodily ties, hence their renunciation of even the most legitimate of the pleasures of this world. As for the Qumran texts, the *Manual of Discipline* says that those who let themselves be guided and inspired by the spirits of truth and light will be blessed in this world and will enjoy eternal gladness in a world without end. The wicked will be punished in the darkness of an everlasting fire (2.8, 4.7-8).

THE GRECO-ROMAN WORLD. The imagination of the ancients endowed the land of Greece with many mouths of the underworld, called the "gates of Hades." For some, these were the paths through which people vanished after death, for others they were the wombs of perpetual rebirth; the Greeks were divided over these two views of the afterlife (André Motte, *Prairies et jardins de la Grèce antique,* Brussels, 1973, p. 239).

Orphism. Monuments to Orpheus are found as early as the sixth century BCE, and allusions to his descent into the underworld appear in the fifth century. Priests who preach salvation in the name of Orpheus and promulgate an initiation that sets people free for their lives in the next world are reported in Classical times. In the Hellenistic period references to Orpheus become more frequent, and Orphism finds fertile ground in Ptolemaic Egypt, where it encounters the cult of Osiris.

Orphism professes the belief in a happy afterlife. The seed of salvation is within man, since his immortal soul is a piece of the divine stuff, and the purpose of life on earth is to come to a permanent choice. The Orphic doctrine of purification allows for the reincarnation of souls. We know from Plato that the Orphians offered rather gloomy descriptions of the torments of the guilty soul and the evils awaiting the damned, plunged into a pool of mud (*Republic* 2.363d).

Early Pythagoreanism. Settling in Magna Graecia in the second half of the sixth century, Pythagoras founded at Croton a brotherhood shrouded in secrecy, which introduced its followers to a new kind of life meant to point the way that led to salvation. In religious matters Pythagoras espoused Orphic views and brought about, as Eliade (1982) has indicated, a large-scale synthesis of archaic elements (some of them "shamanistic") and bold reevaluations of ascetic and contemplative techniques. The Orphic and Pythagorean doctrines regarding the soul display many features in common: immortality, transmigration, punishment in Hades, and the soul's eventual return to heaven. Pythagoreanism, however, developed its teaching independently, in a closed society. For Pythagoras the human soul is immortal; it is held within the body as if in a prison and can live independently of the body. After death, the soul passes into Hades to be purified, and to the extent that it is not completely cleansed it must return to earth and seek a new body.

GNOSTIC RELIGION. The gnostics viewed man as a combination of matter and spirit and saw the body as the prison which holds the soul after its fall. Within this mixture, the soul, an aeon of the same substance as the celestial world, remains intact, for it is incorruptible. The technical term *aphtharsia* ("incorruptibility") is part of the theological vocabulary of all gnostic systems. Incorruptibility is part of the soul's makeup because of its divine origin and is the essence of its immortality, even though by being imprisoned in the body the soul has become steeped in matter.

Salvation consists in the liberation of the soul. A heavenly savior intervenes to stir the captive soul's memory, to remind it of its origin and make it recognize its true "self." This revelation is made through a series of initiatory trials, by the end of which the soul has discovered a luminous vision of its own essence; the vision awakens in it a burning desire to return to its home. Then begins the second stage, that of the return to the "realm of life." The description of this ascension (or *Himmelsreise*) is found in the texts of all the sects; it includes deprivation and release from material bonds, a path passing through many dangers, the presence of a heavenly guide, and a triumphant entry into celestial Paradise for an immortal destiny amid the blessed light. The gathering of all the souls that have been held in bodies reconstitutes the Pleroma.

MANICHAEISM. In the Manichaean scheme, man is a mixture of light and darkness. His body is the work of the archons, but his soul is a divine spark, a portion of the eternal realm of light that has fallen into the material world and been imprisoned in the body by birth. The saving element in the earthbound soul is the *nous,* while the *psuche* is the part that must be saved; this is the task of Gnosis, a hypostatic divine entity from the realm of light. The gnostic message awakens the *psuche,* makes it aware of its divine origin, and stirs in it the desire to return on high. This awakening of the soul is the beginning of salvation. The gnostic strives to realize the separation of light and darkness within himself. By an unceasing choice he carries out a *katharsis* within himself, a preliminary salvation that will take full effect after death, in a final liberation of the radiant and eternal soul.

ISLAM. The proclamation of the Day of Judgment comes at the beginning of the Qur'an, and it is seen from the standpoint of the resurrection, *qiyama.* On that day all the race of Adam will be gathered together, each one to receive judgment and everlasting retribution according to his deeds. Fear of the Last Day and of the punishment of Hell is a fundamental feature of the Prophet's teaching. The chosen ones on the right, the believers, will be called to enjoy Paradise, while the unbelieving will be condemned to torture.

Islamic anthropogony. The Islamic view of the nature of man is not particularly clear. The word *ruh* means *pneuma,* "breath"—the subtle breath that comes from the brain, that is, the mind. In some traditions it dies with the body only to be brought back to life with it. This is the spiritual part of the human being. There is also the *nafs* (Heb., *nefesh*), commonly translated as "soul," the carnal breath that comes "from the viscera."

The spiritualist doctrine of Shiism views the *ruh* as the pure breath of all matter, a spiritual substance that is immortal by nature. In this perspective man is not a body with a soul, but a spirit which temporarily inhabits a body as its instrument. Only on leaving the body does it find its true nature, for it is made to live independently; the soul's pleasure lies in the spiritual world. This tradition sees the spirit as a celestial, radiant substance, imperishable and immortal.

In its teaching on the Last Judgment, the Qur'an constantly talks of "weighing the deeds" of all adult and responsible humans.

PAGE 341

The Christians' belief in the resurrection of Jesus was the basis of their hope for the future.

PAGE 80

As against the spiritualistic tendency of Shiism, the traditional Sunni theologians held that man is rather a compound of substances, body and soul, and entirely material. The central question is this: what happens at the moment of death? For those who take man to be a material composite of body plus soul, the soul "disappears" at death and is brought back to life on the last day, while those who see in the body only a temporary instrument of the soul believe the human soul to be made for the spiritual life, even after its separation from the body. In the first case the resurrection of the body is indispensable, whereas in the second the afterlife can do without it. As may be seen, the possible viewpoints can differ sharply.

CHRISTIANITY. In order to understand the Christian doctrine of immortality, the message of the New Testament must be located within its twofold setting in the biblical tradition of Israel on one hand and the context of religious beliefs and philosophical ideas of the Greco-Roman world on the other. At the time of the birth of Christianity, the Platonic doctrines of the human composite of *soma* and *psuche,* the dissolution of this composite by death, and the immortality and afterlife of the *psuche,* were widely held in Mediterranean thought. With this in mind, the central question concerns not the immortality of the soul as such but the originality of Christian revelation concerning the immortality of man, as he is created in the image of God and redeemed by Christ.

The faith in an individual and eschatological resurrection is clearly attested in the *Book of Daniel* and in the *Second Book of the Maccabees,* in the second century BCE. But where did the idea of bodily resurrection fit into the eschatological thought of Jesus? In an early presentation, Jesus affirms that those who enter the kingdom will receive a share in a life of unending peace and happiness, a point of view both communal and personal. The divine gift of eternal life is one of a spiritual nature; whosoever will enter the kingdom easily will be transformed (*1 Cor.* 15:51). This presentation ends by proclaiming the Messiah's passage through death and the reopening of his kingdom after it. This is the idea behind the earthly pilgrimage of the church, through which Jesus shared his own victory over death with his disciples (*1 Cor.* 15:20).

How did apostolic Christianity interpret the resurrection of Christ? After living first in the hope of the Lord's coming (*1 Cor.* 16:22), the apostles focused on the message of resurrection. Jesus is resurrected as the first fruit of the believers who die before his second coming. Later the church gradually accorded more importance to resurrection for all.

[*See also* Resurrection.]

— JULIEN RIES

TRANSLATED FROM FRENCH BY DAVID M. WEEKS

INCA RELIGION

The pre-Columbian Andean cultures, of which the Inca empire was the final heir, extended over a geographical area that the Inca believed corresponded to the four quarters *(tahuantinsuyu)* of the world. At the time of the Inca empire's fall to Spanish forces under Francisco Pizarro in 1532, the Inca occupied large portions of present-day Ecuador, Peru, Bolivia, and Chile. The great Andean civilizations flourished in this setting of contrasting ecosystems (coastal desert ribbed with fertile valleys, arable highlands at altitudes of more than four kilometers, Amazonian and montane rain forests) that offered resources for pursuing a variety of means of subsistence, including fishing, hunting and gathering, agriculture, and the herding of llamas, guanacos, and alpacas.

INCA COSMOLOGY. The Inca religious system is usually attributed to either the Inca Tupac Yupanqui or his predecessor, the Inca Pachacuti, and dates to at most one hundred years before the European conquest. The expansion of Cuzco, the Inca capital, was carried out in the name of the superiority of its gods over those of other peoples who, once they were assimilated into the empire, left their principal idol (or its replica) in the Inca capital. The colonization, or federation, was founded on a system of reciprocity overseen by Cuzco. Certain cults and temples were richly endowed by the Inca (the title given the head of the empire); others were suppressed. The great social and religious leaders of the empire went regularly to the capital city, and the Inca brought colonies of collaborators *(mitima)* to the temples of the empire and sometimes had himself named priest of honor. The sanctuaries of the provinces paid tribute in kind to Cuzco, contributing, for example, young children to be sacrificed during the Capacocha ceremony. Rites of communion were held periodically to ensure the political and religious cohesion of the empire. Generally, these rites took place at the Temple of the Sun, in the center of the *tahuantinsuyu,* which center was located at the junction of the two rivers of Cuzco.

The inhabitants of the Andean region worshiped a great number of gods, idols, and spirits, which were designated by the generic name *huaca,* a term that was also applied to the shrines. Each family—and, at the higher level, each village and province—claimed to descend from a given *huaca* (a particular man-god, conquering ancestor, founder, or civilizer), who represented a cosmic power and whom they venerated in the form of a mummy, a stone, an animal, or a constellation of stars.

INCA GODS. The kings of Cuzco, reputed to be sons of the Sun, formed a religious, cosmic, and territorial imperial structure in which the Sun reigned over

the Andean highlands and the heavens and the god Pachacámac ruled over the lowlands and the underworld.

The Coricancha, the great Temple of the Sun in Cuzco, was flanked by two golden pumas and its walls were covered with gold and silver plaques. The halls contained statues and cosmic representations, and the mummies—or their replicas—of earlier kings and queens. The temple sheltered a large number of priests (the first priest was a close relative of the Inca) and the "virgins of the Sun" *(aclla),* who dedicated themselves to making cloth and corn beer for the cult of the Sun, and who also served as concubines to the Inca.

From the dark bowels of the cosmos, Pachacámac caused earthquakes and sent pestilence. Illapa, who represented thunderbolts, lightning, rain, hail, snow, and frost, was venerated by a large cult in the highlands. The serpent Amaru represented the striking thunderbolt and also the animal or monster who, according to the myths, rose from the lake and moved toward the upper world.

Women were the principal participants in the cult of Quilla, the Moon, who was the sister and wife of the Sun. The Coya ("queen") was believed to be the daughter of the Moon, just as the Inca was believed to be the son of the Sun. The anthropomorphic statues of Quilla were silver, while those of the Sun were gold. A lunar calendar was used along with a solar calendar. Quilla was associated with the earth and the dead. Traditionally, she pursued dead thieves into the underworld at night. One month of the year was especially sacred to her. Men also worshiped her, in Cuzco and elsewhere, particularly in the temple of Nusta, which was located on an island in Lake Titicaca.

When they were not visible, the stars, like the sun and the moon, were believed to go under the earth. The Milky Way—thought of as two rivers—may have inspired the construction of the Coricancha at the junction of the two rivers of Cuzco. Among the constellations, that of the llama, visible during the dry season, was of special importance to cattle raisers. The Pleiades were associated with the rainy season. If they appeared clearly at the end of May, a good harvest was augured.

After death, one of the two souls that were attributed to a man returned to its place of origin, either before or after a journey strewn with obstacles, and dwelt in the land of the souls, which was not unlike the world of the living. The kind of afterlife enjoyed by this soul was conditional on the type of death, social rank, and virtues of the dead. The other soul remained in the body, which had to be preserved intact, and which had the same needs as the living person.

Viracocha was the supreme god of the Inca. He was also a complex deity and was thought of as both one and many, the principle of transformation. Two others of his names were Con-Ticsi-Viracocha and Pachayachachic ("he who gives order to the world") and he had a large family with several sanctuaries. Viracocha was associated with water and the foam of Lake Titica-

CORICANCHA

The great Temple of the Sun, built at the junction of two rivers in the Incan capital Cuzco, was the sight of sacrificial ceremonies.

> *"Make one of your prayers one sweet sacrifice and lift my soul to heaven."*
>
> WILLIAM SHAKESPEARE, HENRY VIII

ca, whence he had come, and with the foam of rivers and the surface of the ocean, where, according to some myths, he (in human form) disappeared to the northwest, walking on the waves. These attributes associated him with the rainy season, and others made him the representative of the fire of the heavens and of the triumphant Sun.

INCA RITES. The great religious ceremonies were publicly celebrated in Cuzco. The sacrifices were designed to nourish and placate the gods, and offerings were selected from the great complementary ecosystems of nature (plants, birds, shells, the blood of animals—particularly llamas—and men) and culture (maize, coca, pepper, corn beer, cloth, statuettes). At the center of the ceremonial place was the *usnu,* a small edifice on which the Inca sat enthroned and that was pierced at its base by underground canals leading to the temples of Viracocha, the Sun, and Illapa. Here the Sun was given "drink," which acted to placate and balance the powers of the lower and upper worlds. The *usnu* may also have served as an astronomical observatory. The golden statues of Viracocha, the Sun, and Illapa, the silver statue of the Moon, and the mummies of dead sovereigns—or their replicas—were set out on ceremonial occasions.

The performance of these ritual duties was also intended to ward off cataclysms *(pachacuti),* especially those caused by excessive heat ("suns of fire") or water (floods). Such cataclysms were believed to result from the dissatisfaction of the cosmic powers of the upper and lower worlds. They were believed to have occurred before, ushering in new cycles, and it was thought that they could happen again. These ideas, which were based on the observation of the movements of the sun and moon and the oppositions of day and night, dry and rainy seasons, and fire and water, were projected through time to construct an explanation of the history of the world. In any case, the important Quechua word *pacha* means both "time" and "space."

— PIERRE DUVIOLS

TRANSLATED FROM FRENCH BY ERICA MELTZER

INDIAN RELIGIONS

VEDISM

Vedic thought was based on the belief in an inextricable coordination of nature, human society, ritual, and the sphere of myth and the divine; it was also founded on the belief that these spheres influence one another continuously and that men have, by means of ritual, an obligatory part to play in the maintenance of universal order and the furtherance of their common interests. In later times also, Indians have constantly sought correspondences between objects and phenomena belonging to distinct spheres of nature and conceptual systems. Many hymns and individual stanzas of the oldest literary corpus (the *Rgveda Samhita,* an anthology drawn from family traditions) were intended for the cult and used in the liturgy of spectacular solemn *(srauta)* ceremonies, which gradually increased in number, length, and complexity. These ceremonies were to ensure the orderly functioning of the world for the benefit of noble or wealthy patrons. The rites were performed in the open on a specially prepared plot—there were no temples or idols—by specialized officiants. Part of this literature was employed, along with texts from the *Atharvaveda Samhita,* in the domestic or magic ritual performed by a householder or single priest to ensure an individual's health, safety, success, prosperity, and longevity. These texts and the ritual formulas of the *Yajurveda,* which invariably fulfill some ritual function, are collectively called *mantras.* They are believed to be revelations of aspects of the divine, the product of the exalted experiences of sages *(rsis)* and hence constitute sacred and inherently powerful verbal formulas for producing a desired result. Some Vedic *mantras* remained in Hinduist rites, which, however, generally require other ones.

HINDUISM

Some prehistoric forms of Hinduism—the civilization of the Hindus, consisting of their beliefs, practices, and socioreligious institutions—must have existed at the Vedic period, especially in the unrecorded religion of the lower classes, and probably earlier. Domestic ritual, which is entirely different from the solemn rites, consists of many rites that, though described and systematized by brahman authorities in the Vedic Grhyasutras, are in essence not typically Vedic, or rather constitute Vedic varieties of widespread rites of passage, rites of appeasement, cult of the dead, and so on. Later chapters of this literature show markedly non-Vedic and post-Vedic influences.

NON-ARYAN INFLUENCES. How much influence was exerted by the religions of the non-Aryan inhabitants of India on the formation and development of Hinduism is a matter of dispute. Although aborigines may have contributed some elements, their religion is generally different in many respects (e.g., they do not venerate the cow, and they allow their widows to remarry). The Vedic religion had no demonstrable relation with the great civilizations of Harappa, Mohenjo-Daro, and vast regions to the east of the Indus Valley (c. 2500-1500 BCE). As long as the graphic symbols on seals from these sites are not convincingly deciphered and the language is not identified (that it was Dravidian—the name of non-Aryan languages of

BHAGAVADGITA
Beloved Scripture

The *Bhagavadgita* is perhaps the most widely read and beloved scripture in all Indian religious literature. Its power to counsel and inspire its readers has remained undiminished in the almost two thousand years since its composition.

The *Bhagavadgita* (Song of the Blessed Lord) is sacred literature, holy scripture—it is a text that has abundant power in its persistence and its presence. The pious Hindu, even if his piety is mild, will inevitably have access to the book or will be able to recite, or at least paraphrase, a few lines from it. The text is intoned during the initiation ceremony wherein one becomes a *samnyasin* (renunciant); teachers and holy men expound upon it; professors translate it and write about it; the more humble listen to the words that, though heard countless times before, remain vibrant. The text is read by all Hindus, esteemed by Saivas as well as by Vaisnavas, venerated by the lower caste as well as by the high, savored by villagers as well as by the more urbane.

One may dispute whether the *Bhagavadgita* teaches the dualistic Samkhya philosophy or the nondualistic Vedanta, whether it is a call to action or renunciation; but what is beyond dispute is that it teaches devotion to god as a means to liberation, whether that liberation is understood as release from the world or freedom in the world: "Hear again My supreme word, the most secret of all: thou are greatly beloved by Me, hence I will speak for thy good. Center thy mind on Me, be devoted to Me, sacrifice to Me, revere Me, and thou shalt come to Me. I promise thee truly, for thou art dear to Me" (18.64-65).

The individual human being, according to the *Bhagavadgita*, is at once natural (a product of nature caught up in lawlike relations and filled with desires and longings) and spiritual (an embodiment of the divine). The individual human being, Krsna tells Arjuna early on in the text, is also immortal. Possessed of an eternal, unchanging spirit, a person can only appear to be an autonomous actor in the natural world. This appearance derives from an ignorance of the true self. Normally identifying himself as an ego self-sufficiently working within the conditions of his psychophysical nature, a person must reidentify himself at a deeper level of integrated selfhood and thereby understand his true role as a social being.

Ideally each person works out his social career according to the dictates of his own nature *(svadharma)* as this is itself a product of past experience. *Dharma*, *karman* ("action" or "work"), and *samsara* ("rebirth") belong together: action carried over innumerable lives must be informed by a sensitivity to the obligations one has in virtue of one's interdependence with others. Arjuna is a member of the warrior class and must fulfill the duties of this social position—he must fight.

But what is the nature of reality that makes this both possible and imperative? The *Gita's* answer to this is that reality, in its essence, is the presence of a personalized *brahman*, something higher than the impersonal *brahman*, the absolute reality described in the Upanisads. "There are two spirits in this world," Krsna explains, "the perishable and the imperishable." The perishable is all beings and the imperishable is called *kutastha* ("the immovable"). But there is another, the Highest Spirit *(purusottama)*, called the Supreme Self, who, as the imperishable Lord, enters into the three worlds and sustains them. "Since I transcend the perishable and am higher even than the imperishable, I am renowned in the world and in the Veda as the highest Spirit" (15.16-18).

In its analysis of the lower status of the divine, the *Gita* draws heavily upon the Samkhya system of thought. Nature *(prakrti)* is seen as an active organic field constituted by various strands *(gunas)*, which can best be understood as energy systems. Everything in nature, and particularly every individual human being, is constituted by a combination of these forces. *Sattva* represents a state of subtle harmony and equilibrium which is exhibited as clear intelligence, as light. At the other extreme is darkness, *tamas*, the state of lethargy, of heaviness. In between is *rajas*, agitation, restlessness, passion, the motivating force for actions. The *purusa* ("the individual spirit") caught up in *prakrti*, is driven by the *gunas* and is deluded into thinking that, as a given phenomenal fact, it is their master and not their victim.

The aim of human life in the Bhagavadgita is to attain a self-realization that "I" am not a separate, autonomous actor but that "I" am at one with a divine reality, and that my ultimate freedom comes from bringing my actions into accord with that reality. The realization of this aim of life is at the heart of the *Bhagavadgita's* teaching, and has been the most controversial among both modern and traditional interpreters of the text.

Following Sañkara, whose commentary is one of the oldest to have survived, many have argued that the central yoga put forward by the *Bhagavadgita* is the way of knowledge, *jñanayoga*: it alone provides the insight into reality that allows for genuine self-realization. Taking the position of Ramanuga, others have argued that *bhaktiyoga*, the discipline of devotion, remains the highest way for the *Gita; bhakti*, in his understanding of the text, provides the basis for a salvific relationship between the individual person and a loving god with absolute power and supremacy over the world. Still others have seen the *Gita* as a gospel of works, teaching most centrally *karmayoga*, the way of action—of acting without attachment to the fruits of one's acts. This multiplicity of interpretations results from the fact that the *Bhagavadgita* does extol each of these ways at various times.

— ELIOT DEUTSCH AND LEE SIEGEL

Sankara is by far the most outstanding and the most widely known exponent of Vedanta.

PAGE 698

southern India—is still unproved conjecture), most of the conclusions drawn from archaeological material and argumentation regarding links with elements or characteristics of older and even contemporary Hinduism remain as speculative as the hypothesis of a predominantly influential Dravidian substratum.

EARLY HISTORY. The history proper of Hinduism begins with the emergence of the great works on *dharma,* the totality of traditional custom and behavior that, agreeing with standards considered to derive their authority from the Vedas, manifests and maintains order and stability. This is also the age of the epics, especially the *Mahabharata* (c. 300 BCE-300 CE), that "encyclopedia of Hinduism" that shows, even then, what appears to be a varied and confused conglomerate of beliefs and practices. However, there are two main currents, soteriologies when viewed from their doctrinal aspect and religions from the viewpoint of their adherents: Vaisnavism and Saivism. Neither current is in itself a unity. Yet all Vaisnavas are essentially monotheistic, believing in Visnu as their immanent high god (Isvara), although in many contexts he appears as one of the divine polytheistic figures *(devas).* In the Vedas, Visnu represents universal pervasiveness; his beneficent energy, in which all beings abide, reaches the world through the *axis mundi,* the central pillar of the universe. Vaisnavas often worship him through his manifestations or incarnations *(avataras),* such as Rama or Krsna. Preference for an *avatara* is mainly traditional; in the North, Krsna is more often worshiped; in the South, it is Rama, Visnu himself, or Visnu's consort, Sri. The *Bhagavadgita,* an episode of the *Mahabharata* and the most seminal of all Vaisnava works, founded Vaisnava ethics: fulfilling their duties disinterestedly, men should realize God's presence in themselves, love him and their fellow beings devotedly, and dedicate all their actions to him so as to earn the prospect of final emancipation.

The Hinduist worship, in many different groups and currents, of Siva in his various manifestations results from a complex development to which the often malevolent outsider god Rudra of the Vedas has contributed much. (There may also have been Dravidian influences.) Rudra, primarily representing the untamed aspects of uncultivated nature, was called Siva ("the mild one") when the benevolent and auspicious aspects of his nature were emphasized. Saivism is an unsystematic amalgam of pan-Indian Saiva philosophy, local or folk religion, mythological thought, and popular imagery. Siva's many-sided character, to which accreted features of great gods as well as demoniac powers, is split up into many partial manifestations representing aspects of his ambivalent nature. He is both mild and terrible, a creator and destroyer, an ascetic and a sexualist.

BUDDHISM AND JAINISM

The same period saw the spread of two heterodox soteriologies, heterodox because they reject the authority of the Veda and the social prejudices of the brahmans, although they scarcely attack the fundamentals of Hindu belief and practices. The way in which the early Buddhists presented their doctrines has much in common with the oldest Upanisads, which must antedate the spread of the Aryan culture to the south and the activity of Gautama (c. 560-480 BCE). Gautama, the Buddha, first gave an exposition of his basic doctrine in Banaras. He taught that those who wish to be delivered from *samsara* and the automatism of *karman,* which does not rely upon a permanent transmigrating soul (whose existence the Buddha denied), should realize four basic truths: (1) earthly existence is pain; (2) the cause of pain is craving for existence, leading to rebirth; (3) cessation of that craving is cessation of pain; (4) an eightfold path leads to that cessation. Final deliverance is realized only in an ascetic and monastic life by those who, after having successfully observed definite rules of life and reached complete meditation *(samadhi),* experience the undefinable state of *nirvana,* the cessation of all becoming.

As the number of adherents increased, the Buddhist order received large gifts that led to the establishment of monasteries. The multiplying order spread to different parts of India, including the south and Sri Lanka (third century BCE). In the beginning of the fourth century BCE the community began to be split by successive schisms, each of which made its own collection of canonical texts. After about 500 CE, Indian Buddhism began to decline.

The Buddha was not the only illuminated teacher who, after renouncing the world, organized his initiates into a community. In Bihar one of his contemporaries, Vardhamana Mahavira, reformed an existing community and founded the predominantly monastic Jainism, which spread to northern and central India, Gujarat, and the Deccan, and in the last few centuries BCE split into two groups, not on philosophic disagreement but on points of rules for the monks. Jainism is systematic and has never changed in its basic ideology. Its philosophy is dualistic: it posits nonliving entities (including space and time) pervaded by (partly transmigrating, partly emancipated) immaterial and eternal souls; the world, eternal and changeless, is not governed by a supreme being; the system is characterized by the absence of gods *(devas); karman* is the central power that determines the destiny of unemancipated souls. Man has to perfect his soul and that of his fellow creatures; *ahimsa* and universal tolerance are the main duties and cardinal virtues. Whereas the adherents of Buddhism were from a variety of social classes, Jainism attracted the wealthy and influential.

SAIVA RELIGIONS AND TANTRISM

Some religions of India do deviate from common Hinduist traditions and institutions. In contrast to the Saiva Siddhantins of the Tamil-speaking South—who, basing themselves also on the mysticism of the Saiva Tamil saint-poets (Naya-nars), teach that God in the shape of a spiritual guide, or *guru,* graciously permits himself to be realized by the purified soul—the Virasaivas, or Lingayats, in southwestern India (not mentioned before the twelfth century) abandon many traditional elements (e.g., caste, image worship). Doctrinal dissent is always possible. The religio-philosophic idealist and monist Kashmir school of Saivism disagrees in certain important respects with the teaching of Sankara (eighth century), the founder of Advaita monism, derived from the Upanisadic Vedanta as a system of absolute idealism that is mainly followed by the intellectual elite. Sankara, a native of Malabar who resided in Banaras and traveled throughout India, was a superb organizer; he established a monastic order and monasteries *(mathas),* which, like the many hermitages *(asramas)* and the great shrines, became centers of religious activity and contributed to the realization of his ideal of Hindu unity.

From about 500 CE, Tantric ritual and doctrines manifest themselves more or less frequently in Buddhism, Saiva Siddhanta, and Pañcaratra. Tantrism, primarily meant for esoteric circles, yet still an important aspect of Hinduism, is a systematic quest for spiritual excellence or emancipation through realization of the highest principle, the bipolar, bisexual deity, in one's own body. The possibilities of this microcosmos should be activated, sublimated, and made to exert influence on the macrocosmos, with which it is closely connected (physiological processes are thus described with cosmological terminology). Means to this end, partly magical, partly orgiastic, include recitation of *mantras;* contemplation of geometrical cosmic symbols *(mandalas),* leading the performer of the rites to the reintegration of consciousness; appropriate gestures *(mudras);* and meditation. Tantric *puja* is complicated and in many respects differs from conventional ceremonies. Especially in Bengal, Tantrism has tended to merge with the Sakta cult. The term *Tantra* commonly applies to Saiva or Sakta works of the Tantric tradition. Saktism, not always clearly distinguishable from Saivism, is the worship of the Supreme as divine creative energy *(sakti),* a female force that creates, regulates, and destroys the cosmos; when regarded as a person, she usually is Siva's spouse, often the dreadful goddess Durga or Kali.

BUDDHA
Indian Buddhism was widespread in Southern India and Sri Lanka for a thousand years between 500 B.C.E. and 500 C.E.
KIMBELL ART MUSEUM/ CORBIS

VAISNAVA RELIGIONS AND BHAKTI

Although Vaisnavism, less coherent than Saivism, had, in the sixth century, spread all over India, it reached predominance in Tamil Nadu, which became the cradle of important schools and movements that still have many adherents. The tradition known as the Sri Vaisnavas was inaugurated between about 900 and 1130 by Yamuna, the first apologist of Vaisnava theology, and consolidated by the great philosopher Ramanuja (c. 1050-1137). The Sri Vaisnavas introduced into their temple ceremonies the recitation of Tamil hymns of the Alvars, which evince a passionate belief in and love of God. Considering these poets and their great teachers *(acaryas)* integral parts *(amsas)* of God's nature, they often worship images of them in their temples. According to Ramanuja, *brahman* is as a "person" *(purusa)* the sole cause of his own modifications (emanation, existence, and absorption of the universe), immaterial, perfect, omnipotent, the soul of all being, the ultimate goal of all religious effort, to which God induces the devotee who wishes to please him. The purificatory significance of the ritual, meritorious works, disinterested discharge of duties, and *bhakti* are emphasized.

The influential *Bhagavata Purana* (c. 900?), also composed in Tamil Nadu, teaches that God through his incomprehensible creative ability *(maya)* expands himself into the universe, which is his outward appearance. On the basis of this teaching, Bengal Vaisnavism developed the theory of a relation of inconceivable difference in identity and identity in difference between

Probably the most important element in the religious symbolism of the Celts is the number three.

PAGE 127

God and the world, as well as the belief that God's creative activity is his sport *(lila)*. The safest way to God, *bhakti*, is a mystical attitude of mind involving an intuitive, immediate apprehension and loving contemplation of God. This often overshadows the devotee's aspirations to final emancipation and assumes a character of uncontrollable enthusiasm and ecstasy, marked by tears, hysteria, and fainting.

In northern and central India the *bhakti* movement flourished from the thirteenth to the eighteenth century, producing a vast and varied literature in vernacular languages. Even today these areas feel the influence of a long succession of saint-poets, passionate itinerant preachers (among them Caitanya, in Bengal, 1485-1533), and *gurus*.

REACTION TO FOREIGN RELIGIONS

The revival of Hinduism in the south and the spread of the *bhakti* movement also prepared the Indians to withstand the proselytizing of external religions, particularly Islam. From 1000 CE onward, the Muslims conquered the Northwest, made Delhi their capital, and extended their influence to Bengal, the Deccan, and the South, destroying temples and idols and making many converts, particularly among the untouchables. But Islam scarcely affected the Hindu way of life; rather, it provoked a counterreaction in the form of increased adherence to the Hindu *dharma* and the Hindu religions and stricter observance of rites and ceremonies. Nevertheless, the presence of Islam in India involved an age-long conflict between strict monotheism and the various manifestations of Hinduism. In one field, however, Islam and Hinduism could draw near to each other: Muslim and Hindu mystics have in common the idea of an all-embracing unity. To be sure, the Sufis made this idea a channel of islamization, but some Indian spiritual leaders tried to bridge the gulf between Islam and Hinduism.

India's contact with the West, Christianity, and modern life since the early nineteenth century has led to the emergence of many new religious movements and spiritual groups, as diverse in their principles, ideals, and reactions to foreign influences as the personalities of their founders; most distinguish themselves from traditional devotional movements by a more pronounced interest in ethical, social, and national issues. The extent of their influence in India has, however, often been exaggerated in the West, for the beliefs and customs of the Indian masses are still largely traditional.

[*For discussion of specific traditions, see* Hinduism. *For discussion of specific; nonorthodox traditions, see* Buddhism; Jainism; and Sikhism. *On the Indo-European components of Vedic religion, see* Indo-European Religions.]

— JJAN GONDA

INDO-EUROPEAN RELIGIONS

Research has confirmed the relations among languages, in the family now known as Indo-European: Germanic, Celtic, Baltic, Slavic, Armenian, Albanian, Anatolian (chiefly Hittite), and Tokharian (an obscure language found in western China and Turkistan).

Based on linguistic and archaeological research, the ancient Indo-European peoples are generally considered to have been semisettled pastoralists, whose wealth consisted of relatively large herds, including domesticated sheep, pigs, goats, and, most important, cattle. Some agriculture seems to have been practiced, although this was much less important and prestigious an activity than herding or war. The pursuit of warfare, especially the raiding of livestock from neighboring peoples, was facilitated not only by use of chariots but also by an elaborate weaponry built on a single metal, probably copper or bronze.

Linguistic data are insufficient to posit the existence of either a homeland or a proto-Indo-European community, and it is possible to view the similarity of the various Indo-European languages as the cumulative result of complex borrowings, influences, and cultural interrelations between multiple social and ethnic groups over many centuries. Some scholars have sought to employ archaeological evidence to demonstrate a specific point of origin for proto-Indo-European society. Of such theories, the most widely accepted is that of Marija Gimbutas, who has delineated what she calls the Kurgan culture, dating to the middle of the fifth millennium BCE and located in the southern Russian steppes, in the area that stretches from the Urals to the land north of the Black Sea, and including such groups as the Jamna culture of the Ural-Volga region north of the Caspian and the Srednii Stog II culture north of the Black Sea.

MYTHIC LEGITIMATIONS OF SOCIETY, ECONOMY, AND POLITY

It is possible to reconstruct a number of myths that describe the origin, nature, and sometimes problematic interrelationships among the cultures.

Most important of these is the creation myth, a complex, polyphonic story that told how the world was created when the first priest (often bearing the name Man, *Manu) offered his twin brother, the first king (often named Twin, *Yemo), in sacrifice, along with the first ox. From Twin's body, the world was made, in both its material and social components. (The asterisk denotes a reconstructed form unattested in any written source.)

Although we shall return to the cosmic dimensions

of this myth, it is its social contents that concern us now. Among these, the following four should be noted:

1. Society consists of vertically stratified classes, with priests or sovereigns in the first position, warriors in the second, and commoners—those entrusted with the bulk of productive labor—in the third. There is a fourth class of relative outsiders—servants.
2. The characteristic activity of each of these classes is explained and chartered by the part of Twin's body from which they originated. Thus, the intellectuals who direct society by exercise of thought and speech come from his head; those who defend society by their physical prowess come from his chest (heart) and arms; those who produce food, reproduce, and provide material support for the other classes come from the lower body, including belly, loins, legs, and feet.
3. The priest, following the model of Man, has as his prime responsibility the performance of sacrifice, sacrifice being the creative act *par excellence.*
4. The king, following the model of Twin, combines within himself the essence of all social classes and is expected to sacrifice himself for the good of the whole.

Another myth, which has as its central character the first warrior, whose name was Third (*Trito), provided an analysis of the warrior class. Within this story, it was related that cattle originally belonged to Indo-Europeans but were stolen by a monster, a three-headed serpent who was, moreover, specifically identified as a non-Indo-European. Following this theft, it fell to Third to recover the stolen cattle, and he began his quest by invoking the aid of a warrior deity to whom he offered libations of intoxicating drinks. Having won the god's assistance, and himself fortified by the same intoxicant, Third set forth, found the serpent, slew him, and recovered the cattle, which had been imprisoned by the monster.

This myth, which is attested in more reflexes than any other (its traces are still apparent in countless fairy tales), speaks to the eternal themes of wealth and power. It asserts, first, that cattle—the means of production and of exchange in the most ancient Indo-European societies—rightly belong exclusively to Indo-Europeans, falling into other hands only as the result of theft. Theft is condemned here because of its reliance on stealth and treachery, and it is set in contrast to raiding, which—far from being condemned—is heartily endorsed. Raiding emerges as a heroic action sanctioned by the gods, hedged with ritual, and devoted to regaining what rightfully belongs to the Indo-European warrior or his people. Throughout Indo-European history, Third in his various reflexes has remained the model for warriors, who repeatedly cast themselves in his image—raiding, plundering, and killing their non-Indo-European neighbors, con-

COSMOLOGY AND THE GODS
The Link of Above and Below

Deities were characterized as radiant celestial beings. In addition to the **deywo-s,* however, there was another class of divinities associated with the waters beneath the earth's surface and with darkness. These deities—whose names were regularly formed with the preposition signifying downward motion (**ne-,* as in Latin *Neptunus,* Greek *Nereus,* Germanic *Nerthus,* Sanskrit *Nirrti*)—figure in myths that are nothing so much as meditations on the interconnections between "above" and "below," involving immergence into and emersion out of the world ocean.

Speculation on the nature of the cosmos also forms an important part of the creation myth, the social contents of which we touched on above. It must be noted, however, that beyond this social discourse, the myth established a series of homologic relations between parts of the human body and parts of the physical universe—that is to say, an extended parallelism and consubstantiality was posited between the microcosm and the macrocosm. Many texts thus tell of the origin of the sun from the eyes of the first sacrificial victim, stones from his bones, earth from his flesh, wind from his breath, and so forth, while others invert the account.

In these and other texts the elements of the physical universe are converted into the constituent parts of a human body, as cosmogony (a story of the creation of the cosmos) becomes anthropogony (a story of the creation of man). In truth, cosmogony and anthropogony were regarded as separate moments in one continuous process of creation, in which physical matter eternally alternates between microcosmic and macrocosmic modes of existence. Bones thus become stones and stones become bones over and over again, matter and change both being eternal, while the body and the universe are only transient forms, alternate shapes of one another.

— BRUCE LINCOLN

In ancient Greek cosmology, Hades lies within the ocean, perpetually shrouded in clouds and mist.

PAGE 686

vinced all the while that they were engaged in a sacred and rightful activity.

RITUAL ACTION

The myths that we have considered were closely correlated with and regularly represented in numerous ritual forms. Thus, the creation myth was inextricably connected to sacrifice, the most important of all Indo-European rites. Insofar as the first priest created the world through the performance of a sacrifice in which a man and an ox were the victims, so each subsequent priest recreated the cosmos by sacrificing men or cattle. This was accomplished through manipulation of the homologies of macrocosm and microcosm, such that when the victim was dismembered, its material substance was transformed into the corresponding parts of the universe.

The belief in the soul's immortality among the Celts and the Gauls is attested by numerous early witnesses.

PAGE 318

Other rituals were closely related to the myth of Third. Embarking on cattle raids—which were raised to the status of a sacred act as a result of this mythic charter—Indo-European warriors invoked the assistance of martial deities, poured libations, partook of intoxicating drinks, and aspired to states of ecstatic frenzy. Moreover, each young warrior had to pass through certain initiatory rituals before he attained full status as a member of the warrior class. Regularly his first cattle raid was something of a rite of passage for the young warrior, and other initiations were consciously structured on the myth of Third and the serpent.

While the use of intoxicants was an important part of warrior ritual, these had other applications as well. The oldest Indo-European intoxicating beverage was mead, later followed by beer, wine, and a pressed drink known as *soma* to the Indians and *haoma* to the Iranians; the symbolism and ideology surrounding all of these remained relatively constant. In all instances, the drink appears as a heightener of abilities and activities. When consumed by a priest, it increases his powers of vision and insight. Similarly, it makes a poet more eloquent, a warrior more powerful, a king more generous and just.

A large group of rituals served to forge bonds of community and to cement important social relations. Extremely important in this regard were certain formalized reciprocal obligations, including hospitality and gift exchange, whereby individuals, lineages, and even larger units were brought into repeated contact and friendly interchange. Marriage also must be considered as a prolonged exchange relationship between social groups, given the predominant preference for exogamy.

Verbal rituals—including those of vow, oath, and treaty—played a highly important part in the establishment and preservation of social bonds; accordingly, truth and fidelity were cardinal virtues. Initially, this must be related to the lack of literacy among the most ancient Indo-European peoples, a state of affairs that also contributed to the high development of verbal art (epic poetry, for instance) and mnemonic techniques. But even after the introduction of writing among the scattered Indo-European peoples, a marked preference for the oral transmission of religious lore remained.

DEATH, RESURRECTION, AND ESCHATOLOGY

A central issue in Indo-European religions, as in most religions, was what becomes of an individual after death. Although several scholars have devoted attention to certain details of funerary ideology, the full nature of Indo-European thought on this topic remains to be worked out. Among the major contributions thus far are the studies of Hermann Güntert (1919), who showed that there was a goddess *Kolyo ("the coverer") whose physical form incarnated the mixture of fascination and horror evoked by death, for she was seductively beautiful when seen from the front, while hiding a back that was repulsive—moldy and wormeaten—in the extreme. Paul Thieme (1952) has also contributed an important study of the view of death as a reunion with departed ancestors, and Kuno Meyer (1919) has shown that in Ireland as in India it was the first mortal (*Yemo, the twin) who founded the otherworld.

If ideas regarding the fate of the soul are unclear—no reconstructible word approximates the semantic range of the English *soul,* the nearest equivalent being a term for "life-breath"—those on the fate of the body are extremely precise and reveal a remarkable religious content. For death is seen as the last sacrifice that an individual can offer, in which his or her own body is itself the offering. Moreover, that body is transformed into the elements of the physical universe, just as was that of Twin at the time of creation, each death being not only a sacrifice but a representation of the cosmogonic sacrifice.

This is not a final fate, however, for it would seem that nothing within the cosmos was perceived as final. Just as cosmogony was seen to alternate with anthropogony, so also death and resurrection. That matter that assumes its cosmic form when one specific human body dies will once again assume bodily form when that specific cosmos itself dies, as must inevitably happen. Greek, Germanic, and Indo-Iranian evidence permits reconstruction of a temporal scheme involving four world ages, the first of which is most pure and stable, followed by ages in which human virtue and the very order of the cosmos gradually break down. At the end of the fourth world age, there is an apocalyptic collapse, followed by the creation of a new, pure, and regenerated world. One of the cardinal features of the eschatological destruction of the cosmos, however, is the resurrection of the dead, their bodies being formed out of the material substance freed when the cosmos falls apart. The new creation that follows is then in most versions accomplished with an initial act of sacrifice.

— BRUCE LINCOLN

INNER ASIAN RELIGIONS

The peoples of Inner Asia who lived in the tundra and taiga were widely dispersed in small communities and posed no threat to their neighbors. It was the peoples of the steppes, formed in large tribes with vast herds of sheep, goats, camels, cattle, and horses, who were highly mobile and had the organizational ability to lead military excursions against their sedentary neighbors. When these peoples first appear in historical sources, they come from two great steppe regions: the south Russian (or Pontic) steppe and the Mongolian steppe.

SCYTHIANS. The first important Inner Asian people, the Indo-Iranian Scythians, appeared on the south Russian steppe in the eighth century BCE and began to fade out of the historical scene around 175 BCE, although some remnants survived until the third century CE. The Scythians were the first historically known people to use iron, and having defeated the Cimmerians, they assumed full command of the south Russian steppe.

In Persian sources these people were called Saka, and three kinds were enumerated: the Saka beyond the sea, the pointed-hat Saka, and the Saka who revered Hauma. The Scythians of Herodotus lived north of the Black Sea, while the Saka of Persian sources lived beyond the Oxus River (the modern Amu Darya) and south of this area in Iran. The social structure of the Scythians was tripartite: agriculturists, warriors, and priests. They had cities, centers of metallurgy, and a highly developed, stylized animal art.

Animals, particularly horses and cattle, as well as humans were sacrificed as offerings to the gods. Herodotus listed the Scythian gods with what he thought were their Greek equivalents, the supreme deity being Tabiti (Vesta). Images, altars, and temples were used. Scythian soothsayers were called into service when the king was ill; Enarees, womenlike men among the Scythians, practiced divination and elaborate funeral and burial rites. A strong will to protect the tombs of their ancestors, and prescribed ceremonies for oath taking existed. By the late second century BCE, the ethnically and linguistically related nomadic tribes of the Sarmatians began to replace the Scythians, who had reached a degree of civilization perhaps unparalleled by any other Inner Asian empire.

HSIUNG-NU. On the eastern edge of Inner Asia, the Hsiung-nu were the first clearly identifiable and important steppe people to appear on the borders of China, constantly menacing the frontier with raids that sometimes penetrated deep into Chinese territory. Their center of power was the Mongolian steppe. Appearing in Chinese sources around 230 BCE, an account of the Hsiung-nu was provided by the grand historian of China, Ssu-ma Ch'ien (c. 145-86 BCE). By about 56 BCE internal revolts had begun to rack the Hsiung-nu empire and some tribes moved to the west; in 48 CE the Hsiung-nu finally split into two major groups: the Southern Hsiung-nu and the Northern Hsiung-nu. The former continued to be a serious threat to China and finally faded from the historical scene around 400 CE, while the Northern Hsiung-nu remained on the original homeland of the Mongolian steppe. The Northern Hsiung-nu never regained their former power, however, and about 155 CE they were destroyed by another steppe people, the Hsien-pei.

The military power of the Hsiung-nu, like that of the Scythians, lay in their remarkable skill as highly disciplined mounted archers. In fact, Ssu-ma Ch'ien considered warfare their main occupation. The Chinese set up border markets in an attempt to weaken the Hsiung-nu by supplying them with luxuries and fostering a dependence on Chinese goods. Even though there was a hereditary aristocracy within the Hsiung-nu confederation, internal organization was loose, each tribe having its own pastures.

At set times of the year, sacrifices were offered to ancestors, gods, heaven, and earth, while auspicious days were chosen for major events, and the stars and moon were consulted for military maneuvers. Burials were elaborate, particularly for the ruler, with many of his concubines and loyal ministers following him in death. Although condemned by the Chinese for lacking in morals, not understanding court ritual, and not showing respect for the aged, the Hsiung-nu had laws, customs, and manners of their own that contradicted the ethnocentric views of the Chinese.

YÜEH-CHIH, WU-SUN, AND KUSHANS. The Hsiung-nu greatly affected the history of Inner Asia to the west and south of their domains where, in 160 BCE, they inflicted a terrible defeat on the Yüeh-chih, an Indo-European people located on the Chinese border of modern Kansu Province. This caused the Yüeh-chih to divide; the Lesser Yüeh-chih moved to the south while the Greater Yüeh-chih began moving west. As the latter migrated through the Ili River valley, they abandoned the Mongolian steppe to the complete control of the Hsiung-nu, while they themselves displaced the Sai (or Saka) tribes. The majority of the Yüeh-chih

The time for regular sacrifices is determined by the astronomical or vegetative year.

PAGE 588

With a few small exceptions, the Turkic religion has offered structures to all peoples of all social classes in all regions of the Turkic world throughout history.

PAGE 682

continued to move west into the Greek state of Bactria. At about the same time, the Chinese emperor Wu-ti (r. 140-87 BCE) sent Chang Ch'ien to the Greater Yüeh-chih to form an alliance against the Hsiung-nu. Leaving in 139, Chang Ch'ien had to pass through Hsiung-nu territory, where he was detained and held prisoner for more than ten years. Although his mission to the Yüeh-chih failed, he was sent again in 115 to try to form a different alliance against the Hsiung-nu, this time with the Wu-sun, another people probably of Iranian origin. They also refused to cooperate. It was not until the Hsiung-nu empire was disintegrating that the Wu-sun inflicted serious defeats on them.

The Yüeh-chih tribes that settled in Bactria were later united under one tribe, the Kushans, probably in the first century BCE. Besides Bactria, their kingdom included extensive domains in Central Asia and large portions of Northwest India, where centers of Greco-Buddhist art were established at Gandhara and Mathura. The Kushan period is extremely controversial, and the dates and order of kings are widely disputed. But it was during the reign of Kaniska, a patron of Buddhism, that this Indian religion began to spread into Central Asia and China, heralding a new era for the region. Chinese monks began to travel to India and Sri Lanka to obtain the Buddhist *sutras,* passing through Tun-huang, Khotan, and Turfan on the edge of the Tarim Basin, as well as Ferghana and Sogdiana.

HUNS. With the appearance of the Huns toward the end of the fourth century CE, a new movement began on the south Russian steppe. Rumors of invasions spreading fear and panic reached Jerome (c. 311-420) in Palestine, where he wrote that these "wolves of the north"—the Huns—"spared neither religion nor rank nor age." It was with this turmoil on the steppe north of the Sea of Azov that the *Völkerwanderung,* or migration of the peoples, began. Aided by civil wars in Italy that occupied the Roman army, some Hun tribes had established themselves by 409 on the Roman limes and in the Roman province of Pannonia (on the right bank of the Danube). When, in 434, a Hun king named Rua died, he was succeeded by his nephews, Bleda and Attila.

Hun penetration into Europe and the displacing of existing tribes were instrumental in the formation of modern Europe. Aetius, the great fifth-century general and power broker of the Western Roman Empire, provoked some Hun tribes to attack the Burgundians in 437 in order to shatter Germanic power and to strengthen Roman rule in Gaul. The Visigoths, who had been pushed from the east into the Toulouse area, forced the Vandals into Spain and North Africa, an event that caused great consternation to the entire Roman empire. However, Aetius's attempt to use the Huns to defeat the Visigoths failed in 439. Turmoil continued, this time in the Eastern Roman Empire with the Persian decision to attack Byzantium; at the same time, Attila attacked the Byzantines from the north, gaining new treaty concessions. Then in 445 Attila murdered Bleda, thus becoming the sole ruler of the Hun tribes of Pannonia. In the end, a nervous Aetius allied himself with the Visigoths to meet Attila in the Battle of the Catalaunian Plain (451) near Troyes, France, where the Visigoth king Theodoric II lost his life and the Romans withdrew in a battle that left neither Hun nor Roman the victor. With Attila's death in 453, Hun influence on Europe rapidly crumbled.

HSIEN-PEI AND JUAN-JUAN. As already mentioned, the Northern Hsiung-nu state was replaced around 155 CE by that of the Hsien-pei, who probably spoke a Mongol language. Through this victory, the Hsien-pei became the dominant tribal confederacy on the Mongolian steppe. With other nomadic peoples, including the Southern Hsiung-nu and the Wu-huan, they continued attacks on China but were repulsed, particularly by the famous Chinese general Ts'ao Ts'ao. When the Hsien-pei first appeared, during the Wang Mang interregnum (9-23 CE), they had no supreme ruler; unified leadership is not ascribed to them until just before their defeat of the Hsiung-nu: The Hsien-pei failed to create a lasting empire in this fragmented period of steppe history.

From approximately 400 to 550 a new power emerged on the Mongolian steppe: the Juan-juan (or Jou-jan). Their origins are uncertain but future research may clarify their relation to the Hua and to the Avars who appeared in Europe in the fifth century. According to a widely accepted but yet unproven theory, the Juan-juan in the east are identified with the Avars in the west. Personal names, as given in Chinese, do not appear to be either Turkic or Mongol, but it is with the Juan-juan that the title *kaghan* is first used for the ruler.

TÜRK. The appearance of the Türk—the first Inner Asian people whose language is known and the first also to use with certainty a Turkic idiom—marks a turning point in the history of the steppe. According to Chinese sources they were metallurgists employed by the Juan-juan, but it is not clear whether the revolt led by Bumin (d. 552) was social in character or a minority uprising. After Bumin's death the empire split, one group, led by his son, establishing itself on the Mongolian steppe, while the other group, under the leadership of his brother Ishtemi, ruled over the more western part of the empire. Because of its commercial interests in the silk trade—represented mainly by Sogdian merchants—the Western Türk empire then found itself embroiled in the conflict between Persia and Byzantium. Persian attempts to stop silk from reaching Byzantium forced the Türk to go directly to Byzantium by a northern route. It was for this reason that embassies were first exchanged between Türk and Byzantium, opening up entire new horizons for Romans as well as for the Chinese. The Western Türk empire disintegrated around 659.

The Eastern Türk empire, in a semipermanent state of war with China and plagued by internal dissension, was finally defeated in 630. Chinese rule then lasted until 682 when the Türk revolted and again seized power, forming a second Türk empire that was overthrown in 743 by the revolt of three Turkic tribes: the Basmil, the Karluk, and the Uighur.

AVARS, KHAZARS, AND BULGARS. The Greek historian Priscus wrote of a migration of peoples taking place from 461 to 465 on the south Russian steppe. An embassy from the Oghur, Onoghur, and Saroghur had arrived in Byzantium, reporting that they had been pushed by the Sabir, who in turn were being displaced by a people in Central Asia called Avar. For almost a century there was no news of them, but in 558 the Avars, now in the Caucasus, sent an embassy to the Byzantine emperor Justinian I (r. 527-565) requesting land in exchange for military protection. Fleeing from the Western Türk, the Avars were given asylum in the Byzantine empire by Justin II, an act that infuriated the Türk, who considered the Avars their own, fugitive subjects. Settled in the Carpathian Basin, the Avars remained there for some two and a half centuries, becoming an effective wedge between the northern and southern Slavs. When they had arrived in the Carpathian Basin, the Avars found two Germanic tribes, the Gepids, whom they destroyed, and the Lombards, who fled and settled in northern Italy. The Avars also menaced the Byzantines and the Franks. In 626 the Avars and the Persians jointly attacked Constantinople and were defeated only when the Byzantine forces destroyed the Persian fleet as it attempted to cross the Bosphorus.

Meanwhile, the south Russian steppe continued to be a place of turmoil. The Turkic-speaking Khazars became increasingly powerful with the weakening of the western Türk, and by the mid-seventh century achieved independence. Christian and Islamic missionaries had already had some influence among the Khazars, but in 740 the Khazar ruler and his entourage adopted Judaism. A Christian Bulgar prince, Kovrat, and his son Asparukh led other Bulgar tribes, mostly Turkic, to the lower Danube region where Asparukh created a Bulgar state between 679 and 681. Some of the Bulgars settled with the Avars in the Carpathian Basin, but the formation of this Bulgar buffer state between the Avars and Byzantium effectively ended Avar-Byzantine relations by 678. As a result, the Avars led a reasonably quiet life for over a century until they were attacked and greatly weakened (although not defeated) in 791, 795-796, and 803 by Charlemagne.

UIGHURS. The final blow to the Türk empire was delivered by the Uighurs who, as we have seen, had been a part of the Türk confederacy. Their language was basically the same as that of the Türk, with some of their texts written in runic script and some in a script borrowed from the Sogdians, one that would become a major script used in Inner Asia. Unlike the Türk, whom they overthrew in 743, the Uighurs often allied themselves with China; thus, during the reign of Mou-yü the Uighurs helped China to quell the An Lu-shan rebellion (755-757). When Mou-yü visited Lo-yang in 762-763, he was converted to Manichaeism, which had been propagated in China by the Sogdians. A description of his conversion appears on the trilingual inscription (in Uighur, Sogdian, and Chinese) of Karabalghasun, the Uighur capital city. When Mou-yü returned home he took Manichaean priests with him and made Manichaeism the state religion. Thus, the Uighurs became the first Inner Asian people to adopt an institutionalized, major religion. Many Uighurs disliked the influence gained by Sogdians in Uighur affairs and an anti-Sogdian faction, led by the uncle of Mou-yü, revolted and killed the kaghan and his family. There followed a succession of rulers embroiled in family intrigues, plagued by assassinations and suicide. Even so, Sogdian and Manichaean influence remained in a kingdom dominated by Buddhism.

Not absorbed into the new ruling Kirghiz confederacy, the Uighurs moved. Some went to China, settling in today's Kansu Province, where some of their descendants can still be found; the majority moved to the Tarim Basin and created a new state centered on the city of Kocho (850-1250), where a sophisticated, multi-lingual, and multiethnic civilization developed.

MONGOLS. The rise of Mongol power and the domination of the Chinggisid states brought unification to Inner Asia in a way that had not existed since prehistoric times.

A mixture of forests rich in game, agricultural land made fertile by abundant rainfall, and pastures suitable for horse and cattle breeding determined the basic economy of Manchuria. The settled way of life also made pig raising an important feature of all Manchurian civilizations. In the fourth century, the Mongol-speaking Kitan began to gain dominance in the region, entering into relations with China in 468, but by the sixth century, they came under Türk domination. A new Kitan rise to power was signalled by their attack and defeat of the Kirghiz ruling over the Mongolian steppe in 924; they then expanded their rule over North China, adopting the Chinese dynastic title of Liao (927-1125). In 1125 Kitan domination was

"The pity of war, the pity war distilled."

WILFRED OWEN
STRANGE MEETING
1920

replaced by that of the Jurchen, a Tunguz-speaking Manchurian people who had been Kitan subjects. The Jurchen assumed the Chinese dynastic title of Chin (1125-1234) and maintained their rule over northern China until the Mongol conquest. When the Jurchen moved into North China, some Kitan tribes, with the permission of the Uighurs, moved west across the Tarim Basin through the kingdom of Kocho to Central Asia, where a third Kitan state was founded (after those of Manchuria and China), that of the Karakitai (Black Kitan or Kitai) centered at Bala-sagun in the Chu River valley.

Between Central Asia and Manchuria, two major mongolized Turkic tribes, the Naiman and the Kereit, were vying for power in the eleventh century. Both tribes had been strongly influenced by Nestorianism; the conversion of the Kereit around 1000 was related by the Syriac chronicler Bar Hebraeus (fl. thirteenth century). The first united Mongol kingdom ended in the late eleventh century, followed by a period of internecine warfare between Mongol tribes and against the neighboring Tatar tribes. It was not until Chinggis (known as Temüjin before he was elected khan) had defeated all of his rivals that a new and powerful Mongol state emerged.

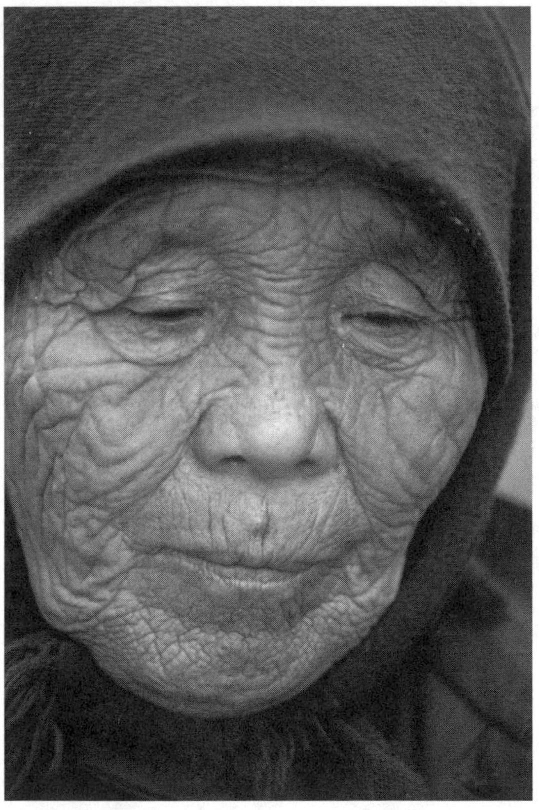

RICH ANCESTRY

The Mongols dominated Asia and Southern Europe from 927 to 1368 C.E. This Mongolian woman, a Chinese citizen, might trace her ancestry to Marco Polo or Chingis Khan.

EARL KOWALL/CORBIS

Chinggis, angered by the Naiman leader Küchlüg, who had defeated the Karakitai in Central Asia, began the great push west, defeating the Naiman in 1218, and then led a punitive campaign against Khorezm aimed at avenging the murder of Mongol envoys. Before Chinggis's death in 1227, Central Asia had been devastated, and the campaigns of the famous Mongol generals Jebe and Sübetei had spilled into Georgia, across the Caucasus, and into Russian territory, where the Russian forces and their Cuman allies were defeated in the Battle of Kalka in the late spring of 1223. The Mongols advanced as far as the city of Bulgar where they were turned back at the very end of the year 1223. With the death of Chinggis, the Mongol empire was to be divided among his four sons. But the eldest son, Jochi, predeceased Chinggis and his appanage of the westernmost Mongols, the so-called Golden Horde, went to his son, Chinggis's grandson, Batu.

Defeating Bulgar in the winter of 1237-1238, the Mongols then swept into eastern and central Europe with a great offensive begun in the winter of 1239-1240. All of Europe now accepted the Mongol threat as real, however, an attitude that opened a period of rapprochement in Mongol-Western relations was begun by Pope Innocent IV (r. 1234-1254) at the Council of Lyons (June 1245). Three groups of papal emissaries were sent to the Mongols: the Dominican Ascelinus, the Dominican Andrew of Longjumeau, and the Franciscan Giovanni da Pian del Carpini, who brought back the first extensive accounts of the Mongols, as did the later Franciscan missionary William of Rubrouck, who journeyed to the Mongols from 1253 to 1255.

With Batu's death in 1256, his brother Berke (r. 1257-1267) became ruler of the Golden Horde. He converted to Islam, thus placing the Golden Horde at odds with the Il-khanids of Persia. The Il-khanids came to power under Hülegü, who sacked Baghdad in 1258 and ended the Abbasid caliphate. The Mamluk sultan Baybars (r. 1259-1277), powerful foe of the Crusaders but also of the Mongols, defeated the Il-khanid forces in the Battle of Ain Jalut (1259), thereby stopping the Mongol conquest of the Arab world. During the reign of the Il-khan Arghun (r. 1284-1291), Buddhism was declared the state religion and close contact was maintained with Europe, particularly with the Vatican and the kings of France and England. Under severe economic pressure, Il-khanid Persia declined and religious tension forced Gazan (r. 1295-1304) to proclaim Islam the official religion. With the death of Abu Sa'id in 1335, Il-khanid Persia fragmented. Meanwhile, the power of the Golden Horde reached its apogee under Özbeg (r. 1313-1341), but attempts to expand its territory brought it into military conflict with ambitious Muscovite princes and the great military leader Timur (Tamarlane; 1336-1405) in Central Asia. Finally, the Golden Horde split into three successor states: the khanates of Kazan, Astrakhan, and the Crimea.

It was Khubilai (r. 1260-1294), the last great Mongol khan, who brought China under Mongol rule (the Yüan dynasty, 1264-1368). With the extended visit of Marco Polo to Khubilai's court (1271-1292) the first reliable information about China came to the West. After the death of Khubilai, Mongol rule in China began to weaken until they were overthrown in 1368 by the Chinese. What remained of Mongol power returned to the steppe where the western Mongols (Oirats, Dzungars, Kalmuks) became a factor in Central Asia, with two successive Oirat states menacing the territory between the western Mongolian steppe and the Caspian Sea from the mid-fifteenth century until their final defeat in 1758 at the hands of the Chinese.

— RUTH I. MESERVE

INQUISITION, THE

THE EARLY MEDIEVAL INQUISITION

During the eleventh century, western European society began a metamorphosis that led to great cultural and social achievements during the twelfth and thirteenth centuries. The church found strong leadership in the reformers who had brought institutional and doctrinal innovations to the eleventh-century papacy. Monastic reform, exemplified by Cluny, provided centers of spiritual and liturgical power throughout the West, while the laity discovered a new consciousness of social cohesion through the Peace and Truce of God movements, church-sponsored attempts to control noble and knightly ravages. In the midst of eleventh-century social and economic expansion, a sense of spiritual unity was born: Europe had become Christendom.

However, this new sense of Christian unity was evident in reactions to heretics, who now seemed, to townspeople and rulers alike, to threaten society itself: hence the public burning of a dozen or so heretics at Orleans in 1022, at the command of King Robert and with public approval. In addition, the three-year-old corpse of a heretic was exhumed and ejected from its Christian burial ground. Heretics were burned by popular demand at Milan about 1028, while Henry III of Germany allowed the hanging of purported Cathari at Goslar in 1052.

In the twelfth century, antiheretical activities on the part of church and lay princes accelerated. The dualist Cathari—some of whom may have been victims of eleventh-century popular violence—were expanding into western Europe from eastern Europe, particularly into regions where secular authority was weak or fragmented by competing powers, as in southern France (Languedoc) and northern Italy (Lombardy). Mobs and secular authorities continued to put heretics to death, as at Soissons, Cologne, and Liège, and the king of Aragon officially decreed burning as the penalty for heresy in 1197.

The church dealt with heresy in several twelfth-century councils (Toulouse, 1119; Second Lateran, 1139; Reims, 1157; Tours, 1163), prescribing as punishments excommunication, confiscation of property, and imprisonment. In 1179, at the Third Lateran Council, Pope Alexander III, called attention to the need to quell the Cathari of Languedoc and to confiscate their lands, and again he requested aid from secular lords. The earlier conciliar legislation had had limited effect, however, and in 1184 Pope Lucius III, in association with Emperor Frederick Barbarossa (d. 1190), issued more specific orders. In the bull *Ad abo-lendam,* Lucius regularized the episcopal inquisition, requiring bishops to visit their parishes and ascertain, through witnesses, who was engaged in heretical activity. The accused were to be apprehended and examined.

In 1199 Pope Innocent III (d. 1216), following the lead of earlier canonists, equated heresy with treason, in the bull *Vergentes in senium.* The obstinate were to be handed over, as traitors to God, to the secular powers for (unspecified) punishment, and their lands were confiscated. Roman concepts of *lèse-majesté,* and appropriate procedures and punishments, were beginning to be absorbed into canonical forms and penances.

The battle against heresy (especially Catharism) during the thirteenth century grew more rigorous and determined under the leadership of powerful popes. Innocent III commissioned Cistercian monks to preach and stir up antiheretical sentiment in Languedoc from 1203 to 1208; he also called upon the French king, Philip II, to mount a crusade against the Cathari in the south. The Albigensian crusade, led by Simon de Montfort, lasted for some twenty years. Many Cathari, and orthodox Christians as well, were killed by the Crusaders, who invaded Languedoc for material as well as spiritual motives.

In the aftermath of the Albigensian crusade, many Cathari returned to Languedoc, but they were far more secretive: they had been driven underground, but not exterminated. Pope Gregory IX was determined to put an end to the heresy and in 1230 he began to enact severe legislation against it. Besides sending out friars as inquisitors, by 1231 he had adopted the canons of the Council of Toulouse (1229) and the punishment of death by fire prescribed by his enemy Emperor Frederick II (in 1224). In 1233 the pope established a tribunal at Toulouse, staffed by legatine-controlled Dominicans, who were to cooperate with the bishop in prosecuting heretics. The popular outcry caused by this inquisition—for its policy of exhuming the corpses of

In 1252 Innocent IV authorized the use of torture by the Inquisition, and Alexander IV (1254-1261) gave it jurisdiction over all cases of sorcery involving heresy. Gradually almost all sorcery came to be included under the rubric of heresy.

PAGE 707

"Distrust all in whom the impulse to punish is power."

FRIEDRICH NIETZSCHE
THUS SPAKE ZARATHUSTRA

purported heretics, for example—was chronicled by William Pelhisson, one of the Dominican inquisitors assigned to the area. Although Gregory faced difficulties in securing the cooperation of many northern Italian cities, and for political reasons had to suspend the inquisition of Toulouse in 1238 (later reinstated), he had established the Inquisition in its basic outlines. In later decades its powers and procedures were to increase in extent and complexity.

The Cathari of Languedoc suffered a major setback— one from which they never really recovered— when their castle of Montségur was stormed in 1244, following the murder of a party of local inquisitors in 1242. More than two hundred Cathar leaders, known as the *perfecti,* were said to have been burned after the lengthy siege.

In the late 1240s Innocent commissioned the first handbook of inquisitorial procedure, which was drawn up by two inquisitors of Languedoc. Such manuals continued to be compiled until the end of the Middle Ages. More significantly, in the bull *Ad extirpanda* (1252), Innocent ordered that heretics handed over to the secular arm should be executed within five days, and he ordained that torture could be used to elicit information for inquisitorial courts. In doing so, Innocent brought the special tribunal of the Inquisition into line with criminal procedure already followed by thirteenth-century lay governments. Not only the revival of Roman law (with its *inquisitio* and use of torture) but also the abolition of the ordeal and other divine aids encouraged a more rigorous application of human agencies to prove guilt in both secular and inquisitorial courts.

THE LATER MEDIEVAL INQUISITION

The heresy of the Cathari, which had helped to bring the Inquisition into being, declined in Languedoc (after a brief revival in the early fourteenth century) and throughout western Europe; by the mid-fourteenth century it had virtually disappeared. At the same time, however, the Inquisition continued to develop in other areas of Europe along procedural lines laid down in the thirteenth century. Under papal leadership it spread into eastern Europe and Germany, though in the latter, local bishops sometimes resisted papal interference. England never accepted the institution, whereas by the later fifteenth century, it had been absorbed into the political machinery of Castile and Aragon and would result in the infamous Spanish Inquisition. The Spanish monarchs Ferdinand and Isabella used the inquisitorial machinery for their own political as well as religious ends. Their attempts to expand their authority through persecution of Moriscos and Marranos were guided by the Grand Inquisitor Tomás de Torquemada (1420-1498). In Italy, though Cathari were no longer a problem, the Waldensians continued to interest inquisitors, whose tasks were made more difficult by political rivalries among Italian city-states, and between these states and the papacy. During the sixteenth-century Counter-Reformation, the Inquisition, or Holy Office, underwent reorganization and centralization at Rome.

Political complications are also evident in France, where King Philip IV (d. 1314), in his conflict with the papacy, was sympathetic toward complaints levied against the Inquisition. By 1307, with a compliant pope, the king had turned the Inquisition against the Order of the Knights Templar, which was dissolved at the Council of Vienne (1312). From the mid-fourteenth century, the Parlement and University of Paris tended to exercise inquisitorial powers. Indeed, throughout its history the Inquisition was rivaled by local ecclesiastical and secular jurisdictions. No matter how determined, no pope ever succeeded in establishing complete control of the institution in western Europe: princes, bishops, civil authorities, and kings vacillated between acceptance and resistance.

Historical judgments on the medieval Inquisition have varied from absolute condemnation to qualified approval of at least some of its characteristics. Only a small portion of those who appeared before the Inquisition were sent to their deaths, and in this respect, it was more lenient than violent mobs or contemporary secular criminal courts; yet even in the thirteenth century, some, such as the lawyers who cautioned against the unrestricted use of torture, doubted whether this ecclesiastical tribunal, with its distinctive procedures, served the interests of Christendom.

— R. C. FINUCANE

INUIT RELIGION

The Inuit (Eskimo) live in the vast Arctic and sub-Arctic area that stretches from the eastern point of Siberia to eastern Greenland. Of the approximately 105,000 Inuit, 43,000 live in Greenland, 25,000 in Arctic Canada, 35,000 (plus 2,000 Aleut) in Alaska, and 1,500 (plus a small number of Aleut) in the Soviet Union.

The word *Eskimo* seems to be of Montagnais origin. The word *Inuit* means "people." Traditionally the Inuit are divided into many geographic groups. The members of each group, or band, were connected through kinship ties, but the band was without formal leadership. The nuclear family was the most important social unit.

RELATIONS BETWEEN MEN AND ANIMALS. According to eastern Inuit religious tradition, each animal had its own *inua* (its "man," "owner," or "spirit") and also its own "soul." Since the Inuit believed that the animals they hunted possessed souls, they treated their game with respect. Seals and whales were commonly offered a drink of fresh water after they had been dragged ashore. Having received such a pleasant welcome as guests in the human world, their souls, according to Inuit belief, would return to the sea and soon become ready to be caught again, and they would also let their fellow animals know that they should not object to being caught.

In southern Greenland the head of a slain polar bear was placed in a house facing the direction from which the bears usually came so that the bear's soul could easily find its way home.

During the days before the whaling party set out, the men slept in the festival house and observed sexual and food taboos.

TABOOS, AMULETS, AND SONGS. Unlike cultic practices in connection with the deities, which had relatively minor significance, taboos, amulets, and songs were fundamentally important to the Inuit. Most taboos were imposed to separate the game from a person who was tabooed because of birth, menstruation, or death. An infringement of a taboo might result in individual hardship (for example, the loss of good fortune in hunting, sickness, or even death), but often, it was feared, the whole community would suffer. Usually a public confession under the guidance of the shaman was believed sufficient to reduce the effect of the transgression of a taboo.

Amulets, which dispensed their powers only to the first owner, were used primarily to secure success in hunting and good health and, to a lesser degree, to ward off negative influences.

Songs were either inherited or bought. If a song was passed on from one generation to the next, all members of the family were free to use it, but once it was sold it became useless to its former owners.

RITES OF PASSAGE. In many localities in Canada and Alaska, women had to give birth alone, isolated in a small hut or tent. The family celebrated particular stages in a child's development, especially in connection with subsistence activities. For example, when a boy killed his first seal, the meat was distributed to all the inhabitants of the settlement, and for each new important species a hunter killed, there was a celebration and ritual distribution.

Death was considered to be a passage to a new existence. There were two lands of the dead: one in the sky and one in the sea (or underground). The Inuit in Greenland considered the land in the sea more attractive because people living there enjoyed perpetual success in whale hunting; those in the sky, on the other hand, led dull existences.

The Bladder Feast, an important calendar feast celebrated in Alaska from Kodiak Island to Point Hope, was held in midwinter. At this feast, the bladders of all the seals that had been caught during the previous year were returned to the sea in order that their souls might come back in new bodies and let themselves be caught again.

SHAMANS. Prospective shamans often learned from skilled shamans how to acquire spirits and to use techniques such as ecstatic trances. In Greenland and Labrador, the apprentice was initiated by being "devoured" by a polar bear or a big dog while being in trance alone in the wilderness. After having revived, he was ready to become master of various spirits. Shamans in Greenland always used a drum to enter a trance. Masks were also instrumental, especially in Alaska, both in secular and religious connections. The shaman might summon his familiar spirits to the house where a séance was taking place, or he might go on a spiritual flight himself. The Canadian shaman might, for example, go down to the *inua* of the sea, that is, the Sea Woman, to get seals.

Shamans also functioned as doctors. For example, they would suck the sick spot where a foreign object had been introduced or try to retrieve a stolen soul.

THE DEITIES. The Inuit of Canada and Greenland believed that the inua of the sea, the Sea Woman, controlled the sea animals and would withhold them to punish people when they had broken a taboo. The Inuit of eastern Baffin Island ritually killed Sea Woman *(Sedna)* during a feast that was held when the autumn storms came and whose purpose was to make sealing possible again. This ceremony included, *inter alia,* a ritual spouse exchange and a tug-of-war, the result of which predicted the weather for the coming winter.

While *Sedna* represented the female principle of the world, the *inua* of the moon, Aningaaq, represented the male principle. An origin myth tells how he was once a man who committed incest with his sister. She became the sun, he the moon.

The air was called Sila, which also means "universe" and "intellect." The *inua* of the air was a rather abstract but feared figure; if it was offended when taboos were broken, it would take revenge by bringing storms and blizzards.

— INGE KLEIVAN

The Inuit have no particular birth goddess, but Sedna, the mistress of the sea animals is in her unclean states a prototype of the woman who is ritually unclean.

PAGE 41

ISLAM

AN OVERVIEW

The root *slm* in Arabic means "to be in peace, to be an integral whole." From this root comes *islam,* meaning "to surrender to God's law and thus to be an integral

I

ISLAM

An Overview

The Muslim tradition, has never ceased to confirm, even to protect, the inaccessibility of God.

PAGE 248

"Do not veil the truth with falsehood, nor conceal the truth knowingly."

THE QUR AN 2:42

whole," and *muslim*, a person who so surrenders. It is important to note that two other key terms used in the Qur'an with high frequency have similar root meanings: *iman* (from *amn*), "to be safe and at peace with oneself," and *taqwa* (from *wqy*), "to protect or save." These definitions give us an insight into the most fundamental religious attitude of Islam: to maintain wholeness and proper order, as the opposite of disintegration, by accepting God's law. It is in this sense that the entire universe and its content are declared by the Qur'an to be *muslim*, that is, endowed with order through obedience to God's law; but whereas nature obeys God's law automatically, humanity ought to obey it by choice. In keeping with this distinction, God's function is to integrate human personality, both individual and corporate: "Be not like those who forgot God, and [eventually] God caused them to forget themselves" (surah 59:19).

Origin and History

Muslims believe that Islam is God's eternal religion, described in the Qur'an as "the primordial nature upon which God created mankind" (30:30). Further, the Qur'an claims that the proper name *Muslim* was given by Abraham (22:78). As a historical phenomenon, however, Islam originated in Arabia in the early seventh century CE. Two broad elements should be distinguished in that immediate religious backdrop: the purely Arab background and the penetration of Judeo-Christian elements. The Qur'an makes a disapproving reference to star worship (41:37), which is said to have come from the Babylonian star cult. For the most part, however, the bedouin were a secular people with little idea of an afterlife. At the sanctuaries *(harams)* that had been established in some parts, fetishism seems to have developed into idol worship; the most important of these sites was the Ka'bah at Mecca.

The bedouin Arabs believed in a blind fate that inescapably determined birth, sustenance (because of the precarious life conditions in the desert), and death. These Arabs also had a code of honor (called *muruwah*, or "manliness") that may be regarded as their real religious ethics; its main constituent was tribal honor—the crown of all their values—encompassing the honor of women, bravery, hospitality, honoring one's promises and pacts, and last but not least, vengeance *(tha'r)*. They believed that the ghost of a slain person would cry out from the grave until his thirst for the blood of vengeance was quenched. According to the code, it was not necessarily the killer who was slain in retaliation, but a person from among his kin equal in value to the person killed. For reasons of economics or honor, infant girls were often slain, and this practice, terminated by the Qur'an, was regarded as having had religious sanction (6:137).

In southwestern Arabia, a rather highly sophisticated civilization had existed since the Sabian period, with a prosperous economy and agriculture. The Sabian religion was, at the beginning, a trinitarian star cult, which was replaced, in the fourth century CE, by the monotheistic cult of al-Rahman (a term that appears to have traveled north and found a prominent place in the Qur'an, where it means "the merciful"). In the sixth century CE, Jewish and Christian ideas and formulas were adopted, with the term *al-Rahman* applied to the first person of the Trinity.

As for the Judeo-Christian tradition, it was not only present where Jewish and Christian populations existed (Jews in Medina—pre-Islamic Yathrib—in the south and in Khaybar in the north; Christians in the south, in Iraq, in Syria, and in certain tribes), but it had percolated in the air, generally speaking. Indeed, there had been Jewish and Christian attempts at proselytizing the Meccans, but these were unsuccessful because the Meccans wanted a new religion and scripture of their own, "whereby they would be better guided than those earlier communities" (35:42, 6:157). In the process, the Meccans had nevertheless come to know a good deal about Judeo-Christian ideas (6:92), and several people in Mecca and elsewhere had arrived at the idea of monotheism. Even so, they could not get rid of the "intermediary gods" for whom they had special cults, and there was still no cult for God, whom they called "Allah," or "the God." In addition to these limitations, there was also a great disparity between the rich and the poor and disenfranchised in the thriving commercial community of Mecca. Both of these issues are strongly emphasized from the beginning of the Qur'anic revelation, making it clear that the primary background of Islam is Arab rather than Judeo-Christian, although the latter tradition has strongly influenced Islam. In its genesis, Islam grew out of the problems existing in an Arab Meccan society.

EARLY DEVELOPMENT OF THE COMMUNITY. During a twelve-year struggle in Mecca (610-622 CE), the prophet Muhammad had gathered a devoted group of followers, largely among the poor but also among the well-to-do merchants. Yet his movement seemed to reach an impasse because of the unflinching opposition of the mercantile aristocracy, which saw in it a threat to both of their vested interests—their Ka'bah-centered religion, from which they benefited as custodians of the sanctuary and recipients of income from the pilgrimage, and their privileged control of trade. After Muhammad and his followers emigrated from Mecca to Medina in 622 (the beginning of the lunar Islamic calendar, called the *hijri*, or "emigration," calendar), at the invitation of the majority of the Arab inhabitants there, he became the head of both the nascent community and the existing polity. However, while he gave laws, waged peace and war, and created social institutions, he never claimed to be a ruler, a lawgiver, a judge, or a general; he referred to himself always as a messenger of God. As a result, not only were Islamic "religious" doctrine and ritual in the narrower sense regarded as Islamic but so were the state, the law, and social institutions. Islam is thus the name of a total way of life and does not merely regulate the individual's private relationship with God.

In Medina, then, the Prophet was able to institute his social reforms through the exercise of the religious and political power that he had been denied in Mecca.

KA'BAH
The House of Allah

The Ka'bah (lit., "cube"), the House of Allah, is located in Mecca. It is the principal Islamic shrine, the *qiblah*, or specific point faced by Muslims when performing the daily ritual prayers *(salat)* anywhere in the world. Located at the center of the great open Haram Mosque, it is the geographical and religious center of the Islamic world, the lifetime goal of Muslims who respond to the Qur'anic obligation to make at least one pilgrimage there. Muslim tradition also locates it directly below the heavenly Ka'bah.

The Ka'bah is constructed of Meccan granite and, as its name indicates, is a cubelike building, measuring more than sixteen meters high, thirteen meters long, and eleven meters wide. Its single door (there are no windows) is located on the northeast side, about two meters above the pavement of the open mosque. On the infrequent occasions when the Ka'bah is opened, mobile stairs give access to its interior. Inside are gold and silver lamps suspended from the ceiling. Three wooden pillars, recently replaced, support the ceiling.

It is, however, the building as a whole, not its contents, that is sacred to Muslims, and the most important object at the Ka'bah is located on the exterior: this is the Black Stone *(al-hajar al-aswad)* embedded in the eastern corner. Actually dark red-brown, and now encased in a massive silver band, the Black Stone is of unknown pre-Islamic origin, possibly meteoric. Myths affirm that it fell from heaven or that it was brought forth by the angels as a white stone to provide the cornerstone for the original Ka'bah; darkened by the touch of humans across the millennia, it serves as a register of human degradation. Muslims commonly refer to it as the "cornerstone of the House" and the "right hand of God on earth," but they are at pains to insist that it is not an idol and not to be worshiped: prayers here are addressed to God, not to the Black Stone. When beginning the rite of circumambulation *(tawaf)* of the Ka'bah, which during the pilgrimage season forms part of the pilgrimage performance, Muslims kiss or touch the Black Stone, as Muhammad is reported to have done. The *tawaf* is performed in the immediate vicinity of the Ka'bah on a broad pavement of polished granite called the mataf, the place of circumambulation.

Between the Black Stone and the raised door is a section of exterior wall known as the *multazam*, where worshipers press their bodies at the conclusion of the circumambulations in order to receive the *barakah* ("blessing, power") associated with the holy house.

The Ka'bah is usually covered by the *kiswah* ("robe"), a thick black and gold embroidered cloth fabricated each year by Meccan artisans. Prior to 1927 it was provided annually by the Egyptians and was brought to Mecca in the pilgrimage caravan from Cairo. The *kiswah* contains wide bands of Arabic calligraphy, mostly verses from the Qur'an.

Near the Ka'bah stands a gilded glass cage (replacing an earlier simple wooden framework) that contains a stone marking the Station of Ibrahim (Abraham). This stone is said to have miraculously preserved the footprint of Ibrahim, who stood on it in order to complete the construction of an earlier Ka'bah: it is, as it were, the builder's mark.

Opposite the corner of the Black Stone is a small building housing the sacred well of Zamzam, from which pilgrims drink water at the conclusion of their circumambulations and prayers. Its origin is mythically associated with Hajar (Hagar) and Isma'il (Ishmael), for whom God provided water in this desert place after commanding Ibrahim to abandon mother and child and promising to care for them in his place.

The historical origin of the Ka'bah is uncertain, but it had undoubtedly existed for several centuries before the birth of Muhammad (c. 570 CE). By his time it was the principal religious shrine of central Arabia and, located at the center of a sacred territory *(haram)*, had the characteristics of a Semitic sanctuary. Islam incorporated it as part of its monotheistic cultus, a process begun by Muhammad, who, upon capturing the Ka'bah, cleansed it of the idols (and perhaps icons) it contained.

The Ka'bah has been severely damaged by fire, flood, earthquake, and attack during its long history. The current building dates from the seventeenth century but contains stones from earlier buildings. As recently as 1958 the Saudi government repaired its walls and roof. Two years earlier it began a remodeling and enlargement of the Haram Mosque that added over 6,000 square meters to its area; the mosque now has a total area of 16,326 square meters and can accommodate 300,000 persons.

— HARRY B. PARTIN

I

ISLAM

Origin and History

PRAYING TO MECCA

The Qur'an declares Mecca to be the anchor of the Muslim Community and the direction for prayer.

UPI/CORBIS-BETTMANN

After three battles in which Muslims gained the upper hand over the Meccans and their allies, Islam, now in rapid ascendancy, was able to take Mecca peacefully in AH 8/630 CE along with a large part, if not the whole, of the Arabian Peninsula. In Medina, too, the Muslim community *(ummah muslimah)* was formally launched in 2/624 as the "median community," the only community consciously established by the founder of a religion for a specific purpose, as the Qur'an speaks of those "who, when we give them power on the earth, shall establish prayers and welfare of the poor and shall command good and forbid evil" (22:41). At the same time, the Qur'an (22:40) provided this community with the instrument of *jihad* (utmost exertion in God's cause, including peaceful means but also cold and hot war). Finally, Mecca was declared to be the goal of annual pilgrimage for the faithful and also the direction *(qiblah)* for prayer instead of Jerusalem. Both the constitution and the anchoring of the community were complete.

After a brief lapse into tribal sovereignty following the Prophet's death, Arab resistance to the acknowledgment of Medina's central authority was broken by force. The tribesmen's energies were turned outward in conquests of neighboring lands under the banner of Islam, which provided the necessary zeal for rapid military and political expansion. Within a century after the Prophet's death, Muslim Arabs were administering an empire stretching from the southern borders of France through North Africa and the Middle East, across Central Asia and into Sind. Muslim rule in the conquered territories was generally tolerant and humane; there was no policy of converting non-Muslims to Islam. The purpose of *jihad* was not conversion but the establishment of Islamic rule. Nonetheless, partly because of certain disabilities imposed by Islamic law on non-Muslim subjects (mainly the *jizyah*, or poll tax—although they were exempt from the *zakat*, or alms tax levied on Muslims, the *jizyah* was the heavier of the two, particularly for the lower strata of the population) and partly because of Islamic egalitarianism, Islam spread quickly after an initial period during which conversions were sometimes even discouraged. This was the first phase of the spread of Islam; later on, as we shall see, Muslim mystics, or the Sufis, were the main vehicles of Islamic expansion in India, Central Asia, and sub-Saharan Africa, although the role of traders in the Indian and Indonesian coastal areas and China must not be minimized. Even in the twentieth century, Turkish soldiers brought Islam to South Korea during the Korean War.

Several major developments in this early period affected the religious texture of the Muslim community as a continuing phenomenon. Less than half a century after the Prophet's death, political dissensions over succession led to civil war. A number of groups called the Kharijis ("those who went out") declared war on the community at large because it tolerated rule by "unrighteous" men; they claimed that a Muslim ceased to be a Muslim by committing a reprehensible act without sincerely repenting, and that other Muslims who did not regard such a person as non-Muslim also became non-Muslim. In reaction to the Kharijis and the ensuing civil strife, the community (both the Sunni mainstream and the Shi'ah, or party of 'Ali) generally adopted a religious stand that not only was tolerant of religious and political deviations from strict Islamic norms but was even positively accommodating toward them. The members of the community who took this stand were known as the Murji'ah (from *irja'*, meaning "postponement," in the sense of not judging a person's religious worth, but leaving it to God's judgment on the Last Day). The net result of this basic development was that excommunication was ruled out so long as a person recognized the community as Muslim and professed that "there is no god but God and Muhammad is his prophet."

This formula created or rationalized accommodation for an amazing range of different religious opinions and practices under one God and Muhammad's prophethood. Oddly enough, the only systematically rigid and illiberal school of doctrine that persecuted its opponents, after it became state creed under the Abbasid caliph al-Ma'mun in the first half of the ninth century, was the liberal rationalist school of the Mu'tazilah. The emergence of this school was largely the result of the impact on the Islamic religion of the wholesale translations of Greek works of science, philosophy, and medicine into Arabic on the orders of al-Ma'mun. The Mu'tazilah tried to create necessary free space by insisting on freedom of human will and God's rational justice, but the Muslim orthodoxy, countering with doctrines of the inefficacy of human will and the absolutism of God's will and divine predeterminism, actually provided more accommodation for varying opinions and human actions and thereby halted the growth of the rationalist school.

With the advent of the Abbasids, there were other political, social, and religious changes as well, among them the improvement of the status of the Iranians, who, under Umayyad rule, were denied an identity of their own as "clients" *(mawali)* of the Arab tribes; and the espousal and implementation of legal measures created by the religious leadership, which had been largely alienated from the Umayyads. All of these developments combined to facilitate the rapid spread of Islam.

MEDIEVAL AND LATER DEVELOPMENTS. With the weakening of the central caliphal authority in Baghdad, the tenth century saw not only the virtual fragmentation of the Abbasid empire and the rise of *de facto* independent rulers (sultans and emirs) in the provinces but the almost ubiquitous rise of the Shi'ah. While Baghdad came under the political and fiscal "management" of the orthodox Twelver Shi'ah through the Persian Buyid family, Egypt and North Africa came under the rule of the Isma'ili Fatimids. But if the Buyids were able to influence Islamic practices in some ways—such as the observance of 'Ashura', the tenth of Muharram (the first month of the Islamic calendar) as the commemoration of the martyrdom of the Prophet's grandson Husayn at the hands of the Umayyad troops—Fatimid rule, by and large, did not leave much of a trace on later Muslim thought and institutions, despite the fact that the Isma'iliyah had offered a revolutionary ideology claiming to usher in a new world order through the establishment of a universal religion. [*See also* Shiism.]

Shiism is a major branch of Islam with numerous subdivisions, all upholding the rights of the family of the Prophet (ahl al-bayt) to the religious and political leadership of the Muslim community.

PAGE 597

In purely religious terms, indeed, it was not so much Shiism as the rise and spread of Sufism that constituted the new and greatest challenge to Islamic orthodoxy, in terms of ideas and spiritual orientation, and indeed, it was Shiism that suffered most, in terms of following, as a result of the new movement. From modest beginnings as an expression of refined piety on the part of a spiritual elite in the eighth and ninth centuries, Sufism became a mass religion from the eleventh century onward. In its origins as a deepening of the inner "life of the heart," Sufism was largely complementary to the outer "life of the law," which was the domain of the *'ulama'*, the religious scholars who functioned as custodians of the *sha'riah* (sacred law) and never claimed to be pastors or custodians of the soul.

In its later development, however, through networks of brotherhoods that spread from the shores of the Atlantic to Southeast Asia, it practically took the place of "official" Islam, particularly in the countryside. Feeding on certain pantheistic ideas of eminent Sufis and generating latitudinarian, indeed protean, tendencies, it served to convert to Islam large populations in the Indian subcontinent, Central Asia, Africa, and Indonesia. A long line of orthodox Sufis, beginning in the eighth and ninth centuries and culminating in the monumental work of al-Ghazali (d. 1111), struggled hard, with a good measure of success, to bring about a synthesis that would ensure a respectable place for Sufi spirituality in the orthodox fold. After the advent of Sufism, and particularly after al-Ghazali's success, the number of converts to Islam expanded dramatically, and the number of Shi'ah shrank equally dramatically, apparently because the demands for an inner life that Shiism had satisfied through its esoteric claims were now satisfied by Sufism. [*See also* Sufism.]

During the thirteenth and fourteenth centuries, Islam penetrated into the Malay archipelago largely through Arab traders, who went first to the coastal areas of Java and Sumatra and afterward to Malaysia. Shortly after the advent of Islam, however, these lands fell under western European domination. Because the structure of British power in Malaysia differed from Dutch colonialism in Indonesia, in that British overlordship was exercised through regional sultans whereas the Dutch ruled directly, Islam was inhibited in Indonesia: a large percentage of the population of the interior remained *abangans,* or "nominal Muslims," whose life is still based on ancient custom *('adat)* under a thin Islamic veneer. Recently, however, a large-scale thrust of islamization has changed this picture considerably. In Djakarta, for example, a little more than a dozen years ago, there were only a few cathedral mosques for Friday services, but now the number has multiplied spectacularly; indeed, there is a mosque attached to every government department. This process of "consolidation in orthodox Islam," necessitated by the initial compromises made by Sufis with local cultures, has been going on for some decades in the Indian subcontinent as well.

"He says Be! and there it is."

THE QUR AN, 36:82

In Africa south of the Sahara, Islam appears to have penetrated through both traders and pilgrims. Although, as noted above, Islam spread there through the influence of Sufi orders, one unique feature of African Islam seems to be the combination of Sufism with militancy, the latter acclaimed as the result of the Islamic teaching on *jihad*, although it is also congruent with the spirit of local tribalism.

Africa is the only continent where Muslims are in the majority, while in Europe, Islam now constitutes the second largest religion, mainly comprising emigrants from Muslim lands but a few Western converts as well. In North America, Muslims are said to number around two million, most of whom are emigrants from Muslim countries. But there is also in the United States a significant phenomenon of conversion among local blacks, originating in the social protest movement against white ascendancy. The earliest group, known as the Black Muslims, called itself the Nation of Islam during the lifetime of its founder, Elijah Muhammad, and was a heterodox movement. After his death in 1973 it moved closer to the rest of the Muslim community, taking the new name of American Islamic Mission and receiving financial help from oil-rich Arab countries such as Saudi Arabia, Libya, and Kuwait. (The organization was dissolved in 1985.) There are also other numerous, though small, Afro-American Muslim groups scattered throughout the United States. [*See* Afro-American Religions, *and sidebar* Malcolm X.]

Arriving at a precise estimate of the Muslim population in China presents a serious problem. According to data collected unofficially by Chinese Muslims in 1939-1940 and extrapolations from these data in terms of population growth, Chinese Muslims might number close to one hundred million in the 1980s. The official Chinese figure given in the early sixties, however, was ten million, a figure revised to between fifteen and twenty million two decades later (religion is a factor not counted in the Chinese census). According to the 1979 United Nations statistics, the world Muslim population is just under one billion.

The Systematic Content of Islam

With the rise of Islamic legal and theological thought in the eighth century CE, a framework had to be articulated within which religious developments were to be set. The most basic sources in this framework were the Qur'an and the *sunnah* of the Prophet.

THE QUR'AN. The God of the Qur'an is a transcendent, powerful, and merciful being. His transcendence ensures his uniqueness and infinitude over and against all other creatures, who are necessarily characterized by finitude of being and potentialities. Hence God is all-powerful, and no creature may share in his divinity (belief in such sharing is called *shirk* and is condemned in the Qur'an as the most heinous and unforgivable sin). This infinite power is expressed, however, through God's equally infinite mercy. The creation of the universe, the fact that there is plenitude of being, rather than emptiness of nothing, is due solely to his mercy. Particularly with reference to humanity, God's creation, sustenance, guidance (in the form of revelations given to the prophets, his messengers), and, finally, judgment, are all manifestations of his power in mercy.

God created nature by his command "Be!" In fact, for whatever God wishes to create, "He says, Be! and there it is" (36:82). But whatever God creates has an orderly nature, and that is why there is a universe rather than chaos. God puts into everything the proper "guidance" or "nature" or laws of behavior to make each part fit into the entire pattern of the universe. "All things are measured" (e.g., 54:49), and only God is the measurer; hence he alone is the commander, and everything else is under his command. This command, which is a fact of automatic obedience in the case of nature (3:83), becomes an "ought" in the case of humans, for whom moral law replaces natural law. Nature is, therefore, a firm, well-knit machine without rupture or dislocations.

Here it is interesting and important to note that while the Qur'an patently accepts miracles of earlier prophets (67:2-3), in response to pressure from Muhammad's opponents for new miracles (e.g., 2:23, 10:38, 11:13), the Qur'an insists that it is itself the Prophet's miracle, and one that cannot be equaled. As for supernatural miracles, they are out of date because they have been ineffective in the past (17:59, 6:33-35).

Nature is, therefore, autonomous but not autocratic, since it did not bring itself into being. God, who brought nature into being, can destroy it as well; even so, although the Qur'an, when speaking of the Day of Judgment, often invokes a cataclysm that strongly suggests destruction (see, for example, surah 81), in many verses it speaks instead of a radical transformation and a realignment of the factors of life (e.g., 56:60-63). Finally, the universe has been created for the benefit of human beings, and all its forces have been "subjugated" to them; of all creatures, only they have been created to serve God alone (e.g., 31:20, 22:65).

In its account of the human race, while the Qur'an holds that humans are among the noblest of God's creatures and that Adam had indeed outstripped the angels in a competition for creative knowledge, a fact testifying to his unique intellectual qualities, it nevertheless criticizes them for their persistent moral failures, which are due to their narrowmindedness, lack of vision, weakness, and smallness of self. All their ills are reducible to this basic deficiency, and the remedy is for them to enlarge the self and to transcend pettiness. This pettiness is often represented by the Qur'an in economic terms, such as greed, fraud, and holding back from spending on the poor (as was the case with the Meccan traders): "If you were to possess [all] the treasures of the mercy of my lord, you would still sit on them out of fear of spending [on the needy]" (17:100). It is Satan who whispers into people's ears that they would be impoverished by spending, while God promises prosperity for such investment (2:268). Instead of establishing usurious accounts to exploit the poor, believers should establish "credit with God" (2:245, 57:11, 57:18 et al.).

In its social doctrine and legislation, the Qur'an makes a general effort to ameliorate the condition of the weak and often abused segments of society, such as the poor, orphans, women, and slaves. People are asked to free slaves on freedom-purchasing contracts, "and if they are poor, you give them from the wealth God has bestowed upon you" (24:33). An egalitarian statement concerning males and females is made, but the husband is recognized as "one degree higher" (2:228) because he earns by his strength and expends on his wife. Polygamy is limited to four wives with the provision that "if you fear you cannot do justice [among them], marry only one" (4:3), and the further admonition that such justice is impossible "no matter how much you desire" (4:129). Kind and generous treatment of wives is repeatedly emphasized; celibacy is strongly discouraged, although not banned outright. The basic equality of all people is proclaimed and ethnic differences discounted: "O you people, we have created [all of] you from a male and a female, and we have made you into different nations and tribes [only] for the purpose of identification—otherwise, the noblest of you in the sight of God is the one who is the most righteous" (49:13).

In the economic field, the widespread practice of usury is prohibited. The *zakat* tax is levied on the well-to-do members of the community; it was meant as a welfare tax to be spent on the poor and the needy in general, but surah 9:60, which details the distribution of *zakat*, is so comprehensive in its scope that it covers practically all fields of social and state life. In general, fair play and justice are repeatedly advised. Detailed inheritance laws are given (4:7ff.), the main feature of which is the introduction of shares to daughters, although these shares are set at half of what sons receive. Communal affairs are to be decided through mutual consultation (*shura baynahum*, 42:38), a principle that has never been institutionalized in Islamic history, however.

One noteworthy feature of the moral teaching of the Qur'an is that it describes all wrong done against anyone as "wrong done against oneself" (*zulm al-nafs*, as in 2:231, 11:101, 11:118). In its teaching on the Last Judgment, the Qur'an constantly talks of "weighing the deeds" of all adult and responsible humans (101:6-11, 7:8 et al.). This doctrine of the "weight" of deeds arises out of the consideration that people normally act for the here and now; in this respect, they are like cattle: they do not take a long-range or "ultimate" *(akhirah)* view of things: "Shall we tell you of those who are the greatest losers in terms of their deeds? Those whose whole effort has been lost [in the pursuit of] this life [i. e., the lower values of life], but they think they have performed prodigies" (18:104). The rationale of the Last Judgment is to bring out the real moral meaning, "the weight" of deeds. But whereas the Last Judgment will turn upon individual performance, the Qur'an also speaks about a "judgment in history," which descends upon peoples, nations, and communities on the basis of their total performance and whether that performance is in accord with the teaching of the divine messages brought by their prophets: many nations have perished because of their persistence in all sorts of disobedience and moral wrong, for "God gives inheritance of the earth [only] to good people" (21:105).

The Qur'an, therefore, declares unequivocally that God has sent his messages to *all* peoples throughout history and has left none without guidance (35:24, 13:7). These messages have been essentially the same: to reject *shirk* (associating anyone with God) and to behave according to the law of God. All messages have emanated from a single source, the "Mother of All Books" (13:39) or the "Hidden Book" (56:78) or the "Preserved Tablet" (85:22), and although every prophet has initially come to his people and addressed them "in their tongue" (14:4), the import of all mes-

"God gives inheritance of the earth only to good people."

THE QUR'AN, 21:105

sages is universal; hence it is incumbent on all people to believe in all prophets, without "separating some from the others." For this reason the Qur'an is severely critical of what it sees as proprietary claims upon God's guidance by Jews and Christians and rejects Jewish claims to special status in strong terms (62:6, 2:94-95, 5:18, et al.). Despite the identity of divine messages, moreover, the Qur'an also posits some sort of development in religious consciousness and asserts that on the Last Day every community will be judged by the standards of its own book and under the witness of its own prophet(s) (4:41, 16:84, et al.). The Qur'an protects, consummates, and transcends earlier revelations, and Muhammad is declared to be the "seal of the prophets" (33:40).

Finally, the Qur'an states five basic constituents of faith *(iman)*: belief in God, in angels, in revealed books, in God's messengers, and in the Last Day. Corresponding to these five items of belief, a fivefold practical doctrine was formulated very early on. These "Five Pillars" include (1) bearing witness in public at least once in one's lifetime that "There is no god but God and Muhammad is his prophet"; (2) praying five times a day (before sunrise, early afternoon, late afternoon, immediately after sunset, and before retiring), while facing the Ka'bah at Mecca; (3) paying *zakat*; (4) fasting during Ramadan (the ninth month of the Islamic lunar year), with no eating, drinking, smoking, or sexual intercourse from dawn until sunset, when the daily fast is broken; and (5) performing the annual pilgrimage to the Ka'bah at least once in one's adult lifetime, provided one can afford the journey and leave enough provisions for one's family.

The pilgrimage is performed during the first ten days of the last month of the Islamic year. One may perform the lesser pilgrimage *('umrah)* at other times of the year, but it is not a substitute for the great pilgrimage *(al-hajj al-akbar)*. The pilgrimage has, through the centuries, played an important role, not only in strengthening general unity in the global Muslim community but also in disseminating religious ideas both orthodox and Sufi, for it provides the occa-

JIHAD
To Endeavor, to Strive, to Struggle

JIHAD is the verbal noun of the Arabic verb jahada, meaning "to endeavor, to strive, to struggle." It is generally used to denote an effort toward a commendable aim. In religious contexts it can mean the struggle against one's evil inclinations or efforts toward the moral uplift of society or toward the spread of Islam.

Jihad in the Qur'an and the Hadith. In about two-thirds of the instances where the verb jahada or its derivatives occur in the Qur'an, it denotes warfare. They are often linked with the phrase "in the way of God" (fi sabil Allah) to underscore the religious character of the struggle.

Many later verses on jihad order the believers to take part in warfare, promise heavenly reward to those who do, and threaten those who do not with severe punishment in the hereafter. Some verses deal with practical matters such as exemption from military service (9:91, 48:17), fighting during the holy months (2:217) and in the holy territory of Mecca (2:191), the fate of prisoners of war (47:4), safe conduct (9:6), and truce (8:61).

There is an abundant body of hadith on jihad. The hadiths deal with the same topics as the Qur'an but place more emphasis on the excellence of jihad as a pious act, on the rewards of martyrdom, and on practical and ethical matters of warfare.

Jihad in Islamic Law. The prescriptions found in the Qur'an and hadith, together with the practice of the early caliphs and army commanders, were, from the latter half of the second century ah on, cast in the mold of a legal doctrine to which a separate chapter in the handbooks on Islamic law was devoted. The central part of this doctrine is that the Muslim community as a whole has the duty to expand the territory and rule of Islam. Consequently, jihad is a collective duty of all Muslims, which means that if a sufficient number take part in it, the whole community has fulfilled its obligation.

The ultimate aim of jihad is "the subjection of the unbelievers" and "the extirpation of unbelief." This is understood, however, in a purely political way as the extension of Islamic rule over the remaining parts of the earth.

The jihad chapters in the legal handbooks contain many practical rules. Warfare must start with the summons in which the enemies are asked to embrace Islam or accept the status of non-Muslim subjects. Only if they refuse may they be attacked.

Jihad in History. Throughout Islamic history the doctrine of jihad has been invoked to justify wars between Muslim and non-Muslim states and even to legitimate wars between Muslims themselves. Examples of jihad movements are the Wahhabiyah in Arabia, founded by Muhammad ibn 'Abd al-Wahhab (1703-1787), the Fulbe jihad in northern Nigeria led by Usuman dan Fodio (1754-1817), the Sanusiyah in Libya and the Sahara, founded by Muhammad ibn 'Ali al-Sanusi, and the Mahdist movement of Muhammad Ahmad in the Sudan (1881-1898). In the twentieth century the jihad doctrine lost much of its importance as a mobilizing ideology in the struggle against colonialism.

— RUDOLPH PETERS

sion for an annual meeting among religious leaders and scholars from different parts of the Muslim world. For the past few decades, it has also served to bring together political leaders and heads of Muslim states. In recent years, too, because of new travel facilities, the number of pilgrims has vastly increased, sometimes exceeding two million each year. [*See also* Qur'an, *articles on* The Text and Its History *and* Its Role in Muslim Piety.]

SUNNAH. The word *sunnah* literally means "a well-trodden path," but it was used before Islam in reference to usage or laws of a tribe and certain norms of intertribal conduct accepted by various tribes as binding. After the rise of Islam, it was used to denote the normative behavior of the Muslim community, putatively derived from the Prophet's teaching and conduct, and from the exemplary teaching of his immediate followers, since the latter was seen as an index of the former. In the Qur'an, there is no mention of the term *sunnah* with reference to the Prophet's extra-Qur'anic precepts or example, but the term *uswah hasanah*, meaning a "good model" or "example" to be followed, is used with reference to Muhammad's conduct as well as the conduct of Abraham and his followers (33:31, 60:4, 60:6). The term *uswah* is certainly much less rigid than *sunnah* and does not mean so much a law to be literally implemented as an example to be matched.

Even so, there is clear evidence that the concept of *sunnah* was flexible in the early decades of Islam because, with hardly any written codifications of the *sunnah* (which was used in the sense of an ongoing practice rather than fixed formulas), there was no question of literal imitation. As political, legal, and theological dissensions and disputes multiplied and all kinds of positions sought self-validation, however, the opinions of the first three generations or so were projected back onto the Prophet to obtain the necessary authority, and the phrase *sunnat al-nabi* (the *sunnah* of the Prophet) gradually took the place of the term *sunnah*.

During the second and third centuries AH, the narration and codification of the *sunnah* into hadith was in full swing. A report that claims to convey a *sunnah* (or *sunnahs*) is called a *hadith*. It is reported that while earlier people used to accept a *hadith* as genuine on trust alone, after the civil wars of the late first to early second centuries AH, a *hadith* was accepted only on the basis of some reliable authority. From this situation emerged the convention of the *isnad*, or the chain of guarantors of *hadith*, extending from the present narrator backward to the Prophet. The *isnad* took the following form: "I, So-and-so, heard it from B, who heard it from C, who said that he heard the Prophet say so-and-so or do such-and-such." Then followed the text *(matn)* of the *hadith*. A whole science called "principles of *hadith*" developed in order to lay down meticulous criteria for judging the reliability of the transmitters of *hadith*, and the discipline stimulated in turn a vast literature of comprehensive biographical dictionaries recording thousands of transmitters' names, their lives, character, and whether a transmitter actually met or could have met the person he claims to transmit from. The canons for criticizing transmitters were applied rigorously, and there is hardly a transmitter who has escaped criticism.

The experts on *hadith* also developed canons of "rational critique" alongside the critique of the chains of transmission, but they applied the former with far less rigor than they did the latter. Although the specialists divided *hadith* into several categories according to their "genuineness" and "reliability," to this day it remains the real desideratum of the science to work out and apply what is called historical criticism to the materials of *hadith*. The six authoritative Sunni collections of *hadith* date from the third century AH, while the famous Shi'i collection of al-Kulini, *Al-kafi* (The Sufficient), dates from the early fourth century. In modern times, the authenticity of *hadith* and hence of the recorded *sunnah* of the Prophet (although not so much the biographies of the Prophet and historical works) has come under general attack at the hands of certain Western scholars and also of some Muslim intellectuals—and this is happening increasingly—but the *'ulama'* have strenuously resisted these attacks because a large majority of Islamic social and political institutions and laws are either based on *hadith* or rationalized through it.

LAW. The well-known dictum among Western Islamicists that, just as theology occupies the central place in Christianity, in Islam the central place belongs to law is essentially correct. Law was the earliest discipline to develop in Islam because the Muslims needed it to administer the huge empire they had built with such astonishing rapidity. Recent research has held that the early materials for Islamic law were largely created by administrators on the basis of *ad hoc* decisions and that, in the second stage, systematic efforts were made by jurists to "islamize" these materials and bring them under the aegis of the Qur'an and the *sunnah*. (The content of the latter, in the form of *hadith*, developed alongside this activity of islamization.) This picture is probably too simplistic, however, and it would be more correct to say that the process of subsuming administrative materials and local custom under the Qur'an and the *sunnah* went hand in hand with the reverse process of deriving law from the Qur'an and whatever existed by way of the *sunnah* in the light of new administrative experiences and local custom.

Although clarification of this issue requires further research, it is certain that up to the early third century AH the schools of law were averse to the large-scale use

The ultimate aim of this quest is always to better align the behavior of the believer to the "correct path" that God wishes him to take

PAGE 248

of *hadith* in the formulation of law and that, in fact, some scholars explicitly warned against the rise of "peripheral *hadith*" and advised the acceptance of only that *hadith* that conformed to the Qur'an. However, the need for the anchoring authority of the Prophet had become so great that in the latter half of the second century AH al-Shafi'i (d. 204/819) made a strong and subsequently successful bid for the wholesale acceptance of "reliable" *hadith*—even if narrated by only one person. As a result, *hadith* multiplied at a far greater rate after al-Shafi'i than before him. Nevertheless, the followers of Abu Hanifah (d. 767) continued to reject a single-chain *hadith* in favor of a "sure, rational proof derived from the *shari'ah* principles," just as the followers of Malik (d. 795) continued to give preference to the early "practice of Medina" over *hadith*.

The final framework of Islamic jurisprudence came to recognize four sources of law, two material and two formal. The first source is the text of the Qur'an, which constitutes an absolute "decisive proof"; the second is *hadith* texts, although these can vary from school to school, particularly between the Sunni and the Twelver Shi'i schools. In new cases, for which a "clear text" *(nass)* is not available, a jurist must make the effort *(ijtihad)* to find a correct answer himself. The instrument of ijtihad is analogical reasoning *(qiyas)*, which consists in (1) finding a text relevant to the new case in the Qur'an or the *hadith*, (2) discerning the essential similarity or *ratio legis* (called *'illat al-hukm*) between the two cases, (3) allowing for differences *(furuq)* and determining that they can be discounted, and (4) extending or interpreting the *ratio legis* to cover the new case. This methodology, although neatly formulated in theory, became very difficult to wield in practice primarily because of the differences of opinion with regard to "relevant texts," particularly in the case of *hadith*.

READING QUR'AN

The text of the Qur'an constitutes absolute "decisive proof" within the framework of Islamic law.

HULTON-DEUTSCH COLLECTION/CORBIS

The fourth source or principle is called *ijma'*, or consensus. Although the concept of consensus in the sense of the informal agreement of the community (for Islam has no churches and no councils to produce formal decisions) has in practice an overriding authority, since even the fact and the authenticity of a Qur'anic revelation are finally guaranteed by it, there is no consensus on the definition of consensus: it varies from the consensus of the *'ulama'*, through that of the *'ulama'* of a certain age, to that of the entire community. There is also a difference of opinion as to whether a certain consensus can be repealed by a subsequent one or not; the reply of the traditionalists is usually, though not always, in the negative, while that of modern reformers is in the positive.

A special category of punishments called *hudud* (sg., *hadd*) was established by jurists and includes penalties specified in the Qur'an for certain crimes: murder, theft, adultery, and false accusation of adultery, to which was later added drunkenness. The theory is that since God himself has laid down these penalties, they cannot be varied. But in view of the severity of the punishments, the jurists defined these crimes very narrowly (adultery, for example, is defined as the penetration of the male organ into the female) and put such stringent conditions on the requisite evidence that it became practically unattainable (for example, in order to prove adultery, four eyewitnesses to the sexual act itself were required). The legal maxim "Ward off *hadd* punishments by any doubt" was also propounded, and the term *doubt* in classical Islamic law had a far wider range than in any other known system of law. In addition, Muslim jurists enunciated two principles to create flexibility in *shari'ah* law and its application: necessity and public interest. The political authority, thanks to these two principles, could promulgate new measures and even suspend the operations of the *shari'ah* law. In later medieval centuries, the Ottoman rulers and others systematically promulgated new laws by invoking these particular principles of the *shari'ah*.

After the concrete and systematic establishment of the schools of law during the fourth and fifth centuries AH, original legal thought in Islam lost vitality; this development is known as "the closure of the door of *ijtihad*." It was not that new thinking was theoretically prohibited but rather that social, intellectual, and political conditions were unfavorable to it. However, a procedure known as *talfiq* (lit., "patchwork") was introduced whereby, if a certain provision in one legal school caused particular hardship, a more liberal provision from another could be borrowed, without necessarily taking over its reasoning. Thus, given the impracticality of the Hanafi school's regulation that a wife whose husband has disappeared must wait more than ninety years before remarrying (according to the reasoning that the wife must wait until her husband can be presumed dead through natural causes), the Maliki school's provision that such a wife may marry after four years of waiting (Malik reasoned that the maximum period of gestation, which he had himself witnessed, was four years) was taken over in practice.

Of the four extant Sunni schools of law, the Hanafi is prevalent in the Indian subcontinent, Central Asia, Turkey, Egypt, Syria, Jordan, and Iraq; the Maliki school in North Africa extends from Libya through Morocco; the Shafi'i, in Southeast Asia, with a considerable following in Egypt; and the Hanbali school, in Saudi Arabia. Within Shi'i jurisprudence, the Ja'fari (Twelver Shi'i) school prevails in Iran. At one time, the "literalist" (Zahiri) school was represented by some highly prominent jurists, but it has practically no following now, while the Khariji school is represented in Oman, and to a limited extent in East and North Africa.

It must finally be pointed out that when we speak of Islamic law, we mean all of human behavior, including, for example, intentions. This law is therefore very different from other systems of law in the strict sense of the term. Islamic law does not draw any line between law and morality, and hence much of it is not enforceable in a court, but only at the bar of conscience. This has had its advantages in that Islamic law is shot through with moral considerations, which in turn have given a moral temper to Muslim society. But it has also suffered from the disadvantage that general moral propositions have very often not been given due weight and have been selectively construed by jurists as mere "recommendations" rather than commands that must be expressed in terms of concrete legislation: the result has been an overemphasis on the specific dos and don'ts of the Qur'an at the expense of general propositions. For example, the Qur'anic verse 4:3, permitting polygamy up to four wives, was given legal force by classical Muslim jurists, but the rider contained in the same verse, that if a person cannot do justice among co-wives, then he must marry only one, was regarded by them as a recommendation to the husband's conscience that he should do justice.

THEOLOGY. At an elementary level, theological speculation in Islam also began very early and was occasioned by the assassination of 'Uthman, the third caliph (d. 665), but its rise and development was totally independent of the law, and the first great theological systems were constructed only in the third and fourth centuries AH. The first question to become the focal point of dispute was the definition of a true Muslim. The earliest political and theological schism was represented by the Kharijis (from *khuruj*, meaning "secession"), who contended that a Muslim ceases to be a Muslim by the commission of a single serious sin such as theft or adultery, no matter how many times that person may recite the profession of faith, "There is no god but God and Muhammad is his prophet," unless he or she repents sincerely. They held that 'Uthman and 'Ali (the fourth caliph) had both become *kafirs* (non-Muslims), since the former was guilty of serious maladministration, including nepotism, and the latter had submitted his claim to rule to human arbitration, even though he had been duly elected caliph. The Kharijis, who were exemplars of piety and utterly egalitarian, and who believed that the only qualification for rule is a person's goodness and piety, without consideration of race, color, or sex, were mostly bedouin, which largely explains both their egalitarianism and their fanaticism. They were "professional rebels" who never united but always fought successive governments in divided groups and were almost entirely crushed out of existence by the middle of the second century AH.

While the Kharijis were not a systematic theological school, a full-fledged school, that of the Mu'tazilah, soon developed from their milieu. These thinkers, who emerged during the second and third centuries AH, held that while grave sinners do not become *kafirs*, neither do they remain Muslims. Their central thesis concerned what they called "God's justice and unity," which they defended to its logical conclusion. God's justice demands that human beings have a free and efficacious will; only then can they be the locus of moral responsibility and deserve praise and blame here and reward and punishment in the hereafter. They carried this belief to the point of holding that just as God, in his justice, cannot punish one who does good, neither can he forgive one who does evil, for otherwise the difference between good and evil would disappear. This position certainly offended religious sensitivities, since the Qur'an repeatedly mentions that God will forgive "whom he will" (2:284, 3:129 et al.).

For the Mu'tazilah, God plays no role in the sphere of human moral acts, except that he gives man moral support provided man does good by himself; God's activity is limited to nature. All anthropomorphic statements in the Qur'an were interpreted by the Mu'tazilah either as metaphors or as Arabic idioms. They rejected *hadith* outright because much of it was anthropomorphic and refused to base law upon it on the ground that *hadith* transmission was unreliable. They further held that good and evil in terms of general principles (but not the positive religious duties) were knowable by human reason without the aid of revela-

"Surely God wrongs not men, but themselves men wrong."

THE QUR'AN 10:44

tion but that revelation supplied the necessary motivation for the pursuit of goodness. In conformity with this view, they believed that one must rationally ponder the purposes of the Qur'anic ordinances, for in laying these down, God had a positive interest in furthering human well-being *(maslahah)*. This presumably means that law should be rationally grounded; there is, however, no evidence that the Mu'tazilah ever attempted to work out a legal system.

On the issue of God's unity, the Mu'tazilah rejected the separation of God's attributes from his essence, for this would entail belief in a multiplicity of eternal beings, amounting to polytheism. They did not deny that God is "living," "knowing," and "willing," as divine activities, but they denied that God is "life," "knowledge," and "will," as substantives. The development of this particular doctrine was possibly influenced by Christian discussions on the nature of the Trinity, and how and whether three hypostases could be one person, because the terms in which it is formulated are all too foreign to the milieu of pristine Islam. As a consequence of this doctrine, the Mu'tazilah also denied the eternity of the Qur'an, the very speech of God, since they denied the substantiality of all divine attributes. When their credo was made state creed under Caliph al-Ma'mun, they persecuted opposition religious leaders such as Ibn Hanbal (d. 855), but because of these very doctrines—denial of God's forgiveness and of the eternity of the Qur'an—they became unpopular, and Caliph al-Mutawakkil (d. 861) brought Sunnism back to ascendancy.

The Mu'tazili schools taught that, starting from creation, human intelligence can and must rise to the affirmation of God even without the help of a new explicit revelation (the Qur'anic preaching) to make this obligatory.

PAGE 250

What is in fact called Sunnism means nothing more than the majority of the community; it had its content defined in large measure as a reaction to the Kharijis and the Mu'tazilah, for Sunni orthodoxy is but a refined and sophisticated form of the popular reaction that crystalized against these groups. There, no small role was played by popular preachers and popular piety, which had already found its way into *hadith*. In doctrinal form, this reaction can be described as Murji'ism (from *irja'*, "postponement"), the belief that once adults have openly professed that there is no God but Allah and Muhammad is his prophet, if there is no reason to suspect that they are lying, mad, or under constraint, then such people are Muslims, irrespective of whether their deeds are good or whether their beliefs quite conform to orthodoxy, and that final judgment on their status must be "postponed" until the Last Day and left to God.

In conscious opposition to the Kharijis and the Mu'tazilah, the Murji'ah were content with minimal knowledge of Islam and Islamic conduct on the part of a believer. On the question of free will, they leaned heavily toward predestinarianism, and some were outright predestinarians. There is evidence that the Umayyad rulers supported the Murji'ah, apparently for their own political ends, since they were interested in discouraging questions about how they had come to power and set up a dynastic rule that abandoned the first four caliphs' model and high moral and political standards. However, it would have been impossible for these rulers to succeed if popular opinion had not swung toward the Murji'ah, particularly in reaction against the Kharijis.

The chief formulator of the Sunni creed was Abu al-Hasan al-Ash'ari (d. 935), a Mu'tazili who later came under the influence of the traditionists *(ahl al-hadith)* and turned the tables on his erstwhile preceptor and fellows among the Mu'tazilah. For al-Ash'ari, people cannot produce their own actions; rather, God does, and neither man nor nature has any powers or potencies before the actual act. At the time of the act, for example, when fire actually burns, God creates a power for that particular act. Thus God creates an action, while human beings "appropriate" or "acquire" *(kasaba)* it and thereby become responsible for "their" acts. The Ash'ari theologians are, therefore, atomists in terms of both time and space, and they reject causation and the entire idea of movement or process. God is under no obligation to do what human beings call justice; on the contrary, whatever God does is just. Justice involves reference to certain norms under which the agent works; since God has no norms to obey, there is no question of doing justice on his part. He also promised in the Qur'an that he will reward those who do good and punish those who do evil, and this is the proper and only assurance we have of the fate of human beings; if he had chosen to do the reverse, no one could question him. It also follows that good and bad are not natural characteristics of human acts, but that acts become good or bad by God's declaration through the revelation that he has been sending since Adam, the first prophet. It is, therefore, futile to probe rationally into the purposes of divine injunctions, for these are the result of God's will.

On the question of divine attributes, al-Ash'ari taught that these are real, although they are "neither God, nor other than God." God has an eternal attribute of "speech," which al-Ash'ari called "psychic speech," manifested in all divinely revealed books. Although the Qur'an as God's "psychic speech" is eternal, as something recited, written, and heard it is also created: one cannot point to a written copy of the Qur'an or its recital and say "This is eternal."

A contemporary of al-Ash'ari, the Central Asian theologian al-Maturidi (d. 944), also formulated an "official" Sunni creed and theology that in some fundamental ways was nearer to the Mu'tazili stance. He recognized "power-before-the-act" in man and also declared good and bad to be natural and knowable by human reason. Whereas al-Ash'ari belonged to the Shafi'i school of law, which was based principally on *hadith*, al-Maturidi was a member of the Hanafi school, which gave greater scope to reason. Yet, in subsequent centuries, the former's views almost completely eclipsed the latter's, although in the Indian subcontinent such prominent thinkers as Ahmad Sirhindi (d. 1624) and Shah Wali Allah of Delhi (d. 1762) criticized Ash'ari theology. The reason behind this sweeping and enduring success of Ash'ari theology seems to be the overwhelming spread of Sufism (particularly in its pantheistic form), which, in theological terms, was much more akin to Ash'ari thought than to that of Mu'tazilah or even the Maturidiyah, in that it sought to obliterate the human self in the all-embracing and all-effacing self of God, the most important nodal point of this conjunction being al-Ghazali.

In the intellectual field, as we shall see, Sufism grew at the expense of theology and utilized the worldview of the Muslim philosophers. On the moral and spiritual planes, however, the powerful corroboration of theology and Sufism stimulated the vehement reaction of the jurist and theologian Ibn Taymiyah (d. 1328). Struggling all his life against popular Sufi superstitions, against worship of saints and their shrines, and against Ash'ari theology, he tried to resurrect the moral activism of the Qur'an and the *sunnah*. He regarded the Mu'tazili denial of God's role in human actions as an error but considered the Ash'ari denial of human free and effective will as extremely dangerous and, in fact, stated that pantheistic Sufis and the Ash'ari theologians were considerably worse than not only the Mu'tazilah but even the Zoroastrians. He held that the Zoroastrians' postulation of two gods was undoubtedly an error but argued that they had been forced into this belief by the undeniable distinction between good and evil that both Ash'ari theology and pantheistic Sufism virtually obliterated, leaving no basis for any worthwhile religion. (As we shall see, a similar argument was conducted within Sufism by a later Indian Sufi, Ahmad Sirhindi.) Ibn Taymiyah sought to solve the perennial problem of free will versus divine omnipotence by saying that the actual application of the principle of divine omnipotence occurs only in the past, while the *shariah* imperatives are relevant only to the future. His teaching remained more or less dormant until the eighteenth century, when it inspired the Wahhabi religious revolution in the Arabian Peninsula.

SUFISM. The mainspring of Sufism lay in the desire to cultivate the inner life and to attain a deeper, personal understanding of Islam. Among the many proposed etymologies of the word *sufi*, the most credible is the one that derives it from *suf*, meaning "coarse wool," a reference to the kind of garb that many Sufis wore. The first phase of this spiritual movement was definitely moral, and the works of most early Sufis, those of the second and third centuries AH, show a preoccupation with constant self-examination and close scrutiny of one's motivation.

Sufi doctrine. The dialectic of the trappings and self-deception of the soul developed by Hakim al-Tirmidhi (d. 898) in his *Khatm al-awliya'* (The Seal of the Saints) provides one extraordinary example of spiritual insight, but this strongly moral trend continues from Hasan al-Basri (d. 728) through al-Muhasibi (d. 857) to his pupil al-Junayd (d. 910). The essence of their doctrine is moral contrition and detachment of the mind from the "good things" of the world *(zuhd)*. But from its very early times, Sufism also had a strong devotional element, as exemplified by the woman saint Rabi'ah al-'Adawiyah (d. 801). The goal of love of God led to the doctrine of *fana'* or "annihilation" (that is, of the human self in God). There were definitely Hellenistic Christian influences at work here. But the annihilation ideal was soon amended into "survival *(baqa')* after annihilation," or (re)gaining of a new self, and this formula was given different interpretations.

Most Sufis taught that, after the destruction of the human attributes (not the self), mortals acquire divine attributes (not the divine self) and "live in" them. The firm view of the orthodox and influential Sufi al-Junayd was that when a person sheds human attributes and these attributes undergo annihilation, that person comes to think that he or she has become God. But God soon gives that person the consciousness of otherness (not alienation) from God, which is extremely painful and is only somewhat relieved by God's also giving the consolation that this is the highest state attainable by human beings. Yet there were also Sufis who, most probably under the influence of Hellenistic Christianity, believed in human transubstantiation into God. In 922, al-Hallaj, a representative of this school, was charged with having uttered the blasphemous statement "I am God" and was crucified in Baghdad. Yet, a somewhat earlier mystic, al-Bistami (d. 874), who is said to have committed even graver blasphemies, was never touched by the law. It may be, as some contend, that the real reasons behind al-Hallaj's execution were political, or it may be related to the fact that al-Hallaj was in the capital, Baghdad, whereas al-Bistami lived in an outlying province.

This example of such divergent interpretations of a fundamental doctrine should warn us that with Sufism we are dealing with a truly protean phenomenon: not only do interpretations differ, but experiences themselves must differ as well. However, under pressure from the *'ulama'*, who refused to acknowledge any objective validity for the Sufi experience, the Sufis for-

One of the truly creative manifestations of religious life in Islam is the mystical tradition, known as Sufism.

PAGE 630

mulated a doctrine of "spiritual stations" *(maqamat)* that adepts successively attained through their progressive spiritual itinerary *(suluk)*. These stations are as objectifiable as any experience can be. Although the various schools have differed in the lists of these stations, they usually enumerate them as follows: detachment from the world *(zuhd)*, patience *(sabr)*, gratitude *(shukr)* for whatever God gives, love *(hubb)*, and pleasure *(rida)* with whatever God desires.

After the violent death of al-Hallaj, another important doctrine of the dialectic of Sufi experience was developed by orthodox Sufis. According to this doctrine, the Sufi alternates between two different types of spiritual states. One type is the experience of unity (where all multiplicity disappears) and of the inner reality. In this state the Sufi is "absent" from the world and is "with God"; this is the state of "intoxication" *(sukr)*. The other state, that of "sobriety" *(sahw)*, occurs when the Sufi "returns" to multiplicity and is "with the world." Whereas many Sufis had earlier contended that "intoxication" is superior to "sobriety" and that, therefore, the saints *(awliya')* are superior to the prophets (who are "with the world" and legislate for society), the orthodox Sufis now asserted the opposite, for the goodness of saints is limited to themselves, whereas the goodness of prophets is transitive, since they save the society as well as themselves.

Ibn 'Arabi is unique because he was both an original thinker and synthesizer.

PAGE 631

On the basis of this doctrine, al-Hallaj's famous statement was rationalized as "one uttered in a state of intoxication" and as such not to be taken at face value. But it was al-Ghazali who effected a meaningful and enduring synthesis of Sufi "innerism" and the orthodox belief system. A follower of al-Ash'ari in theology and of al-Shafi'i in law, al-Ghazali also studied thoroughly the philosophic tradition of Ibn Sina (known in the West as Avicenna, d. 1037), and although he refuted its important theses bearing on religion in the famous work *Tahafut al-falasifah* (The Incoherence of the Philosophers), he was influenced by it in important ways as well. He then adopted Sufism as his "way to God" and composed his magnum opus, *Ihya' 'ulum al-din* (The Revivification of the Sciences of the Faith). His net accomplishment lies in the fact that he tried to infuse a new spiritual life into law and theology on the one hand and to instill sobriety and responsibility into Sufism on the other, for he repudiated the Sufi *shatahat* (intoxicated utterances) as meaningless.

Within a century after al-Ghazali's death, however, a Sufi doctrine based on out-and-out monism was being preached by Ibn al-'Arabi (d. 1240). Born in Spain and educated there and in North Africa, Ibn al-'Arabi eventually traveled to the Muslim East; he lived for many years in Mecca, where he wrote his major work, *Al-futuhat al-makkiyah* (The Meccan Discoveries), and finally settled in Damascus, where he died. Ibn al-'Arabi's writings are the high-water mark of theosophic Sufism, which goes beyond the ascetic or ecstatic Sufism of the earlier period, by laying cognitive claims to a unique, intuitive experience (known as *kashf*, "direct discovery," or *dhawq*, "taste") that was immune from error and radically different from and superior to the rational knowledge of the philosophers and the theologians.

Ibn al-'Arabi's doctrine, known as Unity of Being *(wahdat al-wujud)*, teaches that everything is in one sense God and in another sense not-God. He holds that, given God, the transcendent, another factor that in itself is not describable "either as existent or as nonexistent" comes to play a crucial role in the unfolding of reality. This factor is neither God nor the world; it is a "third thing," but it is God with God and world with the world. It is the stuff of which both the attributes of God (for God as transcendent has no names and no attributes) and the content of the world are made. It is eternal with the eternal and temporal with the temporal; it does not exist partially and divided in things: the whole of it is God, and the whole of it is the world, and the whole of it is everything in the world. This "third thing" turns out finally to be the Perfect or Primordial Human Being (who is identified with the eternal, not the temporal, Muhammad), in whose mirror God sees himself and who sees himself in God's mirror. This immanent God and Human Being are not only interdependent but are the obverse and converse of the same coin. There is little doubt that Ibn al-'Arabi represents a radical humanism, a veritable apotheosis of humanity.

This monistic Sufism found certain devoted and distinguished exponents in Ibn al-'Arabi's school, in both prose and poetry, the most illustrious and influential representative of the latter being Jalal al-Din Rumi (d. 1273), whose *Mathnavi* in Persian has been hailed as the "Qur'an in the Persian language." Through poetry, moreover, it has had a profound and literally incalculable influence on the general intellectual culture of Islam, in terms of a liberal humanism, indeed, latitudinarianism, and among the lower strata of Islamic society even antinomianism. A striking feature of this antinomianism, where orthodoxy was unashamedly scoffed at and ridiculed for its rigidity and narrow confines, is that it was tolerated by the orthodox only when it was expressed in poetry, not in prose. Also, because of the latitude and broad range of Sufi spirituality, from roughly the twelfth century to the impact of modernization in the nineteenth century, the more creative Muslim minds drifted from orthodoxy into the Sufi fold, and philosophy itself, although it remained rational in its methods, became mystical in its goals.

I have already noted the severe reaction against Sufi excesses on the part of Ibn Taymiyah in the fourteenth century. It may be mentioned here that for Ibn Taymiyah the ultimate distinction between good and evil is absolutely necessary for any worthwhile religion that seeks to inculcate moral responsibility, and further, that this distinction is totally dependent upon belief in pure monotheism and the equally absolute distinction between man and God. He sets little value on the formal fact that a person belongs to the Muslim community; he evaluates all human beings on the scale of monotheism. Thus, as seen above, he regards pantheistic Sufis (and, to a large extent, because of their predestinarianism, the Ash'ariyah as well), as being equivalent to polytheists; then come the Shi'ah and Christians because both consider a human being to be a divine incarnation; and last come Zoroastrians and the Mu'tazilah, since both posit two ultimate powers.

Later, the Indian shaykh of the Naqshbandi order, Ahmad Sirhindi (d. 1624), undertook a similar reform of Sufism from within. His massive *Maktubat-i Ahmad Sirhindi* (Letters), the main vehicle of his reform, besides the training of disciples, was twice translated into Ottoman Turkish and was influential in Turkey; in the Arab Middle East, his reformist thought was carried and spread in the nineteenth century. Sirhindi, who accepts Ibn al-'Arabi's philosophical scheme at the metaphysical level, introduces a radical moral dualism at the level of God's attributes and, instead of identifying the temporal world with the stuff of divine attributes, as Ibn al-'Arabi does, regards that world as being essentially evil, but evil that has to be transformed into good through the activity of the divine attributes. The basic error of the common Sufis, for him, is that instead of helping to transform this evil into good, as God wants to do through his attributes, they flee from it. The spiritual heights to which they think they are ascending are, therefore, a pure delusion, for the real good is this evil, "this earth," once it has been transformed. But this realization requires a constant struggle with evil, not a flight from it. It is a prophet, then, not a saint, who undertakes the real divine task, and the true test of a person's ascent to real spiritual heights is whether he or she reenters the earth in order to improve and redeem it. Despite the efforts of Ibn Taymiyah, Sirhindi, and other figures, however, Ibn al-'Arabi's influence has been, until today, very strong in the Muslim world, not just on Sufism but on Islamic poetry as well.

Sufi orders. Up to the twelfth century, Sufism was a matter of limited circles of a spiritual elite that might be aptly described as "schools" with different spiritual techniques and even different spiritual ideologies. From the twelfth century on, however, they developed into networks of orders, involving the masses on a large scale. Systems of Sufi hospices—called variously *zawiyahs* (in Arabic), *tekkes* (in Turkish), and *khanagahs* (in Iran and the Indian subcontinent)—where the Sufi shaykh lived (usually with his family in the interior of the building) and guided his clientele, grew up from Morocco to Southeast Asia. Although in some of the hospices orthodox religious disciplines such as theology and law were taught along with Sufi works, orthodox education was generally carried on in the *madrasahs*, or colleges, while only Sufi works were taught in the Sufi centers.

Sufi orders can be divided into those that are global and those that are regional. The most global is the Qadiri order, named after 'Abd al-Qadir al-Jilani (d. 1166), with branches all over the world that are tied only loosely to the center at Baghdad. Somewhat more regional are the Suhrawardi and the Naqshbandi orders. The latter, which originated in Central Asia in the thirteenth century, formulated an explicit ideology early in its career to try to influence the rulers and their courts, with the result that they have often been politically active. One of its branches, the Khalwatiyah, played a prominent role in modernizing reform in Turkey during the eighteenth and nineteenth centuries. Several of the Sufi orders have been associated with guilds and sometimes, particularly in Ottoman Turkey, have been directly involved in social protests and political rebellions against official oppression and injustice.

Another broad and important division is that between urban and "rustic" orders. The former, particularly the Naqshbandi order and its offshoots, were refined and close to the orthodoxy of the *'ulama'*, with the result that an increasingly large number of the *'ulama'* gradually enrolled themselves in these urban Sufi orders, particularly the orthodox ones. By contrast, many of the rustic orders were without discipline and law *(bi-shar')*, especially in the Indian subcontinent, where they were often indistinguishable from the Hindu *sadhus* (monks). With the spread of modernization, Sufism and Sufi orders have suffered greatly; in Turkey, they were suppressed by Mustafa Kemal Atatürk in the 1920s, and their endowments were confiscated by the government. It is interesting to note, however, that since the mid-twentieth century some orders have experienced a revival in the industrial urban centers of Muslim lands, probably in reaction to the excessively materialistic outlook generated by modernization, while in Central Asia their underground networks are waging anti-Soviet activities in an organized manner. Correspondingly, in the West, several intellectuals, such as Frithjof Schuon and Martin Lings, have actively turned to Sufi devotion to escape the spiritual vacuity created by their own overly materialistic culture.

SECTS. There are two broad divisions within the

"God changes not what is in a people, until they change what is in themselves."

THE QUR'AN 13:11

Muslim community, the Sunnis and the Shi'ah. The theological views and the legal schools of the Sunnis—the majority of the community—have been dealt with above. The Shi'i schism grew out of the claim of the Shi'ah (a word meaning "partisans," in this context "the partisans of 'Ali") that following the Prophet, rule over Muslims belongs rightfully only to 'Ali, Muhammad's cousin and son-in-law, and to his descendants. This doctrine, known as "legitimism," was opposed to the Khariji view that rule is open to any good Muslim on a universal basis and to the Sunni view, which was no more than a rationalization of actual facts, that "rulers must come from the Quraysh," the Prophet's tribe, but not necessarily from his clan or house.

The Twelver Shi'ah today constitute the great majority of the Shi'ah and are often referred to simply by the latter name.

PAGE 598

The Shi'ah, in early Islam, were primarily sociopolitical dissidents, sheltering under the umbrella of "the house of the Prophet" but actually representing various elements of social protest against Umayyad Arab heavy-handedness and injustices. But it was not long before they began establishing an ideological and theological base for themselves. Until well into the third century AH, Shi'i theology was crude and materialistic: it asserted that God was a corporeal being who sat on an actual throne and created space by physical motion. Hisham ibn al-Hakam (d. 814?), among the best known of the early Shi'i theologians, is reported to have said that God was "a little smaller than Mount Abu Qabis." There were several other early Shi'i theologians who attributed some kind of body, including a physical body, to God, but beginning in the latter half of the ninth century, Shi'i theology was radically transformed, inheriting and asserting with increasing force the Mu'tazili doctrine of human free will against the Sunnis.

In the thirteenth century CE, through the work of the philosopher, theologian, and scientist Nasir al-Din Tusi (d. 1273), philosophy entered Shi'i theology, a process that was further facilitated by Tusi's student, the influential theologian al-Hilli (d. 1325). In his work on the creed, *Tajrid al-'aqa'id* (Concise Statement of the Creeds), which was subsequently commented upon by both Shi'i and Sunni theologians, Tusi describes man as "creator of his own actions." Tusi, however, rejects the philosophical thesis of the eternity of the world. Here it is interesting to compare this Shi'i development with the Sunni position that was articulated about three-quarters of a century earlier at the hands of Fakhr al-Din al-Razi (d. 1209), who expanded the official Sunni theology by incorporating into it a discussion of major philosophical themes. But whereas the Shi'ah accepted many philosophical theses into their theology, al-Razi and other Sunnis after him refuted all the philosophical theses point by point, thus erecting a theology that was an exclusive alternative to philosophy. Against this background is probably to be understood the fact that while philosophy was exorcized from the curricula in the Arab world from the thirteenth century on and declined sharply in the rest of the Sunni world, it reached its zenith in Shi'i Iran in the seventeenth century and continues unabated until today, although many of the orthodox Shi'ah continue to oppose it.

In law, the Twelver Shi'i school has long been recognized as valid by the Sunnis, despite differences, the most conspicuous being that Shi'i law recognizes a temporary marriage that may be contracted for a fixed period—a year, a month, a week, or even a day. Among the Shi'ah, the nearest school to Sunnism, particularly in law, is that of the Zaydiyah in Yemen, whose founder Zayd ibn 'Ali (d. 738), a brother of the fifth imam of the Shi'ah, was a theology student of the first Mu'tazili teacher, Wasil ibn 'Ata' (d. 748).

But the most characteristic doctrine of the Shi'ah is their esotericism. This has a practical aspect called *taqiyah*, which means dissimulation of one's real beliefs in a generally hostile atmosphere. This doctrine, apparently adopted in early Islamic times, when the Shi'ah became a subterranean movement, as it were, in the wake of political failure, subsequently became a part of Shi'i dogma. But in its theoretical aspect esotericism is defined by the doctrine that religion, and particularly the Qur'an, has, besides the apparent, "external" meaning, hidden esoteric meanings that can be known only through spiritual contact with the Hidden Imam. In the early centuries of Islam, this principle of esotericism was probably unbridled and fanciful in its application, as is apparent from the ninth- to tenth-century Qur'an commentary of al-Qummi. But as Shiism was progressively permeated by rational thought, esotericism became more systematic, even if it may often seem farfetched (as in certain philosophical interpretations of the Qur'an). As pointed out earlier, the Sufis also patently practiced esotericism in understanding the materials of religion, particularly the Qur'an; the ultimate common source of both Shiism and Sufism lies in gnosticism and other comparable currents of thought, and, indeed, Ibn al-'Arabi's interpretations are often purely the work of his uncontrolled imagination.

Beginning from about the middle of the tenth century, when the Sunni caliph in Baghdad came under the control of the Shi'i Buyid dynasty, there were public commemorations of the martyrdom of Husayn at Karbala on the tenth of Muharram ('Ashura'). These ceremonies caused riots in Baghdad and still do so in some countries such as Pakistan and India today. The commemoration is traditionally marked by public processions in which participants lamenting the death of the Prophet's grandson beat their breasts and backs with heavy iron chains. Scenes of Husayn's death are recreated in passion plays known as *ta'ziyahs*, and he is eulogized in moving sermons and poetry recitals. Fed from childhood with such representational enactments of this event, a Shi'i Muslim is likely to develop a deep sense of tragedy and injustice resulting in an ideal of martyrdom that is capable of being manipulated into outbursts of frenzied emotionalism, like the spectacular events of the Iranian Revolution.

Shii subsects. In the first and second centuries of the Islamic era, Shiism served as an umbrella for all kinds of ideologies, with a general social protest orientation, and the earliest heresiographers enumerate dozens of Shi'i sects, several with extremely heretical and antinomian views. The main surviving body, the Ithna 'Ashariyah, or Twelvers, number probably between fifty and sixty million people. All other sects (except the Zaydiyah of Yemen) are regarded even by the Twelvers themselves as heretical extremists *(ghulat)*. The main one among these, the Isma'iliyah, or Seveners, broke with the Twelvers in a dispute over which son of the sixth imam was to be recognized as the latter's successor: the Twelvers refused to recognize the elder son, Isma'il, because he drank wine, while the Seveners did recognize him (thus the name Isma'ili) and continue to await his return.

The Isma'iliyah established a powerful and prosperous empire in North Africa and Egypt from the tenth to the twelfth centuries. Prior to this, the Isma'iliyah had been an underground revolutionary movement, but once they attained political power, they settled down as part of the status quo. Since the late eleventh century, they have been divided into two branches: the Nizariyah, commonly known by the name Assassins, who were active in Syria and Iran, and in recent years have been followers of a hereditary Aga Khan, and the Musta'liyah, who are mainly centered in Bombay. Isma'ili philosophy, which is reflected in the *Rasa'il Ikhwan al-Safa'* (Epistles of the Brethren of Purity), produced by a secret society in the late ninth century, is essentially based on Neoplatonic thought with influences from gnosticism and occult sects.

The Isma'ili sect, which was organized and propagated through a well-knit network of missionaries *(du'ah)*, adheres to a belief in cyclic universes: each cycle comprises seven Speakers, or Messengers, with a revelation and a law; each Speaker is followed in turn by one of the seven Silent Ones, or Imams. The last imam, when he appears, will abrogate all organized religions and their laws and will institute a new era of a universal religion. During the leadership of the third Aga Khan (d. 1957), the Isma'ili community started drawing closer to the mainstream of Islam, a trend that seems to be gaining further strength at present under Karim Aga Khan's leadership: Isma'ili intellectuals now describe their faith as the "Isma'ili *tariqah* [spiritual order] of Islam." There are other "extremist" subsects within the Shi'ah, including the Druze, Nusayriyah, and 'Alawiyun. Of these, the Druze are the most prominent. This sect arose in the eleventh century as a cult of the eccentric Fatimid ruler al-Hakim, who mysteriously disappeared in 1021.

Later sects. In more recent times, there have been two noteworthy sectarian developments, one within Shi'i Islam in mid-nineteenth-century Iran and the other within Sunni Islam in late nineteenth-century India. During an anticlerical movement in Iran, a certain Muhammad 'Ali of Shiraz claimed to be the Bab, or "Gate," to God. He was executed by the government under pressure from the *'ulama'* in 1850. After him, his two disciples, Subh-i Azal and Baha' Allah, went different ways, and the latter subsequently declared his faith to be an independent religion outside Islam. While the origin of the Baha'i religion was marked by strong eschatological overtones, it later developed an ideology of pacifism and internationalism and won a considerable number of converts in North America early in the twentieth century. In Iran itself, Babis and Baha'is are frequent targets of clerical persecution, and many of them have been executed under the Khomeini regime.

The Sunni sect called the Ahmadiyah arose in the 1880s when Ghulam Ahmad of Qadiyan (a village in East Punjab) laid claim to prophethood. He claimed to be at once a "manifestation" of the prophet Muhammad, the Second Advent of Jesus, and an avatar of Krsna for the Hindus. It is possible that he wanted to unite various religions under his leadership. After his death, his followers constituted themselves as an independent community with an elected *khalifah* (successor; i. e., caliph). When the first caliph died in 1911, the Ahmadiyah split in two: the main body carried on the founder's claim to prophethood under Ahmad's son, Bashir al-Din, while the other, the Lahore group, claimed that Ghulam Ahmad was not a prophet, nor had he claimed to be one, but rather that he was a reformer or "renovator" *(mujaddid)* of Islam. Both groups have been active with missionary zeal, particularly in Europe and America. In 1974, the National Assembly of Pakistan, where the main body had established its headquarters after the creation of the state, declared both groups to be "non-Muslim minorities."

MODERNISM. In the eighteenth century, against a background of general stagnation, a puritanical fundamentalist movement erupted in Arabia under Muhammad ibn 'Abd al-Wahhab (1703-1792). The movement called for a return to the purist Islam of the Qur'an and the *sunnah* and its unadulterated monotheism, uncompromised by the popular cults of saints and their shrines. Ibn 'Abd al-Wahhab married into the family of Sa'ud, a chieftain of Najd, who accepted his teaching and brought all Arabia under his ruling ideol-

The spiritualist doctrine of Shiism views the ruh *as the pure breath of all matter, a spiritual substance that is immortal by nature.*

PAGE 319

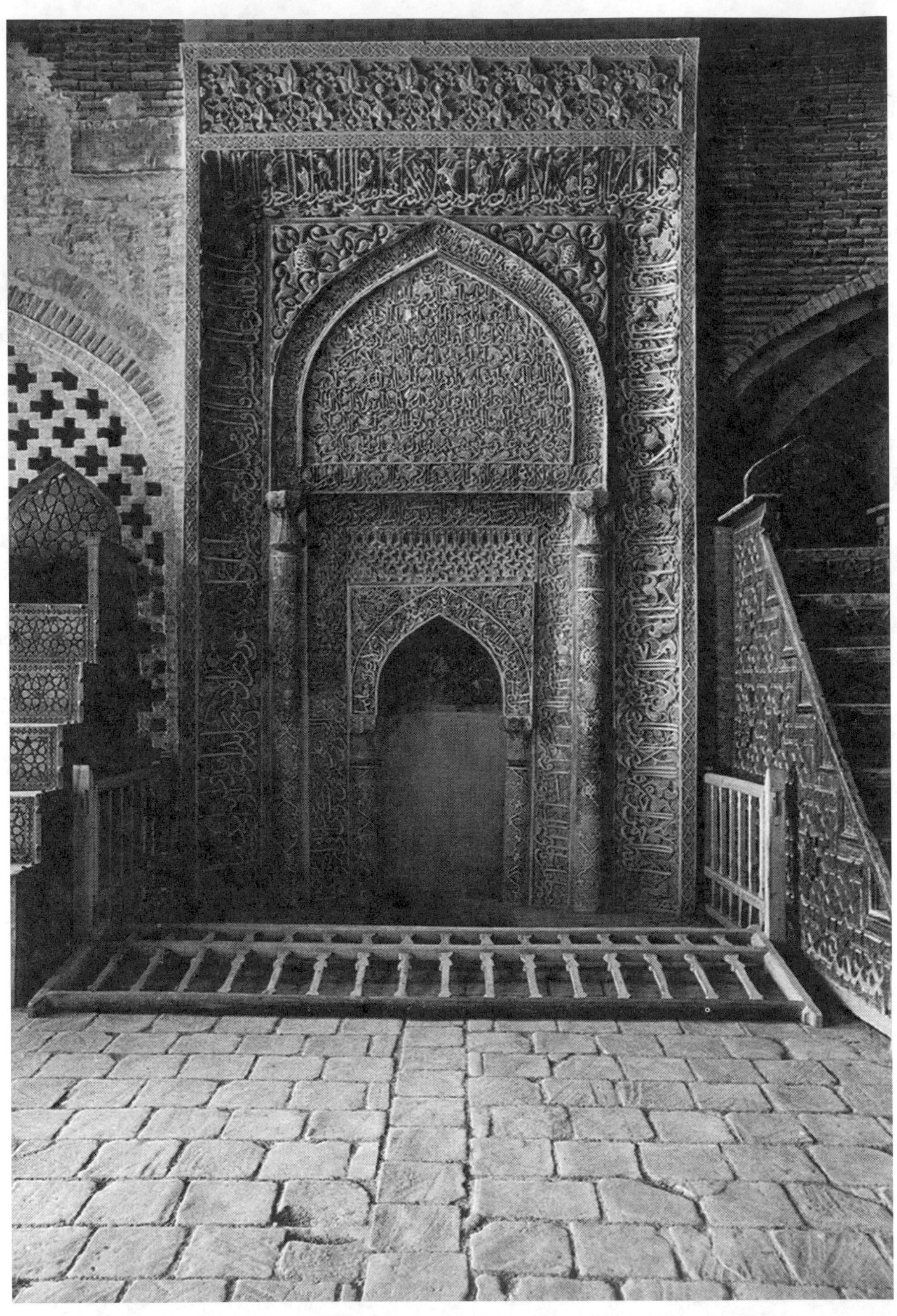

HOLY PLACE *The Friday Mosque in Isfahan, Iran was built during the fourteenth century. The sacred mihrab pictured here was built to face Mecca.* ROGER WOOD/© CORBIS

ogy. At the same time, in the Indian subcontinent, Shah Wali Allah of Delhi, a highly sophisticated intellectual (said to have been a fellow student of Ibn 'Abd al-Wahhab during his stay in Medina), also advocated a return to pristine Islam although, unlike his Arabian contemporary, he was a Sufi at a high spiritual level.

In the nineteenth century a reformist militant group called the Jihad movement arose out of Wali Allah's school, and three more movements followed in Africa—the Sanusi in Libya, the Fulbe in West Africa, and the Mahdists in the Sudan. Although these three movements emerged from different environments, common to all of them was a reformist thrust in terms of the recovery of the "true pristine Islam" of the Qur'an and the Prophet, particularly emphasizing monotheism; an insistence upon *ijtihad*, that is, rejection of the blind following of tradition in both theology and law in favor of an attempt to discover and formulate new solutions to Islamic problems; and finally, resort to militant methods, including the imposition of their reformist ideologies by force. In addition, these movements generally brought to the center of consciousness the necessity of social and moral reforms as such, without recourse to the rewards and punishments of the hereafter. In other words, all three were characterized by a certain positivistic orientation.

While these premodernist reform movements laid great emphasis on *ijtihad*, in practice their *ijtihad* meant that Muslims should be enabled to disengage themselves from their present "degenerate" condition and to recover pristine Islam. Also, it is a general characteristic of all fundamentalist movements that in order to "simplify" religion and make it practical, they debunk the intellectualism of the past and discourage the growth of future intellectualism. In such cases education becomes so simplified that it is virtually sterile, thus leaving little possibility for *ijtihad*. Of the fundamentalist groups I have described above, the progenitors of the Indian and Libyan movements were sophisticated and accomplished scholars, but the leaders of the other three had only a modicum of learning and were primarily activists.

Nonetheless, these movements signaled real stirrings in the soul of Islam and paved the way for the intellectual activity of the Muslim modernists—Muslims who had been exposed to Western ideas and who, by integrating certain key ones among them with the teaching of the Qur'an, produced brilliant solutions to the crucial problems then faced by Islamic society. The influence of premodernist reformism upon the modernists is apparent from the fact that they keep the Qur'an and the tradition of the Prophet as ultimate referents for reform while criticizing or rejecting the medieval heritage. Thus, although their individual views regarding, for example, the relationship between faith and reason differ, all of them insist on the cultivation of positive sciences, appealing to numerous verses of the Qur'an that state that the entire universe has been made subservient to good ends of humankind and that we must study and use it.

MUSLIM POPULATIONS PER WORLD REGION

	Muslim	Total Population**
Africa	1,986,000	748,130,000
Asia	786,991,000	3,513,218,000
Europe*	1,650,000	727,678,000
Latin America	760,000	490,444,000
Northern America	1,365,000	295,677,000
Oceania	323,000	28,973,000
Total	793,075,000	5,804,120,000

*Includes former Soviet Union.
**United Nations Medium Variant Figures, mid 1996
Source: *The 1997 Britannica Book of the Year*

"I believe in any book God may have revealed."

THE QUR'AN 42:15

In the political sphere, citing Qur'an 42:38, which says that Muslims should decide all their affairs through mutual consultation (*shura*, actually a pre-Islamic Arab institution confirmed by the Qur'an), the modernists contended that whereas the Qur'an teaches democracy, the Muslims had deviated from this norm and acquiesced to autocratic rule. Similarly, on the subject of women, the modernists argued that the Qur'an had granted equal rights to men and women (except in certain areas of economic life where the burden of earning and supporting the family is squarely laid on men), but the medieval practice of the Muslims had clearly departed from the Qur'an and ended by depriving women of their rights. Regarding polygamy, the modernists stated that permission for polygamy (up to four wives) had been given under special conditions, with the proviso that if the husband could not do justice among his co-wives then he must marry only one wife, and that finally the Qur'an itself had declared such justice to be impossible to attain (4:129).

Of the half-dozen most prominent names in Islamic modernism, two were *'ulama'*-trained along traditional lines: Jamal al-Din al-Afghani (1839-1897), a fiery activist with a magnetic personality, and his disciple, the Egyptian shaykh Muhammad 'Abduh (1845-1905). Three were lay intellectuals with modern education: the Turk Namik Kemal (1840-1888) and the two Indians Ameer Ali (d. 1928) and Muhammad Iqbal (1877-1938), while the Indian Sayyid Ahmad Khan (1817-1898), the most radical of them all in theological views, was a premodern lay-educated scholar. Yet, despite their differences and the fact that none of them, except for al-Afghani and 'Abduh, ever met any of the others, they shared the basic tenet—*à la* premodernist reform movements—that medieval Islam had deviated on certain crucial points from the normative Islam of the Qur'an; this argument runs through all the issues that they discuss.

However, while these modernists sought reform within their own societies, they also waged controversies with the West on the latter's understanding of Islam, and some of them, particularly Iqbal, argued about the West's own performance on the stage of history. Iqbal bitterly and relentlessly accused the West of cheating humanity of its basic values with the glittering mirage of its technology, of exploiting the territories it colonized in the name of spreading humanitarian values, which it itself flouted by waging internecine wars born of sheer economic savagery, and of dewomanizing the women and dilapidating the family institution in the name of progress. Iqbal was an equally strong critic of the world Muslim society, which for him represented nothing more than a vast graveyard of Islam. He called the whole world to the "true Islam" of the Qur'an and the Prophet, a living, dynamic Islam that believed in the harnessing of the forces of history for the ethical development of mankind.

Organizations such as the Muslim Brotherhood or the jamaat are regarded by some Muslim regimes as dangerous foci of opposition and have thus met with violent repression.

PAGE 475

Iqbal and others, such as the Egyptian Rashid Rida (d. 1935), proved to belong to a transitional stage from modernism to a new attitude, perhaps best described as neofundamentalism, for unlike the fundamentalism of the premodernist reform movements, the current neofundamentalism is, in large measure, a reaction to modernism, but it has also been importantly influenced by modernism. This influence can best be seen on two major issues: first, the contention that Islam is a total way of life, including all fields of human private and public life, and is not restricted to certain religious rites such as the Five Pillars (to which the Islam of the traditionalist *'ulama'* had become practically confined); and, second, that cultivation of scientific knowledge and technology is desirable within Islam.

Besides emphasis on technology (although Iran appears to pay only lip service to science and technology), neofundamentalists have, on the one hand, oversimplified the traditionalist curriculum of Islamic studies, and, on the other, embarked upon a program of "islamization" of Western knowledge. Besides these points, the most basic factor common to the neofundamentalist phenomena is a strong assertion of Islamic identity over and against the West, an assertion that hits equally strongly at most modernist reforms, particularly on the issue of the status and role of women in society. This powerful desire to repudiate the West, therefore, leads the neofundamentalist to emphasize certain points (as a *riposte* to the modernist, who is often seen as a pure and simple westernizer) that would most distinguish Islam from the West. Besides the role of women, which is seen to lie at home, the heaviest emphasis falls on the islamization of economy through the reinstitution of *zakat* and the abolition of bank interest (which is identified with *riba*, or usury, prohibited by the Qur'an). No neofundamentalist government in the Muslim world—including Iran and Pakistan—however, has been successful in implementing either of the two policies, while the Libyan leader Mu'ammar al-Qadhdhafi has declared that the modern banking institution is not covered by the Qur'anic prohibition of *riba*.

Neofundamentalism is by no means a uniform phenomenon. Apart from the fact that there exist, particularly in the Arab Middle East, extremist splinter groups of neofundamentalists that are strikingly reminiscent of the Kharijis of early Islamic times, on most crucial issues, such as democracy or the nature of Islamic legislation, even the mainstream elements are sharply divided. While in Libya, for example, Mu'ammar al-Qadhdhafi has taken a most radical stand on legislation, repudiating the precepts of *hadith* as its source and replacing them with the will of the people, the current rulers of Pakistan and Iran show little confidence in the will of the people. The most interesting attitude in this connection is that of the religious leaders of Iran: while almost all reformers since the mid-nineteenth century—including Shi'i thinkers such as Ameer Ali—have insisted that there can be no theocracy in Islam since Islam has no priesthood, the Iranian religious leaders are asserting precisely the opposite, namely, that Islam does have a priesthood and that this priestly class must rule, a position expounded even prior to the Islamic Revolution by Ayatollah Khomeini, the chief ruler of Iran, in his work *Vilayat-i faqih* (Rule of the Jurist, 1971). [*See also* Muslim Brotherhood.]

Finally, the phenomenon of international Islamic conferences in modern Islam is also to be noted since, in the absence of political unity in the Muslim world, these help the cause of unity of sentiment, if not uniformity of mind. The beginnings of this phenomenon go back to the 1920s, when conferences were held in Cairo and Mecca to deliberate on the possibility of reinstituting the caliphate after Atatürk abolished it with the secularization of the Turkish state. But from the mid-1940s on, as Muslim countries gained independence from European colonial rule, the sentiment for international Muslim gatherings became progressively stronger. In the mid-1960s all the national and international private Islamic organizations became affiliated with the semiofficial Saudi-sponsored Muslim World League (Rabitat al-'Alam al-Islami), headquartered in Mecca; the league finances Islamic causes both in the Muslim world and in Western countries, where large numbers of Muslim settlers are building mosques and Islamic centers and developing Islamic community life, including programs for education.

At the same time, since the 1969 Muslim Summit Conference held in Rabat, Morocco, an Islamic Secretariat has been set up in Jiddah, Saudi Arabia, as the administrative center for the Organization of Islamic Conferences (OIC) on the state level. Besides holding summit meetings, this organization maintains a developmental economic agenda through which interest-free development banks have been set up, financed principally by oil-rich Arab countries to help poorer Muslim countries (this is in addition to the aid given to non-Muslim countries). All these conferences, whether organized by the OIC or the World Muslim League, discuss political problems affecting the Muslim world and try to formulate a common response to them, through the United Nations and its agencies or through other channels.

ISLAM'S ATTITUDE TO OTHER RELIGIONS. According to Qur'anic teaching divine guidance is universal, and God regards all peoples as equal. Every prophet's message, although immediately addressed to a given people, is nevertheless of universal import and must be believed by all humanity. Muhammad himself is made to declare, "I believe in any book God may have revealed" (Qur'an 42:15), and all Muslims are required to do likewise. This is so because God is one; the source of revelation is one, and humankind is also one. The office of prophethood is, in fact, indivisible.

Muslims, however, have, from earliest times, considered Muhammad to be the bearer of the last and consummate revelation. Nevertheless, there is a tension within the Qur'an itself on this issue. In keeping with its fundamental teaching that prophethood is indivisible, the Qur'an, of course, invites Jews and Christians to Islam; it insists on the unity of religion, deplores the diversity of religions and religious communities, which it insists is based on willful neglect of truth, and denounces both Jews and Christians as "partisans, sectarians," with "each sect rejoicing in what itself has" (30:32).

On the other hand, it states that although religion is essentially one, God himself has given different "institutions and approaches" to different communities so that he might "test them in what he has given them," and that they might compete with each other in goodness (5:48), which implies that these different institutional arrangements have positive value and are somehow meant to be permanent. In fact, the Qur'an categorically states that whether a person is a Muslim or a Jew or a Christian or a Sabian, "whosoever believes in God and the Last Day and does good deeds, they shall have their reward with their Lord, shall have nothing to fear, nor shall they come to grief" (2:62; see also 5:69). This tension is probably to be resolved by saying that it is better, indeed incumbent upon humankind to accept Muhammad's message, but that if they do not, then living up to their own prophetic messages will be regarded as adequate even if it does not fulfill the entire divine command.

The organization of Muslims as a community—which was inherent in the message of the Prophet—set in motion its own political and religious dynamics. The Qur'an itself, while strongly repudiating the claims of Jewish and Christian communities to be proprietors of divine truth and guidance, frankly tells Muslims also (for example, in 47:38) that unless they fulfill the message they cannot take God for granted. Soon after the time of the Prophet, however, the community came to be regarded as infallible, and a *hadith* was put into currency that the Prophet had said "My community shall never agree on an error." This development was necessitated partly by intercommunal rivalry, but largely by the internal development of law, since the doctrine of legal consensus had to be made infallible.

In his last years, the Prophet decided on the policy of forcible conversion of Arab pagans to Islam and gave religious and cultural autonomy to Jews and Christians as "people of the Book" (although Jews were driven out of Medina by Muhammad and later from the rest of the Arabian Peninsula by 'Umar I). Muslims had to determine for themselves the status of Zoroastrians, Hindus, and Buddhists when they conquered Iran and parts of Northwest India. It was decided that these populations were also "people of the Book" since they believed in certain scriptures, and consequently they were allowed to keep their religion and culture, like the Jews and Christians, on payment of the poll tax *(jizyah)*. In contrast with their stance toward Jews and Christians however, Muslims were prohibited from having social intercourse or intermarrying with these other groups.

Indeed, when the community became an imperium, further developments took place that had little to do with the Qur'an or the *sunnah* of the Prophet but rather were dictated by the logic of the empire itself. The law of apostasy, for example, which states that a Muslim apostate should be given three chances to repent and in the case of nonrepentance must be executed, has nothing to do with the Qur'an, which speaks of "those who believed and then disbelieved, then once again believed and disbelieved—and then became entrenched in disbelief" (4:137; see also 3:90), thus clearly envisaging repeated conversions and apostasies without invoking any penalty in this world. It is, therefore, important to make these distinctions and to treat historic Islam not as one seamless garment but rather as a mosaic made up of different pieces.

Islam was asserted to be the true religion of Abraham, from which Jews and Christians had deviated.

PAGE 472

Traditional Islamic doctrine regards the words of the Qur'an as the actual speech of God, for which Muhammad was only a passive channel of transmission.

PAGE 473

There are numerous other laws that are the product neither of the Qur'an nor of the Prophet's *sunnah*, but of the Islamic imperium, such as the inadmissibility of evidence of a non-Muslim against a Muslim in a criminal case. In this legal genre also falls the juristic doctrine that the world consists of three zones: the Abode of Islam *(dar al-Islam)*, where Muslims rule; the Abode of Peace *(dar al-sulh)*, those countries or powers with whom Muslims have peace pacts; and the Abode of War *(dar al-harb)*, the rest of the world. This doctrine was definitely the result of the early Islamic conquests and the initial Islamic law of war and peace resulting from them. But during the later Abbasid period, the concept of *jihad* was formulated in defensive terms, because the task then was the consolidation of the empire rather than the gaining of further territory through conquest. To this general problem also belongs the consideration advanced by several Western scholars that Islam cannot authentically be a minority religion because the presumption of political power is built into its very texture as a religion. What is true is that Islam requires a state to work out its sociopolitical ideals and programs, but this does not mean that Muslims cannot live as a minority; indeed they have done so throughout history. The Qur'an, in fact, envisages some sort of close cooperation between Judaism, Christianity, and Islam, and it invites Jews and Christians to join Muslims in such a goal: "O People of the Book! Let us come together on a platform that is common between us, that we shall serve naught save God" (3:64).

— FAZLUR RAHMAN

ISLAMIC LAW

Shari'ah is an Arabic term used to designate Islamic law. In the case of Islamic law, the way is one that leads the righteous believer to Paradise in the afterlife. The *shari'ah* is not deemed a religious law by virtue of the subject matters it covers, for these range far beyond the sphere of religious concerns strictly speaking and extend to the mundane affairs of everyday life. Rather, its religious character is due to the Muslim belief that it derives from divinely inspired sources and represents God's plan for the proper ordering of all human activities. Although Muslims agree that they are bound by the *shari'ah,* the interpretations of its requirements have differed historically according to sectarian and school divisions and, in modern times, also according to differing views of how the *shari'ah* applies in the changed circumstances of present-day societies.

ORIGINS AND NATURE. The historical origin of the *shari'ah* lies in the revelation that Muslims believe was given to the prophet Muhammad by God through the vehicle of the archangel Gabriel in the last decades before the Prophet's death in 632 CE. This divine revelation was later recorded in a text known as the Qur'an. Although only a small portion of the Qur'an concerns strictly legal questions, it sets forth a number of general principles regarding how Muslims are to conduct themselves.

The *shari'ah* grew into a vast corpus of law. *Shari'ah* rules were part of the positive law applied by the government of the early Muslim community, which was originally conceived as an entity where political and religious loyalties would be coterminous. At the same time, the *shari'ah* was also understood as a system of moral guidance for the individual believer.

In the Islamic view, governments exist only to ensure that the *shari'ah* is properly administered and enforced. Governments are subordinate to the *shari'ah* and must execute its commands and prohibitions. On the Day of Judgment each Muslim will be held to account for any personal failures to comply with the commands and prohibitions of the *shari'ah.*

Classification of acts. The dual nature of the *shari'ah* as positive law and deontology, serving the combined functions of law and of what in some other religious systems might be moral philosophy, is reflected in the fact that Muslim jurists distinguish between two fundamentally different ways of classifying human acts. One way is to assess the moral character of acts, an assessment that corresponds to the deontological quality of the *shari'ah.* For this task there exists a five-fold scheme of classification, according to which an act may be mandatory, recommended, neutral (that is, entailing no moral consequences), blameworthy, or prohibited. Knowledge of this classification scheme enables pious Muslims to follow a meritorious course of conduct that will ensure their salvation on the Day of Judgment.

The second way of classifying acts reflects the fact that the *shari'ah* is meant to be used as the positive law of Muslim societies. The fundamental distinction made by Muslim jurists in this connection is between acts that are legally binding and valid and those that are of no legal effect or invalid. They also distinguish between licit acts and illicit acts warranting the imposition of penalties or exposing the actor (and potentially persons in privity with the actor) to legal liability.

Principal divisions. The two principal divisions of the *shari'ah* are based on the subject categories of legal rules. The first category is that of the *'ibadat,* or strictly religious obligations. These comprise the believer's duties vis-à-vis the deity. In this category one finds very extensive rules regarding precisely how to carry out the acts of worship and religious observances incumbent on the individual Muslim.

The other main category of *shari'ah* rules is that of the *mu'amalat,* which regulate the conduct of interpersonal relations rather than the relationship of the believer to the deity. There is considerable diversity among the sects and schools regarding the *shari'ah* rules in this category. Today there is also significant controversy about the degree to which these rules, originally formulated by medieval jurists, need to be updated and reformed in the light of modern circumstances.

HISTORICAL DEVELOPMENT. The question of the historical development of the *shari'ah* cannot be fairly discussed without acknowledging the deep and persistent cleavage between the views set forth in modern Western scholarship and the views of the majority of Muslim scholars. The nature of the differing views and their implications will be explained in what follows.

The relation of the Qur'an to previous law. As already noted, the Qur'an provided the original kernel of *shari'ah* law. Most of the Qur'anic verses dealing with legal questions were transmitted to the Prophet in the decade after the Hijrah, or flight from Mecca to Medina (622 CE).

An unresolved dispute in Islamic jurisprudence stems from the question of whether the rules set forth in the Qur'an should be regarded as a break with the preexisting system of western Arabian customary law or whether the revelations came to modify and reform some aspects of that law while otherwise retaining it. Some Muslim scholars have concluded that the great unevenness in depth of coverage of different topics in Qur'anic legislation should be taken to imply that the resulting gaps were intended to be filled by reference to those pre-Islamic customary laws that were not changed by the Qur'an, while others see in it a fresh starting point for legal development.

The Sunni-Shi'i division. The death of the prophet Muhammad in 632 CE marked the end of the period of Qur'anic revelation to the Muslim community. Until the Umayyad dynasty (661-750) came to power, the community was ruled by four leaders known as the Rashidun, or the "Rightly Guided [Caliphs]." The assumption of leadership by the Umayyads had great consequences for both sectarian and legal developments. Repudiating the Umayyads, the Shi'i and Khariji factions both broke away from the main body of Muslims, who came to be called Sunnis, and their respective legal orientations thenceforth diverged. The Kharijis (also known as the Ibadiyah) believed that the leadership of the Muslim community should be determined by elections and that Muslims had the right to rebel against an unqualified ruler. The Shi'i faction believed that the first three caliphs had usurped the rule of the community, which in their view should have passed to the fourth of the Rashidun, 'Ali ibn Abi Talib (d. 661), a cousin and son-in-law of the Prophet.

Not only did the Shi'ah believe that the caliph 'Ali had been the rightful successor of the Prophet, but they also believed that leadership of the community rightfully still belonged to Ali's blood descendants after the civil war that resulted in his death and the establishment of a hereditary monarchy by the victorious Umayyads. Those of the caliph 'Ali's descendants who inherited his authority were known as imams, and like him they were believed by the Shi'ah to share the same divine inspiration that had enabled the Prophet, while himself not divine, to make authoritative pronouncements on *shari'ah* law. The Shi'i community subsequently split into subsects over questions of who was entitled to succeed to the position of imam. The largest of the subsects, the Twelvers, believes that the last imam, who disappeared in 874, went into a state of occultation from which he is expected eventually to return, while the other subsects follow lines of imams whose descent has continued into the modern era.

The earliest stage of shari'ah law. For Sunnis the possibility of divine revelation and the making of new Islamic law ceased with the death of the Prophet. Subsequent generations of Muslims who were concerned with how to establish a legal system on an Islamic basis were thus faced with a problem of scarce source material. *Ad hoc* measures and a spirit of pragmatism appear to have characterized much of the decision making of the early political leaders, who also served as judges.

The view of Western scholarship is that as the new empire absorbed its early conquests of Syria, Iraq, Egypt, and Iran, it was also exposed to influences from the local civilizations, which included the very highly developed legal cultures of Romano-Byzantine law, Jewish law, Sasanid law, and the law of the Eastern Christian churches. Most Muslim scholars absolutely reject this view and take the position that *shari'ah* law owes no debt whatsoever to any non-Islamic tradition.

Ancient law schools. The jurisprudence of the Sunni branch of *shari'ah* law had its beginnings in what are called the ancient schools of law. Within a century of the Prophet's death there were prominent law schools in various cities in Iraq, Syria, and the Hejaz. It appears that the scholars in these ancient schools felt free to resort to ratiocination to develop legal rules for new situations and that they may also have been influenced in their approach to legal questions by the judicial practice of the tribunals set up by the Umayyad rulers.

The traditionist movement. Meanwhile, a second movement was under way, that of the traditionists, who began to make their influence felt in the course of the second century after the Prophet's death. The traditionists did not accept the authority of the *sunnah* of the ancient schools, nor did they accept the practice of the scholars of those ancient schools who relied on juristic opinion to resolve legal questions. Instead, the traditionists proposed that accounts relating the sayings and doings of the Prophet should be treated as

With the weakening of the central caliphal authority in Baghdad, the tenth century saw the almost ubiquitous rise of the Shi'ah.

PAGE 339

legally binding statements of law. The traditionists collected traditions, known as *hadith* (pl., *ahadith*), which purported to record the Prophet's sayings and his reactions to the different situations he had confronted.

The genuineness of the *hadith* literature is yet another point on which modern Western scholars tend to find themselves in disagreement with many of their Muslim counterparts. The prevailing view among Western scholars has been that most, if not all, of the *hadith* are pious forgeries put into circulation by traditionists of the first and second Muslim centuries with a view to creating Islamic pedigrees for rules of law that had originally been the products of juristic reasoning or judicial practice, that were inherited from Arabian customary law, or that were borrowed from other legal cultures. Western scholarship has generally evaluated the traditional science of *hadith* criticism as inadequate for differentiating historically accurate accounts from later fabrications. In the view of most Muslims, including those who have reservations about the genuineness of some of the *hadith* and the adequacy of *hadith* scholarship, these Western criticisms are excessively harsh.

The beginnings of the classical law schools. Despite the initial resistance that it encountered, the traditionists' position steadily gained ground at the expense of the influence of the ancient schools of law in the second century after the death of the Prophet. The ancient schools did not disappear but adapted in differing degrees to the new trends in legal thought. It is in the second century AH (ninth century CE) that the foundations were laid for the development of what were subsequently to become the classical *shari'ah* schools.

The oldest of the classical Sunni schools is the Maliki, which originated in Medina and was named after the prominent legal scholar and traditionist Malik ibn Anas (d. 795). Respect for the *sunnah* of Medina as the place most closely associated with the mission of the Prophet and the first Muslim community persisted in the legal thought of the Maliki school.

The Hanafi school was meanwhile developing in the context of the legal community in Kufa in southern Iraq. Although the school was named after a prominent local jurist, Abu Hanifah (d. 767), its followers actually often showed greater deference to the views of two of his disciples, Abu Yusuf (d. 798) and al-Shaybani (d. 805). The Hanafi school bore many traces of influences from the Iraqi environment in which it developed. Ha-nafi jurists attached great importance to systematic consistency in legal thought and the refinement of legal principles.

Muhammad ibn Idris al-Shafi'i (d. 820), the founder of the school that bears his name, was associated with the city of Medina. He ranks among the foremost figures in the history of Islamic legal thought and was, more than any other person, responsible for the

SUNNI LAW SCHOOLS

Sunni Muslims, like those shown here, believe that the possibility of divine revelation and the making of new Islamic law ceased with the prophet. Their ancestors created ancient law schools to develop legal rules for new situations.

HULTON-DEUTSCH COLLECTION/CORBIS

eventual triumph of the traditionist thesis in classical Islamic legal thought. According to al-Shafi'i, the *sunnah* of the Prophet as embodied in the *hadith* totally superseded the *sunnah* of the ancient schools as a normative legal standard. Al-Shafi'i thus elevated the *sunnah* of the Prophet to the status of a source of law coequal with the Qur'an. He articulated the view, which subsequently found widespread acceptance, that the *sunnah* of the Prophet explained the meaning of the Qur'an.

Having established the Qur'an and the much more extensive corpus of *hadith* literature as the material sources of the *shari'ah,* al-Shafi'i rejected the use of juristic opinion or speculative reasoning in formulating legal principles and insisted that jurists be restricted to the use of analogical reasoning *(qiyas),* to extend principles in the sources to cover problems not explicitly addressed in the texts of the Qur'an and *hadith.* In his view, only by insisting that jurists limit themselves to such careful, piecemeal extensions of principles in the texts could one be sure that the jurists were not injecting undue subjective elements into their interpretations of *shari'ah* requirements or distorting the rules set forth in the sources. Al-Shafi'i also refused to accord any weight to juristic consensus and held that the only binding consensus would be one among all members of the Muslim community.

The last of the classical Sunni schools crystalized around Ahmad ibn Hanbal (d. 855), a traditionist from Baghdad who traveled widely among different centers of learning. Subsequent members of the Hanbali school have shared Ibn Hanbal's traditionist orientation and his concern for the consensus of the companions of the Prophet, but individual Hanbali scholars have taken diverging opinions on questions of jurisprudence.

Usul al-fiqh. With the development of the classical schools of Islamic law came the articulation of the principles of *usul al-fiqh,* the roots or sources of jurisprudence. Although the *usul* are often called sources of the *shari'ah,* only the Qur'an and the *sunnah* are material sources. Ultimately, the study of *usul al-fiqh* is concerned with establishing a science of proofs of the Islamic derivation of substantive legal principles, thus enabling the jurist to discern which legal rules are correct statements of *shari'ah* principles. The rules shown by this science to be authentically Islamic are known as the *furu' al-fiqh,* the branches of jurisprudence. The study of *usul* has been one of the major preoccupations of Muslim jurists over the centuries and continues to be so today. As the subsequent history of the development of the *shari'ah* demonstrates, the influence of al-Shafi'i on the fomulation of the classical Sunni theory of *usul al-fiqh*—a formulation that was basically complete by the ninth century—was considerable.

The first root of the *fiqh* is the Qur'an. In the prevailing view, it is to be treated as the eternal and uncreated word of God, part of his essence. Muslim jurists developed an elaborate methodology to interpret the Qur'an. Some differences in the legal principles derived from the Qur'an relate to the sectarian divisions of Islam; perhaps the most striking example lies in the laws of intestate succession among the Sunnis and the Twelver branch of the Shi'ah. In the Sunni view, the Qur'an meant to retain, with only limited modifications, the pre-Islamic Arabian scheme of agnatic succession, in which males inheriting through the male line got a major part of the estate. By contrast, the Twelver Shi'i jurists held that, in designating inheritance shares for females and the children and parents of the deceased, the Qur'an was implicitly repudiating the customary law of pre-Islamic Arabia and setting forth a completely different scheme of succession.

Al-Shafi'i succeeded in persuading subsequent jurists that the *sunnah* of the Prophet should be treated as the second root of Islamic jurisprudence and a source co-equal with the Qur'an. It is generally accepted among Muslims not only that the Prophet was a perfect human being and thus worthy of emulation, but also that he enjoyed divine inspiration and thus could make no error in matters of religion or *shari'ah* law. As noted, challenges to the authenticity of the *hadith* literature on which the understanding of the Prophet's *sunnah* rested generated a science of *hadith* criticism to weed out unsound or dubious accounts. In addition, methodologies were worked out to reconcile seeming contradictions and inconsistencies in different *hadith* and between *hadith* and verses of the Qur'an. As in the case of the Qur'an, reading the *hadith* literature without a grasp of how orthodox Islamic scholarship interprets the legal implications of the *hadith* and the relevant jurisprudence can lead to erroneous conclusions.

Qiyas, reasoning by analogy, is a method for expanding the rules in the Qur'an and *sunnah* to cover problems not expressly addressed in the sources. Most Sunnis accept *qiyas* as the third root of *fiqh. Qiyas* involves the application of a legal ruling from a case mentioned in the Qur'an or *sunnah* to a subcase not mentioned in the text but sufficiently related to permit coverage by analogical extension. The extension of rules through *qiyas* ultimately involves human judgment, since it is first necessary to identify the reason underlying the original rule set forth in the text. In practice, jurists have been far from unanimous in their identification of these underlying reasons, with the result that they have extended the rules of the Qur'an and *sunnah* in different ways.

Twelver Shi'i jurists do not accept the Sunni model of *qiyas.* Many of them use forms of juristic reasoning that are not limited to drawing analogies in order to construe the meaning of the Qur'an and *sunnah.*

Just as theology occupies the central place in Christianity, in Islam the central place belongs to law.

PAGE 341

When we speak of Islamic law, we mean all of human behavior, including, for example, intentions.

PAGE 345

Known as the Usuliyah, Twelver Shi'i jurists who believe that *shari'ah* rules can be extended by human reason have historically been opposed by another faction of jurists, the Akhbariyah, who insist that rules generated by human reason cannot be binding statements of *shari'ah* law and argue that the Qur'an and the *sunnah* of the Prophet and the Shi'i imams alone provide trustworthy guidance.

Ijma' refers to the retroactive ratification of the correctness of an interpretation of *shari'ah* requirements. Most Sunnis treat *ijma'*, which is constituted by the consensus of all the jurists of one generation, as the fourth root of *fiqh*. According to the majority Sunni position, once a legal principle has won such unanimous endorsement, it becomes definitively established and cannot be challenged by subsequent generations. Among the critics of the Sunni view of *ijma'* are the Twelver Shi'ah, who have historically taken a variety of positions on the significance of *ijma'* and how it is constituted.

Jurists and the development of the shari'ah. With the foundation of the classical schools of Islamic law and the formulation of the fundamental principles of *usul al-fiqh*, the *shari'ah* became a jurists' law, and exhaustive training in law and ancillary disciplines was essential for interpreting how the shari'ah applied to a given problem. The jurist, or *faqih* (pl., *fuqaha'*), came to enjoy great prestige as a result of his monopoly of expertise regarding the sacred law.

The task of interpreting the requirements of the *shari'ah* is termed *ijtihad*, and the person performing the interpretation is termed a *mujtahid*. The exercise of *ijtihad* by the early jurists defined the basic contours of the *shari'ah* by the start of the tenth century CE. It has been widely believed that at that point in Sunni jurisprudence, the *fuqaha'* were held to be bound by the solutions to legal problems reached by jurists of earlier generations on the grounds that the latter, being closer in time to the prophet Muhammad, were less likely to fall into error than scholars of later generations. This bar to reexamination of previously decided questions of *shari'ah* law has been termed "the closing of the door of *ijtihad*." Never recognized by Twelver Shi'i law, it may have inhibited innovative thought and retarded legal reform in Sunni circles, although not in the Hanbali school, where many jurists denied that they could be bound by the *ijtihad* of their predecessors. However, the common supposition that the corollary doctrine of *taqlid*, or obedience to established legal authority, immutably fixed *shari'ah* doctrines at an early stage and had a stultifying impact on the evolution of *shari'ah* law has never been conclusively established; the necessary scientific examination of the actual historical effect of *taqlid* on the ability of jurists to adjust legal doctrines and respond to the exigencies of the changing environment has not been undertaken.

THE MATURE CLASSICAL LAW SCHOOLS. From the tenth century until the disruptive impact of European imperialism made itself felt in India in the eighteenth century, and in the other parts of the Muslim world in the nineteenth century, there was no major discontinuity in the development of doctrines of the classical law schools. Instead, one could say that this period was devoted to refining and amplifying the early treatments of Islamic jurisprudence.

As the schools matured, their doctrines became more elaborate—often, as already noted, deviating from the views of their eponymous founders. Although the schools did not require that all members adhere to precisely the same doctrines, within each school there tended to be a core of doctrines that enjoyed widespread acceptance and that embodied a distinctive approach to the resolution of legal problems.

One of the ancillary subjects essential for aspiring *fuqaha'* to master was classical Arabic, the language of God's speech in the Qur'an and the language of the *hadith*. Arabic has continued to be the essential language for the study of the *shari'ah*. No translated versions of the Qur'an or the *hadith* are adequate for use in scholarly investigations. All of the classical *fiqh* works are also in Arabic. Although recently some have become available in translations, these are of very uneven quality and must be used with great caution.

The schools spread far from their original settings. Adherence to one school or another, as well as sectarian allegiances, changed in accordance with the many political upheavals and vicissitudes suffered by the different parts of the Muslim world over the centuries, and the patterns of school and sect distribution varied significantly at different eras of Islamic history.

It should be recalled that all of the four classical Sunni schools are considered equally orthodox. Although concerns for doctrinal consistency and coherence mandated that a jurist follow the established doctrine of his school, it was not unusual for jurists to study the *fiqh* of other Sunni schools or even to refer extensively to the opinions of other schools in treatises.

Comparisons of the rules of the classical fiqh. In detail the rules of the various Sunni schools are often different enough to affect the outcome of a legal dispute. On the average legal question, the degree of doctrinal difference between a given Sunni school and a Shi'i school is often not much greater. Notwithstanding the different approaches that Sunni and Shi'i *fiqh* purport to have to the sources of law, aside from their differences regarding who should rule the Muslim community one finds few major divergencies except on some points of religious ritual and worship, certain rules of marriage and divorce, and the laws of inheritance.

PRINCIPAL FIGURES. The founders of the schools of Sunni law and the imams of the Shi'i sects, who enjoyed the same capacity as the prophet Muhammad to make authoritative pronouncements regarding the requirements of the *shari'ah*, would have to be ranked in the fore-front of the principal figures in the history of Islamic law. Given the vast corpus of writings on the *shari'ah*, it is impossible to present any summary treatment without risking unfair omissions of outstanding figures. The following list must therefore be understood to be only a selection of persons who are representative of some of the important aspects of the Islamic legal heritage and suggestive of its variety and richness.

An early jurist who is notable for a conception of the role of the *shari'ah* different from that of his more orthodox contemporaries was Ibn al-Muqaffa' (d. 756). He unsuccessfully urged the Abbasid caliph al-Mansur to end the confusion and disparities in the *shari'ah* resulting from conflicting interpretations by the jurists of the early law schools by systematizing and codifying the *shari'ah*. He argued that the *shari'ah* should be enacted into uniform legislation that would apply throughout the caliph's domain; his failure to convince others of the correctness of his ideas meant that the *shari'ah* continued to be viewed as a jurist's law independent from and untouchable by political authorities.

Before its extinction, the once-influential Zahiri school enjoyed a flowering in Muslim Spain. The most famous and distinguished Zahiri thinker was Ibn Hazm (d. 1065), a vigorous polemicist who made many enemies in the course of his harsh attacks on the doctrines of other law schools. He challenged the authenticity of much of the *hadith* literature, rejected *qiyas* and the rules it produced, limited *ijma'* to that of the companions of the Prophet, and insisted that, in the absence of explicit commands in the Qur'an and *sunnah*, all conduct should be regarded as outside the concern of religious law.

One of the most eminent figures in Islamic intellectual history, al-Ghazali (d. 1111) examined the teachings of the *shari'ah* in relation to his own theological and philosophical views. Although he is best known for his searching inquiry into the theological fundamentals of Islam, al-Ghazali also wrote a number of important books of Shafi'i *fiqh*. In his greatest work, *Ihya' 'ulum al-din* (The Revivification of Religious Sciences), al-Ghazali sought to achieve a synthesis of the teachings of Islam and to define the role of the shari'ah in relation to other aspects of religion. His work may constitute the most accomplished statement of what passed for Sunni orthodoxy in medieval Islam.

One of the most original medieval jurists was the Hanbali Ibn Taymiyah (d. 1328), who had an influential disciple in Ibn Qayyim al-Jawziyah (d. 1350). Ibn Taymiyah strongly attacked the doctrine of *taqlid* that bound Muslims to the interpretations of the early jurists. He argued that qualified Muslim thinkers should be free to return to the Qur'an, *sunnah*, and consensus of the companions of the Prophet and interpret them afresh. Muhammad ibn 'Abd al-Wahhab (d. 1792), the leader of the puritanical Wahhabi reform movement that won many followers in Arabia and elsewhere, invoked Ibn Taymiyah's ideas in his rejection of the authority of the classical law schools and his insistence on fresh *ijtihad*.

Theories about the need to identify and follow the fundamental policies underlying *shari'ah* provisions and to interpret these provisions in a manner responsive to social needs were developed by the Maliki jurist al-Shatibi (d. 1388). Ibn Nujaym (d. 1562) was a Hanafi jurist who extracted what he saw as the fundamental *shari'ah* principles from the specific instances of applications of rules set forth in the *fiqh*. While not himself a jurist, the Mughal emperor Awrangzib 'Alamgir (d. 1707) made his mark on Islamic legal history by ordering the composition of the famous *Fatawa 'Alamgiriyah*, a thorough compilation of Hanafi *fiqh*.

Muhammad 'Abduh (d. 1905) served as Grand Mufti of Egypt and in that capacity and in his writings on Islamic law proposed rationalist and liberal reformist interpretations of the *shari'ah*. The influential Salafiyah movement inspired by 'Abduh and led by his disciple Rashid Rida advocated a return to a purified version of the *shari'ah* meant to be more authentic than the versions developed in the course of the centuries devoted to the study of medieval *fiqh*. An example of 'Abduh's approach may be seen in his famous argument that the *shari'ah* prohibits polygamy. Dismissing traditional support for polygamy among the *fuqaha'*, 'Abduh returned to the Qur'an and offered a novel reading of two critical verses, which he claimed were to be taken together, although they had previously been held to apply to different issues. Surah 4:3 of the Qur'an was traditionally interpreted to allow a man to wed up to four women at a time, with a moral injunction to marry only one if he could not treat additional wives justly. Surah 4:129, which says it is not possible for a man to deal equally with his wives, was traditionally interpreted as offering reassurance to the polygamous husband that he was not sinning if he felt stronger attraction to and affection for one of his wives. Treating the injunction to deal equally with wives in the earlier verse as a legally binding precondition for a valid marriage, 'Abduh used the later verse as evidence that this precondition could not in practice be met, so that in the *shari'ah*, no polygamous marriage could be valid. 'Abduh's practice of interpreting *shari'ah* rules to serve the ends of enlightened social policies had far-reaching

Muslim theologians such as al-Ghazali participated in a golden age of theology.

PAGE 209

With the development of the classical schools of Islamic law came the articulation of the principles of usul al-fiqh, *the roots or sources of jurisprudence.*

PAGE 359

intellectual repercussions. His ideas encouraged many Middle Eastern Muslims in the first half of the twentieth century to accommodate liberal political, economic, and social reforms in their interpretations of Islamic law.

Among the principal figures of Twelver Shiʻi jurisprudence, Muhammad ibn al-Hasan al-Tusi (d. 1067) wrote a number of works that became treated as classic statements of principles of Shiʻi *fiqh*, as were the writings of Muhaqqiq al-Hilli (d. 1277). An important representative of the Akhbari faction of Twelver Shiism was Muhammad Baqir al-Majlisi (d. 1699), who, in addition to producing an encyclopedic statement of *fiqh*, also served as a judge and became the most powerful judicial figure under the Safavids. After the Safavids made Twelver Shiism the state religion of Iran, he, like many major Shiʻi jurists, attempted to define the proper political relationship between the Shiʻi clergy and the state. Al-Majlisi conceived of a powerful, independent political role for the clergy. A jurist of similar eminence, but representing very different tendencies in Twelver thought, was Murtada Ansari (d. 1864). A member of the Usuli school, which predominated in Iran in the nineteenth century, he wrote a major treatise on the Usuli theory of sources. His writings promoted the view that each layperson was bound to follow the legal interpretations of the most learned of living jurists, the *marjaʻ-i taqlid*, whose *ijtihad* became absolutely binding on his followers. He took the view that public law was not a true concern of the *shariʻah* and stressed instead its ethical dimensions. The single most important Ismaʻili jurist is Qadi al-Nuʻman (d. 974), who served as the highest judge in the Fatimid empire and also wrote a great treatise of Ismaʻili law.

Principal subjects. Classical *fiqh* works have similar, although not always identical, subject divisions. They begin with a section on the very extensive *ʻibadat*, the obligations of the individual to God. The remaining subjects belong to the *muʻamalat* category, including (in a representative, though not exhaustive, list) marriage, divorce, manumission of slaves, oaths, criminal penalties, relations between the Muslim community and non-Muslims, treasure troves, missing persons, partnership, religious trusts, sales, guarantee contracts, transfers of debts, rules for judges, evidence, legal claims, acknowledgments of legal obligations, gifts, hire, the purchase of freedom by slaves, the defense of compulsion, incapacity, usurpation and damage of property, preemptive purchases, partition, agency, contracts for cultivation of agricultural land, slaughter of animals (for food), animal sacrifice, hateful practices, cultivation of waste lands, prohibited drinks, hunting and racing competitions, pledge, personal injuries, blood money and fines, intestate succession, and wills.

THE SITUATION IN RECENT TIMES. The situation of the *shariʻah* in recent times has two significant dimensions, corresponding to its dual nature as a positive law and a deontology.

Beginning in the nineteenth century, the *shariʻah* was increasingly supplanted as a positive law in the legal systems of Muslim countries by borrowed European law. Historically, substantive *shariʻah* rules survived in the legal systems of modern Muslim countries in rough proportion to the importance traditionally accorded to the subject area involved, but even in those areas where the *shariʻah* was able to maintain itself, it was nonetheless subjected to some reforms. In the twentieth century, *shariʻah* reform became one of the major legal problems faced by Muslim societies and provoked protracted political and intellectual controversies. Despite popular and clerical support for retention of the *shariʻah*, governments have generally moved as quickly as political constraints permit in the direction of westernization. In the 1970s the political influence of forces favoring the retention and/or renewal of the *shariʻah* began to make itself felt, and a process of abrogating westernizing reforms and reinstating *shariʻah* law began in Libya, Iran, Pakistan, Egypt, Sudan, and Kuwait. How far the process of islamization will proceed and what the future role of the *shariʻah* as a positive law will be are at present uncertain.

Also in the twentieth century, Muslim intellectuals concerned with questions of *fiqh* subjected the medieval versions of the *shariʻah* to critical reexamination and brought new interpretive approaches to the *shariʻah* sources. The variety in modern approaches to the *shariʻah* is reminiscent of the situation prevailing in the first centuries after the death of the Prophet, before the doctrines of the classical schools coalesced. There are still many conservative thinkers who defend the validity of the medieval *fiqh*. Arrayed against them are many who support new interpretations of what the *shariʻah* means. Adding to the fragmentation of legal doctrines is the fact that with the spread of educational opportunities and the increase in literacy, many Muslims who are educated but have not pursued a traditional course of study at a religious institution are contributing interpretations of the *shariʻah*. In other words, laypersons who belong to the modern educated elite do not necessarily feel that they must defer to the specialized knowledge of the *fuqaha'* and are prepared to challenge the monopoly formerly enjoyed by the *fuqaha'* to make authoritative statements on *shariʻah* law. As a result, it has become very difficult to make generalizations about contemporary *shariʻah* doctrines.

The westernization of legal systems in the Muslim world. The westernization of the legal systems of Muslim countries began with the impact of European imperialism on Muslim societies in the eighteenth and nineteenth centuries. The legal systems of Muslim

IRANIAN WOMEN

The status of women in Islamic society has varied dramatically throughout history. Neofundamentalists believe that women should remain covered when appearing outside the home.

DEAN CONGER/CORBIS

societies subjected to direct colonial rule underwent distinctive transformations in relation to the legal culture of the colonizing power. Thus, there developed in Muslim parts of India under British rule a peculiar blend of common law and elements of the *shari'ah* that became known as Anglo-Muhammadan law. This unique, hybrid law was progressively reformed to eliminate what were regarded as the more archaic features of the shari'ah elements, and it remained influential in the legal systems of India and Pakistan after they achieved independence in 1947. Algeria was part of France from 1830 until independence in 1962, and as a French colony, it also developed a hybrid legal system, known as *le droit musulman algérien*, which incorporated many French features.

Eager to strengthen their relatively backward and weak societies in the face of threatened European domination, most elites in the independent countries of the Muslim world tended to see the *shari'ah* as an obstacle to the achievement of essential modernization. Governments first replaced those parts of the shari'ah that were viewed as impeding economic transformation, such as *shari'ah* commercial law, or those possessing features that seemed particularly archaic by modern standards, as in the cases of *shari'ah* procedural and criminal law.

It was not always the substance of *shari'ah* rules that troubled modernizers. Their arcane formulation and their diffuse mode of presentation in medieval *fiqh* treatises meant that only specialists with a mastery of medieval legal Arabic and an extensive traditional training could find answers to legal questions in a reasonably efficient manner. The cumbersome form of the *fiqh* works could be compared with the streamlined, systematized legal compendia to be found in nineteenth-century continental European codes. Growing impatience with the *fiqh* works encouraged a definite preference for codified law.

At the early stages of this legal reform process, one possibility for saving the *shari'ah* from eclipse by Western law seemed to be that of vastly simplifying and systematizing its presentation. Attempts were made to codify the *shari'ah* in the late nineteenth century, the most notable accomplishment being the promulgation of the Ottoman Majalla in 1877. Starting with some general principles of *shari'ah* law taken from Ibn Nujaym, the Majalla presents a codification of the law of obligations derived from the views of various Hanafi jurists. The Majalla proved its utility, surviving for decades in former Ottoman territories well after they had obtained their independence from the empire. A later code, the Ottoman Family Rights Law of 1917, constituted an original attempt to codify *shari'ah* law on that subject by reference to the doctrines of more than one Sunni law school. This was the first important instance of the application of the technique of *takhayyur*, or picking and choosing the most apt principles from the doctrines of different schools and combining them in an arrangement that had no precedent in the classical *fiqh*. However, the preference for wholesale importation of Western law codes was ultimately so strong that there was soon lit-

Besides the role of women, which is seen to lie at home, the heaviest emphasis falls on the islamization of economy.

PAGE 354

tle incentive to pursue projects for devising further codes on a *shari'ah* basis.

Another factor mandating change from the old *shari'ah*-based system of law was the international political setting. The rulers of Muslim states in the nineteenth and twentieth centuries were obliged to deal with a historical reality that was vastly different from what had been contemplated in early *shari'ah* theory. The *shari'ah* was originally conceived as a law whose application would be coextensive with religious affiliation. The world was to be converted to Islam, and there would result one community of believers with a common political allegiance and a common obligation to follow the shari'ah. This conception did not envisage the appearance of obstacles in the way of the realization of this ideal, such as the fragmentation of the Muslim community into separate and mutually hostile political units, the development of national identities and the rise of modern nationalism, the failure of large non-Muslim communities within the Muslim world to convert, and the need to deal with non-Muslim countries possessed of greater economic and military resources.

Muslims in China have always been predominantly Sunni, but in the sixteenth century Sufism reached China through Central Asia.

PAGE 140

The continued existence of non-Muslim communities had necessitated one legal adaptation at an early stage of Islamic history, namely, the allowance of separate religious laws and courts for minority communities. Members of the minority religious communities on Muslim territory were permitted to follow their own religious laws in matters of personal status and in transactions between themselves while remaining subject to the *shari'ah* in their interactions with outsiders or in their public activities. This practice was highly developed under the Ottoman empire, where it was known as the *millet* system.

Under outside pressures, this system was further modified by a practice of according a special legal status to non-Muslims from the powerful European states: from the medieval period onward, certain states exacted from Muslim governments agreements, or "capitulations," according extraterritorial status to their nationals. Originally granted only by way of exception, capitulatory privileges were expanded apace with growing European influence. An example of the resulting system of extraterritoriality can be seen in the powerful Mixed Courts of Egypt, set up in 1875, expanded after the British occupation in 1882, and continuing until 1949. Originally established as alternatives to the "native courts" for cases involving foreigners, the Mixed Courts were able to extend their jurisdiction to a wide variety of cases, including those involving Egyptians, in instances where the courts detected some "foreign interest" in the outcome. One reason for the exaction of these concessions, the demands for which became increasingly onerous as Muslim power and wealth declined and that of the West grew, was the Western perception that the substantive provisions of the *shari'ah* were "primitive" and "barbaric" by modern European legal standards, and that the justice meted out by the traditional courts was arbitrary. European powers also objected to the inferior legal status accorded to non-Muslims under the *shari'ah* and exploited this as a pretext for political intervention. In attempts to forestall such intervention, the Ottoman sultan promulgated the Hatt-i Serïf of Gülhane in 1839 and the Hatt-i Humâyûn of 1856, officially establishing the principle that Ottoman citizens regardless of their religion should be equal in terms of their legal rights and obligations.

Retention of *shari'ah* law as the law of the land in these political circumstances thus presented obstacles to setting up a unified national legal system and entailed exposure to risks of compromising the sovereignty and national dignity of the Muslim states. The reluctance of governments to continue to make such sacrifices provided an impetus for law reform that would place legal systems in Muslim countries on a par with the emerging modern international standard.

The formation of modern nation-states in the Muslim world starting in the nineteenth century and the subsequent collapse of the Ottoman empire in World War I prompted Muslims to reassess the relationship between the *shari'ah* law and the new political entities into which the Muslim world had been divided. Although the claims of the Ottoman sultans to be the legitimate successors of the Prophet had been based on tenuous legal and historical arguments, some Sunnis saw in the sultan-caliphs an embodiment of the original *shari'ah* notion that religious allegiance—not nationality—should determine political loyalties. With the ouster of the last of the Ottoman sultan-caliphs in 1924, there ended any real chance in the Sunni world of preserving an Islamic caliphate, a government under which all Muslims would share a common political and religious allegiance.

Iran's *'ulama'* faced a momentous question at the turn of the twentieth century, when a growing movement favored the establishment of a democratic government, and the Constitutional Revolution of 1905-1909, led to the overthrow of the Qajar dynasty. To the *'ulama'*, accepting this revolution meant acknowledging the legitimacy of a government based on the principle of popular sovereignty and the law-making authority of the people's representatives. Such changes were seen by some as a challenge to the theoretical primacy of the imamate and the exclusive prerogative of the *'ulama'* to determine and declare the law. Other important jurists, such as Muhammad Na'ini (d. 1936), however, took the position that, pending the return of the Hidden Imam from the state of occultation, it was impossible to have a government that truly accorded with *shari'ah* ideals and that it was therefore permissible for Iran to adopt a constitutional form of government in the interim.

The acceptance of the idea in the Sunni and Shi'i camps that laws should be enacted on a national basis by representatives of the people did not by itself entail a reduction of the role of the *shari'ah*. However, the attendant pressures for systematic uniformity meant that statutes enacted by the state inevitably replaced the old, decentralized system of jurists' law. Thus, the realization that laws would henceforth be made by national governments encouraged the acceptance of the idea that there should be neutral, secular laws that could apply to all persons on the national soil. The typical pattern in Muslim countries in the nineteenth century, and more particularly in the twentieth century, was to abandon the *shari'ah* in favor of imported European law save in matters of personal status and religious trusts, and occasional token provisions in other fields such as the law of contracts.

The timing of the adoptions of Western law was related to the chronology and extent of various countries' exposure to European imperialism. The Ottoman empire was therefore the first Muslim state to adopt Western laws, followed shortly by the semiautonomous province of Egypt. The first French-based codes to be introduced in the Ottoman empire were in the areas of commercial law (1850), penal law (1858), and commercial procedure (1861). The countries that remained most insulated from such influences—Afghanistan, the Yemen, and Saudi Arabia—were the last to undertake westernization of their legal systems. In most countries, legal westernization was largely completed by the 1950s. Alone among Muslim countries, Turkey, under the leadership of Kemal Atatürk after the collapse of the Ottoman empire, abandoned the *shari'ah* in favor of a completely secular legal system. At the opposite extreme, Saudi Arabia has retained the *shari'ah*, or more specifically, Hanbali *fiqh*, as the official norm, which has prevented the government from openly undertaking legislative activity, including the enactment of a constitution.

In contemporary Muslim countries the desire on the part of the governments for legal modernization combined with the need to show respect for the *shari'ah* has resulted in various compromises. In the area of personal status, a number of reforms, by and large modest ones, have been enacted in Muslim countries with a view to improving the status of women in matters of marriage, divorce, support, and child custody. The boldest reforms in this area were enacted in the Tunisian Code of Personal Status of 1956, the Iranian Family Protection Law of 1967 (since abrogated by the revolutionary government), and the South Yemen Family Law of 1974. Only a few very cautious reforms of aspects of the *shari'ah* law of intestate succession have been undertaken.

Even Muslim states with westernized legal systems generally enshrine Islam in the national constitution as the state religion and stipulate that the *shari'ah* is a source of law or even the source of all laws. In some constitutions there are provisions stating that laws must accord with the *shari'ah* or that they may be reviewed and nullified if they are found to violate the *shari'ah*. In the past such provisions often had little more than symbolic significance, but as supporters of the shari'ah gained political strength in the 1970s throughout the Islamic world, there was increasing pressure for reinstatement of *shari'ah* rules and the abrogation of imported laws that conflict with *shari'ah* principles. Thus, the *shari'ah* is tending to be treated more and more as a fundamental law in the legal systems of Muslim countries

— ANN ELIZABETH MAYER

ISLAMIC STUDIES

These studies encompass the study of the religion of Islam and of Islamic aspects of Muslim cultures and societies. At the outset we must recognize that the word *Islam* itself is used in very different senses by faithful Muslims, for whom it is a norm and an ideal, and by scholars (Muslim and non-Muslim Islamicists), who refer to it as a subject of study or a kind of symbol for the focus of their inquiry, as well as by the larger public in the West who are outsiders and give different appreciations of what is felt by them to be "foreign." By extension, a sharp distinction must be made between normative Islam (the prescriptions, norms, and values that are recognized by the community as embodiments of divine guidance) and actual Islam (all those forms and movements, practices and ideas that have in fact existed in the many Muslim communities in different times and places). In other words, Islamic data sought for the sake of scholarly understanding are not the same as the ideals that Muslims as adherents of Islam attach to them, the meaning they attribute to them, or the truth they recognize in them.

The Scope of Islamic Studies

On the basis of these distinctions, it is possible to identify three different enterprises that come under the general rubric of Islamic studies:

1. *The normative study of Islamic religion* is generally carried out by Muslims in order to acquire knowledge of religious truth. It implies the study of the Islamic religious sciences: Qur'anic exegesis *(tafsir)*, the science of traditions *('ilm al-hadith)*, jurispru-

In Turkey the Ottomans (1281-1922) made a major contribution with the centralized mosque, dominated both inside and outside by a massive dome.

PAGE 471

The Eucharist, also known as the Mass, Communion service, Lord's Supper, and Divine Liturgy, among other names, is the central act of Christian worship, practiced by almost all denominations of Christians.

PAGE 216

dence *(fiqh),* and metaphysical theology *(kalam).* Traditionally pursued in mosques and special religious colleges *(madrasahs),* it is now usually carried out in faculties of religious law *(shari'ah)* and of religious sciences *('ulum al-din)* at universities or special Islamic institutes in Muslim countries.

2. *The nonnormative study of Islamic religion* is usually done in universities and covers both what is considered by Muslims to be true Islam (the Islamic religious sciences in particular) and what is considered to be living Islam (the factual religious expressions of Muslims).
3. *The nonnormative study of Islamic aspects of Muslim cultures and societies* in a broader sense is not directed toward Islam as such. It takes a wider context into consideration, approaching things Islamic from the point of view of history and literature or cultural anthropology and sociology, and not specifically from the perspective of the study of religion.

My focus in this essay is on the two nonnormative forms of study, which we may call Islamic studies in the narrower (2) and the wider (3) sense. In the narrower sense of Islamic studies, the focus is on Islamic religion as an entity in itself; the wider sense of Islamic studies deals with data that are part of given Muslim communities and are culled from the Islamic experience but that may or may not possess a religious (i. e., Islamic) significance for particular Muslim groups.

ISLAMIC STUDIES AS PART OF ORIENTAL STUDIES

The development of Islamic studies in the nineteenth century was part of the general development of Oriental studies, commonly called "Orientalism." Oriental studies were largely patterned after the classical studies that had arisen in the sixteenth century; they were based on philology in the broad sense of the term, that is, the study of a particular culture through its texts. Islamic studies in this sense lead to nonnormative accounts of Islamic religion as described under (2), above. The field has always been a demanding one, presupposing an intensive study of Arabic and other "Islamic" languages, on the basis of which text editions can be prepared and textual studies, including textual criticism and literary history, can be carried out. Familiarity with the texts, in its turn, is a prerequisite for the further study of history. Supplemented by the study of other Islamic expressions in art and architecture and in present-day religious life, textual, historical, and anthropological research together prepare the way for the study of Islamic culture and religion.

Within the Orientalist tradition, Islamic studies were conceived of as a cultural discipline and exhibited certain assumptions of European civilization of the time, notably the superiority of Western civilization and the excellence of its scholarship. Stress has generally been laid on the differences between Islamic civilization and European culture, with an ethnocentric bias toward the latter. Beyond the interest in its origins, a certain predilection can be discerned for the "classical" period of Islamic civilization, a preference that can also be observed in other branches of Oriental studies. Specialization increasingly led to detailed studies, and the ideal of a comprehensive view of Islam often came down simply to mastering an extraordinary mass of facts.

THE NONNORMATIVE STUDY OF ISLAMIC RELIGION. The history of Islamic religion has been approached in three basic ways. A great number of historians, following the example set by Julius Wellhausen (1844-1918) in his various studies on the early Islamic period, have focused on the external history of Islam.

Another kind of historical research concentrates rather on what may be called the inner developments in Islamic religion and culture. This approach was introduced by one of the major figures in the field, Ignácz Goldziher (1850-1921), who tried to establish the basic framework of an intellectual history of Islam.

Somewhere between the general historians and the historians of religion are cultural historians of the medieval period such as Carl Heinrich Becker (1876-1933), Jörg Kraemer (1917-1961), and Gustav Edmund von Grunebaum (1909-1972), all of whom set religious developments within wider cultural frameworks, which were related in turn to political and military history. The name of Marshall G. S. Hodgson (1921-1968) should also be mentioned here because of his efforts to situate the total history of Islam within a culturally oriented world history.

Muhammad. Various approaches have developed since the mid-nineteenth-century biographies mentioned earlier. In a two-volume biography, *Mohammed* (1892-1895), Hubert Grimme gave an account of the social factors in Muhammad's life and stressed the Prophet's aspect as social reformer; Frants Buhl assembled all historical materials available at the time for a substantial biography of Muhammad in *Das Leben Muhammed* (1930; 2d ed., 1955). Tor Andrae studied later Muslim views of Muhammad as a prophet and paradigmatic figure in his *Die person Muhammeds in lehre und glauben seiner gemeinde* (1918). A breakthrough in establishing the context of Muhammad's life and work is W. Montgomery Watt's two-volume study, *Muhammad at Mecca* (1953) and *Muhammad at Medina* (1956), which focuses attention on the social and economic changes in Arabia (Mecca) that Muhammad tried to address in his prophetic activity. Maxime Rodinson's thought-provoking biography, *Mohammed* (1961; Eng. trans., 1971), interprets historical data from a similar perspective but adds a psychological dimension.

The Qur'an. After the important translation into English by George Sale (1697?-1736), published in 1734 with a famous "preliminary discourse," a great number of translations of the Qur'an have seen the light. I may mention those by Richard Bell (1937), A. J. Arberry (1955), and Marmaduke Pickthall (1930), this last being recognized by Muslims. The classic study of the Qur'anic text remains that of Theodor Nöldeke in its three-volume second edition (1909-1938), enlarged and revised with the help of colleagues. Arthur Jeffery published two important studies, *The Textual History of the Qur'an* (1937) and *The Foreign Vocabulary of the Qur'an* (1938). Rudi Paret's conscientious German translation (1962) was subsequently accompanied by his important commentary (1971). Important is Angelika Neuwirth's *Studien zur Komposition der mekkanischen Suren* (1981). John Wansbrough's *Quranic Studies* (1977) has brought the accepted theory on the early collation of the Qur'anic text into question.

The study of the Qur'an implies that of Muslim commentaries *(tafsirs)* of the Qur'an. See Helmut Gätje's *Koran und Koranexegese* (1971) and compare Mohammed Arkoun's *Lectures du Coran* (1982).

Hadith. Goldziher's critical stand in *Muhammedanische Studien,* vol. 2 (1890; Eng. trans., 1971), with regard to the historical dating of *hadiths* ("traditions") that were ascribed to Muhammad or his companions but were in fact later creations, was carried further by Joseph Schacht (1902-1969) in *The Origins of Muhammadan Jurisprudence* (1950) and led to a debate on their authenticity. Since the *sunnah* (consisting of hadiths) is the second source, after the Qur'an, of religious knowledge and law in Islam, here too Muslims are particularly sensitive to scholarly criticism from outside. See G. H. A. Juynboll's *The Authenticity of the Tradition Literature: Discussions in Modern Egypt* (1969).

Law. The structure of religious law (shari'ah) in Islam, its ideal character, and the rules of juridical reasoning by Muslim jurists were first elucidated by Goldziher and by Christiaan Snouck Hurgronje (1857-1936), who also studied its application, side by side with customary law, in Indonesia. Current trends toward islamicization in Muslim countries are again arousing interest in its juridical aspects. Among the scholars who have worked on changes in the application of the *shari'ah* in modern Muslim states, the names of J. N. D. Anderson and Noel J. A. Coulson deserve particular mention.

Metaphysical theology. An important study on early Muslim creeds is A. J. Wensinck's *The Muslim Creed* (1933). Georges Anawati and Louis Gardet's *Introduction a la théologie musulmane* (1948) demonstrates the structural similarity of medieval Islamic and Christian theological treatises. Here and in other works these authors stress the apologetic character of Islamic theology. On the other hand, Harry A. Wolfson, in *The Philosophy of the Kalam* (1976) is attentive to parallels between Islamic, Christian, and Jewish theological thought.

Islamic philosophy. It has become clear that there are philosophical traditions of a gnostic nature in Islam, which can be found in Shi'i intellectual circles, both Iranian Twelvers and Isma'ili Seveners. We owe this discovery mainly to the investigations of Henry Corbin (1903-1978), whose works, such as *En islam iranien* (4 vols., 1971-1972), revealed hidden but still living spiritual worlds.

Mysticism. Muslim mystical thought and experience have attracted serious scholarly attention in the West only in the course of the twentieth century, especially through the work of Reynold A. Nicholson (1868-1945) and Louis Massignon (1883-1962). The former concentrated on certain major works and their authors, such as *The Mathnawi* of Jalal al-Din Rumi; the latter focused on the development of mystical terminology and produced a four-volume biography of the tenth-century mystic al-Hallaj (1922; Eng. trans., 1982).

Islamic art and architecture. This field deserves a separate status among the disciplines making up Islamic studies, since it deals with materials other than texts and is linked with art history in general. Among scholars who deserve mention are K. A. C. Creswell (1879-1974), and Richard Ettinghausen (1906-1979), and at present Oleg Grabar and Robert Hillenbrand.

Religious institutions. In recent decades important breakthroughs have been made in the understanding of the relationships between Islamic religious institutions and the societies in which they function. In *La cité musulmane* (1954), Louis Gardet attempted to sketch the outline of the ideal society in terms of orthodox Islam, while H. A. R. Gibb and Harold Bowen addressed the eighteenth-century Muslim "religious structure," especially with regard to processes of modernization in parts 1 and 2 of *Islamic Society and the West* (1950-1957). Considerable attention has been paid to religious authorities (*'ulama',* Sufi shaykhs) with their different roles in society. Important in this respect is A. C. Eccel's study *Egypt, Islam and Social Change: Al-Azhar in Conflict and Accommodation* (1984).

Modern developments in Islam. It has become clear that recent developments should be described according to the country within which they occur and that although certain patterns can be established as valid for nearly all Muslim countries, in each country various groups, including the government, have their own articulation of Islam. A major contribution to this formulation is *Der Islam in der Gegenwart,* edited by

The first systematic history of the lives of Sufi mystics is ascribed to Abu 'Abd al-Rahman al-Azdi al-Sulami.

PAGE 631

Werner Ende and Udo Steinbach (1984). Events in revolutionary Iran have shown, moreover, that Islamicists in the Orientalist tradition simply have not been adequately equipped to interpret what happens in Muslim countries. On the other hand, *Religion in the Middle East: Three Religions in Concord and Conflict*, edited by A. J. Arberry (2 vols., 1969), may be mentioned here as an example of objective and impartial information about the three major religions that coexist in the Middle East.

Present-Day Islamic Studies in the Wider Sense

As in other scholarly fields and disciplines, new issues have come under discussion in Islamic studies.

METHODOLOGICAL ISSUES. Intense epistemological debates seem to have been absent from Islamic studies until the 1960s, chiefly because of the inherited pattern established by the scholarly tradition. Yet there have been other currents in Islamic studies too, and with the incorporation of textual research within a larger cultural and even religious perspective, scholars such as Louis Massignon, Gustav E. von Grunebaum, Wilfred Cantwell Smith, and Clifford Geertz have been able to see the Islamic universe in new ways. We shall point here to three matters of paramount importance: (1) the questioning of Islamic identities, (2) the increased assertion of Islamic identities, and (3) Islam as a living religion and faith.

“Traditionary religion” has defined itself and its faith on the basis of received tradition.

PAGE 224

Questioning Islamic identities. Among Western scholars who have reevaluated accepted readings of the Islamic tradition, John Wansbrough has opened up critical research with regard to the text of the Qur'an in the aforementioned *Quranic Studies* and has extended this inquiry to early Islamic history in *The Sectarian Milieu* (1978). In an even more controversial work, *Hagarism: The Making of the Islamic World* (1977), Patricia Crone and Michael Cook have argued that the historical formation of Islamic religion and civilization can be explained in terms of a complex network of Jewish-Arab relations.

Asserting Islamic identities. An intention to assert Islamic identities becomes evident in books such as *Islamic Perspectives: Studies in Honor of Sayyid Abul Ala Mawdudi*, edited by Khurshid Ahmad and Zafar Ishaq Ansari (1979), and *Islam and Contemporary Society*, edited by Salem Azzam (1982). One important contribution of Muslim scholars is that of making Muslim forms of understanding available to other Islamicists; their work should lead, moreover, to discussions within the Muslim community. Noteworthy, for instance, is Mohammed Arkoun's semiotic approach in *Lectures du Coran* (1983) and Fazlur Rahman's studies on the history of Islamic thought, for instance in his *Prophecy in Islam: Philosophy and Orthodoxy* (1979).

Islam as a living religion. Recent methodological and epistemological concerns have been stimulated in large part by a growing interest in Islam as a living religion and faith, which is connected with certain political solidarities and social and economic issues. As a result, the meaning of events and processes in Muslim countries is studied more and more in their contemporary cultural and Islamic framework. Three questions are paramount in these Islamic studies in the wider sense:

1. Which kinds of groups support and transmit various particular interpretations of Islam, and who are the leaders of these groups?
2. How do particular changes occurring in the religious institutions (or in institutions legitimized by religion) relate to changes in society at large, and what are the consequences of such social changes for the institutions concerned (and vice versa)?
3. What general social functions do various Islamic ideas and practices perform within particular Muslim societies, apart from the specifically religious meaning they are meant to have?

Such questions can also be asked about Muslim societies of the past, provided that historical data are available to answer them. Indeed, it is a mark of epistemological progress that subjects excluded from investigation fifty years ago for lack of methodological tools can now come under the purview of Islamic studies.

Tradition in a wider sense. The notion of tradition, too, has attracted new attention in Islamic studies among both historians and anthropologists, who recognize that successive generations of Muslims have interpreted their lives, their world, and history through the religious and cultural framework, or “tradition,” of the society into which they have been born. On the one hand, we have the normative “great” tradition with elements ranging from the Qur'an and parts of the *shari'ah* to particular creeds, practices of worship, and paradigmatic figures and episodes in Islamic history. On the other hand, for each region we must add numerous elements of the local “little” tradition, including legendary events in the history of the region, miracles and blessings of particular saints, the meritorious effect of particular practices, and so on, all of which constitute local, popular religion.

NEW TOPICS OF RESEARCH. As a result of these and other methodological issues, new topics of research have come within our horizon, of which the following may be mentioned as examples.

Revitalization of Islam. Different forms of Islamic revitalization have been signaled by both Muslim and non-Muslim observers in a number of countries. While the media have addressed the political and “exotic,” even abhorrent dimensions of this revitalization, scholarly investigation is needed to distinguish various sectors of life and society in which such revitalization takes place (as well as its religious from its nonreligious aspects) according to both Islamic criteria and criteria developed by the scientific study of religion. Preceding movements of reform and renewal should be taken into account.

Ideologization of Islam. During the last hundred years a great number of Islamic ideologies have developed; what for centuries was considered a religion based on revelation seems to have evolved in certain quarters into an Islamic system or ideology of a cognitive nature, in which the dimension of faith and religious knowledge seems to have given place to a definite set of convictions and values. This ideologization responds to a need for rationalization and may serve apologetic purposes, against criticism from the West, for instance, or against secularizing trends within society. Often the predicate "Islamic" suggests that a correspondence is sought between the older cultural and religious tradition and the solutions proposed for the problems of the present.

Islam, political action, and social and economic behavior. After a period of Western domination in which a political articulation of Islam was mostly impossible, Islam has again come to play various political roles, in both more conservative and more progressive quarters, usually bypassing the authority of those schooled in religious law (the *'ulama'*). So the question arises: what are the possibilities and the limits of the political, social, and economic use and abuse of Islam? Islam has permitted very different economic systems (including a form of capitalism) as Maxime Rodinson (1966) has demonstrated. We may go on to ask in what ways Islam can be related positively or negatively to economic development, and to determine what basic values economic development is subordinated to within the Islamic framework. That Islam is articulated basically as a way of life and as social behavior has become evident again, for instance, by the recurrence of the veil and by expressions of solidarity with Muslims in other parts of the world.

Muslim self-interpretations. In the course of the history of Islamic studies, serious hermeneutical mistakes, that is, errors of interpretation, have been made. Western scholars for instance tended to reify Islam, forgetting that "Islam" in itself does not exist, that "Islam" is always Islam *interpreted*, and that Muslims keep this interpretive process going. Much more attention should be paid to what Muslim authors, speakers, groups, and movements actually mean when they express themselves in particular situations, free from interpretations or explanations imposed from outside. Carrying out study in collaboration with Muslim researchers is appropriate here as in many fields.

Interaction and image formation. It is perhaps a sign of renewal of Islamic studies that Islam is no longer studied only as an isolated culture, tradition, and religion that may have assimilated outside influences, but that more attention is given to the spread of Islam, processes of interaction with other communities, and Muslim images of other religions and of the non-Muslim world generally. This direction of inquiry is evidenced first by works of Arab scholars like Albert Hourani, Abdallah Laroui, and others, as well as by publications like Bernard Lewis's T*he Muslim Discovery of Europe* (1982) and *Euro-Arab Dialogue: Relations between the Two Cultures,* edited by Derek Hopwood (1985). This area of study has been opened up as a consequence of the recognition of Islamic religion and culture as an autonomous partner in international religious and cultural relations, which are linked, in turn, to political and other relationships. The recent establishment of considerable Muslim communities living side by side with a non-Muslim majority in a number of Western societies may also have made both North America and Western Europe more sensitive to the plurality of religions and cultures in daily life.

— JACQUES WAARDENBURG

ISRAELITE RELIGION

GENERAL FEATURES

Unique in many ways, Israelite religion is most remarkable for its monotheism. The difference between monotheism and polytheism is not only in number—one god versus a plurality of gods—but in the character and nature of the deity. In contradistinction to the polytheistic system according to which gods are subject to biological rules (the existence of male and female in the divine sphere, which means procreation, struggle for survival, etc.), the God of Israel is transcendent, that is, beyond the sphere of nature and therefore not subject to physical and biological principles.

The transcendence of God explains the absence of mythology in the religion of Israel. The transcendent character of the God of Israel explains, too, the objection of Israelite religion to magic, which was so prominent in polytheistic religions. God's will cannot be revealed unless he himself wishes to do so; his will cannot be revealed through magic, which draws its power from mystic powers not subordinated to the deity.

It is true that the biblical stories as well as the biblical cult contain magical elements. There are many allusions to the marvelous transformation of objects: the staffs of Moses and Aaron become serpents (*Ex.* 4:2-4, 7:9-10); Moses divides the sea with his staff (*Ex.*

The life and death of Malcolm X helped to increase interest in Islam among black Americans.

PAGE 20

14:16); Elisha's staff is supposed to revive the Shunammite's son (2 *Kgs.* 4:29); and the three arrows that Joash, the king of Israel, drove into the ground gave him three victories over Aram (*2 Kgs.* 13:14-19). However, all these acts are considered wondrous signs from God. The wonder is seen as "the hand" and power of God and not as originating in the action itself or in the power of the sorcerer, as was the case in pagan religions (cf. *Ex.* 4:1-4, 7:8-10, et al.). Thus, for example, Elisha's staff performs wonders only when accompanied by prayer (contrast *2 Kgs.* 4:29-31 with 4:32-35).

Another transcendent feature of Israelite monotheism is the prohibition against representing God by visual symbol or image: "You shall not make for yourself a sculptured image [pesel] or any likeness" (*Ex.* 20:4, *Dt.* 5:8, et al.).The god which is beyond nature and cosmos cannot be represented by anything earthly and natural.

"You shall not make for yourself a sculpted image or any likeness."

EXODUS 20:4

It is this feature which makes the Israelite religion philosophical, as conceived by the Greeks. For example, it was the observation of Theophrastus (c. 372-287 BCE), a disciple of Aristotle, that "being philosophers by race, [the Jews] converse with each other about 'the Divine' [to *theion*]" (Menachem Stern, *Greek and Latin Authors on Jews and Judaism,* vol. 1, 1974, p. 10). "The Divine" denotes here the philosophical concept of the one force that governs the world in contrast to the popular belief in various mythical deities.

HISTORICAL DEVELOPMENT UNTIL THE TEMPLE CULT

THE RELIGION OF THE PATRIARCHS. Tradition considers Abraham the father of Yahvistic monotheism but this has no basis in the Bible itself. On the contrary, the biblical documents show an awareness of a gap between the religion of the patriarchs and the Yahvistic national religion of Israel. The name of God, *Yahveh* (preserved only unvocalized in the texts, i. e., YHVH) is not known before Moses (*Ex.* 3:13f., 6:2ff.), and the nature of the patriarchal creed is completely different from that of Moses and later Israelites. The god of the patriarchs is tied to person and family; the god is called God of Abraham, Isaac, or Jacob or "the God of the father" (*Gn.* 26:24, 28:13, 31:42, 32:10, 46:3, 49:25), as is appropriate to a wandering family.

HISTORICAL CIRCUMSTANCES OF THE BIRTH OF MONOTHEISM. As is well known, the term *Hebrews ('Ivrim)* is associated with the term *Habiru,* which designates the nomadic population in the ancient Near East during the second millennium BCE. The "god of the Hebrews" was worshiped by all sorts of nomads in the area of Sinai and the Negev: the Midianites and Kenites, as well as the Israelites. Most important in this respect is the new, extrabiblical evidence which came to light in the last decades. In the Egyptian topographical lists of King Amenhotep III (1417-1379 BCE) discovered in the temple of Amon at Soleb in Nubia as well as in the list of King Ramses II (1304-1237 BCE) discovered at Amarah West, we find "the land of nomads [of] Yahveh," along with "the land of nomads [of] Seir" (see Raphael Gibeon, *Les bédouins Shosu des documents égyptiens,* Leiden, 1971, nos. 6a, 16a). A land of nomads associated with Yahveh alongside the land of Edom (Seir) reminds us of the old traditions of Israel, according to which Yahveh appeared from Sinai, Edom, Teman, Paran, and Midian (*Dt.* 33:2, *Jgs.* 5:4, *Hb.* 3:3-7). The fact that Yahveh's revelation is associated with places scattered over the whole Sinai Peninsula as well as over the Edomite territory east of Sinai seems to indicate that Yahveh was venerated by many nomads of Sinai and southern Palestine and that "the land of nomads of Yahveh" refers to the whole desert to the east of the delta. To be sure, the god revealed to Moses and adopted by the Israelites reflects a unique phenomenon. Monotheism did come out of Israel and not out of Edom or Midian. However, in the light of the new evidence, one must consider the existence of some kind of proto-Israelite belief in Yahveh in the wilderness region of Sinai and Edom (cf. S. Herrmann, "Der Name Jhw in den Inschriften von Soleb." *Fourth World Congress of Jewish Studies,* vol. 1, Jerusalem, 1967, pp. 213-216; B. Mazar, "Yahveh came out from Sinai," *Temples and High Places in Biblical Times: Proceedings of the Colloquium in Honor of the Centennial of Hebrew Union College-Jewish Institute of Religion, Jerusalem, 14-16 March 1977,* ed. A. Biran, 1981, pp. 5-9).

All this shows that there were close relations between the Israelites and other nomads in the desert, and, as we have indicated above, Yahveh's appellation in *Exodus,* "the god of the Hebrews," seems to support this notion.

EXODUS FROM EGYPT. Among the nomadic tribes in the land of Yahveh (that is, the Sinai Peninsula), the Israelites were under Egyptian control, and, as I have indicated, the religion of Israel actually took shape in the course of a struggle with Egyptian religion and culture. The struggle of the Israelite tribes with the Egyptians comes to full expression in the story about the liberation of Israel from "the house of bondage"—that is, the Exodus, which became the hallowed Israelite epic.

EARLY CULTIC WORSHIP. According to Pentateuchal sources, God revealed himself to the people on a specific mountain called Sinai or Horeb. However, ancient poems hail several places in the Sinai Desert as places of theophany. For example, *Deuteronomy* 33 speaks of YHVH coming from Sinai, Seir, and Mount Paran (33:2; cf. *Jgs.* 5:4-8). In *Habakkuk* 3 we read that God comes from Teman and from Mount Paran, and in the continuation of this poem Cushan and Midian are also mentioned. In all of these instances God sets out from his holy abode (on the mountain) to save his people, not to give laws as in the later prosaic sources. Furthermore, in these poems the deity sets out not from a single hallowed place (e.g., Sinai or Horeb) but from various places scattered throughout the Sinai Peninsula and the northwestern Arabian Desert. It seems that there were several holy mountains in this area that served the nomads who venerated YHVH.

Excavational findings suggest that the Sinai Desert was the site of a long tradition of cultic practices; Mount Sinai was only one of many cultic sites. The elaborate biblical descriptions of the cultic practices at Mount Sinai may reveal aspects of worship at such sites throughout the desert. The center of the tribal worship was the Mountain of God, ascent to which was allowed only to the priesthood and the elders (*Ex.* 24:1-2, 24:9, 24:14). Access to the godhead was the privilege of the prophet Moses alone (*Ex.* 3:5, 19:9-13, 19:20-22, 24:15, 33:21-23, 34:2ff.).

COVENANT BETWEEN GOD AND ISRAEL. The covenant of Sinai, which became so central in the religion of Israel, denotes not a bilateral agreement between the deity and the people but rather a commitment by the people to keep the law of YHVH as it is inscribed on tablets and found in the "Book of the Covenant" (*Ex.* 24:3-8). The word *covenant* (Heb., *berit*) means a bond or obligation that is accompanied by a pledge or oath and that is validated by sanctions, dramatized curses, threats, and the like performed in specific cultic rites.

A very old Mosaic cultic rite not repeated in later periods is the blood covenant as described in *Exodus* 24:3-8. After Moses builds an altar at the foot of Mount Sinai and erects twelve stone pillars, he prepares sacrifices and uses the blood of the animal sacrifices for the covenantal ceremonies. Half of the blood he sprinkles on the altar (and, apparently, on the stone pillars), and the other half he puts into basins in order to sprinkle it over the people. Then he declares: "This is the blood of the covenant that the Lord [YHVH] has cut with you" (*Ex.* 24:8). The fact that the blood ritual is found only in the Sinaitic ceremony may teach us that it belongs to the ancient nomadic reality and therefore reflects a Mosaic background.

REVELATION AT SINAI. In the description of the Sinaitic cult we find a clear distinction between the place of revelation on Mount Sinai and the place of worship below the mountain. This situation is reflected in the tradition about the tent of meeting *(ohel mo'ed)* at Sinai. According to *Exodus* 33:7-11, Moses pitches the tent of meeting outside the camp, and there it serves as a place of encounter between God and Moses. This contrasts with the later description of the Tabernacle by the Priestly source, which conceives the tent of meeting as the sanctuary in the middle of the camp, where Moses meets God (cf. *Ex.* 29:42-43; 40:34-35). The two phenomena, revelation and cult, which previously existed separately, amalgamated here, a situation which prevailed in later times when prophecy and cult joined hands in the Israelite and Judahite temples.

The place of revelation, be it the top of the mountain or the tent outside the camp, was out of bounds to the people. Indeed, according to the Sinaitic tradition it was Moses alone who received the words of God (the Decalogue), and as mediator, he delivered them afterward to the people.

COVENANT OF SINAI

The covenant from the Godhead to Moses is central to the religion of Israel. It represents a commitment by the people to keep the law of Yahveh.

CORBIS-BETTMANN

That the words written on the tablets of the covenant are identical with the commandments of *Exodus* 20 is explicitly said in *Deuteronomy* 5:19, 9:10, and 10:4, and there is no reason to suppose that this was differently understood in former times. A series of cultic commandments in *Exodus* 23:10-19 (paralleled in *Exodus* 34:10-26) has been considered the original Decalogue by some scholars, who see the traditional Decalogue (*Ex.* 20:1-14) as a later ethical decalogue inspired by prophetic circles. But there is no warrant for this supposition. The division of the series of laws in *Exodus* 23:10-19 and 34:10-26 into ten discrete commandments is highly controversial, and the idea that a "cultic decalogue" should be more ancient than an "ethical" one has no basis at all.

The human partners swore to abide by certain stipulations, the penalty for disobedience being calamitous curses on the community and ultimately its exile.

PAGE 193

THE TEN COMMANDMENTS: THEIR ESSENCE AND FUNCTION. From the point of view of content and form there is no difference between the Ten Commandments and other laws. The various law codes of the Bible contain the same injunctions which are attested in the Decalogue in both its versions. The prohibitions against idolatry and swearing falsely, the observance of the Sabbath, the honoring of parents, and the prohibitions against murder, adultery theft, and false witness—all these appear again and again in the various laws of the Pentateuch. The only exception is the injunction against coveting a neighbor's property, and this is indeed indicative of the particular nature of the Decalogue.

Though we do not have clear evidence of when the Decalogue was crystallized and accepted, it seems to be very old. It is referred to by the eighth century BCE prophet Hosea (*Hos.* 4:2) and later by Jeremiah (*Jer.* 7:9) and is cited in two ancient psalms (*Ps.* 50:7, 50:18-19, 81:9-11), and one cannot deny that it might date from the beginning of Israelite history; it may even be traced back to Moses, the founder of Israel's religious polity.

A clear parallel in the ancient world to such a phenomenon as Moses, the prophet who reveals divine commands to the people, is to be found in a Greek document of the Hellenistic period. In a private shrine of the goddess Agdistis in Philadelphia (modern-day Alasehir), in Asia Minor, an oath inscribed in a foundation stone of the sanctuary was found which contains injunctions similar to the ethical part of the Decalogue: not to steal, not to murder, not to commit adultery, and so on. These were revealed in a dream by the goddess Agdistis to the prophet Dionysius, who inscribed them on the stela of the sanctuary (see F. Sokolowski, *Lois sacrées de l'Asie Mineure,* 1955, no. 20, ll. 20ff.). It is also said in the inscription that whoever will violate one of the mentioned commandments will not be allowed to enter the shrine. Although this document is of late origin (first century BCE), it undoubtedly reveals ancient religious practice which is typologically similar to that of the Decalogue: a concise

TEN COMMANDMENTS
Revelation at Sinai

The Ten Commandments (or the Decalogue) appear twice in the Hebrew scriptures, at *Exodus* 20:1-17 and at *Deuteronomy* 5:6-21. There are differences between the two listings, but the order and the general contents are substantially identical. The commandments may be grouped as follows:

- Commandments 1-3: God's self-identification, followed by commandments against the worship of other gods, idolatry, and misuse of the divine name (*Ex.* 20:1-7, *Dt.* 5:6-11).
- Commandments 4-5: Positive commands to observe the Sabbath and to honor parents (*Ex.* 20:8-12, *Dt.* 5:12-16).
- Commandments 6-7: Prohibitions of violent acts against neighbors, namely, killing and adultery (*Ex.* 20:13-14, *Dt.* 5:17-18).
- Commandments 8-10: Prohibitions of crimes against community life, namely, stealing, testifying falsely, and hankering after the life and goods of neighbors (*Ex.* 20:15-17, *Dt.* 5:19-21).

In the Jewish and Christian communities the order has occasionally varied, and the numbering has varied considerably, especially in the different Christian communions.

The Ten Commandments are alluded to in a number of places in the Hebrew scriptures, in the Qumran literature, and in the New Testament, although they are rarely quoted exactly and do not appear at all in a complete listing outside of *Exodus* and *Deuteronomy.* The prologue is found in a number of places (*Hos.* 13:4, *Ps.* 81:10/11), and there are lists of some of the prohibitions in several places (*Hos.* 4:2, *Mk.* 10:17-22 and parallels). But the fundamental outlook of the Ten Commandments is characteristic for the Jewish and Christian communities through the centuries. God will not have the divine name and selfhood profaned, for the Creator remains free and sovereign over against the creation. God demands rest from labor as well as labor, and he will not tolerate the mistreatment of elderly parents by adult children. God claims authority over human life and demands respect for life on the part of all. God will not permit the violation of the extended life of human beings in their social and institutional relations.

The Ten Commandments became a fixed part of Christian catechetical practice and worship. Less prominent in Islam, they are implicit in much that Muhammad taught. In the course of Christian history they have frequently contributed to narrowness of vision and legalism. Yet it seems likely that they have contributed much more by way of positive guidance to the community. Negatively put categorical statements of this sort provide moral orientation of the community, the defining characteristics of a people, showing what is simply not allowed. The Ten Commandments require positive statements of what idolatry means, what murder is, how the Sabbath is to be observed, and the like. They constitute not so much a constriction of human freedom as an invitation to the community to claim its proper freedom within the confines of what would be ruinous for it.

— WALTER HARRELSON

set of commandments revealed by a god to his prophet, who is to transmit them to the believers.

COVENANT BETWEEN GOD AND ISRAEL. The obligation of Israel toward God to keep his law equals the pledge to show loyalty to him. Besides the Mosaic covenant, which is based on the promise to observe the laws, we find in *Joshua* 24 a covenant which stipulates exclusive loyalty to the one God. Joshua's covenant, which took place in Shechem, modern-day Nablus (cf. *Dt.* 27 and *Jos.* 8:30-35), is mainly concerned with the choice of the God of Israel and the observance of strict loyalty toward him: "He is a jealous God. . . . if you forsake the Lord and serve alien gods, . . . he will make an end of you" (*Jos.* 24:19-20). This covenant, which was concerned with loyalty and made at the entrance to the Promised Land, was especially necessary because of the exposure to Canaanite religion and the danger of religious contamination.

In fact, the Shechemite covenant described in *Joshua,* which is associated—as indicated—with the foundation ceremony between mounts Gerizim and Ebal (cf. *Dt.* 27, *Jos.* 8:30-35), is close in its character to the covenant of the plains of Moab, presented in *Deuteronomy.* This covenant takes place before the crossing into the Promised Land and is defined as an act of establishing a relationship between God and Israel (*Dt.* 26:17-19, 27:9-10, 29:12; see especially *Dt.* 27:9: "This day you have become a people belonging to the Lord your God").

The two covenants presented in the Pentateuch, the one at Sinai (*Ex.* 19-24) and the other at the plains of Moab in *Deuteronomy,* were patterned after the type of covenant prevalent in the ancient Near East between suzerains and vassals.

The notion of exclusive loyalty that is characteristic of the monotheistic belief has been dressed not only in the metaphor of the relationship between suzerain and vassal but also in the metaphor of the relationships between father and son and husband and wife. Just as one can be faithful only to one suzerain, to one father, and to one husband, so one can be faithful only to the God of Israel and not to other gods as well. The prophets elaborated the husband-wife metaphor in describing the relations between God and Israel (*Hos.* 3, *Jer.* 3:1 10, *Ez.* 16, 23).

CENTRALIZATION OF THE CULT: THE GREAT TURNING POINT

Although there had existed in Israel a central shrine since the times of the Judges (cf. the temple at Shiloh, *1 Samuel* 1-2), small chapels and altars were also allowed. We hear about the patriarchs building altars in various places in the land of Canaan (*Gn.* 12:7-8, 13:18, 26:25), and we also find that during the time of the judges altars were built in the fields and on rocks (*Jgs.* 6:24, 13:19; *1 Sam.* 19:35). These other shrines were not prohibited; on the contrary, from Elijah's words at his encounter with God at Horeb (*1 Kgs.* 19:10, 19:14), we learn that the destruction of an altar dedicated to Yahveh is tantamount to killing a prophet of Yahveh. Elijah himself is praised because of his restoration of an altar to Yahveh on Mount Carmel (*1 Kgs.* 18).

The act of Hezekiah was actually the culmination of a process which started in the northern kingdom of Israel in the ninth century. That was the period of the struggle initiated by the prophets against the Tyrian god, Baal (*1 Kgs.* 17-19, *2 Kgs.* 9-10). From this struggle emerged the polemic against the golden calves erected in Dan and in Bethel (*1 Kgs.* 12:28ff.) and, finally, an iconoclastic tendency which affected the high places and altars all over the country, developing further a tendency to purge Israelite religion of pagan elements.

The abolition of the provincial sites created the proper atmosphere for the spiritualization of worship as reflected in *Deuteronomy.* Even the Temple in Jerusalem was now conceived not as the physical house of the Lord but as the house in which God establishes his name (*Dt.* 12:11, 12:21, et al.). Furthermore in the reform movement of Hezekiah and Josiah, which is reflected in *Deuteronomy,* there is a shift from sacrificial ritual to prayer. The author of *Deuteronomy* is not concerned with the cultic activities in the Temple, such as daily offerings, burning incense, kindling the lamp, and so on. On the other hand, he is very interested in worship that involves prayer (*Dt.* 21:7-9, 26:5-10, 26:13-15), because he sees in liturgy the most important form of worship.

THE RELIGION OF THE BOOK: SCRIBES AND WISE MEN. Hallowed as the "book of the torah" *(sefer ha-torah)* written by Moses (*Dt.* 31:9), *Deuteronomy* became the authoritative, sanctified guidebook for Israel. It was the first book canonized by royal authority and by a covenant between God and the nation, established by the people gathered in Jerusalem in 622 BCE, under the auspices of King Josiah (*2 Kgs.* 23:1-3). Only after other books were appended to *Deuteronomy* did the term Torah refer to the whole Pentateuch.

The sanctification of the holy writ brought with it the need for scribes and scholars who had the ability to deal with written documents. It is in the period of the canonization of *Deuteronomy* that we hear about scribes *(soferim)* and wise men *(hakhamim)* preoccupied with the written Torah (*Jer.* 8:8). After the return to Judah of many Jews from exile in Babylonia, the man who brought with him the book of the Torah and disseminated it in Judah was Ezra the scribe (*Ezr.* 7:6, 7:11). Since the scribes and wise men were preoccupied with education in general, they did not limit themselves to sacred literature but also taught wisdom literature. The

"This day you have became a people belonging to the Lord your God."

DEUTERONOMY 27:9

Prayer is a necessity of the human condition.

PAGE 551

latter consists of didactic instructions on the one hand and speculative treatises on justice in the world (e.g., the *Book of Job*) and the meaning of life (e.g., *Ecclesiastes*) on the other. It is true that wisdom literature is cosmopolitan in nature and therefore addresses man as such and does not refer at all to Israel or to other sacred national concepts. However, this did not deter the scribes and wise men in Israel from incorporating this literature into their lore.

Wisdom literature was canonized and turned into an integral part of the holy writ. Furthermore, it was identified with the revealed Torah (cf. *Sir.* 24). *Deuteronomy,* in which the subject of education plays a central role, defines *torah* as wisdom (*Dt.* 4:6), and as has been shown (Weinfeld, 1972, pp. 260ff.), contains a great many precepts borrowed from wisdom tradition. The amalgamation of the divine word of Torah with the rational values of wisdom turned the law of Israel, especially the Deuteronomic law, into a guide of high moral and humane standards.

THE CRYSTALLIZATION OF JUDAISM: THE POSTEXILIC PERIOD. The period of exile and restoration left its deep marks on the people and changed their spiritual character. Because the exiles were deprived of sacrificial worship as a result of the principle of centralization of worship in Jerusalem, the spiritual, abstract nature of the religion was enhanced. The shift from sacrifice to prayer was facilitated by the very act of centralization, as shown above; however, as long as sacrifice was being practiced in the chosen place in Jerusalem, religion was still tied to the Temple. In the religious vacuum created following the destruction of the First Temple, stress came to be laid on the spiritual side of religion, and thus the way was paved for the institution of the synagogue, which is based on prayer and the recital of holy scripture. All this leaves no doubt that the synagogue service was already taking shape in the fifth century BCE.

Another important factor which shaped the character of Second-Temple Judaism was the impact of prophecy. The fact that prophets of the First-Temple period had predicted the return to Zion after a period of exile added to the glorification of the prophets and to the trust in their words. People began to believe that the prophecies about Jerusalem as the spiritual center of the world would also be realized and that the nations would recognize the God of Israel and finally abandon their idolatrous vanities.

Observance of the Torah. The exiles took seriously not only the demand for exclusive loyalty to the God of Israel, which meant complete abolition of idolatry and syncretism, but also the positive commands of God embodied in the law of Moses. They felt obliged not only to fulfill the law in a general sense but to do exactly as written in the book.

At this time the Tetrateuch, the first four books of the Pentateuch, was added to the "Book of the Torah," or *Deuteronomy,* which had been sanctified before the exile, with the reform of Josiah in 622 BCE. The Tetrateuch was composed of ancient documents that had already been codified in literary sources, such as the Yahvistic-Elohistic source and the Priestly code. After adding these sources to *Deuteronomy,* the name "Book of the Torah" was extended to the whole of the Pentateuch, namely, the Torah, which was thus also taken as comprising the "Book of Moses."

The Pentateuch, then, comprised various codes representing different schools or traditions and different periods which sometimes contradicted each other. However, all of them were equally obligatory. How then would one fulfill two contradictory laws? According to the Priestly code, for example, one has to set aside a tenth of his crop for the Levites (*Nm.* 18:21f.), while the Deuteronomic code (written after centralization of the cult) commands one to bring the tithe to Jerusalem and consume it in the presence of the Lord (*Dt.* 14:22ff.). These laws reflect different social and historical circumstances, but since both were considered to belong to the law of Moses, both were authoritative.

No less a problem was the exact definition of the ancient law in order to apply it to life circumstances. Thus, for example, the commandment "you shall not do any work on the seventh day" (*Ex.* 20:9) is quite vague. What does work mean? Is drawing water from the well considered work (as in *Jubilees* 50.8)? Interpretation of the law split the people into sects; the most practical were the Pharisees, who fixed thirty-nine chief labors forbidden on the Sabbath (*Shab.* 7.2), and thus tried to adjust the law to life. The Essenes, however, were much more stringent in their understanding of work forbidden on the Sabbath. Before the Maccabean Revolt (166-164 BCE), making war was forbidden on the Sabbath; in the Maccabean times, when the nation fought for its existence, the people learned that it could not survive without permitting themselves to fight on the Sabbath.

The struggle for the correct interpretation of the Torah was actually the struggle to fulfill the will of the Lord, and in this goal all Jews were united.

— MOSHE WEINFELD

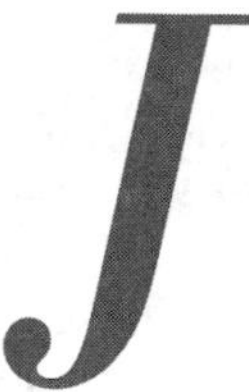

JAINISM

HISTORY. There remains no objective document concerning the beginnings of Jainism. The date of Maha-vira's death ("entry into *nirvana*"), which is the starting point of the traditional Jain chronology, corresponds to 527/526 BCE, but some scholars believe it occurred about one century later. In any case, the Jain community was probably not "founded" solely by Mahavira. Rather, his adherents merged with the followers of a previous prophet (Parsva); reorganizations and reforms ensued and a fifth commandment was added to the older code, as was the practice of confession and repentance; nakedness came to be recommended to those among the believers who took the religious vows, although apparently it was not imposed on Parsva's disciples.

In 79 CE, the community split into two main churches—the Digambara, "sky-clad" (and thus naked), and the Svetambara, "white-clad." By the time of the separation, however, the doctrine had been fixed for the whole community; this accounts for the fundamental agreement in the main tenets professed by the Svetambaras and the Digambaras. On the other hand, epigraphic and literary records prove that religious "companies" *(gana)* already existed, subdivided into *sakhas* ("branches") and *kulas* ("families" or "schools"). The remarkable organization of Mahavira's church has proved a firm foundation for the welfare and survival of his followers. The community of the monks and nuns is said to have been entrusted by Mahavira to eleven chief disciples, or *ganadharas* ("company leaders"). The chief among them was Gautama Indrabhuti, while his colleague Sudharman allegedly taught his own pupil Jambu the words spoken by the Jina. Thus the canon of the Svetambaras goes back to Sudharman through uninterrupted lines of religious masters *(acaryas)*.

After Mahavira's time the Jain community spread along the caravan routes from Magadha (Bihar) to the west and south. They claim to have enjoyed the favor of numerous rulers. Notwithstanding possible exaggerations, they probably were supported by a number of princes. By the fifth century (or earlier), the Digambaras were influential in the Deccan, especially in Karnataka. Under the Ganga, Rastrakuta, and other dynasties Jain culture undoubtedly flourished. Numerous sects were founded, among them the brilliant Yapaniya, now extinct. In the tenth century, however, Vaisnavism and Saivism crushed Jainism in the Tamil area, and in the twelfth century they triumphed over Jainism in Karnataka as well.

As for the Svetambaras, they were especially successful in Gujarat where one of their famous pontifs, Hemacandra (1089-1172), served as minister to the Calukya king Kumarapala (1144-1173) and enforced some Jain rules in the kingdom. Decline was to follow soon after his death, which was hastened by the Muslim invasions. Jain activities did not cease with his

JAINIST LITERATURE
All Set for Polemic Discourse

From early times the Jains have been engaged in a variety of literary activities. Their works, whether intended for their own adherents or composed with rival groups in view, generally have an edifying, proselytizing, or apologetic purpose. The languages used vary to suit the audience and the epoch.

All of the oldest texts are composed in varieties of Prakrits (i. e., Middle Indo-Aryan), more or less akin to the languages in current use among the people of northern India at the time of the first sermons.

The Jain traditions, while considering that the fourteen Purvas have been lost, contend that part of the material they included was incorporated into later books. The Digambaras boldly assert that some sections are the immediate basis of two of their early treatises (c. first century CE) whereas, according to the Svetambaras, the teachings of the Purvas were embedded in the so-called twelfth Anga of their canon, now considered lost. The earliest extant documents are the canonical scriptures of the Svetambaras and the systematic treatises *(prakaranas)* of the Digambaras.

— COLETTE CAILLAT

Vardhamana Mahavira, reformed an existing community and founded the predominantly monastic Jainism,

PAGE 324

Confession in Jainism (alocana *and, more generally,* pratikramana) *is mainly a monastic institution, performed twice daily.*

PAGE 174

demise, however. Elaborate sanctuaries were erected, such as that on Mount Abu, now in Rajasthan. The rise of several reformist sects testifies to the vitality of the Svetambaras, who even succeeded in interesting the Moghul emperor Akbar (r. 1555-1605) in the Jain doctrine.

Although the Jain community never regained its former splendor, it did not disappear entirely; nowadays, the Digambaras are firmly established in Maharashtra and Karnataka and the Svetambaras in Panjab, Rajasthan, and Gujarat.

The Digambaras rely on *prakaranas,* of which the oldest are written in a third variety of Prakrit. Their authors include Vattakera, author of the *Mulacara* (Basic Conduct; approximately 1,250 stanzas) and Kundakunda, a prolific writer and much admired mystic, and author of *Samayasara,* (Essence of the Doctrine).

These books mark the beginning of an important literary genre that was also cultivated by the Svetambaras. One of the fundamental treatises in this category is by Umasvati (c. second century; most likely a Svetambara): with small variants, both churches accept the authority of his *Tattvarthadhigama Sutra* (Sutra for Attaining the Meaning of the Principles), a doctrinal synthesis composed of 350 aphorisms written in Sanskrit. This linguistic selection shows that the Jains were prepared to engage in polemics with other schools of thought and to engage the brahmans with Brahmanic terminology and words of discourse.

RELIGIOUS PRACTICES. The practices observed among the Jains are dependent on two main factors: specific Jain convictions and the general Indian environment. They reflect, in fact, many parallels with the rules and observances of Brahmanic ascetics and Buddhist monks.

All Jains are members of the four-fold congregation *(samgha),* composed of monks and nuns, laymen and laywomen. They share a common belief in the *triratna* ("three jewels"): *samyagdarsana* ("right faith"), *samyagjñana* ("right knowledge"), and *samyakcaritra* ("right conduct"). Observance of the "three jewels" provides the conditions for the attainment of the goal, that is, liberation from bondage. Deliverance can be attained only by the *nirgrantha,* the Jain monk "free from bonds" both external and internal. The ideal practices therefore are those in force in the (male) religious community.

The monks and nuns take the five "great vows" *(mahavratas).* The life of Mahavira is regarded as an ideal model.

Religious age and hierarchy play a great role: elders look to the material and spiritual welfare of the company; the *upadhyaya* is a specialist in teaching the scriptures; the *acarya* acts as spiritual master. Full ordination takes place after a short novitiate that lasts approximately four months. Admission as a novice is subject to prior examination. At his departure from home, the novice abandons all property and his head is shaved.

Right religious conduct is minutely defined, giving

JAIN TEMPLE

Cultic Practices and temple worship are tolerated by the Jain church, despite their belief that such rituals imply violence.

HANS GEORG ROTH/CORBIS

rules for habitation and wandering, begging, study, confession, and penances. During the four months of the rainy season the religious groups remain in one locality; nowadays fixed places of shelter *(upasrayas)* are prepared for them, often near a temple, where householders visit, ask advice, and listen to teachings.

Called *sravakas* ("listeners") or *upasakas* ("servants"), the lay believers also take five main vows, similar to (but milder than) the *mahavratas,* and hence termed *anuvratas* ("lesser vows"). These include *ahimsa* ("nonviolence") and *satya* ("truthfulness"). They are complemented by three "strengthening vows" and four "vows of spiritual discipline," of which the last, but not the least, is *dana* ("charity").

These practices are evidently relevant in a doctrine that emphasizes individual exertion, and that considers the Jinas to be inaccessible, liberated souls. On the other hand, the Jain church has not been able to ignore the devotional aspirations of the laity, who are also attracted by Hindu ritual. Hence, although temple worship (with the burning and waving of lamps, plucked flowers and fruit, preparation of sandal paste, etc.) implies violence, cultic practices are tolerated, being considered ultimately of help to the worshiper's progress.

MYTHOLOGY AND COSMOLOGY. The Jain representation of the cosmos *(loka)* is akin to (though not identical with) the standard Brahmanical descriptions. The cosmos is composed of three main parts: the lower, middle, and upper worlds. It is often represented as a colossal upright human figure, the enormous base of which is formed by seven hells (populated by beings whose past actions were violent and cruel and who consequently suffer terrible torments).

Next is the "middle world". Though small, it has a great importance: there, in a few circumscribed areas, time and the law of retribution prevail, different kinds of men live (among them the civilized *aryas*), and spiritual awakening and perfection can be achieved.

Beginning far above the stars, the upper world appears as a gradually purer and purer counterpart of the lower world. Finally, near the top of the *loka* lies the place, shaped like an inverted umbrella (or the crescent moon) where the *siddhas* ("perfected ones," i. e., liberated souls) are assembled.

Divinities are found in the three worlds, and fall into four main classes. Only mankind, however, can give birth to the Jain prophets, who are called *tirthamkaras,* literally, "ford-makers" across the ocean of rebirths.

Like other Indian systems, Jainism compares the cyclic course of time *(kala)* to the movement of a wheel, and divides it into recurring periods called *kalpas* ("eons").

DOCTRINE. The tenets of Jainism are well delineated in the Svetambara canon and the Digambara procanonical books, and are systematically presented in the *Tattvarthadhigama Sutra.*

Knowledge *(jñana),* of which the Jains distinguish five kinds, is an essential attribute of the soul *(jiva).* It culminates in *kevala-jñana,* absolute and perfect omniscience.

The Jain system of logic is characterized by the complementary theories of *syadvada* ("[different] possibilities") and of *nayavada* ("[method of] approach"). The first affirms that a statement about an object is valid not absolutely but under one of "several conditions" (hence its other name, *anekantavada);* considering that an object "can be" *(syad)* such, not such, and so forth, seven modes of assertion are distinguished. The *nayavada* defines seven main points of view (generic, specific, etc.) from which to consider an object. The Jains adopt an empirical standpoint.

Jainism is a pluralist substantialism that insists on the reality of change. The world and non-world are basically constituted from five *astikayas* ("masses of being"). Matter furnishes to the souls a body in which to be incorporated and the possibility of corporeal functions. There are five kinds of bodies, each having different functions. All corporeal beings possess at least two of them, the "karmic" and the "fiery" (the latter for digestion).

Bondage occurs because the subtle matter resulting from anterior intentions and volitions is attracted to the soul through the vibration of its "soul-points"; this attraction (called *yoga*) is exercised by means of the material elements of speech, body, and mind. The subtle matter that has been so attracted becomes *karman* when entering the soul. The pious Jain strives to rid the latter of these material extrinsic elements. When life ends, the *jiva,* if it has recovered its essential nature, immediately rejoins the other *siddhas* at the pinnacle of the universe.

ETHICS. The essentials of Jain ethics are contained in the sets of vows to be taken by the monks and nuns on the one hand, and by the lay believers on the other. Monks and householders further observe other series of prohibitions and engagements that are meant to favor spiritual progress.

The monks cultivate *samvara,* the spiritual path defined by the cessation of karmic influx, by means of established ethical and behavioral practices. The monk finally sheds the residues of *karman* by means of steadfast and thorough asceticism *(tapas).*

Lists of the virtues required of the householder have received much attention in Jain tradition and literatures. Some lists include as many as thirty-five ethical imperatives incumbent on the nonclerical Jain, but all include five *anuvratas* ("small vows," as opposed to the monks' *mahavratas,* or "great vows"): *(ahimsa),* truthfulness and honesty in all business affairs *(satya),*

In Jainism, spiritual power is understood to reside especially in the monastic communities, that is, among those monks and nuns who have left ordinary secular life to pursue spiritual perfection through ascetic practices.

PAGE 538

that material wealth be gained only through legitimate transactions (*asteya,* lit., "non-stealing"), restraint from all illicit sexual activities *(brahma),* and renunciation of one's attachment to material wealth *(aparigraha).* Moreover, the householder or business person should progress through the higher stages of renunciation involving increasingly complete performance of these vows. Thus, he can come closer and closer to fulfilling the monk's vows as well, and ultimately can attain the purity of the "wise man's death."

The actual path to liberation *(moksa)* is described by Jains as one that includes fourteen "stages of qualification" *(guna-sthana).* Leaving the state characterized by "wrong views," the path leads ultimately to the elimination of all passions and culminates in omniscience.

Jain ascetics fasted while on pilgrimage and in preparation for certain festivals.

PAGE 225

CULTIC STRUCTURES. It is a specific aspect of the householder's religious life that he is allowed to take part in temple rituals and to worship temple images.

The structure of the Jain temple is on the whole similar to the Hindu temple. [*See* Temple.] The distinctive feature of the Jain shrine is the image of the *tirthamkara* to whom it is dedicated and the idols of the prophets who flank him or occupy the various surrounding niches. Secondary divinities are frequently added (and are very popular); there are also auspicious and symbolic diagrams: the wheel of the Jain law, and the "Five Supreme Ones": *arhats, siddhas, acaryas, upadhyayas,* and *sadhus.* There are also conventional representations of continents, of holy places, and of the great festive congregation *(samavasarana)* in the middle of which the Jina is said to have delivered his sermon for the benefit of all creatures. The offerings placed on the offering plates or planks by the faithful with the rice grains he has brought to the shrine are symbols of the three jewels (three dots), which provide escape from the cycle of bondage (the *svastika*) and lead to *siddhi* (a crescent at the top of the figure).

The example set by great men other than the *tirthamkaras* is also commemorated: homage is paid to the "footprints" *(padukas)* in stone of the great teachers. Above all, Bahubali is a source of inspiration to the Digambaras: "sky-clad" on the crest of the Indragiri hill in Sravana Belgola, his colossal monolithic statue (fifty-seven feet high, erected c. 980) attracts streams of pilgrims, and has been reproduced at several other sites.

PROMINENT JAIN PERSONALITIES. Jain achievements are due to the energy and courage of a comparatively united community. Certain brilliant and outstanding individuals, however, have influenced the movement. Recently, Mohandas Gandhi himself paid homage to the Jain jeweller and poet Raychandbhai Mehta (1868-1901). [*See also the biography of Mohandas Gandhi.*] This is the epoch when, after two to three centuries of relative stagnation, a reawakening took place thanks to enlightened monks and householders. Among those who took part in this renewal, Vijaya Dharma Suri (1868-1922) is one of the best known, both in India and in the West. Among the many others who deserve mention are two Digambara scholars, Hiralal Jain (1898-1973) and A. N. Upadhye (1906-1975), or, on the Svetambara side, those whose collaboration made the foundation of the Lalbhai Dalpatbhai Institute of Indology in Ahmedabad possible: the Muni Punyavijaya (1895-1971), Kasturbhai Lalbhai, and Pandit D. M. Malvania (a pupil of the philosopher Sukhlalji, 1880-1978).

— COLETTE CAILLAT

JAPANESE RELIGION

Like many other ethnic groups throughout the world, the earliest inhabitants of the Japanese archipelago had from time immemorial their own unique way of viewing the world and the meaning of human existence and their own characteristic rituals for celebrating various events and phases of their individual and corporate life. To them the whole of life was permeated by religious symbols and authenticated by myths. From this tradition an indigenous religious form, which came to be designated as Shinto, or "the way of *kami,*" developed in the early historic period. Many aspects of the archaic tradition have also been preserved as basic features of an unorganized folk religion. Meanwhile, through contacts with Korea and China, Japan came under the impact of religious and cultural influences from the continent of Asia. Invariably, Japanese religion was greatly enriched as it appropriated the concepts, symbols, rituals, and art forms of Confucianism, Taoism, the Yin-yang school, and Buddhism. Although these religious and semireligious systems kept a measure of their own identity, they are by no means to be considered mutually exclusive; to all intents and purposes they became facets of the nebulous but enduring religious tradition that may be referred to as "Japanese religion."

It is worth noting in this connection that the term *shukyo* ("religion") was not used until the nineteenth century. In Japanese traditions, religious schools are usually referred to as *do, to,* or *michi* ("way"), as in Butsudo ("the way of the Buddha") or Shinto ("the way of *kami*"), implying that these are complementary ways or paths within the overarching Japanese religion. Various branches of art were also called *do* or *michi*, as in *chado* (also *sado,* "the way of tea"). This usage reflects the close affinity in Japan between religious and aesthetic traditions.

EARLY HISTORICAL PERIOD

Prior to the introduction of Sino-Korean civilization and Buddhism, Japanese religion was not a well-structured institutional system. The early Japanese took it for granted that the world was the Japanese islands where they lived. They also accepted the notion that the natural world was a "given." Thus, they did not look for another order of meaning behind the natural world. Although the early Japanese did not speculate on the metaphysical meaning of the cosmos, they felt they were an integral part of the cosmos, which to them was a community of living beings, all sharing *kami* (sacred) nature.

Equally central to the early Japanese outlook was the notion of *uji* ("lineage group, clan"), which provided the basic framework for social solidarity. Each *uji* had clansmen *(ujibito),* groups of professional persons *(be)* who were not blood relations of the clansmen, and slaves *(nuhi),* all of whom were ruled by the *uji* chieftain *(uji no kami).* Each *uji* was not only a social, economic, and political unit but also a unit of religious solidarity centering around the *kami.*

IMPACT OF CHINESE CIVILIZATION AND BUDDHISM ON JAPANESE RELIGION. With the gradual penetration of Chinese civilization—or, more strictly, Sino-Korean civilization—and Buddhism during the fifth and sixth centuries, Japanese religion was destined to feel the impact of alien ways of viewing the world and interpreting the meaning of human existence. Sensing the need to create a designation for their hitherto unsystematized religious, cultural, and political tradition, the Japanese borrowed two Chinese characters—*shen* (Jpn., *shin*) for *kami,* and *tao* (Jpn., *to* or *do*) for "the way." Inevitably, the effort to create almost artificially a religious system out of a nebulous, though all-embracing, way of life left many age-old beliefs and practices out of the new system.

There is little doubt that the introduction of Chinese script and Buddhist images greatly aided the rapid penetration of Chinese civilization and Buddhism. As the Japanese had not developed their own script, the task of adopting the Chinese script, with its highly developed ideographs and phonetic compounds, to Japanese words was a complex one. There were many educated Korean and Chinese immigrants who served as instructors, interpreters, artists, technicians, and scribes for the imperial court and influential *uji* leaders of the growing nation. The Japanese intelligentsia over the course of time learned the use of literary Chinese and for many centuries used it for writing historical and official records.

Through written media the Japanese came to know the mystical tradition of philosophical Taoism, which enriched the Japanese aesthetic tradition. The Japanese also learned of the Yin-yang school's concepts of the two principles (*yin* and *yang*), the five elements (metal, wood, water, fire, and earth), and the orderly rotation of these elements in the formation of nature, seasons, and the human being. The Yin-yang school thus provided cosmological theories to hitherto nonspeculative Japanese religion. It was also through written Chinese works that Japanese society, which had been based on archaic communal rules and the *uji* system, appropriated certain features of Confucian ethical principles, social and political theories, and legal and educational systems.

PRINCE SHOTOKU. The regency of Prince Shotoku (573-621), who served under his aunt, Empress Suiko (r. 592-628), marks a new chapter in the history of Japanese religion. To protect Japan's survival in the precarious international scene, Shotoku and his advisers attempted to strengthen the fabric of national community by working out a multireligious policy reconciling the particularistic Japanese religious tradition with the universal principles of Confucianism and Buddhism. Shotoku himself was a pious Buddhist and is reputed to have delivered learned lectures on certain Buddhist scriptures. Moreover, he held the Confucian notion of *li* ("propriety") as the key to right relations among ruler, ministers, and people. Shotoku was convinced that his policy was in keeping with the will of the *kami.* In his edict of 607 he states how his imperial ancestors had venerated the heavenly and earthly *kami* and thus "the winter [*yin,* negative cosmic force] and summer [*yang,* positive cosmic force] elements were kept in harmony, and their creative powers blended together," and he urged his ministers to do the same.

Prince Shotoku took the initiative in reestablishing diplomatic contact with China by sending an envoy to the Sui court. He also sent a number of talented young scholars and monks to China to study. Although Shotoku's reform measures remained unfulfilled at his untimely death, the talented youths he sent to China played important roles in the development of Japanese religion and national affairs upon their return.

THE RITSURYO SYNTHESIS. Prince Shotoku's death was followed by a series of bloody power struggles, including the coup d'état of 645, which strengthened the position of the throne. During the second half of the seventh century the government, utilizing the talents of those who had studied in China, sponsored the compilation of a written law. Significantly, those penal codes (*ritsu;* Chin., *lü*) and civil statutes (*ryo;* Chin., *ling*), which were modeled after Chinese legal systems, were issued in the name of the emperor as the will of the *kami.* The government structure thus developed during the late seventh century is referred to as the Ritsuryo ("imperial rescript") state. Although the

"The combined essences of heaven and earth became the yin and yang."

HUAI-NAN TZU

In ancient Japanese the word kami was used adjectivally to mean something mysterious, supernatural, or sacred.

PAGE 599

basic principle of the Ritsuryo state was in a sense a logical implementation of Prince Shotoku's vision, which itself was a synthesis of Buddhist, Confucian, and Japanese traditions, it turned out to be in effect a form of "immanental theocracy," in which the universal principles of Tao and Dharma were domesticated to serve the will of the sovereign, who now was elevated to the status of living or manifest *kami.*

NARA PERIOD

During the eighth century Japanese religion reached an important stage of maturity under Chinese and Buddhist inspirations. It was a golden age for the Ritsuryo state and the imperial court. In contrast to earlier periods, when Korean forms of Buddhism influenced Japan, early eighth-century Japan felt the strong impact of Chinese Buddhism. In 710 the first capital, modeled after the Chinese capital of Ch'angan, was established in Nara, which was designed to serve as the religious as well as the political center of the nation. During the Nara period the imperial court was eager to promote Buddhism as the religion best suited for the protection of the state. Accordingly, the government established in every province state-sponsored temples *(kokubunji)* and nunneries *(kokubunniji).* In the capital city the national cathedral, Todaiji, was built as the home of the gigantic bronze statue of the Buddha Vairocana. The government sponsored and supported six schools of Chinese Buddhism. Of the six, the Ritsu (Vinaya) school was concerned primarily with monastic disciplines.

Despite such encouragement and support from the government, Buddhism did not have much impact on the populace. More important were three new religious forms that developed out of the fusion between the Japanese religious heritage and Buddhism.

The first new form was the Nature Wisdom school (Jinenchishu), which sought enlightenment by meditation or austere physical discipline in the mountains and forests. Those who followed the path, including some official monks, affirmed the superiority of enlightenment through nature to the traditional Buddhist disciplines and doctrines. The indigenous Japanese acceptance of the sacrality of nature was thus reaffirmed.

Second is the emergence of a variety of folk religious leaders, variously called private monks *(shidoso)* and unordained monks who appropriated many features of Buddhism and taught simple and syncretistic "folk Buddhism" among the lower strata of society.

A third new form came out of an amalgamation of Buddhism and Shinto called Tyobu Shinto.

KAMI
Divine Forces

The Japanese term kami, often translated as "gods," or "divine forces," denotes the focus of Shinto worship.

In the *Kojiki* (Records of Ancient Matters), compiled in 712 CE, and the *Nihonshoki* (Chronicles of Japan), compiled in 720 CE, there are two types of kami. Kami of the first and most important type figure anthropomorphically in the early myths. For example, the first three kami were said to have revealed themselves in the High Celestial Plain (according to the *Kojiki*) or among marsh reeds between heaven and earth (according to the *Nihonshoki*). Kami of the second type appear as offspring of earlier kami. Most "nature" kami, stones, mountains, rivers, and trees, and the ancestral kami as well, belong to this second category. Entities in nature, including human beings, are individually considered to be kami. Kami, therefore, can be regarded as the spiritual nature of each individual existence. The number of kami is infinite, although only a finite number of them are actually enshrined. The Japanese emperor, believed to be the direct descendant of both the sun goddess Amaterasu and the "high life-giving kami," Takamimusubi, has been especially venerated.

After Buddhism came to Japan in the sixth century, a gradual change took place in the understanding of kami. At first, the Buddha was accepted as a foreign kami, but with the support of the imperial household the Buddha attained an independent status politically and socially equal to that of the traditional kami. From the ninth century on the syncretization of Buddhism and Shinto was promoted by the Buddhist clergy. Subsequently, kami were treated as guardians of the Buddha and were sometimes given the title bodhisattva. As a result, Buddhist sutras were commonly recited in Shinto shrines for the salvation of kami. Moreover, although Shinto originally produced no iconic representations of kami, statues of kami began to appear during the thirteenth century at some shrines in imitation of Buddhism.

Today, the Association of Shinto Shrines rejects any monotheistic interpretation that could detract from the independent dignity of individual kami in the Shinto pantheon. Shinto is a polytheistic religion, permitting worship of many kami at the same time, although Amaterasu retains the central and highest position.

— UEDA KENJ

Because of the excessive support of religion and culture by the court, which benefited only the aristocracy, the capital of Nara during the second half of the eighth century was doomed by political corruption, ecclesiastical intrigue, and financial bankruptcy. Therefore the capital was moved in 794 from Nara to a remote place and then ten years later to the present Kyoto.

EROSION OF THE RITSURYO IDEAL. The new capital in Kyoto, Heiankyo ("capital of peace and tranquillity"), was also modeled after the Chinese capital. Freed from ecclesiastical interference, the leaders of the Kyoto regime were eager to restore the integrity of the Ritsuryo system, and they forbade the Nara Buddhist schools to move into the new capital. Instead, the imperial court favored, side by side with Shinto, two new Buddhist schools, Tendai (Chin., T'ien-t'ai) and Shingon (Chin., Chen-yen).

The foundation of the Ritsuryo system was the sacred monarchy. Ironically, during the Heian period the two institutions that were most closely related to the throne, namely, the Fujiwara regency and rule by retired monarchs *(insei)*, undercut the structure of the Ritsuryo system. The regency had been exercised before the ninth century only by members of the royal family and only in times when the reigning monarch needed such assistance. But from the late ninth century to the mid-eleventh century the nation was actually ruled by the regency of the powerful Fujiwara family. The institutionalization of the regency implied a significant redefinition of the Ritsuryo system by the aristocracy. The aristocratic families acknowledged the sacrality of the throne, but they expected the emperor to "reign" only as the manifest *kami* and not to interfere with the actual operation of the government.

The Heian period witnessed the phenomenal growth of wealth and political influence of ecclesiastical institutions, both Shinto and Buddhist, equipped with lucrative manors and armed guards.

This period, and the elegant culture it produced, vanished in the late twelfth century in a series of bloody battles involving both courtiers and warriors. Then came a new age dominated by warrior rulers.

RELIGIOUS ETHOS DURING THE KAMAKURA PERIOD

That the nation was "ruled" by warrior-rulers from the thirteenth to the nineteenth century, even though the emperor continued to "reign" throughout these centuries, is a matter of considerable significance for the development of Japanese religion. There were three such feudal warrior regimes (*bakufu* or shogunates): (1) the Kama-kura regime (1192-1333), (2) the Ashikaga regime (1338-1573), and (3) the Tokugawa regime (1603-1867). Unlike the Ritsuryo state, with its elaborate penal and civil codes, the warrior rule—at least under the first two regimes—was based on a much simpler legal system, which allowed established Shinto and Buddhist institutions more freedom than they had under the cumbersome structure of the Ritsuryo state. It also set the stage for the development of new religious movements, many with roots in the folk tradition.

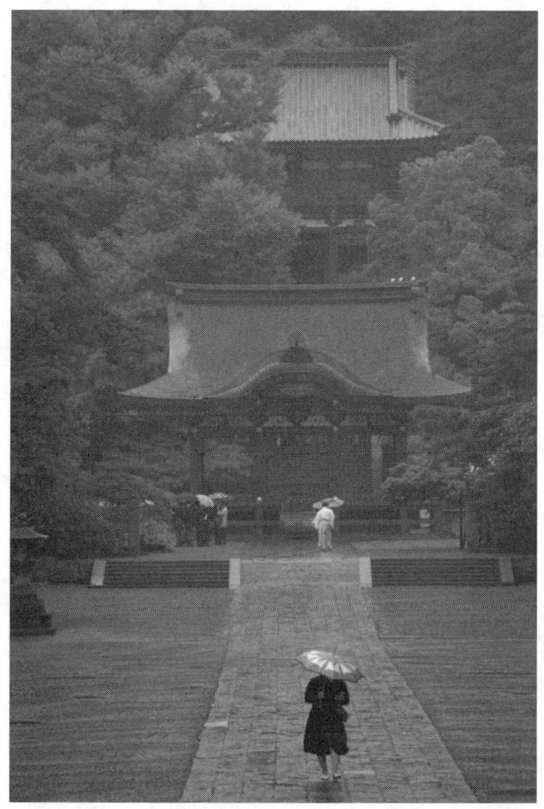

SHINTO SHRINE

The term kami, often translated as "gods" or "divine forces," represents the focus of Shinto—the indigenous religion of Japan.

MICHAEL S. YAMASHITA/CORBIS

The warriors for the most part were not sophisticated in cultural and religious matters. Many of them, however, combined simple Buddhist piety with devotion to the pre-Buddhist indigenous tutelary *kami* of warrior families rather than those of the imperial Shinto tradition. At the same time, the peasantry, artisans, and small merchants, whose living standard improved a little under the Kamakura regime, were attracted to new religious movements that promised an easier path to salvation in the dreaded age of degeneration *(mappo)*.

The most important surviving Buddhist temple compound of early Japan is Horyuji, located just south of modern-day Nara.

PAGE 660

New religious leaders became instrumental in the establishment of the three Pure Land (Amida's Western Paradise) traditions. They were Honen (Genku, 1133-1212) of the Jodo (Pure Land) sect, who is often compared with Martin Luther; Shinran (1173-1262) of the Jodo Shin (True Pure Land) sect, a disciple of Honen, who among other things initiated the tradition of a married priesthood; and Ippen (Chishin, 1239-1289) of the Ji (Time) sect, so named because of its practice of reciting hymns to Amida six times a day.

On the other hand, Nichiren (1222-1282), founder of the school bearing his name and a charismatic

"Kami and the Buddha differ in name, but their meaning is one."

EDICT OF 1614

prophet, developed his own interpretation of the *Hokekyo* (Lotus Sutra), the *Saddharmapundarika Sutra,* as the only path toward salvation for the Japanese nation.

In contrast to the paths of salvation advocated by the Pure Land and Nichiren schools, the experience of enlightenment *(satori)* was stressed by Eisai (Yosai, 1141-1215), who introduced the Rinzai (Chin., Lin-chi) Zen tradition, and Dogen (1200-1253), who established the Soto (Chin., Ts'ao-tung) Zen tradition. Zen was welcomed by Kamakura leaders partly because it could counterbalance the powerful and wealthy established Buddhist institutions and partly because it was accompanied by other features of Sung Chinese culture, including Neo-Confucian learning. The Zen movement was greatly aided by a number of émigré Ch'an monks who settled in Japan. [*See* Zen.]

Despite the growth of new religious movements, old religious establishments, both Shinto and Buddhist, remained powerful during this period; for example, both gave military support to the royalist cause against the Kamakura regime during the abortive Jokyu rebellion in 1221. On the other hand, confronted by a national crisis during the Mongol invasions of 1274 and 1281, both Shinto shrines and Buddhist monasteries solidly supported the Kamakura regime by offering prayers and incantations for the protection of Japan.

ZEN, NEO-CONFUCIANISM, AND KIRISHITAN DURING THE ASHIKAGA PERIOD

Unlike the first feudal regime at Kamakura, the Ashikaga regime established its *bakufu* in Kyoto, the seat of the imperial court. Accordingly, religious and cultural development during the Ashikaga period (1338-1573, also referred to as the Muromachi period) blended various features of warrior and courtier traditions, Zen, and Chinese cultural influences. This blending in turn fostered a closer interpenetration of religious and aesthetic values. All these religious and cultural developments took place at a time when social and political order was threatened not only by a series of bloody power struggles within the *bakufu* but also by famines and epidemics that led to peasant uprisings and, further, by the devastating Onin War (1467-1478) that accelerated the erosion of Ashikaga hegemony and the rise of competing daimyo, the so-called *sengoku daimyo* ("feudal lords of warring states"), in the provinces. In this situation, villages and towns developed something analogous to self-rule. Merchants and artisans formed guilds *(za)* that were usually affiliated with established Buddhist temples and Shinto shrines, whereas adherents of Pure Land and Nichiren sects were willing to defend themselves as armed religious societies. Into this complex religious, cultural, social, and political topography, European missionaries of Roman Catholicism, then known as Kirishitan, brought a new gospel of salvation.

Throughout the Ashikaga period established institutions of older Buddhist schools and Shinto (for example, the Tendai monastery at Mount Hiei, the Shingon monastery at Mount Koya, and the Kasuga shrine at Nara) remained both politically and economically powerful. However, the new religious groups that had begun to attract the lower strata of society during the Kamakura period continued to expand their influence, often competing among themselves.

ZEN AND NEO-CONFUCIANISM. By far the most influential religious sect during the Ashikaga period was Zen, especially the Rinzai Zen tradition, which became *de facto* the official religion. Many Zen priests served as advisers to administrative offices of the regime. They earned reputations as monk-poets or monk-painters, and Gozan temples became centers of cultural and artistic activities.

Zen priests, including émigré Chinese Ch'an monks, also made contributions as transmitters of Neo-Confucianism, a complex philosophical system incorporating not only classical Confucian thought but also features of Buddhist and Taoist traditions that had developed in China during the Sung (960-1127) and Southern Sung (1127-1279) periods.

The combined inspiration of Japanese and Sung Chinese aesthetics, Zen, and Pure Land traditions, coupled with the enthusiastic patronage of shoguns, made possible the growth of a variety of elegant and sophisticated art: painting, calligraphy, *renga* (dialogical poetry or linked verse), stylized *no* drama, comical *kyogen* plays, flower arrangement, and the cult of tea.

THE TOKUGAWA SYNTHESIS. The Tokugawa regime, which was to hold political power until the Meiji restoration in 1867, was more than another feudal regime; it was a comprehensive sixfold order—political, social, legal, philosophical, religious, and moral—with the shogun in its pivotal position.

The religious policy of the Tokugawa regime was firmly established by the first shogun, who held that all religious, philosophical, and ethical systems were to uphold and cooperate with the government's objective, namely, the establishment of a harmonious society. Following the eclectic tradition of Japanese religion, which had appropriated various religious symbols and concepts, the first shogun stated in an edict of 1614: "Japan is called the land of the Buddha and not without reason. . . . *Kami* and the Buddha differ in name, but their meaning is one." Accordingly, he surrounded himself with a variety of advisers, including Buddhist clerics and Confucian scholars, and shared their view that the Kirishitan (Roman Catholicism) religion

THE COMING OF KIRISHITAN

Christianity, Buddhism, and Political Power

When the Onin War ended in 1478 the Ashikaga regime could no longer control the ambitious provincial daimyo who were consolidating their own territories. By the sixteenth century Portugal was expanding its overseas empire in Asia. The chance arrival of shipwrecked Portuguese merchants at Tanegashima Island, south of Kyushu, in 1543 was followed by the arrival in Kyushu in 1549 of the famous Jesuit Francis Xavier. Although Xavier stayed only two years in Japan, he initiated vigorous proselytizing activities during that time.

The cause of Kirishitan (as Roman Catholicism was then called in Japanese) was greatly aided by a strongman, Oda Nobunaga (1534-1582), who succeeded in taking control of the capital in 1568. Angry that established Buddhist institutions were resisting his scheme of national unification, Nobunaga took harsh measures; he burned the Tendai monastery at Mount Hiei, killed thousands of Ikko (True Pure Land) followers, and attacked rebellious priests at Mount Koya in order to destroy their power. At the same time, ostensibly to counteract the residual influence of Buddhism, he encouraged Kirishitan activities. Ironically, this policy was reversed after his death. Nevertheless, by the time Nobunaga was assassinated, 150,000 Japanese Catholics, including several daimyo, were reported to be among the Japanese population.

The initial success of Catholicism in Japan was due to the Jesuits' policy of accommodation. Xavier himself adopted the name *Dainichi* (the Great Sun Buddha, the supreme deity of the Shingon school) as the designation of God; later, however, this was changed to *Deus*. Jesuits also used the Buddhist terms *jodo* ("pure land") for heaven and *so* ("monk") for the title *padre*. Moreover, Kirishitan groups followed the general pattern of tightly knit religious societies practiced by the Nichiren and Pure Land groups. Missionaries also followed the common Japanese approach in securing the favor of the ruling class to expedite their evangelistic and philanthropic activities. Conversely, trade-hungry daimyo eagerly befriended missionaries, knowing that the latter had influence over Portuguese traders. In fact, one Christian daimyo donated the port of Nagasaki to the Society of Jesus in 1580 hoping to attract Portuguese ships to the port, which would in turn benefit him. Inevitably, however, Jesuit-inspired missionary work aroused strong opposition not only from anti-Kirishitan daimyo and Buddhist clerics but from jealous Franciscans and other Catholic orders as well. Furthermore, the Portuguese traders who supported the Jesuits were now threatened by the arrival of the Spanish in 1592, via Mexico and the Philippines, and of the Dutch in 1600.

Meanwhile, following the death of Oda Nobunaga, one of his generals, Toyotomi Hideyoshi (1536-1598), endeavored to complete the task of national unification. Determined to eliminate the power of Buddhist institutions, he not only attacked rebellious monastic communities, such as those in Negoro and Saiga, but also conducted a thorough sword hunt in various monastic communities. Hideyoshi was interested in foreign trade, but he took a dim view of Catholicism because of its potential danger to the cause of national unification. He was incensed by what he saw in Nagasaki, a port that was then ruled by the Jesuits and the Portuguese. In 1587 he issued an edict banishing missionaries, but he did not enforce it until 1596 when he heard a rumor that the Spanish monarch was plotting to subjugate Japan with the help of Japanese Christians. Thus in 1597 he had some twenty-six Franciscans and Japanese converts crucified. The following year Hideyoshi himself died in the midst of his abortive invasion of Korea. [See also Christianity, article on Christianity in Asia.]

— JOSEPH M. KITAGAWA

could not be incorporated into the framework of Japanese religion and would be detrimental to the cause of social and political harmony. Nevertheless, the Tokugawa regime's initial attitude toward Catholicism was restrained; perhaps this was because the regime did not wish to lose foreign trade by overt anti-Kirishitan measures. But in 1614 the edict banning Kirishitan was issued, followed two years later by a stricter edict.

BUDDHISM AND THE TOKUGAWA REGIME. The Tokugawa regime's anti-Kirishitan measures required every Japanese citizen to become, at least nominally, Buddhist. Accordingly, the number of Buddhist temples suddenly increased from 13,037 (the number of temples during the Kamakura period) to 469,934. Under Tokugawa rule a comprehensive parochial system was created, with Buddhist clerics serving as arms of the ruling regime in charge of thought control. In turn, Buddhist temples were tightly controlled by the regime, which tolerated internal doctrinal disputes but not deviation from official policy. The only new sect that emerged during the Tokugawa period was the Obaku sect of Zen, which was introduced from China in the mid-seventeenth century.

CONFUCIANISM AND SHINTO. Neo-Confucianism was promoted by Zen Buddhists prior to the Tokugawa period. Thus, that Neo-Confucian scholars were also Zen clerics was taken for granted. Fujiwara Seika (1561-1619) first advocated the independence of Neo-Confucianism from Zen. By his recommendation, Hayashi Razan (1583-1657), one of Seika's disciples, became the Confucian adviser to the first shogun. Not surprisingly, Razan and many Neo-Confucians expressed outspoken anti-Buddhist sentiments, and some Confucian scholars became interested in Shinto. Razan, himself an ardent follower of the Shushi (Chu Hsi) tradition, tried to relate the *ri* (Chin., *li,* "reason, principle") of Neo-Confucianism with Shinto. The Shushi school was acknowledged as the official guiding ideology of the regime and was promoted by powerful members of the Tokugawa family.

Like his teacher, Hayashi Razan had studied Zen but was soon drawn to the orthodox teachings of Chu Hsi.

PAGE 185

The second tradition of Neo-Confucianism, Oyomeigaku or Yomeigaku (the school of Wang Yang-ming), held that the individual mind was the manifestation of the universal Mind. Quite different from the traditions of Shushi and Oyomei was the Kogaku ("ancient learning") tradition, which aspired to return to the classical sources of Confucianism.

Throughout the Tokugawa period, Confucian scholars, particularly those of the Shushigaku, Oyomeigaku, and Kogaku schools, exerted lasting influence on the warriors-turned-administrators.

SHINTO REVIVAL AND THE DECLINE OF THE TOKUGAWA REGIME. With the encouragement of anti-Buddhist Confucianists, especially those of Suika Shinto, Shinto leaders who were overshadowed by their Buddhist counterparts during the early Tokugawa period began to assert themselves. The nationalistic sentiment generated by the leaders of the Shinto revival, National Learning, and pro-Shinto Confucians began to turn against the already weakening Tokugawa regime in favor of the emerging royalist cause. The authority of the regime was threatened further by the demands of Western powers to reopen Japan for trade. Inevitably, the loosening of the shogunate's control resulted in political and social disintegration, which in turn precipitated the emergence of messianic cults from the soil of folk religious traditions.

MODERN PERIOD

The checkered development of Japanese religion in the modern period reflects a series of political, social, and cultural changes that have taken place within the Japanese nation. These changes include the toppling of the Tokugawa regime (1867), followed by the restoration of imperial rule under the Meiji emperor (r. 1867-1912); the rising influence of Western thought and civilization as well as Christianity; the Sino-Japanese War (1894-1895); the Russo-Japanese War (1904-1905); the annexation of Korea (1910); World War I, followed by a short-lived "Taisho Democracy"; an economic crisis followed by the rise of militarism in the 1930s; the Japanese invasion of Manchuria and China followed by World War II; Japan's surrender to the Allied forces (1945); the Allied occupation of Japan; and postwar adjustment. The particular path of development of Japanese religion was, of course, most directly affected by the government's religious policies.

MEIJI ERA. Although the architects of modern Japan welcomed many features of Western civilization, the Meiji regime was determined to restore the ancient principle of the "unity of religion and government" and the immanental theocratic state. The model was the Ritsuryo system of the seventh and eighth centuries. Accordingly, sacred kingship served as the pivot of national policy *(kokutai)*. Thus, while the constitution nominally guaranteed religious freedom and the historic ban against Christianity was lifted, the government created an overarching new religious form called State Shinto, which was designed to supersede all other religious groups. In order to create such a new official religion out of the ancient Japanese religious heritage an edict separating Shinto and Buddhism *(Shin-Butsu hanzen rei)* was issued. The government's feeling was that the Shinto-Buddhist amalgam of the preceding ten centuries was contrary to indigenous religious tradition. After the abortive Taikyo Sempu ("dissemination of the great doctrine") movement and the compulsory registration of Shinto parishioners, the government decided to utilize various other means, especially military training and public education, to promote the sacred "legacy of the *kami* way" *(kannagara)*: hence the promulgation of the Imperial Rescript to Soldiers and Sailors (1882) and the Imperial Rescript on Education (1890). Significantly, from 1882 until the end of World War II Shinto priests were prohibited by law from preaching during Shinto ceremonies, although they were responsible—as arms of the government bureaucracy—for the preservation of State Shinto.

Furthermore, in order to keep State Shinto from becoming involved in overtly sectarian activities, the government created between 1882 and 1908 a new category of Kyoha ("sect") Shinto and recognized thirteen such groups, including Kurozumikyo, Konkokyo, and Tenrikyo, which had emerged in the late Tokugawa period. Like Buddhist sects and Christian denominations, these groups depended on nongovernmental, private initiative for their propagation, organization, and financial support. Actually, Kyoha Shinto groups have very little in common. Some of them consider themselves genuinely Shinto in beliefs and practices, whereas some of them are marked by strong Confucian features. Still others betray characteristic features of folk religious tradition such as the veneration of sacred mountains, cults of mental and physical purification, utopian beliefs, and faith healing.

Buddhism. Understandably Buddhism was destined to undergo many traumatic experiences in the modern period. The Meiji regime's edict separating Shinto and Buddhism precipitated a popular anti-Buddhist movement that reached its climax around 1871. In various districts temples were destroyed, monks and nuns were laicized, and the parochial system, the legacy of the Tokugawa period, eroded. Moreover, the short-lived Taikyo Sempu movement mobilized Buddhist monks to propagate Taikyo, or government-concocted "Shinto" doctrines. Naturally, faithful Buddhists resented the Shinto-dominated Taikyo movement, and they advocated the principle of religious freedom. Thus, four branches of the True Pure Land sect managed to secure permission to leave the Taikyo movement, and shortly afterward the ill-fated movement itself was abolished. In the meantime, enlightened Buddhist leaders, determined to meet the challenge of Western thought and scholarship, sent able young monks to Western universities. Exposure to European Buddhological scholarship and contacts with other Buddhist traditions in Asia greatly broadened the vista of previously insulated Japanese Buddhists.

The government's grudging decision to succumb to the pressure of Western powers and lift the ban against Christianity was an emotional blow to Buddhism, which had been charged with the task of carrying out the anti-Kirishitan policy of the Tokugawa regime. Thus, many Buddhists, including those who had advocated religious freedom, allied themselves with Shinto, Confucian, and nationalist leaders in an emotional anti-Christian campaign called *haja kensei* ("refutation of evil religion and the exaltation of righteous religion"). After the promulgation of the Imperial Rescript on Education in 1890, many Buddhists equated patriotism with nationalism, thus becoming willing defenders and spokesmen of the emperor cult that symbolized the unique national polity *(kokutai)*. Although many Buddhists had no intention of restoring the historic form of the Shinto-Buddhist amalgam, until the end of World War II they accepted completely Buddhism's subordinate role in the nebulous but overarching super-religion of State Shinto.

Confucianism. Confucians, too, were disappointed by the turn of events during the early days of the Meiji era. It is well to recall that Confucians were the influential guardians of the Tokugawa regime's official ideology but that in latter Tokugawa days many of them cooperated with Shinto and nationalist leaders and prepared the ground for the new Japan. Indeed, Confucianism was an intellectual bridge between the premodern and modern periods. And although the new regime depended heavily on Confucian ethical principles in its formulation of imperial ideology and the principles of sacred national polity, sensitive Confucians felt that those Confucian features had been dissolved into a new overarching framework with heavy imprints of Shinto and National Learning (Kokugaku). Confucians also resented the new regime's policy of organizing the educational system on Western models and welcoming Western learning *(yogaku)* at the expense of, so they felt, traditionally important Confucian learning (Jugaku). After a decade of infatuation with things Western, however, a conservative mood returned, much to the comfort of Confucians. With the promulgation of the Imperial Rescript on Education and the adoption of compulsory "moral teaching" *(shushin)* in school systems, Confucian values were domesticated and presented as indigenous moral values. The historic Chinese Confucian notion of wang-tao ("the way of true kingship") was recast into the framework of *kodo* ("the imperial way"), and its ethical universalism was transformed into *nihon-shugi* ("Japaneseism"). As such, "nonreligious" Confucian ethics supported "super-religious" State Shinto until the end of World War II.

Christianity. The appearance—or reappearance, as far as Roman Catholicism was concerned—of Christianity in Japan was due to the convergence of several factors. These included pressures both external and internal, both from Western powers and from enlightened Buddhist leaders who demanded religious freedom. Initially, the Meiji regime, in its eagerness to restore the ancient indigenous polity, arrested over three thousand "hidden Kirishitan" in Kyushu and sent them into exile in various parts of the country. However, foreign ministers strongly advised the Meiji regime, which was then eager to improve its treaties with Western nations, to change its anti-Christian policy. Feeling these pressures, the government lifted its ban against the "forbidden religion." This opened the door to missionary activity by Protestant as well as Roman Catholic and Russian Orthodox churches. From that time until 1945, Christian movements in Japan walked a tightrope between their own religious affirmation and the demands of the nation's inherent immanental theocratic principle.

The meaning of "religious freedom" was stated by Ito Hirobumi (1841-1909), the chief architect of the Meiji Constitution, as follows:

> *No believer in this or that religion has the right to place himself outside the pale of the law of the Empire, on the ground that he is serving his god. . . . Thus, although freedom of religious belief is complete and exempt from all restrictions, so long as manifestations of it are confined to the mind; yet with regard to external matters such as forms of worship and the mode of propagandism, certain necessary restrictions of law or regulations must be provided for, and besides, the general duties of subjects must be observed.*

Even today, many Japanese pay homage to Shinto shrines at the same time that they are associated with Buddhist temples.

PAGE 103

This understanding of religious freedom was interpreted even more narrowly after the promulgation of the Imperial Rescript on Education; spokesmen of anti-Christian groups stressed that the Christian doctrine of universal love was incompatible with the national virtues of loyalty and filial piety taught explicitly in the Rescript. Some Christian leaders responded by stressing the compatibility of their faith and patriotism. Although a small group of Christian socialists and pacifists protested during the Sino-Japanese and Russo-Japanese wars, most Christians passively supported the war effort.

Another burden that the Christian movement has carried from the Meiji era to the present is its "foreignness." The anti-Kirishitan policy and all-embracing, unified meaning-structure of the Tokugawa synthesis that had lasted over two and a half centuries resulted in an exclusivistic mental attitude among the Japanese populace. A new religion thus found it difficult to penetrate from the outside. However, during the time of infatuation with things Western, curious or iconoclastic youths in urban areas were attracted by Christianity because of its foreignness. As a result, Westernized intellectuals, lesser bureaucrats, and technicians became the core of the Christian community. Through them, and through church-related schools and philanthropic activities, the Christian influence made a far greater impact on Japan than many people realize.

Christianity in Japan, however, has also paid a high price for its foreignness. As might be expected, Christian churches in Japan, many of which had close relationships with their respective counterparts in the West, experienced difficult times in the 1930s. Under combined heavy pressure from militarists and Shinto leaders, both the Congregatio de Propanganda Fide in Rome and the National Christian Council of the Protestant Churches in Japan accepted the government's interpretation of State Shinto as "nonreligious." According to their view, obeisance at the State Shinto shrines as a nonreligious, patriotic act could be performed by all Japanese subjects. In 1939 all aspects of religion were placed under strict government control. In 1940 thirty-four Protestant churches were compelled to unite as the "Church of Christ in Japan." This church and the Roman Catholic church remained the only recognized Christian groups during World War II. During the war all religious groups were exploited by the government as ideological weapons. Individual religious leaders who did not cooperate with the government were jailed, intimidated, or tortured. Christians learned the bitter lesson that under the immanental theocratic system created in modern Japan the only religious freedom was, as stated by Ito Hirobumi, "confined to the mind."

After World War II, the Occupation authorities ordered the Japanese government to sever all official affiliation with Shinto shrines and to cease all financial support for the shrines from public funds.

PAGE 602

JAPANESE RELIGION TODAY. In the modern world the destiny of any nation is as greatly influenced by external events as by domestic events. As far as modern Japan was concerned, such external events as the Chinese Revolution in 1912, World War I, the Russian Revolution, and the worldwide depression intermingled with events at home and propelled Japan to the world stage. Ironically, although World War I benefited the wealthy elite, the economic imbalance it produced drove desperate masses to rice riots and workers to labor strikes. Marxist student organizations were formed, and some serious college students joined the Communist party. Many people in lower social strata, benefiting little from modern civilization or industrial economy and neglected by institutionalized religions, turned to messianic and healing cults of the folk religious tradition. Thus, in spite of the government's determined effort to control religious groups and to prevent the emergence of new religions, it was reported that the number of quasi religions *(ruiji shukyo)* increased from 98 in 1924 to 414 in 1930 and then to over one thousand in 1935. Many of them experienced harassment, intervention, and persecution by the government, and some of them chose for the sake of survival to affiliate with Buddhist or Kyoha Shinto sects. Important among the quasi-religious groups were Omotokyo, founded by Deguchi Nao (1836-1918); Hito no Michi, founded by Miki Tokuharu (1871-1938); and Reiyukai, founded jointly by Kubo Kakutaro (1890-1944) and Kotani Kimi (1901-1971). After the end of World War II these quasi-religious groups and their spiritual cousins became the so-called new religions *(shinko shukyo)*. [*See* New Religions.]

The end of World War II and the Allied occupation of Japan brought full-scale religious freedom, with far-reaching consequences. In December 1945 the Occupation force issued the Shinto Directive dismantling the official structure of State Shinto; on New Year's Day 1946 the emperor publicly denied his divinity. Understandably, the loss of the sacral kingship and State Shinto undercut the mytho-historical foundation of Japanese religion that had endured from time immemorial. The new civil code of 1947 effectively abolished the traditional system of interlocking households *(ie seido)* as a legal institution, so that individuals were no longer bound by the religious affiliation of their households. The erosion of family cohesion greatly weakened the Buddhist parish system *(danka)* as well as the Shinto parish systems *(ujiko)*.

The abrogation of the ill-famed Religious Organizations Law (enacted in 1939 and enforced in 1940) also radically altered the religious scene. Assured of religious freedom and separation of religion and state by the Religious Corporations Ordinance, all religious groups (Buddhist, Christian, Shinto—now called

Shrine Shinto—and others) began energetic activities. This turn of events made it possible for quasi religions and Buddhist or Sect Shinto splinter groups to become independent. Sect Shinto, which comprised 13 groups before the war, developed into 75 groups by 1949. With the emergence of other new religions the total number of religious groups reached 742 by 1950. However, with the enactment of the Religious Juridical Persons Law (Shukyo hojin ho) in 1951, the number was reduced to 379—142 in the Shinto tradition, 169 Buddhist groups, 38 Christian denominations, and 30 miscellaneous groups.

In the immediate postwar period, when many people suffered from uncertainty, poverty, and loss of confidence, many men and women were attracted by what the new religions claimed to offer: mundane happiness, tightly knit religious organizations, healing, and readily accessible earthly deities or divine agents.

It has not been easy for older Buddhist groups to adjust to the changing social situation, especially since many of them lost their traditional financial support in the immediate postwar period. Also, religious freedom unwittingly fostered schisms among some of them. Nevertheless, the strength of the older Buddhist groups lies in their following among the intelligentsia and the rural population. Japanese Buddhological scholarship deservedly enjoys an international reputation. Japanese Buddhist leaders are taking increasingly active roles in pan-Asian and global Buddhist affairs while at the same time attending to such issues as peace and disarmament at home.

— JOSEPH M. KITAGAWA

JAVANESE RELIGION

The Javanese occupy the central and eastern parts of Java, a moderately sized island over twelve hundred kilometers long and five hundred kilometers wide. The island constitutes only about 7 percent of the total land area of the Indonesian archipelago, which now constitutes the Republic of Indonesia.

HISTORY. Hinduism probably came to Java during the fourth century of the common era through the trade routes from South India, although the earliest traces of a Hindu-Javanese civilization can only be dated to the eighth century. During that period Javanese Buddhism also developed, and the remnants of ancient religious structures such as the Hindu Prambanan and the Buddhist Borobudur seem to indicate that Javanese Hinduism and Javanese Buddhism coexisted peacefully.

Islam also came to Java through the trade routes, via North Sumatra and the Malay Peninsula between the fourteenth and seventeenth centuries. Islam in Java exhibits an emphasis on mystical ideas. Indeed, Islamic mysticism seems to have found fertile ground in Java because of the existing mystical elements in Javanese Hinduism: Muslim literary works written during the early period of Javanese islamization show the importance of mystical Islam, or Sufism (Arab., *tasawwuf*).

As a new religion, Islam initially influenced the port towns and harbor states of Java's north coast, which subsequently became prosperous and powerful and undermined the declining power of the Majapahit empire of East Java. In the following period zealous Muslim missionaries who became holy men, called *wali* (Arab., *wali;* "saint, guardian") in Javanese folklore, spread Islam through the interior regions of East and Central Java.

The court center of the Central Javanese empire, Mataram, traditionally resisted the penetration of Islam from the interior of Java. During the second half of the eighteenth century, however, Islam reached the heartland of the ancient Central Javanese civilization, although not always through peaceful means.

AGAMI JAWI. The Agami Jawi belief system includes an extensive range of concepts, views, and values, many of which are Muslim in origin: the belief in God Almighty *(Gusti Allah),* the belief in the prophet Muhammad *(kanjeng nabi Muhammad),* and the belief in other prophets *(para ambiya).* All human actions as well as important decisions are done "in the name of God" *(bismillah),* a formula pronounced many times a day to inaugurate any small or large endeavor.

Divine Beings. God is conceptualized as the totality of nature: he is a tiny divine being, so small that he can enter any human heart, yet in reality as wide as the oceans, as endless as space, and manifested in the colors that make and symbolize everything that exists on earth. In addition to the belief in God and the prophets, the Agami Jawi Javanese also believe in saints. Included among these holy persons are the nine semihistorical "apostles" *(wali sanga),* or first missionaries of Islam, religious teachers, and certain semihistorical figures who were known to the people through the Babad literature.

Many other elements, such as the belief in a great number of deities *(dewata),* are of Hindu-Buddhist origin, as one can see from their Sanskritic names. However, the roles and functions of several of the deities are different from those of the original ones. Dewi Sri, for instance, who originated from Sri, the wife of the Hindu god Visnu, is in Javanese culture the goddess of fertility and rice. Bathara Kala was derived from the Hindu concept of time *(kala),* and this destructive aspect of Siva the creator is in Javanese culture the god of death and calamity.

AGAMI ISLAM SANTRI. The Agami Islam Santri

During the thirteenth and fourteenth centuries, Islam penetrated into the Malay archipelago largely through Arab traders.

PAGE 339

belief system of both rural and urban Javanese is composed of puritanical Islamic concepts about God, the prophet Muhammad, creation, personal ethics, death and afterlife, eschatology, the day of resurrection, and so forth. These concepts are all clearly determined by dogmatic creed. In addition to having memorized certain parts of the Qur'an, many have also been exposed to the exegetical literature *(tafsir),* and prophetic tradition *(hadith)* during their education in more advanced religious schools *(pesantren).* The Muslim belief system is organized and systematized in the *shari'ah* (Islamic law); the dominant legal school *(madhhab)* in Java, and throughout Indonesia, is that of al-Shafi'i (d. 820).

Most of the Islamic calendrical ceremonial celebrations are observed by the Santri Javanese who also perform rites to celebrate certain events in the life cycle of the individual. However, unlike the Agami Jawi Javanese, who hold numerous *slametan* ceremonies, they prefer to give *sedhekah* sacrifices in accordance with the *shari'ah.* Their funerary ceremonies do not differ significantly from those of the Agami Jawi.

SPIRITUAL AND RELIGIOUS MOVEMENTS. There have always been adherents of Agami Jawi for whom recurrent *slametan* rituals, *sajen* offerings at fixed periods, and routine visits to graves represent a superficial, meaningless, and unsatisfactory religious life. Therefore, they search for a deeper understanding of the essence of life and spiritual existence. One response to the demand for a more spiritually meaningful life are the numerous *kebatinan kejawen* spiritual movements, which have emerged and disappeared, but have retained a constant following in the course of Javanese history. The term *kebatinan* refers to the search for truth, *batin* (Arab., *batin*). Since the late 1960s, the number of these movements has increased significantly.

[*See also* Southeast Asian Religions *and* Islam.]

— R. M. KOENTJARANINGRAT

"Ye are my witnesses, saith the Lord."

ISAIAH 43:10

JEHOVAH'S WITNESSES

Along with the Mormons, the Christian Scientists, and perhaps a few other groups, Jehovah's Witnesses is one of the few truly American expressions of religion. Like these others, Jehovah's Witnesses developed from a humble start into a worldwide religious movement. From its inception in 1872 with a handful of believers, it had increased by the 1980s to a membership of more than two million people in about two hundred countries. Powered by distinctive biblical beliefs, made effective by an efficient social organization, and fired by the conviction that the end of the historical era is at hand, the movement has maintained its distinctive appeal.

The organization's name is based on the assumption that the proper name for the Judeo-Christian deity is Jehovah. In their *New World Translation of the Holy Scriptures* (Brooklyn, N. Y., 1961), the Witnesses render as *Jehovah* the more than six thousand references in the Hebrew scriptures to the deity. Employing a variety of scriptural references (such as *Isaiah* 42:8, 43:10-11; *John* 18:37; and *Hebrews* 12:1), the Witnesses also conclude that the proper term for the followers of Jehovah is not *Christians* but *Witnesses.*

HISTORY

Jehovah's Witnesses was founded in Allegheny, Pennsylvania (now a suburb of Pittsburgh), by Charles Taze Russell, born in Pittsburgh in 1852 as the second son of Joseph L. and Eliza (Birney) Russell. Brought up as a Presbyterian, Russell came under the influence of the adventist teachings of William Miller (founder of the "Millerites") and others. Russell was prevented from obtaining an extensive education because of responsibilities in his father's chain of clothing stores, but he possessed a keen appreciation of the Bible and an engaging manner, which helped him in forming a small group to study the Bible from the perspective of the second coming of Christ. Russell's group grew, and in time other groups were formed and a publication was organized, *Zion's Watch Tower and Herald of Christ's Presence* (later called simply *The Watchtower*). The watchtower theme, appearing in various forms, has been central to the Witnesses' nomenclature. By 1884 the Zion's Watch Tower Tract Society was formed, later to become the Watch Tower Bible and Tract Society. By 1888 about fifty persons were working full-time to spread Russell's views on the Bible and the anticipated end of the age. Within a few years, groups arose throughout the United States and in a number of other countries. In 1909, finding increased acceptance, the Witnesses moved its headquarters to Brooklyn, New York, from which its international operations have been directed ever since. Russell ably led in the development of the movement despite several setbacks, including the divorce action of his wife Maria Ackley Russell in 1913. He died en route to Kansas on 31 October 1916.

Russell was succeeded by Joseph Franklin Rutherford. Born into a farm family in Morgan County, Missouri, in 1869, Rutherford was admitted to the Missouri bar at twenty-two after having been tutored in the law by a local judge. He joined the Jehovah's Witnesses in 1906 and soon shared public platforms with Russell. At a time when the Witnesses were increasingly involved in litigation, Rutherford's talents became ever more valuable. Two months after Russell's death, Rutherford was elected president of the society. He and other Witnesses believed that the "gentile times" had ended in 1914, ushering in Christ's millennial rule. Since that time, the movement has believed that Satan is the ruler of the nations and that it is therefore proper to assume a neutralist (not pacifist) stance. During World War I, Rutherford and seven other Witnesses were convicted under the Espionage Act and sent to prison, where they organized Bible studies. They were released when wartime emotions subsided.

Rutherford was an able organizer, and he persuaded the movement to use modern methods of advertising and communicating. Under his leadership the Witnesses greatly expanded their membership, the volume of their publications, the number of their full-time workers, and their international scope. In the last twelve years of his life Rutherford grew increasingly aloof from the organization, spending his time in a mansion in San Diego, California, that the society had built to house Abraham and the prophets upon their return to earth. He died at the age of seventy-two in 1942 and was interred in Rossville (Staten Island), New York.

The third president of the society was Nathan Homer Knorr, born in Bethlehem, Pennsylvania, on 23 April 1905. In his youth Knorr attended a Dutch Reformed church, but at sixteen he was attracted to the Witnesses and soon thereafter became a full-time worker. He worked in the printing plant in Brooklyn, was promoted to a higher position in the shipping department, and shortly thereafter became head of all printing operations. In 1935 he became vice-president of the society. Under his leadership, the Jehovah's Witnesses grew even more rapidly. Knorr was an indefatigable worker, an effective preacher, a world traveler for the cause, and an able administrator. He died in June 1977.

ORGANIZATION AND FINANCING

Although Knorr was succeeded by Frederick W. Franz as president, administrative leadership shifted to the Governing Body, in which no one person enjoys supreme authority. The Governing Body consists of six central committees and the lower administrative units, the branch committees. A new and more bureaucratic era had arrived. Since 1927 the society's voluminous literature has been produced in an eight-story factory building in Brooklyn, New York. The international headquarters there includes six additional buildings as well as nearby homes to house the workers needed for the printing and other activities of the society. Near Wallkill, New York, a combination farm and factory produces the two principal magazines (*The Watchtower* and *Awake!*) and food for the society's full-time workers. Aside from room and board, these workers receive a small monthly allowance for incidental expenses. The backbone of support for the society in all its activities is the voluntarism of its members.

BELIEFS AND PRACTICES

Although the Witnesses' beliefs appear to be based upon the Judeo-Christian Bible and within that context seem to represent an American fundamentalist outlook, they are indeed distinctive. All that they believe is based on the Bible. They "proof text" (that is, supply a biblical citation to support) almost every statement of faith, taking for granted the authority of the Bible, which entirely supplants tradition.

For the Witnesses, God, properly addressed as Jehovah, is the one supreme and universal deity. Jesus is thought to be God's son, but he is held as definitely inferior to Jehovah. Yet Christ holds a special place in Witness theology: he is the first of God's creations; his human life was paid as a ransom for salvation; he died on a stake (not a cross), was raised from the dead as an immortal spirit person, and is present in the world as a spirit. He is the focus of congregational gatherings; the Witnesses pray to Jehovah only through Christ.

Witnesses believe that history has run its course and that the "time of the end" is very close. Until that end, Satan rules the world. For several decades various of the society's publications have used the same title: *Millions Now Living Will Never Die.* The end is that close. Until the end, a Witness must keep apart from the world and must obey only those secular laws and follow only those practices of faith that are in conformity with the society's understanding of the Bible. In this regard, several negative requirements must be upheld. Images must not be used in worship. Spiritualism must be shunned. Witnesses must not participate in interfaith movements. Taking blood into the body, through the mouth or by transfusion, is contrary to Jehovah's laws. A clergy class and distinctive titles are prohibited. No national flag is to be saluted and no pledge of allegiance to a nation is permitted. In maintaining these requirements, the Witnesses in some countries have been prosecuted by civil authorities and at times martyred. Adherence to their beliefs in opposition to the laws of various countries has won admiration from a wide spectrum of civil libertarians, although the society does not aim at extending human freedom, but rather at expressing its own deeply held religious convictions.

Although the Witnesses uphold the doctrine of the virgin birth of Jesus, they refuse to celebrate Christmas, believing that the holiday is of pagan origin. They say that the Bible nowhere teaches that Christ's birth, or indeed, anyone's birthday, should be celebrated. (Actually, the Witnesses believe that Christ was born on 1 October, 2 BC.) They also recognize neither Lent nor Easter. They do, however, have a Lord's Meal ceremony, which takes place once a year.

Witnesses believe that baptism by immersion

The major functional attributes of scripture are bound up with the power felt to be inherent in scriptural word.

PAGE 594

symbolizes dedication. They deny the obligation of Sunday worship, asserting that the observance of the Sabbath day was pertinent to Old Testament religion only and that this requirement ended with the fulfillment of Mosaic law in Jesus. The Witnesses do, however, conform to social norms in accepting Sunday as a day of rest and worship. They meet in "kingdom halls" for study and worship, as well as in members' homes.

The Witnesses believe that the end of history will begin with a great battle (which the Witnesses call Har-Magedon) between the forces of good and evil. Historical circumstances as heretofore known will be destroyed and a new order created. Satan will be vanquished and wicked human beings eternally destroyed; hell is humankind's common grave. But although human death is a consequence of Adam's sin there is hope of resurrection. Those whom Jehovah approves will receive eternal life. But only a small flock of 144,000 true believers from the whole of history will be born again as spiritual children of God and will go to heaven to rule with Christ.

Christian belief began with the need to specify the significance of the person of Jesus, seen as the "Christ."

PAGE 162

On earth, however, Christ will establish a new kingdom and will rule in righteousness and peace. Ideal living conditions will be established and the earth will be environmentally restored to perfection, never again to be destroyed or depopulated. In effect, heaven will be established on earth; those who inhabit it will enjoy all good. In the meantime, the Witnesses must give public testimony to the truth of the movement's teachings. This they do through a voluminous publishing program, worldwide efforts at conversion, a variety of weekly meetings and mass celebrations, and—as they have become known to countless non-Witnesses—through door-to-door visitations.

— HERBERT HEWITT STROUP

JESUS

More fully Jesus of Nazareth, (c. 7/6 BC–c. AD 30), called Christ; founder of Christianity.

LIFE AND WORK

A basic history of Jesus would include at least the following items. He was a Galilean Jew, the son of a woman called Mary who was married to Joseph, a carpenter. Jesus was baptized by John, began to preach and teach, associated in a special way with public sinners and other outcasts, called disciples to follow him, worked miracles, and taught some memorable parables. His challenge to given forms of piety (*Mt.* 6:1-18), his desire to correct certain traditions (*Mk.* 7:1-23), his violation of some Sabbath observances (*Mk.* 2:23-27), his attitude toward the Temple in Jerusalem (*Mk.* 14:58, 15:29 and parallels), and other offenses aroused the antagonism of some Jewish leaders and teachers. In Jerusalem (where he had come for the Passover celebration) he was betrayed, arrested, interrogated by members of the Sanhedrin, condemned by Pontius Pilate, executed on a cross (which bore an inscription giving the charge against Jesus as a messianic pretender), and buried later the same day.

MINISTRY. Hardly anything is more certain about Jesus' ministry than that through his words and deeds he proclaimed the kingdom, or rule, of God. He understood his activity to be initiating a new, powerful, and final offer of salvation (e.g., *Mt.* 4:23, 9:35: 12:28). Faced with this offer, his audience was called to repent (e.g., *Mk.* 1:15) and accept the divine pardon that Jesus himself communicated in his own person (*Mk.* 2:17 and parallels). Through words of forgiveness (*Mk.* 2:5, *Lk.* 7:48), parables of mercy (e.g., *Lk.* 15:11-32), and table fellowship with outcasts (e.g., *Mt.* 11:19), he aimed to bring sinners back into God's company.

In doing all this, Jesus acted with a striking sense of personal authority (*Mk.* 1:22) that did not hesitate to go beyond the divine law received by Moses (*Mk.* 10:2-9). His call for radical conversion (e.g., *Mt.* 5;1-7:27, *Lk.* 6:20-49) entailed transforming in his own name that law and carrying to the ultimate its inmost spirit (*Mt.* 5:21-48).

How did Jesus assess and describe his own identity? To begin with, he thought of himself as a spiritual physician (*Mk.* 2:17), a shepherd to his people (*Mt.* 15:24), and a divinely authorized prophet (*Lk.* 13:33). Then around seventy times in the synoptic Gospels Jesus calls himself (the) "Son of man," a term that in its Semitic background either was a circumlocution for oneself as speaker (e.g., *Mt.* 8:20) or simply meant "a human being" or "someone." What is not quite certain is whether by the time of Jesus himself "Son of man" was also a clearly defined title associated with a deliverer expected to come in the last times. However, the three contexts in which Jesus designated himself as "Son of man" carried their own distinct meanings. This self-designation was used of Jesus' earthly work and condition (e.g., *Mk.* 2:10, 2:28; *Mt.* 11:19 and parallel); of his suffering, death, and resurrection (*Mk.* 8:31, 9:31, 10:33-34); and of his coming in future glory as a redeemer-judge (e.g., *Mk.* 8:38, 13:26; *Mt.* 24:27 and parallel).

CRUCIFIXION. Jesus' ministry ended in Jerusalem when he was betrayed by Judas, put on trial before members of the Sanhedrin, convicted (for despising the law and blasphemously claiming messianic authority?), handed over to Pilate, and executed as a threat to the public order. Did Jesus anticipate and interpret in advance such a violent death?

JESUS OF NAZARETH *The Agony of the Garden by Garofalo is a striking portrayal of Jesus' anticipation of his violent death.*
THE NATIONAL GALLERY, LONDON/CORBIS

It was, or at least became, obvious to Jesus—and for that matter to any moderately intelligent observer—that fidelity to his mission would bring deadly opposition from the public authorities (e.g., *Lk.* 11:47, 11:49-50, 13:33-34). Among other things, the fate of John the Baptist suggested such a danger. Then Jesus' demonstrative entry into Jerusalem (*Mk.* 11:1-11) and cleansing of the Temple (*Mk.* 11:15-18) increased the danger from Caiaphas and other leading Sadducees, who under the Roman army retained some power in the capital. This and further evidence (e.g., from the Last Supper and the agony in the garden of Gethsemane) point to the conclusion that Jesus anticipated and accepted his violent end.

RESURRECTION. As far as the historical evidence goes, the Christian movement began with the simple announcement that the crucified Jesus had been raised to new life and had appeared to some witnesses. At first, individuals who had seen him risen from the dead guaranteed the truth of the resurrection (e.g., *1 Cor.* 15:5, 15:7, 15:8; *Lk.* 24:34). Then the Christian community as such professed this truth (see, for example, the formulations cited in *1 Thessalonians* 4:14, *Romans* 1:3-4, and *Romans* 10:9). The discovery of the empty tomb by Mary Magdalene, accompanied perhaps by other women (*Mk.* 16:1-8; *Jn.* 20:1, 20:11-13; *Lk.* 24:10, 24:23), served as a confirmatory sign. But the New Testament shows a clear awareness that an empty tomb simply by itself did not establish Jesus' resurrection (e.g., *Jn.* 20:2, *Mt.* 28:11-15).

"The Lord has been taken from the Tomb!"

JOHN 20:2

It is not surprising that, together with their claims about Jesus' resurrection, Christians defined God in terms of the risen Christ. Repeatedly Paul cited a formula from the early tradition that identified God as "having raised Jesus from the dead" (e.g., *Gal.* 1:1, *Rom.* 10:9, *1 Cor.* 6:14). Hence, to be wrong about the resurrection would be to "misrepresent" God (*1 Cor.* 15;15). [*See also* Resurrection.]

CHRISTOLOGICAL DEVELOPMENTS

COUNCILS OF THE CHURCH. In the development of Christology, progress often occurred in reaction to views rejected as heterodox. Thus the occasion for the first ecumenical council, the Council of Nicaea (325), came with the teachings of Arius (c. 250-336). To preserve the oneness of God, while at the same time affirming the uniqueness of Jesus Christ, Arius asserted that the Son was a perfect creature, at most a kind of demigod subordinated to the Father. To combat Arius, the council adopted a term that had been used by Origen (c. 185-c. 254) to indicate that Christ shared one common divine being with the Father; *homoousios* ("of one substance"). This teaching on Christ's divinity raised a question: how could believers then maintain Christ's true humanity? One supporter of Nicaea, Apollinaris of Laodicea (c. 310-c. 390), reduced Christ's full humanity by apparently suggesting that at the incarnation the divine Logos (or Word of God) assumed only a body and itself took the place of the human spirit. Against Apollinaris the First Council of Constantinople (381) taught that Christ had a true human soul.

Defenders of the unity between Christ's divinity and humanity went to another extreme. Eutyches of Constantinople (c. 378-454) seemed to maintain that Christ's divinity absorbed his humanity—the so-called monophysite heresy, according to which the one divine nature *(phusis)* swallowed up Christ's humanity. The Council of Chalcedon (451) reacted by acknowledging in Christ "two natures in one person [*prosopon*] or acting subject [*hupostasis*]." This personal unity left the divine and human natures quite intact and in no way confused or intermingled them with each other.

Chalcedon said nothing about Christ's crucifixion and resurrection. In the centuries that followed, an all-absorbing theology of the incarnation generally monopolized attention. In one important development the Third Council of Constantinople (680) condemned monothelitism, or the view that acknowledged only one will in Christ. The council held for a divine and human will; the duality of Christ's natures entailed a duality of wills.

THE MIDDLE AGES. When theology tended to represent Christ largely in terms of his divinity, church art, popular belief, and widespread devotions often defended his truly human existence and experience. Icons, the Christmas crib, carols, the stations of the cross, and later the success of Luther's hymns and Roman Catholic devotion to the Sacred Heart witnessed to the instinctive attachment of ordinary Christians to the real humanity of Jesus.

In his *Cur Deus homo* (1098), Anselm of Canterbury became the first Christian writer to devote a whole work to the redemptive activity of Christ. According to Anselm, sin offended God's honor, and either satisfaction or punishment had to follow that offense. By making satisfaction, Jesus restored the divine honor, and punishment was not involved. Unfortunately, those who drew on *Cur Deus homo*—from Thomas Aquinas, through John Calvin (1509-1564), down to Karl Barth (1886-1968) and others—added punitive elements to Anselm's version of redemption. Nowadays his soteriology, or doctrine of salvation, has fallen on hard times and is often dismissed as legalistic and concerned with the divine honor rather than with God's love. However, John McIntyre, Gispert Greshake, and Walter Kasper have defended Anselm's theology of satisfaction for appreciating the divine fidelity to creation and the moral order.

MODERN TIMES. From the eighteenth century onward Christology began to be deeply affected by the rise of critical methods in historical and biblical research. Scientific history became and in many ways has remained the dominant partner in dialogue with theological thinking about Jesus' person and saving work.

The historical Jesus. In the classical period for the historical study of Jesus' life, writers like David Friedrich Strauss (1808-1874), Ernest Renan (1823-1892), and Adolf von Harnack (1851-1930) attempted to penetrate behind the christological doctrines of Paul and the early church and get back to Jesus of Nazareth as he actually was. They hoped to recover by scientific, unprejudiced use of the earliest sources—in particular Mark's gospel—an authentic picture of the real Jesus.

Despite the work of these scholars, however, no common, scientifically established picture of Jesus emerged. By the time Albert Schweitzer wrote his classic study of this nineteenth-century enterprise, *The Quest of the Historical Jesus* (1906), it had become clear that many had been portraying Jesus largely in the light of their own personal presuppositions and the convictions of their society. Schweitzer protested against all these attempts to modernize Jesus and insisted that the key was to be found in Jesus' eschatology, or views about the end of history.

Contemporary approaches. From Thomas Aquinas in the Middle Ages down to Karl Barth in the twentieth century, classic Christology began its theological interpretation with God. The essential question for this approach was "How did the preexistent Son of God 'come down' and enter this world?" In place of this Christology "from above," much recent thinking has begun "from below," using as its starting point the historical, human situation of Jesus in this world. The key question for such a Christology "from below" is "What does it mean to say that a particular man from Nazareth was both universal savior and 'God among us'?" How could a human being have been such and been recognizable as such?

Wolfhart Pannenberg, who originally championed a Christology "from below" in *Jesus: God and Man* (1964), in the second volume of *Grundfragen systematischer Theologie* (1980) came to question the correctness of setting up sharp alternatives. In *Jesus the Christ* (1974) Walter Kasper sees the two approaches ("from above" and "from below") as complementing each other.

A second major distinction in contemporary Christology concerns its center. For some (e.g., John A. T. Robinson and Pierre Teilhard de Chardin), evolving creation provides the primary focus. Jean Galot, Karl Rahner, and others organize matters around the incarnation. In their varying ways, yet other scholars (e.g., Hans Küng, James Mackey, Edward Schillebeeckx, and Jon Sobrino) have taken the synoptic Gospels' account of the ministry as the center.

Right from the birth of Christianity the convictions embodied in worship supported the centrality of the Easter mystery. Believers expressed liturgically, especially through baptism (Rom. 6:3-5) and the Eucharist (1 Cor. 11:26), the sense that Jesus' crucifixion and resurrection were the heart of the matter. From such a midpoint, Christology can look in one direction (through Jesus' life, the incarnation, and the history of the Israelites) back to creation, and in the other direction (through the coming of the Holy Spirit, the life of the church, and the history of humanity) forward to the future consummation of all things.

ISSUES

THE RESURRECTION. In the late nineteenth and early twentieth century Wilhelm Bousset, James G. Frazer, and others connected Jesus with myths of dying and rising gods, frequently those of the mystery religions of Greece and the ancient Near East. Belief in the resurrection of the crucified Jesus was taken to be simply another projection of the human need to cope with the changing seasons and common challenges of life.

Subsequently it was maintained that the message of the resurrection was not a statement that claimed to present a fact about Jesus himself but simply functioned to declare a personal commitment of the early Christians to a new way of life (e.g., Paul M. Van Buren in *The Secular Meaning of the Gospel,* 1963).

It has sometimes been argued that the disciples "saw" and announced Jesus risen from the dead simply because they needed his resurrection to cope psychologically and religiously with the horror of his crucifixion. In *The Resurrection of Jesus of Nazareth* (1968), Willi Marxsen takes "resurrection" to have been no more than one possible way of interpreting the experience of "seeing" Jesus and finding faith.

SUFFERING AND REDEMPTION. Moltmann (in *The Crucified God*) and other theologians have developed various kinds of post-Holocaust Christologies that draw partly on the theme of God's pain and sorrow over human sin, which is to be found in the Hebrew scriptures (e.g., *Gen.* 6:6, *Is.* 63:10) and in rabbinic literature. This approach was anticipated by certain English and Russian kenotic Christologies of the nineteenth and early twentieth centuries, in which the Son of God's self-emptying *(Phil.* 2:7) enabled him to enter into a radical solidarity with the alienated and dehumanized of this world.

The interpretation of the scriptural texts to which these Christologies appeal (e.g., *Mk.* 15:34, *Rom.* 8:32, *Jn.* 3:16) has been widely challenged. The notion of God

Just as Christ died and rose again, the fellowship with him cannot be broken by death.

PAGE 576

J

JUDAISM

From the Bible to Rabbinic Judaism

"You shall conceive and bear a son and give him the name Jesus."

LUKE 1:31

being open as such to suffering and change through an event of this world (the crucifixion) runs into philosophical and theological difficulties, at least for many schools of thought. The alternative to Moltmann's history of the triune God's suffering is not necessarily a detached God who remains indifferent to human pain and misery. Rather, it can be a belief in a compassionate God whose boundless love freely revealed itself in human history—above all, in the passion and death of Jesus.

VIRGINAL CONCEPTION. On the basis of the infancy narratives of Matthew and Luke (*Mt.* 1-2, *Lk.* 1-2), Christian tradition has held that Jesus had no human father but was conceived through the power of the Holy Spirit. Challenges to this tradition have come on a number of grounds. Some rule it out as part of their general rejection of any such miraculous intervention by God. Others maintain that early Christians were under pressure to invent the story of the virginal conception, once Jewish critics began to claim that Jesus was illegitimate. Still others have argued that myths about male gods impregnating earthly women prompted Christians (who already believed in Jesus' divinity) to develop the legend of this virginal conception. Then there are those who think that Christians have misinterpreted the intentions of Matthew and Luke in their infancy narratives.

These challenges to the tradition of the virginal conception are balanced by other arguments. Any adequate discussion of the rejection of divine miraculous intervention would require an enormous parenthesis on the nature and role of miracles. The challenge that the doctrine is a defense against the charge of illegitimacy is weakened by the argument of Raymond E. Brown in *The Birth of the Messiah* (1977). Brown shows that the charge of illegitimacy, which appeared in the second century, may have emerged only after the composition of the gospels of Matthew and Luke and perhaps even as a reaction to their narratives of the virginal conception. In that case the story of the virginal conception would not have arisen as a Christian response to a charge of illegitimacy that was already in circulation.

With regard to the challenge that Christians have misinterpreted the intentions of Matthew and Luke, Brown argues that while we cannot scientifically trace the way the tradition(s) of the virginal conception originated, were transmitted in the early Christian communities, and reached the evangelists, it seems that "both Matthew and Luke regarded the virginal conception as historical," even if "the modern intensity about historicity was not theirs" (*Birth of the Messiah,* p. 517). The two evangelists refer to the conception of Jesus from different standpoints—Matthew from that of Joseph, Luke from that of Mary—but both agree that the conception came about without human intercourse and through the power of the Holy Spirit.

[*For further discussion of Christian reflection on the life and ministry of Jesus, see* Trinity.]

— GERALD O'COLLINS, S. J.

JEWS AND JUDAISM

[*See article* Judaism *below.*]

JUDAISM

Neither of the sacred Jewish classics, the Bible or the Talmud, speaks of "Judaism." Hellenistic Jews created this Greek word to describe their uncommon way of serving God (2 *Mc.* 2:21, 8:1, 14:38; *Gal.* 1:13-14). All such mediating terms, because they utilize alien categories as the means of self-representation, necessarily distort as much as they explain. Thus, while the Jews of the first century CE integrated their ethnicity and their religion, Paul, writing *Galatians* for gentile readers, must sunder faith from folk in order to communicate.

Contemporary Jewish thinkers radically disagree as to the nature of Judaism and even the advisability of employing the term. Interpretations of Judaism today range from steadfast traditionalism to radical universalism. The traditionalists themselves differ strongly on accommodation to modernity. The right-wing Orthodox resist accommodation, while the Modern Orthodox accept any cultural good not forbidden by God's revelation. Debates over the role of mysticism add further diversity. Other contemporary Jews have rejected Orthodoxy because they deem it incompatible with the practice of democracy and the findings of the natural and social sciences, especially critical history.

Among nonreligious Jews, some are humanists who assimilate their Jewishness to contemporary culture, especially ethics. Others identify Judaism with Jewish folk culture. Zionism and the state of Israel represent the secularization of Judaism at its fullest.

Among liberal—that is, non-Orthodox—religious Jews, four differing emphases occur. (1) Jews who have an ethnic attachment to Judaism often find that it acquires a core of universal spirituality that, in turn, revitalizes their attachment. (2) Jews seeking a more disciplined Jewish religiosity direct their ethnic life through Jewish law, dynamically interpreted, as a historically evolving structure. (3) Jews concerned with the demands of rationality assert that Judaism uniquely comprehends the idea of ethical monotheism, a universal truth that is reinforced by their sense of ethnicity. (4) Jews who adopt a personalist approach conceptualize Judaism as a relationship, a covenant mutually created by God and the Jewish people and recreated in every generation. This article describes postbiblical Judaism in terms of the evolving expression of the Jewish people's covenant with God, understood in liberal religious terms.

FROM THE BIBLE TO RABBINIC JUDAISM

We have little hard data by which to trace the progress from biblical to rabbinic Judaism, despite some help from the biblical *Book of Daniel*. From Ezra and Nehemiah (Hebrew leaders of the mid-fifth century BCE) to the earliest rabbis (the authorities mentioned in the Talmud) in the first half of the first century CE, the sources in Jewish tradition that are considered authoritative provide little reliable historical information. Learned conjectures can fill this gap, but as their validity rests on hermeneutic foundations that often shift, all such speculations are best left to historians.

The rabbis themselves affirmed an unbroken transmission of authoritative tradition, of Torah in the broad sense, from Moses to Joshua to the elders, the prophets, and thence to the immediate predecessors of the rabbis (*Avot* 1.1). By this they meant that along with the written Torah (the first five books of the Bible, also known as the Pentateuch or Law) Moses also delivered the oral Torah, or oral law, which contained substantive teaching (legal and nonlegal) as well as the proper methods for the further development of the Torah tradition. As inheritors and students of the oral (and written) law, the rabbis knew themselves to be the authoritative developers of Judaism.

Modern critical scholarship universally rejects this view. For one thing, the Bible makes no mention of oral law. Then, too, it is reasonable to think of Torah as undergoing historical development. When, over the centuries, Judaism grew and changed, later generations validated this unconscious process by introducing, retroactively, the doctrine of the oral law.

We may see rabbinic Judaism's mix of continuity and creativity more clearly if we briefly note these same features in their late biblical predecessors. Ezra and Nehemiah believe that God and the Jewish people have an ancient pact, and they seek to be faithful to it by their lives. Though they acknowledge that God rules the whole world, they and their fellow Babylonian Jews manifest a deep loyalty to a geographic center returning from an apparently more prosperous land to resettle Jerusalem and restore God's Temple there. They are ethnic separatists, rejecting offers of help from the Samaritans and requiring Jewish males to give up their gentile wives. They carefully restore the Temple cult and insist on observance of the Sabbath. But their Judaism involves sensibility as well as statute. When Nehemiah discovers people collecting debts in a time of hardship, he denounces such hard-heartedness as incompatible with covenant loyalty, and they desist.

Ezra and Nehemiah also evidence a new religious concern: acting in accordance with "the book of God's Torah" (*Neh.* 9:3). In a great public ceremony, the book is read to all the people, men, women, and children, and explained to them in detail. By the mid-fifth century BCE, then, a written tradition has taken the place formerly occupied by divination, prophecy, and priestly teaching. [*See* Israelite Religion.]

Nearly three centuries later, *Daniel* gives us another glimpse of late biblical Judaism. Daniel, the paradigmatic Jew, lives outside the Land of Israel, among idolaters. He perseveres in the prescribed Jewish patterns of eating, drinking, and praying, despite the threat of severe punishment. A heavy eschatological focus distinguishes this book, as do its bizarre visions and their cryptic interpretations. After calamitous persecutions of the holy people, including wars against them by foreign powers, God intervenes, sending one who defeats their foes and establishes their kingdom forever. A time of cosmic judgment follows that dooms the wicked to eternal reprobation while the righteous live on forever. The biblical prophets' expectations of an ideal king, descended from King David, who would one day establish worldwide justice, compassion, and recognition of God have here been radically extended.

THE JUDAISM OF THE RABBIS

Rabbinic Judaism appears as a mature development in its earliest datable document, the Mishnah, a compilation of Jewish traditions redacted about 200 CE. We can flesh out its sparely written text by consulting the more extensive classic works of rabbinism, the Talmud and the Midrash. The Talmud—essentially a collection of rabbinic discussions on the Mishnah—exists in two forms: the Jerusalem Talmud *(Yerushalmi)*, redacted about 400 CE, and the Babylonian Talmud *(Bavli)*, redacted about 500 CE and considered the more authoritative of the two. [*See* Talmud.] The Midrash is a body of homiletic and other exegeses of the Bible, of which the earliest compilations date from the third to the sixth centuries CE. The rabbis proceed on the assumption that the Temple, destroyed by the Romans in 70 CE, will be rebuilt only in "the days of the Messiah." They refer to the Temple cult mainly as the stuff of memory and hope and as material for study. Their Judaism centers about the Torah, particularly the oral Torah. To the critical eye, the distinctive features of rabbinic Judaism reflect creative development as much as reverent continuity with the past.

A structural innovation of the rabbis provides a

The collection of writings that we call "Torah" or "the Torah of Moses" comprises the first five books of the Bible.

PAGE 670

convenient entry into their Judaism. They utilize parallel, mutually reinforcing modes of instruction, *halakhah* ("the way," the law, the required pattern of living) and *aggadah* (all else, including lore, preachment, speculation, and theology). Both are considered Torah, which literally means God's own instruction. In rabbinic texts they are often found organically intertwined, but they carry different degrees of authority. When dealing with *halakhah*, the rabbis, for all their disagreement and debate, seek to attain coherence and to decide what constitutes lawful practice. (The rabbis' courts can inflict severe penalties on transgressors.) By contrast, the realm of the *aggadah* is unregulated. The rabbis appear to delight in finding ingenious ways to amaze their colleagues with their imaginative exegeses and dicta. In all their contradiction and contrariety, these teachings too are part of the oral law.

Halakhah, in the general sense of the word, is the entire body of Jewish law, from scripture to the latest rabbinical rulings.

PAGE 259

Way of the Rabbis

For the rabbis, the covenant entails the adoption of a way of life faithful to God more than acquiescence to a specific doctrine. All later varieties of Judaism—including, despite radical differences, the modern ones—have echoed these spiritual priorities. A description of Judaism, therefore, should begin with some highlights of the rabbinic way. What follows represents the norms stated in authoritative rabbinic texts much more than it does the realities of community practice of the rabbinic era, about which we have no direct independent data.

RESPONSIBILITY OF THE INDIVIDUAL. The bulk of rabbinic literature concentrates on how the ordinary Jewish man ought to conduct himself so as to sanctify his life. Feminists have correctly pointed out that the rabbis take men to be the primary focus of God's instruction, with women essentially considered to be their adjuncts. Thus, men make all the halakhic decisions about women's duties, and though any man might qualify to render such decisions, traditionally no woman can. The rabbis did assign women a comparatively high personal and communal status. Nonetheless, by egalitarian standards, the differentiation of women's duties from those of men, which are viewed as the norm, imposes on women a loss of dignity and worth.

The troubling issue of sexism aside, rabbinic Judaism is remarkably democratic. It calls all Jews to the same attainable virtues: righteousness in deed, piety of heart, and education of the mind. It may derogate the wicked and the ignorant, but it never denies they might change and attain the highest sanctity. The sacred elite, the rabbinate, remains open to any man and recognizes no substantial barriers between rabbis and other Jews.

With the Temple destroyed, rabbinic Judaism made the ordinary Jew a "priest" by transforming many rituals once connected with the Temple cult so that they became a way of sanctifying one's everyday life at home or in the marketplace. Before eating or after excreting, one was to wash one's hands ritually and recite an appropriate blessing. Each morning and afternoon—the times of the Temple sacrifices—men worshiped in a prescribed liturgical structure. (An evening service was added later.) In the morning, men said their prayers wearing head and arm phylacteries (Heb., *tefillin*), small leather boxes that contain biblical citations. (The very pious wore them all day.) The doorpost of a Jewish home bore its own small container, the *mezuzah*, which contained Torah texts. A special fringe on the corner of a man's garment served as a reminder of his responsibility to God.

The Jew's table became an altar. What came to it had to be ritually acceptable, *kasher*. The list of foods proscribed by the Torah was amplified by rabbinic interpretation. Animals had to be slaughtered in a religiously acceptable, humane manner, and their carcasses had to be examined for diseases. Rabbinic law extended the biblical prohibition against boiling a kid in its mother's milk to prohibit mixing any meat with any milk product. It also mandated various blessings to be recited prior to eating bread, fruit, grain, vegetables, and other foods. After a meal, a longer, preferably communal grace was to be said.

The recitation of blessings was a constant part of the Jew's day. Hearing good news or bad news; seeing the sea, or a flowering tree, or an odd-looking person, or a meteor; smelling spices; acquiring something new; passing a place where a miracle had been done—all such occasions, and many more, required brief words of prayer.

The conduct of business also exhibited this intermingling of the commonplace with the transcendent. The rabbis spelled out in detail their religious equivalent of what Western civilization calls civil law. The covenant embraced such issues of justice as the proper treatment by employers of workers and the responsibilities of workers to their employers; the definition of reasonable inducements to customers and of illegitimate restriction of trade; the extent of a fair profit and a seller's responsibility in the face of changing prices; the duty to testify in the rabbinic court and the form in which contracts were to be written. Disputes between Jews on any of these matters were to be taken to the rabbinic court, which had detailed standards for administering justice.

The rabbis made daily study—for its own sake and as a ritual observance—a religious responsibility of the highest significance. The minimum requirement could be satisfied by studying selected biblical verses and rabbinic passages, but even the liturgy included numerous study texts and regular Torah readings. Besides, the acquisition of knowledge was a source of community esteem, a typical example of social custom strengthening rabbinic ideals. The rabbis endowed Jewish religiosity with its bookish cast, and their argumentative, analytic form of study made Jewish life uncommonly verbal and cerebral.

Because much that the rabbis valued could not usefully be made law, they surrounded their precepts with their individual opinions about what constitutes the good person and the ideal community. Like the Bible's authors, they abominate lying, stealing, sexual immorality, violence, and bloodshed. They decry gossip, slander, faithlessness, injustice, hard-heartedness, arrogance, and pride. They glorify industry, honesty, compassion, charity, trustworthiness, humility, forgiveness, piety, and the fear of God. Believing in the Jewish community's good sense, they urge individuals to acquire a "good name."

They do not underestimate the difficulties involved in striving to be a good Jew—yet they never doubt that, with God's help, one can be more righteous than wicked. They picture humans as being in perpetual conflict between their *yetser ha-ra'* ("urge to do evil") and their *yetser tov* ("urge to do good"). The former they describe as a relentless, wily, indefatigable foe that seeks to dominate human consciousness and easily infects human sexuality and that can be defeated only momentarily. Realists that they were, the rabbis acknowledge that the evil urge often leads to good. Its driving energy causes people to marry, build homes, engage in useful commerce, and the like. Though one ought never to underestimate its destructiveness or one's own vulnerability, human beings can harness some of its strength for their own good and to do God's work.

One can best fight off or sublimate the "urge to do evil" by studying, remaining pious, keeping good companions, and above all by observing the Torah. However, nothing guarantees its defeat, and self-righteousness practically invites its victory. Death alone terminates the struggle, and only at the "end of days" will the "urge to do evil" be destroyed. Until then, Jews continually beseech God's help, confident that, as the Bible teaches and the rabbis continually reiterate, God will aid them in their striving for purity.

The rabbis do not expect anyone to remain sinless. (Even Moses, their model, was not sinless.) Having sinned, one should do *teshuvah*, "turning" or "repentance." Elaborating on a biblical theme, the rabbis specify the stages by which sinners right their relationship with God. One begins by becoming conscious of having sinned and feeling remorse. That should lead to a confession of one's sin before God and thus to confrontation with one's guilt. But morbidity leaves no energy for sanctification. Instead, guilt should motivate one to recompense those one has wronged and ask their forgiveness. Having firmly resolved never to repeat the iniquity, one may then beseech God's mercy with confidence, for God loves this effort of the human will and graciously accepts each sincere initiative, granting atonement.

One need not be Jewish to do *teshuvah*, and the rabbis directed that the *Book of Jonah* be read on the annual Day of Atonement to remind Jews that even the wicked Ninevites had once done so. Even for Jews *teshuvah* involves no special rites or sanctified personnel. Rather, each day's dynamic of striving but often failing to fulfill the Torah involves the individual in practicing *teshuvah*. (On Yom Kippur, the Day of Atonement, the Jewish people, in a unique sequence of four worship services, carries out a corporate *teshuvah*.)]

> *"Perhaps I may be able to make atonement for your sin."*
>
> MOSES
> EXODUS 32:30

FAMILY IN RABBINIC JUDAISM. The rabbis usually think of individuals not as isolated entities but as organically connected to their families and their people. For the rabbis the Jewish way primarily involves an ethnic group's unique covenant with God and its consequences for the lives of the individuals who constitute the group. The Jewish family replicates in miniature the greater covenant community.

The rabbis consider marriage a cardinal religious obligation, though they tolerate some exceptions. Through marriage one carries out the biblical command to have children. Because marriages were arranged in their era, the rabbis provide much counsel about this important process. They strongly urge that men marry early and that they take a wife from a good family who has a pleasant personality. They favor monogamy but do not require it (it was finally made obligatory by the medieval sages). They subordinate good looks, love, sexual pleasure, and even fecundity—in all of which they delight—to their goal of family well-being, *shalom*, which comes from a couple's mutual dedication to the Torah.

The rabbis hope that a deep love will arise between the spouses, on whom they enjoin sexual fidelity. (Talmudic law defines such fidelity in terms of the wife's behavior; medieval writers tend to apply similar standards to husbands.) They expect male dominance in the household, but counsel the temperate use of power by husbands and fathers. They also display a canny sense of the critical, even decisive, role the wife/mother plays in family affairs.

Despite this exaltation of marriage in their sacred way of living, the rabbis provided for the possibility of divorce. Though they decried the breakup of a family, they did not make divorce administratively impractical. Divorced men and women often remarried.

From biblical times, Jews experienced infertility as

The most venerated explanation for the foundation of the synagogue traces its foundation to the Jews taken captive to Babylon in the sixth century BCE. In the absence of the Temple, the exiles gathered for worship and spiritual instruction, creating proto-synagogues.

PAGE 653

grievous suffering. If Jews have no offspring, the covenant expires. Through future generations all prior Jewish devotion hopes to reach completion. Children—particularly sons, in the rabbinic view—therefore come as a great blessing, and if they grow up to be good people, respected in the community, their parents enjoy inestimable fulfillment. Should they be wicked, their parents consider it a major judgment on themselves. Some rabbis identify suffering caused by one's children as the worst of divine visitations.

Only occasionally do the rabbis discuss parents' obligations to their children, perhaps because they believed that natural sentiment, guided by Jewish folkways, would adequately direct them. By contrast, they say much about children's duties toward their parents. The rabbis' amplification of the Fifth Commandment—"Honor your father and mother"—not only reflects their regard for wisdom and experience but testifies to the covenant between the generations that revivifies the covenant between God and Israel. Jewish personal names add to this intimacy, for one is called the "son (or daughter) of so-and-so" and thus carries one's parent in one's personhood all one's life.

These relationships functioned within the Jewish home, the primary scene of ongoing Jewish observance. Particularly since it might also be one's place of business, the home brought the diverse aspects of Jewish life together in mutually strengthening integrity.

JEWISH COMMUNITY AND JEWISH PEOPLE. In rabbinic times most Jews lived away from the Land of Israel, in the Diaspora, and from about the fifth to the tenth century CE, Babylonian Jewry exercised preeminent religious authority. To carry on their faith, the Jews who were scattered across the Parthian and Roman empires found it helpful to live near other Jews. The experience of anti-Semitism also brought Jews together. As always, the social and the sacred interpenetrated.

The responsibility of the Jewish community to uphold the covenant received its most visible expression in the liturgy of the daily worship services at which communal prayer was offered. (Obligatory individual prayer derives from this corporate duty.) A quorum of at least ten adult males, representing the entire Jewish people, was required to be present. At the morning service on Mondays, Thursdays, Sabbaths, and festivals, and on Sabbath afternoons, the group read a portion of the Torah scroll, often followed by a selection from the prophetic books. If a particularly learned man were in the congregation, he might give a sermon.

Any man with the requisite knowledge could lead the service or read from the scroll. Various religious functionaries enhanced the community's life, but a rabbi was not a requirement. Both a ritual slaughterer (so there could be kosher meat) and a teacher for the children took priority. Devoted volunteers attended and buried the dead and took care of other such communal duties.

Rabbis in the Talmudic period were not employed by the Jewish community but, like other Jews, worked at some ordinary occupation. When the community did have a rabbi, he functioned as both scholar and judge. He exemplified the Jewish duty to study and he answered questions about Jewish law, when necessary convening a rabbinical court *(beit din)*. Decisions of the *beit din* were considered part of the oral law and hence carried divine authority, yet they could be appealed by writing to a greater scholar elsewhere who might, by the authority of his knowledge and piety, indicate that the ruling was faulty.

Corporate life turned about several institutions. One, the synagogue, which may have predated the earliest generations of rabbis, was recognized by them as a surrogate for the destroyed Temple, with prayer as a fully adequate substitute for sacrifice and laymen in the place of priests. The rabbis also made it possible for a synagogue to function anywhere a quorum met, including a private home. A populous settlement might have many congregations. A prosperous community would erect an appropriate building to house synagogue activities.

Another institution was the study house, where those devoted to learning would find a place to study and to meet with other students of Torah. Often this was a room in the synagogue.

The rabbinical court, which was composed of three learned men, did more than hear significant cases. It bore responsibility for the community's spiritual well-being. In special situations, its executive power had few limits, and it could enact decrees that were binding on the community.

The community's rabbinical authorities shared power with its lay leadership. Jewish communities in the Diaspora often possessed considerable legal independence, and their gentile rulers expected the community leaders to collect taxes, regulate the markets, and generally supervise Jewish internal affairs. All these matters were handled by applying the Torah's teaching to the immediate social and political realities.

Community leaders, carrying out a prime Jewish obligation, collected and disbursed charity (the Hebrew term, *tsedaqah*, literally means "justice"). Every Jew had obligations toward every other Jew, particularly those who needed help. Gathering and distributing the funds were among the most honored community tasks. Many communities so esteemed *tsedaqah* that even its recipients gave to others.

Geography and cultural differences produced variations in Jewish practice between the two leading cen-

PASSOVER

Celebration of Freedom

PASSOVER is the joyous Jewish festival of freedom that celebrates the Exodus of the Jews from their bondage in Egypt. Beginning on the fifteenth day of the spring month of Nisan, the festival lasts for seven days (eight days for Jews outside Israel). The Hebrew name for Passover, Pesah, refers to the paschal lamb offered as a family sacrifice in Temple times (*Ex.* 12:1-28, 12:43-49; *Dt.* 16:1-8), and the festival is so called because God "passed over" (*pasah*) the houses of the Israelites when he slew the Egyptian firstborn (*Ex.* 12:23). The annual event is called Hag ha-Pesah, the Feast of the Passover, in the Bible (*Ex.* 34:25). Another biblical name for it is Hag ha-Matsot or the Feast of the Unleavened Bread, after the command to eat unleavened bread and to refrain from eating leaven (*Ex.* 23:15, *Lv.* 23:6, *Dt.* 16:16). The critical view is that the two names are for two originally separate festivals, which were later combined. Hag ha-Pesah was a pastoral festival, whereas Hag ha-Matsot was an agricultural festival. In any event, the paschal lamb ceased to be offered when the Temple was destroyed in 70 CE, and although the name Passover is still used, the holiday is now chiefly marked by the laws concerning leaven and, especially, by the home celebration held on the first night—the Seder ("order, arrangement").

Prohibition on Leavening. On the night before the festival the house is searched thoroughly for leavened bread. Any found is gathered together and removed from the house during the morning of 14 Nisan. This is based on the biblical injunction that not only is it forbidden to eat leaven, but no leaven may remain in the house (*Ex.* 12:15, 12:19). On Passover, observant Jews do not employ utensils used during the rest of the year for food that contains leaven. Either they have special Passover utensils or they remove the leaven in the walls of their regular utensils by firing or boiling them in hot water. Only food products completely free from even the smallest particle of leaven are eaten. In many communities, rabbis supervise the manufacture of packaged Passover foods to verify that they are completely free from leaven, after which they attach their seal of fitness to the product.

The biblical reason given for eating unleavened bread (*matsah*) and refraining from eating leaven (*hamets*) is that during the Exodus the Israelites, having left Egypt in haste, were obliged to eat unleavened bread because their dough had had insufficient time to rise (*Ex.* 12:39). *Matsah* is therefore the symbol of freedom. A later idea is that leaven—bread that has risen and become fermented—represents pride and corruption, whereas unleavened bread represents humility and purity.

Synagogue Service. The synagogue liturgy for Passover contains additional prayers and hymns suffused with the themes of freedom and renewal. On the first day there is a prayer for dew; the rainy season now over, supplication is made for the more gentle dew to assist the growth of the produce in the fields. The scriptural readings are from passages dealing with Passover. On the seventh day, the anniversary of the parting of the sea (*Ex.* 14:17-15:26), the relevant passage is read; some Jews perform a symbolic reenactment to further dramatize the event.

The Seder and the Haggadah. The Seder, celebrated in the home on the first night of Passover (outside Israel, also on the second night), is a festive meal during which various rituals are carried out and the Haggadah is read or chanted. The Haggadah ("telling") is the traditional collection of hymns, stories, and poems recited in obedience to the command for parents to tell their children of God's mighty deeds in delivering the people from Egyptian bondage (*Ex.* 13:8). The main features of the Haggadah are already found in outline in the Mishnah (*Pes.* 10) with some of the material going back to Temple times. It assumed its present form in the Middle Ages, with a few more recent additions. The emphasis in the Haggadah is on God alone as the deliverer from bondage. It is he and no other, neither messenger nor angel, who brings his people out from Egypt. Even Moses is mentioned by name only once in the Haggadah, and then only incidentally, at the end of a verse quoted for other purposes.

A special dish is placed on the Seder table upon which rest the symbolic foods required for the rituals. These are three *matsot,* covered with a cloth; *maror,* bitter herbs that serve as a reminder of the way the Egyptian taskmasters embittered the lives of their slaves (*Ex.* 1:14); *haroset,* a paste made of almonds, apples, and wine, symbolic of the mortar the slaves used as well as of the sweetness of redemption; a bowl of salt water, symbolic of the tears of the oppressed; parsley or other vegetables for a symbolic dipping in the salt water; a roasted bone as a reminder of the paschal lamb; and a roasted egg as a reminder of the animal sacrifice, the *hagigah* offered in Temple times on Passover, Shavu'ot, and Sukkot.

Certain traditional Seder dishes symbolize the tears of the slaves in Egypt and their hard bondage. Commentators to the Haggadah have read into this theme various mystical ideas about the survival of Israel and the ultimate overcoming of death itself in eternal life. All join in singing these songs, for which there are many traditional melodies. This night is said to be one of God's special protection so that the usual night prayers on retiring to bed, supplicating God for his protection, are not recited since that protection is granted in any event.

— LOUIS JACOBS

ters of Jewry, one in the Land of Israel (under Roman rule) and the other in Babylonia (under Parthian and, after 226 CE, Sasanid rule). No single agency existed to enforce uniformity in practice or theory. Instead, a relatively loose pattern of authority emerged. From time to time, certain institutions or individuals arose whose scholarship and piety commanded the respect of many Jews. In time, their teachings established precedents for later Jewry.

Despite the open texture of the Judaism of this era, the rabbis exhibited a clear-cut sense of the unity and identity of the Jewish people, who were the sole recipients of God's law and thus bore unique witness to God. They detested the idolatry and immorality they saw all about them. Hence they consciously sought to distinguish and separate Jews from the nations. But most rabbis happily accepted sincere converts. The isolation of the Jews made hospitality to strangers critical: Jews on a journey could always expect to find a welcome in other Jewish communities, which, despite variations in custom, clearly followed the same Torah in the same basic way.

Within the Judaic tradition only one day of fasting was imposed by Mosaic law, Yom Kippur, the Day of Atonement.

PAGE 225

THREE RHYTHMS OF JEWISH TIME. Jews live in three interrelated dimensions of time: the personal, the annual-historical, and the eschatological. The critical passages of each individual's life are marked by sacred rites. On the eighth day after his birth, a newborn boy receives the physical sign of the covenant in the ceremony of circumcision. At thirteen he assumes personal responsibility for performing the commandments, becoming *bar mitsvah*. Should he complete the study of a classic text, he marks the occasion with a small celebration. Marriage is preceded by formal betrothal. The wedding itself is as elaborate as the family's means and the community's standards will allow. The birth of children, the experience of bereavement and mourning, the dissolution of marriage in divorce are all social acts that involve community participation; many of them are also sanctified by prayer and ritual.

Prayer and ritual similarly mark the great moments of each year. The six workdays climax in the rest, worship, study, and feasting of the Sabbath. On Friday eve (in the Jewish calendar, the day begins at sundown) it is traditional that women light the Sabbath candles and say a blessing over them. Before the special Sabbath meal is eaten, a prayer of sanctification is recited over a cup of wine. When the Sabbath has ended, its "holy time" is demarcated from the "profane time" of the weekday by the recitation of blessings over wine, spices, and a multi-wicked flame in a ritual called Havdalah ("separation").

The year begins in the autumn during the period of the High Holy Days. The solemn synagogal rites of Ro'sh ha-Shanah celebrate God's sovereignty, justice, and mercy. The ensuing ten days of penitence are climaxed by the all-day fast and worship service of Yom Kippur, the Day of Atonement, in which the congregation beseeches God's promised forgiveness. In the course of the year there are three "pilgrimage" festivals, Passover, Shavu'ot (Weeks or Pentecost), and Sukkot (Tabernacles; Feast of Booths). Originally these were agricultural festivals during which all Jews came on pilgrimage to the Temple in Jerusalem, but they were transformed by the rabbis into historical symbols: Passover celebrates the Exodus from slavery in Egypt, Shavu'ot the giving of the Torah, and Sukkot God's providential care of the Israelites in the wilderness. Thus, the undeviating cycle of the year becomes a reminder and renewal of the Jewish people's unique historical experience.

Rabbinic creativity likewise embellished the minor festivals of the year. The rabbis established a ceremony of special psalms, prayers, and a reading from the Torah scroll to greet the beginning of each lunar month. For the fast day of Tish'ah be-Av, commemorating the destruction of the Temple, they enjoined a reading of the *Book of Lamentations*. They memorialized other tragic events with lesser fasts. The salvation of ancient Persian Jewry, recounted in the *Book of Esther*, is remembered on the feast of Purim. The Maccabees' rededication of the Temple in 164 BCE, after its desecration by the Hellenistic ruler of Syria, Antiochus IV, is celebrated as Hanukkah at about the time of the winter solstice with a ritual that includes the kindling of lights in the home over the course of eight nights.

The number of each Jewish year indicates the time since creation, according to rabbinic calculation, even as the rhythm of the year directs attention toward history's promised climax, God's manifest rule on earth. A messianic hopefulness infuses all Jewish observance, for the end might begin at any moment; yet the Jews' heartbreaking experience with premature messiahs—particularly Bar Kokhba in the rebellion against Rome of 132-135 CE—indicated that the Messiah would come only at the "end of days."

We can surmise something of the tone and quality of the rabbis' Judaism from what their traditions tell us about the way they lived. Their teachings show that they can be wildly playful, though they are usually highly serious; exuberant in celebration, yet careful of minutiae; free in opinion, yet obedient to discipline; guilt-stricken at sinning, yet confident of forgiveness; desirous of intention in the performance of *mitsvot* (the commandments), yet content with the deed itself; highly individualistic, yet absorbed in community; concerned with the practical, yet oriented toward the eschatological. They were simultaneously mystic and rationalistic, emotionally demonstrative and devoted to order, foolish sinners and pious martyrs. They were ordinary people who might be one's neighbors, yet they

were saintly, endowing their spirituality with intellect and a communal and personal activism. And the communities that were guided by their teachings seem much like them, human and holy at once.

Above all, the rabbis have a passion for this mundane life, despite the finer one to come. They delight in its opportunities to serve God through the routines specified by Torah. Yet they insist that in order to save a life, all the laws of the Torah could—indeed, must—be broken (except the prohibitions against idolatry, murder, and sexual sin). Similarly, when the survival of the Jewish people seems to be at risk, the rabbis find ways to accommodate reality, but not by compromising principle. For they believe, above all, that the world was created for the sanctification of life, and that only through holy Jewish living can it hope to endure and reach completion.

Beliefs of the Rabbis

It is characteristic of the rabbis that their faith is inseparable from their way of life. Their test for heresy was behavioral, not creedal. Their explicit statements of belief are generally more poetic than precise, more fragmentary than general, and they exhibit little interest in systemic coherence.

While acknowledging the notorious elusiveness of what they call rabbinic theology, some modern scholars have yet found it possible to explicate some of its major themes. The rabbis' theological creativity operates mainly in their reshaping of the multitudinous ideas and images of biblical belief. In this process they continue the millennial Jewish experience of reinterpreting the covenant as times change and as their own intellectuality and religious sensitivity demand.

The primacy of continuity in rabbinic belief helps explain what modern readers often consider the rabbis' surprisingly modest response to the Temple's destruction. Though they were deeply traumatized, the rabbis did not see the loss of the Temple as a disaster requiring major theological reconstruction; rather, they found it a confirmation of the Bible's teaching. God had done what God had promised to do and had done once before (in 587/6 BCE). Sin eventually begets punishment, even to the destruction of God's Temple and the exile of God's people. But the punishment has a covenant purpose, to bring the people back to God's service. In due course, the rabbis believed, God would again restore the holy people and their Temple. Continuing the faith of the Bible as they understood it, the rabbis indomitably transcended profane history.

GOD. Monotheism anchors the rabbis' faith, just as it anchors the later biblical writings. The rabbis abominate idolatry and passionately oppose the notion that there are "two powers" in heaven. That does not prevent their speaking of God's heavenly retinue, the subordinates by whom God's governance of the universe usually proceeds. Similarly, they exhibit no inhibition about using metaphors to describe God. These may be abstract names, such as "the Place," "the Power," "the Holy," or images drawn from human life,

WAILING WALL

In Rabbinic Judaism, the rabbis believe that the world was created for the sanctification of life, and that only through holy Jewish living can it hope to endure and reach completion. This believer at the Wailing Wall in Jerusalem continues this tradition.

RICHARD T. NOWITZ/CORBIS

such as references to God's phylacteries, or daily schedule, or emotions.

Another typical rabbinic dialectic moves between the utter greatness and the immediate availability of God. The ineffably glorious Sovereign of all universes attends and responds to a human whisper or fleeting meditation.

Rabbinic theology often pivots about God's justice and mercy. The declaration "There is no Judge and no justice" seems to be the rabbinic equivalent of atheism, but the rabbis give elaborate validations of the reliability of God's justice. They believe that the world could not survive if God were absolutely just: human fallibility and willfulness make such stringency impractical. For people freely to come to righteousness, God must also be merciful and compassionate. But if there were mercy without justice, this same rebellious humankind would never become responsible for its own actions. Undaunted by the paradoxes, the rabbis affirm that the one and only God is both just and merciful, demanding and forgiving, the ultimate idealist and realist in one.

The rabbis are committed to the propositions that God is One, creator of heaven and earth; that he rewards those who obey his will and punishes those who disobey.

PAGE 243

Much of what other people might take to be evil the rabbis steadfastly consider the subtle working-out of God's justice. They do not deny that unmerited suffering occurs. Sometimes they explain this as "chastisements of love," torment given to the pious in this world so that rewards will await them in the afterlife. Sometimes they merely ascribe it to God's inexplicable will, God's "harsh decree." (Parallel reasons are offered by the rabbis for the gift of God's unmerited blessing—that is, it comes because of the "merit of the patriarchs," or simply because God loves or chooses to bless the recipient.) Less frequently, the rabbis will picture God, as it were, as somehow unable to prevent a tragedy or as lamenting its occurrence. With reason or without, they hold God to be the ultimate source of evil as well as good and so call for the recitation of a blessing upon hearing evil tidings. They devoutly trust God, whom they know they cannot hope to understand despite all their study and piety.

Perhaps they evince such confidence because they have a strong, full belief in life after death. Several stages of the afterlife may be identified in rabbinic traditions. At death, the soul is taken from the body for preliminary judgment and purification and stays with God until the general bodily resurrection that will take place at the "end of days." Then the soul, rejoined to its purified body, receives judgment. The wicked are utterly destroyed, and the less culpable receive a limited term of expiatory punishment. Finally, the individual enters the "future to come," the blissful but indescribable reward God has promised the righteous.

HUMANKIND AND HUMAN DESTINY. The rabbis' conception of humankind stands behind their Jewish self-understanding. Human beings literally

SHABBAT
The Day of Rest

The Hebrew word shabbat is from a root meaning "to desist" or "to rest," that is, from work and labor. The Sabbath is the day of rest each week after six days of work. The command to keep the Sabbath holy is found in both versions of the Decalogue (Ex. 20:8-11, Dt. 5:12-15), but the reasons given for Sabbath observance differ. In Exodus the creation motif is stressed: "For in six days the Lord made heaven and earth and sea, and all that is in them, and he rested on the seventh day." In Deuteronomy the social motivation is prominent. Man must rest on the Sabbath and allow his slaves to rest with him.

The nature of the "work" *(mela'khah)* that is forbidden on the Sabbath has received many different interpretations in the course of Jewish history. In addition, various restrictions were introduced by the rabbis, as on the handling of money or of objects normally used for work, and all business activities.

Reform Judaism largely ignores the rabbinic rules governing acts forbidden on the Sabbath, preferring to understand "work" as gainful occupation alone, and the spiritual atmosphere of the Sabbath as generated chiefly by means of rituals in the home and services in the synagogue. Orthodox Judaism follows the traditional regulations in their entirety.

The ideas of honoring the Sabbath and taking delight in it are expressed in the wearing of special clothes, having a well-lit home, forgetting worldly worries and anxieties (for this reason petitionary prayers are not recited on the Sabbath), the study of the Torah, three meals, and the union of husband and wife.

The central feature of the synagogue service on the Sabbath is the reading of the Torah from a handwritten scroll—the Sefer Torah (Book of the Law). The Torah is divided into portions, one section *(sidrah)* of which is read each Sabbath. The whole Torah is completed in this way each year, and then the cycle begins anew.

There are a number of special Sabbaths marked by additions to the standard liturgy and by relevant Prophetic and extra Torah readings. The earliest of these are the four Sabbaths of the weeks before Passover.

— LOUIS JACOBS

constitute a family since God created them from one pair of progenitors. And God made and maintains a covenant with all the descendants of Noah. Under it, God promised that there would be no more annihilatory floods and commanded all people to obey seven laws: six negative—not to blaspheme God, or worship idols, or steal, or murder, or commit sexual offenses, or eat the limb of a living animal—and one positive—to set up courts of justice.

Human nature being so torn between its evil and good urges, people regularly transgress these simple laws. So God brought a special nation into being, the Jews, to serve God devotedly by accepting a covenant of 613 commandments. In the rabbinic sociology of religion, people are either Jews, faithful servants of the only God, or part of "the nations," idolaters and therefore sinners. The Jews' experience of anti-Semitism reinforced this view and strengthened the Jewish commitment to separatism for God's sake.

The customary strife between the nations and the people of Israel will greatly intensify as the "end of days" nears. But God will send the Messiah, a human, Davidic king descended from King David, to lead God's people to victory. Once again, the rabbinic accounts grow hazy and irreconcilable. Some see the nations converting to Judaism; others see them accepting Jewish leadership. There is little elaboration of the biblical poems that prophesy a time of universal justice, peace, contentment, and lack of fear. However, the rabbis anticipate that at the final judgment the nations will be found guilty of wickedness and denied entry to the "future to come." Some rabbis mitigate this attitude by teaching that individuals who are "pious among the nations of the world have a share in the world to come."

Of course, any sinner might become righteous by repenting. The rabbis tell—occasionally with considerable envy—of a number of gentiles and Jews who by a heartfelt act of *teshuvah* immediately gained the life of the world to come.

Most of these matters became part of rabbinic law concerning non-Jews. Hence this doctrine, in general, may be said to be authoritative rabbinic teaching.

RABBINIC THEORY OF TORAH. Radical theological creativity appears starkly in the rabbis' doctrine of the oral law. Unlike some of their other distinctive ideas, such as repentance, the Messiah, and resurrection, the notion of the oral law has no explicit biblical foundation. Since it undergirds all of rabbinic Judaism, it may be said to be the rabbis' most characteristic doctrine. To reiterate what has been said above, the rabbis taught that God gave Moses not only the first five books of the Bible (and, by implication, the rest of it) but also unrecorded verbal instructions, including specific duties and the methods for educing further oral law.

The rabbis also delimit the content of the written law in its broader sense of holy scripture, that is, the Hebrew scriptures. They apparently inherited fixed versions of the five books of the Torah and of the Prophets (including *Joshua, Judges, Samuel,* and *Kings*) and they determined what would be included in the Writings, admitting *Ecclesiastes,* for example, but rejecting *Ben Sira*. With these three divisions (Torah, Prophets, Writings; abbreviated in Hebrew as *Tanakh*) they closed the canon, for they believed that revelation ended with *Haggai, Zechariah,* and *Malachi* and that the books of the Writings had preceded these prophetical books. Though the rabbis occasionally hear a "heavenly echo" concerning matters under discussion, they may disregard it. Effectively, therefore, postbiblical Judaism derives from the rabbis' delimitation of the written law and their continuing explication of the oral law.

God excepted, no aspect of Jewish belief arouses the rabbis' awe as does Torah. They describe it as existing before creation, as God's guide to creation, and as God's most treasured possession, one so precious the angels tried to keep it from being taken to earth. The people of Israel, by virtue of having been given and having accepted the Torah, have become infinitely precious to God and central to human history. The rabbis acknowledge that wisdom may be found among the nations, but for them Torah contains God's fullest truth for humankind, making it the arbiter of all wisdom.

The rabbis do not detail the correct means or institutional structure for amplifying the oral law. Rather, the living practice of the master (*rabbi* means "my master") sets the model for his disciples. From time to time various institutions have emerged that temporarily exercised some general authority, but none lasted or created a form that later generations utilized. We have no way of gauging the extent to which Jews accepted the rabbis' leadership even in their own time. It seems paradoxical to seek control and integrity with such lack of structure and tolerance of diversity, but the arrangement has persisted to the present day.

With God's teaching available in verbal form, learning became a major Jewish religious activity. On a simple level, study motivated Jewish duty and specified its content. On a more advanced level, pondering God's instructions—even those of only theoretical relevance, like the rules for the Temple service—enabled one to have intellectual communion, as it were, with God. Gifted men sought to become rabbis, perhaps even to have their teachings cited by others, but always to set a living example for other Jews. Often reports of a master's deeds themselves became part of the oral law.

This heavy intellectual emphasis should not be divorced from its religious context. The intellectually keenest rabbis are also depicted as deeply pious, passionate in prayer, caring and virtuous in their dealings with people, intimately involved in the ordinary activi-

More fully called the Torah of Moses, the Torah comprises the first five books of the biblical canon, usually known in English as the Pentateuch: Genesis, Exodus, Leviticus, Numbers, and Deuteronomy.

PAGE 169

ties of life. Many also were mystics, though we have only hints about their esoteric spirituality.

The rabbinic doctrine of Torah brought fresh dynamism to Judaism. By authorizing new and open forms of authority and practice it enabled the Jewish people to keep the covenant vital, no matter what changes were brought by time and dispersion. With Judaism now centered on the individual and communal practice of Torah rather than on the Temple cult in Jerusalem, one could live as a faithful Jew anywhere. And as life created new problems, one only needed to find or become a learned Jew to determine what God wanted now, God's continuing command, and hence feel God's continuing care and concern. This oversimplifies a highly sophisticated process, but also conveys its providential gist.

"The Lord thy God hath chosen thee to be a special people unto himself."

JUDGES 7:6

THE JEWS AS GOD'S TREASURED PEOPLE. The people of Israel uniquely serve the one God of the universe by living by God's teachings. Whatever superiority the people of Israel might claim over the gentiles derives from their faithfulness in living according to the covenant. Having the Torah does not exempt the Jews from God's demand for righteousness; if anything, because they have more commandments to fulfill they bear more responsibility before God. At the same time, God has a special love for the people of the covenant. When the people of Israel sin, God patiently waits for them to repent and helps them do so, sometimes by punishing them to remind them of their responsibilities.

The rabbis directly applied these beliefs to their situation, with the Temple destroyed and Jewish life in the Land of Israel degenerating. They lamented the calamities of their time: their inability to fulfill the commandments regarding God's cult and the material and spiritual distress brought on by dispersion and Roman rule. But their faith did not waver. They held that this people had been justly punished for its sins, though they often pictured God as pained at having had to execute so dire a sentence. To the rabbis, this new exile came because of the covenant and not as its negation; God had fulfilled what the covenant called for in response to egregious iniquity.

The Jews' political and social insignificance in the Roman empire did not negate their faith in their continuing spiritual uniqueness. Rather, the idolatry and immorality of the Romans proved them unworthy of Jewish admiration and God's esteem. To keep their service of God uncontaminated, the Jews set a distance between themselves and the nations. They also lived in the hope that their stubborn loyalty to God would one day be vindicated before all humankind. The eschatological savior described in the *Book of Daniel* had become an important figure in rabbinic Judaism, the King Messiah. One day—perhaps today—God would send him to restore the holy people to its land, defeat its enemies, reestablish its throne, rebuild its Temple and reconstitute its cult, institute a world order of justice and compassion, and usher in a time when all the promise of creation and the covenant would be fulfilled.

This was a human and historical expectation. As a consequence, some Jews would, from time to time, declare one or another figure of their day to be the anticipated Son of David, in the hope that the Jewish people had so lived up to its covenant responsibilities that God had sent the Messiah. Even if the folk did not merit him, it was understood that God would, in God's own time, send redemption. In either case, the rabbis could only fantasize as to what God would then do to transform and perfect creation. They imagined nature pacified and responsive, the nations admiring of the Torah or even converted to Judaism. Diverse as these conceptions were, all the rabbis agreed that this glorious time will be succeeded by the resurrection of the dead, the final judgment, and the climactic but indescribable "future to come."

The rabbis taught the people of Israel to remain confident of God's rule and favor and to await in history and beyond it God's sure deliverance and blessing—a faith that carried them through history until modern times.

FROM TALMUDIC TO MODERN TIMES

After the editing of the Talmud, countless variations of the rabbis' way appeared as Jews lived in diverse countries, cultures, social orders, and historical circumstances. Mostly they added observances; some of these became generally accepted, such as the holiday of Simhat Torah (Joy of Torah), which became the ninth day of the festival of Sukkot, and the *yohrtsayt*, the later Ashkenazic practice of memorializing a close relative's day of death. A selective factor also operated, as in the abandonment of the triennial cycle of reading the Torah scroll during worship services in favor of an annual cycle. The range of this cultural creativity was greatly extended by the folk or ethnic nature of the Jews.

Two major cultural streams emerged. The Sefardic tradition (from the medieval Hebrew word *Sefarad* for the Iberian Peninsula) chiefly embraced the Jews of the Mediterranean Basin, many of whom were descended from families exiled from Spain in 1492, as well as those in Arab countries. The Ashkenazic tradition (from the medieval word *Ashkenaz* for northern France and Germany) encompassed the Jews of northern and eastern Europe, from whom most Jews in North America descend. Sefardic rabbis led Jewry throughout the Diaspora from the eleventh through the sixteenth century; meanwhile, the Ashkenazic sages created a halakhic scholarship that eventually brought them to the fore in Jewish life.

Each cultural style encompassed diverse national and local ways of living that changed over the centuries. Sefardic spokesmen have often taken pride in their community's urbanity, its respect for form and decorum, its devotion to liturgy, and its esteem of clear intellectuality. Similarly, Ashkenazic leaders have proudly noted their group's passionate energy, its fierce individuality, its dedication to study, and its love of Talmudic erudition.

Developing the Rabbinic Way

We know little about the actual practices of Jews for much of this period, though we know much about what rabbis said ought to be done. But the quasi-institutional means that evolved to control the development of Jewish life so evidences the spirit of Judaism that it deserves description. In their far-flung Diaspora, Jews recognized no institution or group as universally authoritative. Yet despite the slowness of communication, or lack of it, among the Jewish communities, and the immense diversity in local practice, the Jews remained and recognized one another as one covenant people.

Persecution intensified this sense of identity. With the rise of Islam early in the seventh century, Jews, living mostly in Islamic lands, became a group tolerated, but given second-class social and legal status. Among Christians, the occasional anti-Jewish outbreaks of the early centuries gave way after the First Crusade (1096 CE) to nearly seven centuries of harassment, including economic limitations, forced conversions, pogroms and riots, and communal expulsions, culminating about 1500 CE in the formal creation of the ghetto, the walled-in Jewish quarter of European cities. This pariah status strongly affected Jewish practices and attitudes and helped give rise to an elemental spiritual resistance founded on the certainty of possessing God's revelation and favor. The immediate contrast between their way of life and that of their oppressors empowered Jews to live and die steadfast in their faith.

Jewish communities vested authority in those whose learning and piety evoked it. Early on, the geonim, leaders of the Babylonian academies *(yeshivot)* that produced the Babylonian Talmud, began responding to questions addressed to them by distant Jews. This pattern of questions and answers, *she'elot u-teshuvot*, established itself as a way to get and give authoritative guidance. To this day, *teshuvot*, also known as *responsa*, remain the preeminent device for Jewish legal development. The power of a *teshuvah* derives entirely from the prestige and scholarship of its author. Many *teshuvot* became academic additions to the body of Jewish "case law." Others became widely authoritative, like one of Rav Amram, gaon of the *yeshivah* in Sura, Babylonia, from 856 to 874 CE. His lengthy answer to a question from Spanish Jews about liturgical practice established the prototype for Jewish prayer books.

The geonim and other sages sometimes wrote commentaries to portions of the Talmud or composed treatises on an aspect of the law. Eventually, the growing accretion of law led some teachers to compile codes. Each code became the subject of critical commentaries, some of which are printed alongside the code text in modern editions. The *Shulhan 'arukh* of Yosef Karo (1488-1575), a Sefardic master, published in 1565 CE, became generally accepted among Ashkenazic Jews as well after Mosheh Isserles (c. 1525-1572) wrote glosses to it that reflected Ashkenazic practice. To this day, the *Shulhan 'arukh* remains the authoritative code of Jewish law, though scholars continue to rework some of its sections.

Only one serious internal challenge to rabbinic Judaism emerged in the medieval period: the Karaite (biblicist) movement, which rejected the authority of the oral law and created a pattern of practice based on the Bible alone. Beginning in the eighth century CE in the Middle East, it reached the peak of its appeal and literary productivity in the eleventh and twelfth centuries. By then rabbinic authorities had declared Karaism heretical and prohibited intermarriage with Karaites. Some few thousand Karaites still exist, largely in the state of Israel.

In many other fields, as well as law, the range of Jewish study continually expanded. Biblical exegesis, homilies, poetry, mystical accounts, chronicles, polemics, explorations of piety, handbooks for good conduct, philosophy—every period produced its books and the students to ponder them. The invention of printing added further impetus to Jewish learning.

New Ideas and Their Effect on Practice

Four particularly significant, if not always distinguishable, intellectual currents moved through much of the Jewish world during the Middle Ages: pietism, mysticism, philosophy, and polemic. It will help to consider pietism, the most popular, first, though mysticism, an elitist enterprise, predates it.

MEDIEVAL PIETISM. The Talmud and Midrash devote much attention to the virtues a Jew should manifest, but do so only in passing. About the eleventh century, a popular, specifically pietistic literature known as *musar* began to appear. Well into modern times, large numbers of Jews read and sought to live by the high spiritual standards its authors advocated.

The title of the early, exemplary *musar* book, *Duties of the Heart*, written in Arabic by Bahye ibn Paquda in the late eleventh century, epitomizes the movement's

The period of exile and restoration left its deep marks on the people and changed their spiritual character.

PAGE 374

Jewish mysticism shows an unparalleled variety of forms ranging from deep speculation to purely emotional experience.

PAGE 477

aims. While the Talmud focused on the good Jew's acts, Bahye stressed the inner life as the basis for action. He and other pietists called attention to the need for intimacy between the individual and God, stressing the humility of the one and the greatness of the other. Consciousness of this relationship, they said, should strongly motivate one to cultivate personal holiness, particularly through loving behavior to others—an emphasis so pronounced that the pietists' writings are often called "ethical" books.

Two concerns of *musar* teachers gradually became common in most medieval Jewish writing. First, the pietists strongly contrast the purity of the soul with the grossness of the body. This duality, alluded to in both the Bible and the Talmud, became central and intense in *musar* piety. With corporeality the soul's antagonist, the pietists commend a measure of asceticism and social withdrawal. Yet they do not go so far as to become full-fledged dualists, for they believe that God created the body and ordained social life.

Second, the pietists express great anxiety about sinning and cultivate the fear of incurring guilt. How can anyone who is intensely aware of God's greatness not find the idea of defying God utterly reprehensible? One of the most common *musar* strategies for avoiding or surmounting temptation is to remember the punishment awaiting the wicked in the next world. The *musar* writers therefore urge heartfelt remorse and repentance for every sin, even suggesting compensatory atonements one might undertake. In no small measure, the conflict between the values of modern life and the values of premodern Judaism arose from disagreement over these matters.

MATURATION OF JEWISH MYSTICISM. Whereas pietism reached out to ordinary Jews, mysticism limited itself to select individuals who were initiated into an esoteric doctrine by masters who often concealed as much as they revealed.

The Jewish mystical writings describe and exhibit phenomena that are associated with mysticism in many cultures: stringent spiritual discipline, bizarre language and exalted spiritual expression, techniques for gaining mystical experience, visions of the heavenly realm, physical images of God coupled with assertions of God's utter ineffability, longing for religious consummation and ways of hastening it—all these and more appear refracted in perplexing and fascinating fashion through sensitive temperaments affected by highly diverse situations.

The main tradition of Jewish mysticism is known as Qabbalah. Developed in response to God's revelation of a holy way of life, it has a highly cognitive content that is concerned with cosmogony and theosophy. Its most significant document, the *Zohar* (Book of Splendor), written primarily in Aramaic in late thirteenth-century Spain, is a commentary on the Torah that elaborates a mystical doctrine of God's complex nature. Ultimately, God is Ein Sof, "without limit," hence the one about whom nothing at all can be said. Yet God is also intimately known, contemplated, and related to through interacting loci of divine energy, the *sefirot* (lit., "spheres" or "numbers"; in qabbalistic terminology, emanations from God's inner being). The mystics speak of the *sefirot* with a freedom of metaphor that is almost limitless, not even excluding sexual anthropomorphisms. Feminine metaphors for God, rare in the Bible and occasional in the Talmud, now come into full use alongside masculine metaphors in explications of God's nature.

The Jewish mystics, for all the immediacy of their relationship with God, believe that Torah—the written and oral law—remains primary to Judaism. They therefore eschew antinomianism—the idea that faith, not law, is sufficient—and cultivate meticulous observance. By ascribing supernal significance to commandments and customs that reason cannot explain, they easily provide absolute justification for them.

Two late developments in Jewish mysticism have had continuing repercussions. The first was the qabbalistic thought of Isaac Luria (1534-1572). According to his cosmogonic explanation of evil, creation began with an act of divine self-contraction that produced an outflow of generative light. God projected this light into the vessels, or material forms, that had been prepared for it. These vessels proved too fragile and shattered, leaving unsanctified shards or husks that contain only sparks of God's creative, transformative light. By observing God's commandments, people can free the heavenly sparks from their husks and mend the broken vessels, thus restoring the world and rescuing it from evil. God appears passive in this process, as it is human action that brings the Messiah—a striking anticipation of modern liberalism.

In the eighteenth century, in southern Poland and the Ukraine, the Hasidic movement transformed qabbalistic tradition through a radical appropriation of God's accessibility (prompting charges by their opponents that the Hasidim were pantheists). To the Hasidim, God's nearness implied that life should be lived with joy and enthusiasm. For cleaving to God, one need not be a spiritual virtuoso but only give God one's heart. This attitude encouraged new practices and fervent observance, though its opponents claimed that its emphasis on spontaneity and inner experience led to laxity in ritual.

Hasidism became a mass movement that carried a dialectical tension. On the one hand, the humblest person could live the mystical life. The Hasidic leaders encouraged this egalitarianism by putting many of their teachings in exoteric form, as tales, stories, and popular preaching, and by promoting a close community life. On the other hand, Hasidism established a religious elite. Each community was led by a *tsaddiq*, or *rebe*. The *tsaddiqim* represent Hasidism's esoteric side, privately practicing an exalted mysticism and serving as the intermediary between their followers and heaven. Their followers believed that the *tsaddiqim* could work wonders and thus beseeched their intercession on every personal problem. Since each community thought its own *tsaddiq* the most powerful, some Hasidic communities isolated themselves even from other Hasidim.

Later, Hasidism became institutionalized around dynasties and antagonistic to modernity. The groups that managed to survive the Holocaust have had a resurgence in the state of Israel and the United States. They have gained recruits from Jews who, disillusioned with secular culture, seek out the intensity of immersion in a separatist Jewish esoteric community.

THE ENCOUNTER WITH PHILOSOPHY. The Talmud knows nothing of Philo Judaeus of Alexandria (fl. first century CE) or any other Hellenistic Jewish philosopher. Certain that they possessed God's revelation, the rabbis spurned formal Greek philosophy, which they associated with idolatry. In the ninth century CE, Jews encountered Muslim philosophy, which claimed that it taught the purest monotheism because its doctrine of God had been refined through rational argument. For the next seven centuries—that is, as long as cultural involvement with the Muslims persisted—a tiny Jewish intellectual aristocracy created Jewish philosophy. Their work had little direct impact on Jewish life, though some of their ideas—for example, Moses Maimonides' excoriation of anthropomorphism—became widely influential.

The early philosophical thinkers, such as Sa'adyah Gaon (882-942), adduced proofs for God's creation of the world, from which they deduced God's unity and sovereign power. On this basis they sought to give rational justification to such problems as miracles, providence, evil, and why Judaism was the true revelation. The rational defense of certain inexplicable commands of the Torah evoked considerable philosophic ingenuity.

In the course of time, most medieval Jewish philosophical thought came to employ Aristotelian categories. The occasional Neoplatonic voice found little

That God is the creator of the universe is accepted as axiomatic by all the medieval thinkers.

PAGE 244

MOSES MAIMONIDES

A Quest to Integrate Halakhah and Philosophy

MAIMONIDES, MOSES (c. 1135/8-1204), hellenized name of Mosheh ben Maimon; also known by the acronym RaMBaM (Rabbi Mosheh ben Maimon); distinguished Talmudist, philosopher, and physician, and one of the most illustrious figures of Jewish history. He had a profound and pervasive impact on Jewish life and thought, and his commanding influence has been widely recognized by non-Jews as well as Jews. His epoch-making works in the central areas of Jewish law *(halakhah)* and religious philosophy are considered to be unique by virtue of their unprecedented comprehensiveness, massive erudition, and remarkable originality and profundity. Their extraordinary conjunction of halakhic authority and philosophic prestige has been widely acknowledged. While the generations before the age of Maimonides produced philosophically trained Talmudists—scholars well versed in both Greek science and rabbinic lore—the extent to which Maimonides thoroughly and creatively amalgamated these disciplines and commitments is most striking.

The natural integration of traditional Torah study and philosophy is a pivot of his massive literary achievement and an axiom of his understanding of Judaism. His creativity reflects a strong pedagogic drive. His youthful works (*Millot ha-higgayon*, on logic, and *Ma'amar ha-'ibbur*, on the astronomical principles of the Jewish calendar) were composed in response to specific requests. Throughout his life he wrote hundreds of *responsa (teshuvot)*—decisions concerning the interpretation or application of the law—and letters of advice, comfort, or arbitration to all parts of the world, including Yemen, Baghdad, Aleppo, Damascus, Jerusalem, Alexandria, Marseilles, and Lunel. *Iggeret ha-shemad* (Epistle on Conversion) and *Iggeret Teiman* (Epistle to Yemen) are especially noteworthy. His code of law was intended for "small and great"; indeed, law for him was an educative force leading to ethical and intellectual perfection, and his code was intended to be not only a manual of commands but an instrument of education and instruction.

Maimonides' major works are the *Perush ha-Mishnah* (Commentary on the Mishnah), *Sefer ha-mitsvot* (Book of the Commandments), *Mishneh Torah* (Review of the Torah; also known as *Yad ha-hazaqah*), and *Moreh nevukhim* (Guide of the Perplexed). He also wrote some ten medical treatises that illustrate his vast erudition and the high ethical standards he brought to medicine. They are based to a large extent on Arabic medical literature. One of them deals with Galen and contains a rejoinder to Galen's criticisms of the Mosaic Torah.

— ISADORE TWERSKY

philosophic resonance, though the mystics found the Neoplatonic concept of emanation congenial to their notion of levels of being. Sometimes, as in the case of Yehudah ha-Levi (c. 1075-1141), a thinker became critical of philosophy and subordinated reason to revelation, rather than making it an equal or senior partner.

Modern thought rejects the medieval concept of causality, and the philosophy based on it remains of interest mainly to academic specialists. However, the contemporary clash between reason and faith seems

MOSES MAIMONIDES

One of the most illustrious figures in Jewish history, Maimonides' axiom was the natural integration of traditional Torah study and philosophy.

CORBIS-BETTMANN

prefigured in the writings of Moses Maimonides (Mosheh ben Maimon, 1135/8-1204), the preeminent Jewish philosopher. The author of the first great code of Jewish law, the *Mishneh Torah* (lit., "Second Torah"), he gained incomparable stature among Jews. He faced an intellectual crisis: the resolution of the Torah's teachings with the views of Aristotle, who had denied the idea of creation and affirmed the eternity of the universe. Maimonides refused to repudiate the demands either of reason or of faith, and his masterful effort to harmonize Judaism with a scientific view of reality became the model for all later rationalist validations of religious faith. But when, at the end of the fifteenth century, the Jews were expelled from Spain and Portugal, where philosophy was an important part of the culture, this fruitful intellectual enterprise came largely to an end.

"In the realm of Nature there is nothing purposeless, trivial, or unnecessary."

MOSES MAIMONIDES
THE GUIDE FOR THE PERPLEXED

The intellectual defense of Judaism took a more popular form in the polemics against Christianity that circulated from the twelfth century on. The Talmud contains remnants of earlier polemics, but not until major Jewish centers suffered under Christian religious oppression did Jewish books criticizing Christianity appear. (Fewer polemical works were directed against Islam, whose treatment of Jews as inferiors was based on sociopolitical stratification rather than harassment and was often mitigated by pragmatic considerations. Relatively quiescent relations existed between Muslims and Jews after the early centuries of Muslim conquest.)

Jewish teachers could elaborate their faith without reference to Christianity or Islam, though the Bible and Talmud are replete with attacks on idolatry. Besides, the Christian claim that Jesus of Nazareth was the Messiah seemed, to the Jews, self-refuting, as the world remained radically unredeemed. But as the church increasingly attacked Jewish belief, Jewish leaders found it necessary to refute the church's claims and invalidate its doctrines.

Jewish polemics sought to demonstrate Christian misinterpretation of biblical texts by citing the original Hebrew texts and the traditional Jewish understanding of them. Christian converts from Judaism countered these arguments by citing Talmudic and Midrashic passages that were alleged to prove Jesus' messiahship. The Jewish disputants attacked the credibility of the conflicting gospel accounts of Jesus' life and the evangelists' ignorance of Talmudic law (which they assumed to have been operative in Jesus' time). They also caustically exposed the irrationality of such Christian doctrines as the virgin birth, the incarnation, and the Eucharist. By contrast, they contended, Judaism was a religion a rational man could accept. It was a theme that Jews would continue to find persuasive into modern times.

JEWISH POPULATIONS PER WORLD REGION

	Jewish	Total Population
Africa	165,000	748,130,000
Asia	4,257,000	3,513,218,000
Europe*	2,432,000	801, 819,000
Latin America	1,084,000	727,678,000
Northern America	5,836,000	490.444,000
Oceania	92,000	28,973,000
Total	13,866,000	5,804,120,000

*Includes former Soviet Union.
**United Nations Medium Variant Figures—mid 1996
Source: *The 1997 Britannica Book of the Year*

MODERNITY: OPPORTUNITY AND PERIL

Emancipation, the fitful process by which the segregation and oppression of European Jewry was encouraged to end, began in earnest with the French Revolution. Gradually, as nationality was severed from membership in an official Christian faith, Jews and other minority denominations received equal political rights and social opportunity. As a result, most modern Jews, despite their religious heritage, have avidly supported keeping government and civil society neutral with regard to religion. Because their politics and religion are closely intermixed, the Islamic nations that granted Jews complete equality were among the last states to do so.

After some fifteen hundred years of degradation and centuries of grinding oppression, most European Jews enthusiastically welcomed equality. To those raised in the ghettoes or in the *shtetls* (Yi., "villages") of eastern Europe, every new freedom, no matter how hedged by limitations or by secularized forms of anti-Semitism, came as a near fulfillment of messianic hopes. A politicized, humanistic hope now became the dominant tone of Jewish existence.

But the price of equality was conformity to the larger culture. European society did not allow for much cultural diversity, and although the accepted social conventions were ostensibly secular, they often reflected their Christian origins.

As emancipation proceeded, the consequences for rabbinic Judaism were devastating. One group of Jews rejected modernization altogether, another group rejected the major doctrines of Judaism. Most Jews found these reactions too extreme, preferring a middle way.

A small minority of traditionalists, rather than surrender anything that they felt God asked of them, spurned modernization. Many pious eastern European Jews long refused to immigrate to America with the hundreds of thousands of Jews who began to do so in the last decades of the nineteenth century. This produced a social situation unique in Jewish history. Elsewhere, long established Orthodox institutions formed the basis of community life. The non-Orthodox movements that arose with the coming of modernity were reactions to them. In the United States, non-Orthodox institutions became well established in the late nineteenth and early twentieth centuries, and only after World War I did Orthodox institutions slowly come to prominence.

Most Jews rejected this strategy of separatism for pragmatic and intuitive reasons. Practically, emancipation offered Jews a dignity they had known only sporadically for two thousand years. Hence their embrace of modernity can be understood as an existentially transformed way of keeping the covenant, arising from the intuition that Western civilization, as evidenced by its movement toward liberation, contained a considerable measure of the universal truth of Judaism.

Some Jews carried this appreciation to the point of urging Jews to assimilate fully and allow their "parochial" faith to die so that they might participate in humankind's emerging universal culture. Again, most Jews demurred. Given their passion for modernity, their insistence on also remaining Jewish has been difficult to explain, especially since no single philosophy of modern Jewish living has ever become widely accepted. Anti-Semitism has kept some Jews Jewish—yet its continuing virulence seems more a reason to defect than to stay. Moreover, even in the absence of overt hatred of Jews, many Jews have refused to assimilate. Modernist believers see this as an act of persistent loyalty to the covenant: Jews remain personally faithful to their ancient pact even if uncertain about how to live it, while God, in some inexplicable but familiar way, does not let them go.

Postemancipation Jewry has chosen to be both modern and Jewish, thus fixing its continuing agenda: first, establishing a less separatistic, more adaptive way of living; and second, validating the authenticity of that way in Jewish and modern terms.

Since the beginning of the nineteenth century, Jewish religion has lost even the semblance of uniformity that it once had.

PAGE 569

Sundering the Unity of the Way

Modernity made religion a private affair and defined religious groups in terms derived from Christianity—that is, as communities united by common faith and ritual practice. Nationality was dissociated from religion and subordinated to the nation-state, an arrangement that can still cause social unrest in multinational countries. On both counts, Judaism could not maintain itself as a religio-ethnic entity (the hybrid designation modernity has forced upon students of Judaism). As a result, an unprecedented dichotomy came into Jewish life: one group of Jews defined their Judaism as "religious," while another group defined theirs in secular terms, as an ethnicity.

RELIGIOUS WAYS OF LIBERAL JEWS. Faced with the unacceptable options of either staying Jewish but in an isolated manner—as though still within ghetto walls—or joining modern society by converting to Christianity, some early nineteenth-century German Jewish laymen began experimenting with a Judaism adapted to European modes of religiosity. In that spirit, they reformed synagogue worship. Essentially, they adorned it with a new aesthetic, eliminating liturgical repetitions and poetic embellishments and introducing solemn group decorum, vernacular prayers, sermons, and contemporary musical styles (including the use of a pipe organ and female as well as male singers). They also abolished the halakhic requirement of the separation of the sexes at services, allowing families to sit together in worship.

This early version of Reform Judaism paved the way for subsequent non-Orthodox Jewish movements. The early reformers justified their form of Judaism with the notion, derived from contemporary German culture, that eternal essences take on transient forms. The essence of Judaism, in their view, is ethical monotheism, which its rituals and customs serve to transmit and strengthen. When times change and old forms no longer function well, they should be altered or abandoned and new forms created.

Most modern Jews have accepted moral duty as the core of Jewish obligation. Many believe that the Jewish people have a mission to teach humankind the religious primacy of universal ethics. In any case, modern Jews often reduce the teachings of the Torah to ethics and, though allowing much else in rabbinic Judaism to atrophy, devote themselves to the moral transformation of society. This universalized sense of covenant responsibility accounts for the astonishing record of modern Jewish contributions to the improvement of human welfare.

In the United States, Conservative Judaism was formally launched in 1886 with the founding of the Jewish Theological Seminary of America.

PAGE 189

In the latter part of the nineteenth century, a new movement emerged: Conservative Judaism. Many eastern European immigrants to America found that their sense of Jewish modernity was not satisfied by the adaptive tone and the essentially ethical content of Reform Judaism, which had been brought over by earlier immigrants from Germany. While seeking to be modern, these Russian and Polish Jews also wanted to preserve a considerable measure of particular Jewish practice. Devotion to the Jewish people as the dynamic creator of Jewish law was their counterpoise to the Reform concentration on ethics. Over the decades, smaller movements have also arisen, positioning themselves essentially in relation to these central communal groups. The most significant of these is Reconstructionism, a movement which derives from the theory of Mordecai Kaplan (1881-1983) that the Jewish community, acting in democratic fashion, ought to be authoritative with regard to Jewish practice.

By the 1970s, the denominational lines had become blurred. Most American Jews, regardless of affiliation, now follow one of several patterns of liberal Jewish living. These vary in their loyalty to classic observance and spirituality, but show considerable similarity in the cultural activities they integrate into their Judaism—especially participation in higher education, civic affairs, and the arts, music, and literature. But the interplay between Judaism and modernity can best be illustrated by the devotion of Jews to interpersonal relationships. American Jews today express the longstanding rabbinic commitment to family and community by their disproportionate involvement in the helping professions (such as teaching, social work, and psychotherapy) and their intense concern for family relationships. In these areas they demonstrate a dedication lacking in their observance of the halakhic dietary laws and laws governing sexual relations between spouses. They seem to believe that sanctifying life, their covenant goal, now requires giving these general human activities priority in Jewish duty.

Despite this heavy cultural borrowing, American Jews manifest a significant measure of particular Jewish action. Even at the humanist end of the religious spectrum, the concern with ethics and other universal issues is reinforced by an attachment to the Jewish folk. Such Jews invest energy and self in Jewish charity, organized defense against anti-Semitism, support of the state of Israel, and occasional ritual acts, most notably those associated with life-cycle events, High Holy Day services, and the home Seder, the Passover meal. In this group one sees clearly a problem that continues to bedevil all liberal Jews: the freedom not to be Orthodox is often taken as a license to do and care little about Judaism altogether.

At the other end of the liberal religious spectrum stands a small minority of Jews whose lives are substantially guided by Jewish tradition, interpreted through a modern ethical and cultural sensibility. They exhibit the rabbinic devotion to self, family, people, and God, seeking to live by rabbinic law wherever they can. They constitute the spiritual heart of non-Orthodox Judaism, whose viability depends upon its acceptance of their leadership in combining modernity and tradition.

The outstanding achievements of liberal Judaism derive from its pursuit of a mediating spirituality. It has radically enlarged the horizon of Jewish duty by its dedication to ethics and democracy. It has revolutionized the study of Judaism by its insistence upon the adoption of modern scholarly methods. Above all, it has convinced most of the Jewish community that modernity and Judaism can successfully be integrated. What many in a prior generation passionately feared and fought, most Jews now consider of great benefit to Judaism.

Nothing so well illustrates the continuing promise and problem of liberal Judaism as its response to feminism. Early in the nineteenth century, the German reformers recognized an ethical imperative to break with the Jewish laws and customs that discriminate against women. But it took more than a century for Reform congregations to elect women officers and until 1972 for the first American woman to be ordained a rabbi; women cantors followed quickly. Since then, the Reconstructionist and Conservative movements have accepted both innovations.

Much of the community has welcomed this development, but it is not clear how far it will tolerate alter-

ation of the old patterns—for example, removing the sexist language of the prayer book, or allowing the genuine sharing of power between men and women. If liberal Jewish daring in this matter eventually becomes part of the accepted covenant way, then its experimentation will again have taught Jews a new way of sanctifying Jewish existence. Orthodox critics rejoin that in breaking with the traditional rabbinic understanding of the Torah which defines separate roles for the sexes, the liberals are more likely to dilute Judaism than to win its future.

RELIGIOUS WAYS OF ORTHODOX JEWS. As a self-conscious movement, Jewish Orthodoxy arose in response to liberal Judaism with the purpose of correctly delineating Jewish authenticity. Traditional Judaism knows only one standard of faithfulness to God: loyalty to God's law as expounded in the Torah, especially the oral law in its continuing development by contemporary sages. The Torah has absolute primacy. Modernity can come into Judaism only as the Torah allows. Hence the lives of believing Orthodox Jews display religious continuity more than religious change. Variations in observance among Orthodox Jews derive from local custom, from the differences between Ashkenazim and Sefardim, Hasidim and other Orthodox Jews, and from the variety of opinion passed down by various sages.

The major forms of Orthodoxy can be distinguished by the degree to which they are open to modernity. They stand united, however, in defense of the Torah against what they consider the faithlessness of most other Jews. Even innovations permissible under Jewish law are often resisted lest they give credence to other Jews' radical departures from tradition.

Orthodox attitudes toward the acceptance of modernity range from antagonistic to embracing. The Hasidic sects visibly project their hostility to modernity and their distance from the gentile world (and other Jews) by their distinctive dress, hair, and body language. Several Orthodox groups also seek to reconstitute the cultural isolation of eastern European Jewry, but in less separatistic ways—a goal more easily accomplished in the state of Israel than elsewhere. The continued use of Yiddish, the Judeo-German vernacular of eastern

HANUKKAH
A Festival of Lights

HANUKKAH ("dedication") is the Jewish winter festival that falls on the twenty-fifth of the month of Kislev and lasts for eight days. It celebrates the victory of the Maccabees over the forces of Antiochus after a three-year battle in the second century BCE. The major sources on the festival's origin are two apocryphal books, *1 Maccabees* and *2 Maccabees.* It is stated there (*2 Mc.* 10:6-8) that the altar was rededicated and the festival of eight days introduced because during the war the Jews were unable to celebrate the eight-day festival of Sukkot. Thus in the earliest period there is no reference to Hanukkah as a feast of lights. That it became such is due to the Talmudic legend (B. T., *Shab.* 21b) that the Maccabees found only one small jar of oil for the kindling of the *menorah* ("candelabrum") in the Temple. This was sealed with the seal of the high priest but contained only sufficient oil to burn for a single night. By a miracle the oil lasted for eight nights. It was consequently ordained that lights be kindled on the eight nights of Hanukkah. However, it is stated in the Talmud (B. T., *Shab.* 21b) that the Shammaites and Hillelites, at the beginning of the present era, debated whether the lights were to be kindled in descending order (eight the first night, seven the second, etc.) or in ascending order (one the first night, two the second, etc.). If this statement is historically correct, it demonstrates either that the legend of the oil was already known at that time or that, at least, there was an association of Hanukkah and light even at this early period. According to some historians, the origin of the festival is to be found in pagan festivals of light in midwinter. The prayers for Hanukkah refer only to the victory, but in practice the kindling of the lights is the main feature of the festival.

It has long been the custom for each member of the household to kindle the Hanukkah lights in an eight-branched candelabrum frequently called a menorah (though the *menorah* in the Temple had only seven branches) but nowadays also known as a *hanukkiyyah.* The lights are kindled in the synagogue as well as in the home. One light is kindled on the first night, two on the second night, three on the third night, and so on until all eight are lit. In order to avoid lighting the candles one from the other, an additional candle known as the *shammash* ("retainer") is used to light the others. A declaration is recited:

> We kindle these lights on account of the miracles, the deliverances, and the wonders which thou didst work for our ancestors, by means of thy holy priests. During all the eight days of Hanukkah these lights are sacred, neither is it permitted to make any profane use of them; but we are only to look at them, in order that we may give thanks unto thy name for thy miracles, deliverances, and wonders.

— LOUIS JACOBS

"What is hateful to you do not do to your neighbor. That is the whole Torah."

HILLEL
TALMUD SHABATH

European Jewry, characterizes this entire wing of Orthodoxy. Its antagonism to modernity does not prevent the pious from utilizing technological advances that enhance observance of the commandments or from having contacts with gentiles when necessary, as in commerce. Some groups have marginal affiliates who live in more modern fashion but maintain their ties to the group by keeping some of its special customs, visiting its communities, and giving financial support.

Another wing, known as Modern Orthodoxy, contends that Jewish law allows, and many sages exemplify, the virtue of embracing any cultural good that enhances human existence as the Torah delineates it. The Modern Orthodox have been most innovative in creating two new instruments for Jewish education, the Jewish university and day school, which feature the sciences and sports, both once considered un-Jewish. They generally speak the vernacular (English in America, Hebrew in Israel), not Yiddish, and their only distinguishing visual sign is the small, often knitted skullcap (Yi., *yarmulke*; Heb., *kippah*) worn by males.

HANUKKAH CELEBRATION

The Jewish winter festival celebrates the victory of the Macabees over the forces of Antiochus. Roughly coinciding with the Christian Christmas season, Hanukkah has become a popular secular holiday.

MARK THIESSEN/© CORBIS

But their disciplined loyalty to the Torah appears in such matters as prayer, diet, study, and Sabbath and festival observance.

Orthodoxy has enjoyed a significant resurgence as the twentieth century moves toward its end. Some Jews have lost their once great confidence in Western civilization and have withdrawn from it somewhat by adopting a more distinctive practice of Judaism. A minority have joined the separatistic Jewish sects. Most Orthodox Jews have rejected self-ghettoization, choosing to live a dedicated Jewish life as part of an observant community so as to differentiate themselves from an ofttimes pagan society. Their approach to living the life of Torah has nonetheless carried a modern overlay their Orthodox great-grandparents would probably have opposed; even so, the movement to greater Jewish authenticity has debilitated Modern Orthodoxy's innovative zeal.

The large number of Jews who are only nominally Orthodox testifies to the continuing influence of modernity. Despite their affiliation, these Jews are only sporadically observant and their faith fluctuates or is inconsistent. They often consider their private preferences in Jewish law to be genuine Judaism, a heresy in the eyes of Orthodox sages.

Orthodoxy has notable accomplishments to its credit. Despite dire predictions of its death from the effects of modernity, it has created a cadre of Jews whose personal piety and communal life demonstrate the continuing religious power of rabbinic Judaism. It has kept alive and advanced eastern European Jewry's exalted standards of the study of Jewish law. Particularly in the field of bioethics, but in other areas as well, it has shown the continuing vitality of the oral law.

As with liberal Judaism, the issue of feminism best clarifies the continuing promise and problems of Orthodox Judaism. In refusing to grant women substantial legal equality, contemporary sages have defended the integrity of God's law as they received and understand it. Considering how modernity has shattered family life, they do not deem it to possess a wisdom superior to that of Torah. Rather, every genuine faith demands some sacrifice, and Judaism, abandoned by so many and in such worldwide peril, deserves the obedient dedication of all who wish it to remain true to itself and God.

Many Orthodox authorities have long acknowledged that some laws regarding women create suffering—for example, the woman who, because she cannot meet certain technical criteria, is barred from receiving a Jewish divorce. Liberal Jews perceive the inability of contemporary Orthodox sages to institute legal remedies for this situation as a telling indication that, good will notwithstanding, the laws' inequities are still operative. Feminists cannot believe that, with most Orthodox Jews committed to the general self-fulfillment of women, Orthodox women will long be content with sex-segregated duties and roles. However, Orthodox Judaism has shown no significant loss of membership from its defense of classic Judaism in this matter.

CULTURE AS "TORAH" OF SECULAR JEWS. In late nineteenth-century Europe and mid-twentieth-century America, as Jews became university educated and urban dwelling, they secularized. They believed that modernization meant the acceptance of the idea that there is no God and the end of practices that differentiated Jews from their neighbors. Yet, as they became thoroughly secularized, they generally did not do so to the point of assimilation. Large numbers retained a connection with the Jewish people, if only by discovering that many of the humanitarians they enjoyed associating with were also secularized Jews. Two interrelated major patterns of secular Jewish living arose from this process, one cultural, the other political.

The early foes of emancipation argued that the Jews could not modernize because they had no capacity for high culture. Liberal Jews sought to refute them by aestheticizing Jewish worship. Secular Jews did the same by devoting their lives to literature and the arts, often achieving uncommon success in these areas. Existentially, secular Jews made high culture their "Torah," bringing to it the intense dedication they had once given to faith, for it now validated their existence.

To keep the Jewish people alive, some European Jewish secularists suggested that Jews participate in universal culture through the development of a secular Jewish literature, initially in Hebrew, but later in Yiddish as well. This movement toward Haskalah (Enlightenment) revived the Hebrew language, which had long been used only for traditional scholarship and religious purposes. The long-range hopes of the leaders of Haskalah did not survive the realities of anti-Semitism, acculturation, and migration. Only in the state of Israel, where Jews have created a national culture, has the Hebrew language successfully been used as a means for the modernization of Jewish life. In the Diaspora, few Jews now maintain their Jewishness by utilizing Hebrew or Yiddish to pursue humanism. Yet Diaspora Jews and those of the state of Israel commonly consider a positive attitude to culture an integral part of their Jewishness.

Jewish secularity also directed itself to ethical politics, that is, redeeming the world through the achievement of social justice. Jews became advocates of the rights of labor and the virtues of socialism, seeing in the struggles for civil rights and civil liberties their own cause as it affected other minorities. Prayer and piety no longer seemed effective responses to social injustice. Being politically informed and involved therefore became for Jews the modern equivalent of a commandment.

This movement's effects have been felt both in general society and in the Jewish community. Jewish politicians and Jewish activists have been a significant influence in humanizing modern society. Simultaneously, the notion of pluralistic democracy has reshaped Jewish life in America. The American Jewish community now operates on a fully voluntary basis and features a broad inclusiveness, diverse organizations, and a dynamism undaunted by emergency or changing times. It has raised more money for Jewish charity than any other voluntary philanthropic effort in history. In the midst of secularization, the lineaments of the covenant appear.

NATIONALISM: ZIONISM AND THE STATE OF ISRAEL. The cultural and political drives in Jewish secularization climaxed in Zionism, the movement that reinterpreted Judaism as Jewish nationalism. Organized on a worldwide basis by Theodor Herzl (1860-1904) in 1897, the Zionists began a crusade to liberate Jews on two levels. First, they sought freedom from persecution by acquiring a land where the Jewish masses might find economic opportunity and political security. Second, they wanted to create a genuinely Jewish culture that would express, in an untrammeled way, the Jewish people's spirit.

Many liberal and Orthodox Jews initially opposed Zionism for religious reasons. The former found its secularism Jewishly aberrant and its nationalism a threat to Jewish emancipation in the Diaspora. The latter objected to its notion of a Jewish state independent of the Torah and found its nationalistic activism a usurpation of God's role in bringing the Messiah. Vestiges of these anti-Zionist attitudes still exist, but most religious Jews now ardently support the state of Israel.

Before the founding of the state of Israel in 1948, Zionism generated a new form of Jewish living in the Diaspora, one built on political activity, immigration and the preparation for it, and participation in the renewal of Hebrew culture. The barbarity of Nazi Germany and the callousness of the rest of the world toward the Jews in the 1930s and 1940s gave Zionism an additional concern: acquiring one place in the world to which Jews could immigrate without restriction.

With the birth and growth of Israel, Jews could return to a way of living they had not known for nearly two millennia: as a Jewish community living on the Jewish homeland in Jewish self-determination. Israel is a secular state—though Orthodox Judaism retains special rights in it—and its ethos is democratic and welfare-oriented. Its extraordinary effort, amid the most trying political circumstances, to hold itself to ethical standards higher than those pursued by most other nations has won it the admiration and identification of world Jewry. Nothing in postemancipation Jewish life has remotely approached its ability to arouse Jewish devotion and action.

Israeli Jews, the great majority of whom consider themselves nonreligious (that is, non-Orthodox), live by the rhythm of the Jewish calendar and draw their ideals from the Bible, the great national saga. Their everyday language is Hebrew and their culture increas-

Religious Zionists make up roughly 10 percent of the Jewish population but are in some sense the symbol of contemporary Israel.

PAGE 540

ingly reflects the concerns of individuals and a society facing the awesome dilemmas of modern existence. In every human dimension, Jews living in the state of Israel are, even without thinking about it, living Jewishly. And for those who carry on Orthodox Judaism or the tiny minority who are Reform or Conservative Jews, the reconstituted Jewish society provides an incomparable context for religious existence.

Outside the state of Israel, Zionism as a total way of life has virtually disappeared. Most Diaspora Jews do not carry on a Jewish cultural life in Hebrew or plan to immigrate to Israel. They may be deeply emotionally attached to Israel, but it does not provide the essential content of their Jewish lives. Zionism has had an incomparable triumph in the high human and Jewish accomplishment of the state of Israel. Yet Zionism's thorough secularization of the covenant has apparently rendered it incapable of guiding Diaspora Jewish life.

The commitment of Reform Judaism to Zionism deepened in the postwar period.

PAGE 574

Philosophic Grounds of Modern Jewish Life

Judaism makes its claims upon the Jew in the name of God and the Jewish people's corporate experience—but modernity radically individualizes authority. A modern philosophy of Judaism must mediate between autonomy and tradition and do justice to each of them.

Contemporary Orthodoxy does not wait for each individual to make a decision about what constitutes Jewish duty. Orthodoxy begins with faith and has felt no pressing need for theoretical expositions of its beliefs. It has therefore largely left to liberal Jews the task of constructing systematic Jewish theologies. Five distinctive intellectual statements have gained continuing attention—six, if Zionist ideology can be considered an equivalent system.

TWO RATIONALIST INTERPRETATIONS. Rationalism had an irresistible appeal to nineteenth-century Jewish modernizers. It compellingly distinguished between the lastingly valuable essence of Judaism, ethical monotheism, and its transient historical expression in ceremony and ritual. This early liberal criterion of continuity and change first attained sophisticated statement in the work of Hermann Cohen (1842-1918), the famed Marburg Neo-Kantian philosopher.

In rigorous academic works, Cohen delineated the religion a rational person could accept. Cohen sought to demonstrate that rationality requires a philosophical idea of God to integrate its disparate scientific, ethical, and aesthetic modes of thinking. His system was dominated by ethics and he argued that this ethical monotheism appeared for the first time in history in the work of the biblical prophets. As the earliest and purest proponent of ethical monotheism, the Jewish people had a mission to humankind: to teach the universal truth of rational religion. Messianism could no longer be the miraculous advent of God's regent, but became humankind's task of ethically perfecting itself. (This view led Cohen to oppose Zionism as a constriction of the Jewish ethical horizon.) All customs that strengthened Jewish ethical sensitivity or kept Jews faithful to their mission ought to be maintained; those that thwarted them ought to be abandoned. In greatly diluted fashion, Cohen's ethical reworking of Judaism became the accepted ideology of modern Jews.

Leo Baeck (1873-1956), the German thinker who remained closest to Cohen's Judaism of reason, felt the need to supplement reason with the experience of mystery, even though that meant sacrificing Cohen's logical rigor. Baeck pointed to religious consciousness as the deepest foundation of ethical monotheism. He evocatively described the sense human beings have of being creations yet also ethical creators, of being utterly transient yet linked in spirit with that which is eternal.

However, Baeck's rationalism remained sovereign. Fearing the dangers of romanticism, he insisted that religious consciousness should lead to action only as ethics permitted. Thus, while authorizing some nonrational commandments, he ruled out anything that smacked of superstition and bigotry. He also conducted a vigorous polemic against Christianity and Buddhism, finding both of them deficient in their ethics and monotheism. He so closely identified Judaism with a universal rational faith that he alone among modern Jewish thinkers urged Jews to seek converts.

Baeck called for a broad horizon of Jewish obligation. He believed the Jewish people to be so historically identified with the idea of ethical monotheism that should Judaism die, ethical monotheism would also die. The Jewish people, therefore, must survive. To keep it alive, the Jewish people continually create group practices that strengthen and protect the people from the perils it encounters in history.

RATIONAL VALIDATIONS FOR THE PRIMACY OF PEOPLEHOOD. Zionist ideologists proclaimed the Jews a nation, not a religion, and looked forward to a renewal of Judaism as the communal life of the Jewish folk resettled on its ancient soil. They demythologized the biblical interpretation of exile—which Jewish mystics had applied metaphorically even to God—and made it a purely sociopolitical concept. Redemption would not come by a Messiah but with geographic relocation, cultural self-expression, and political reconstitution.

One early Zionist debate still roils the community: is modern Jewish nationalism rigorously secular, and thus free of religious and ethnic values, or is it distinctively Jewish? No one raised this issue more penetratingly than the essayist Ahad ha-'Am ("one of the people," pseudonym of Asher Ginzberg, 1856-1927).

Ahad ha-'Am's Zionism drew on the ninteenth-century concepts of folk psychology and cultural nationalism to assert that Jews, like other peoples, had a folk "character" to which they needed to be true. The Jewish national soul exhibited a talent for ethics and high culture with a devotion to absolute justice as the central theme of great literature and other arts, as the Bible indicates. Jewish nationalism, therefore, had to work for the recreation of an ethically and aesthetically elevated Jewish culture. A renascent Jewish state could serve as its worldwide spiritual center, and Diaspora Jewish communities would survive spiritually by participating in its cultural life.

Most Zionist ideologists simply assumed that Zionism mandated humanistic values and rarely sought to explicate them. Besides, crises in Jewish life followed so hard upon one another in the twentieth century that arguing such abstractions seemed frivolous. But various events in the life of the state of Israel have kept the issue alive. Its very persistence testifies to its unusual combination of secularity and religiosity. The Israeli courts, in rulings on the legal definition of Jewishness and other issues, have refused to sever the connectionbetween Jewish nationalism and Jewish religion. Some thinkers therefore insist that, for all its putative secularity, the state of Israel can best be understood as an eccentric development of classic Jewish ethnic religiosity.

An American thinker, Mordecai M. Kaplan (1881-1983), created another distinctive Jewish rationalism in terms of philosophic naturalism. Basing his thinking on ideas derived from the recently developed science of sociology, Kaplan held that for Jewish life today to be meaningful, it must reflect the scientific worldview and democratic commitment of modernity. Kaplan therefore carried on a vigorous polemic against supernaturalism in Judaism. He inverted the central idea of traditional Judaism: that God gave the Torah to the Jewish people (thus giving it its distinctive character). Kaplan now claimed, arguing from the perspective of sociology, that the Jewish people had created Judaism, which he defined as an ethnic civilization, based on a land, a language, a history, a calendar, heroes, institutions, arts, values, and much else, with religion at its core. Through its concept of God, Jewish civilization expressed its highest values. The Jewish people's health could be restored only by fully reconstructing its folk life; hence Kaplan called his movement Reconstructionism. The involvement of American Jews in Jewish art, music, and other cultural forms owes much to Kaplan. Kaplan also called for the Jewish community to reorganize itself institutionally so that the community, not a given religious movement or synagogue, would be the focus of Jewish affiliation. Though pluralistic, it could then democratically seek to legislate for its members and meet the full range of religious, political, cultural, and social needs of a healthy ethnic group. But no Jewish community has yet so reconstituted itself.

Kaplan proposed a daring definition of God as the power (or process) that makes for "salvation," by which he meant "human fulfillment." Speaking of God in impersonal, naturalistic terms indicates the purely symbolic status of folk anthropomorphisms and the modern rejection of miracles, verbal revelation, and the idea of the chosen people. Equally important, defining God in finite terms—as that aspect of nature that abets human self-development—solves the theological problem of evil. Kaplan's God does not bring evil, only good. We can now maturely see evil as caused by nature and take it as a challenge to our moral creativity.

Kaplan's bold recasting of Judaism won him a small but enthusiastic following. However, his equation of modernity with scientific rationality lost its appeal in the Jewish community as the interest in nonrationalist Jewish thinkers heightened.

NONRATIONALIST JEWISH THINKERS. After World War I, Franz Rosenzweig (1886-1929), the youthful German author of a magisterial work on Hegel, pioneered Jewish existentialism with his effort to situate Judaism in selfhood rather than in acts or ideas. Rosenzweig connected being Jewish with acting Jewishly—that is, observing the law insofar as one was existentially able to acknowledge it as possessing the quality of commandment. He thus specified, but never fully clarified, a greatly appealing balance between duty and freedom, bequeathing to later liberal Jewish thought one of its central issues.

Martin Buber (1878-1965), an older contemporary and sometime collaborator of Rosenzweig's, created a more extensive system. He suggested that human existence is dynamically relational, occurring either in an objectifying mode he called I-It, or a value-conferring mode of personal openness and mutuality he called I-Thou, which he carefully differentiated from romanticism and mysticism. Romanticism involves an I-It of emotion or experience; mysticism, a loss of self in the One. Buber had in mind something as subtle yet much more common.

Like all significant personal involvements, an I-Thou relationship with God (the "Eternal Thou") evokes responsive action—it "commands." Transgression of such duty involves guilt and the need to atone. All this has a corporate dimension, for whenever two persons truly meet, God is present as well. Consequently, the I-Thou experience directs us to create true human community, a society of Thou's.

Religions arise when relationships with God take on social forms. In time, this process of institutionalization, instead of expediting living contact with God, obstructs it. Institutionalized faiths may designate one

Martin Buber, the best-known of Jewish religious existentialists, stresses the personal aspects of the deity.

PAGE 245

sphere of life as holy, leaving the rest to be profane. But the I-Thou relationship knows no limits, and all life should be lived on its terms. Hence Buber opposed all "religion."

According to Buber, the Hebrew Bible recounts the I-Thou experiences of the Jewish people with God, which, over centuries, created an indissoluble relationship between them—the covenant. No other ethnic group has ever so identified its corporate existence with loyalty to God. Because of its covenant, the Jewish folk undertook the messianic task of creating community among its members and thus, eventually, among humankind. While Jews sometimes lost sight of this task, it could never be completely lost, as indicated by early Hasidism and by Zionism. During Buber's decades of residence in Israel, his public insistence that the state should live up to his ideal of the covenant made him a figure of considerable controversy there.

"The Holocaust is a central event in many people's lives, but has also become a metaphor for our century."

AAHRON APPELFELD
NEW YORK TIMES
NOVEMBER 15, 1986

Another great system builder, Abraham Joshua Heschel (1907-1972), integrated much of twentieth-century Jewish experience in his own life. The scion of a Polish Hasidic dynasty, he took a doctorate in Berlin, and escaped World War II by going to the United States to teach at the Reform rabbinical school (Hebrew Union College) in Cincinnati. He later taught a near-Orthodox theology at the Conservative seminary in New York.

Heschel faulted the existentialists for defining religion as the movement of people toward God. Modern Jewry's very skepticism, he said, should make it awestruck at the power Someone has given humankind. When such "radical amazement" opens people to the reality of the giver, it becomes apparent, as the Bible indicates, that God pursues humankind, forcing upon it God's self-revelation, and that the biblical prophets accurately transmit God's message.

The meaning of the prophets, Heschel said, is clear: God is a God of pathos, one who suffers when people transgress and who rejoices when they achieve holiness. To argue that God would be more perfect if God had no feelings reflects a Stoic, that is, a Roman point of view, not that of the Bible. Revelation proceeds by "sympathos," by uncommonly gifted individuals coming to feel what God feels. They may verbalize this understanding in different ways, but they do not interpose themselves between God and humankind. The commandments transmitted by Moses and the sages accurately reflect God's injunctions. They are the divinely sanctioned media for meeting God by doing God's will.

Two themes in Heschel's thought mitigate his absolute acceptance of Jewish tradition. First, he emphasized the paucity of revelation compared with the subsequent plethora of interpretation, thereby suggesting the virtue of continuing development. Second, he carefully documented the prophets' intense ethical devotion, implying, perhaps, that human considerations should predominate in interpreting the Torah. He nobly exemplified this in his participation in the civil rights and antiwar struggles of the 1960s. But he never indicated whether he would advocate changes in Jewish law for these or other reasons.

Since the articulation of these six positions, much theological writing and discussion has gone on, but no distinctive new pattern has won substantial acceptance.

Confronting the Holocaust

For reasons still debated, not until the mid-1960s did Jewish thinkers confront the theoretical implications of the Nazi murder of six million Jews. With the emergence of the short-lived "death of God" movement, some Jewish philosophers demanded that a Jewish theology be created that would focus on the reality revealed at Auschwitz, the most notorious of the Nazi death camps and the symbol of the Holocaust. Where the revelation at Sinai spoke of God's rule, God's justice, and God's help to the people of Israel, Auschwitz now spoke of God's absence, of the world's injustice, and of the terrible abandonment of the Jewish people. But it was in the creation of the state of Israel that the Jewish people had given its deepest response to Nazi destructiveness: it was the expression of an intense determination to survive with high human dignity. The Arab-Israeli Six-Day War of 1967 which threatened Israel's (and therefore Jewish) existence catalyzed Jewry worldwide to identify even more intensely with the state of Israel. Israel, therefore, for all its secularity, took on a numinous quality for those who strove to maintain the covenant.

The survival of the Jewish people now became a central preoccupation of Diaspora Jews and a major motive for individuals to assume or extend their Jewish responsibilities. Associated with this was a reassessment of the values of the emancipation. Because of the messianic hope that emancipation had awakened, Jews had surrendered much of their traditional way of life. Now, even as Western civilization began to lose its ultimate confidence in science, technology, education, and culture—in utter human capability—so Jews started to approach their tradition with new receptivity. For some, this partial withdrawal from universal concerns led back to Orthodoxy. Most Jews found that though their social activism could no longer take on redemptive guise, they still could not spurn the ethical lessons of the emancipation, especially with regard to feminism. The critical challenge now facing such chastened liberal Jews is the delineation of their duty and the creation of communities to live it, a concern giving rise to considerable experimentation.

The theoretical response to the Holocaust had an

ironic outcome. Experience made substituting Auschwitz for Sinai unacceptable to most Jews. Despite the mass depravity that continues to plague the twentieth century, the revelation of God's absence and of humanity's depravity in the Holocaust does not constitute the norm of human or Jewish existence. Sanctifying the routine without forgetting the extraordinary remains the Jew's fundamental responsibility, as the revelation at Sinai taught. The primary response to the Holocaust, Jews agree, must be an intensification of human responsibility.

Some Orthodox leaders, like the *rebe* of the Lubavitch Hasidic sect, say, in the tradition of the *Book of Deuteronomy*, that in the Holocaust God grievously punished a sinful generation. Most Jews find it impossible to view the Holocaust as an act of divine justice. Alternatively, rationalist teachers assert that God has only finite power and was incapable of preventing the Holocaust, so humankind must actively help God bring the Messiah. Others have come to a Job-like stance. They remain stunned that God can entrust humans with the freedom to become as heartless as the Nazis did. They admit they do not understand God's ways. Nonetheless, they accept God's sovereignty and seek to build their lives on it.

All these views of evil circulated in the Jewish community well before the Holocaust, leading some to suggest that what truly died in the Holocaust was the Enlightenment's surrogate god, the infinitely competent human spirit. As a result of the loss of absolute faith in humankind, a small minority of modern Jews have sought answers in Jewish mysticism. For others, Orthodoxy has gained fresh appeal. For most Jews, the emancipation has only been qualified, not negated. Mediating between Judaism and modernity continues to be the central spiritual concern of the people who believe themselves to stand in covenant with God, working and waiting for the realization of God's rule on earth.

[*For further discussion of the mainstream movements in contemporary Judaism, see* Hasidism.]

— EUGENE B. BOROWITZ

KONGO RELIGION

The Kikongo-speaking peoples of the Niger-Congo linguistic group represent a rich and diverse cultural heritage associated with the ancient kingdom of Kongo.

There are a number of basic Kongo religious concepts that have persisted amid the profound viscissitudes of Kongo history. Among them is the belief in a supreme being, known as Nzambi Kalunga or Nzambi Mpungu Tulendo, who is thought to be omnipotent. Although Nzambi Kalunga is the creator and the ultimate source of power, lesser spirits and ancestors mediate between humanity and the supreme being. Evil, disorder, and injustice are believed to be the result of such base human motives as greed, envy, or maliciousness. As constant sources of life and well-being, both the land and the matrilineal ancestors buried in it form the basis of the preoccupation in Kongo thought with fertility and the continuity of the community. Patrifilial relations and other alliances formed in the public sphere bring forth in Kongo religion a concern with the nature of power, its sources, applications, and the consequences of beneficent and malevolent uses of it.

Kongo cultic history may be seen as a veritable tradition of renewal, either at the local lineage level, the national level, or in terms of a specific focus. Often the appeal is for restoration of public morality and order; individualized charms are commanded to be destroyed, the ancestors' tombs are restored, cemeteries purified, and group authority is renewed.

Especially important in the context of Kongo religious leaders is the twentieth-century Kongo prophet Simon Kimbangu, whose widely influential teachings eventually gave rise to the largest independent church in Africa.

Mission Christianity, implanted during the Free State and subsequent colonial era by British, Swedish, and American Protestant groups and by Belgian, French, and Portuguese Catholics has given rise to many congregations and conferences, as well as to schools, hospitals, seminaries, and other specialized institutions. Furthermore, it has brought about the far-reaching christianization of the Kongo populace. Many Kongo-speakers in the late twentieth century are nominal Christians. However, paradoxically, most Kongo Christians still subscribe to the fundamental tenets of the Kongo religion and worldview.

Kongo religion is more complex and profound than any single doctrine or congregation represented within it. It is a set of perspectives about life, of symbolic traditions and roles that have formed over centuries of human experience at the mouth of the Kongo River. This experience includes the adversities of the slave trade, massive depopulation, epidemics, colonialism, and droughts, as well as the challenges of christianization and independence. Kongo religion is at the heart of one of the great historic, yet living, human civilizations.

— JOHN M. JANZEN

KOREAN RELIGION

Confucianism, Taoism, and Buddhism, often said to be Korea's major religions, all came to Korea from or through China. Another faith, indigenous to Korea, has usually been considered superstition rather than religion because it lacks an explicitly formulated, elaborated, and rationalized body of doctrine. Yet this indigenous creed possesses a rich set of supernatural beliefs, a mythology, and a variety of ritual practices. In recent years, therefore, an increasing number of scholars have come to recognize this folk system of beliefs and rites as another of Korea's major religious traditions.

Affiliation with a traditional Korean religion entailed participation at some of its rites or acceptance of at least part of its ideology rather than exclusive membership in a church organization. As a result, participants at rituals usually include already existing social groups—such as family, village, or extended kinship group—rather than a specially constituted church congregation. Another result has been a religious eclecticism constrained not by feelings of commitment to one faith or sense of contradiction between disparate beliefs but by traditional role expectations of men and women. In many Korean families, men perform ancestor rites and consult geomancers whereas women make offerings to household gods and confer with fortune-tellers, but even this gender division of labor is not rigidly observed.

The absence of church congregations not only facilitated eclecticism and adaptation but also allowed significant regional, social, and even interpersonal

But it was Yi Hwang (1501–1570), better known as T'oegye, who brought Korean Neo-Confucianism to maturity.

PAGE 187

K

KOREAN RELIGION

Indigenous Folk Religion

"Let no one pay me honor with tears, nor celebrate my funeral rites with weeping."

QUINTUS ENNIUS
CICERO

variations in religious belief and practice. Nowhere is this more evident than in Korea's indigenous folk religion, where the lack of written scripture further encouraged diversity.

INDIGENOUS FOLK RELIGION. The earliest source on the rituals of Korea's folk religion appears in the *Tongguk Yi Sangguk chip*, a collection of poems and essays by Yi Kyu-bo (1168-1241). One of his poems describes some folk religious practices only briefly, but the description corresponds with the rites presently performed by *mudang* in Kyonggi Province, located in the western-central part of the Korean Peninsula.

Religious Specialists. Though different regional terms also exist, the term *mudang* is used throughout Korea to designate the specialists of Korea's folk religion. It is usually translated into English as "shaman," but this translation is problematic because several different definitions have been advanced for the term *shaman.* Moreover, there are two types of mudang—possessed *(kangsin mu)* and hereditary *(sesup mu)*—and only the former fits some of the better-known definitions.

Pantheon. The pantheon of Korea's folk religion is polytheistic. A variety of gods are available to aid supplicants, bring them good fortune, and help them avoid misfortune. Some of these deities are known only in particular regions, but the following are known throughout Korea and are among those that most often receive rites: Mountain God, Earth God, Dragon King God, Smallpox God, Seven-Star God, God of Luck (Chesok), God of the House Site, Kitchen God, and Birth God. These represent only a small fraction of the total pantheon, however.

The deities are not thought to be inherently good or evil; whether they are helpful or harmful depends on the circumstances. If they are treated with regular offerings, they bring good fortune; otherwise, they inflict punishment.

ANCESTOR WORSHIP. The history of Korean ancestor worship is better documented than the history of Korean folk religion, though it too suffers from a paucity of written records before the end of the Koryo dynasty (918-1392). Some form of rites for the dead probably existed in prehistoric times, and Buddhism was closely involved with such rites at the time of its importation from China in the fourth century CE. By the end of the Koryo dynasty, both Buddhist and *mudang* rites for the dead evidently existed. Such rites can still be seen today, and traces of Buddhist teachings are still evident in Korean funeral customs.

The establishment of the Choson dynasty (1392-1910) brought the adoption of Neo-Confucianism as Korea's official ideology and government efforts to transform ancestor rites to a Neo-Confucian format. Particularly seminal was the *Chu-tzu chia-li,* a ritual manual attributed to the Chinese philosopher Chu Hsi. By the end of the Choson dynasty, Neo-Confucian ancestor rites, with modifications, became generally accepted throughout most of the population. Even today, many Korean households have etiquette books with instructions for ancestor rites derived in some measure from the *Chu-tzu chia-li.*

Rituals. The kind of ritual activity directed toward an ancestor depends largely on the length of time that has elapsed since his or her death. A funeral usually begins with calling out the name of the deceased while setting forth shoes and rice for the death messenger(s) who come to escort the souls of the deceased along a difficult journey to face judgment in the underworld. The remainder of the funeral, during which visitors make condolence calls and the corpse is prepared for burial, usually lasts three days: the day of death, the following day, and the day of burial.

After the funeral is completed, a spirit shrine is erected at the home of the deceased. There his or her soul is said to reside for the duration of the formal mourning period.

Ritual attention is given to ancestors on yet other occasions. When a bride first enters her husband's family, for example, she bows before the tablets of the ancestors regularly commemorated by his household.

Ideas about the Afterlife. Rites for ancestors take place in three different contexts, each implying a different location for the soul: before ancestor tablets, at graves, and at seances to which ancestors "come" from the otherworld. When pressed, individuals can justify these seemingly disparate practices by reciting the well-known saying that each person has three souls.

In general, the dead are thought to remain in the same condition as they were at the time of death and thus to retain the same need for clothing, shelter, and, especially, food. To meet these needs, sets of clothing are occasionally offered at *mudang* rites, graves are maintained, and food offerings are presented at Neo-Confucian rites.

DIVINATION AND FORTUNE-TELLING. Most of the divination practiced by professional fortune-tellers falls into two major categories: spirit divination and horoscope reading. The first is used by possessed *mudang* and possessed diviners. Though the latter, unlike *mudang,* do not perform *kut,* their divination techniques are the same. Speaking through the mouth of either a *mudang* or diviner, a supernatural being makes a revelation about the cause of a present misfortune or predicts a future event or condition. Often the fortune-teller mimics the spirit that is providing the revelation, speaking like a child, for example, when possessed by a dead child.

Horoscope reading, the other major form of fortune-telling practiced by professional diviners, is espe-

cially prevalent in cities. Based on the theory that the time of a person's birth determines the main course of his or her life, horoscope reading utilizes the system of reckoning time according to the sexegenary cycle. Each year, month, day, and two-hour period is designated by one of sixty pairs of Chinese characters; and combining the four pairs associated with a person's year, month, day, and hour of birth yields eight characters. These are translated into predictions according to a variety of complex methods described in several printed manuals.

CHRISTIANITY. Korea's first known contact with Christianity came during the late sixteenth century. A Jesuit missionary accompanied the Japanese army that invaded Korea at that time, but there is no evidence to indicate that his visit had any influence on Korean religion.

Christianity first had an influence in Korea during the following century, when Korean envoys to the Chinese court in Peking encountered some of the ideas brought there by Jesuit missionaries. A few of these attracted the interest of some noted Korean intellectuals of the seventeenth and eighteenth centuries. By the last quarter of the eighteenth century, a few Korean literati had formed study groups to examine and discuss Catholicism, and a few individuals even announced their conversion to the new religion.

The Choson dynasty court soon viewed Catholicism as a threat to Korea's established social order, primarily because of Catholic opposition to ancestor rites. Any challenge to filial piety, whether toward living parents or deceased predecessors, had serious political implications. Thus the new religion was officially proscribed by the mid-1780s, and a few executions soon followed. This antipathy toward Catholicism was exacerbated in 1801 by the involvement of some Korean Catholics in an attempt to draw Chinese and Western military forces into Korea in order to ensure freedom for their religion. The incident provoked further persecutions and imprisonment of Catholics. Yet despite bloody, if sporadic, persecutions, Catholicism continued to grow throughout the nineteenth century, largely through the efforts of French missionaries and church officials in Peking.

The growth of Catholicism in Korea was later eclipsed by the successes of Protestant missionaries. Though sustained Protestant missionary efforts began only in the penultimate decade of the nineteenth century, by the mid-1980s Protestants outnumbered Catholics by about four to one in South Korea. Though published statistics vary widely, depending on their sources, Catholics appeared to number about 1.5 million and Protestants about 5.5 million at that time.

NEW RELIGIONS. Like similar movements elsewhere in the world, Korea's new religions have tended to flourish in times of greatest personal distress and social disorder. The final decades of the Choson dynasty and the years following World War II, during which many of these religions emerged and grew, were periods of especially intense social, economic, and political turmoil. In both eras, moreover, threatened or actual foreign military intervention exacerbated Korea's internal difficulties.

Some present-day new religions teach that Korea will eventually become the most important of the world's nations, or they display the South Korean flag prominently during their services.

Though the doctrines of the new religions vary, most are directed toward the resolution of economic or health problems rather than a concern for the afterlife. Many of the new religions offer their followers the promise of utopia on earth. As in Korean folk religion, wealth is not viewed as a hindrance to happiness but rather as a blessing to be actively sought.

— YIM SUK-JAY, ROGER L. JANELLI, AND DAWNHEE YIM JANELLI

American missionaries in Korea sympathized deeply with Korean national aspirations and were opposed, though quietly and discreetly, to Japanese colonial enterprise.

PAGE 452

L

LATTER-DAY SAINTS

[*See article* Mormonism.]

LORD'S PRAYER

When his disciples asked Jesus to teach them to pray, *Luke* 11:2-4 records the Master's reply in words similar to the teaching in the Sermon on the Mount at *Matthew* 6:9-13. In a slightly simplified tabulation, the two versions of the text may be compared as follows, with the Matthean surplus and variations in brackets and two particularly difficult expressions in parentheses:

> [Our] Father [who art in heaven],
> Hallowed be thy name,
> Thy kingdom come,
> [Thy will be done,
> On earth as it is in heaven].
> Give us [this day] our (daily) bread,
> And forgive us our sins [Mt.: debts],
> For [Mt.: As] we [have] forgive[n] our debtor[s],
> And lead us not into (temptation)
> [But deliver us from evil].

USE IN CHRISTIAN WORSHIP. The church has taken the Lord's Prayer as indicating both the spirit of Christian prayer and a formula to be employed in worship. The Matthean form is at almost all points the more usual in the liturgy. Liturgical use is the probable source of the concluding doxology, "For thine is the kingdom, the power, and the glory for ever," which is found—though not yet with the addition of the word *kingdom*—in a text that is as early as the first- or second-century church manual the *Didache* (8.2). The Lord's Prayer has been used, formally and informally, in daily worship as well as in the eucharistic liturgy. In the latter case, its place has usually been between the great prayer of thanksgiving and the Communion, whither it was doubtlessly attracted by the bread to be consumed.

CLASSICAL COMMENTARIES. The early Fathers taught the prayer's meaning to their catechumens, and it has remained a favorite subject of exposition by spiritual writers. Tertullian and, in his wake, Cyprian both wrote pastoral tracts entitled *On (the Lord's) prayer.* Origen dealt with it in his theological treatise *On Prayer* (chaps. 18-30). Cyril of Jerusalem expounded it to the newly baptized in his *Mystagogical Catechesis* 5.11-18, while Augustine of Hippo preached sermons 56-59 on it to the *competentes* (candidates for baptism) and also treated it as part of his commentary *The Sermon on the Mount* (2.4.15-2.11.39) and elsewhere. John Chrysostom devoted to the Lord's Prayer his *Nineteenth Homily on the Gospel of Matthew.* Gregory of Nyssa discoursed on it in his five *Sermons on the Lord's Prayer.* Conferences on it are ascribed to Thomas Aquinas. Luther explained the prayer in his Large and Small Catechisms and in other writings, such as *A Simple Way to Pray,* written in 1535 for his barber. Calvin presented it in the first edition of his *Institutes of the Christian Religion* (1536; cf. 3.20.34-49 in the final edition of 1559) and commented on it in his *Harmony of the Gospels* (1555). Teresa of Ávila used the Lord's Prayer to instruct her religious communities in *The Way of Perfection* (chaps. 27-42). John Wesley devoted to the prayer one of his Standard Sermons (numbered variously 21 or 26) and versified it in the hymn "Father of All, Whose Powerful Voice." Karl Barth treated it in his 1947-1949 seminar notes entitled *Prayer* and developed the address and the first two petitions in the unfinished part 4.4 of his *Church Dogmatics.* Simone Weil's thoughts on the subject are contained in her *Waiting on God.*

A CONTEMPORARY EXEGESIS. The best contemporary exegesis of the Lord's Prayer is that of Raymond E. Brown, who interprets it as an eschatological prayer. Jesus announced the coming of the kingdom of God. His followers prayed for the definite establishment of God's eternal rule and intimated their own desire to be part of it. They requested a place at the messianic banquet and asked for forgiveness in the divine judgment as well as for deliverance from the mighty struggle with Satan that still stood between the community and the final realization of its prayer. As hopes for the imminent advent of the final kingdom faded, interpreters adapted the prayer to continuing life in the present age with the assurance that God's kingdom had at least begun its entry into the world through the life, death, and resurrection of Jesus.

RECURRENT THEMES OF ANALYSIS. The Lord's Prayer opens with a bold filial salutation. To

"We praise the majesty of your name."

I CHRONICLES 29:13

LORD'S PRAYER

Recurrent Themes of Analysis

address almighty God as "Abba, Father" (*Rom.* 8:14, *Gal.* 4:6) is to share by grace a privilege that Jesus enjoyed by nature (*Mk.* 14:36, cf. *Mt.* 11:25-27). Liturgically, believers do in fact proclaim that they "make bold to say" *(audemus dicere)* this prayer. The heavenly Father is near. Moreover, to address the Father as "*our* Father" is to acknowledge that the Christian faith is a communal matter with brothers and sisters who are, at least potentially, as numerous as the human race. After this opening address six petitions follow, which typically attract the kind of comments next summarized.

*1. **Hallowed be thy name.*** God is by definition holy, and strictly speaking, only God can hallow the divine name: he does so in history by vindicating his holiness (*Ez.* 36:22-27, *Jn.* 12:28). But humans join in by not despising the Lord's name (*Ex.* 20:7 and, identically, *Dt.* 5:11), by praising the name of the Lord (*1 Chr.* 29:13 and often in *Psalms*), by calling on the name of the Lord for salvation (*Jl.* 2:32, *Acts* 2:21, *Rom.* 10:13), and by living in accord with the name put upon them in baptism (Augustine, sermon 59; cf. *1 Cor.* 6:11).

In the classic formulation of Martin Luther, "to 'have a god' is nothing else than to trust and believe him with our whole heart."

PAGE 223

*2. **Thy kingdom come.*** Instead of "Thy kingdom come" a minor variant reads "May thy Holy Spirit come upon us and purify us." Here outcrops the common view that God's rule may at least begin in the present in human lives. Yet the primary agency in establishing the kingdom remains God's.

*3. **Thy will be done.*** In the garden of Gethsemane, Jesus accepted the Father's will (*Mk.* 14:36, *Mt.* 26:39, 26:42; cf. *Jn.* 6:38, *Heb.* 10:7-10). Thereby God's eternal will for salvation was implemented (*Eph.* 1:5, 1:9, 1:11). Humans benefit through faithful and obedient participation. The scope of God's plan is no less than heaven and earth.

*4. **Give us this day our daily bread.*** The adjective qualifying bread (Gr., *epiousios*) is otherwise practically unknown. Suggested possibilities for its meaning include: food "suited to our spiritual nature" (Origen); the bread "we need" for our "everyday" lives (Syriac and Old Latin traditions—cf. *Mt.* 6:34); an "excellent" bread surpassing all substances (the Vulgate's *supersubstantialis*). The original eschatological tone of the prayer favors the reading "tomorrow's bread," as in some Egyptian versions and in Jerome's report on the "Gospel of the Hebrews" wherein he employs the Latin word *crastinus* ("for tomorrow"); it is an urgent prayer for the feast of the age to come. Whatever their interpretation of *epiousios,* commentators regularly emphasize the graciousness of the divine provision and the human obligation to share the blessings of God, and most of them make a link with the eucharistic Communion.

*5. **Forgive us our sins.*** The parable of the unforgiving servant in *Matthew* 18:23-35 suggests that the final execution of God's will to forgive sinners depends on the sinner's readiness to forgive others (cf. *Mt.* 6:14f., *Lk.* 6:37). While humans cannot compel God's gracious forgiveness, they can be prevented from receiving it by their own unforgiving spirit.

*6. **Lead us not into temptation.*** Commentators have stressed the indirect character of God's testing of humans (*Jas.* 1:12-14) and insisted that God "will not let you be tempted beyond your strength" (*1 Cor.* 10:13). Some modern liturgical translations have restored the strictly eschatological character of the petition: "Save us from the time of trial" (cf. *Rv.* 3:10). In the present, the devil still "prowls around like a roaring lion, seeking whom he may devour" (*1 Pt.* 5:8; cf. *Eph.* 6:11-13, 1 *Jn.* 5:19), but his defeat has already been assured by Christ, and the deliverance of believers is certain (*2 Thes.* 3:3, *Jn.* 17:15).

— GEOFFREY WAINWRIGHT

LUTHER, MARTIN

Martin Luther (1483-1546), the German theologian and reformer of the Christian church, was born in Eisleben on 10 November. After initial schooling, he matriculated at the University of Erfurt to pursue the customary study of the seven liberal arts. Upon receiving the master's degree in 1505 Luther began the study of law. Less than two months later, however, the experience of a terrifying thunderstorm near Stotterheim prompted his vow to Saint Anne to become a monk. Two years later, on 27 February 1507, Luther was ordained to the priesthood. Completing his doctorate in theology at Wittenberg in October 1512, he assumed the *lectura in Biblia,* the professorship in Bible studies endowed by the Augustinian order.

In 1515 he became preacher at the parish church in Wittenberg and was appointed district vicar of his order. The latter position entailed the administrative oversight of the Augustinian monasteries in Saxony.

In his later years Luther spoke of having had a profound spiritual experience or insight (dubbed by scholars his "evangelical discovery"), and intensive scholarly preoccupation has sought to identify its exact date and nature. Two basic views regarding the time have emerged. One dates the experience, which Luther himself related to the proper understanding of the concept of the "righteousness of God" (*Rom.* 1:17), as having occurred about 1514, the other in about 1518. The matter remains inconclusive, partly because nowhere do Luther's writings of the time echo the dramatic notions that the reformer in later years associated with his experience. The import of the issue lies both in the precise understanding of what it was that alienated Luther from the Catholic church, and in understanding the theological frame of mind with which Luther entered the indulgences controversy of 1517.

The Ninety-five Theses of 31 October 1517 (the traditional notion that Luther nailed them to the door of the Wittenberg castle church has recently been questioned) catapulted Luther into the limelight. These theses pertained to the ecclesiastical practice of indulgences that had not as yet been dogmatically defined by the church. Luther's exploration of the practice was therefore a probing inquiry.

Almost immediately after the appearance of the Ninety-five Theses, a controversy ensued. Undoubtedly it was fanned by the fact that Luther had focused not merely on a theological topic but had also cited a number of the popular grievances against Rome, thus touching upon a political issue. In addition to sending copies of the theses to several friends, Luther sent a copy to Archbishop Albert of Hohenzollern, whom he held responsible

DOCTRINES AND WORSHIP

Christ is the Center

Luther's doctrine of "justification through grace by faith alone, apart from works of law," echoing Paul in his letter to the Romans (3:28), forms the core of Lutheranism. A person is right with God (i. e., "justified") by completely trusting the work of Christ (i. e., "by faith") and not by making any human effort to appease God (i. e., "apart from works of law"). Christ's atonement is communicated both verbally, in preaching and teaching, and visibly, in the celebration of the sacraments. Thus to Luther the doctrine of justification was not one among many doctrines, as medieval theology taught, but was the "chief article of faith" that establishes the norm for Christian faith and life.

In worship, Lutherans have tried to be faithful to the ecumenical tradition of the Mass by regarding its center, the sacrament of Holy Communion, as the means of grace that strengthens and sustains Christians in a world of sin, death, and evil. Luther changed little in the liturgy of the Roman Mass, removing only what he called the "sacrifice of the Mass," namely, the prayers of thanksgiving that surround the act of consecrating bread and wine.

Lutherans recognize only two sacraments, baptism and the Lord's Supper, because Luther could find no clear evidence that Christ instituted any other sacraments.

The core of Luther's reform movement was the proposal that the church return to the Christocentric stance that he had found in scripture and in the early church fathers.

The doctrine of baptism proved to be the most revolutionary aspect of Lutheranism, since it allowed Luther to invite territorial princes to become "emergency bishops" of the new churches. Thus German princes interested in liberating themselves from the domination of Rome established Lutheranism in their own territories and encouraged it to spread. Princes, peasants, patricians, priests, and even bishops joined the Lutheran cause, mainly to break from Rome. Danish and Swedish kings declared Lutheranism the religion of their lands.

The Formula of Concord used medieval scholastic terminology and Aristotelian philosophical categories to provide a theological system to protect Lutheranism from both Catholic and Calvinist influences. The result was a systematic, rational interpretation of the doctrines of sin, law, and grace, the cornerstones of a Lutheran theology grounded in the forensic notion that God declared humankind righteous by faith in Christ. The Formula rejected both the Catholic notion of cooperation between human nature and divine grace through free will and Calvin's doctrine of Christ's spiritual (not real or bodily) presence in the Lord's Supper.

Between 1580 and 1680, German Lutherans favored a uniform religion that fused pure doctrine with Christian laws. The resulting alliance between church and state created seventeenth-century Lutheran orthodoxy. Assisted by orthodox theologians, territorial princes dictated what people should believe and how they should behave, and obedience to political authority became the core of Christian ethics. But Lutheran orthodoxy gave rise to a new reform movement, nicknamed "pietist," which stressed a "religion of the heart" rather than the prevalent "religion of the head." Lutheran Pietism emphasized individual conversion, lay ministry, and a morality distinct from worldly ethics. By the nineteenth century, the pietist impulse had created an "inner mission" movement in Germany that established a female diaconate, built hospitals and orphanages, instituted educational programs, cared for the mentally retarded, and advocated prison reform.

In the United States, Henry Melchior Mühlenberg (1711-1787), who had come from Halle to Philadelphia, organized the first American Lutheran synod in Pennsylvania in 1748. Lutheran theological seminaries, colleges, and journals were soon founded in regions where Lutherans predominated. During the Civil War, the United Lutheran Synod of the South was formed. But it was not until after World War I that Lutherans in the United States managed to form larger denominations through mergers.

After World War II, some 184 delegates representing about 80 million Lutherans from 49 churches in 22 countries organized the Lutheran World Federation in 1947. Headquartered in Geneva (which is also the headquarters of the World Council of Churches) the Lutheran World Federation unites Lutheran churches from around the world in common social-action projects and in regular world assemblies but otherwise has no authority over the churches.

— ERIC W. GRITSCH

L

LUTHER, MARTIN

MARTIN LUTHER

The ecclesiastical reformer and theologian Martin Luther's notion of justification by grace and faith alone is his major legacy to the Protestant tradition.

LIBRARY OF CONGRESS/ CORBIS

for a vulgar sale of indulgences in the vicinity of Wittenberg, together with a fervent plea to stop the sale. The ensuing debate therefore became a public one, eventually allowing for the formation of a popular movement.

In April 1518 Luther presented a summary of his theological thought, which he called the "theology of the cross," at a meeting of the Augustinian order in Heidelberg. In presenting a caricature of scholastic theology, Luther appropriately emphasized its one-sidednesses. Soon afterward he was ordered to appear in Rome in conjunction with the proceedings against him, but the intervention of his territorial ruler, Elector Frederick, caused the interrogation to take place in Augsburg, Germany. With Cardinal Legate Cajetan representing the Curia, the meeting proved unsuccessful, since Luther refused to recant. Luther fled from Augsburg and, upon his return to Wittenberg, he was inadvertently drawn into a disputation held in Leipzig in July 1519. Luther's opponent, Johann Eck, professor of theology at Ingolstadt, was intent on branding him a heretic.

Luther's "theology of the cross" affirmed that God always works contrary to experience.

PAGE 570

After the election of Charles V as the new emperor, which had preoccupied the Curia for some time, official proceedings against Luther were resumed.

Luther soon after disappeared from the public scene. A period of self-doubt, it was also an exceedingly creative time, part of which he spent in translating the New Testament from Greek into German. He returned to Wittenberg in March 1522 to calm the restlessness that had surfaced there over the nature of the reform movement. In a series of sermons he enunciated a conservative notion of ecclesiastical reform, and his stance left its imprint on the subsequent course of the Reformation.

His own theological formation was essentially complete by 1521; his theological work thereafter consisted in amplification and clarification.

The year 1525 proved to be a major theological and personal watershed for Luther: he became embroiled in two major controversies—with Erasmus and Thomas Müntzer—that resulted in a marked division in the reform movement. On 13 June of that same year he married Katharina von Bora, a former nun who had left her convent the previous year. Even though the marriage—coming as it did on the heels of the German Peasants' War—was a subject of notoriety among Luther's enemies, it set the tone for a Protestant definition of Christian marriage.

As a political outlaw, he stayed at Coburg (as far south as he was able to travel on Saxon territory), and his close associate Philipp Melanchthon functioned as spokesman for the Lutherans. Several of Luther's most insightful publications appeared during that summer—a tract on translating, an exposition of Psalm 118, and *Exhortation That Children Should Be Sent to School.*

Luther's final years were overshadowed by his growing antagonism toward the papal church. He died on 16 February, 1546.

Not surprisingly, Martin Luther has received considerable scholarly and theological attention throughout the centuries. Assessments of Luther have always been staunchly partisan, with a clear demarcation between Protestant and Catholic evaluations. A key theme in Luther's theology is that of the sole authority of scripture, formulated as the notion of *sola scriptura;* this notion, because it implied the possibility of a divergence of tradition from scripture, raised a startling new question. Late medieval theology had formulated the issue of authority in terms of the possible divergency of pope and council. A related theme in Luther's theology was the relationship of law and gospel, which provided the key to the understanding of scripture. God reveals himself as both a demanding and a giving God, two qualities that Luther loosely assigned to the Old and New Testaments respectively; but in truth, so Luther asserted, grace is found in the Old Testament even as law is found in the New.

The notion of justification by faith is traditionally cited as the heart of Luther's thought. It is, in fact, his major legacy to the Protestant tradition. In contradistinction to the medieval notion of a cooperative effort between man and God, between works and grace, Luther only stressed grace and God. Such grace is appropriated by faith, which affirms the reality of the grace of forgiveness, despite the reality of sin. Luther's "theology of the cross" affirmed that God always works contrary to experience.

— HANS J. HILLERBRAND

M

MAORI RELIGION

GODS AND THEIR INFLUENCE

In common with other Polynesians, the Maori conceived of reality as divided into two realms: the world of physical existence *(te ao marama,* "the world of light") and the world of supernatural beings (comprising both *rangi,* "the heavens," and *po,* "the underworld"). Communication between the two realms was frequent.

Gods or spirits, termed *atuas,* were frequent visitors to the physical world, where they were extremely active. Indeed, any event for which no physical cause was immediately apparent was attributed to the gods. This included winds, thunder and lightning, the growth of plants, physical or mental illness, menstruation, involuntary twitches in the muscles, the fear that gripped a normally brave warrior before battle, the skill of an artist, even—after the arrival of Europeans—the operation of windmills.

Another critical concept in traditional Maori religion is *tapu* (a term widespread in the Pacific, often rendered in English as "taboo"). Numerous definitions of the Maori *tapu* have been advanced. Perhaps the most useful view is that of the nineteenth-century magistrate and physician Edward Shortland, who defined *tapu* simply as the state of being under the influence of some *atua.* Because the influencing *atua* might be of any nature, from a protecting and strengthening god to an unwelcome, disease-dealing demon, the condition of a *tapu* person or thing could be anything from sacred to uncommonly powerful or brave; from dangerous to sick, deranged, or dead.

ESTABLISHING TAPU. One common way of instilling *tapu* (that is, inviting the gods to extend their influence over someone or something) was through ritual incantations called *karakia.*

Another means of attracting *atuas* and disposing them to lend their influence to human affairs was to give them gifts. Many Maori rituals included the preparation of several ovens; the food cooked in one of them was reserved for the gods. When an important new canoe was launched, the heart of a human sacrifice might be offered to the gods for protection of the craft.

The influence of *atuas* was considered to be highly contagious, readily spreading from things that were *tapu* to things that were not. One common pathway was physical contact. Death was highly *tapu,* and anything that came in contact with a corpse—the tree on which it was exposed during decomposition, the people who scraped the bones a year after death, the place where the bones were finally deposited—became *tapu* as well.

The principles of *tapu* contagion were used ritually to introduce godly influence into places or situations where it was desired. One means of doing this was to put rudely carved stone images in sweet potato fields during the growing season. These *taumata atuas* were resting-places that attracted the gods, whose influence would then permeate the field and stimulate the growth of the crop.

"The glorious gifts of the gods are not to be cast aside."

HOMER
THE ILIAD

DISPELLING TAPU. *Tapu* was by no means an invariably desirable state. Disease, as I have already noted, was thought to be the work of certain gods or demons noted for their maliciousness. Well-known mischief workers in the Rotorua area were Te Makawe, an *atua* who caused people to be scalded by geysers or hot pools, and the *atua* Tatariki, who rejoiced in swelling people's toes and ankles.

The Maori had a number of means for terminating the *tapu* state. One was simply to leave the area; many *atuas* were limited in their activities to a certain locale.

Water was thought to remove *atua* influence by washing it away. Those who had handled a corpse or who had been involved in the *tapu* activity of teaching or learning sacred lore might immerse themselves in water, preferably the flowing water of a stream.

Women frequently played important roles in *whakanoa* rituals designed to dispel *tapu.* A war party might be released from *tapu* by a rite in which a woman would eat the ear of the first enemy they had killed. Because women were thought to attract *atuas,* the female—specifically her genitalia—represented a passageway between the two realms of existence. When brought in proximity with a woman, an *atua* would be drawn into and through her, and thereby repatriated to the spiritual realm.

In the Pacific Islands, prayers are offered to ancestors and to symbolic beings whose invisible presence is still felt.

PAGE 534

The remaining *whakanoa* agent to be discussed is the latrine. Built on the edge of a cliff or brow of a hill, the Maori latrine was made with a low horizontal beam supported by two upright, often carved, posts. The user placed his feet on the beam while squatting, preserving his balance by grasping hand grips planted

Classic Maya stelae–accurately dated, erected at fixed intervals, and containing long hieroglyphic texts–display profile and frontal portraits of the great Maya dynasts.

PAGE 303

in the ground in front of the beam. A person could be ritually released from a *tapu* state by biting the latrine's horizontal beam.

The latrine beam marked a sharp line of separation: before it was the village, humming with life; behind it was a silent, shunned area where excrement fell and where people ventured only for murderous purposes, such as to learn witchcraft.

— F. ALLAN HANSON

MAYA RELIGION

The religion of Classic Maya civilization (300-900 CE) flourished in the Petén lowlands of northern Guatemala, producing a distinctive cosmology and worldview that still persist. Today, more than three million descendants of the Classic Maya occupy the area stretching from the Yucatán Peninsula in the north to the highlands of Guatemala and Chiapas, Mexico, in the south.

CLASSIC MAYA RELIGION. A concern with the passage of time led the Maya to chart the motion and phases of the sun, moon, Venus, and various constellations. By calculating the duration of different celestial cycles in terms of whole-day units (e.g., 149 lunations = 4,400 days), Classic Maya astronomers were able to compute lunar periods, the length of the solar year, and the revolutions of Venus, all to within minutes of their modern values. These calculations were greatly facilitated by the invention of a system of place-value arithmetic, an achievement that the Maya share only with the ancient Mesopotamians. The coalescence in Maya thought of time, astronomy, mathematics, and writing finds expression in Itzamná, the principal deity of the Classic Maya: he was alternately the creator god, the sun, and the first priest who invented writing and books.

Classic Maya religion, however, involved more than time and astronomy. Figures in Classic inscriptions once thought to depict deities are now known to represent actual Maya rulers, and the dynastic histories of such sites as Yaxchilan, Tikal, and Palenque have been reconstructed. Ancestor worship and the apotheosis of deceased rulers were essential aspects of Classic Maya religion. Some archaeologists further suggest that the impressive temples and pyramids that dominate Maya sites were funerary monuments to these deified rulers. The magnificent tomb of Lord Pacal (603-683 CE) found beneath the Temple of Inscriptions at Palenque clearly supports this theory.

POSTCLASSIC MAYA RELIGION. Despite the rapid decline of Classic Maya civilization after 900 CE, Maya religion survived in the Postclassic states of Yucatán and highland Guatemala (900-1530 CE). Old agricultural deities such as the *chacs* (rain gods), the *balams* (guardians of field and hearth), Kauil (the maize god), and Ixchel (the moon goddess and patroness of weaving, medicine, and childbirth) undoubtedly also survived intact. The Spanish conquest of the Maya area (1524-1540 CE) came as only another in a series of foreign incursions that never quite obliterated the distinctiveness of Maya culture and religion.

CONTEMPORARY MAYA RELIGION. Contemporary Maya religion has been transformed by Roman Catholicism, but strong continuities with the pre-Hispanic past persist. The motion of the sun still defines Maya cosmology, making the eastern and western horizons the primary cardinal directions. The circular paths of the sun and moon unite the various layers of the cosmos above and below the earth's surface. The preeminence of the sun as "Our Father" or "Our Grandfather" is reflected in its identification with God or, more frequently, Christ. Similarly, the moon is often associated with the Virgin Mary and called "Our Mother" or "Our Grandmother." In quotidian affairs, Catholic saints have become the supernatural guardians of field, hearth, and health, although in Yucatán the old *balams* still persist, and in some highland communities autochthonous ancestral deities remain important.

Human destiny also involves the welfare of the soul. Unlike the eternal Christian soul, Maya souls are largely involved with the here and now, since the soul represents the seat of reason, most concretely expressed in articulate speech and proper social behavior. In their very essence, individuals are enmeshed in their community and the social morality that it presupposes. Individuals can lose all or part of their soul through illness, through experiencing strong emotions such as anger or fright, or through other forms of culturally inappropriate behavior. Saving one's soul requires the constant attention to one's relations with fellow community members rather than merely purity of action and intent.

Individuals serve the saints by joining *cofradías* ("brotherhoods"), where for one year they care for the saint's image and perform the proper rituals, often at considerable personal expense. In return, individuals gain social prestige and access to higher political and religious offices. Outside the *cofradías,* traditional Maya religion recognizes no formal institutions.

— JOHN M. WATANABE

MENNONITES

The Mennonites, a Christian denomination, were first called Menists, or Mennonites, in 1541 by Countess Anna of Friesland after the group's primary leader,

Menno Simons (1496-1561). She used this name in order to distinguish the Mennonites, as peaceful settlers whom she welcomed in her lands, from other, revolutionary, groups. Historically and theologically, Mennonites are the direct descendants of sixteenth-century Anabaptists, a radical reform group in Europe.

EARLY HISTORY AND DOCTRINE

One of the most significant influences upon Mennonite history and identity has been the experience of decades of persecution during the sixteenth and seventeenth centuries. Numerous martyrologies, including the classic *Martyrs' Mirror* (1660), testify to this experience. The Mennonites lived in an age that was not ready for religious or social pluralism. In their insistence upon a church constituted of believers only, and in their embodiment of the principles of voluntary church membership and the separation of church and state, they represented a counterculture that society could not tolerate. In their reading of the Bible, however, they found these principles to be self-evident, particularly in the teaching and example of Jesus Christ. In keeping with the vision of their Anabaptist forebears, the Mennonites also shared the vision of a New Testament church restored both in essence and in form.

A church-world dualism was implicit in the Mennonites' theology and social view. It had been given early expression in the "Brotherly Union" of 1527, sometimes called the Schleitheim Confession of Faith, article 4 of which states:

> *Now there is nothing else in the world and all creation than good or evil, believing and unbelieving, darkness and light, the world and those who are [come] out of the world, God's temple and idols, Christ and Belial, and none will have part with the other.*

Toleration came to the Mennonites first in the Netherlands in the 1570s and somewhat later in other parts of Europe, except in Switzerland, where severe restrictions against them remained until the eighteenth century. Increasing freedom in the north led to rapid growth in membership, until by 1700 the Dutch congregations included 160,000 members. The sectarian virtues of frugality and hard work led to considerable affluence and to urbanization. Soon Mennonites became prominent patrons of the arts in the Netherlands. Numerous artists, poets, and writers from among their ranks achieved lasting fame. But the Enlightenment spirit of rationalism and secularism was also a part of these developments, and by 1837 there were only 15,300 members left in the Netherlands. Late-nineteenth- and twentieth-century developments resulted in another increase in membership.

The early pattern of survival through withdrawal from society led to numerous migrations. Records indicate that emigration from the Netherlands eastward to Hamburg and along the coast to Danzig (present-day Gdansk) began as early as 1534. Eventually large settlements developed in the Vistula delta. In 1788, migrations began from there to the Ukraine. By 1835 some 1,600 families had settled on Russian lands. By 1920 this population had grown to 120,000. But migration began again, this time from Russia beginning in the 1870s, primarily to North America.

A similar pattern prevailed among the Swiss and South German Mennonites. Many escaped Swiss persecution by migrating to the Palatinate or to central Germany. Others immigrated to the United States and Canada, beginning in 1663. The first permanent Mennonite settlement in the United States was established at Germantown, six miles north of Philadelphia, in 1683. Yet the total number of western European Mennonites coming to North America did not exceed 8,000, which, along with the approximately 55,000 immigrants from Prussian, Polish, and Russian lands, contributed to a core immigration to North America of no more than 70,000 up to the mid-1980s. There have also been migrations from North America, primarily from Canada to Mexico, Paraguay, Bolivia, and other Latin American locations. Thus pilgrimage has been central to Mennonite identity.

While Mennonites are noncreedal and affirm the Bible as their final authority for faith and life, they have written numerous confessions throughout their history. Chief among these are the Brotherly Union (1527) and the Dordrecht Confession of Faith (1632). In these the nature of the church as a believing, covenanting, caring, and obedient fellowship is central, as would be in keeping with the vision of restoring the New Testament church. The importance of the new birth and the authority of the Bible are stressed. Peace, including absolute pacifism, is considered an integral part of the gospel and, therefore, part of the discipleship of the believer. This discipleship is possible within the context of an Arminian theology, which acknowledges free will rather than Augustinian determinism. The second Adam, Christ, has undone the damage of the first Adam, making possible a gradual transformation of the disciple's life into the image of Christ himself. Ethics is a part of the Good News. Grace is necessary for discipleship rather than being antithetical to it. The believer who has experienced this grace is ready to receive baptism as a covenanting member of the "Believers' Church," a term commonly used since the 1950s to refer to noninfant baptizers.

LATER DEVELOPMENTS

Partly through migration and natural increase, but particularly through twentieth-century missionary activi-

The Anabaptist-Mennonite tradition, from its sixteenth-century origins has stressed the radical call of discipleship, believer's baptism, and a committed, inflexible following of the radical ethical demands of the gospel.

PAGE 150

Anabaptism originated formally in Zurich among young humanist associates of Zwingli.

PAGE 571

ties, Mennonites were scattered across the globe by the late twentieth century. In 1984 their total membership was approximately 700,000. The Mennonite World Conference, begun in 1925, meets every five or six years for fellowship and the sharing of ideas, as well as for worship and celebration. It is not a delegate conference, and no decisions binding upon world membership are made.

The extent to which contemporary Mennonites hold to the doctrines of early Anabaptism varies from nation to nation, from group to group, and even from congregation to congregation. Mennonites do form regional and national conferences, but they are basically congregational in polity. The Amish, who split off from Swiss and Alsatian Mennonites in 1693-1697, as well as the Hutterites and some conservative Mennonites, do not form conferences. Historically, pietism, more than other socioreligious movements, has influenced Mennonite theology; fundamentalism has also had an impact in North America. Both movements strengthen the inner, personal, and experiential aspect of faith but weaken social concern, pacifism, and the inherent church-world dualism of the sixteenth century. An enthusiastic recovery of the "Anabaptist vision," led by Harold S. Bender (1897-1962), has modified these influences since the 1940s.

Anabaptists Four Centuries Later (Kauffman and Harder, 1975) provides a profile of late-twentieth-century North American Mennonite religious attitudes and practices. In relation to two doctrinal orthodoxy scales established in the study, 90 percent of the respondents chose the most orthodox response on a liberal-orthodox continuum. About 80 percent of the members could identify a specific conversion experience. The practice of daily personal prayer ranged from a low of 73 percent in one conference to a high of 82 percent in another. More than 80 percent reported regular Sunday school participation, with teenagers having the highest rating. Fewer than 2 percent of the membership had experienced divorce or separation. Some 85 percent considered sexual intercourse before marriage as always wrong. The early emphasis on church-world dualism, pacifism, not taking oaths, and church discipline was affirmed by a range of from 60 to 80 percent, depending upon the conference.

This religious stance is nurtured through worship, attendance at denominational schools, devotional practices, small-group Bible study, and involvement in mission and service projects. Church buildings are generally functional and relatively austere. Worship services are usually sermon-centered. Most congregations enjoy singing, often *a cappella.* The Lord's Supper is celebrated two to four times annually. Some congregations practice the rite of foot washing.

Numerous liberal arts colleges are maintained in North America; they were established originally to train workers for church vocations. Seminaries, Bible schools, secondary schools, and other church institutions are maintained by Mennonites around the world as political and economic conditions permit. Retirement centers, community mental health centers, and medical and disaster aid services are maintained particularly in North America and Europe. The concern for united help for needy people around the world led to organization of the Mennonite Central Committee (MCC) in North America in 1920. A Dutch Mennonite relief agency had been organized two hundred years earlier. In 1983, the MCC had a cash and material aid budget in excess of $25 million, of which over $20 million was spent abroad and the balance on projects in North America. In the same year, a total of 944 workers were involved in fifty-five countries. Approximately one-third of these workers were non-Mennonite.

These activities are a direct extension of the Mennonite conviction that word and deed must be one and that love must be visible. It may, however, also be that these and related activities serve the less altruistic function of legitimizing the social significance and usefulness of a traditionally pacifist and persecuted people. Nevertheless, most Mennonites are deeply concerned about the futility of war and nuclear weapons, as well as about global poverty and the need for peaceful steps toward economic and social justice. These concerns are part of the total global mission to which Mennonites continue to feel committed.

— CORNELIUS J. DYCK

METHODIST CHURCHES

Methodism arose from the search of John Wesley and his brother Charles for a deepened religious life within the ordered ways of the Church of England, which John described as "the best constituted national church in the world." He sought no drastic reform in doctrines but rather a greater emphasis upon a personal experience of God's saving and perfecting grace and more opportunity for a spiritual quest within Christian groups, undeterred by denominational barriers. He downplayed the divisive element of his movement, publishing in 1742 an elaboration of Clement of Alexandria's description of a perfect Christian as *The Character of a Methodist* and offering this simple definition in his *Complete English Dictionary* (1753): "A Methodist, one that lives according to the method laid down in the Bible."

John Wesley, both as the living leader and later as the almost legendary "Mr. Wesley" of "the people called Methodists," so greatly influenced the developing thought and churchmanship of Methodism that he demands a far greater proportion of attention than if he had been the mere titular founder of a new denomination.

After his heart was "strangely warmed" on 24 May 1738, Wesley began to preach salvation by faith with the conviction of personal experience, and he gathered around him an organized society in London, the first of many that spread throughout the British Isles. These societies were intended to supplement, not supplant, the worship of the church. In his *Rules* (1743) he argued that a society was simply "a company of men 'having the form, and seeking the power of godliness,' united in order to pray together, to receive the word of exhortation, and to watch over one another in love, that they may help each other to work out their salvation." There was only one condition for membership, "a desire . . . to be saved from [their] sins." To test and reinforce his followers' sincerity, however, the *Rules* insisted that members should avoid evil, do good, and seek holiness, for which illustrative examples were given in all three categories.

In order to proclaim his message and administer his societies Wesley enrolled a steadily increasing number of lay preachers to join the handful of sympathetic clergy who engaged in an itinerant evangelical ministry under his supervision. In 1744 he called these together in London to confer about doctrine and organization. This was the first annual conference of Wesley's Methodism, although the Welsh Calvinistic wing of the movement, who looked to George Whitefield as their chief inspirer, had been holding their "Associations" for several years.

The primary purpose of the Conferences of 1744-1747 was to formulate the major doctrinal emphases of Methodist preaching: salvation by grace through faith, confirmed and exemplified by good works; the witness of the Holy Spirit to a person's salvation from the penalties of past sin and to his power over present temptations to sin; and the theoretical possibility of personal triumph over temptation, under the title of Christian perfection, which Wesley defined as perfect love to God and man, though consistent with human error and with no guarantee of permanence. These doctrines, as taught and illustrated in Wesley's first four volumes of *Sermons* (1744-1760) and his *Explanatory Notes upon the New Testament* (1755), formed the basis of all Methodist preaching.

Meanwhile British immigrants, especially from Ireland, brought Methodism to America, where it became so firmly rooted that Wesley responded to their plea for help by sending out matched pairs of itinerant preach-

Millenarianism is the belief that the end of the world is at hand and that in its wake will appear a new harmonious world.

PAGE 431

THE METHODIST CONFERENCES

Only Connect

Early Conferences, held 1744–47, consolidated the organization of Methodism into a "connexion," a network of societies served by lay preachers itinerating regularly on a circuit, or round, covering a district such as a county in tours lasting from four to six weeks, but also itinerating between circuits periodically—at first every three months, then every six, and eventually every year. Each year Wesley's own preaching and administrative journeys took him over most of England. In 1747 Ireland was added to his tour, and in 1751, Scotland. Wesley and his itinerant preachers developed a strong family identity among the societies.

This connexional unity became so strong that in 1749 Wesley published two sets of extracts from the minutes of his conferences, each with the same title—*Minutes of Some Late Conversations between the Revd. Mr. Wesleys and Others*—one summarizing Methodist teaching, the other Methodist organization. In effect they constituted a declaration that Methodism had become an established ecclesiastical body. Inevitably this process of consolidation aroused much criticism of Methodism: the preachers' teaching, so unfamiliar to non-Methodists, was incorrectly described as unorthodox; their vigor, warmth, and ebullience were pejoratively labeled "enthusiasm"; and Wesley's unconventional preaching in the open air and in other men's parishes, and, worse still, his authorizing laymen to preach, were regarded by even sympathetic clergy as a grave breach of ecclesiastical order. Preachers and people were occasionally mobbed, but the somewhat quiescent church authorities took no concerted action.

The chief threat, indeed, came from within the movement. The people's desire to receive the sacraments from their preachers fed the preachers' natural ambitions to improve their status and to transform the society into a church. John Wesley was inclined to let things run their course, but the vehement opposition of his brother Charles led him to tighten the rein on his preachers, most of whom from 1752 onward signed agreements "never to leave the communion of the Church of England without the consent of all whose names are subjoined." Avowed separation from the church was narrowly averted at the Conference of 1755, when all agreed "that (whether it was *lawful* or not) it was no ways *expedient.*" This deferred any open separation for almost thirty years.

— FRANK BAKER

M

METHODIST CHURCHES

The decision to employ the term bishop in American Methodism probably arose from the determination to assert independence from Anglicanism.

PAGE 441

ers in 1769, 1771, 1773, and 1774, of whom by far the best known and most influential was Francis Asbury, who remained throughout the Revolutionary War (1775-1783). With some difficulty Asbury persuaded the American Methodists not to sever their ties with Wesley in their eagerness for religious independence, and thus Wesley himself was able to assist Americans in the birth of the first independent church within Methodism.

The year 1784 was "that grand climacteric year of Methodism." Aided by Dr. Thomas Coke, Wesley prepared a deed poll that legally defined the term *Conference,* and made that body heir to British Methodism after Wesley's death. Wesley also entrusted to Coke a major part in publishing a revision of *The Book of Common Prayer* for the use of American Methodists, and discussed with him a complementary plan for securing a threefold ministry in American Methodism. Already convinced that in any ecclesiastical emergency the power of ordination resided in presbyters, Wesley ordained two of his preachers, first as deacons and then as elders. With their assistance he then commissioned Coke as "superintendent" of the American flock, with instructions to share his new authority with Asbury upon his arrival in America.

At the "Christmas Conference" in Baltimore (1784-1785) with Wesley's blessing, a new denomination was launched, the Methodist Episcopal Church. In England Methodism still remained a society, governed by a presbyter of the Church of England and at least theoretically within the fold of that church. After Wesley's death in 1791, however, under the terms of his deed poll, the Conference of preachers became the ruling body, with a modified presbyterian system of government rather than the modified episcopalian polity that was being developed in America. Although some of Wesley's Anglican friends had occasionally referred to "the Methodist church" during his lifetime, not until 1893 did the class tickets indicating membership in the Wesleyan Methodist Society carry the word *church.*

"I look upon the world as my parish."

JOHN WESLEY
JUNE 11, 1739 JOURNAL

When in 1739 Wesley had written, "I look upon *all the world as my parish,*" he was defending his disregard of ecclesiastical boundaries in Britain, but in fact he did also cherish a vision of a world renewed in the image of Christ, and was convinced that his liberal, pragmatic approach to theology and to churchmanship should make good missionaries of his people—as indeed it did. He heartily supported Coke's missionary plans, and a month before his death wrote to a native American preacher, "Lose no opportunity of declaring to all men that the Methodists are one people in all the world." Within a century after Wesley's death immigrants and missionaries from both sides of the Atlantic had planted Methodism on each continent and in almost every country.

Methodist missionary expansion during the nineteenth century varied little whether it came from the British or the American type of church polity, because polity was overshadowed by ethos, and the ethos sprang from Wesley. Methodists everywhere remained within a tightly knit "connexion" governed by a conference. They followed Wesley in assigning major responsibilities to laymen, and were progressive in enrolling women as leaders, and even as preachers. They emphasized evangelical preaching and continued to experiment with an adventurous and flexible organization. While making good use of their rich heritage of Charles Wesley's hymns they observed those almost uniquely Methodist forms of worship, the watch-night, the covenant service, and the lovefeast, as well as the close fellowship of the class-meeting and the bands, with their cherished tickets of membership. They constantly remembered their early rules, by "avoiding evil of every kind—especially that which is most generally practised," and by "doing good of every possible sort, and as far as is possible to all men."

It is true that the full appreciation of some of these features fell off even during the nineteenth century, and a few were almost forgotten in the twentieth, such as Wesley's constant charge, "Press on to perfection." Human frailty brought about fragmentation into many independent denominations, a process furthered during the twentieth century by the hiving off of national churches from the parent bodies.

The first major division in England, the Methodist New Connexion (1797), was a revolt against the autocracy of the leading Wesleyan preachers, but the Primitive Methodists (1811) and Bible Christians (1819), though also favoring more lay leadership, left because they wished to restore evangelism. The Wesleyan Methodist hierarchy came under increasing attack from 1849 onward in a disruptive pamphlet warfare that led to eventual democratic reforms at the cost of losing many thousands of members. Happily, some of these breaches were progressively healed through the formation of the United Methodist Free Churches in 1857, the United Methodist Church in 1907, and the Methodist Church in 1932.

In America, where membership had almost drawn level with that in the British Isles by Wesley's death, Methodism expanded and divided far more rapidly than in Britain during the nineteenth and twentieth centuries. The controversy over the institution of slavery and other disruptive forces similar to those in England were at work in America. Coke and Asbury had unsuccessfully sought to eradicate slavery from the Methodist Episcopal Church, but even in the abolitionist strongholds of New York and Philadelphia race remained an issue among Methodists. There, blacks forsook their second-class membership to form their own congregations, which eventually became the African Methodist Episcopal Church (1816) and the African Methodist Episcopal Zion Church (1820), each with a community of over a million in the 1980s. In 1844 the whole Methodist Episcopal Church split into north and south over the issue, though other factors also were at work, including varying views of the episcopacy. In 1870 the Methodist Episcopal Church South blessed the incorporation of their own black members into the Colored (now "Christian") Methodist Episcopal Church. Slavery was also a factor in the formation of the Wesleyan Methodist Connection (1843), which did not name itself a "church" until 1947, and which also sought a return to earlier Wesleyan evangelism and the abolition of the episcopacy. The Free Methodist Church (1860) arose after lengthy preliminaries from a widespread desire to recover Wesley's teaching upon Christian perfection. A similar emphasis within American Methodism upon the need to recover scriptural holiness led to the piecemeal formation of the Church of the Nazarene.

In American Methodism and its missions, as well as in the British Commonwealth, a measure of consolidation took place during the nineteenth and twentieth centuries, notably in the union of the northern and southern churches with the Protestant Methodists in 1939 to form the Methodist Church, which in 1968 united with the Evangelical United Brethren (itself a union of churches with a German-speaking background) to form the United Methodist Church, with a membership of eleven million out of a total world Methodist community of something like fifty million.

These and other unions were consummated largely because of the coming together in Christian fellowship of representatives from dozens of autonomous Methodist churches and missions from all over the world, first decennially from 1881 in the Ecumenical Methodist Conference, then quinquennially from 1951 in the World Methodist Council. Welcome guests at these gatherings are representatives from churches where Methodism has subsumed its identity in an interdenominational union, such as the United Church of Canada (1925), the Churches of North and South India, the Uniting Church in Australia, or other such unions in Belgium, China, Ecuador, Japan, Pakistan, the Philippines, and Zambia. As an important element in the World Council of Churches, Methodism remains true to the spirit of its founder, who gloried in the catholicity of his early societies, open to persons of all creeds, and who firmly maintained, in spite of attacks by his critics, that "orthodoxy, or right opinions, is at best but a very slender part of religion."

— FRANK BAKER

MILLENARIANISM

Millenarianism, known also as millennialism, is the belief that the end of this world is at hand and that in its wake will appear a New World, inexhaustibly fertile, harmonious, sanctified, and just. The more exclusive the concern with the End itself, the more such belief shades off toward the catastrophic; the more exclusive the concern with the New World, the nearer it approaches the utopian.

MILLENARIAN THOUGHT

Complexity in millenarian thought derives from questions of sign, sequence, duration, and human agency. What are the marks of the End? At what stage are we now? Exactly how much time do we have? What should we do? Although warranted by cosmology, prophecy, or ancestral myth, the End usually stands in sudden proximity to the immediate era. The trail of events may at last have been tracked to the cliff's edge, or recent insight may have cleared the brier from some ancient oracle.

Crowded into ghettos in a hostile and foreign environment, black migrants sought security in the church.

PAGE 18

The root term, *millennium,* refers to a first-century eastern Mediterranean text, the *Apocalypse of John* or *Book of Revelation,* itself a rich source of disputes about the End.

In theory, as a speculative poetic enterprise, millenarianism is properly an adjunct of eschatology, the study of last things. In practice, millenarianism is distinguished by close scrutiny of the present, from which arise urgent issues of human agency. Once the fateful coincidence between history and prophecy has been confirmed, must good people sit tight, or must they gather together, withdraw to a refuge? Should they enter the wilderness to construct a holy city, or should they directly engage the chaos of the End, confront the regiments of evil? Millenarians answer with many voices, rephrasing their positions as they come to terms with an End less imminent or less cataclysmic. Where their image of the New World is that of a golden age, they begin with a restorative ethos, seeking a return to a lost purity. Where their image is that of the land of the happy dead or a distant galaxy of glory, their ethos is initially retributive, seeking to balance an unfortunate past against a fortunate future. Few millenarians remain entirely passive, quietly awaiting a supernatural transformation of the world.

A millenarian's sense of time, consequently, is neither strictly cyclical nor linear. However much the millennium is to be the capstone to time, as in Christian and Islamic traditions, it is also in character and affect the return of that carefree era posited for the start of things. However much the millennium is to be an impost between two of the infinite arches of time, as in Aztec and Mahayana Buddhist traditions, it is for all mortal purposes a release from pain and chaos for many generations.

M

MILLENARIANISM

Typologies of Millenarian Movements

A strongly ritualistic religion, Zoroastrianism marked the year with a series of fixed holidays, thus incorporating traditional ways and customs that were hard to eradicate.

PAGE 721

To the uninitiated, the millenarian mathematics of time may seem mysteriously scaled: how can one account for that arbitrary algebra that assigns the value 3,500 years to the locution "a time, and times, and half a time" (*Rv.* 12:14)? Millenarian thought is figurative in both senses of that word—metaphorical and numerological. Intricate play with numbers of years is founded upon a faith in the impending aesthetic wholeness of the world-historical process. Millenarian searches for laws of historical correspondence between the individually human and the universally human bear a formal similarity to one another, whether the searchers are nineteenth-century social visionaries or twelfth-century monastics. Each discerns a pattern of historical ages that promises both completion and recapitulation.

World religions have known two deep reservoirs of millenarian thought, one noumenal and gnostic, the other phenomenal and nomothetic. When the reservoirs empty into each other—when mathematicians allude to secret knowledge or contemplatives allude to laws of physics (as in fifth-century southern China, seventeenth-century Western Europe, twentieth-century North America)—millenarianism waxes strong.

Among the world religions we can locate two constellations of millenarian thought about an epochal pulsing of time, one Zoroastrian-Jewish-Greek-Christian, the other Hindu-Buddhist-Taoist-Confucian. In the Mediterranean littoral, an epochal aesthetic was elaborated by scribal elites who were resistant first to Greek rule, then Roman rule, and finally to Muslim rule. Feasting upon a cosmopolitan diet of Zoroastrian cosmology, Jewish notions of Sabbath, and Greco-Roman ideas of historical recurrence, these literati stamped the disturbing flux of empires with the template of the divine creative week, which they saw being played out again at length in human history through a reassuringly predictable series of world kingdoms over a period of six or seven thousand years. At the end lay a millennial sabbath, transposed from a time of perpetual rest to a time of truce and earthly reward prior to the final onslaughts of the dragon, tyrant, or false messiah.

Across East Asia, a millenarian aesthetic developed within contexts far less adversarial, and we find no figure antiphonal to the universal perfect ruler (the Hindu *cakravartin,* the Buddhist Rudra Cakin, the Javanese hybrid *Ratu Adil*) or to the future incarnate savior (the Hindu Kalkin, the Maitreya Buddha, a reborn Laotzu). Furthermore, the epochal scheme was overwhelmingly degenerative: it fixed all recorded history within the last of the four increasingly chaotic eras *(yugas)* of the aeon *(kalpa)*. The problem here was not to expand the prophetic horizon but to foreshorten the 4.3 million-year Indian *kalpa* cycle so that hundreds of thousands of distressing years of the fourth era, the *kaliyuga,* did not still lie ahead.

Each *kalpa* was to end in a cosmic disaster that would, after some blank time, initiate a new cycle whose first *yuga* was always a golden age. Strategic foreshortening brought present catastrophe stern to snout with a renewed world. The foreshortening began in northern India with early Mahayana Buddhist images of *bodhisattvas,* compassionate enlightened beings who chose to work in this world for the benefit of others rather than withdraw into final *nirvana.* Almost simultaneously, Chinese commentators during the Later Han period (25-220 CE) alloyed the Confucian golden age of antiquity, the Ta-t'ung, to the T'aip'ing golden age, which according to Taoist sexagenary cycles could be both ancient and imminent, as the Yellow Turban rebels in 184 sincerely hoped. By the sixth century, the colossal four-cycle Indian cosmology had collapsed under the weight of Taoist alchemy, pietist Pure Land Buddhism, and popular Chinese worship of the Eternal Mother (Wu-sheng Lao-mu) and the *bodhisattva* Prince Moonlight (Yüeh-kuang T'ung-tzu).

There were then three accessible ages, associated cosmologically with the Taoist Former, Middle, and Latter Heavens, typologically with the three Buddhas (Lamplighter, Sakyamuni, and Maitreya), and synecdochically with the Buddhas' lotus thrones of azure, red, and white. Each age begins with a new Buddha and then declines, again in triplets: True Doctrine, or Dharma; Counterfeit Doctrine; and Last Days of Doctrine. Since the days of the historical Buddha, Sakyamuni (and, traditionally, of Confucius and Lao-tzu), we have squatted uncomfortably in the dissolute Last Days, awaiting Maitreya or his predecessor, Prince Moonlight, who is due to sweep in at the height of catastrophes one thousand years after Sakyamuni's *parinirvana.*

Common to millenarian aesthetics in all the world religions is this epochal scenario: a calm inaugural and a riotous finale to each act; the circling of two protagonists near the End, one imperial, the other sacramental; and a time at the End that is at once encore, intermezzo, and the throwing open of the doors.

Though flood, plague, famine, or war may summon visions of collective death, millenarians promise more than an accurate prediction of catastrophe. They promise an earth lifted beyond safety to grace. Even at their most catastrophic, millenarians insist that a classical tragedy must be fought through only to reach a genuinely good time.

TYPOLOGIES OF MILLENARIAN MOVEMENTS

Altogether, as a system of thought and social movement, millenarianism spins on two axes: golden age or new era; primitive paradise or promised land. This oscillation leads perplexed observers to depict mil-

lenarian movements as volatile, metamorphic, undirected, and ephemeral. Journalistic or academic, administrative or missiological, works on the subject abound with images that have shaped policy. Millenarianism is described in five iconic sets:

1. a contagion to be quarantined (as with Mormonism in Utah in the later 1800s);
2. a quicksand to be fenced off (as in the legal actions against the American Shakers in the early 1800s and the present-day anticult campaigns against the Unification Church);
3. a simmering stew to be watched, on the premise that a watched pot never boils (as in police surveillance of the group surrounding Catherine Théot in Paris in 1793 and 1794);

CHAOS

Millenarians promise more than a prediction of catastrophe, they promise earth lifted beyond safety to grace.

CORBIS-BETTMANN

4. a boil to be lanced (as in the English kidnapping of the prophet Birsa from Munda country in northeastern India in 1895 or the Belgian imprisonment of Simon Kimbangu and his first disciples from 1921 to 1957);
5. an explosion to be contained (the German war against the Maji Maji of German East Africa [modern-day Tanzania] in 1905 and 1906 or the Jamaican government's preemption of Rastafarian music and rhetoric in the last two decades).

"And ye shall hear of wars and rumours of wars."

MATTHEW 24: 6-7

Millenarianism appears here as an epiphenomenon, a symptom of or a pretext for something more sinister. These images (and policies) have an august history. Church councils in Latin, Byzantine, and Protestant Christianity, legal scholars of Sunni Islam and rabbinic Judaism, the presiding monks of Buddhist *samghas*—all have long regarded millenarianism as a disguised attack on codes of behavior that are meant to govern faith and cult. Rulers and their bureaucracies—Confucian, Islamic, Hindu—have regarded millenarianism as a ritual mask worn by crafty rebels.

Present-day typologists are somewhat more sympathetic. For them, millenarianism is emblematic, a ceremonial flag waved furiously over swamps of injustice. Such an interpretation was codified by the French and German Enlightenments, then refurbished by liberals in the nineteenth century until positivist denials of a religious instinct made religion itself seem epiphenomenal. Latter-day social scientists have made millenarianism doubly emblematic, for they describe it as the sign of transition from a religious to a secular society.

Current typologies work along three scales: temporal focus, soteriology, and sociopolitical engagement. On the first scale, typologists range those movements oriented toward (1) the reconstitution of an earlier social structure (called nativist, traditionalist, conservationist, restorative), (2) the imaginative making of peace with change (called acculturative, adjustive, perpetuative, revitalist, reformative), and (3) the creation of an ideal future society (called messianic or utopian). The second scale runs from those movements concerned exclusively with individual salvation (called redemptive, revivalist, thaumaturgic) to those that demand an overhaul of economy and etiquette (called transformative or revolutionary). The third scale starts at total isolation and finishes with collective assault on the state. This scale especially has been plodded and plowed by rhetoric (reactionary/progressive, passive/active, prepolitical/political, mythological/ideological). Like mule teams, these binary terms are hardworking but perpetually sterile, since millenarians delight in the yoking of opposites.

Dynamic typologies, plotted by such scholars as Mary Douglas (1970), James W. Fernandez, (1964), and Wim M. J. van Binsbergen (1981), are quadrivalent, balancing social pressures against social structures. Douglas uses two variables, social cohesion and shared symbolic systems. Fernandez takes acculturation as his ordinate, instrumentality as his abscissa. Van Binsbergen considers both the source of disequilibrium (infrastructural, superstructural) and the nature of the threat ("peasantization," "proletarianization"). Such typologies, more appreciative of the complexity of millenarian movements, still hesitate before the phase shifts through which most movements go.

Motives for the fabrication of typologies may themselves be classified as prophylactic or exploitative. Most typologies mean to be prophylactic. Political scientists, for example, may hope to forestall the rise of charismatic tyranny; anthropologists in colonial settings may want to persuade authorities to handle millenarian movements more reasonably and with less show of force; missionaries may wish to avoid spawning highly independent churches or syncretic cults. Other typologies are exploitative. Marxist and capitalist alike place millenarians on a sociohistorical ladder so as to direct their obvious energies upward, toward national liberation and socialism or toward modern industrialism and oligopoly. Occultists and irenic church people place millenarians on one rung of the ladder of spiritual evolution so as to draw them toward higher consciousness, the Aquarian age, or one broad faith.

EXPLANATIONS FOR MILLENARIAN MOVEMENTS

Despite the many typologies, there are but two current scholarly explanations for the birth of millenarian movements. The first asserts that millenarianism arises from feelings of relative deprivation in matters of status, wealth, security, or self-esteem. Millenarian movements appear in periods of crisis, when such feelings become most painful. The crisis may be as blatant and acute as the sack of a city or as subtle and prolonged as the passage from isolated agrarian community to industrial megalopolis. Whichever it is, the crisis engenders personal fantasies of invulnerability and escape, which are transformed by charismatic individuals who are often members of displaced elites. These prophets shape public expressions of protest at a time when more straightforward political action seems useless. In the necessarily unsuccessful aftermath, millenarians master the cognitive dissonance between expectation and failure by perpetuating millenarian beliefs within a revised chronology and a new missionary plan. The underlying causes for feelings of deprivation will not have been resolved, so a millenarian tradition, halfway between social banditry and the politics of party, burns on.

The second, complementary explanation says that

millenarian movements spring from contact between two cultures when one is technologically far superior to the other. Millenarianism spreads within the settled, inferior culture, whose polity is critically threatened. The newcomers, usually white and literate, disrupt traditional systems of kinship, healing, and land rights. Most wrenching are the factorial economics introduced by the newcomers, whose quantitative uses of time and money rasp across the qualitative webs of social reciprocity. The indigenes must redefine their notions of power, status, and law, or they must stave off the well-armed traders, their navies, and their missionaries. Acknowledging the superiority of the newcomers' technology but not that of their ethic of possessive individualism, the indigenes begin to speculate about the true origin of the goods and gods of the stingy, secretive newcomers. The result is the contact cult (also called a "crisis cult" or "cargo cult") devoted to frenzied preparation for the receipt of shiploads of goods (cargo) that will dock unaccompanied by whites or in the company of fair-skinned but unselfish ancestors. Already under intense pressure, the people ceremonially destroy sacred objects and standing crops. They believe that this world is ending and a new one must begin, best with the newcomers gone and themselves masters of the secret of wealth.

Contact is the sociology for which deprivation is the psychology. Contact leads to millenarianism when one group feels unalterably deprived vis-à-vis a new other. The two explanations, compatible with stock images of eruption and contagion, rely on the premise of a closed system. At the millenarian core lies frustration; out of frustration squirms fantasy, and fantasy breeds violence. Early Freudian analyses of hysteria, psychosis, and schizophrenia have been employed here to wire the circuit between individual fireworks and collective explosion.

Deprivation theories prevail despite decades of criticism for their being slackly predictive. Scholars have noted that relative deprivation does not account specifically for millenarianism; it may as easily induce fracas, sabotage, or personal depression. Conversely, millenarian movements have not "burst out" where relative deprivation has been most apparent: eighteenth-century Ireland, nineteenth-century Ethiopia, the southeastern coast of modern India. Indeed, as critics may add, where across this imperfect world has relative deprivation ever been absent or a crisis lacking?

At this point, theorists invoke a *homo ex machina*, the charismatic prophet who processes the raw stuff of frustration. As a person whose life portends or echoes social crises, the prophet articulates the myth-dream of the people and so becomes invested with the power to direct its expression. Wherever gambols a weak social theory about religious movements, sure to follow is the fleece of charisma. For face-to-face groups, as W. R. Bion showed in his *Experiences in Groups* (New York, 1961), prophetic leaders may embody group fantasies of rebirth. For larger groups—like most millenarian movements—charisma becomes narcotic, a controlled substance rather than a theory of social relations.

Theorists have given particularly short shrift to the remarkable prominence of women as millenarian prophets. In all but Islam and Judaism, women have stridden at the head of millenarian movements, with men as their scribes, publicists, and ideologues. The list is long; a few examples must do: Priscilla and Maximilla of the New Prophecy (the Montanists) in Asia Minor in the late second century; Guglielma of Milan and her women disciples in the late thirteenth century; Dona Béatrice's Antonine movement in the Lower Congo from 1703 to 1706; Joanna Southcott with perhaps twenty thousand followers in England before her death in 1814; Ellen Gould White, chief oracle of the Seventh-day Adventists in the United States, in the late nineteenth century; Jacobina Maurer of the Brazilian Muckers movement from 1872 to 1898; the visionary Gaidaliu in Assam from 1929 to 1930 and 1961 to 1965; Mai Chaza's Guta ra Jehova (City of Jehovah) in Rhodesia from 1954 to 1960; Kitamura Sayo's Dancing Religion (Tensho Kotai Jingukyo) founded in Japan in 1945.

Deprivation theories maintain that women, an injured group, use religion as a means to power otherwise denied them by patriarchies. This makes religion a negative (compensatory) vehicle for women and a positive (creative) vehicle for men, and it fails to explain the power that women gain over men through millenarian movements. There is as yet no sufficient discussion of female charisma. Indeed, where prophetic leadership is male, analysis customarily proceeds from the instrumental, socioeconomic background to doctrine and political tactics; where female, it proceeds from affective, sexual background to ritual and spirit possession. Active men, reactive women: a contact theory of the sexes.

Contact theories are tricky. Amazed by discoveries of previously unknown tribes in the Amazon region and in the Philippines, industrial societies exaggerate the isolation of nonindustrial people. Nonetheless, contact is always a matter of degree: from armies with bulldozers abruptly grading runways in Melanesia to pandemics of smallpox hundreds of miles from (European) vectors. Contact is never so much a shock that some prophecy or other has not already accumulated around a piece of strangeness that years before drifted in on a storm tide or fell from the clouds.

In addition, we have sparse evidence that a number of peoples—the Guaraní of South America, the Karen of Burma, the Lakalai of the island of New Britain, and perhaps the Pacific Northwest Indians—had myths, rituals, and cults whose motifs were millenarian and whose origins were prior to contact with an in-pressing "superior" (Eurasian) culture.

Furthermore, not every uneven contact lights a millenarian "fuse." While the same material imbalance between Europeans and natives faced both Polynesians and Melanesians, millenarian movements have been infrequent among the politically stratified societies of Polynesia. More loosely bunched and socially fluid, Melanesians had inadequate etiquette by which to carry out diplomacy between distinctly separate orders. The customary structure of discourse, not contact itself, seems to have been a key variable in the general absence of cargo cults in Polynesia and their flowering in Melanesia, where consistently powerful Europeans could not be dealt with as easily as could another and analogous order.

One of the most widespread millenarian movements in sub-Saharan Africa is the Church of the Watchtower, or Kitawala.

PAGE 9

At best, deprivation predisposes, contact precipitates. There are six other factors whose presence predisposes to millenarian movements:

1. permeable monastic communities and lay sodalities that extend loyalties beyond the family;
2. itinerant homeopathic healers who carry ritual and rumor across regional borders;
3. a mythopoetic tradition in popular drama and folktale, which makes history prophetic and the people the bearers of prophecy;
4. numerology and astrology, which encourage people habitually to search out relationships between number, event, and time;
5. rituals of inversion, such as carnival or exhaustive mourning, in which endings and beginnings are willfully confused;
6. migration myths that call for the return to an ancestral land or for the return of the dead to a renewed land.

There are negatively prejudicial factors as well. Millenarian movements are least likely at the extremes of the economic spectrum—that is, among those who have complete freedom of mobility and among those absolutely constrained. No millenarian movements occur within groups whose positions are secure, comfortable, and protected by mechanisms of caste (classical North Indian, Japanese, and Roman aristocracies). Nor do millenarian movements occur within groups whose mobility has been severely restricted by political oppression (prisoners, inmates of concentration camps), economic oppression (slaves), physical illness (hospital patients, the starving), or mental illness (asylum inmates, the autistic).

This verges on tautology: millenarian movements happen where physical movement is possible. But the near tautology is suggestive. Where cultural ideals of physical movement differ, so, correspondingly, may the nature of social movements. For example, to be harshly schematic, Western Europeans have stressed vertical, direct, outbound motion in their sports, their dancing, their tools, and their manners; the head and shoulders lead, with the mass of the body in tow. Sub-Saharan Africans such as the Dogon have a kinesthetic of orchestral, highly oppositional, polyrhythmic motion in which the body twists at the hips. The northern Chinese have in their martial arts, their medicine and calligraphy a kinesthetic of sustained circular motion, an integrated body linked to the flow of universal energy. These differences may be expressed in the European proclivity for a tight echelon of prophets leading an undifferentiated millenarian body, the African tendency toward coextensive and fissiparous leadership, the Chinese history of generational continuity from one guiding millenarian family to the next. Kinesthetic differences may also determine the relative importance of the precipitants of millenarianism: where a society looks for whole-body motion, the triggering instances must affect the entire society; where a society looks for articulated or isolated motions, the triggering instances may be more local.

The following four factors recur cross-culturally as major precipitants of millenarian movements:

1. the evangelism of foreign missionaries whose success requires the reordering of native patterns of marriage, family, diet, and calendar;
2. displacement by refugees or invaders, or as a result of persecution, economic decline, or natural calamity;
3. confusion about landholdings due to shifting settlement, the superposition of a new legal grid, or the advent of new technologies, as foreshadowed most particularly by census taking, geological surveys, rail laying, and road building;
4. generational distortion, where the traditional transfer of loyalties and moral authority is profoundly disturbed by war deaths, schooling, long-distance migrations, or urbanization.

These are, of course, related. Threaded throughout are anxieties about inheritance, boundaries, and language (its intelligibility, its capacity for truth-telling). Set within a matrix of predisposing factors, granted some rumors and good weather, these anxieties should specifically engage the wheels of millenarianism, with its special freight of ages, places, and figures of speech. Expansive millenarianism occurs when believers are imperiled or impressed by forces within their society; astringent millenarianism occurs when the forces seem foreign.

PATTERNS OF MILLENARIAN MOVEMENTS IN WORLD HISTORY

The world's great religions share a larger historical pattern of millenarian activity (although Vedanta Hinduism may be a partial exception). Founded on the fringes of empire or at the fracture line between competing kingdoms, these religions find themselves several centuries later at the center of an empire. Millenarian thought then appears in canonical form, drawing its impetus from those forces of imperial expansion that compel the recalculation of calendars, histories, distances, and sacred geography. The new arithmetic signals a shift in scales of measurement, mediated as much by mystics as by scientists. When an empire seems to have reached its limits, millenarian movements flourish, usually several generations before the dynastic collapse.

When the millennium does not arrive, or when millenarian movements are co-opted by a new dynasty, as in Ming China or Safavid Iran, millenarianism does not fade away. End-of-the-world images linger in the dreams and speech of the people, and end-time ideas

ANTICIPATING 2000

Why Are We So Fixated on the End?

Why does millenarianism presently seem in such need of some kind of covering law? The answers to this question have to do with the characteristics of the North Atlantic ecumene, which is responsible for most of the law making.

A first answer is that millenarians tend not to fall within the bell of the ecumene's emotional curve. Although sternly depressed about current affairs, millenarians are at the same time exultant about the prospects for a New World. European and North American psychologists interpret ambivalence as a symptom of inner discord; the greater the ambivalence, the more serious the illness. But "sensible" middle-class citizens join UFO cults, buy fifteen million copies of Hal Lindsey's *The Late Great Planet Earth* (Grand Rapids, Mich., 1970), and order bulk goods from End Time Foods, Inc., in Virginia. Why?

A second answer is that millenarians threaten the stability of the ecumene, upsetting the development of outlying colonies. Millenarians seem haphazardly amused by industrial investment and international tariffs. Why do they keep popping up to make a hash of foreign policy, and why do they prefer the "magical" to the "practical"?

A third answer is that the wars of this century have burned the mark of the beast on North Atlantic arts, philosophy, and history. The beast roared through the no-man's-lands of World War I and the gas chambers and radioactive cinders of World War II. Apocalypse has lost its reference to millennium; it has become simply a synonym for disaster.

We can also trace the growth of a catastrophic mood in North Atlantic science over a century of work in astronomy, cosmology, ecology, climatology, and, recently, morphogenetics and mathematics (the last two united by catastrophe theory, which accounts topologically for instant changes of state). The mood has prevailed in popular science from Henry Adams's 1909 essay on the second law of thermodynamics ("The Rule of Phase Applied to History") to the syzygy scare of the so-called Jupiter effect (1974-1982).

A fourth, more upbeat answer is that archaeology, theology, politics, and the Gregorian calendar have conspired to regenerate the utopian side of millenarianism. Although no millenarian movements and exceedingly few prophecies were geared to the year 1000 (few then used such a calendar), the historical myth persists because it seems to many that the year 2000 will be truly millennial. The discovery of the Dead Sea Scrolls since 1947 has underscored the contention, popularized by Albert Schweitzer in 1906, that eschatological hope was vital at the time of apostolic Christianity and should therefore be part of all true Christian belief. Israel's statehood in 1948 and its 1967 reunification of Jerusalem have convinced fundamentalist Christians of the nearness of the Second Coming, for which a principal sign is the Jews' return to Zion. So we see in the ecumene a telephone hot line for news of the latest scriptural prophecies fulfilled, an international conference on end-of-world prophecies (in Jerusalem in 1971), and a perfume called Millennium: "In the life of every woman's skin there comes a turning point, a time when her face begins to look older. Now there is an alternative."

Outside the ecumene, detached from Christian dates, Hindu and Buddhist revivalists (Hare Krishna, Divine Light Mission, Soka Gakkai) preach the last era, the kaliyuga or mappo. Shi'is awaiting the Mahdi at century's end (AH 1399/1979-1980 CE) experienced instead the Iranian revolution. Mexican intellectuals of the Movement of the Reappearance of Anauak, following the Aztec calendar, find this a time of cataclysm. Marxists, flipping through an economic almanac, tear off the leaves of late capitalism.

The fifth answer, then, is that from within and without the ecumene, notions of change have taken on a prepotently millenarian cast.

— HILLEL SCHWARTZ

are filtered through monasteries, lay brotherhoods, and scientific communities. As these are gradually attracted to the nodes of political power, millenarian movements reappear either as adjuncts of conquest or as resistance to it. Millenarian activity peaks again when the limits of territorial coherence are felt within the empire and along its colonial periphery.

This sequence may obtain for other than the great world religions (e.g., for the Aztec, Iroquois, and Bakongo), but materials are lacking that would sustain such an argument for the many preliterate cultures. It is tempting, in the same way that millenarianism itself is tempting, to offer a global explanation—such as climatic cycles—for its rhythms. The quest for global explanations, however, like the quest for a fountain of youth, tells more about the explorers than it does about the territory.

— HILLEL SCHWARTZ

"Imitate me as I imitate Christ."

SAINT PAUL
I CORINTHIANS II:I

MINISTRY

The term *ministry* traditionally refers to offices of leadership in the Christian church, but there has been a growing recognition that it also describes the way the mission of the whole church is conducted. Both in terms of specific offices (ministers) and in terms of the work of the church in general, ministry has biblical roots. In Hebrew, *sheret* ("to serve") applies to temple officers and was normally translated *leitourgein* in the Septuagint. This use was carried over into the New Testament, where the various linguistic forms of *leitourgein* are used not only for general acts of service to others (*Rom.* 15:27, *2 Cor.* 9:12, *Phil.* 2:30) but also for worship (*Acts* 13:3) and particularly for priestly and Levitical functions under the Old Covenant (*Lk.* 1:23; *Heb.* 8:2, 8:6, 9:21, 10:11). But the New Testament introduced the words *diakonia* ("service") and *diakonein* ("to serve"), referring to the menial work done by a *diakonos* ("servant") or *doulos* ("slave") to indicate the quality of ministry in the church. These words represent not status but the serving relationship of the minister to the one served: following the example of Christ (and, subsequently, the example of the apostle Paul) is at the heart of the Christian understanding of ministry (*Jn.* 13:1-20; *1 Cor.* 4:16, 11:1; *Phil.* 3:17).

Scholars dispute how far the New Testament reflects a uniform and obligatory pattern of ministerial orders. Roman Catholic scholars generally hold that it does, but most Protestant scholars believe that the New Testament offers several patterns of ministry (*Eph.* 4:11-12; *1 Cor.* 12:27-31; *1 Tm.* 3:1-13, 4:11-16, 5:3-10, 5:17-22). The former view maintains that the orders of ministry are fixed by tradition and that their authority is transmitted by historical succession from the apostles through bishops or the pope as the vicar of Christ (apostolic succession). The latter view regards ministerial orders as essentially functional and focused on faithful transmission of the apostolic testimony.

There is, however, agreement that all ministry traces its authority to Jesus Christ and to the apostles who testified to his saving work and resurrection (*Mt.* 16:13-24, 18:18, 28:18-20; *Jn.* 20:23). Although the apostle Paul could not claim personal connection with the Galilean ministry, he did claim commission from Jesus Christ as the heart of his own call to apostleship (*Gal.* 1:1, 1:11-24, 2:1-21). Churches also generally agree that officers in the church's ministry (i. e., the clergy) have particular responsibility for preaching, for administration of the sacraments (or ordinances), and for the oversight and nurture of their congregations.

By the beginning of the second century, three principal orders of ministry—bishop or pastor *(episcopos,* "overseer"), presbyter or priest *(presbuteros,* "elder"), and deacon *(diakonos,* "servant")—had become widely accepted, and although various confessional groups may not agree how far or when these orders became dependent on the Roman pontiff, the primacy of the pope seems to have been widely acknowledged by the time of Leo I (d. 461) and continued in the West until the Reformation. In the Eastern church the break with Rome, the Great Schism, is often given the date 1054, but scholars recognize that this was the end of a process of estrangement over centuries. However, the threefold ministry remained unchanged in both halves of Christendom through a millennium of Christian history. [*See* Priesthood *and* Papacy.]

Catholic branches of the church claim unbroken succession with this earlier history and believe that these offices are prescribed (i. e., *iure divino*) and guaranteed by apostolic succession. Ordination is a sacrament whereby the Holy Spirit is transmitted through the bishop's imposition of hands, which imparts special grace to administer the sacraments and to exercise authority in the church. In the Roman Catholic church these powers derive ultimately from the pope, while among the Orthodox it is exercised by the bishop within the corporate authority of the Orthodox community. Old Catholics and Anglo-Catholics hold a position on apostolic succession close to that of Rome but do not acknowledge the infallible authority of the papacy.

The sixteenth-century Reformation challenged the absolute authority of ecclesiastical tradition and its priesthood. Protestants turned from papal authority to the authority of the Bible, which led to revisions in their understanding of the church and its ministry. In the main, they claimed to restore the New Testament pattern, and in reaction to ecclesiastical legalism they tended to appeal to the Bible as a divine law book. New Testament "restorationism" appears in the early Luther, based on a primary appeal to scripture and on scripture exegeted by "the priesthood of all believers." Luther may be described as advocating a form of "evangelical pragmatism," since he accepted any pattern consistent with scripture that served the effective preaching of the word and the proper administration of the sacraments. Lutheranism has therefore adopted episcopal, consistorial, and congregational forms of churchmanship. [*See* Reformation.]

Attempts to restore a more biblical pattern of church and ministry are to be found in almost every form of Reformation church, and not least the Reformed church. Differences between Ulrich Zwingli (1484-1531) and the Anabaptists (Swiss Brethren) were not over the primacy of scripture but over its interpretation. John Calvin (1509-1564) systematized the Reformed position, claiming that church and ministry are of divine institution (*Institutes* 4.1, 4.3). Like many in his day, he regarded apostles, prophets, and evangelists as peculiar to the apostolic age, although he recognized that they might be revived "as the need of the times demands." Pastors and teachers, he argued, were indispensable. Pastors exercised general oversight discipline and preached and administered the sacraments; teachers were responsible for doctrine. Calvin also recognized the New Testament office of deacon in care of the poor (within which he included the office of the "widow"). He insisted on both the inward call of a minister and the recognition by the church of that call. In matters of discipline the pastor was to share power with a consistory of elders so that power would not be exclusively in the hands of a single person.

Calvin's fourfold ordering of ministry was taken over by the Reformed church and the Puritans in the British Isles and colonial America in the Presbyterian and Congregational churches. Similar forms of ministry arose out of English Separatism (e.g., Baptist churches) and the Christian Church (Disciples of Christ) movement of the American frontier. Differences between the classic Reformation positions and later restoration movements turned not so much on the appeal to the Bible as on other matters affecting scriptural interpretation: the relationship of the church to civil authorities, insistence on the church's purity, ministerial training, and how far literal appeal to scripture may be modified by the Holy Spirit revealed in scripture. Extreme restorationists reject any deviation from the New Testament pattern; at the other extreme, the Society of Friends (Quakers) claims that the spirit of the scriptures requires no specially ordained ministers.

A different modification of the church's ministry is seen in the Anglican settlement. In the sixteenth century, Henry VIII sought to separate from Rome without changing the shape of the national church, and his daughter, Elizabeth I, followed his lead. She wooed English Catholics by maintaining traditional vestments, liturgy, and forms of church government (episcopal). From the first the Church of England tried to reconcile appeal to scripture and to church tradition. Originally the settlement was based on the authority of the crown (the divine right of kings), but at the turn of the seventeenth century appeals to the divine right of the episcopacy began to appear. Differences concerning the role of the episcopacy are reflected in the so-called high church (Anglo-Catholic), broad church (Latitudinarian), and low church (Evangelical) traditions within Anglicanism. [*See* Anglicanism.]

In the eighteenth century, John Wesley, founder of Methodism, refused to separate from the Church of England. He finally became convinced that priests and bishops were of the same order in the New Testament and that he had the right to ordain ministers for America, but he refused to designate bishops and instead appointed superintendents. The decision to employ the term *bishop* in American Methodism probably arose from the determination to assert independence from Anglicanism. But although Wesley believed that the threefold order of ministry is scriptural, he offered an essentially pragmatic interpretation of these offices. His position was fundamentally the evangelical pragmatism seen in Luther. [*See* Methodist Churches.]

By the mid-1980s there was no acceptance of the ordination of women in the Roman Catholic and Orthodox branches of the church, but a growing acceptance of women into the ordained ministry of Protestant denominations and in some provinces of Anglicanism was evident. Protestant and Anglican practices stem from the theological belief that the call to ministry is open to all God's people. The ecumenical movement has also prompted many churches to reexamine earlier claims and to recognize that they have much to learn from each other. Statements on ministry prepared for the Consultation on Church Union (1984), which reflected the views of ten American Protestant denominations, and by the World Council of Churches (1982) indicate a significant and growing consensus. This consensus reveals an emphasis on the servanthood of ministry as evidenced in the ministry of Jesus; an awareness that the whole church is the proper context in which the ordained ministry should be considered; an awareness that the doctrines of church and ministry cannot be separated; and a recognition that the traditional threefold ordering of ministry should not be lightly discarded. This growing consensus shows that many Christian churches seek to manifest their essential unity and to arrive at a point where their ministries may be mutually recognized.

— ROBERT S. PAUL

Elizabeth's settlement remains the foundation of Anglicanism.

PAGE 35

Although traditionally any male Christian could aspire to become a priest or minister, in recent years many Christian denominations have begun to ordain women clergy

PAGE 538

M

MIRACLES

Miracles in the Mediterranean World

Apollonius of Tyana frequently performed miracles that included acts of healing, magical disappearances, and even raising the dead.

PAGE 267

MIRACLES

The history of religions has preserved the record of miracles, that is, events, actions, and states taken to be so unusual, extraordinary, and supernatural that the normal level of human consciousness finds them hard to accept rationally. These miracles are usually taken as manifestations of the supernatural power of the divine being fulfilling his purpose in history, but they are also caused to occur "naturally" by charismatic figures who have succeeded in controlling their consciousness through visions, dreams, or the practices of meditation.

MIRACLES IN THE MEDITERRANEAN WORLD. In archaic Greece, Pythagoras is especially noteworthy. Pythagoras was a "divine man" *(theios aner),* combining the figure of the popular miracle worker, the portrait of the philosopher, and the idealized image of the practical statesman. His image as miracle worker was enhanced by several recurring motifs: (1) Pythagoras was seen in two cities at the same time; (2) he could recall his previous existences; (3) he was endowed with the ability to stop an eagle in flight; and (4) he could predict events in the future. It is highly probable that, as Neo-Pythagoreanism gained popularity among ordinary people, the image of Pythagoras the thaumaturge was promoted by a circle of followers quite distinct from those who wished to cultivate his reputation as a philosopher and scientist.

Apollonius of Tyana described exorcisms and instances of healing the blind, the lame, and the paralytic in India (see Philostratus, *The Life of Apollonius of Tyana* 3.38-39); more important than that, he performed similar miracles himself. Apollonius reportedly performed even the miracle of raising the dead while he was in Rome (4.45).

The figure of Moses was one of the most important propaganda instruments that Jews of the Hellenistic period used in their competition with non-Jewish schools and cults. In *Deuteronomy* 34:10-12, Moses is described as the greatest prophet in Israel, known for his signs and wonders as well as for his mighty powers and great and terrible deeds.

There are many stories in late Judaism narrating how rabbis worked miracles of healing. The best known, perhaps, is the healing of the son of Yohanan ben Zakk'ai by Hanina' ben Dosa'. Both rabbis lived in Palestine around 70 CE. Hanina' ben Dosa' went to study the Torah with Yohanan ben Zakk'ai, whose son was seriously ill. Yohanan requested: "Hanina', my son, pray for mercy for him that he may live." Hanina' ben Dosa' laid his head between his knees and prayed, and then the boy was cured (B. T., *Ber.* 34).

Throughout late antiquity, Epidaurus was a holy site especially celebrated for the epiphany of Asklepios, the divine healer. According to Strabo, Asklepios was believed to "cure diseases of every kind." His temple was always full of the sick as well as containing the votive tablets on which treatments were recorded (*Geography* 8.6.15).

The Mediterranean world knew Egypt as the home of thaumaturgy, theosophy, and esoteric wisdom. There, the goddess Isis was praised for her miraculous healings; she was credited with bringing the arts of healing to men and, once she had attained immortality, taking pleasure in miraculously healing those who incubated themselves in her temple (Diodorus Siculus, *The Library of History* 1.25.2-5). At her hands the maimed were healed and the blind received their eyesight.

YOGINS, TAOIST CONTEMPLATIVES, AND YAMABUSHI. Indian ascetics practicing Yoga are well known for their miraculous powers. [*See* Yoga.]

The yogin acquires the "miraculous powers" *(siddhis)* when he has reached a particular stage of his meditational discipline called *samyama,* referring, more specifically, to the last stages of yogic technique, that is, concentration *(dharana),* meditation *(dhyana),* and samadhi. For example, by practicing *samyama* in regard to the subconscious residues *(samskaras),* the yogin knows his previous existences; this enables him to ideally relive his former existences. Some of the yogin's "miraculous powers" are even more extraordinary: he can make himself invisible by practicing *samyama* concerning the form of the body.

Taoists in ancient China are convinced that man can become an "immortal".

The practice of meditation essential for attaining immortality leads inevitably to the possession of miraculous powers. According to the *Pao-p'u-tzu,* the Taoist immortal Ko Hsüan, one of Ko Hung's paternal uncles, would stay at the bottom of a deep pond for almost a whole day in hot summer weather. This "miracle" was possible because of his mastery of "embryonic respiration": he was able to accumulate his breaths and to breathe like a fetus in its mother's womb.

Mountain ascetics in Japan known as *yamabushi* acquired magico-religious powers through a series of disciplines. The *yamabushi* was the master of heat and fire; he walked barefoot on red hot charcoals without injury; he proved his extraordinary power when, with only a white robe on his naked body, he entered a bath of boiling water and came out entirely unscathed; and he surprised his spectators by climbing a ladder of swords, the sharp edge facing upward.

MIRACLES IN FOUNDED RELIGIONS. The founders of three major religions of the world—Buddhism, Christianity, and Islam—have each taken a different attitude toward miracle.

Buddhism. The Buddha was well aware that the practice of meditation essential for attaining enlightenment leads eventually to the possession of "miraculous

power" (Skt., *siddhi;* Pali, *iddhi*). But he did not encourage his disciples to seek *siddhis.* The true task was not to acquire miraculous powers but to transcend the world of pain and suffering and to attain the state of enlightenment.

According to biographical sources, however, the Buddha was sometimes led to work miracles; for example, when he returned to his native city, Kapilavastu, for the first time after attaining enlightenment, he rose in the air, emitted flames of fire and streams of water from his body, and walked in the sky (see *Mahavastu* 3.115). According to Asvaghosa's *Buddhacarita* (19.12-13), in order to convince his relatives of his spiritual capacities and prepare them for conversion, the Buddha rose in the air, cut his body to pieces, let his head and limbs fall to the ground, and then joined them together again before the amazed eyes of the spectators. Among the eminent disciples of the Buddha, Moggallana (Skt., Maudgalyayana) was well known as the "chief of those endowed with miraculous powers."

Christianity. Jesus Christ performed the miracles of healing and exorcism. In the miracle stories that, together with his sayings and passion narratives, occupy an important place in the synoptic Gospels, Jesus of Nazareth is presented as the supreme thaumaturge, the great miracle worker, the magician.

Typically, the miracle stories of healing and exorcism in the synoptic Gospels all emphasize three motifs: (1) the history of the illness, (2) the actual process or techniques of the healing, and (3) a demonstration of the cure to the satisfaction of spectators.

Particularly interesting are the techniques that Jesus employed for healing and exorcism. There is no question that he considered prayer to be essential for working miracles (*Mk.* 9:29). But, as a thaumaturge, he had to work up his emotions; in healing a leper Jesus was moved with "anger" *(orgistheis),* stretched out his hand, and touched him (*Mk.* 1:40-45). Jesus displayed the emotional frenzy of the thaumaturge (see also *Lk.* 4:39). In the story of the deaf and mute man (*Mk.* 7:32-37), Jesus puts his fingers into his ears, spits and touches his tongue. Looking up to heaven, he sighs and says to him, "Ephphatha" ("Be opened"). In *Mk.* 8:22-26 Jesus heals a blind man by spitting on his eyes and laying his hands on them.

Especially interesting is a cycle of miracle stories in the *Gospel of Mark* (4:35-5:43) that includes the stories of the Gerasene demoniac, the woman with an issue of blood, and the daughter of Jairus. Each of these has all the characteristics of the popular miracle story, and each contributes to the impression that Jesus is a "divine man," tempting New Testament scholars to talk about the development of "divine man Christology" in the *Gospel of Mark.*

In the subsequent history of Christianity, charisma or divine gift of "power" was represented on earth by a limited number of exceptional charismatic figures, such as the martyrs of the second and third centuries, the bishops of the late third century, and, finally, the succession of great Christian saints.

Islam. Muhammad, the "seal of the prophets," rejected every request to pose as a miracle worker; in contrast to Moses and other Hebrew prophets, as well as Jesus, who all worked miracles *(mu'jizat),* Muhammad made no attempt to advance his religious authority by performing miracles, although people demanded them.

However, Muhammad is presented in the traditions *(hadiths)* as having worked miracles in public on many occasions. It was especially Sufi saints who performed miracles *(karamat).* Often called the "friends of God" *(awliya',* sg. *wali),* they worked miracles by divine grace. On the one hand, it is often said by the Sufis that saints must not seek after the gift of miracle working, which might become a serious obstacle in the path to the union with God. On the other hand, the biographies of leading Sufis abound in miracle stories that certainly have been utilized for evangelical purposes: saints traveled a long distance in a short time; walked on water and in the air; talked with such inanimate objects as stones, as well as with animals; miraculously produced food, clothing, and other necessities of life; and made predictions of future events.

— MANABU WAIDA

"I do will it. Be cured."

JESUS
MARK 1:41

MISSIONS

MISSIONARY ACTIVITY

FOUNDATIONS AND MOTIVATIONS. It is possible to venture some generalizations about missionary activity that seem relevant for all the great missionizing religions. The first point is that missionizing religions are religions that, impelled by a unique revelation or a great discovery about the nature of being, or a momentous social transformation and revitalization of purpose sparked by spiritual impulses, have generated a salvific metaphysical-moral vision that they believe to be of universal import for humanity. This vision induces a passion for transcendence that intellectually, morally, and emotionally frees its adherents from local deities and cults, from familial, tribal, clan, caste, or ethnic loyalties, from fixed political-economic conditions, and from traditional "paganisms." The missionary impulse is to become "homeless," for it finds its true home in a transcendent realm that relativizes all that is understood to be "natural." It further evokes a desire to bring about the universal

M

MISSIONS

Missionary Activity

Theravada accounts record that Asoka sponsored Buddhist missions that traveled beyond the frontiers of his considerable empire.

PAGE 664

acceptance and application of the vision, which it holds to be universally true in principle.

Every missionizing religion, thus, is by definition transcultural; where it is not entirely transmundane, it is cosmopolitan. It endows its advocates with a transcendental, ecumenical, cross-cultural, and global perspective, which understands humanity as trapped in chaotic conditions of spiritual and/or physical oppression from which humanity must be delivered by accepting a new foundation of meaning and a new discipline, one that liberates from evil and falsehood and binds to good and truth.

A missionary is one who seizes or is seized by a universalistic vision and who feels a mandate, a commission, a vocation to bring the vision and its benefits to "all." Thus, missionary activity, both domestic and foreign, is most intense in those moments when the metaphysical-moral vision of a religion is engendered or revitalized and held to be pertinent to new conditions. "Home" missions often take the form of new programs for youth, "purification" of religious and cultural practice, proselytism of marginal groups, protest against lax practices among the social elite (including the established clergy), and, often, moral or spiritual attempts to put domestic social, political, and economic policies on a new foundation. "Foreign" missions attempt to take the vision beyond the land of origin and thereby to lay the foundations for a new spiritual world order by transforming the souls and minds of individuals and the social habits of their society. Missionary activity always to some degree alienates its converts from previous belief and practice, for it introduces a different way of organizing faith and life. Both domestic and foreign missionary activity is marked by intense intellectual activity, for the whole of reality has to be reconsidered from the new perspective.

One or another universalistic vision has provided the foundations and motivations for Buddhism, Christianity, Islam, and that new secular civil religion, communism, to name but four of the most obvious missionizing religions. Certain strands and periods of Judaism, Zoroastrianism, and "syncretistic" religions such as Baha'i, Sikhism, and the Unification Church (Moonies) have a similar dynamic. A universalistic metaphysical-moral vision is less pronounced, however, in the beliefs of the tribal religions and Shinto, and less overt in many strands of Confucianism, Judaism, and Zoroastrianism. However great their spiritual, moral, and intellectual achievements, these latter religions are constitutively tied to specific sociopolitical contexts and, often, to ethnic particularities. These religions may also claim to possess a universalistic message; they may welcome converts, and their metaphysical-moral visions may be espoused by other religions; but they are spread more by the migrations of peoples or by the gradual incorporation of immediate neighbors than by organized missionary activities. Hinduism represents a special and exceedingly complex case, for while it is similar to nonmissionizing traditions in many respects, and while it seems to have spread essentially by a process called sanskritization—the gradual adoption of Vedic practices and brahmanic authority by non-Aryan peoples on the Indian subcontinent (see Srinivas, [1952] 1978)—it has had periods of vigorous missionary activity. Indeed, today, active missions are being carried out by "evangelical" forms of Hinduism such as the Rama-krishna Mission, ISKCON (Hare Krishna), and the Transcendental Meditation movement of Maharishi Mahesh Yogi.

SOME DYNAMICS OF MISSIONARY ACTIVITY. As a population is missionized, new patterns of educational, familial, cultural, and political-economic conditions are routinized into a transformed "tradition" on new foundations. The tendency to identify the universalistic message with the newly established local or regional patterns of life within particular groups is widespread. The vision "for all" once again becomes "our" vision, "for us," until such time as a new burst of piety and learning renews the awareness of the universalistic vision and revitalizes missionary efforts, demanding a purging of false tendencies to syncretism. Missionary religions are continually or episodically engaged in religious renewal and reformation from within. The great missionizing religions are in part to be contrasted with the occasionally proselytizing, primal, and localistic religions precisely by the enduring and recurring vitality of their universalizing, in contrast to the particularizing and syncretizing tendencies of the localistic religions. It is not surprising that missionary religions are those with an authoritative scripture and "orthodox" doctrine that serve as the standards for periodic renewal.

The great universalistic teachings of the missionizing religions are, however, always treasures borne in "earthen vessels," to paraphrase Paul, the model of all Christian missionaries. And the line between the treasure and the vessel is frequently extremely fine. Early Buddhist missionaries, to cite another example, were sent out presumably armed with nothing but the pure and unadulterated message of Gautama's great discovery of the secret of true enlightenment. Wittingly or not, however, they carried with them both the philosophical presuppositions of Indian religious thought, which were the terms in which and through which the Buddha found his truth, and the political, social, and cultural patterns of Indian society. Theravada Buddhism, as it missionized in Sri Lanka, Burma, and Thailand, brought with it sociopolitical principles that derived from Hindu traditions and which, in part, the Buddha sought to overcome and transcend. (See

Smith, 1978.) In Mahayana Buddhism as well, careful scholars can speak of the "Indianization of China." (See Hu, 1937.)

Later, when this stream of Buddhism became wedded to motifs from Confucian and Taoist sources, its movement into Korea and Japan carried powerful elements from these traditions with it. And it is well known that both Christianity and Islam carried Greco-Roman patterns of thought, medicine, and political theory—as well as Hebraic understandings of ethical monotheism—with them as they expanded in the medieval periods. Islam has also always borne a certain Arabic cultural stamp wherever it goes, and communism today bears everywhere the marks of Germanic philosophy, Enlightenment social theory, Western technological hopes from the days of the industrial revolution, and often something of Soviet nationalism. Along with the Gospel, modern Christian missions transmit Western definitions of human rights and scientific methods in the fields of education, technology, management, and agriculture.

MISSIONS AND CULTURAL IMPERIALISM. Two factors differentiate missionary expansion from cultural imperialism. First, the truly religious missionary recognizes a distinction between the message and the accoutrements, the universalistic kernel and the incidental husk. However difficult it is to distinguish the two, the primary concern is with the former. Transformation of the latter is allowed in terms of and for the sake of the former. The imperialist understands the message only in terms of its sociocultural trappings in highly particularist ways. Such imperialism obtains when, for example, Buddhism in Burma becomes identical with the prerogatives of the Burman as opposed to those of the Chin, Kachin, or other Burmese peoples; when Christianity becomes German in the Nazi period or Afrikaner in South Africa; when Islam in, for instance, Iran, is understood to be coterminous with the fate of the country itself; or when communism is thought to be identical with "socialism in one country" and allied with a personality cult. These domestic forms of cultural imperialism have had their vicious international corollaries wherever particular social traditions, political expansions, or opportunities for economic exploitation are confused with a universalistic religious message and spread by coercive means among colonialized peoples abroad in the name of religion.

Second, missionary activity is rooted in the fundamental assumptions that, once people are exposed to "the truth" that has been proclaimed, they will choose this truth and that they ought to be free to encounter and choose even "foreign" truth. Missions presuppose that a truly universalistic vision is convincing to the mind and compelling to the will. Missions thus require, or provoke, a situation in which some degree of freedom of thought, speech, and religious organization is allowed, where the will and the mind can be exercised in accordance with conscience and conviction. However much missionary activity has been carried out hand in hand with military power, economic opportunism, "brainwashing," and forced conversion, there has been and remains in principle a sharp tension between missionary efforts and imperialistic imposition of religion by force, or "mind-control," a fact increasingly documented by missiologists examining the relative validity of the charge that missions are but the ideological instrument of colonial practice. Those incapable of imagining the transformation of values, attitudes, and habits in conversion to a new truth, however, always attribute the change to nefarious forces.

It is certainly true that every missionizing religion has had periods during which something like the classic Islamic pattern could be documented: H. A. R. Gibb writes of Islam that "while the faith itself was not spread by the sword, it was under the wing of Muslim dominance that its missionaries found most favorable conditions for their activities of conversion. This view of Islam . . . was universally held by its adherents; the theologians found justification for it in the Koran, the jurists made it the basis of their expositions of Muslim law, and the mass of the people accepted it as a self-evident fact" (Gibb, 1932, p. 56; cf. Bulliet, 1979).

REACTIONS OF MISSIONIZED PEOPLE. Every missionary religion must be received as well as proclaimed. Where it is not received, missionary activity dies out, and doubt about the universality of the originating vision sets in. Where it is received under coercion, and not in the heart, mind, or customs of the people, the indigenous religion goes underground, eventually resurfacing as a revitalized indigenous religion and rallying point to overthrow those who hold power or as a heterodox or heretical religion in contention with the one brought by missions. Where the missionary religion is received in the heart and mind, newly converted people soon send out their own missionaries. But it is almost never received as given. It is filtered through the philosophical, sociopolitical, and historical perspectives of the recipients. Thereby, it is inevitably modified by its reception and, over time, at least partially purged of those missionary-borne incidental elements that can be seen as "merely" cultural or sociopolitical.

One of the most fascinating studies of the reception of a religion is the study by Kenneth Ch'en (1973) of the way in which Buddhism was modified, acculturated, and indigenized in China. A message, such as that exported from Indian Buddhism, that called for the breaking of family ties and demanded that kings give honor to monks simply did not make sense in a culture

Zealous Muslim missionaries spread Islam through the interior regions of East and Central Java.

PAGE 387

where filial piety and homage to the emperor were absolutely central to both belief and social order. Ch'en demonstrates that, as one speaks of the "indianization of China" with the spread of Buddhism, one must also speak of the "sinicization of Buddhism." In China key Buddhist texts were given fresh interpretation; apologetic literature, new poems, and new laws and regulations were promulgated that modified and, indeed, transformed aspects of the Buddhist message so that it could graft onto, and in some ways revitalize, dimensions of the indigenous folk religions and of the Confucianism and Taoism of that land. Comparable stories can be told of every missionizing religion: the Christianity of Eastern Orthodoxy in Greece is not the same as that of the Kimbanguists of central Africa; the Islam of Tunisia differs from that of Mindanao in significant ways; Communism in Moscow is distinct from that of "Euro-communism" or that of Marxist-inspired movements in Central America. Today, the degree to which this "contextualization" or indigenization is valid is the subject of heated debate within many of the great world religions.

In this connection, it must be noted that some religions engage in missionary activity precisely as a result of being invited, sought, or adopted with great eagerness. Robin Horton (1975) has shown, for example, that in Africa where traditional systems have been displaced by exploitative cultural contact, war, crop failure, or the failure of a social system to survive its own internal strains, missionary groups bearing universalistic messages are readily embraced, for they offer fresh symbolic and cognitive models by which life and its perplexities may be interpreted. Often, the appropriation of a new religion is accompanied by a rational quest for new technological, educational, and sociopolitical frameworks for organizing the common life. Missionaries often agree that such a quest is at the core of their metaphysical-moral vision. Certainly a comparable phenomenon has occurred in quite different locales, as Garrett (1982) has shown in regard to the Pacific Islands, and Downs (1983) has demonstrated concerning the christianization of tribal peoples of Assam in the last century. More ancient examples are the historic reception in the sixth and seventh centuries of Chinese Buddhism into Japan at the hands of the imperial court (along with Confucian ideals of a well-organized society); the reception in the ninth to eleventh centuries of Eastern Orthodox Christianity into Russia, bringing with it Byzantine art, literature, and political theory; and the reception in the twelfth to fifteenth centuries of Islam (as mediated through India) in the Malay archipelago, accom-

MISSIONS, MERCHANTS, AND SOLDIERS

Cross-cultural Traders

The earliest, unofficial missionaries are, more often than not, traders. One does not have to accept the Marxist interpretation of the relationship between commercial exploitation and religion to observe that, indeed, the spreading of a new religious insight repeatedly follows commercial traffic lanes and that this insight is frequently borne by merchants. Further, it must be noted that both commercial and missionary activities can only be conducted in conditions of relative peace and political stability. Such conditions often obtain, and when they do not, soldiers are frequently brought in to establish them, accompanied by new waves of missionaries. Since traders and soldiers vary widely in their behavior, from the simply marauding to the relatively benevolent, missionary activity has often been conducted within a network of shifting alliances, both economic and military, on the far end of trade routes. It is not possible to make any single generalization about these relationships, however, for missionaries have resisted exploitative trade as often as they have endorsed it and have fought imperial military "pacification" as often as they have embraced it. (See, e.g., Christensen and Hutchison, 1982; cf. Reed, 1983.)

The cross-cultural frequency of missionary activity by merchants, however, invites speculation as to why this general class has played so significant a role in missionizing. Perhaps it is because merchants are people who seek increased opportunity by taking the risk of leaving the settled and accepted patterns of life at home. The very act of engaging in trade on a cross-cultural basis, haowever crass the individual motivation might be, requires a somewhat more cosmopolitan perspective on the world than is frequently present in those societies where religion and morality run in channels circumscribed by fixed economic roles and duties for people of each specific ethnic, gender, age and class status. In addition, those societies that send merchants farthest and equip caravans or ships the most extensively for trade are usually the more highly developed economically, politically, militarily, and socially. It would not be strange for them to hold the view that their "superiority" in this respect is due in substantial part at least to the "superior" religious, spiritual, and ethical foundations of their faith.

—MAX L. STACKHOUSE

panied by aspects of mysticism and caste-related political order.

In almost no instance, however, is a new religion received without some resistance. This resistance is sometimes easily overcome. When the indigenous faith is a highly literate and complex religion, however, the resistance is usually prolonged and powerful. The fact that Buddhism originated in India and at one time had nearly swept the subcontinent, but now can scarcely be found there, is one of the dramatic examples of this resistance. Hinduism reasserted itself by a ten-century-long process involving the adoption of some aspects of Buddhism (especially the revitalization of devotional practice in *bhakti*), by the bloody slaughter of Buddhist monks, by extensive philosophical argumentation, and by out-organizing and out-teaching Buddhism among the people. Similarly, Confucianism reasserted itself in China during the "neo-Confucian" period of renewal in the ninth century by a similar process—one that relegated the Buddhists to a somewhat inferior status. Islam encountered intellectual and military resistance when it threatened expansion into Europe from the time of Charlemagne through the Crusades, and the Christianity that expanded into western Asia is now weak and scattered because of Islamic resistance. And most Western Jews and Christians today resist the Hindu, Islamic, and Buddhist missions, as well as the host of hybrid or syncretistic cults rooted in these, or in some heterodox Christian faith, that are to be found in most of the major cities of the West today. (See Needleman and Baker, 1978; Barker, 1981.)

TYPES OF MISSIONARIES. In surveying mission and missionary activity, however, one must not only note the primacy of the metaphysical-moral vision—its relationship to social and cultural patterns, its patterns of reception, and resistances to it—one must also consider certain similarities of institutional form that are characteristic of missionary activity. What groups or classes of people undertake missionary activity, and how do they organize to do so?

New religions are seldom, if ever, however, fully developed in a new location by the sometimes quite unholy alliance of missionaries, merchants, and soldiers, or by general processes of cultural diffusion that accompany them. The introduction of a religion through commercial channels (the character and quality of which influence reception and/or resistance) has everywhere been succeeded by the arrival of professional missionaries. For most religions throughout most of history, the professional missionary has been monastic, that is, organized into ascetic, trained, and disciplined religious orders intentionally "homeless" for the sake of the metaphysical-moral vision held to be universally true.

Missionary monks and nuns attempt to spread their religious convictions by public proclamation and commentary on sacred texts at both popular and learned levels; by teaching hymns, chants, and prayers; by establishing new centers of worship where the truth they know can be celebrated; and by service—that is, by medical, educational, pastoral, and social relief and social advocacy. Needless to say, all missionary religions have relied on "wondrous," magical, or technological demonstrations of "spiritual" power from time to time. The stories well known in the West about saintly missionary monks such as Patrick, Columba, Boniface, Ramón Lull, and Francis Xavier are paralleled in the lore of Buddhism, in the formation of the *mathas* as a Hindu reaction to the challenge posed by Buddhism, and in the roles played by the "schools" of jurists and even more by the Sufi orders of Islam. (In Eastern Europe, accounts of the "dedicated heroes, martyrs, and organizers" of communist proletarian movements are written for children and young people.)

One of the definitions of "faith" is "credo" (which is the Latin for "I believe").

PAGE 224

To carry out their tasks, missionaries have four requirements. First, they must have a dedication, a commitment, a piety, if you will, linked to learning. Missionaries must be able to articulate the faith and to interpret it in intellectual and cultural terms that are foreign to them. They must be able to understand and put into perspective whatever they encounter in the course of their work. It is no accident that several sciences, including modern comparative linguistics and anthropology, to a large extent have their roots in missionary activity. Everywhere, professional missionaries are given to literary activity; they have published apologetics, propaganda, tracts, commentaries, and they are responsible for the composition and dissemination of poetry, song, and history. (See Kopf, 1969.)

Second, missionary professionals require a reliable institutional foundation, a polity, to sustain them. Missionary orders and societies are surely among the world's first transnational, nonprofit corporations. These polities, however, are ever subject to incorporation into the existing polities of the host countries. Thus, the Buddhist *samgha*, spread under the protectorate of kings, is ever tempted to become simply an instrument of state. Converted Christian communities in India are always in peril of becoming more a subcaste than a church; and the *tariqahs* of Islam tend to become simply trade guilds or sanctified tribal brotherhoods. (See Trimingham, 1971.)

Economic support may derive from state funds, charitable bequests, the establishment of plantations, handicraft manufacturing centers, agricultural communes, and religious taxes. The economic ties of a missionary enterprise with its country of origin or with the elites of the host country are the source of enormous distrust of missionary activity. (See Reed, 1983.)

And fourth, missionaries must have a clear policy,

one that coordinates strategies and tactics and prevents divergent teachings from confusing potential converts. These policies must cover such matters as how much of the indigenous culture to allow and what to disallow, how to deal with marriage practices, "pagan" festivals, various "fraternities" that are marginally stamped with traditional religious practices, and the like.

MODERN PRACTICES. Modern missionary efforts have been pursued not so much by monastic orders (although these orders continue to missionize around the world) as by nonmonastic missionary "societies." This situation is prompted primarily by the rather unique developments of "free-church" Protestant polities, economic support systems, and policies. While the established churches in Europe had been sending out monastic missionaries for centuries, and the Moravians anticipated later developments, the formation of the London Missionary Society in 1795 inaugurated a new form of paraecclesial organization that continues to this day and is now being emulated by non-Christian missionaries. Missionary societies, of which there are now hundreds, raise funds by free-will contributions and form nonmonastic "voluntary associations" staffed by a combination of nonparochial clergy, lay professionals, and volunteers, not only to save souls from "paganism" but to sweep away superstition and oppression, to offer agricultural, technical, medical, and educational assistance, and to engender a desire for democratic institutions, human dignity, self-sufficiency, and social liberation. Some modern theorists, indeed, suggest that these efforts at social service and social change are the very core of missionizing. (See Dunn, 1980; Yuzon, 1983.)

"Go monks, preach the noble Doctrine."

BUDDHA

A notable example of the side effects of this recent pattern can be illustrated by reference to the Young Men's Christian Association. Formed in England in 1844 as a part of a "home mission" voluntary association for youth flocking to the cities to get jobs in factories, and attempting to provide a wholesome place where young men could find physical, mental, social, and spiritual benefit on a biblical foundation, the movement spread to North America and to most of the countries around the world where missions were active. It was often the agent of evangelization and the womb of efforts at social change by young men who came under its influence. Other religions responded by forming counterorganizations on a comparable basis. Today, one can find not only the YMCA but the Young Men's Buddhist Association, the Young Men's Hebrew Association, and the Young Men's Muslim Association, as well as youth hostels for Hindus and for communists, scattered throughout much of Asia; some also are to be found in Africa and South America.

Today, the great Asian religions are not at their peak in terms of missionary activity, although Buddhist and Islamic groups in Southeast Asia have formed a few missionary centers to repropagate the faith in the People's Republic of China, now that the doors of trade and travel are partially open again. Christianity, Islam, and communism are very active, with the latter two having the closest ties to the spread of political control and Christianity again moving along channels established by international commerce. All continue to make major gains in areas where none of the great missionizing religions has established a sustained foothold, with more modest, but significant, gains among "overseas" peoples of Hindu or Confucian background—the Indians of Malaysia and the Chinese of Indonesia, for example.

Increasingly, the great missionizing religions are confronting not only adherents of primal or folk religions but one another. Thus far, missionary efforts to convert adherents of the other great missionary religions have been only marginally successful. This is in part because severe restrictions on missionary activities by other faiths are frequent in Islamic and communist lands.

Although some theorists have argued that these religions are moving toward a great synthesis of world faiths (an essentially Hindu argument), and while others have attempted to find the common moral and symbolic patterns present in all human religions as the clue to their hidden unity (a humanist argument), the way in which these religions will deal with one another in the future is not at all certain. (See Oxtoby, 1983.) None of the great missionary faiths can be satisfied with relativism, the view that what is ultimately true for some is not true for others. The main possibilities are, thus, direct confrontation (with each backed by the political, military, and economic power of the regions where they are predominant), dialogic exchange of perspective in a common quest for transcultural religious truth, and/or openness to redoubled efforts to mutual conversion by allowing free and open debate among the peoples of the world.

— MAX L. STACKHOUSE

BUDDHIST MISSIONS

According to an ancient tradition, the Buddha himself sent out the first group of disciples to spread the new faith: "Go, monks, preach the noble Doctrine, . . . let not two of you go into the same direction!" This canonical saying illustrates both the missionary ideal that has inspired Buddhism from the earliest times and the way in which it was to be carried out: not by any large-scale planned missionary movement, but rather by the individual efforts of itinerant monks and preachers. And this, in fact, is our general impression of the way in which Buddhism grew from a minor monastic movement in northern India in the fifth century BCE into a world religion covering, at its heyday, a territory that reached from Sri Lanka to Mongolia, and from Iran to Japan. Apart from the missionary ideal and the prescribed inherent mobility of the clergy, its dissemination outside its homeland was no doubt facilitated by three other features of Buddhism. In the first place, the members of the order, "who had gone into the homeless state" and thereby rejected all worldly distinctions, stood outside the caste system. Unlike brahman priests, they were free to associate with people of every description, including foreigners, without fear of ritual pollution. Second, Buddhism, especially Mahayana Buddhism, had a liberal attitude toward all religions. Thus it easily accepted non-Buddhist creeds as preliminary and partial revelations of truth, a tendency toward adaptation and syncretism that also appears in its readiness to incorporate non-Buddhist deities into its pantheon. Third, the scriptural tradition of Buddhism—unlike that of Brahmanism—is not associated with any sacred or canonical language, so that its holy texts could freely be translated into any language. In fact, especially in China, the most prominent foreign missionaries were all active as translators, usually with the help of bilingual collaborators.

THE PATTERN OF DIFFUSION. The general picture of the spread of Buddhism is one of gradual dissemination at grassroots level, inspired by the Buddha's exhortation and carried out by wandering monks who preached "for the benefit of all beings" (an ideal that became even more explicit in Mahayana Buddhism) and who established monastic centers in the new territories they entered. As the clergy was wholly dependent on the contributions of lay believers, these monastic settlements *(viharas)* tended to be established near the larger cities and to branch out along the major highways that connected them. The spread of Buddhism was also closely related to the development of long-distance trade: it was carried all over Asia by monks who attached themselves to trade caravans and merchant vessels. To some extent, it was also carried by the pilgrims and students who came to India to visit the holy places, to collect texts, and to study under Indian masters.

HISTORY OF DIFFUSION FROM INDIA. This pattern of diffusion accounts for the slow pace of the process, for it took Buddhism some twenty centuries to spread over Asia, from its first propagation in the Ganges basin about 400 BCE to its last major conquest, the conversion of the Mongols in the sixteenth century. By the third century BCE it had spread over India and into Sri Lanka. Under the Kushan rulers in the northwest, in the first and second centuries CE, it reached Parthia (modern-day Iran) and the region of Bukhara and Samarkand. About the same time it was propagated via the oasis kingdoms of Central Asia to China, where it is attested for the first time in 65 CE. The earliest known missionaries and translators (Parthians, Kushans, Sogdians, and Indians) arrived at the Chinese capital Lo-yang in the middle of the second century CE by the transcontinental Silk Road, the main artery of trade between the Chinese Han empire and the Roman orient. Just as Buddhism was carried to China by caravan trade, the development of Indian seaborne trade to the coastal regions of Southeast Asia from the second century CE onward provided the channel through which it started to expand in that direction. From the second to the fifth centuries, commercial contacts and the diffusion of Indian culture led to the rise of several more or less Indianized kingdoms in which Buddhism flourished: the Thaton region in southern Burma; the kingdom of Funan with its center on the lower Mekong; that of Champa in southeastern Vietnam; the Malay Peninsula; and the Indonesian archipelago, where Palembang on Sumatra was already an important Buddhist center by 400 CE.

SECONDARY CENTERS OF DIFFUSION: CHINA AND TIBET. By 600 CE, when China after centuries of disunity had been reunited under the Sui and T'ang dynasties (589-906 CE), Buddhism in many forms had become a major religion in all parts of China and an important element in the cultural life of all social strata. China had thereby become a secondary center of diffusion, from which Buddhism was spread to Korea, Japan, and northern Vietnam. In all these regions, various types of Chinese Buddhism were introduced as part of a general process of the sinicization of these regions. In the fifth century Buddhism reached Korea and became popular among the ruling elite. The transplantation of Chinese Buddhist sects and schools went on throughout Korean history. From Korea, Buddhism reached Japan about the middle of the sixth century, but the real influx of Chinese-type Buddhism into the emerging island empire began in the early seventh century, when the Japanese court embarked on its remarkable program of massive borrowing of Chinese culture and institutions. Between 625 and 847, all early schools of T'ang Buddhism were transplanted to Japan through the deliberate efforts of prominent scholarly monks, most of whom were sent to China as members of "cultural embassies" from the Japanese court. Much later, in the twelfth century, other Chinese schools—notably the devotional cult of the Buddha Amitabha (Ching-t'u, Pure Land Buddhism, known in Japan as Jodo) and the Ch'an (Jpn., Zen) or Meditation sect—were introduced. To the present day, Japan has remained the stronghold of Buddhism in countless varieties.

The last wave of expansion is associated with the propagation of Buddhism in Tibet and Mongolia,

Once outside its country of origin, the propagation of Buddhism assumed the character of long-distance diffusion in various directions.

PAGE 106

where it eventually developed into the mainly Tantric creed known as Lamaism. Buddhism penetrated the Tibetan kingdom around 650 CE, but became dominant only in the eleventh century. It was from Tibet that Lamaism finally spread to the nomads of the Mongolian steppe in the sixteenth century.

PILGRIMAGE AND STUDY IN INDIA AND CHINA. The diffusion of Buddhism from India was for centuries accompanied by a reverse process: the steady flow of pilgrims and scholars to India. Apart from the many inscriptions that they left, the process is documented mainly by the invaluable travelogues of Chinese pilgrims: Fa-hsien, who left China in 399 and spent six years in India; Hui-sheng, who visited northwestern India in 518-522; I-ching, who spent twenty-four years (671-695) in India and Southeast Asia, and above all, the great scholar Hsüan-tsang (c. 596-664), who left a detailed description of his stupendous journey (621-645) in his *Hsi-yü chi* (Record of the Western Regions). India was the holy land of Buddhism, and the desire to make a pilgrimage certainly played a role in the decision of these travelers to undertake their journeys. It should be stressed, however, that the travelers were at least as much motivated by scholastic as by religious considerations: to collect texts, and to study the Doctrine at Indian centers of learning such as Pataliputra (modern Patna) and Nalanda. They knew what they were looking for, and they came back loaded with canonical and scholastic texts that they later translated.

"Blessed are they which are persecuted for righteousness sake: theirs is the kingdom of heaven."

MATTHEW 5:10

But as we have seen, in T'ang times China itself became a center of diffusion and there the pattern was repeated by countless Korean and Japanese monks who came to China to collect Chinese Buddhist texts and to study Buddhism in its vastly modified Chinese forms. After their return from China, some of these monks became prominent "Masters of the Doctrine" whose names are linked with the most influential trends in Japanese Buddhism. Saicho introduced the Tendai (Chin., T'ien-t'ai) sect in 804; two years later, Kukai brought Esoteric (Tantric) Buddhism to Japan; and Ennin, apart from his fame as a transmitter of the Doctrine, left an extensive diary of his nine-year stay on the continent (838-849), a diary that presents a fascinating panorama of Buddhist life in T'ang China.

For centuries, India continued to draw pilgrims and students from all over the Buddhist world; the flow came to an end only with the decline of Buddhism in India itself and, finally, with the destruction of the holy places by the Muslim invasions of around 1200. However, Chinese inscriptions found at Bodh Gaya do show that as late as the eleventh century some Chinese pilgrims still followed the examples of Fa-hsien and Hsüan-tsang. For the next seven centuries, Buddhism was nonexistent in its country of origin, to the extent that its holy places became completely forgotten and had to be rediscovered by modern archaeologists. However, as the result of the (still rather modest) revival of Buddhism in India in the twentieth century, pilgrimage has been resumed and is growing steadily.

[*For a fuller account of the dissemination and propagation of Buddhism outside of India, see* Buddhism.]

— ERIK ZÜRCHER

CHRISTIAN MISSIONS

THE EARLY FOLLOWERS OF JESUS. The earliest followers of Jesus seem to have understood the universal dimension of their faith as the fulfillment of Old Testament prophecy (Isaiah, Zechariah), according to which all nations would come up to Jerusalem to receive the law of the Lord in the form of the new covenant in Jesus. Two new factors reversed this original Christian understanding. The first was persecution, which led to many Christians being dispersed from Jerusalem. The second was the adventurous spirit of certain Greek-speaking Jews who crossed over a well-marked boundary and in Antioch began to proclaim the gospel to non-Jews, apparently with considerable success. This new Christian perspective was rationalized by Saul of Tarsus, also called Paul, who, believing that he had received a commission as apostle of the gentiles, worked out a master plan for establishing Christian groups in all the main centers of the Greco-Roman world. He looked to Rome, and beyond that even to Spain, the western limit of the Mediterranean world.

So great a project was far beyond the strength of one man, but the impulse given by Paul never died. The Christian proclamation was carried out almost entirely anonymously; indeed, the names of the founders of the great churches of the Roman empire remain for the most part unrecorded. Yet this early work had surprisingly rapid success. Within a century of the death of the founder, churches came into existence in many parts of Asia Minor, in Greece, in Italy, in Egypt, almost certainly in France and Spain, and perhaps even as far away as India. To this day, the Thomas Christians in Kerala claim that their church was founded by the apostle Thomas in person.

Whence this rapid success? By around AD 100, many more Jews lived outside Palestine than within its borders. The strict monotheism of the Jewish faith, and the high moral standards inculcated by their law, had attracted many to at least a partial acceptance of the Jewish faith, and this served for some as a preparation for the Christian gospel. In that hard and often cruel world, a fellowship of people who really loved one another and cared for one another's needs clearly had attractive power. The fervent expectations of the

Christians, both for the world and for the individual, must have come as a message of hope to those who had none. Jesus became known as the Savior of the world.

PERSECUTION AND STABILIZATION. The persecutions to which the early Christians were periodically exposed seem to have done little to hinder the advance of their faith. Not all Christians were being persecuted all the time, and the number of martyrs was greatly exaggerated in tradition. To be sure, there were signs of hysteria among the faithful, and some failed to stand fast. But persecution often undermined its own purpose because the courage, dignity, and charity shown by martyrs often won the allegiance and admiration of some who might otherwise have remained indifferent.

The great change in the Christian situation came in 313 when Constantine made Christianity the religion of the empire at a time when its followers cannot have numbered more than about 10 percent of the population. From that time on, the resemblance between Christianity and the other missionary religions has been startlingly close. From the time of Asoka in India (third century BC) to Sri Lanka and Thailand in 1983, Buddhism has always maintained close relations with the ruling powers. In all Muslim countries, and in all those which have come under Marxist domination, the identification of the state with religion or ideology has been undisguised and taken for granted. But since Christians claim to be followers of the Prince of Peace, close connections between interests of state and interests of religion have proved a burden and an embarrassment rather than a help. Justinian, who reigned from 527 to 565, seems to have been the first Roman emperor to accept coercion as a legitimate instrument of conversion to Christianity.

By the year 600, the Mediterranean world was almost entirely Christian, with outliers among the Goths, in the approaches to Inner Asia, in Ethiopia, and in what is now Sudan. At the end of the century, Gregory the Great (540-604) saw the importance of the world which lay north of the Alps and which was yet to be converted. Hence the pope's mission to the Angles in Kent. This was the first mission of the church to be officially organized; it paved the way for the central control over the missions which Rome exercised for many centuries.

A LONG PERIOD OF UNCERTAINTY. In the year 600, it might have seemed that the gospel was destined to carry all before it. Then suddenly everything went into reverse. In 610 an obscure prophet named Muhammad began to preach a new faith to the tribes of Arabia. By the time of his death he had given to these tribes unity, a simple demanding creed, and a sense of destiny. Only a century later, the Muslim armies were at Tours, in the very heart of France, and were repelled only by the vigor and military skill of Charles Martel (685-741). By that time the Christian churches had almost disappeared in Palestine, Syria, and Egypt, and were gravely threatened in Persia, North Africa, and large parts of Asia Minor. In 1453, the Turks succeeded in capturing Constantinople and destroying the Eastern Empire, which for a thousand years had been the bulwark of the Christian world. Many causes have been adduced for the disappearance of so many churches. Military weakness was no doubt one, but there were others as well: dissensions among Christians, the rise of national feeling in Egypt and elsewhere, and the superficiality of conversion in such areas as North Africa, where the church had failed to express Christian truth in the languages of the local people.

In this period, the wisdom of Gregory was vindicated. During the centuries between 632 and 1232, the Christian faith spread west, north, and east until the conversion of Europe was complete. There was a dark side to this advance. When at the end of the eighth century Charlemagne succeeded in conquering the long-refractory Saxons, he agreed to spare their lives on the condition that they accept baptism. It was only one of many regions in which cross and sword went together. In Scandinavia, conversion proceeded more easily. In many areas the ruler was the first to accept the faith, and this brought about a quiet revolution. Iceland seems to have been unique in accepting the faith (around AD 1000) by genuinely democratic methods. With the conversion of Jagiello (1383), king of the Lithuanians, conversion seems to have reached its natural term.

Monks and nuns played a creative part in the building of churches. In the remote places where they settled they introduced better methods of agriculture and new crops. They laid the foundations of literature in the languages of Europe. They gave to isolated peoples a sense of belonging to one great unity: the catholic church. Out of these beginnings grew the splendid cultures of medieval Europe.

Missionary activity sometimes took on the form of conflict between the old and the new. Such actions as Boniface's felling the oak of Thor at Geismar must not be misinterpreted as mere missionary vandalism. The people of that time believed that the powerful spirit who inhabited the oak would be able to take condign vengeance on any intruder, thus they expected Boniface to fall dead upon the spot. When he survived, they concluded that the god whom he preached was more powerful than their own.

The Eastern church, with its base in Constantinople, beginning with the conversion in 988 of Vladimir, grand duke of Kiev, created the great Slavonic cultures, the Christian origins of which are not disputed even by

The powerful Irish Christianity that shaped the civilization of northern Europe may be regarded as the direct descendant of the Coptic church.

PAGE 192

Marxist opponents of religion. These cultures survived the fall of Constantinople. During the fifteenth century, the faith was received by more remote peoples to the east and north, a process that continued until by the end of the nineteenth century it had reached the shores of the Pacific Ocean.

With the great Franciscan and Dominican movements of the thirteenth century, the missionary enterprise of the Western church looked beyond the limits of Europe; the "friars travelling abroad in the service of Christ" reached strange lands far afield. One of their most remarkable achievements was the creation of an archbishopric in Peking; the first archbishop to fill the post, John of Monte Corvino, lived there from 1294 to 1328, greatly respected by all. But the church's hope of converting the Inner Asian peoples was frustrated by the Muslims' success in winning them to the Islamic faith. The lines of communication with Inner Asia were too tenuous, however, and in the fifteenth century the mission to China faded away. For the moment Christian expansion seemed to be at an end.

The growth of Catholicism in Korea was later eclipsed by the successes of Protestant. missionaries.

PAGE 421

THE COLONIAL PERIOD. The last decade of the fifteenth century saw the discovery of America by Columbus in 1492 and the opening up of the sea route to India by Vasco da Gama in 1498. These two events changed the relationships between the nations of the world and in time gravely affected the presentation of the Christian gospel to the non-Christian world.

Roman Catholic monopoly. For two centuries the greater part of the missionary enterprise of the Western church was in the hands of the Portuguese, who, following the precedent of Muslim evangelism in Europe, expected their converts to accept Portuguese names, manners, and customs. There was, however, never total adoption of this principle. By the end of the sixteenth century, the Portuguese had on their hands three considerable blocks of Indian Christianity. In those possessions which they directly controlled, the process of Europeanization was almost complete. The Thomas Christians in Kerala and the Parava converts on the coast of Coromandel, on the other hand, declared and maintained their intention to be and to remain Indian Christians, a stance from which they have not departed in four centuries.

Moreover, in these years two notable attempts were made to adapt Christian thought to the ideas and ways of Asia. The Italian Matteo Ricci in 1601 succeeded in reaching Peking. He and his Jesuit colleagues, by mastering the Chinese language, winning the favor of the emperor and other leaders by their skill in astronomy and other sciences, and by adapting Christian faith to Chinese ideas, were able to maintain their mission, albeit with varying fortunes, through nearly three centuries. In southern India another Italian, Roberto de Nobili, learned Tamil and Sanskrit, and in order to win

INTERNATIONAL MISSION WORK

Strains Arise in Church-Colonizer Relations

The Lutherans sent their first missionaries to India in 1706. In 1794 the English Baptists, represented by their great pioneer William Carey and his colleagues, set up their work in Bengal. Thus the enormous resources of the English-speaking world, followed by those of the Dutch, the Swiss, and Scandinavians, were let loose throughout the world.

From this time on, relations between the Western governments and Christian missionary forces became unimaginably complicated. On the whole, the British maintained an attitude of lofty neutrality toward missionary activity, modified by the personal interest of a number of Christian government officials. But as government financial aid became available for educational and medical programs and for other forms of service, the Christian missionaries in the forefront of such enterprises profited greatly, perhaps excessively, from the provision of such aid. On the other hand, in British India the Indian rulers prohibited all Christian propaganda in their areas; religious freedom in India was proclaimed not by the British but by the government of independent India after 1947. In northern Nigeria, the British clearly favored Islam at the expense of Christianity.

In German, Dutch, and Belgian colonies, the association of governments with missions was undesirably close. In China, because of Napoleon III's decision that all missionaries, of whatever nationality, must be in possession of French passports, Roman Catholic missions were inevitably stigmatized as dangerous and foreign. By contrast, Hudson Taylor, the director of the largest Protestant mission, instructed his missionaries that in case of trouble they were to turn not to consular authorities but to the local representatives of the Chinese governments.

A new factor emerged when the Japanese government showed itself as the great colonial power in the East. American missionaries in Korea sympathized deeply with Korean national aspirations and were opposed, though quietly and discreetly, to Japanese colonial enterprise.

—STEPHEN C. NEILL

over the brahmans turned himself into a brahman, and not without success. Unfortunately, in 1744 Rome condemned all such efforts at adaptation, thereby sterilizing the Roman mission for the next two hundred years.

— STEPHEN C. NEILL

Varieties of missionary enterprise. Over two centuries there has been significant diversification of missionary enterprise, including the activities of women missionaries, which indeed have been far more numerous and diverse than those of men. Almost every conceivable means of communication has been employed. Education, on the basis of the Christian conviction that all truth and all knowledge are from God, has been emphasized. Together with this priority has gone the widespread distribution of Christian literature in countless languages. Medical and social services were conceived and have been rendered by Christians, not as propaganda but as manifestations of the universal love of Christ, and they were perceived as such by many who were served. Public lectures to interested non-Christians have in many areas left deep impressions on the minds of the hearers, though debates between the adherents of different religious systems have tended more to exacerbation than to conviction. Preaching in the open air in villages and public places has made many hearers aware of the existence of alternative systems of belief. Quiet study groups, under the guidance of sympathetic Christians, have helped to clarify questions about Christian belief. Where no open propaganda has been permitted, the mere presence of loving Christians as neighbors has proved remarkably effective as witness to the faith.

The nature of conversion. No full and scientific study of the process of conversion in the non-Christian world has as yet been written. Undoubtedly in a number of cases the desire for social advancement and a better manner of life has played a powerful part. But is this a blameworthy motive in the case of those who have been subjected for centuries to ruthless oppression reinforced by religious sanction? For many in the twentieth century, as in the first, the gospel comes with promise of deliverance from the power of evil forces which are believed at all times to threaten and beleaguer the well-being of humans. For some, the gospel represents an immense simplification of religion. It has been stated that in India more people have been converted to Christianity by reading the first three chapters of Genesis than in any other way, for the majestic simplicity of these chapters appeals deeply to those perplexed by the complexity of Hindu mythology. Other converts, oppressed by the burden of sin, are drawn by the promise of forgiveness in Christ, so different from the inexorable law of *karman* in Hinduism. Others, conscious of moral infirmity, have come to believe that Christ can offer the inner rehabilitation which they feel they need. Yet others have been impressed by the intensity of mutual love manifest in the society of Christian believers. Varied as the process may be, in all there is a central unity. Christ himself stands at the center of everything. Only when the risen Christ is seen as friend, example, savior, and lord can genuine Christian conversion be expected to take place. Conversion to Christ is not necessarily identical with acceptance of the church; but in the vast majority of cases this follows, though this second acceptance may prove to be more difficult than the first.

Missionary motives. For more than four centuries the Western powers have exercised a dominating influence on the destinies of the rest of the world. Since so many people, especially in Muslim countries, have identified the West with the Christian West, there has been a natural tendency to regard Christian missionary enterprise as no more than an expression of Western aggression and imperialism. How far is there any adequate basis for this equation?

Many careful studies of missionary motivation have been made. Clearly no human motives are entirely pure. But only in a minority of cases can it be shown that national and imperialistic motives have played a strong part in missionary devotion. More frequently the glory of Christ has been the central and dominant motive. Some missionaries have gone so far in identifying with those they have come to serve as to renounce their own nation and to accept naturalization in the countries they have made their own. All have accepted some measure of acculturation in new surroundings. All who have served long years in alien lands have accepted with equanimity the destiny of becoming strangers in their own homes. The number of missionary martyrs is legion, their sacrifice equaled only by the devotion of their friends in many nations around the world who have also given their lives in the service of Christ.

THE TWENTIETH CENTURY. When in 1910 the first World Missionary Conference was held at Edinburgh, twelve hundred delegates from all over the world (including, however, no Roman Catholic or Orthodox Christians) could look back on a century of almost unimpeded progress. Converts had been won from every form of religion. In almost every country—a notable exception being Tibet—churches had come into existence, and the process by which the foreign mission was being transformed into the independent self-governing church was well advanced.

The years which followed were marked by a number of major setbacks to Christian missionization, such as the Russian revolution and the fading of religion in many Western communities. Yet the *World Christian Encyclopedia*, edited by David B. Barrett (1982) makes

In the nineteenth century, surnamed "the great century" in the leading history of Christian missions, most of the major Christian denominations of the West, Protestant as well as Roman Catholic, set out to evangelize the globe.

PAGE 160

Since 1949 Chinese religions have increasingly prospered in Taiwan, particularly at the popular level. The same can be said for Chinese popular religion in Hong Kong and Singapore.

PAGE 145

it plain that the achievements of the prior seventy years had been greater than those of the preceding century. For the first time in history the possibility of a universal religion appeared a reality. Roughly one-third of the inhabitants of the world had come to call themselves Christians. The progress of Christian missions continues in almost every area of the world. In India, Christians, already the third largest religious community after Hindus and Muslims, are also the most rapidly increasing in number.

Hostile critics of the Christian enterprise have maintained that the gospel has failed to touch deeply the mind and conscience of peoples outside the West, that the Christian churches in these areas are fragile and exotic blooms that came with the colonial powers, have been dependent exclusively on foreign aid and support, and that with the disappearance of the colonial powers these churches will also disappear. The twentieth century has shown that there is no ground at all for these expectations. After the communist takeover in China (1949), it was held even by a number of Christians that "missionary Christianity" in China had no roots and that there was little if any chance of its survival. When relaxation of government control occurred in 1980, however, it was revealed that several million Chinese had remained faithful to the Christian church. Chinese Christians have made known their determination to be fully independent of every kind of foreign control and to work out for themselves a form of Christian faith which will be genuinely Chinese. Elsewhere, if all foreign support has been compulsorily withdrawn, as in Burma, the churches have simply declared their maturity and have planned for a future of self-support and radical independence. Where this has taken place, accessions to the Christian faith have been more numerous than they were in the flourishing colonial days.

Changing world order. As a world phenomenon, the Christian church has not remained unaffected by the violent changes that have taken place in the troubled twentieth century. During the nineteenth century the dominant nations and the churches which were dependent on them assumed that they could plant Christian missions wherever they pleased, sometimes imposing their will by force on unwilling peoples. In the twentieth century all this has changed. A number of nations (e.g., Burma, Guinea, Saudi Arabia) prohibit all religious activity by foreigners which is directed at native citizens. A number of others make it very difficult for missionaries to obtain visas or residence permits. Yet others (e.g., Nepal) admit missionaries with few restrictions, but only on condition that they engage in what the government regards as nation-building activities (such as educational or medical services). Where all access is made impossible, churches in neighboring areas fall back upon the help that can be rendered by prayer alone.

The churches have gladly accepted the claim of these nations to independence and national dignity. No case is on record of a missionary leaving his or her assignment through unwillingness to accept the changed conditions of service. Christian witnesses have desired to stay on and to become in fact what they always wanted to be—servants of those to whom they came to minister. Even in China missionaries stayed on until it became clear that there was no longer any useful service that they could render. From Burma and other areas, foreigners withdrew because they felt that their work was done, since the local churches could carry on without their aid, and that their continued presence might embarrass—and possibly endanger—their Christian friends. Some have been deported, at very short notice, for political reasons.

Anti-Western sentiments and resentments have been strong in many countries of the world since the end of the nineteenth century. Since 1947, decolonization has taken place with quite unexpected rapidity. Yet wounds remain. Some nations have desired to emancipate themselves from Western influences, but this has proved impossible. The more far-sighted leaders have seen it as their task to retain all that is valuable in the Western inheritance and at the same time to assert or to rediscover the integrity of their own national traditions.

From foreign mission to independent church. The major change in the twentieth century was the process of transfer of power from foreign mission to independent local church, a process almost complete by the end of the century in almost every country in the world. The churches in some emerging nations think that the process has not gone fast enough or far enough; that it is on the way cannot be doubted by any observer of the process of change. Where churches are still wrestling with the problems and the prejudices of the past, they may be unwilling to accept the help of foreigners. Where they have reached maturity, as in India and Korea, and are becoming aware of the immense tasks still before them, they are in many cases glad to accept the help of foreigners, provided that these are prepared to keep their proper place and to accept only such responsibilities for service or leadership as the local church may lay upon them. Nor need it be supposed that all missionaries will be from the Western world; missionary interchange among developing nations is one of the most interesting features of the contemporary situation.

The independence of churches outside Europe and North America is increasingly shown in a number of remarkable ways. One that has attracted considerable attention is the rise of African independent churches, all of which have grown out of the mission-controlled

MONASTICISM

churches of the past. Some of these are unorthodox. But the great majority desire to remain part of the main lines of the Christian tradition and have yet to create for themselves a place in which to feel at home, to think out the gospel for themselves, and to decide for themselves which of the ancient traditions of Africa can be retained within the Christian structure. Many Christians, even in the mainstream churches outside the West, are rethinking their own past in the light of divine providence, expecting to find signs of the working of God no less in their own pre-Christian history than in the special history of which the Old and New Testaments are the record. Some in India, for example, have suggested that the Upanisads are the real "old testament" of the Indian Christian and should take rank at least on the same level as the Hebrew scriptures. The nature of this quest is neatly summed up in the title of a book by Raimundo Panikkar, *The Unknown Christ of Hinduism* (New York, 1981). Genuinely indigenous theology is still in its beginnings, and it has to be confessed that the reapings in this field are still rather scanty; but what there is gives promise of a richer harvest in days to come.

One reason for the Christian quest to discover Christ beyond the historical bounds of Christendom is to be found in the remarkable resuscitation in the twentieth century of the ancient non-Christian faiths. Rediscovering the treasures of their own past, non-Christians feel able to approach Christians with renewed confidence and a sense of security. The Buddhist knows himself to be in contact with the great mystery of nothingness, the Hindu to be in contact with the unchangeable mystery of infinite being, the Muslim with the mystery of the infinite exaltation of God. There need be no Christian doubt about the greatness of these religions. Christian and non-Christian alike have much to teach one another in a manner different from that of the past.

The basis of this approach is a conventional rationale of mutual respect. Through centuries millions of men and women have lived by the teachings that they have received in these various religions, and, therefore, these may not be treated as though they did not matter, even though some of their teachings may be displeasing to the adherents of other religions. So one who engages in dialogue with those of faiths other than his own must come to it in the spirit Chaucer described in the words "gladly would he learn and gladly teach." Confident in the value of what he has experienced through his own faith, the Christian is able to delight in everything that he learns from others of what is true and good and beautiful, and at the same time maintain his hope that those who have seen in their own faith what he must judge to be partial may come to find the full-orbed reality of the true, the good, and the beautiful as he himself has seen it in Jesus Christ. If mission is understood in this sense, some of the asperities of the missionary approach in the past may be mitigated.

A NEW UNDERSTANDING OF MISSION. Almost all Christians who are members of churches outside Europe and North America are conscious of belonging to a single great worldwide fellowship, regardless of the denominational label they may bear. Several, though not all, are ardent supporters of contemporary ecumenical movements for the unity and renewal of the church. But they too are almost at one in holding that reconsideration of the meaning of the term *mission* is long overdue. Those who have traveled in the lands of older Christian traditions and sensed the decay in Christian allegiance of many in these countries are inclined to think that mission should be labeled as a product intended for universal and international export. In the past, the gospel traveled across continents and oceans almost exclusively in one direction. Has not the time come to establish two-way traffic, to have the gospel travel across continents and oceans in many directions? If this is true, the word *mission* may be in need of new and contemporary definition.

[*For further discussion of Christian missions, see* Christianity.]

— STEPHEN C. NEILL

"Gladly would he learn and gladly teach."

CHAUCER

MONASTICISM

The Greek word *monos,* from which *monasticism* and all its cognates derive, means "one, alone." According to this etymology, therefore, the basic monastic person may be a hermit, a wandering ascetic, or simply someone who is not married or a member of a household. However, the term *monastic* normally refers to people living in community and thus embraces the cenobitic as well as the eremitic and peripatetic lifestyles. In Western societies, the definition of *monasticism* has often been restricted to its classic manifestations, especially the Benedictine tradition. By this definition clergy who adopt some aspects of monastic life and rule (canons regular or regular clerks), mendicant orders (Franciscan, Dominican, and like associations), and other religious orders are not properly called "monastic." Furthermore, within the classic definition one might be able to include some kinds of non-Christian monasticism—that is, those with goals and life patterns fairly similar to the Benedictines—but not others.

Nevertheless, many religious traditions feature (with varying degrees of formal institutionalization) a recognizable type of social structure for which *monasticism* is an appropriate name. The Buddhist *samgha,* the Christian religious and monastic orders, Jain monasti-

cism, and Hindu *sadhus* or *samnyasins* provide the most obvious examples.

DEFINING FEATURES. First and most prominent of the essential features of monasticism is the monastic's distinctive social status and pattern of social relationships. The monastic person is identified as one whose self-perception and public role include membership in a special religious category of persons, a status which is deliberate and extraordinary.

The second defining feature of the monastic situation is a specific program or discipline of life. The most obvious examples of formal regulations for the monastic life are the Vinaya of Buddhism and the Benedictine rule, but even less clearly defined categories set up expectations concerning appropriate behavior and activities for monastics. Monastic life, in contrast to the rest of human life, is entirely oriented toward a personal religious goal.

Monastic status is differentiated from other religious roles, offices, and functions in that it is not primarily based on performing some service to others in the religious tradition or to the larger society but on the more private cultivation of a path of transformation. A minister, priest, shaman, or similar expert in sacred procedures exhibits a kind of religious leadership dependent on a community to which sacred values are transmitted. Certainly these roles can be merged: some religious professionals also live like monastics.

Finally, it is important to note the presence of a larger religious tradition and set of institutions within which the monastic phenomenon takes place. Christianity can exist without monasticism because, in the "secular" priesthood and episcopal office, it has a social structure and forms of leadership independent of monastic patterns. Such patterns are even less central in Islam, where much of the tradition disowns monasticism completely. By contrast, monasticism is central to Buddhism and Jainism.

EREMITISM

A Solitary, Consecrated Life

EREMITISM is a form of monastic life characterized by solitariness. (The term derives from the Greek *eremos,* "wilderness, uninhabited regions," whence comes the English *eremite,* "solitary.") In this type of life, the social dimension of human existence is totally or largely sacrificed to the primacy of religious experience. It is thus understandable that Christianity has traditionally regarded eremitism as the purest and most perfect form of a life consecrated to God. While other forms of monasticism or of the religious life have striven to bring religious experience to bear on human relationships (Western Christianity especially emphasizes external service), eremitism has always been purely contemplative in thrust. Hermits live only in order to cultivate their spiritual life in prayer, meditation, reading, silence, asceticism, manual work, and, perhaps, in intellectual pursuits. In eremitism, the celibacy characteristically practiced in monachism extends to the suppression of all social relationships. While Christian monks have always stressed charity in relationships within the monastic group and, in the Middle Ages especially, written treatises on Christian friendship, Buddhist monks have emphasized the necessity for freedom from every affective relationship that might hinder the achievement of enlightenment.

While isolation for a limited period of time is common in many religions, especially as part of a process of initiation or as a special time dedicated to prayer and reflection, eremitism as a permanent vocation or prolonged phase of asceticism is found only in those religions that grant monasticism an established and determinative role. The religions in question are salvation religions, whether in the sense of self-liberation or of redemption. In Buddhism, Jainism, and Christianity religiosity has a personal character as opposed to a merely societal character (religion as a series of beliefs and rites of a tribe, *polis,* or state). Buddhism, Jainism, and Manichaeism are essentially monastic religions, owing to the importance they attach to the pursuit of the self-liberation of the human being. Christian hermits, too, often went into the wilderness in hopes of finding there the answer to the all-absorbing question: "How can I attain salvation?"

Eremitism in Islam. In Islam, eremitism is regarded as an exceptional type of life. In general, the religious life is lived either in the bosom of the family or in a community made up of a master and a number of disciples. However, a radical form of Sufism is found among itinerant monks, who express their estrangement from the world in a manner somewhat reminiscent of Hindu or Syrian practitioners of pilgrimage. Many Sufis, even if they do not fully profess this type of life, spend a certain number of years traveling throughout the Muslim world in search of a spiritual master. The ideal of the Muslim spiritual masters is "solitude in the midst of the multitude" *(kalwat dar anjuman),* that is, a state of remaining habitually in the presence of God without being touched by the tumult of one's surroundings. As means for achieving this state spiritual masters recommend detachment, silence, and interior peace.

— JUAN MANUEL LOZANO

FREQUENT CHARACTERISTICS. Even though the most careful definition of *monasticism* could not include communal life as a necessary factor, there can be no doubt that monastic existence is rarely completely solitary. Even wandering or hermit monks assemble periodically.

Sometimes monastic status is lifelong; this would seem to be the normal implication of the initiation into a higher realm. Christian religious orders often have some arrangement whereby lay people can become affiliated with the order without becoming full members. The third order of the Franciscan tradition and the Benedictine oblates are two such orders. In some instances a residential oblate may live just like the other members of the community or order.

Another important aspect of much monasticism, yet one not essential to it, is poverty or simplicity of lifestyle. Accumulation of wealth, as well as other factors that may lead to a change in the character of a monastic community's life over a period of time, have produced successive reforms within long monastic traditions. Benedictine history is a story of reforms: the first notable one took place under the aegis of Benedict of Aniane about three hundred years after Benedict of Nursia founded the order. This was followed by the reform programs of Cluny, the Cistercians, the Trappists, and so on.

Some monastic work involves intellectual activity. Benedict's rule emphasizes reading *(lectio divina)* as a major component of the monastic life along with prayer and work. The path to perfection or religious transformation is often an intellectual path that requires a new understanding of the self and the world. Reading and study in the monastic context is a means of salvation, a technique for the reconstruction of one's worldview. Also, because the rule, religious texts, and other written guides to meditation, prayer, and discipline must be available to monastics, much of their effort has been put to copying, studying, and teaching these materials.

In some situations charitable acts are held to be more important for the monastic than more individual disciplines. A distinction is made within Christian communities between contemplative orders, where activities like those mentioned above predominate, and active orders, where emphasis is placed on work with beneficial effects for others. A monastic belonging to an active order may be a teacher, nurse, priest, or support person in some beneficial institution, but with an interest or investment in the work that is beyond that of nonmonastic colleagues. For the monastic such work is part of a discipline or rule, a means toward a religious goal.

CONTEMPORARY MONASTICISM. In recent decades monastics from various religious traditions have become more aware of each other. Toward the end of his life the famous Trappist monk Thomas Merton wrote and spoke of the many similarities among the world's monastic systems. Roman Catholic monasteries in traditionally non-Christian areas have been interested in this consanguinity and have produced some writing on monasticism as an interreligious phenomenon. Since 1960 an organization known as Aide Inter-Monastères has encouraged dialogue between monastics of various religions. Some Christian monastics and monasteries now practice techniques borrowed from Hinduism and Buddhism.

In the United States many experimental as well as traditional new religious communities have been established. A monastic impulse seems to have been a part of the "counterculture" revolution of the sixties and seventies. Monasticism apparently continues to be a persistent and beneficial social and religious structure. In the seriousness with which the monastic reexamines life and its goals, in the rigor with which a discipline of life is pursued, the monastic phenomenon offers an alternative way of life and view of the world to the rest of society.

— GEORGE WECKMAN

MONGOL RELIGIONS

If stereotypical reports from early times are taken into account, the religious forms of the Mongols have been influenced by the religions professed by all ethnic groups who have lived in what later was to become Mongolian territory prior to the emergence of the Mongols. The oldest of these religious forms was shamanism. It remains the perennial dominant religious practice of the Mongols.

Mongol shamanism developed into its current state in various phases. In the original phase, fear of natural powers that were thought to be caused by evil forces led to the worship of the spirits of ancestors. The functions of shamanism, as explained by the shamans themselves, are to invoke the *ongons,* to shamanize with their help, to intercede on behalf of ill persons, to exorcize evil and the powers creating calamities and illness, to expel these into effigies that are then destroyed, and to pronounce charms and prognostications by scapulimancy and other divinatory methods.

In the thirteenth century Mongol shamanism was influenced by administrative measures when the first Mongol emperor in China, Khubilai Khan (r. 1260-1294), established by imperial decree the office of the state shamans. These shamans were responsible for offerings in memory of Chinggis Khan and his house as well as for the worship of fire. According to the *Yüan shih,* the official Chinese history of the Yüan dynasty, these shamans pronounced their prayers and invoca-

With the extended visit of Marco Polo to Khubilai's court (1271–1292) the first reliable information about China came to the West.

PAGE 333

CORBIS-BETTMANN

tions in the Mongolian language. Judged by the evident longevity of the Mongolian oral tradition and its extraordinary reliability, it seems certain that some of the prayers still used today at the so-called Eight White Yurts, the center of worship of the deified Chinggis Khan in the Ordos territory, contain remnants of these early shamanic prayers and supplications.

The ephemeral contacts of Buddhism with the ruling strata of the Mongol nobility during the twelfth and thirteenth centuries and later did not lead to any decisive intrusion of Buddhist notions into the religious conceptions of the bulk of the Mongol populations. Shamanism remained dominant. Only when Buddhist missionary work began among the Mongols in the sixteenth century did shamanism come under heavy attacks. Princes and overlords sustained the missionaries by donating horses and cows to converts while burning the confiscated shamanic idols in iconoclastic purges. Thousands of the idols were destroyed in this period, and the shamans had to renounce their profession and faith. Many fled during the sixteenth century into more remote regions.

CHINGGIS KHAN

A Emperor Who Became a God

Chinggis Khan (1162?-1227), the great Mongol leader and founder of a vast empire in Asia, s a striking example of an emperor who became a god.

Born in Mongolia, northeast of present-day Ulan Bator, and called Temüjin in his youth, he was the eldest son of a chieftain of the Mongol Borjigit clan. Having succeeded in uniting the Mongol and Turkic tribes of the area, he adopted the title of Chinggis Khan and set out to conquer the world. He subdued the Chin empire in North China, the Hsi-hsia kingdom northeast of Tibet, the Turkic states in Turkistan, and the empire of Khorezm, comprising Transoxiana as well as Afghanistan and Eastern Iran. Mongol units even advanced as far as India and the Crimea. When Chinggis Khan died in 1227 near Ning-hsia, capital of Hsi-hsia, he left the broad foundations of an empire that would extend, under his sons and grandsons, from Korea to the Near East and southern Europe and from southern Siberia to Indochina.

The thirteenth-century *Secret History of the Mongols,* the first work of Mongolian literature, patterns Chinggis Khan's biography after the model of the hero-king, and thus reflects the indispensable qualities of a ruler and the hopes set upon him. Chinggis Khan possesses the mandate of Heaven and Heaven's support to restore law, order, and peace on earth. He is of noble totemistic descent. Born on the holy mountain, the center of the world, Chinggis Khan goes forth to conquer nations and peoples in all directions, and to this same place his dead body returns. He has a good wife, a good horse, and good companions, and he finds himself in a situation favorable for his activities.

After Chinggis Khan's death, his character develops in three ways: Chinggis Khan becomes a means of political identification, a figure of political theology, and a deity. Chinggis Khan is used as a means of political identification by the Mongols as well as by the Chinese. To the Mongols, as the founder of their unified state, he is a symbol of Mongol national independence, or at least autonomy. To the Chinese, he is the glorious first emperor of a Chinese dynasty of Mongol nationality, a symbol of the multinational character of Chinese history.

Three aspects portray the deification of Chinggis Khan. First, he became the ancestral deity of the ruling Borjigit clan, the state, and the whole Mongol people, guarding them against all evil. Second, Chinggis was incorporated into the Lamaist-Buddhist pantheon as a local guardian deity of comparatively low rank. In the practice of folk religion he became fused with the ancestral deity. Third, traits of an initiatory god were imputed to Chinggis Khan; as this deity, he introduced marriage customs, seasonal festivals connected with the nomadic economy, and certain ritual practices of daily life. [*See also* Inner Asian Religions.]

— KLAUS SAGASTER

Considered by both the Lamaist clergy and most princes to be a meritorious deed that would further the spread of Buddhism, such persecution has been repeated again and again up to the beginning of the twentieth century. Cases of rounding up, mistreating, and burning shamans were reported among the eastern Khalkha Mongols in the nineteenth century and in the remote northwest of Mongolia in 1904. Yet shamanism and related forms of popular religious worship have not been totally subdued. Forced during the periods of worst suppression into some camouflaged forms, it found a new, more syncretic expression by adding and adapting objects and forms of Buddhist veneration.

In more recent times the healing activities of the shamans have been more and more predominant, the shaman personnel being divided into real shamans *(böge/udaghan)* and non-shamanic healers and singers. The method of healing employed tends toward a kind of group therapeutic treatment of psychic illness *(andai),* which consists of shamans, helpers, and a crowd of laymen singing and arguing with the patient as a means of restoring him to his normal psychic state. In eastern Mongolia this singing therapy has been practiced since at least the mid-nineteenth century.

[*See also* Buddhism.]

— WALTHER HEISSIG

MORAVIANS

The Moravian church, as the Unitas Fratrum (Unity of Brethren) is popularly known, is a Protestant denomination with roots in the fifteenth-century Hussite reformation and the eighteenth-century German Pietist movement. By the late nineteenth century, these influences had coalesced to give the denomination its contemporary form and character.

The Unity of Brethren was founded in March 1457 in Kunwald, Bohemia as the Jednota Bratrská ("Society of Brethren"), but the issues behind this event stretch back more than a century. From the mid-fourteenth century there had been growing demands for reform within the Roman Catholic church of Bohemia and neighboring Moravia. The reform movement was centered in the capital city of Prague and the newly established Charles University (1348). Persistent Waldensian influences as well as newer Wyclifite influences from England were evident in this movement.

The calls for reform finally found their most eloquent voice in Jan Hus, priest, university professor, and popular preacher. Although attracted to the doctrines of Wyclif, Hus claimed to advocate independently a return to apostolic simplicity in the church, and he vigorously attacked the lax morality of the clergy. As Hus's popularity increased, so did controversy about his ideas and his difficulties with the hierarchy. He was excommunicated by Pope John XXIII in 1411 but eventually appealed his case to the Council of Constance then in session. After his trial, deemed irregular by later historians, he was burned at the stake on 6 July 1415 as a heretic.

Hus's death served to arouse his followers in Bohemia. His ideas soon became entwined with a developing Bohemian nationalism, and Hus himself became something of a folk hero. When civil war erupted, a series of unsuccessful crusades were launched, with the blessings of the papacy, in an attempt to subdue the heretics. Among the most ardent Bohemians, highly respected for their military zeal, were a group of radical religious and political reformers headquartered in the town of Tabor. Although they were destroyed as a separate party by the late 1430s, many of their religious ideas lingered on in the population. Bohemia's political situation would remain unstable for a century after Hus's death until 1526, when the crown was acquired by the Habsburg Ferdinand I.

Upheavals occurred also in the religious life of the Bohemians and Moravians as several groups claiming the heritage of Hus emerged alongside the Roman Catholic church. One such group, the Utraquists, represented a conservative attempt at reformation, finally insisting only on the right of all believers to receive the bread and wine at Communion and continuing to hope for a reunion with a purified Roman Catholic church. It was the Utraquist archbishop-elect Jan z Rokycan (c. 1390-1471) whose preaching inspired one of the founders of the Brethren, his nephew Gregory (d. 1474), to pursue more vigorously the goal of reformation. Jan z Rokycan also introduced Gregory to the writings of the radical reformer Petr Chelcicky (c. 1380-c. 1460).

Within ten years of the founding of their society, the Brethren felt the need to establish their own clerical orders to insure the efficaciousness of their ministry. They chose deacons, presbyters, and bishops from among their membership. One of the candidates was a former Roman Catholic priest, and some Waldensians may have participated in the establishment of the new orders. Modern historians see in these events an attempt by the Brethren to reconstitute the style of ministry of the New Testament church. Any attempt by the Brethren to claim apostolic succession as traditionally understood must be laid to a faulty reading of Waldensian history on their part. The orders established in 1467 have been carried on into the contemporary Moravian church.

The first decades of the Brethren organization were marked by sectarian characteristics including pacifism,

"O holy simplicity!"

JAN HUS
HIS LAST WORDS 1415

Methodism remains true to the spirit of its founder, who gloried in the catholicity of his early societies, who firmly maintained, in spite of attacks by his critics, that "orthodoxy, or right opinions, is at best but a very slender part of religion."

PAGE 433

rejection of oaths, communal organization, use of the titles "Brother" and "Sister" for all members, suspicion of advanced education, reluctance to admit members of the nobility to membership, and a preference for rural living. This trend was reversed under the leadership of Bishop Luke of Prague (c. 1460-1528), who succeeded in 1494 in having the works of Chelcicky and Gregory reduced to nondogmatic status. The group gave up much of their exclusiveness and moved into the mainstream of society, though not without the defection of a conservative minority. The majority, although retaining a strict church discipline, grew rapidly. It has been estimated that by the 1520s there were from 150,000 to 200,000 members located in 400 congregations in Bohemia and Moravia.

Under the leadership of such bishops as Jan Augusta (1500-1572) and Jan Blahoslav (1523-1571), the Brethren maintained generally friendly contacts with Luther (who wrote favorably about them) and later with leaders of the Reformed churches. Although ecumenical in spirit and experiencing strong influences from first Lutheran and later Reformed theology, the Brethren maintained their own course. They structured their church with dioceses headed by bishops, abandoned clerical celibacy, and eventually accepted a general Reformed understanding of the sacraments of baptism and the Eucharist.

In worship, while ritual was simplified, the church year was retained and lay involvement encouraged through the publication of hymnals and the Czech-language Kralitz Bible (1579-1593) in six volumes with commentary. The church sponsored schools and encouraged the training of clergy in foreign universities.

Since their legal status was often in doubt, the Brethren endured periodic persecutions by the Utraquists and the Roman Catholics. But they continued to maintain their vitality and established congregations in Poland, which later merged with the Reformed church.

The involvement in political affairs of members who were of the nobility helped to bring about disastrous consequences for the Brethren in the opening phase of the Thirty Years' War (1618-1648). With the defeat of the Protestant forces at the Battle of the White Mountain (1620), suppression of Protestantism in Bohemia and Moravia began. The events of this era are highlighted in the career of Bishop Johannes Amos Comenius (1592-1670), the renowned educational theorist. He spent much of his life in exile developing his reforms of education and despite several personal tragedies never lost his belief in the power of the educated mind to serve God's purposes for humanity.

The traditions of the Brethren survived in Bohemia and Moravia through secret meetings and the laxity of government officials in enforcing conformity. Sporadic contacts with Lutherans in border areas also helped to sustain morale.

A group of these secret Brethren were led in 1722 to the German estate of Count Nikolaus Zinzendorf (1700-1760) by the lay evangelist Christian David (1690-1751). There they established the village of Herrnhut. A creative theologian and gifted leader, Zinzendorf became the driving force behind the merger of the Brethren's traditions with the emphases of the Pietist movement.

After initial difficulties, the growing community experienced a series of unifying experiences in the summer of 1727, culminating in a service of Holy Communion on 13 August. The fellowship now developed the unique characteristics that would mark its second phase. The residents were organized into residential groups based on age, sex, and marital status ("the choirs"). The intent was to foster spiritual experience appropriate to one's stage in life and to utilize the resources of a concentrated labor force. From Zinzendorf's Christocentric emphasis flowed a rich liturgical life with stress upon the Advent-Christmas and Holy Week-Easter cycles. The Moravian understanding of the joyous nature of the relationship between the believer and the Savior enabled them to develop education and the arts in his praise, sponsoring schools and producing musicians and artists of note. The Brethren's clerical orders were continued through new ordinations by the two remaining bishops in exile. Since the church developed a conferential form of government, however, the bishops became primarily spiritual leaders.

Worship was characterized by a simplified liturgical ritual that observed the festivals of the Christian calendar with particular attention to the Advent-Christmas and Holy Week-Easter cycles. Unique features included the singing of many hymns, with the minister clad in a surplice for the celebration of the sacraments of baptism and Holy Communion. The Lovefeast, patterned after the agape meals of the early Christians, developed as a significant service. In it participants were served a simple meal as an expression of their fellowship with one another.

Under the leadership of Zinzendorf and his *de facto* successor Bishop Augustus Gottlieb Spangenberg (1703-1792), Herrnhut became the model for some twenty similar communities established in Europe, England, and the eastern United States. These self-sufficient "settlement congregations" were to serve as the home base for two types of outreach developed by the Brethren.

Beginning in 1727 the Moravians sent forth members to serve in their "diaspora" through establishing Pietist renewal societies within existing state churches. This practice is supported by European Moravians today. In 1732, after Zinzendorf's presentation of the plight of the West Indian slaves to the community, the Brethren Leonard Dober (1706-1766) and David Nitschmann (1696-1772) went to Saint Thomas. By 1760 the Moravians had sent out 226 missionaries to the non-European world. This effort introduced into Protestantism the idea that missionary outreach is the responsibility of the whole church, brought the Moravians into significant ecumenical contacts, such as that with John Wesley (1703-1791) in Georgia and England, and helped shape the contemporary Moravian church.

By the mid-nineteenth century, the settlement congregations were given up as no longer viable and the towns opened to all who wished to settle in them. German and Scandinavian immigration to North America in the last century brought new Moravian congregations into being in the eastern and midwestern United States and western Canada. The end of World War II found Herrnhut and the older settlements in East Germany and, through the movement of refugees, a stronger Moravian presence in western Europe. Immigration continues to affect the Moravian church through the recent movements of Surinamese members to the Netherlands and Caribbean-area members to cities in England and North America.

The Moravians have also experienced constitutional changes as they have moved beyond their European origins. The British and American areas of the church gained independence from the German in the mid-nineteenth century, but the foreign missions continued under control of an international board that met in Germany until the end of World War I. Responsibility for the work was then divided among the European, British, and American areas of the church. A major constitutional change in 1957 resulted in the creation of the present seventeen autonomous provinces located in Europe, England, North America, Central America, and Africa, and the undertaking of educational work in India and Israel. The provinces constitute the "Moravian Unity" and send delegates to periodic meetings of the "Unity Synod." The late twentieth century has witnessed the rapid growth of the church in Africa and Central America. In America, the Moravian church did not experience significant growth until after the mid-nineteenth century. Earlier attempts at "diaspora"-style outreach had proved unsuited to America, since there was no religious establishment within which to work. Groups gathered by "diaspora" workers simply became congregations of other denominations. The retention of the exclusive settlement congregations until the 1840s also retarded outreach.

The church has continued to honor many of its traditions of worship and practice. While eschewing a formal dogmatic theological tradition of its own, it affirms the historic creeds of the Christian faith, continues to emphasize the believer's relationship with Christ, and to encourage fellowship among its members. Both men and women are ordained as pastors. The church's historical ecumenical stance is reflected in its participation as a founding member of the World Council of Churches and in the activities of the various provinces in regional councils of churches. Total membership recorded in December 1982 was 457,523.

— DAVID A. SCHATTSCHNEIDER

MORMONISM

The religious movement popularly known as Mormonism encompasses several denominations and sects, the largest of which is the Church of Jesus Christ of Latter-day Saints with headquarters in Salt Lake City, Utah. The second-largest organization, with headquarters in Independence, Missouri, is the Reorganized Church of Jesus Christ of Latter Day Saints.

Mormonism had its beginnings in western New York in the 1820s when a mingling of spiritual and physical developments left many Americans bewildered and confused. Among those passed by in the rush for progress was Joseph Smith. According to a later, official church account, it was in the spring of 1820 that the boy, aged fourteen, retired to a grove on his father's farm, where he prayed for divine guidance. In a vision he beheld God the Father and Jesus Christ

Many Christian churches seek to manifest their essential unity and to arrive at a point where their ministries may be mutually recognized.

PAGE 441

JOSEPH SMITH

Smith, founder of the Mormon Church and "interpreter" of the Book of Mormon, was a charismatic but controversial leader.

LIBRARY OF CONGRESS/CORBIS

JOSEPH SMITH
Charismatic Founder of the Mormon Church

SMITH, JOSEPH, (1805-1844), the founder of the Church of Jesus Christ of Latter-day Saints, popularly known as the Mormons.

Born in Sharon, Vermont, on 23 December 1805, Smith was the third of the nine children of Joseph and Lucy Mack Smith. He grew up in the unchurched and dissenting, but God-fearing, tradition of a New England Protestant biblical culture, which attracted many of those whose economic standing in established society had been eroded. In 1816, plagued by hard times and misfortune, the sturdy, self-reliant, and closely-knit Smith family left New England for western New York in search of economic betterment; they settled in the village of Palmyra, along the route of the Erie Canal.

During the 1820s, as the Smiths continued to struggle against economic reversals, the religiously inclined young man had a number of visions and revelations. These convinced him that he was to be the divinely appointed instrument for the restoration of the gospel, which in the opinion of many of his contemporaries had been corrupted. Under the guidance of an angel he unearthed a set of golden plates from a hill near his parents' farm. He translated these golden plates with divine aid and published the result in 1830 as the *Book of Mormon.* Smith claimed that this book, named after its ancient American author and compiler, was the sacred history of the pre-Columbian inhabitants of America, migrants from the Near East, some of whom were the ancestors of the American Indians. In 1829, divine messengers had conferred the priesthood—the authority to baptize and act in the name of God—on Smith and his associate Oliver Cowdery. Shortly after the publication of the *Book of Mormon*, Smith and Cowdery officially organized the Church of Christ in Fayette, New York, on 6 April 1830. In 1838, the name was changed to the Church of Jesus Christ of Latter-day Saints.

Prominent among those attracted to Smith's teachings was Sidney Rigdon, erstwhile associate of Alexander Campbell. Rigdon invited Smith and his New York followers to establish a Mormon settlement in Kirtland, Ohio. It was there that Smith greatly amplified and broadened his theological and organizational principles in a series of revelations (first published in 1833 as the *Book of Commandments*, and later enlarged into the current, canonical *Doctrine and Covenants*). The Saints were enjoined to gather in communities as God's chosen people under an egalitarian economic system called the Law of Consecration and Stewardship. They were also directed to build a temple as the sacred center of the community. These revelations initiated a patriarchal order that harkened back to Old Testament traditions.

In the meantime, Smith also established settlements in Missouri, which he regarded as the center of a future Zion. In 1838, economic difficulties and internal dissension forced Smith to give up the Kirtland settlement. His intention of gathering all the Saints in Missouri, however, had to be deferred after the Mormons were ruthlessly driven from the state in 1839. It was in Nauvoo, a settlement founded in 1839 on the Mississippi River, that Smith further expanded his ambitious vision of a Mormon empire that was to be both spiritual and temporal. By 1844, Nauvoo had become the largest city in Illinois, with a population of about eleven thousand. This city was under the full religious, social, economic, and political control of the Mormon kingdom, with Joseph Smith as its charismatic leader.

Some historians suggest that he may have become touched by megalomania; he assumed leadership of the Mormon militia in the resplendent uniform of a lieutenant general and announced his candidacy for the presidency of the United States. Smith ostensibly made his gesture toward the presidency in order to avoid making a politically difficult choice between the two major parties, but he was also imbued with the millennial belief that if God wanted him to be president and establish Mormon dominion in the United States, no one could hinder him. Innovative ordinances, such as baptism for the dead, and especially plural marriage—with Smith and his closest associates secretly taking numerous wives—offended the religious sensibilities of many Mormons. Likewise, controversial doctrines such as pre-existence, metaphysical materialism, eternal progression, the plurality of gods, and man's ability to become divine through the principles of Mormonism, failed to gain universal acceptance among the Saints. A group of alarmed anti-Mormons effectively capitalized on internal dissent and were able to organize a mob that killed Smith and his brother Hyrum on 27 June 1844.

It was Smith's spirituality, imagination, ego, drive, and charisma that not only started Mormonism but kept it going in the face of nearly insurmountable internal and external opposition. At the same time, these were the very characteristics that had generated much of that opposition. Smith's was a multifaceted and contradictory personality. Reports of encounters with him by both non-Mormons and believers give the impression of a tall, well-built, handsome man whose visionary side was tempered by Yankee practicality, geniality, and a sense of humor that engendered loyalty in willing followers. Though after his death his followers could not all agree on precisely what he had taught and split into several factions, they all accepted Smith's central messages of the restoration of the gospel and the divine status of the *Book of Mormon*, continuing revelation by prophets, and the establishment of the kingdom of God with Christ as its head.

— KLAUS J. HANSEN

and was told to join none of the existing denominations, for they were "all wrong."

As young Joseph matured, he had a number of subsequent visions and revelations. In preparation for this restoration, he was directed by an angel to unearth a set of golden records from a hill near his parents' farm. He then translated these records with divine aid and published them in 1830 as the *Book of Mormon,* a sacred history of three groups of pre-Columbian migrants to America, including the ancestors of the American Indians. According to the *Book of Mormon,* Christ had visited the inhabitants of the Western Hemisphere after his crucifixion, taught the gospel, and instituted a church "to the convincing of the Jew and Gentile that Jesus is the Christ, the Eternal God, manifesting himself to all nations." Although accepted as scripture by believing Mormons and popularly called the Mormon bible by nonbelievers, Smith regarded the *Book of Mormon* as a supplement rather than a substitute for the Bible.

Although the new religion called Church of Jesus Christ of Latter-Day Saints initially met with skepticism and persecution, it succeeded in attracting a substantial following among restorationists who saw in

BRIGHAM YOUNG
Creator of the Kingdom

YOUNG, BRIGHAM (1801-1877), second president of the Church of Jesus Christ of Latter-day Saints (hereafter LDS); chief architect of the form of Mormonism that flourished in the intermountain region of the western United States in the nineteenth century and expanded throughout the United States and into many other countries.

Young became a follower of the Mormon prophet, Joseph Smith, in 1832, when the character of the new movement was becoming as Hebraic as it was Christian, given the emphasis being placed on its "gathering" doctrine, its temple-building plans, its patriarchal office, and its assertion that Mormons are God's only chosen people. Convinced that these elements separating Mormonism from traditional Christianity were scripturally correct, Young accepted them wholeheartedly. Moreover, when temple ordinances were introduced that added plural marriage and baptism for the dead to Mormonism, and when the movement organized itself into a political kingdom, he accepted these innovations as well, albeit somewhat less enthusiastically.

After his rebaptism, Young devoted his entire energies to Mormonism. Following a preaching mission in the eastern United States, he moved to Ohio, assisting with the construction of the Kirtland temple and much else. He went with Zion's Camp, a paramilitary expedition that failed to rescue beleaguered Missouri Saints from their enemies, but nevertheless tested the mettle of future LDS leaders. Called to the highest council in Mormondom, the Quorum of the Twelve, in 1835, and made its president in 1841, Young rendered signal service, particularly in organizing the exodus when the Saints were driven from Missouri in 1839 and in establishing a successful Mormon mission in England in the early 1840s. In Nauvoo, Illinois, during the final years of Smith's life, Young served in the prophet's inner circle as the LDS political kingdom was organized and the secret practice of plural marriage instituted.

The struggle for succession to LDS leadership after Smith's murder in 1844 intensified a division within the movement. On one side were Saints who, regarding Mormonism as an idiosyncratic version of primitive Christianity, opposed plural marriage and the political organization of a kingdom in an Old Testament mode; on the other were Saints who supported these innovations as a part of the restoration of the "ancient order of things." Although most historical accounts present Young as the clear winner in this succession struggle, recent demographic studies reveal that he was the acknowledged leader of the latter group, but that he by no means led the whole of the LDS community after Smith's death.

For the thousands who followed him, however, Young managed to effect the transfer of Mormon culture from Illinois to the Great Salt Lake Valley while preserving the vision of Mormonism that Joseph Smith held at the end of his life. He did this by assuming ecclesiastical, political, and spiritual leadership of his followers. In Nauvoo, he took practical charge of the chaotic situation and arranged the departure of the Saints. In 1847, he was sustained as president of the church by those who went west with him. In 1851, the federal government recognized his leadership by appointing him as governor of Utah Territory. From these dual positions of power, he established a new "Israel in the tops of the mountains" in which, in the manner of Solomon of old, he reigned supreme as prophet, church president, and political leader. Unlike Joseph Smith, however, Young was not a prophet who delivered new revelations and added lasting theological elements to the movement he headed. His great contribution was realizing Smith's vision through the creation of a literal LDS kingdom. Even changed, as it was at the end of the nineteenth century, this kingdom continues to animate and inspire Mormonism in much the same way that Solomon's kingdom has animated and inspired Judaism and Christianity across the ages.

— JAN SHIPPS

Mormonism the fulfillment of the awaited return of the true church of Christ, led by a divinely ordained priesthood. Perhaps the most prominent and influential of these converts was Sidney Rigdon, who brought virtually his entire Ohio congregation over to the new religion, thus inducing Smith and most of his New York followers to establish a Mormon settlement in 1831 in Kirtland, Ohio. It was there that Smith greatly amplified and broadened his theological and organizational principles in a series of revelations first published in 1833 as the *Book of Commandments* and later enlarged into the canonical *Doctrine and Covenants.* The Saints were enjoined to gather in communities as God's chosen people under an egalitarian economic order called the Law of Consecration and Stewardship and to build a temple that was, literally and symbolically, the sacred center of the community.

"This is the place!"

BRIGHAM YOUNG
ON FIRST SEEING THE VALLEY OF THE GREAT SALT LAKE 1847

These innovations began to arouse the hostility of non-Mormons. The Saints were forced to leave Kirtland in 1838, primarily because of opposition to their kingdom. Internal conflict also intensified as Smith continued to move beyond his early restorationist impulse in favor of a kingdom of God that achieved its fullest expression in Nauvoo. Nauvoo, a settlement founded in 1839 for refugees from Missouri, had become Illinois's largest city, with a population of about eleven thousand by 1844. It was a city under the full religious, social, economic, and political control of the Mormon kingdom.

The success of Nauvoo may well have led Smith to overreach himself. He assumed the leadership of the Mormon militia and announced his candidacy for the presidency of the United States. A group of alarmed anti-Mormons effectively capitalized on internal dissent and formed a mob that killed Smith and his brother Hyrum on 27 June 1844.

BRIGHAM YOUNG

In 1847, most Saints followed Brigham Young to the Great Salt Lake where they built an inland empire.

CORBIS-BETTMANN

History has shown the killers of the Mormon prophet wrong in thinking that they had delivered a mortal blow to Mormonism. As early as 1834, Smith had organized some of his most loyal lieutenants into a council of twelve apostles in restorationist emulation of the primitive church. In 1840, Brigham Young became president of this powerful and prestigious group. It was in this capacity that he was sustained as leader by those Mormons who had unquestioningly accepted Smith's Nauvoo innovations. Most of those devotees followed Young to Great Salt Lake in July 1847 and immediately began to survey a site for a city, with a temple at the center. Aided by a steady stream of immigrants, Young built an inland empire including Utah and parts of Idaho, Wyoming, Arizona, and Nevada that boasted a population of over one hundred thousand by the time of his death in 1877.

When the Saints voted on 6 October 1890 to jettison some of their most distinctive institutions and beliefs—economic communitarianism, plural marriage, and the political kingdom—they followed their erstwhile evangelical adversaries into the pluralistic American cultural mainstream, joining what historian Martin Marty has called "a nation of behavers." In search of new boundaries and symbols of identification, the Mormons, much like the evangelicals, adopted strict codes of behavior: abstinence from alcohol, tobacco, tea and coffee; acceptance of regulated dress norms; adherence to a strict code of sexual morality.

Mormons found these values equally congenial in their own adaptation to a competitive, individualistic social and economic order, and they prepared the rising generation to meet this change. Religious commitment thus became a springboard for social and economic success in the world, which was further facilitated by the Mormons' increasing commitment to education; nearly thirty thousand Latter-day Saints attended Brigham Young University by 1984, and many thousands more were studying at secular universities throughout the United States and the Western world. Mormons serve in prominent positions in the federal government, in the military, in major business corporations, and in major universities.

Mormonism continues to appeal to many socially and culturally disoriented members of society. They are attracted by a lay church that offers active participation to all of its members and provides an instant, socially cohesive group whose authoritarian male leaders set boundaries while providing recognition for behavior that conforms to group standards. Many converts are especially drawn to the Mormon family ideal.

— KLAUS J. HANSEN

MOSES

LITERARY TRADITION. The traditions about Moses are contained in the Peutateuch from *Exodus* to *Deuteronomy,* and all other biblical references to Moses are probably dependent upon these. The view of most critical scholars for the past century has been that the Pentateuch's presentation of Moses is not the result of a single author but the combination of at least four sources, known as the Yahvist (J), the Elohist (E), Deuteronomy (D), and the Priestly writer (P), and composed in that order. A long period of time separates any historical figure from the written presentation of Moses in the Bible. To bridge this gap one is faced with evaluating the diversity of traditions within the Moses legend and with tracing their history of transmission prior to their use by the later authors, as well as with considering the shape and color the authors themselves gave to the Moses tradition as a reflection of their own times and concerns.

Moses as Deliverer from Egypt. The general background for the deliverance of the people through Moses is the theme of the oppression and enslavement in Egypt.

Within the tradition of enslavement the JE writer introduces a special theme of attempted genocide (*Ex.* 1:8-22), which provides the context for the story of Moses' birth and his rescue from the Nile by the Egyptian princess (*Ex.* 2:1-10). But once this story is told, the theme of genocide disappears, and the issue becomes again that of enslavement and hard labor. The story of Moses as a threatened child rescued from the basket of reeds and reared under the very nose of Pharaoh to become the deliverer of his people corresponds to a very common folkloric motif of antiquity.

The story of Moses' experience of the burning bush theophany at Sinai/Horeb, in the land of Midian (*Ex.* 3-4), has all the marks of a new beginning. It resembles that of the prophetic-call narratives in which the prophet experiences a theophany and then is given his commission (*Is.* 6, *Ez.* 1-3). The primary concern in the dialogue between Moses and Yahveh is in Moses' role as a spokesman whom the people will believe and who can speak on behalf of the people to the foreign ruler. The author (JE) has drawn upon both the tradition of classical prophecy and the literary history of Gideon and Saul to fashion his rather composite presentation of Moses' call and commission as Israel's deliverer.

The climax of Israel's deliverance is at the Red Sea (*Ex.* 13:17-14:31), and here again Moses' role is to announce judgment on the Egyptians and salvation for Israel. In the JE account Moses and Israel do nothing but witness the divine rescue, while in the P version Moses, at God's command, splits the sea with his rod to create a path for the Israelites and, again at divine command, makes the sea come back upon their pursuers. It is remarkable that except for one late addition to *Deuteronomy* (11:4) there are no references to the Red Sea event in this source even though the Exodus is mentioned many times. This suggests that the Red Sea episode is really secondary to the Exodus tradition.

Moses as Leader. Apart from an initial contact with Israel's elders in Egypt, which did not turn out very well (*Ex.* 5), Moses' direct leadership of the people begins only when they depart from Egypt. As their leader he is the one to whom the people complain about their hardships in the wilderness. But it is always God who meets their needs, with manna from heaven, or quails, or water from a rock.

On a few occasions the Israelites are involved in military encounters, but Moses' role in these is very limited. Moses appears to lead the forces in the D account, but in JE he recedes into the background. Moses is not a military hero in these traditions.

Moses as Lawgiver. The theme of Moses as lawgiver is more closely associated with the theophany at Sinai/Horeb (*Ex.* 19-20, *Dt.* 4-5), and with the prolonged stay at the mountain of God, during which the Law was given to Israel through Moses. Many scholars have argued that the giving of the Law at Sinai originated as a separate tradition.

MOSES

Moses is revered as the founder of the Israelite religion, author of the Pentateuch, great teacher and prophet.

CHRIS HELLIER/CORBIS

Nevertheless Moses has often been viewed as the author of the Ten Commandments. But the two forms, in *Deuteronomy* 5 and *Exodus* 20, are in the sources D and P respectively, and their language is so characteristic of D that there seems little reason to believe that they are any older than the seventh century BCE.

Deuteronomy largely summarizes discourses of Moses and is marked by its own characteristic style and theological tendency.

PAGE 69

"Go and show yourself to the priest and offer the gift Moses prescribed."

MATTHEW 8:4

MOSES AS THE FOUNDER OF ISRAELITE RELIGION. Many scholars believe that Moses is the founder of Israel's religion, at least in the form of a worship of Yahveh alone and, ultimately, in the form of monotheism. This position is based upon a number of arguments. The P source explicitly states (*Ex.* 6:2-3) that the name of Yahveh was not known before the time of Moses and that the forefathers worshiped God as El Shaddai. In Genesis there are also frequent references to forms of El worship among the patriarchs. Yet the JE corpus clearly regards the patriarchs as worshipers of Yahveh and the El epithets as merely titles for Yahveh. This and other aspects of the Moses tradition continue to heat debate about his place in Isrealite Religion.

RABBINIC VIEW OF MOSES. The rabbinic tradition represents a vast array of sources from the second century to the Middle Ages, containing a wide spectrum of belief and opinion.

In the legal tradition *(halakhah)* Moses represents the great "teacher" by which Israel was instructed in the Torah. This includes not only the laws of the Pentateuch but all the subsequent oral Torah, which was handed down from Moses to Joshua and in succession to the rabbis. All students of the law were really disciples of Moses. The homiletic tradition *(aggadah)* brought to the fore those other aspects of the Moses tradition that were a part of Jewish piety. It continued to embellish the biography of Moses as the "man of God," but more central is his role as the servant of God.

There is also a tradition within the *aggadah* about Moses' heavenly ascent at Sinai that elaborates on his vision of God and his struggles with the angels to acquire the Torah for Israel. There was a certain reticence expressed by some rabbis toward this form of piety and the rather speculative character of its traditions.

MOSES IN THE NEW TESTAMENT. The New Testament accepts Moses as the author of the Pentateuch (*Mt.* 8:4, *Mk.* 7:10, *Jn.* 1:17), but the real significance of the Pentateuch is as a prophecy that discloses the origins of Christianity (*Lk.* 24:25-27). Yet the whole of the institutional and ritual forms of Judaism as well as the Pharisaic-rabbinic tradition is associated with Moses, so that Moses reflects the ambivalent feelings of Christianity's continuity and discontinuity with Judaism.

MOSES IN ISLAM. Moses is highly regarded in Islam as the great prophet who foretold the coming of Muhammad, his successor. Details about Moses' life from the *aggadah* are to be found in the Qur'an, but there are additional details with parallels from folklore as well as borrowed from other biblical stories and applied to Moses (see especially surah 28:4-43; also 7:104-158, 20:10-98, 26:11-69).

— JOHN VAN SETERS

MOSQUE

HISTORY AND TRADITION

NAME. The word *mosque*, anglicized from the French *mosquée*, comes through the Spanish *mezquita* from the Arabic *masjid*, meaning "a place where one prostrates oneself [in front of God]." The term *masjid* (same in Persian, Urdu, and Turkish) was already found in Aramaic, where it was used in reference to Nabatean and Abyssinian sacred places; it was also a common word in pre-Islamic Arabia.

The *masjid* is frequently mentioned in the Qur'an (principally 2:144, 9:17-18, 9:107-108, 22:40, 62:1, 72:17); there it is applied generally to sanctuaries where God is worshiped but does not refer to a specifically new kind of Muslim building. Whenever a precisely Muslim identification was needed, the term was used in a compound construct, as in *masjid al-haram* in Mecca or *masjid al-aqsa* in Jerusalem. A celebrated *hadith* ("tradition") indicates that a *masjid* exists wherever one prays and thus makes the existence of a Muslim building unnecessary. However, all Muslims are obliged to perform prayers collectively once a week on Fridays at noon, when they also swear allegiance to the Prophet's successor. The great mosque in which the community *(jama'ah)* of worshipers attended the Friday *(jum'ah)* service took the name *masjid al-jama'ah*, or *masjid al-jum'ah*, or *masjid al-jami'* ("place of assembly"), usually called simply *al-jami'*. Subsequently, the word *jami'* has been reserved for large congregational mosques where the Friday *khutbah* ("sermon") is delivered, whereas the word *masjid* refers to small private mosques of daily prayer (with the exception of the mosques of Mecca, Medina, and Jerusalem, which have kept their traditional Qur'anic names of *masjids*). This distinction is still clearly observed in Turkey where the respective terms are correctly used.

DEFINITION. In simple terms, the mosque is a building large enough to contain the community of the believers, laid out with a covered space for prayer and an open space for gatherings, and oriented toward Mecca. The structure, in spite of chronological developments and stylistic and regional variations, has remained unchanged in its essentials. All mosques are built on an axis oriented in the direction of Mecca, the focus of prayer established in the Qur'an (2:139). They all have a prayer hall parallel to the wall of the *qiblah* (the direction of Mecca) where Muslim men, on an egalitarian basis, rich or poor, noble or humble, stand in rows to perform their prayers behind the imam. Women, who are expected to say prayers at home, may join in certain mosques but are expected to use a separate place specially screened off for them. Otherwise, Muslim men from all four Sunni legal schools (Shafi'i,

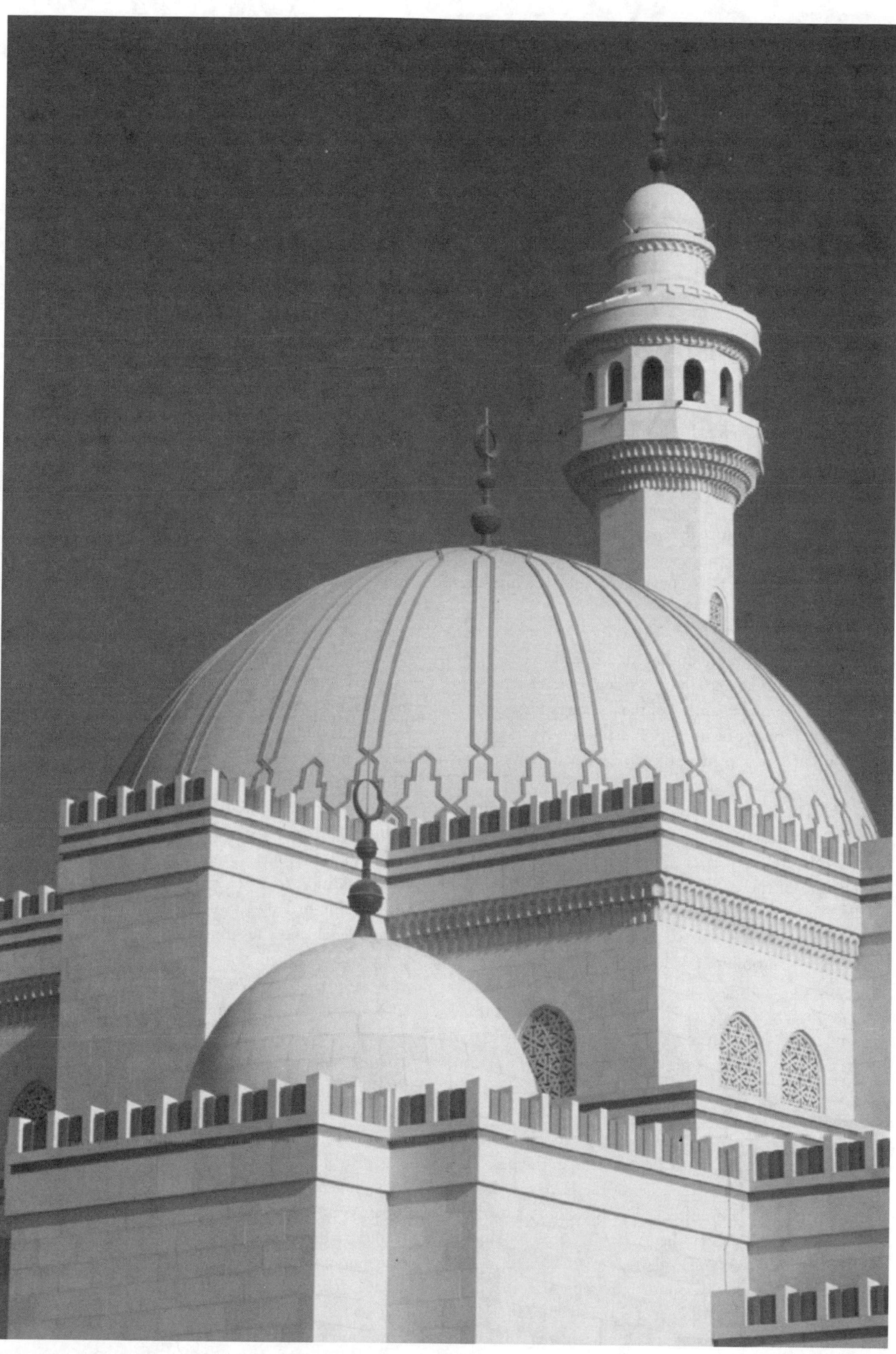

GRAND MOSQUE *All Muslims are obliged to perform collective prayers every Friday at noon during which they also swear allegiance to the Prophet's successor.* ADAM WOOLFITT/CORBIS

M

MOSQUE

History and Tradition

Personal prayer, regarded as the act of persons pouring forth their hearts to God, has been considered by many as the truest form.

PAGE 552

Hanafi, Maliki, and Hanbali) go to the same mosque. Shi'i Muslims, on the other hand, pray in mosques of their own.

The building proper has few characteristic symbols that identify it with the requirements of the faith: on the outside, a fountain for ablutions is provided so the Muslims can pray in ritual cleanliness, and a minaret serves to call the believers for prayer, while inside, a small, empty niche *(mihrab)* in the center of the *qiblah* wall indicates the direction of prayer, and in communal Friday mosques *(jami's)* a pulpit *(minbar)* is placed to the right of the *mihrab* for the prayer leader *(khatib)* to deliver his sermon. Other optional features are an enclosed area for the ruler *(maqsurah)*, the respondent's platform *(dikkah)*, and a cantor's lectern *(kursi)*.

It must be stressed that the mosque is not an exclusively religious space. Rather, like the Greek agora or the Roman forum, the court of the mosque has also been the favored place of public assembly, where the Friday *khutbah* has always addressed issues of politics, war, religion, and so forth, the community has acclaimed caliphs and governors, judges have held court, the treasury has been kept, and teaching has taken place.

OFFICIALS. Historically, mosques have been maintained through endowed properties (*waqf*, pl. *awqaf*) administered by a warden *(nazir)* who also oversees the management of the mosque's finances and the appointment of its staff. Since Islam has no clergy and no liturgy, mosque officials are few in number and their functions are simple and clear.

1. The imam, or prayer leader, is the most important appointee. In the early days the ruler himself filled this role; he was leader *(imam)* of the government, of war, and of the common *salat* ("ritual prayer"). Under the Abbasids, when the caliph no longer conducted prayers on a regular basis, a paid imam was appointed. While any prominent or learned Muslim can have the honor of leading prayers, each mosque specifically appoints a man well versed in theological matters to act as its imam. He is in charge of the religious activities of the mosque, and it is his duty to conduct prayers five times a day in front of the *mihrab*. The office is not a profession, for an imam usually has another occupation, such as judge, schoolteacher, or shopkeeper, and the title remains with the job rather than the person.

2. The *khatib*, or preacher of the Friday sermon, is also a religious appointee. The office, like that of the imam, evolved when the Abbasid caliph no longer delivered *khutbahs* on Fridays. A man learned in religious matters was appointed to represent the ruler. *Qadis* ("judges") have been frequently chosen as *khatibs*, and the office is usually hereditary. In large mosques, a number of *khatibs* are appointed to relieve one another, while in smaller mosques the offices of *khatib* and imam can be combined. Besides the *khatib*, the *wa'iz* and the *qass* act as edifying preachers without set forms.

3. The muezzin *(mu'adhdhin)* announces to the faithful the five daily prayers and the Friday noon service. According to tradition, the *adhan* ("announcement") was instituted in the first year of the Muslim era, and Bilal, the Prophet's freed Abyssinian servant (known for his sweet voice), was the first muezzin to convoke the believers to prayer. Originally called out from the top of the mosque, the *adhan* quickly acquired a formal locale in the *ma'dhanah* (minaret). Until the twentieth century, the muezzin climbed to the top of the minaret five times a day to issue the call to prayer, but with the introduction of electrical loudspeakers and recorded *adhans*, the highly developed art of the muezzin is no longer a prerequisite. The muezzins, whose office has sometimes been hereditary, are organized under chiefs *(ru'asa')* who are next to the imam in importance. At times they also perform the role of *muwaqqit*, the astronomer who ascertains the *qiblah*.

INSTITUTIONS. In early times, mosque construction was viewed as an obligation of the ruler, but with the spread of Islam, governors assumed that role in the provinces and were followed by private individuals. Once the building of mosques came to be regarded as a religious and social obligation—one *hadith* reported that the Prophet said, "For him who builds a mosque, God will build a home in Paradise"—and as a reflection of prestige, their number increased dramatically. Chronicles and travelers report, for instance, 3,000 mosques for tenth-century Baghdad, 300 for tenth-century Palermo, 241 for twelfth-century Damascus, and 12,000 for fourteenth-century Alexandria.

In addition to its religious and political functions, the mosque had always served as a center of administrative, legal, and educational activity. While the actual work of government was transferred early on from the mosque to a special *diwan* ("office") or *majlis* ("council"), matters of public finance continued to be transacted at the mosque, and the community treasury *(bayt al-mal)* was kept there. Similarly, in the time of the Prophet, legal questions were settled in the mosque; as early as 644/5 the *qadi* of Fustat held his sessions in the mosque, and in tenth-century Damascus the vice-*qadi* occupied a special *riwaq* ("aisle") in the court of the Umayyad mosque. When the judges officially moved to law courts, the mosque remained the center of legal studies. Finally, the mosque has served as the most continuous center of education in Islam, with study circles *(halaqat)* traditionally gathering around the teachers in the courtyard and at the base of columns. Some mosques, such as that of al-Mansur in Baghdad or those in Isfahan, Mashhad, Qom, Damascus, and Cairo, became centers of learning for students from all over the world. Teaching in mosques continued even after the proliferation of *madrasahs* where permanent, state-approved, and state-financed teaching took place. In modern times, the political, administrative, social, and educational functions of the community mosque have been taken over by specialized institutions.

— HAYAT SALAM-LIEBICH

ARCHITECTURAL ASPECTS

LITURGICAL ELEMENTS. The obligation to perform prayers is of seminal importance for the form of the mosque. The ritualized prayer *(salat)*, a sequence of standing, kneeling, and prostrating postures, is repeated five times daily and performed facing the spiritual center of the Muslim world, the Ka'bah in Mecca. This orientation, the *qiblah*, is the central organizing feature of the mosque. The singular importance of the *qiblah* was evidenced in the practice of Muhammad's armies when out in the field. At the hour of prayer a long line at right angles to the direction of Mecca was drawn in the sand, and ranks of soldiers lined up behind it to pray. As the first row of worshipers enjoyed greater proximity to Mecca, the source of blessing, the tendency was for the line to be broadly drawn. In the mosque likewise, the sanctuary was wide and shallow, in contrast to the narrow and deep configuration of the Christian church. The *qiblah* wall, the broad one turned toward Mecca, marked by an elaborate niche *(mihrab)* in its center, is the architectural culmination and focus of the entire mosque.

Prayer also requires an open, ritually purified floor area. Thus the simplest places of prayer *(musallas)*, used for large outdoor gatherings, are merely open areas with an indicated *qiblah* line or wall. Worshipers bring their own mats or prayer rugs to maintain ritual cleanliness and to define their individual space. For the same reason mosque interiors are generally carpeted and require baring the feet to avoid ritual defilement. To keep interior space open toward the *qiblah* wall, multiple-columned or "hypostyle" halls were the earliest and still prominent solution. Such halls can easily be expanded with additional rows of columns to accommodate a growing population. The hypostyle hall also reflects the equality of supplicants in prayer; lacking a priesthood, the mosques long maintained a communal rather than a hieratic organization. As the diversity of congregations grew, interiors were often elaborated with specially configured rows of pillars or ancillary *mihrab* niches spatially distinguishing areas for the different groups and quarters of the town.

Though prayer is often performed in isolation, the celebration of the *ummah*, or polity, is a concept basic to the mosque. Since Islam does not distinguish between spiritual and temporal power, the congregational or Friday mosque was generally (until the nineteenth century and the institution of colonial civil governments) the center for secular as well as religious practice. At the Friday noon prayer, the main weekly service, the entire adult community assembles at the congregational mosque for the reading of the sermon *(khutbah)*, a compilation of financial and political news. The congregational mosque often forms the core of a major urban center, a complex that can include markets, caravanseries, a government administration center, public baths, saints' shrines, and schools.

The small local or community mosques, simple oratories for daily prayer and without the more complex furnishings of the congregational mosque, are identified with the patrons, prominent families, charitable foundations, or communities. In an urban framework the local mosque establishes the identity of neighborhood quarters. Permission to build such a mosque constitutes official recognition of a community or group. While the congregational mosque and the simpler oratory mosque were originally two discrete types, the distinction is often lost today.

One final requirement for the performance of prayer is sequestration from the profane world. The words of God as spoken in the Qur'an are the subject of prayer and revelation. The mosque concretizes this contemplative arena in a building most often lacking exterior embellishment or elaborate facades. The architectural focus is rather on the secluded realm of the courtyard and the sanctuary. Furthermore, Muslims very early on rejected the depiction of animate objects or human figures in religious environments as degrading to the transcendental state of prayer. The subject of the ornamentation is thus the word itself. Domes, portals, and *mihrabs* are lavishly embellished with Qur'anic passages in stylized calligraphy.

The earliest building used for prayer and an important symbolic and functional precedent for the organization of the mosque was the prophet Muhammad's house in Medina (dating from the Hijrah or Emigration of 622) where his followers gathered for discussion and prayer. A rudimentary courtyard house, enclosed by a high wall with a shaded porch supported by palm trunks along one wall, it became the basis for the early hypostyle mosques of the seventh century. With its square courtyard *(sahn)* and covered sanctuary facing Mecca, the hypostyle plan established two basic features: the division of the mosque into court and sanctuary, and the intersection of the *qiblah* wall with the direction of Mecca. Functionally, it exemplified the dual role of Muhammad's house, and subsequently the mosque, as both an oratory for prayer and a social and political center for the community.

ARCHITECTURAL ELEMENTS AND FURNISHINGS. With the accession of the Umayyad

The most typical and certainly the most widely used means of conveying the Islamic message was and still is calligraphy.

PAGE 314

M

MOSQUE

Architectural Aspects

Africa is the only continent where Muslims are in the majority, while in Europe, Islam now constitutes the second largest religion.

PAGE 340

caliphate (661-750) and the expansion of the empire west into Syria, Palestine, Iraq, North Africa, and Spain, the influence of Hellenism and the development of a formalized liturgy resulted in a more elaborate assembly of parts. Primary among these, the *mihrab*, a niche evoking the symbolic presence of the Prophet, marks the direction of Mecca in the *qiblah* wall and is the symbolic culmination of the mosque. The *mihrab* is typically of an arched apsidal shape, lavishly ornamented and flanked by colonnettes. It may be surmounted by a window to show its directional position or fronted by a dome.

The *minbar*, a stepped pulpit that is as much a symbol of authority as an object for acoustical elevation, is located to the right of the *mihrab*. The top step of the *minbar* is reserved for the Prophet; the imam, or prayer leader, stands on the second step and uses the top one as a seat. After reading the *khutbah*, the imam descends the pulpit to lead the prayer standing before the *mihrab* as member of the assembly, a demonstration of his double role as both lawgiver and religious leader. *Minbars* are usually of wood and encrusted with nacre and ivory, though marble is also used.

The dome is of minor liturgical significance but is, along with the *mihrab*, the object of the most lavish architectural embellishment. Domes are often placed adjacent to the *qiblah* wall, emphasizing it from the exterior and washing it with light inside.

The minaret *(manarah)* evolved from the need for the call to prayer. In contrast to the Jewish use of the shofar (ram's horn) or the Christian use of wooden clappers, in Islam a specially delegated muezzin *(mu'adhdhan)* gives the call to prayer *(adhan)*. In Damascus, an early Muslim conquest, the old church tower was adapted to raise the call above the rooftops, a practice subsequently spurring the design of specially built towers. With the addition of a platform or a peripheral balcony the muezzin could broadcast the *adhan* to all corners of the city. Lighter and more slender than church towers encumbered with heavy bells, minarets took a variety of forms, from the square fortresslike towers of North Africa to the slender spires of Ottoman Turkey.

The fountain for ablutions is commonly located in the center of the courtyard. Tradition requires that the worshiper use running water and wash hands, feet, and face. An elevated step or stool may be provided to remove the cleansed supplicant from the impure floor or courtyard pavement. An additional marble jar may be found inside the mosque, a provision for the elderly who cannot be safely exposed to inclement weather. At the entrance to the mosque a low screen demarcates the boundary between ritually pure and impure areas.

The *dikkah*, somewhat analogous to the church choir, is a raised platform holding a group of respondents *(muballighun)* who echo the imam's prayers and postures, transmitting the liturgy to those unable to see or hear the imam himself. In widespread use by the eighth century, the *dikkah* was invented as a means of communicating the prayers among increasingly large congregations. It usually straddles the *qiblah* axis in the middle of the mosque, though it may sit off-axis so the officiant can be seen more readily. With the installation of electronic amplification systems, it has largely fallen into disuse.

A final piece of mosque furniture, the *kursi*, is a lectern for the recitation of the Qur'an. Usually made of wood and placed next to the *dikkah*, the *kursi* is lavishly ornamented and holds a platform for the Qur'an reciter *(qari)* to kneel while facing the *qiblah*. Sometimes it has a V-shaped slot to hold the very large Qur'ans that are often used.

HISTORICAL DEVELOPMENT. The hypostyle mosque had a pervasive influence over the first six Muslim centuries (seventh to twelfth centuries CE), spreading throughout the Middle East and the southern Mediterranean. The shaded porticoes, interior courtyards, and vast columned or arcuated halls were well suited to the native building practices, climatic conditions, and Hellenistic architectural heritage of the region. To the east a second major mosque tradition arose from indigenous Iranian building and coalesced during the Seljuk dynasty (1038-1194). Like the hypostyle mosque, the *iwan* plan derived from a courtyard house plan, one so culturally predominant in Iran that it was applied interchangeably to house, *madrasah*, and caravansary. The major focus and organizing feature of the plan is the central courtyard, which is faced with four vaulted, open porches *(iwans)*, one in the center of each side, and each encompassed by a giant portal *(pishtaq)*, providing functional, shaded outdoor areas and monumental entryways. Generally, the *iwan* leading to the sanctuary precedes a domed bay directly fronting the *mihrab*. Subsidiary rooms and spaces open off of an arcade surrounding the courtyard. This *iwan* plan yielded a distinctive mosque type featuring large domed spaces, slender round minarets, elaborate decorative brickwork, and polychromed mosaic ornamentation. The *iwan* mosque flourished in Iran, Afghanistan, and Central Asia through the seventeenth century.

Throughout the history of Islam the basic features of the mosque have been repeatedly reinterpreted and adapted to a wide range of geographical, cultural, and historical contexts. Egyptian mosques with richly decorated street facades took on a strong public presence beginning already in the Fatimid era (969-1171). The *iwan* mosque and Seljuk influence penetrated Egypt under the rule of Salah al-Din (Saladin) and his Ayyubid dynasty (1171-1250). Under the patronage of the Mamluk sultans (1250-1517), elaborate mosque complexes with monumental portals and towering domes and minarets delineated in carved and polychrome masonry marked the power, prestige, and material wealth of the rulers and their entourage.

When the Seljuks conquered India in the twelfth century, *iwan* mosques were transformed by a highly sophisticated Hindu building tradition of trabeated stone construction and elaborate inlay and ornamental stone carving into a host of regional developments. In the Indo-Islamic style of the Mughal period (1526-1858), the Hindu influence emerged in a courtyard that was frequently the primary spatial element and a sanctuary reduced to an elaborated pavilion or arcade wall. The giant *iwan* of the sanctuary, the portals, and the arcades were articulated with ogee arches, onion domes, and polychromed masonry bearing the ornamental lineage of both traditions.

In Turkey the Ottomans (1281-1922) made a major contribution with the centralized mosque, dominated both inside and outside by a massive dome. The earlier Seljuk rulers had brought the *iwan* plan to the cold climate of the Anatolian highlands, where the courtyard was soon engulfed by a pillared hall, a skylit dome over the ablution fountain, and a second dome over the *mihrab* bay. Under the Ottomans the *iwan* plan was monumentalized and merged with the Byzantine centralized basilica plan. The courtyard and sanctuary each assumed a square configuration, the courtyard open to the sky and surrounded by domed porches, the sanctuary sheltered beneath a single circular dome buttressed by semidomes. This ascending mountain of domes flanked by two or four needlelike minarets introduced a monumentality into the urban landscape that was alien to the hypostyle mosque.

In sub-Saharan Africa Islam arrived by way of the caravan routes around the year 1000. Along its path a synthesis of Muslim and African architectural concepts evolved. The Sudanic mosques merge indigenous mud architecture with the hypostyle mosque of North Africa in a range of ethnic variations. The Djenné Mosque has been rebuilt repeatedly in its history, most recently in 1909. Engulfing the hypostyle interior the pinnacled and buttressed facade integrates three square, symmetrically ordered minarets reflecting the indigenous monumental design. Projecting wooden dentils serve both as scaffolding for repairs to the adobe surface and as an ornamental motif. Male and female fertility symbols that ornament the towers and buttresses and the twin *mihrabs* and *minbars* are also a reflection of traditional religious beliefs.

The mosques of Southeast Asia and China were largely incorporated into existing building traditions. In China mosque design was influenced by Central Asian precedents but became increasingly sinicized through the centuries. With the first Muslim communities during the T'ang dynasty (618-907), the Central Asian masonry techniques employing domes, vaults, and arches was uniformly adopted. But already by the Laio dynasty (907-1125), the indigenous character of Chinese design asserted itself on both a national and a regional level. In the Niu-chieh Mosque in Peking (962), the prayer hall and ancillary pavilions sit within the confines of a traditional series of axial courtyards and gateways, while the wooden pavilions themselves feature elaborate bracket systems and tiled roofs with the characteristic upward-sloping corners.

In its long history the mosque has been subject to an ever-changing series of contingencies. Like Islam itself, the vitality of the mosque tradition must be seen as tied to its syncretic potential. While its contemplative and liturgical functions have barely altered through time, its specific political and social roles have varied widely according to the historical and cultural context. So, too, have climatic and technical exigencies continuously reshaped and delimited its exterior form. The aesthetic component, coordinating and unifying these diverse elements, has given expression to the particular significance of the mosque in space and time. Today the evolution of the mosque continues as the techniques of modern technology and contemporary society interact with ancient traditions of Islam.

— SUSAN HENDERSON

MUHAMMAD

Muhammad (c. 570-632 CE) was the Prophet or, as Muslims usually call him, the Messenger of God from whose activity the religion of Islam developed.

LIFE AND CAREER

Muhammad was a political as well as a religious leader, and it is convenient to look first at the external and political aspects of his career before considering the religious aspect in more detail; the latter, of course, cannot be completely excluded at any point.

FIRST PREACHING OF ISLAM. It was presumably the frustrations he faced in the years before his marriage that made Muhammad especially sensitive to the community of Mecca. He had skill in handling people and great intellectual gifts, and yet he was unable to use these qualities in trading because of his lack of capital. He is said to have spent a month each year in a cave near Mecca meditating on spiritual matters, including conditions in Mecca itself. About the year 610 he had some strange experiences. As a result of these he became convinced that he had been called to be the "Messenger of God" *(rasul Allah)* who would bear messages or revelations from God to the people of

The Qur'an is the scripture of the Muslim community. It comprises the revelations "sent down" to the prophet Muhammad over a period of approximately twenty-two years.

PAGE 564

M

MUHAMMAD

Life and Career

"I am only a warner, and a bringer of good tidings to a people who believe."

THE QUR'AN 7:188

Mecca. He was also convinced that these messages, which he "found in his heart," came from God and were not the product of his own thinking. After his death the messages were collected to form the book still in our hands, the Qur'an.

The messages which were earliest, so far as we can tell, spoke of God's power and his goodness to human beings, called on them to acknowledge their dependence on God and to be generous with their wealth, and warned them that all would appear before God on the Day of Judgment and be assigned to Paradise or Hell according to whether their deeds were good or bad. These messages were clearly relevant to the situation in Mecca. The great merchants thought they could control everything because of their wealth and expertise and that they could flout traditional nomadic moral standards with impunity, especially in such matters as the use of their wealth.

At first Muhammad communicated the messages only to his own household and a few close friends, but gradually an increasing number of people accepted the messages as true. A wealthy young man called al-Arqam offered his house as a meeting place, and the believers gathered there daily. Then, about three years after receiving the call to be Messenger of God, Muhammad began to preach publicly. By this time he had at least fifty followers (whose names have been preserved), and enough was generally known about the content of the messages for bitter opposition to have been aroused among the wealthy merchants.

THE PROPHET

Muslims often refer to the Prophet Muhammed, founder of Islam, as the Messenger of God.

CORBIS-BETTMANN

REJECTION AT MECCA. Muhammad and his followers deeply resented the treatment they received at the hands of their opponents in Mecca, perhaps chiefly because in the end this made it impossible for Muhammad to continue preaching and gaining disciples there. In themselves many of the measures were not serious, although slaves and those without clan protection could suffer bodily harm. Muhammad himself experienced verbal taunts and petty insults. That Muhammad was able to go on preaching in Mecca as long as he did was due to the fact that his own clan of Hashim continued, as custom and honor required, to protect him, although most of them did not accept what he preached. Attempts were made to persuade the clan either to stop the preaching or to refuse further protection, but Abu Talib, as clan chief, would do neither. In consequence, about 616, most of the clans of Quraysh joined together to boycott Hashim by refusing trade dealings and intermarriage.

When Muhammed learned there was a plot to kill him in Mecca, he and cousin Abu Bakr set out secretly, eluded pursuit from Mecca by various ruses, and reached Medina safely on 24 September 622. Medina, about 250 miles north of Mecca, was an oasis in which dates and cereals were grown. The inhabitants included various groups of Jews and Arabs. The groups who were called Jewish had intermarried to a considerable extent with Arabs and had adopted Arab customs, while still following Jewish religious practices. It was probably they who had developed agriculture in the oasis, and for a time they had been politically dominant.

RELATIONSHIPS WITH JEWS AND CHRISTIANS. When Muhammad made the Hijrah to Medina he hoped that the Jews there would accept him as a prophet, since he had been told that the messages or revelations he was receiving were identical in content with those of the biblical prophets. One or two Jews did so accept him and became Muslims, but the majority merely rejected his claim. At the same time Muhammad was coming to rely more on an anti-Jewish party in Medina. Islam was asserted to be the true religion of Abraham, from which Jews and Christians had deviated. It was pointed out that Abraham was neither a Jew nor a Christian (which is true) but a *hanif,* which the Qur'an takes to be one who believes in God without being attached to either Judaism or Christianity.

This ideological "break with the Jews" was followed over the next four years by physical attacks. After this there remained in Medina only a few small groups of Jews, now thoroughly chastened and very dependent on their Arab allies. Finally, soon after the expedition which led to the treaty of al-Hudaybiyah, Muhammad led an attack against the Jews of Khaybar, who had been trying to bribe Arab nomads to join them in attacking the Muslims.

There were few Christians in either Mecca or Medina. After the welcome given to the Muslims who immigrated to Abyssinia, Christians in general were accounted friends (as is shown by surah 5:82). In the last years of Muhammad's life, however, the Muslims had to fight against hostile Christian tribes along the route to Syria, and attitudes changed. Some of the Qur'anic arguments against Jews were also used against Christians, and there were also arguments against specifically Christian doctrines.

PROPHETHOOD

THE CALL TO BE A PROPHET. The experiences which led Muhammad to believe that he was called to be a messenger of God or prophet began with two visions which are briefly described in the Qur'an (53:1-18). In the first, he saw a mighty being on the horizon, who then came nearer; in the second, he saw the same being in mysterious circumstances. At first he appears to have thought that this being was God, but later he concluded it must have been the angel Gabriel. The early biographers of Muhammad present accounts of how the angel Gabriel appeared to him and said, "You are the Messenger of God," and then continued, "Recite in the name of your Lord . . ." (the beginning of surah 96, said to be the first revealed). Other accounts make the first revelation "Rise and warn . . ." (74:1-7). Both versions may well be only the conjectures of later scholars.

Many verses imply that Muhammad was a prophet to the Arabs, but there are also suggestions that his mission was universal, such as the title "Mercy to the Worlds" (21:107).

THE NATURE OF REVELATION. Traditional Islamic doctrine regards the words of the Qur'an as the actual speech of God, for which Muhammad was only a passive channel of transmission. He himself believed that he could distinguish such revelations from his own thinking, and in this his sincerity must be accepted. The insistence of Muslim scholars that Muhammad's personality contributed nothing to the Qur'an does not entirely rule out the possibility that the messages came somehow or other from Muhammad's unconscious.

THE PROPHET AS POLITICAL AND RELIGIOUS LEADER. It does not belong to the conception of messenger as such that he should also be political leader of his community. In the earlier passages of the Qur'an Muhammad is spoken of as a "warner" *(nadhir, mudhakkir),* whose function it was to "warn" his fellows that they would all have to appear before God to be judged on the Last Day. When Muhammad went to Medina, it was not part of the formal agreement that he was to be head of state; he was only one clan head out of nine. There was always, however, a readiness among the Arabs, even among his opponents at Mecca, to regard someone capable of receiving messages from God as being the person best able to guide the affairs of his community wisely. Muhammad's political power grew as he came to be respected more by the people of Medina; and the success of most of his expeditions contributed to that growth of respect. In his later years, too, many nomads who came to settle in Medina were attached to the "clan" of Emigrants, so that it became relatively more powerful. If at the end of his life Muhammad was ruling a large part of Arabia, that did not follow automatically from his being a prophet, but was due to his personal qualities. It is also to be noted that it was not his practice to seek revelations in order to solve political problems.

What has not been so clearly recognized is that much of the establishment of Islam as a religion is due to him personally, even in the Islamic view that he contributed nothing to the Qur'an. Although some justification can be found in the Qur'an for the religious institutions of Islam (such as the profession of faith, the five daily prayers, the fast, and the pilgrimage), they are by no means clearly defined there; they derive their precise shape from the practice of Muhammad and the early Muslims, and this was in part recognized by the later use of the *hadith* to justify these institutions.

— W. MONTGOMERY WATT

MUSLIM BROTHERHOOD

Founded in 1928 by Hasan al-Banna' (1906-1949), the Society of Muslim Brothers (al-Ikhwan al-Muslimun) was created to bring Egyptian Muslims back to an awareness of the objectives of religion within a society that had, in the view of al-Banna', been corrupted by alien ideologies and a materialist philosophy imported from the West.

HISTORICAL BACKGROUND

The British occupation of Egypt in 1882 had fueled a nationalist movement seeking independence from British rule; these aspirations culminated in the revolt of 1919 under the leadership of the aging politician Sa'd Zaghlul and the newly formed Wafd ("delegation") party. The decade of the 1920s offered the Egyptians constitutional government and hopes of an impending settlement between Britain and Egypt through a negotiated treaty. When Zaghlul died in 1927, these hopes were eroded, and a number of movements appeared as alternatives to the liberal

The most basic factor common to the neofundamentalist phenomena is a strong assertion of Islamic identity over and against the West.

PAGE 354

notions of government that had not been successful, partly through interference on the part of the king and the British authorities in Egypt and partly through ineptness on the part of the parliamentarians. In addition to the fascists and the communists, these movements included the Society of Muslim Brothers, who believed that the path of reforming the country's social and political problems lay in the islamization of institutions.

Hasan al-Banna', a primary school teacher who was the son of a small-town religious teacher, was early attracted to Sufism, which, along with classical Islamic studies, formed his major intellectual foundations and became the linchpins of his group. He described the Muslim Brotherhood as a "Salafiyah movement [espousing return to the early principles of Islam], a Sunni [orthodox] way, a Sufi [mystical] truth, a political organization, an athletic group, a cultural and educational union, an economic company, and a social idea." The movement spread rapidly, representing every segment of society from newly urbanized rural immigrants to high government officials. In its heyday in the 1940s, the Muslim Brotherhood claimed to represent one million members; later estimates are difficult to establish.

Muslims believe that Islam is God's eternal religion, described in the Qur'an as "the primordial nature upon which God created mankind."

PAGE 336

The structure of the organization was spelled out in the Fundamental Law of the Organization of the Muslim Brothers, promulgated in 1945 and later amended. Leading the organization was the general guide, who chaired the General Guidance Council (the policy-making body) and the Consultative or General Assembly, both of which were elective bodies. A secretary general was in charge of a secretariat linking the council and the rest of the organization. Two further subdivisions dealt with various committees (press, peasants, students, etc.) and with an administrative body supervising branches outside the capital. A chain of command was thus established over the entire membership.

SPREAD OF THE MOVEMENT

Weekly lectures, preaching in mosques, and periodic conferences allowed for popular participation, and the establishment of a press soon spread the message of the Society of Muslim Brothers further. Unconcerned with doctrinal differences, the participants concentrated on growth, action, and organization, and by 1939 they were ready for political activity. The war years were to provide them with a forum.

Nationalist agitation against the British continued with labor strikes and student demonstrations until, in 1942, the British threatened King Faruq (Farouk) with deposition and forced him to appoint a Wafd government under Mustafa al-Nahhas. This incident generated further support for the Muslim Brotherhood, by then the only other grouping with a mass base to rival the Wafd. Even among the Wafd leadership there were many who approved of the society as a bulwark against the spread of communism among the working class. For the next few years the society established links with disaffected officers within the army (who were later to carry out the revolution of 1952), and, unknown to even his closest colleagues, al-Banna' stockpiled weapons and created a secret apparatus trained in the use of armed violence for tactical operations.

With the end of the war, agitation for the evacuation of British forces from Egypt started once again, with frequent student demonstrations and acts of violence until the British garrison was finally withdrawn to the Canal Zone. The situation in Palestine and the war against Israel in 1948 provided the Muslim Brotherhood with an opportunity to collect more arms as members volunteered during the war and remained in the forefront of the fighting until their organization was dissolved in December 1948. The immediate cause for the government's action against the society was the death of the Egyptian chief of police, Salim Zaki, who was killed by a bomb thrown at him during student demonstrations protesting the armistice with Israel. Mass arrests followed as the government, fearing the society's growing influence, sought to proscribe it. Three weeks later, the prime minister, Mahmud Fahmi al-Nuqrashi, was assassinated by a Muslim Brother. In February 1949 Hasan al-Banna' was himself assassinated, probably with the complicity, if not the actual participation, of the government of the day.

After the Muslim Brotherhood was proscribed, its property confiscated, and its members put on trial, many of its remaining members fled to other Arab countries, where they founded autonomous branches of the society. In 1951 a Wafd government, seeking a buffer against rising leftist movements, allowed the society to reconvene. A judge with palace connections, Hasan Isma'il al-Hudaybi, was chosen as new leader. That same year the Wafd government unilaterally abrogated the treaty of 1936 with England, and Egyptian youth, including the Muslim Brothers, were encouraged to harass British camps in the Canal Zone. In January 1952 British forces attacked the Ismailia police station, and forty Egyptian policemen were killed. On the following day Cairo was set on fire in a monstrous riot that gutted the heart of the city. The Muslim Brothers were suspected of planning the riot, which they had not, although some of them were among the many participants. From then on the country was virtually without effective government until 23 July 1952, when the Free Officers movement, which included future Egyptian presidents Jamal 'Abd al-Nasir (Gamal Abdel Nasser) and Anwar al-Sadat, seized power and three days later sent the king into exile.

There had been strong links between the Muslim Brotherhood and the Free Officers—Nasser and Sadat had both been members of the society. Once all political parties had been disbanded, the only focus for mass support lay with the society. Nasser knew that it represented the lone challenge to his authority and that its leaders expected to share power with the officers; a power struggle was inevitable. In 1954 a member of the Muslim Brotherhood allegedly attempted to shoot Nasser during a public rally, and once again the society was proscribed and its members arrested.

The society remained underground throughout the Nasser era. When Sadat came to power in 1970 all prisoners were released, including the Muslim Brothers, and, to combat the Nasserite current, Sadat allowed the society to reestablish itself under the leadership of an *'alim* (religious scholar), Shaykh al-Tilimsani, and to publish its own newspapers. Meanwhile newer associations patterned after the society, the Islamic *jamaat* ("groups"), had appeared. Some of these were extensions of the Muslim Brotherhood; others regarded the society as retrograde and beholden to the government. It was a member of one of the latter, more extremist groups who assassinated Sadat in 1981.

DOCTRINES AND IMPACT

According to the program of al-Banna', the Society of Muslim Brothers was given a mission to restore the rule of the *shariah* (Islamic law) to Egypt, and to all other Muslim countries where their missionary activities had set up affiliates. Rule of the *shariah* rendered inadmissible the separation of church and state, for the state, they believed, existed in order to serve religion and to facilitate the fulfillment of Islamic religious duties. The Islamic state had the Qur'an as its constitution; its government operated through *shura,* or consultation, and the executive branch, guided by the will of the people, ruled through Islamic principles. The ruler, chosen by the people, was responsible to them and not above the law, with no special privileges. Should he fail in his duties he was to be ousted. Freedom of thought, of worship, and of expression were vital, as was freedom of education. Finally, freedom of possessions was to be maintained within the limits set by Islamic law, which frowns upon the excessive accumulation of wealth and enjoins *zakat* ("alms") as a basic religious duty. Social justice was to be the guiding principle of government.

The significance of the Society of Muslim Brothers and of its modern offshoots, the *jamaat,* is that they represent a protest movement couched in a traditional Islamic idiom that expresses the ethos of a people. The society arose in protest against a foreign occupation that threatened the identity of a people and the dissolution of its culture and religion. It spoke to people in the language they understood and appreciated, that of Islam and its historical past, and it did not posit newfangled notions derived from a Western idiom, although the society did use Western techniques of mass communications and of assembly, even ideas of government, which were garbed in Muslim idiom. As such it was comprehensible to the masses who suffered political discrimination and economic exploitation by a government that was largely indifferent to their welfare, especially during periods of economic recession. Those who were disillusioned with Western ideologies and their ability to solve Egypt's problems, or indeed the problems of any Muslim country, turned to the precepts of the society, or to similar movements that they identified with their roots and cultural authenticity *(asa-lah),* for guidance and spiritual consolation. The same phenomenon was reproduced during the Sadat regime (1970-1981) when the "Open Door" *(infitah)* policy disrupted society and led to rampant consumerism, which, exacerbated by the influx of oil money, raised fears of becoming engulfed by westernization.

Organizations such as the Muslim Brotherhood or the *jamaat* are regarded by some Muslim regimes as dangerous foci of opposition and have thus met with violent repression. In Syria the regime of Hafiz al-Asad has been in conflict with the Muslim Brotherhood since 1976. In 1982 the army shelled the city of Hama, a Muslim Brotherhood stronghold; portions of the city were leveled and casualties were variously estimated at ten thousand to twenty thousand. Similar attacks were repeated in Aleppo, Homs, and Latakia. In Iraq the regime of Sadam Husayn waged a relentless campaign against the Shi'i group al-Da'wah al-Islamiyah. In Saudi Arabia Muslim militants seized the Grand Mosque in Mecca for several days in 1979. In Sudan the Muslim Brotherhood forced the regime of Muhammad Ja'far al-Numayri (Numeiri) to adopt Islamic policies in 1977. Comparable militant groups have spread to most Muslim countries irrespective of their forms of government.

— AFAF LUTFI AL-SAYYID MARSOT

The historical origin of the shari'ah lies in the revelation that Muslims believe was given to the prophet Muhammad by God.

PAGE 354

MYSTICISM

No definition could be both meaningful and sufficiently comprehensive to include all experiences that, at some point or other, have been described as "mystical." In 1899 Dean W. R. Inge listed twenty-five definitions. Since then the study of world religions has considerably expanded, and new, allegedly mystical cults have sprung up everywhere. The etymological lineage of the term provides little assistance in formulating an unambiguous definition.

MYSTICISM OF THE SELF

Mysticism belongs to the core of all religion. Those religions that had a historical founder all started with a powerful personal experience of immediate contact. But all religions, regardless of their origin, retain their vitality only as long as their members continue to believe in a transcendent reality with which they can in some way communicate by direct experience. The significance of such an experience, though present in all religion, varies in importance. Christianity, especially in its reformed churches, attaches less significance to the element of experience than other faiths do. In Vedantic and Samkhya Hinduism, on the contrary, religion itself coincides with the kind of insight that can come only from mystical experience. Their particular concept of redemption consists in a liberation from change and from the vicissitudes of birth and death. Their craving for a state of changeless permanence aims not at some sort of unending protraction of the present life but rather at the extinction of all desire in this life. Hindu spirituality in all its forms displays an uncommonly strong awareness of the sorrowful quality of the human condition.

"Work out your salvation with diligence."

THE PALI CANON 6:10

The original Vedic religion with its emphasis on sacrifice and rite appears rather remote from what we usually associate with the term *mysticism.* Yet two elements in its development strongly influenced the later, more obviously mystical direction. First, forms of meditation became at some point acceptable substitutes for the performance of the actual sacrifice and were held to yield equally desirable benefits. Though such forms of concentration had little in common with what we understand today by contemplation, they nevertheless initiated an interiorization that Hinduism would pursue further than any other religion (Dasgupta, 1972, p. 19). Second, the term *brahman,* which originally referred to the sacred power present in ritual and sacrifice, gradually came to mean a single, abstractly conceived Absolute.

An upanisad is literally a mystical–often "secret"–connection, interpreted as a teaching of mystical homologies.

PAGE 274

In the Upanisads (eighth to fifth century BCE) the unifying and the spiritualizing tendencies eventually merged in the idea of an inner soul (atman), the Absolute at the heart of all reality to which only the mind has access. This is not a metaphysical theory, but a mystical path to liberation. It requires ascetical training and mental discipline to overcome the desires, oppositions, and limitations of individual selfhood. "As a man, when in the embrace of a beloved wife, knows nothing within or without, so this person, when in the embrace of the intelligent Soul, knows nothing within or without" (*Brha-daranyaka* 4,3.22). Here lies the origin of the *advaita* (nondualist monism that would become dominant in classical Hinduism).

THE MYSTICISM OF EMPTINESS: BUDDHISM

It seems difficult to conceive of two religious doctrines more different from one another than Hinduism, especially Samkhya, and Buddhism. In one, we find a quest for an absolute self *(atman, purusa);* in the other, the obliteration of the self (*anatman/anatta*—no soul). Yet upon closer inspection the two appear to have a great deal in common. Both are systems of salvation, rooted in a profoundly pessimistic attitude about the changing world of everyday existence, and they aim at a condition of changelessness that surpasses that existence. The Buddhist description both of the experience and of the path that leads to it is characterized by a spare simplicity as well as by a persistent reluctance to use any but negative predicates. Their development varies from the Hinayana to the Mahayana doctrines. But even in the Theravada tradition, the Eightfold Path of virtue concludes with "right concentration," which, in turn, must be obtained in eight successive forms of mental discipline (the *dhyanas*). Once again we are confronted with a faith that from its origins is headed in a mystical direction. The three negative terms—nonattainment, nonassertion, nonreliance—define a state of utmost emptiness by which Nagarjuna's Madhyamika school (150 CE) described enlightenment.

The ways to emptiness vary. Mental training by the confrontation of paradoxes has been mentioned. Other ways, especially Yogacara Buddhism, emphasize the attainment of "pure thought." This consists not in thinking *about* something but rather in the insight that thought is not in any object but in a subject free of all objects. Yogacara pursues the basic truth of emptiness in a practical rather than a logico-metaphysical way.

Of particular importance here is Ch'an (Jpn., Zen) Buddhism, a doctrine imported into China by the Indian Bodhidharma that later spread to Japan. Most consistent of all in its pursuit of emptiness, it rejected all dependence (nonreliance), including the one based on the Buddha's own words.

Most typical of that final state of emptiness as Zen Buddhists conceive of it is that it results not in a withdrawal from the real but in an enhanced ability to see the real as it is and to act in it unhampered by passion and attachment. Thus emptiness creates a new worldliness.

MYSTICISM OF THE IMAGE: EASTERN AND EARLY WESTERN CHRISTIANITY

Unlike some other religions, Christianity has never equated its ideal of holiness with the attainment of mystical states. Nor did it encourage seeking such

states for their own sake. Nevertheless, a mystical impulse undeniably propelled it in its origin and determined much of its later development.

The mystical quality of Jesus' life is most clearly stated in the Fourth Gospel. Some of the words attributed to him may have originated in theological reflection rather than in his own expression. But they thereby witness all the more powerfully to the mystical impulse he was able to transmit to his followers.

The first attempt at a systematic theology of the mystical life in Christ was written by Origen. In his *Twenty-seventh Homily on Numbers* Origen compares spiritual life to the Jews' exodus through the desert of Egypt. Having withdrawn from the pagan idols of vice, the soul crosses the Red Sea in a new baptism of conversion. She passes next through the bitter waters of temptation and the distorted visions of utopia until, fully purged and illuminated, she reaches Terah, the place of union with God. In his commentary on the *Song of Songs,* Origen initiated a long tradition of mystical interpretations that see in the erotic biblical poem just such a divine union. His commentary also presents the first developed theology of the image: the soul is an image of God because she houses the primal image of God that is the divine Word. The entire mystical process thus comes to consist in a conversion to the image, that is, to ever greater identity with the indwelling Word. The emphasis on the ontological character of the image of God in man (as opposed to the external copy) persists throughout the entire Christian tradition and holds the secret of its amazing mystical power.

Augustine (354-430), the towering figure who stands at the beginning of all Western theology (also, and especially, spiritual theology), described the divine image rather in psychological terms. His treatise *On the Trinity* abounds with speculations on the soul's similarity to the Trinity, such as her constituting one mind out of the three faculties of intellect, will, and memory. They would amount to no more than superficial analogies were it not that God's presence in that same inner realm invites the soul to turn inward and convert the static resemblance into an ecstatic union. "Now this Trinity of the mind is God's image, not because the mind resembles, understands, and loves itself [the superficial analogy], but because it has the power also to remember, understand, and love its Maker" (*On the Trinity* 14.12.15). In actualizing the divine potential of its external resemblance, in allowing it to be directed to its archetype, the soul is gradually united with God.

Johannes Eckhart, possibly the most powerful mystical theologian of the Christian Middle Ages, synthesized the Greek and Augustinian theories of the image with a daring negative theology in one grandiose system. God is Being, and being in the strict sense is only God. With this bold principle, Eckhart reinterprets a Thomist tradition that "analogously" attributed being to God and finite existence. For Eckhart, the creature *qua* creature does not exist. Whatever being it possesses is not its own, but remains God's property. Both its limited essence (what determines it as this being rather than that) and its contingent existence (that it happens to be) are no more than the negative limits of its capacity to receive God's own being. "Every creature," Eckhart wrote, "radically and positively possesses Being, life and wisdom from and in God, and not in itself."

The soul's being is generated in an eternal now with (indeed, within) the divine Word: "The Father bears his Son in eternity like himself. 'The Word was with God, and God was the Word' (Jn 1:1): the same in the same nature. I say more: He has borne him in my soul. Not only is she with him and he equally with her, but he is in her: the Father in eternity, and no differently" (ibid., p. 135). The mystical process then consists in a person's becoming conscious of his divine being.

"Now this Trinity of the mind is God's image, not because the mind resembles, understands, and loves itself [the superficial analogy], but because it has the power also to remember, understand, and love its Maker"

AUGUSTINE DE TRINITATE

MYSTICISM OF LOVE: MODERN CHRISTIAN MYSTICISM AND SUFISM

Some time during the twelfth century, Christian piety underwent a basic change: its approach to God became more human and affective. Love had, of course, always been an essential ingredient. But now it became the whole thing. At first it appeared in conjunction with the newly recovered trinitarian mysticism. The same Cistercians who reintroduced the Greek theology of the image to the West also initiated love mysticism.

The emphasis on love is part of a more general tendency to involve the entire personality in the religious act. The new spiritual humanism (partly influenced by the Spanish Islamic culture) would revive interest in the psychological theory of Augustine and pay an unprecedented spiritual attention to the created world. The first great name to emerge was Bernard of Clairvaux. No Christian mystic has ever surpassed "the mellifluous doctor," as he is called, in the eloquent praise of spiritual love.

The humanization of man's relation to God transforms man's attitude toward a creation in which God now comes to be more intimately present. An interpersonal, and hence more creaturely, relation to God is ready to accept each creature on its own terms and for its own sake. In this respect its attitude differs essentially from the image mysticism that holds the creature worthy of spiritual love only in its divine core, where it remains rooted in God. The love mystic also cherishes its finite, imperfect being, which, resulting from a divine act of creation, is endowed with a sacred quality of its own. The mystery of the divine incarnation here attains a more universal level of meaning, as if Christians suddenly understood how much the creation must matter to a God who himself has become flesh.

Sufism. With its stern emphasis on law and orthodoxy, Islam hardly seems to present a fertile soil for intensive personal experience of the love of God. Yet Islam assumes the entire social system, *shari'ah* (the way), into a privileged communal relation with God. Moreover, the Qur'an states that, next to the ordinary believers who serve their creator according to the precepts of the law, there are some to whom God communicates his essential mystery inwardly in peace of the soul and friendship with God (Qur'an 17:27). Here the Prophet allows for the possibility of a realm of personal religion. The possibility was soon actualized and eventually flowered into unparalleled mystical beauty. Even the unique authority of the Qur'an has in an indirect way contributed to Islam's mystical wealth, for precisely because it remains the supreme norm of its interpretation, pious readers may find in it whatever meaning divinely inspired insight *(istinbat)* privately reveals to them. Only when personal interpretation openly clashes with established doctrine (especially its rigorous monotheism) could religious authorities interfere. Thus, paradoxically, Islam, the "religion of the book," allows greater freedom of interpretation than religions that place less emphasis on the written word. Though early Muslim mysticism stayed in close connection with the Islamic community, conflicts arose. Already at the time of Hasan al-Basri (d. 728), the patriarch of Islamic mysticism, Sunni traditionalists objected to his attempt to go beyond the letter of law and doctrine. Thus began the opposition between "internal" and "external" religion that, from the tenth century on, led to increasingly severe confrontations. Nevertheless, a deep personal piety remained an essential element of Islam that substantially contributed to rendering it a world religion.

CHRISTIAN MYSTIC

Bernard of Clairvaux, also known as the "mellifluous doctor," praised spiritual love as part of a general tendency to involve the entire personality in the religious act. This is the cloister of Saint Bernard Clairvaux, a church dedicated in his honor.

LEE SNIDER/CORBIS

Sufi piety reached a temporary truce with orthodox learning in al-Ghazali (d. 1111), the greatest of the theologians. Bypassing the antinomian trends that had emerged, he returned to a more traditional attempt to emphasize experience over the letter of the law. With Ibn al-'Arabi (d. 1240) the dependence on Neoplatonism (especially the so-called *Theology of Aristotle*) and, with it, the movement toward monism became more pronounced than ever. He provided the link between Western classical culture and Eastern Islamic mysticism that culminated in Jalal al-Din Rumi. Sufi mysticism, however much inclined toward monism, never abandoned the language and imagery of love. Ibn al'Arabi, with al-Ghazali the most philosophical of all Muslim mystics, never ceases to integrate his Neoplatonic vision with the Qur'an's dualistic doctrine of man's relation to God. The Absolute for him is an indistinct One that, overcome by the desire to be known, projects itself through creative imagination into apparent otherness. In this projection the relation of the One to the created world, specifically to man, determines that of the Absolute to the differentiated idea of God, the intellectual pole as opposed to the cosmic pole of finite being. All that the creature is, is divine, yet God always exceeds creation. Through man's mediation the dependent, created world returns to its primordial unity. As the image of God, man imposes that image upon the cosmos and reflects it back to its original.

Millenarianism is properly an adjunct of eschatology, the study of last things.

PAGE 433

ESCHATOLOGICAL MYSTICISM: JEWISH MYSTICS

Judaism has produced forms of mysticism so unlike any other and so variant among themselves that no common characteristic marks them all. At most we can say that they "commune" with one another, not that they share an identical spirit. Gershom Scholem wisely embedded this irreducible diversity, reflective of a spiritual Diaspora, in the very title of his authoritative work *Major Trends in Jewish Mysticism* (1941). The closest he comes to a general characteristic is the point at which he draws attention to the persistent presence of eschatological traits in Jewish mysticism: "This eschatological nature of mystical knowledge becomes of paramount importance in the writings of many Jewish mystics, from the anonymous authors of the early He-khaloth tracts to Rabbi Naham of Brazlav" (p. 20). The eschatological element most clearly appears in the earliest trend: the often gnostically influenced mythical speculation on Ezekiel's vision of the throne-chariot, the *merkavah.* Mysticism around this theme began in the first centuries of the common era. It consisted of an attempt to ascend to the divine throne beyond the various intermediate spheres (the *heikhalot*). Except for its biblical starting point (first developed in the Ethiopic *Apocalypse of Enoch*), the impact of gnostic *pleroma* mythology dominates this spiritual "throne world." But also the typically Hellenistic connection of mysticism and magic appears to have been strong. *Merkavah* mysticism declined after the seventh century, but enjoyed a steady revival in Italy in the ninth and tenth centuries, which, in turn, may have influenced medieval German Hasidism.

Hasidic "theology" shows a resemblance to Neoplatonism even in its Greek Christian development. God's glory *(kavod)* is distinct from God's being as a first manifestation of his presence *(shekhinah),* which mediates between this hidden essence and the fully manifest creation. The Hasidim indulged in elaborate speculation about the inner and outer glory of God, and about the kingdom of his created yet hidden presence.

These daring speculations seldom developed into a coherent theology. In that respect they differed from the spiritual movement that, from the fourteenth century on, would largely replace it—Qabbalah. It absorbed the Neoplatonic currents that had swept through the Arabic and Jewish culture of twelfth- and thirteenth-century Spain. Considering the hazardous nature of its thought, its relation to normative tradition and official authority remained, on the whole, remarkably peaceful, if not always amiable. Indeed, the branch that produced the most daring speculation found its expression mostly in traditional rabbinical commentaries on the sacred text. They all aim at assisting the soul to untie the "knots" that bind it to this world of multiplicity and to allow it to return to its original unity (surprisingly named after Aristotle's Agent Intellect). This union may be attained through contemplation of a sufficiently abstract object, such as the letters of the Hebrew alphabet. Any combination of letters results in word figures that in some way refer to the sacred tetragrammaton of the divine name, YHVH.

The theophysical mysticism that resulted in that unsurpassed masterpiece of mystical speculation, is the *Zohar* (Book of Splendor). The writer, familiar with the philosophies of Maimonides and of Neoplatonism, has, above all, undergone the influence of unknown gnostic sources. Synthesizing all qabbalistic writings of the century, he attempts to stem the rationalist trend by giving traditional Judaism a hidden mystical interpretation. Thus this highly esoteric work was, in fact, written for the enlightened Jewish intelligentsia of late-fourteenth-century Spain. Central in the *Zohar* doctrine is the theology of the *sefirot,* the ten "regions" into which the divine emanation extends itself. Importantly, the divine *pleroma* of these *sefirot* does not emanate *from* God: it remains within God as his manifest being, in contrast to the "hidden God."

Jewish mysticism shows an unparalleled variety of forms ranging from deep speculation to purely emotional experience. It consistently appeals to scriptural authority, yet no mystical movement ever strayed further from theological orthodoxy than late messianic Qabbalah.

— LOUIS DUPRÉ

NEW CALEDONIA RELIGION

New Caledonia religion is best known from the work of Maurice Leenhardt, a former Protestant missionary (Société des Missions Évangéliques Pratique de Paris), who was Marcel Mauss's successor as professor of comparative religions at the École Pratique des Hautes Études.

Because each local group (*mwaro*) in New Caledonia is linked with an animal or plant or other natural phenomenon, Western observers have described the religion of the island as "totemism." Though this term is now less fashionable than it was in the period from 1880 to 1940, it can still, for convenience' sake, be applied to the New Caledonia religious system. The local groups have divided among themselves all the aspects of nature that either can be utilized or need to be feared, with each group becoming the master of a particular aspect. Within each group, one of the members of the most junior line, referred to as the group's "master," is in charge of performing the ritual that will protect or benefit all the *mwaro*. Thus, the master of the yam ensures a good crop over the whole of the valley. Along the sea one finds masters of the trade winds, the shark, the whale, or the mosquito, while masters of the thunder are to be found nearer the mountain range.

Each master not only ensures prosperity and wards off natural disasters, but also controls the specific sickness thought to be linked with the totemic entity assigned to him. If someone is ailing, word is sent to a seer, who divines the cause of the sickness. A messenger is then sent to the master in charge of the force responsible for the sickness. The master prays and gives the necessary herbal remedies to the patient; many of these medications are quite effective in treating at least those illnesses that were not brought by Europeans.

The natures of the New Caledonia gods are complex, and Leenhardt spent considerable time attempting to understand them. R. H. Codrington, in *The Melanesians* (1891), distinguished two principal types of gods: those who were once human and those who have never been human. The New Caledonians, however, make no linguistical distinction, both types of gods being referred to either as *bao* or *due.* The two kinds of deities are linked in the figure of Teê Pijopac, a god who has himself never been human but who controls the subterranean or submarine land of the dead, where all must go. According to local belief, the dead reach the entrances to this land by following ridges that lead down to the sea. At one of these entrances, known as Pucangge (near Bourail), the goddess Nyôwau examines all those who wish to enter to make sure that their left earlobe is pierced. She pierces any unpierced lobe with the mussel-shell knife that she also uses to peel yams.

"The voice of the dead was a living voice to me."

ALFRED TENNYSON
IN THE VALLEY OF THE CAUTERETZ 1847

There is constant communication between the living and the dead. The dead can be seen and spoken with when needed. They can be called upon to help in a crisis such as sickness or war, or to favor the results of family labors. Myths speak of the living going to the land of the dead and of the dead acting in the land of the living. There are, for example, various versions of a myth in which a loving husband attempts to bring his young wife back from the land of the dead. He either succeeds in his quest through the help of a bird (a common link for communication with the dead), or he fails. Among the stories about people from the underworld acting among the living there are those that describe an unsuspecting husband who might find, for example, that his new wife snores at night, or that she is double-jointed, both of which are characteristics of people from the underworld. There are also numerous versions of a myth about a goddess, usually Toririhnan, who, after drowning the pregnant wife of a chief, disguises herself as the wife by filling her belly with pots. The true wife, however, is saved by a miracle and taken away to a distant island. Later, this woman returns with her grown sons; their identity is revealed, and the usurper is killed.

Ancestors are one of the many types of spirits recognized by Melanesian tribal peoples.

PAGE 30

Other gods preside over agriculture, such as Kapwangwa Kapwicalo, who protects irrigated taro terraces in the Gomen area, or Toririhnan, who causes it to rain each time she blows her nose at the top of the Hienghène Valley. There are also a great number of gods whose function is the protection of a given clan, protection that is often traced back to the clan's mythical origin. Gods can have sexual relations with humans, an event that either can have terrifying consequences—such as the death of the mortal or the turning backward of his head—or can resemble normal human sexual acts. Myths in which families trace their origins to instances of intercourse between gods and humans record both types of occurrences.

The term underworld *refers to the subterranean region inhabited by the dead.*

PAGE 685

Indeed in Melanesia, as in Polynesia, all genealogies have divine origins, and although the religion of New Caledonia is totemistic in appearance there is no available evidence that any of the kinship groups believe that they are descended from the animal species or natural phenomenon with which they are spiritually associated. These totem entities—called *rhë re* (sg., *rhë e*)—represent the "spiritual belonging" of the group and are passed along through the male line. When a woman marries outside of her totem group, her *rhë e* is sometimes said to follow her. This does not mean, however, that the *rhë e* has left its original abode; because mythical beings are understood to be ubiquitous they are thought to be able to dwell in the two places at once.

There are occasions on which the *rhë re* and the *bao* (who were formerly human) meet. Such a meeting will take place in part of the landscape that is outside of human control, such as the bush, the forest, or the mountain range. The dead, those *bao* who were formerly human, can merge with the *rhë e* that is linked with their clan. Thus, for example, if thunder is associated with a particular group, the rumbling of the thunder is also the voice of the dead of that clan. Also in accordance with this pattern, no ancestor of the octopus group, for example, will appear in the form of a shark, unless they have what early authors referred to as "linked totems," that is, clusters of symbols all of which are linked to a certain *mwaro.* In some cases a group's *rhë e* will manifest itself in various forms depending on the setting: thus, for some chiefly families of the so-called Naacuwe-Cidopwaan group the *rhë e* takes the form of a lizard if seen inland, but becomes a water-snake on the beach, or a shark in the sea, and is also thought of as a masked male dancer said to emerge from the sea.

Missionaries who worked among the New Caledonians attempted to find the natives' idols in order to destroy them; they discovered objects resembling idols that had been carefully preserved by clan leaders over the course of centuries. Pierre Lambert (1900) has published illustrations of some of these items. They are stones of various shapes about which little is actually known except that they turn up from time to time in yam gardens, are linked with the clan's totem entity, and are in some way connected with success in farming, fishing, weather control, and so forth, as were the thunderstones (meteorites) of the Europeans of old. It has been observed that when these artifacts are used as repositories of the divine presence for sacramental purposes—and not as representations of gods—they can be replaced if lost or confiscated. This provision allows for the indefinite preservation of this type of link with the divine.

It is important to recognize that the mythical systems of the hundreds of different clans are highly diversified, a diversity that appears most clearly in the origin myths of the various groups. Some clans believe their spiritual origin to be the mountain that is called Souma (in the Ajië language) or Caumyë (in the Paici language). The vernacular texts obtained by Leenhardt demonstrated that the mountain had a connection with the creation of mankind and that its importance stems from the gods who live in the various principal mountains. For instance, Ka To Souma, the god associated with Souma, guards one of the possible entrances to the subterranean land of the dead. So great is the respect for, and fear of, this god that his proper name (Gomawe or Kavere) is never uttered. Other clans, usually those living near the watershed, claim a spiritual link with one or another of the forms of thunder. These different forms are grouped in distinctive ways according to the local theology, thereby giving each clan a powerful mythical protector. We can thus classify clans according to their myths; conversely, mythical beings in charge of protecting the various clans may be classified according to the patrilineal marriage moieties with which they are associated in the Paici area or, in the north, according to the political phratries to which they belong.

The nearby Loyalty Islands (Uvéa, Lifou, and Maré) present a different set of problems. Although the inhabitants have been Christians for a century and a half (twice as long as the natives of New Caledonia proper) sacred groves still exist there, the old deities are remembered, and the cult of the dead continues to surface from time to time. However, the distribution of mythical beings among the families of the islands is significantly different from what prevails in New Caledonia. One essential aspect of the religion of the Loyalty Islands is that direct relations with the invisible world are the prerogative of the oldest established clans. These privileged clans, called *ten adro* (on Lifou), *wäi* (on Uvéa), or *èlè-tok* (on Maré), act as hosts to visiting gods. It is this status as host to the gods that provides legitimacy to the chiefly lines of today. The senior clans are also, however, the wardens of the invisible road along which the dead travel, eventually diving into the sea and reaching the island of Heo (Beautemps-Beaupré), where the entrance to the world of the dead is located. At the court of each of the paramount chiefs, a special person (called Atesi on Lifou and, on Maré, Acania) has the role of being the representative of these clans. He acts as their intermediary, for neither they nor their yams can enter a chief's house since their presence would endanger his life. On these islands there is thus a formalized distinction between families having the privilege of communicating with the divine world—each *ten adro* has its own god, to which only it can pray—and those who must be satisfied with praying to their own dead. The latter use diviners to discover whom they must negotiate with in order to ward off any invisible power which is causing injury to the clan.

— JEAN GUIART

taken, assumptions. They show that modern people are not necessarily less religious than their ancestors, that religious innovation is no more likely to be progressive than conservative, that religion is not the exclusive prerogative of church-type organizations, and that the dynamics of new religious movements cannot be separated from social change.

— JAMES A. BECKFORD

NEW RELIGIONS

AN OVERVIEW

THE CONCEPT. Terms such as *new religion, new religious movement,* and *cult* are used in widely differing ways, yet their application is not arbitrary: it is conditioned by historical and theological, as well as academic, considerations. While there seems to be agreement that "new religions" are adaptations of such ancient traditions as Shinto, Buddhism, Hinduism, and the primal religions of Africa, the definition of *new religious movement* is much looser. In fact it serves as an umbrella term for a stunning diversity of phenomena ranging from doctrinal deviation within world religions and major churches to passing fads and spiritual enthusiasms of a questionably religious kind. *Cult* also lends itself to different meanings but is further complicated by pejorative connotations of exoticism and insignificance. In the study of new or "cult" forms of religion, it is important to recognize that disagreement over definitions and concepts is endemic, and that the empirical diversity of these phenomena defies the selection of any single, all-purpose term. Attempts to legislate usage are doomed, but the search for distinctions in usage can help to explain what is taken for granted about the old and the new in different religious traditions.

MEANING. The importance of the study of new religious movements and cults has been established on several grounds. First, it indicates the extent to which established religious organizations are challenged, both for the allegiance of their members and because of the influence that they wield. Second, the conditions in which people are prepared to participate in new movements are revealing in that they display the shifting lines of tension or fracture in social and cultural structures. Third, the controversies which surround many new movements reflect deep-rooted assumptions and prejudices. In short, the main reasons for studying such movements have to do less with what they represent in themselves and more to do with what they indirectly reveal about the state of society, other religious bodies, or structures of meaning.

Systematic studies of new religious movements and cults have helped to scotch several common, but mis-

NEW RELIGIONS AND CULTS IN THE UNITED STATES

Since the 1960s the United States has been experiencing conspicuous spiritual ferment and innovation, which has been compared by some observers to the "Great Awakenings" of the eighteenth and nineteenth centuries. Four principal elements seem to have contributed to the present ferment: (1) a substantial growth of "Eastern" mystical religions (e.g., Hinduism, Buddhism, Sufism); (2) a similiar spread of quasi-religious, therapeutic or "human potential" movements such as Scientology, est (Erhard Seminars Training), Arica, and Silva Mind Control, whose philosophies are often composites of Eastern mysticism and pop psychology; (3) a parallel surge of evangelical, pentecostal, and fundamentalist movements both within established churches and as new independent churches and fellowships; and (4) the growth of a number of controversial authoritarian sects or "cults."

Types of Groups

"CULTS. " The term *cult* is frequently employed to refer to deviant or marginal religious or therapeutic groups; however, the term really has no precise concensual meaning. Several writers have tried to distinguish between "cults" and "sects" and thereby to assimilate the concept of cult within traditional "church-sect theory" in the sociology of religion. Three partly incompatible conceptions of what constitutes a cult seem to have emerged.

1. Authoritarianism and the related notion of "totalism" appear to be defining properites of "cults" in much popular and journalistic literature
2. Looseness and diffuseness of organization and an absence of clear "boundaries."
3. Deviancy.

CRITICAL AND NORMATIVE TYPOLOGIES. Adaptive movements, we found, promote the assimilation of converts to conventional vocation, educational, and familial roles, and are often associated with other "integrative" outcomes such as drug rehabilitation. In contrast, converts to marginal movements tend to drop

The Unification Church had become one of the most widely known and controversial of the contemporary wave of new religious movements.

PAGE 688

N

NEW RELIGIONS

New Religions and Cults in Europe

"There are in every man two simultaneous postulations, one towards God, the other towards Satan."

CHARLES BAUDELAIRE
MON COEUR MIS À NU, 1887

out of conventional structures and become encapsulated in self-sufficient and authoritarian communal institutions. Marginal groups are more likely to evoke hostility from the relatives of converts and from other parties.

Well-known marginal groups include the Unification Church, the Children of God, The Way, the Alamo Foundation, ISKCON, and Love Israel. Clearly adaptive groups include followers of Meher Baba, Transcendental Meditation, and est.

Monistic and dualistic systems. Monistic meaning systems employ concepts from Eastern mysticism and affirm the essential "oneness" of reality, the ultimately illusory quality of the phenomenal world, the ideas of reincarnation and karma, and the primacy of inner consciousness and its refinement through enlightenment, although not all essentially monistic groups entail every one of these traits. Generally monistic groups include such "Eastern" groups as the Divine Light Mission, ISKCON, Happy-Healthy-Holy (3HO), the followers of Rajneesh, Meher Baba, and Baba Muktananda, and Tibetan and Zen Buddhist groups as well as such implicitly monistic religiotherapeutic movements as est, Scientology, and Arica.

Implicit in monistic perspectives is a qualified moral relativism and a rejection of absolute polarities in human experience. Dualistic systems, on the other hand, revolve around absolute dualities and the immediate, urgent, and inescapable choices that must be made between right and wrong, God and Satan, and so on. Dualistic religion generally affirms the radical transcendence of the godhead and the ever-present tension between the divine creator and the corrupted human creation. Monism, however, affirms a universal order immanent in the depths of consciousness—a latent universal self—in which all priorities are resolved and transcended.

Univocal vs. multivocal cognitive styles. There is a distinction between one-level and two-level monism related to a broad distinction between univocal and multivocal conceptions of reality. The rationalization of culture has as its linguistic dimension the hegemony of "rational discourse" involving terms that are fixed, precise, and context-free in their meaning and that are clear and specific in their empirical referents. Multivocal symbols give way to univocal signs. Ambiguous metaphysical and supernatural (supraempirical) terms are excluded from rational discourse and rationalized culture. To use Max Weber's term, the world is "disenchanted." However, the symbolic impoverishment of the dominant rationalized culture frustrates human needs for multivocal enchantment and thus engenders spiritual ferment and an alternative culture of multivocal mystiques aimed at reenchanting the world.

A reduction of symbolic conceptions to univocal rationalism can thus transpire simultaneously with a protest against the rationalized "reduction" of religion: that is, the same movements and mystiques can both protest against and embody the cognitive style of univocal rationality. Assuming that reductionism is objectionable and that the recovery of spiritual enchantment is desirable, the distinctions between univocal and multivocal religious conceptions, between monism and dualism, and between technical and charismatic religiosity may lay the foundation for a critical typology of contemporary religious movements (Anthony, Ecker, and Wilber, 1983).

— THOMAS ROBBINS AND DICK ANTHONY

NEW RELIGIONS AND CULTS IN EUROPE

The new religious movements with which this article is concerned are those which first appeared, or became noticeable, in Europe during the second half of the twentieth century, especially during the late sixties and the seventies. Many, indeed most of them, have their roots in other religions, but they are termed "new" because they arose in a new form, with a new facet to their beliefs, or with a new organization or leadership which renounced more orthodox beliefs and/or ways of life. Some of the movements have been denied, or have themselves rejected the label *religious.* No attempt will be made here to argue what a "real" religion should or should not consist of. The term *new religious movements* is employed merely as a somewhat arbitrary, but usefully general, term by which to refer to a multitude of movements which might be termed cults, sects, spiritual groups, or alternative belief systems by others.

ORIGINS AND CLASSIFICATIONS. The vast majority of the new movements were not indigenous to Europe. Most can be traced to the United States (frequently California) or Asia (mainly India, but also Japan, Korea, and other parts of Asia). There are also a few groups that have come from Africa, most of these finding their home among the black populations residing in Europe.

In order to try to create some sense of order among the myriad movements, a number of different classificatory systems have been proposed. One of the simplest divisions is based on the origin of the movement.

Those new religions from the mainly Indian tradition of the East include Ananda Marga, Brahma Kumaris, the Divine Light Mission, ISKCON, followers of Meher Baba and of Sathya Sai Baba, the Rajneesh Foundation (Bhagwan Shree Rajneesh), and Transcendental Meditation. Those from Japan include Nichiren Shoshu (Soka Gakkai) and Rissho Koseikai; and from Korea comes the Unification Church. The movements originating in America tend to be either

Christian derivatives (or deviations) such as The Way International, Armstrongism (The World Wide Church of God), Bible Speaks, and The Children of God (The Family of Love), or, alternatively, groups connected with the human potential movement like est (Erhard Seminars Training), Exegesis, Silva Mind Control, P. S. I. (People Searching Inside and the Kundalini Research Institute of Canada), and the Rebirth Society. Occasionally techniques offered primarily for self-improvement are transferred into (and sometimes back from) a movement claiming to be a new religion. Dianetics' transformation into the Church of Scientology (and back into Dianetics) is a case in point. Also from America come innumerable New Age groups and those which deal in the occult, neopaganism, witchcraft, and magic. These are joined by similar, indigenous groups which are most prolific in northern Europe, especially in parts of Scandinavia and Britain. Such groups range from highly secret fellowships practicing ritual "sex magick," to orthodox covens, to the English Gnostic Church (founded in Chicago in 1979), to astrological groups, Druid gatherings, and Aquarian festivals. From Africa come the Aladura churches, and from Jamaica has come the Rastafarian movement, which has gained considerable popularity among the West Indian population in Britain. Among

INTERNATIONAL SOCIETY FOR KRISHNA CONSCIOUSNESS
Hare Krishna

International Society for Krishna Consciousness (ISKCON) is the missionary form of devotional Hinduism brought to the United States in 1965 by a pious devotee of Krsna who wanted to convert the English-speaking world to "God-consciousness." In less than two decades ISKCON became an international movement with more than two hundred centers worldwide (sixty-one in the United States).

The founding *guru,* A. C. Bhaktivedanta Swami Prabhupada, was born Abhay Charan De in 1896 in Calcutta. Educated in a Viasnava school and later in Scottish Church College, he was a sporadically successful businessman in the pharmaceutical industry. However, after he was initiated in 1922 by Bhaktisiddhanta Sa-rasvati, a Gaudiya (Bengali) Vaisnava in the line of the sixteenth-century saint and reformer Caitanya, he began increasingly to invest time and money in his religious interests. In 1944 Bhaktivedanta established the magazine *Back to Godhead,* and in 1952 he formed the Jhansi League of Devotees. He gave up his life as a householder *(grhasthin)* in 1954 and in 1959 took the formal vows of an ascetic *(samnyasin).*

In September 1965, at the age of sixty-nine, Bhaktivedanta arrived in New York City with a suitcase full of his translations of the *Srimad Bhagavatam* and less than ten dollars in his pocket. He lived with various Indian and American supporters in Manhattan, where he set out daily to chant and sing the praises of Krsna to anyone who would listen. Bhaktivedanta's lectures and devotional services slowly attracted a following, primarily counterculture youths, and preaching centers were eventually established in Los Angeles, Berkeley, Boston, and Montreal. By the late 1960s Los Angeles had become the headquarters of ISKCON and home of its publishing office, which has printed more than fifty different volumes of translations and original works by Bhaktivedanta.

From the earliest years of the movement, Bhaktivedanta's disciples have been known for their public chanting *(sankirtan)* of the Hare Krsna *mantra* and their distribution of *Back to Godhead* as well as Bhaktivedanta's books. Like his Indian predecessors, Bhaktivedanta believed that the recitation of God's name was sufficient for salvation. Further, his *guru* had instructed him to make known "Krishna consciousness" to the English-speaking world. Consequently, the "Hare Krishnas" in India and America have been both visible and very missionary-minded.

Bhaktivedanta circled the globe several times in his twelve years of missionary activity and established temples in England and continental Europe. Just before his death, he appointed eleven disciples as initiating *gurus* to keep the Caitanya chain of disciples unbroken and to missionize the rest of the world. (In 1982 the number was expanded to thirteen.) By the early 1980s his disciples had established forty-five temples or farms in Europe, ten in Africa, thirty-five in Asia, and forty in South America. Whereas the full-time membership of the American temples remained fairly constant after 1977, ISKCON branches grew rapidly overseas, where they often found more tolerant environments.

ISKCON has encountered opposition from anticult groups such as the Citizens Freedom Foundation, but the movement has also experienced challenges from within. In 1970 a group of devotees questioned Bhaktivedanta's disciplic authority, and in 1982 one of his appointed successors left the organization to follow another guru. The movement's practices and techniques of book distribution and proselytizing have most often been at the heart of both external and internal criticism. Yet these practices shaped by the unbounded enthusiasm and organizational inconsistencies of the early years of ISKCON are now being molded by processes of institutionalization and accommodation that are well under way in ISKCON throughout the world.

— LARRY D. SHINN

the groups indigenous to Europe there is the Pentecostal Earmark Trust, the Bugbrooke (Christian) Community, Ishvara (an offshoot of the Divine Light Mission), and the Emin, an esoteric group founded by "Leo" (Raymond Armin/Scherlenlieb).

One of the more useful ways in which new religious movements have been classified is by Roy Wallis's threefold distinction between world-rejecting movements,

CHARISMATIC LEADER

Reverend Sun Myung Moon, founder of the Unification Church, claims that on Easter Day 1936 Jesus appeared and asked him to assume responsibility for the mission of establishing God's kingdom on earth.

UPI/CORBIS-BETTMANN

such as the People's Temple, ISKCON, and the Children of God, which see society being in need of and/or about to experience radical change; world-affirming movements, such as Scientology and the human potential groups, which might be called quasi-religious in that, although they pursue transcendental goals by largely metaphysical means, they concentrate on techniques for improvement of the individual's lot within contemporary society, and thus "straddle a vague boundary between religion and psychology"; and, last, world-accommodating movements, such as Neo-Pentecostalism and western branches of Soka Gakkai, which concentrate on providing religion for their followers' personal, interior lives, and which tend to be unconcerned with their followers' social lives.

— EILEEN BARKER

Like similar movements elsewhere in the world, Korea's new religions have tended to flourish in times of greatest personal distress and social disorder.

PAGE 421

NEW RELIGIONS IN JAPAN

The modern era has been a prolific period for new religious movements in Japan. A new religion will have most or all of the following attributes:

1. Founding by a charismatic figure whose career often recalls the shamanistic model: supernatural calling, initiatory ordeal, wandering, oracular deliverances from the spiritual world.
2. Tendency toward monotheism or a single, monistic source of spiritual power and value. Against the background of the spiritual pluralism of popular Shinto and Buddhism, the new movements set one deity, one founder, and one revelation as definitive.
3. Syncretism, drawing from several strands of religion and culture.
4. A definite, this-worldly eschatology. The new religions usually teach that rapid change is afoot and a divine new age imminent.
5. A sacred center, often an entire sacred city, to which pilgrimage is made, where the faith is headquartered, and which represents a foretaste of the coming paradise.
6. Emphasis on healing.
7. A tendency toward "mentalism," that is, the belief that through the power of affirmative thinking one can heal mind and body and control one's own destiny.
8. A single, simple, sure technique for attaining and employing the special spiritual power offered by the religion. One practice, whether the Daimoku of the Nichirenshu or the *jorei* of World Messianity, is presented as the key to unlock spiritual power.
9. A simple but definite process of entry, suggesting that the religion is open to all but requires a personal decision and act of commitment.

— ROBERT S. ELLWOOD

NORTH AMERICAN INDIAN RELIGIONS

INDIANS OF THE FAR NORTH

The North American sub-Arctic extends from Alaska to Labrador, a vast region comprising several vegetation zones. The tundra covers the area along the Arctic coast, a strip of treeless wilderness between one and four hundred miles wide, which protrudes deep into the interior in northern Alaska and in Canada west of Hudson Bay.

ADAPTATION TO CLIMATE. The inhospitable

climate of the region, with its long, severe winters and short summers, shaped the culture of the native inhabitants. Since any form of cultivation was impossible, human existence was dependent on hunting and fishing. And here natural factors proved to be of some assistance. Large deer, such as caribou and moose, sought refuge in the forest zone in the autumn, then wandered back into the northern tundra in spring. This movement back and forth set huge herds of migrating caribou into motion, which facilitated big-game hunting and the accumulation of food reserves. In late winter, however, hunting was limited to stalking of small packs or isolated animals. Extensive river networks that abounded in fish, particularly salmon, provided food in the summer. Hunting and fishing, two seasonally varying activities—the one with lance and arrow, the other with hook and net—formed the basis of the sub-Arctic economy so long as the native population was isolated from outside influences. This alternation in economic life led to nomadism, which often involved a short-term relocation of housing. A round, dome-shaped house covered with bark or straw was erected in the winter; a rectangular, gabled lodge was preferred in the summer. Today these structures have given way to the conical tent, which in turn is beginning to be replaced by the log cabin.

The advancing Europeans encountered tribes belonging to three linguistic families: the Inuit (Eskimo) along the Arctic Ocean, the Athapascan in western Canada, and the Algonquian in eastern Canada. Among the Algonquian we also include the Abnaki of New Brunswick and Maine (Micmac, Malecite, Passamaquoddy, Penobscot, Abnaki), who have preserved vestiges of their sub-Arctic way of life up to the present. The non-Indian Inuit will not be treated here, as they are the subject of a separate article. [*See* Inuit Religion.]

The usual division leaves us twenty-four groups or tribes of Athapascan provenance and thirteen of Algonquian provenance. All are unmistakably shaped by the sub-Arctic way of life with its alternation between forest and water, its absence of any cultivation, and its big-game hunting in winter and fishing in summer.

Human existence in the sub-Arctic has always revolved around surviving the winters. January and February witness the worst side of the cold season: the temperature reaches its lowest point, the reserves are exhausted, the short days limit the hunter's range of movement, and the last caribou and moose in the vicinity of the winter camps have already been hunted down. This is a time of extreme hardship. The isolation of families—each has its own hunting grounds—is a hindrance to mutual help and support. The earliest reports tell of famine and starvation and of whole bands fatalistically facing their death.

By way of comparison, the Inuit cultures along the Arctic coast mastered every environmental difficulty: of their inventions one need only think of the igloo, fur clothing, seal hunting at the breathing holes on the ice, and oil lamps—a utilization of natural conditions not to be found among the Athapascan and the Algonquian.

AGES OF THE WORLD. The mythical chronology falls into three stages (see Rand, 1894; Osgood, 1932; and Pliny Earle Goddard, "The Beaver Indians," *Anthropological Papers of the American Museum of Natural History* 10, 1916). In the earliest period there were no divisions between living creatures; each could assume any animal's form and discard it again at will. All moving creatures spoke a single language; no barriers stood in the way of understanding. The second period began with the birth of the culture hero, the great teacher and leader of mankind. Material and spiritual knowledge derived from him. The house, tent, snowshoe, sled, bark canoe, bow, arrow, lance, and knife—in short, all man's appurtenances—stem from him, as does knowledge of the land of the dead, the stars and constellations, the sun, the moon, and the calendar months. It was also he who had the muskrat dive into the waters after the Deluge and who then created a new world from the mud that was brought up, thus becoming a second creator (if there had been a first).

The present era is within the third epoch. Although the hero has disappeared, the special position of mankind remains and begins to expand. Only the shamans are able to cross the boundaries between the human and the extrahuman.

Individual tribes expand this universal chronology. The Koyukon, for example, the northwesternmost Athapascan tribe in Alaska, speak of no less than five world periods: (1) the hazy time before there was light on the earth; (2) the epoch when man could change into animals, and animals into men; (3) the time when the culture hero created the present state; (4) the past time of legends; and (5) the present as far back as memory reaches (*Handbook*, vol. 6, p. 595).

Unity of life. The sequence of world epochs is more than a faded memory. It lives on today in traditional beliefs and customs that recall the events or conditions of those epochs—especially the earliest period, with its basic idea of the world family and the unity of all living creatures. Thus the Kutchin, a northern Athapascan tribe that inhabits the territory between the Mackenzie River delta and the upper Yukon, possess a special relationship with the caribou; every man, they believe, carries a small piece of caribou heart within himself, and every caribou a portion of human heart. Hence, each of these partners knows what the other feels and thinks (*Handbook*, vol. 6, p. 526). The Sekani

"From winter, plague, and pestilence, good lord deliver us!"

THOMAS NASHE
1592

of British Columbia believe that a mystical bond links man and animal (*Handbook*, vol. 6, p. 439); the Koyukon call the bear "Grandfather" and the wolf "Brother" (*Handbook*, vol. 6, p. 593); and the Chipewyan, who live west of Hudson Bay, identify with the wolf (*Handbook*, vol. 6, p. 279).

The names of certain Athapascan tribal groups—Beaver, Dogrib, Hare—point to familial ties with certain animals. In all of these examples we hear an echo of the earliest epoch, when a common language prevailed and all creatures had the ability to transform themselves and thus to overcome every barrier between them.

Also, the game that is killed is treated respectfully. The animal is addressed in familial terms; its death is mourned; its bones are protected from the dogs. Otherwise, the spirit "master" of the particular type of animal will withhold game from the hunter, subjecting him to hunger. The very concept of a master of the game teaches the Indians to show a religious reverence toward the nonhuman creatures of the world. They know that every animal form has a spirit protector and helper to whom the souls of the killed animals return and, if warranted, make complaints about ill treatment. They know that no game returns to earth without the consent of the master. Finally, they know that this consent is dependent on the keeping of certain religious prescriptions. Thus the activity of the hunter is a religious act: he is constantly aware of being watched by extrahuman beings.

THE SUPREME BEING. In general, research on religions of sub-Arctic Indians tends to assume the absence of a belief in a supreme being. Lane's statement on the Chilcotin of British Columbia—"There was no belief in a supreme being" (*Handbook*, vol. 6, p. 408)—is supposed to be applicable to all Athapascan and Algonquian groups. Any hints of such a belief that do occur are assumed to be due to Christian influence.

This simplistic assumption might never have arisen had its supporters referred to the dictionary compiled by the French priest Émile Petitot (1876). Under the entry "Dieu" Petitot distinguishes between native terms for the deity and those that came into circulation as a result

THE CULTURE HERO
Bringer of Abundance

The culture hero remains the most powerful figure within the cosmic hierarchy. To the hunter, this heroic figure is an ideal that cannot be equaled. The Ojibwa on the northern side of Lake Superior liken this master to the captain of a steamboat or to the government in Ottawa; he directs all lesser masters (Diamond Jenness, The Ojibwa Indians of Parry Island, 1935, p. 30).

The culture hero is responsible, too, for the abundance and richness of sub-Arctic mythology. Around the camp fire or in the tent, the deeds of the hero, teacher, and friend of mankind provide the most important story-telling material. Other mythical figures are patterned after him, so there is a continuous expansion of the cycles of myths. The Koyukon are said to have "a highly developed and sophisticated repertory of myth and legend" (*Handbook*, vol. 6, p. 595); other groups are said to have a "deep respect for and attachment to their mythology" (*Handbook*, vol. 6, p. 195). The oral tradition is not understood merely as entertainment; the mythical stories confer a sacral dimension on it, which is still recognized by the Indians.

The figure of the hero is most clearly developed among the Algonquians of the Atlantic coast. The Micmac of Cape Breton Island, for example, call the teacher of mankind Kuloscap ("liar" or "deceiver") because he always does the opposite of what he says he will do. The stations of his life can still be read in the natural features of the landscape: Cape Breton Island abounds in references to the hero. Every large rock, every river, every waterfall, testifies to his deeds. All the sub-Arctic Indians have a similar mythical geography.

To the west of the Micmac other names for the culture hero appear. Among the Montagnais-Naskapi of Labrador he is called Little Man or Perfect Man; among the Cree on either side of James Bay, the One Set in Flames or the Burning One; among the Chipewyan, Raised by His Grandmother; among the Beaver Indians, He Goes along the Shore.

This last example brings us to the group of names found in northern Athapascan mythologies, which pay particular attention to the hero's unflagging wanderlust. In the regions around the large Canadian lakes, the Kutchin, Koyukon, and Kolchan speak of the Wanderer, Ferryman, Celestial Traveler, He Who Paddled the Wrong Way, He Who Went Off Visiting by Canoe, or One Who Is Paddling Around, designations that refer to a particular task of the hero. He is said to labor continuously to combat giants, cannibals, and monsters for the benefit of mankind. The mass of fantasy figures in whose deeds the mythologies abound—such minor heroes as Moon Boy, Moon Dweller, Shrew, Moss Child, Wonder Child, White Horizon, the Hero with the Magic Wand—follow the same path as the tireless figure of the Wanderer.

— WERNER MÜLLER
TRANSLATED FROM THE GERMAN
BY ANNE HERITAGE
AND PAUL KREMMEL

of missionary activity, some time after 1850. Among the first category are found the following: *The One by Whom One Swears, Vault of the Sky, The One through Whom Earth Exists, Eagle, Sitting in the Zenith, The One Who Sees Forward and Backward, Having Made the Earth, The One through Whom We Become Human.* Alongside these early native names appear the Christian terms *Creator, Father of Mankind, The One Who Dwells in Heaven,* but the first two Christian terms are also found among the early native designations, and Petitot includes them in both categories. He evidently wanted to indicate that the designations *Creator* and *Father of Mankind* existed before the missionaries arrived.

This shifting of basic values, that is, the eradication of the supreme being and the ascendancy of the hero, must have begun long before the first contact with Europeans, for the attempt to degrade the creator can be seen even in the names for the deity. Names that recall Janus figures, like *The One Who Looks Forward and Backward*, are totally unsuitable for a supreme being who has relinquished the function of world-orderer to the culture hero. Likewise, the name *Boatsman* is linked to the wandering hero but not to the regent of the universe.

The contrariness of these two key religious figures is quite evident. The hero is closely identified with man and with man's goals and purposes. The supreme god, however, encompasses the world in its entirety; he is the cosmos itself. "He is in the sun, moon, stars, clouds of heaven, mountains, and even the trees of the earth," according to the Penobscot (Speck, "Penobscot Tales," p. 4). The Naskapi likewise declare, "He is a spirit like the sun, moon, and stars, who created everything including them" (Speck, 1935, p. 29).

SHAMANISM. The all-encompassing rituals mentioned above form the bulwark of human life in more southerly latitudes. They incorporate everyone into the cosmic unity of life. These universal celebrations provide an indestructible shelter within the world house and prevent isolation of the individual. In the taiga and tundra, however, the individual is dependent on himself. When he needs help, the sub-Arctic Indian turns to the shaman. It is he who provides the only help when bad weather spoils the hunt, when the game withdraws into inaccessible places, when fewer fish swim upstream, when disease announces the loss of the soul, and when continued misfortune bespeaks the attack of a hostile shaman.

Dreams, songs, and journeys. The shaman's important and essential characteristics are attained through dreams. The visions befall selected candidates. The chosen must have a "peculiar aptitude" (*Handbook*, vol. 6, p. 607), but family inheritance can also play a role. The strength of a shaman depends on spirit helpers that are either acquired through dreams or inherited from his father or his maternal uncle. Every hunter has one such helper, acquired in the years of childhood through dream-fasting, but the shaman has at least half a dozen. The spirits manifest themselves in the form of animals, in natural phenomena such as the sun and the moon, or in the souls of deceased shamans (*Handbook*, vol. 6, p. 409).

Every spirit helper has its own song, and when a shaman incants a spirit's song, the spirit addressed hurries to help his master. The activity of the shaman alleviates much more than everyday cares. It is believed that his spirit leaves his body every night, travels on lengthy visits to the sky, and learns there everything he desires to know. When his spirit returns from its flight accompanied by the shaman's helpers, the drum on the wall begins to sound without being touched. His song is heard far and wide, and his body dances six inches above the ground (John Alden Mason, *Notes on the Indians of the Great Slave Lake Area,* 1946, p. 40).

These "journeys" establish the reputation of a shaman. While his body lies rigid and motionless on the floor, his soul hastens through far-off spaces and unknown lands, encounters mythical figures, and receives their instruction. The few reports we have indicate that the images in these dream experiences are the same as those found in the tribal mythologies. The visionary sees in his trance only what he knows. His dream journeys revitalize religious knowledge; without the continual confirmation through dreams, the mythical images would be forgotten. The shaman is thus the most important preserver of tribal traditions.

The shaman's drum. Pictorial representations are mostly to be found on the drum, the most important accessory of the shaman. Physically the drum consists of a skin-covered wooden hoop. The upper side is painted with numerous figures, all illustrations of dream experiences. Animal tendon into which pieces of bone have been twisted is stretched across the drumhead. When the drum is beaten with a wooden stick, the bone fragments begin to vibrate; they "sing."

The drum is used to induce a trance in the drummer; the vibrating and buzzing sound dulls the consciousness and opens the way for the "journey." At the same time the drum beckons the helping spirits.

The shaking tent. In addition to the drum, the eastern Canadian Algonquians use another device to communicate with the spirits: the shaking tent, which is a specially built cylindrical structure with a framework of thick poles. The top of the tent remains open so that the spirits can enter. As soon as the shaman crawls into the tent and begins to sing, the posts, which are dug in deeply, start to shake. The beckoned spirits can be heard rushing by; animal cries arise; the shaman

According to the religious beliefs of the Arctic peoples, the whole world is filled with spirits: mountains, trees, and other landmarks have their spirits, and animals have their spirit masters.

PAGE 40

asks questions; and the spirits respond. The séance ends when all the participants are satisfied (*Handbook*, vol. 6, p. 251).

— WERNER MÜLLER
TRANSLATED FROM GERMAN BY
ANNE HERITAGE AND PAUL KREMMEL

INDIANS OF THE NORTHEAST WOODLANDS

The Northeast Woodlands peoples occupy an area within 90° to 70° west longitude and 35° to 47° north latitude. The region can be divided into three smaller geographical areas: (1) the upper Great Lakes and Ohio River Valley region, (2) the lower Great Lakes, and (3) the coastal region.

The most prominent tribes, divided according to language group, are (1) Algonquian-speaking (Southern Ojibwa, Ottawa, Potawatomi, Menomini, Sauk, Fox, Kickapoo, Miami, Illinois, Shawnee, Narraganset, Mohican, Delaware, Nanticoke, and Powhatan), (2) Iroquoian-speaking (Huron, Erie, Neutral, Petun, Seneca, Oneida, Onondaga, Cayuga, Mohawk, and Tuscarora), and (3) Siouan-speaking (Winnebago, Tutelo).

"What is life? The breath of a buffalo in the wintertime."

CROWFOOT
1890

COSMOLOGICAL BELIEFS. The cosmological beliefs of the Northeast Woodlands peoples involve the concept of power as manifested in the land, in the dialectic of the sacred and the profane, and in patterns of space and time. According to the mythic thought of these peoples, power is that transformative presence most clearly seen in the cycles of the day and the seasons, in the fecund earth, and in the visions and deeds of spirits, ancestors, and living people. This numinous power is so manifestly present that no verbal explanation of it is adequate; rather it is itself the explanation of all transformations in life. While generally regarded as neutral, power may be used for good or ill by individuals.

Power. This all-pervasive power is expressed among Algonquian-speaking tribes by the word *manitou* or one of its linguistic variants. *Manitou* is a personal revelatory experience usually manifested in dreams or in visions of a spirit who is capable of transformation into a specific human or animal form. The efficacy of power is symbolized as "medicine," either as a tangible object reverently kept in a bundle or as an intangible "charm" possessed internally.

The belief in *manitou* can be found among the coastal Algonquians from New England to North Carolina. Similarities may be seen in the name for the Great Manitou: for the Narraganset he was Kautantowwit and for the Penobscot, Ktahandowit. The Delaware worshiped as Great Manitou a spirit called Keetan'to-wit, who had eleven assistants *(manitowuks)*, each having control over one of eleven hierarchically organized "heavens." The most ancient of the *manitou* was Our Grandfather, the great tortoise who carries the earth on his back. The Virginia Algonquians called those *manitou* who were benevolent *quiyoughcosuck*; this was also the name given to their priests. The evil *manitou* were called *tagkanysough*. Southeast Woodlands influences led to the depiction of *manitou* in carvings and statues, usually found in the sacred architecture of the North Carolina and Virginia Algonquians.

The Huron concept of *oki* referred both to a superabundance of power or ability and to spirit-forces of the cosmos, or guardian spirits. An *oki* could be either benevolent or malevolent. The supreme *oki*, Iouskeha, dwelt in the sky, watched over the seasons and the affairs of humans, witnessed to vows, made crops grow, and owned the animals. He had an evil brother, Tawiskaron.

The Iroquois *orenda*, a magico-religious force, was exercised by spirit-forces called Otkon and Oyaron; it was present in humans, animals, or objects that displayed excessive power, great ability, or large size. The Iroquois had a dualistic system whereby all of the spirit-forces deemed good were associated with the Good Twin and all of those deemed evil with his brother the Evil Twin.

The land. In many of the mythologies of the peoples of the Northeast Woodlands this cosmic power was intimately connected with the land. Both the Algonquian speakers and the Siouan-speaking Winnebago developed cosmologies in which the heavens above and the earth regions below were seen as layered in hierarchies of beneficial and harmful spirits. The highest power was the supreme being called Great Spirit by the Potawatomi, Ottawa, Miami, and Ojibwa; Master of Life by the Menomini, Sauk, and Fox; Finisher by the Shawnee and Kickapoo; and Earthmaker by the Winnebago. This "great mysterious" presence maintained a unique relationship with the last and weakest members of creation, namely, human beings.

CEREMONIAL PRACTICES. Some understanding of the rich and complex ritual life of the Northeast Woodlands peoples can be obtained by considering selected ceremonies concerned with subsistence, life cycles, and personal, clan, and society visions.

Subsistence. Through subsistence rituals, tribes contacted power to ensure the success of hunting, fishing, or trapping; gathering of herbs, fruits, or root crops; and agricultural endeavors. Among the Sauk and Menomini there were both private and public ceremonials for hunting that focused on sacred objects generically labeled "medicine." The large public medicine-bundles of three types were believed to have

SPIRIT-FORCES
Mixing the Scared and Profane

Power and guidance entered human existence from the cosmic spirit-forces, from the guardian spirits of individuals and medicine societies, and from spirits of charms, bundles, and masks. Dreams, in particular, were a vehicle for contacting power and thus gaining guidance for political and military decisions. New songs, dances, and customs were often received by the dreamer and were used to energize and reorder cultural life; dreams channeled power as consolation and hope during times of crisis, and often initiated contact between visionary power and the shamans. One means of describing the human experience of this cosmic power is through the dialectic of the sacred and the profane.

This dialectic is useful even though the Northeast Woodlands peoples did not draw a sharp distinction between the sacred and profane. The dialectic refers to the inner logic of the manifestation of numinous power through certain symbols. Profane objects, events, or persons might become embodiments of the sacred in moments of hierophany. This manifestation of the sacred in and through the profane frequently became the inspiration for sacred stories and mythologies that narrated the tribal lore. Among the Winnebago and other Northeast Woodlands peoples, narrative stories were distinguished as *worak* ("what is recounted") and *waika* ("what is sacred"). Telling the *worak* stories of heroes, human tragedy, and memorable events was a profane event, whereas narrating the *waika* stories evoked the spirits and was therefore a sacred ritual. Thus the ordinary act of speaking could become the hierophany that manifests power. Not only narrative but also the interweaving of sacred space and time gave real dimensions to cosmic power.

— JOHN A. GRIM AND DONALD P. ST. JOHN

been obtained by the trickster-culture hero Manabus from the Grandfathers, or *manitou* spirits. The first hunting bundle, called Misasakiwis, helped to defeat the malicious medicine people who tried to foil the hunter's success. Both the second bundle, Kitagasa Muskiki (made of a fawn's skin), and the third (a bundle with deer, wolf, and owl skins), fostered hunting success. Each bundle might contain a variety of power objects such as animal skins, miniature hunting implements, wooden figures, herbal preparations, and often an actual scent to lure animals. The bundle's owner obtained the right to assemble or purchase such a bundle from a personal vision. Songs, especially, evoked the powers of the bundle; these songs often recalled the agreement between the visionary and the *manitou* as well as the prohibitions and obligations that impinged upon the owner of a bundle. In this way the bundle owner, and the hunters he aided, thwarted the evil ones and contacted the *manitou* masters of the hunted animals. Thus power objects from the environment, the empowered hunters, and the ritually imaged *manitou*-spirits, functioned together to bring sustenance to the people.

Although the growing season varied within the Northeast, most of these peoples practiced some form of agriculture. With the introduction of agriculture new symbol complexes developed, giving meaning and power to this new subsistence activity and integrating it into the larger cosmic order. The northern Iroquois, for example, linked together woman, earth, moon, and the cycles of birth and death.

The domestic ceremony of apology for taking life is found among all these Northeast Woodlands people. This simple ceremony illustrates the moral character of the force that was believed to bind the cosmos together. The ceremony consisted of a spoken apology and a gift of sacred tobacco for the disturbance caused to the web of life by cutting trees, gathering plants, or taking minerals. This ceremony is both a thanksgiving for the blessing of a material boon and an acknowledgment of the environmental morality that binds the human and natural worlds.

Life cycles. Life-cycle rites of passage are illuminating examples of these peoples' recognition that the passage through life's stages required a structured encounter with power. These ceremonies included private actions that invoked power at liminal moments such as menstruation, marriage, and birth. Other life-cycle ceremonials, however, were marked by elaborate ritual activities, such as naming, puberty, and death ceremonies.

Birth and early childhood. Naming ceremonies arise both from the belief that humans are born weak and require power for growth and survival as well as a belief that new life should be introduced into the cosmos. Generally, two types of naming ceremonies have been found. Among the Southeast Woodlands tribes a child was given an ancestral clan name. This situated that child in the clan lineage and empowered the child by directly connecting him or her to the ancestral vision embodied in the clan medicine bundles. Another ceremony associated with the Menomini, Potawatomi, Ojib-

Tricksters everywhere are deceitful, cunning, amoral, sexually hyperactive, taboo-breaking, voracious, thieving, adventurous, vainglorious—yet not truly evil or malicious.

PAGE 675

wa, and Ottawa, but occasionally practiced by the other groups, involved naming by virtue of a dream vision. In this ritual a person was chosen by the parents to undergo a fast or a sweat lodge purification so that they might receive a name for the child from the *manitou.*

Among the Iroquois and Delaware the naming ceremony, which was conducted in the longhouse, was the most significant ritual of early childhood. Delaware parents were attentive to their dreams for a revelation of the name. They would give their child to an elder in the big house who would announce the child's name and offer prayers of blessing for it. A similar ceremony would be conducted for an adult who decided to change his or her name due to a significant deed or because the first name no longer seemed appropriate. The Huron pierced the ears of the child and named it shortly after birth; the child's name then belonged to the clan and could not be used by another member of the tribe. The Iroquois named their children either at the Green Corn ceremony in the summer or before the Midwinter ceremonies. A child who resembled a dead ancestor might be given his or her name since it was believed that the name might have some of the ancestor's personality. The name remained the child's exclusive privilege and the focus of his or her early spiritual formation until the puberty ceremonials.

Among the Iroquois, the Algonquians to the south of the Great Lakes, there are second funerals, involving the burial of the disinterred bones in a common grave or funeral urn.

PAGE 315

Puberty. It is uncertain whether the puberty rites of the Algonquians of Virginia and North Carolina involved a vision quest. However, the vision quest was part of the puberty rites of all of the upper Great Lakes peoples with variations according to the tribe. Some southern Ohio River groups such as the Shawnee emphasized less ecstatic experiences such as a boy's first kill. Among the Potawatomi, however, on specially designated mornings the parents or grandparents would offer a youth in his or her early teens a choice of food or charcoal. Encouraged to choose the charcoal and to blacken their faces, the youngsters were taken to an isolated place, often to perch in the limbs of a tree. There, alone, they fasted for dream visions. Although boys and girls might undertake vision quests, many tribes in this area had special ceremonies for girls.

The northern Iroquois, the Delaware, and the coastal Algonquians secluded girls in huts during their first menstruation. Among the Delaware the girls observed strict rules regarding food, drink, and bodily care; while in seclusion they wore blankets over their heads, and they were not permitted to leave the huts until their second menstrual period. This rite signified a girl's eligibility for marriage. There is evidence that some northern Iroquoians did not seclude their women during menstruation, although certain taboos had to be observed.

One of the most striking puberty rites was the Huskanawe of the Algonquians of Virginia. This rite was undergone by boys selected to be future chiefs and priests, positions of great importance in a highly stratified society. The ceremony began with the ritual tearing away of the children from their mothers and fathers, who had to accept them thenceforth as "dead." The boys were taken into the forest and were sequestered together in a small hut. For months they were given little to eat and were made to drink intoxicating potions and take emetics. At the end of this period of mental and emotional disorientation, they completely forgot who they were, and they were unable to understand or speak the language they had known. When the initiators were sure that the boys had been deconditioned, they took them back to the village. Under close supervision from their guides, the boys formed a new identity; they relearned how to speak and were taught what to wear and the intricacies of the new roles now assigned to them. As rulers or priests they had to be free from all attachments to family and friends. Their minds had been cleansed and reshaped so that they might see clearly and act wisely. Their claim to authority and their power to lead others rested on their successful ritual transition to a sacred condition.

Death. The form of death rites varied widely among the Northeast Woodlands peoples. In the tribes of the upper Great Lakes area, bodies were usually disposed of according to the individual's wishes or clan prerogatives for scaffold exposure, ground burial, or cremation. Among the Fox, death was a highly ritualized event announced to the village by a crier. The members of the deceased's clan gathered for a night of mourning. The clan leader addressed the corpse, advising it not to look back with envy on those still alive but to persevere in its journey to the ancestors in the west. After burial there were the rituals of building a grave shed and installing a clan post as a marker. A six-month period of mourning then followed, during which time a tribesperson was ceremoniously adopted to substitute for the deceased person, especially at memorial feasts.

Burial practices differed among the peoples of the lower Great Lakes and coastal region. The Algonquians of Carolina buried common people individually in shallow graves. The Algonquians of Virginia wrapped the bodies of common people in skins and placed them on scaffolds; after the decay of the flesh was complete, the bones were buried. The rulers of both peoples, however, were treated differently. After death their bodies were disemboweled and the flesh was removed, but the sinews were left attached to the bones. The skin was then sewn back on to the skeleton, after being packed with white sand or occasionally ornaments. Oil kept the body from drying. The corpses were placed on a platform at the western end of the temple and attended by priests.

The Nanticoke and other tribes of the southern Maryland and Delaware peninsula area practiced a second ossuary interment, in some cases preceded by an inhumation and in others by scaffold burials. The rulers of most of these tribes were treated like those of the Algonquians of Virginia and North Carolina. Some of the southern Delaware also had a second ossuary burial, but the main tribal group had one inhumation only; no special treatment for chiefs was noted.

These life-cycle ceremonials were an integral part of every tribesperson's passage through life. Indeed, in the Winnebago Medicine rite the image of human aging in four steps is presented as a paradigm of all life. However, such ceremonial rites of passage can be distinguished from certain personal, clan, and group rituals.

Individual, clan, and group. Power objects given by the *manitou*, such as medicine bundles, charms, and face-paintings, became the focus of personal rituals, songs, and dances. An individual evoked his or her spirit and identified with it by means of rhythmic singing, drumming, rattling, or chanting; one would then channel the power brought by the spirit to a specific need such as hunting, the healing of sick people, or, in some cases, toward more selfish ends.

The Huron owned power charms *(aaskouandy)*. Many of these were found in the entrails of game animals, especially those who were difficult to kill. Charms could be small stones, tufts of hair, and so on. One of the abilities of a power charm was to change its own shape, so that a stone, for example, might become a bean or a bird's beak. *Aaskouandy* were of two types: (1) those that brought general good luck and (2) those that were good for one particular task. The particular use of a charm would be revealed to its owner in a dream.

An individual or family might collect a number of charms and keep them in a bundle consisting of, for example, tufts of hair, bones or claws of animals, stones, and miniature masks. The owner was periodically obliged to offer a feast to his charms, during which he and his friends would sing to the charms and show them honor. The owner usually established a relationship to the charm spirit, similar to that between an individual and a guardian spirit, although charm spirits were known to be more unpredictable and dangerous than guardian spirits. An individual or family who wished to get rid of a charm had to conduct a ritual and bury it; even then uneasiness surrounded the event.

Among the Huron and Iroquois, there were masks that had to be cared for in addition to a charm or bundle. A person acquired a mask through dreaming of it or having it prescribed by a shaman. A carver would go into the forest and search for a living tree; basswood, cucumber, and willow were the preferred woods. While burning tobacco, he recited prayers to the tree spirit and the False Face spirits. The mask was carved into the tree and then removed in one piece. The finishing touches, including the eye-holes (which were surrounded with metal) and the mouth hole, were added later. If the tree had been found in the morning, the mask would be painted red; if in the afternoon, black. The hair attached to the mask was horsetail.

Personal power could overwhelm individuals, causing them to seek only self-aggrandizement. The Shawnee have myths that relate the origin of witchcraft to that mythic time when a crocodile's heart, which was the embodiment of evil, was cut out and carried home to the village by unwitting tribespeople. While the tribes of the Northeast fostered belief in contact with power, they also condemned the misuse of such power in sorcery. They tried to control their exceptional personalities by threatening the return of all evil machinations to the perpetrator. Nonetheless,

IROQUOIS FACE MASK

The Iroquois and Huron tribespeople were inspired to carve elaborate masks from living trees which would then become an important ceremonial element.

RICHARD A. COOKE/CORBIS

witch societies have been prominent in Menomini history. Even though these destructive medicine practices were at times pervasive among the Northeast Woodlands tribes, their many religious societies never completely abandoned the constructive use of power.

The Miami and Winnebago each had religious societies formed around clan war-bundles. The Kickapoo still have clan societies that hold spring renewals centered on their ancestral bundles. Vision societies also developed among individual Winnebago, Sauk, Fox, Kickapoo, Illinois, Miami, and Shawnee people

"I hear the eagle bird pulling the blanket back off from the eastern sky."

IROQUOIS INVITATION SONG

who had received vision revelations from the same *manitou* spirit. Throughout this region societies also formed around those warriors or braves whose heroic acts in battle were seen as special signs of personal power. So also the Potawatomi Southern Dance temporarily brought together tribespeople who still grieved for deceased relatives. The medicine societies and other groups, such as the Dream Dance (or Drum Dance) and the Native American Church, admitted tribespeople who felt called to these societies and were willing to submit to the societies' ethics.

RELIGIOUS PERSONALITIES. The shaman is the most important religious figure among the upper Great Lakes and Ohio River native peoples. Primarily a healer and diviner, the shaman contacts power by means of a trance and channels that power to specific needs. Shamans are known by a variety of names derived from the calls to their vocation they have received by way of visions, as well as from their particular healing functions. Generally, four shamanic vocations are found among the northeastern Algonquian peoples. There are also a number of shamanic techniques. Both the shamanic vocations and techniques are documented from the seventeenth century.

The manipulation of fire for healing purposes is an ancient shamanic vocation; the Ojibwa call this healer *wabeno*, the Menomini called him *wapanows*, and the Potawatomi, *wapno*. The traditional call to this vocation came from Morning Star, who was imaged as a *manitou* with horns. The *wabeno*, working individually or in a group, healed by using the heat of burning embers to massage and fascinate his patients.

Shamanism among the Huron and the Iroquois of the seventeenth century was primarily an individual enterprise, although a few societies did exist. In subsequent centuries the Iroquois channeled shamanistic powers and skills into the growing number of medicine societies, as described above. The central concern of the Huron shamans was the curing of illness. Illness was caused by either (1) natural events, (2) witchcraft, or (3) desires of the soul. The first could be handled by an herbalist or other practitioner. The second and third required the diagnostic and healing abilities of a shaman *(arendiwane)*, including divining, interpreting dreams, sucking, blowing ashes, and juggling hot coals.

The *ocata* was a shaman skilled in diagnosis. In the case of a hidden desire of the soul whose frustration was causing illness he would seek to have a vision of what was desired. To do this he might gaze into a basin of water until the object appeared or enter into a trancelike state to see the object or lie down in a small dark tent to contact his spiritual allies to assist him.

The spirit-ally *(oki)* was won after a long fast and isolation in the forest; it could take the form of a human, an animal, or a bird such as a raven or eagle. Sometimes the power and skill needed to cure would come through a dream. There were shamanic specialists who handled hot coals or plunged their arms into boiling water without injury; frequently a power song, which allowed the person to accomplish this, was sung. Other shamans cured by blowing hot ashes over a person or by rubbing the person's skin with ashes.

Witchcraft was combatted by the *aretsan*; usually the *aretsan* would suck out the evil spell that the witch had magically injected into his victim. Still other shamans could see things at a distance, cause rain, persuade animal guardian spirits to release game, or give advice on military or political matters.

Outside of these established vocations, certain shamanic techniques were available to all lay people among the tribes of the Northeast. These included tattooing, naming, divining, bloodletting, induced vomiting as a cure, weather control, and herbal healing. However, at times individual shamans or shamanic societies were so strong that they absorbed these and other curing practices as their exclusive prerogative.

Other outstanding religious personalities included the war chiefs, who led war bundle ceremonies and war parties, and the peace chiefs, who did not go to fight but who acted as mediators, working for peace within the tribe as well as between separate tribes. The Menomini chose hereditary war chiefs from the Bear clan and peace chiefs from the Thunderer clan. All Northeast Woodlands tribes used a war and peace chief system, but the clan totems from which these leaders were selected often differed from band to band.

Northeast Woodlands peoples have struggled to maintain their traditions into the present period. Not only have they endured the cultural inroads of a variety of Christian missionaries, but these native traditions have also persisted in the face of tribal fragmentation and degradation. This struggle was reflected in the life of the Seneca leader Handsome Lake; he was able to give focus to his people's plight by drawing on the spiritual power of dreams that came to him during an illness brought on by drunkenness and despair. The traditional sanction of dreams and visions in native Northeast Woodlands religions continues into the present revitalization of the sweat lodge, the vision quest, and medicine-wheel gatherings. The relevance of these traditional ceremonies to contemporary needs is highlighted by the growing participation of non-Indians in these meditative rituals

— JOHN A. GRIM AND DONALD P. ST. JOHN

INDIANS OF THE SOUTHEAST WOODLANDS

The Indians who were the aboriginal inhabitants of the southeastern United States lived in a region whose boundaries were approximately the same as those of the contemporary South, that is, extending from about 95° west longitude eastward to the Atlantic coast and from about 37° north latitude southward to the Gulf of Mexico. The Indians of the Southeast Woodlands were linguistically diverse. Muskogean was the most important language family, but four additional language families were present: Iroquoian, Siouan, Algonquian, and Caddoan. Both prehistoric and historical forces shaped the cultural and social characteristics of the Southeast Indians.

Various estimates of the Indian population of the Southeast Woodlands have been proposed for the period just prior to European exploration in the sixteenth century. They range from a low of 170,000 to a high of perhaps 1.7 million. But whatever the Indians' aboriginal population, beginning in the sixteenth century they began to suffer from a series of European epidemic diseases that caused very heavy loss of life. By 1755, they may have numbered only about 50,000 to 70,000. It is clear that this demographic collapse caused extensive social and cultural change. The Indians' social structure became less stratified, and their religious and ritual life was simplified. The most detailed information on Southeast Indian religious beliefs and practices was collected in the late nineteenth and early twentieth centuries, although some good information was collected by eighteenth-century observers, and this is complemented by scattered information from the sixteenth and seventeenth centuries. Some threads of continuity can be discerned among beliefs and practices throughout this four-hundred-year period.

THE BELIEF SYSTEM. The Southeast Indian conception of the cosmos resembled, in its broad outlines, the cosmologies of many other New World peoples. The Southeast Indians believed, for example, that this world—the earth on which they lived—was a circular island that rested upon the waters. The sky above was thought to be a vault of stone, in the form of an inverted bowl. At dawn and at dusk, the bowl rose so that the sun and the moon, two principal deities, could pass beneath it at the beginning and end of their transit through the heavens.

In addition to the earth on which they stood and the world in which they lived, the Indians believed that an upperworld existed above the sky vault and that an underworld existed beneath the earth and the waters. The upperworld was peopled by the sun and the moon, and by large, perfect archetypes of all the creatures that lived on the earth. The underworld was peopled by spirits and monsters living in a chaotic world full of novelty and invention.

For the Southeast Indians, the upperworld was a place of structure, regularity, and perfect order. Its opposite was the underworld, a place of chaos and disorder, as well as fecundity. The Indians appear to have attempted to steer a middle course between the compulsive order of the upperworld and the mad chaos of the underworld. They believed, for example, that in the beginning there were only two worlds, the upperworld

CHEROKEE BEAR DANCE

In Cherokee mythology, the bear is a buffoon who failed in his attempt to act as a humans act. He is, after all, an animal.

LEONARD DE SELVA/CORBIS

The main religious ceremony is the maize harvest ceremony, called the Busk.

PAGE 530

and the underworld, and that this world had been created when soft mud was brought up from beneath the waters to form the island earth. Moreover, they believed that the island was suspended rather precariously from the sky vault by four cords, one in each of the four cardinal directions. They appear to have believed that man's inability to behave strictly in accordance with moral and religious precepts weakened the cords, and thus they feared that the earth would one day sink beneath the waters.

The Southeast Indians believed that certain kinds of beings were more pure, more sacred, than others. Sacred beings were those that seemed able to resist or to stand above natural, mundane constraints.

The sun, the chief upperworld deity, was represented on earth by sacred fire. The smoke that rose from sacred fire connected this earthly world with the upperworld. The Southeast Indians believed that when they behaved badly in the presence of sacred fire, their behavior was immediately known to the sun. The medium that connected people in this world with the underworld was the water in creeks and rivers, which were thought to be avenues or roads to the underworld. The Cherokee personified rivers and streams, calling them "the long person." Fire and water were considered opposites. As such, fire and water were one of an extensive series of opposed forces and beings in the Southeast Indian belief system.

The Cherokee, and probably other Southeast Indians, classified living beings into large categories, and the relationships among these categories were important structural features of their belief system. The three categories of living beings were people, animals, and plants.

Each of these three categories was further subdivided into smaller categories. People were divided into matrilineal clans. Plants were classified in terms of an elaborate taxonomy. Animals were divided into birds, four-footed animals, and vermin, the latter category including fish, snakes, and other creatures inhabiting the watery realm. Many of these animals were invested with symbolic value. In Southeast Indian thought, each of these three animal categories was epitomized by a particular species. The rattlesnake, the most feared venomous snake in the Southeast, was the epitome of the vermin category, and the Virginia deer, the region's most important game animal, was the epitome of the four-footed animals. Birds may have been epitomized by two creatures—the bald eagle, the supreme bird of peace, and the peregrine falcon, the supreme bird of war. If frequency of occurrence in late prehistoric art is a reliable measure of symbolic importance, then the peregrine falcon was clearly the more important of the two birds.

In addition to the animals that epitomized the normal categories, the Southeast Indian belief system recognized an extensive series of anomalous beings that did not fit neatly into a single category. In each case, these anomalies were given special symbolic value. For example, the Venus's-flytrap *(Dionaea muscipula)* and the pitcher plant *(Sarracenia purpurea)*, because they "catch" and "digest" insects, were considered to be plants that behave like animals. The Cherokee believed that the roots of both plants possessed extraordinary magical powers.

The bear was considered anomalous because it is a four-footed animal that possesses certain characteristics reminiscent of people: it is capable of bipedal locomotion; the skeletal structure of its foot closely resembles the human foot; it is as omnivorous in its diet as people are; and its feces resemble human feces. In Cherokee mythology the bear is depicted as a buffoon who attempts to act as humans act, but who fails because of his clumsiness and because he is, after all, an animal.

The most anomalous being in the Southeast Indian belief system was a monster formed of the parts of many creatures. There is evidence that the Indians considered this monster to be an actual being, not a creature whose existence was exclusively spiritual. The Cherokee called this monster the *uktena*. Its body was like that of a rattlesnake, only much larger, the size of a tree trunk. It was believed to live on the margins of the known world, in deep pools of water and near high mountain passes. If a person merely saw an *uktena*, it could cause misfortune, and to smell the breath of an *uktena* brought death.

RITUALS. The Southeast Indians acted out their beliefs about the world in rituals at both small and large junctures in their lives.

Immersion in water was a ritual that all Southeast Indians were supposed to perform each day, although some practiced it more faithfully than others. One was supposed to go to a moving stream at dawn and immerse oneself in the life-renewing water, even if ice was on the water. This ritual appears to have been kept most strictly by males, and particularly by younger males, upon whose vigor the defense of the society depended.

All important transitions of life were underscored by rites of passage. Mothers generally gave birth in the small houses where women sequestered themselves during menstruation. Before the newborn baby was allowed to suckle, it was taken to a creek or a spring and dipped into the water. Then bear oil was rubbed all over the baby's body. The father of a newborn baby was required to fast for four days.

Marriages were sealed by a series of exchanges. The kinsmen of the groom first collected gifts that were then presented to the kinsmen of the bride. In the marriage ceremony itself, the most essential acts were the killing of a deer or a bear by the groom, symbolizing his role as meat producer, and the cooking of a corn dish by the bride to symbolize her role as corn producer.

The principal concern of young men in the aboriginal Southeast was acquiring war honors, which they earned by meritorious deeds of valor. At each juncture in their military careers, a new name was bestowed upon them at a ceremony in their honor. The young men to be honored rubbed bear oil over their bodies and wore special clothing. The beloved old men delivered orations on the valor of the young men, and they admonished others to observe sacred precepts.

In curing illness, Southeast Indian priests and medicine men relied upon rituals as much as upon herbal medicines. As has been seen, they believed that many diseases were caused by vengeful spirits of the animals they had slain. If, for example, a medicine man concluded that his patient's disease had been caused by a vengeful fish spirit, he might invoke a kingfisher spirit or heron spirit to fly down and snatch away the offending fish spirit. Or if the illness happened to be rheumatism caused by an angry deer spirit, the medicine man might require the patient to drink a medicine made of several different ferns, and he would then invoke a terrapin spirit to come and loosen the rheumatism from the patient's bones.

Individuals consult witch doctors to obtain relief from disease or other misfortunes attributed to witchcraft.

PAGE 705

Funerals were the rites of passage around which the Southeast Indians organized their most elaborate rituals. In the late prehistoric era, and in some places even in the early historical era, the death of an important person could cause several other people to submit to voluntary death so that they could accompany the dead person to the otherworld. The interment of an important person's body was the occasion of a solemn ceremonial with much mourning. Months later the body was dug up and the bones cleaned and placed in a basket or box that was kept in the temple. Less important people received less elaborate treatment, but even they might be buried with some of their possessions, as well as with containers of food for their journey to the otherworld. In some cases, favorite pets were killed and interred with their masters.

In addition to a multitude of everyday taboos and avoidances, life-crisis rituals, and rites of passage, the Southeast Indians organized periodic ceremonials that were performed on behalf of the entire society. There is evidence that the Southeast Indians in the late prehistoric period performed a series of such rituals throughout the year. But by the eighteenth century only one of these was widely performed—the Green Corn ceremony, was a first-fruits ceremony and a rite of thanksgiving. It was also an important vehicle in the Southeast Indians' never-ending quest for purity. In fact, the

WITCHCRAFT
Stealers of Human Time

The Southeast Indians explained many of the events in their lives as reward and punishment meted out by spiritual beings who acted according to known standards of behavior. For example, young men who were too careless or headstrong to observe certain taboos and rules of behavior could endanger their own safety and the safety of their comrades in warfare. And women were required to segregate themselves during their menses; if they failed to do so, their mere presence was thought to be polluting and could spoil any serious enterprise. Thus the Southeast Indians explained some of the misfortunes in their lives as having emanated from a just principle—bad things happened when people behaved badly.

In Cherokee myths witches are depicted as irredeemably evil people who can take on the appearance of any person, four-footed animal, or bird. Witches are thought particularly likely to assume the appearance of a horned owl or a raven. The Cherokee took pains to stay up all night at the bedside of anyone who was seriously ill because they believed that witches were especially likely to attack such weak and defenseless people. They believed that witches stole the remaining days, months, or years of life of the ill person, extending their own lives by adding this time to their own. For this reason, the Cherokee believed that witches were often old people.

The Cherokee believed that witches' activities could sometimes be discovered through divination. This was especially necessary in the case of people who were ill. The medicine man who was taking care of the afflicted person would rake up a cone-shaped mound of coals in the fireplace and then sprinkle some pulverized tobacco *(Nicotiana rustica)* on the cone. Using the mound of coals as a kind of compass, the medicine man would recognize the direction of a witch's presence by the place on the cone where the sparks flared. If the particles clung together and flared with a loud burst, the witch was just outside the house. The Cherokee believed that a witch could be killed merely by learning his or her identity. Deceit and deception were at the core of witchcraft, and without these a witch could not exist.

— CHARLES HUDSON

"Soldiers of Christ, arise, and put your armor on."

CHARLES WESLEY
1749

Green Corn ceremony was a ritual means of purifying an entire society.

CHRISTIAN MISSIONS AND MODERN RELIGIOUS MOVEMENTS. The christianization of the Southeast Indians began in the late sixteenth century, when the Spanish built a mission system along the Georgia coast and in northern Florida. An early missionizing attempt by the Jesuits failed, but beginning in 1583 the Franciscans laid the groundwork for a mission system that endured until the late seventeenth and early eighteenth centuries. The Spanish friars taught the mission Indians Roman Catholic dogma, and they taught some of them to speak Spanish; a few Indians even became literate in the language. The missionaries also introduced European grains, vegetables, and fruits. The friars were able to maintain their missions only in the coastal regions; they were never able to missionize effectively in the interior, although a few attempts were made.

The Spanish mission system was rapidly destroyed after the British founded the colony of South Carolina in 1670. In their new colony the British quickly set about building plantations to be worked with slave labor. They armed Indian mercenaries to aid in their attacks on the Spanish missions. They enslaved many of the Indians and put them to work alongside the African slaves. By 1705, the Spanish mission system among the Southeast Indians had been completely destroyed.

Throughout the eighteenth century the Southeast Indians were caught up in the competition among the British, French, and Spanish for supremacy in the Southeast. The French sent a few missionaries to the Indians, but they were relatively ineffective. In the British colonies the Anglican Society for the Propagation of the Gospel did some mission work, although never with great enthusiasm. John and Charles Wesley also attempted for a time to missionize the Indians of the Georgia colony, but without success.

The first serious attempt after the Spanish to missionize the Southeast Indians came in the late eighteenth and early nineteenth centuries, when several Protestant groups began working among the Indians. It was also at this time that a nativistic movement swept through one group of Southeast Indians, the Upper Creek, with disastrous results. Partly stimulated by a visit from the Shawnee leader Tecumseh, who attempted to unite the Indians against the Americans, a number of prophets arose among the Upper Creek who believed that they could expel the Americans through combining religious and military action. This led to the Creek War of 1813-1814, which ended in a decisive defeat of the Indians.

At the very time when nineteenth-century Protestant missionaries were trying to "civilize" the Southeast Indians by teaching them not only Christianity but also modern agricultural and mechanical arts, pressure was building among southern planters to "remove" the Indians from their land. Ultimately the planters had their way, and beginning in the 1830s almost all the Indians of the Southeast Woodlands were forced to migrate to the Indian Territory, now Oklahoma.

Although fragments of the old Southeast Indian belief system have lingered on, often in an underground way, such beliefs have become curiosities in the twentieth century. In some places descendants of the Southeast Indians attend "stomp dances," but similar dances are performed by many modern American Indians. In a few places the Green Corn ceremony continues to be performed, although it lacks the powerful and pervasive meaning it once had.

— CHARLES HUDSON

INDIANS OF THE PLAINS

Plains Indian religion is as varied and complex as the various peoples who inhabit the Plains region, an area delineated by the Rocky Mountains on the west; the Canadian provinces of Alberta, Saskatchewan, and Manitoba on the north; the Mississippi River on the east; and the Gulf of Mexico on the south. The Great Plains measure 1,125,000 square miles, an area roughly equal to one-third the land mass of the United States, and serve as the home for more than thirty American Indian ethnic groups, conventionally known as bands, tribes, nations, and confederacies. The Plains present linguistic as well as ethnic complexity; seven distinct language families are found.

Although population figures are difficult to ascertain, there are currently 225,000 Indians on the Plains, and most authorities believe that, following a dangerous population decline at the turn of the twentieth century, the present-day Indian population equals or surpasses precontact figures.

The Plains culture essentially comprises a potpourri of religious ideas from other parts of the United States and Canada, and it is useful to see the Plains as a point of synthesis of various customs, beliefs, and rituals that amalgamate as a result of emigration and, ultimately, diffusion. Nearly all the basic religious ideas found in other parts of native North America are found on the Plains. If the focus is on the historical period, these basic religious ideas can be seen to fall into three major categories.

The first category may be regarded as tribal religion, idiosyncratic beliefs and rituals that are perceived by their adepts to be unique to their own tribe.

The second category is made up of pantribal religion, beliefs and rituals acknowledged to have been diffused usually from a known single source. Frequent-

LANGUAGE FAMILIES OF THE PLAINS INDIANS

Language	Tribes
Algonquian	the Northern Arapaho of Wyoming the Southern Arapaho of Oklahoma the Atsina (or Gros Ventre of the Prairies) the Blackfeet Confederacy: Siksika, Kainah (or the Blood)
Piegan	the Northern Cheyenne of Montana the Southern Cheyenne of Oklahoma the Plains Cree the Plains Ojibwa (or Chippewa or Bungi)
Athapascan	the Lipan Apache the Kiowa Apache of Oklahoma the Sarsi of Alberta*
Caddoan	the the Arikara (or Ree) the Caddo the Kichai the Pawnee the Wichita
Kiowa-Tanoan	the Kiowa of Oklahoma
Siouan	the Assiniboin (known in Canada as the Stoney) the Crow (or Absoroka) of Montana the Deghiha family: Kansa (or Kaw), Omaha, Osage, Ponca, Quapaw) of Oklahoma the Hidatsa (or Gros Ventre of the River) the Iowa the Oto the Missouri the Mandan the Arikara the Dakota (or Santee) the Lakota (or Teton) the Nakota (or Yankton)
Tonkawan	the Tonkawa of Oklahoma
Uto-Aztecan	the Commanche of Oklahoma

* Counted with the Blackfeet Confederacy despite the difference in language.

ly there is a conscious effort made to learn a new religion from a foreign ethnic group.

A third category falls somewhere between the first two and consists mainly of two ubiquitous religious institutions, the vision quest and the Sweat Lodge ceremony, as well as a number of other beliefs and practices that, although present in all Plains tribes, are still considered by their followers to be unique to each.

RITUAL PRACTITIONERS. The most important figure in Plains religion is the ritual leader, who is known by a variety of names depending on his or her specialization. Normally, a shaman cures people of symbolic illness by ritual means, such as singing, dancing, or praying, while a medicine man or woman is a specialist in herbal curing. In most cases both types of ritual leaders employ the knowledge of the other, and frequently the medicine man or woman relies on supernatural aid in the selection of the proper herb, just as the shaman occasionally uses herbal teas and other concoctions in the course of a shamanic ceremony. Although *shaman* is a preferred term among scholars who study ritual behavior that is highly individualistic and informal, most Plains Indians refer, in English, to both ritual curers and herbalists as "medicine men." In the native languages, however, discrete terms are used.

Each ritual practitioner is well known in a tribal community and achieves high status by performing cures for his patients and by conducting the important ceremonies. He is often a conjurer or magician capable of amazing his adepts with his mystical abilities. The ritual practitioner is usually well paid for his services, previously in horses, buffalo robes, or blankets, now in food and money, although most shamans admit that payment is not required. Part of the popularity of the ritual practitioner is predicated on his success rate with patients and the particular way he conducts the important public ceremonies. Frequently the greatest difference in technique between shamans is stylistic: there are many variants of public and private ceremonies since they are conducted and performed according to instructions received in visions by individual shamans. In many cases, the popular shaman is simply the one who can put on the most interesting performance, but showmanship is not seen as a detraction from the sincerity of the performances.

Although witchcraft and sorcery are not common on the Plains, several tribes have such beliefs. The Plains Cree and Plains Ojibwa brought from their Great Lakes homeland a number of ceremonies, and although they quickly learned the Sun Dance from the Assiniboin, they continued to bury their dead in the ground and conduct an annual Feast of the Dead. They were particularly frightened of witchcraft and sorcery and had one ceremony, probably related to the cere-

The major New Year ceremony is the Sun Dance, during which asceticism, dancing, praying, and curing take place.

PAGE 530

The most widespread iconographic trickster type is theriomorphic: Raven, Coyote, or Rabbit.

PAGE 301

monies of the Midewiwin, or Great Medicine society, in the Great Lakes, in which a shaman was bound hand and foot and placed in a lone tipi. It was believed that spirits entered the tipi, untied the shaman, and taught him how to cure the sick and find lost articles. Sometimes to the amazement of the devotees, the tent began to shake while the shaman was being untied and frequently he was found in a ridiculous position, sometimes wedged in between the tipi poles. For this reason, this particular ceremony (called a "shamanic cult institution" in the anthropological literature) is referred to as the Shaking Tent rite. Modified forms of this ceremony are still popular on the northern Plains among the Arapaho, Cheyenne, Lakota, and others. The Lakota call the ritual Yuwipi, a term referring to the act of rolling up into a ball the rope with which the shaman is tied.

THE SUPERNATURAL. The notions of sacredness and taboo are common to Plains religion. Both designate states, desirable or not, that may be changed through the mediation of prayer, song, dance, or general propitiation of the proper spirits. The idea of the holy is most often expressed by native terms such as the Lakota *wakan*; the Algonquian variants of *manitu*; the Ponca *xube*; and Comanche *puha*. All animate and inanimate objects are capable of serving as a receptacle for this sacred state. The rituals employed to transform persons or objects from a profane state to a sacred one have frequently but erroneously been called in English "medicine," or "making medicine." Frequently the source of a medicine man's personal power is kept in a "medicine bundle." *Medicine* is here a misnomer for *sacred power*.

All Plains people distinguish in their respective languages between power and sacredness. *Great Mystery* and *Great Spirit* are also English terms associated with the Plains belief in a creator god or prime mover, a belief that led to the Christian interpretation that Plains Indians believed in a monotheistic god prior to European contact.

The Plains culture hero or trickster who figures importantly as the mediator between the supernaturals and humankind goes by a number of names—Inktomi ("spider") among the Lakota; Great White Hare among the Algonquian speakers; and Old Man or Coyote among the Crow. In the creation myths this being teaches humans about culture after the establishment of the earth. He also plays another important role in the mythology of the Plains people: he is the principal character in a cycle of morality stories in which positive values of the Indian people are taught through negative examples, that is, the hero always makes mistakes and demonstrates poor judgment. Children are told not to behave as the trickster.

Taboos associated with sexual intercourse, menstruation, and food are as prominent on the Plains as they are elsewhere in American Indian culture, although recent evidence shows that menstrual taboos are positive, in their reinforcement of the female biological role, as well as negative, in their reinforcement of the male fear of "pollution."

THE HEREAFTER. The hereafter was described as a hazy duplicate of the living world. There people dwelled in tipi camps, hunted buffalo, sang, feasted, danced, and were reunited with their kin. Enemies also abounded, and one had to beware of vengeance from the spirit of a slain enemy. It is alleged that the practice of scalping prevented the enemy spirit from going to the spirit camp after death.

The most common forms of burial on the Plains were scaffold and tree burials. The deceased was dressed in fine clothing and wrapped in a buffalo hide. Then the body was placed in the scaffold or tree and secured tightly; it remained there until it decomposed. Most Indians were generally fearful that the spirit of the deceased haunted the place of its burial, so burial grounds were usually avoided. At the time of the burial, however, close relatives of the deceased would come and linger near the corpse. They prepared foods for the spirit's journey to the hereafter and placed new hunting and fighting implements near the scaffold. Frequently a favorite horse was killed and placed at the foot of the scaffold so that the spirit of the deceased could ride that of the horse in the other world.

It was commonly believed that when a person died, its ghost would attempt to entice a close relative to join it in death. These ghosts heralded their presence in numerous ways and some believed that if they heard a baby crying outside in the night or a wolf howl or a rooster crow, it was some boundless spirit calling someone to die. When this occurred members of the family would fire guns to frighten away the spirit. Shamans would burn incense with an aroma that was displeasing to these angry ghosts. Belief in ghosts was common, and it was accepted that ghosts were capable of advising humans about the welfare of the tribe. Shamans were believed to commune with ghosts at night. The shamans freely asked the advice of ghosts about how to cure people, and the ghosts predicted certain events in the lives of the living. Ghosts were also capable of finding lost or stolen articles and in some cases were capable of taking another life.

MAJOR SYMBOLS. Perhaps there is no more universal a symbol of Plains Indian religion than the long-stemmed pipe, sometimes called the "peace pipe." The pipe is essentially a medium of prayer, and when people pray with the pipe it is believed that the smoke rising from the pipe will carry the message of the supplicants to the spirits above. Pipe smoking is a necessary prelude to every important religious ceremony. In the past a pipe was also frequently smoked when deliberations had to be made over hunting or warfare. Normally, each man owned his own pipe and carried it in an elaborate bag or bundle.

Several types of Indian tobacco are smoked in the pipe, and it too is considered to have certain sacred powers. It is often wrapped in pouches and hung in trees as offerings to the supernaturals. Prior to the Indians' confinement to the reservation, there were various types of commercial tobacco traded between traders and Indians, as well as indigenous types cultivated by tribes such as the Crow.

The eagle was regarded by most tribes as the chief of all birds because of its perceived ability to fly higher than any other bird. It was believed that the bird was the paramount messenger of the Great Spirit, and thus its feathers were highly prized for ceremonial purposes and to indicate prestige, as in the famous Plains headdress, the warbonnet.

The Hidatsa are the best known of the Plains tribes for their ability to trap eagles. Eagle trapping was regarded as both a sacred and a dangerous event. Late in the fall the eagle trappers would build a camp a mile or so from the village. High atop hills each trapper dug a pit about three feet deep that he covered with grass and twigs to form a blind. Using a rabbit or small fox for bait, the man climbed into the pit and waited for an eagle to soar overhead and spot the bait. When the eagle landed on top of the pit, the man thrust his hands upward and grabbed the eagle by its legs, pulling it down into the pit, and strangling it. After the feathers were secured there was sometimes a ceremony in which the eagle's body was buried and offerings made to its spirit.

CREATION MYTHS. The sedentary tribes that lived in permanent villages devoted much time to elaborate rituals and accompanying belief systems. The Pawnee seemed to have been great religious innovators, having established one of the most comprehensive philosophies of all the Plains Indians.

The Pawnee elaborated a series of myths that described the creation of the world, the origin of humans, and the power of the gods. The Pawnee believed that Tirawa, the supreme being, was married to the Vault of Heaven, and both reigned somewhere in the heavens in a place beyond the clouds. Yet they were purely spiritual beings and took no earthly shape. Tirawa sent his commands to humans through a number of lesser gods and messengers who manifested themselves to the Pawnee.

Next in importance to Tirawa and his wife was Tcuperika ("evening star"), who was personified as a young maiden. Evening Star was keeper of a garden in the west that was the source of all food. She had four assistants, Wind, Cloud, Lightning, and Thunder. She married Oprikata ("morning star"), and from them was born the first human being on earth. Morning Star was perceived as a strong warrior who drove the rest of the stars before him. In some Pawnee ceremonies, the sacrifice of a young captive girl was offered to him, suggesting some relationship between Pawnee religion and the religions of central Mexico where human sacrifice was also known.

Of lesser status were the gods of the four directions, the northeast, southeast, southwest, and northwest, and next in rank to the four directions were the three gods of the north: North Star, chief of all the stars; North Wind, who gave the buffalo to humans; and Hikus ("breath"), who gave life itself to the people. Next in line came Sun and Moon, who were married and produced an offspring, the second person on earth, whose marriage to the offspring of Morning Star and Evening Star gave rise to the first humans.

MAJOR CORPORATE RITUALS. Not only were the philosophy and mythology of the Pawnee rich, but their ceremonies were many and varied. There were ceremonies to Thunder, to Morning Star and Evening Star, for the planting and harvesting of Mother Corn, as well as lesser ceremonies for the general welfare of the people.

The Hako. One of the best documented rituals of the Plains, the Hako was performed so that the tribe might increase and be strong, and so that the people would enjoy long life, happiness, and peace. The ceremony was conducted by a man called the *kurahus* ("man of years") who was venerated for his knowledge and experience. To him was entrusted the supervision of the songs and prayers, which had to be performed precisely in the same order each time. The Hako was usually performed in the spring when birds were nesting, or in the fall when they were flocking because it was believed that when prayers were offered for life, strength, and growth of the people it must be done when all life was stirring.

Those taking part in the ceremony were divided into two groups, the fathers who sponsored the ceremony and the children who received the intentions, prayers, and gifts from the fathers. The head of the fathers' group, called Father, was responsible for employing the *kurahus*. The head of the children's group, called Son, also played an important part in the ceremony, acting on behalf of the other children.

The most important paraphernalia used in the Hako were the sacred feathered wands resembling pipe stems without the bowls attached. The ceremony took three days and three nights during which time twenty-seven rituals were performed, each ritual and song unveiling Pawnee sacred lore. At the end of the ceremony, the wands were waved over the children, thus sealing the bond between fathers and children.

Sacred Arrow Renewal. In addition to the Sun

The number four has various cosmological aspects: four cardinal points, four winds, four lunar phases, four seasons, and the four rivers at the beginning of the world.

PAGE 196

Dance there were other public ceremonies that Plains tribes participated in. One of the most important for the Cheyenne was the Sacred Arrow Renewal.

The Cheyenne believe that long ago their supreme being, Maiyun, gave four sacred arrows to the mythological hero Sweet Medicine in a cave in what are now called the Black Hills of South Dakota. Sweet Medicine taught them about the ritual of the sacred arrows. The arrows have been kept in a fox-skin bundle, which has been handed down from one generation to another and guarded by a person known as the sacred-arrow keeper. In alternate years an individual pledges to sponsor a Sacred Arrow Renewal ceremony and the arrows are unwrapped and displayed to all the male members of the tribe. The man making the pledge does so in order to fulfill a vow, such as is the case with the Sun Dance. The vow was originally made when a warrior was threatened during a fight, or someone became sick and was fearful of dying. Although only one person makes the pledge, the ceremony is given on behalf of all Cheyenne, so that they will be ensured of a long and prosperous life.

The Sacred Arrow Renewal ceremony traditionally took four days to perform. On the second day the sacred arrows were obtained from the keeper and the bundle was opened and examined. If the flight feathers of the arrows were in any way damaged, a man known for his bravery was chosen to replace the feathers. On the third day the arrows were renewed and each of the counting sticks was passed over incense to bless all the families in the tribe. On the last day the arrows were exhibited to the male members of the tribe. The Cheyenne said that it was difficult to look directly at the arrows because they gave off a blinding light.

The Ghost Dance. Although missionaries provided Christianity as a viable option to native Indian religions, Plains Indian traditional religions persist in most parts of the Plains. After missions had been established for only a few years, there was one last attempt to rebel against white domination in a pacifistic movement called the Ghost Dance. It began in the state of Nevada when a Paiute Indian named Wovoka had a vision that the white man would disappear from the face of the earth in a cataclysmic event:

THE SUN DANCE
Pierced Hearts Aloft

The most characteristic religious ceremony of the Plains was the well-known Sun Dance, usually performed in the early summer in conjunction with the annual communal buffalo hunt. It owes its name to the fact that certain men who had taken vows to participate danced for several days gazing at the sun, or more precisely, in the direction of the sun. It is useful to note that the Sun Dance was held also in cloudy and even rainy weather, and there is some speculation that the progenitor of the dance may actually have been performed at night during the time of a full moon.

There is some agreement that the oldest form of the Sun Dance originated among the Mandan. Unlike the sun dances of other tribes, the Mandan Sun Dance, called Okipa, was held indoors in the tribe's medicine lodge. The ceremony lasted for four days, during which time the dancers were actually suspended by skewers through their chest from the lodge rafters and the bodies spun around by helpers below. The dance was usually done in advance of warriors going out on a war party.

In other tribes, dancers had skewers of wood placed through the fleshy part of their chest; the skewers were attached to rawhide thong ropes that were tied to a center pole. The dancers pulled backward as they bobbed in time with drum beats until they tore the flesh, thus releasing themselves from the thongs. The Lakota philosophized that the only thing that one could offer to the Great Spirit was one's own body since it was the only thing that a human being really owned. The Sun Dance was one form of making such an offering, the skewering of the dancer also being equated with being in a state of ignorance, and the breaking free as symbolic of attaining knowledge.

The Blackfeet form of the Sun Dance was unlike that of other tribes inasmuch as it centered around a woman known for her industry who vowed to lead the dancers and who bore the title "medicine woman." While she did not go through tortures like her male counterparts in other tribes, she did participate in a number of elaborate ceremonies that preceded the actual dance. Two important ceremonies over which she presided were the Buffalo Tongues and the Sweat Lodge ceremonies. Before the Sun Dance, people in the camp were asked to bring buffalo tongues to a certain lodge erected for that purpose. In the lodge the tongues were ceremoniously skinned, cleaned, and boiled and then distributed to the remainder of the people in camp. Later a special sweat lodge was constructed from one hundred willow saplings, which were placed in the ground and tied together at the tops like those of an ordinary sweat lodge. The dancers then fasted and joined in the Sweat Lodge ceremony before dancing.

— WILLIAM K. POWERS

the earth would turn over, taking all the white men with it. All the old Indians who had died, as well as the buffalo, now all but extinct, would return to live the old way of life. Wovoka claimed that in his vision he visited with these spirits of the deceased Indians and they taught him a dance that would bring about the destruction of the whites. Wovoka preached to other tribes that it was useless to fight with the white man anymore, for soon this cataclysm would be upon them and they would disappear.

After the teachings of this Indian messiah, who had been raised by a Bible-reading white family, the Ghost Dance spread rapidly throughout the Plains, spilling over occasionally into bordering culture areas. All but the Comanche, who preferred their own, more individualistic form of religion, participated.

During the dance the dancers performed for long periods of time until they went into trances. When they awoke they sang of great meetings with their dead kin and of how glad they were that the old way of life would soon return.

But the cataclysm did not come. Instead, the federal government, fearing that the Ghost Dance would serve to engender hostilities among the Indians, ordered all dancing stopped. On 29 December 1890 a band of Ghost Dancers under the leadership of Chief Big Foot was halted on Wounded Knee Creek on the present-day location of the Pine Ridge Indian reservation. Shots rang out, and 260 men, women, and children were massacred, thus ending the short-lived movement.

THE NATIVE AMERICAN CHURCH. A pantribal religion that has become popular since the turn of the twentieth century is the Native American Church, better known in the anthropological literature as the peyote cult.

The majority of peyotists are found among the southern Plains tribes, though members of almost all tribes on the Plains as well as other culture areas belong.

Peyotism is strongly influenced by Christianity and individual tribal beliefs; thus there are minor differences in the ceremonies from one tribe to the next. There are two major divisions, analogous to denominations: the Half Moon, by far the most popular, and the Cross Fire. The rituals of the two divisions differ somewhat, the greatest ideological difference being that the Cross Fire uses the Bible in its ceremonies. Peyote ceremonies are likely to vary also from one tribe to the next, or even from one practitioner to the next. If all members attending a meeting are from the same tribe, it is likely that the native language will be used. If members from several tribes congregate, English is used as the religious lingua franca. Despite the many variations of peyotism, however, there are some customs, rituals, and paraphernalia that are common to all.

GHOST DANCE

The Ghost Dance was a metaphoric dance with spirits that would bring about the destruction of the white man. The ceremony was banned and brutally suppressed by the federal government.

CORBIS-BETTMANN

Peyote meetings are held on Saturday nights, usually from sundown to sunup on Sunday. The ceremony takes place in a traditionally shaped tipi made from canvas. It is especially erected for the occasion and dismantled after the meeting is concluded. The doorway of the tipi faces east, and inside an altar is built containing a fireplace in the center of the lodge behind which is a crescent-shaped earthen altar. On top of the altar is placed a large peyote button called Father, or Chief Peyote. Between the fire and the altar is another crescent made from ashes. Between the fireplace and the doorway of the lodge are placed food and water that later will be ceremonially consumed.

> *"Ten thousand saw I at a glance, tossing their heads in sprightly dance."*
>
> WILLIAM WORDSWORTH
> I WANDERED LONELY AS A CLOUD 1807

The principal leaders of the meeting are assigned special seats inside the tipi. The peyote chief, also known as the "roadman" or "road chief," sits directly opposite the doorway, in what is for most Plains tribes the traditional seat of honor. On his right sits the drum chief, the keeper of the special drum used in the ceremony. To his left sits the cedar chief. Next to the doorway sits the fire boy. The remainder of the congregation are interspersed between the ritual leaders around the perimeter of the tipi. If a Bible is used it is placed between the earth altar and the peyote chief.

Peyote meetings may be held for special purposes such as curing ceremonies, birthday celebrations, funerals, memorial services, or on occasions when persons leave the Indian community to travel great dis-

Peyotism spread through the Basin despite the resistance of many traditionalists.

PAGE 514

tances or return from the armed services. Some are simply prayer meetings conducted on a regular schedule similar to Christian services. Persons wishing to participate in the ceremony arrive at the home of the sponsor, who provides all the peyote buttons for consumption during the meeting as well as the food that will be shared by the participants at the conclusion.

As the drum resounds, the peyote chief sings the opening song of the ceremony. This is a rather standardized song at all peyote meetings, no matter what tribe. He sings it four times, the sacred number for most Plains tribes. When he finishes, each member in turn eats some of the peyote buttons and sings four songs. The man on the right of the singer plays the drum while the singer shakes the gourd rattle. In this manner the ritual of eating and singing progresses around the tipi clockwise. The particularly fast drumming on the water drum and the rapid phrasing of the peyote songs may have a great deal to do with creating the hallucinatory effects experienced in peyote meetings.

Concurrent with the visionary experience is the feeling of a closeness with God. Because peyotism is now greatly influenced by Christianity, the members pray to Jesus Christ, equate the consumption of the peyote button with Holy Communion, and espouse the basic tenets of the Christian churches in their prayers and songs.

The praying, eating of peyote, and singing continue until midnight, when there is a special ceremony. The fire boy informs the peyote chief that it is midnight and then leaves the tipi to get a bucket of water. He returns with the water and presents it to the peyote chief, who dips a feather into the bucket and splashes water on the people in the tipi. After smoking and praying, the water is passed around to the members so that each may drink. During this part of the ceremony another standard song is sung. After the water drinking at midnight, the bucket is removed and it is time to resume the peyote eating and singing.

Despite its Christian aspects, peyotism is frowned on by many missionaries. Yet the Native American Church thrives. It has already become increasingly popular among tribes who were once adherents of their native religions or outright Christians. In the early years peyotism was extremely popular with adjacent communities of black Americans, and today many other non-Indians are joining the Native American Church.

— WILLIAM K. POWERS

INDIANS OF THE NORTHWEST COAST

The peoples of the Pacific Northwest Coast of North America lived along a narrow strip of land that extends from the mouth of the Columbia River north to Yakutat Bay in Alaska.

For the sake of convenience, the Northwest Coast culture area has been divided into three subareas: the northern area was inhabited by the Tlingit, Haida, and Tsimshian peoples; the central by the Bella Coola, Nootka, and Kwakiutl groups; and the southern by the Coast Salish and Chinookan tribes of the Washington and Oregon coasts. While the cultures within each subarea shared some basic traits that distinguished them from one another, the bewildering variety of linguistic, social, political, and ideological variations within each area implied numerous migrations, acculturations, and cultural borrowings that make any retrospective synthesis of Northwest Coast culture a formidable task.

MATERIAL CULTURE. The lives of the Northwest Coast Indians were entirely oriented toward the sea, on whose bounty they depended. The staple food of the area was salmon; varieties of salmon were smoked and stockpiled in immense quantities. However, many other types of fish, sea mammals, large land mammals, water birds, shellfish, and varieties of wild plants were also collected. Though food was plentiful, the rugged topography of the land limited access to food-collecting sites. Access to these sites was also controlled by an oligarchy of hereditary nobles (called "chiefs") who maintained their power primarily through ritual performances that legitimized their claims.

Northwest Coast technology was based on a complex of wood and animal products. Wood and tree bark, especially from cedars, were the fundamental materials and were used ubiquitously. Humans lived in houses, traveled in canoes, caught fish with hooks, trapped salmon in weirs, stored their belongings and were themselves interred in boxes, and wore clothing and ceremonial costumes all made from wood products. A system of symbolic correspondences between objects underlay the entire ceremonial system. Skins, flesh, and bones from animals were also used and played a critical symbolic role in religious activities.

SOCIAL ORGANIZATION. The basic principles of Northwest Coast social organization have been the object of much theoretical controversy. Traditional tribal appellations may lump together groups with similar languages but very different customs, and vice versa. Essentially the basic unit of social and political organization was the independent extended local family, defined by some degree of lineal descent and by coresidence in a single communal household in a single winter ceremonial village. (Winter was the season in which virtually all ceremonies were held.) Group membership was defined less by kinship than by concerted economic and ceremonial activity, though in the northern subarea suprafamilial kin groups played a role in setting the boundaries of a group. The head of each household was its political and spiritual leader, the inheritor and custodian of the house's aristocratic titles, and its ambassador to both human and supernatural worlds. All aristocratic titles in each area were ranked hierarchically for all ceremonial activities. Whether or not the hierarchical system created a class structure as well as a rank structure is a controversial theoretical question. While there was some social mobility, social position was primarily ascribed and inherited. As one goes north within the area, hierarchical systems seem to increase in importance and are firmly embedded in a religious matrix. The peoples of the southern subarea seemed to put little emphasis on hierarchy and exhibited a social structure and religious ideology with more similarities to peoples of the Plateau and California areas than to the coastal peoples to their north.

BELIEF AND RITUAL. There was little synthesis of religious ideas and institutions on the Northwest Coast. Rituals and myths developed into a multiplicity of local traditions that directly integrated local history and geographical features with the more universal elements of creation. Different families and different individuals within families might have conflicting accounts of family history and its mythic events, giving the religion an atomistic quality that permitted a continual restructuring of ceremonies and renegotiating of meanings. However, much of the cognitive conflict that might arise from such discrepancies was mitigated by the fact that although there was an extraordinary amount of public ceremony most rituals were performed in secret and were known only to the rankholder and his heir.

Like the religions of other native North American peoples, the beliefs of the Northwest Coast Indians focused on the critical relationship of hunter to prey and on the set of moral principles that permitted that relationship to continue. Humans were thought to be essentially inferior to the rest of the world's inhabitants and were dependent on other creatures' good will for survival. Humans were important as mediators between different spirit realms because supernatural beings had granted them gifts of knowledge and insight about how the world operates and how they fit into the world. The features unique to Northwest Coast religion centered on the private possession and inherited control of the religious institutions by titled aristocrats. Access to the supernatural beings (called "spirits" by anthropologists because of their essential rather than corporeal nature) and their power was strictly under the control of chiefs, as was access to food.

Spirits. The origin of all power—both the power to control and, more importantly, the power to become aware—was in the spirit world, and the actions of spirit power, which gave form and purpose to everything, were visible everywhere. All objects, ideas, forces, and beings were believed to have inherent power that could be released and directed into human affairs, if correctly integrated into ritual action. The world was seen as filled with spirit power that could be reified in human rituals. Spirits, the personified categories of power, were less characters than ineffable forces. As a salmon could be brought into the human world when caught in a properly constructed net, so could spirit power be brought into the human world when caught in a net of properly constructed ritual action. Humans could never perceive the true nature of spirits, but they could see that the costumes—created as coverings for the spirits—became animated when the spirits covered themselves with them and danced.

The peoples of the Northwest Coast saw their world as one in which myriad personified forces were at work, competing for a limited supply of food and souls. Every human, every group, every species, and every spirit-being had its own needs, its own specialized niche in the food chain. All of their conflicting demands and needs had to be balanced against one another, and this could be achieved only through ritual, which was seen as a method of mediation between the various creatures of the universe. The world was filled with a seemingly endless variety of raptorial creatures who feed on human flesh and souls just as humans feed on salmon flesh. Man-eating birds and other animals, ogres, dwarves, giants, and monsters were believed to prey upon humans as raptorial birds prey upon mice (a frequent image in Northwest Coast myths).

Animals, which were seen as the material representations of spiritual beings, sacrificed themselves for the benefit of human survival because humans had agreed to sacrifice themselves for the benefit of the spirits. The metaphors of Northwest Coast ritual continually repeat the image of the responsibility of humans to support the spirit world. Humans and spirits, living off each other's dead, were intertwined in a reincarnational web. By eating the substance of each other's bodies, they freed the souls and permitted their reincarnation. If any link in the ritual chain was lost, the entire system of reincarnation broke down.

Food. Food was thus a sacramental substance, and meals were inherently ceremonial occasions. Northwest Coast religion placed a heavy emphasis on the control of food-related behavior, on the denial of hunger (which was thought to be a polluting desire), and on the ritual distribution of food and other material substances. The rules, taboos, and rituals associated with food are ubiquitous and enormous in number.

Of all the ceremonies directed toward the propitiation of the animals on which humans feed, those

The Northwest Coast Indians are the most conspicuous users of totem symbols.

PAGE 301

known collectively as the first-salmon ceremonies were the most widespread. These were sets of rituals performed every year in each area over the first part of the salmon catch of each species. Similar ceremonies existed for other species as well. The fish were addressed as if they were chiefs of high rank and were killed, prepared, and served in a ceremonious manner. Their released souls returned to the land of their compatriots to inform them of the proper treatment that they had been accorded. Like most other Northwest Coast rituals, these ceremonies were the property of individual chiefs, who performed them for the benefit of all of the people. All hunting was imbued with ceremony, since success in the hunt was strictly a matter of the proper ritual relationship to the hunted animal. The ceremonies associated with hunting were an important part of a family's inheritance.

Shamanism. Connections to the spirit world could be made through inheritance or by acquiring, through a vision, the power to cure disease. All illnesses and death were considered a sickness of the spirit that was caused either by the magical intrusion of a foreign substance into the body or by the wandering or the loss of the soul. When methods for reestablishing one's spiritual purity failed to alleviate the symptoms, a curer (or "shaman") was called in. A shaman cured an illness by going into a trance during which his guardian spirits would fight with the soul of the disease or of the witch who had sent the disease. When the shaman came out of his trance, he was able to display a small object that symbolically represented the empty husk of the diseased spirit body. Shamanic paraphernalia, like other ritual objects, were formed and moved so as to direct the spirit power in the proper ways to effect a cure. Shamanic performances were dramatic events, with much stage illusion as well as singing, dancing, and praying.

Shamans acted as intermediaries between humans and the forces of nature and the supernatural, and were thought to be able to foretell the future, control the weather, bring success in war or in hunting, communicate with other shamans at a distance, and, most importantly, cure illnesses and restore souls stolen by

GUARDIAN SPIRITS
Shared Destinies and Souls

In theory, a person could obtain a guardian spirit by dedication to a regimen of self-mortification, abstinence, fasting, prayer, and ritual bathing. However, the most powerful contracts with the spirits were obtained in mythic times through the group's ancestors, and these contracts formed the basis of the rank system. Every ranked position was actually an embodiment of a spiritual contract—a covenant between the rankholder and the spirit world. The relationship between the ancestor and the spirit was the primary element of a family's patrimony and was constantly reaffirmed in ritual. As the living representative of the ancestor, the rankholder acted as an intermediary to the spirits on secular occasions and as an impersonator or embodiment of a spirit on sacred occasions.

The relationships between particular aristocrats and particular spirits were manifested in a system of "crests," which were images of spirits that have become allied with individual families. Through the crest, the identity of the aristocrat was connected to that of the spirit being, and through this connection the aristocrat's self expanded to a more cosmic identity. The widespread use of crest objects was graphic proof of the extent to which religious ideas permeated the entire fabric of Northwest Coast culture.

In addition to having shared destinies, humans and spirits were interrelated in that all creatures were considered to be human and to possess human souls. Each lived in its own place in one of the levels of the universe, where it inhabited a house, performed ceremonies, and otherwise acted like a human being. At the proper season, the spirits donned costumes and visited the world of humans, where they appeared in their transformed identity. Similarly, humans who appeared to themselves as humans put on costumes and appeared to the spirits as spirits.

With the exception of Frederica De Laguna's account of Tlingit culture (1972), Northwest Coast Indian ideas of the self, its components, and its relationship to the spirits are not well documented. It is clear that the soul was believed to have several material manifestations as well as several incorporeal components. A person was viewed as a combination of life forces and parts from different planes of existence, and therefore as having spiritual connections in many directions. Whatever their component parts, souls were thought to exist in only limited numbers, to undergo metempsychosis, to be transferred from one species to another, and to be reincarnated alternately in first a human and then either a spirit or animal being. A human death freed a soul for an animal or spirit, and vice versa, linking humans, animals, and spirits in a cycle of mutual dependency. Ideas about the soul and its nature seem to have been better codified among the Northern peoples, though this impression may be an artifact of the high quality of De Laguna's ethnography.

— STANLEY WALENS

witches or maleficent spirits. The shaman was believed both to control and to be inspired by the spirits with whom he was connected. Among the Tlingit, shamanic rituals were usually inherited, but among the central tribes they were obtained through visions.

Witches. Northwest Coast Indian beliefs about shamans were complemented by their beliefs about witchcraft. Witches were thought to be motivated by envy and jealousy, either conscious or unconscious, and there was no act, no matter how terrible, of which they were thought incapable. Patterns of witchcraft among the Northwest Coast Indians were parallel to those of other North American groups: it seems likely that few if any people practiced witchcraft, but accusations of witchcraft were an important means of articulating rivalry and competition. Among the central tribes, witches were generally thought to be shamans from enemy tribes; among the northern groups, where fear of witches was more prevalent, witches were thought to belong to the same kin group as their victims. Witches were thought to be under the compulsion of a possessive spirit, from whose influence the witch could be freed by torture.

The causal principle underlying the ideas of the Northwest Coast Indians on the effectiveness of ritual lay in the idea that under the proper analogical conditions, the patterned motions or words of human beings have an inherent ability to coerce the spirits into parallel actions. Thus a human action could be magnified and intensified into a power that alters the state of the world. Human beings were conduits for supernatural power: although they possess no powers themselves, humans could become the vehicles of supernatural power if they observed the proper ritual actions. In creating analogies between themselves and the spirits, humans gained the ability to influence the actions of those more powerful than themselves.

Creation. Supporting the social and ritual systems was an extensive and varied body of myths and tales (which, except in the work of Claude Lévi-Strauss, have been little analyzed). There were few myths about the creation of the world as such, since the world was seen as a place of innumerable eternal forces and essences. Like other North American groups, the Indians of the Northwest Coast were less interested in how the world was created as material substance than in how it was made moral or how the inherent powers of the universe could be controlled for the benefit of its inhabitants. The creation of material phenomena—the sun and moon, human beings, animal species—is always secondary to the moral dilemmas presented in the myths and the resolution (or lack thereof) of those dilemmas. For example, though there are no myths about the sun being created out of nothing, there are many myths about the sun being placed in the sky, in order to fulfill its proper role by enabling people to see—reminding them of the continual motion and flux of the world and of the balance of light and darkness.

Transformers. Although there are few myths about a creator spirit (and those possibly developed after contact with whites), there are cycles of myths about a transformer or trickster figure who through his actions places the forces of the world in balance. The most detailed and integral of these is the Raven cycle found among the Tlingit (though each tribe had some form of trickster or transformer cycle, not always associated with Raven). Raven is a creature of uncontrollable desires and excesses, and in the act of trying to satisfy his desires, he inadvertently creates moral order and constraint. Incidental to each act of moral creation is the creation of some physical attribute of the world—a mountain or other geographical feature, or the color of a mallard's head or an ermine's tail—that serves to remind people of the myth and its moral import. Thus the world is made up of signs and images of mythic significance for those who know the stories behind them.

Myths of origin. Every feature of the geographic, social, and ceremonial world had an origin myth that encapsulated it into the basic structure of power and ideology, and these myths formed the basic material for Northwest Coast religion and ceremony. No public ceremony occurred without the retelling—either in recital or a dance reenactment—of the origin myths of the people involved, which is to say that no ceremony took place without the reenergizing of the connection between humans and spirits. Clan and family myths were integrated individually into the larger corpus of hero mythology, so that every family and person of title was in some specific way linked to the events and forces of the universe. Myth is a depiction of the interaction of universal forces, and the retelling of the myth reactivates and redirects those forces.

Northwest Coast rituals, like myths, developed into a multiplicity of local traditions, resulting in the direct linking of local history to the more cosmic elements of creation. Ceremonies were always changing as new rituals were acquired through war, marriage, new visions, or the emigration of families. There was a constant renegotiation of the meanings and structure of all rituals and stories, as traditions coalesced, melded, or broke apart; conflicting versions of stories were constantly being reworked.

Winter ceremonials. Spirit power was an essential part of the success of any task; thus there was ceremony in all human endeavor. Even so, there was a clear division of the year into secular (summer) and sacred (winter) seasons. Large-scale ceremonial performances were given in the winter. These were most important among the Kwakiutl and Nootka. Among the southern tribes there was a ceremony of spirit-possession and

"Myth is the secret opening through which the energies of the cosmos pour into human cultural manifestations."

JOSEPH CAMPBELL
THE HERO WITH A THOUSAND FACES 1949

occasional rituals of world renewal similar to those of the peoples of northern California.

The narrative structure of the Kwakiutl winter ceremonials, like that of the family origin myths, was based on a simple set of images that were endlessly elaborated: a hero cuts himself off from the material world of humans, seeks or is kidnapped by spirits who take him to their home, learns the rituals of the spirits, obtains some of the spirits' power, and then brings the rituals back to the human world. These rituals were performed in the most sensationalistic fashion, with elaborate stage effects and illusions, masked performances, complicated props, and stunning displays of strength and athletic agility.

The rituals of the winter ceremonials were under the jurisdiction of groups called "dance societies" or "secret societies." Membership in these groups was inherited and strictly limited. A new member could be invested only upon the retirement of his predecessor, but there were many stages of initiation and many years of preparation before complete initiation. Most of the ceremonies of the dance societies were performed away from public scrutiny, to maintain private ownership of the rituals and to prevent the uninitiated from being harmed by the presence of immense spirit power. A small proportion of the ceremonies were performed only for members of the dance society or for a small group of aristocrats, and a very few were performed for the entire village. Yet even this small proportion of rituals went on for hours every day over a period of four or five months. In essence, then, the entire winter period was given over to ceremony—a fact that belies the usual claim by anthropologists that the peoples of the Northwest Coast were primarily interested in status.

The animal ceremonialism is focused on the sea fauna, and there are many sea spirits in animal forms.

PAGE 530

Of all the winter-ceremonial performances, the most famous and widely discussed is the Hamatsa dance, which the Kwakiutl considered to be their most powerful ceremony. The Hamatsa dance seems to best encapsulate the ethos of Northwest Coast religious ideology. The *hamatsa* was a human who had been carried away by those supernatural creatures who preyed on the flesh and substance of human beings; while living with these supernatural creatures in their ceremonial house, the *hamatsa* took on their spiritual qualities (especially their affinity with death and killing); and when he returned to the land of human beings, he was possessed with the wild desire to eat human flesh. In a long series of rites, the members of the tribe gradually tamed his wildness through a series of pledges to sacrifice their wealth and (when they eventually died) their souls, to feed the spirits so that the world would remain in equilibrium. The violence and energy with which the *hamatsa* acted was a potent representation of the intensity of the struggle or task that humans had to accept if the world were to be kept moral. The burden of spiritual power demanded not a quiet acceptance but energetic activity, a ferocity for right action.

KWAKIUTL MASK

The Kwatkiutl of the Northwest Coast would perform sensational winter ceremonies with elaborate stage effects, illusions and masked performances.

CONCLUSION. Although founded on the same basic philosophical principles as that of other native North American religions, Northwest Coast religion developed those ideas into a distinct set of social and religious institutions that were adaptable to the changing fortunes and histories of each village and its individual members. It was a system in which atomistic elements could be separated from their original relationships with each other and reformed in new combinations dealing in a powerful, cohesive, creative, and poetic way with the purposes and dilemmas of human existence.

Unfortunately, much of Northwest Coast culture was irrevocably altered or destroyed in the course of the nineteenth and early twentieth centuries. All Northwest Coast religion was illegal in Canada from 1876 to 1951, though enforcement of applicable laws was uneven, and some ceremonial life persisted. In the last several decades, there has been a new emphasis on the traditional rituals, but how much they retain of their original character and the place they hold in the lives of the people today are questions that remain to be answered. As North American Indians and scholars both reexamine the historical record to determine the significance of the Northwest Coast religion for the present, it can only be hoped that there will be new interpretations and understandings of what is unquestionably one of the most vibrant and fascinating of the world's tribal religions.

— STANLEY WALENS

INDIANS OF CALIFORNIA AND THE INTERMOUNTAIN REGION

The Intermountain Region of North America is framed on the east by the Rocky Mountains of Canada and the United States and on the west by the Cascade and the Sierra Nevada ranges. Ethnographers customarily divide this region into two indigenous "culture areas," the Plateau and the Great Basin. The Plateau is bounded on the north by the boreal forests beyond the Fraser Plateau of British Columbia and on the south by the Bitterroot Mountains of Idaho and the arid highlands of southern Oregon and northwestern Montana. It includes the Columbia River's plateau and drainage in Washington, Oregon, and a small portion of northern California. The Great Basin is the area of steppe-desert lying primarily in Nevada and Utah but including parts of southern Idaho, western Wyoming, and western Colorado. It runs south from the Salmon and Snake rivers of Idaho to the Colorado Plateau, is bounded by the Colorado River on the south, and includes the interior deserts of southwestern California.

General Themes

The pervasiveness of religious concerns and behavior in the daily lives of all of these peoples is suggested by the range of religious themes that are common to the three areas, despite the diverse, area-specific expressions given them.

POWER. Significant contacts with European influences occurred in the three areas beginning in the eighteenth century and had achieved devastating impact by the mid-nineteenth century. As will be seen, European influence tended to elevate concepts of anthropomorphic creator figures to new eminence. Before contact, however, a widespread perception of a diffuse, generalized, and impersonal cosmic force, often referred to today as "power," was far more significant. This energic field of all potentials is a neutral, amoral, and generative presence that produces all things.

Mythology. In some cases, power was first manifested by a world creator who, through it, brought the world into its present form. Such creators might be culture heroes and transformers, such as Komokums among the Modoc, a people interstitial between California and the Plateau. Komokums and many others like him acted in conjunction with earth divers to form the earth from a bit of soil raised from the depths of a primordial sea. In other cases, especially in north-central California, world creators are likely to be true creator gods, thinking the world into existence or bringing it forth with a word. In southern California we find creation myths of great metaphysical complexity and subtlety, such as those of the Luiseño, for whom creation arose by steps, out of an absolute void. Even here, however, we find a transformer, Wiyot, shaping the present world from an earth that preceded his existence, and this seems the more typical pattern. Such gods and heroes tend to become otiose after their work is accomplished, rather than lingering on as moral overseers.

Unlike the Californians, neither the peoples of the Basin nor those of the Plateau seem to have been much concerned with world origins. Yet they shared with Californians a profound concern for a variety of pre-human spirits—usually animals, but also celestial beings, monsters, and others—who aided in bringing the world to its present shape and in establishing culture. Thus, throughout the region one finds arrays of such prehuman beings, each exercising power for good or ill according to its innate proclivities. The actions of each are recounted in a broad spectrum of myths and stories.

SPIRITS AND PERSONAL POWER. Many animal spirits, including tricksters, remained in the world as sources of specialized powers for human beings. Other unique power potentials might reside in celestial and landscape features and in common, manufactured objects. People might encounter such spirits, usually in their anthropomorphic forms, in visions or in dreams. Through such encounters individuals gained spirit-helpers, enhancing the power innate in themselves and gaining particular powers that, through volitional control, brought success in specific endeavors. Vision quests in many different forms are found throughout the three areas.

Seeking increased, specialized power and protection through intentional encounters with spirit-beings was a primary concern of the religions of the Plateau. In the Basin, visions and personal powers tended to come to individuals spontaneously, at the spirits' will, and were not often sought through formal quests. In California, spirit encounters sometimes resulted from stringent austerities and Plateau-style questing, as among the Achomawi and Atsugewi in the northeast. Often they were sought through participation in initiatory "schools" of pubescent boys seeking power collectively under the tutelage of older initiates. Such schools were central to the visionary religions of the south and the elaborate dance and healing societies of northern California.

More generally, both males and females had access to the spirits and, thus, to personal power. In the Plateau, young boys and girls alike often sought visions, although boys did so more frequently than girls. In the Basin, both males and females could receive spirit powers at any time during their lives, although it appears that men were more often so favored. The situation in California was more complex. In each of three major subareas, women were initiated into some groups but not into others and, among these groups, there were often varying, ranked degrees of male and female spirit acquisition and initiation.

Throughout the three culture areas, the specific spirits that one might encounter and the powers that they enabled were varied. Hunting or fishing skill, the

The most powerful contracts with the spirits were obtained in mythic times through the group's ancestors.

PAGE 506

"So certainly is there nothing, nothing in spiritual things, perfect in this world."

JOHN DONNE
1626

ability to cure and to injure, success in courting and in fighting, finesse in crafts and in song making, gambling luck, wealth, wisdom, and many other potentials might be realized.

Although increased and specialized powers could be acquired and maximized through contacts with spirits, they could also be lost by offending those spirits through failure to adhere to taboos imposed in vision or dream; through misuse of songs, rituals, or power objects; through more general breach of custom, or simply through baffling happenstance. Every increase in an individual's power had its price.

SHAMANS. The shamans were the most powerful of people, the most respected for their spirit contacts, and the most feared. It was they who paid the highest price for their acumen. (*Shaman* here means a healer who obtains and exercises his powers through direct contact with spiritual beings.) In the Plateau, special effort was not usually exerted to obtain the guardian spirits that brought shamanic powers. Here, as in the Basin, both men and women could receive shamanic powers, although male shamans predominated. The same was largely true of Californians, although shamans among Shoshoni, Salinan, and some Yokuts groups were exclusively male, whereas in northwestern California female shamans vastly predominated, those who were the daughters and granddaughters of shamans having the greatest proclivity toward acquiring such powers.

Throughout the three areas, initial encounters with spirits capable of bestowing shamanic powers (sometimes volitionally sought in California and, to a lesser extent, in the Basin) were followed by intensive and often longterm training in the control of the spirit-power and an apprenticeship in its use under a recognized shaman. Such training might include initiation in the secrets of legerdemain, fire handling, and ventriloquism, on which shamanic performances often depended for their dramatic impact. Yet although shamans everywhere were expected to display their powers in such feats, and occasionally to best other shamans in public power contests, their primary function was as curative specialists, and the tricks of the trade were subordinate to success in this important function.

Theories of disease were fairly uniform. Illness came through magical objects projected into the sufferer's body by human sorcery or witchcraft. Again, ghosts or spirits whose rules for conduct had been ignored or whose special places had been defiled might make people ill. The spiritual essence of the patient could be called away by unseen beings or injured by a sorcerer or witch. Finally, one could be poisoned by a witch, either psychically or physically. In the Plateau all such power-related disease was distinguished from natural, physical illness; shamans treated only the former, whereas the latter were treated through exoteric remedies, often by lay specialists. Among the Washo of the Basin, however, all death was attributed to sorcerers.

Shamans in most groups acquired other, noncurative powers and specialties as well. In the Great Basin, in southern California, and north through the central California subarea, rattlesnake handling was practiced by shamans specially related to this powerful creature and capable of curing its bites. Weather shamans who both caused and stopped rains were found in these areas as well. In the Basin, shamans served as hunt leaders, dreaming of quarry such as antelope, leading drives, and charming the game into enclosures. Other specialties abounded. Paiute shamans in the Basin and many in central and northern California became "bear doctors," imitating these animals and using their powers for both benign and malign ends. Others might gain the power to find lost objects, to predict the future, or to conjure, as among the Colville and the Kutenai of the Plateau, whose rites were similar to the shaking tent rites more common far to the east. Virtually everywhere, even among the Plateau and Basin groups whose shamans first obtained their powers without special questing, such practitioners often sought to augment their acumen through gaining additional spirit helpers, often seeking these in special places.

FIRST-FRUITS RITES. First-fruits rites, celebrated for a variety of resources throughout the region, were often conducted by shamans. This was true, for example, of the small, local first-salmon rites that were common along many of the rivers and streams of the Plateau, along the northern California coast south to San Francisco Bay, and among the Pyramid Lake Paviosto, the Lemhi Shoshoni, and some other groups in the northern Great Basin. In some cases, however, first-salmon and other first-fruits rites were incorporated into larger-scale renewal ceremonies, as in northwestern California, and were directed by specialized priests—intermediaries between the human and nonhuman worlds who, as holders of inherited and appointed offices, recited codified liturgies.

GIRLS' PUBERTY AND MENSTRUAL SECLUSION. The ritual initiation of females into adulthood at menarche and, often, the public celebration of this event constitute a second widespread ritual element in the religions of the three culture areas. In general, throughout the region women were isolated at menarche and placed under a variety of restrictions, their conduct during the time being thought to presage their future. Emphasis on girls' puberty tended to be greater among peoples more dependent on hunting than on gathering. Thus, periods of training might be as short as five days, as among the peoples of the western Basin, or extended as long as four years, as among the Carrier Indians of the northern Plateau. In coastal southern California, puberty was a community concern, and all young women reaching menarche during a given year were secluded and instructed together, sometimes being "cooked" in heated pits in a way reminiscent of the training of novice shamans to the north in California. Indeed, it can be argued that puberty rites in many groups represent a female equivalent of male spirit quests and sodality initiations. Such "cooking" of pubescent girls is found elsewhere, as among the Gosiute of the Basin. Communal rites are paralleled in the Plateau, where the Chilcotin, the Southern Okanogen, the Tenino, and the Nez Perce utilized communal seclusion huts for the initiation of young girls.

The prevalence of concern for female puberty in the three areas is clearly related to a concern for menstruation in general. Menstrual blood was viewed as among the most powerful of substances, highly dangerous if not properly controlled and, although often of positive virture to the woman herself, inimical to the welfare of others, especially males. The isolation and restriction of girls at menarche was thus widely repeated—although with far less elaboration—at each menses. Communal menstrual shelters were found in some Plateau communities and perhaps in parts of California. Elsewhere, a small hut for the individual menstruant was constructed, as in much of the Basin, or her movements were restricted to the family's dwelling, as among the River Yuman groups. Menstrual seclusion and dietary and other restrictions varied in duration from the time of the flow up to ten or twelve days, as in northwestern California.

Major Religious Systems

In each area, and often in specifiable subareas, the general themes outlined above were manifested within the context of—and were given particular ideological inflections by—area-specific religious systems.

THE GREAT BASIN. Basin religion was largely an individual or small-band concern, and shamans provided spiritual leadership sufficient to the needs of most bands. Rituals, such as girls' puberty celebrations, that in other areas served as foci for large gatherings here tended to be small, family affairs. The healing performances of shamans might provide occasions for shared ritual participation, but such gatherings, too, were small, limited to band members, and not held according to a fixed schedule.

Large-scale Big Times did occur with some regularity among the Washo and Paiute of the western Great Basin, several bands gathering together for harvest of the more abundant wild crops (such as piñon nuts) for ritual, and for recreation. The Paiute reciprocated such Big Times with the Mono and Miwok of California. Interband antelope drives, sometimes in conjunction with Big Times, were ritually prepared and imbued with religious significance, as suggested by the many Basin rocks displaying petroglyphs and pictographs that date from the remote past through the nineteenth century.

The Big Times of the western Great Basin and California were supplanted in the eastern portion of the Basin area by other sorts of events. Ute and Shoshoni bands convened several times a year for "round dances." Among the Ute, a more ritually focused Bear Dance, marking the return of bears from hibernation and thus the renewal of the world in spring, was performed annually in late winter.

THE PLATEAU. In the Plateau the common western theme of personal spirit-power was honed to its greatest refinement and served as the basis for an areal religious system keynoted by collective "winter spirit-dances." Although there were a great many variations in the specifics of individual guardian-spirit quests and of winter dances among Plateau tribes, a generalized account may be offered as an introduction.

Among the Sanpoil-Nespelem and most other Salish groups, boys and many young girls began spirit questing at or before puberty, often when they were as young as six or eight. (Sahaptin groups placed less emphasis on spirit quests, and others, such as the Carrier, restricted them to certain males.) The child was sent out to fast, scour himself with rough foliage, bathe in cold pools, and keep vigils in isolated places. In dreams, as among the Carrier, or in visions, the supplicant was visited by an animal spirit or the spirit of an object or place. The spirit instructed the person in a song that often had an associated dance step, and sometimes revealed power objects. In many groups, the supplicant, on returning from a successful quest, "forgot" both encounter and song. (The Kutenai, whose youths sought only a single, immediately effective spirit, present an exception.) Among the Salish, when the individual reached full adulthood, usually about age twenty-five for men, the spirit returned, often causing illness. With the aid of a shaman, the individual "remembered" the song and spirit. Once fully accepted, one's spirit became an intrinsic aspect of one's being, like a soul, a "partner" whose loss was life-threatening. Throughout their lives, people might seek different, additional spirits with associated powers and specialties.

During a two-month period in the winter, anyone who had a guardian spirit—a shaman or a layman—might sponsor a spirit dance. The dances, held in a winter lodge, lasted two or three nights and were scheduled so that people of a given locale might attend several in a winter. Under the supervision of shamans, dancers imitated their own guardian spirits, singing

The Sanemá of the Brazilian-Venezuelan frontier region recognize eight different kinds of invisible beings, or hekula.

PAGE 612

Life-cycle rites of passage are illuminating examples of these peoples' recognition that the passage through life's stages required a structured encounter with power.

PAGE 491

their songs and performing their dance steps. New initiates to whom spirits had recently returned used the occasion to legitimize their relationships with their spirits. Other components of the dances included feasting and the giving of gifts to visitors, the offering of gifts to spirits at a center pole, and shamans' displays and contests. The conduct of the audience was rigidly controlled during the dances, and in some groups their behavior was policed by officiants.

Among the Sanpoil, Colville, Kutenai, Kalispel, Spokan, Coeur d'Alene, and Flathead, a society of men possessing Bluejay as guardian spirit served this policing function. These "Bluejay shamans" identified entirely with Bluejay during the winter dance period, painting their faces black, keeping to themselves, and scavenging food. The Bluejay shamans perched in the rafters of dance houses during performances, swooping down on those who broke the rules of conduct. They also performed services as finders of lost objects and as curers, and were ritually returned to a normal state at the end of the dance period. Although the Bluejay shamans suggest an at least latent sodality structure in the southeastern Plateau, such sodalities were fully developed only in California.

CALIFORNIA. There were four major subareal ritual complexes in aboriginal California.

Toloache. From the Yuman tribes of the south, north through the Yokuts and, in diminished forms, to the Miwok, the use of *Datura stramonium*—jimsonweed, or *toloache* (from the Nahuatl and Spanish)—was a common and central feature of religious practice. A psychotropic decoction was made from the root of this highly toxic plant and carefully administered to initiates by shamans or by specialized priests. After a period of unconsciousness the initiates awoke to a trancelike state of long duration during which, guided by adepts, they acquired animal or celestial spirit-helpers. Such collective, drug-induced vision questing was often undertaken by males at puberty and in the context of an extended "school," as among the Luiseño-Juaneño, the Cahuilla, the Ipai-Tipai, the Cupeño, and the Gabrielino. Schooling included severe physical ordeals, instruction in mythic cosmology carried out through dry painting, and in some cases the creation of rock art. In such groups as the Chumash and the Serrano, training was restricted to the sons of an elite. In all cases, the group of initiated men, and—among the Monache and the Yokuts—women, formed a sodality that bore defined religious, economic, and political responsibilities. Among the Chumash, such an organization provided the basis for a highly complex, elite socioreligious guild, *Iantap*, led by priest-astronomers. Throughout the subarea, shamans made use of *toloache* in achieving curing trances.

Mourning anniversaries. With their stress on ritual death and rebirth, the *toloache* religions of southern and central California reflected an overriding concern with personal and cosmic death and renewal. A second feature, the "mourning anniversary," accompanied the *toloache* complex. In broad outline, mourning anniversaries were large public gatherings in which effigies of the year's dead, together with large quantities of property, were burned on poles erected in circular brush shelters, the assembled audience mourning its collective losses. The occasion often served as a vehicle for girls' puberty celebrations, for the giving of new names, for honoring chiefs, and for expressing reciprocity between kin groups. Often an Eagle (or Condor) Dance, in which shamans displayed their power by slowly killing a sacrificial bird, formed an important part of the event.

The mourning anniversary, with many local variations, was practiced by the Basin peoples of the southern portion of contemporary California—the Cheme-huevi, the Panamint, the Kawaiisu, and the Tubatulabal—as well as by virtually all groups in the southern California culture area. The practice extended northward through the *toloache*-using groups and beyond, being performed by the Maidu and Nisenan of northern California in conjunction with another religious complex, the Kuksu cult.

Kuksu. The term Kuksu derives from the Pomo name for a creator-hero who is impersonated by masked dancers in the periodic performances that are the focus of the religious system. A parallel figure, Hesi, was prominent in the performances of groups in the Sacramento Valley and the Sierra Nevada foothills. The Hill Maidu expression of the complex featured a third such figure, Aki, who is found together with Hesi among the Northwestern Maidu. Kuksu and Hesi are sometimes found together among other groups.

Masked and costumed dancers impersonated these and other spirits and mythic figures in elaborate ceremonials performed in dance houses before large audiences during gatherings that lasted several days. Dances at various ceremonial centers were reciprocally supported. As with *toloache* religions, the various Kuksu religions provided collective "schools" for pubescent initiates who were, through cultic indoctrination and participation, conducted into secret, often ranked sodalities. Such sodalities could exercise great political and economic influence, as well as spiritual power. The Kuksu dances themselves returned the world to its pristine, mythic condition and often included first-fruits and curing elements in their scope. Intergroup trading, gambling, shamans' contests, and recreation were features of the Big Times that usually followed Kuksu performances.

Among groups that had both Kuksu and Hesi

sodalities, as well as some others, participation was open to young men and also to some young women, as among the Cahto and the Yuki. More commonly, membership in such sodalities was restricted to males. In some groups, membership was further restricted to elite cadres who worked their way up through the sodality's ranked levels, as among the Pomo-speaking groups. In such groups a second sodality, the Ghost society, was open to all young men, as among the Patwin, and sometimes to women as well, as among the Eastern Pomo. These less prestigious sodalities presented masked dances that paralleled those of the Kuksu type and emphasized the honoring of the departed, the curing of ghostdisease, and the continuity of generations. Such themes were present in the mourning anniversaries prevalent to the south. Thus, the Ghost society was not found among groups in the Kuksu subarea (such as the Maidu and the Nisenan) that practiced mourning anniversaries.

Postcontact Religious Change

The religions of California, the Great Basin, and the Plateau have undergone thousands of years of slow change and development. They were probably changed most suddenly and drastically by the direct and indirect influences of Europeans and Euro-Americans that began in the eighteenth century.

The Roman Catholic missionization of California, beginning in 1769, had largely disastrous effects on the native populations of the area. Voluntary conversions took place, but forced baptism and forced residence in mission communities were more common. Ultimately, the successes of Catholic missionization north to San Francisco Bay were negated by the fearsome toll exacted by the diseases fostered by overcrowded missions and forced labor under the Spanish *encomienda* system. Success measured in lasting conversions was modest, and negative in terms of human welfare, but the missionaries contributed to native religious revitalization.

Other missionaries, primarily Protestant and Mormon, also made extended efforts in the nineteenth century in California, the Basin, and the Plateau. Yet the effects of later missionization were broadly similar: rather than supplanting native religions, Christianity provided symbolic means through which native religions found new forms to cope with the radically changing circumstances of life.

However, the effects of conquest were not limited to innovations informed by Christian ideology. The introduction of the horse onto the Plains and thence

WORLD RENEWAL
Staving Off Global Chaos

Mythic reenactment, collective mourning, generational continuity, and world renewal are all motives present in the Kuksu religion that found other expressions in northwestern California, where a fourth areal ritual complex, the World Renewal cult, flourished. This complex featured cyclic ten-day ceremonials within more extended periods of ritual activity performed by specialized officiants. The various dances were given reciprocally at two- to three-year intervals at perhaps thirteen ceremonial centers in Yurok, Karok, and Hupa territories. Close equivalents of these World Renewal dances were held by Tolowa-Tututni, Wiyot, Chilula, and Shasta groups as well. The focal occasions were religious festivals, extended periods of public and private ritual, dancing, feasting, and communality that at times attracted several thousand participants. World Renewal festivals thus replaced both Big Times and mourning anniversaries in the northwestern subarea. However, the primary purpose of these large gatherings was the prevention of world disorder and the reaffirmation of interdependency. The world, potentially imbalanced by the weight of human misconduct, was "fixed" or "balanced" through the Jump Dance, the interdependence and abundance of all life reaffirmed and ensured through the Deerskin Dance. In both, teams of dancers displayed finery and power objects emblematic of the spiritual ascendency of their sponsors, and it was in this sense that such costumes and objects were considered "wealth."

The World Renewal religion was given different inflections by the different participating groups: the Yurok incorporated first-salmon rites and collective fishing as well as the rebuilding of a sacred structure; the Karok included "new fire" (new year) elements, as well as a first-salmon rite; and the Hupa celebrated a first-acorn rite, the rebuilding of a cosmographic structure, and so on. All stressed the reenactment, by priests, of the origins of the dances and their attendant rituals. The recitation of long, codified mythic scenarios was a central feature. School-like organizations of "helpers" were instructed by the priests. These organizations were similar to the initiatory sodalities of south and central California and included both men and women. Neither priests and their assistants nor dancers impersonated spirit beings, however, as was done in Kuksu performances or the spirit dances of the Plateau.

— THOMAS BUCKLEY

On 29 December 1890 a band of Ghost Dancers under the leadership of Chief Big Foot was halted on Wounded Knee Creek. Shots rang out, and 260 men, women, and children were massacred, thus ending the short-lived movement.

PAGE 503

into the Plateau and the northwestern Basin in the early eighteenth century had an important impact on the peoples of these areas. Together with the horse came other Plains influences. Military sodalities were integrated into the religions of the Kutenai and the Flathead, as was the Sun Dance. The Sun Dance also spread to the Great Basin, where it was taken up by the Wind River Shoshoni and the Bannock and was introduced to the Utes by the Kiowa as late as 1890.

The preponderant contact phenomena evidenced in the religious life of all three areas, however, were the millenarian crisis cults inspired by a variety of "prophets" whose visions had been shaped by Christian influences. Typically, such visions occurred in deathlike states in which prophets met God or his emissary and received word of the coming millennium and the practices and moral codes that would ensure Indians' survival of it. Perhaps the best known of such crisis cults are the Paiute Ghost Dances of 1870 and 1890.

The first of these, initiated by the prophet Wodziwob in 1870, moved through the Basin and into central California. It was taken up by a number of California groups and moved north to the Shasta. The Ghost Dance doctrine stressed the destruction of the whites by the Creator, the return of the Indian dead, and the restoration of the earth to its pristine, precontact condition. It inspired a number of variants in the years following 1870. Most of these represented fusions of Kuksu-type and Ghost society dances with the new millenarianism. Such cults included the Earth Lodge religion practiced by many central and northern California peoples. Adherents awaited the millennium in large, semisubterranean dance houses. Other cults inspired by the 1870 Ghost Dance included the Big Head and Bole-Maru cults of the Hill Patwin, the Maidu, and the Pomo-speaking groups, and a succession of other local cults led by various "dreamers."

The 1890 Ghost Dance, initiated in 1889 by the Paiute prophet Wovoka, again spread through the Basin, this time moving east onto the Plains. It directly affected neither California nor the Plateau.

The two Ghost Dances are but the better known of a large number of similar efforts toward religious revitalization that flourished, particularly in the Plateau area, in the nineteenth century. In the 1830s, many prophets, not acting in concert, spread the Prophet Dance through the central and southern Plateau. This round dance, always performed on Sundays and reflecting belief in a high god, showed Christian influence, although some have argued that it had aboriginal precedents as well. The dance took many forms under the guidance of many prophets and dreamers, of whom the best known is perhaps Smohalla, a Sahaptin dreamer who revived the Prophet Dance in the 1870s in a form that spread widely.

In 1881 a Salish Indian from Puget Sound named John Slocum underwent what was by that time the established visionary experience of a prophet. Together with his wife Mary he inaugurated the Indian Shaker church, a Christian church in which the presence of God's power, signified by physical trembling ("the shake"), was used by congregants to cure the sick. This mixture of Christian and native shamanistic elements proved highly appealing, and the Indian Shaker church spread into the Plateau, where it was accepted by Yakima, Umatilla, Wasco-Tenino, Klamath, and, to a lesser extent, Nez Perce Indians. In northwestern California in 1926, churches were built by Yurok, Tolowa, and Hupa congregations. The Shakers' popularity in California began to wane in the 1950s, the result of internal schism, competition with evangelical Christian churches, and increasing stress on "Indianness" and the accompanying return to old ways.

These two apparently conflicting ideologies, based on the salvific powers of Jesus Christ, on the one hand, and on an Indian identity perceived as traditional, on the other, seem to have reached mutual accommodation in peyotism and its institutionalized expression, the Native American Church. The Peyote Way has been accepted by a large number of Basin Indians, spreading among the Ute, Paiute, Gosiute, and Shoshoni in the early twentieth century, its acceptance perhaps facilitated by the collapse of the 1890 Ghost Dance. The Washo received peyote from Ute believers in 1936.

Peyotism spread through the Basin despite the resistance of many traditionalists, becoming itself the basis for a new traditionalism. It was not, however, established in California, although Indians from such cities as San Francisco make frequent trips to take part in peyote meetings sponsored by the Washo and others in Nevada.

Many other postcontact religious systems, including the Sun Dance, continue to be enacted. Chingichngish remains central to religious life on the Rincon and Pauma reservations in southern California; Smohalla's Prophet Dance is still practiced as the basis of the Pom Pom religion of the Yakima and Warm Springs Indians; and Bole-Maru and other postcontact transformations of Kuksu religions are viable among Pomo and other central Californian groups. The Indian Shaker church survives in many communities.

Since the 1960s Indians of all three culture areas have made concerted efforts to reassert religious, as well as political, autonomy; indeed, the two realms continue to be closely intertwined. Traditional religious specialists and, in many cases, collective ritual activities have survived both conquest and christianization. Younger Indians are increasingly turning to elderly specialists and investing themselves in old ritual practices. Annual mourning ceremonies are still prominent in parts of southern California; northwestern Californians continue to dance in World Renewal rituals; and shamanism survives in the Basin, as does spirit questing on the Plateau. A myriad of other native ritual events and private practices continue throughout the region. Such state agencies as California's Native American Heritage Commission, as well as federal legislation such as the 1978 American Indian Religious Freedom Act, support these efforts to a degree. Withal, one can see the durability of the ancient ways, their persistence, and their ability to continue through modern transformations.

— THOMAS BUCKLEY

INDIANS OF THE SOUTHWEST

From the southern end of the Rocky Mountains in Colorado, the Southwest culture area extends southward through the mountains, high sandstone mesas, and deep canyons of northern New Mexico and Arizona, and dips over the Mogollon Rim—the southern edge of the Colorado Plateau—into the arid, flat, and sparsely vegetated, low-lying deserts of southern New Mexico and Arizona and northwestern Mexico, to the warm shores of the Gulf of California. It is interspersed throughout with mountain ranges, some bearing dense forests and large game animals. Major rivers are few: the Colorado, its tributaries, and the Rio Grande are the primary sources of water for large sectors of the southwestern ecosystem.

Given the variegation in topography, vegetation, and climate, it is not surprising that the Southwest should contain an equal cultural variety. Four major language families (Uto-Aztecan, Hokan, Athapascan, Tanoan) are represented by a large number of peoples, and two other languages (Zuni and Keres) comprise language isolates. But it should not be thought that language boundaries are a guide to cultural boundaries. The thirty-one pueblos of New Mexico and Arizona include speakers of six mutually unintelligible languages from four language groups. Yet they share numerous cultural, and specifically religious, features. On the other hand, among the groups speaking Uto-Aztecan languages are found sociocultural forms as disparate as the hunter-gatherer bands of Shoshoneans in the north and the great Aztec state to the south of the Southwest culture area.

ECONOMIC PATTERNS. Edward Spicer (1962) has suggested four major divisions according to distinctive economic types at the time of European contact: rancheria peoples, village peoples, band peoples, and nonagricultural bands. The rancheria peoples all traditionally practiced agriculture based on the North American crop triumvirate of maize, beans, and squash. They lived in scattered settlements with households, or "small ranches," separated by some distance from each other. This general economic pattern was followed by groups as disparate as the Tarahumara and Concho in the Sierra Madre of Chihuahua, the Pima and Papago of southern Arizona, the Yaqui and the Mayo concentrated in the river deltas along the Sonoran coast of the Gulf of California, and the riverine and upland Yuman groups.

The village peoples of Spicer's classification are, by contrast, sedentary communities with tightly integrated populations in permanent villages of stone and adobe construction. These are the Pueblo peoples, who have come to be regarded as the archetypical indigenous agriculturalists of the Southwest. The Tanoan Pueblos include the Tiwa, Tewa, and Towa, whose villages stretch up and down the upper portion of the Rio Grande in New Mexico. Also living for the most part along the Rio Grande or its tributaries are several Keresan Pueblos, with linguistically close Laguna and Acoma a little farther west, on the San Jose River. Moving west across the Continental Divide lies the pueblo of Zuni on a tributary of the Little Colorado River. At the western edge of Pueblo country, on the fingerlike mesas that extend southwestward from Black Mesa of the Colorado Plateau, are the eleven Hopi villages, whose inhabitants speak Hopi, a Uto-Aztecan language. Also located in this vicinity is one Tewa village, Hano, settled by refugees from the Rio Grande valley after the Great Pueblo Revolt of 1680.

The Pueblos are intensive agriculturalists. Among the Eastern Pueblos (those occupying the Rio Grande area) and in Acoma, Laguna, and Zuni (which with the Hopi constitute the Western Pueblos), agriculture is based on a variety of irrigation techniques. Hopi country has no permanent watercourses, and agriculture there is practiced by dry farming. Their sedentariness is a striking feature of the village peoples: Acoma and the Hopi village of Oraibi vie for the status of oldest continuously inhabited community in North America, with ceramic and tree-ring dates suggesting occupation from at least as far back as the twelfth century CE.

Spicer's third subtype is that of the band peoples, all Athapascan speakers. These consist of the Navajo and the several Apache peoples. These Athapascans migrated into the Southwest, probably via the Plains, from northwestern Canada not long before the arrival of Spanish colonists at the turn of the sixteenth century. They variously modified a traditional hunting and gathering economy with the addition of agriculture from the Pueblos (Navajo and Western Apache) and of sheep (Navajo) and horses (all groups) from the Spanish. The means of acquisition of these economic increments—through raiding of the pueblos and Spanish

Human representations can also signify the heroes or founders of cults; such is the case with many images on Pueblo altars and other representations on Northwest Coast poles.

PAGE 302

settlements—points up another important feature of Apache economies.

The fourth economic subtype Spicer refers to as non-agricultural bands. The Seri of the northwestern coastline of the Mexican State of Sonora are the primary representatives of this subtype. Traditionally, they hunted small game, fished and caught sea turtles, and gathered wild plant resources along the desert coast of the Gulf of California.

Variations in economy do not, of course, suggest variations in religious structure and orientation *tout court*. Still, modes of environmental adaptation do, within certain bounds, constrain the possibilities of social complexity. Southwest Indian religious patterns frequently do reflect forms of environmental adaptation because of a prevailing notion of social rootedness within a local environmental setting. Since many of the religious concerns of Southwest peoples pertain to man's relationship with environmental forces, the interplay between economic and religious spheres is fundamental.

Religion penetrates all aspects of Pueblo life. A rich set of ceremonies that mark the divisions of the year are conducted by different religious societies.

PAGE 531

RELIGIOUS PATTERNS. Among the panoply of indigenous Southwestern cultures, two general patterns of religious action are evident: that focusing on the curing of sickness and that celebrating, reaffirming, and sanctifying man's relationship with the cyclical forces of nature. Religious actions of the former type are usually shamanic performances whose participants include an individual patient and an individual ritual specialist (or a small group of specialists). The latter type includes communal rituals involving large groups of participants under the direction of cadres of hereditary priests. These two general forms are present in the Southwest in a variety of combinations and permutations. Among the Yumans, the Tarahumara, and the Apache, shamanistic curing is the prevalent religious form, and little emphasis is placed on communal agricultural rituals. (The Havasupai, who until the turn of the century held masked ceremonial performances at stages of the agricultural cycle—a practice probably borrowed from their near neighbors, the Hopi—provide a partial exception.) Historically the Pima and Papago peoples held communal agricultural rituals as well as shamanic performances, but with sociocultural change the former have passed from existence while the latter, by themselves, have come to represent traditional religion. At the other end of the continuum, the Pueblos devote most religious attention to the calendrical cycle and have even communalized their curing ceremonies by creating medicine societies to fill the role played in less communally oriented societies by the individual shaman. (The Hopi are an exception, in that they still recognize individual medicine men and women.)

SEVERAL CAVEATS TO STUDENTS OF SOUTHWEST RELIGIONS. A key problem facing the student of Southwest Indian religions is sociocultural change. The Spanish conquest and colonization of the sixteenth and seventeenth centuries affected all Southwest cultures, though individual peoples were treated differently. Our knowledge of indigenous religious beliefs and practices is in some cases (for example, the Seri) severely limited by the wholesale abandonment of indigenous beliefs and their replacement with Christian concepts. Syncretism of traditional and introduced forms is, as among the Yaqui and Mayo, so historically entrenched that it is impossible to isolate the threads of precontact religious life. The traditional Yaqui and Mayo system of three religious sodalities fused in the seventeenth century with Jesuit beliefs and came to embody largely Christian notions, but these peoples' version of Christian ceremonies, such as the rituals recapitulating the Passion of Christ, incorporate traditional figures with clear similarities to the kachinas and clowns of the Pueblos. Since such syncretic processes began long before careful ethnographic records were made of indigenous belief and practice, the "pure forms" are simply irretrievable.

The Pueblos, the Navajo, and the Apache have maintained more of their traditional religious systems intact than other Southwest peoples. Of these groups, the Pueblos have the most complex religious systems, which in many instances preserve indigenous forms intact and distinct from religious elements introduced by Europeans. Hence I shall focus upon the Pueblos in this essay. The persistence of Pueblo religious patterns, despite almost four hundred years of colonial domination, is remarkable. The presence of Puebloan peoples in the Southwest, and of the earlier so-called Basket Makers, with whom there is a clear cultural continuity in the archaeological record, reaches far back into antiquity. The remains found in New Mexico's Chaco Canyon and Colorado's Mesa Verde of the civilization of the Anasazi are simply the better-known evidences of this socially complex and culturally sophisticated people, the direct ancestors of the historical Pueblos. The height of Anasazi culture (twelfth and thirteenth centuries CE) is represented by monumental architecture and elaborately constellated settlement patterns that suggest extensive social networks over large regions. For reasons we can only guess at—perhaps drought, war, disease, population pressure, internal social strife, or all of these in concert—the larger Anasazi pueblos had given way to the smaller pueblos by the time of the earliest historical records (c. 1540).

How much change and persistence have occurred in religion is an unfathomable problem. Nevertheless, the religious conservatism of the modern Pueblos, as well as archaeological indications (such as certain petroglyphs) suggest that more than a few Pueblo reli-

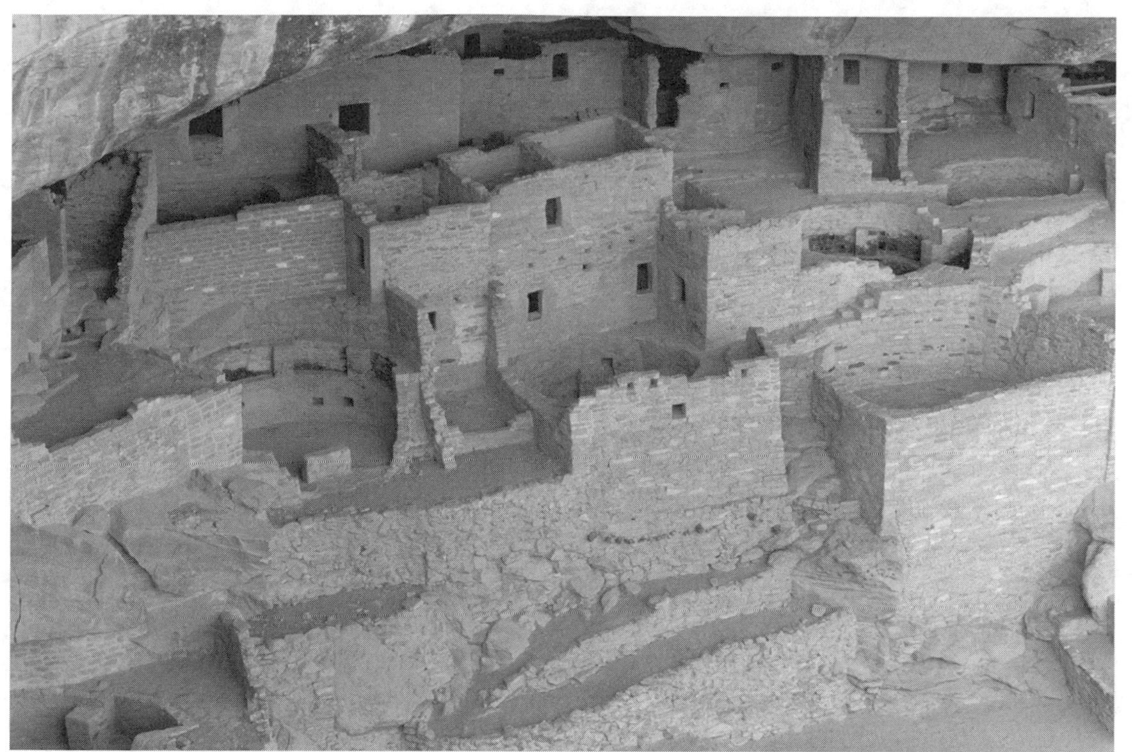

ANASAZI PUEBLOS

The Pueblo Indians have been and remain today an extremely reticent, unwilling to reveal anything beyond superficial aspects of their religious life.

KEVIN FLEMING/© CORBIS

gious practices have persisted for a very long time. These two factors—the conservatism and antiquity of Pueblo religious practices—reflect another prominent characteristic: that the more important Pueblo beliefs and ritual practices are deliberately and rigorously preserved by an all-encompassing cloak of secrecy. The Pueblos have been and remain today extremely reluctant to reveal anything beyond the superficial aspects of their religious life. No anthropologists, apart from native Pueblo individuals, have been allowed to conduct extended resident field research by any of the Eastern Pueblos. Questions about religion meet with evasion or a purposive silence. Often information obtained by outsiders has been gathered in unusual ways, such as by interviewing individuals in hotel rooms distant from their pueblos. Only limited aspects of Pueblo religious performances are public; no non-Indian outsider has been permitted to witness a *kachina* performance in any of the Rio Grande pueblos since the seventeenth century.

Secrecy is pervasive not simply to preserve the integrity of traditional religion from the corrupting influences of the outside world, but also to protect the religious practices' integrity within the pueblos themselves. Initiates into religious societies are inculcated with the idea that their disclosure of secret, ritually imparted knowledge will have dire supernatural (their own or their relatives' deaths) and social (their ostracism from the pueblo) consequences. The result is that knowledge of Pueblo religion is fragmentary, flimsy, and in some cases inaccurate. We do know something of the surface contours of Pueblo religion, and these are discussed below. In deference to the Pueblos' rights to maintain their religions as they see fit, perhaps this surface level is as far as we may conscionably prosecute our inquiries.

THE PUEBLO COSMOS. In Pueblo thought generally, there is no absolute origin of life or of human beings. Although there have been a number of transformations since the earliest times, the earth and the people have always existed. Accordingly, there is less concern with primordial origins than with the process through which human beings were transformed into their present state of being from previous states.

Southwest peoples in general envision a multilayered cosmos whose structure is basically tripartite: "below," "this level," and "above." Each level has subdivisions, but the number and character of the subdivisions vary from culture to culture. All the Pueblos believe themselves to have originated beneath the present earth's surface. The layer below is characterized as a previous world, or as several previous worlds (or "wombs") stacked one atop another. The Zuni and the Keresans conceive of four previous worlds, the Hopi of three, and the Tewa only one. The last world "below" lies under a lake or under the earth's surface. At the beginning of the present age, the people were impelled—by supernatural signs in some versions of the Emergence story, by the need to flee evil in other versions—to seek a new life in the world above. By methods that vary from story to story (in some versions by climbing a tree, in others a giant reed), the people

Mysterious occurrences and beings that habitually or occasionally impinge upon our everyday experience are called "supernatural."

PAGE 632

ascended to this level. The earth's condition was soft, and it required hardening. This was accomplished with the supernatural aid of the War Twins, who are found among all the Pueblo groups, or it was done by a human being with special powers—for example by the Winter Chief, who in the Tewa story hardened the ground with cold.

The timing and methods of the creation of natural phenomena vary, but the trajectory of human progress is the same throughout the various Pueblo traditions. After their emergence onto the earth's surface through an opening referred to as an "earth navel," the people migrated over the earth, stopping at locations that are identified by oral tradition with the numerous ruins throughout the Southwest, before reaching their final destination in the present-day villages. Variant migration patterns reflect differing forms of social organization: the matrilineal clans of the Hopi migrated independently and arrived at the present Hopi towns as separate units, whereas the two moieties of the Tewa— Winter and Summer—migrated down opposite banks of the Rio Grande from their Emergence point in the north.

Hence Pueblo origin myths emphasize the process of becoming the Pueblo peoples of the present. Each pueblo is highly independent, and, but for exceptional occasions requiring dire responses (such as in the Pueblo Revolt of 1680 or during severe famines), there is no political unity among pueblos whatsoever. Such independence is reflected in Pueblo worldview: each pueblo regards itself as the center of the bounded universe. Forces radiate both centripetally from the outer limits and centrifugally from a shrine at the pueblo's center, which is represented as the heart of the cosmos. Thus the Zuni are "the people of the middle place," the Hopi of Second Mesa live at the universe center, and each of the various Tewa villages lies about its "earth-mother earth-navel middle place" (Ortiz, 1969, p. 21). The outer limits of the world are marked variously. Among the Eastern Pueblos and the Acoma and Laguna, the world is a rectangular flat surface (although of course broken by topography) bounded by sacred mountains in the cardinal directions. For the Zuni, the surface is circular and is surrounded by oceans that are connected by underworld rivers. The Hopi world is more abstractly bounded, although sacred mountains and rivers act as circumscribing features.

All Pueblo worlds are rigorously aligned by six cardinal directions, four of which correspond to our north, west, south, and east (or, in the Hopi case, sunrise and sunset points on the horizon at the solstices—roughly northwest, southwest, southeast, and northeast) and the zenith and nadir. From the viewpoint of its inhabitants, each pueblo lies at the center formed by the intersection of the axes of opposed directions. The directions are symbolized by numerous devices: colors, mammals, birds, snakes, trees, shells, sacred lakes, deity houses, and so forth.

The Zuni and the Tewa seem to have elaborated the axial schema to the greatest extent. For the Zuni, the six directions serve as a multipurpose organizational model for society—in terms of matrilineal clan groupings, priesthood sodalities, kiva (ceremonial chamber) groupings—and for nature, in that the taxonomy of species is directionally framed. The fourfold plan (i. e., excluding the vertical axis) of the earth's surface is represented by the Tewa as a series of concentric tetrads, which are marked by four mountains at their extremities and by four flat-topped hills, four directional shrines, and four village plazas as the center is approached. Neither is this a static abstraction in Tewa belief: ritual dancers in the plazas must face the four directions; songs have four parts; and so forth. Each of the physical features marking the corners of the concentric boundaries (the four mountains, hills, shrines, and plazas) is a place of power. Each contains an "earth navel" that connects the three levels of the cosmos and that is presided over by particular supernaturals.

THE PUEBLO PANTHEON. Associated with the levels and sectors of the Pueblo world is a panoply of supernatural beings. Elsie C. Parsons (1939) divides these beings into collective and individualized categories.

Collective supernaturals. The collective category signally includes clouds, the dead, and the *kachinas*. Clouds and the dead have an explicit association: the specific destiny of the deceased person depends upon the role he played during life, but in general the dead become clouds. The cloud beings are classified according to the directions and, accordingly, associated with colors. *Kachina* is a fluid spiritual concept that refers both to supernatural beings and to their masked impersonators at Pueblo ceremonies. *Kachinas* appear in numerous guises and represent many features of the natural and supernatural worlds. They are dramatized in masked impersonation and in stories, where they appear in the forms of animals, plants, birds, the sun, and stars and as spirits such as the War Twins, sky deities, culture heroes, and so on. Some *kachinas* also represent game animals, and *kachinas* associated with the directions are also linked with hunting. *Kachinas* dwell in locations on the edges of the bounded world: in mountains, for instance, or in lakes or other sites associated with the powers of moisture. The three concepts of the dead, the clouds, and the *kachinas* overlap: the dead may become *kachinas*, and *kachinas* may manifest themselves as clouds. The interrelation among clouds, the dead, and *kachinas* points up a significant concern of Pueblo beliefs and ritual practices: the importance of rainfall in this largely arid environment is paramount, and the *kachinas*, as rain spirits, have the power to bring rain to nourish the crops—the central link in the Pueblo chain of being.

Individualized supernaturals. In some respects, individualized supernaturals reflect the arrangement of the cosmos into levels. Thus among the Hopi, Sootukw-nangw ("star-cumulus cloud"), the zenith deity, is associated with lightning and powerful rain; Muyingwu, an earth deity associated with the nadir, is the spirit of maize, germination, and vegetation; and Maasawu is the guardian of this level, the surface of the earth. But each of these figures has multiple aspects and cannot be neatly slotted into an abstract cosmic layer. Through his power to shoot lightning like arrows, Sootukw-nangw is also an important war deity, and Maasawu, especially, has a cluster of characteristics. He is associated with fire, war, death, and the night, and he looks and behaves in a more manlike fashion than do the deities of above and below. Supernaturals associated with cosmic features also embody moral principles (Maasawu represents humility, conservatism, lack of avarice, serious commitment to the duties of life, and the terrifying consequences of excessive individualism) and biological principles (Sootukw-nangw's lightning arrows are associated with male fertilization). Further, there is a plethora of other supernaturals who are not arranged hierarchically but who crystallize a number of religious concerns. The Pueblo pantheon lacks systematization: supernaturals often overlap in meaning and function, and this is further evident in the pattern of religious organization. Discrete segments of Pueblo society often focus exclusively upon the sets of supernaturals under their control; individuals not in a particular social segment do not have rights of appeal to its set of deities, and they risk severe social repercussions for unauthorized attempts at intercourse with such deities.

The sun, regarded everywhere as male, is a powerful fertilizing force, the father in relation to the earth, who is the mother. Traditionally, every individual was expected to offer cornmeal and to say a prayer to the sun at dawn, when the sun leaves his house (or *kiva*) at the eastern edge of the world and begins his journey to his western house. Prayers to the sun refer to the desire for a long and untroubled path of life for each individual. After a period of seclusion in darkness, the newborn Pueblo infant is taken out and shown to the sun to request a long and happy life and the sun's beneficent attention. As Father, the sun is equated with the care and spiritual nurturance of his children. Songs are addressed to him to ask for his life-giving powers of light and warmth, kept in balance so as not to burn the crops or dry them out. Sun is also a deity of hunting and war; the Keresans, Tiwa, and Hopi seek his assistance in these endeavors.

Other celestial deities. Less significant by comparison, other celestial deities include, first, the moon, who is variously female (Zuni, where Moonlight-Giving Mother is the sun's wife) and male (Tewa, Towa, Tiwa). Moon is rarely addressed in prayer or song. In association with the sun and some constellations, however, the moon's movements and phases are utilized to plan the calendrical cycle of ceremonies. The antiquity of such practices is suggested by the numerous lunar and solar marking devices found in prehistoric Puebloan sites, such as the well-known Sun-Dagger petroglyphs in Chaco Canyon.

The morning star and the constellations Orion and the Pleiades have associations with war and with the timing of ceremonies. The movement of celestial phenomena is critically linked to the seasonal passage of the year. The ceremonial moiety division of the Tewa into Winter and Summer people, each of which has ritual and political charge of half the year, is an indication of the thoroughgoing nature of seasonal principles. The Hopi and Zuni divide their seasons by the solstices, the Tewa by the equinoxes, but the pattern of opposed dual principles is pervasive.

Dawn is deified in the form of Dawn Youths (Tewa), Dawn Mothers (Zuni), and Dawn Woman (Hopi). At Hopi, Dawn Woman is linked with another female deity, Huruingwuuti ("hard substances woman"), who has a formative role in the cosmogonic process. In the Keresan pueblos, she seems to have a counterpart in Thought Woman, whose every thought became manifest into substance. Thought Woman mythologically precedes Iyatiku, a chthonic being who is the mother of people, *kachinas*, game, and maize and who occupies the most prominent role in the Keresan pantheon. Iyatiku is in some respects parallel to Muyingwu, the Hopi maize and germination deity of the below. The principle of human and animal fertility is represented at Hopi by Tiikuywuuti ("child-water woman"), who is Muyin-gwu's sister.

Other common supernaturals. This group includes the War Twins, who are war gods, culture heroes, and patrons of gamblers; the maternal spirit animating the earth (whose body parts may be represented by vegetation, hills, and canyons); the Feathered and Horned Serpent, who lives in the water forms of the earth—springs, pools, rivers, the oceans—and who is a dangerous, powerful water deity responsible for floods and earthquakes; Spider Grandmother, a cosmogonic creator whom the Hopi consider grandmother of the War Twins; Salt Woman or Salt Man, deities of salt lakes and other salt sources; Fire Old Woman, Ash Man, and Ash Boy, with obvious associations; a giant eagle, or Knife Wing (Zuni), one of several war deities; Poseyemu, generally father of the curing societies, a miracle worker, and a possible syncretic counterpart of Christ; the master spirits of particular

The Hopi portray the Sun, Taawa, anthropomorphically but, in keeping with Hopi iconography, he wears a mask that consists of a circular disc fringed with radiating feathers and horsehair.

PAGE 301

animals, such as Bear, Badger, Mountain Lion, Wolf, and Coyote, who are patrons of specific curing societies; the sun's children, patrons of the clown societies; and many others.

Each of these supernatural entities embodies a different form of power. They are, however, discrete forms and not subsumable under a concept of pervasive supernatural power such as *mana* or *orenda.* They may be harnessed by human beings and used to transform events and states in the world. Access to power is, however, strictly limited in these societies and is based upon initiation into a religious sodality and, especially, a priestly office. There is no vision quest whereby power (at least for males) is democratically accessible.

Perhaps the best way to appreciate the influence of practical religion is to look at the rituals that accompany the life cycle.

PAGE 615

RELIGIOUS ORGANIZATION AND RITUAL PRACTICE. The basic form of religious organization in the pueblos consists of ritual societies, which serve a variety of purposes. Pueblo religion focuses on a number of issues: agricultural fertility and productivity, human fertility, fertility and productivity of game animals, war, and curing. These major issues are further divisible into aspects. Thus agricultural concerns are trained on the attainment of adequate—but not excessive—moisture, adequate heat and light, and the effective prevention of many crop pests and of excessive wind and cold. Rituals concerning game animals and hunting may be divided according to the species pursued. War society rituals are prophylactic, ensuring strength and success, as well as being celebrations of victory and rituals of purifying and sacralizing scalps taken in battle. Curing societies are organized according to the types of sicknesses they cure. "Bear medicine," "Badger medicine," and so forth are sympathetically and contagiously associated with particular ailments and are used by societies of the same names to produce cures. Typically, societies are composed of small numbers of priests and some lay members, and each society follows an annual cycle of ritual undertakings. In their most spectacular forms, such undertakings climax in dramatic public performances at specified times of the calendrical cycle.

The ceremonial cycle. The public dimension of each society's activities is concentrated at particular points in an annual liturgy. The beginning of the year, which is reckoned in lunar months, falls from late October to late November and is marked by the manhood society ceremonies. Following an eight-day retreat in the kivas (semisubterranean ceremonial chambers), which involves private rituals, two of the societies (the Wuwtsim and the Singers) process slowly around the village in two facing columns. (Members of both societies are in each column.) The columns are "guarded" at both ends by some members of the Two-Horn society. The Wuwtsim and Singers sing songs composed for the occasion, some of which

HOPI RELIGIOUS SOCIETIES

A Supernatural Hierarchy

An examination of Hopi religious societies provides insight into the structure of such societies in Pueblo cultures generally. In Hopi thought, the religious societies have different degrees of importance and confer different degrees of power on the initiated. A ranking of the societies into three orders of ascending importance may be constructed as follows (translations are given where Hopi names are translatable): Kachina and Powamuy are third-order societies; Blue Flute, Gray Flute, Snake, Antelope, Lakon, and Owaqöl are second-order societies; and Wuwtsim, One Horn, Two Horn, Singers, Soyalangw, and Maraw are first-order societies.

Each of these societies focuses upon a different set of supernatural beings and a different set of specific concerns. The ranking into three orders parallels the age requirements for initiation into particular societies. All children aged six to ten (male and female) are initiated into either (the choice is their parents') the Kachina or the Powamuy society. After this initiation, they are eligible to join second-order societies, although not all individuals will actually join. (Second-order societies are distinguished by sex: Lakon and Owaqöl are female; the rest male.) At about age sixteen, all males (traditionally) are initiated into one of the four manhood societies (Wuwtsim, One-Horn, Two-Horn, Singers) and females into the Maraw (womanhood) society. Initiation into one of the manhood societies, together with birthright, is prerequisite to participation in the Soyalangw society; since this society carries no formal initiation, it can be regarded as a more exclusive extension of the manhood societies.

— PETER M. WHITELEY

poke fun at the sexual proclivities of the Maraw society (the women's counterpart to the Wuwtsim society). The remaining members of the Two-Horn society and all the One-Horns are meanwhile continuing with private rituals in their respective *kivas.* After the final circuit of the Wuwtsim and Singers, all the Two-Horn and One-Horn members, in two separate processions (which are dramatic although unaccompanied by song) visit a series of shrines around the village and deposit offerings. Each manhood society is regarded as complementary to the other three, and

each is associated with a particular religious concern: the Wuwtsim and Singers with fertility, the Two-Horns with hunting and game animals, and the One-Horns with the dead and with supernatural protection of the village.

A month later, at the time of the winter solstice, the Soyalangw ceremony occurs. This is one of the most complex Hopi ceremonies and involves the participation of the most important priests in the village. They ritually plan the events of the coming year and perform a variety of ritual activities concerned with reversing the northward movement of the sun and with the regeneration of human, floral (both wild and cultivated), faunal (wild and domestic), and meteorological harmony. Several key themes of Hopi religious concern are sounded in this winter solstice ceremony, which renews and reorients the world and man's position within it. After Soyalangw, game animal dances are held (nowadays particularly Buffalo Dances). These are regarded as "social" dances, as are a group of dances performed in September, which include, among others, Butterfly Dances and "Navajo Dances." The distinction between social dances and sacred performances is not completely clear; songs sung at social dances frequently express desires for beneficial climatic conditions, and in general the social dances evince continuity with the religious concerns of the sacred performances. Clearly, however, the social dances are regarded with less solemnity, and there are only minor religious proscriptions on the performers.

The Soyalangw ceremony opens the *kachina* "season." *Kachinas* are impersonated in repeated public performances from January to July. As has been noted, the *kachina* concept is multiple. The *kachina* costume worn by impersonator-performers includes a mask (there are more than three hundred kinds) and specific garments and body paints. The Hopi regard the masked representations of *kachinas* to be fully efficacious manifestations of the *kachina* spirits; when speaking English, they avoid the term *mask* because of the implication that "masking" is somehow less than real. Many *kachinas* have distinct emblematic calls and stylized body movements. *Kachina* performers represent a great variety of spirits, including those of plant and animal species, deities, and mythological figures of both benign (e.g., the "mudheads") and severe (e.g., the cannibal ogres) countenance. Positive and negative social values are sometimes fused in the same *kachina*. Often a *kachina* represents many elements and practices simultaneously and contains a thick condensation of symbolic devices. Some *kachinas* ("chief *kachinas*") are more important than others and are "owned" by particular clans and regarded as significant clan deities. Usually from January through March *kachinas* appear in groups to dance at night in the *kivas*; for the remainder of the *kachina* season, they appear during the day to

Harmonious relations with the supernatural world could be restored by the dramatic imitation of the creation, often in an annual rite.

PAGE 528

HOPI RITUAL

At age sixteen, Hopi males are initiated into one of four manhood societies while females are inducted into the Maraw (womanhood) society.

UPI/CORBIS-BETTMANN

dance in the village plaza. During daytime performances, the *kachinas* may be accompanied by a group of unmasked sacred clowns, who conduct a ceremony in parallel to the *kachina* performance. Clowns are given broad license and are social commentators *par excellence*. They expose numerous social aberrancies on the part of village members and poke fun at everything from sacred ceremonial actions to current events.

The two most important *kachina* ceremonies occur in February (Powamuy, "the bean dance") and in July (Niman, "the home dance"). At Powamuy, children may be initiated into either the Kachina or Powamuy society in an evening ceremony inside a *kiva*. During the day a large and multifarious assemblage of *kachinas* proceeds in ceremonial circuits around the village. This facinating and beautiful pageant features a series of minipageants occurring in different parts of the village simultaneously. Powamuy purifies the earth and also prefigures the planting season. Beans are germinated in soil boxes in the *kivas* by the artificial warmth of constant fires. During the day of the public pageant, the bean plants are distributed by *kachinas* to each household, where they are cooked in a stew. At the same time the kachinas distribute painted wooden *kachina* dolls and basketry plaques to girls and painted bows and arrows to boys, ensuring their futures as fertile mothers and brave warrior-hunters.

Corn is the plant most commonly visualized. The representation can simply refer to the plant itself, but frequently a maize deity is being invoked.

PAGE 301

The Niman ("homegoing") ceremony, marks the last *kachina* performance of the year. At the close of Niman, the *kachinas* are formally "sent" by several priests back to their mountainous homes in the San Francisco Peaks and elsewhere. They are requested to take the prayers of the people back with them and to present them to the community of *kachina* spirits.

The *kachina* season is followed by the season of "unmasked" ceremonies. In August occur the Snake-Antelope ceremonies or the Flute ceremonies, the performance of which alternates from year to year. In either case, the two societies from which the ceremonies take their names come together at this time to perform complex rituals that last nine days. The Snake-Antelope rites include a public performance in which the Snake men slowly dance in pairs around the plaza while the Antelope men form a horseshoe-shaped line around them and intone chants. The Snake-Antelope and the Flute ceremonies are densely expressive. Both include a magical attempt to bring clouds over the fields to give rain to the crops; both mark the sun's passage; and both dramatize the mythological entrance of particular clans into the village.

Following these ceremonies in the annual liturgy come the ceremonies of the women's societies. The Lakon and Owaqöl, both referred to in English as Basket Dances, feature a circular dance in the plaza. Selected society members run in and out of the circle throwing gifts to the men, who throng the edges of the circle and dispute over the gifts. Both Lakon and Owaqöl women hold basketry plaques in front of them while they sing. The Maraw society's ceremony features a similar circle in which women hold long prayer-sticks. A number of other rites occur during the nine-day Maraw, including burlesques of male ceremonial activities. Maraw rites relate to war and fertility; Lakon and Owaqöl rites stress fertility and the celebration of the harvest.

This bare outline of the Hopi ceremonial cycle reveals some basic concerns of Pueblo religion. The timing of ceremonies is intimately connected with the annual progress of nature. The *kachina* performances are especially related to the life cycle of cultivated plants, and they occur at critical points in this cycle. The first ceremonies of the year prefigure the planting and successful fruition of crops; they are designed to bring snow and rain to saturate the earth with moisture, which will remain there until planting occurs in April. The daytime *kachina* performances likewise seek rainfall to help the crops grow. Niman, the Homegoing, signals the end of the early phases of crop maturation; the kachinas' departure suggests that the spirits of the crops are sufficiently mature no longer to require the *kachinas'* nurturance. The Snake-Antelope and Flute ceremonies complete the course of metaphysical encouragement and nourishment of the crops. Coming at the hottest, driest time of the year, they invoke powerful forces to bring one last bout of rain to ensure the full maturing of the crops and to prevent the sun's fierce gaze from withering them. The women's society Basket Dances celebrate the success of the harvest by the joyful distribution of basketry plaques and household goods.

Private rituals. All ceremonies include private rituals in *kivas* prior to the public performance. Typically such private rituals include the construction of an altar, which consists of a rectangular sand painting in front of a vertical assemblage of painted and carved wooden pieces that incorporate symbolic designs of birds, animals, and supernaturals. The sand painting also incorporates many symbolic elements. Long songs are incanted over the altar, and tobacco is ceremonially smoked and blown to portray clouds. (Smoking binds together the hearts of the priests as they pass the pipe around a circle and gives them a collective power to express their prayers more forcefully.) The *kiva* itself is a multiplex symbol: it is axially oriented by the directions, and at its center is a hole representing the *sipapu*, the place of emergence from the world below. The *kiva's* four levels, from the underfloor to the roof, are identified with the worlds through which man has ascended; the passage into this world is portrayed by the *sipapu* and the *kiva* ladder that leads to the roof.

Maize symbolism and ritual. Maize is the dominant, pervasive symbol of Hopi religious life. Maize is regarded as the mother of people, since it is the primary sustainer of human life. "Corn is life," the Hopi say. Two perfect ears of white maize are given to a newborn child as its "mothers"; when a person dies, ears of blue maize similarly accompany him on his journey beyond life. Maize seeds, ears, tassels, milk, pollen, and meal all serve as sacramental elements in differing contexts. Moreover, other important symbols are related to the maize cycle. Clouds, rains, lightning, feathered serpents, and various species associated with water, such as frogs, ducks, reeds, and so forth, all underline a paramount interest in securing water for maize.

Two devices, above all others, serve as mechanisms for establishing holiness or for communicating with supernatural forces: cornmeal and prayer feathers. Corn-meal is an all-purpose sanctifying substance; it is sprinkled on *kachina* dancers, used to form spiritual paths for *kachinas* and the dead, offered to the sun and to one's own field of growing maize plants, and accompanies all forms of private and public prayer. The act of making a prayer to various supernatural forms with the sprinkled offering of cornmeal may be considered the most fundamental religious act for the Hopi as for all the Pueblos.

Feathers of many different bird species are used in innumerable ways in Hopi ritual; they are worn in the hair and around arms and ankles, and they decorate *kachina* masks, altars, and religious society emblems. Prayer sticks and prayer feathers are the two basic forms of feather offerings. Prayer sticks, carved in human or supernatural forms, are living manifestations of prayer and are simultaneously petitions for aid. Feathers are regarded as particularly effective vehicles for conveying messages to supernaturals: they "carry" the prayers of people with them.

COMPARISONS. It is evident from the Hopi situation that religious action is multiple. There is no single set of activities we can demarcate as "Hopi religion" as distinct from Hopi agriculture or even Hopi politics, since political activity goes on even within the context of private ceremonial gatherings. Also, the exclusiveness of religious societies above the third order suggests

THE ZUNI CULT SYSTEM

The Significant Six

Other Pueblo groups depart significantly from the Hopi scheme yet still exhibit similarities that suggest some common patterns of belief and practice. Ethnologists have identified six major types of cults or societies among the Zuni.

1. *The Sun cult.* Responsibility for the important religiopolitical officer called the *pekwin* (Sun priest) belongs to the Sun cult. Membership is restricted to males, and the sodality conducts its ceremonies at the solstices.

2. *The Uwanami ("rainmakers") cult.* This cult is composed of twelve distinct priesthoods of from two to six members each. Membership is hereditary within certain matrilineal families. Each priesthood holds retreats (but no public ceremonies) during the summer months from July through September.

3. *The Kachina cult.* Unlike the Hopi Kachina society, membership in the Zuni Kachina society is not open to females. The cult has six divisions, which are associated with the six directions and are accordingly headquartered in six *kivas*. Each *kiva* group dances at least three times per year: in summer, in winter following the solstice, and following the Shalako ceremony in late November or early December.

4. *The cult of the kachina priests.* Whereas the Kachina society is primarily concerned with rain and moisture, the cult of the *kachina* priests focuses on fecundity—of human beings and game animals. The *kachina* priests are responsible for the six Shalako *kachinas*, the ten-foot-tall, birdlike figures whose appearance marks the most spectacular of Zuni religious dramas, and for the *koyemsi* ("mudhead") *kachinas*, who are at once dangerously powerful beings and foolish clowns. Other *kachinas* under the charge of the *kachina* priests appear at solstice ceremonies, at the Shalako ceremonies, and every fourth year at the time when newcomers are initiated into the general Kachina cult.

5. *The War Gods cult.* The Bow priesthood, which is exclusively male, controls the War Gods cult. Traditionally, initiation required the taking of an enemy's scalp. The Bow priests are leaders in war and protectors of the village, and they serve as the executive arm of the religiopolitical hierarchy, in which role they prosecute witches. (The extinct Momtsit society may have been the Hopi counterpart of the Bow priests.)

6. *The Beast Gods cult.* The cult is overseen by twelve curing societies, and membership is open to both men and women. Each society focuses on a particular source of supernatural power, which is embodied in the bear, mountain lion, or another predatory animal. The individual societies practice general medicine, but each also specializes in healing specific afflictions. The collective ceremonies of the societies are held in the fall and winter.

— PETER M. WHITELY

a socially fragmented pattern of religious belief and practice. Religious knowledge is highly valued and tightly guarded, and it serves as the primary means of making status distinctions in Hopi society. Hopi explanations of the diversity of their religious activities point to historical circumstances: each cult is identified with a particular clan that introduced it when the clan negotiated admission to the village in the distant past. Although lay cult members may be from any clan, the chief priests should always be of the clan which "owns" the ceremony. In part, then, ceremonial performances celebrate separate clan identities and mark off particular ritual activities as the exclusive prerogative of particular clans. This pattern of closed ceremonial societies with exclusive rights in certain forms of religious action is a fundamental characteristic of Pueblo religion.

Keresan Pueblo religious practice. Among the Keresan Pueblos—Acoma and Laguna to the west, Santo Domingo, Cochiti, San Felipe, Santa Ana, and Zia to the east on the Rio Grande and its tributaries—the chief religious organizations are referred to as "medicine societies." With variations from pueblo to pueblo, the basic pattern consists of four major medicine societies—Flint, Cikame (an untranslatable Keresan word), Giant, and Fire—and a number of minor societies, including Ant, Bear, Eagle, and Lizard. The medicine societies conduct a communal curing ceremony in the spring, echoing a theme of the Hopi Bean Dance, and they hold performances throughout the year to effect the cure of individual patients. The societies also have rainmaking functions, which they fulfill at private ritual retreats during the summer months. Reportedly, these societies erect altars and construct sand paintings similar to those described for the Hopi and the Zuni. The same major sacramental elements—prayer sticks and cornmeal—are central vehicles for religious action, and extensive songs and prayers designed to make unseen power manifest in the world are a key part of ceremonial content. The medicine societies also have important roles in solstitial ceremonies aimed at reversing the course of the sun.

Among the American Indian peoples we find a conception of the soul that forms the basis of their beliefs in immortality.

PAGE 315

Other important Keresan societies include a paired group: the Koshare, which is a clown society parallel in many ways to Hopi clown societies, and the Kwirena, which is primarily associated with weather control. A Hunters society, with a permanently installed "hunt chief," and a Warriors society, composed of scalp-takers, are other important societies that traditionally held ceremonies during the winter. A village-wide Kachina society is divided into two ceremonial moieties, Turquoise and Squash, associated with the two kivas in the village. *Kachina* performances by both moieties occur during fall and winter, but especially during the summer immediately following the rainmaking retreats of the medicine societies. These retreats include a supernatural journey to the *sipapu*, from which the *kachinas* are brought back to the village. As among other Pueblo groups, ritual activities among the Keresans are dominated by males; although both sexes may join medicine societies, women serve as secondary assistants, and only men may perform as *kachinas*.

The climatic and ecological situation of the Keresan Pueblos is of much greater reliability than that of the Hopi. The Keresans' religious concern with the agricultural cycle is evident, but, since the Keresans have irrigation and more plentiful precipitation, they put less emphasis on the agricultural and more on the curing functions of religious societies. A primary function of the more important medicine societies is to combat witchcraft by evil-hearted human beings and evil supernaturals, which is believed to be the cause of illness. Witchcraft is, and has been historically, a profound concern of Hopi and Zuni also, although at Hopi the concern receives less concerted attention from the major religious societies.

The theme of dualism, which appears at Hopi and Zuni in the form of the solstitial switching of ritual emphases, is manifested at the Keresan Pueblos with the division of the ceremonial organization into moieties centered in two *kivas*.

Tewa, Tiwa, and Towa religious systems. The theme of dualism in Southwest religion achieves perhaps its maximum expression in the religious life of the six Tewa pueblos: San Juan, Santa Clara, San Ildefonso, Tesuque, Nambe, and Pojoaque. The division of people into Winter and Summer ceremonial moieties is part of a thoroughgoing dual scheme phrased in terms of seasonal opposition. The division of significance among the Tewa is by equinoxes; the seasonal transfer ceremony that is held (roughly) at each equinox places one or the other of the ceremonial moieties in charge of the village for the following season. Hence there are two overarching religious leaders, or caciques, each the head of a moiety. The calendar of religious activities is planned in accordance with the division into summer (agricultural activities) and winter (nonagricultural activities).

Typically, each Tewa pueblo has two *kivas* in which the ceremonial moieties are headquartered. There are eight religious societies in all: the Winter and Summer moiety societies, each headed by a moiety priest; the Bear Medicine society; the Kwirena ("cold clowns") and Kossa ("warm clowns") societies; the Hunt society; the Scalp society; and the Women's society. The most intensive ritual activity occurs between the autumnal and vernal equinoxes. This contrasts with the Hopi model, in which the most active part of the cycle occurs from the winter to the summer solstice (and just thereafter). Parallel elements are otherwise clear: religious-society orga-

TAOS PUEBLO

Taos rituals emphasize game animals and hunting which reflects their close cultural ties to the Plains.

WOLFGANG KAEHLER/CORBIS

nization among the Tewa is reminiscent of the nearby Keresans. Religious concerns, too, are similar between the Tewa and Keresan Pueblos, though the Tewa Pueblos place less emphasis on curing. The main sacraments are the same; the *kachina* performance is a fundamental religious practice, though more restricted here than among the Hopi, Zuni, and western Keresans.

The traditional religious practices of the Tiwa pueblos—Taos and Picuris in the north and Sandia and Isleta in the south—are the least well known. Taos, in particular, has been most effective in protecting matters it regards as not appropriate for public consumption. At Taos, each of the six *kivas* (which are divided into three on the "north side" and three on the "south side" of the pueblo) houses a religious society. *Kiva* society initiation involves a set of rituals prolonged over a number of years and is restricted by inheritance to a select group. The *kiva* organization at Taos seems to serve the same purpose as religious societies at other pueblos. At Taos, there is greater ritual emphasis upon game animals and hunting, in line with the pueblo's close cultural ties with Plains peoples, than there is upon the agricultural cycle. Taos may be the only pueblo in which *kachinas* are not represented in masked performances. Picuris seems traditionally to have done so, and it otherwise exhibits more religious similarity with the Tewa pueblos than it does with Taos, its close linguistic neighbor. *Kachinas* do occur, however, in Taos myths.

The southern Tiwa in Isleta pueblo have a system of ceremonial moieties divided into Winter (Black Eyes) and Summer (Red Eyes), each with its "moiety house" (which is equivalent to a *kiva*). In addition, Isleta Pueblo's five Corn groups, associated with directions and colors, seem to parallel *kiva* organizations at Taos. The moieties conduct seasonal transfer ceremonies similar to those at Tewa pueblos, and likewise each moiety controls the ritual activities for the season over which it presides. The ceremonial cycle is attenuated in comparison with that at other pueblos; there is a Land Turtle Dance in the spring and a Water Turtle Dance in the fall. Although unverified, it has been reported that *kachina* performances are conducted by a colony of Laguna Pueblo people who have lived in Isleta since the late nineteenth century.

Nearly all the basic religious ideas found in other parts of native North America are found on the Plains.

PAGE 498

Jemez, the only modern representative of the Towa Pueblos, exhibits an extraordinarily complex ceremonial organization, with twenty-three religious societies and two *kiva* moieties. Every Jemez male is initiated into either the Eagle society or the Arrow society; other societies are more exclusive. Societies can be classified according to function: curing, rainmaking and weather control, fertility, war and protection, and hunting. The Jemez ceremonial cycle includes a series of retreats by the different religious societies. In the summer, these celebrate agricultural growth; in the fall the ripening of crops; in the winter war, rain, ice, snow, and game animals; and in the spring the renewal of the forces of life. The two ceremonial *kiva* moieties are Turquoise and Squash, the same as among the eastern Keresans, and although the principle of dualism is in evidence it is not so pronounced as among the Tewa.

LIFE, DEATH, AND BEYOND. The Pueblos hold that an individual's life follows a path, or plan, that is present in his fate from birth. A long, good life and a peaceful death in old age are the main requests contained in prayers delivered at the birth of a new person. Through the course of maturation, the person becomes increasingly incorporated, in a ritual sense, into the world. So the Tewa, for example, perform a series of childhood baptismal rites—"name giving," "water giving," "water pouring," and "finishing"—that progressively fix and identify the individual in relation to the forces of society and the cosmos. Religious society initiations and marriage mark further passages in the individual's path of life.

Beliefs about and rituals surrounding death reveal some of the most essential features of Pueblo conceptions of the nature of existence. I have noted above the association between the dead, clouds, and *kachina* spirits. In general, Pueblos believe that when a person dies, the spirit, or breath, returns to the place of the Emergence and becomes transformed into cloud. Cloud spirits have myriad conceptual associations, and the dead (or certain of them) may likewise be given special associations. So, although clouds are generally regarded as the spirits of all the ancestral dead, distinctions are also made between different afterlife destinations, which vary according to the status the deceased person held while alive.

"O our Mother the Earth, O our Father the Sky, your children are we, and with tired backs we bring you gifts."

TEWA
SONG OF THE SKY LOOM

All the Pueblos distinguish between two kinds of people: those who hold important religious offices (or who are initiated members of religious societies) and everyone else. The former are regarded as supernaturally and socially powerful, ritually significant people; the latter are commoners. For the Tewa, the distinction is between "made," or "completed," people and "dry food" people; for the Zuni, the distinction is between valuable and ceremonially poor, or unvaluable, people; among the Keresans the term *sishti* ("commoners") denotes those without ceremonial affiliation; and for the Hopi, the distinction is between *pavansinom* ("powerful" or "completed" people) and *sukavungsinom* (common people).

The afterlife fate of these different categories may vary from one Pueblo group to another. Deceased members of the Hopi Two-Horn and One-Horn societies judge the newly dead at the house of the dead. Witches, suffering a different fate from that enjoyed by the righteous, may be transformed into stinkbugs! Zuni rain priests join the *uwanami* spirits who live in the waters, whereas Zuni Bow priests join their spiritual counterparts in the world above as makers of lightning. Other religious society members return to the place of the Emergence, but Zuni commoners go to "*kachina* village," the home of the *kachinas*, which is at a distance of two days' walk to the west of Zuni. In short, the social and religious organization in life is replicated in the organization of the dead,

SYNCRETISM AND CHANGE. The Pueblos were first exposed to Christian practices through the Franciscan friars who accompanied Francisco Vasquez de Coronado during his exploration of the Southwest (1540-1542). When the Province of New Mexico was made a colony of Spain in 1598, the Franciscan order was given special jurisdiction over the souls of the Indians. Missions were built in most of the pueblos; tributes were exacted; strenuous discipline was enforced; and extremely brutal punishments were levied for infractions of the total ban on indigenous religious practices. In reaction to this colonial domination, and especially to the religious oppression, all the pueblos united in an uprising in 1680, under the leadership of Popé, a Tewa priest. Many Spanish priests and colonists were killed, and the rest were forced to withdraw from New Mexico. Most of the pueblos immediately dismantled their missions. The Oraibi Hopi record that in the Great Pueblo Revolt the Roman Catholic priests were actually killed by warrior *kachinas*, symbolically demonstrating the spiritual rectitude of the action and the greater power of the indigenous religion.

Removed from the mainstream of Spanish settlements, the Hopi never allowed Spanish missions to be built among them again, and their religious practices remained free of Franciscan influence. The other Pueblos all suffered the reestablishment of missions after the Spanish reconquest of the 1690s. The influence of the missions depended upon the regularity and zeal with which they were staffed. At Zuni, a desultory missionary presence seems to have had little impact on traditional religious forms. The Rio Grande pueblos, on the other hand, came under a great deal of Franciscan influence. These pueblos are all nominally Catholic and observe many ceremonies of the Christian calendar. Each town has a patron saint and holds a large dance—called a Corn Dance or Tablita Dance—to celebrate the saint's day. The dance is thoroughly indigenous in character; however, a Christian shrine honoring the saint stands at one side of the plaza during the dance. At the conclusion of the dance, all the participants enter the church and offer prayers and thanks in a Christian fashion. Thus the two traditions coexist in a "compartmentalized" fashion. In some areas, such as rites of passage, Christian practices have supplanted indigenous Pueblo forms, especially in those pueblos that have become increasingly acculturated during the twentieth century (Pojoaque, Isleta, Picuris, and Laguna are examples). Many Eastern Pueblos have also taken over Spanish and Mexican religious dramas, such as the Matachine performances, which are also practiced among the Yaqui, Mayo, and Tarahumara.

Protestant churches have been attempting to proselytize the Pueblos since the latter nineteenth century, though in general without much success. Despite sustained longterm efforts by the Mennonites, Baptists, Methodists, Roman Catholics, Mormons, and Jehovah's Witnesses among the Hopi, their rate of conversion to Christianity has remained below 10 percent. On the other hand, major Christian holidays such as Christmas and Easter are popular occasions and may be having some impact on traditional religion. A *kachina* dance is regularly scheduled for Easter weekend nowadays, and the array of presents they bring the *kachinas* includes baskets of colored eggs. Regarding other nontraditional religions, only at Taos has peyotism to some extent been adopted, and even there its practice is evidently kept compartmentalized and apart from both indigenous religious practice and Catholicism.

CONCLUSION. The religious traditions of other Indians of the Southwest contain their own conceptual and historical complexities. I have chosen to focus upon the Pueblos here because of the richness of their extant religious practices and because of the separate treatment that the Apache and the Navajo receive in this study. This does not imply that Pueblo religions are somehow representative of the religions of other native Southwest peoples, though certain Pueblo themes are echoed in different ways among non-Pueblo peoples. Sodalities and clown societies exist among the Yaqui and Mayo; sand painting is practiced by the Navajo, Pima, and Papago; and masked impersonators of supernatural beings perform rainmaking dances among the Havasupai, Yavapai, Pima, and Papago: but these common threads occur in cloths of quite different weaves. Let me emphasize at the last that the indigenous Southwest is enormously diverse. The sheer complexity of its religious practices belies any attempt to standardize these into a meaningful common pattern.

— PETER M. WHITELEY

NORTH AMERICAN RELIGIONS

Main Religious Features

North America is a continent with many diverse cultures, and it is therefore meaningless to speak about North American religion as a unified aggregate of beliefs, myths, and rituals. Still, there are several religious traits that are basically common to all the Indians but variously formalized and interpreted among different peoples. Two characteristics are, however, typically Amerindian: the dependence on visions and dreams, which can modify old traditional rituals, and an intricate and time-consuming ceremonialism that sometimes almost conceals the cognitive message of rituals.

SPIRIT WORLD. To these common elements belongs the idea of another dimension of existence that permeates life and yet is different from normal, everyday existence. Concepts such as the Lakota *wakan* and the Algonquian *manitou* refer to this consciousness of another world, the world of spirits, gods, and wonders.

Supreme being. The supernatural world is primarily expressed through the spiritual powers residing in a host of gods, spirits, and ghosts. In many American tribes prayers are directed to a collectivity of divine or spiritual beings, as in the pipe ceremony. Foremost among these divinities is, in most tribes, a sky god who represents all other supernatural beings or stands as their superior and the ruler of the universe. The Pawnee Indians in Nebraska, for instance, know a hierarchy of star gods and spirits, all of them subservient to the high god in the sky, Tirawa.

The supreme being is closely associated with the axis mundi, or world pillar. The Delaware Indians say that he grasps the pole that holds up the sky and is the center of the world. In ceremonial life the world pole, or world tree, is the central cultic symbol in the great annual rites of peoples of the Eastern Woodlands, the Plains, the Basin, and the Plateau. At this annual celebration the Indians thank the supreme being for the year that has been. In California, a region of frequent earthquakes, similar world renewal rituals have as their main aim the stabilizing of the universe. In the east, the Delaware Big House ceremony is an adaptation of the hunters' annual ceremony to the cultural world of more settled maize-growing peoples: the sacred pillar is here built into a ceremonial house.

The culture hero. The connection of the supreme being with creation is often concealed by the fact that in mythology another supernatural being, the culture hero, is invested with creative powers. His true mission is to deliver cultural institutions, including religious ceremonies, to the first human beings, but he is sometimes an assistant creator as well. In this quality he competes with the Great Spirit and appears as a ludicrous figure, a trickster, or an antagonist of the Great Spirit, an emergent "devil."

Spirits and ghosts. The other beings of the supernatural world—and they are innumerable, vary from tribe to tribe

There are powers such as the dead, who operate in different places in different types of cultures. There is everywhere a belief in ghosts on earth, who are often heard whistling in the night. Independent of these

People might encounter such spirits, usually in their anthropomorphic forms, in visions or in dreams.

PAGE 509

"Quarry mine, blessed am I in the luck of the chase. Comes the deer to my singing."

NAVAHO HUNTING SONG

beliefs is a ubiquitous idea of reincarnation or transmigration into animals.

Guardian spirits and vision quests. Other spirits are the guardian spirits acquired in fasting visions by youths of the Plateau and the Northeast Woodlands and by both boys and men of the Plains and the Basin. These spirits are mostly zoomorphic. They may be animal spirits or spirits that show themselves in animal disguise. Everywhere except among the pueblo-dwelling peoples of the Southwest it has been the individual hunter's ambition to acquire one or several of these guardian spirits. They usually appear to the person after a vision quest during which he has spent several days and nights in fasting and isolation at some lonely spot in the wilderness. The spirit endows his client with a particular "medicine," that is, supernatural power (to hunt, to run, to make love, to cure).

Medicine men and medicine societies. The medicine man is a visionary who has succeeded in receiving power to cure people. However, visionaries with other extraordinary powers, such as the capacity to find lost things or divine the future, have also been labeled "medicine men." In cultures with more complicated social organizations, medicine men may join together, exchanging experiences and working out a common, secret ideology. An example of this is the Midewiwin, or Great Medicine society, of the Ojibwa, which is organized like a secret order society and has four or eight hierarchical grades.

RITUAL ACTS. Harmony or spiritual balance is what North American Indians want to achieve in their relations with the supernatural powers. A harmonious balance can be reached through prayers and offerings or through imitative representation of supernatural events.

Prayers and offerings. Prayers range from a few words at meal offerings to detailed ritual prayers, from casual petitions of blessing to deeply emotional cries for help and sustenance. Indeed, Navajo prayer has been characterized by one researcher as "compulsive words," by another as "creative words."

There are many kinds of offerings. A simple form is throwing tobacco or food into the fire or onto the ground at mealtimes. Another example is the placing of tobacco pouches on the ground at the beginning of dangerous passages, such as crossing a lake or walking over a mountain ridge.

When hunters killed game they usually performed rites over the body. True sacrifices were not common, but did occur in the Northeast Woodlands, where white dogs were sacrificed to the powers. In many places the skins of animals (and, later, pieces of cloth as well) served as offerings. There was religious cannibalism in the East, even endocannibalism (the eating of one's family dead) in ancient times. Mutilations of fingers and other cases of self-mutilation as offerings occurred in the Sun Dance of the Lakota and in the closely related Mandan Okipa ceremony.

Ritual representations. Harmonious relations with the supernatural world could be restored by the dramatic imitation of the creation, often in an annual rite, as, for instance, the Sun Dance. In the enactment of mythical drama, performers assumed the roles of supernatural beings, as in the representation of the *kachina,* cloud and rain spirits, and spirits of the dead in the Pueblo Indian Kachina Dances. In the Pawnee sacrifice to Morning Star, a young captive girl was tied to a frame and shot with arrows; she was supposed to represent Evening Star, a personification of the vegetation whose death promotes the growth of plants. Even today a Navajo patient sits in the middle of a sand painting symbolizing the cosmos and its powers while the practitioner pours colored sand over him.

Historical Survey

Most North American religions express the worldview typical of hunters and gatherers. This is natural, since the first immigrants who arrived perhaps forty to sixty thousands years ago were Paleolithic hunters who came by way of the Bering Strait. This origin in northern Asia explains why so much of American Indian religion bears an Arctic or sub-Arctic stamp, and why so many features even in more temperate areas seem to be derived from northern cultures.

The languages of the North American Indians are enormously diverse, and with the exception of the relatively lately arrived Athapascan groups none seem related to known Old World languages. The common factor joining them all is their polysynthetic structure, whereby many sentence elements are included in a single word by compounding and adding prefixes and suffixes. Paul Radin suggested many years ago that there may be a genetic relationship between most of these languages, except those of the Aleut and Inuit, who differ from the mainstream of American aborigines in race, culture, and religion.

The Paleo-Indians of eastern North America were big-game hunters, concentrating on animals like the mammoth, the giant bison, the three-toed horse, and the camel. In all likelihood the inherited concepts of animal ceremonialism and the master of the animals were applied to these animals. Only one big animal—the bear—survived and continued to be the focus of special rites. The ritual around the slaying of the bear, distributed from the Saami (Lapps) of Scandinavia to the Ainu of northern Japan, and, in North America, from the Inuit and Athapascans in the north and west to the Delaware in the east and the Pueblo Indians in the south, seem to be a leftover from these Paleolithic and Mesolithic days.

The old hunting culture slowly disintegrated into a series of more specialized regional cultures about 7000-5000 BCE, and there are reasons to presume that the religious structures changed accordingly.

An exceptional development took place in the south. In the increasingly arid regions of the Great Basin, the Southwest, and parts of California a so-called desert tradition was established, with heavy dependence on wild plants, seeds, and nuts. The corresponding religious system survived in late Great Basin religions, and part of it was also preserved in many Californian Indian religions. In the Southwest, the Basket Making culture, while an example of the desert tradition, also served as a link to horticultural development.

It seems fairly certain that the cultivation of tobacco spread from Mexico into North America with maize, for maize and tobacco cultivation share the same general distribution within the eastern regions of North America. In the Southwest, however, while maize was cultivated, tobacco was gathered wild.

The introduction of maize into North America occurred in two places, the Southwest and the Southeast. From all appearances it was known earlier in the Southwest, where it is recorded from 3000 to 2000 BCE in the wooded highland valleys of New Mexico. Village agriculture was firmly established about the time of the birth of Christ, and was effective after 500 CE.

The most important evidence of the cultural influence from the south is the architectural planning of the towns: irrigation canals, oval ball courts for ritual games, and platform mounds of earth or adobe serving as substructures for temples with hearths and altars.

The Mexican influence on religion can also be seen in the neighboring Anasazi or Pueblo cultures down to our own time. Mesoamerican symbols appear in the bird designs that decorate Hopi pottery.

The maize complex entered the Southeast slightly later than the Southwest, perhaps sometime after 1000 BCE.

A major change took place with the introduction of the so-called Mississippian tradition about 700 CE. Large rectangular and flat-topped mounds of unprecedented size were arranged around rectangular plazas. The mounds served as foundations of temples, whence the name Temple Mound, also used to designate these cultures. Intensive agriculture belonged to this new tradition, which flourished in the lower and middle Mississippi Valley but was particularly anchored in the Southeast.

The agricultural religions rarely reached such an advanced stage of development in eastern North America, but they spread from the Southeastern hearth in different directions. Mississippian traits mingled with older Woodland traits in the Iroquois culture in the north and, after 1000 CE, with Plains hunting religions in the river valleys to the west.

A Regional Survey

The religions of the indigenous peoples in North America have developed on the foundations that have just been described. However, factors other than historical have contributed to the differentiation in religious profiles that occurs in every region.

As Clark Wissler and others have noted, the geographic regions and the cultural areas correspond closely to each other. Since geographical and ecological factors have influenced religious forms, each region reveals unique features.

ARCTIC. The barren country around the Arctic coasts is sparsely inhabited by the Inuit and, on the Aleutian Islands, their kinsmen the Aleut. Inuit religion carries all marks of a hunting religion, concentrating on beliefs and rituals related to animals and on shamanism. The hunting rituals are rather intricate, in particular in Alaska where they focus on the whale (whale feasts are also found among the Nootka of the Northwest Coast and the Chukchi and Koriak of Siberia). [*See* Inuit Religion.]

SUB-ARCTIC. A vast region of the coniferous forests, lakes, and swamps in interior Alaska and Canada, the sub-Arctic is sparsely inhabited by Athapascan-speaking Indians in its western half and Algonquian-speaking Indians in its eastern half. The Athapascans are latecomers from Siberia, arriving perhaps around 9000 BCE; their linguistic affiliations are with the Sino-Tibetan tongues. The Algonquian tribes conserve religious traits that associate them closely with the circumpolar culture.

The region is inhabited by hunting cultures, with inland game, in particular the caribou and the moose, as food resources.

Religion is dominated by hunting ceremonialism and, to a certain extent, by shamanism. Bear ceremonialism is widespread, and hunting taboos are very common. Sweat baths grant their practitioners ritual purity before hunting or important ceremonies. The vision and guardian-spirit quest is fairly common.

NORTHEAST WOODLANDS. Formerly covered by mixed coniferous and deciduous trees, the Northeast Woodlands held a large population of Algonquian-, Iroquoian-, and Siouan-speaking tribes. In historical and protohistorical times both agriculture and hunting were practiced, particularly by the Iroquoian groups; the Algonquian tribes were hunters with only limited horticulture.

The double economic heritage is to some extent mirrored in the religious pattern. The hunters concentrate on hunting rituals and vision quests, the planters on rituals and beliefs surrounding the crops. The Iro-

Next to the supreme being, the most important spirits of the upper world are the Sun, the Moon, and the thunder spirits.

PAGE 40

N

NORTH AMERICAN RELIGIONS

A Regional Survey

quois, for instance, have a series of calendar rites celebrating the planting, ripening, and harvesting of the "three sisters": maize, squash, and beans.

SOUTHEAST WOODLANDS. In the southern deciduous forests, with their savannas and swamps, the tribes of Muskogean stock, interspersed with Siouan groups and the Iroquoian-speaking Cherokee, kept up a peripheral high culture, the last vestiges of the prehistoric Mississippian culture. The Southeastern Indians were, at least at the beginning of the historical era, predominantly engaged in agriculture, and their sociopolitical organization was adjusted to this fact. Thus, the Creek had a maternal clan system, with clans subordinated to both phratries and moieties. Characteristic of Creek religion is the emphasis laid on ceremonialism and priestly functions.

Both prehistoric and historical forces shaped the cultural and social characteristics of the Southeast Indians.

PAGE 495

The main religious ceremony is the maize harvest ceremony, called the Busk. It is also a New Year ritual, in which old fires are extinguished and a new fire is kindled and people ritually cleanse themselves through washing and the drinking of an emetic.

PRAIRIES AND PLAINS. The tall-grass area between the woodlands in the east and the high Plains in the west is known as the Prairies. The Plains are the short-grass steppe country, too dry for agriculture, that stretches toward the mountains and semideserts in the far West.

The historical cultures were formed during the seventeenth and eighteenth centuries when the acquisition of horses made the wide-open spaces easily accessible to surrounding tribes and white expansion forced woodland Indians to leave their home country for the dry, treeless areas. Algonquian and Siouan tribes immigrated from the east and northeast, Caddoan tribes from the south. Several groups ceased practicing horticulture (the Crow and Cheyenne) and turned into buffalo hunters, but they kept parts of their old social and political organization. In the west, Shoshonean groups held the ground they had traditionally occupied, and groups of Athapascans—for example, the Apache—forced their way to the southern parts of the region.

Whereas the Prairies could be regarded as a periphery of the Eastern Woodlands, the Plains region offers a late cultural and religious complex of its own. The religion is a mixture of derived agricultural ceremonialism and hunters' belief systems. The major New Year ceremony is the Sun Dance, during which asceticism, dancing, praying, and curing take place. Other forms of ritualism center around tribal and clan bundles, and the sacred ritual known as the Calumet Dance, or Pipe Dance.

NORTHWEST COAST. The broken coastline, high mountains, and deep fjords of the Northwest Coast were the home of the Tlingit, Haida, Tsimshian, and Wakashan tribes and some Coast Salish and Chinookan groups in the south. With their totem poles, their plank houses and canoes, and their headgear reminiscent of East Asian conic hats, these Indians make an un-American impression. The basic substratum seems to be a fishing culture that developed on both sides of the North Pacific and gave rise to both Inuit and Northwest Coast cultures.

The religion is characterized partly by its association with the activities of hunters and fishermen, partly by its secret societies adapted to the complicated social structure. The animal ceremonialism is focused on the sea fauna, and there are many sea spirits in animal forms.

PLATEAU. The Intermountain area, which includes both the Columbia and the Fraser river drainages, is known as the Plateau; it was inhabited by Salish and Shahaptin tribes that lived on fish and, secondarily, on land animals and roots. In their religion the Plateau Indians stressed the visionary complex and food ceremonies. The vision quests were undertaken at puberty by both sexes. The relation between the guardian spirit and his client was displayed in the Winter Dance, or Spirit Dance, a ceremony, under the supervision of a medicine man, in which the spirit was impersonated.

GREAT BASIN. A dry region of sands and semideserts, the Great Basin was inhabited by Shoshonean (Numic) groups, some of them, like the Gosiute, the most impoverished of North American groups. Seeds, nuts, and rodents provided the principal food. The religious pattern was closely adapted to a lifestyle based on the bare necessities. Hunters had to be blessed by spirits in visions in order to be successful, but there was little elaboration of guardian-spirit beliefs. Medicine men had specialized powers.

CALIFORNIA. The central valleys and coastland of California constituted a separate cultural area, known as the California region, densely populated by Penutian, Hokan, and Numic groups. These natives, living in a mild climate, dedicated themselves to collecting, hunting, and fishing. In this diversified culture area religious expressions were most varied. North-central California is known for its lofty concept of a supreme being and for its initiation of youths into religious societies. In the southern part of the area, initiation ceremonies were accompanied by the drinking of drugs prepared from jimsonweed and by various symbolic acts referring to death and rebirth. In some places there were great commemorative ceremonies for the dead.

THE SOUTHWEST. A magnificent desert country with some oases, particularly along the Rio Grande, the Southwest was populated by hunting and farming groups of Piman and Yuman descent, by former hunters like the Athapascan Apache and Navajo—who did not arrive here until about 1500 CE—and by the Pueblo peoples, intensive agriculturists mostly belonging to the Tanoan and Keresan linguistic families.

Religion penetrates all aspects of Pueblo life. A rich set of ceremonies that mark the divisions of the year are conducted by different religious societies. Their overall aim is to create harmony with the powers of rain and fertility, symbolized by the ancestors, the rain and cloud spirits, and the Sun. Each society has its priesthood, its attendants, its sacred bundles, and its ceremonial cycle. There are also medicine societies for the curing of diseases—the inspired, visionary medicine man has no place in this collectivistic, priestly culture.

— ÅKE HULTKRANTZ

OCCULTISM

The term *occultism* is properly used to refer to a large number of practices, ranging from astrology and alchemy to occult medicine and magic, that are based in one way or another on the homo-analogical principle, or doctrine of correspondences. According to this principle, things that are similar exert an influence on one another by virtue of the correspondences that unite all visible things to one another and to invisible realities as well. The practices based upon this essentially esoteric principle express a living and dynamic reality, a web of cosmic and divine analogies and homologies that become manifest through the operation of the active imagination.

Occultism, as a group of practices, is to be distinguished from esotericism, which is, roughly speaking, the theory that makes these practices possible. We may therefore accept the following distinction proposed by the sociologist Edward A. Tirya-kian:

> *By "occult," I understand intentional practices, techniques, or procedures which (a) draw upon hidden and concealed forces in nature or the cosmos that cannot be measured or recognized by the instruments of modern science, and (b) which have as their desired or intended consequences empirical results, such as obtaining knowledge of the empirical course of events or altering them from what they would have been without this intervention. . . . By "esoteric" I refer to those religio-philosophic belief systems which underlie occult techniques and practices; that is, it refers to the more comprehensive cognitive mappings of nature and the cosmos, the epistomological and ontological reflections of ultimate reality, which mappings constitute a stock of knowledge that provides the ground for occult procedures. By way of analogy, esoteric knowledge is to occult practices as the corpus of theoretical physics is to engineering applications.*
>
> *(Tiryakian, 1972, pp. 498–499)*

OCCULTISM BEFORE OCCULTISM

The first instances of something that can be called occultism appear in the early centuries of the Christian era, combined with esoteric and theosophical teachings. Theurgy can be found in the teachings of the fourth-century *Chaldean Oracles;* in the Alexandrine Hermetism of the *Corpus Hermeticum,* from the second and third centuries; and in the third-century Neoplatonism of Porphyry, that of Iamblichus in the fourth century, and that of Proclus in the fifth. Alchemy flourished at Alexandria until the seventh century. [*See* Alchemy.] Even Stoicism had an occult aspect, insofar as it emphasized the necessity of knowing the concrete universe by harmoniously combining science and technique, and adopted an open attitude toward popular religion, especially toward all kinds of divination.

In the thirteenth century, Albertus Magnus wrote a treatise on minerals and referred to both alchemy and magic. Thomas Aquinas himself believed in alchemy and attributed its efficacy to the occult forces of the heavenly bodies. Roger Bacon, too, took a close interest in the occult, since for him "experimental science" meant a secret and traditional science; that is, a concrete science, but one inseparable from holy scripture.

In the Renaissance, we begin to hear of the "occult sciences," an expression that is common in the works of Blaise de Vigenère. Central to these sciences is the symbolic image of the two books: the "book of nature" and the "book of revelation," or, in other words, the universe and the Bible.

The link between alchemy and gnosticism and Hermetism is most tangibly documented in the occult literature of Hellenistic Egypt.

PAGE 23

OCCULTISM AND MODERNITY

The industrial revolution naturally gave rise to an increasingly marked interest in the "miracles" of science. It promoted the invasion of daily life by utilitarian and socioeconomic preoccupations of all kinds. Along with smoking factory chimneys came both the literature of the fantastic and the new phenomenon of spiritualism. These two possess a common characteristic: each takes the real world in its most concrete form as its point of departure, and then postulates the existence of another, supernatural world, separated from the first by a more or less impermeable partition. It is interesting that occultism in its modern form—that of the nineteenth century—appeared at the same time as fantastic literature and spiritualism.

The taste for magic in all its forms finds a psychological outlet in fantasy films (Roman Polansky's *Rosemary's Baby* is one example among hundreds). Occultist sects have proliferated as rapidly as the films, offering themselves as a similar sort of spectacle for the world at large.

"Esoteric knowledge is to occult practices as the corpus of theoretical physics is to engineering applications."

TIRYAKIAN

O

OCEANIC RELIGIONS

An Overview

Such cults are in a sense the manifestations of the desire to explore the unknown.

Occultism, like esotericism in general, has been the object of a great number of scholarly works, especially in the last generation or two. Today, historians such as Alain Mercier, Guy Michaud, and Jean Richer are throwing new light on the relationships between occultism, literature, and philosophy. Thus, like the popularization of occultism by the media, current erudition too contributes a new facet to the subject: its sociocultural dimension.

— ANTOINE FAIVRE

TRANSLATED FROM FRENCH BY KRISTINE ANDERSON

OCEANIC RELIGIONS

AN OVERVIEW

Ancestors are one of many types of spirits recognized by Melanesian tribal peoples.

PAGE 30

The Pacific islands are dispersed over the widest expanse of sea in our world. They comprise semicontinents (such as New Guinea), strings of large mountainous islands (along the curve of the Melanesian chain), and groups of more isolated larger and smaller islands further east, with many of those islets or islands arranged as atolls, or, more rarely, organized into whole archipelagoes such as the Tuamotus and the Carolines. The classic view is that one should distinguish between three large cultural areas: Micronesia in the northwest, Melanesia in the south, and Polynesia in the east. The reality is that while Micronesia is somewhat distinct in that its cultures display the influences of constant Asian contacts, Melanesia and Polynesia are artificial concepts created by Western powers. The Europeans settled and christianized Tahiti and eastern Polynesia, using the peoples of these islands to contact and control islands further west—as soldiers, Christian teachers, and petty civil servants who were accorded a status slightly higher than that of the so-called "cruel" Melanesian savages. In Polynesia the islanders resisted incursion settlement, and land transfers to Europeans were often obtained through marriages with the locals: these practices provided support for the queer conception that the islanders of the east were closer to their colonizers in terms of civilization, while those of the west were uncouth and dangerous.

Hereditary chieftainships exist, and chiefs are often surrounded by such formal behavior and etiquette that Westerners gave the title "king" to all such titular heads of social groups without checking to see if these "kings" in fact had kingdoms.

All things alive (social, biological, or material) are accounted for either by the actions of the dead (who hold, collectively or individually, enormous power), or by those of the so-called culture heroes of the cosmogonic or semicosmogonic myths. Religious concepts are usually a means of justifying the way in which a society and culture function, and thus support institutionalization and not change. Autochthonous Oceanic beliefs are responsible, even now, for stability in the societies of this area. Experience over recent decades has shown that aboriginal religious beliefs and concepts are far from dead in the Pacific islands, although the whole area is nominally Christian. Prayers are still offered to ancestors and to symbolic beings whose invisible presence is still felt.

In the nineteenth century, after research in Vanuatu (formerly New Hebrides) and the Solomon Islands, R. H. Codrington (1891) came to understand that there were two kinds of gods, those who had lived as human beings and those who had never been human. Maurice Leenhardt (1947) later confirmed that most of the so-called gods were believed to have once been human. The transformation from human to god began with their deaths. Their corpses, called *bao* (which is also the word for "human being," and is often translated as "spirit"), were from then on named in prayers.

STATUS, POWER, AND ANCESTRY. Localization is the key to understanding how status and power systems function in the islands. Part of the status, independence, and prestige of each lineage involves its ownership, or mastery, of a portion of the universe. It is the function of each lineage to act in ways prescribed by the tradition so as to make the universe run smoothly and so that each group will benefit from the ritual actions of all of the others and will reciprocate through its own. Such mythical endowment, however, always includes both positive and negative powers.

Belief in a god of creation who is different from the culture heroes is common throughout Oceania. He seems to be a *deus otiosus,* however, who no longer deals with human problems.

INITIATION. One of the most imprecise terms used in accounts of Oceanic religions is *initiation.* It is well known that, throughout the Pacific islands, male teenagers are taken away from their mothers and kept in seclusion for a number of weeks. During this time they are given special food (without relish, and roasted instead of boiled). Their mettle is tested through painful experiences such as the incision of the foreskin—rarely complete circumcision—or scarification or tattooing. Older men teach the teenagers the traditional songs. The young men are taught the verse and the prose of their vernacular traditions, and are informed as to what can and cannot be said in the presence of women and children. They perform plays and dances dealing with the mythical beings associated with their local groups, and they learn to play musical instruments. Some Highland New Guinea youths start at this point to learn the technique of swallowing a rattan vine through the nose as a means of purifying the body of all bad influences. Generally youths are either beaten with stinging nettles or threatened with death if they talk to anybody about what they have been through.

These rites actually represent only a partial initiation, one that highlights the cohesion of allied groups and that teaches what can be told in front of a number of people of different lineages. Another important part of the traditional lore will be taught, over the years, by the mother, the father, the father's sister, the mother's brother, and the grandparents. The key to the lessons of this multiple process of tuition lies in the numerous place names that must be remembered. Each myth, each piece of oral lore is rooted somewhere, belonging not only to a specific social group but also to a specific point in space where—and only where—its story can be told.

Some of the powers and ritual formulas might be kept by the father until his deathbed, because he has waited to transmit them until almost his last breath.

DIVINATION AND WITCHCRAFT. Individuals pray directly to their own dead relatives for help, but on occasions when they are in need of greater help—to obtain the favors of a woman, for example, or to discover who has been sending sickness to a next of kin—they go to see a clairvoyant, who may be a man but is often a woman.

Witchcraft is used for retribution when full-scale war is not in order. However, many ideas about witchcraft as a negative institution are entirely wrong. The "sorcerer" is always an ambiguous person. He will heal as well as cause sickness or death, and he protects his own lineage against dangers.

MATERIAL ASPECTS OF RELIGION. In most instances, the contact between man and god was secretive, without any witness. Only in the cases of widely established institutions such as meetings between numerous interlocked lineages do we find large-scale public ceremonies, which had always as much a political as a religious meaning.

One important question regarding the material

DEATH IN OCEANIC CULTURES
Tracing the Path of the Dead

The link between men and women and their dead is one of the keys for the understanding of Pacific islanders' religious behavior. The dead are believed to be living in another form of existence in some faraway place, under the sea or under the earth, where they have arrived after following a set path and after one of that group of gods who have never been human ordains their life in the afterworld. The path that the dead follow can be mapped: it may go from one island to another—so that the dead require, as in Vanuatu, the ghost of a canoe, which transports those from Malekula across to Ambrim—or it may follow, as between Lifou and Uvéa in the Loyalty Islands, some subterranean route where maiden temptresses will try to stop the dead person so as to devour him. When the path follows a known route to the sea or to the underworld, its protection is the responsibility of a given lineage, which will derive prestige and authority from such a privilege.

The geographical location of the dead is not always a precise one. Melanesian groups recognize different openings of the afterworld on each of the coasts of their principal islands, and these places are marked by names such as *Devil's Rock* or *Devil's Point*.

Corpses receive all sorts of ritual treatment. They may be laid in a grave or buried fetuslike in the ground, with the head sticking out; the head might later be removed for use in special mortuary rites. Mortuary techniques vary from place to place, and change according to fashion. For instance, the custom of eating parts of the dead body, particularly the brain, and of rubbing newborn children with the dead person's fat, was introduced into the Fore area of the New Guinea Highlands only four generations ago.

Very generally, a special rite often occurs ten days after death, during which the deceased person is reverentially asked to depart his lifelong place of residence and to go to join the other dead in their abode, where he now belongs.

Some of the dead are unwelcome at all times, since they can only be harmful; these include, for instance, the dead of another group, who should not be allowed to stray out of their own territory, and, especially, the ghosts of those who were left without normal burials, or of women who died in childbirth and who do not have their children—or carved representations of their babies—with them (New Caledonia).

When one looks at the texts of prayers, chants, or invocations *(such as the Maori karakia)*, one always finds, directly or indirectly, the mention of the dead and their powers, or of superior beings. These beings often cannot be named because the *tapu* against saying their exact, or secret, name is too high for it to be uttered without great danger. The hints or roundabout ways that vernacular texts have of addressing the dead or superior beings are often incomprehensible even to those Europeans knowledgeable in Oceanic languages.

— JEAN GUIART

aspects of Oceanic religions involves the role of monumental stone or wooden carvings, or of the small carved pieces depicting the human figure and popularly called *tiki.* The first missionaries thought that these human carvings represented gods and were cult objects, dismissing them all as "heathen" idols. The only role of the monumental carvings was, however, architectural: they represented a way of conceiving space that took the sky into account. The smaller carved pieces were kept at home, carefully wrapped in rolls of tapa cloth and not taken out much more than once a year. The key to understanding these objects comes from Fiji, where small carvings of human figures, in wood or whaletooth ivory, circulated in pre-European days.

A single principle is general throughout this area: a carved figure can be the repository of a godly presence, when it must, but the god has no obligation whatsoever to choose this particular abode. Monumental carvings are rarely thought of as possible repositories for godly presences, with the exception of the Hawaiian wickerwork figures covered with parrot feathers that were carried to battle as representations of Ku-ka'ili-moku, the god of war.

— JEAN GUIART

Every missionary religion must be received as well as proclaimed. But it is almost never received as given.

PAGE 445

MISSIONARY MOVEMENTS

While nearly all Pacific islanders today are Christians—except for the natives of inland New Guinea, where Christianity has made only partial inroads—one can still find here and there a village, family, or individual happily clinging to a "heathen" religion. Although Christianity is deeply entrenched in the Pacific, it is lived even now as only one of the several planes on which the islanders simultaneously exist without any sense of contradiction.

The Christianity of the Pacific islanders has a predominantly mythical quality. Even today, many islanders believe the biblical narrative is merely a story and that Jerusalem and other holy places have only a symbolic existence.

HISTORY OF CHRISTIAN MISSIONS IN THE PACIFIC. Both Protestant and Catholic communities exist on most of the Pacific islands (with adherents of the Protestant churches usually being in the majority). The most recent missions have been those of the Seventh-day Adventists, Jehovah's Witnesses, Latter-Day Saints (Mormons), and Baha'is. Of these only the Seventh-day Adventists and the Mormons have had substantial success. In Hawaii, Tahiti, and the Tuamotus, Mormon missionary activity has even given rise to a breakaway church, the Kanito (or Sanito) movement.

Roman Catholic missions have rarely been the first to arrive in any area of Oceania, which explains why Catholics are in the minority in most places.

The history of christianization shows some regularities inasmuch as all of the missionary bodies, Protestant and Catholic, have used the same technique: mass conversions were precipitated through the conversion of members of the local aristocracy. Rival chiefs adopted different faiths, and there have been full-fledged Christian religious wars in Samoa, Tonga, Wallis, Fiji, and the Loyalty Islands, especially between Catholic and Protestant converts. The Seventh-day Adventists, to the discomfort of the well-established churches, have thrived by converting groups whose politics do not agree with those of the majority church in any given area. The Assemblies of God, the Jehovah's Witnesses, and to a lesser extent the Mormons, have recently made gains in similar fashions.

Christian missions in the Pacific frequently became involved in local disputes over land and social status. Missionaries were often used by one party to thwart the ambitions of another.

In order to consolidate the effects of sometimes hurried conversions, missionaries established programs to educate native youths as future leaders in the movement to spread the Christian faith.

— JEAN GUIART

HISTORY OF STUDY

Oceania is conventionally defined in terms of the three major cultural divisions of the Pacific islanders: Polynesia, Micronesia, and Melanesia. The best nineteenth-century sources are largely the works of administrators and other longterm residents, such as Abraham Fornander's *An Account of the Polynesian Race* (1878-1885; reprint, Rutland, Vt., 1969) and George Grey's *Polynesian Mythology and Ancient Traditional History of the Maori as Told by Their Priests and Chiefs* (1855; reprint, New York, 1970).

Despite this growing wealth of information about Oceanic cultures, the systematic study of Oceanic religions remained largely undeveloped before the advent of anthropology in the latter part of the nineteenth century.

A major goal of early anthropology was the creation of typological schemes to lay the basis for the reconstruction of evolutionary stages from savagery to civilization. One consequence of this essentially typological orientation was that apparent commonalities tended to be stressed at the expense of the distinctive features of particular religious systems, fostering a spurious sense of uniformity.

Anthropology from the mid-1970s forward witnessed a growing interest in processes of symbolization, and this development, coupled with the impact of previous work, prompted a number of detailed studies placing religion once again at the heart of anthropology in the Pacific.

Two of the most significant recent trends in the study of Oceanic religions are the incorporation of a view that accords to symbols an active role in transforming experience and a concern to come to grips with the dynamism of religious life. These orientations grow out of general anthropological preoccupations and at the same time reflect the necessity of coming to terms with history. Pacific pagans are now few and far between, and the last century has seen the emergence of Christianity as the dominant religious form in Oceania.

— DAN W. JORGENSEN

ORDINATION

Ordination here refers to the practice in many religions of publicly designating and setting apart certain persons for special religious service and leadership, granting them religious authority and power to be exercised for the welfare of the community. The way each religious community practices ordination depends on that community's worldview and religious beliefs. For example, in traditions that emphasize a direct relationship with the divine being or beings, the ordained person may be thought of primarily as a mediator or priest. Communities that consider human beings to be especially troubled by evil spirits or witchcraft look to shamans or exorcists to counteract the evil influences. In religions that present a goal of inner enlightenment and purified life, the ordained person will be a monk or nun leading the way toward this goal of enlightenment. And religious communities that place much emphasis on living in accordance with the divinely given law set certain persons apart as religious scholars and judges.

Each religion sets up qualifications that candidates must meet before they can be ordained. Sometimes ordination is based on heredity. In many religions the candidate must be male, although some roles are specified for women; other traditions allow both male and female candidates to be ordained. While aptness for the religious role is always a requirement, in some traditions the person must already have demonstrated his suitability for that role before being chosen, while in others it is assumed that the office will be learned through a period of training. Every religion presupposes some kind of divine call or inner motivation on the part of the candidate.

An authority and power not possessed by the ordinary people of the community are conferred on the candidate through ordination. The source of that authority and power may be the divine powers, the consent of the community, or those who have already been ordained. Upon ordination, the person receives a new religious title. The English term priest can be used in many religious traditions to designate those who have been ordained or set apart, but a variety of other terms is sometimes preferred, such as *shaman, medicine man, monk or nun, rabbi, bishop, presbyter, deacon, minister,* or *imam.*

ORDINATION IN ANCIENT AND TRADITIONAL SOCIETIES. Numerous ancient or traditional societies have beliefs and practices according to which they set apart certain persons, endowing them with special authority and power for the performance of essential religious services, such as serving the gods and spirits, sacrificing, communicating with spiritual powers, warding off evil powers, healing, and the like. Among the great diversity of roles dealing with spiritual power, some basic types are priests, shamans, and medicine men.

The term *priest* generally designates a person ordained with authority to practice the cult of certain divinities or spirits. The priesthood may be hereditary, or priests may be called or chosen by the divinity. After selection or calling, the aspiring priest undergoes a period of purification and training.

Shamans (male and female) are commonly thought to be elected directly by tutelary spirits, who in a visionary experience initiate the future shaman.

ZOROASTRIAN AND HINDU ORDINATION. Among Indo-Europeans the priesthood was an important class, as evidenced in the priesthoods of the ancient Romans, Greeks, Celts, Persians, Aryans, and others. The present-day Zoroastrians (Parsis in India) and the Hindus have continued this emphasis on a class of priests ordained to perform the important purifications, sacrifices, and other ceremonies for the maintenance of a healthy relationship between humans and the eternal divine order of the universe.

The religion of the ancient Persians, as transformed by the prophet Zarathushtra (Zoroaster) into Zoroastrianism, is practiced today in Iran and India.

In Hinduism, brahman priests have always played an important role. In ancient Vedic times they were thought to uphold the whole social order through their mediation, by virtue of their mastery of the sacred rituals, sacrifices, and formulas. Today, especially for people of the high castes, it is important to have a brahman household priest *(purohita)* perform the traditional rituals and chant the Vedic texts properly so that the cosmic order will continue with its health and goodness for each according to his or her place in the total order. Some brahmans prepare to be priests of temple worship, where rituals center on the ceremonial treatment of the images of the gods—although many functions of temple worship can be performed by the people without priestly help.

Priests are inducted into their office through ordination.

PAGE 554

ORDINATION AMONG JAINS AND BUDDHISTS. Two religions that grew up in India along with Hinduism are Jainism and Buddhism, and in these religious traditions spiritual power is understood to reside especially in the monastic communities, that is, among those monks and nuns who have left ordinary secular life to pursue spiritual perfection through ascetic practices. The monks and nuns are primarily devoted to their own spiritual perfection; yet because they possess great power they can perform religious service for the laypeople, such as chanting scripture, performing funeral rites, and teaching.

ORDINATION OF PRIESTS IN TAOISM AND SHINTO. Priests in Chinese religious Taoism function as ritual and liturgical specialists, but they also act as exorcists and healers, expelling and pacifying demons. Taoist priests *(tao-shih)* are often designated on the basis of heredity. Since the ritual of Taoism is esoteric, that is, not directly to be understood and witnessed by the laypeople, usually the aspiring priest will join the entourage of a recognized master who knows the important formulas and hidden aspects of ritual Taoism.

"Hear this, O priests. It is you who are called to judgment."

HOSEA 5:1

The main function of Japanese Shinto priests *(shinshoku)* of all ranks is to worship and serve the *kami,* the spiritual beings associated with the powerful forces of nature and the ancestors. The priests maintain good relations with the *kami* for the divine protection and welfare of the human community.

Priests often come from families with long and strong traditions of Shinto worship. In ancient times a few priestly families supplied most of the priests, although in modern times the priesthood is open to candidates from nonpriestly families also.

ORDINATION IN JUDAISM. The religion of Judaism after the Babylonian exile and especially after the destruction of the Temple in the Roman period moved away from a sacrificial temple cult and, consequently, the most important religious leaders became those ordained as rabbis. They functioned as judges, scholars, teachers, and expounders of the Torah and Talmud; in modern times, rabbis also function as worship leaders, officiants at marriage and burial ceremonies, and spiritual heads of local communities of Jews.

Some groups have traditional schools *(yeshivot)* that give the traditional *semikhah* ordination with its emphasis on training in the Talmud and Jewish codes. Other groups have seminaries that see preparation for the rabbinate as including not only knowledge of the Talmud and codes but also professional training to function as a synagogue rabbi within modern society.

ORDINATION IN CHRISTIANITY. Christians hold that Jesus Christ is the great high priest, the real mediator between God and humans, and that all Christians as members of his body participate in his priesthood. While some Christians conclude that there is no need for specially ordained leaders, most Christian groups have recognized the need for ordained priests or ministers to lead the Christian community.

Although traditionally any male Christian could aspire to become a priest or minister, in recent years many Christian denominations have begun to ordain women clergy also, while some denominations, such as the Roman Catholic church, continue to ordain male candidates only. Candidates are given a course of study and training in a theological seminary before being certified and presented to the church denominational authorities for ordination.

Those set apart for special service are given many different titles: priest, minister, pastor, presbyter, bishop, and deacon are the most common among those designating the clergy.

APPOINTING SPIRITUAL LEADERS IN ISLAM. In Islam, every Muslim can perform the religious rites, so there is no class or profession of ordained clergy. Yet there are religious leaders who are recognized for their learning and their ability to lead communities of Muslims in prayer, study, and living according to the teaching of the Qur'an and Muslim law. These religious leaders belong to the learned group of orthodox Muslim scholars and jurists known as the *'ulama'* (*'alim* in the singular). They have studied at recognized schools of Islamic learning and have secured appointments as mosque functionaries, teachers, jurisconsults, or judges.

The religious leader who is contracted by a local community of Muslims to lead the community in public worship, preach at the Friday mosque prayer, teach, and give advice on religious matters on the local level is called the imam, belonging to the broad group of *'ulama'.*

— THEODORE M. LUDWIG

ORTHODOX JUDAISM

Orthodox Judaism is the branch of Judaism that adheres most strictly to the tenets of the religious law.

PAGE 441

Orthodox Judaism is the branch of Judaism that adheres most strictly to the tenets of the religious law *(halakhah).* Its forebears may be identified in the eighteenth century, by which time the *qehillah,* the Jewish communal organization in each locality, had lost much of its authority in central and western Europe and its prestige in eastern Europe. This, in turn, undermined religious authority, which had heretofore relied not only on the faith of each Jew but also on communal consensus and the formal authority and prestige of communal leaders. The breakdown of the traditional community, coupled with the hope and expectation of political emancipation, encouraged new interpretations of Jewish life and new conceptions of appropriate relationships between Jews and non-Jews. These began to emerge by the end of the eighteenth century in central and western Europe and somewhat later in eastern Europe. Orthodoxy was born as the ideological and organizational response to these new conceptions.

The major tenets of Orthodoxy, like those of traditional Judaism, include the dogma that the Torah was "given from Heaven," that the *halakhah* derives directly or indirectly from an act of revelation, and that Jews are obligated to live in accordance with the *halakhah* as interpreted by rabbinic authority. But unlike traditional Judaism, Orthodoxy is conscious of the spiritual and cultural challenges of the modern world and especially of rival formulations of the meaning and consequences of being Jewish. Orthodoxy, in all its various manifestations and expressions, has never recognized any alternative conception of Judaism as legitimate. But it is aware of itself as a party, generally a minority party, within the Jewish world.

Orthodoxy arose in eastern Europe at the end of the nineteenth century, primarily in response to secular interpretations of Jewish life rather than in opposition to religious reform. The most important centers of Orthodoxy today are in Israel and the United States.

HUNGARIAN ORTHODOXY. The ideological and programmatic outlines of Hungarian Orthodoxy were formulated by Rabbi Mosheh Sofer (1762-1839), better known as the Hatam Sofer, the title of his seven-volume *responsa* to halakhic questions. This earliest variety of Orthodoxy is best described by the term *neotraditionalism* because it rejects any attempt at change and adaptation of the tradition. According to the Hatam Sofer, "all that is new is forbidden by the Torah"; the phrase is a play on the words of an injunction prohibiting consumption of "new" grain from each year's harvest until a portion is offered in the Temple in Jerusalem. Unlike some of his followers, the Hatam Sofer did not oppose all forms of secular education. A knowledge of some secular subjects, for example, is helpful in resolving certain halakhic problems. But in characteristically neotraditional fashion, he legitimated secular education in utilitarian terms, not as an end in itself.

The Hatam Sofer favored immigration to the Land of Israel. Many who favored immigration in those days were reacting to the reformers' rejection of nationalist elements in Judaism. The Hatam Sofer's espousal of an early form of Jewish nationalism and his projection of the importance of the Land of Israel in the Jewish tradition may also have been related to his negative attitude toward political emancipation. He feared its threat to religious authority.

The distinctive instrument of Hungarian Orthodoxy in furthering its neotraditional objectives was the independent communal organization. In 1868 the Hungarian government convened a General Jewish Congress in order to define the basis for the autonomous organization of the Jewish community. The majority of the delegates were sympathetic to religious reform (Neologs), and most of the Orthodox delegates withdrew from the Congress. In 1870 the Hungarian parliament permitted the Orthodox to organize themselves in separate communal frameworks, which might coexist in the same locality with a Neolog community or a Status Quo community (the latter was composed of those who refused to join either the Orthodox or the Neolog community).

Hungarian Orthodoxy included both Hasidic and non-Hasidic elements. Hasidism, which originated in the eighteenth century, was bitterly opposed by the traditional religious elite, who feared that its folkishness, pietism, and ambivalence toward the central importance of Talmudic study undermined the tradition itself. Orthodoxy might have been born in opposition to Hasidism if not for leaders like the Hatam Sofer who sought a *modus vivendi,* recognizing that Hasidic leaders were no less antagonistic to basic changes in tradition than were the traditional religious elite. In fact, by the end of the century, the centers of Hasidic influence in the smaller Jewish communities remained least compromising in their attitude toward modernity.

GERMAN ORTHODOXY. The year 1850 marks the emergence of German Orthodoxy, with the establishment of the Israelitische Religionsgesellschaft in Frankfurt am Main, a congregation led by Samson Raphael Hirsch from 1851 until his death. But the distinctive ideological formulation of German Orthodoxy (often known as Neo-Orthodoxy) dates, at least in embryo, from the publication of Hirsch's *Nineteen Letters on Judaism* in 1836. The publication a few years later of an Orthodox weekly by Ya'aqov Ettlinger (1798-1871) is also of significance.

Hirsch was the foremost proponent of the idea that Torah-true Judaism (to borrow a popular phrase of German Orthodoxy) was compatible with modern culture and political emancipation. Hirsch envisaged a divine order revealed in nature in which Jews could and should participate. But the divine order was also revealed in the Torah, many of whose commands were specific to Jews. The effect of Hirsch's conception, though not his intent, was the compartmentalization of life for the Orthodox Jew. Modern culture, patriotism, civil law—all become legitimate spheres for Jewish involvement since they were perceived as falling outside the realm proscribed by *halakhah.*

Reform Judaism, as a self-conscious movement in Jewish life, began in Germany with the establishment of the Hamburg temple in 1818. In the first few decades of the century it seemed that Reform conceptions of Judaism would replace those of traditional

As a self-conscious movement, Jewish Orthodoxy arose in response to liberal Judaism with the purpose of correctly delineating Jewish authenticity.

PAGE 411

Many in the Orthodox community have attempted to resort to legal measures in the civil courts to force compliance with halakhah.

PAGE 261

Judaism in Germany. What Hirsch never forgot was that the attraction of reform was an outgrowth of Jewish desire for emancipation and acceptance, that traditional Judaism appeared to be an obstacle to this goal, and that unless it could be reformulated as compatible with emancipation and modern culture, it had no future in Germany.

ORTHODOXY IN EASTERN EUROPE. The vast majority of eastern European Jews continued to live in accordance with the religious tradition throughout the nineteenth century, although the institutions of traditional Judaism were severely undermined. Government law had destroyed many of the traditional privileges and responsibilities of the Jewish community.

ORTHODOXY IN ISRAEL. Most Orthodox Jews today reside in Israel or the United States. Religiously observant Jews make up 15 to 20 percent of the Jewish population of Israel. The neotraditionalists, once quite marginal to Israeli society, play an increasingly important role. The most colorful and controversial group within their ranks is the successor to the old yishuv, the 'Edah Haredit (Community of the Pious), consisting of a few thousand families with thousands of sympathizers located primarily in Jerusalem and Benei Beraq (on the outskirts of Tel Aviv). These are the most intransigent of the neotraditionalists. They relate to the state of Israel with varying degrees of hostility. They refuse to participate in its elections, the more extreme refuse to bear Israeli identification cards or utilize the state's services (their schools, for example, refuse government support), and the most extreme seek the imposition of Arab rule.

The religious Zionists are in a different category. They make up roughly 10 percent of the Jewish population but are in some sense the symbol of contemporary Israel. Israel's political culture, particularly since the 1970s, focuses on the Jewish people, the Jewish tradition, and the Land of Israel as objects of ultimate value. Symbols of traditional religion, though not traditional theology, pervade Israeli life. Religious Zionists are viewed by many of the nonreligious as most committed to and most comfortable with these values and symbols.

The political elite, in particular, has been strongly influenced by the religious Zionist. In no other society do Orthodox Jews, religious Zionists in particular, feel quite so much at home. They are separated from the non-Orthodox population by their distinctive cultural and educational institutions (in the advanced religious Zionist *yeshivot,* students are required to fulfill their military obligations but generally do so in selected units) and their own friendship groups.

But most religious Zionists not only feel that they fully participate as equal members of the society but also sense a wholeness to their lives that they find missing outside of Israel. Nevertheless, they, too, confront the tension between tradition and modernity.

The state of Israel provides basic religious services such as religious schools, supervision over the *kashrut* of foods, religious courts, an established rabbinate with responsibility for marriage and divorce of Jews, ritual baths, and subsidies for synagogue construction and rabbis' salaries. The religious political parties act as intermediaries in the provision of welfare and educational services. Hence, although the role of the synagogues proliferate in Israel, there is probably no country in the world where they play a less important role in the life of the Orthodox Jew.

ORTHODOXY IN THE UNITED STATES. American Orthodoxy bears the mark of two waves of immigrants and a native generation that combines characteristics of each. Many of the eastern European immigrants who came to the United States during the great wave of Jewish immigration between 1881 and 1924 were traditionalists. In the confrontation with American culture and the challenge of finding a livelihood, they abandoned many traditional patterns of religious observance. The dominant Orthodox strategy that emerged in the United States was adaptationism. In fact, in the first few decades of the century it appeared as though the difference between American Orthodox and Conservative Judaism was really the degree or pace of adaptation. The institutions and ideology of American Orthodoxy were severely challenged by neotraditionalist immigrants who arrived just prior to and immediately following World War II. They established their own *yeshivot,* Hasidic *rebeyim* among them reestablished their courts of followers, and they expressed disdain for the modern Orthodox rabbi. He was likely to be a graduate of Yeshiva University, the major institution for the training of Orthodox rabbis in the United States, where rabbinical students are required to have earned a college degree. The neotraditionalists were zealous and very supportive of their own institutions. In addition, they clustered in a few neighborhoods of the largest cities. Their concentration and discipline provided their leaders with political influence, which, in the heydays of the welfare programs of the 1960s and 1970s, was translated into various forms of government assistance.

The neotraditionalist challenge to modern Orthodoxy has had a decided impact on the native generation raised in modern Orthodox homes, and the American environment has left its mark on the generation raised in neotraditionalist homes. The American-born Orthodox Jew, regardless of the home in which he was raised, tends to be punctilious in religious observance, more so than his parents, and hostile to what he considers deviant forms of Judaism (i. e., Conservative or Reform). But he is sympathetic to many aspects of

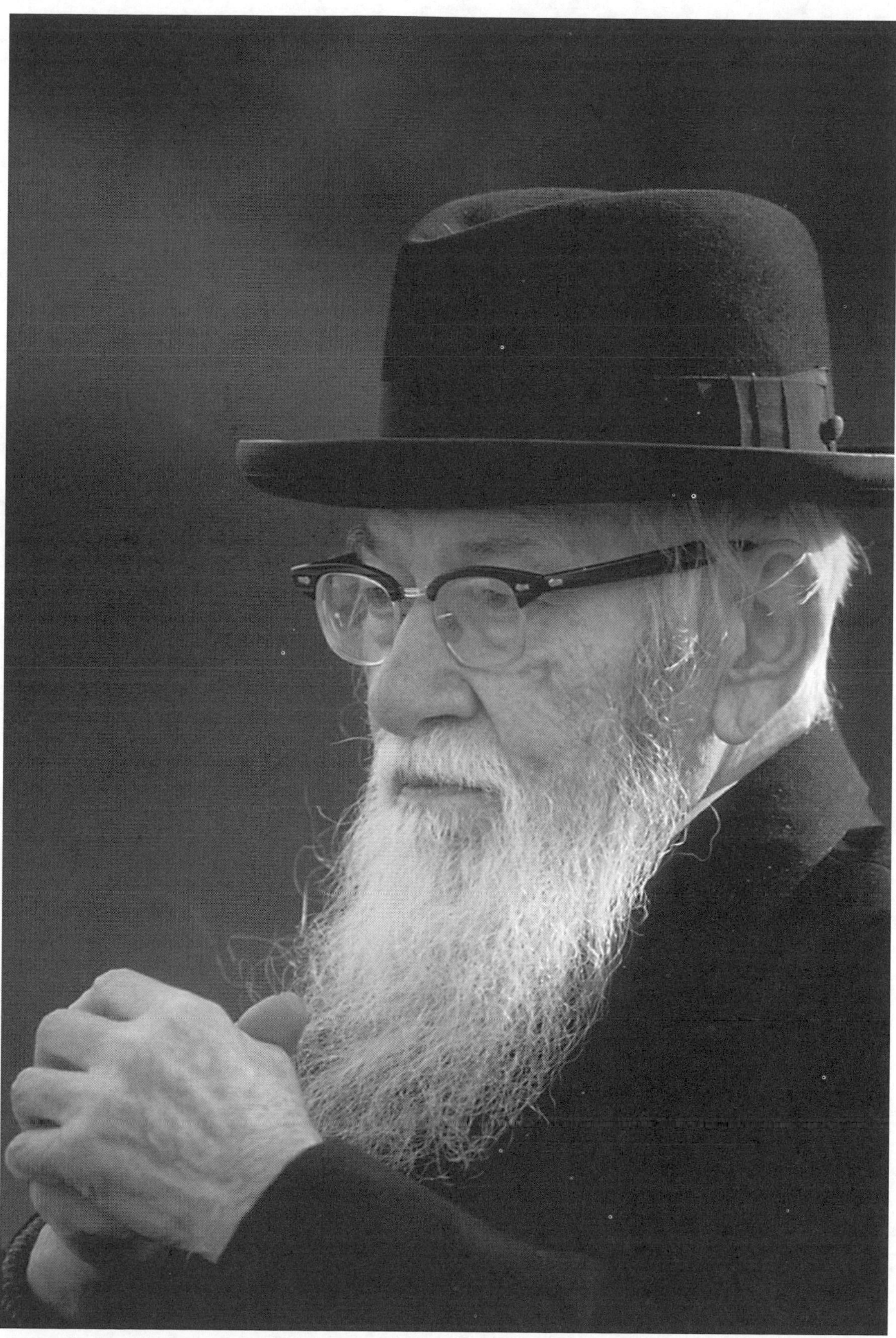

ORTHODOXY *Most Orthodox Jews today reside in Israel or in the United States. The dominant trend in Orthodoxy throughout the world has been punctilious religious observance and less accommodation to contemporary culture and values.* PAUL A. SOUDERS/CORBIS

contemporary culture and accepting of secular education, if only for purposes of economic advancement. Finally, there is a general willingness among most American Orthodox Jews to work with the non-Orthodox on behalf of general Jewish interests, those of Israel in particular.

ORTHODOX JUDAISM TODAY. The dominant trend in Orthodoxy throughout the world, since the end of World War II, has been increased religious zealotry, punctiliousness in religious observance, and, with some exceptions, less explicit accommodation to modern values and contemporary culture. This is, at least in part, a result of the direction in which modern values and culture have moved. Increased permissiveness; challenges to authority, order, and tradition in general; and affirmation of self are inimical to all historical religions. But Orthodoxy has become far more skilled, after a century of experience, in developing institutions—such as schools, synagogues, political organizations, a press, and summer camps—to mute the threats of secularism and modernity. In some respects this means that Orthodoxy is more at ease with the world and tolerates certain forms of accommodation (advanced secular education is the outstanding example) that many Orthodox circles denounced in the past. But it also means an increased self-confidence and an absence of fear on the part of Orthodoxy to challenge and reject some of the basic behavioral and ideological assumptions upon which most of modern culture rests.

— CHARLES S. LIEBMAN

P

PAPACY

The papacy is the central governing institution of the Roman Catholic church under the leadership of the pope, the bishop of Rome. The word *papacy* (Lat., *papatus*) is medieval in origin and derives from the Latin *papa,* an affectionate term for "father."

THE EARLY PERIOD

This era, extending from the biblical origins of Christianity to the fifth century, was marked by the ever-increasing power and prestige of the bishop of Rome within the universal church and the Roman empire.

SCRIPTURAL FOUNDATION. Traditional Roman Catholic teaching holds that Jesus Christ directly bestowed upon the apostle Peter the fullness of ruling and teaching authority. He made Peter the first holder of supreme power in the universal church, a power passed on to his successors, the bishops of Rome. Peter had a preeminent role in the New Testament, where he is described as the most prominent apostolic witness and missionary among the Twelve. He is the model of the shepherd-pastor, the receiver of a special revelation, and the teacher of the true faith. Gradually Christians, through the providential direction of the Holy Spirit, recognized the papacy, the office of headship in the church, to be the continuation of that ministry given by Christ to Peter.

FIRST THREE CENTURIES. The early Christian churches were not organized internationally. Yet Rome, almost from the beginning, was accorded a unique position, and understandably so: Rome was the only apostolic see in the West; it was the place where Peter and Paul were martyred; and it was the capital of the empire.

The exact structure of the very early Roman church is not known, but it seems that by the middle of the second century monepiscopacy (the rule of one bishop) was well established. The bishops of Rome in the third century claimed a universal primacy, even though it would be another 150 years before this idea was doctrinally formulated. Rome attracted both orthodox and heterodox teachers—some to have their views heard, others to seek confirmation. More and more, the bishop of Rome, either on his own initiative or by request, settled doctrinal and disciplinary disputes in other churches. Roman influence was felt as far away as Spain, Gaul, North Africa, and Asia Minor. The see of Peter was looked upon as the guarantor of doctrinal purity.

FOURTH AND FIFTH CENTURIES. With the Edict of Milan (313) the empire granted toleration of all religions and allowed Christians to worship freely. This policy ended the era of persecution, increased the number of Christians, and shaped the institutional development of the papacy. Once Emperor Constantine decided to move the seat of the empire to Constantinople in 324, the papacy began to play a larger role in the West. By the time Christianity became the official religion of the empire in 381, several popes were already affirming papal primatial authority. The critical period in the doctrinal systematization of Roman primacy took place in the years between Damasus I (366-384) and Leo I (440-461). In that period, the popes explicitly claimed that the bishop of Rome was the head of the entire church and that his authority derived from Peter.

Damasus I, the first pope to call Rome the apostolic see, made Latin the principal liturgical language in Rome and commissioned Jerome to revise the old Latin version of the New Testament. His successor, Siricius (384-399), whose decretal letters are the earliest extant, promoted Rome's primatial position and imposed his decisions on many bishops outside Italy.

It was Leo I, the first of three popes to be called the Great, who laid the theoretical foundation of papal primacy. Leo took the title Pontifex Maximus, which the emperors no longer used, and claimed to possess the fullness of power (*plenitudo potestatis*). Governing the church through a tumultuous period of barbarian invasions and internal disputes, he relentlessly defended the rights of the Roman see. He rejected Canon 28 of the Council of Chalcedon (451), which gave the bishop of New Rome (Constantinople) privileges equal to those of the bishop of Old Rome and a rank second only to that of the pope. Leo believed that Peter's successors have "the care of all the churches" (*Sermons* 3.4), and he exercised his authority over Christian churches in Italy, Africa, and Gaul. The Western Roman empire ended in 476.

THE MEDIEVAL PAPACY

The eventful period from the sixth to the fifteenth century demonstrated the unusual adaptability of the papal office.

There are more than one-half billion Catholics worldwide, by far the largest body of Christians.

PAGE 576

Roman Catholic moral theology recognizes a special teaching office in matters of faith and morals that is given to, specifically, the pope and the bishops.

147

P

PAPACY

The Medieval Papacy

The most nearly universal discipline among the world's priesthoods is probably the discipline of meditation.

PAGE 556

THE STRUGGLE FOR INDEPENDENCE. The popes of the sixth and seventh centuries resisted excessive encroachments but were still subservient to the power of the emperor. The most notable pope at this time was Gregory I, the Great (590-604), a deeply spiritual man who called himself "the servant of the servants of God." A skilled negotiator, he was able to conclude a peace treaty with the Lombards, who threatened Rome; the people of Rome and the adjacent regions considered him their protector. Gregory was respectful of the rights of individual bishops, but he insisted, nevertheless, that all churches, including Constantinople, were subject to the apostolic see of Rome.

The break with the East began when Gregory II (715-731) condemned the iconoclastic decrees of Emperor Leo I, who had prohibited the use of images in liturgical ceremonies. The gap widened when Stephen II (752-757), the first pope to cross the Alps, met with Pépin, king of the Franks. Pépin agreed to defend the pope against the invading Lombards and apparently promised him sovereignty over large areas in central Italy. The Donation of Pépin was an epoch-making event; it marked the beginning of the Papal States, in existence until 1870. Stephen became the first of a long line of popes to claim temporal rule. Through his alliance with the Frankish kingdom, Stephen was virtually able to free the papacy from the domination of Constantinople. The last step in the division of Rome from the Eastern Empire was when Pope Leo III (795-816) crowned Charlemagne emperor of the West at Saint Peter's Basilica in 800. The primatial prominence of Rome increased when the Muslim conquests destroyed the church in North Africa and ended the strong influence of Rome's great rivals: the patriarchates of Alexandria, Antioch, and Jerusalem.

The tenth century was a bleak one for the papacy. The so-called Ottonian privilege restricted the freedom of papal electors and allowed the emperor the right of ratification. There were some two dozen popes and antipopes during this period, many of low moral caliber.

THE REFORM MOVEMENT. Advocates of reform found a dedicated leader in Leo IX (1049-1054). He traveled extensively throughout Italy, France, and Germany, presiding over synods that issued strong decrees dealing with clerical marriage, simony, and episcopal elections. Only six months of his entire pontificate were spent in Rome. Further reforms were made under Nicholas II (1059-1061). His decree on papal elections (1059), which made cardinal bishops the sole electors, had a twofold purpose: to safeguard the reformed papacy through free and peaceful elections and to eliminate coercion by the empire or the aristocracy.

The most famous of the reform popes was Gregory VII (1073-1085), surnamed Hildebrand. His ambitious program of reform focused on three areas: to restore prestige to the papacy; to reform clerical corruption; and to reform lay investiture—a practice whereby feudal lords, princes, and emperors bestowed spiritual office through the selection of pastors, abbots, and bishops. Henceforth, the papacy exercised a new style of leadership; the pope emerged not only as the undisputed head of the church but also as the unifying force in medieval western Europe.

THE HEIGHT OF PAPAL AUTHORITY. The papacy reached its zenith in the twelfth and thirteenth centuries. Six general councils between 1123 and 1274 issued many doctrinal and disciplinary decrees aimed at reform and left no doubt that the popes were firmly in control of church policy. During the pontificate of Innocent III (1198-1216), one of the most brilliant of all the popes, the papacy reached the summit of its universal power and supervised the religious, social, and political life of the West. Honorius III (1216-1227) further centralized papal administration and finances and approved the establishment of the Franciscan and Dominican orders. In theory, papal authority extended also to non-Christians. Innocent IV (1243-1254) believed that every creature is subject to the pope—even infidels, Christ's sheep by creation though not members of the church. This idea of a world theocracy under the popes was to be part of the theological and political justification for the Crusades.

Two significant changes were made in the procedures for papal elections. At the Third Lateran Council (1179), Alexander III (1159-1181) decreed that all cardinals—not just cardinal bishops—could vote and that a two-thirds majority was required. The Second Council of Lyons (1274), under Gregory X (1271-1276), established the law of the conclave, whereby the cardinal electors had to assemble in the papal palace and remain in a locked room until the election was completed.

DECLINE OF THE PAPACY. Several factors contributed to the decline of the papacy: high taxation, the inappropriate conferral and control of benefices, corruption in the Roman bureaucracy, and, above all, the failure of the popes to foresee the effect of nationalism on church-state relations.

In 1308, Clement V (1305-1314) moved the papal residence to Avignon, which then belonged to the king of Naples, a vassal of the pope. Several factors prompted this decision: the upcoming general council of Vienne (1311-1312); the tension between the pope and the king of France; and the unsafe and chaotic political situation in Rome and Italy. The popes remained in Avignon for seventy years. During their so-called Babylonian Captivity, the popes were French, but the papacy was not a puppet of the French rulers. Centralization and administrative complexity increased, especially under John XXII (1316-1334). The cardinals assumed greater power that at times bordered on oligarchy. They introduced the practice of capitulation—an agreement made by electors of the pope to limit the authority of the person chosen to be pope—and thus tried to restrict papal primacy.

No sooner had Gregory XI (1370-1378) returned to Rome in 1377 than the papacy faced another crisis, the great Western schism. The election of Urban VI (1378-1389) was later disputed by some of the cardinals, who claimed coercion. Five months after Urban's election, they rejected him and elected Clement VII (1378-1394), who went back to Avignon. The two popes had their own cardinals, curial staffs, and adherents among the faithful. A council was held at Pisa in 1409 to resolve the problem, but instead still another pope was elected, Alexander V, who in less than a year was succeeded by John XXIII (1410-1415). The general council of Constance (1414-1418) confronted the scandal of three would-be popes and pledged to reform the church in head and members. Unity was restored with the election of Martin V (1417-1431).

FROM THE RENAISSANCE TO THE ENLIGHTENMENT

Papal authority was severely challenged between the fifteenth and eighteenth centuries.

THE RENAISSANCE. Martin V tried to fulfill the provisions of the decree *Frequens* (1417) that emanated from the Council of Constance, which mandated that a general council should be held in five years, another seven years later, and then one regularly every ten years. He convened a council at Siena that later moved to Pavia (1423-1424), but the plague forced its dissolution. Seven years later another council was held, meeting first at Basel and later at Ferrara and Florence (1431-1445), under Eugene IV (1431-1447). Greek and Latin prelates attended, and they were able to agree on several thorny doctrinal issues including the primacy of the pope.

Nicholas V (1447-1455) and his successors made Rome a center of the arts and scholarship. Pius II (1458-1464), one of the most notable examples of papal humanism, in the bull *Exsecrabilis* (1460) prohibited any appeals to future general councils, thus striking at conciliarism. Sixtus IV (1471-1484) concerned himself mostly with the restoration of Rome and the expansion of the Papal States; he is responsible for building the magnificent Sistine Chapel in the Vatican. The most famous of the warrior popes was Julius II (1503-1513), known as Il Terribile. A capable and energetic leader, Julius became the patron of Michelangelo, Raphael, and Bramante; he commissioned the construction of the new basilica of Saint Peter's. Adrian VI (1522-1523) was an exception among the Renaissance popes; in his short pontificate he tried to introduce reform measures, but these met persistent opposition from both civil rulers and highly placed ecclesiastics. In sum, the Renaissance popes were generally more interested in politics, the arts, and the ostentatious display of wealth than in providing genuine religious leadership.

THE REFORMATION AND COUNTER-REFORMATION. By the beginning of the sixteenth century the papacy was severely weakened by internal decay and a loss of supernatural vision. The faithful throughout Europe were asked to contribute alms to the extravagant building projects in Rome. These factors, coupled with deep-seated religious, social, and economic unrest in Europe, set the stage for the Protestant Reformation. Martin Luther's challenge in 1517 caught the papacy unprepared. Leo X (1513-1521) and his successors badly underestimated the extent and intensity of antipapal sentiment in Europe. The popes neither adequately comprehended the religious intentions of Luther nor understood the appeal that the reformers' ideas had for many who were outraged at both the policies and the conduct of church leaders. What began in the Reformation as a movement to restore genuine apostolic integrity to the church of Rome ended with the creation of a separate church; by the time of Clement VII (1523-1534), millions of Catholics in Germany, Scandinavia, the Low Countries, Switzerland, and Britain had departed from the Roman communion.

The rapid rise of Protestantism had a sobering effect on the papacy: it forced the popes to concentrate on church affairs. Paul III (1534-1549), for example, appointed competent cardinals to administrative posts, authorized the establishment of the Society of Jesus (1540), and reformed the Roman Inquisition (1542). The church's most wide-ranging answer to the Protestant Reformation was the Council of Trent (1545-1563), convoked by Paul III and concluded by Pius IV (1559-1565). In its twenty-five sessions, the council discussed the authority of scripture and of tradition, original sin and justification, the sacraments, and specific reform legislation. It did not, strangely enough, treat explicitly the theology of the church or the papacy.

One of the effects of the Tridentine reform was a reorganization of the church's central administrative system. The Curia Romana, which had existed, at least functionally, since the first century, was plagued by nepotism, greed, and abuse of authority. Sixtus V (1585-1590), who was committed to a reform of the Curia, established fifteen congregations of cardinals to carry out church administration. The popes endeavored to consider moral character and ability in select-

"The Papacy is nothing other than the Ghost of the deceased Roman Empire."

THOMAS HOBBES
LEVIATHAN

TABLE 1. THE POPES

A Roman numeral in parentheses after a pope's name indicates differences in the historical sources. The names of the antipopes and their dates are given in brackets. The first date for each pope refers to his election; the second date refers to his death, deposition, or resignation. Dates for the first two hundred years are uncertain. Abbreviations: Bl. = Blessed; St. = Saint. [1164-1168]

NAMES	DATES	NAMES	DATES	NAMES	DATES
St. Peter	?-64/7	[Lawrence]	[498; 501-505]	Gregory IV	827-844
St. Linus	64/7-79?	St. Hormisdas	514-523	[John]	[844]
St. Anacletus (Cletus)	79?-90/2	St. John I	523-526	Sergius II	844-847
St. Clement I	90/2-99/101	St. Felix IV (III)	526-530	St. Leo IV	847-855
St. Evaristus	99/101-107?	Boniface II	530-532	Benedict III	855-858
St. Alexander I	107?-116?	[Dioscorus]	[530]	[Anastasius]	[855]
St. Sixtus I	116?-125?	John II	533-535	St. Nicholas I, the Great	858-867
St. Telesphorus	125?-136?	St. Agapitus I	535-536	Adrian II	867-872
St. Hyginus	136?-140/2	St. Silverius	536-537	John VIII	872-882
St. Pius I	140/2-154/5	Vigilius	537-555	Marinus I	882-884
St. Anicetus	154/5-166?	Pelagius I	556-561	St. Adrian III	884-885
St. Soter	166?-174?	John III	561-574	Stephen V (VI)	885-891
St. Eleutherius	174?-189?	Benedict I	575-579	Formosus	891-896
St. Victor I	189?-198?	Pelagius II	579-590	Boniface VI	896
St. Zephyrinus	198?-217?	St. Gregory I, the Great	590-604	Stephen VI (VII)	896- 897
St. Callistus I	217?-222	Sabinian	604-606	Romanus	897
[St. Hippolytus]	[217?-235]	Boniface III	607	Theodore II	897
St. Urban I	222-230	St. Boniface IV	608-615	John IX	898-900
St. Pontian	230-235	St. Deusdedit (Adeodatus I)	615-618	Benedict IV	900-903
St. Anterus	235-236	Boniface V	619-625	Leo V	903
St. Fabian	236-250	Honorius I	625-638	[Christopher]	[903-904]
St. Cornelius	251-253	Severinus	640	Sergius III	904-911
[Novatian]	[251-258?]	John IV	640-642	Anastasius III	913
St. Lucius I	253-254	Theodore I	642-649	Lando	914
St. Stephen I	254-257	St. Martin I	649-655	John X	914-928
St. Sixtus II	257-258	St. Eugene I	654-657	Leo VI	928
St. Dionysius	259-268	St. Vitalian	657-672	Stephen VII (VIII)	928-931
St. Felix I	269-274	Adeodatus II	672-676	John XI	931-935
St. Eutychian	275-283	Donus	676-678	Leo VII	936-39
St. Gaius (Caius)	283-296	St. Agatho	678-681	Stephen VIII (IX)	939-942
St. Marcellinus	296-304	St. Leo II	682-683	Marinus II	942-946
St. Marcellus I	308-309	St. Benedict II	684- 685	Agapetus II	946-955
St. Eusebius	309	John V	685-686	John XII	955-964
St. Miltiades	311-314	Conon	686-687	Leo VIII	963-965
St. Sylvester I	314-335	[Theodore]	[687]	Benedict V	964
St. Mark	336	[Paschal]	[687]	John XIII	965-972
St. Julius I	337-352	St. Sergius I	687-701	Benedict VI	973-974
Liberius	352-366	John VI	701-705	[Boniface VII]	[974;
[Felix II]	[355-365]	John VII	705-707		984-985]
St. Damasus I	366-384	Sisinnius	708	Benedict VII	974-983
[Ursinus]	[366-367]	Constantine	708-715	John XIV	983-984
St. Siricius	384-399	St. Gregory II	715-731	John XV	985-996
St. Anastasius I	399-401	St. Gregory III	731-741	Gregory V	996-999
St. Innocent I	401-417	St. Zachary	741-752	[John XVI]	[997-998]
St. Zosimus	417-418	Stephen (II)	752	Sylvester II	999-1003
St. Boniface I	418-422	Stephen II (III)	752-757	John XVII	1003
[Eulalius]	[418-419]	St. Paul I	757-767	John XVIII	1004-1009
St. Celestine I	422-32	[Constantine II]	[767-769]	Sergius IV	1009-1012
St. Sixtus III	432-440	[Philip]	[768]	Benedict VIII	1012-1024
St. Leo I, the Great	440-461	Stephen III (IV)	768-772	[Gregory]	[1012]
St. Hilary	461-468	Adrian I	772-795	John XIX	1024-1032
St. Simplicius	468-483	St. Leo III	795-816	Benedict IX (first time)	1032-1044
St. Felix III (II)	483-492	Stephen IV (V)	816-817	Sylvester III	1045
St. Gelasius I	492-496	St. Paschal I	817-824	Benedict IX (second time)	1045
Anastasius II	496-498	Eugene II	824-827	Gregory VI	1045-1046
St. Symmachus	498-514	Valentine	827	Clement II	1046-1047

TABLE 1. THE POPES

NAMES	DATES	NAMES	DATES	NAMES	DATES
Benedict IX (third time)	1047-1048	Urban IV	1261-1264	Paul III	1534-1549
Damasus II	1048	Clement IV	1265-1268	Julius III	1550-1555
St. Leo IX	1049-1054	Bl. Gregory X	1271-1276	Marcellus II	1555
Victor II	1055-1057	Bl. Innocent V	1276	Paul IV	1555-1559
Stephen IX (X)	1057-1058	Adrian V	1276	Plus IV	1559-1565
[Benedict X]	[1058-1059]	John XXI	1276-1277	St. Pius V	1566-1572
Nicholas II	1059-1061	Nicholas III	1277-1280	Gregory XIII	1572-1585
Alexander II	1061-1073	Martin IV	1281-1285	Sixtus V	1585-1590
[Honorius II]	[1061-1072]	Honorius IV	1285-1287	Urban VII	1590
St. Gregory VII	1073-1085	Nicholas IV	1288-1292	Gregory XIV	1590-1591
[Clement III]	[1080-1100]	St. Celestine V	1294	Innocent IX	1591
Bl. Victor III	1086-1087	Boniface VIII	1294-1303	Clement VIII	1592-1605
Bl. Urban II	1088-1099	Bl. Benedict XI	1303-1304	Leo XI	1605
Paschal II	1099-1118	Clement V	1305-1314	Paul V	1605-1621
[Theodoric]	[1100]	John XXII	1316-1334	Gregory XV	1621-1623
[Albert]	[1102]	[Nicholas V]	[1328-1330]	Urban VIII	1623-1644
[Sylvester IV]	[1105-1111]	Benedict XII	1334-1342	Innocent X	1644-1655
Gelasius II	1118-1119	Clement VI	1342-1352	Alexander VII	1655-1667
[Gregory VIII]	[1118-1121]	Innocent VI	1352-1362	Clement IX	1667-1669
Callistus II	1119-1124	Bl. Urban V	1362-1370	Clement X	1670-1676
Honorius II	1124-1130	Gregory XI	1370-1378	Bl. Innocent XI	1676-1689
[Celestine II]	[1124]	Urban VI	1378-1389	Alexander VIII	1689-1691
Innocent II	1130-1143	Boniface IX	1389-1404	Innocent XII	1691-1700
[Anacletus II]	[1130-1138]	Innocent VII	1404-1406	Clement XI	1700-1721
[Victor IV]	[1138]	Gregory XII	1406-1415	Innocent XIII	1721-1724
Celestine II	1143-1144	[Clement VII, Avignon]	[1378-1394]	Benedict XIII	1724-1730
Lucius II	1144-1145	[Benedict XIII, Avignon]	[1394-1423]	Clement XII	1730-1740
Bl. Eugene III	1145-1153	[Clement VIII, Avignon]	[1423-1429]	Benedict XIV	1740-1758
Anastasius IV	1153-1154	[Benedict XIV, Avignon]	[1425-1430]	Clement XIII	1758-1769
Adrian IV	1154-1159	[Alexander V, Pisa]	[1409-1410]	Clement XIV	1769-1774
Alexander III	1159-1181	[John XXIII, Pisa]	[1410-1415]	Pius VI	1775-1799
[Victor IV]	[1159-1164]	Martin V	1417-1431	Pius VII	1800-1823
[Paschal III]	[1164-1168]	Eugene IV	1431-1447	Leo XII	1823-1829
[Callistus III]	[1168-1178]	[Felix V]	[1439-1449]	Pius VIII	1829-1830
[Innocent III]	[1179-1180]	Nicholas V	1447-1455	Gregory XVI	1831-1846
Lucius III	1181-1185	Callistus III	1455-1458	Pius IX	1846-1878
Urban III	1185-187	Plus II	1458-1464	Leo XIII	1878-1903
Gregory VIII	1187	Paul II	1464-1471	St. Pius X	1903-1914
Clement III	1187-1191	Sixtus IV	1471-1484	Benedict XV	1914-1922
Celestine III	1191-1198	Innocent VIII	1484-1492	Pius XI	1922-1939
Innocent III	1198-1216	Alexander VI	1492-1503	Pius XII	1939-1958
Honorius III	1216-1227	Pius III	1503	John XXIII	1958-1963
Gregory IX	1227-1241	Julius II	1503-1513	Paul VI	1963-1978
Celestine IV	1241	Leo X	1513-1521	John Paul I	1978
Innocent IV	1243-1254	Adrian VI	1522-1523	John Paul II	1978-
Alexander IV	1254-1261	Clement VII	1523-1534		

NOTE

For centuries the popes did not change their names. The first name change occurred when a Roman called Mercury, having been elected pope, chose the more suitable appellation of John II (533-535). From the time of Sergius IV (1009-1012)—his name had been Peter Buccaporca (Peter Pigmouth)—the taking of a new name has continued to the present, with two exceptions: Adrian VI (1522-1523) and Marcellus II (1555). The most popular papal names have been John, Gregory, Benedict, Clement, Innocent, Leo, and Pius. There has never been a Peter II or a John XX. John Paul I was the first pope to select a double name. The legend that a woman pope—Pope Joan—reigned between Leo IV (847-855) and Benedict III (855-858) has long been rejected by historians.

The foregoing list is based generally on the catalog of popes given in the Annuario pontificio, the official Vatican yearbook, with some changes dictated by recent scholarly research. It should be noted that the legitimacy of certain popes—for example, Dioscorus (530), Leo VIII (963-965), Benedict V (964), Gregory VI (1045-1046), and Clement II (1046-1047)—is still controverted. Although Stephen (752) is mentioned in the list, he died three days after his election without being consecrated a bishop.

ing cardinals, whose number was set at seventy in 1588. Under Gregory XIII (1572-1585), papal nuncios to Catholic countries proved most valuable in implementing the ideals of Trent and in supervising the activities of the local bishops. The bishops of dioceses, who now had to submit regular reports to Rome and visit it at specified intervals, became much less independent. The success of the Counter-Reformation resulted from sound papal governance and the extraordinary contributions of the Jesuits and other religious orders.

SEVENTEENTH AND EIGHTEENTH CENTURIES. Skepticism, rationalism, and secularism became pervasive during the Enlightenment, and many intellectuals were violently opposed to the Catholic church and the papacy.

"Private property is a natural fruit of labor, a product of intense activity of man."

POPE PIUS XII
SEPTEMBER 1, 1944

The Thirty Years War (1618-1648), a series of religious and dynastic wars that involved most of Europe, embroiled the papacy in conflict. Paul V and Gregory XV (1621-1623) had little influence on the conduct of Catholic rulers. Innocent X (1644-1655) protested, albeit futilely, against the Peace of Westphalia (1648), because he felt that Catholics were treated unjustly. This war and its aftermath showed how ineffective the papacy had become in European politics.

During the following decades the popes were active in many areas. In the theological area, Innocent X repudiated five propositions on the theology of grace found in the writings of the Flemish bishop Cornelis Jansen; Alexander VII (1655-1667) rejected laxism as a moral system; and Alexander VIII (1689-1691) acted similarly against rigorism. The most dramatic papal action of the eighteenth century occurred when Clement XIV (1769-1774), bending to pressure from the Bourbon monarchies and fearing possible schism in France and Spain, suppressed the Society of Jesus in 1773.

THE MODERN PERIOD

Dramatic shifts in the prestige and authority of the papacy have occurred between the era of the French Revolution and the twentieth century.

REVOLUTION AND RESTORATION. The French Revolution, which began in 1789, and the subsequent actions of Napoleon created a new political order in Europe that adversely affected the Roman Catholic church. Pius VI (1775-1799), who had little sympathy with the ideals of the revolution, was unable to deal effectively with such vehement defiance of the Holy See and such massive threats to the very existence of religion. At times it seemed as if the papacy itself would be destroyed. The octogenarian and infirm Pius was taken prisoner by Napoleon and died in exile on his way to Paris. Resistance to Napoleonic aggression continued during the pontificate of Pius VII (1800-1823). The Concordat of 1801 with Napoleon, which for over a century regulated the relationship between France and the church, revealed that Pius was willing to make concessions for the sake of peace. Yet in 1809 Napoleon captured Rome, annexed the Papal States, and arrested the pope and held him prisoner until 1814. The Catholic restoration began after the defeat of Napoleon: the Congress of Vienna (1814-1815) returned most of the papal territory to the church, and in 1814 Pius restored the Society of Jesus.

The thirty-two-year pontificate of Pius IX (1846-1878), the longest in history, was significant. Initially hailed as a liberal, he soon showed his advocacy of ultramontanism. He restored the Catholic hierarchies of England (1850) and the Netherlands (1853), began a renewal of Marian devotion by his definition of the Immaculate Conception of Mary (1854), and supported extensive missionary activity. His greatest disappointment was the loss of the Papal States in 1870, which ended a millennium of temporal sovereignty. Pius's greatest triumph was the First Vatican Council (1869-1870), which ended abruptly when Italian troops occupied Rome. It produced two constitutions: *Dei filius*, a reaffirmation of the centrality of revelation, and *Pastor aeternus*, a definition of papal primacy and infallibility.

VATICAN I AND MODERNITY. The most formal and detailed exposition of papal prerogatives is found in *Pastor aeternus*. In regard to primacy it taught that Jesus conferred upon Peter a primacy of both honor and jurisdiction; that by divine right Peter has perpetual successors in primacy over the universal church; that the Roman pontiff is the successor of Peter and has supreme, ordinary (not delegated), and immediate power and jurisdiction over the church and its members; and that the Roman pontiff is the supreme judge who is not subject to review by anyone. In regard to infallibility, Vatican I taught that by divine assistance the pope is immune from error when he speaks *ex cathedra*—that is, when "by virtue of his supreme apostolic authority he defines a doctrine concerning faith or morals to be held by the universal church." The formidable conception of the papacy at Vatican I was a victory for ultramontanism. Using juridical and monarchical language, it asserted the universal spiritual authority of the pope.

The popes between Vatican I and Vatican II, individuals of superior quality, had much in common. First, they were all committed to the spiritual restoration of Catholicism, using their magisterial and jurisdictional authority to that end. Second, the popes continued to centralize church administration in Rome by increasing the power of the Roman Curia and the diplomatic corps. Third, the papal office actively promoted missionary endeavors. Fourth, the popes, at times reluctantly and unsuccessfully, tried to respond to the demands of a changing world. They sought amicable relations with secular governments, especially through concordats, and worked devotedly for social justice and peace.

The popes of this period continued the ultramontanist policies of the nineteenth century, but with a difference. Leo XIII (1878-1903), for example, was more open to the positive aspects of modernity. His successor, Pius X (1903-1914), desired to renew the interior life of the church, as is shown by his teachings on the Eucharist, the liturgy, and seminary education. During World War I, the complete impartiality of Benedict XV (1914-1922) brought criticism from all sides. In 1917 he promulgated the first Code of Canon Law. The pope of the interwar years was Pius XI (1922-1939), noted for his encyclicals on marriage (*Casti connubii,* 1930) and social thought (*Quadragesimo anno,* 1931). Finally, Pius XII (1939-1958), a trained diplomat with broad interests, addressed almost every aspect of church life, and in a prodigious number of pronouncements applied Catholic doctrine to contemporary problems.

VATICAN II AND POSTCONCILIAR DEVELOPMENTS. John XXIII (1958-1963), elected when he was nearly seventy-seven, began a new era for Roman Catholicism. His open style of papal leadership, enhanced by his appealing personality, was warmly welcomed by Catholics and non-Catholics alike. Although he is well known for his efforts in promoting ecumenism and world peace (*Pacem in terris,* 1963), the pope's greatest accomplishment was the unexpected convocation of the Second Vatican Council (1962-1965). John designed the council to foster reform and reunion, believing that a contemporary reformulation of the Christian tradition would revitalize the Catholic church and ultimately benefit all humankind. Paul VI (1963-1978) skillfully maintained the council's pastoral orientation. To implement its program, he established the Synod of Bishops, internationalized and increased the number of cardinals, reformed the Curia, and promoted liturgical reform. He made nine trips outside Italy.

Vatican II supplied what was lacking in Vatican I. Its doctrine of collegiality described the relationship between the pope and the bishops. The Constitution on the Church (*Lumen gentium*) stated: "Together with its head, the Roman Pontiff, and never without this head, the episcopal order is the subject of supreme and full power in relation to the universal church. But this power can be exercised only with the consent of the Roman Pontiff" (Article 22). The college of bishops, then, exists only under the leadership of the pope, himself a bishop. The pope is not the executor of the bishops' wishes (Gallicanism), nor are the bishops vicars of the pope (papal absolutism). Both the papacy and the episcopacy have their own legitimate authority, and the purpose of collegiality is to unite the bishops with the pope.

The theory of collegiality has altered the style of papal leadership, making it far less monarchical. The closer relationship between the pope and the bishops is best exemplified by the Synod of Bishops, a consultative body that meets once every three years. Collegiality has made the papacy less objectionable to other Christians since it fosters the idea of authority as service and not domination. This aspect has been noted in the fifth dialogue of the Lutheran-Roman Catholic

POPE PAUL VI

John Paul VI implemented the spirit of Vatican II by establishing the Synod of Bishops, internationalizing and increasing the number of cardinals and promoting liturgical reform.

DAVID LEES/© CORBIS

discussions (1974) and in the Final Report of the Anglican-Roman Catholic International Commission (1982). Both groups recognized the value of a universal Petrine ministry of unity in the Christian church and foresaw the possibility of the bishop of Rome exercising that function for all Christians in the future.

In 1978 two popes died and two were elected. The pontificate of John Paul I, the successor of Paul VI, lasted only thirty-three days. Breaking a tradition that had endured for more than nine hundred years, John Paul I was not installed by a rite of coronation or enthronement. He rejected the obvious symbols of temporal and monarchical authority and was inaugurated at a solemn mass. Instead of the tiara, he was given the pallium, a white woolen stole symbolizing his spiritual and pastoral ministry. His successor, John Paul II, became the first non-Italian pope in 456 years, the first Polish pope, and the first pope from a Communist country. The most-traveled pope in history, John Paul

The Second Vatican Council greatly influenced the renewal of moral theology.

PAGE 148

II earned huge popular appeal with his international pastoral visits.

[*For related discussions, see* Crusades; Inquisition, The; Reformation, The; Vatican Councils]

— PATRICK GRANFIELD

Following Dagan come seven Baals. The name Baal is derived from the common Semitic noun meaning "lord, master, husband."

PAGE 116/117

PHILISTINE RELIGION

Although many questions about the Philistines remain unanswered, including questions about Philistine religion, a variety of sources provide a modicum of evidence on this intriguing people. Most important among these are the Old Testament (Hebrew scriptures), the Egyptian texts, and archaeological materials from Palestine.

The Philistines were a warlike people who migrated from somewhere in the Aegean basin to the southern coastal plain of Palestine; the most important and best-documented phase of this migration took place in the early part of the twelfth century BCE. The Philistine invasion of the southeastern Levant is well known from the artistic and literary accounts at Medinet Habu in Egypt, where Ramses III left a record of his military encounter (c. 1190 BCE) with two groups of "Sea Peoples," the Tjekker and the Peleset. The Egyptians repelled the invasion, and some of the Sea Peoples settled in southern Palestine. This region was called Philistia, and the Greek name for the Philistines, *Palastinoi,* later evolved into *Palestine,* the modern name for the land as a whole. The major cities of the Philistines were Gaza, Ashdod, Ashqelon, Gath, and Ekron, the so-called Philistine pentapolis. Because of their expansion into the hinterland of Canaan, the Philistines (Heb., *pelishtim*) were major rivals of the Israelites during the Israelite conquest, settlement, and early monarchy, although the Philistine threat waned after their military defeat by King David (c. 950 BCE).

There is some evidence concerning Philistine origins in the archaeological record and the nonbiblical literature (e.g., the tendency to associate the Philistine migration with the ethnic upheaval at the end of the Greek Bronze Age, around 1200 BCE). But it is the Old Testament that contains the most direct statements concerning the Philistines' ancestral homeland. Several passages linking the Philistines with Caphtor, or Crete (cf. *Dt.* 2:23, *Jer.* 47:4, *Am.* 9:7), are among the many indications pointing to an Aegean background. *Genesis* 10:14 and *1 Chronicles* 1:12 identify Egypt as the Philistines' place of origin, but this can be understood in light of the Philistine migration route.

Excavations at numerous Palestinian sites, most of which are located in the coastal plain or the Shephelah (the western foothills of the Judean mountains), have yielded significant remains of Philistine material culture; the beautiful and distinctive painted pottery of the Philistines is undoubtedly the best-known aspect of their civilization. Unfortunately—and surprisingly—there is no written text that can be attributed to the Philistines with any degree of certainty. While this dearth of Philistine literature may be eliminated as archaeological research continues, it is obvious that any attempt to describe Philistine religion is severely limited by a lack of primary Philistine texts on the subject. Nevertheless, we are not totally ignorant of the Philistine pantheon and cult, since the Old Testament and the archaeological data can be gleaned for relevant details.

In her important study *The Philistines and Their Material Culture,* Trude Dothan has provided archaeologists with a thorough analysis of the types and groups into which Philistine pottery (found at some thirty Palestinian sites) can be divided. Dothan's summary statement concerning this pottery serves as a general introduction to Philistine religion as well: "Typologically, Philistine pottery reflects the Sea Peoples' Aegean background, plus certain Cypriot, Egyptian, and local Canaanite elements" (p. 94). A careful investigation of Philistine religion reveals a similar potpourri that points to the eclectic or assimilative nature of Philistine religion. Such assimilation is evident in the Philistines' pantheon, religious practices, temples, and cult objects.

PANTHEON. The members of the Philistine pantheon about whom we possess specific information—Dagon (or Dagan), Baalzebub (or Baalzebul), and Ashtoret (or Ashtaroth)—were all deities worshiped for centuries by the pre-Philistine occupants of Canaan. According to the biblical record, Dagon was the supreme god of the Philistine pantheon (*1 Sm.* 5:1-7, *1 Chr.* 10:10). Like many ancient high gods, he was probably understood as a god of war, since we read about the Philistines giving thanks to this deity after victory over two of their archenemies, Samson and Saul (*Jgs.* 16:23-24, *1 Chr.* 10:10). Dagon had temples in Gaza (*Jgs.* 16:21, 23-30), Ashdod (*1 Sm.* 5:1-7; *1 Mc.* 10:83-85, 11:4), and probably in Beth-shan (*1 Chr.* 10:10; cf. *1 Sm.* 31:10). The Ashdod temple housed a statue of Dagon. Interestingly, the biblical account points to the Philistine acknowledgment of the superiority of Yahveh over Dagon. As noted above, Dagon was an important god in the ancient Semitic pantheon (his name appears in Canaanite toponyms). He is known to have been worshiped at Ugarit, and, in fact, he was honored at ancient Ebla as early as the second half of the third millennium BCE.

Baalzebub, another member of the ancient Semitic pantheon, was closely associated with the Philistine town of Ekron (probably Tel Miqne): *2 Kings* 1:2-16 informs us that Baalzebub was consulted by an oracle and was in some way associated with healing. Baalzebul was a name used at Ugarit for Baal. Texts from the time of Ramses III indicate that the Philistines knew the god Baal when they invaded Egypt.

In addition to these members of the Semitic pantheon, there is evidence that the Philistines worshiped Egyptian deities. The wholesale assimilation apparent in the Philistine pantheon may indicate that the Philistine settlement in Palestine was a more gradual process than has previously been imagined. It should be remembered, however, that such borrowing of divine names and/or epithets was a common practice in ancient Near Eastern religions. Indeed, the Old Testament contains frequent denunciations of the Israelites' attraction toward and participation in religious practices of their neighbors, including the Philistines (*Jgs.* 10:6).

RELIGIOUS PRACTICES AND FUNCTIONARIES. According to *Judges* 16:23-24, the Philistines and their leaders gathered together for sacrifices and festivals. In fact, the Old Testament records an occasion when the Philistines sent a guilt offering to the God of Israel, since they had learned to respect this other national deity (*1 Sm.* 4:6, 5:1-6:21). Apparently, the Philistines carried or wore portable idols or amulets into battle (*2 Sm.* 5:21; cf. *2 Mc.* 12:40). The advice of priests and diviners was sought (*1 Sm.* 5:5, 6:2-9; cf. *2 Kgs.* 1:2), and the art of soothsaying was developed (*Is.* 2:6). With regard to burial customs, several Philistine sites have yielded whole or fragmentary anthropoid clay coffins, use of which was probably borrowed from the Egyptians.

Clearly, the religious practices of the Philistines were similar to those of their Semitic neighbors; the absence of circumcision seems to be the one exception (*Jgs.* 14:3; *1 Sm.* 17:26, 17:36, 18:25). Indeed, the Philistines' failure to practice this ritual enabled the Israelites to refer to their archenemies as "the uncircumcised" (*Jgs.* 15:18; *1 Sm.* 14:6, 31:4).

TEMPLES AND CULT OBJECTS. A large number and wide variety of cult objects have been recovered in the excavations of Philistine strata, especially at Gezer, Ashdod, and Tell Qasile. They include kernos rings and bowls, decorated bowls and vases, zoomorphic and anthropomorphic figurines, ritual stands, rhytons, and so on. Of special interest are the numerous kernos rings and bowls, especially since these Early Iron Age Philistine objects show affinities to objects from the final years of Mycenaean culture. Also important is a series of lion-headed libation cups from Philistine sites in Palestine, vessels that have similarities with rhytons from the Mycenaean-Minoan tradition.

Without a doubt, the most frequently discussed cult object associated with the Philistines is the stylized female figurine called the Ashdoda (so named after the site where it was found). The Ashdoda looks like a throne or couch into which human body parts—a head, elongated neck, armless torso, and molded breasts—have been merged; the entire figurine is elaborately painted. According to Trude Dothan, this figurine is probably "a schematic representation of a female deity and throne" (p. 234), an object with clear-cut Aegean antecedents. It is part of a group of Ashdodas, now fragmentary, found in strata at Ashdod that date from the twelfth to the eighth century BCE.

The Ashdoda, together with other artifacts and features of Philistine material culture and religion, has prompted many scholars to view Philistine religion in terms of its Aegean background. Here the term *Aegean* is used broadly and includes Crete, Cyprus, and the Greek islands and mainland. Yet it is also clear that the Philistines assimilated much—including a number of religious beliefs and practices—from their Semitic neighbors.

— GERALD L. MATTINGLY

PRAYER

Prayer, understood as the human communication with divine and spiritual entities, has been present in most of the religions in human history. Viewed from most religious perspectives, prayer is a necessity of the human condition.

PRAYER AS TEXT

Prayer is thought of most commonly as the specific words of the human-spiritual communication, that is, as the text of this communication, such as the Lord's Prayer (Christian), the Qaddish (Jewish), and the prayers of *salat* (Muslim).

A common basic typology of prayer has been formulated by discerning what distinguishes the character and intent expressed by the words of prayer texts. This kind of typology includes a number of classes, all easily distinguished by their descriptive designations. It includes petition, invocation, thanksgiving (praise or adoration), dedication, supplication, intercession, confession, penitence, and benediction. Such types may constitute whole prayers or they may be strung together to form a structurally more complex prayer.

In perhaps the most extensive comparative study of prayer, *Prayer: A Study in the History and Psychology of Religion* (1932), Friedrich Heiler understood prayer as a pouring out of the heart before God. However, when the understanding of prayer as a free and spontaneous "living communion of man with God" (Heiler) is conjoined with the general restriction of prayer to the text

The Christian church has taken the Lord's Prayer as indicating both the spirit of prayer and a formula to be employed in worship.

PAGE 423

form, incongruency, confusion, and dilemma arise. Prayer texts, almost without exception and to a degree as part of their nature, are formulaic, repetitive, and static in character, much in contrast with the expected free and spontaneous character of prayer.

Heiler held that prayer texts were, in fact, not true prayers, but were rather artificially composed for the purpose of edifying, instructing, and influencing people in the matters of dogma, belief, and tradition.

Due to the nature of the materials available, prayers must often be considered primarily, if not solely, as texts, whose study is limited to the semantic, informational, and literary aspects of the language that constitutes them. Despite such limitations, the texts of prayers reflect theological, doctrinal, cultural, historical, aesthetic, and creedal dimensions of a religious culture.

"A single thankful thought towards heaven is the most perfect of all prayers."

GOTTHOLD EPHRAIM LESSING
MINNA VON BARNHELM

PRAYER AS ACT

Intuitively prayer is an act of communication. In its most common performance, prayer is an act of speech.

The distinction between personal and ritual prayer has often been made when viewing prayer as act. Personal prayer, regarded as the act of persons pouring forth their hearts to God, has been considered by many as the truest form, even the only true form, of prayer. Yet, the data available for the study of personal prayer are scant. Still, the record of personal prayers found in letters, biographies, and diaries suggests a strong correlation and interdependence of personal prayer with ritual and liturgical prayer in language, form, style, and physical attitude. A person praying privately is invariably a person who is part of a religious and cultural tradition in which ritual or public prayer is practiced.

Ritual prayer, by not conforming to the naive notions of the spontaneity and free form of prayer, has often been set aside. It can be shown that prayer when formulaic, repetitive, and redundant in message can be a true act of communication, even heartfelt. In recent years a range of studies has developed showing the performative power of language and speech acts. Simply put, these studies show that language and other forms of human action not only say things, that is, impart information, they also do things. Ordinary language acts may persuade, name, commit, promise, declare, affirm, and so on; and these functions are often more primary than that of transmitting information.

When prayer is considered as act, the unresponsive and noncreative dimensions that seem inseparable from the rigidity of words tend to dissolve, for a prayer act always involves one praying in a historical, cultural, social, and psychological setting. These ever-changing contextual elements are necessarily a part of the act. In some prayer traditions, the Navajo of North America for example, it has been shown that highly formulaic constituents of prayer are ordered in patterns and conjoined with familiar ritual elements in combinations that express very specifically the heartfelt needs and motivations of a single person for whom the prayer is uttered. Analogous to ordinary language where familiar words can be ordered according to a single set of grammatical principles in infinite ways to be creative and expressive, prayer passages may be ordered in conjunction with ritual elements to achieve the same communicative capabilities.

When prayer is considered as act, a whole range of powerful characteristics and religious functions may be discerned. Here the issue is not primarily to show that prayer is communication with the spiritual or divine, or even necessarily to discern what is communicated, but rather to direct attention to the comprehension and appreciation of the power and effectiveness of communication acts that are human-divine communications.

PRAYER AS SUBJECT

Prayer is also a subject that is much written and talked about. It is the subject of theory, of theology, of sermons, of doctrine, of devotional guides, of prescribed ways of worship and ways of life, and of descriptions of methods of prayer. The extent of literature in religious traditions about prayer is massive and ranges from personal meditations on the "way of prayer" to formal theologies and philosophies of prayer. In these writings, prayer becomes the subject by which to articulate the principles and character of a religious tradition or a strain within a tradition.

— SAM D. GILL

PREHISTORIC RELIGIONS

The term *prehistory* refers to the vast period of time between the appearance of humanity's early hominid ancestors and the beginning of the historical period. Since the invention of writing is used to mark the transition between prehistory and history, the date of this boundary varies greatly from region to region. The study of prehistoric religion, therefore, can refer to religious beliefs and practices from as early as 60,000 BCE to almost the present day. Generally, however, the term *prehistory* is defined by its European application and hence refers to the period from the Paleolithic period, which occurred during the Pleistocene epoch, to the protohistoric Neolithic period and the Bronze and Iron ages.

Access to a prehistoric culture is highly problematic. And when one attempts to understand a phenomenon such as religion, the problem becomes acute. We understand religion primarily in terms of "language," that is, its principal characteristics are its interpretive meanings and valuations. The wordless archaeological remains of prehistoric religion—cultic or ceremonial artifacts and sites, pictures and symbols, sacrifices—have provided limited access to the religious "language" of prehistoric cultures. For example, knowledge of how corpses were disposed during the Neolithic period does not reveal why they were so disposed. Consequently, even when there is clear evidence of a prehistoric religious practice, interpretation of the nature of prehistoric religions remains highly speculative and disproportionately dependent upon analogies to contemporary "primitive" cultures.

Our knowledge of prehistoric religion is therefore the product of reconstructing a "language" from its silent material accessories. Among the oldest material forms of cultic practice are burial sites, dating from the Middle Paleolithic. One can trace, from the Upper Paleolithic on, a growing richness and diversity of grave goods that reach extravagant proportions during the Iron Age. The practices of second burials, the burning of bodies, and the ritual disposition of skulls are also common. Megalithic graves date back to the Neolithic period. Despite the cultic implications of these massive stone constructions (e.g., ancestor cults), a uniform religious meaning remains undemonstrated.

Evidences of sacrifices from the Middle Paleolithic period in the form of varied quantities of animal bones near burial sites suggest offerings to the dead. Sacrificial traditions that were associated with game (e.g., bear ceremonialism) date back to the Upper Paleolithic. There is no evidence of human sacrifice prior to the Neolithic period, and hence this practice is associated with the transition from a hunter-gatherer culture to an agrarian culture and, consequently, with the domestication of plants and animals. [*See* Sacrifice.]

Prehistoric works of art dating back to the Paleolithic period—paintings, drawings, engravings, and sculpture—are the richest form of access to prehistoric religion. The primary subjects of these earliest examples of graphic art were animals; humans, rarely depicted, were often drawn with animal attributes. The intimate and unique role of animals in the physical and mental lives of these early hunter-gatherers is clearly demonstrated. (This role is also evidenced in the sacrificial traditions.) Though some form of animalism is suggested, the religious significance of these animal figures is difficult to interpret.

Shamanistic practices are also reflected in this art, especially in the paintings of birds and of animals that have projectiles drawn through their bodies. Common in prehistoric sculpture is the female statuette. Although frequently related to fertility, these figurines are open to numerous interpretations of equal plausibility (e.g., spirit abodes, ancestor representations, house gods, as well as spirit rulers over animals, lands and other physical or spiritual regions, hunting practices, and natural forces).

It is unlikely that we shall ever be able adequately to interpret the "language" of prehistoric religion. The material evidence is too scarce and the nature of religious phenomena too complex. There is, however, a meaning in these wordless fragments that is itself significant for any study of religion. The power and depth of these silent archaeological remains cause one to recognize the limitation of written language as a purveyor of religious meaning. The connections one is able, however tenuously, to draw between the evidences of religious life among prehistoric peoples and the beliefs and practices of their descendants address the conditions that have inspired human beings, from our beginnings, to express our deepest selves in art and ritual.

— MARY EDWARDSEN AND JAMES WALLER

PRESBYTERIANISM, REFORMED

Presbyterians are Catholic in their affirmation of the triune God and of the creeds of the ancient Catholic Church: the Apostles' Creed, the Nicene Creed, and the Chalcedonian definition. They are Protestant in the sense of Martin Luther's treatises of 1520. Their Reformed roots are in the Reformation at Zurich, under the leadership of Ulrich Zwingli (1484-1531) and Heinrich Bullinger (1504-1575); at Strasbourg, under Martin Bucer (1491-1551); and at Geneva, with the work of John Calvin (1509-1564).

REFORMED THEOLOGY AT THE TIME OF THE REFORMATION. Reformed theology was a type of Protestantism—as distinct from Lutheranism, Anglicanism, and the theology of the radical Reformation—that originated in Switzerland, the upper Rhineland, and France. Most of the early Reformed theologians had a background in Christian humanism. The Reformed church insisted upon positive scriptural warrant for all church practice.

Reformed theology was characterized by its emphasis upon the doctrine of God, who was conceived not so much as beauty or truth but as energy, activity, power, intentionality, and moral purpose. Reformed theologians believed that all of life and history is rooted in the decrees or purposes of God. They emphasized the lordship of God in history and in the salvation of the Christian as emphasized in the doctrine of predestination. John Calvin, the most influential of Reformed theologians, was not a speculative

An urbane French lawyer and humanist by background, John Calvin was the embodiment of both the differentiation of Reformation views and of its European dimension.

PAGE 571

thinker. While rejecting curiosity as destructive of faith, Calvin insisted that Christians should know what they believed; the way a person thinks determines action. Calvin also placed high value upon verbal expressions of faith. The sermon became the focus of Reformed worship.

REFORMED LITURGY. In liturgy the Reformed churches placed a premium upon intelligibility and edification. As with life generally, Calvin insisted that worship should be simple, free from theatrical trifles. The sacraments were limited to the Lord's Supper and baptism, which were believed to have been instituted by Jesus Christ. Among the more prominent documents of the liturgical tradition are Huldrych Zwingli's *Liturgy of the Word,* Guillaume Farel's *The Order Observed in Preaching,* Calvin's *The Form of Church Prayers,* and John Knox's *The Form of Prayers.*

PRESBYTERIAN POLITY. Presbyterianism is not a fixed pattern of church life but a developing pattern that has both continuity and diversity. Many features of the system vary from time to time and from place to place. In the United States, for example, Presbyterianism developed from the congregation to the presbytery, to the synod, to the General Assembly. In Scotland, Presbyterianism grew out of a gradually evolving notion of how the church should be governed, out of conflict with episcopacy, and from the General Assembly down to the congregation.

The English term priest can be used in many religious traditions to designate those who have been ordained or set apart.

PAGE 537

Presbyterians find the roots of their polity in the reforming activity of Calvin. In his doctrine of the church, Calvin's primary emphasis was on the action of the Holy Spirit, who created the church through word and sacrament. Jesus Christ is the only head of the church, and under him all are equal. In addition, Calvin struggled all his life for a church that was independent of state control. He held to the notion of a Christian society with a magistrate whose work in the civil order is a vocation from God, but ideally Calvin wanted church and state to work together under God yet in independence of each other organizationally. Calvin placed great emphasis on the minister, who interprets and applies the word of God.

There are four basic principles of presbyterian polity. The first is the authority of scripture. The other three principles of presbyterian polity relate to form of governance and relations among clergy and between clergy and laity.

— JOHN H. LEITH

PRIESTHOOD

USAGE IN THE WEST. The strict sense of the meaning of *priest* prevailed prior to modern times, while looser and more inclusive applications of the term have come into use more recently. This development has to do with religious and conceptual horizons of the Christian West, in which the vocabulary of Latin and its derivatives has been dominant. In the traditions of the Judeo-Christian West, our point will become clear when we consider circumstances in which the term *priest* has not been used. The two principal cases are the Jewish and the Protestant.

For Judaism, priesthood is a well-defined and central role in the biblical tradition. The performance of sacrifices was one of its essential characteristics. The priests carried out the sacrificial ritual at altars, and from the seventh century BCE onward such ceremony was centralized at the temple in Jerusalem. Religious leadership in the synagogue, which replaced the temple, passed to the rabbis in their role as teachers. As far as the Hebraic context is concerned, the terms we translate by *priest* regularly imply the performance of sacrifice, and in the absence of the sacrifice the concept has been considered inapplicable.

Protestants do not generally refer to their clergy as "priests" either. But Protestants do have a conception of priesthood, referred to as "the priesthood of all believers." In avoiding the term *priest* as a designation of their own clergy, most Protestants have implied a repudiation of the notion that priestly ordination should elevate any man above his fellow human beings or confer on him any access to the divine that is denied others. Protestants did differ from Rome on the senses in which the Lord's Supper, the eucharistic meal of the Mass, might be considered in itself a sacrifice, for they held that Jesus' self-sacrifice was commemorated rather than repeated. But the truly sore point was the privileged, controlling status enjoyed by the officiating Roman clergy.

DESCRIPTION OF PRIESTHOOD IN NON-WESTERN RELIGION. A great many other activities and attributes of priests in the European Christian tradition have built up a range of connotations. Priests in the West generally wear ceremonial robes while officiating and have distinctive details of street clothing; hence, Western visitors to Japan, for instance, termed the robed personnel of temples "priests," whether Shinto or Buddhist. Priests in the Latin Christian tradition are unmarried; hence the disposition of visitors to Sri Lanka, Burma, or Thailand sometimes to refer to Buddhist monks as "priests," even if the status of their ritual as a sacrifice is debatable. Priests are inducted into their office through ordination; hence the tendency to view tribal societies' ritually initiated specialists in divination, exorcism, healing, and the like as priests. Priests deliver sermons and moral injuctions; hence, presumably, occasional references to the *'ulama',* or religious scholars of traditional Islamic lands, as

BUDDHIST PRIESTS

Western visitors to Southeast Asia sometimes refer to Buddhist monks as "priests" because clerics in the west generally wear ceremonial robes while officiating.

THE PURCELL TEAM/CORBIS

priests, despite the fact that they are neither ordained nor do they perform ritual sacrifice.

ELIGIBILITY FOR PRIESTHOOD. The world's priests in various traditions can be divided into what one might term *hereditary* priesthoods and *vocational* priesthoods. In the first case, the priestly prerogatives and duties are the special heritage of particular family or tribal lineages. The ancient Hebrew priesthood, for example, was reserved to the Levites, or descendants of Levi. Similarly, hereditary is the priesthood in Zoroastrianism. Traditionally, fathers who were practicing priests trained their sons in the proper recitation of the prayers.

It is generally expected that the clergy in hereditary priesthoods will marry, so that the line may be perpetuated. Indeed, the genealogical awareness of hereditary priesthoods is often as carefully documented as is that of royalty, and for similar reasons.

What one may call a vocational priesthood, on the other hand, recruits its members from the pool of promising young people in the community. Celibacy is something that a tradition of vocational priesthood can require, as does the Roman Catholic Church, but many vocational priesthoods still permit marriage, such as those of the Greek Orthodox, Russian Orthodox, and other Eastern Christian churches.

In the vast majority of the world's religious traditions, eligibility for priesthood has been restricted to males. The Hindu, Buddhist, Taoist, Zoroastrian, and Christian traditions have had exclusively male clergy until modern times. Judaism likewise restricted the rabbinate (its equivalent to the more inclusive current sense of the term *priest*) to males. In today's world various branches of both Christianity and Judaism have begun to ordain women to serve as the ritual and spiritual leaders of congregations.

Another feature of eligibility for priesthood is a sound physical and mental condition. Traditional Roman Catholic custom has required in particular that the hands of a priest, which perform the sacrament, be without deformity.

"A man with God is always in the majority."

JOHN KNOX

TRAINING AND ORDINATION. A wide variety of instruction, training, and initiation for work as a priest exists among the world's religious traditions. [*See* Ordination.] The content of the training is generally a blend of three components that one could term the practical, the theoretical, and the disciplinary.

The practical side of a priest's training includes most saliently the skills the community expects for correct performance of ritual. In a great many traditional settings the efficacy of a prayer or incantation has been held to depend on the acoustic correctness of its utterance. The Hindu concept of *mantra* as a verbal formula entails such training on the part of those who will pronounce *mantras,* and in the view of many Zoroastrians the exactness of the priests' pronunciation of the liturgical prayers in the Avestan language is what makes the prayers effective.

Besides the formulas of the ritual text itself there is much else for a priest to learn: where the ceremonial objects and the officiant should be placed; how the right time for an observance is to be determined; and so on. Where the celebration of a ritual has depended for its timing on direct observation of the sun, moon, or stars, the training of a priest has necessitated mastering a certain amount of practical astronomy. Where the means of divination have included the bones or entrails of animals, the priest has of necessity had to be a practical veterinary surgeon. Indeed, it is instructive to observe in the history of cultures that many professions that became independent specializations have had their origin as branches of priestly learning.

What can be termed theoretical training stands at the other end of the spectrum. Training for priesthood thus may contain a substantial component of historical and philosophical study, in which the prospective congregational leader is given at least a rudimentary exposure to the results of scriptural and doctrinal scholarship.

Dramatic shifts in the prestige and authority of the papacy have occurred between the era of the French Revolution and the twentieth century.

PAGE 548

The perceived need for competence in theoretical matters has generally led religious communities to develop courses of formal academic instruction for their priests (or comparable personnel) in theological studies. Throughout the Islamic world, religious scholarship flourished in a type of school known as a *madrasah* meaning etymologically "place of study." In medieval Europe, the origin of universities as institutions was frequently closely tied to the need to educate the Christian clergy, and in a number of northern European countries since the Protestant Reformation both Protestant and Roman Catholic theological faculties have continued to be integral parts of the older universities.

Under the heading of "discipline" can be considered a third kind of preparation for priesthood. In various cultures, from tribal to modern, the priest-to-be is expected to undertake regimes of physical or spiritual self-cultivation—the better to be worthy of, or effective in, the practice of his role.

Celibacy for priests is a discipline for which a number of rationales have been offered. There is, of course, the notion of sexual activity as a physical pollution. Beyond this may lie a cosmological or metaphysical view most characteristic of gnostic and Manichaean thinking, that the very perpetuation of physical existence in this world hinders the eventual release of pure spirit from its imprisonment in inherently evil matter.

The most nearly universal discipline among the world's priesthoods is probably the discipline of meditation. The priest in his exercise of his role may be expected to lead others in meditation; in his training, he is prepared by its practice. A general feeling of well-being or decisiveness can be a personal benefit of meditation to those who practice it; but as a spiritual discipline, meditation needs to serve an unselfish goal, the control of the self and dedication of the priest's personal identity to a power or cause beyond himself.

Upon completion of his training, the priest is ceremonially inducted into the exercise of his role, a process to which Westerners often apply the Christian term *ordination.* Among Christians, the notion of "apostolic succession" implies that each priest has a pedigree of ordination going back to the apostles. Buddhist lineages are similar in that monks or pupils trace their ordination back for centuries to earlier teachers.

THE FUTURE OF PRIESTHOOD. The challenge of maintaining an ancient ritual tradition in a modern secular and technological age is a major one. In most of the modern world's religious communities, recruitment of priests is a pressing problem. The celibate life, for instance, surely deters many Roman Catholic males from opting for a priestly vocation. Economic considerations are also a factor: the offerings of the faithful sometimes no longer support a priest in the comfort, compared with other lines of work, that they once afforded. Priests have been reduced to mendicant roles even in those communities which have not characteristically expected priests to be poor. Among the Zoroastrian Parsis of India, most priests are paid on a piecework basis for prayers said, as opposed to being salaried.

Even more serious than this is a widespread decline in intellectual respect for priests throughout the contemporary world. Modern secularist criticism of traditional religious affirmations has to a certain extent called the content of the priest's affirmations into question, and the response from the pulpit has unfortunately sometimes been pietistic obscurantism. But at least as important has been the sociological fact of the growth of other skills and professions around the world. Today it is not unusual for the spiritual leader of a congregation to count among his flock scientists, engineers, or other professionals whose training is much more highly focused than his own. The challenge of life's ultimate questions, however, persists. Priesthood will probably attract able personnel in significant and perhaps sufficient numbers for many generations to come.

[*See also* Ministry.]

— WILLARD G. OXTOBY

PROTESTANTISM

Protestantism is a worldwide movement that derives from sixteenth-century reforms of Western Christianity. As a movement it is both a set of church bodies and a less well defined ethos, spirit, and cultural achievement. Thus, one speaks of Reformed or Methodist churches as being Protestant, just as one may speak of a "Protestant ethic" or a "Protestant nation."

FOUR PROTESTANT CLUSTERS. For demographic purposes, David B. Barrett in his *World Christian Encyclopedia* (1982) tries to bring some order to definitional chaos by classifying the non-Roman Catholic and non-Orthodox part of the Christian world into five families, or blocs, which he calls "Protestant," "nonwhite indigenous," "Anglican," "marginal Protestant," and "Catholic (non-Roman)." All but the last of these have some sort of Protestant ties. The mainstream Protestant category includes long-established Northern Hemisphere churches such as the Congregationalist and Baptist. The Anglican family includes plural, low church, high church, evangelical, Anglo-Catholic, and central (or Broad church) traditions. The category of marginal Protestants includes Jehovah's Witnesses, Mormons, Religious Science, and Unitarian, Spiritualist, and British-Israelite churches.

PROTESTANT DIVERSITY AND COHERENCE. The first perception of both old and new Protestantism has always been its diversity. Barrett claims that the one billion and more practicing Christians of the world belong to 20,780 distinct denominations. While more than half the Christians are Catholic, the vast majority of these 20,780 denominations would be classed as part of the Protestant movement. Thus, in classic Protestantism, in 1980 there were almost 345 million people in 7,889 of these distinct bodies in 212 nations. The nonwhite indigenous versions, almost all of them Protestant, were located in 10,065 distinct bodies. There were also 225 Anglican denominations and 1,345 "marginal Protestant" groups. Indeed, this diversity and this fertility at creating new, unrelated bodies were long used as a criticism of Protestantism by Roman Catholicism, which united under the Roman pope, and by Orthodoxy, which was divided more into national jurisdictions but saw itself as united in holy tradition.

It is possible to move behind this first perception of the chaos of unrelated bodies to see some forms of coherence. Great numbers of Protestant bodies, along with many Orthodox ones, are members of the World Council of Churches, established in 1948, which has a uniting confessional theme around the lordship of Jesus Christ. In many nations there are national councils or federations of cooperating churches, which allow for positive interaction even where there is not organic unity. World confessional families of Lutherans, Reformed, Baptists, and others throughout the twentieth century have brought into some concord these churches that have family resemblances. Finally, there have been significant mergers of Protestant churches both within families, such as Lutheran with Lutheran, Presbyterian with Presbyterian, and across

COMMON GROUND
Rites that Protestants Share

While the resistance to papal claims is a uniting factor, it is not likely that many people ever choose to remain loyal to Protestantism on such marginal and confining grounds alone. The first common mark of Protestantism is historically clear and clean; virtually all Protestant groups derive from movements that began in the sixteenth century. When later groups were formed, as were the Disciples of Christ in nineteenth-century America, they may not have seen themselves as working out the logic of earlier Protestantism; yet historians at once traced the roots of this typical new group to various older Presbyterian and Baptist forms, among others.

A very few Protestant groups can also trace their lineage back to pre-Reformation times. Modern Waldensians, for example, are heirs of a movement begun under Pierre Valdès (Peter Waldo) in the twelfth century, and some modern Czech churches are heirs of traditions that go back to the Hussite Jednota Bratrská (Society of Brethren, known in Latin as Unitas Fratrum) of the fifteenth century. At another point on the spectrum is the Church of England, or Anglicanism. Most of its articulators stress that they remain the church Catholic as it has been on English soil since the christianization of England. Although it has kept faith in the apostolic succession of bishops and has retained many pre-Reformation practices, the Anglican communion as it has existed since the break with Rome under Henry VIII in the sixteenth century is vastly different from the Catholic church under Roman papal obedience in England before and since the Reformation. In short, the Waldensians, the Czech groups, and the Anglicans alike were, and were seen to be, part of the Protestant revolt from both the viewpoints of Roman Catholic leadership and historical scholarship ever since. Individual groups may have parentage in the Middle Ages or may have sprung up late in the twentieth century, yet the sixteenth-century breach in Christendom is the event by which Protestant existence is somehow measured.

—MARTIN E. MARTY

The Protestant rejection of the authority of the pope is closely joined to a redefinition of the nature of the church.

PAGE 166

family lines, as in America's United Church of Christ, which blended a New England Congregationalist tradition with a German Reformed heritage.

— MARTIN E. MARTY

GOD IN PROTESTANTISM. All Christian movements, unlike some other religions, focus finally on their witness to God. Protestantism is theistic. There have been momentary expressions by theological elites of a "Christian atheism," but these have been dismissed by the Protestant public as idiosyncratic, personal forms of witness or philosophical expression.

At the left wing of marginal Protestantism stand some former Protestant groups that have retained certain elements of the Protestant tradition. Among these are Unitarianisms of humanistic sorts and Ethical Culture movements, which grew up on Jewish soil in America but acquired some Protestant traits.

"All Protestantism, even the most cold and passive, is a sort of dissent."

EDMUND BURKE
MARCH 22, 1775

If Protestants are not humanistic or atheistic, they also are not pantheistic. Individual pantheists may exist as mystics, and there have been pantheistic Protestant heresies, so regarded both by those who have innovated with them and by those who have excluded their advocates. In some formal theological circles, one sometimes hears advocated teachings that seem to verge on pantheism, the proposition that the world and God are coextensive, identical. Yet articulators of such teachings usually take pains to distance themselves from pure pantheism.

Protestantism on occasion has had deistic proponents, agents of a natural religion that made no room for a personal God, special revelation, or reasons to pray to an unresponsive, divine, originating, but now absentee force. Yet deism has consistently in due course been seen as a deviation from, not a part of, the Protestant impulse.

AUTHORITY AND STRUCTURE: THE SCRIPTURES. The Bible of Protestantism is the canon of the Old and New Testaments, and almost never the Apocrypha, which has special status in the Orthodox and Catholic traditions. The canon is theoretically open; it is conceivable that a book could still be added to it. While the Bible has become the only document used and useful for uniting Protestant witness or helping determine Protestant theological argument—it provides at least something of the genetic programming of Protestantism, or the ground rules for their games—there is here as so often a very broad spectrum of approaches to its authority. Most Protestants have accepted the Lutheran mark *sola scriptura,* that the Bible alone is the authority; but this formula tells all too little about how to regard the book.

At one extreme, conservative Protestants who have resisted modern historical criticism of biblical texts stress that the Bible is somehow not only inspired but infallible and inerrant. At the other end of the spectrum are a minority of Protestants, chiefly in academic centers, who have completely adopted post-Enlightenment views of biblical criticism. They have thus treated the biblical text as they would any other ancient literary text. They grant no special status to the inspiration of biblical authors. For them the Bible still has authority as a document that both reflects and promotes the norms of the Christian community. Many schools of interpretation, even among those who have immersed themselves in historical and literary criticism, find that the Bible "discloses," or potentially discloses, what God would reveal.

THE AUTHORITY OF THE CHURCH. Lacking paper authority as they do, and unwilling as they are for the most part to yield to bishops as having a determinative role in dispensing tradition, how do Protestants see the authority of the church? The vast majority of Protestants in all ages, though they be churched and faithful, have rendered secondary to the Bible all other church authority, creeds, confessions, and forms of polity. When they are serious and are seriously confronted, most Protestants characteristically will say that they get authority for teaching and practice from the Bible alone.

Despite this claim, reflective Protestants will also admit that over the centuries they have spilled much ink in treatises on churchly authority. As much as Catholics, they may have exacted sweat and blood from people who ran afoul of church authorities, who tested the bounds of orthodoxy, or who came under ecclesiastical discipline. Protestantism, in other words, may seem chaotic to the outsider who sees its many groupings and varieties, but to most confessors and members the chaos is minimized, because they are ordinarily touched only by the authority system of which they are a part, that of their own church.

Once one insists on making churchly authority secondary, other values come to be dominant in association with the church. The church on Protestant soil is a fellowship, a congregation of people who have like minds or similar purposes. The church may be seen as "the body of Christ" or "the communion of saints" before it is an authority to compel conformity in teaching or practice. Yet once one assigns values to the group, even in forms of Protestantism that accent the right of private judgment or go to extremes of individualism, there must be and in practice have been many subtle ways to assert authority and to effect discipline. A small congregation's authority on Baptist or Congregational soil can be felt more immediately, for instance, than might Catholic authority asserted from the distance between Rome and India by a not always efficient and always pluralistic church.

PROTESTANT CHURCH POLITIES. Protestantism presents a broad spectrum of often mutually incompatible polities. Most Protestant churches have preserved elements of the polity that came with their birth, transformed by exigencies of local, contemporary demands and, in the modern world, adjustments to the managerial and bureaucratic impulse.

On one end of this spectrum are churches like the Anglican church or the Lutheran church in Sweden, which insist on apostolic succession in an episcopacy that is of the essence (displays the *esse*) of the church. Elsewhere, as in Methodism and much of Lutheranism, bishops belong to the *bene esse* of the church; they are beneficial for its order but theoretically could be replaced in a different polity. Many Reformed churches rely on synodical or connectional and associational patterns under the rule of presbyters or elders. From the days of the radical reformation in the sixteenth century through various later Baptist and Congregational witnesses into modern times, and especially in burgeoning nonwhite indigenous Protestantism, the authority and even the autonomy of the local congregation is asserted.

Those Protestants at the "catholic" end of the spectrum, who regard bishops as of the *esse* of the church, have been least ready to see their polity as negotiable in an ecumenical age. Presbyterian, synodical, and congregational bodies, while emphatically cherishing and defending their polities, have shown more signs of flexibility.

CIVIL GOVERNMENT. In the late twentieth century, most of the new nations in which nonwhite indigenous Protestantism prospered had undergone experiences of modernization that, whatever else these meant, provided no room for fusion of church and state or an interwoven pattern of religious and civil authority. Similarly, it was on the soil of largely Protestant nations such as the United States that the greatest degree of constitutional separation between the two authorities first occurred. Yet political philosopher Hannah Arendt is correct to chide Protestants for claiming that modern democracy with its religious freedom is simply a Christian invention. Some Christians have found it easy to reach into their repository of options to find impetus for supporting republicanism based on Enlightenment principles and practical support of equity and civil peace whenever pluralism has been strong.

Historical Protestantism in almost all its mainstream and dominant forms first simply carried over authority patterns from medieval Catholicism. In the Church of England, the Presbyterian church in Scotland, the Lutheran churches of Scandinavia, the Lutheran and Reformed churches of Germany, Switzerland, and the Netherlands, and wherever else leaders had the power to do so, they naturally clung to establishment. They simply broke from Roman Catholic establishment to form Protestant versions.

Despite all these establishmentarian dimensions, it is also fair to say that Protestantism did contain the seed that helped disestablishment and separation of church and state develop. A religion of the word, Protestantism called for that word to separate people from attachment to the culture as it evoked decision. So the boundaries of the church and the state could not be coextensive, as they aspired then to be in Catholicism. Whatever "the priesthood of all believers," "the right of private judgment," and the call to conscience in biblical interpretation meant theologically, they had as their practical consequence an honoring of individualism and personal profession of faith. Both of these would become confined were there an official and authoritative church.

PROTESTANT SUBSTANCE. Original or classic Protestantism was more ready to see itself as distinctive in the content of faith than is modern pluralist Protestantism. In the sixteenth century, late medieval Catholicism presented what to Protestant eyes was an egregious violation of God's system of approach to human beings. Catholicism had generated, or degenerated into, a system that progressively depended more and more upon human achievement. Key words were human *merit* or humanly gained *righteousness.* Elaborate schemes, for example, the sale of indulgences to help make up the required number of merits to assure salvation, had been devised. These led to abuses, which contemporary Catholic reformers and later historians have agreed made Protestant revolt plausible.

Protestantism across the board held to generally extreme views of human finitude, limits, "fallenness," and need. Mainstream and marginal reformers alike were not convinced by claims that human beings retained enough of the image of God upon which to build so that their own works or merits would suffice to appease a wrathful God. They exaggerated the way Catholicism had diminished the role of Jesus Christ as giver of a gift or imparter of grace upon the wholly undeserving.

In the sixteenth century, there were many variations on this theme, and Martin Luther's proclamation of "justification by grace through faith," while at home in all of Protestantism, was not necessarily the chosen formula for all Protestants. Yet all did accent divine initiative, human limits, the gifts of God in Jesus Christ, and the new condition of humanity as a result of divine forgiveness.

Protestantism has considered the church always to be reforming, never reformed; Catholicism and Protestantism alike, many would say, stand in need of being reformed, and from time to time they move past rigid,

Justification by faith active in love stands at the heart of Lutheran theology and is opposed to merit, justification by works, and legalism.

PAGE 149

"A few honest men are better than numbers."

OLIVER CROMWELL
SEPTEMBER 1643

older identities and formulas. Such moves are not incongruent with the Protestant ethos and spirit.

PROTESTANT WORSHIP. In describing baptism (whether sprinkling of infants or immersion of adults), the Lord's Supper, and the act of preaching and the uses of the word, the outlines of Protestant worship become generally clear. To these should be added that Protestants characteristically have gathered for worship in buildings set aside for that purpose. While they believe that the gathered community may effectively baptize, eat and drink, hear and pray under the sky or in secular buildings, they have had an impulse to set aside and consecrate a sacred space, which symbolically, not actually, becomes a house of God.

The sacred space usually accents a place for preaching, a baptismal font or pool, and a table or altar for the Lord's Supper. Around these the people gather, in pews or on chairs. The gathering occurs to recognize the presence of God, to follow divine commands to congregate for purposes of praise, to build the morale of the group for purposes outside the sanctuary, and to celebrate the seasons of the church year, the events of the week, and the passages of life.

With few exceptions, Protestantism is also a singing religion. It took the act of praising in song, which had become largely a preserve of clergy and choir, and enlarged it to include the congregation.

Except in Seventh-day Adventism, Protestant worship almost always occurs on Sunday, the Lord's Day, the Day of Resurrection, although believers are urged to worship at any time or place. Most Protestants observe the inherited Catholic church year but have purged it of many of its occasions. That is, they annually follow the life of Christ from Advent and Christmas, with its birth rites, through another season of repentance and preparation, Lent, on the way to a climax at Good Friday and Easter weekend, and then a festival of the Holy Spirit at Pentecost. The more Puritan forms of Protestantism, however, saw something "papist" in these seasonal observances and did away with almost all of them, sometimes including Christmas itself. The rest of Protestantism, which kept the church year of observances, also honored biblical saints like Paul and John on special days but rejected most postbiblical saints. Thus in the United States many observe a Thanksgiving Day, Mother's Day and Father's Day, Stewardship Sunday, Lay Sunday, and the like. The impulse to ritualize life is strong even on the purging, purifying, and simplifying soil of Protestantism.

PROTESTANT EXPRESSION. In general, Protestantism has been less fertile than Catholic Christianity in affirming the literary and artistic worlds. Sometimes this has resulted from a certain suspicion about the validity of the earthly venture for the sake of salvation.

Protestantism seemed most productive in the field of music, perhaps because the kinetic character of music seemed to be congruent with a word-centered, iconoclastic tradition. One thinks here of the musical poets of Protestantism, most notably the composer Johann Sebastian Bach. In literature there have been John Milton and John Bunyan, but in the contemporary world Protestantism has seldom helped produce anything approaching modern classics. In the visual arts geniuses like Lucas Cranach or, supremely, Rembrandt, have given expression to their evangelical sympathies and Protestant outlook.

[*For discussion of the dispersion of Protestantism, see regional surveys under* Christianity. *For discussion of particular manifestations of Protestantism, see* Anglicanism; Baptist Churches; Christian Science; Lutheranism, *sidebar* Luther, Martin; Mennonites; Methodist Churches; Moravians; Mormonism; Presbyterianism, Reformed; Puritanism; Quakers; Seventh-day Adventism; Shakers; *and* Unitarian Universalist Association.]

— MARTIN E. MARTY

PURITANISM

The first stirrings of Puritan reform came in the reign of Elizabeth from a group of former Marian exiles, clergy and laity. Initial protests focused on outward signs and ceremonies of the church such as the wearing of vestments, the physical position of church furnishings, and matters of nomenclature. The usage of the establishment, in the view of its critics, symbolized belief in a sacrificial priesthood, a real presence of Christ in the Eucharist, and other elements of Roman Catholic faith and practice.

Clerical opposition to the dictates of the queen and her archbishop of Canterbury, Matthew Parker (1559-1575), caught the public's attention. Puritanism drew the support of laity as distinguished as members of the queen's Privy Council and tapped deep wells of popular support in town and village, so much so that in some cases of the nonuse of vestments it was lay pressure that strengthened the will of a Puritan clergyman rather than pressure from a clergyman stirring up popular discontent.

Puritan hopes for early reform were bolstered when Edmund Grindal (1519-1583) succeeded Parker as archbishop of Canterbury in 1575. A progressive bishop, although not a Puritan, Grindal promoted efforts to upgrade the education of the clergy and to reform ecclesiastical abuses, positions strongly supported by Puritans but advocated by progressive members of the establishment as well. When Grindal refused to carry out the queen's desire to suppress prophesyings (clerical conferences designed to promote the continuing education of the participants), Elizabeth suspended him, and the division within the church widened.

In the last years of Elizabeth's reign and during the rule of James I (1603-1625), a new generation of religious thinkers began to articulate their theologies. One group reflected an accommodation to the views of the Dutch theologian Jacobus Arminius (1559-1609), and stressed the authority of king and bishops, the efficacy of the sacraments in the process of salvation, and the return to a more elaborate use of liturgical ceremony. In contrast to this evolving "new orthodoxy," John Preston (1587-1628), William Perkins (1558-1602), and William Ames (1576-1633) spelled out the essentials of Puritan belief that would characterize the seventeenth-century history of the movement in England and in the New England in America. The lines of demarcation between "orthodox" and Puritan members of the church became more sharply defined, and compromise became less likely.

The starting point for Puritan theology was an emphasis on the majesty, righteousness, and sovereignty of God. In their speculation about the means whereby God reached out to elect certain souls for the gift of salvation, the Puritans developed elements of traditional Calvinism. Puritan theologians, William Perkins in particular, made concepts of the covenant central to their evangelism and moralism. Believing in predestination, they explained that all human beings were pledged by the covenant of works to adhere to the divine law and were justly condemned for failure to adhere to it. The covenant of works depended on human action, while the covenant of grace required a faith that God himself enabled the elect to grasp.

The task of redeeming England seemed more difficult than ever as the reign of James I gave way to that of Charles I (1625-1649). Puritan clergymen were hauled before ecclesiastical courts, deprived of their livings, and harried out of the land.

Having failed to reform England by their written or spoken word, some Puritan leaders conceived the idea of persuading their countrymen by the example of a model Puritan community. This was the goal of many who joined in the Great Migration to New England in the 1630s. Massachusetts and her sister commonwealths of Connecticut (founded in 1636) and New Haven (1637) and the moderate Separatist colony of Plymouth represented an orthodoxy that was designated the New England Way. Their social and political fabric was knit from ideas of Christian organicism owing much to English rural traditions as well as to the corporate strain in Puritan thought. In matters of religion the orthodox developed a congregational church structure with all residents required to attend service but with full membership and its privileges reserved for those who could persuade their peers that they had experienced saving grace.

In England, while political stability was provided by the rise of Oliver Cromwell (1599-1658) as lord protector in 1649, religious diversity did not come to an end. Cromwell did, however, make progress toward the establishment of a Puritan state church uniting moderate Congregationalists. The return of the Stuart monarchy with the Restoration of Charles II (1660-1685) in 1660 saw the casting out of Puritanism from the Church of England. What had been a reform movement within Anglicanism became nonconformity in the shape of Presbyterian, Congregational, and Baptist denominations.

— FRANCIS J. BREMER

The Puritans were to be a major element in English history until the second half of the seventeenth century.

PAGE 572

QUAKERS

The Quakers, or the Religious Society of Friends, arose in seventeenth-century England and America out of a shared experience of the Light and Spirit of God within each person. This source of worship, insight, and power they identify as the Spirit of Christ that also guided the biblical prophets and apostles. Quakers also affirm each person's ability to recognize and respond to truth and to obey the Light perfectly through the leading of an inner witness, or "Seed," called by some Quakers "Christ reborn in us" and by others "that of God in every man," out of which transformed personalities can grow. They therefore ask of each other, and of human society, uncompromising honesty, simplicity of life, nonviolence, and justice.

The early Friends, as Quakers were named (from *Jn.* 15:5) by their first leader George Fox, arose in England during the Puritan Commonwealth under Oliver Cromwell, manifesting an inward intensification of radical and spiritual forms of Puritanism. Quakers held distinctive ideas on the purely inward nature of true baptism and Communion, on the ministry of all laymen and women, on God's power judging and working within hearts and history, and on the need for biblical events to be fulfilled within each person's life-story.

The early Quaker mission throughout England, in 1654-1656, was presented as the "Day of Visitation" by the Lord to each town or region; newly transformed Friends spoke in markets and parish churches despite mobbing and arrests. In New England, Quakers challenging the "biblical commonwealth" were banished on pain of death, and Mary Dyer and three men were hanged in Boston. To persecution for these offenses under the Puritans was added, after the restoration of Charles II, mass arrests—due to the Anglicans' Conventicle Acts of 1664 and 1670. Out of fifty thousand Friends, five hundred died in jail. Quaker courage won over to Quakerism such leaders as William Penn, the mystic Isaac Penington, and the theologian Robert Barclay.

The formal network of Quaker Meetings for Business, held monthly for a town, quarterly for a county, or yearly for a state or nation, was set up to replace reliance on individual leaders. The duties of these Meetings were to register births, marriages, and burials and to aid prisoners, widows, and poor Friends. Fox insisted after 1670 on independent Women's Meetings for Business throughout Quakerism. The monthly Meeting for Sufferings in London and local Meetings recorded imprisonments, oversaw publication of Quaker books, and disowned actions untrue to Quaker norms.

Quaker governments were set up in 1675 and 1682 by Edward Billing and Penn in their new colonies of West New Jersey and Pennsylvania; the charters of these governments mandated toleration and political and legal rights for all men including the Delaware Indians.

Friendship with the American Indians was a Quaker policy: a Quaker committee shared in peace negotiations in 1756-1758 and 1763-1768, and others set up schools and mediation for the New York Senecas and for the Shawnees and other tribes evicted from Ohio and sent to Oklahoma after 1830. In the 1870s, President Grant asked Friends to administer the Indian Agencies of Kansas-Nebraska.

Change and growth characterized Quaker activities during the eighteenth and nineteenth centuries. Eighteenth-century English industry, banking, and science were increasingly led by the interbred Quaker families of Darbys, Barclays, Lloyds, and Gurneys, who (notably Elizabeth Fry) also pioneered in reforming prisons, mental hospitals, and education for Quaker youth and the poor. Philadelphia Friends emulated them.

Quaker organization and worship, not greatly changed since 1690, were now centered in the American Midwest on revivals and hymns and hence on pas-

The Society of Friends (Quakers) claims that the spirit of the scriptures requires no specially ordained ministers.

PAGE 441

MARY DYER

The Quaker martyr Mary Dyer was executed in the mid seventeenth century for challenging the "biblical commonwealth."

CORBIS-BETTMANN

tors and superintendents, led by John Henry Douglas in Iowa and Oregon. By 1898 half the Meetings, even in Indiana, supported pastors and programmed worship with sermons and hymns and biblical Sunday schools. The Richmond Conference of 1887 gathered all orthodox Friends to look at these new patterns and to restrain David Updegraff's advocacy of water baptism. The Richmond Declaration of Faith reaffirmed evangelical orthodoxy. Concern for unity led in 1902 to a formally gathered Five Years Meeting, which since 1960 has been called Friends United Meeting, and is still centered in Richmond, Indiana. It currently includes seven Orthodox (evangelical) American Yearly Meetings (mostly midwestern); the reunited Baltimore, Canadian, New England, New York, and Southeastern Yearly Meetings; three Yearly Meetings in Kenya; and one each in Cuba, Jamaica, and Palestine arising from missions. Their total 1997 membership was estimated at 83,761 in North America.

In 1985, there remained 18,500 Friends in England and Scotland, 1,750 in Ireland, 2,000 in English communities in Australia, New Zealand, and South Africa, and 20 to 400 each in eight post-1918 Yearly Meetings in nations of continental Europe.

[*See also* Puritanism.]

— HUGH BARBOUR

Mistrusting the source of his revelation and fearing he was possessed by jinn or devils, Muhammad was about to throw himself off a mountain when Jibril (Gabriel) appeared and confirmed him as God's prophet.

PAGE 33

QUR'AN

THE TEXT AND ITS HISTORY

The Qur'an is the scripture of the Muslim community. It comprises the revelations "sent down" to the prophet Muhammad over a period of approximately twenty-two years (from 610 to 632 CE); these ecstatic utterances were collected, ordered, and made into a book sometime after Muhammad's death. Muslims look upon the Qur'an as the very words of God himself, which convey a divine message of saving guidance for those who submit. In consequence the Qur'an has a place of unparalleled importance at the very center of Muslim religious life and practice. Qur'anic teachings are the guide both to personal and social life and to religious responsibility. Indeed, it may be claimed that all Muslim religious thought and activity, and much else besides, are but extended commentaries on the Qur'anic revelation and on the life of the Prophet, who was the agent of its delivery.

The Prophet and the Qur'an

The Qur'an and the Muslim understanding of it are both inextricably interwoven with the experience of the Prophet through whom the holy book was delivered. It was solely the fact of being chosen as a messenger (*rasul*) to humankind (to deliver the Qur'an) that constituted Muhammad's prophethood; he had no other claim to authority and obedience. The experience of receiving the Qur'anic revelations transformed Muhammad from an ordinary citizen of Mecca into a religious visionary who subsequently became not only the leader of his people but one of the most influential individuals in all of history.

Once the revelations began, they continued to come with more or less frequency throughout Muhammad's lifetime except for a short period early on in his career (known as the *fatrah*, or pause) that caused him much soul-searching and doubt. The fragmentary nature of the revelations, the fact that they came in bits and

THE CALL TO PROPHETHOOD

"Recite in the Name of Thy Lord"

By temperament Muhammad was a reflective person with a strong disposition toward religiosity. Tradition records that prior to his prophetic call he cultivated the habit of retiring into isolation in the hills surrounding Mecca to practice *tahannuth*, or devotional exercises, including perhaps prayer, vigils, fasting, and mild austerities. During one of his night vigils in about his fortieth year, according to tradition, Muhammad experienced the call to prophethood. In the traditional account the call came as the vision of the angel Gabriel, who said, "O, Muhammad, thou art the Messenger of God," and commanded Muhammad, "Recite." At first Muhammad replied, "I cannot recite" (or "What shall I recite?" according to the way one understands the words). Thereupon, Gabriel seized him and squeezed him violently three times until, in one version of the story, Muhammad "thought it was death," and again the angel ordered "Recite in the name of thy Lord." Muhammad then recited the verses the constitute the first part of surah (chapter) 96 of the Qur'an:

> Recite in the name of thy Lord who created
> Created man from a clot
> Recite; thy Lord is most generous,
> Who taught by the pen
> Taught man what he knew not.

— CHARLES J. ADAMS

pieces, rather than all at once, is among their most notable features. The Qur'an is not a straightforwardly organized treatise; rather it moves without transition from one subject to another, often returning after many pages to a subject discussed earlier; it is repetitious, and it leaves many matters of great importance quite incomplete. The fragmentariness may be explained in terms of the Prophet's responses to the circumstances and problems that he and his community faced: as new situations arose, posing new questions or difficulties, the revelation provided guidance and answers.

THE NAMES OF THE REVELATION. Several different terms are employed in the Qur'an as names or designations of the revelations. It is of some importance to consider these terms for the light they throw on the Muslim holy book.

Qur'an. We may begin with the word *qur'an* itself. As used in the text it is clear that the word cannot refer to the structured book that we know today by that name, since the revelations came at intervals, bit by bit, over a period of more than twenty years and were not complete until they ceased with Muhammad's death. Further, the historical tradition is unanimous in holding that the Qur'an (the book) did not achieve its final form until some time after the Prophet's demise.

The noun *qur'an* is normally said to be derived from the Arabic verb *qara'a*, meaning "to read" or "to recite." Most often it is Muhammad who recites, and what he recites is the *qur'an* (i. e., the recitation). In other cases, however, God recites the revelations to Muhammad as in the instance of verse 75:17.

Scholars generally have accepted the view that *qur'an* is non-Arabic in origin, deriving from a Syriac word that means a scripture lesson or reading, something to be recited in connection with worship. Hence, such statements as "Behold, we have made it [the Book] an Arabic *qur'an*" (43.3) and "We have sent it down as an Arabic *qur'an*" (12:2) were likely understood by Muhammad and his contemporaries as signifying that he was bringing to the Arabs a body of verbal formulas that might be recited or read in a liturgical context just as other communities, notably the Christians and Jews, possessed scriptures that they used in this way. Indeed, the word is employed in certain passages that clearly indicate a liturgical setting for the recitation.

Muhammad may have caused portions of the revelations to be written down, but it is unlikely that he wrote them for himself: his primary function was to recite what had been made known to him in the revelation experiences. He also urged the recitation of the revelations upon others as an expression of piety, associating the recitation with prayer. Recitation, therefore, was a means of preserving the revelations and a way of conditioning the community to their significance as well as one of the most praiseworthy acts of submission to the divine will. The role played by recitation of the revelations in the community's early life has continued through the centuries as a fundamental element of religious expression.

Kitab. Another word for the revelation that often occurs in conjunction with *qur'an* is *kitab*, which is found more than 250 times in the Muslim scripture. Literally, it means something written, any piece of writing, such as a letter or a document, and there are instances of this use in the text. The word also occurs in connection with the Final Judgment when each person will be given his *kitab*, the book or record of his deeds (17:71 et al.), in his right or left hand or behind his back according to the moral quality of his life. In perhaps the most general sense the term conveys God's knowledge and control of all that will happen; the destinies of human beings and the world are decreed and written down beforehand in a book. "Naught of disaster befalleth in the earth or in yourselves but it is in a Book before we bring it into being." (57:22).

The most frequent use of *kitab* is in conjunction with the idea of scripture, both the scripture given to Muhammad in the revelations and that given to others in previous times, the "peoples of the book." In this sense the *kitab* is identical with the revelation. Further, the scripture given to Muhammad is confirmed in the scriptures of these other religious communities and in its turn confirms them; all, therefore, originate from God. *Kitab* as scripture in one sense also appears to be synonymous with *qur'an* inasmuch as both are revelation, but in certain passages *kitab* is a broader term, *qur'an* being only those parts of the heavenly kitab that have been sent down to Muhammad in Arabic.

Other names. Other words used to indicate the revelations are *tanzil*, *dhikr*, and other forms of the same root, such as *furqan*. *Tanzil* is the verbal noun from the verb *nazzala*, "to send down" or "to cause to send down"; *tanzil* may be rendered, therefore, either as "sending down" or as "something sent down." *Dhikr* means either "mention" or "reminder," and its significance as a name of the revelation is to indicate that the revelation is an admonition and a warning; the point is underlined by references to Muhammad as an admonisher. In the text itself the coming of the *furqan* is associated with the Battle of Badr, and Alford Welch has suggested that the designation became current because it was at about that time that the Muslims first began to differentiate clearly between their community and scripture and those of the Christians and Jews. The *furqan* would thus have been understood as the basis of the distinction between Muslims and these others.

Chronology of the Qur'an

There are many reasons other than a general historical interest why it is important to establish the chronology

Muhammad became convinced that he had been called to be the "Messenger of God" (rasul Allah) who would bear messages or revelations from God to the people of Mecca.

PAGE 471

"Behold, we have made it (the Book) an Arabic qur'an."

THE QUR'AN 43.3

of the revelations. In making decisions about the abrogating and abrogated verses, for example, the dating of passages and individual verses is essential. Likewise, a reliable chronology would be an invaluable aid for the historian in tracing the development of the prophetic consciousness and the outlook of the early community.

MUSLIM DATING. First, attention should be called to the existence of a traditional Muslim dating of the chapters of the Qur'an. In printed versions there is customarily a heading for each chapter which, among other information, indicates that the chapter is either Meccan or Medinan. At the same time Muslim scholars recognize that some chapters of the Qur'an are composite, that they may contain material from different periods with Meccan material sometimes being inserted in the midst of a largely Medinan chapter and vice versa. There are also traditional lists of the order in which the chapters are assumed to have been revealed. All of these Muslim datings rest upon traditions reported of Muhammad or traditions that relate to the *asbab al-nuzul.* Although one cannot hope to obtain precise dating of any particular passage or verse from this traditional scheme, its divisions of the material into Meccan and Medinan chapters has, with only few exceptions, been borne out by modern scholarship.

The entire universe and its content are declared by the Qur'an to be muslim, that is, endowed with order through obedience to God's law

PAGE 336

MODERN DATING. The leaders in modern study of Qur'anic chronology have been Theodor Nöldeke and Richard Bell. In his *Geschichte des Qorans Nöldeke*, argued that the chapters of the Qur'an fall into four discernible periods, three in Mecca and one in Medina. He mounted his argument on the basis of internal evidence from the Qur'an including both style and subject matter. Assuming that Muhammad's prophetic inspiration would have been at its most intense in the beginning of his career, Nöldeke held that the short chapters, which exhibit great force of expression and strong emotion and have a marked rhythm and rhyme, must have been the first to come to the Prophet. In the Medinan situation, where Muhammad had all the responsibilities of rule, the revelations would have been characterized by attention to practical matters and been more expository in nature.

The Scottish scholar Richard Bell believed that the revelations were given in much smaller units, often consisting of only a verse or two or three. A proper dating of the revelations, he reasoned, should concern itself with these smaller units, and he set out to divide the chapters as they presently exist into what he considered to be their component parts. By a complex process of analysis he then attempted to give a date to each of the pericopes into which he had divided the text. In some instances he found portions of what he thought to be a single revelation widely separated and inserted into different chapters. Despite Bell's minute verse-by-verse consideration of the Qur'an, he could not assign precise dates to a majority of verses, and there is uncertainty about numerous others. The entire question of the dating of the revelations remains, therefore, undecided.

— CHARLES J. ADAMS

ITS ROLE IN MUSLIM PIETY

For more than fourteen hundred years, Muslims of all schools of thought have interiorized the Qur'an as the transcendent word of God, infinite in meaning and significance for all times and places. The Qur'an has permeated every facet and stage of the life of Muslim society and that of every Muslim believer. It is, however, particularly evident in Shi'i piety, since much of Shi'i theology is based on a hagiography in which the Qur'an as well as the imams figure prominently. With its words, the newborn child is welcomed into the world, as the father utters certain popular verses into its ear. As the sixth Shi'i imam, Ja'far al-Sadiq, declared, "Whoever recites the Qur'an while yet a youth and has faith, the Qur'an becomes intermingled with his flesh and blood" (Ayoub, vol. 1, p. 12).

LANGUAGE. The Qur'an addresses Muslims in various styles and on various levels of eloquence. Its brief and cryptic verses present in sharp contrasts the portents, fears, and torments of the Day of Judgment and the bliss and pleasures of Paradise. Its longer and more didactic verses address the day-to-day life of the community—its social relations, political loyalties, and legal problems.

Qur'anic language is at times rhapsodic. The opening verses of surah 36 (*Yasin*, the names of two Arabic letters), for instance, move rapidly and with great dramatic force in relating unknown stories of bygone ages and the dramatic encounter of human beings with God on the Day of Judgment; its awe-inducing power is such that it is recited over the dead. In other places the language is smooth and calming, as in surah 55 (*al-Rah-man*, The Merciful), which describes the flowing rivers of Paradise, only imperfectly realized on earth, and which has been recognized to have hypnotic qualities.

Among the most popular and most frequently repeated passages of the Qur'an, recited by Muslim men and women in times of crisis, fear, or uncertainty, are the Fatihah (the opening surah), the throne verse (2:255), and the surah of sincere faith (112). It is a widespread custom, for instance, that when the parents of a young man and woman agree on uniting their children in marriage, the agreement is sealed with the recitation of the Fatihah; business deals and other transactions are blessed in the same way. The Fatihah is the basic Muslim prayer, for the Prophet declared: "There is no prayer except by the opening of the

THE QUR'AN AS POETRY

From Sura XCIX—The Earthquake

In the Name of God, the Compassionate,
the Merciful

When the Earth with her quaking shall
quake

And the Earth shall cast forth her burdens,

And man shall say, What aileth her?

On that day shall she tell out her tidings,

Because thy Lord shall have inspired her.

On that day shall men come forward in
throngs to behold their works,

And whosoever shall have wrought an
atom's weight of good shall behold it,

And whosoever shall have wrought an
atom's weight of evil shall behold it.

— EVERYMAN'S LIBRARY,
TRANSLATED BY J. M. RODWELL.

Book." It is composed of seven brief verses which present two distinct but closely related themes: in the first half, thanksgiving, praise, and recognition of God's mercy ("In the name of God, the All-merciful, the Compassionate/Master of the Day of Judgment/You alone do we worship"), and in the second half, a plea for guidance ("and you alone do we beseech for help/Guide us on the straight way/The way of those upon whom you have bestowed your favor, not of those who have incurred your wrath or those who have gone astray").

POWER. The powers of the Qur'an have been used in Muslim folklore to heal and to inflict harm, to cause strange natural occurrences, and even to charm snakes and find lost animals. In amulets it serves to protect a child from the evil eye or any other mishap and to strengthen or break the bond of love between two people.

In times of sickness and adversity, believers turn to the Qur'an as a source of "healing and mercy for the people of faith" (17:82); the Fatihah in particular is called *al-shafiyah* (the surah of healing).

COMFORT. The Qur'an also serves as a source of strength and reassurance in the face of the unknown. For the pious, the Qur'an provides the means of controlling future events or mitigating their outcome through *istikharah*, seeking a good omen in the text. *Istikharah* represents the choice of what God has chosen; it is carried out by averting the face, opening the book, and letting it speak directly to one's need or condition. The action is usually accompanied by elaborate prayers and rituals.

The Qur'an is a source of blessing and comfort to the dead as well as the living. Often before a pious person dies, he or she stipulates that the Qur'an be recited at the grave for three days to ensure the rest of his or her soul. Whenever a deceased person is remembered by friends or family, the Fatihah is recited; it is considered a gift to the dead, a fragrant breeze from Paradise to lighten the great hardship of the grave. It is, however, the portions of the Qur'an learned in this world which will bring believers great merit in the hereafter. As a consolation for the followers (*shi'ah*) of the family of the Prophet, Imam Ja'far al-Sadiq promised that "Any one of our Shi'ah, or those who accept our authority (*wilayah*), who dies without having attained a good knowledge of the Qur'an shall be taught it in his grave, in order that God may raise his station in paradise, because the number of stations in paradise is equal to the number of the verses of the Qur'an" (Majlisi, vol. 39, p. 188).

RECITATION. Because the Qur'an is an object of great reverence, we are told, no one should touch it unless he is pure (56:79), nor should anyone recite it unless he is in a state of ritual purity. Before beginning to recite, he must clean his teeth and purify his mouth, for he will become the "path" of the Qur'an. The Qur'an reciter must put on his best attire, as he would when standing before a king, for he is in fact speaking with God.

Likewise, because the Qur'an is the essence of Islamic prayer, the reciter should face the *qiblah*, or direction of prayer toward Mecca. Anyone who begins to yawn in the course of reciting is obliged to stop, because yawning is caused by Satan.

The Qur'an is not a book with a beginning, middle, and end. Every portion, or even every verse, is a Qur'an, as the entire book is the Qur'an, properly speaking. Thus reciting the complete text over a period of days, weeks, or months may be considered a journey through an infinite world of meaning, a journey in and with the Qur'an. The primary purpose of this sacred journey is to form one's character and life according to the word of God, to achieve true righteousness (*taqwa*). The task of reciting the Qur'an is in itself a source of blessing.

According to prophetic tradition, the best of men is he who studies the Qur'an and teaches it to others. In a tradition related on the authority of Abu Hurayrah, the Prophet is said to have declared: "There are no people assembled in one of the houses of God to recite the book of God and study it together but that the *sakinah* (divine tranquillity) descends upon them. Mercy covers

The God of the Qur'an is al-'Azim, the Inaccessible well beyond the bounds of human understanding.

PAGE 248

them, angels draw near to them, and God remembers them in the company of those who are with him" (Ayoub, vol. 1, pp. 8-9). Indeed, the highest merit for which a person can hope in the world to come is that of engaging with others in the study of the Qur'an.

LITERARY LEGACY. In its written form, the Qur'an has set the standard for Arabic language and literature as the proper and indeed the highest expression of literary Arabic. Its style of storytelling, its similes and metaphors have shaped classical Arabic literature and have even had their influence on the modern writers. Even daily conversation, whether on weighty or mundane matters, is interspersed with Qur'anic words and phrases, and Qur'anic verses are beautifully calligraphed to decorate mosques, schools, and the homes of the pious.

— MAHMOUD M. AYOUB

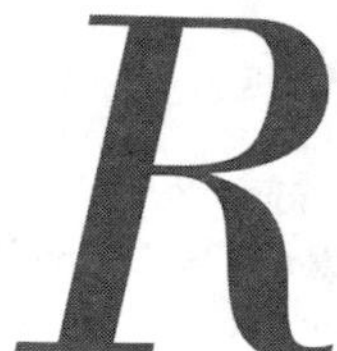

RABBINATE

The term *rabbinate* derives from the Hebrew title *rabbi* ("my master, my teacher"), which came into use in the first century of the common era.

LATE ANTIQUITY. Tradition holds that from the time of Moses there has been an unbroken succession of "laying on of hands" that conferred rabbinical status. Even Moses is referred to frequently as "our rabbi." But we have no instance of anyone being designated rabbi in a specific ceremony of ordination in ancient times, nor is the rabbinate decisively connected with the two Hebrew roots that designated the putative ceremony of ordination, *smkh* and *mnh.*

In the New Testament, the term *rabbi* is not often encountered in the synoptic Gospels. The term is, however, used particularly in the *Gospel of John,* but only in the equivalent of any teacher of disciples.

Rabbis during the Talmudic period were, above all, teachers and interpreters of the Torah. The rabbis of these centuries created the Jewish calendar out of biblical materials and ensured that the Jewish calendar would be a kind of temporal catechism. These same rabbis fixed the biblical canon and the synagogue liturgy. As against Jewish Christians, agnostics, and a mixed bag of dissidents whom the rabbis termed *minim,* the Jewish community became unified and distinguished through rabbinic definitions and "fences."

THE MIDDLE AGES AND EARLY MODERN PERIOD. By profession the Talmudic rabbi was a woodsman, a farmer, a shoemaker, a shepherd, or the like. He worked for a living and served as a rabbi only in his spare time. Not until the Middle Ages was the rabbinate decisively professionalized.

The increasingly professional rabbi confronted the organized Jewish community leadership as colleague, employee, and/or competitor. The rabbi was, after all, in a sense a layman, since he possessed no sacramental or charismatic advantage, yet his role increasingly led to a collision course with the lay establishment in his town. Wealthy lay leadership often chose the judiciary, dominated weak rabbis, and threatened strong ones. The rabbis were not without their own discrete powers. They supervised the ritual life of the community and had prerogatives as authors and educators. They had the final weapon of excommunication, a sword better and more often sheathed than recklessly employed. But they were often torn between various lay factions, and they had to face the practical issues of tenure and dismissal.

The Jewish community slowly and steadily achieved increasing autonomy from the Middle Ages until the eighteenth century, but this strengthened the power of laymen, who had their own agenda and their own ambitions, often at the expense of the rabbinate. The rabbi was generally honored and respected during the Middle Ages. He was called *morenu*, "our teacher," when invited to the Torah reading, and he had a seat of honor in the synagogue. Prominent rabbis often constituted a court of appeal for decisions made by lower, lay-controlled judiciaries, and rabbis gave permission for Jews to utilize otherwise forbidden secular courts. They also delivered a kind of *nihil obstat* to authorize publication of books.

"Rabbi, we know you are a teacher come from God."

NICODEMUS
JOHN 3:2

Rabbinical duties in the Middle Ages were both the same as and different in nuance from those of the Talmudic period. The rabbi taught, judged, and officiated at marriages and funerals. He circumcised newborn boys and preached at least twice a year and, in some communities, more regularly. He sometimes administered burial societies and poor funds. One of the rabbi's chief responsibilities was private study.

THE MODERN PERIOD. In modern times, pressures to establish a professional rabbinate continued to grow. The community nominated, and the government named, chief rabbis in Britain and France, as well as in British-mandated Palestine.

Since the beginning of the nineteenth century, Jewish religion has lost even the semblance of uniformity that it once had. Reform, or Liberal, Judaism appeared as an early reaction to modern thinking and citizenship in western European countries, followed quickly by what came to be called Conservatism and Neo-Orthodoxy. In each of these denominations, the rabbi took on, more and more, the characteristics of a Protestant minister. Salaries of rabbis tended to rise; the status of the rabbi often paralleled that of his Christian clerical counterpart, who was also, in a new sense, his colleague. The older functions of the rabbi—teaching, learning, judging, and the like—remained crucial in Orthodoxy.

The question of the extent of scriptural law versus rabbinic law was deeply debated among the medieval Jewish jurists.

PAGE 259

New kinds of learning did not prevent the modern rabbi from suffering a crisis of authority. The modern rabbi could not claim to be a sole, or even a principal, authority in his milieu. In some countries, the community hired rabbis to serve a whole town or a designated part of it. But in America, for instance, rabbis are almost always hired by individual congregations, thus finding themselves in the anomalous position of being the employees of the very people they are expected to lead.

At the present time there are new as well as many old issues of rabbinical function. The Reform, Reconstructionist, and Conservative movements have begun to ordain women, to the dismay of Orthodoxy. Traditionally, a woman cannot serve as a witness or judge, but there is no halakhic reason why she cannot preach or teach or administer a congregation.

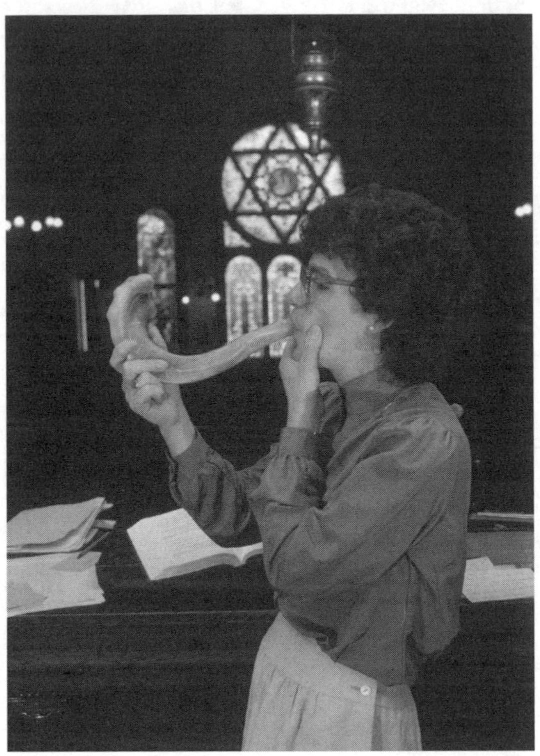

DIVERSE RABBINATE

The Reform, Reconstructionist and Conservative movements of Judaism have begun to ordain women. Here a Rabbi blows the shofar.

DAVIS H. WELLS/CORBIS

The modern rabbi is the true inheritor of a millennial tradition but is also very much a product of the modern world.

[*For further discussion of the role of the rabbi in various movements within Judaism, see* Reform Judaism and Hasidism.]

— ARNOLD JACOB WOLF

Luther's "theology of the cross" affirmed that God always works contrary to experience.

PAGE 426

REFORMATION

BACKGROUND. The traditional view, from the Protestant perspective, has been that in the early sixteenth century, church and society were in a state of crisis. The church was seen as suffering from various moral and theological abuses and the Reformation was a necessary reaction against that state of affairs.

The Catholic church stood in the center of society. It had extensive land holdings. It controlled education. It possessed its own legal system. It provided the ethical principles on which society was based and which were meant to guide it. Above all, the church, as the guardian of eternal truth, mediated salvation. There is no doubt that, on the eve of the Reformation, the church possessed a great vitality, especially in Germany, and that it commanded considerable loyalty and devotion.

Along with these manifestations of vitality, there were also problems. The hierarchy seemed distant and too cumbersome to deal with the spiritual needs of the people. The higher clergy, notably the bishops, were mainly recruited from the nobility and viewed their office as a source of prestige and power. This was particularly true in Germany, where many bishops were political rulers as well as spiritual rulers.

In this setting many voices pleaded for church reform. Despite criticism and anticlericalism, the call was for change and reform, not for disruption and revolution.

CONTROVERSY OVER INDULGENCES. The Reformation originated in a controversy over indulgences precipitated by Martin Luther's Ninety-five Theses of 31 October 1517. Indulgences, originally remissions of certain ecclesiastical penalties, had by the early sixteenth century come to be understood as offering forgiveness of sins in exchange for certain payments. Luther's misgivings about a singularly vulgar sale of indulgences by the Dominican monk Johann Tetzel found expression in a probing of the theology of indulgences. In a letter to Archbishop Albert of Hohenzollern, Luther pleaded for the discontinuance of the sale. What was meant as an academic and pastoral matter quickly became a public one, however, primarily because Luther sent out several copies of the theses, and the positive response of the recipients helped to propagate them. [*See also the biography of Luther.*]

By early 1518 Luther had been cited as a suspected heretic. The Edict of Worms declared Luther a political outlaw. He was excommunicated that year.

BEGINNING OF THE REFORMATION. At Luther's formal condemnation in 1521 the nature of events changed. With Luther removed from the scene (many thought him dead), the message of reform was spread by an increasing number of comrades-in-arms and supporters. By that time consequences of the new message and its call for reform were beginning to emerge.

The message is evident in the multitude of pamphlets published between 1517 and 1525. Their themes were simple: of a religion of substance rather than form, of inner integrity rather than outward conformity, of freedom rather than rules. The impact of the reformers was so strong because they deliberately took their arguments to the people whom they knew to be interested in the issues discussed. The issues propounded were not merely religious ones; they encompassed a wide variety of social and political concerns that made for an intertwining of religious and nonreligious motifs.

By the end of the 1520s the reform movement had firmly established itself, especially in southern and central Germany. Two themes were dominant in the years between the Diet of Speyer (1526) and the Peace of Augsburg (1555): the expansion of the Reformation and the pursuit of reconciliation (or coexistence) between the two sides. The theme of Protestant expansion found striking expression in the spread throughout Europe and, in Germany, of the acceptance of the Reformation by a majority of the imperial cities.

The 1530s brought continued Protestant expansion in Germany. At the end of the decade new attempts were made to explore the possibility of theological agreement. At the Colloquy of Worms (1539), agreement was reached concerning justification, which had been the main point of controversy between the two sides. In the end, however, disagreement prevailed, and the attempt to resolve the controversy by theological conciliation failed.

Catholic Charles V was now determined to use force. Upon concluding peace with France in 1544, he was ready to face the Protestants. War broke out in 1546 and despite a good deal of blundering, Charles emerged successful, winning the decisive Battle of Muhlberg in 1547. The victorious emperor convened a diet at Augsburg in 1548 to impose his religious settlement on the Protestants. The result was the Augsburg Interim, which afforded the Protestants two temporary concessions—use of the communion cup and the married clergy—but left little doubt about the emperor's determination to restore Catholicism fully in the end. At the same time, Charles V sought also, through an ambitious constitutional reform project, to enhance imperial power in Germany.

Charles faced increasingly formidable opposition from the territorial rulers, Protestant and Catholic alike, and he had to acknowledge that Protestantism was firmly entrenched in Germany.

DIFFERENTIATION OF REFORMATION VIEWS. As the Reformation movement spread, it became evident that the reformers' common opposition to the Catholic church did not entail a common theological position. The first incidence of differentiation came in 1522, when Andreas Karlstadt, a colleague of Luther's at the University of Wittenberg, publicly disagreed with Luther. Two years later Thomas Müntzer, minister at Allstedt, not far from Wittenberg, published two pamphlets in which he dramatically indicted Luther's notion of reform. In the spring of 1525, Müntzer joined the rebellious peasants in central Germany and became their spiritual leader. The pamphlets that issued from his pen were vitriolic and categorical: the true church would be realized only through suffering and by a resolute opposition to the godless rulers.

The major division within the ranks of the reformers is associated with the Swiss reformer Huldrych (Ulrich) Zwingli, of Zurich. The specific issue that was to divide the Reformation was the interpretation of the Lord's Supper. Luther, while rejecting the Catholic doctrine of transubstantiation, affirmed the real presence of Christ in the elements of bread and wine, while Zwingli affirmed a spiritual presence. The controversy between the two men erupted in 1525 and continued, with increasing vehemence, for years to come. By 1529 political overtones to the theological disagreement had surfaced. Since military action against the Protestants was a possibility, the internal disagreement weakened the Protestant position. It became clear that the future of the Reformation lay in political strength.

A second major division within the ranks of the Reformation pertained to a heterogeneous group whom contemporaries called "Anabaptists." This term, derived from a Greek word meaning "rebaptizer," indicated the Anabaptists' most prominent assertion: that baptism should be performed in adulthood as the outgrowth of an individual's decision. Anabaptism originated formally in Zurich among young humanist associates of Zwingli who, influenced by Müntzer and Karlstadt, were disenchanted with the slow progress of reform. Their attempt to impose their own vision of speedier and more comprehensive reform on the course of events proved unsuccessful. They broke with Zwingli, administered believer's baptism early in 1525, and found themselves promptly persecuted, since the authorities were unwilling to tolerate diverse forms of religion in their midst.

These rebaptizers were scandalously denying the validity of that first baptism, setting themselves up as a truer church if not, indeed, the true church.

PAGE 68

Although some of the intellectual roots of Antitrinitarianism can be traced to the late Middle Ages, the catalytic influence of the Reformation was paramount in the movement. The atmosphere of challenge of established opinion and the stress on the Bible as sole authority seemed to call for the repudiation of the doctrine of the Trinity. A most dramatic event, in the early 1530s, was the publication of two staunchly antitrinitarian tracts by a Spanish lay theologian and physician, Michael Servetus.

An urbane French lawyer and humanist by background, John Calvin was the embodiment of both the differentiation of Reformation views and of its European dimension. Calvin had left his native country for Switzerland to arrange for the publication of his brief summary statement of Reformation theology, *Institutes*

"Give peace in our time, O Lord."

THE BOOK OF COMMON PRAYER

Many of the corruptions that had acted as tinder for the Reformation received the careful attention of the Roman Catholic council fathers.

PAGE 157

of the Christian Religion. Passing by chance through Geneva in 1536, the twenty-seven-year-old scholar was pressured into staying to take part in the reform there. His first attempt to implement reform led to conflict with the city authorities and to his expulsion in 1538. Three years later, however, he was invited to return and he remained there until his death in 1564. [*See* Christian Ethics, *sidebar* John Calvin.]

The central thesis of *Institutes of the Christian Religion* echoed in many variations, is the majesty of God, from which man's eternal destiny—predestination to salvation or to damnation—is reasoned. While Calvin always wished to emphasize God's majesty as the overarching theme of biblical religion, the concept of predestination emerged as the characteristic feature of Calvin's thought. Calvin's determination to implement his vision of God's law brought him into conflict with influential Genevans.

EUROPEAN DIMENSION OF THE REFORMATION. At the time the Reformation movement broke out in Germany, reform notions were already strong in France. While Francis I was himself a humanist by disposition, political prudence led him to take a Catholic and papal course. He responded with persecution and a stern censorship of books. His successor, Henry II, continued this policy.

Henry's unexpected death in 1559 precipitated a constitutional crisis over the exercise of regency during the minority of the new king, Francis II. Cardinal Guise summarily assumed the regency, but his move was opposed by the prestigious Bourbon family, which argued for a council of regency. The constitutional issue had religious overtones, since the Guises were staunch Catholics, while the Bourbons had Protestant leanings.

The Wars of Religion, which began in 1562, sought to resolve the issue of political power. The Edict of Nantes (1598) ended the struggle. Protestants failed in their effort to win acceptance of their religion by France, but they were given freedom of worship.

In the 1520s England underwent a period of lively agitation against the Roman Catholic church. This atmosphere of religious agitation was complicated by Henry's sudden desire for an annulment of his marriage to Catherine of Aragon (his deceased brother's widow) on the grounds that the marriage violated canon law. Extensive efforts to obtain a favorable papal decision proved unsuccessful. In 1533 Parliament passed the Act in Restraint of Appeals to Rome, which declared England an "empire" whose sovereign could adjudge all spiritual and temporal matters in his realm. This act kept the judicial resolution over Henry's "divorce" in England. The king had broken with the papal church. [*See also* Anglicanism.]

Concomitant ecclesiastical changes in England were initially few, however, and pertained mainly to jurisdictional and organizational matters. Despite his own Catholic temperament, Henry actively encouraged anti-Catholic propaganda throughout the 1530s.

When Henry died in 1547 religious affairs were thus in a precarious balance, neither strongly Protestant nor strongly Catholic. The official religion of the land veered in the direction of Protestantism. Under the aegis of Archbishop Cranmer, a new order for worship *(The Book of Common Prayer)* was promulgated in 1549. Drawing on the rich liturgical heritage of the medieval church, this order for worship, with the beauty of its language and its structure of the divine office, proved to be an immensely enriching contribution to English Christendom. The theological tone of the prayer book was conservative in that it espoused a Lutheran view of Communion. A revision of the book, three years later, embraced a Zwinglian view.

PURITANISM. Critics argued that too many vestiges of Catholicism remained in the English church. They wanted a "pure" church, and before long they came to be called "Puritans." The Puritans were to be a major element in English history until the second half of the seventeenth century. Puritanism underwent significant changes in the course of its lengthy history. Toward the end of the sixteenth century it became increasingly diverse and sectarian, some strands determined to break with the established church. It also became increasingly political. [*See* Puritanism.] In England, their separatist sentiment came to fruition during that time with the emergence of different groupings, of which several—Congregationalists, Baptists, and Quakers—were to become ecclesiastical traditions in Anglo-Saxon Christendom.

THE CATHOLIC REACTION. The initial reaction of the Catholic church to Luther was astoundingly swift and categorical. By 1520 the position of the church had been delineated: Luther's understanding of the Christian faith was declared heretical and his notion of reform rejected. It was to be of profound import for subsequent events that despite this condemnation, the Catholic church possessed neither a comprehensive policy for reform nor a clear perception of how to execute the judgment against Luther or halt the increasing defections. Moreover, the papacy had its own priorities, which were slow to focus on the Lutheran affair and the Protestant Reformation.

When a council eventually convened at Trent in 1545, it was clear that it could have no other function than to sharpen the true Catholic position on a wide variety of issues. Thus the council, which met intermittently until 1563, possessed significance only for the Catholic church. Its canons and decrees were consciously anti-Protestant and offered conciliatory views only with respect to issues contested within Catholicism.

— HANS J. HILLERBRAND

REFORM JUDAISM

Reform Judaism is the branch of the Jewish faith that has been most adaptive, in belief and practice, to the norms of modern thought and society. It is also sometimes called Liberal Judaism or Progressive Judaism. By *Reform* is meant not a single reformation but an ongoing process of development.

BELIEFS AND PRACTICES. Unlike more traditional forms of the Jewish faith, Reform Judaism does not hold that either the written law (Torah) or the oral law (Talmud) was revealed literally by God to Moses at Sinai. It accepts biblical and other historical criticism as legitimate, understanding scripture and tradition as a human reflection of revelation rather than its literal embodiment. While theologies among Reform Jews vary greatly, from the traditional to the humanistic, concepts of God strike a balance between universal and particular elements, with somewhat more stress upon the former than among other religious Jews. Like other branches of Judaism, Reform recognizes the close connection between religion and ethics.

The doctrine that most significantly sets Reform Judaism apart from more traditional currents is the conception of progressive revelation. Reform Jews hold that revelation is ongoing with the progress of human knowledge and religious sensitivity. The freedom of the individual Jew to be selective, to draw from Jewish tradition those elements of belief and practice that he or she finds the most personally meaningful, is far greater among Reform Jews than among either Orthodox or Conservative.

At most Reform congregations in America the main religious service of the week is held after dinner on Friday evenings; men and women sit together, participating equally in the service. Only in recent years have many rabbis, some male congregants, and a much smaller number of women begun to wear the ritual head covering (*kippah* or *yarmulke*) during worship.

Outside the synagogue Reform Jews practice their faith by attempting to guide their lives according to the moral precepts of Judaism. A large percentage practices some Jewish rituals in the home, especially the lighting of the Sabbath candles on Friday evening, the Passover eve ceremony, or Seder, and the celebration of Hanukkah. Once especially aware of their religious differences from traditional Jews, today Reform Jews emphasize to a greater extent their common ethnic identity and the faith shared by all religious Jews, limiting the significance of denominational differences.

THE MOVEMENT IN EUROPE. Reform Jews have often pointed out that religious reform was inherent in Judaism from its beginnings. They have noted that the prophets were critics of contemporary religious practices, that the Talmud includes reforms of earlier biblical legislation, and that even later legal scholars were willing to alter received beliefs and practices. Such willingness to adjust to historical change waned only under the pressure of persecution and the isolation of the ghetto. Latter-day Jews seeking religious reform thus sought, and to a degree found, precedent for their programs in earlier layers of Jewish tradition. However, they soon became aware that most of their fellow Jews, and especially the established rabbinical leadership, did not share such views. The result was a movement for reform, originally intended to harmonize all aspects of Jewish life with the modern world into which European Jews increasingly entered beginning with the later eighteenth century. Only gradually did the movement come to focus specifically on the religious realm, and only after a generation did it separate itself as a differentiable religious current with a more or less fixed religious philosophy. In discussing origins, it is therefore more accurate to speak of the "Reform movement in Judaism" than of Reform Judaism. Even this terminology, however, requires the qualification that self-conscious awareness of being a movement with definite goals came only gradually with the coalescence of various elements of belief and practice.

AMERICANIZATION. Reform Judaism has enjoyed its greatest success in the United States. In Europe it was repeatedly forced to assert itself against an entrenched Orthodoxy, sometimes supported by the government; in the New World it faced no such established institutions. The United States lacked officially recognized Jewish communities, like the German *Gemeinde* with its powers of taxation and centralized control over Jewish affairs. The complete separation of church and state, the numerous Christian denominations existing side by side, and the prevalent notion that religious activity was strictly a matter of free choice created an atmosphere most conducive to Jewish religious fragmentation. Moreover, it was difficult for an immigrant Jew in nineteenth-century America to make a living while still observing all the inherited traditions. Given also the large influx of Jews from Germany in the second third of the nineteenth century—among them some who had had experience with religious reform, as well as a number of Reform rabbis—it is understandable that until the massive Jewish immigration from eastern Europe in the last decades of the century, Reform Judaism should play the dominant role in American Jewry. In the freer atmosphere of America, Reform soon took on a considerably more radical character than its counterpart in Europe.

DEVELOPMENTS SINCE WORLD WAR II. In the immediate postwar years Reform Judaism in the United States enjoyed remarkable growth. The Christian religious revival of the 1950s produced renewed

The Reform, Reconstructionist, and Conservative movements have begun to ordain women, to the dismay of Orthodoxy.

PAGE 570

interest in Jewish theology. The well-known biblical archaeologist Nelson Glueck, as president of the Hebrew Union College from 1947 to his death in 1971, was able to achieve a merger with the Jewish Institute of Religion and to bring about considerable expansion of the combined institution.

Reform Judaism now engaged itself vigorously with the moral issues troubling American society. Rabbis and laity participated actively in the civil rights movement and later in the organized opposition to the Vietnam War. In 1961 the UAHC established the Religious Action Center in Washington, D. C., with the intent of making a direct impact on legislation of Jewish and general religious or moral concern, as well as educating the Reform constituency as to questions under current legislative consideration. In the spirit of ecumenism, the UAHC developed a department dealing with interfaith activities.

Frank Rosenzweig connected being Jewish with acting Jewishly–that is, observing the law insofar as one was existentially able to acknowledge it as possessing the quality of commandment.

PAGE 415

Reform theology in this recent period grew increasingly diverse. A group of Reform rabbis, who became known as "covenant theologians," favored a more personalist and existential grounding of their faith. Influenced by the twentieth-century European Jewish thinkers Franz Rosenzweig and Martin Buber, they eschewed the earlier idealist theology based on progressive revelation in favor of the notion of divine-human encounter as represented both by the testimony of the Torah and by contemporary religious experience. At the same time, however, there arose a significant rationalist and even humanist faction within the movement. Its members stressed the impact of biblical criticism and psychoanalysis upon religion, as well as the difficult theological questions that the Holocaust had raised for Jewish theism.

Jewish education among Reform Jews became more comprehensive in the 1970s. In place of the customary two hours per week of Sunday school instruction, most temples now offered twice-weekly classes, supplemented by weekends or summer sessions at a camp. The National Federation of Temple Youth introduced study programs for Reform teenagers beyond religious-school age, and rabbinical education was extended to women, the first woman (Sally Preisand) being ordained by HUC-JIR in 1972.

The commitment of Reform Judaism to Zionism deepened in the postwar period. Reform Jews welcomed the establishment of the state of Israel in 1948, shared feelings of crisis and relief during its Six Day War, and increasingly appropriated its cultural impact. Israeli melodies entered the synagogues, religious schools, and summer camps. The CCAR declared Israeli Independence Day a religious holiday, and beginning in 1970 HUC-JIR required all entering rabbinical students to spend the first year of their study at its campus in Jerusalem.

The centrality of Jewish peoplehood, symbolized by the state of Israel, found clear expression in the most recent platform of Reform Judaism. Called "A Centenary Perspective" because it was composed about one hundred years after the creation of the first national institutions of American Reform Judaism, it was adopted by the CCAR in 1976. The statement was the work of a committee chaired by Rabbi Eugene Borowitz, a professor at the New York school of HUC-JIR and one of the most influential contemporary theologians of the movement. Unlike previous platforms, it does not seek to define Judaism as a whole dogmatically, but only to give a brief historical account of Reform Judaism—what it has taught and what it has learned—and to describe its present spiritual convictions. Recognizing and affirming the diversity of theology and practice in contemporary Reform, it points to those broad conceptions and values shared by most Reform Jews. In the wake of the Holocaust and recognizing the physically precarious situation of Israeli Jewry and the assimilatory forces operative on American Judaism, the statement gives prominence to the value of ethnic survival, an element not highlighted in earlier platforms. It affirms the reality of God, without setting forth any specific theology, and defines the people of Israel as inseparable from its religion.

[*See also* Judaism.]

— MICHAEL A. MEYER

REINCARNATION

The doctrine of reincarnation concerns the rebirth of the soul or self in a series of physical or preternatural embodiments, which are customarily human or animal in nature but are in some instances divine, angelic, demonic, vegetative, or astrological (i. e., are associated with the sun, moon, stars, or planets).

ARCHAIC CULTURES. A belief in reincarnation in some form or another is to be found in non-literate cultures all over the world. Besides central Australia, in which this precept is noticeably present, are West Africa (among the Ewe, Edo, Igbo, and Yoruba), southern Africa (among the Bantu-speakers and the Zulu), Indonesia, Oceania, New Guinea, and both North and South America (among selected ethnic groups).

In sub-Saharan Africa, for example, reincarnation is not only viewed positively, but failure to be reborn and thereby gain yet another opportunity to improve the world of the living is regarded as an evil (as is the state of childlessness).

Among the Yoruba and Edo peoples, the belief in the rebirth of the departed ancestors remains a strong and vibrant cultural force to the present day. It is their custom to name each boy child "Father Has Returned" and each girl child "Mother Has Returned."

According to Australian Aboriginal religious beliefs, a deceased ancestor, after a sojourn of an unspecified length of time in the land of the dead, returns to the world of the living by entering the body of a mother at the moment of conception. The father is believed to play no direct role in impregnating the mother. Instead, the mother-to-be conceives new life by coming into the proximity of an *oknanikilla,* or local totem center, in which a spirit being *(alcheringa)* or soul of a deceased ancestor is lying in wait to be reborn.

HINDUISM. The whole of the Hindu ethical code laid down in the ancient law books (e.g., *Laws of Manu*) presupposes the survival of the soul after death and assumes that the present life is fundamentally a preparation for the life to come. According to the Hindu conception of transmigration or rebirth (samsara, "a course or succession of states of existence"), the circumstances of any given lifetime are automatically determined by the net results of good and evil actions in previous existences. This, in short, is the law of karman (action), a universal law of nature that works according to its own inherent necessity.

The succession of finite births has traditionally been regarded by Hindus pessimistically, as an existential misfortune and not as a series of "second chances" to improve one's lot, as it is often viewed in the West. Life is regarded not only as "rough, brutish, and short" but as filled with misery *(duhkha)*. Thus, the multiplication of births within this "vale of tears" merely augments and intensifies the suffering that is the lot of all creatures.

BUDDHISM. Sakyamuni Buddha, like his philosophical and spiritual predecessors, believed that birth and death recur in successive cycles for the person who lives in the grip of ignorance about the true nature of the world. However, he undercut the Vedantic position by denying that the world of evanescent entities is undergirded and suffused by an eternal and unalterable Self or "soul-stuff" *(atman)*. In place of the doctrine of absolute self, he propagated the precept of "no-self" *(anatman)*, namely, that the human person, along with everything else that constitutes the empirical universe, is the offspring *(phala)* of an unbroken, everfluctuating process of creation and destruction and birth and extinction according to the principle of Dependent Co-origination (*pratitya-samutpada;* Pali, *paticca-samuppada*).

JAINISM. According to the teachings of Mahavira (c. 599-527 BCE), the founder of Jainism, the unenlightened soul is bound to follow a course of transmigration that is beginningless and one that will persist for an unimaginable length of time. The soul becomes defiled by involvement in desire-laden actions and thereby attracts increasingly burdensome quantities of karmic matter upon itself. This polluting material, in turn, promotes the further corruption of the soul and causes its inevitable movement through countless incarnations.

CONCLUSION. There is no question but that the twin doctrines of *karman* and reincarnation have done more to shape the whole of Asian thought than any other concept or concepts. Ironically, the notion of reincarnation is beginning to make inroads into contemporary Western thought (particularly in theology, the philosophy of religion, and psychology) by way of a number of circuitous routes. One of the most curious manifestations of the belief in reincarnation in modern times is a new approach to psychotherapy that operates in the United States under the rubric of "rebirthing analysis," which purports to help the client deal with current psychological and spiritual problems by recalling personal experiences during numerous past lifetimes with the aid of meditation, hypnosis, and in some cases, consciousness-altering drugs.

[*See also* Immortality.]

— J. BRUCE LONG

RESURRECTION

The term *resurrection* is so intricately bound up with Christian ideas that it is extremely difficult to decide when it should be used for similar ideas in other religions.

TAOISM. In Chinese Taoism there is frequent mention of prolonging life and strengthening the vital force, but there is no uniform doctrine on this subject. We are told of various practices—meditation, use of alcoholic beverages, magical rites—through which the lower and mortal elements in man can be replaced by higher and immortal ones and the vital principle can be strengthened so as not to be separated from the body. In this way man can achieve immortality and ascend to the heavenly world. But this is hardly resurrection in the strict sense of the word.

INDIA. The Vedic language possesses several words that have been thought to denote the "soul" as an immortal spiritual substance in man: *manas* ("thought, thinking"), *asu* ("life"), *atman* ("breath"), *tanu* ("body, self"). But the equation of any of these words with "soul" is hardly correct. In the *Rgveda* there are hints that at death the various parts of the body merge with natural phenomena of a similar kind: the flesh goes to the earth, the blood to the water, the breath to the wind, the eye to the sun, the mind *(manas)* to the moon, and so on. Although this belief differs consider-

The nature of the soul can be seen in the Vedic attitude toward death, for the dead are simply the shadows of the living.

PAGE 317

"For since by man came death, by man came also the resurrection of the dead."

I CORINITHIANS 15:20

ably from the Christian idea of resurrection, it may perhaps be described by this term.

EGYPT. The Egyptian view of man presupposes two incorporeal elements, neither corresponding to any modern concept of the soul. When a person dies, his *ba* (soul) leaves the body but hovers near the corpse. The *ka* combines the ideas of vital force, nourishment, double, and genius. *Ba* and *ka* cannot exist without a bodily substrate. Therefore the body is embalmed to secure their existence. In addition, the funerary rites transform the deceased into an *akh,* a "shining" or "transformed" sprit. In this capacity the deceased lives on in the realm of Osiris, the god of the netherworld, who once died but was revived again as the ruler of the dead.

ZOROASTRIANISM. The earliest documents of Zoroastrian religion do not mention the resurrection of the body but rather the soul's ascent to paradise. But in the later parts of the Avesta there is at least one reference to resurrection: "When the dead rise, the Living Incorruptible One will come and life will be transfigured" (*Yashts* 19.11). The Living One is the savior, Saoṣhyant (Pahl., Soshans), who is to come at the end of the present era. Another passage (*Yashts* 13.11), which speaks of joining together bones, hairs, flesh, bowels, feet, and genitals, refers not to resurrection, as has been maintained, but to birth.

JUDAISM. The Hebrew scriptures (Old Testament) as a whole have no doctrine of resurrection. Usually the scriptures assert that "if a man dies, he will not live again" (*Jb.* 14:14) or that "he who goes down to She'ol does not come up" (7:9).

The only clear reference to resurrection is found in the *Book of Daniel* (c. 165 BCE). There we read: "Many of those who sleep in the dust will awake, some to eternal life, others to eternal shame" (12:2).

Similar statements are found in *4 Ezra* 7:32 : "The earth shall give up those who sleep in it, and the dust those who rest there in silence, and the storehouses shall give back the souls entrusted to them." The mention of the souls seems to indicate that death is the separation of body and soul (cf. 7:78) and that resurrection means they are reunited.

CHRISTIANITY. In primitive Christianity the resurrection of Christ was the fundamental fact; belief in it was even regarded as a prerequisite of salvation.

The first Christians expected the second coming of Christ (the Parousia) to happen in their lifetime. But as several Christians died without having experienced the Parousia, questions arose as to the reliability of the Christian hope. Paul answers such questions in *1 Thessalonians* 4:13-18, asserting that just as Christ died and rose again, the fellowship with him cannot be broken by death: first those who have died in Christ will rise when "the archangel calls and the trumpet sounds," then those who are still alive will be taken away to heaven to Christ.

ISLAM. Islam shares with Christianity the belief in a general resurrection followed by a judgment. The stress is rather on the latter. In the Qur'an the last day is referred to as "the day of resurrection" *(yawm al-qiyamah)*, but also as "the day of judgment" *(yawm ad-din)*, "the day of reckoning" *(yawm al-hisab)*, or "the day of awakening" *(yawm al-ba'th)*. In the Qur'an there are several very graphic descriptions of the day of resurrection, focusing on the natural phenomena that accompany it and on the outcome of the judgment—the believers entering paradise and the unbelievers being thrown into the fire of hell. It is a day "when the trumpet is blown" (cf. *Mt.* 24:31, *1 Thes.* 4:16) and men "shall come in troops, and heaven is opened and the mountains are set in motion" (surah 78:18-20; cf. 18:99), a day "when heaven is rent asunder . . . when earth is stretched out and casts forth what is in it" (84:1-4; cf. 99:1-2).

— HELMER RINGGREN

ROMAN CATHOLICISM

Roman Catholicism refers both to a church (or, more accurately, a college of churches that together constitute the universal Catholic church) and to a tradition. As a church, Roman Catholicism exists at both the local level and the universal level. In the canon law of the Roman Catholic church, the term "local church" (more often rendered as "particular church") applies primarily to a diocese and secondarily to a parish. The universal Roman Catholic church, on the other hand, is constituted by a union, or college, of all the local Catholic churches throughout the world. There are more than one-half billion Catholics worldwide, by far the largest body of Christians. [*See* Papacy.]

As a tradition Roman Catholicism is marked by several different doctrinal and theological emphases. These are its radically positive estimation of the created order, because everything comes from the hand of God, is providentially sustained by God, and is continually transformed and elevated by God's active presence within it; its concern for history; its stress on mediation; and, finally, its affirmation of the communal dimension of salvation and of every religious relationship with God

CATHOLIC VISION AND CATHOLIC VALUES

The church's belief in and commitment to the reality of God is focused in its fundamental attitude toward Jesus Christ (the *Christian* core). For Catholics, as for every

Christian, the old order has passed away, and they are a "new creation" in Christ, for God has "reconciled us to himself through Christ" (*2 Cor.* 5:17, 5:19). "Catholic," therefore, is a qualification of "Christian," of "religious," and of the human.

To be Catholic is, before all else, to be human. Catholicism is an understanding and affirmation of human existence before it is a corporate conviction about the pope, or the seven sacraments, or even about Jesus Christ. But Catholicism is also more than a corporate understanding and affirmation of what it means to be human. Thomas Aquinas affirms that all reality is rooted in the creative, loving power of that which is most real *(ens realissimum)*. Catholicism answers the question of meaning in terms of the reality of God. In brief, Catholicism is a religious perspective, and not simply a philosophical or anthropological one.

Catholicism's view of and commitment to God is radically shaped by its view of and commitment to Jesus Christ. For the Christian, the ultimate dimension of human experience is a triune God: a God who creates and sustains, a God who draws near to and identifies with the human historical condition, and a God who empowers people to live according to the vocation to which they have been called. More specifically, the God of Christians is the God of Jesus Christ. But just as Jesus Christ gives access to God, so, for the Catholic, the church gives access to Jesus Christ.

Roman Catholicism is distinguished from other Christian traditions and churches in its understanding of, commitment to, and exercise of the principles of sacramentality, mediation, and communion.

SACRAMENTALITY. The Catholic sacramental vision "sees" God in and through all things: other people, communities, movements, events, places, objects, the world at large, the whole cosmos. The great sacrament of our encounter with God, and of God's encounter with us, is Jesus Christ. The church, in turn, is the key sacrament of our encounter with Christ, and of Christ with us; and the sacraments, in turn, are the signs and instruments by which that ecclesial encounter with Christ is expressed, celebrated, and made effective for the glory of God and the salvation of men and women.

For the Catholic, the world is essentially good, though fallen, because it comes from the creative hand of God. And for the Catholic, the world, although fallen, is redeemable because of the redemptive work of God in Jesus Christ.

MEDIATION. A kind of corollary of the principle of sacramentality is the principle of mediation. A sacrament not only signifies; it also causes what it signifies. Indeed, as the Council of Trent officially taught, sacraments cause grace precisely insofar as they signify it. If the church, therefore, is not a credible sign of God's and Christ's presence in the world, if the church is not obviously the "temple of the Holy Spirit," it cannot achieve its missionary purposes. It "causes" grace (i. e., effectively moves the world toward its final destiny in the kingdom of God) to the extent that it signifies the reality toward which it presumes to direct the world. For the Catholic, God is not only present in the sacramental action; God actually achieves something in and through that action.

The principle of mediation also explains Catholicism's historic emphasis on the place of Mary, the mother of Jesus Christ. The Catholic readily engages in the veneration (not worship) of Mary, not because Catholicism perceives Mary as some kind of goddess or supercreature or rival of the Lord himself, but because she is a symbol or image of God. [See Christianity, *sidebar* Mary.]

COMMUNION. Finally, Catholicism affirms the principle of communion: the human way to God, and God's way to humankind, is not only a mediated but a communal way. Even when the divine-human encounter is most personal and individual, it is still communal, in that the encounter is made possible by the mediation of a community of faith. Catholics have always emphasized the place of the church as the sacrament of Christ, which mediates salvation through sacraments, ministries, and other institutional elements and forms, and as the communion of saints and the people of God.

POPE JOHN XXIII AND THE SECOND VATICAN COUNCIL

John XXIII first announced his council on 25 January 1959 and officially convoked it on 25 December 1961. In his address at the council's solemn opening on 11 October 1962, he revealed again his spirit of fundamental hope. He believed that "Divine Providence is leading us to a new order of human relations." The purpose of the council, therefore, would be the promotion of "concord, just peace and the brotherly unity of all."

Although John XXIII died between the first two sessions of the council, his successor, Paul VI, carried his program to fulfillment.

PROVISOS OF VATICAN II

1. The church is the people of God, a community of disciples. The hierarchy is part of the people of God, not separate from it.
2. The church must read the signs of the times and interpret them in light of the gospel.
3. Christian unity requires renewal and reform. Both sides were to blame for the divisions of the Reformation; therefore both sides have to be open to change.

John XXIII (1958-1963), elected when he was nearly seventy-seven, began a new era for Roman Catholicism.

PAGE 549

4. The word of God is communicated through sacred scripture, sacred tradition, and the teaching authority of the church, all linked together and guided by the Holy Spirit.
5. The church proclaims the gospel not only in word but also in sacrament: the signs (i.e., language and rituals) must be intelligible.
6. No one is to be forced in any way to embrace Christian or Catholic faith. This principle is rooted in human dignity and the freedom of the act of faith.
7. God speaks also through other religions. The church should engage in dialogue and other collaborative efforts with them.

After four sessions the Second Vatican Council adjourned in December 1965. The story of Catholicism since the council—through the pontificates of Paul VI (1963-1978), John Paul I (1978), and John Paul II (1978-)—has been shaped largely, if not entirely, by the church's efforts to come to terms with the various challenges and opportunities which that council presented: specifically, how can the church remain faithful to its distinctively Catholic heritage even as it continues to affirm and assimilate such modern values as ecumenism, pluralism, and secularity?

POPE JOHN XXIII

John XXIII (r. 1958–1963) convened the Second Vatican Council. His open style of leadership made him extremely popular with Catholics and non-Catholics alike.

UPI/CORBIS-BETTMANN

THEOLOGY AND DOCTRINE

The principles of sacramentality, mediation, and communion frame Catholic thinking and teaching about every significant theological question.

REVELATION AND FAITH. Catholics share with other Christians the conviction that God has somehow communicated with humankind in the history of Israel; supremely in Jesus Christ, the Son of God; then through the apostles and evangelists; and, in a different way, through nature, human events, and personal relationships. Fundamentally, all Christians, conservative and liberal alike, are united in the belief that Jesus Christ, as both person and event, provides the fullest disclosure of God. Christian faith is the acceptance of Jesus Christ as the Lord and Savior of the world and as the great sacrament of God's presence among us.

CREATION AND ORIGINAL SIN. Roman Catholics adhere to the ancient Christian creeds, which professed their belief in one God, the Almighty Creator, who made the heavens and the earth, and all things visible and invisible. And they adhere as well to the later councils of the church, which added that God freely created the world from nothing at the beginning of time in order to share his own goodness, to manifest his own glory, and to sanctify humankind. Jesus Christ is not only the head of the whole human race but also is himself the summit of all creation.

Original sin is the state in which all people are born precisely because they are members of the human race. As such, we are situated in a sinful history that affects our capacity to love God above all and to become the kind of people God destined us to be. What is important to remember, Catholics insist, is that we came forth from the hand of God essentially good, not essentially evil. Humankind is redeemable because men and women are radically good. [*For discussion of sin and related issues in broad religious perspective, see* Evil.]

NATURE AND GRACE. Roman Catholics have never endorsed the view that people are saved by their own power. To be in the state of grace means to be open to the presence of God, and of the Holy Spirit in particular. This indwelling of the Spirit really transforms us. Our sins are not merely "covered over." They are obliterated by an act of divine forgiveness and generosity, on the sole condition that we are truly sorry for having offended God in the first place.

JESUS CHRIST AND REDEMPTION. Roman Catholics share with other Christians the central conviction of Christian faith that Jesus of Nazareth is the Lord of history (*Phil.* 2:5-11), that he was crucified for our sins, was raised from the dead on the third day, was exalted as Lord of all, is present to history now in and through the church.

Jesus Christ is both human and divine in nature, yet one person. "Born of a woman" (*Gal.* 4:4), he is like us in all things save sin (*Heb.* 4:15). At the same time, he is of the very being of God, Son of the Father, the light of God in the world. He is, in the words of the Second Vatican Council, "the key, the focal point, and the goal of all human history".

EXCOMMUNICATION
Cut Off From Communion

To excommunicate means "to cut off from communion" or "to exclude from fellowship in a community." In a Christian setting, the term *excommunication* also applies to exclusion from Holy Communion, or the Eucharist.

As a medicinal, or healing, penalty, excommunication under Roman Catholic law may be incurred only if a serious sin has been committed, or if the person is obstinate in a position after being given formal warnings and time to repent. Reflecting medieval and later developments, some excommunications are automatic *(latae sententiae)*, incurred by committing a specified act, such as abortion or physically striking the pope. Other excommunications are imposed *(ferendae sententiae)* after an administrative or judicial investigation. Excommunication must always be lifted as soon as the delinquent repents and seeks peace with the church.

An excommunicated person loses basic rights in the church, but not the effects of baptism, which can never be lost. In the revision of the code carried out after Vatican II the effects of excommunication were clarified, and the distinction of *vitandi* and *tolerati* was dropped. Instead, all are treated as *tolerati* so far as the effects are concerned.

Generally, a person who is excommunicated is denied any role in administering the sacraments, especially the Eucharist. He may not receive any of the sacraments or administer sacramentals, such as burials, and he is forbidden to exercise any church offices or functions.

Under the reform of the law, automatic excommunication can be incurred in only six instances, including abortion. It may be imposed for a limited number of other crimes against faith, the Eucharist, or the seal of the confessional in the sacrament of penance. If imposed by a sentence or public declaration, excommunication can be lifted only by a public authority in the church, usually the local diocesan bishop.

— JAMES H. PROVOST

HOLY SPIRIT AND TRINITY. The Holy Spirit is God's self-communication as love and as the power of healing, reconciliation, and new life. The divinity of the Holy Spirit was defined by the First Council of Constantinople in 381. The Spirit has the same divine essence as the Father and the Son and yet is distinct from them both. Within the Trinity, the Spirit proceeds from the Father *through* the Son.

CATHOLIC MORALITY. For Catholicism, morality is a matter of thinking and acting in accordance with the person and the community one has become in Christ. Catholic morality is characterized by a both/and rather than an either/or approach. It is not nature or grace, but graced nature; not reason or faith, but reason illumined by faith; not law or gospel, but law inspired by the gospel; not scripture or tradition, but normative tradition within scripture; not faith or works, but faith issuing in works and works as expressions of faith; not authority or freedom, but authority in the service of freedom; not the past versus the present, but the present in continuity with the past; not stability or change, but change in fidelity to stable principle, and principle fashioned and refined in response to change; not unity or diversity, but unity in diversity, and diversity that prevents uniformity, the antithesis of unity.

POLITY

Just as the universal church is composed of an international college of local churches, so the universality of the church is expressed through the collegial relationship of the bishops, one to another. The bishop of Rome serves as the head and center of this collegial network. Bishops participate in the governance of the church through synods. The college of cardinals constitutes a special college of bishops within the larger episcopal college.

At the diocesan level there are bishops, auxiliary bishops, vicars general, chancellors, marriage courts, diocesan pastoral councils, and the like. At the parish level there are pastors, associate pastors, pastoral ministers, extraordinary ministers of the Eucharist, parish councils, and the like.

— RICHARD P. MCBRIEN

"Come, Holy Spirit, and send out from heaven the beam of your light."

ARCHBISHOP STEPHEN LANGTON
1228

ROMAN RELIGION

The Roman state's extraordinary and unexpected transformation from one that had hegemony over the greater part of Italy into a world state in the second and first centuries BCE had implications for Roman religion which are not easy to grasp. After all, Christianity, a religion wholly "foreign" in its origins, arose from this period of Roman ascendancy. To begin, then, to understand the religious system of imperial Rome, it is best to confine ourselves to three elementary and obviously related facts.

The first is that the old Roman practice of inviting

the chief gods of their enemies to become gods of Rome (*evocatio*) played little or no part in the new stage of imperialism.

The second fact is that while it was conquering the Hellenistic world Rome was involved in a massive absorption of Greek language, literature, and religion, with the consequence that the Roman gods became victorious over Greece at precisely the time that they came to be identified with Greek gods. As the gods were expected to take sides and to favor their own worshipers, this must have created some problems.

The third fact is that the conquest of Africa, Spain, and, ultimately, Gaul produced the opposite phenomenon of a large, though by no means systematic, identification of Punic, Iberian, and Celtic gods with Roman gods. This, in turn, is connected with two opposite aspects of the Roman conquest of the West. On the one hand, the Romans had little sympathy and understanding for the religion of their Western subjects. On the other hand, northern Africa, outside Egypt, and western Europe were deeply latinized in language and romanized in institutions, thereby creating the conditions for the assimilation of native gods to Roman gods.

In its most fundamental meaning, faith has been defined as faithfulness, and as such, it has been taken as an attribute both of the divine and of believers in the divine.

PAGE 223

Yet the Mars, the Mercurius, and even the Jupiter and the Diana we meet so frequently in Gaul under the Romans are not exactly the same as in Rome. The assimilation of the native god is often revealed by an accompanying adjective (in Gaul, Mars Lenus, Mercurius Dumiatis, etc.,). An analogous phenomenon had occurred in the East under the Hellenistic monarchies: native, especially Semitic, gods were assimilated to Greek gods, especially to Zeus and Apollo. The Eastern assimilation went on under Roman rule (as seen, for example, with Zeus Panamaros in Caria).

The Romans also turned certain gods of Greek origin into gods of victory. As early as 145 BCE L. Mummius dedicated a temple to Hercules Victor after his triumph over Greece. After a victory, generals often offered 10 percent of their booty to Hercules, and Hercules Invictus was a favorite god of Pompey. Apollo was connected with Victory as early as 212 BCE.

IMPERIAL ATTITUDES TOWARD AND USES OF RELIGION. Augustus and his contemporaries thought, or perhaps in some cases wanted other people to think, that the preceding age (roughly the period from the Gracchi to Caesar) had seen a decline in the ancient Roman care for gods. Augustus himself stated in the autobiographical record known as the *Res gestae* that he and his friends had restored eighty-two temples. He revived cults and religious associations, such as the Arval Brothers and the fraternity of the Titii, and appointed a *flamen dialis,* a priestly office that had been left vacant since 87 BCE.

Marius was accompanied in his campaigns by a Syrian prophetess. Sulla apparently brought from Cappadocia the goddess Ma, soon identified with Bellona, whose orgiastic and prophetic cult had wide appeal. Furthermore, he developed a personal devotion to Venus and Fortuna and set an example for Caesar, who claimed Venus as the ancestress of the *gens Julia.* As *pontifex maximus* for twenty years, Caesar reformed not only individual cults but also the calendar, which had great religious significance.

Unusual religious attitudes were not confined to leaders. A Roman senator, Nigidius Figulus, made religious combinations of his own both in his writings and in his practice: magic, astrology, and Pythagoreanism were some of the ingredients. Cicero, above all, epitomized the search of educated men of the first century BCE for the right balance between respect for the ancestral cults and the requirements of philosophy.

The Augustan restoration discouraged philosophical speculation about the nature of the gods: Lucretius's *De rerum natura* remains characteristic of the age of Caesar. Augustan poets (Horace, Tibullus, Propertius, and Ovid) evoked obsolescent rites and emphasized piety. Vergil interpreted the Roman past in religious terms. Nevertheless, the combined effect of the initiatives of Caesar and Augustus amounted to a new religious situation.

For centuries the aristocracy in Rome had controlled what was called *ius sacrum* ("sacred law"), the religious aspect of Roman life, but the association of priesthood with political magistracy, though frequent and obviously convenient, had never been institutionalized. In 27 BCE the assumption by Octavian of the permanent title *augustus* implied, though not very clearly, permanent approval of the gods (*augustus* may connote a holder of permanent favorable auspices). In 12 BCE Augustus assumed the position of *pontifex maximus,* which became permanently associated with the figure of the emperor *(imperator)*, the new head for life of the Roman state. Augustus's new role resulted in an identification of religious with political power

As the head of Roman religion, the Roman emperor was therefore in the paradoxical situation of being responsible not only for relations between the Roman state and the gods but also for a fair assessment of his own qualifications to be considered a god, if not after his life, at least while he was alive.

Within the city of Rome, the emperor was in virtual control of the public cults. As a Greek god, Apollo had been kept outside of the *pomerium* since his introduction into Rome: his temple was in the Campus Martius. Under Augustus, however, Apollo received a temple inside the *pomerium* on the Palatine in recognition of the special protection he had offered to Octavian. The Sibylline Books, an ancient collection of prophecies that had been previously preserved on the Capitol, were now transferred to the new temple. Later, Augustus

demonstrated his preference for Mars as a family god, and a temple to Mars Ultor (the avenger of Caesar's murder) was built. Another example of these changes inside Rome is the full romanization of the Etruscan haruspices performed by the emperor Claudius in 47 CE (Tacitus, *Annals* 11.15).

A further step was the admission of Oriental gods to the official religion of Rome, such as the building of a temple to Isis under Gaius. Jupiter Dolichenus, an Oriental god popular among soldiers, was probably given a temple on the Aventine in the second century CE.

Coins and medals, insofar as they were issued under the control of the central government, provide some indication of imperial preferences in the matter of gods and cults. They allow us to say when and how certain Oriental cults (such as that of Isis, as reflected on coins of Vespasian) or certain attributes of a specific god were considered helpful to the empire and altogether suitable for the man in the street who used coins. But since as a rule it avoided references to cults of rulers, coinage can be misleading if taken alone. Imperial cult and Oriental cults are, in fact, two of the most important features of Roman religion in the imperial period. But we also have to take into consideration popular, not easily definable trends; the religious beliefs or disbeliefs of the intellectuals; the greater participation of women in religious and in intellectual life generally; and, finally, the peculiar problems presented by the persecution of Christianity.

THE IMPERIAL CULT. Imperial cult was many things to many people. The emperor never became a complete god, even if he was considered a god, because he was not requested to produce miracles, even for supposed deliverance from peril. Ultimately, the cult of the living emperor mattered more.

The cult of Roman provincial governors disappeared with Augustus, to the exclusive benefit of the emperor and his family. When he did not directly encourage the ruler cult, the emperor still had to approve, limit, and occasionally to refuse it. Although he had to be worshiped, he also had to remain a man in order to live on social terms with the Roman aristocracy, of which he was supposed to be the *princeps.* It was a delicate balancing act. It is probably fair to say that during his lifetime the emperor was a god more in proportion to his remoteness, rather than his proximity, and that the success (for success it was) of the imperial cult in the provinces was due to the presence it endowed to an absent and alien sovereign. His statues, his temples, and his priests, as well as the games, sacri-

WALL MURAL, POMPEII

This wall mural showing the Dionysian Cult in the Villa of Mysteries, Pompeii is a striking example of the Roman assimilation of Greek gods.

MIMMO JODICE/CORBIS

fices, and other ceremonial acts, helped make the emperor present; they also helped people to express their interest in the preservation of the world in which they lived.

Schematically it can be said that in Rome and Italy Augustus favored the association of the cult of his life spirit *(genius)* with the old cult of the public lares of the crossroads *(lares compitales)*: such a combined cult was in the hands of humble people. Similar associations (Augustales) developed along various lines in Italy and gave respectability to the freedmen who ran them. Augustus's birthday was considered a public holiday. His *genius* was included in public oaths between Jupiter Optimus Maximus and the *penates.* In Augustus's last years Tiberius dedicated an altar to the *numen Augusti* in Rome; the four great priestly colleges had to make yearly sacrifices at it.

"A civilization is destroyed only when its gods are destroyed."

E.M. CIORAN
THE NEW GODS 1969

Augustus's successors tended to be worshiped either individually, without the addition of Roma, or collectively with past emperors. In Asia Minor the last individual emperor known to have received a personal priesthood or temple is Caracalla. In this province—though not necessarily elsewhere—the imperial cult petered out at the end of the third century. Nevertheless, Constantine, in the fourth century, authorized the building of a temple for the *gens Flavia* (his own family).

When the imperial cult died out, the emperor had to be justified as the choice of god; he became emperor by the grace of god. Thus Diocletian and Maximian, the persecutors of Christianity, present themselves not as Jupiter and Hercules but as Jovius and Herculius, that is, the protégés of Jupiter and Hercules. It must be added that during the first centuries of the empire the divinization of the emperor was accompanied by a multiplication of divinizations of private individuals, in the West often of humble origin. Such divinization took the form of identifying the dead, and occasionally the living, with a known hero or god. Sometimes the divinization was nothing more than an expression of affection by relatives or friends. But it indicated a tendency to reduce the distance between men and gods, which helped the fortunes of the imperial cult.

ORIENTAL INFLUENCES. Oriental cults penetrated the Roman empire at various dates, in different circumstances, and with varying appeal. They tended, though not in equal measure, to present themselves as mystery cults.

Cybele, the first Oriental divinity to be found acceptable in Rome since the end of the third century BCE, was long an oddity in the city. As the Magna Mater ("great mother"), she had been imported by governmental decision, she had a temple within the *pomerium,* and she was under the protection of members of the highest Roman aristocracy. Yet her professional priests, singing in Greek and living by their temple, were considered alien fanatics even in imperial times. What is worse, the goddess also had servants, the Galli, who had castrated themselves to express their devotion to her.

Although Isis appealed to men as well as to women— and indeed her priests were male—it seems clear that her prestige as a goddess was due to the unusual powers she was supposed to have as a woman. In association with Osiris or Sarapis, Isis seems to have become the object of a mystery cult in the first century CE; as such she appears in Apuleius's *Metamorphoses.*

Late in the first century CE, Mithraism began to spread throughout the Roman empire, especially in the Danubian countries and in Italy (in particular, as far as we know, in Ostia and Rome). A developed mystery cult, it had ranks of initiation and leadership and was, to the best of our present knowledge, reserved to men. The environment of the Mithraic cult, as revealed in numerous extant chapels, was one of darkness, secrecy, dramatic lighting effects, and magic.

The cult of Sabazios may have been originally Phrygian. Sabazios appears in Athens in the fifth century BCE as an orgiastic god. He was known to Aristophanes, and later the orator Aeschines became his priest. In Rome his cult left a particularly curious document in the tomb of Vincentius, located in the catacomb of Praetextatus; it includes scenes of banquets and of judgment after death. Whether this is evidence of mystery ceremonies or of Christian influence remains uncertain. (See Erwin R. Goodenough, *Jewish Symbols in the Greco-Roman Period,* vol. 2, 1953, p. 45, for a description.)

Another popular Oriental god occupies a place by himself. This is Jupiter Dolichenus, who emerged from Doliche in Commagene in the first century CE and for whom we have about six hundred monuments. Of the Oriental gods, he seems to have been the least sophisticated and to have disappeared earliest (in the third century). He was ignored by Christian polemicists. While he circulated in the empire, he preserved his native attributes: he is depicted as a warrior with Phrygian cap, double ax, and lightning bolt, standing erect over a bull.

EXTENT OF SYNCRETISM. We are in constant danger of either overrating or underrating the influence of these Oriental cults on the fabric of the Roman empire. If, for instance, Mithraists knew of the Zoroastrian deity Angra Mainyu, what did he mean to them? How did this knowledge affect the larger society? At a superficial level we can take these cults as an antidote to the imperial cult, an attempt to retreat from the public sphere of political allegiance to the private sphere of small, free associations. The need for small loyalties was widely felt during the imperial peace. Tavern keepers devoted to their wine god and poor people meeting regularly in burial clubs are examples of such associations *(collegia)*. Ritualization of ordinary life emerged from their activities. Nor is it surprising that what to one was religion was superstition to another. Although allegiance to the local gods (and respect for them, if one happened to be a visitor) was deeply rooted, people were experimenting with new private gods and finding satisfaction in them. Concern with magic and astrology, with dreams and demons, seems ubiquitous. Conviviality was part of religion.

It remains a puzzle how, and how much, ordinary people were supposed to know about official Roman religion. The same problem exists concerning the Greeks in relation to the religions of individual Greek cities. But in Greek cities the collective education of adolescents, as *epheboi,* implied participation in religious activities (for instance, singing hymns in festivals) which were a form of religious education. In the Latin-speaking world, however, there is no indication of generalized practices of this kind.

Another element difficult to evaluate is the continuous, and perhaps increased, appeal of impersonal gods within Roman religion. There is no indication that Faith (Fides) and Hope (Spes) increased their appeal. (They came to play a different part in Christianity by combining with Jewish and Greek ideas.) At best, Fides gained prestige as a symbol of return to loyalty and good faith during the reign of Augustus. But Fortuna, Tutela, and Virtus were popular; the typology of Virtus on coins seems to be identical with that of Roma.

A third element of complication is what is called syncretism, by which we really mean two different things. One is the positive identification of two or more gods; the other is the tendency to mix different cults by using symbols of other gods in the sanctuary of one god, with the result that the presence of Sarapis, Juno, and even Isis was implied in the shrine of Jupiter Dolichenus on the Aventine in Rome. In either form, syncretism may have encouraged the idea that all gods are aspects, or manifestations, of one god.

ROLE OF WOMEN. Women seem to have taken a more active, and perhaps a more creative, part in the religious life of the imperial period. This was connected with the considerable freedom of movement and of administration of one's own estate which women, and especially wealthy women, had in the Roman empire. Roman empresses of Oriental origin (Julia Domna, wife of Septimius Severus, and Julia Mamaea, mother of Severus Alexander) contributed to the diffusion out-

LITERARY EVIDENCE
Clues among the Great Books

Epigraphy and archaeology have taught us much, but the religion of the Roman empire survives mainly through writings in Latin, Greek, Syriac, and Coptic (not to speak of other languages): biographies, philosophical disputations, epic poems, antiquarian books, exchanges of letters, novels, and specific religious books. The Stoic Lucan in his *Pharsalia,* a poem on the civil wars, excludes the gods but admits fate and fortune, magic and divination. Two generations later, Silius Italicus wrote an optimistic poem, centering on Scipio as a Roman Herakles supported by his father, Jupiter. More or less at the same time, Plutarch was reflecting on new and old cults, on the delays in divine justice, and (if the work in question is indeed his) on superstition.

The variety of moods and experiences conveyed by these texts, from the skeptical to the mystical, from the egotistic to the political in the old Greek sense, gives us an approximate notion of the thoughts of educated people on religious subjects. These books provide the background for an understanding of the Christian apologists who wrote for the pagan upper class. Conversely, we are compelled to ask how much of pagan religious thinking was conditioned by the presence of Jews and, even more, of Christians in the neighborhood. The anti-Jewish attitudes of a Tacitus or of a Juvenal offer no special problem: they are explicit.

The most problematic texts are perhaps those which try to formulate explicit religious beliefs. Even a simple military religious calendar (such as the third-century Feriale Duranum, copied for the benefit of the garrison of Dura-Europos) raises the question of its purpose and validity: how many of these old-fashioned Roman festivals were still respected? When we come to such books as the *Chaldean Oracles* (late second century?) or the Hermetic texts, composed in Greek at various dates in Egypt (and clearly showing the influence of Jewish ideas), it is difficult to decide who believed in them and to what extent. Such texts present themselves as revealed: they speak of man's soul imprisoned in the body, of fate, and of demonic power with only a minimum of coherence. They are distantly related to what modern scholars call gnosticism, a creed with many variants which was supposed to be a deviation from Christianity and, as such, was fought by early Christian apologists.

— ARNALDO MOMIGLIANO

These developments culminated in the best-preserved of all Roman temples, the Pantheon in Rome, built by the emperor Hadrian (117-138)

PAGE 663

side Africa of the cult of Caelestis, who received a temple on the Capitol in Rome. The wife of a Roman consul, Pompeia Agrippinilla, managed to put together a private association of about four hundred devotees of Liber-Dionysos in the Roman Campagna in the middle of the second century CE. (See the inscription published by Achille Vogliano in the *American Journal of Archaeology* 37, 1933, p. 215.) Women could be asked to act as *theologoi,* that is, to preach about gods in ceremonies, even those of a mystery nature.

Dedications of religious and philosophical books by men to women appear in the imperial period. Plutarch dedicated his treatise on Isis and Osiris to Clea, a priestess of Delphi; Diogenes Laertius dedicated his book on Greek philosophers (which has anti-Christian implications) to a female Platonist. Philostratus claims that Julia Domna encouraged him to write the life of Apollonius of Tyana.

STATE REPRESSION AND PERSECUTION. The Roman state had always interfered with the freedom to teach and worship. In republican times astrologers, magicians, philosophers, and even rhetoricians, not to speak of adepts of certain religious groups, had been victims of such intrusion. Under which precise legal category this interference was exercised remains a question, except perhaps in cases of sacrilege. Augustus prohibited Roman citizens from participating in druidic cults, and Claudius prohibited the cult of the druids altogether. Details are not clear, and consequences not obvious, though one hears little of the druids from this time on.

This being said, we must emphasize how unusual it was for the Roman government to come to such decisions. Existing cults might or might not be encouraged, but they were seldom persecuted. Even Jews and Egyptians were ordinarily protected in their cults, although there were exceptions. The long-standing conflict between the Christians and the Roman state—even taking into account that persecution was desultory—remains unique for several reasons which depended more on Christian than on imperial behavior. First, the Christians obviously did not yield or retreat, as did the druids. Second, the Christians hardly ever became outright enemies of, or rebels against, the Roman state. The providential character of the Roman state was a basic assumption of Christianity. The workings of providence were shown, for Christians, by the fact that Jesus was born under Roman rule, while the Roman state had destroyed the Temple of Jerusalem and dispersed the Jews, thus making the church the heiress to the Temple. Third, the Christians were interested in what we may call classical culture. Their debate with the pagans became, increasingly, a debate within the terms of reference of classical culture; the Jews, however, soon lost their contact with classical thought and even with such men as Philo, who had represented them in the dialogue with classical culture. Fourth, Christianity and its ecclesiastical organization provided what could alternatively be either a rival or a subsidiary structure to the imperial government; the choice was left to the Roman government, which under Constantine chose the church as a subsidiary institution (without quite knowing on what conditions).

The novelty of the conflict explains the novelty of the solution—not tolerance but conversion. The emperor had to become Christian and to accept the implications of his conversion. It took about eighty years to turn the pagan state into a Christian state. The process took the form of a series of decisions about public non-Christian acts of worship. The first prohibition of pagan sacrifices seems to have been enacted in 341 (*Codex Theodosianus* 16.10.2). Closing of the pagan temples and prohibition of sacrifices in public places under penalty of death was stated or restated at an uncertain date between 346 and 354 (ibid., 16.10.4).

— ARNALDO MOMIGLIANO

RUSSIAN ORTHODOX CHURCH

Vladimir I, grand prince of Kiev, was baptized in 988. Having sent ambassadors to investigate the religions of his day, Vladimir was persuaded to embrace Greek Christianity when, according to the Russian *Primary Chronicle,* his envoys reported that at the liturgy in Constantinople they did not know whether they were in heaven or on earth. Vladimir's marriage to the Byzantine princess Anna and his economic dealings with the empire also played a significant part in his decision to align his principality with the imperial church of Byzantium.

After the baptism of the Kievan peoples, Orthodox Christianity flourished in the lands of Rus'. Before the Tatar devastations in the thirteenth century, Kiev was a cosmopolitan city with commercial and cultural ties with Europe and the East. Its spiritual center was the Kievan Monastery of the Caves, which provided for the first literary and historical, as well as religious, writings in the Russian lands; for centuries it served as the theological and spiritual center of Ukrainian church life. In the early years of Christian Kiev, several remarkable churches were constructed. The leader of church life was the bishop of Kiev.

After the devastation of Kiev by the Tatars in 1240, the center of Russian political and ecclesiastical life shifted to Moscow. The ascendancy of Moscow could

R

RUSSIAN ORTHODOX CHURCH

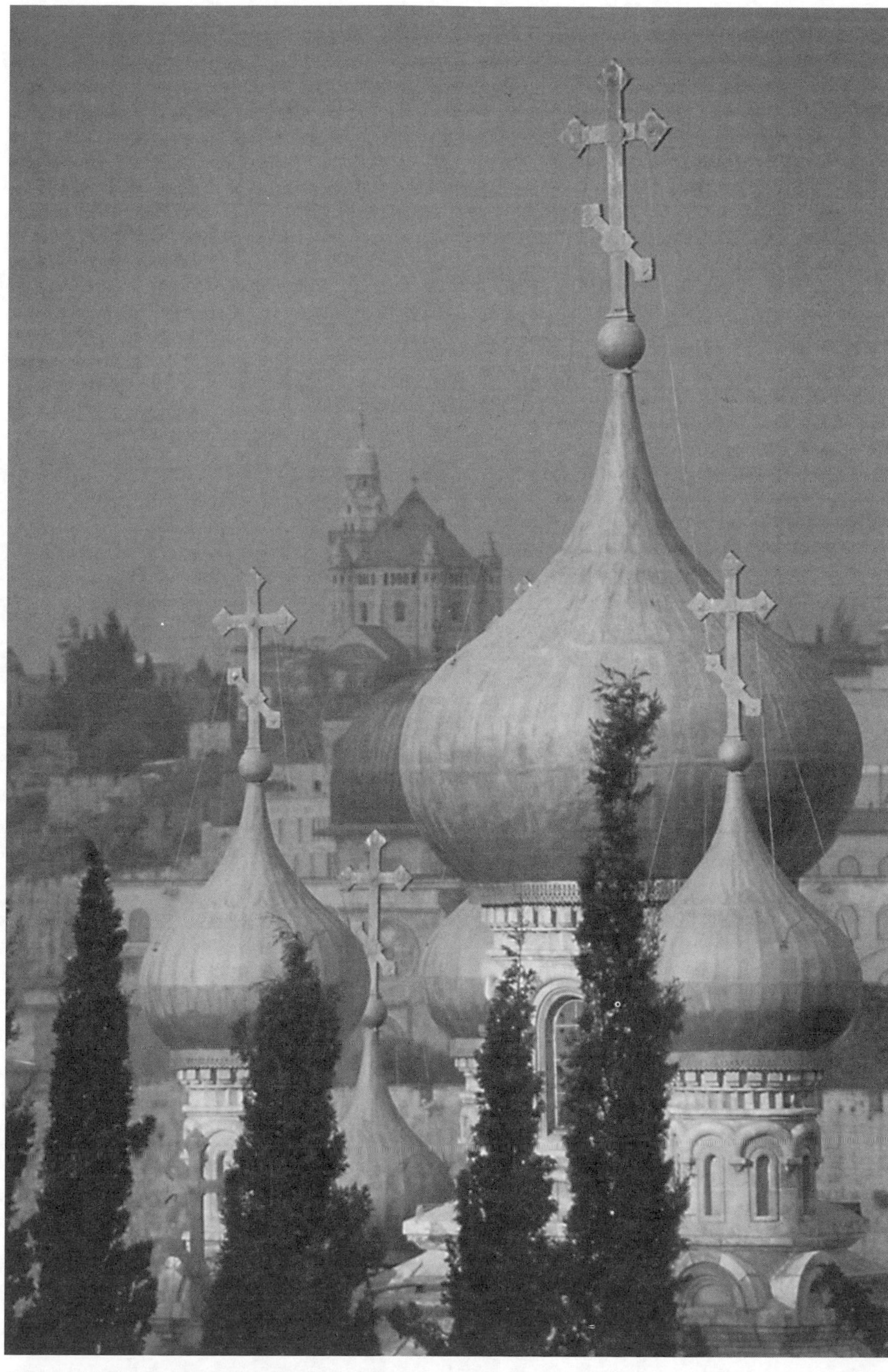

SAINT MARY MAGDELENE, JERUSALEM *Domes, perceived as a symbol of heaven, are considered to be the divine made visible in the Russian Orthodox Church.* DAVE BARTRUFF/CORBIS

The church in Russia went on producing saints and scholars, and through the icons and the liturgy it suffused the faith and life of the common people with the meaning of the Christian faith.

PAGE 158

not have occurred without the efforts of church leaders, particularly the metropolitans such as Alexis (d. 1378), who for a time served as governing regent, and the abbot Sergii of Radonezh (d. 1392). Sergii is considered by many to be Russia's greatest saint and the "builder" of the nation. A simple monk who became famous for his ascetic labors and mystical gifts, he was appointed abbot of the Saint Sergius Trinity Monastery, which he founded in the wilderness north of Moscow (in present-day Zagorsk). The monastery soon became the center of social and economic as well as religious and spiritual life in the region.

In the fifteenth century, with the fall of Constantinople to the Turks (1453), the theory developed that Moscow was the "third Rome," the last center of true Christianity on earth. Job, the metropolitan of Moscow, was named patriarch by Jeremias II of Constantinople in 1589, thus giving the Russian church a status of self-governance and honor equal to that of the ancient patriarchates of the Christian empire. The patriarchate existed in Russia until the time of Peter the Great, who in 1721 issued the Ecclesiastical Regulation, which created a synodical form of church government patterned after that of the Protestant churches of Europe.

In the seventeenth century Patriarch Nikon (d. 1681) attempted to reform the Russian church according to the practices of the church of Constantinople. During the time of the westernization of Russia under Peter the Great and subsequent tsars, the Russian church became the virtual captive of the state. The patriarchate was abolished and replaced by the Holy Synod, consisting of bishops, presbyters, and laymen. Church councils were forbidden, ecclesiastical properties were appropriated and secularized, and church schools began to teach in Latin and to propagate Roman Catholic and Protestant doctrines.

In the eighteenth and nineteenth centuries the missionary efforts of the Russian church were extensive. The scriptures and services of the church were translated into many Siberian languages and Alaskan dialects as the Eastern regions of the empire were settled and evangelized. Russian missionaries reached the Aleutian Islands in Alaska in 1794, thus beginning the history of Russian Orthodoxy in the New World. The monk Herman (d. 1830), a member of the original missionary party, was canonized a saint of the church in 1970 by both the Russian church and the Orthodox Church in America.

These centuries also saw a revival of traditional Orthodox ascetical and mystical life uninfluenced by the westernizing tendencies of the ecclesiastical institutions. Paisii Velichkovskii (d. 1794) brought the hesychast method of mystical prayer, rooted in the invocation of the name of Jesus, into the Ukraine and Russia. He translated into Church Slavonic many ancient texts, including the anthology of writings on the spiritual life by the church fathers called the *Philokalia (Dobrotoliubie).*

During this same period a tradition of spiritual eldership (*starchestvo*) emerged in Russia, the most famous center of which was the hermitage of Optina, where such elders (*startsy*) as Leonid, Macarius, and Ambrose spent several hours each day instructing and counseling people of all classes, including many philosophers, intellectuals, and statesmen, among whom were Tolstoi, Dostoevskii, Solov'ev, and Leont'ev.

The turn of the century also saw a revival of patristic studies and a recapturing of the authentic Orthodox theological and liturgical tradition in the ecclesiastical schools, as well as a religious renaissance on the part of a significant number of Russian intellectuals, many of whom either perished in Stalin's prison camps, like Pavel Florenskii, or were exiled to the West, including the philosopher Nikolai Berdiaev (d. 1948) and the theologian Sergei Bulgakov (d. 1944) who served as dean of the émigré Russian Orthodox Theological Institute of Saint Serge in Paris.

— THOMAS HOPKO

S

SACRIFICE

The term *sacrifice,* from the Latin *sacrificium* (*sacer,* "holy"; *facere,* "to make"), carries the connotation of the religious act in the highest, or fullest sense; it can also be understood as the act of sanctifying or consecrating an object.

Sacrifice differs from other cultic actions. The external elements of prayer are simply words and gestures (bodily attitudes), not external objects comparable to the gifts of sacrifice. Eliminatory rites, though they may include the slaying of a living being or the destruction of an inanimate object, are not directed to a personal recipient and thus should not be described as sacrifices. The same is true of ritual slayings in which there is no supernatural being as recipient, as in slayings by which companions are provided for the dead (joint burials) or that are part of the dramatic representation of an event in primordial time.

THE SACRIFICER. The sacrificer may be the head of a family or clan, an elder, or the leader of a band of hunters; in matrilineal societies, the sacrificer may be a woman. This is true especially of hunting and food-gathering cultures as well as nomadic pastoral cultures; even when these include individuals with specific ritual functions (medicine men, sorcerers, soothsayers, shamans), the function of offering sacrifice is not reserved to them. Food-planting cultures, on the other hand, commonly have cultic functionaries to whom the offering of sacrifice is reserved (e.g., the "earth-chiefs" in West African cultures).

The more fully articulated the divisions in a society, the more often there is a class of cultic ministers to whom the offering of sacrifice is reserved. In this situation, tensions and changing relations of power can arise between king and priests, as in ancient Egypt.

MATERIAL OF THE OBLATION. Perhaps we may say that originally what was sacrificed was either something living or an element or symbol of life; in other words, it was not primarily food that was surrendered, but life itself. Yet inanimate things were also included in the material for sacrifice. (But do not archaic cultures regard a great deal as living that to the modern scientific mind is inanimate? Some scholars emphasize not the life but the power of the object.) Only by including inanimate objects is it possible to establish a certain classification of sacrificial objects, as for example, on the one hand, plants and inanimate objects (bloodless offerings), and, on the other, human beings and animals (blood offerings).

Bloodless offerings. Bloodless offerings include, in the first place, vegetative materials. Thus food-gatherers offer a (symbolic) portion of the foodstuffs they have collected. Among herders milk and milk products (e.g., koumiss, a drink derived from milk and slightly fermented, used in Inner Asia) play a similar role, especially in firstlings sacrifices (see below). In the ritual pouring (and especially in other ritual uses) of water, the intention is often not sacrifice but either some other type of rite (lustration, purification, or expiation) or sympathetic magic (e.g., pouring water in order to bring on rain). The offering of flowers or of a sweet fragrance otherwise produced (as in the widespread use of incense, or, among the American Indians, of tobacco smoke) also serves to please the gods or other higher beings.

"So Abraham went and took the ram and offered it up as a holocaust in place of his son."

GENESIS 22:13

Blood offerings. When animals or human beings serve as the sacrificial gift, the shedding of blood may become an essential part of the sacrificial action. Thus *ritual* slaying makes its appearance among cultivators and herders. The most extensive development of ritual slaying is found among cultivators. Here blood plays a significant role as a power-laden substance that brings fertility; it is sprinkled on the fields in order to promote crop yield. Head-hunting, cannibalism, and human sacrifice belong to the same complex of ideas and rites; human sacrifice is also seen as a means of maintaining the cosmic order. Blood sacrifices, however, consist primarily of domesticated animals.

Substitutes. Blood sacrifices, especially those in which human beings were offered, were often replaced at a later stage by other sacrificial gifts, as, for example, "part-for-the-whole" sacrifices, like the offering of fingers, hair, or blood drawn through self-inflicted wounds. Some authors would thus classify so-called chastity sacrifices and include under this heading very disparate and sometimes even opposed practices such as, on the one hand, sexual abandon (sacral prostitution) and, on the other, sexual renunciation, castration, and circumcision.

Animal sacrifices can replace human sacrifices, as seen in well-known examples from Greek myth, epic, and history, and in the Hebrew scriptures (Old Testament; *Gn.* 22:1-19).

Divine offerings. In the examples given under the

previous heading, a sacrificial gift is replaced by another of lesser value. The opposite occurs when the sacrificial gift itself is regarded as divine. This divine status may result from the idea that the sacrificial action repeats a mythical primordial sacrifice in which a god sacrificed either himself or some other god to yet a third god. In other cases the sacrificial object becomes divinized in the sacrificial action itself or in the preparation of the gifts. Thus among the Aztec the prisoner of war who was sacrificed was identified with the recipient of the sacrifice, the god Tezcatlipoca; moreover images of dough, kneaded with the blood of the sacrificed human, were identified with the sun god Huitzilopochtli and ritually eaten.

PLACE AND TIME OF SACRIFICE. The place of offering is not always an altar set aside for the purpose. Thus sacrifices to the dead are often offered at their graves, and sacrifices to the spirits of nature are made beside trees or bushes, in caves, at springs, and so on. Artificial altars in the form of tables are relatively rare. Far more frequently, natural stones or heaps of stones or earthen mounds serve as altars.

The time for regular sacrifices is determined by the astronomical or vegetative year; thus there will be daily, weekly, and monthly sacrifices (especially in higher cultures in which service in the temple is organized like service at a royal court). Sowing and harvest and the transition from one season to the next are widely recognized occasions for sacrifice; in nomadic cultures this is true especially of spring, the season of birth among animals and of abundance of milk.

Extraordinary occasions for sacrifice are provided by special occurrences in the life of the community or the individual. These occurrences may be joyous, as, for example, the erection of a building (especially a temple), the accession of a new ruler, the successful termination of a military campaign or other undertaking, or any event that is interpreted as a manifestation of divine favor. Even more frequently, however, it is critical situations that occasion extraordinary sacrifices: illnesses (especially epidemics or livestock diseases) and droughts or other natural disasters.

INTENTIONS OF SACRIFICE. Theologians usually distinguish four intentions of sacrifice: praise

HUMAN SACRIFICE
The Ultimate Sacrifice

E. B. Tylor (1832-1917) theorized that the origin of religion lay in the primitive tendency to "animate" the entire world with "soul-ghosts." Human sacrifice released these soul-ghosts so that they might join their ancestors and function as a gift to gain particular ends, as homage to a deity, or as a form of renunciation.

Nine basic purposes of human sacrifice have been commonly cited; (1) humans are sacrificed in order to release souls for the service of the dead ancestors; (2) human sacrifice is a gift that binds deities to people in an exchange or that serves to propitiate the gods ; (3) human sacrifice is a communion meal in which the power of life is assimilated and thus regenerated; (4) the offering of human sacrifice serves as an expiation of past transgressions and has a redemptive character; (5) it brings about atonement, (6) the regeneration of earthly fertility, or (7) immortality; (8) it transforms human conditions; and (9) it unifies the divine and mortal.

The burials at Chan Chan (fourteenth-fifteenth centuries) in Peru are illustrative of the theme of soul-release and kinship with the dead. The themes of expiation, redemption, and communion were central in the sacrificial tradition of the early Christian church. Themes of redemption and abnegation can also be found in the self-sacrifices of the samurai in Japan.

In the Hawaiian Islands, sacrifice stands for transformation, communion, and the capacity to reorder what has been disordered.

The evidence for human sacrifice in Vedic India (c. 1500-600 BCE) is still largely contested. However, by drawing on both textual and archaeological sources, Asko Parpola has suggested that rituals that were precursors of the Agnicayana (Vedic fire sacrifice) included the killing of humans.

The themes of order and disorder play a role in Aztec sacrifice as does the theme of sacrificial exchange.

Human sacrifice may seem remote to civilized sensibilities. Nevertheless, as a human act it must be at least partly intelligible to other humans. On 18 November 1978, in Jonestown, Guyana, 914 members of the People's Temple took their own lives by means of a cyanide-laced fruit drink. Most of them did so willingly. The complex reasons for this massive sacrifice of human lives are both disturbing and challenging to one's capacity to understand. Yet some familiar themes may be recognized. The people of Jonestown, like the Christian martyrs, believed in a utopian world on "the other side." Like the samurai, they chose death as a "revolutionary act" to protest against the racism that they had failed to overcome, and like the Aztecs, they preferred to choose the time and place of their own deaths. As Jim Jones said during that "white night": "I haven't seen anybody yet didn't die. And I like to choose my own kind of death for a change."

— KAY A. READ

(acknowledgment, homage), thanksgiving, supplication, and expiation.

Praise (homage). Pure sacrifices of praise that express nothing but homage and veneration and involve no other intention are rarely found. They occur chiefly where a regular sacrificial cult is practiced that resembles in large measure the ceremonial of a royal court.

Thanksgiving. Sacrifices of thanksgiving are more frequent. According to the best explanation of firstlings sacrifices, these, in the diverse forms they have taken in various cultures, belong to this category. Votive sacrifices likewise belong here, insofar as the fulfillment of the vow is an act of thanksgiving for the favor granted.

Supplication. Sacrifices of supplication (petition) include all those sacrifices that, in addition to establishing or consolidating the link with the world of the sacred (which is a function of every sacrifice), are intended to have some special effect. Such effects include the maintenance of the cosmic order; the strengthening of the powers on which this order depends (e.g., by the gift of blood, as in the human sacrifices of the Aztec); and the sacralization or consecration of places, objects, and buildings (construction sacrifices, dedication of boundary stones, idols, temples), of individual human beings, and of human communities and their relationships (ratification of treaties). Sacrifices are also offered for highly specialized purposes, for example, in order to foretell the future by examining the entrails of the sacrificial animal.

Expiation. Expiation means simply the removal of what has roused (or might rouse) the anger of spirits and demons, so that they will leave humans in peace; no relationship of goodwill or friendship is created or sought. On the other hand, the higher beings may be regarded as inherently benevolent, so that any disturbance of a good relationship with them is attributed to a human fault; the normal good relationship must therefore be restored by an expiatory sacrifice or other human action; in these cases we speak of atonement, conciliation, or propitiation. The human fault in question may be moral, but it may also be purely ritual, unintentional, or even unconscious.

— JOSEPH HENNINGER

TRANSLATED FROM GERMAN BY MATTHEW J. O'CONNELL

SALVATION ARMY

The Salvation Army is described in its official statements as a "fellowship of people who have accepted Jesus Christ as their personal Savior and Lord" whose "primary aim is to preach the gospel of Jesus Christ to men and women untouched by ordinary religious efforts." The movement is a denomination of the Church of Christ; its members—called Salvationists—are officially required to subscribe to eleven doctrines, which are fundamentalist, evangelical, and Protestant. The Army's theological position is based on that of John Wesley (1703-1791), the founder of Methodism, and in particular is a restatement of the orthodox belief that love is the single motive for all true Christian endeavor: as God loved his children and sent his Son to die for them, so his children desire to love God and to show love to each other and to all people, especially the unsaved. Salvationists show this love through aggressive evangelism and through a broad range of charitable and socially ameliorative activities. Except for the omission of sacramental observances, the doctrinal beliefs of the Salvation Army have excited little controversy.

HISTORY AND AIMS

The doctrinal positions, objectives, and military structure of the Salvation Army have not changed since its beginning in 1878, and in many aspects even its methods of operation have changed but slightly. The movement was the brainchild of William Booth (1829-1912), an English evangelist, and his wife Catherine (1829-1890). The founders' influence over the contemporary Army remains strong, although they are long dead and the last member of their family to hold an important position of leadership—their daughter Evangeline (1865-1950)—retired in 1939.

The forerunner of the Salvation Army was a preaching mission, called the Christian Mission, that the Booths established in the East End of London in 1865 to evangelize the urban poor. Booth and his associates believed that this segment of the population had been ignored by the organized religious bodies of their day. While this is not strictly true, Booth's efforts developed into the first systematic and large-scale program to reach London's poor with the gospel. A degree of social conscience was characteristic of the Christian Mission almost from the beginning. Efforts to relieve the destitution of those who attended their religious services were a natural outgrowth of the missionaries' evangelical zeal: alms and hospitality were commanded by Christ, and on the practical level, hunger and cold kept many potential converts from attending to the gospel. By 1867 four small-scale charitable activities, including a soup kitchen, were listed in the mission's annual report.

The military structure, by which the Christian Mission was transformed into an army, was the inspiration of a moment, although Booth and his closest associates had been dissatisfied with the conference system of governing the mission for some time. While preparing the mission's annual report for 1878 Booth

Some holiness groups, most notably the Salvation Army, founded in England in 1865, combined their evangelism with extensive charitable work among the needy.

PAGE 217

deleted the term *volunteer army* in describing the work and substituted *Salvation Army*. The term was catalytic. Booth became the "General"; full-time mission workers became "officers" and adopted a variety of military titles; converts and members became "soldiers." Brass bands, long popular with the English working class and especially well suited to the Army's street-corner evangelism, were added in 1879, along with a weekly devotional and news publication suitably called *The War Cry*. In 1880 the first regulation uniform was issued to George S. Railton (1849-1913) as he departed for the United States to establish the Army's first official overseas mission. Comrades who died were "promoted to Glory," and children born into Army families were hailed as "reinforcements." Since 1890 soldiers have been required to subscribe to the "Articles of War," a statement of doctrine, allegiance, and zeal for the "salvation war."

As the statement of a truth, doctrine has a philosophical cast; as a teaching, it suggests something more practical.

PAGE 206

Booth and his officers were driven by an overpowering sense of urgency. The new Salvation Army grew rapidly. Its social relief activities did not reflect any commitment to bringing about change in the social structure, however; the great work was not revolution but rescue, while time yet remained. The Army's most frequent self-portrayal, which appeared in posters, on *The War Cry* covers, and in songs, was as a lifeboat or a lighthouse, with eager Salvationists shown snatching the lost from the waves of drunkenness, crime, and vice. The thrill of losing oneself in a triumphant crusade, the military pomp, and a constantly expanding scheme of social relief proved irresistible to large numbers of the poor, and to many working- and middle-class persons as well. Despite legal obstructionism from municipal authorities and ridicule from the movement's opponents, by 1887 there were a thousand corps (i. e., stations) in Britain, and by the end of the decade work had been started in twenty-four other countries and British colonies.

DOCTRINES AND PRACTICES

The Salvation Army held its converts at least partly on the strength of its doctrines, which were formally established by an Act of Parliament in 1878. The Army's doctrinal statement proclaims, on the one hand, both the atonement of Christ and the necessity of radical conversion and, on the other hand, the "privilege of holiness." In Army terms holiness means that the sincere believer can live for love, in adoration of Christ, in joyful fellowship within the ranks of the Army, and in kindly service to a dying world. Salvationists see religious questions in stark and simple terms; anything that is not deemed absolutely essential to salvation or helpful to evangelism or that is regarded as inherently confusing to unlettered converts is simply jettisoned. It was partly for these reasons that the Booths abandoned sacramental observances; in addition, they had committed their movement almost from the start to the temperance (abstinence) crusade, which disallowed the use of sacramental wine.

As appealing as the doctrines of the Salvation Army may be, however, they are neither original nor unique, and they only partly explain its strength as a religious movement. The rest of the explanation has been the use to which the Army puts its members, its system of discipline, and its social relief program. Converts are put promptly to work giving testimony about their own conversion, distributing *The War Cry*, playing a band instrument at indoor and outdoor religious meetings, or visiting prisoners, the elderly, and the sick. Soldiers expect a lifetime of such service, and occasional natural disasters add to the ordinary demands on local Army personnel. In addition, a number of entertaining and useful programs have been developed to utilize the energy of young people. Parades, military regalia, and an effective use of music augment, where they do not actually create, joy and pride in being part of the "Army of God."

Salvationists are comfortable within the Army's autocratic structure, which emphasizes obedience, loyalty, and efficiency; the system has changed little in fact, and not at all in spirit, since 1878. The single major alteration in the absolute autocracy established by William Booth came in 1929 (the Act of Parliament was formally amended in 1931), when the general's privileges of serving for life and naming his own successor were abolished. The generalship became an elective office at the disposal of a council of all territorial commanders, and the leader so chosen serves only until a certain age. Once a general is installed, however, his powers differ little from those of the founder; every subordinate officer is expected to obey without question the orders of a superior, and much the same is required of the soldiers.

Aside from its religious and operational distinctiveness, the second part of what the Salvation Army calls its "balanced ministry" is the vast system of social welfare activities that has grown up under its auspices. There were important beginnings in the 1880s in England, America, and elsewhere, but the turning point in the development of the Army's social welfare program came in 1890 with the publication of General Booth's manifesto entitled *In Darkest England and the Way Out*. The book, and the scheme it offered for relieving the sufferings of the "submerged tenth" of Victorian society, attracted considerable publicity, controversy, and in the end financial support. Food and shelter depots, industrial rehabilitation centers, rescue homes for converted prostitutes, hospitals for unwed mothers, orphanages, day-care centers, halfway houses for released convicts, programs for alcoholics and drug addicts, camping trips for poor city children, a variety of family relief and counseling—all have grown up since 1890, especially in the American branch of the Army.

By 1982 the Salvation Army was operating in eighty-six countries. Its greatest strength is in English-speaking countries and Scandinavia; just over 50 percent of all active officers and 70 percent of all lay employees are found in five countries: the United States, Great Britain, Canada, Australia, and New Zealand. Although the international headquarters remains in London, the American branch is by far the largest.

The Army in the United States is divided into four territorial commands, each with its own headquarters and training school; the officers who command these territorial operations report to the national commander, whose headquarters is in Verona, New Jersey. The large majority of the 3,600 Salvation Army officers in the United States are engaged in "field work"; they serve as ministers to the 1,056 local corps congregations and direct the numerous social services that flow from the typical corps. Officers not in field work serve in staff and educational appointments or as administrators of the Army's many social institutions. The Men's Social Service Department, which offers residential care and alcoholic rehabilitation to transient alcoholic men (and in a few places to women), is particularly well developed.

— EDWARD H. MCKINLEY

SATAN

Although the name *Satan* sometimes has been connected with the Hebrew verb *sut,* which means "to roam" (perhaps suggesting that Satan acts as God's spy), it is more commonly derived from the root *satan,* which means "to oppose, to plot against." In the New Testament, Satan as the Devil is called the "great dragon" and "ancient serpent" (*Rv.* 12:9). In the *Book of Job,* Satan belongs to the court of God and, with God's permission, tests Job. By contrast, in a second occurrence (*Zec.* 3), Satan, on his own initiative, opposes Joshua.

The figure of Satan in noncanonical Hebrew literature intensifies his identification with evil. He not only emerges as an adversary of God, but, as such apocalyptic works as *Jubilees,* the *Testament of Reuben,* the *Book of the Secrets of Enoch (2 Enoch),* and the Qumran documents show, he is also the leader of the fallen angels.

Christianity synthesized Greek and Jewish concepts of the Devil. The word *devil* is actually derived from the Greek *diabolos,* which has the dual sense of "accuser" and "obstructor." If the Old Testament, according to later tradition, implicates Satan in the fall of man, the New Testament refers clearly to the fall of Satan himself in *2 Peter* 2:4 and in *Revelation* 12:7-9. Again, in contrast with the Old Testament, the power of the Devil is often mentioned (e.g., Lk. 4:6). He is also identified with other names: *Beelzebul* ("lord of flies"), *Beelzebub* ("lord of dung"), and, with somewhat less critical certainty, *Lucifer.*

In the ministry of Jesus Christ, "there is a constant campaign against Satan from the temptation after Jesus' Baptism until his death on the cross, and, in each act of healing or exorcism, there is anticipated the ultimate defeat of Satan and the manifestation of the power of the new age." (Davis, 1984, p. 952)

Satan's name appears as *Shaytan* in the Qur'an, although it is not clear whether the name is Arabic or not. Shaytan shares certain functions of the Judeo-Christian Satan, such as leading people astray (4:83), but there is a significant extension of this view in that Satan is accused of tampering with divine verbal revelation (22.52). However, it is in his role as Iblis (2:34, etc.) that al-Shaytan is most striking (Watt, 1970, p. 155). He is deposed for refusing to bow before man as the other angels had done, but is allowed, after his refusal, to tempt mortals. In Islam, the figure of Satan is more or less exclusively associated with evil and the underworld. This association may help "account for the Western tradition that Satan is not only Lord of evil and of death but is also associated with fertility and sexuality, a trait evident in the witches' orgy and in the horns the Devil often wears" (Russell, 1977, p. 64).

The serpent or snake is perhaps the best-known

AL-SHAYTAN

Satan's name appears as Shaytan in the Qur'an. He is deposed for refusing to bow before man as the other angels had done.

CHRIS HELLIER/CORBIS

"When the devil had finished all the tempting he left him, to await another opportunity."

LUKE 4:13

S

SCRIPTURE

Origins and Development of the Concept

The completed canon of the Hebrew Bible exerted a profound influence, first upon the Jewish people that produced it, and then upon a large section of the rest of humanity.

PAGE 69

symbol associated with Satan. *Genesis* (3:1ff.) mentions the serpent but not Satan; in *Romans* (16:20), however, Paul suggests that the serpent was Satan, an association already made in apocalyptic literature. This would imply that Satan tempted Adam, but the consensus of early Christian tradition was that Satan fell after Adam (Russell, 1977, p. 232). There may be good reason for believing that not until Origen in the third century CE was it clearly established that Satan's sin was pride, that he fell before Adam's creation, and that he was the serpent in the garden of Eden.

Satan is persistently, if not consistently, associated with the serpent. Leaving aside the question of the actual nature of Satan as formulated by the Council of Toledo (447), or the tendency to consider him an imaginative personification of evil, the association with the serpent needs to be accounted for. Several views have been advanced. At a homiletic level, the serpent has been taken to represent cunning. At a psychoanalytic level, the serpent has been associated with emergent sexuality.

[*For further discussion of the symbolism, philosophy, and theology associated with the figure of Satan, see* Evil *and* Witchcraft.]

— ARVIND SHARMA

SCRIPTURE

Scripture is the generic concept used in the modern West and, increasingly, worldwide, to designate texts that are revered as especially sacred and authoritative in all major and many other religious traditions.

ORIGINS AND DEVELOPMENT OF THE CONCEPT

Whatever the subtleties and difficulties of defining it, scripture is a major phenomenon in the history of religion and thus an important concept in the study of religion.

THE IDEA OF A HEAVENLY BOOK. The development of the concept of a scriptural book is often linked to the notion of a heavenly book. The idea of a heavenly book containing divine knowledge or decrees is an ancient and persistent one found primarily in the ancient Near Eastern and Greco-Roman worlds and in subsequent Jewish, Christian, and Islamic traditions. As Leo Koep points out in *Das himmlische Buch in Antike und Christentum* (Bonn, 1952), it can take one of several forms, typically that of a book of wisdom, book of destinies, book of works, or book of life. References to a celestial book or tablet of divine wisdom appear in ancient Babylonia and ancient Egypt and recur in almost all subsequent Near Eastern traditions, apparently as an expression of divine omniscience.

THE IDEA OF A SACRED BOOK. The quintessential "book religions" are those that trace their lineage in some fashion to the Hebrews, the prototypical "people of the book." We do not yet fully understand how Judaic ideas of the sacred or heavenly book joined historically with influences from other sectors of the ancient Near Eastern world and the growing status of the book in later antiquity to set in motion the "book religion" that plays so large a role in Christianity, Manichaeism, and, most spectacularly and pronouncedly, in Islam. Christianity's increasing emphasis on authoritative writings, the point of departure for which was Jewish reverence for the Torah, was especially decisive in this development. Mani's self-conscious effort to produce books of scriptural authority reflects the degree to which by his time (third century CE) a religious movement had to have its own scriptures. It was the Qur'an's insistence upon the centrality of the divine book, given now in final form as a recitation, that carried the development of book religion to its apogee in the early seventh century.

SEMANTIC BACKGROUND. The most basic meaning of *scripture,* as of its Indo-European cognates (Ger., *Schrift;* Ital., *scrittura;* Fr., *écriture;* etc.), is "a writing, something written." It is derived from the Latin *scriptura,* "a writing" (pl., *scripturae*). In the Mediterranean world of later antiquity, pagan, Jewish, and Christian writers used these words (or their plurals) to refer to various kinds of written texts in the Hebrew Bible, the Greek Septuagint, and the Old Testament books of the Latin Vulgate (e.g., *Ex.* 32:16, *Tob.* 8:24, *Ps.* 86:6). By the time of the Christian New Testament writers, however, the terms had gradually come to be used especially for sacred books, above all the three divisions of the Hebrew scriptures, the Pentateuch (Torah), Prophets (Nevi'im), and (other) Writings (Ketuvim).

In the New Testament (e.g., *Rom.* 1:2, 2 *Tm.* 3:15) and in the works of the Christian fathers, and as well as in Philo and Josephus, various adjectives were added to the words for "scripture(s)" and "book(s)" to emphasize their special, holy character: for example, *hieros, hagios, sanctus* ("holy"); *theios, divinus* ("divine"); *theopneustos* ("divinely inspired"); *kuriakos* ("of the Lord").

GENERALIZATION OF THE CONCEPT. In these ways, the Jewish and Christian worlds gradually appropriated the use of such terms as *scripture, holy scripture(s), books, sacred books,* and so forth, primarily as proper-noun designations for their own holy texts. In particular, as Christian culture and religion triumphed in the Mediterranean, especially in southern Europe, *(sacred) scripture* came to mean specifically the Christian Bible.

Such Western generalization of the concept of scripture was, to be sure, hardly novel. In the Muslim world, the concept of sacred "scripture" *(kitab)* had already been generalized in the Qur'an, where especially Jews and Christians are spoken of as "people of scripture" *(ahl al-kitab)*.

The extended use of the term *scripture* for any particularly sacred text is now common in modern Western usage and widely current internationally. Even the word *Bible* has been used, albeit less often, in a similarly general sense to refer to any sacred scripture (cf. Franklin Edgerton's reference to the *Bhagavadgita* as "India's favorite Bible" in *The Bhagavad Gita, or Song of the Blessed One,* Chicago, 1925).

CHARACTERISTIC ROLES

Scriptural texts function in a variety of ways in a religious tradition. Some of their major functions are discussed below.

SCRIPTURE AS HOLY WRIT. The significance of the written word of scripture is difficult to exaggerate. With the important exception of the Hindu world, the writing down of the major religious text(s) of a community is an epochal event in its history, one that is often linked to the crystallization of religious organization and systematic theological speculation, as well as to the achievement of a high level of culture. The written scriptural text symbolizes or embodies religious authority in many traditions (often replacing the living authority of a religious founder such as Muhammad or the Buddha).

Although the fixity and authority of the physical text have been felt particularly strongly in the last two thousand years in the West, the idea of an authoritative sacred writing is not limited to one global region. Veneration for the sacred word as book has also been important, if not always central, in most of the Buddhist world of Southeast and East Asia. It has been suggested, for example, that there was an early Mahayana cult of the book *(sutra)* that vied with the *stupa* relic cult, and high esteem for the written *sutras* has been generally prominent in Mahayana tradition. Furthermore, it was in India, not the West, that the veneration of the written text reached one of its heights in the Sikh movement.

One of the overt ways in which the importance of the written text is revealed is in the religious valuation of the act of copying and embellishing a sacred text. Christian and, still more, Jewish and Islamic scriptures boast especially strong calligraphic traditions.

SCRIPTURE AS SPOKEN WORD. Recitation or reading aloud of scripture is a common feature of piety, whether in Islamic, Sikh, Jewish, or other traditions. Many scriptures have primary or secondary schemes of division according to the needs of recitation or reading aloud in the community (e.g., the 154 divisions of the Torah for synagogal reading over a three-year span). Great esteem is given to the person who knows all of the sacred scripture "by heart"—in the Muslim case, such a person is honored with the special epithet *hafiz,* "keeper, protector, memorizer [of the Word]". In the early synagogue and in the early Christian church, the reading aloud of scripture in worship was fundamental to religious life (Ismar Elbogen, *Der jüdische Gottesdienst,* Leipzig, 1913, chap. 3; Paul Glaue, *Die Vorlesung heiliger Schriften im Gottesdienst,* Berlin, 1907; but cf. Walter Bauer, *Das Wortgottesdienst der ältesten Christen,* Tübingen, 1930), just as it was in pagan cults of the Hellenistic Mediterranean, such as that of Isis (Leipoldt and Morenz, 1953, p. 96). The Jews call both the reading of scripture and the passage read *miqra'* (*Neh.* 8:8), "what is recited, read aloud, a reading." In Talmudic usage , the term came to refer to the Torah (Pentateuch), the Prophets, and the Writings that make up the Tankakh, or Hebrew scriptures.

In other traditions, notably the Islamic and Buddhist, the recitation of the sacred word is even more central to religious practice, despite the frequently massive importance of veneration of the written text in the same traditions. In Hindu practice, the oral, recited word completely eclipses the importance of any written form of it and presents the most vivid instance of the all but exclusively oral function of scripture.

SCRIPTURE IN PUBLIC RITUAL. Whether the written or the oral text of a scriptural book predominates, the most visible religious role of a scripture is in public worship. In some instances a scripture is explicitly a ritual text that orders and explains the rite itself, as in the case of the Brahmanas in Vedic tradition. In other cases it is a sacred text either recited in ritual acts (e.g., the Qur'an, the Zoroastrian *Gathas,* the Vedic *mantras,* and the Shinto *norito,* or ritual prayers taken from the Engi-shiki) or read aloud from a written copy in communal worship, as in Jewish or Christian practice. Such recitation or reading is often a major if not the central element in worship.

Ritually important passages of a scriptural text are sometimes pulled together into special anthologies or collections that serve the liturgical needs of the community, as in the Christian breviary, psalter, lectionary, or evangeliarium; the Patimokkha selection from the Vinaya that is recited as a regular part of Buddhist monastic life; or the *Blue Sutra,* an abridgement of the *Lotus Sutra* that is used in the ritual of the modern Reiyukai Buddhist sect in Japan (Helen Hardacre, *Lay Buddhism in Contemporary Japan,* Princeton, 1984).

SCRIPTURE IN DEVOTIONAL AND SPIRITUAL LIFE. Recitation and reading aloud are not only central to formal worship (see above), but also to pri-

The Hebrew scriptures and Hebrew Bible have been traditionally accepted by Jews and Christians alike as having been divinely inspired and, as such, authoritative in shaping their respective faiths and practices.

PAGE 69

SCRIPTURE

Characteristic Attributes of Scripture

"I go for refuge to the Buddha. I go for refuge to the Doctrine."

THE PALI-CANON

The Qur'an has a place of unparalleled importance at the very center of Muslim religious faith and practice.

PAGE 564

vate devotion and the practice of diverse spiritual disciplines. *Meditatio* in the Christian tradition was from the start basically an oral activity of learning the text "by heart" through reciting with concentrated attention and reflection. In turn, as Jean Leclercq has eloquently stated in *The Love of Learning and the Desire for God* [1957] 1974), meditation formed the basis of the monastic *lectio divina,* the active, oral reading of and reflecting on scripture upon which the monk's discipline was based in Pachomian, Benedictine, and other rules.

Closely related to meditative practices involving scriptural texts are the recitation of and meditation upon formulas derived from scripture. The chanting of Hindu and Buddhist *mantras* and of Buddhist *dharanis,* as well as the recitation of Sufi *dhikr* litanies (many of which are Qur'anic) are major examples of formulaic use of scripture in devotional life.

CHARACTERISTIC ATTRIBUTES OF SCRIPTURE

The scriptures of any given religious tradition possess a number of characteristic attributes. Some of the most important are as follows.

POWER. The major functional attributes of scripture are bound up with the power felt to be inherent in scriptural word. Both the written and the spoken word carry a seemingly innate power in human life. At the most basic level, a word is an action: words do not signify so much as they perform. Hence to speak a name ritually is in some measure to control or to summon the one named. For the faithful, a sacred word is not merely a word, but an operative, salvific word. Its unique, transformative power often rests upon its being spoken (or written) by a god (as in Jewish, Christian, or Muslim tradition). In other cases, the sound itself is holy (as in India), or the message or teaching embodied in the scriptural word is considered to be salvific truth, with little or no reference to a divine origin (as in many Buddhist traditions).

AUTHORITY AND SACRALITY. The authoritative character of scripture is most vivid in those cases in which a sacred text provides the legal basis of communal order. This is especially evident in the Jewish tradition, where the written Torah is the pediment upon which the entire edifice of Jewish life is built, and in the Islamic tradition, where the minimal legal prescriptions and much larger body of moral injunctions found in the Qur'an are viewed as the ultimate bases of the *shari'ah.* It is also evident in the role of the Vinaya ("discipline") section of the Tripitaka, the "law" of Buddhist monasticism.

The extraordinary sacrality of scripture is seen in almost every facet of its use in communal life. The way in which a scriptural text is handled, the formulas of respect that accompany its mention, citation, recitation, or reading, and the theological doctrines that are developed to set it apart ontologically from all other texts are common evidence of such sacrality.

UNICITY. A further quality of scripture is its perceived unicity of source, content, and authority in the community involved with it (see especially Leipolt and Morenz, 1953). No matter what the historical origins or textual development of its constituent parts, and no matter how diverse those parts, a scriptural corpus is commonly conceived of as a unified whole, both in its ontological origin as sacred word and its authoritativeness and internal consistency as sacred truth. The many originally separate texts that were collected into the Egyptian *Book of Going Forth by Day,* the diverse "holy scriptures" of the Hebrew or Christian Bible, the myriad *sutras* of the Chinese Buddhist canon, or the various kinds of Vedic texts revered as *sruti*—these and other bodies of sacred texts are each conceived as an ontological and conceptual unity, whether that unity is one of God's holy word (as in ancient Egypt or Islam), the Buddha-word, or the "sound" (Skt., *sabda;* Chin., *sheng*) of ultimate truth or wisdom heard by the ancient Indian and ancient Chinese sages.

INSPIRATION AND ETERNALITY/ANTIQUITY. The tendency to see one's own formal or informal canon of scriptures as a unified whole is closely linked to the characteristic development of a theory of inspiration, revelation, or some other kind of suprahuman and primordial origin for its words. All of the prophets and teachers whose words become part of scripture are held to have been inspired in their speech (as with the Hebrew prophets), to have been given God's direct revelation to their fellows (as with Muhammad and Mani), or to have had an experience in which they transcended the contingent world to grasp ultimate reality (as in the Buddha's enlightenment).

The divine word is also commonly held to be eternal, as in the role of Vac ("speech") as primordial being or goddess in Vedic thought, in the Hindu concept of the eternal Veda (cf. *Laws of Manu* 12.94, 12.99), in the Muslim doctrine of the uncreated, eternal Word of the Qur'an (which, as God's very Word, is an eternal divine attribute), in the Sikh concept of the *bani* ("word") that preexists and extends beyond the gurus and the Adi *Granth* (W. Owen Cole and Piara S. Sambhi, *The Sikhs,* London, 1978, p. 44), and in Buddhist ideas of the eternal Dharma or the *buddhavacana* ("Buddha word") in Mahayana thought.

A scripture is virtually always conceived to be, if not eternal, at least of great antiquity. The Japanese *Kojiki* and *Nihongi,* the Avesta, and the Five Classics of China are all prime examples of sacred texts to which hoary antiquity is ascribed.

— WILLIAM A. GRAHAM

SEVENTH-DAY ADVENTISM

The origins of Seventh-day Adventism run back to the interdenominational Millerite movement in the United States in the early 1840s, when William Miller, a Baptist lay minister and farmer, sought to rekindle a second awakening by predicting that Christ would soon return to earth. Following a series of failed time-settings, Millerites fixed their hopes for the second advent of Christ on 22 October 1844, the Day of Atonement. The "great disappointment" that resulted from this miscalculation splintered the movement into several factions. The majority, including Miller, admitted their exegetical error but continued to expect Christ's imminent return.

Early beliefs that 22 October marked the date when God shut the "door of mercy" on all who had rejected the Millerite message gradually gave rise to an open-door theology and to evangelization. The observance of Saturday as sabbath, as required by the Ten Commandments and practiced by the Seventh Day Baptists, became the most obvious symbol of Seventh-day Adventist distinctiveness and served as a means by which legalistic members sought to attain the higher morality expected of God's people at the close of history.

In many respects Seventh-day Adventism developed as a typical nineteenth-century American sect, characterized by millenarianism, biblicism, restorationism, and legalism. By 1850 sabbatarian Adventists, still looking for the soon appearance of Christ, composed a "scattered flock" of about two hundred loosely structured sectarians who sought to restore such primitive Christian practices as foot-washing, greeting with the "holy kiss," and calling each other "brother" and "sister." The institutionalization of Seventh-day Adventism was well under way. In 1859 the Adventists adopted a plan of "systematic benevolence" to support a clergy; the next year they selected the name Seventh-day Adventist; by 1863 there were 125 churches with about 3,500 members.

Adventist theology shifted in the 1880s, when two West Coast editors, Ellet J. Waggoner and Alonzo T. Jones, both still in their thirties, challenged the legalistic emphasis that had come to characterize the sect. In opposition to General Conference leaders, who maintained that salvation depended upon observing the Ten Commandments, especially the fourth, Waggoner and Jones followed evangelical Christians in arguing that righteousness came by accepting Christ, not by keeping the law.

For decades Adventists confined their evangelistic efforts almost exclusively to North America until church leaders became convinced that they had an obligation to carry their message "into all the world". By 1900 the Adventists were supporting nearly five hundred foreign missionaries. To train medical personnel for service at home and abroad, Adventists in 1895 opened the American Medical Missionary College, with campuses in Battle Creek and Chicago. Battle Creek soon grew into the administrative, publishing, medical, and educational center of Adventism. Such centralization and concentration of power concerned church leader Ellen White, who recommended dismantling the Battle Creek colony. As a result, Battle Creek College (now Andrews University) was moved in 1902 to rural southwestern Michigan and administrative and publishing activities were moved to the outskirts of Washington, D. C.

In 1915 Ellen White died, leaving a church of more than 136,000 members. By 1980 membership had swelled to nearly 3.5 million, roughly 85 percent of whom lived outside of North America.

— JONATHAN M. BUTLER AND RONALD L. NUMBERS

Millenarianism, known also as millennialism, is the belief that the end of this world is at hand and that in its wake will appear a New World, inexhaustibly fertile.

PAGE 433

SHAKERS

Members of the American religious group the United Society of Believers in Christ's Second Appearing are popularly called Shakers. One of the longest-lived and most influential religious communitarian groups in America, the Shakers originated in 1747 near Manchester, England, in a breakaway from the Quakers led by Jane and James Wardley. The group may also have been influenced by Camisard millenarians who had fled from France to England to escape the persecutions that followed revocation of the Edict of Nantes in 1685. The nickname Shaking Quaker, or Shaker, was applied to the movement because of its unstructured and highly emotional services, during which members sang, shouted, danced, spoke in tongues, and literally shook with emotion. Under the leadership of Ann Lee, a Manchester factory worker who became convinced that celibacy was essential for salvation, the core of the Shakers emigrated to America in 1774 and settled two years later near Albany, New York. Until Lee's death in 1784 the Shakers remained a loosely knit group that adhered to Lee's personal leadership and to what they viewed as a millenarian restoration and fulfillment of the early Christian faith.

During the 1780s and 1790s under the leadership of two of Ann Lee's American converts, Joseph Meacham and Lucy Wright, Shakerism developed from a charismatic movement into a more routinized organization. Meacham and Wright oversaw the establishment of parallel and equal men's and women's orders. Adherents lived together in celibate communities and practiced communal ownership of property inspired by the Christian communism of *Acts* 2:44-45. Supreme authority was vested in the ministry at New Lebanon, New York, usually two men and two women, one of whom headed the entire society. Each settlement was divided into "families"—smaller, relatively self-sufficient communities of thirty to one hundred men and women living together under the same roof but strictly separated in all their activities. By 1800 eleven settlements with sixteen hundred members were functioning in New York, Massachusetts, Connecticut, New Hampshire, and Maine. A second wave of expansion, inspired by the Kentucky Revival and drawing heavily on the indefatigable Richard McNemar, a "new light" Presbyterian minister who converted to Shakerism, led to the establishment of seven additional settlements, in Ohio, Kentucky, and Indiana, by 1826.

Together with his wife Mary, John Slocum inaugurated the Indian Shaker church, a Christian church in which the presence of God's power, signified by physical trembling ("the shake"), was used by congregants to cure the sick.

PAGE 514

The high point of Shaker membership and the last major effort to revitalize the society came during the decade of "spiritual manifestations" that began in 1837. Frequently called "Mother Ann's work" because many of the revelations purportedly came from the spirit of Ann Lee and showed her continuing concern for her followers, the period saw a rich outpouring of creativity in new forms of worship, song, and dance, including extreme trance and visionary phenomena. Following the great Millerite disappointments of 1843 and 1844 when the world failed to come to a literal end, hundreds of Millerites joined the Shakers, bringing membership to a peak of some six thousand by the late 1840s. Thereafter the group entered into a long, slow decline. The loss of internal momentum and the changing conditions of external society led the Shakers to be viewed increasingly not as a dynamic religious movement but as a pleasant anachronism in which individuals who could not function in the larger society could find refuge. As late as 1900 there were more than one thousand Shakers, but today the group has dwindled to virtual extinction.

As the largest and most successful religious communitarian group in nineteenth-century America, the Shakers attracted the attention of numerous visitors, writers, and creators of more ephemeral communal experiments. The Shakers were known for their neat, well-planned, and successful villages; their functional architecture, simple furniture, and fine crafts; their distinctive songs, dances, and rituals; and their ingenuity in agriculture and mechanical invention. They also were sometimes criticized because of their sophisticated and highly unorthodox theology, which stressed a dual godhead combining male and female elements equally; perfectionism and continuing revelation; and the necessity of celibacy for the highest religious life. They were unique among American religious groups in giving women formal equality with men at every level of religious leadership, and they created a fully integrated subculture that has increasingly come to be viewed with interest and respect.

— LAWRENCE FOSTER

SHAKER VILLAGE

Shaker settlements like the (restored) Shaker Village of Pleasant Hill in Harrodsburg, Kentucky were divided into small self-sufficient communities each strictly segregated and celibate.

KEVIN R. MORRIS/© CORBIS

SHIISM

Shiism is a major branch of Islam with numerous subdivisions, all upholding the rights of the family of the Prophet *(ahl al-bayt)* to the religious and political leadership of the Muslim community.

ORIGINS AND EARLY DEVELOPMENT

Historically, the Shi'ah emerged in support of the caliphate of 'Ali (AH 35-40/656-661 CE) during the First Civil War. After the murder of 'Ali and the abdication of his eldest son, Hasan, in 661, the Shi'ah continued a latent opposition to the Umayyad caliphate from their center in 'Ali's former capital of Kufa in Iraq. Their attachment to the family of the Prophet, and especially to 'Ali's sons and descendants, reflected local resentment of both the loss of the caliphate to Damascus and the Umayyad denigration of 'Ali and his caliphate.

KUFAN REVOLTS. After the death of the caliph Mu'awiyah, the Kufan Shi'ah invited Husayn from Medina, promising to back his claim to the caliphate. The Umayyad governor gained control of the situation, however. A Penitents movement arose in Kufa; they lamented the death of the Prophet's grandson at his grave in Karbala and sought revenge from those responsible. In 685 the leadership of the Penitents was taken over by al-Mukhtar ibn Abi 'Ubayd, who revolted in Kufa and proclaimed another son of 'Ali, Muhammad, to be the imam and Mahdi, the messianic Restorer of Islam. The movement backing him was called the Kaysaniyah after Abu 'Amrah Kaysan, chief of al-Mukhtar's guard and leader of the non-Arab clients *(mawali)* in Kufa. Local Semites and Persians now joined the Shi'ah in large numbers for the first time, although the leading role in the movement was still played by Arabs.

The Kaysaniyah movement condemned the first three caliphs before 'Ali as illegitimate usurpers and considered 'Ali and his three sons, Hasan, Husayn, and Muhammad, as successive, divinely appointed imams endowed with supernatural qualities. They taught *raj'ah,* the return of many of the dead at the time of the coming of the Mahdi for retribution before the Resurrection, and *bada',* the possibility of a change in the decisions of God.

ABBASID REVOLUTION. A branch of the Kaysaniyah known as the Hashimiyah continued the line of imams to Muhammad ibn al-Hanafiyah's son Abu Hashim, who, in contrast to his father, took an active part in the leadership and organization of the movement. After his death in about 717 or 718 the Hashimiyah split into several groups over the succession. The majority recognized Muhammad ibn 'Ali, a descendant of the Prophet's uncle 'Abbas. The Abbasids initially espoused the Shi'i cause, establishing the reign of the family of the Prophet and demanding revenge for 'Ali and his wronged descendants. Soon, however, they distanced themselves from their mostly extremist Shi'i followers to seek broader support in the Muslim community, but they disintegrated soon afterward.

EXTREMISTS AND MODERATES. Other minor offshoots of the Hashimiyah were notable for their extremist doctrine: metempsychosis, the preexistence of human souls as shadows *(azillah),* metaphorical interpretation of the resurrection, judgment, paradise, and hell. Such teaching became characteristic of many groups of extremists *(ghulat)* excommunicated by the mainstream Shi'ah in the following centuries.

The increasing prominence of the Husaynid imams within the Shi'ah was connected with a shift in the function of the imam. With the rise of legal and theological schools espousing conflicting doctrines in the late Umayyad period, many of the Shi'ah sought the guidance of the imam as an authoritative, divinely inspired teacher rather than as a charismatic leader. The first to perform this new role was Muhammad al-Baqir (d. 735?), a grandson of Husayn who was widely respected for his learning among both the Shi'ah and non-Shi'ah. His teaching of religious law and Qur'an exegesis attracted a large number of the Kufan Shi'ah.

The Buyids were able to influence Islamic practices—such as the observance of 'Ashura

PAGE 597

THE IMAMIYAH AND TWELVER SHI'AH

The Imamiyah became a significant religious community with a distinctive law, ritual, and religious doctrine under Ja'far al-Sadiq (d. 765), the foremost scholar and teacher among their imams. In recognition of his role, Imami law is sometimes called the Ja'fari legal school. In theology, some of his statements upheld intermediate positions on controversial questions such as human free will versus predestination, and the nature of the Qur'an.

THE IMAMATE. The constitutive element of the Imami community is its doctrine of the imamate, which was definitely formulated in this age. It was based on the belief that humanity is at all times in need of a divinely appointed and guided leader and authoritative teacher in all religious matters. Without such a leader, according to Imam Ja'far, the world could never exist for a moment. In order to fulfill his divine mission, this leader must be endowed with full immunity *('ismah)* from sin and error. Following the age of the prophets, which came to a close with Muhammad, the imams continue their prophetic mission in every respect except that they do not bring a new scripture. The imamate is thus raised to the rank of prophethood. Imam Ja'far did not aspire to rule and forbade his followers from engaging in revolutionary activity on his behalf. He predicted that the imams would not regain their rightful position until the emergence of

S

SHIISM

The Imamiyah and Twelver Shi'ah

Shi'ah is esotericism as defined by the doctrine that religion, and particularly the Qur'an, has hidden esoteric meanings that can only be known through spiritual contact with the Hidden Imam.

PAGE 350

the Qa'im (lit. "riser," i. e., the Mahdi) from among them to rule the world.

The succession to Ja'far al-Sadiq was disputed and led to a schism among the Imamiyah. A group of his followers considered the designation as irreversible, however, and either denied Isma'il's death or recognized Isma'il's son Muhammad as the imam. They became the founders of the Isma'iliyah. In the absence of a new designation, they turned to his brother Musa al-Kazim, the seventh imam of the Twelver Shi'ah. Some of them, however, continued to recognize 'Abd Allah, Ja'fara's son, the rightful imam. They were known as the Fathiyah and constituted a sizable sect in Kufa until the late fourth century AH (tenth century CE). Musa was arrested later in his life by Caliph Harun al-Rashid and died in prison in Baghdad in 799. His death was denied by many of his followers, who considered his position as seventh imam to be of momentous significance and expected his return as the Mahdi. They did not recognize 'Ali al-Rida, the eighth imam of the Twelver Shi'ah, although some of them considered him and his successors as lieutenants *(khulafa')* of the Mahdi until his return. They also formed a sizable sect known as the Waqifah and competed with the group which was to become the Twelver Shi'ah.

The succession after al-Rida down to the eleventh imam, Hasan al-'Askari, produced only minor schisms, but the death of the latter in 874, apparently without a son, left his followers in disarray. The main body, henceforth known as the Twelver Shi'ah (the Ithna 'Ashariyah in Arabic), eventually came to affirm that a son had been born to him before his death but had been hidden. This son had become the twelfth imam and continued to live in concealment. Identified with the Qa'im and the Mahdi, he was expected to reappear in glory to rule the world and make the cause of the Shi'ah triumphant. He continues to live unrecognized on earth, however, and may occasionally identify himself to one of his followers or otherwise intervene in the fortunes of his community.

INTELLECTUAL CURRENTS. The absence of the imam strengthened the position of the scholars *('ulama')* in the Shi'i community as transmitters and guardians of the teaching of the imams. They now undertook to gather, examine, and systematize this teaching. For the most part, the first transmitters of the statements of the imams had been Kufans, while the compilation and sifting of the traditions into more comprehensive collections was the work of the school of Qom in northwestern Iran. The traditionist school of Qom reached its peak in the works of Abu Ja'far al-Kulayni of Rayy (d. 941) and Ibn Babawayhi al-Saduq of Qom (d. 991/2).

A rival school in Baghdad progressively adopted the rationalist theology of the Mu'tazilah, who espoused human free will and an anti-anthropomorphist, abstract concept of God in sharp conflict with the predominant theology of Sunni Islam. The Baghdad school rejected Mu'tazili doctrine, however, where it clashed with the basic Imami beliefs about the imamate; thus it repudiated the Mu'tazili thesis of the unconditional, eternal punishment of the unrepentant sinner in the hereafter, affirming the effectiveness of the intercession of the imams for sinners among their faithful followers. In fact, faith in the power of the imams' intercessions was a vital motive for the visits to their shrines which have always been a major aspect of popular Shi'i piety. Twelver Shi'i theologians also maintained, against the Mu'tazili position, that the opponents of the imams occupied the status of infidels and that the imamate was, like prophecy, a rational necessity, not merely a revealed legal requirement.

The Twelver Shi'ah today constitute the great majority of the Shi'ah and are often referred to simply by the latter name.

THE ISMA'ILIYAH

An offshoot of the Imamiyah, the Isma'iliyah first became historically important after the middle of the ninth century as a secret revolutionary movement promising the impending advent of Muhammad ibn Isma'il, grandson of Ja'far al-Sadiq, as the Mahdi. The movement soon split into two. One of its branches recognized the hidden leaders of the movement as imams descended from Muhammad ibn Isma'il. With backing of this branch, the leaders rose to rule as the Fatimid caliphate (909-1171). The other branch, commonly known as the Qaramitah, broke with the leadership and refused to recognize the imamate of the Fatimid caliphs. Their establishment of a Qarmati state in eastern Arabia lasted from 899 until 1076.

The Fatimid branch was rent by a schism during the caliphate of al-Hakim (996-1021), whose divinity was proclaimed by a group of enthusiastic followers. The sect arising from this deviation is known as the Druze. After the death of the caliph al-Mustansir in 1094 the Persian Isma'ili communities recognized his eldest son, Nizar, who did not succeed to the caliphate, as their imam. Known as the Nizariyah, they established their headquarters, and later the seat of their imams, in the mountain stronghold of Alamut in the Elburz mountains. The main line of Nizari imams has continued down to the Aga Khans in modern times.

THE ZAYDIYAH

Retaining the politically militant and religiously moderate attitude predominant among the early Kufan Shi'ah, the Zaydiyah developed a doctrine of the imamate distinctly at variance with Imami beliefs. They neither accepted a hereditary line of imams nor considered the imam as divinely protected from sin and error. Rather they held that any descendant of Hasan or Husayn qualified by religious learning could claim the imamate by armed rising against the illegitimate rulers and would then be entitled to the allegiance and backing of the faithful. Thus there were often long periods without legitimate Zaydi imams.

The unity of the Zaydi community in Yemen was rent in the eleventh century by the rise of two heterodox sects, the Mutarrifiyah and the Husayniyah. Both sects disappeared by the fourteenth century. The Zaydi community in Yemen, living mostly in the northern highlands, has survived to the present.

— WILFERD MADELUNG

SHINTO

Shinto is the name given to the traditional religion of Japan, a religion that has existed continuously from before the founding of the Japanese nation until the present.

GENERAL CHARACTERISTICS

The ancient Japanese did not themselves have a name for their ethnic religion, but when in the sixth century of the common era Buddhism was officially introduced from the Asian continent, the word *Shinto* ("the way of the *kami*") was used to distinguish the traditional religion from Buddhism (*Butsudo,* "the way of the Buddha"). The first literary usage of the word *Shinto* is found in the *Nihonshoki* (720).

DEFINITION. One representative prewar scholar of Shinto, Kono Seizo, defined Shinto as the way of the *kami,* the principle of the life of the Japanese people, as inherited from time immemorial. Shinto is a "national religion," practiced for the most part by Japanese (including overseas immigrants), and which, with the exception of several sects, has no founder but instead developed naturally. Shinto's concept of *kami* is basically polytheistic, and Shinto includes prayer to the *kami,* festivals *(matsuri),* ascetic disciplines, social service, and other elements.

TYPOLOGY. In modern times, Shinto can be classified into three broad types, all of which are mutually interrelated:

Shrine Shinto (Jinja Shinto). Shrine Shinto, consisting principally of worship of the *kami* at local shrines *(jinja),* dates from the beginning of Japanese history to the present day and constitutes the main current of Shinto tradition. It has played an important role in the unification and solidarity of the nation and of rural society. While Shrine Shinto has no founder, it possesses an organization based on believers, (parishioners) and others, festivals and other religious practices, doctrines rooted in Shinto traditions, and Japanese myth, all centered upon the shrines' spiritual unification.

Sect Shinto (Kyoha Shinto). Also known as Shuha Shinto, Sect Shinto is the term for the Shinto movement centering upon thirteen groups formed during the nineteenth century. The distinguishing feature of Sect Shinto is the fact that each of its sects has founders or organizers, that for the most part their founders or organizers established groups among the common people, and that in addition these sects were developed from an individual's religious experience or upon the basis of Fukko ("revival") Shinto. Generally, these groups do not have shrines but instead use churches as their centers of religious activity.

Folk Shinto (Minzoku Shinto). Folk belief exists among the common people at the bottom of the social pyramid and has no systematic thought that could be called doctrine or dogma, nor does it feature church organization. Japanese folk belief derives from three sources: survival of ancient traditions, customs of abstinence and purification and the cult of house and field deities, and fragments of foreign religion such as Taoism, Buddhism, and medieval Catholicism.

HISTORICAL OUTLINE

ANCIENT SHINTO. By ancient Shinto is meant Shinto in the period before it came to be influenced by Confucianism, Buddhism, and other foreign religions. It is difficult to give precise dates, but one can say that the ancient period lasted from the seventh to the early eighth century, while partially overlapping with the next period.

The character of Japanese religion in prehistory is unclear. In ancient Japan many small principalities were formed in various areas. These various principalities were loosely unified into a single nation, predominantly by the ancestors of the present-day imperial household. On the evidence of continental epigraphs, we can surmise that this unification probably took place before the mid-fourth century. However, even taking into consideration these early archaeological findings, it is not until the early eighth century, with the first appearance of Shinto texts, that we can grasp the actual situation of ancient Shinto.

In ancient Japanese the word *kami* was used adjectivally to mean something mysterious, supernatural, or sacred. According to Muraoka Tsunetsugu and Miyaji Naoichi, the ancient *kami* may be divided into three categories: (1) natural deities (deities dwelling in natural objects or natural phenomena, or deities that control these objects or phenomena); (2) anthropomorphic deities (heroes, great personages, and deified ancestors); (3) conceptual deities (deities who serve an ideal or symbolize an abstract power).

Although the early Japanese did not speculate on the metaphysical meaning of the cosmos, they felt they were an integral part of the cosmos, which to them was a community of living beings, all sharing kami (sacred) nature.

PAGE 379

S

SHINTO

General Characteristics

At different times and places, man has given names to the transcendent power or reality that is the source of all blessings.

PAGE 86

Shinto originally had no shrines. Instead its rites were carried out at places regarded as sacred, such as at the foot of a beautiful mountain, beside a pure river or stream, in a mysterious grove, or a place providing the temporary seat of the deity, such as an evergreen tree *(himorogi)* or a rock in its natural setting *(iwakura)*. Because Japan's primary mode of subsistence until the nineteenth century was agriculture, the main rites of ancient Shinto concerned agriculture. Among these, the spring Prayer for Good Harvest (Kinensai) and the autumn Shinto Thanksgiving (Niinamesai) were especially important.

Two cosmologies existed simultaneously. The first conceived of the world as having a vertical pattern, featuring three planes, namely, Takamanohara ("plain of high heaven"), the world of the gods; Nakatsukuni ("middle land"), the world of humankind; and Yomi ("underworld"), the land of the dead. The second cosmology saw the universe as a horizontal, two-tiered structure in which Tokoyo ("perpetual land") exists at the edge of the phenomenal world. Tokoyo was believed to be a utopian country far beyond the sea.

Under the influence of continental culture, ancient Shinto began to develop in many ways. One such development is the ethical consciousness that came about through the influence of Chinese culture, introduced to Japan around the fifth century. People began to seek a standard in the myths and to pattern their lives upon the will and action of the *kami*. *Magokoro* (purity of mind or sincerity) was valued highly in the days of ancient Shinto, and as time went on it became more and more highly valued.

With the appearance of a unified nation, Amaterasu Omikami, previously the tutelary deity of the imperial clan, came to be worshiped outside the imperial palace as the protective deity of the nation and its people. At the same time, the clan deities of the great clans, in addition to their original functions, were made protective deities of the entire nation, and every year offerings were devoted to them by the central government.

The national system of Shinto rites was completed in the early Heian period (late eighth century to late twelfth century). At the beginning of the tenth century, there were nearly three thousand shrines receiving offerings from the government.

AMALGAMATION OF BUDDHISM AND SHINTO. From around the time of the Taika Reforms until the early Heian period, Chinese influence in thought, ethics, law, literature, technology, and industry was very great, but in religion Buddhism's influence and power of permeation increased quickly following its introduction in 538. Initially, the Buddha was thought of as "the neighboring country's [i. e., China's] *kami*" and was not rigorously distinguished from the *kami* of Japan. However, Buddhist art, worship, and notions of transience eventually won the hearts of the people, beginning with the ruling elites. However, because Shinto continued to live on strongly as a religion of the people, many connections between the two religions were formed.

Three stages in the assimilation of Buddhism and Shinto can be distinguished. The first was that in which the *kami* were made protectors of the Buddhas; from the middle of the eighth century Shinto tutelary deities were worshiped in Buddhist temples. The second stage coincided in time with the first. Among the Buddhist clergy arose the idea that in the Ten Realms of Beings (ten levels of karmically determined existence, ranging from denizens of the various Buddhist hells to Buddhas) the *kami* correspond to the Buddhist *devas* ("gods"), who occupy the highest position in the Realm of Ignorance.

The third stage, beginning at the end of the eighth century, held that *kami* are *avataras,* or incarnations, of *bodhisattvas* and assigned *bodhisattva* titles to the *kami.* Later, it was held that Buddhas are the original form of *kami,* while *kami* are phenomenal manifestations of the Buddhas.

Buddhist Shinto was based on the concepts of *kami* held by the Buddhist clergy. These concepts were fully developed by the Kamakura period (late twelfth century to early fourteenth century). Typical examples of Buddhist Shinto were Tendai Shinto and Shingon Shinto. In Tendai's philosophy of ultimate reality, primordial Buddha nature as represented by Sakyamuni Buddha was held to be the reality behind all phenomena, including the *kami.*

In Shingon thought Mahavairocana ("great illuminator"), symbolized by the sun, is held to be the source of the universe and all existence, uniting its two aspects, the Diamond cycle *(kongokai)* and the Womb-store cycle *(taizokai)*. It was held in accordance with this principle that the original form of the deity of the Inner Shrine at Ise, Amaterasu Omikami, was the Womb-store cycle (the feminine aspect), and that the original form of the deity of the Outer Shrine was Mahavairocana, of the Diamond cycle.

The situation described above continued until the end of the Edo period (1603-1867), and it is estimated that Buddhist priests were in charge of over half of all the Shinto shrines in the country by that time. But a movement in opposition began as far back as the early Kamakura period. Ise, or Watarai, Shinto, while continuing to be influenced by Shingon Shinto, developed among the priests of the Grand Shrine at Ise, and was the first anti-Buddhist Shinto. One of its theories held that *konton,* or chaos, was the original form of all phenomena.

Yoshida Shinto was founded by Urabe Kanetomo (1435-1511), priest of the Yoshida Shrine in Kyoto, in the latter half of the fifteenth century. According to him, the fundamental god of the universe, Taigen Sonjin ("great exalted one"), is identical to the *kami* that appears at the beginning of the *Nihonshoki,* Kuni no Toko-dachi no Mikoto. Yoshida held that all beings originate from this deity.

CONFUCIAN SHINTO. In the early Edo period it was Confucian Shinto that made the greatest strides philosophically at this time. Confucian scholars tried to interpret Shinto in terms of Neo-Confucianism as expounded by Chu Hsi and Wang Yang-ming and proclaimed that Shinto and Confucianism are one. The two main schools promoting this view were Yoshikawa Shinto and Suiga (also read Suika) Shinto. Yoshikawa Koretaru (1616-1694) emphasized Shinto's usefulness as a philosophy for governing the realm. At birth, the heart-mind has within it *ri* (Chin., *li*), the source of all existence that is this deity, but if at the same time the *ki* (Chin., *ch'i;* the physical element) is not purified, the *kami's* divine wisdom will be obstructed by egoistic desire and will fail to be activated. Therefore, he held, it is necessary to pray and to purify heart and flesh in order to recover humanity's original oneness with the deity by eradicating egotism.

Suiga Shinto was founded by Yamazaki Ansai (1618-1682). Although he had sometimes farfetched explanations, his teachings were accompanied by the emphasis on reverential exactitude *(tsutsushimi)*, purity of mind, prayer, fervent loyalty to the imperial house, and so on. They later became one of the sources of the political movement to overthrow the shogunate.

REVIVAL OF SHINTO. Kokugaku (the school of National Learning), arising in the atmosphere of free scholarship, of the early Edo period (late seventeenth century), sought to recover and clarify the ethos of ancient Japan through exacting literary research. Established by Motoori Norinaga, Revival Shinto (Fukko Shinto) refers to the Shinto research and religious movement that was based on Kokugaku. Motoori criticized the syncretistic theories linking Shinto with Buddhism and Confucianism and urged that through study of the classics the spirit of ancient Shinto be revived.

Among Motoori's disciples, Hirata Atsutane (1776-1843) was the most important successor in the field of Shinto. Hirata's view of humanity held that human nature is originally good, but that this world is only a temporary one that *kami* have established to test us. He goes on to claim that there will be retribution for past bad deeds in the next world. These Catholic influences were continued by some of Hirata's disciples, but in later Shinto they were unable to command significant following.

However, Hirata's doctrines laid the theoretical groundwork for Shinto funerals among the people through his idea of the otherworld. Hirata also promoted domestic rites and composed many prayers. He furthermore propounded the notion that Japan is the center of the world and advocated emperor worship.

ESTABLISHMENT OF SECT SHINTO. The thirteen sects of Shinto developed out of Shinto, Confucianism, Buddhism, Taoism, Shugendo, and folk beliefs. These groups show a variety of patterns of development, patterns on the one hand growing out of the teachings and actions of a religious leader looked upon as founder by believers, or developing from Revival Shinto, or from the conflation of a number of related, preexisting groups. The reasons for the development of these groups included the shock felt by the people in the face of the social and political changes surrounding the end of the Edo Period and the Meiji Restoration, the impotence of Buddhism when it lost the support of the shogunate, the impact of Revival Shinto, and the necessity of autonomous proselytization on a grass roots level after the failure of the Great Promulgation Movement.

BELIEFS, TEACHINGS, ORGANIZATION

CONCEPT OF KAMI. The core of Shinto is the belief in the profound and mysterious power of the *kami* (*musubi,* namely, the power of harmony and creation) as well as the way of the *kami* or the "will" of the *kami* (*makoto,* namely, truth or truthfulness). The essence of *kami* transcends the ability of words to explain and is an ineffable existence far beyond humanity's powers of comprehension. However, devoted believers are able to know the will and the existence of *kami* through faith.

THE NATURE OF HUMANITY. The fundamental assumption of Shinto's conception of the nature of man is the idea that "human beings are the children of *kami.*" Since man is believed to have received life from the *kami,* man has within him the sacrality that is the essence of *kami.*

INSTITUTIONS. The main facilities of Shrine Shinto are, of course, shrines. Sect Shinto and Shinto-derived new religions, however, make use of "churches," structures specifically designed for formal, congregational worship.

Shrines, in their several architectural styles, combine with their surrounding forests to fulfill their functions and to give the appearance appropriate to these functions. Therefore, the entire precinct should be considered as the shrine. At the entrance to the shrine stands the *torii,* the classic Shinto double-linteled gateway, demarcating the boundary between the sacred place and the secular world. As one proceeds along the approach, one finds the ablution basin, where visitors wash their hands and rinse their mouths. In its vicinity are the shrine office, the gathering hall, the purification

The biannual Shinto ceremony of Oho-harahi resembles a rite of confession, but it is only a recitation of a complete list of possible sins or impurities by the nakatomi, a high dignitary, or by other priests.

PAGE 174

hall, the treasury, and other buildings. Most people who worship at shrines make a small offering before the hall of worship and pray. Occasionally, they might ask a priest to perform rites of passage or give special prayers, announcements, and thanksgiving.

BELIEVERS' ORGANIZATIONS. Sociologically, there are many patterns of organization in Shinto believers' associations *(sukeishakai)*. In the case of the Shinto sects and the new religions, these are all, in the words of Joachim Wach, "specifically religious groups." In contrast, in Shrine Shinto we find both specifically religious groups and "identical religious groups," in which "natural" and religious groupings are identical. In the latter case we find that such natural groups as branch and stem family groups, territorial groups, age groups, and professional groups have become the units for the performance of festivals, and even in modern times this phenomenon is frequently found in agricultural areas.

In December 1945 the Occupation force issued the Shinto Directive dismantling the official structure of State Shinto.

PAGE 386

SOCIAL FUNCTIONS AND THE PRESENT SITUATION

Historically, Shinto's functions may be divided into two broad categories. The first concerns the search for the meaning of life and the solution to basic human problems of individual and family life. The second is the ability to nurture in people the feeling of mutual belonging and solidarity as members of regional society, and to unify them as citizens in the larger, national society. The second of these functions is particularly conspicuous in Shrine Shinto.

Considered from social and political perspectives, the duty of the emperor and other authorities in ancient times was not limited to ordinary politics but included service to the gods. The expression *saisei itchi*, meaning, "Shinto ceremonies and political affairs are one and the same," belongs to a later epoch. But also demanded of those in power was equality in government, true-hearted government based on a religious sincerity under the protection of the gods and the worship of them.

Under the influence of these traditions, the Meiji government revived the tenth-century system of national shrines. The Constitution of 1889 guaranteed the conditional freedom of religion (i. e., to the extent that this freedom did not infringe upon one's performance of patriotic duties), but Shinto was favored as a cornerstone of the nation's structure. Shinto education was carried out in public schools, and most national holidays coincided with Shinto festivals. As of 1945, there were 218 national shrines, including 14 overseas, and 110,000 local shrines.

After World War II, the Occupation authorities ordered the Japanese government to sever all official affiliation with Shinto shrines and to cease all financial support for the shrines from public funds. Shrine Shinto experienced a period of economic, social, and political difficulty. However, through the private support of the people, ruined shrines have been rebuilt, and *matsuri* and various rites of passage have been revived. According to statistics of the Agency for Cultural Affairs, in 1982 there were 79,700 shrines. Most of these belong to the Association of Shinto Shrines. Of these, 570 are independent or belong to small religious organizations. The number of Shrine Shinto believers stands at 74,660,000.

Shinto is intimately connected with the cultural and social life of the Japanese people

[*See also* Priesthood, New Religions *and* Japanese Religion.]

— HIRAI NAOFUSA

TRANSLATED FROM JAPANESE BY HELEN HARDACRE

SIKHISM

Sikhism was a later offshoot of the *bhakti* (devotional) cult of Vaisnava Hinduism, which developed in Tamil Nadu and was based upon the teachings of Alvar and Adiyar saints. Its chief propagators were Adi Sankara (eighth century), who expounded *kevaladvaita* (pure monism), and, later, Ramananda (1360-1470) and Kabir (1398-1518), who were influenced by Islam and accepted Muslim disciples.

Nanak, the founder of Sikhism, was the Punjab's chief propounder of the *bhakti* tradition. A mystical experience at age twenty-nine was the turning point in Nanak's life. While bathing in a nearby rivulet, he disappeared from view and was given up as drowned. According to the Janamsakhis ("life stories"), he was summoned by God and charged with his mission: "Go in the world to pray and to teach mankind how to pray."

Abandoning worldly pursuits, Nanak undertook four long voyages. On the first, he went eastward as far as Assam, visiting Hindu places of pilgrimage and meeting and discussing spiritual problems with ascetics and holy men.

He returned to his home for a short time before setting out on another long tour. This time he went southward, through Tamil Nadu and as far as Sri Lanka. His third journey was to the northern regions of the Himalayas; his fourth and last of the long journeys began in 1518. This time he went westward to Mecca, Medina, and as far as Basra and Baghdad. By the time Nanak returned home, he was too old to undertake any more strenuous journeys. He decided to settle down at Kartarpur and instruct people who came to him. Large numbers of peasants—both Hindus and Muslims—flocked to hear him. Many became his disciples, or *sisyas,* from which the Punjabi word *Sikh* is derived.

Nanak accepted most of the traditional beliefs of Hinduism pertaining to the origin of creation and its dissolution. He likewise accepted the theory of *samsara*—of birth, death, and rebirth.

Nanak's God was one, omnipotent, and omniscient. God was *sat* (both "truth" and "reality"), as opposed to *asat* ("falsehood") and *mithya* ("illusion"). He thus not only made God a spiritual concept but also based principles of social behavior on this concept. In other words, if God is truth, to speak an untruth is to be ungodly.

His God is ineffable because he is *nirankar,* or "formless." The best one can do is to admit the impossibility of defining him. But the fact that God cannot be defined should not inhibit us from learning about truth and reality. This we can do by following the path of righteousness.

Nanak made the institution of "guruship" the pivot of his religious system. Without the *guru* as a guide, he insisted, no one can attain *moksa* ("release"). The *guru* keeps his followers on the path of truth; he acts as a goad stick, keeping man, who is like a rogue elephant, from running amok. The *guru* is to be consulted, respected, and cherished—but not worshiped. He is a teacher, not a reincarnation of God, an *avatara,* or a messiah. Nanak constantly referred to himself as the bard *(dhadi),* slave, and servant of God.

Nanak believed that all human beings have a basic fund of goodness that, like the pearl in the oyster, only awaits the opening of the shell to emerge and enrich them. The chief task of the guru is to make man aware of the treasure within him and then help him unlock the jewel box.

— KHUSHWANT SINGH

SLAVIC RELIGION

The exact origin of the Slavs, an indigenous European people, is not known, but by about 800 BCE pockets of Slavs were scattered in a region east of the Vistula and the Carpathians and west of the Don. Around the sixth century CE the Slavs began separating into three groups, the West, South, and East Slavs. The West Slavs lived in a region reaching beyond the Elbe and were bounded on the west by Germanic tribes. The South Slavs, covering the area east of the Adriatic, south of the Danube, and west of the Black Sea, had the Magyars and Vlachs as their northern and eastern neighbors. The ancestors of today's Russians, Belorussians, and Ukrainians, the East Slavs lived in an area bounded by Lake Ladoga, the upper Volga and Don, and the Dnieper.

SIKHS

Sikhism is an offshoot of the Bhakti cult of Vaisnava Hinduism influenced by Islam. It evolved into a non-Hindu, non-Muslim movement on its own.

NAZIMA KOWALL/CORBIS

S

SLAVIC RELIGION

Formation of Slavic Religion

"Slow but sure moves the might of the gods."

EURIPIDES
THE BACCHAE 407 B.C.

FORMATION OF SLAVIC RELIGION

The term *Slavic religion* can be used to refer to the mythology and cultic life common to all Slavs from the sixth to the tenth century. Three important factors must be borne in mind in regard to Slavic religion. First, literacy came to the Slavs in the aftermath of christianization; songs, fairy tales, and oral epics represent pagan religious traditions. The second important factor in the formation of the Slavic religion was the close contact of the Slavs with neighboring peoples, especially the Balts and Indo-Iranians, attested to by some words that have clear affinities with Iranian. The third and most essential factor is the heritage of mythological images. In the tradition of Celtic, Baltic, Greek, and other related mythologies of Europe, Slavic beliefs strongly preserved very ancient pre-Indo-European images typical of an agricultural, matrifocal, and matrilinear culture.

TEMPLES AND IDOLS. The most precise descriptions of temples and idols come from the eleventh through the thirteenth century in the area of the northwestern Slavs, present-day Germany. The best-documented site is Arkona, a citadel-temple of the god Sventovit, which was destroyed in 1168 by Christian Danes. Carl Schuchhardt's excavation in 1921 proved the existence of the temple.

The earliest source, Thietmar (1014), describes a similar temple on the castle hill of Riedegost or Radigast (Rethra). It contained several hand-sculpted idols dressed in helmets and armor and each dedicated to a god, the most important being that of Zuarasici (Svarozhich). Carl Schuchhardt, who excavated Rethra in 1922, concluded that Riedegost was principal among all the local temples. People came to it with homage before going to war, and with offerings on their return. The priests determined reconciliation offerings by means of dice and horse oracles. it was apparently the sanctuary for the entire Lutici confederation, of which the Retharii were one tribe.

At Wolin, according to Monarchus Prieflingensis, Bishop Otto of Bramberg found a temple with a sacred spear that, as legend had it, had been placed there in memory of Julius Caesar. The practice of building a church on the site of a pagan sanctuary was one of the most effective, and most commonly employed, methods of combating paganism all over the Slavic area. It attracted the people to whom the place itself was still holy, and it removed all traces of the worship previously performed there.

A ruined temple, perhaps of Perun, was discovered in 1951 near Novgorod in a place called Peryn. The wooden structure itself was not preserved, but the floor plan, an octagonal rosette shape, was clearly evident. In the center was charcoal, indicating where the idol and a place for fire had probably been located. Nearby was a flat stone, apparently a part of an altar. In 1958, at Staraia Ladoga, a wooden effigy of a god with mustache and beard and wearing a conical helmet was found in a layer dated to the ninth or tenth century.

Idols were dedicated to various gods. In the West Slavic area, the richest temples belonged to the warrior god of "heavenly light" in his various aspects (Svarozhich, Iarovit, Sventovit), whereas the thunder god (Perun) was worshiped outdoors. It is clear that at the time when Christianity arrived, the official religion was dominated by warrior gods of Indo-European heritage.

GODS OF INDO-EUROPEAN HERITAGE

Three divine archetypes of the Indo-European religious tradition are clearly represented in the Slavic pantheon: the god of heavenly light, the god of death and the underworld, and the thunder god. The first two stand in opposition to each other, but the relationship of the three deities is triangular, not hierarchical.

THE GOD OF HEAVENLY LIGHT. Many different names identify the god of heavenly light. The personified sun appears throughout Slavic folklore: each morning he rides out from his golden palace in the east in a two-wheeled chariot drawn by horses. He begins the day as a youth and dies each night as an old man. He is attended by two lovely virgins (the morning and evening stars), seven judges (the planets), and seven messengers (the comets).

Certain Slavic myths give an anthropomorphic interpretation to the relationship between the sun and the moon. The Russian word for "moon," mesiats, is masculine, but many legends portray the moon as a beautiful young woman whom the sun marries at the beginning of summer, abandons in winter, and returns to in spring. In other myths, the moon is the husband and the sun is his wife, as in Baltic mythology.

THE GOD OF DEATH AND THE UNDERWORLD. The names *Veles* and *Volos* apparently represent two aspects of the same god: (1) a sorcerer god of death, related to music and poetry, and (2) a god of cattle, wealth, and commerce.

Veles was degraded to a devil at the beginning of Christian times. All that remains of this god are such expressions as *k Velesu za more* ("to Veles in the otherworld"). Place-names incorporating *Veles* imply sites where this god was worshiped, such as Titov Veles in Macedonia.

Volos was merged with the image of Saint Blasius (Vlasii) and also partly with that of Saint Nicholas (Nikola), the patrons of flocks and crops. He was honored as such up to the twentieth century on his holiday, 11 February.

THE THUNDER GOD. Overseer of justice and order, purifier and fructifier, and adversary of the devil, Perun is feared to this day in some Slavic areas. His presence and actions are perceived in lightning and thunder. Parallels in other Indo-European mythologies, such as the Baltic Perkons and Perkunas and the Germanic Þórr (Thor), attest to the antiquity of this god. With the onset of Christianity, Perun gradually merged with Saint Elijah (Il'ia), who is portrayed in Russian icons crossing the heavens in a chariot. Bull sacrifice and a communal feast on Saint Il'ia's Day, 20 July, were recorded in northern Russia in 1907.

HOUSEHOLD GUARDIANS. Slavic names for household guardians—Russian *ded, dedushka* (dim.), and *domovoi;* Ukrainian *did, didko,* and *domovyk;* Czech *dedek;* and Bulgarian *stopan*—have the meaning "grandfather" or "house lord," suggesting their origins in ancestor worship within a patrilineal culture. He cared for animal herds and protected the entire home and its occupants from misfortune.

The Russian forest spirit, Leshii or Lesovik (from *les",* "forest"), also appears as an old man or an animal. His principal function is to guard forests and animals.

Ancestor worship, a prominent practice among all pre-Christian Slavs, is evidenced in gifts presented to the dead. A strong belief in life after death is indicated by prehistoric and even modern burial rites. Food offerings are made in cemeteries to this day. Everything deemed necessary for the afterlife—weapons, tools, clothing, wives, slaves, horses, hunting dogs, food—was buried in the grave or was burned if the deceased was cremated.

MYTHIC IMAGES ROOTED IN OLD EUROPEAN RELIGION

The primary figures of the oldest stratum of Slavic culture are predominantly female: Fates, Death, Baba Yaga, Moist Mother Earth, and a host of nymphs and goblins.

LIFE-GIVING AND LIFE-TAKING GODDESSES AND THEIR ASSOCIATES. In folk beliefs, Mokysha, or Mokusha, has a large head and long arms; at night she spins flax and shears sheep. Her name is related to spinning and plaiting and to moisture. The life-giving and life-taking goddess, or Fate, was the spinner of the thread of life and the dispenser of the water of life. Up to the twentieth century, it was believed that fate took the form of birth fairies who appeared at the bedside of a newborn baby. Three Fates of different ages were believed to appear. They determined the infant's destiny and invisibly inscribed it upon his or her forehead.

The Russian *dolia* and the Serbian *sreca* represent the fate of a person's material life. There were good and bad *dolias* and *srecas.* The benevolent spirit protected her favorites and served them faithfully from birth to death. The malevolent spirit, *nedolia* or *nesreca,* usually personified as a poor and ugly woman, capable of transforming herself into various shapes, bestowed bad luck.

Associates of the life-giving and life-taking goddesses were female spirits filled with passionate sensuality. The Bohemians called them *divozenky,* the Poles *dziwozony,* the Slovaks *divja davojke,* and the Bulgarians *divi-te zheny* ("wild women"). They often took care of neglected babies and punished bad mothers.

BABA YAGA AND VED'MA. The Old European goddess of death and regeneration is reflected in the Slavic deity Baba Yaga, who has been preserved in folk tales as a witch. She was said to live in darkness and to devour humans, but she was also believed to have a gift for prophecy. She was usually old and ugly, with bony legs, a long nose, and disheveled hair, but she might also appear as a young woman, or as two sisters.

Ved'ma ("witch") is a demonized goddess. She can be seen flying beneath the clouds and over the mountains and valleys on a broom or a rake. She can make herself invisible, turn into a ball of yarn, and move rapidly. She knows the magical properties of plants and is the keeper of the water of life and death.

MOIST MOTHER EARTH AND CORN MOTHER. The sacred deity known as Moist Mother Earth (Mati Syra Zemlia) was perceived as pure, powerful, and pregnant. Up to the twentieth century peasants believed that in springtime it was a grave sin to strike the earth with anything before 25 March, because during that time the earth was pregnant.

The corn (i. e., grain) spirit was personified as the Corn Mother or as the Old Rye (Barley, Wheat, or Oat) Woman. She made crops grow. At harvest, it was believed that she was present in the last stalks of grain left standing in the field.

NYMPHS. Two types of nymph were known to the Slavs:

Vilas. Many Slavs believed that *vilas* originated like blossoms with the morning dew or that they were born when the sun shone through the rain. Because she is so beautiful, she cannot tolerate the presence of anyone more beautiful than she. There are three kinds of *vila,* associated with mountains, with water, and with clouds.

Rusalkas. Descriptions of *rusalkas* vary from region to region. They are sometimes said to live in the forest, but in most accounts they are reported to live at the bottom of lakes and rivers, in the deepest water. The *rusalka* is seen as the mistress of water, the female counterpart of the male spirit of water, the *vodianoi.* The *rusalka* is depicted as a beautiful young woman with a white body and long, loose, green or gold hair that she combs while sitting on a riverbank. Always naked, she loves to swing on branches and to play, sing, and dance. She entices men off forest paths or lures

"Nymph, in thy orisons, Be all my sins remembered."

WILLIAM SHAKESPEARE
HAMLET

The physical form of the Indo-European goddess Kolyo (the coverer) incarnated the mixture of fascination and horror evoked by death. She was seductively beautiful from the front while hiding a back that was repulsive in the extreme.

328

them into her dance so as to tickle them to death and carry them into the water.

GOBLINS. In the West and South Slavic areas, goblins were perceived as little men (dwarfs) who, if they were fed and cared for, brought good harvests and money. The Bohemian *setek* or *sotek* stayed in sheep sheds or hid in pea patches or wild pear trees. The Slovak *skratak,* Polish *skrzat* or *skrzatek,* and Slovene *skrat* (cf. German *Schrat*) appeared as a small bird emitting sparks. The Polish *latawiec* ("flying goblin") took the shape of a bird or a snake.

[*For discussion of Slavic religion in broader context, see* Indo-European Religions. *See also* Germanic Religion.]

— MARIJA GIMBUTAS

All religions, regardless of their origin, retain their vitality only as long as their members continue to believe in a transcendent reality with which they can in some way communicate by direct experience.

PAGE 476

SOUTH AMERICAN INDIANS

INDIANS OF THE ANDES

The Andean region is formed by the Andes mountain range, which extends the entire length of western South America. This region can be divided into three geographically contrasting subareas: the highlands, the coast, and the eastern cordillera. In the highlands the intermontane valleys lie at altitudes of between three and four thousand meters. These valleys were the places in which the Chavín (tenth to first centuries BCE), Tiahuanaco-Huari (eighth to tenth centuries CE), and Inca (fifteenth century CE) cultures flourished. In the region along the Pacific coast, composed mostly of low-lying desert plains, life was concentrated out of necessity in the valleys formed by the rivers that drain from the highlands into the ocean. The coastal valleys in the Peruvian sector of the Andes region were the cradles of cultures such as the Moche (second to eighth centuries CE), the Paracas-Nazca (second to eighth centuries CE), and the Chimú (twelfth to fifteenth centuries CE), who devised colossal irrigation works that enabled them to bring extensive areas of desert under cultivation. The dramatic, abruptly changing topography of the eastern cordillera is covered by dense tropical vegetation. Peoples of the intermontane valleys entered this region and built the cities of Machu Picchu and Pajatén, and they terraced vast areas of the rugged, wooded hillsides to gain land for cultivation and to prevent erosion.

The sheltered agricultural cultures of the Andes have interrelated since ancient times. The areas where such cultures did not develop, although geographically "Andean," are not considered part of the Andean *cultural* region. The territory of the central Andes—basically equivalent to present-day Peru—became the center of the Andean cultural process. The northern Andes (parts of present-day Colombia and Ecuador) was the scene of the Quimbaya and Muisca (Chibcha) cultures and of the earlier Valdivia culture, which may have given the initial impulse to the entire high-Andean culture.

More than ten thousand years have passed since human beings first trod the Andes. The earliest settlers were hunters and Neolithic agriculturalists. By the third millennium BCE there appear incipient signs of complex cultures, such as that of Aldas on the northern coast of Peru, whose people built monumental temples. During the second and first millennia BCE, the appearance of Valdivia and Chavín represented the first flowering of developed culture, which set the foundation for the developments that eventually culminated in the Inca empire. By the time that Europeans arrived in the Americas, the Inca empire stretched for more than four thousand miles along the western part of South America, from southern Colombia in the north to Maule, in south central Chile, in the south. The empire passed into Spanish dominion in 1532, when Atahuallpa, the thirteenth and last of the Inca sovereigns, was beheaded. From then on, the breakdown of indigenous Andean cultural values is apparent.

SUBSISTENCE AND RELIGION. The peoples of the Andes are predisposed toward mysticism and ceremonial; even today, Andeans are steeped in an elaborate religious tradition. A significant part of their intense religiosity may be explained by ecological factors: no other agricultural society in the world has had to face a more hostile environment than that of the Andes region, with its vast areas of desert, its enormous wastes, and the heavy tropical vegetation that covers the mountains' rugged eastern flanks. All physical effort, all organization of human labor, and all technological solutions are insufficient to counter the environment, to whose ordinary harshness are added nature's frequent scourges, especially droughts. This endemic state of crisis could only be exorcised, it seems, through intense magico-religious practices; only through manipulation of supernatural powers have Andean peoples believed it possible to guarantee their existence.

The dramatic situation imposed by the environment perhaps explains why Andean religiosity appears to have been unencumbered by the moralizing of other religious traditions. Rules like "Thou shalt not steal" and "Thou shalt not commit adultery" were of course enforced, but theft and adultery were considered social offenses: it was the duty of the administrators of state law to punish offenders. There was no concept of a future expiation. The relationship between religion and morality was closest in regard to behavior toward the deities; if their worship was not properly carried out, they were affronted, resulting in a series of calamities that could be checked through prayers, weeping, and sacrifices. The hostility of nature in the Andes led to a permanently febrile state of religiosity.

GODS OF SUSTENANCE. Andean deities jointly governed both individual and collective existence by providing sustenance. Soil fertility plays a significant role in Andean religion, as demonstrated by the profuse worship given to the deities that personified and controlled the forces of nature. The gods, though individualized, form a hieratic unit and share one focus: the economic state of the people. They are conceived in the image of nature, which simultaneously separates and conjoins the creative forces, masculine and feminine. Thus the first basic division appears in the opposition of Inti-Viracocha-Pachacámac and Quilla-Pachamama. Both of these deity-configurations are creative forces, but in accordance with the social order of the sexes, the supremacy of the former, masculine element is asserted. The powerful Illapa ("thunder, weather") is also integrated into the sphere of Inti-Viracocha-Pachacámac, but, above all his other functions, Illapa directly provides life-giving rain.

Viracocha. Glimpses of a culture hero on whom divine attributes have been superimposed can be seen in the figure of Viracocha, and therefore Pierre Duviols (1977) and María Rostworowski de Diez Canseco (1983) corectly deny him the character of a creator god. Because of these same divine attributes, however, Viracocha was thought by the sixteenth-century Spaniards to resemble the God of Christianity, although Christian-Andean syncretism preserved some aspects of Viracocha's indigenous origin. Thus, according to the stories told about him, Viracocha molded men in clay or sculpted them in stone. (They finally spring from the womb of Pachamama, "mother earth," which is sometimes represented as a cave.) On the other hand, stories about Viracocha also portray him as entering into confrontations with other divine beings and as engaged in other tasks ordinarily associated with culture heroes (for example, "teaching the created people").

Pachacámac. The myth of Pachacámac ("animator of the world") links this Andean deity even more strongly than Viracocha with the creation of the first generation of human beings. This deity is characterized, above all, as bringing to mankind the food necessary for survival as a result of the entreaties of a primordial woman, Mother Earth. The provision of edible plants is shown in other myths: in one of these, Pachacámac disguises himself, taking the form of the sun (in some instances, the son, the brother, or even the father of Pachacámac, according to the chronicler Francisco Lopez de Gómara), who with his rays fertilizes the primordial woman, perhaps the incarnation of Pachamama. In another myth, Pachacámac kills what he has created, and this action may be interpreted as the institution of human sacrifice to nourish the food and fertility deities. When the victim is buried, his teeth sprout maize, his bones become manioc, and so on.

Inti. According to both the surviving mythic literature and the images discovered by archaeologists, the masculine creative force was incarnated in Inti, the sun. He offers heat and light, and his rays possess fertilizing powers, as is evident in the myth of Pachacámac. Mythic literature testifies to the Andeans' reliance on the power of the sun and to their anxiety that he may disappear, causing cataclysm and the destruction of mankind (an event that would be followed by the creation of a new generation of men). This anxiety explains the redoubled prayers and supplications during solar eclipses—rituals that ended with loud cries and lamentations (even domestic animals were whipped to make them howl!). Archaeological evidence of another form of magico-religious defense against this premonition of the tragic disappearance of the sun is found in stone altars called *intihuatanas*, a word revealingly translated as "the place where the sun is tied." Inti was also associated with fertility through water, as when the sun ceases to give light.

PACHAMAMA-QUILLA. Pachamama ("mother earth") symbolized the feminine element of divinity for the Andeans. Pachamama is incarnated as the primordial mother of mythic literature, and she is personified as Quilla, the moon. In this connection she is symbolized by silver; with this metal many representations of Pachamama were made, especially in the form of the half-moon (called *tumi*), which was one of the most important religious symbols of the Andes. The cult of Pachamama was, and still is, extensive (Mariscotti de Görlitz, 1978). Pachamama was held to be the producer of food, animals, and the first man. As primordial mother, she creates through the fertilizing action of the Sun, and she later becomes co-donor of food plants, especially maize.

The mythological literature tells of several female supernatural beings. These are likely regional versions of Pachamama. Among them are Chaupiñanca, the primordial mother of Huarochirí mythology; Illa, who appears in the mythic traditions of the Ecuadorian Andes; and Urpihuáchac, sister and wife of Pachacámac, who seems to be an expression of Cochamama, the marine form of Pachamama. To Cochamama is attributed the creation of fish and of seabirds such as the guanay, which latter act is in turn related to agricultural productivity because of the use of guano to fertilize crops.

Ancient documents show that Pachamama was individualized *ad infinitum* to guarantee the abundance

The central Andes of pre-Columbian times is characterized by a belief in high gods and their respective cults, by the worship of ancestors and of the dead, and by agrarian rites directed to a female earth deity.

PAGE 625

"The thirsty earth soaks up the rain, and drinks and gapes for drink again."

ABRAHAM COWLEY
ANACREON II 1656

of specific produce—maize, for example. Andean iconography offers representations of Pachamama incarnated in specific vegetable forms: multiple ears of maize, for instance, or groups of potatoes. In other instances these agricultural products metaphorically acquire human aspects, and they are also portrayed as being fertilized by a supernatural, anthropomorphic personage. Pachamama in her Cochamama aspect also appears to symbolize the presence of abundant water—essential for fertilizing the agricultural fields.

The symbolism of Pachamama has implications regarding the social status of women: as compared with the male element of divinity, Pachamama, the female, is clearly a passive and subaltern being. The attitude of sexual modesty is to be seen in the many representations that appear to show versions of Pachamama, from the archaic terracotta figures of Valdivia to those of the late Chancay civilization of the central coast of Peru. In all these, sexual characteristics are not pronounced: the figures seem to represent almost asexual beings, and they remind one of the existence of non-Christian sexual taboos (see Kauffmann Doig, 1979a). Not only do these figures rarely stress sexual characteristics, but, curiously, they seldom portray pregnant women or women giving birth.

Pachamama still plays an important role in the deeply rooted peasant magic of today's Andean people. She is even venerated in Christian churches. In the Peruvian village of Huaylas, for example, Saramama (a version of Pachamama) is venerated in the form of two female saints who are joined in a single sculpture—like Siamese twins—to give visual representation to a pathetic fallacy: the symbolization of abundance that is identified in the double or multiple ears of grain that maize plants often generously produce.

Illapa. The deity Illapa (generally translated as "thunder," "lightning," or "weather") occupies a preferential place in the Andean pantheon. Much of the mythological literature makes reference to Illapa, who takes on regional names and is expressed in varying forms: Yaro, Ñamoc, Libiac, Catequil, Pariacaca, Thunapa (possibly), and so on. To refer to these beings as if they were separate would be artificially to crowd the Andean pantheon by creating too great a number of distinct deities—a trap into which many interpreters, both early and recent, have fallen. Illapa may be seen as the incarnation of Inti, the sun, in Illapa's primary mythic form of a hawk or eagle (*indi* means "bird" in Quechua), a form to which were added human and feline attributes; thus Inti-Illapa may be said to be a true binomial in the Andean pantheon.

Associated with meteorological phenomena such as thunder, lightning, clouds, and rainbows, Illapa personifies rain, the element that fecundates the earth. As the direct source of sustenance—giving rains to the highlands and rivers and rich alluvial soils to the coastal valleys—Illapa is revered in a special and universal way.

After the Conquest, Andeans fused Illapa with images of James the Apostle, a syncretism perhaps suggested by earlier Spanish traditions. In the realm of folklore, Illapa's cult may be said still to flourish in the veneration of hills and high mountains, which are the nesting places of the *huamani* (falcons) sacred to this deity. Also associated with Illapa are the *apus*, the spirits of the mountains, and the spirits of the lakes, which, if they are not worshiped, make the waves rise destructively, and which are offended if approached by someone not protected by the sacred coca leaf.

When he appears as an incarnation of, or as joined to, Inti, Illapa may be represented by a male feline with human and avian attributes. According to iconographic studies, Illapa's image as the "flying feline," or "tiger bird" (Kauffmann Doig, 1967; 1983, p. 225) is still current in the Andes, as witnessed in the oral documentation collected by Bernard Mishkin (1963) regarding Qoa, a god who is ruler of meteorological phenomena. Qoa still appears as a flying cat, his eyes throwing out lightning and his urine transformed into fertilizing rain. Pictorial representations of the "tiger bird," which have been made since the formative period, especially in Chavín and allied art (see below) have recently been related to Qoa by Johan Reinhard (1985, pp. 19-20).

FORMS OF WORSHIP. Through acts of worship, the sphere of the sacred could be manipulated to benefit mankind. The effectiveness of human intervention into the realm of the supernatural powers depended on the intensity with which the rites were performed. In the Andean world, where natural factors put agricultural production and even existence itself to a constant test, worship assumed an extraordinary intensity and richness of form. The calamities that endangered personal and collective welfare were believed to have been caused by offenses to supernatural beings and especially to a lack of intensity in worship. Offerings to the gods of sustenance and to other supernatural beings related to them complemented the cultic display. Cruel sacrifices were necessary to worship's efficacy; in times of crisis they were performed lavishly and included human sacrifices.

The popular form of communication with *huaca* (i. e.. the entire supernatural world) was effected through the *muchay* ("worship, reverence"). *Muchay* was performed by removing one's sandals, gesticulating, throwing kisses, murmuring supplications, bowing one's shoulders in humility, puffing out one's cheeks to blow in the direction of the object worshiped, and so on. Other forms of contact with supernatural beings were made through oracles, whose traditions go back to early forms of Andean cultures, like the Chavín.

Oracles were represented in the form of idols located in sanctuaries such as the famous one of Pachacámac, near Lima; these oracles rendered predictions about important future events to shamans and priests.

To make an offering was an act of paying tribute. Offerings were made voluntarily, but they were also collected in the form of compulsory tribute, the administration of which was centralized in temples. A widespread, popular offering was *mullo*, a powder made of ground seashells, which by association was linked to fertility through water; another was coca (*Erythroxylon coca*) in the form of a masticated wad. Stone cairns in the high passes were places of worship; wads of coca would be thrown in a ritual act called Togana. The mummified dead were offered special jars containing grains, fruits, and liquids. Guinea pigs and llamas served as important sacrificial offerings.

Among sacrifices, that of young boys and girls was the most important; sometimes human sacrifice was performed by walling up a living female person. It appears that among the Inca the sacrifice of boys and girls was received as a form of tribute, called the *capaccocha*, from the provinces. The person who was to serve as the *capaccocha* was delivered to the capital city of Cuzco in great pomp; after his death, his remains were returned to his homeland and mummified; the mummy acquired votive rank and was the object of supplications for health and agricultural welfare. Necropompa (Span., "death rite") was a special type of human sacrifice that consisted of immolations (voluntary or not) that were performed on the occasion of the death of an illustrious person (Aranībar, 1961). Decapitation of human sacrificial victims had been performed since ancient times: the Sechín stone sculpture of northern Peru depicting this practice is over three thousand years old. Head shrinking was rare and there

ANDEAN ICONOGRAPHY

Of Cats and Birds

Iconographic portrayal of supernatural beings is abundant and dates back more than three thousand years.

The image of a conspicuously superior being is found in the initial stages of high Andean civilization (especially in Chavín and related cultures). This image, typically a human form with feline and raptorial-bird attributes, is repeated in practically all the Andean cultures that succeeded Chavín, with variations of secondary importance. At Chavín, such hierarchal figures of the highest order appear on the Raimondi Stela; although lacking human elements, the figures on the Tello Obelisk and the Yauya Stela, both Chavín in style, may also be considered as representations of the highest level of being, because of their monumental stature and fine execution. The central figure of the Door of the Sun at Tiahuanaco is an almost anthropomorphic representation of the highest-ranking god. Attributes of a culture hero are perhaps also incorporated here.

A frequently encountered image of what was perhaps the same god as the one described above (but represented in a clearer and more accessible form) is that of a hybrid being that also had a form somewhere between a feline and a bird of prey (a falcon?), represented naturalistically, in which elements of human anatomy are sometimes completely absent. This "winged feline" may be the most ancient and authentic representation known to us of an Andean god. The convoluted, baroque style of Chavín art is responsible for the fact the the "winged feline" has sometimes been identified as a caiman and sometimes as a lobster, a shrimp, or even a spider. These animals, however, do not appear in relation to the divine sphere at any later stage of Andean culture.

Supernatural beings of the highest category are to be found in representations of the culture-heroes/gods Ai-apaec and Ñaymlap and of the gods at Tiahuanaco and Paracas-Nazca. All are anthropomorphic beings that combine traits of both bird and feline; in this context they imply an evolutionary development of the older "winged feline" of Chavín. In the archetypical versions of Ai-apaec, the figure bears wings (Kauffmann Doig, 1976; 1983, pp. 362, 624). At Paracas-Nazca, one figure seems to represent an evolution from a purely birdlike body into one that incorporates human elements (Kauffmann Doig, 1983, pp. 303, 325, 331-332). Feline and ornithomorphic ingredients are evident in the large figures at Tiahuanaco and Huari; from their eyes fall large tears in the form of birds, which, since Eugenio Yacovleff (1932) and even before, have been interpreted as symbolic of the fertilizing rainwater of Pachamama (Mamapacha).

Connubial gods in which the male element radiates fertilizing solar rays are found especially in the iconography derived from Huari and, more particularly, in the valleys of Huara, Pativilca, and Casma on the coast of Peru (Kauffmann Doig, 1979a, pp. 6, 60). The examples of Inca art that have survived have but scant votive content. But both the feline and the falcon continue to occupy their place of honor among iconographic elements, as may be seen in the "heraldic shield" of the Inca rulers drawn by Guaman Poma.

—FEDERICO KAUFFMANN DOIG
TRANSLATED FROM THE SPANISH BY
MARY NICKERSON

ANDEAN SHRINE

Natural shrines such as this near Cuzco, Peru were popular destinations for Andean pilgrims.

WOLFGANG KAEHLER/CORBIS

is no evidence of cannibalism in the Andean region. (Though in the myths there are a number of supernatural beings, such as Carhuincho, Carhuallo, and Achké, who are anthropophagous.) Human sacrifice, performed to achieve greater agricultural fertility, drew its rationale from the principle that the Andeans believed governed nature: death engenders life.

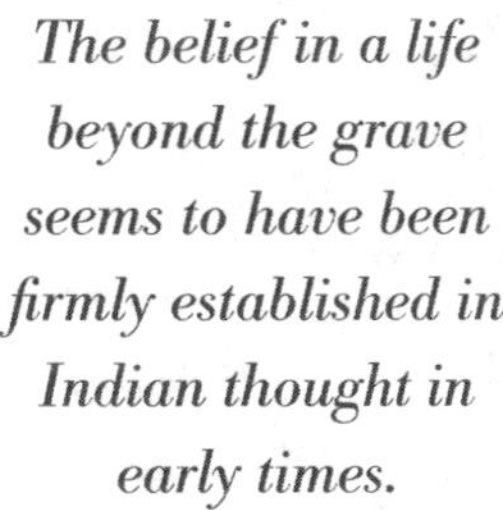

The belief in a life beyond the grave seems to have been firmly established in Indian thought in early times.

PAGE 315

The dead, mummified and revered, were expected to implore the supernatural powers for sustenance, soil fertility, abundant water, and the multiplication of domestic animals. Often bodies were buried in the cultivated fields in order to enrich them. As has recently been reported from Ayacucho, Peru, this practice survives in secret, isolated cases even to the present day: a mentally ill person is selected, intoxicated with liquor, thrown into a pit, and buried alive. Such "strenghening" rites were, according to sixteenth-century chroniclers, also practiced in laying the foundations of houses and bridges, and traces of these rites also have been recently reported from the central Andes.

Funeral rites included expressions of grief such as loud sobbing intermingled with chants in praise of the deceased; a practice that also survives in isolated areas of the Andes. The dead were mummified and taken to their tombs on stretchers. With few exceptions (e.g., among the Moche), bodies were buried in seated positions. Frequently the hands held the head, perhaps to simulate the fetal position. These "living" corpses were surrounded with food and drink, weapons, and other belongings meant to serve as provisions in the hereafter; some were buried with their mouths open, both to express the terror of sacrifice and to voice supplications to the gods for success in agriculture.

Religious festivals were celebrated continuously in the great plazas of Cuzco and at temples such as the Coricancha, the temple of the sun. Festivals dedicated to specific themes, especially in the context of food production, were held monthly with great pomp; the sovereign Inca presided, and guests were invited at his expense. Great quantities of *chicha* (maize beer) were consumed, drunk from ceremonial wooden vessels *(queros)*.

Andeans have made pilgrimages since the remote times of Chavín, and one of the favorite *huacas*, or shrines, was the sanctuary of Pachacámac. "Natural" shrines such as those on the peaks of high mountains were also popular with pilgrims. The Collur Riti festival, a celebration that coincides with the Feast of Corpus Christi, follows ancient rites. Originally, the Collur Riti was dedicated to water, and even today pilgrims return to their homes with pieces of ice carved from the mountain glaciers, symbolizing the fertility imparted by water. In the past, pilgrims fasted for variable periods of time, abstaining from maize beer, *ají (Capsicum anuum)*, and sexual intercourse.

MEDICINE AND MAGIC. Shamans use maracas in their healing rites, a practice carried on into the present by Andean *curanderos* (Span., "healers"). The *curanderos* also use hallucinogenic substances to cause them to enter the trance state. The San Pedro cactus *(Trichocereus pabhanoi)* is a powerful hallucinogen used particularly on the Peruvian coast; it gives the *curandero* the ability to discover the cause of an illness. In the highlands the diagnosis is still made by rubbing the body of a sick person with a guinea pig or with substances such as maize powder. The cure was effected through the use of medicinal plants. Today, *curanderos* complement their ancient remedies with modern pharmaceutical products.

Divination was often performed under the influence of hallucinogens or coca. Several studies, among them those of Alana Cordy-Collins (1977) and Ralph Cané (1985) speculate that the intricate art of Chavín originated in hallucinogenic experiences.

Institutionalized worship gave rise to a rich range of folk magic. Thus, for example, there were magic love-stones *(guacangui)*. Small stone sculptures of domestic animals, used to propitiate the spirits of abundance, are still produced. Ceramic figures representing vigorous bulls *(toritos de Pucará)* are still placed on rooftops, where they signify prosperity and fertility and offer magical protection of the home.

MESSIANISM. Andean mysticism and ritual experienced a vigorous rejuvenescence some thirty years after the Spanish conquest in the form of the nativistic movement called Taqui Oncoy (see Duviols, 1977; Millones, 1964; Ossio, 1973; Curatola, 1977; Urbano, 1981). The aims of this sixteenth-century messianic movement were to drive the white invaders from the land and to reinstate the structures of the lost Inca past. The movement's power was based on the worship of *huacas*, the popular form of Andean religiosity after the Sun had lost its credibility with the defeat inflicted by the Christian God. By a kind of magic purification, Taqui Oncoy sought to free the land from European intrusion after it was no longer possible to do so by force of arms. The movement's adherents believed that, with intensified supplications and increased offerings, the *huacas* could become powerful enough to help reestablish the old order. This movement declined after ten years, but the hope of a return to the Inca past is still alive, although it is confined more and more to middle-class intellectual circles in Peru and Bolivia.

The messianic myth of Inkarri (from Span., *Inca rey*, "Inca king") should also be mentioned here. Originally recorded by José María Arguedas (1956), the myth centers on a figure, Inkarri, who is the son of the Sun and a "wild woman." According to Nathan Wachtel (1977), this archetypal "vision of a conquered people," although of native extraction, seems to be immersed in syncretism. The cult of Inkarri lacks the action that characterized the Taqui Oncoy movement. Inkarri is not an Andean god but rather a pale memory of the deified sovereign of ancient times, who after patient waiting will rise to life to vindicate the Andean world.

— FEDERICO KAUFFMANN DOIG
TRANSLATED FROM SPANISH BY MARY NICKERSON

INDIANS OF THE TROPICAL FOREST

The vast region of lowland South America, mostly drained by the Amazon and Orinoco river systems and mainly covered in tropical forest, presents at first glance an area of exceptional uniformity, but in fact it is comprised of a bewildering variety of microenvironments. The Indian societies that inhabit the region are likewise characterized by great variety masked by apparent uniformity. They have in common such features as the reliance for subsistence on shifting cultivation, hunting, fishing, and gathering, but at the same time they exhibit numerous minute variations. However, these differences are kaleidoscopic patterns put together from similar pieces. It is only because this is so that it is possible to make generalizations about the religions of lowland South America.

Today when one talks about the Indian societies of lowland South America one is referring to relatively small groups—a population of ten thousand is large, and most groups number only a few hundred—dwelling in tiny settlements away from the main waterways. In the past, things were different. Estimates of the pre-Conquest population vary between one and ten million, but whatever the actual number, it is certain that the population declined abruptly, perhaps by as much as 95 percent overall, beginning with the arrival of Europeans at the end of the fifteenth century. At that time, the coasts and main rivers, today virtually without an aboriginal population, were densely inhabited, and in contrast to modern Indian villages, there were large settlements of one thousand or more inhabitants. From this it is relatively safe to surmise that the Indians' social, political, and economic organizations were different from those observable today among extant groups. Despite the fact that the latter are in many cases the fugitive remnants of earlier groups, it is difficult to identify in them features that might be transformations of earlier, more complex forms of organization. However, in one area of culture, that of religion, there is some discernible continuity with the past, for in early accounts by missionaries and travelers we find descriptions of ideas and practices that have their modern counterparts. For example, Pierre Barrère, writing of the Carib of the Guiana coast in 1743, describes religious beliefs and practices very similar to those observable among the modern Carib-speakers at the headwaters of the Guiana rivers.

FUNDAMENTAL RELIGIOUS IDEAS. Although

In the Plateau the common western theme of personal spirit-power was honed to its greatest refinement.

PAGE 511

S

SOUTH AMERICAN INDIANS

Indians of the Tropical Forest

claims have been made for the existence of monotheistic beliefs within the region, there is no evidence that any group worships a single divine being. Where such claims do arise, the reference is, at best, to some otiose culture hero responsible for the creation of the universe or to some primordial power or essence that is the driving force behind the universe. For example, among the Tucanoan-speaking peoples of the northwest Amazon the Primal Sun, or Sun Father, was the creator of the universe; he was considered a primal creative force that is not the same as the sun seen in the sky today.

Among the Carib-speaking Acawai of the Guyana-Venezuelan frontier, the existence of a supreme being is the result of Christian influence, although there appears to have been some traditional, abstract notion of "brightness" associated with the sun; the term for this idea means "light" and "life" and is the root of the word meaning "soul" or "spirit."

It is through myths that Indians make statements about the fundamental nature of the world in which they live.

PAGE 614

It is necessary to look elsewhere for Indian religion, and as a rough guide we may take E. B. Tylor's nineteenth-century definition of religion as animism, that is, the belief in spiritual beings. This concept needs some careful refining, and a first step in this task can be taken by considering the cosmology of the Indians. On this topic there is a remarkable degree of agreement among the various tribes. The universe has three layers: the sky, the earth, and a watery underworld. Each level may be further subdivided. [*See* South American Religions.] The three different layers are peopled by assorted beings, some of whom appear as recognizable denizens of the environment, whereas others are monstrous and fantastic. Thus the underworld is inhabited by aquatic creatures who are exemplified by the largest of such animals, the anaconda or the caiman. The earth is inhabited not only by people but also by forest-dwelling creatures, in particular the jaguar. The sky is the realm of the birds, for which the king vulture or the harpy eagle is often taken to be representative. Although one may refer to these beings as identifiable zoological species, it is unwise to regard them as absolutely or necessarily of an animal nature. It is often difficult to distinguish between them and people, and myths and rituals that refer to the origin of the universe frequently do not make this distinction.

Most human beings are not normally in a position to visit the other layers of the cosmos, although they may obtain experience of them under specified conditions. In many societies, houses are held to be models of the universe—microcosms—in which it is possible, through ritual, to collapse the coordinates of space and time into a unity.

In addition to the three cosmological layers, the world is also constituted of two parts, one visible, the other invisible, although the latter is visible to people with special skills and may in fact reveal itself to any person at any time. It is mistaken to see this duality as involving two separate worlds, for the seen and the unseen are really two aspects of one intermingled world and are counterparts to each other. The unseen reality is often as important as or even more important than what is revealed to the eye. Indeed, everyday events, apparently random and chaotic, can only be fully understood by reference to the invisible. Thus, the Jivaroan Indians of Ecuador regard it as essential for everyone, sometimes even hunting dogs, to have experience of the other world, experience achieved in the case of the Jivaroan people by the use of hallucinogenic substances. Dreams are another avenue of access to the invisible realm.

Power, which for the Indian lies outside society and within the invisible world, is ambiguous—that is, it can be used for good or evil—and needs, like a strong electric current, to be handled with care.

INVISIBLE BEINGS. All the layers of the universe are inhabited by invisible beings. In many cases, these are the invisible counterparts of visible objects, both animate and inanimate. Some peoples consider virtually everything to have an invisible aspect, although only certain of these unseen objects are likely to be endowed with any great importance or to seriously impinge on human affairs. However, invisible beings are notorious for their unpredictability, so it is considered wise to take precautions. Their appearance, in visible form, to a human is thought to portend misfortune.

There are a great number of these invisible beings, and they take numerous forms. For example, the Sanemá of the Brazilian-Venezuelan frontier region recognize eight different kinds of invisible beings, or *hekula*. These include *hekula* of animals, humans, plants, artifacts, mythical ancestors of animal species, mythical ancestors of human social groups, sky people, and evil spirits. All *hekula*, regardless of origin, are humanoid in appearance. Each society has its own way of classifying the inhabitants of the invisible world, but in each case the classification is likely to reflect the nature of the relationship between the invisible beings and human society.

Masters of animals. There is a widespread belief in "owners" or "masters" who govern the animals. The Tucano-Desána of the northwest Amazon believe that there are two such masters, one for animals of the forest and one for fish. The former lives in the rocky hills, the latter in the rocks that form the falls and rapids in the rivers. Here, in a larger-than-life, prototypical form, the animals and fish live in huge longhouses, like people. It is the master of the animals who lets out animals for Indians to hunt, but he does so only in return for human souls, which are used to replenish the supply of animals.

The masters of animals may appear in a variety of

guises, either as a normal animal or as a monstrous man or animal. They sometimes appear to people, especially after dark in the forest. Some of them are definitely regarded as dangerous, others as little more than mischievous. These "bush spirits," as they are often referred to in the literature, are not to be confused with men who take on monstrous form in order to kill or bewitch other men, such as the *kanaima* of the Guyana region.

Ancestral spirits. In some societies the invisible beings most central to the continued existence and well-being of society are the ancestral spirits. Among the Tucano-Barasana of the northwest Amazon, the ancestral spirits are associated with the He instruments. These sacred flutes and trumpets form the local manifestation of a widely distributed cult popularly known as Yurupary. The term He does not refer just to these instruments but also means "ancestral" or "mythical," and conceptually it has much in common with the Dreaming of the Australian Aborigines. It is timeless, and although created long ago, He persists as an alternative aspect of reality. There are also He people and animals, the first ancestors (anacondas in the case of the Barasana). It is through ritual contact with the original creation and with He, its generative force, that society continues and reproduces itself. The names of living people are those of the first ancestors, which are passed on through alternate generations, a person taking the name of a dead grandparent. The soul is considered to be inherited in the same way.

This recycling of soul-matter is another common theme in lowland South America, although by no means universal (it is mainly restricted to the Tropical Forest area). Throughout the lowlands the soul is considered to be another invisible entity, one that is crucial in the organization of everyday life. An individual is often regarded as having more than one soul and as having several different sorts of soul whose activities differ in this life and in the afterlife. Most people believe that the soul is detachable from the body and that during sleep or a trance it may leave the body and wander by itself. Many illnesses are attributed to soul-loss, often as a result of a soul being captured while wandering alone, and death is the result of the final detachment of the soul from the body.

The ghosts—that is, the souls of the dead—have many parts to play: they may be benevolent to the living, as among the Akwe-Xavante of central Brazil; they may be of no concern to the living, as among the Ge-speaking Suyá of the same area; or they may be menacing, as among the Waiwai of Guyana. The notion of reincarnation in the strict sense of the word does not seem to exist. It is not that an individual has a second life, but that the soul-matter energizes a new and different individual.

RELIGIOUS PRACTITIONERS. The main religious practitioner throughout the region is the shaman. Shamans are usually but not always men. South American shamanism shares many characteristics with its Siberian prototype. It is often the one specialized role to be found in Indian societies, and although the actual functions vary from one society to another, shamans everywhere depend on similar basic skills: the ability to see the invisible aspect of the world, to communicate with it, and to travel to different cosmic layers while in a state of trance. The role of the shaman is that of cosmic mediator, and in this role he often acts as a transformer through whom the generative forces of the invisible world are transmitted to the everyday world for the benefit of its inhabitants. The shaman is assisted by spirit helpers, or familiars. To gain contact with the invisible world and to travel to the different cosmic levels, the shaman normally enters into a trance induced by a narcotic or hallucinogenic substance. In some societies it is expected that all adults will have firsthand experience of the invisible through the ingestion of such substances, and accordingly will have some shamanic competence. Among the Guaraní, for example, the men and women were divided into four hierarchically graded categories based on shamanic knowledge, with women were allowed membership in all but the highest grade. However, even in situations such as this a class of "true shamans" is recognized, and shamans do not lose their preeminent role. It is the true shaman's task to guide the more or less skilled laymen through their experiences and to interpret these experiences for them, since unlike the shaman such people tend to have only a passive and not a manipulative relationship with the other world.

Shamanism. The ability to see, contact, and operate in the other world gives the shaman considerable power, and in some societies shamanic and ritual knowledge are the basis of political authority. However, the roles of spiritual and secular leader are not everywhere necessarily conjoined. When separate, their duties parallel each other: the secular leader defends his community from the dangers of the visible world, while the shaman wards off mystical attacks.

Given the ambiguity that characterizes the Indian concept of power, it is not surprising that a similar ambiguity characterizes those who hold power. It is occasionally suggested that there are two kinds of shaman—good and bad, or those who cure and those who kill. However, in most societies there is only one kind, whose power may be used for good or bad ends, depending on his relative position. A shaman in one's own community is considered good, while those in other, distant communities are considered bad and are held responsible for the misfortunes, illnesses, and deaths that result from mystical attacks. It is the home

"Dust as we are, the immortal spirit grow like harmony in music."

WILLIAM WORDSWORTH
THE PRELUDE 1799-1805

Throughout South America outside the Andean region, the shaman remains the pillar of the religious life.

PAGE 626

shaman's job to ward off such attacks and to mount counterattacks. The possession of power, because it can be used for good or bad ends, brings with it occupational hazards. It is reported from the Tupian-speaking Mundurucú and Tapirapé of Brazil that in the face of severe misfortune blame is assigned to a powerful shaman who is then killed.

Even so, there are societies in which two different types of shaman are found. For example, among the Jivaroan people of Ecuador there are both curing and bewitching shamans.

The functions of the shaman are varied. He is best known as a curer, although in practice this is but one aspect of his general ability to contact the invisible world. This point can be understood only if it is appreciated that sickness is not seen solely as a physiological phenomenon but also as a social disorder, the cause of which lies in the invisible world and results from either human or spirit activity. The job of the shaman as medical practitioner is to cure both aspects of the sickness. Curing techniques may include blowing tobacco smoke over the patient, sucking out spirit weapons, or going into a trance to obtain the advice or help of familiars in fighting hostile spirits who have captured the patient's soul. Such séances often take place in the dark, either at night or in a specially constructed hide enclosure. Séances are usually public and dramatic performances in which the audience can hear, if not see, the shaman in communication with his spirit helpers. In some societies curing sessions may take place outside the house during daylight hours.

The shaman's other tasks include prophecy; control over the weather, especially storms (a close association between shamans and thunder is common); the interpretation of omens and dreams; and maintenance of the supply of game animals. To fulfill the latter duty, the shaman either goes to negotiate with the master of animals for the release of game or is himself directly responsible for the supply. Powerful Tapirapé shamans secure game by visiting the home of wild pigs and having sexual intercourse with the sows. A further commonly reported duty of the shaman is the preparation of food, a mystical process parallel to the normal culinary techniques that render food edible.

Finally, there is the role of the shaman in major rituals, when a number of shamans may act together or be assisted by other ritual specialists. Among the Tucano-Barasana of the northwest Amazon, a group of such specialists, the dancer/chanters, perform a vital role complementary to that of the shaman: they represent the ancestors making their original creative journey.

One can also compare the dancer/chanters of the northwest Amazon with certain other lower-order religious specialists found elsewhere. For example, the Carib-speaking Kalapalo of the upper Xingu River in central Brazil give recognition to the role of exceptionally learned men and women who know the ceremonial songs, can make the ceremonial gear, and know how a ritual should be performed. In the same society there are also members directly responsible for the sponsoring of certain ceremonies

Prophets. Prophets also occur from time to time in some Indian societies. There is evidence that such figures existed in Indian societies prior to the arrival of Europeans. The great treks undertaken by the Tupi-speaking peoples across the continent in the fifteenth and sixteenth centuries appear to have been millennial in nature and led by prophets. In more recent times, the appearance of prophets has been closely associated with the influence of Christian missionary teaching. A well-known and well-documented messianic cult led by prophets is Hallelujah, found among the Carib-speaking Acawai and Patamona of Guyana. Hallelujah is concerned with contact with the ultimate source of power, God; while incorporating something akin to Christian worship, it has clearly borrowed from the shamanistic tradition, which still flourishes as the means of communication with the spirit world.

MYTHS AND RITUAL. Myths of lowland South America have received a great deal of attention in the last two decades as a result of Claude Lévi-Strauss's magnum opus, the four volumes of *Mythologiques* (translated as *Introduction to a Science of Mythology*, 1969-1981). Lévi-Strauss ranges far and wide—often without regard for social context—to reveal universal structures of the human mind. Despite numerous criticisms of these studies, some unfairly dismissive, there is no doubt that Lévi-Strauss's impact on the study of Indian myth has been profound and probably permanent. More recent authors have employed a modified form of his structuralism as an interpretative device with which to obtain a better understanding of the society under examination.

It is through myths that Indians make statements about the fundamental nature of the world in which they live. Myths are indeed a form of knowledge, but it would be wrong to assume that they can be read as simple charters or explanations of social institutions, cultural practices, or natural phenomena. The relationships between myths, between myths and rites, and between rites are dialectical, and the contents of one myth may only be explicable by reference to certain other myths and even practices. At the same time myths, rites, and everyday activities all call on a common set of cultural categories. In other words, religious ideas and practices are embedded in social and cultural activities, and to separate either from the other is to lessen the chance of understanding both.

The ritual and myths of the area make abundant metaphorical use of the environment and its features.

This use of cultural categories and natural objects to make abstract statements underlies the Indians' religious ideas. Given that the same major animals are distributed throughout lowland South America, it is not too surprising to find them recurring repeatedly in the myths of the area. Thus, the anaconda, caiman, jaguar, tapir, peccary, king vulture, harpy eagle, and many other animals, as well as the sun, moon, and constellations, figure regularly in the myths. The specific choice of animals made by a society for this purpose depends on the particularities of wildlife distribution, while the meanings that certain animals hold for different groups vary with the ways in which these animals are juxtaposed and contrasted. Within these limits it would be difficult to argue that the choice of these characters and of their meanings is purely arbitrary. Variability is limited to some extent by the cosmological framework; if the anaconda is substituted for the caiman, for example, their common association with water and thus with the underworld remains unchanged. Likewise the behaviors and habits of creatures do not vary. The weird sounds of the howler monkey, the defecatory practices of the sloth, or the peculiar qualities of the tortoise are the same wherever these animals are found, and as such are appropriate for conveying, within a restricted range, a common set of meanings.

Myths record the differentiation that took place at the beginning of time. But this is not a once-and-for-all event, for mythic time is not historical time; it persists as another aspect of reality. Through ritual, which may involve the chanting of myths, contact is made with this other temporal dimension in which human beings, animals, and ancestors remain undifferentiated. This confounding of categories is a common feature of rituals, which attempt to transcend this mundane world and to draw on the generative forces outside it. Thus among the Carib-speaking Trio of Surinam the ritual festivals are periods in which mythical unity is achieved and the empirical diversity and contradictions of everyday life are suppressed. It is through ritual that society is able both to register its continuity and to reproduce itself.

Another feature of ritual in lowland religions is that it produces a high degree of dependency. It has been noted that at an individual level no one has mastery of all the required ritual techniques and thus everyone has to depend on someone else. But this extends beyond individual requirements because many rituals, and not just the ritual aspect of technical activities, require the cooperation and participation of several people. Some rituals are preceded by collective hunting, and there are ceremonies in which crucial roles must be performed by outsiders. In functional terms, then, ritual can be seen as providing a counterweight to atomistic tendencies—that is, it forces individuals or groups who may dislike or suspect one another to interact for the benefit of society.

PRACTICAL RELIGION. Religion in lowland South American societies is not an institution that can be dealt with in isolation, since it is deeply embedded in other aspects of social, political, and economic life. This will have become apparent from earlier references to the ritual aspect of many everyday activities. Ritual acts are performed by individuals as a precaution against the unpredictable reactions of invisible beings. Some of these rituals involve the recital of a simple formula (rather like saying "God bless you" when someone sneezes) or the avoidance of a particular action (like not allowing a pot to boil over). More elaborate rituals are necessary under certain circumstances—for example, when food has to be treated by the shaman in order to be considered edible.

Perhaps the best way to appreciate the influence of practical religion is to look at the rituals that accompany the life cycle. Lowland South America is often regarded as the area in which the ritual phenomenon known as couvade (often wrongly described as "male childbed," the imitation by fathers of the experience of childbirth) reaches its greatest development. These rites require the parents of a newborn child to observe prohibitions on their diet and activities until such time as the infant's soul becomes properly secured to him. This may be expressed as a direct transfer of soul-matter from parents to child or, as in the case of the Ge-speaking Apinagé of central Brazil, it may be achieved through the increase of blood as the child grows naturally, which is considered to be directly responsible for the formation of the body and soul.

The creation of the individual as a combination of body and soul often has to be taken further in order to provide the person with a third entity, a social persona. This may be achieved through name-giving ceremonies, of which the Ge-speaking peoples provide some of the most elaborate examples. Their name-giving ceremonies involve the public transmission of whole sets of names between people in specifically defined relationships. Ownership of a set of names bestows membership in certain social groupings, such as a moiety. Thus these rituals not only create social beings but at the same time ensure social continuity through the reproduction of social groupings. In the case of the Ge these rituals have a rather secular character compared with the male initiation rites of the Tucano peoples. While the same result is achieved—that is, boys are turned into full members of society and the lineage's continuity is affirmed—the ritual more obviously involves contact with the invisible world, for the boys are born again not only as adults but also as direct descendants of mythical ancestors.

Funerary practices. Funerary practices in lowland

The basic form of religious organization in the pueblos consists of ritual societies, which serve a variety of purposes.

PAGE 520

S

SOUTH AMERICAN INDIANS

Indians of the Tropical Forest

South America range from simple burial to elaborate secondary rites involving endocannibalism and extended feasting. Common throughout the area is the tendency for mortuary practices to reflect the status of the deceased. Even where only simple interment occurs, the death of a village leader results in the abandonment of his settlement—an event unlikely to follow on the death of an individual of lower status. The corpse of a shaman may be treated differently from that of a layman; among the Carib-speaking Waiwai of Guyana the layman was traditionally cremated, while shamans were buried. Among the Carib-speaking Kalapalo of the upper Xingu River there are two social ranks, chiefs and commoners, and their respective statuses are reflected in the ways in which their corpses are disposed of. Chiefs are buried in more elaborate graves, and their funerary rites consist of a series of ceremonies spread over a long period and involve participants from other villages.

Funerary rites are mainly concerned with the separation of the deceased from the living (and also the separation of one part of the body from another—for example, flesh from bone) and with the individual's incorporation among the dead. In addition, they often entail an inquest whose aim is to divine the identity of the person responsible for the death and to direct sorcery against him in revenge.

Ideas about the location of the afterlife or the village of the dead are hazy and, not surprisingly, even Indians from the same community provide rather different descriptions. However, one feature that ethnographers have frequently noted is that life hereafter is envisioned as a negation or reversal of certain aspects of life on earth (e.g., it is day in the afterworld while it is night on earth, and vice versa).

SYNCRETISM. Few Indian systems of belief have escaped modification by the activities of Christian missionaries. The Spanish and Portuguese colonial powers employed representatives of the Roman Catholic church as their main agents for contact with and pacification of the Indians. However, as a result both of factionalism within the church and of antagonism between the church and colonists, it was rare that the influence of any one missionary order was long and sustained. An important exception to this was the Jesuit reductions of the Guaraní, which came to an end

MULTIPLE SOULS

From the Ordinary to the Achieved and Avenging

Multiple souls. Perhaps one of the best examples of the influence of ideas about souls and the other world on social life is provided by the Jivaroan people of eastern Ecuador. These Indians recognize the existence of three forms of soul. These are the "ordinary" soul; an "achieved" soul, of which an individual may possess up to two at any one time; and an "avenging" soul. Every living Jivaroan has an ordinary soul that is obtained at birth and lost at death. It is identified with the blood, and after death it goes through various transformations before finally taking on the form of mist.

The achieved soul is obtained through a vision that involves contact with the other world. Only a few women possess achieved souls, but it is regarded as essential for a man to obtain one by puberty or soon after if he is to survive. While a man is in possession of an achieved soul he is immune to death by certain causes, including violence and sorcery; if he has two, he is immune to death by any cause. The first soul is achieved through a vision quest in which the individual seeks out and touches a monstrous being. In order to become eligible to obtain another achieved soul, an individual first has to kill; only after he has done this can he seek a new soul and thus render himself invulnerable.

The rapid acquisition of the new soul locks in the remnants of the old soul, so that while no man may have more than two achieved souls at the same time, it is possible for him to accumulate power from any number of souls. However, a soul that has been with the same person for a long time will begin to wander, exposing itself to capture, which renders the individual vulnerable. The achieved soul of the Jivaroan appears to have much in common with Western notions of prestige and reputation.

The third soul of the Jivaroan is the avenging soul. This soul comes into existence when a person who has at one point had an achieved soul is killed, and its function is to avenge the death of the individual. This it does by turning itself into a demon and causing the murderer, or a close relative of the murderer, to have an accident. The Jivaroan practice of shrinking heads is associated with the idea of the avenging soul. The soul is trapped inside the head by this means, and after its power is extracted from it by ritual, it is sent back to the locality of its owner.

This case has been considered in some detail because it illustrates particularly well the elaboration of beliefs about the soul and the way in which these beliefs are directly tied to certain forms of social behavior.

— PETER RIVIÈRE

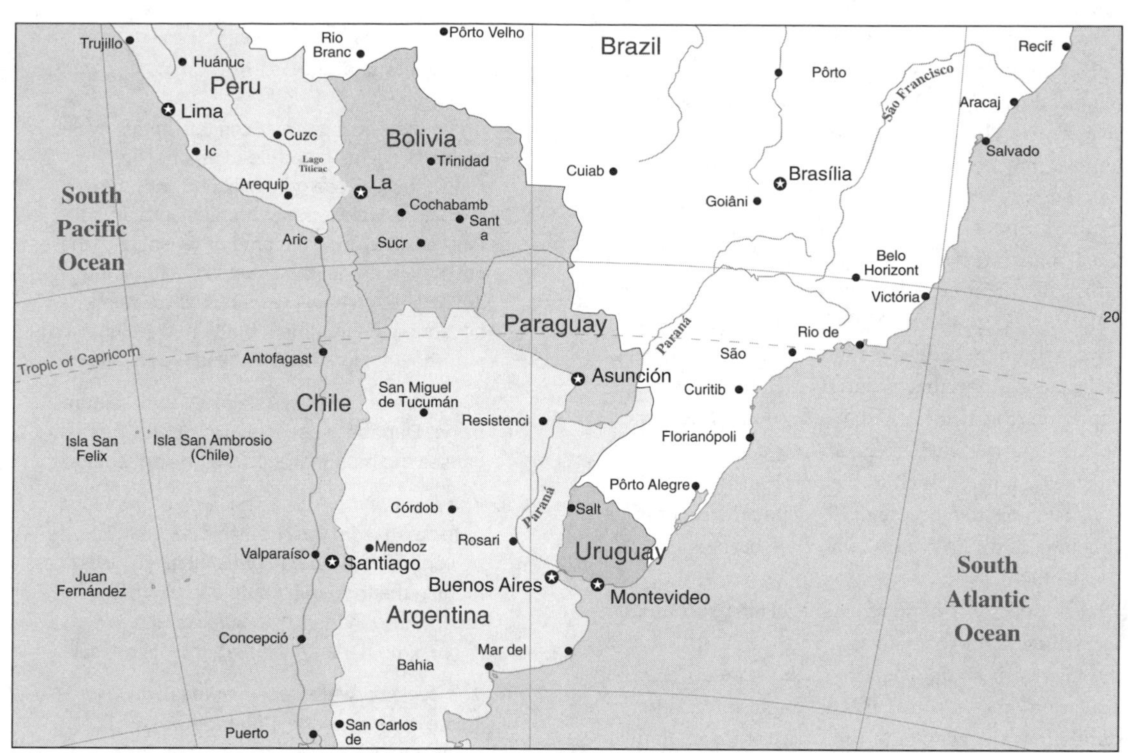

GRAN CHACO

The Gran Chaco is a 725,000 square kilometer region in South America. It lies between the Andes in the west and Paraná river in the east, and between Southern Brazil to the north and Cordoba, Argentina to the south.

ILLUSTRATOR MAGELLAN GEOGRAPHIX/CORBIS

with the expulsion of the order in 1767 after nearly two centuries of contact.

In more recent times, various Protestant missions, in particular those of fundamentalist churches, have been active in lowland South America. The techniques and policies pursued by different missionary organizations, the conditions under which evangelization takes place, and the nature and degree of intactness of indigenous societies are all variables that prevent any simple statement about the effects of evangelization. Some missionary organizations have concentrated on trying to integrate the Indians into the national society by teaching them the national language and introducing a monetarized Western economy in place of the subsistence economy. The teaching of the Christian scriptures is not necessarily combined with attempts to eliminate traces of traditional beliefs and practices. The alternative approach is to teach entirely in the native language and to eliminate all practices that appear to fall foul of particular scriptural interpretations without making a purposeful effort to change the economic way of life. This policy is often associated with attempts to isolate the Indians from contact with the national society.

It is not at present clear why neighboring groups exposed to similar missionary attention have reacted in entirely different ways, one rejecting the teaching, the other accepting it. Under some conditions a form of syncretism has taken place, but elsewhere there has been little more than a smear of Christianity added on top of traditional beliefs. The study of lowland Indian syncretic religions is still an underresearched field. Some work has been done in this direction, in particular on the Hallelujah cult of the Carib-speaking Kapon and Pemón Indians, but a great deal remains to be done. Given the traditional association between religious and medical ideas in the lowlands, the syncretism of folk medicine and Western medical science is also a topic that falls within this general field and deserves further research.

— PETER RIVIÈRE

INDIANS OF THE GRAN CHACO

The Gran Chaco (*chaco*, derived from Quechua, means "hunting land") is an arid alluvial plain in the lowlands of south-central South America. Approximately 725,000 square kilometers in area, it lies between the Andes in the west and the Paraguay and Paraná rivers in the east, and between the Mato Grosso to the north and the Pampas to the south. The scrub forests and grasslands of the Gran Chaco, though sparsely populated, were the home of numerous indigenous groups. In the main they were hunters, fishers, and gatherers, moving seasonally in search of food and practicing supplementary farming. Few still follow their traditional way of life.

The religion of the indigenous groups of the Gran Chaco can be understood through an examination of their mythic narratives, which contain their primary

"There is nothing impossible in the existence of the supernatural."

GEORGE SANTAYANA
THE GENTEEL TRADITION AT BAY 1931

structures of meaning. These myths give an account of a primordial time in which an ontological modification was produced by the actions of various supernatural beings who shaped present-day cultural reality. This rupture may be caused by a lawgiver (who frequently has the appearance of a trickster), or it may be the result of infractions by ancestors or by the transformations of ancestors. Numerous supernatural beings with avowedly demonic characteristics monopolize the realm of fear and danger; their ambivalent intentions toward human beings are usually resolved through malevolent action that manifests itself in illness, culminating in the death of the individual. The general notion of power, such as the *la-ka-áyah* of the Mataco, or specific powers, such as the *uhopié* of the Ayoré, are the structures that ontologically define the supernatural beings as well as people who have been consecrated by them.

The spectrum of supernatural beings encompasses everything from shamans and witches, in the cases of the Guiacurú or the Mataco, to the state of "amorous exaltation" known to the Pilagá. For an integral understanding of the peoples of the Chaco it is important to consider the contributions of these special personages and states of being, which contribute a unique cultural identity to each group's cosmology. In almost all the ethnic groups of the Gran Chaco the shaman occupies the central role in religious tasks, sometimes defending and protecting, and, at other times, injuring. When engaged in healing practices, he can combine various techniques, such as singing, shaking rattles, blowing, and sucking, and can command the collaboration of familiar spirits who are generally powerful owing to their demonic nature. An important aspect of Gran Chaco religions is the idea that one or many souls are incarnated in an individual. Once the individual is dead, these souls, or spirits, enter a demonic state. Although they are directed to an established underworld, they continue to prey upon human communities.

The Zamuco Family

The two members of the Zamuco language group are the Ayoré and the Chamacoco of Paraguay, in the northeastern Chaco.

THE AYORÉ. The religion of the Ayoré (Ayoreo, Ayoreode) is expressed primarily in an extensive set of myths. All natural and cultural beings have their origins related in mythic tales, and in certain cases in various parallel myths. The morphology of the myths centers upon the metamorphosis of an ancestral figure into an entity of current reality. Each tale narrates events that occurred in primordial times and is accompanied by one or more songs, which may be used for therapeutic *(saude)* or preventive *(paragapidí)* purposes.

Despite the abundance of tales, it is possible to classify the Ayoré myths in different cycles as they relate to a particular supernatural being or theme:

1. *The cycle of ancestors.* Each tale in this cycle recounts events in the life of an ancestor *(nanibahai).* These generally end with the ancestor's violent transformation into an artifact, plant, animal, or some other entity of the cosmos, and with the establishment by the ancestor of cultural prescriptions *(puyák)* governing the treatment of the new being and punishments for ignoring these prescriptions.
2. *The cycle of Dupáde.* A celestial supernatural being, Dupáde is associated with the sun; he causes the metamorphosis of the ancestors.
3. *The cycle of the Flood.* The tales of the Flood *(gedekesnasóri)* describe an offense inflicted on lightning by the *nanibahai*, their punishment in the form of a continual rain that inundated the world, and the survival of a few Ayoré, who became the first aquatic animals.
4. *The cycle of "water that washes away."* These tales describe a flood *(yotedidekesnasóri)* similar to that that appears in the preceding cycle, which was caused by Diesná ("cricket"), the ruler of water.
5. *The cycle of the Asohsná bird.* This bird *(Caprimulgidae spp)* is surrounded by numerous *puyák*. The central tale of this cycle relates the life of the female ancestor who created this bird. Asohsná is a supernatural being who established the annual ceremony that divides the year into two segments, one of which is characterized by an incalculable quantity of restrictions.
6. *The cycle of Asningái.* This cycle relates the courage of an ancestor named Asningái ("courage"), who threw himself onto the fire, transforming himself into an animal with certain morphological characteristics. It also established the meaning of slaughter, an important institution among the Ayoré, since an individual could rise to the status of chief *(asuté)* through contamination by spilled blood.

THE CHAMACOCO. The narrative of the Chamacoco, which recounts sacred events, is called "The Word of Esnuwérta." This tale constitutes the secret mythology of those men who have undergone initiatory ordeals and contains the social and religious knowledge of the group. Esnuwérta is the primordial mother. The myth is connected to the women of primordial times who were surprised by harmful supernatural beings *(axnábsero)*. "The Word of Esnuwérta" includes the actions of these *axnábsero*, characters to whom Chamacoco reality is subordinated. The physiognomy of these supernatural beings is similar to that of the Ayoré ancestors in that current reality originates from their transformations and their deaths. The distinctive characteristic of the *axnábsero* is their malignant power *(wozós)* over people.

The foundation of the social order is presented in this myth, since Esnuwérta instituted the clans as well as the male initiation ceremonies in which the participants identify themselves with the principal deities of the myth.

The Chamacoco shaman *(konsáxa)* exercises a power appropriate to a specific region of the cosmos; for this reason there are shamans of the sky, of the water, and of the jungle. The shaman initiation begins with a vision of Esnuwérta, who reveals the cosmos as well as the practices appropriate to the work of the shamans. Another custom originating from Esnuwérta is called *kaamták* and has to do with a ritual offering of food; it relates to the impurity of blood, among other themes.

The Tupi-Guaraní Family

The Tupi-Guaraní language family includes the Chiriguano of Bolivia and the Tapuí of Paraguay.

THE CHIRIGUANO. The tale of the mythical twins Yanderú Túmpa and Áña Túmpa is the most prevalent myth among the Chiriguano (Miá) and appears in conjunction with lunar mythology. The celestial supernatural being Yanderú Túmpa made the cosmos and bestowed its goods on the Chiriguano, at the same time instructing them in cultural practices. He conceived and made Áña Túmpa, who, because of envy, attempts to undermine all Yanderú Túmpa's works. Áña Túmpa received from his maker power *(imbapwére)*, which he in turn gives to other beings *(áñas)* who aid him in his malignant activities. As a result the world has undergone a profound alteration. It is now the actions of the áñas that determine the condition of the Chiriguano world, and they have introduced calamities such as illness and death. The expression *túmpa* is difficult to comprehend, but it appears to designate a quality that transforms the various entities into "state beings." The terms *áña* and *túmpa* define the supernatural nature of these beings, that is to say, they emphasize that they are extraordinary.

TAPUÍ AND GUASURANGWE. The religion of the Tapuí and the Guasurangwe, or Tapieté (an offshoot of the former), does not differ essentially from that of the Chiriguano; the same structures of meaning and the same supernatural beings may be observed.

Lengua-Mascoy Family

The Lengua-Mascoy language group of Paraguay includes the Angaité, Lengua, Kaskihá, and Sanapaná peoples.

THE ANGAITÉ. The religious nature of the Angaité (Chananesmá) has undergone syncretism owing to their proximity to the Mascoy and Guaranian groups. Their mythology makes reference to three levels—the underworld, the terrestrial world, and the celestial world—all of which are inhabited by supernatural beings characterized by their ambivalent actions toward humans. The deity of the dead, Moksohanák, governs a legion of demonic beings, the *enzlép*, who pursue the sick, imprison them, and carry them to the "country of the dead," which is situated in the west. At night it is even possible for them to overpower passersby. The *gabioamá* or *iliabün* act as the spirit familiars of the shaman, and with him their role is ambivalent in a positive sense. For example, they are in charge of recapturing and restoring the souls of the sick.

According to Angaité myth, fire was obtained by a theft in which a bird was the intermediary; it was stolen from a forest demon, one of the *iek'amá*, who are anthropomorphic but have only one leg. Also anthropomorphic is the soul-shadow *(abiosná)*, whose eyes are its distinguishing feature. The concept of corporal material as such does not exist, except for the *iek'amá* ("living cadaver" or "skeleton"), which is what remains after death.

During the initiation process, the shaman goes into the depths of the forest or to the banks of the river, where the familiar spirits (*pateaskóp* or *enzlép*) come to him in a dream. He communicates with the familiars through ecstatic dreams and songs. His therapeutic labors include sucking harmful agents from the bodies of the sick and applying vegetable concoctions whose efficacy resides in their "bad smell." There are shamans with purely malignant intentions, such as the *mamohót*, who are responsible for tragic deaths among members of the group. The benevolent shaman is responsible for discovering the identity of the bewitching shaman and for quartering and burning the body of the victim as a restorative vengeance. The Angaité do not have "lords" or "fathers" of the species; the figures closest to this theme are Nekéñe and Nanticá, male and female supernatural beings respectively, who are anthropomorphic and whose realm is the depths of the waters.

THE LENGUA. The anthropogenic myth of the Lengua (Enlhít, Enslet) attributes the formation of giant supernatural beings and the ancestors of the Lengua to Beetle, who utilized mud as primary material. After giving these beings a human form, he placed the bodies of the first *enlhíts* to dry on the bank of a lake, but he set them so close together that they stuck to one another. Once granted life, they could not defend themselves against the attacks of the powerful giants, and Beetle, as supreme deity, separated the two groups. Eventually the inability of the *enlhíts* to resist pursuit and mistreatment by the giants became so

The most revered god of the Guaraní-Apapocuvá is the creator Nanderuvuçu ("our great father").

PAGE 623

grave that Beetle took away the giants' bodies. The giants' souls gave birth to *kilikháma* who fought to regain control of the missing bodies, and it is for this reason that they torment present-day humans.

The important Lengua myths include the origin of plants and fire and the fall of the world. Ritual dramatizations of the myths are part of the celebrations for female puberty *(yanmána)*, male puberty *(waínkya)*, the spring and autumn equinoxes, the summer solstice, war, the arrival of foreigners, marriage, and mourning.

THE KASKIHÁ. The "masked celebration" of the Kaskihá is of particular interest. It is based on a myth that describes the origin of the festive attire following the quartering of the water deity Iyenaník. The practice of *kindáian*, which is a dance, is the only medium for invoking the power of such deities.

Ancestor worship is clearly linked to an ethic of filial piety and obedience to elders.

PAGE 29

THE SANAPANÁ. The rich mythic narrative of the Sanapaná focuses on the war between the heavenly world, inhabited by the ancestors *(inyakahpanamé)*, and the terrestrial world, inhabited by the fox *(maalék)*. The ancestors, who differ morphologically from present-day humanity, introduced the majority of cultural goods. Among the fundamental structures distinguished by the Sanapaná is the "dream," the soul's life in its wanderings separate from the body. Death is understood as theft of the soul by demonic forces, the souls of the dead that stalk during the night in forests and marshes. The demonic spirits are anthropomorphic. Some are malignant, including those whose mere appearance can cause immediate death. There are also benevolent spirits who are the familiars of shamans *(kiltongkamák)*. The shaman's initiation involves fasting and other tests.

Mataco-Makká Family

The Mataco-Makká language family of the central Chaco includes the Mataco, Chulupí, Choroti, and Makká.

THE MATACO. The religious universe of the Mataco (Wichí) centers on the notion of power *(la-ka-áyah)*, which is the property of innumerable supernatural beings of demonic *(ahát)* or human *(wichí)* nature, personifications of such phenomena as the sun, moon, stars, and thunder. The Mataco recognize a dualism of body *(opisán)* and spirit *(o'nusék)* in humans. Death changes the *o'nusék* into a malevolent supernatural being.

The central character in Mataco mythic narrative *(pahlalís)*, Tokhwáh, is the one who imposes cosmic and ontological order on the present-day world. The actions of this supernatural being, who has a demonic nature, are incorporated in his trickster aspect; nonetheless, he is perceived by the Mataco as a suffering and sad being. In his lawgiving role he introduces economic practices and tools; humanizes the women who descend from the sky by eliminating their vaginal teeth; institutes marriage; and teaches the people how to get drunk, to fight, and to make war. He also introduces demonic spirits who cause illnesses *(aités)* and establishes the shamanic institution *(hayawú)* and death. The most important Mataco ceremony is carried out by the shamans, in both individual and communal form, with the objective of expelling illnesses according to Tokhwáh's teachings.

THE CHULUPÍ. The mythology of the Chulupí (Nivaklé, Asluslây) comprises three narrative cycles on the deities who acted in primordial times, but who then distanced themselves from humanity and the earthly world. The Xitscittsammee cycle describes a supernatural being comparable to an almost forgotten *deus otiosus*. The cycle of the supernatural being Fitsók Exíts includes prescriptions for the rites of female initiation; myths recounting the origin of women, of the spots on the moon, and of honey, among other things; and the tale of the expulsion from the universe of the supernatural creator. The Kufiál cycle relates the cataclysmic events accompanying the fall of heaven and the subsequent actions of the demiurge Kufiál, to name a few of its themes.

A structure essential to the Chulupí religion is *sic'ee*, or ultimate power, which defines and dominates a vast group of beings and actions. In effect, *sic'ee* is the strange made powerful, which can manifest itself in unexpected guises—in human or animal form, by means of a sound or a movement like a whirlwind, or as master of the spirits of the forest. The *sic'ee* plays a significant role in the initiation of the shaman *(toyék)*: he appears to the shaman in the guise of an old man, for example, who offers the shaman power and grants him the spirit familiars called *wat'akwáis*. By fasting, enduring solitude in the woods, and drinking potions made of various plants, the initiate achieves a revelatory experience rich in visions, many of which are terrifying. The Chulupí idea of animistic reality is extremely complicated and varied, given that the soul can appear in any number of manifestations.

THE CHOROTI. The principle cycles of the Choroti are five in number. The cycle of Kixwét describes a supernatural being, of human appearance but gigantic, whose role comprises the duplicity of both the demiurge and the trickster. The cycle of Ahóusa, the Hawk, the culture hero *par excellence*, recounts how he defeated the beings of primordial times, stealing and distributing fire and teaching humans the technique of fishing and the making of artifacts. The cycle of Woíki, the Fox, who partakes of the intrinsic nature of Kixwét and is a very important figure in indigenous cultures, contains myths describing his creation of various beings and modalities of the present-day world. The cycle of We'la, the Moon, relates the formation of the world.

The cycle of Tsematakí alludes to a feminine figure characterized by her ill will toward men and her uncontainable cannibalism.

The Choroti shaman *(aíew)* receives power *(i-tóksi)* from the supernatural beings *(thlamó)*, and the strength of his abilities depends on the number of familiars *(inxuélai)* he has.

THE MAKKÁ. The Makká mythology can be classified as eclectic, as it demonstrates cultural contact with almost all the other indigenous groups of the Gran Chaco. The Makká cycle of the fox is similar to the narrative cycle surrounding the Mataco supernatural being Tokhwáh and demonstrates similar themes, such as the origin of women and the toothed vagina. The Makká hero Tippá, who possesses an immense penis, is somewhat reminiscent of Wéla, the Mataco moon deity.

In earlier times, power *(t'un)* was obtained by capturing a scalp, after which a complex ceremony was held in which the scalp was discarded but the soul *(le sinkál)* of the dead enemy was retained as a personal familiar, or spirit helper. This familiar would manifest itself during sleep by means of a song that even today is sung during drinking bouts. Ceremonies of drinking bouts among adults permit the regulation of power among people. The ceremony of female initiation is also important, as is true throughout most of the Gran Chaco.

Guiacurú-Caduveo Family

The Guiacurú-Caduveo language family of the Gran Chaco and Brazil includes the tribes known as the Pilagá, the Toba, the Caduveo, and the Mocoví.

THE PILAGÁ. Certain mythic cycles may be distinguished in the Pilagá mythology. One cycle describes the celestial deity Dapici, to whom is attributed the inversion of the cosmic planes and the transference of some animals and plants to the sky. In the past, prayers were offered for his help in the most diverse activities. Another cycle describes Wayaykaláciyi, who introduced death, made the animals wild, and established hunting techniques, modifying the Edenic habits of an earlier time. Among the eminent supernatural beings is Nesóge, a cannibalistic woman who determines the practices of the witches *(kọnánagaẹ)*. Such characters and themes as the Star Woman and the origin of women appear in Pilagá myths.

Among the significant structures, the payák is the most important. This notion defines nonhuman nature, which is peculiar to supernatural beings, shamans *(pyogonák)*, animals, plants, and some objects. Relations with the *payák* determine conditions in the indigenous world. Either people acquire *payáks* as familiars who aid them in their customary activities, or the *payáks* inflict suffering on them in the form of illness, the death of domestic animals, the destruction of farms, or a poor harvest of fruit from wild plants. Such concepts as the "master-dependent" *(logót-lamasék)* and the "center-periphery" *(laiñí-laíl)* allow the Pilagá to classify beings and entities according to a hierarchy of power.

THE TOBA. The principal themes of Toba (Kom) narrative are celestial cosmology and mythology, which appear in stories about Dapici and the Pleiades; cataclysms; the origin of specific entities; stories of animals; stories of the trickster Wahayaka'lacigu, the lawgiver Ta'ankí, and Asien, a supernatural being with a repulsive appearance; and encounters between Toba people and the supernatural being Nowét. The morphology of these characters, all of whom were powerful in the primordial times, fluctuates between the human and the animal.

For the Toba, the central structure of the cosmology is *nowét*, which appears in the forms of the masters of animals and of the spheres. Nowét, as a supernatural being, initiates the shamans *(pi'ogonák)* and grants them power that can be used equally to heal or to harm. Outside the shamanic sphere, all special skills—hunting, fishing, dancing, and so on—derive from power given by Nowét. Dreams are structures that have importance in the relations between man and Nowét. Shamanic power is established by the possession of spirit familiars *(ltawá)*, who help shamans cure serious illnesses, which are considered intentional and also material. Therapy combines singing, blowing, and sucking as methods of removing the harmful agent from the victim's body.

Some of the important ceremonies of the Toba are name giving, the initiation of young boys, the offering of prayers to Dapici, matutinal prayers to the heavenly beings, and the supplications of the hunters to some supernatural being in a nowét state.

THE CADUVEO. Go-neno-hodi is the central deity of Caduveo mythology; he is maker of all people and of a great number of the cultural goods. His appearance is that of a Caduveo, and he is without evil intention. In his benevolence, he granted the Caduveo, in ancient times, an abundant supply of food, clothes, and utensils, as well as eternal life, but the intervention of Hawk, astute and malicious, made Go-neno-hodi modify the primordial order. Nibetád is a mythical hero identifiedwith the Pleiades; he greeted the ancestors during the ceremony celebrating the annual reappearance of this cluster of stars and the maturation of the algaroba (mesquite).

The shamanic institution is actualized in two different individuals: the *nikyienígi* ("father"), who protects and benefits the community, and the *otxikanrígi*, the cause of all deaths, illnesses, and misfortunes in the group. Celebrations that are particularly worthy of note

The pre-Columbian Andean cultures extended over a geographical area that the Inca believed corresponded to the four quarters (tahuantinsuyu) of the world.

PAGE 320

The bones of the Island Arawak dead, especially the bones of their leaders and great men, were thought to have power in and of themselves.

PAGE 121

are the lunar ceremonies, the rites celebrating the birth of the chief's son, and the initiations of young men and women.

THE MOCOVÍ. Prominent in the scattered Mocoví material is the myth of an enormous tree that reached to the sky. By climbing its branches, one ascended to lakes and to a river. An angry old woman cut down the tree, extinguishing the valuable connection between heaven and earth.

Gdsapidolgaté, a benevolent supernatural being, presides over the world of the living. His activity contrasts with that of the witches. Healing practices among the Mocoví are the same as those of the other shamans of the Gran Chaco, with the addition of bloodletting. The Mocoví, like all the Guiacurú, believe in the honor of war and value dying in combat as much as killing. When they return from a battle they hang the heads of the vanquished on posts in the center of town and they sing and shout around them.

Arawak Family

The extensive Arawak family of languages includes the Chané of Argentina. Fundamental distinctions cannot be made between the corpus of Chané myths and that of the Chiriguano; similarities abound between them, particularly with respect to the figure of the shaman. There are two kinds of shamans: one with benevolent power (the ipáye) and another dedicated exclusively to malevolent actions that cause death (the ipayepóci). The mbaidwá ("knower, investigator") has dominion over the individual destinies of humans.

— MARIO CALIFANO

TRANSLATED FROM SPANISH BY TANYA FAYEN

SOUTH AMERICAN RELIGIONS

Since the Indians of South America do not conform culturally, there is no religious uniformity among them. Despite this inconsistency, an acceptable overview can be achieved by subdividing the continent's large, geographically distinct regions into the following cultural areas.

1. *The Andes.* This mountain range stretches from present-day Colombia to Chile. Among the most significant of these cultures was the Inca empire, which extended into the dawn of historical times. Direct descendants of earlier Andean cultures, the Quechua and Aymara peoples inhabit present-day Peru and Bolivia.

2. *Amazon and Orinoco rivers.* These jungle- and savanna-covered regions were conquered by tropical farming cultures. From the standpoint of cultural history, this area also includes the mountainous sections of present-day Guyana. As in the past, it is now inhabited by tribes belonging to a number of linguistic families, both small and large (Tupi, Carib, Arawak, Tucano, and Pano), and by a number of linguistically isolated tribes.

3. *Mountains of eastern Brazil.* This region is occupied by groups of the Ge linguistic family, who practice rudimentary farming methods; they settled in these hinterlands of the Atlantic coast region, joining indigenous hunting tribes.

4. *The Gran Chaco.* The bush and grass steppes of this area stretch from the Paraguay River west to the foothills of the Andes. A series of more or less acculturated groups of the Guiacurú linguistic family (the Mataco and the Mascoy) may still be encountered at the present time.

5. *The Pampas and Patagonia.* Hunting groups wandered through these flatlands of the southern regions of South America. The extinct Pampa and Tehuelche Indians were among the peoples of this region. The Tierra del Fuego archipelago, near the Strait of Magellan, is also included within this territory.

6. *Southern Andes.* This area, especially its middle and southernmost regions, is populated by the agrarian Araucanians of Chile, who have prospered up to the present time. Their success has been attributed to their development of a self-sufficient culture a few decades before the Spanish invasicn in the early sixteenth century.

DEITIES, CULTURE HEROES, AND ANCESTORS

The tradition of a creator as the prime mover and teacher of mankind is universal among the Indians of South America (Métraux, 1949). Under certain conditions, a creator, a culture hero, or an ancestor may rise to the position of a deity or supreme being. Such a case occurred in the old cultures of Peru with the religious figure Viracocha.

CULTURE HERO AS SUPREME BEING. Konrad T. Preuss was convinced that Moma ("father") was the paramount, indeed, the only true god of the Witóto of the Putumayo area of the northwestern Amazon and that he was identified with the moon. According to creation legends among these people, Moma came into existence from the "word," that is, he was a product of magico-religious incantations and myths that are endowed with supernatural powers. He was also the personification of the "word," which he bestowed upon human beings, and the "word" was the doctrine that represented the driving force behind all religious ceremonies that Moma introduced.

Among the Witóto, such a representation demonstrates intensely the character of a particular form of culture hero, that is, one who is at the same time a supreme entity. Alfred E. Jensen applied the term *dema deity* in describing such a culture hero among the Marind-anim of New Guinea (Jensen, 1951).

WARÍKYANA SUPREME BEING. A supreme god is also manifested among the Waríkyana (Arikena), a Carib-speaking tribe of the Brazilian Guianas. The highest deity in the religion of the Waríkyana is Pura (a name that, according to the Franciscan missionary Albert Kruse, means "God"). With his servant Mura, Pura stands on the zenith of heaven's mountains and observes all things that take place below (Kruse, 1955). At the command of Pura, the rain is sent from the sky. Pura and Mura are small men with red skin and are ageless and immortal. Pura is considered to be a "primordial man" or culture hero (ibid.).

YANOAMA AND MUNDURUCÚ SUPREME BEINGS. Kruse's work stimulated Josef Haekel to write an article about monotheistic tendencies among Carib-speakers and other Indian groups in the Guianas. According to Haekel's findings, reference to the name *Pura* in connection with a supreme being occurred in no other Carib-speaking tribe except the Waríkyana. To the west of their territory in the Guianas, however, the expression is used with only slight variation, even among different linguistic groups such as the isolated Yanoama (Yanomami) on the Venezuelan and Brazilian borders. According to the beliefs of some groups in Brazil, *Pore* is the name of a supreme being who descended to earth (Becher, 1974).

There are strong similarities between the supreme being, Pura, of the Waríkyana and the figure of Karusakaibe, the "father of the Mundurucú" (an expression coined by Kruse, who was also a missionary among this central Tupi tribe). Karusakaibe once lived on earth and created human souls, the sky, the stars, game animals, fish, and cultivated plants, together with all their respective guardian spirits, and he made the trees and plants fruitful. Martin Gusinde (1960) is of the opinion that Karusakaibe was once a superior god among the Mundurucú. Later his status changed to that of a culture hero.

TUPI-GUARANÍ SUPREME BEINGS. Resonances of a supreme being concept among the Tupi-Guaraní linguistic groups are mentioned by Alfred Métraux, who was the most important specialist in their religious systems (Métraux, 1949). Among these groups, the creator often has the characteristics of a transformer, and as a rule he is also the lawgiver and teacher of early mankind. After he fulfills these tasks, he journeys westward to the end of the world, where he rules over the shades of the dead.

The most revered god of the Guaraní-Apapocuvá according to Curt Nimuendajú, the outstanding authority on this tribe at the beginning of the twentieth century, is the creator Nanderuvuçu ("our great father"). Nanderuvuçu has withdrawn to a remote region of eternal darkness that is illuminated solely by the light that radiates from his breast (Nimuendajú, 1914).

GE SOLAR AND LUNAR GODS. In the eastern Brazilian area, the majority of the northwestern and central Ge tribes (Apinagé, Canella, and Xerente) hold that the Sun and Moon are the only true gods. Both Sun and Moon are masculine. Though not related to each other, they are companions; the Sun, however, is predominant.

At the beginning of the harvest season, a four-day Apinagé dance festival is celebrated in honor of the Sun at which the dancers apply red paint to themselves in patterns representative of the sun. The Canella also publicly implore the heavenly gods, the Sun and the Moon, for rain, the safety of the game animals, the success of their harvest, and an abundance of wild fruit.

SUPREME BEINGS OF TIERRA DEL FUEGO. Among the people living in the southern regions of the continent, a belief in a supreme being is common in hunting and fishing tribes, especially the Selk'nam (Ona) of Tierra del Fuego and the Yahgan and Alacaluf of the Tierra del Fuego archipelago. They, along with the Alacaluf (Halakwulip), maintain belief in a supreme being who is an invisible, omnipotent, and omniscient spirit living in heaven, beyond the stars. He has no physical body and is immortal; having neither wife nor children, he has no material desires.

SUPREME BEINGS OF THE PAMPAS, PATAGONIA, AND THE SOUTHERN ANDES. Although our knowledge of the religious practices and beliefs of the earlier inhabitants of the Pampas and Patagonia is sparse and relatively superficial, it is almost certain that the Tehuelche had a supreme being. Like Témaukel of the Selk'nam, the god of the Tehuelche was characterized by his lack of interest in worldly activities; he was also lord of the dead. This supreme being was, in general, sympathetic toward human beings, but there is no proof of a public cult devoted to him. Traditionally he was called Soychu. A benevolent supreme being of the same name was also found in the religious beliefs of the Pampa Indians, at least after the eighteenth century.

It would appear that the tribal religions of the southern areas of South America were, in general, marked by a belief in a supreme god. The Araucanians of the southern Andes, and in particular the Mapuche, have left behind traces of the concept of a superior god, as well as a devout veneration of him that survived well into the eighteenth century. In most instances the supreme being is referred to as either Ngenechen ("lord of mankind") or Ngenemapun ("lord of the land"). Other, more feminine descriptions may reveal an androgynous character. Ngenechen is thought of as liv-

"Nor dim nor red, like God's own head, the glorious Sun uprist."

SAMUEL TAYLOR COLERIDGE
RIME OF THE ANCIENT MARINER.

ing in heaven or in the sun and is credited with being the creator of the world as well as the provider of life and of the fruits of the earth.

NATURE SPIRITS, HUNTING RITUALS, AND VEGETATION RITES

Owing to the fact that hunting belongs to one of the oldest phases of human history, gods who are associated with this category of subsistence represent archaic beliefs. Not only do the Indians of South America believe in a master of all animals but they frequently display a belief in supernatural protectors of the various animal species. From the standpoint of cultural history, they are related to the lord of all beasts and have affinities with him that stem from the same hunting and fishing mentality.

The image of a conspicuously superior being is found in the initial stages of high Andean civilization.

PAGE 609

TUPI MASTER OF THE ANIMALS. The most important representation of a master of the animals in the tropical lowlands is the forest spirit Korupira, or Kaapora. Although the use of two names creates the impression that Korupira and Kaapora are two separate mythical figures, they are so closely related as to be nearly indistinguishable. Korupira, the master of the animals, is the protecting spirit of the beasts as well as of the forest; he punishes those who maliciously destroy the game and rewards those who obey him or those on whom he takes pity. For a portion of tobacco, Korupira will lift the restrictions that he places on the killing of his animals. Encounters in recent times with a small isolated Tupi tribe, the Pauserna Guarasug'wä, who live in eastern Bolivia, have shown that the belief in Korupira/Kaapora has survived. Kaapora originated as a human being—that is, he was created from the soul of a Guarasu Indian. He is the lord of all animals of the forest and has put his mark somewhere on each of the wild animals, usually on its ear. A hunter must turn to him with a plea to release part of the game, but he is only allowed to kill as many as he will absolutely need for the moment. In thanksgiving for his success, the hunter will leave the skin, the feet, or the entrails of the slain animal behind when he leaves the forest: by doing so he begs forgiveness from the animal for having killed it. After such reconciliations, the soul of the animal returns home to Kaapora.

Kurupi-vyra of the Guarasug'wä is a part-animal, part-human forest spirit, but not a lord of the animals. He is, however, a possible source of help for hunters in emergencies.

MUNDURUCÚ PROTECTIVE MOTHER SPIRIT. In the Amazon region, the idea of a lord of all animals is sometimes replaced by the belief in a lord or master of each individual animal species, and sometimes both concepts occur. Starting from the basic Tupi premise that every object in nature possesses a mother *(cy)*, the Mundurucú, a Tupi-speaking group, recognize and venerate a maternal spirit of all game. She is the protector of the animal kingdom against mankind and maintains a mother-child relationship between herself and the beasts.

HUNTING DANCES. The Taulipáng and the Arecuná of the inland regions of the Guianas believe that each individual animal type has a father *(podole)*, who is envisioned as either a real or a gigantic, legendary representative of that particular species, and who displays supernatural qualities. Two "animal fathers" are especially meaningful for their hunting ritual: the father of the peccary and the father of the fish. In the Parischerá, a long chain of participants, wearing palm-leaf costumes and representing a grunting peccary herd, dance to the booming of cane trumpets or clarinets. Performing the Parischerá ensures a plentiful supply of four-legged animals, just as the Tukui dance guarantees a sufficient supply of birds and fish.

Animal dances devoted to the attainment of game and fish are found among other tribes of the Amazon area and the Gran Chaco. Instead of focusing on the controlling master of the animals, however, they are often directed at the soul of the animal itself.

PLANT FERTILITY RITES. The most impressive religious celebrations of the tribes in the lowlands of the Amazon are those held for the vegetation demons by the peoples in the northwestern section of this region. Among the Tucanoan and Arawakan groups of the upper Rio Negro and the basin of the Uaupés River, the Yurupary rites take place at the time when certain palm fruits particularly favored by the Indians are ripe. At the beginning of the festival, baskets of these fruits are ceremonially escorted into the village by men blowing giant trumpets. These sacred instruments, which represent the voices of the vegetation demons, are hidden from the women and children, who must therefore remain within the huts at this time. During the first part of the ceremony, in which the men scourge one another with long rods, the women are also obligated to remain within their houses. After the secret part of the ritual has ended, however, the women may join the men in feasting and drinking, which continues for several days. The purpose of this feast is to thank the demons for a good harvest and to beg them to provide a rich yield in the coming season.

HUMAN AND PLANT FERTILITY. Among the Kaua (an Arawakan group) and the Cubeo (a Tucano group) in the northwestern Amazon region, fertility rites are obviously connected with a human generative power. At the end of the masked dances, in which the dancers represent animals, the participants unite to perform the Naädö (phallus dance).

Among the Jivaroan people in Ecuador, the cult of the earth mother Nunkwi is restricted to those culti-

vated plants whose soul is believed to be feminine—for example, manioc. The soul of the earth mother resides within a strangely shaped stone *(nantara)* that has the power to summon Nunkwi. The association between fertility of human females and the growth of plants considered to be feminine receives obvious expression through the rule that every woman who plants a manioc cutting must sit on a manioc tuber. The same theme is expressed in the ritual for the first manioc cutting that is taken from a field whose yield is intended to be used at the Tobacco festival. The cutting is painted red, and the woman to be honored places it against her groin.

The Quechua and Aymara peoples of the central Andes region frequently call upon Pachamama, the goddess of the earth, who is essentially responsible for the fertility of plants and who is believed to live underground. In addition to being connected with many celebrations, she is also associated with many daily rituals. The cult devoted to her originated in pre-Hispanic times and has survived to the present.

CONCLUSION

The central Andes of pre-Columbian times is characterized by a belief in high gods and their respective cults, by the worship of ancestors and of the dead, and by agrarian rites directed to a female earth deity. The peoples of the region of the Amazon and Orinoco rivers occasionally display signs of high-god worship (Witóto, Tupi-Guaraní). Along with the vegetation cults (northwestern Amazon) that are typical of crop-cultivating peoples, there is a markedly large number of ceremonies and rites assoicated with deities of the hunt and of wild animals (including fish). The Ge of eastern Brazil exhibit clear signs of worship of astral deities—the Sun and Moon. The cults of the dead and of ancestors dominate much of their religious life. The Gran Chaco, by contrast, is noticeably lacking in religious ceremonies and rites in the narrow sense. First-fruit ceremonies related to hunting and fishing predominate; there are no agrarian rites. In the Pampas and Patagonia region a number of socioreligious

THE SOUL, THE DEAD, AND ANCESTORS

Driving Out the Death Demons

Most of the Indian groups of South America believe that a human being has several souls, each residing in a different part of the body and responsible for numerous aspects of life. After death, each of these souls meets a different fate.

Research on a number of Indian tribes indicates that meticulous preservation of the bones of the dead is a widespread practice. Such action, which is similar to the preservation of the bones of hunted game, can be traced to the belief that residual elements of the soul remain in the bones after death.

Honoring the dead was an essential component within the religions of old Peru, as exemplified by the care that mummies of the ancestors were given by priests (Métraux, 1949) and by the sacrificial victims brought to them. Mummies were also taken on procession at certain festivals.

The combination of a memorial service for the recently dead and a commemorative ceremony for the legendary tribal ancestors can be seen in the Kwarup ritual of the Camayura, a Tupi group of the upper Xingu. The Kwarup (from *kuat,* "sun" and *yerup,* "my ancestor") centers around a number of posts, each about three feet high, outfitted and ornamented as human beings and carved from the sacred camiriva wood from which the creator, Mavutsine, allegedly fabricated the first Camayura. The chant given as people dance around these posts is the same one that Mavutsine sang as he created mankind. In the Kwarup ritual the ancestors return symbolically for the purpose of welcoming those who have recently died.

Death cults and ancestor worship also play an important role in the eastern Brazilian cultural area, particularly among the Boróro. This tribe makes a sharp distinction between nature spirits and spirits of the dead. The Boróro believe that the souls of their ancestors *(aroe)* hold a close relationship to mankind that influences and maintains its daily life. On certain social occasions, the spirits of the dead are ceremonially invoked by special shamans to whom the spirits appear and whom they enlighten in dreams. As a result of this important attachment to the spirits, the funeral rites of the Boróro are highly developed and complex.

A cult of the dead among the indigenous people in the southern regions of South America, including the Gran Chaco and the southern Andes, contains few authentic religious elements. At a funeral, the surviving family members sponsor a large feast in honor of the dead relative. The various ceremonies that take place during this feast—for example, eating and drinking bouts, lamenting, playing of music, feigned attacks, riding games, and speeches—are intended to drive from the village the dreaded spirits of the dead or the death demons, who are responsible for the death of the tribal member, to prevent them from causing more harm.

— OTTO ZERRIES

rites are attested. The Selk'nam and Yahgan of Tierra del Fuego Archipelago believe in a high god, but there is little indication of cult worship. The regions of southern and central Andes share many aspects of religious life. The high-god cult (Ngenechen) is associated with a cultivation and fertility ritual. A highly developed form of shamanism is also prominent. Throughout South America outside the Andean region, the shaman remains the pillar of the religious life.

— OTTO ZERRIES

TRANSLATED FROM GERMAN BY JOHN MARESSA

The job of the shaman as medical practitioner is to cure both aspects of the sickness.

PAGE 614

SOUTHEAST ASIAN RELIGIONS

MAINLAND CULTURES

Mainland Southeast Asia has been termed the "crossroad of religions," for in this region, today divided into the countries of Burma, Thailand, and Laos, Cambodia (Kampuchea), and Vietnam, a large diversity of autochthonous tribal religions are intermingled with Hinduism, Theravada and Mahayana Buddhism, Taoism, Confucianism, Islam, and Christianity, as well as the modern secular faith of Marxist-Leninism. Beneath this diversity there are many religious practices and beliefs that have common roots in the prehistoric past of peoples of the region.

Mainland Southeast Asia is not only a region of religious diversity; it is also a veritable Babel. Insofar as historical linguistics permits us to reconstruct the past, it would appear that most of the earliest inhabitants of the region spoke Austroasiatic languages ancestral to such modern-day descendants as Khmer and Mon.

Prehistoric Foundations

People have lived in mainland Southeast Asia for as long as there have been *Homo sapiens,* and there is evidence of *Homo erectus* and even earlier hominid forms in the region as well. The first significant evidence we have of religious beliefs and practices in mainland Southeast Asia comes from the period when humans in the region first began to live in settled agricultural communities. The domestication of rice, which may have taken place in mainland Southeast Asia before 4,000 BCE, led to the emergence of a powerful image that was to become incorporated in almost all of the religious traditions of the region.

Neolithic burial sites, many only recently discovered, are proving to be sources of knowledge about prehistoric religions in Southeast Asia. The very existence of such sites suggests that those who took so much trouble to dispose of the physical remains of the dead must have had well-formed ideas about the afterlife and about the connection between the states of the dead and the living.

YOUNG BUDDHISTS

These Budhhist Monk initiates in Thailand represent just one faith in Southeast Asia. the "crossroad of religion." Hinduism, Taoism, Confucianism, Islam and several tribal religions are intermingled in the region.

KEVIN R. MORRIS/© CORBIS

In a Neolithic burial site in western Thailand, the grave of an old man was found to contain a perforated stone disk and an antler with the tines sawed off. Per Sørensen, the archaeologist who excavated the site, believes these items may represent the headdress of a shaman; if so, they would be the earliest evidence of shamanism in mainland Southeast Asia.

Peoples of the region in late prehistoric times were often isolated from each other by the numerous ranges of hills and must have developed distinctive religious traditions. An older generation of scholars, best represented by Robert Heine-Geldern, posited an underlying unity of prehistoric Southeast Asian religions that stemmed from the diffusion of a cultural complex from a single European source. While there were certainly contacts among peoples widely separated in Southeast Asia in prehistoric times, and while these contacts resulted in the diffusion of some practices and beliefs, most basic similarities must be understood to reflect the ordering of similar experiences that follow universal modes of human thought.

Drawing on later historical data as well as ethnographic analogy, Paul Mus, a distinguished student of Southeast Asian civilizations, argued that the autochthonous religions of protohistoric Southeast Asia coalesced around cults he termed "cadastral." These cadastral cults constituted the religions of agricultural peoples who had long since made rice their staple, although some cultivated it by swidden or slash-and-burn methods and others cultivated by irrigation. Rice was believed to possess a vital spirit.

The cosmologies of protohistoric Southeast Asian farmers, like those of primitive peoples throughout the world, were structured around fundamental oppositions. In Southeast Asia, the oscillation between the rainy rice-growing season and the dry fallow season found expression in such religious imagery. The fertility of the rainy season is widely associated with a female deity, the "rice mother," although a male image, that of the *naga,* or dragon, and sometimes a crocodile, is also found in many traditions.

The world in which protohistoric peoples lived was marked by uncertainty: crops might fail as a consequence of late rains or devastating floods; women might be barren, die in childbirth, or lose child after child; and both men and women might die young. Hence, people wished to influence the spirits and cosmic forces that controlled fertility and life. The fundamental method of gaining the favor of spiritual powers was through sacrifices. In tribal groups such as those in Burma and northeastern India, those men who organized large-scale sacrifices and the so-called feasts of merit associated with them acquired not only the esteem of their fellows but also a spiritual quality that was believed to persist even after their death. Such tribal chiefs are assumed to be similar to what O. W. Wolters calls "men of prowess." Rough stone monuments associated with early Cham culture in southern Vietnam and upright stones found together with the prehistoric stone jars in Laos have been interpreted, by analogy with the practice by such modern tribal peoples as Chin of Burma and related groups in northeastern India, as monuments that perpetuated and localized the potency of men who had succeeded during their lifetimes in effecting a relationship between the society and the cosmos.

Historical Transformations

Prior to the adoption of Indian or Chinese models, there appears to have been no priesthood in any Southeast Asian society capable of enforcing an orthopraxy among peoples living over a wide area. As the ritual effectiveness of men of prowess waxed and waned, so did the relative power of the polities they headed, thus giving rise to a classic pattern of oscillation between "democratic" and "autocratic" communities found among tribal peoples such as the Kachin of Burma even in recent years.

SINITIC INFLUENCES. Chinese influences appear first in conjunction with the Han conquest of what is now northern Vietnam. This sense of belonging to a Chinese world remained even after the Vietnamese gained independence from China in the eleventh century. The Chinese model was most significant for literati—the Confucian mandarinate, Mahayana Buddhist monks, and even some Taoist priests—who derived their cultural understanding of the world from Chinese and Sino-Vietnamese texts. Those Vietnamese who moved out of the Red River delta in the "push to the south" that began in the thirteenth century and continued into recent times came into contact with other traditions—those of the hinduized Cham and Khmer, the Buddhist Khmer, and local tribal peoples. Many of the religiously inspired peasant rebellions originating in southern Vietnam as well as some modern syncretic popular religons have drawn inspiration from non-Chinese sources. This said, Vietnamese religion in all parts of the country has assumed a distinctly Sinitic cast, being organized primarily around ancestor worship in the Chinese mode.

INDIAN INFLUENCES. The earliest monuments of indianized civilization in Southeast Asia appeared in significant numbers between the fourth and eighth century CE. Particular examples are Siva *linga* of the Cham in southern Vietnam, the Buddhist *sema* (Skt., *sima*) or boundary markers with scenes from the life of the Buddha or from the Jatakas in bas-relief found in Dvaravati sites in northeastern Thailand, and the stupas at Beikthano and Sriksetra in central Burma, Thaton in lower Burma, and Nakhon Pathom in central

The Han emperor Wu devoted much effort to attaining immortality, as had his Ch'in predecessor.

PAGE 136

The spread of Buddhism was also closely related to the development of long-distance trade: it was carried all over Asia by monks who attached themselves to trade caravans and merchant vessels.

PAGE 449

Thailand. These monuments can best be interpreted as having been put up to elevate a man of prowess to a divine form.

The process of indianization in Southeast Asia included identifying a power believed to be embodied in a local shrine with divine or cosmic powers known in Indian texts. This made possible the creation of larger polities, since peoples in very different parts of a realm saw themselves as part of the same cosmos and worshiped the same gods, often gods who were also equated with the rulers.

On the western side of mainland Southeast Asia, Burmese kings also succeeded in establishing a *mandala* (circle of a king) that between the eleventh and thirteenth centuries rivaled the splendor and power of Angkor. It produced both funerary monuments in which the kings became immortalized, albeit in this case in Buddhist terms, and recreations of the sacred cosmos.

The cult of the relics of the Buddha does not constitute the whole of Buddhism as practiced in Southeast Asia. Between the thirteenth and fifteenth centuries, missionary monks established a Theravada Buddhist orthodoxy among the majority of peoples, both rural and urban, living in what are today Burma, Thailand, Laos, and Cambodia. In a sense, orthodox Buddhism made sense to Southeast Asians because of the pre-Buddhist idea that religious virtue is not a product solely of descent from particular ancestors but also a consequence of one's own religiously effective actions.

The success of Theravada Buddhism led to a much sharper distinction between the religious traditions of the peoples of the western part of mainland Southeast Asia and those east of the Annamite cordillera. Not only were the Vietnamese becoming increasingly sinicized, but the Cham, who had once had an important indianized culture in southern Vietnam, turned from this tradition and embraced Islam, a religion that was becoming established among other Austronesian-speaking peoples in major societies of the Indonesian archipelago and on the Malay Peninsula.

Missionization—not only by Christians but in recent years by Buddhists—and the spread of modern systems of compulsory education have rendered tribal religions increasingly peripheral. So, too, have improved health care and secular education undermined beliefs in spirits that were previously elements of the religions of Southeast Asian Buddhists and Vietnamese. Moreover, as agriculture has been transformed by large-scale irrigation works and the introduction of new technology and new high-yield varieties of rice, peoples in the region have become less inclined to credit supernatural powers with the control over fertility.

[*See also* Buddhism *and* Islam, *article on* Islam in Southeast Asia.]

— CHARLES F. KEYES

INSULAR CULTURES

The cultures of insular Southeast Asia are made up predominantly of peoples speaking Austronesian languages, and the traditional religions of the area, despite substantial diversity and extensive borrowing from other sources, retain significant features that reflect a common origin. The initial expansion of the Austronesians began in the third millennium BCE and proceeded, by stages, through the Philippines and the islands of Indonesia, then east to the islands of the Pacific, and eventually west as far as the island of Madagascar.

In the course of migration, natural ecological variation as well as numerous outside influences led to the development, emphasis, or even abandonment of different elements of a general Neolithic culture. In the equatorial zones, for example, reliance on rice and millet gave way to a greater dependence on tubers and on fruit- and starch-gathering activities. During most of their protohistory, Austronesian populations lived in impermanent settlements and combined shifting cultivation with hunting and gathering. The development toward centralized states began on Java, on the coast of Sumatra, and in several other coastal areas that were open to trade and outside influences. Chief among these influences were religious ideas and inspiration that derived variously, at different periods, from Hinduism, Buddhism, Islam, and Christianity.

At present, 88 to 89 percent of the Indonesian population is classified as Muslim. In the Philippines, approximately 84 percent of the population is Catholic. In Indonesia, Bali forms a traditional Hindu-Buddhist enclave but there has occurred a recent resurgence of Hinduism on Java and elsewhere.

The tribal religions of the region vary according to the groups that continue to practice them. These groups include small, often isolated peoples whose economy is based primarily on hunting and gathering with limited cultivation. Examples of such groups are the Sakkudei of the island of Siberut off the coast of western Sumatra; various wandering bands of Kubu scattered in the interior forests of Sumatra; groups of a similar kind in Kalimantan who are referred to generically as Punan; as well as a variety of other small-scale societies on other islands.

Some of these Indonesian populations have formally established religious associations to preserve their traditional practices and some have come to be identified as followers of Hindu-Dharma. In the Philippines, a majority of the indigenous peoples in the mountains of northern Luzon in Mondoro and in the interior of

Mindanao have retained their traditional religions despite increasing missionary efforts.

Studies of traditional religion, many of which have been written by missionaries or colonial administrators, document beliefs and practices that have since been either abandoned or modified through the process of conversion. Significant evidence on traditional religion is also derived from present practices and general conceptions that have been incorporated and retained: (1) the prevalence of complementary duality; (2) the belief in the immanence of life and in the interdependence of life and death; (3) the reliance on specific rituals to mark stages in the processes of life and death; and (4) the celebration of spiritual differentiation. All of these notions may be regarded as part of a common Austronesian conceptual heritage.

THE PREVALENCE OF COMPLEMENTARY DUALITY. Forms of complementary dualism are singularly pervasive in the religions of the region. Such dualism figures prominently, in a wide variety of myths of the origin of the cosmos that combine themes of reproduction and destruction. As well, ideas of complementary duality are reflected in ideas about the principal divinity, who is often conceived of as a paired being; in ideas about the division of sacred space: upperworld and underworld, upstream and downstream, mountainward and seaward, or inside and outside; and above all, in ideas about classes of persons and the order of participants in the performance of rituals. Major celebrations based on this complementarity can become a form of ritual combat that reenacts the reproductive antagonisms of creation.

Conceptions of complementary dualism continue to pervade even those societies that have adopted Hinduism, Islam, or Christianity. Balinese society is replete with dualism. The opposition between Barong and Rangda, which forms one of Bali's best-known dramatic temple performances, is a particularly striking example of complementary dualism. The Javanese *wayang,* or shadow theater, is similarly based on forms of dual opposition.

BELIEF IN THE IMMANENCE OF LIFE. Virtually all of the traditional religions of the region are predicated on a belief in the immanence of life. In the literature this concept is often simplistically referred to as "animism." In traditional mythologies, creation did not occur *ex nihilo:* the cosmos was violently quickened into life and all that exists is thus part of a living cosmic whole. Commonly, humans either descended from a heavenly sphere or emerged from earth or sea.

The traditional religions differ markedly, however, in their classification of categories or classes of beings. Priests of the Ifugao, for example, are reported to be able to distinguish over fifteen hundred spirits or deities, who are divided into forty classes. By contrast, the Rotinese recognize two broad classes of spirits—those of the inside and those of the outside—and are only concerned with naming the spirits of the inside. The traditional religions also differ significantly in attitudes to the spirit world. For some, all spirits are potentially malevolent and must be placated; in others, benevolent spirits are called upon to intervene against troublesome spirits.

A fundamental feature of the traditional religions is their recognition that life depends upon death, that creation derives from dissolution. Moreover, since life comes from death, the ancestral dead or specific deceased persons, whose lives were marked by notable attainments, are regarded as capable of bestowing life-giving potency. Thus the dead figure prominently in the religious activities of the living and the tombs of the dead are often sources of religious benefit.

The chief sacrificial animals in the traditional religions are the chicken, the dog, and the pig (although among those populations that keep them the water buffalo is by far the most important sacrificial animal). The entrails of chickens and the livers of pigs frequently provide a means of divination within a sacrificial context.

RITUALS OF LIFE AND DEATH. Life-cycle rituals mark the process of life and death. They may be seen to begin with marriage—the union of male and female—and proceed through specific stages. Prominent among these rituals are those that mark the seventh month of a woman's pregnancy, haircutting, tooth filing, circumcision (which may have had a pre-Islamic origin but has been given increased significance through the influence of Islam), the coming of adulthood through marriage, and the formation of an autonomous household.

Death rituals are part of the same process as those of life and in general are celebrated throughout the region with great elaboration. Death rituals are also performed in stages commencing with burial and continuing sometimes for years. Often the groups involved in performing these mortuary rituals complete and reverse the exchanges that began at the marriage ceremony of the parents of the deceased, thus ending one phase and beginning the next phase of a continuing cycle

Headhunting was once a prominent feature of the social life of many of the peoples of the region. Although this form of limited warfare was given various cultural interpretations, headhunting was frequently linked in rituals to the general cycle of death and renewal. In this sense, headhunting was a form of "harvest" in which particular individuals were able to achieve great renown.

THE CELEBRATION OF SPIRITUAL DIFFERENTIATION. The tendency in most traditional reli-

"Com, you spirits that tend on mortal thought."

WILLIAM SHAKESPEARE
MACBETH

The mainspring of Sufism lay in the desire to cultivate the inner life and to attain a deeper, personal understanding of Islam.

PAGE 347

gions is to personalize whatever may be considered a manifestation of life. Included among such manifestations are the heavenly spheres—the sun, moon, and stars; the forces of nature—thunder, lightning, or great winds; points of geographical prominence—high mountain peaks, volcanic craters, waterfalls, caves, or old trees; places endowed with unusual significance as the result of past occurrences—sites of abandoned settlement, a former meeting place of some spirit, or the point of a past, powerful dream; and simpler iconic representations of life—ancient ancestral possessions, royal regalia, amulets, and other objects of specially conceived potency.

In social terms, these spiritual premises are conducive to notions of precedence and hierarchy. No society in the region is without some form of social differentiation. Even in the simplest of tribal societies the birth order of the children of the same parents becomes a means for such distinctions. Equally, the same spiritual premises may promote notions of achievement.

Literally and spiritually, individuals are distinguished by their journeys. Rank, prowess, and the attainment of wealth can be taken as evident signs of individual enhancement in a life's odyssey, and this enhancement may be celebrated through major rituals, both in life and after death. In many traditional religions, mortuary rituals and the feasting that generally accompanies them are the primary indicators of a person's social and spiritual position and are intended to translate this position into a similarly enhanced position in the afterlife.

Today throughout insular Southeast Asia, the basic premises of traditional religions are under challenge from religions such as Islam and Christianity that preach transcendence in place of the immanence of life and assert spiritual equality rather than celebrate spiritual differentiation.

[*See* Javanese Religion. *See also* Buddhism and Islam.]

— JAMES J. FOX

SUFISM

ORIGINS

One of the truly creative manifestations of religious life in Islam is the mystical tradition, known as Sufism. The terms *Sufi* and *Sufism* evoke complex layers of meaning in Islam, including the denial of the world, close association with the Prophet and his message, and a spiritual attainment that raises one to a rank of unique intimacy with God.

Some earlier Western scholars of Sufism concluded that mysticism is incompatible with the Muslim perception of an almighty, transcendent God with whom one shares little intimacy. In their opinion Sufi mysticism was born of Islam's contact with other major world religions, especially Christianity and Buddhism. This theory is no longer considered viable.

The experience of mystical union need not be seen as foreign to Islam. On the contrary, interior spiritual development becomes a concern at a relatively early date in the writings of important Qur'an commentators. Of the two traditional methods of Qur'anic exegesis predominating in Islam, *tafsir* emphasizes the exoteric elements of the text: grammar, philology, history, dogma, and the like, while *ta'wil* stresses the search for hidden meanings, the esoteric dimensions of the Qur'anic text. It is among Sufis (and Shi'i Muslims) that *ta'wil* has found special favor.

THE ASCETIC MOVEMENT. The early catalysts for the development of mysticism in Islam, however, were not all spiritual in nature. The dramatic social and political changes brought about by the establishment of the Umayyad dynasty in the mid-seventh century also played a pivotal role. The capital of the empire was moved from Medina to the more opulent and cosmopolitan Damascus, and the rapid spread of Islam introduced enormous wealth and ethnic diversity into what had originally been a spartan, Arab movement. In reaction to the worldliness of the Umayyads, individual ascetics arose to preach a return to the heroic values of the Qur'an through the abandonment of both riches and the trappings of earthly power. The three major centers of the ascetic movement in the eighth and ninth centuries were Iraq, especially the cities of Basra, Kufa, and Baghdad; the province of Khorasan, especially the city of Balkh; and Egypt.

MYSTICAL ECSTASY. The evolution of ascetic and theoretical principles to guide the Sufi wayfarer, and the growing sophistication of aesthetic expressions of love mysticism were not the only signs of a maturing mystical tradition in Islam. An additional area of creative exploration by a number of ninth- and tenth-century Sufis centered on refining the understanding of what actually constitutes the goal of mystical experience.

MYSTICAL LITERATURE

The science of opposites, with its rich symbolism and provocative speculation, appealed only to a small number of Sufis because of the level of intellectual sophistication it demanded and because of its esoteric quality. In contrast, beginning in the late ninth century, a number of texts began to appear that were aimed at a broader spectrum of the Muslim faithful and functioned as training guides for men and women interested in cultivating mystical experience.

THE MANUAL TRADITION. The emphasis of the

manuals was not on the arcane dimensions of Sufism, but on its accessibility and its conformity with Islamic orthodoxy.

One of the earliest manuals addressed to a Sufi novice is the *Kitab al-ri'ayah* (Book of Consideration) of Abu 'Abd Allah al-Harith ibn Asad al-Muhasibi (d. 857). He is remembered particularly for his skill in developing the examination of conscience as an effective tool for advancement in the spiritual life.

Among the classics of this genre of religious literature in Sufism are the *Kitab al-ta 'arruf* (Book of Knowledge) of Abu Bakr Muhammad al-Kalabadhi (d. 990 or 995), the *Kitab al-luma'* (Book of Concise Remarks) of Abu Nasr 'Abd Allah ibn 'Ali al-Sarraj (d. 988), *Al-risalah al-qushayriyah* (The Qushayrian Letter) of Abu al-Qasim 'Abd al-Karim al-Qushayri (d. 1074), the *Kashf al-mahjub* (Unveiling of the Veiled) of 'Ali ibn 'Uthman al-Jullabi al-Hujwiri (d. 1071/2?), and the *Qut al-qulub* (Nourishment of the Heart) of Abu Talib Muhammad ibn 'Ali ibn 'Atiyah al-Harithi al-Makki (d. 996).

OTHER GENRES. In addition to the Sufi manuals, other important genres of mystical literature developed in the classical period. Fables, epigrams, epic poems, poetry, aphorisms, all were creative vehicles for mystical expression. Early Qur'an commentators and street preachers had focused on the lives of the prophets for inspiration. This spawned the *Qisas al-anbiya'* (Tales of the Prophets), collections of lively didactic stories, often with moral themes.These hagiographic compendia are crucial for our knowledge of the lives and teachings of the great masters of classical Sufism.

The first systematic history of the lives of Sufi mystics is ascribed to Abu 'Abd al-Rahman al-Azdi al-Sulami (d. 1021). His *Tabaqat al-sufiyah* (Generations of the Sufis) became the basis for the expanded versions of two later Sufis, the *Tabaqat al-sufiyah* of Abu Isma'il Abd Allah Ansari (d. 1089) and the *Nafahat al-uns* (Wafts of Pleasure) of Nur al-Din 'Abd al-Rahman ibn Ahmad Jami (d. 1492). The most comprehensive work of Sufi hagiography, however, is the prodigious, multivolume *Hilyat al-awliya'* (Necklace of Saints) of Abu Nu'aym al-Isfahani (d. 1037).

GNOSIS AND IBN 'ARABI

The history of mysticism in Islam is replete with individuals of brilliance and creativity. Among these exceptional personalities, however, one stands out from the rest because of his unique genius. Abu Bakr Muhammad ibn al-'Arabi al-Hatimi al-Ta'i received the greater part of his education in the traditional Islamic religious disciplines. A great deal of his mystical insight, evolved from visionary experiences, the first occurring during an illness in his youth. Throughout his life he continued to have visions on which he placed a great deal of reliance.

Ibn 'Arabi's visionary bent is equally evident in his claim to have been initiated into Sufism by the mythic figure Khidr, a mysterious being, said to be immortal, associated with a Qur'anic fable (surah 18) and pre-Islamic legends.

In his early twenties Ibn 'Arabi traveled extensively throughout Spain and North Africa and broadened his intellectual perspectives. He describes a unique meeting in Cordova with the greatest of the Muslim Aristotelian philosophers, Ibn Rushd (known as Averroës in the Latin West). The encounter is heavy with symbolism, for Ibn Rushd represents the total reliance of philosophers on reason *('aql)*, while Ibn 'Arabi champions gnosis *(ma'rifah)* as the only means to experience the fullness of truth.

Ibn 'Arabi is unique because he was both an original thinker and synthesizer. Many of his ideas resonate with earlier intellectual developments in Sufism and in philosophical theology. His greatness, however, lies in his ability to systematize Sufi theory into a coherent whole with solid metaphysical underpinnings. The corpus of Ibn 'Arabi's work is massive, which complicates considerably any attempt at a comprehensive analysis of his thought. In addition his style is often dense, reflecting the esoteric nature of his ideas. Two of his most influential works are *Al-futuhat al-makkiyah* (The Meccan Revelations), which he was ordered to write in a visionary experience while on pilgrimage, and *Fusus al-hikam* (The Bezels of Wisdom).

SUFI FRATERNITIES

The history of Sufism is much more than the history of mystical theory and expression. There is a significant social dimension to Islamic mysticism. Fluid interaction among Sufis soon evolved into the more structured relationship of master and disciple, adding a new level of social complexity. Not only would disciples visit their masters, but many also took up residence with them. The earliest formal Sufi convent seems to date from the latter part of the eighth century CE, on the island of Abadan.

By the thirteenth century, several types of Sufi establishments had evolved, each with a different general purpose. The more serious training took place in the *zawiyahs,* which usually housed a teaching shaykh.

By the thirteenth century, many Sufi groups became self-perpetuating social organizations whose central focus was the founder and his teaching. No longer was the survival of the group dependent on a particular living shaykh; authority was passed from shaykh to disciple, thus providing a stable structural basis for the continued growth and development of the community.

SILSILAHS. These stable social organizations

Portraits of Sufis and dervishes are frequent in the later Middle Ages.

PAGE 313

came to be called *tariqahs* ("ways"), known in English as Sufi orders, fraternities or brotherhoods. Each founding shaykh had his *silsilah* ("chain"), his spiritual lineage which contributed substantially to his stature in the Sufi community. The *silsilah* is, more precisely, a genealogy, tracing the names of one's master, of one's master's master, and so on back through history. Often a prominent shaykh would have been initiated more than once, by a number of illustrious Sufis, thus adding additional stature to his spiritual pedigree.

The centrality of *silsilahs* in Sufi fraternities is not completely unique. One discovers an analogous emphasis in the *hadith* literature, where the literary structure of a *hadith* has two parts: the chain of transmitters *(isnad)* and the body of the text *(matn)*. But, the importance of *isnads* for Muslims is to ground *hadiths* solidly in the period of the original revelation. Thus there can be no question that the teachings of the *hadiths* are innovations; rather *hadiths* are but more detailed insights into God's will already expressed in general terms in the Qur'an.

Associated with the levels and sectors of the Pueblo world is a panoply of supernatural beings. Elsie C. Parsons (1939) divides these beings into collective and individualized categories.

PAGE 518

VENERATION OF SAINTS. The institutionalization of *tariqahs* and the emphasis on *silsilahs* enhanced substantially the religious and political position of the master. The shaykhs of the great Sufi orders, therefore, took on superhuman qualities. They became known as *awliya'* (sg., *wali*), intimates or friends of God. Many of the shaykhs of important orders were acknowledged by their followers as the *qutb,* the "pole" or "axis" around which the cosmos revolves, the Perfect Human Being, the point at which the divine Creative Imagination most fully manifests itself in the world of illusion. The perfected shaykhs are objects of veneration both during their lives and after their deaths.

RITUAL PRACTICE. The full members of the fraternities committed themselves in obedience to the shaykh, who initiated them into the order and bestowed upon them the patched frock *(khirqah)*, the sign of their entry onto the Sufi path. They were encouraged to subject themselves completely to the master's will, to be like dead bodies in the hands of the body-washers.

Common to most of the Sufi fraternities were ritual practices called *dhikr* ("remembrance") and *sama'* ("audition").

Dhikr. The impetus for the practice of *dhikr* is derived from those Qur'anic verses that enjoin the faithful to remember God often. Among Sufis this duty evolved into a complex exercise performed by an individual or group. Many fraternities put their own particular stamp on the *dhikr* exercise. Most *dhikr* techniques, however, involve the rhythmic repetition of a phrase, often Qur'anic, in which one of the names of God appears. In Islam, Allah has one hundred names, ninety-nine of which are known; the hundredth name is hidden. Certain Sufis who ascribed to themselves the rank of *qutb* claimed to have been blessed with this most precious secret. The more sophisticated methods of *dhikr* usually involve breath control, body movements, and a number of other complex techniques to gain control over the five senses as well the psyche and imagination.

Sama'. Like *dhikr, sama'* has become identified with Sufi ritual practice. It involves listening to music, usually with a group. The music is often accompanied by Qur'an chants and/or the singing of mystical poetry. The recital is intended to spark a mystical experience within the auditors. Those most affected by the *sama'* rise up to dance in unison with the music. Depending on the Sufi group, the dance can be a marvel of esthetic movement or the frenetic writhings of the seemingly possessed.

The emphasis on *dhikr* and *sama'* has helped to blur the distinction in popular Sufism between mystical experience that is attained after serious spiritual training and experience that is self-induced. Unsophisticated sessions of *dhikr* and *sama',* to this day, often consist of self-hypnosis, hysteria, drug-induced states, and other violent emotions that pass for mystical experience. Despite accusations of vulgarization, *dhikr* and *sama'* remain important emotional outlets in the Muslim community and are unique sociological events during which various levels of society find themselves interacting on an equal footing.

— PETER J. AWN

SUPERNATURAL, THE

Mysterious occurrences and beings that habitually or occasionally impinge upon our everyday experience are called "supernatural."

HISTORICAL DEVELOPMENT OF THE NOTION

The term *supernatural* was given wide currency by Thomas Aquinas (1225-1274) and the Scholastics, but it had numerous antecedents in the idiom of the Hellenistic thinkers and church fathers. Neoplatonists in particular accumulated superlatives to speak of the realm of the divine: it was above the highest heaven, beyond the world, and even beyond being. This link between grace and the supernatural became firmly entrenched in scholastic theology.

The word *supernatural,* however, became associated with the unusual, the marvelous, the surprising. While medieval theologians had used the term *supernatural* to refer to the moral and spiritual dynamics of salvation, ordinary Christians came to call supernatural any extraordinary occurrence that could not be accounted for by the usual explanations at hand.

Baroque taste spread in Christian lands. What was infinite, awesome, powerful, overwhelming, and stunning was considered to convey a sense of God. Religious architecture and furniture became calculatedly impressive; oratory became stately. Miracles as powerful disruptions of nature's laws appeared, then, necessary to the cause of religion. Many theologians thus taught that human beings must regard the supernatural as contrary to nature: God, they said, intervenes providentially, and occasionally suspends the course of nature; he also reveals supernatural truths that we must obediently accept even though their truth is not manifest to our unaided reason.

APPLICATION OF THE NOTION TO THE STUDY OF RELIGIOUS AND CULTURAL SYSTEMS

Among scholars of the nineteenth century it came to be commonly admitted that belief in what Herbert Spencer has called "the supernatural genesis of phenomena" characterized religious people. All religions were said to feature belief in supernatural beings. Lucien Lévy-Bruhl (1857-1939) in his early influential work argued that the primitive mind believed in "mystical," not "physical," influences, whereas practically all contemporaries recognize a clear line of demarcation between the supernatural (rejected by all except the credulous) and the data furnished by everyday ordinary sense experience and the broad light of day. Paul Radin (1883-1959) argued against Lévy-Bruhl and spoke of the supernatural as arising against a background of inevitable fears (stemming from economic and psychic insecurity) that he found to be present in all human beings, primitive and modern. He saw in the modern West a decline in religion and in recourse to supernatural beings for help, because other means of emphasizing and maintaining life values were available and on the ascendant.

Rodney Needham (1972) has successfully argued that statements of belief are the only evidence we have of the phenomenon. Both theologians and anthropologists, he maintains, have taken too much for granted and have been too quick to specify what beliefs other people have and what difference these beliefs make. Belief in anything, including supernatural beings, is thus a very elusive phenomenon. It would be safer to characterize religion by attitudinal factors and ritual practice rather than by belief. And any statement of belief should be taken with a grain of salt. The highly imaginative stories of primitives abound in wit and irony and cannot be pinned down with the psychology of belief common among sober scientists (whose thinking often reflects the easy and moralistic recourse to expressions of belief characteristic of early modern theologians).

SYSTEMATIC CONSIDERATIONS

The human being has in his favor a quick mobile mind, but he is frail and his body is destined to contract disease and, ultimately, to die. Men and women are thus constantly the potential victims of aleatory events that can be painful to them. Fearful of impending disasters, they seek the protection of stronger human beings. As infants and children they start life with such protection. Later they attach themselves to strong persons whom they count on to be successful and wise so that they themselves can live in a secure world, one without interstices from which unpredictable attacks might come. Priests, who are typical examples of strong ones, are also thinkers. They teach survival skills and provide ritual and verbal comfort when these skills fail, as necessarily they must. Strong ones are therefore in touch with suitable explanations that ideally can help us in those boundary situations that occur when our ordinary world falls apart.

Our modern concept of nature and natural causes firmly supports a reality principle: when physically sick (or, today, even when anxious) we mainly turn to scientific medicine. Fear of and belief in supernatural agencies do not color in any significant way our sense of what is feasible in our embodied condition. But we hold on to some nonscientific health lore passed on through oral, unofficial channels, and we nostalgically transmit recipes for more natural care of the human body and its ailments.

Human beings want both to be believed and to be understood, but usually not at the same time and not by the same people. Individuals want their words and their symbols (1) to be believed and accepted and (2) to create reality, a safe common reality that is not limited to the individual alone. The characteristic feature of modern society is not fewer beliefs in supernatural beings but the variety of strong ones we turn to and include in our world for different purposes and at different times, and the variety of the structures of plausibility that buttress them. And, heroic or not, we, like the hero of many folk tales, have no permanent master to guide our steps through all the perils of life.

— MICHEL DESPLAND

In rural Voodoo, the ideal is to serve the spirits as simply as possible because simplicity of ritual is said to reflect real power and the true African way of doing things.

PAGE 702

SYNAGOGUE

The term *synagogue,* derived from the Greek *sunagoge* ("assembly"), refers primarily to a congregation rather than to a place of meeting. The origins of the synagogue are shrouded in obscurity. Rabbinic tradition

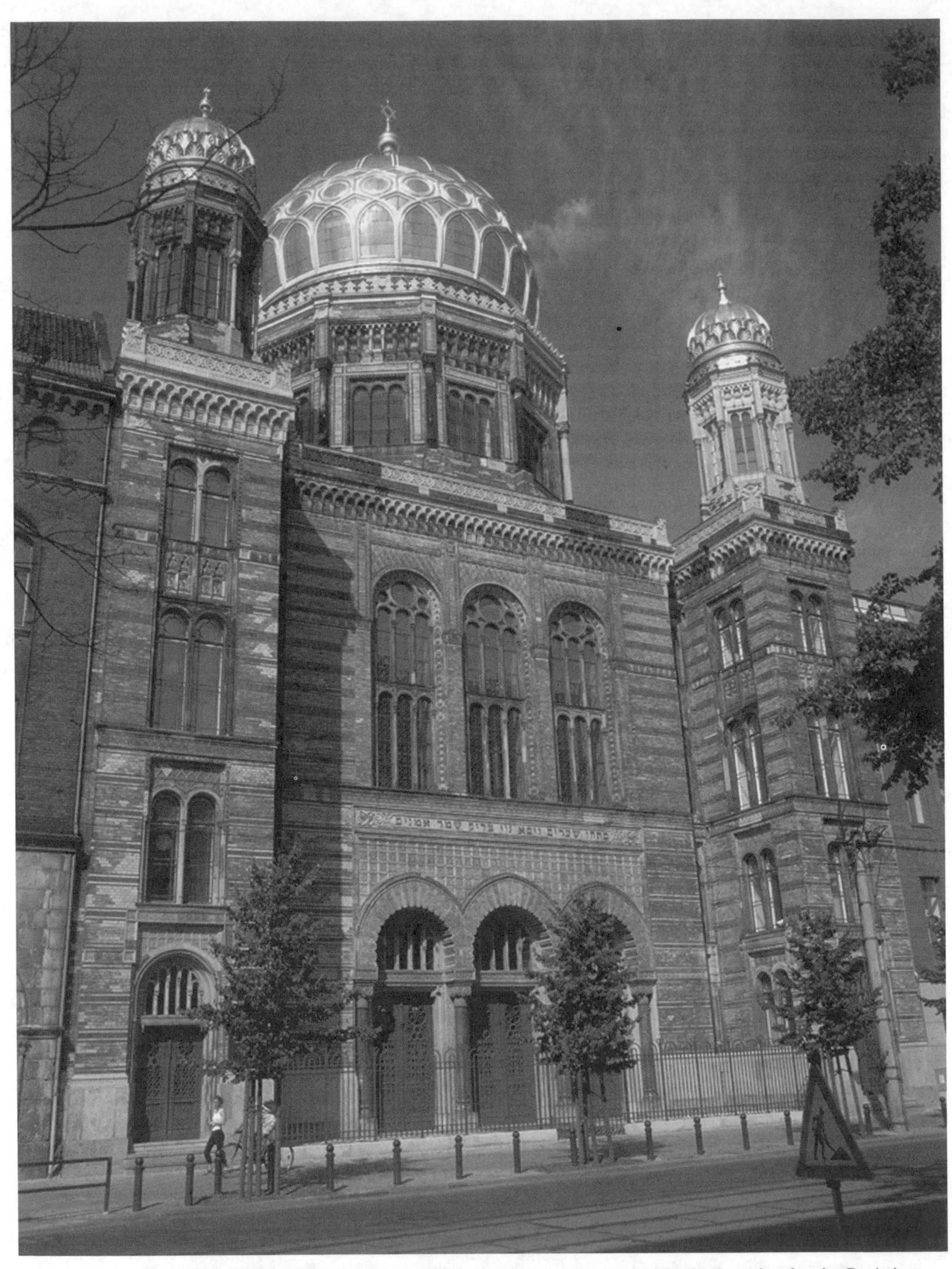

NEUE SYNAGOGE, BERLIN *The term synagogue refers primarily to a congregation rather than a place of meeting. Despite its grandeur, the Neue Synagoge is a humble community of members gathered in a tradition dating back a thousand years.* EYE UBIQUITOUS/CORBIS

attributes its foundation to Moses, yet it is nowhere explicitly mentioned in the Hebrew scriptures, though its existence is sometimes inferred from instances of biblical prayer.

The most venerated explanation traces the synagogue to the Jews taken captive to Babylon in the sixth century BCE. It suggests that in the absence of the Temple, the exiles gathered for worship and spiritual instruction, thereby creating proto-synagogues.

The distinctive nature of the synagogue is best understood in contrast with the Jerusalem Temple. The Temple was a centralized institution. At least from the perspective of its ruling elite, it was the only legitimate Temple. The synagogue, on the other hand, was a decentralized institution. Legitimate synagogues could be established wherever there were enough men to constitute a *minyan* (quorum). The traditional quorum of ten men dates back at least to the first century CE.

It is clear that the synagogue had coexisted with the Temple prior to the Temple's destruction in 70 CE, either as a complement to the Temple or, more likely, as an alternative to it. The Pharisees were lay oriented and critical of the operation of the Temple, both ritually and politically. In its orgins and development, the synagogue coheres with the Pharisees' lay orientation.

Not until the first century CE, well into the period of Pharisaic hegemony, does the synagogue in its present form appear in literary and archaeological evidence. The present practice of three daily worship services (with an additional service [Musaf] on holidays and Sabbaths) was not made obligatory until Gamli'el of Yavneh (c. 83-c. 115), who also regularized the basic order of prayers and gave the Passover Haggadah its classical form.

After the destruction of the Temple, the synagogue was said to have acquired the holiness that had inhered in the Temple, and its prayer service was regarded to have taken the place of the sacrificial service.

THE SYNAGOGUE OF THE ORGANIC COMMUNITY

The synagogue was the central institution in Jewish life during the centuries when, first under the pagan Romans and subsequently under Sasanid, Christian, or Muslim rule, Jews were permitted to live in quasi-autonomous or organic communities. The individual synagogue enjoyed less autonomy in large, centralized areas like Muslim Iberia and more in smaller organic communities like those in European feudal states. But to one degree or another, the synagogue of the organic community, the almost totally self-sufficient Jewish community in which the Talmudic heritage pervaded and guided society, could be found in many places in Europe and in parts of Africa and Asia and elsewhere, well into the twentieth century. In this phase of Jewish history, the synagogue reinforced the basic values which even in the darkness of persecution perpetuated the optimism, morality, creativity, and compassion which traditionally have shaped Jewish life. Socially it was the place where Jews met, commented on events, communicated their needs, planned their charities, adjudicated their disputes, and held their life cycle events. Out of the synagogue emerged the traditional Jewish service organizations, including the *hakhnasat orehim,* for welcoming strangers; *hakhnasat kallah,* for dowering brides; *biqqur holim,* for visiting the sick; and *hevrah qaddisha'* for attending to the dead.

The synagogue was always concerned with education and was often, in smaller communities, the sole locus of learning; among Ashkenazic Jews the synagogue is often called *shul,* a Yiddish word for school, and in Italy *scuola,* the Italian equivalent. Traditionally, the first goal of Jewish education was proficiency in reading the prayer book. The synagogue typically housed popular study groups in Mishnah and Talmud. Through such traditional study, and the discussion of external intellectual challenges as well, the synagogue reinforced the fundamentals of Jewish belief and spurred their more sophisticated formulation.

Psychologically, the synagogue bred respect for the nobility of the individual and the purposefulness of living, reinforcing these sentiments through ritual observances, the bestowing of honors, and liturgical creativity in music and poetry. Further enhancing life were the regular Sabbath and festival sermons, often delivered by resident preachers in the vernacular, including Yiddish for central and eastern Europeans and Ladino for the Sefardim of the eastern Mediterranean.

No less sustaining were the secret synagogues of Jews and prospective Jews, notably the Portugese and Spanish New Christians (Marranos), in areas where Judaism was proscribed. Removed from the mainstream of Jewish life, these secret synagogues developed their own rituals and clergy out of an extraordinary blend of biblical tradition, available to them through the Church, and rabbinic practice known to them only in diminished and garbled form, after the erosion of generations of oral transmission.

THE SYNAGOGUE IN THE MODERN WORLD

By the end of the eighteenth century, two adjectives, "Orthodox" and "Reform," had appeared as designations of the synagogue's polar alternatives. The former described those synagogues that maintained a principled adherence to traditional rituals and theology, the latter those committed to various degrees of change. The adjective "Conservative" emerged before the middle of the nineteenth century to describe commitment

"Make not my Father's house a house of merchandise."

JOHN 2:16

to the historical tradition with some changes but not radical ones. And in the twentieth century, from out of the American Conservative wing has come the Reconstructionist movement whose synagogue rituals are informed by an essentially humanist philosophy.

For all their differences, then, modern synagogues manifest important similarities that distinguish all of them from synagogues of the organic community. The modern synagogue has had to walk a tightrope between change toward assimilation and retention of tradition, all the while remaining mindful of its problematic distinctiveness from the majority culture and of its marginal adherents, whose desire for economic, political, and social acculturation has often occasioned their apathy toward the synagogue and even their defection from it.

Consequently, all modern synagogues have to a greater or lesser extent adjusted traditional attitudes, activities, and articulations. Socially they have espoused the egalitarianism and compassion of the liberal wings of the surrounding culture, clothing them with traditional language, especially that of the biblical prophets. Theologically, they have adopted the prevailing moods of the broader culture, dominantly rational until the late nineteenth century and thereafter increasingly antirational in many religious and some secular circles. They have also dwelt on concepts, like God and covenant, common to the religions in the surrounding cultures even though differently interpreted by them.

Although the modern world has spurred some to flee the synagogue, the impossibility of complete societal acceptance has moved others to synagogue affiliation, particularly in democratic countries.

— MARTIN A. COHEN

T

TAIWANESE RELIGIONS

Taiwan is an offshore island 100 miles southeast of the Chinese mainland. Three groups of people currently inhabit the island: mountain aborigines, Taiwanese natives (themselves originally émigrés from the mainland), and Chinese mainlanders. The mountain aborigines, the earliest inhabitants, migrated from Indochina and the Philippines in prehistoric times. (But some archaeological evidence suggests that the Philippines were inhabited by émigrés from Taiwan.) The Taiwanese natives are the descendants of Chinese who immigrated from South China before the end of World War II. The Chinese mainlanders are the Chinese who fled Mao Tse-tung's forces and took refuge on the island in 1949. Owing to ethnic differences and historical changes, the religions of Taiwan are multifarious and complex. They can best be described in terms of their historical development, which can be divided into five major periods: (1) the prehistoric period, before 1622 CE, (2) the period of Dutch and Spanish rule, 1622-1661, (3) the period of Koxinga and Manchu rule, 1661-1895, (4) the period of Japanese rule, 1895-1945, and (5) the modern period, 1945 to the present.

PREHISTORIC PERIOD. The island of Taiwan was originally connected to the Chinese mainland. Many archaeological artifacts on Taiwan can thus be linked to those on the Asian continent. It has been hypothesized that during Neolithic times (c. 3000-2000 BCE) Oceanic Negroids brought in horticulture from Southeast Asia, followed by Mongoloids with millet from northern China, and Indochinese with Bronze Age culture. About 300 BCE a Megalithic and Iron Age culture was introduced by peoples from the Philippines. The descendants of these ethnic groups have survived and now dwell mainly in the mountain regions. Known collectively as the mountain aborigines, they are divided into ten tribes: Atayla, Saisiat, Banun, Tsou, Rukai, Paiwan, Puyuma, Ami, Yami, and the Plains (or Ping-pu).

Each of these tribes has its own language and culture, and so it is rather arbitrary to generalize about their traditional practices and religion, but certain common elements do exist. While some of these groups are matrilineal and others are patrilineal, all tend to feature a hierarchy based on kinship and role. The chieftain, normally chosen from the eldest male members of the family with the most ancient lineage, plays the role of tribal chief and high priest. The medicine man and woman, who conduct shamanic rituals of healing, divination, exorcism, and magic, are next to the chief in prestige. The House of Ancestral Spirits, built at the center of the clan village, is used for communal worship of the tribal ancestors. The "public house," or "men's house," is for the administration of community affairs. The "youth house" is for the education of young people, which is supervised by the chief and elders. All members of society are divided into cooperative groups and perform various community functions such as field work, hunting, warfare, construction, and preparation for ceremonies.

The mountain tribes have a very rich collection of myths, legends, and genealogies. Myths of creation, the origin of man, celestial phenomena, gods and spirits, culture heroes, and sacred animals are popular among all the tribes. Many myths have etiological motifs identifying the sacred origins of cultural events and ritual actions. Besides these myths, fairly extensive legends and genealogies of tribal history and geography have been preserved. Rites of passage are common to all tribes and are normally observed by all members of the society. Communal rites of opening up the land, sowing and planting, weeding and purification, picking the first crop, harvest, and thanksgiving are observed by all the tribes. Rites of animal hunting and head-hunting are conducted on special occasions. During the rituals, myths are recited and mythic events are reenacted to strengthen the people's sense of identity and harmony with their environment.

The mountain aborigines were able to maintain their traditional culture and religion intact until the arrival of the Dutch, Spaniards, and Chinese in the seventeenth century. Their attitude toward foreigners was alternately hostile and conciliatory. The plains tribes, who lived on the western coastal plains, were conciliatory to the Dutch and Spanish and to their Christian missions. Many of them accepted Christianity, and others were influenced by Chinese religion. However, the remaining aborigines were hostile to foreigners and engaged in head-hunting to resist foreign intrusion. Their primitive weapons were no match for firearms, however, and they had to withdraw into higher mountain regions for protection.

Life-cycle rituals mark the process of life and death.

PAGE 629

Christian and non-Christian alike have much to teach one another in a manner different from that of the past.

PAGE 455

"All that is comes from the mind, it is based on the mind, it is fashioned by the mind."

THE PALI-CANON

During the period of Japanese rule (1895-1945), the Japanese government tried to introduce Japanese culture and religion to the aborigines, but this came to an end in 1945 when the Japanese withdrew from Taiwan. Since the end of World War II, Christian missionaries have been active among the aborigines. As of the late 1970s almost 90 percent have become Christians and more than seven hundred churches have been built in their villages. Many aborigines have been ordained as ministers. With recent rapid changes in society and culture, it is doubtful that the mountain aborigines will be able to maintain their traditional way of life.

DUTCH AND SPANISH RULE. In the course of establishing new trade with China, the Portuguese discovered Taiwan and named it Ilha Formosa ("the beautiful island"). The Dutch and Spanish followed the Portuguese to the Far East, but when they could not establish trade directly with China, they set up a trade base on the island of Formosa. Thus a colonial government was established in southern Formosa by the Dutch in 1622 and in northern Formosa by the Spanish in 1626. As a part of their colonial policy, the Dutch brought in Protestant missions and the Spanish, Catholic missions. They were able to subdue the plains aborigines and convert them.

In order to build their fortresses and exploit the land, the European colonists hired many Chinese workers from South China. As these workers increased, they began to form their own communities and practice the traditional Chinese religions of Confucianism, Taoism, and Buddhism as well as the folk religion. In 1641 the Dutch were able to take control of northern Formosa from the Spanish and so united its rule. However, Dutch rule of Formosa was brought to an abrupt end by the invasion of Koxinga (Cheng Ch'eng-kung), thus halting Christian missions as well. However, a Dominican mission returned in 1859, and a Presbyterian mission in 1865.

KOXINGA AND MANCHU RULE. In 1661, retreating from the invasion of the Manchus into China, Koxinga, the last loyal general of the Ming dynasty, led his army and navy to invade the island of Formosa and expelled the Dutch. He changed the name of the island to Taiwan ("terraced bay") and made Tainan the capital. Soon massive Chinese migrations to Taiwan from the provinces of Fukien and Kwangtung began. These immigrants opened up new land and pushed the aborigines farther back into the mountain regions. As their towns and cities grew in number, they also built many shrines, temples, and monasteries. Often the temples became the centers of Taiwanese communities.

After Koxinga died suddenly in 1662, his successors were unable to carry out his mission to restore the Ming dynasty in China, and in 1692 the Manchurian navy took over control of Taiwan. During the early rule of the Manchu (or Ch'ing) dynasty, Taiwanese who were still loyal to the Ming revolted against the Manchus. Many secret societies such as the White Lotus Society and the T'ien-ti Society were introduced from China and organized in Taiwan to carry out uprisings. However, as the rebellions were gradually subdued and the welfare of the common people was improved by Manchu administration, the latter period of Manchu rule was peaceable.

The religion of the Taiwanese can be divided into two types, the family cult and the community cult. The family cult, which consists of ancestor worship, worship at the family shrine, and rites of passage, is observed by almost all Taiwanese. The community cults include the state cult, the religions associated with the Confucian shrine, the Buddhist monastery, the Taoist temple, the folk temple, and the individual cults of various religious associations. The state cult was established by the government in order to promote political stability and to provide a place for official ceremonies. Temples were erected in Tainan and other cities to commemorate the achievements of Koxinga. Many Confucian shrines were built with the sponsorship of the government to promote Confucian learning and to commemorate the merits of Confucius and Confucian worthies. Many of the earlier Buddhist monasteries were also built by the government in order to provide a retreat for officials.

Buddhism in Taiwan is divided into monastic Buddhism and lay Buddhism (the Chai religion). Monastic Buddhism, practiced by monks and nuns living in monasteries, is chiefly supported by the government and the elite. Two major schools of monastic Buddhism in Taiwan are Pure Land and Ch'an. While monastic Buddhism is isolated from the common people, lay Buddhism has the widespread support of the populace. Called Chai ("purity") religion because it stresses the purification of the mind and the practice of vegetarianism, it has three branches in Taiwan: the Lung-hua, Chin-chung, and Hsien-t'ien. All claim descent from the Southern Ch'an school of the Sixth Patriarch Hui-neng (638-713). However, elements from Confucian moral teachings, Taoist rites, and folk religious practices can also be seen in all three branches. Each branch is organized into a hierarchy consisting of patriach, instructors, lay leaders, and lay devotees. Lay Buddhists believe in the imminent end of the world and expect the swift coming of the Maitreya Buddha, who will bring them into the new era. Because of their strong eschatological beliefs, they have rebelled from time to time against corrupt government, and, in turn, censorship and oppression of their members have been frequent and harsh.

The religious Taoism founded by Chang Tao-ling during the second century CE in China was brought to Taiwan by Chinese immigrants. There it developed into five major sects: the Ling-pao, Lao-chün, Yü-chia, T'ien-shih, and San-nai. The Taoist priests *(tao-shih)* are divided into two groups, the Black Turbans, who are empowered to celebrate the all-important rite of cosmic renewal *(chiao),* and the Red Turbans, who officiate at a host of lesser popular ceremonials. These priests set up altars in their family shops to serve for both private and communal rites. They worship, among others, the Supreme Originator (Yüan-shih T'ien-ts'un), Lao-tzu, Chang Tao-ling, the North Star, the earth gods *(she),* the gods of the ditch *(ch'eng-huang),* and the god of the hearth (Tsao-kung). As the chief religious functionaries of the Taoist community, the priests have various duties, including exorcism, public ritual for the success of the community, religious instruction, the fabrication of charms and amulets for personal use, and the traditional practices of meditation and internal alchemy prescribed in the various texts of the Taoist canon.

The folk religion of Taiwanese natives is polytheistic and syncretic, its rituals complex, and its temples multifarious. Each temple has its own favorite gods, its own holy days and special ceremonies. The folk temple, supported by the common people and supervised by a trustee from among lay leaders, is very often the center of community affairs both sacred and secular. There are also innumerable voluntary religious associations organized by lay devotees for special purposes. Some of these are affiliated with a folk temple; others have their own meeting places. They choose a favorite deity to worship and conduct special rites. While a majority are primarily concerned with religious matters, some associations turn into secret societies and engage in political struggles. The Society of Heaven and Earth (T'ien-ti Hui) was one of the most active of these. Because of their insurgent activities, secret societies are often branded as heretical by the government and are thus the subjects of harsh repression. However, they always seem to revive at times of crises.

JAPANESE RULE. After China's defeat in the Sino-Japanese War in 1895, Taiwan was ceded to Japan. The Japanese colonial government, intending to make Taiwan a stepping stone in its advance toward Southeast Asia, promoted Japanese education and industries in Taiwan. As part of this attempt to establish cultural dominion over the region, the Japanese introduced State Shinto into Taiwan, and the mountain aborigines and Taiwanese natives were forced to take part in Shinto worship. Sixty-three grand shrines and 116 local shrines were built by the government all over the island. In addition to State Shinto, Shinto sects such as Tenrikyo, Shinpikyo, and Konkokyo, and various Buddhist schools such as Tendai, Shingon, Jodo, Zen, Shin, and Nichiren were also introduced into Taiwan. However, most of their adherents were Japanese immigrants; the sects did not have much following among the Taiwanese people. Under Japanese imperial rule, the leaders of traditional Chinese religions suffered oppression, and many folk temples were closed by the government. After World War II, Japan returned Taiwan to China, and thus Shinto also ended on the island. However, the influences of Japanese Buddhism are still visible in Taiwan.

MODERN PERIOD. After World War II, the traditional religions of Taiwan underwent a strong revival. Many ruined temples were rebuilt, and ceremonial parades and pilgrimages became very popular. Conversion to Christianity continued to take place among the mountain aborigines. In the meantime, because of the Communist takeover of the mainland in 1949 and its initial religious persecutions, many religious leaders were among those who took refuge in Taiwan. These included K'ung Te-cheng, a descendant of Confucius; Yin Shun, an eminent Buddhist abbot; the Thirty-seventh Heavenly Master of Taoism; Lama Kangyurwa Hutukhtu, the nineteenth reincarnation of the Living Buddha of Kangyur monastery; and Archbishop Joseph Kuo and Cardinal Tien of the Roman Catholic church. About twenty thousand Muslims and innumerable Buddhists, Catholics, Protestants, Taoists, and Confucianists came to Taiwan, turning it into a rich showcase of world religions.

In 1982 the following religious associations with significant memberships existed in Taiwan: the Confucian and Mencian Academy, the National Taoist Association, the Buddhist Association of the Republic of China, the Chinese Muslim Federation, the Catholic Archdiocese of Taiwan, the Presbyterian Church in Taiwan and about forty-five other Protestant denominations, and Li Chiao and Hsuan-yüan Chiao, two newly established religions.

[*For further discussion of the origins, thought, and practice of the religious traditions of Taiwanese natives and Chinese mainlanders on Taiwan, see* Chinese Religion; Taoism; Buddhism; *and* Christianity.]

— MILTON M. CHIU

TALMUD

In form, the Talmud is an extended, multivolume elaboration of selected tractates of the Mishnah, but it must be emphasized that the contents of the Talmud go far beyond its ostensible base. No subject of interest to the ancient rabbis failed to find its way into this

The Taoist priesthood is active in Taiwan, supported by the presence of hereditary Celestial Masters from the mainland who provide ordinations and legitimacy.

PAGE 145

The Talmud ("study") is an authoritative compilation of expositions of the law and applications of it to particular circumstances.

PAGE 209

immense body of teaching, and for that reason no question arising in later centuries was deemed outside the range that Talmudic teaching might legitimately claim to resolve. A document that seemed merely to elucidate an older text eventually became the all-embracing constitution of medieval Jewish life.

As noted, the Mishnah supplied the overall format for the Talmud. Like the former, the Talmud is divided into tractates, which in turn are divided into chapters and then into paragraphs. Each phrase of the Mishnah is discussed, analyzed, and applied for as long as the editors of the Talmud have materials to supply; when such materials are exhausted (sometimes after very long and quite wide-ranging digressions), the discussion simply moves on to the next phrase or paragraph. The digressions can be such that one loses track of the Mishnaic passage under discussion for pages at a time, but the Talmud always picks up again from its base text when the next section begins.

ORIGINS AND DEVELOPMENT

Very soon after it began to circulate, the Mishnah of Yehudah ha-Nasi' (compiled c. 200 CE) assumed a central place in rabbinic study. As time went on, the structure and content of the Mishnah—the meaning and the sequence of its paragraphs—determined the manner in which the growing accumulation of rabbinic lore was organized. Non-Mishnaic legal materials (the so-called outside traditions; Aram., *baraitot*) were studied primarily in connection with their Mishnaic parallels, and an entire supplementary collection (Tosefta) that followed the Mishnah's own sequence of orders, tractates, and chapters was compiled. Similarly, post-Mishnaic rabbinic teachings—of law, morality, theology, and so forth—were remembered and discussed primarily as the consecutive study of Mishnaic tractates called them to mind, so that most such teachings eventually came to be linked with one or another specific passage (or, occasionally, several) in the earlier collection.

In this way, great compilations of rabbinic teaching, each in the form of a loose exposition of the Mishnah, came into being. Evidence suggests that various centers of rabbinic study developed their own such collections, though in the end only one overall collection was redacted for the Palestinian centers and one for Babylonia. For several generations, the collections remained fluid. Materials were added, revised, or shifted. Free association led to the production of extended discourses or sets of sayings that at times had little to do with the Mishnaic passage serving as point of departure. Early materials tended to be brief explanations of the Mishnah or citations of parallel texts, but later rabbis commented as much on remarks of their predecessors that were not included in the Mishnah or were subsequent to it as on the Mishnah itself. Numerous recent scholars have seen in the developing tradition two sorts of material: brief, apodictic statements of law and much longer dialectical explanations of the specific laws and their underlying principles. Such discussions in turn eventually gave rise to a new generation of legal dicta, and these in turn provoked new efforts at dialectical complication. Thus the Talmudic tradition grew.

The Hebrew word *talmud* and its Aramaic equivalent, *gemara'*, both mean "study." Each term had other meanings at various times, but in the end *gemara'* came to be the name of the vast Mishnah commentary that had taken shape, and *talmud* the name of the combined text (Mishnah plus *gemara'*) that eventually emerged. The rabbis of the immediate post-Mishnaic period (third to fifth centuries CE) are called amoraim (from the Aramaic *'mr*, "say, discuss"), because their characteristic contribution to the developing tradition was the extended discussion of the Mishnah they produced.

Through a process that can no longer be traced with certainty, the text of the *gemara'* underwent periodic reshaping until finally the two Talmuds as we now know them came into being. It should be emphasized that early rabbinic Torah study was oral, so that the *gemara'* was not so much a fixed text as a more-or-less accepted formulation of accumulated lore. There is therefore no reason to assume that there ever was an authorized "original text" of the Talmud, although there may have been parallel recensions of these collections from the earliest stages of their history preserved in different localities. There is still no altogether accepted standard text, and even the relatively uniform wording of recent centuries has much to do with the eventual predominance of European over Asian and North African Jewry and the standardization that inevitably followed the invention of printing.

THE JERUSALEM, OR PALESTINIAN, TALMUD. The so-called Jerusalem Talmud (Heb., *Talmud Yerushalmi*) is really the work of the rabbinic academies of the Galilee; it was substantially completed by the middle of the fifth century. The Jerusalem Talmud covers the first four orders of the Mishnah with the exception of two tractates (*Avot* and *'Eduyyot*); in the last two orders, only half of tractate *Niddah* has Palestinian *gemara'*. The Jerusalem Talmud is characterized in general by brevity and an absence of editorial transitions and clarifications. Its discussions frequently seem laconic and elliptical and often take the form of terse remarks attributed to one or another amora with no connective phrasing at all between them. Occasionally, however, such comments are built up into a more integrated dialectical treatment, with objections raised and answered, contradictions cited and resolved, and biblical proof texts adduced as the editors see fit.

THE BABYLONIAN TALMUD. According to tradition, the redaction of the Babylonian Talmud (Heb., *Talmud Bavli*) was completed by the amoraim Ashi and Ravina' around the year 500. It is clear, however, that the distinctive features of this Talmud in contrast to the other are the work of several generations of rabbis who came after these authorities and are collectively known as the savoraim (from the Aramaic root *svr*, "consider, hold an opinion"), that is, those who reconsidered the Talmudic text and established its final version. Thanks to the labors of these latter revisers, the Babylonian Talmud is far more thoroughly worked out than the Palestinian. Its arguments are replete with a sophisticated technical terminology for introducing source materials, considering objections and counterobjections, offering refutations and defending against them, and so forth. In addition to their detailed contributions, the savoraim also composed entire sections of the Talmud; in particular, the first extended discussion, at the beginning of many tractates, is attributed to them. In general, the literary superiority of the Babylonian Talmud, its far greater logical clarity, and its considerably larger bulk can be attributed to the savoraim of the sixth and seventh centuries. The Talmud as we now have it did not exist until these had done their work.

While the Jerusalem Talmud treats the entire first order of the Mishnah, the Babylonian Talmud has *gemara'* only for the first tractate *(Berakhot)*, which deals with liturgy; the rest of the order treats agricultural rules that were not considered applicable outside the Holy Land. On the other hand, and harder to explain, the great bulk of the fifth order, which regulates the Temple cult and is not to be found in the Jerusalem Talmud, has very substantial Babylonian *gemara'*. Otherwise, with minor exceptions, the two Talmuds cover the same parts of the Mishnah.

LATER DEVELOPMENTS

Over the several centuries following the appearance of the two Talmuds, the Babylonian Talmud gradually eclipsed the other. This predominance was rationalized by the claim that the Babylonian Talmud was the more recent, so that its editors already knew the Jerusalem Talmud and could include its acceptable teachings in their own work and suppress those portions for any reason found unworthy. In retrospect, however, it is clear that such a claim was part of the propaganda of the Babylonian geonim of the last centuries of the first millennium CE in favor of their own authority and against the rival authority of the rabbis of the Land of Israel. The eventual predominance of the Babylonian Talmud throughout the Diaspora and even in the Land of Israel probably is to be explained through reference to such factors as the relatively stronger ties of the rising communities of North Africa and Spain to Babylonian Jewry and the relatively more severe decline of Palestinian Jewry, especially under the onslaught of the Crusades. Those parts of Europe, especially Italy, that retained strong ties with the community in the Land of Israel apparently maintained a tradition of study of the Jerusalem Talmud, but by the beginning of the second millennium this process had run its course. From then on, "the Talmud" always meant the Babylonian. It was taken for granted that issues of Jewish law should be resolved by reference to the Babylonian Talmud, not the Palestinian, and that the latter could provide rulings only in cases where the Babylonian Talmud was silent or ambiguous.

Once the primacy of the Babylonian Talmud was established, it was continually reinforced. The Babylonian Talmud received more attention. It was studied by more scholars, it became the subject of more and of better commentaries; it was copied more often and more carefully by larger numbers of scribes. The result is that modern scholars have a more solidly established text of the Babylonian Talmud and a more fully developed exegetical tradition with which to work. Modern critical study of the Jerusalem Talmud has much more fundamental analytical and restorative work to accomplish before a reliable and comprehensible text becomes available.

It should be noted as well that the power of the medieval Christian church affected the development of the Talmud in two important ways. Periodic waves of seizure and destruction reduced the number of Talmud manuscripts available in certain parts of Europe. The most important of these waves took place in thirteenth-century France and in Italy at the time of the Counter-Reformation; the last burning of the Talmud occurred in Poland in 1757. Occasionally thousands of copies of the Talmud or of Talmudic digests and commentaries were destroyed at a time. In addition, Jewish efforts to avoid such destruction often led to voluntary or involuntary submission of the Talmud to censorship by church authorities. As a result, much early rabbinic discussion of Jesus or the Christian religion has been lost or must now be recovered from scattered manuscripts.

TALMUDIC RELIGION

Despite its vast size and scope, the Talmud is not without focus. Certain themes and certain styles of argument and discourse strongly predominate in its pages, and as a result both the religion of the Talmudic sages themselves and the forms of Judaism based on the Talmud that flourished during the Middle Ages are more compatible with certain types of spirituality than with others.

THE ROLE OF LAW. Well more than half of the Babylonian Talmud and more than three quarters of

Early on, the geonim, leaders of the Babylonian academies (yeshivot) that produced the Babylonian Talmud, began responding to questions addressed to them by distant Jews.

PAGE 405

Halakhah, in the general sense of the word, is the entire body of Jewish law, from scripture to the latest rabbinical rulings.

PAGE 259

"Whoever destroys a single life is as guilty as though he had destroyed the entire world."

TALMUD.

the Jerusalem Talmud are devoted to questions of law. The Mishnah itself takes the form of a law code, and Talmudic discussions are chiefly concerned with clarifying, extending, and finding new applications for the provisions of Mishnaic law. This concentration on law is related to the ancient rabbis' role in their communities where they usually served as judges, teachers, or public administrators. Rabbinic piety came to be organized around gratitude for the law and joy in its fulfillment. The law was understood to be a divine gift, and observance of its provisions was seen as the appropriate response to this generosity. To observe the law meant to strengthen one's link to its giver, and in developing the law into a huge accumulation of detailed regulations covering all aspects of day-to-day living, rabbinic teachers were seeking to multiply occasions for strengthening this link. Study of the law was both the highest intellectual activity in which a Jew might engage and also a practical activity designed to further this expansion of opportunity. Enlarging the scope of the law was not felt to be adding to an already heavy burden; on the contrary, it increased the portion of one's life that could be conducted in response to the voice of God.

THE ROLE OF STUDY AND INTELLECT. While the Mishnah looks like a law code, in fact it is probably something other; its numerous unresolved disputes, its sporadic use of biblical proof texts, and its occasional narratives all reflect the value of study as a religious ritual in its own right, and eventually the activity of studying God's law was as important in Talmudic religion as was the content of that study. With respect to Talmudic law, this enhancement of study as religious rite led to the creation of an elaborate set of legal corpora, most of which are identified by the name of the master to whom the discrete opinions in each corpus were attributed. The well-known Talmudic penchant for hair-splitting dialectics reflects the rabbis' concern that each of these sets of teachings be internally consistent on the one hand and significantly different from any other such set on the other. Hence the frequency with which the Talmud records the chains of transmission by which individual sayings were passed on. Hence the steadily growing integration of teachings from widely disparate fields of law into a single web, and the often forced effort to find unifying principles behind teachings that seem to have nothing to do with one another. Hence, as well, the relative lack of personal interest in the personalities of early masters, except, paradoxically, for those few who became the subject of frequently incredible legends.

This intellectual tendency had several important consequences for Talmudic religion. It gave rabbinic studiousness a scholastic tinge that continued to sharpen as later centuries wore on. It made text commentary an important genre of religious literature; a standard edition of the Talmud even today contains several classical commentaries on the page along with the text and many, many more at the back of the volume. Rabbinic intellectualism turned into disciplined argument; the interplay of proof and refutation, into a holy activity. It also gave primacy to the correct formulation of the wording of sacred texts and recitations over the manner or the circumstances in which they were pronounced; this in turn had important effects on Talmudic and post-Talmudic conceptions of prayer, meditation, and inward spirituality.

TALMUDIC LEARNING AND RELIGIOUS AUTHORITY

In the ancient rabbis' view there was a connection between their emphasis on learning and the role of leadership to which they aspired. It was taken for granted that only the Torah, when properly and sufficiently studied and understood, could enable the people of Israel to become the "kingdom of priests and holy nation" (*Ex.* 19:16) that God intended them to be. This in turn meant that only those properly and sufficiently learned in Torah should be allowed to assume leadership over the community, since only such leaders could be trusted to guide the people in a divinely ordained direction.

Inherent in Talmudic and post-Talmudic Judaism is the assumption that Torah learning (once the Talmud was complete, this meant Talmudic learning) is the only proper criterion by which the leaders of the community should be selected. Whenever conditions permitted, rabbis sought to institutionalize their authority over the community. In the early period, this meant reaching an accommodation with the real rulers of the community (e.g., the Roman empire or, in Babylonia, the allegedly Davidic dynasty of the exilarchs). Later, it meant assuring that internal Jewish courts should be dominated by rabbis and that Talmudic law should govern those aspects of life where Jews maintained internal autonomy (marriage and divorce, religious ritual, educational institutions). Although rabbinical authority was not without challengers, it was never overthrown in principle until the breakdown of Jewish self-government, which began in the late eighteenth century and continued into the nineteenth.

TALMUD STUDY AS RELIGIOUS EXPERIENCE

Rabbis saw their own teaching as "oral Torah." They believed the contents of the Talmud represented a part of the revelation to Moses that had been kept oral but faithfully transmitted for centuries before its inclusion in the text of the Talmud. The name *Tal-*

mud, in fact, can be understood as a short form of the common phrase *talmud Torah*, or "Torah study." Thus to study Talmud was in fact to let oneself hear the word of God, and to add to the accumulation of commentaries, digests, codes, and the like was to make one's own contribution to the spread of divine revelation in the world. To learn Torah was thus a kind of sober mysticism, a reliving of the events at Sinai, while to add to the growing body of "oral" law was to share in a divine activity. Already in the Talmud God is depicted as studying Torah several hours a day (B. T., A. Z. 3b), but the kinship between the rabbi and God was felt to be even stronger. By increasing the amount of Torah in the world, the rabbi could do what previously only God had been held able to accomplish.

Thus the text of the Talmud became the center of an activity believed to be the most Godlike available to human experience. Everyone could study some Torah, and no one was considered incapable of adding a few original thoughts to a study session. In this way, Talmud study became a widespread activity among later Jewish communities. The degree of commitment to this activity might vary, from the ascetic twenty-hour-a-day devotion of the closeted scholar to one-hour-a-week popular learning on Sabbath afternoons. The climax of a boy's education was the point at which he was ready to learn *gemara'*. Such "learning" continues even in our own time, even after the functioning authority of Talmudic law has all but disappeared. It represents the most powerful and the longest-lived inheritance of classical Judaism.

— ROBERT GOLDENBERG

TANTRISM

AN OVERVIEW

An objective and scientific assessment of Tantrism is not easy, for the subject is controversial and perplexing. Not only do authorities give different definitions of Tantrism, but its very existence has sometimes been denied. (These uncertainties apply more to Hindu Tantrism than to Buddhist Tantrism.)

The word *Tantrism* was coined in the nineteenth century from the Sanskrit *tantra*, meaning "warp" or "loom," hence a doctrine, and hence again a work, treatise, or handbook teaching some doctrine, though not necessarily a Tantric one. But it so happened that it was in works known as *tantra* that Western scholars first discovered doctrines and practices different from those of Brahmanism and classical Hinduism, which were then believed to be the whole of Hindu religion. These texts also differed from what was known of ancient Buddhism and of Mahayana philosophy. So the Western experts adopted the word *Tantrism* for that particular and for them very peculiar, even repulsive, aspect of Indian religion.

There is no word in Sanskrit for Tantrism. There are texts called Tantras. There is *tantrasastra*: the teaching of the Tantras. There is also the adjective *tantrika* (Tantric), which is used as distinct from *vaidika* (Vedic) to contrast an aspect of the religious-cum-ritual Hindu tradition not with Vedism properly so called but with the "orthodox" non-Tantric Hinduism that continues down to our own day, mostly in private (as opposed to temple) ritual, and especially in the "sacraments" *(samskara)* enjoined on all twice-born male Hindus (the three highest classes).

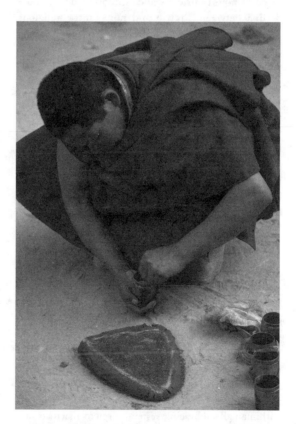

The Tantric tradition thus appears as a revelation differing from that of the Vedas and Upanisads, and especially as having different rites and practices. It is not necessarily opposed to the Vedic tradition, which it often refers to as authoritative, but differs from it in being more adapted than Vedism to the present age of mankind, and in procuring benefits, worldly or nonworldly, that the other cannot give. Tantric Buddhism also opens up new ways and perspectives, but its relationship to the older doctrine is of another kind in that the status of the teaching of the Buddha, for the Buddhists, is different from that of the Veda for the Hin-

Esoteric or Tantric modes of religion also were a significant part of cultural Buddhism in East Asia.

PAGE 95

TANTRIC RITUAL

Ritual is fundamental to Tantrism. All aspects of energy, especially in nature and in the human body, are essential.

CHARLES & JOSETTE LENARS/CORBIS

T

TANTRISM

An Overview

Much of Tantric literature is ritualistic in nature, manifesting Brahmanic influence by the use of incantations (mantra) and the burnt offering (homa).

PAGE 110

dus. But both Hindu and Buddhist Tantrism can be described as reinterpretations, in a new spirit, of their respective traditions.

The complex and ambiguous relationship of Tantrism to Hinduism generally was not realized at first. Even though some scholars perceived that they themselves were partly responsible for the creation of a new category (Arthur Avalon wrote in 1922 that "the adjective *tantric* is largely a Western term"), they believed Tantrism to be limited and specific enough to be conceived of as only a particular, even a rather exceptional, aspect of Hinduism (or of Buddhism). But the progress of research brought the realization that, far from being exceptional, Tantrism was in fact very widespread and indeed the common property of all the religions of "medieval" India.

There is a specific Tantric aspect of Indian religions that, though it is often mixed up inextricably with the rest, does also exist in itself as something more than merely technical and ritual. This appears when one reads the literature, for the texts (Agamas, Tantras, etc.) often distinguish between their teachings and those of non-Tantric, "Vedic" schools. True, the borderline between Tantric and non-Tantric religious groups in Hinduism is difficult to determine clearly; there are common traits on both sides. Still, one can admit Tantrism as a category of its own and define it generally as a practical path to supernatural powers and to liberation, consisting in the use of specific practices and techniques—ritual, bodily, mental—that are always associated with a particular doctrine. These practices are intrinsically grounded in the doctrine that gives them their aim and meaning and organizes them into a pattern. Elements of the doctrine as well as of practices may also be found elsewhere in Indian religions, but when both are associated and welded into a practical worldview, Tantrism is there.

The doctrinal aspect of Tantrism can be summed up, using Madeleine Biardeau's words, as "an attempt to place *kama*, desire, in every meaning of the word, in the service of liberation . . . not to sacrifice this world for liberation's sake, but to reinstate it, in varying ways, within the perspective of salvation." This use of *kama* and of all aspects of this world to gain both worldly and supernatural enjoyments *(bhukti)* and powers *(siddhi)*, and to obtain liberation in this life *(jivanmukti)*, implies a particular attitude on the part of the Tantric adept toward the cosmos, whereby he feels integrated within an all-embracing system of micro-macrocosmic correlations. In Hinduism, these correlations, inherited from the Veda, were further developed in the Upanisads and culminated with Tantrism in a vast theo-anthropocosmic synthesis. This does not apply to Tantric Buddhism, whose philosophy is different, but both Hindu and Buddhist Tantrism share an analogous psycho-mental approach and a number of common practices, all grounded in the idea of using cosmic energy—especially as it is present in the "subtle body" within the adept's physical one—for transcendental ends, where the attainment of supernatural powers is inseparable from progress toward final release. The conception of energy, *sakti*, is not the same in the two religions, but still, just as the illuminated Buddhist realizes the equivalence of *samsara* and *nirvana*, so the Hindu Tantric, on attaining liberation in life, will enjoy this world while being free from it because he has realized the true nature of the supreme reality: the realization, the *coincidentia oppositorum*, is of the same type and is in both cases reached through a reversal of some of the traditionally accepted forms of conduct.

There is also in both religions an extraordinary multiplicity of practices, mental, physical, and ritual, in which rites and yoga are inseparable. This ritual proliferation is all the more remarkable as the Buddha expressly condemned all rites and as, in Hinduism, those who renounce the world for salvation are supposed to forsake all ritual. Here, on the contrary, ritual is fundamental. Equally characteristic is a proliferating pantheon, with a marked insistence on terrifying deities whose role is largely linked to the adept's use of the "lowest" or more "dangerous" human tendencies: lust, anger, and the like. This is found in the *krodhavesa* (possession by frenzy) of Kalacakra Buddhism, as well as in several antinomian practices of Hinduism. Sexual practices also (which, though important and characteristic, are not the main element in Tantrism) are to be understood in terms of the harnessing of "lower" impulses for "higher" aims. The impulse is here all the more important because it repeats at a human level the activity of the divine couple, whose creative bliss is echoed and possibly even reproduced by the human pair.

The essential role of all aspects of energy, especially in nature and in the human body, may explain the place in Tantrism of traditional medicine and still more of alchemy, which occupies an important place in all Tantric literature, both Buddhist and Hindu.

Tantrism, Buddhist as well as Hindu (and Jain, as there is also a Jain Tantrism, or Tantric elements in Jainism), insists on the role of the spiritual master, a role linked to the emphasis on initiation and secrecy. A Tantric adept is necessarily the initiated disciple of a master and must keep the teaching secret (hence the obscurity of most Tantric texts). This is linked to the sectarian aspect of Tantrism and may help to explain why Tantrism, in all religions, seems always to have been a matter of small groups, of "active minorities," to use Louis Renou's phrase, which usefully suggests the contrast between, on the one hand, the small number of Tantric initiates together with the secrecy imposed upon them, and, on the other hand, the enormous impact of Tantrism on all Indian religions and the mass of its textual and artistic production. But Tantrism, however carefully one may attempt to trace and define it, remains in many respects a puzzle to the scientific mind.

— ANDRÉ PADOUX

HINDU TANTRISM

Tantrism may be briefly characterized as a practical way to attain supernatural powers and liberation in this life through the use of specific and complex techniques based on a particular ideology, that of a cosmic reintegration by means of which the adept is established in a position of power, freed from worldly fetters, while remaining in this world and dominating it by union with (or proximity to) a godhead who is the supreme power itself. All practices and notions constituting the Tantric way correspond to a particular conception of the deity, polarized as masculine and feminine, and of the universe and man, both imbued with this divine power. Thus it may be said that, for a Tantric adept, the quest for liberation and the acquisition of supernatural powers result from a tapping, a manipulating of this ubiquitous power.

HISTORY. The history of Hindu Tantrism is impossible to write owing to the scarcity of data, especially for the earlier period. Little epigraphical evidence is available, and there are few datable ancient manuscripts, whereas many texts are still awaiting study. Most likely, a number of works remain to be discovered. Moreover, the dates of formation of Tantric groups, sects, or schools and their interrelationships are usually obscure.

The origin of Hindu Tantrism certainly goes back to an ancient store of beliefs and practices. Some sources are to be found in the Vedas (the *Atharvaveda* and *Yajurveda* notably, on magic and the role of speech or phonetic practices), in the Aranyakas and Brahmanas, and in the earlier Upanisads. This Vedic esotericism was modified and further developed by the adjunction of other elements belonging to autochthonous cults, perhaps Dravidian, certainly an ancient fund whose existence is presumed rather than known. But although we cannot precisely define this fund, we may safely surmise that it existed and played a role in the rise of Hindu Tantrism. Despite these autochthonous and perhaps "popular" roots, Hindu Tantrism cannot be considered a popular form of religion in contrast to a "higher," non-Tantric Hinduism. Indeed, the fact that the main texts are in Sanskrit, and that learned brahmans are among the authors, proves the role played by Brahmanic circles, or at least by the higher castes. Tantrism, in fact, like the whole of Hinduism, has always been divided into practices for the higher and the lower castes. And though renunciates, ascetics, and saints did play an important part in its genesis and development, the fact that these people were on the margins of the Hindu social system does not mean that they were popular figures, still less revolutionaries. Socially speaking, Tantrism, even if theoretically equalitarian (in principle, all, once initiated, have access to its teachings, irrespective of caste or sex), is conservative. Its equalitarianism, like that of *bhakti*, has a ritual, religious scope, not a social one.

Granted that the history of Hindu Tantrism cannot yet be written, the following brief statements may be made:

1. There was no Tantrism in Vedic and Brahmanic times, but merely elements that later evolved and became part of Tantrism. References to the Vedic tradition in Tantric texts must not be taken as proof either of the "Vedic" nature of Tantrism or of direct links with the Veda. Quite likely such references were introduced later to facilitate the acceptance of Tantric texts or sects by orthodox circles.
2. Tantrism as such must have taken shape during the first centuries CE following an internal evolution of Brahmanism: a change whose cause and form escape us, but that can fairly reasonably be attributed in part to an influence of autochthonous elements.
3. Even if the oldest datable documents are Buddhist (they are Chinese, not Indian), Hindu Tantrism, in all likelihood and for several reasons, surely preceded Tantric Buddhism, even if both later interacted.
4. Tantrism appears well established in Hindu India from at least the sixth or seventh century CE. The Gangdhar stone inscription (424 CE) proves that Tantric deities were already worshiped in the fifth century, a period to which some Agamas may possibly belong.

The sixth century and those following were the great creative period during which Hinduism—Puranic and Tantric—took shape.

Texts of all sorts, temples, ritual implements, and works of art continued to be produced until the eighteenth century, testifying to the vitality of Hindu Tantrism. It has been remarked that during this period the texts appear to come more and more from Brahmanic official circles. This may be proof of an increasing hold by Tantrism on the traditional centers of Hindu culture and learning. The steady flow of production, textual or otherwise, has continued until the present, but has yielded little of worth. Practically all ritual manuals and booklets on the practice of *puja* now

From its start Tantrism represented a style and outlook that placed the Goddess at the center of its "extensions."

PAGE 286

T

TANTRISM

Hindu Tantrism

sold in India reflect influences of the Tantric cult. This is not surprising, considering that postmedieval sectarian Hinduism has incorporated many of the ideas and practices of Tantrism. Accordingly, much of the Hindu pantheon is composed of Tantric deities. We must note, however, that the majority of sectarian Hindus using these publications do not regard themselves as Tantrists.

Effective practice by Tantric believers has not disappeared from India. In fact, in recent years, with the interest evinced in the West for Tantrism, and with a change in mental attitude among many Indians, a somewhat larger number of people (not only in Bengal) admit to being Tantric. Some periodicals and many books are published on the subject. Some Tantric and Sakta centers are openly active as such, in addition to the other traditional Tantric groups—no doubt more authentic and effective if less publicized. Hindu Tantrism obviously remains a matter of small groups, but their importance is far from negligible.

Tantric practice (sadhana) addresses itself to experiencing the unity of purusa and prakrti (purusa being both "soul" and deity, prakrti being both "matter" and Goddess).

PAGE 286

Yet despite the prevalence of Tantric ideas and practices in Hinduism, it is unlikely that they ever concerned the majority of Hindus. Tantrics produced an enormous mass of doctrinal, ritual, and technical texts. They elaborated or at least influenced most of the Hindu ritual, both public and, to a lesser extent, private. Their imprint on traditional arts, techniques, and activities was also important (temples are still being built, adorned, and furnished with implements in accordance with the teachings of the Agamas). In all likelihood, however, most Hindus who practiced or attended such rituals, or visited such temples, were not Tantric.

GEOGRAPHY. It is difficult to situate the dual Indian root—Vedic and autochthonous—of Tantrism in any precise area of India, still less in some region beyond the subcontinent. China, Tibet, and even the Middle East have been suggested as possible places of origin of Tantric ideas, or as having exerted a significant influence on them, but no convincing evidence has been put forward to substantiate this. Admittedly, the frontier areas of Indian civilization, such as Kashmir (or Swat) and Bengal-Assam, have been among the main centers of Tantrism. But so has Kerala. So were also regions such as Madhya Pradesh and Orissa (where the few surviving temples to the Yoginis are to be found and where cults to the Goddess still seem very active). Among the non-Aryan elements that contributed to the shaping of Hindu Tantrism, some may have come from the shamanic cultures of Central Asia. The importance of the Himalayan region in the subsequent history of Tantric Hinduism, as proved by the cults still practiced there, by the civilization of Nepal, and by the numerous Tantric manuscripts from these parts necessarily implies an influence of the cultures of these northern border regions, but their real impact is not easy to assess.

On the other hand, Tantric Hinduism spread beyond India, especially in Cambodia, as attested by important iconographic and epigraphic evidence. The Sdo-Kak-Thom inscription of 1052 CE, for example, mentions several Tantras as having been introduced into Cambodia in the early ninth century. Tantric practice based on Tantric texts is still followed in Bali.

SECTARIAN VARIATIONS. Tantrism is essentially sectarian. It has always been divided into sects, mutually exclusive and sometimes hostile. The rare religious persecutions in Hindu India were perpetrated by Tantrics. The divisions differ according to the deities worshiped and the ritual practices followed. In this respect, the spirit of Tantrism is opposed to that of *bhakti*, although it, too, possesses the element of devotion.

The main division of sects is made between worshipers of Visnu (Vaisnavas), of Siva (Saivas), and of the Goddess (Saktas), the last two groups being sometimes difficult to distinguish clearly, if only because Siva and Sakti are metaphysically inseparable and therefore necessarily conceived, even in temples, in some relationship. There are also, or have been, Sauras (worshipers of Surya, the Sun) and Ganapatyas (worshipers of Ganapati, or Ganesa). Among Vaisnavas, the main group is that of the Pañcaratra, although it does not consider itself Tantric nowadays. At least one other and more extreme group from Bengal, the Vaisnava-Sahajiyas, must be mentioned, with their peculiar erotic mysticism, a related modern form of which can be found with the Bauls.

Saiva or Sakta sects are unquestionably Tantric. Among them were such groups as the Kapalikas and Kalamukhas, or the Nathas, a notable Saiva group that transgresses the limits of Hinduism. Most important is the Kula (or Kaula) sect, also found in Buddhism and divided into several subgroups, but its precise nature and scope (sect or school? Saiva or Sakta?) are difficult to assess. The classification into Saiva and Sakta groups is generally a difficult matter, for several traditional divisions exist, corresponding to different criteria and impossible to reconcile with one another. Divisions are made between "currents" *(srotas)*, usually three—"right" *(daksina)*, "left" *(vama)*, and "accepted" *siddhanta)*—although sometimes five srotas are mentioned; or between "remembrances" *(amnayas)*, from five to seven in number; or between "doctrines" or "convictions" *(matas)*, corresponding to the methods of worship or to the main deity, for example Kubjika, Tripura, Kali. There is also a more doctrinal division into "teachings" *(sastras)*, such as Pratyabhijña, Spanda, and Krama of Kashmir Saivism, or Kula and Vamakesvara. But these classification terms are often used loosely. Kula, for instance, is indifferently called *mata*, *sastra*, or *amnaya*. There exists also a "geographical" division into "steps" *(krantas)*, and, finally, the well-known division into "conducts" *(acaras)*: *vama* and *daksina*, "left" and "right," to which is sometimes added *samaya*. The overall picture is confusing. Further research may perhaps clarify it, although there always were, and still are, isolated ascetics or small groups that do not fit into any classification.

DOCTRINES. There is no coherent body of Hindu Tantric doctrine. It varies according to sect or school. Some ideological features, however, coupled with particular practices, are characteristic. Agamas, Tantras, and Samhitas are not philosophical works. Even when they include a "section on knowledge," which one would expect to treat doctrinal matters, one seldom finds there a complete and well-defined system. Some Tantric authors, especially those from Kashmir, did write metaphysical works, but they were of different persuasions, hence the absence of a unified doctrine. Tantric ideology, furthermore, is not original nor does it differ completely from that of non-Tantric Hinduism: it comes from the same source, being largely made up of elements from the classical Indian systems (the Darsanas). Tantric linguistic or metalinguistic speculations depend on those of the Mimamsa. The cosmology is based on the categories *(tattvas)* of the Samkhya. There are also elements of Yoga. Tantric metaphysics are of a Vedantic type: dualist, semidualist, or nondualist, though mostly the last, which is more adapted to the Tantric conception of man and the cosmos. If, however, Tantrism has not been very inventive, it has given new meanings to old notions and organized them into a new pattern.

Regarding Tantric doctrine itself, the following remarks may be made. Although the Ultimate transcends all duality, the Godhead is conceived as having two aspects, masculine and feminine, whose conjunction, described as a sexual union, is the first and necessary step, within God, toward cosmic evolution, the active principle being the feminine. In Sakta sects, where the main deity is the Goddess, the feminine element clearly predominates, but in all sects it is energy, *sakti*, which produces, pervades, sustains, and finally reabsorbs the universe. She (Sakti) is thus the ultimate cause of human bondage and liberation. She is *maya*, cosmic illusion, but is also equated with God's grace, which is sometimes characteristically called *saktipata*, "descent of energy" into the world. Man's response to grace is devotion, *bhakti*, which plays an important role in many Tantric schools. Though the spirit of Tantrism is in many ways opposed to that of bhakti, both can be reconciled and are even promiscuously associated by the Vaisnava-Sahajiyas.

The energetic process giving rise to the world is one of emanation. It is the outward manifestation, the shining forth, of what exists potentially in the Godhead, starting from the first principle and ending with this world, by a transformation, a condensation, from subtle to gross through a series of stages or cosmic categories (the *tattvas*). These usually number thirty-six, but the count is sometimes more or less, as the *tattvas* added to those twenty-five of the Samkhya are not exactly the same in all Tantric schools. The Pañcaratra has its own system of the unfolding *(vyuha)* of creation from the supreme Lord, Visnu. In such systems, there is no discontinuity in the cosmic process: a stir, an imperceptible movement, appears within the Absolute and is then transmitted to the lowest levels of creation. When cosmic resorption sets in, the process is reversed and flows back to its source. *Maya*, in this perspective, is less the great illusion than the mainspring of the infinite diversity of the world, the play of the gods, who manifest the cosmos in a purely gratuitous way. This element of joy and playfulness *(lila)* may also be found in a non-Tantric context, but is one of the main components of the Hindu Tantric vision. It is especially important in the Krsna cults, and is one of the fields where Tantrism and *bhakti* meet.

With such a philosophy, the Tantric adept feels he lives in a world suffused with divine energy, whose elements, even those apparently the humblest, may be used to gain liberation in this life *(jivanmukti)*, a liberation that is not a renunciation but a realization of the plenitude of the world. The Tantric system of micro-macrocosmic correspondences is inherent in this conception. The divine cosmic energy is the *prana*, the cosmic "breath" symbolized especially by *kundalini*, which is the Goddess in her cosmic play and as present in the subtle body of man. Divine energy is also the word *(vac)* or sound *(sabda)*. This is very important, as Tantric practices related to the uses of the sounds of language play an essential role. *Vac* is a fundamental aspect of energy, both the most powerful and effective and the most usable. Some Tantric schools, especially in Kashmir, have worked out a complex cosmogony whereby all levels of the cosmos are manifested just as the letters of the Sanskrit alphabet appear within the deity in their grammatical order. A particular way to liberation corresponds to this phonetic process.

With the universal pervasion of energy, the quest for liberation necessarily involves the use of this power. Consequently, the possession of supernatural powers *(siddhi)* is a normal result of this quest, when successful. Even if the adept does not use them and concentrates on final release, these powers are there. Fully merged in the deity (in nondualist sects), the adept naturally partakes of all divine powers. This adept—often called sadhaka ("efficient, skillful")—does not necessarily look for salvation. He may seek enjoyment

"If the radiance of a thousand suns were to burst forth at once in the sky, that would be the splendor of the Mighty One (Krishna)."

BHAGAVAD GITA II:I2

(perhaps the most normal case, in fact), or he may look for both. All three are legitimate aims for three different types of adepts, though supernatural attainments are always essential.

PRACTICES. Practice is the main aspect of Tantrism. The most characteristic practices are those associated with the use of sacred and ritual formulas, *mantras* and *bijas* (phonic "germs"). These linguistic or phonetic elements—sentences, words, letters, sounds—symbolize spiritual entities and are believed to embody the very power of the main deity. Such formulas are used at all times and in all types of Tantric practice, initiatic and religious rites as well as usual duties or activities. There is no life for a Tantric adept (nor of any Hindu, but this is a Tantric trait) without *mantras*. Indeed, *mantrasastra*, the teaching of *mantras*, is often taken as meaning *tantrasastra*, the teaching of the Tantras.

Tantric texts stress that these practices are to be carried out within a circle of adepts and supervised by a male and female pair of "lords of the circle."

PAGE 286

Mantras are often accompanied by diagrams (*mandalas*, *yantras*, or *cakras*); geometrical cosmic symbols used for ritual and meditation. Symbolic gestures *(mudras)* expressing metaphysical or theological concepts are also used in most ritual practices.

Mantras, *yantras*, and the like must be assimilated spiritually by the adept and put into practice by way of a complex and often long process that is usually both physical and mental. Such are the *mantrasadhana* serving to master a *mantra* and the practices of Tantric yoga. These depend on the Tantric conception of sakti and micro-macrocosmic correlations. They usually consist in awakening, with the help of *mantras*, the *kunda lini* energy that lies dormant, coiled like a (female) serpent in the subtle body of the adept, and leading her up to the point where she unites with the Supreme while the adept merges into the Ultimate. This is done through *hathayoga* methods combining bodily postures and control of breathing with mental exercises leading ultimately to *samadhi* (enstasis) and realization of the essence of the *mantra* and of the deity. Mental exercises are mainly *dhyana*, which here means precise visualizations of the centers of the subtle body (the *cakras*) and of deities residing within or without them. The main and highest means to such a goal is *bhavana*, an intense meditation that brings into existence the subject of meditation: a deity, a cosmic entity, a state of consciousness. All this results in spiritual union with a deity, identification of the individual's mind and body with cosmic entities, and physical and mental integration into the cosmos. There is thus a "mystical physiology" that "cosmizes" the body, as well as a "mystical geography," traditional places of pilgrimage being integrated within. The resulting transformation of the body image changes the attitude of the adept to himself and to the world.

The assignment of various parts of the body, physical or subtle, to *mantras* and other entities in order to divinize them, follows a ritual technique using *dhyana*, *mantra*, and *mudra*, called *nyasa* ("setting down, placing"). Mantras are used for every goal, whether mystical, magical, or ritual. They are used in ritual curing in Tantric medicine (still practiced now) or for alchemy (important in Tantrism) or astrology.

Among the powers of a Tantric adept are the "six actions" *(satkarmani)* whereby it is possible, with *mantras* and rites, to appease, fascinate, bind, drive away, create enmity, kill, and so on. However typical of Tantrism magic may appear to be, it is not by far its main aspect. Nevertheless, in modern India especially, Tantrics are commonly considered magicians or sorcerers and are mostly disapproved of. This is also largely due to the antinomian practices to which they sometimes resort. Tantric doctrine justifies the use of all aspects of life to attain salvation or powers. Hence the use of physical and mental techniques to deviate cravings and impulses—especially the sexual impulse—toward different aims. Hence the use of alcoholic beverages, which enhances energy and shows that the adept transcends normal rules. Hence also repulsive or frightening practices that prove the Tantric is above fear and disgust and is able to use the lowest objects for the highest aims. However, though these practices are part and parcel of Hindu Tantrism, their importance should not be exaggerated. All practices are acted in a ritual context. The whole of Hindu life, in fact, is ritualized, and this ritual is either Tantric or tantricized. This is particularly true of the worship or cult *(puja)* of divinities.

The Tantric *puja* is not only the worship of a god or goddess. It is the transformation (played out rather than mystically effected) of the worshiper into that deity—a transformation deemed indispensable, for "only a god may worship a god." Several rites lead to this "change of ontological status." *Dhyana*, *mantra*, *nyasa*, and *mudra* transform the worshiper's body into a divine one. A "purification of the elements" *(bhutasuddhi)* and a replacement of the limited self *(atman)* by that of the deity are undergone. This is followed by an "inner sacrifice" *(antaryaga)*, an exercise in Tantric yoga whereby the deity is experienced as being present in the adept's body and all the customary services of the cult are imagined and visualized as offered to it there. Then comes the "external" worship. This may be done with an image, although a diagram may be preferred. First it is drawn according to ritual; then the main deity and attendant deities are visualized and mentally placed on the diagram and are instilled with the *prana* that will make them fit for worship. This "breath" or energy is often conceived as springing from the heart of the previously deified worshiper. *Nyasa* (there can be up to thirty series of *nyasas* in a *puja*), *dhyana*, and repetitions of *mantras (japa)* are used. Yoga and mantric practices are integral parts of Tantric worship.

Not always present but typical is the use of the "five elements" *(pañcatattva)* in this worship: alcohol, meat, fish (the second and third elements imply animal sacrifices), *mudra* (usually parched grains), and sexual intercourse *(maithuna)*. The first four items are offered to the deity, then partaken of by the worshiper. The last one is, or can be, a ritual sexual union with a woman previously initiated and "transformed" by *nyasa* and such rites. This may also take place in a collective worship called cakrapuja, "cult made in a ring," where the rite is performed by participants arranged in a ring, in pairs of male and female. This is considered very secret and is reserved for higher initiates. A woman or girl may also be worshiped *(kumaripuja)* as a form of the Goddess, with or without sexual union. The female organ *(yoni)* is in such case equated with the Vedic altar on which the male seed is the offering. Another "secret" worship is done with a corpse. It is used to achieve particular goals, usually evil. *Pujas* made with a special intent *(kamyapuja)* may be used for black magic (especially the "six actions") but can also serve any other end, good or bad: *sakti* as such has no moral connotation. Though sexual symbolism is encountered everywhere and magic is part of the Tantric vision, none of these rites is a compulsory part of Tantric practice.

PANTHEON. Several features of the Hindu pantheon (which has continued to evolve throughout the centuries) are Tantric in form or nature. No complete and systematic study of the Tantric pantheon, as distinct from the epic and Puranic ones, seems to have been carried out so far. Nevertheless, it can be said to be marked by a proliferation of deities emanating from a main supreme god—Visnu, Siva, the Goddess—in a complex hierarchy wherein feminine entities are especially numerous and even predominant, as befits a system in which the whole cosmic process is the work of the feminine energy *(sakti)* in her different forms. The importance in Hinduism of terrifying deities may also be attributed to Tantric influence. The myths and legends of these deities, particularly those of the Goddess in her various aspects, are present in a considerable part of the Tantric texts.

Deities are all the more numerous as the main gods have several forms and secondary divinities sometimes emanate from them in long series. Even the attributes, qualities, or aspects of the different deities are divinized. Siva, for instance, has various aspects and names: Sadasiva, Bhairava, Mahesvara, Kamesvara, and so on. He is said to have five "faces," each being also a divine form. He holds at least four attributes or "weapons" and has six "limbs"; all are deified. The energies emanating from him through Sakti, starting with Vama, Jyestha, Raudri, and Ambika (there are still others), are goddesses, who engender other deities. Entities can thus multiply almost indefinitely. Similarly, a number of divinities emanate from Visnu through the agency of his *sakti*, starting with the four *vyuhas*: Vasudeva, Samkarsana, Pradyumna, and Aniruddha. He, too, has Tantric forms, such as Hayagriva. The main aspect of Siva in the Agamas is Sadasiva; in the Tantras, it is Bhairava. A curious composite form of Surya (the sun god) and Visnu is Martanda-Bhairava. In the Agamas and Tantras, Surya is a form of Siva. Ganesa is also important in the Tantric pantheon.

The Goddess, omnipresent in higher as in "popular" Hinduism, appears under several forms and names. Her nature being ambivalent, some forms are benevolent, such as Gauri, Uma, and Parvati; others are terrifying, such as Durga or Kali. She is worshiped as supreme goddess under several names: Tripura, Kubjika, Malini, and others. As the *sakti* of Visnu or Narayana, she is Sri or Laksmi. She is also manifested in many other ways, all of which constitute forms, or her "emanations" (i. e., like rays emanating from the sun), at different levels of cosmic energy. Her various cosmic activities are accomplished through these aspects, some of which can be her supreme form in certain schools. Such are the sixteen *nityas*, one of which is Tripurasundari, the main deity of the Tripura school. Or the ten Mahavidyas: Kali, Tara, and others. In the Krama school, there exists a "wheel" of twelve Kalis in charge of the different cosmic processes. Mention should also be made of the Mothers (Matr) numbering seven, eight, or nine. The fifty "Little Mothers" (Matrka) are deities of the Sanskrit phonemes over which preside also the eight Mothers. There are usually sixty-four Yoginis, powerful and often terrible, forming a circle, or circles, around Siva or Bhairava. Their number varies, however, sometimes reaching 640 million. All these are found in Saiva and Sakta contexts, but very similar deities or divinized forms of energy playing analogous cosmic roles exist in the Pañcaratra.

There are corresponding hierarchies for male gods, if only because in Tantric Hinduism deities always come in couples, so as to be able to create. This abundance sometimes results from the division of one entity into several others. Such, for instance, is the case of the eight Bhairavas (Asitanga, Ruru, Unmatta, etc.), who, together with Siva, are often associated with the nine Durgas (Navadurga). The Rudras (gods of Vedic origin, in fact), who normally number ten or eleven, can also be fifty and then become male deities of the alphabet, coupled with the Matrkas. There are also 118 Rudras. The Ganas, or Ganesas, headed by Ganesa or Vinayaka, elephant-headed gods, are associated, together with their *saktis*, with the fifty *pithas*, the places of pilgrimage marked by the parts of the dismembered body of Sati, Siva's consort. The Ganas are

The "three forms" of the Absolute: Brahma the creator, Siva the destroyer, and Visnu the preserver.

PAGE 283

also associated with the Sanskrit phonemes, which are also linked with fifty Visnus. Although the *mantras* (sometimes said to number seventy million) are primarily ritual and mystical formulas, they are also considered gods, and then Lords of Mantras (Mantresvara) and Great Lords (Mantramahesvara) are added to the pantheon. Also divinized are the ritual gestures *(mudras)* or the supernatural powers *(siddhis)* and even the three daily acts of worship *(sandhyas)*. All these entities are often said to be distributed in concentric rings (especially in cosmic diagrams such as the *sri-cakra*) surrounding in hierarchical order the main deity at the center. A host of godlings, spirits, demons, ghosts (*pisaca, vetala, preta, bhuta*), and the like play inferior but not unimportant roles in the religious and still more in the magical beliefs and practices of Tantric Hinduism.

— ANDRÉ PADOUX

The other major early book devoted to discussing the Tao behind all things is the early third-century BCE *Tao-te ching (The Way and Its Inner Power).*

PAGE 134

TAOISM

It is no easy task to define Taoism, for throughout its history this philosophical and religious system assumed very different aspects. The period of the Warring States (403-221 BCE) produced a wide variety of philosophical currents, an obvious source of embarrassment for the philologists and bibliographers of the Han dynasty (202 BCE-220 CE), who set themselves the task of ordering this abundant literature. In contrast to the Confucian classics, the writings of the "hundred philosophers" were not easy to classify.

Ancient thinkers were not always aware of belonging to any specific school. Rather, the classification of ancient writings into various ill-defined schools was mainly the work of Han scholars. The philosophers classified under the rubric "Taoist school" (Tao-chia) formed rather small circles comprising a master and a limited number of disciples. Since most of the writings of these Taoist circles were lost, the Taoism of that (the pre-Ch'in) era is essentially represented by the teachings expounded in the *Tao-te ching,* attributed to Lao-tzu, and the *Chuang-tzu,* so named for its putative author.

FORMATIVE CONCEPTS

It has become customary to distinguish the Taoism of the philosophers of the fourth and third centuries BCE from the religious Taoism that presumably appeared in the second and third centuries of our era. In Chinese the former is call Tao-chia (Doka in Japanese) and the latter, Tao-chiao (Dokyo). This distinction was often accompanied by a value judgment wherein much profundity was attributed to the philosophical authors, while religious Taoism was perceived as a mixture of superstition and magic. Recent studies have attempted to rectify this relatively simplistic view. The complex development of religious Taoism gave birth to numerous "schools" or currents, which were in general rather open, despite the esoteric character of their teachings.

In its development, religious Taoism did not break with the fundamental conceptions of the philosophers, although it remains true that these concepts were much transformed. The various Taoist currents shared the quest for longevity, even immortality; it was only their methods that distinguished them.

CONCEPTION OF THE WORLD: MACROCOSM AND MICROCOSM. To understand Taoist theories and practices, one must first understand what the Taoists regarded as the general principles governing the world and man.

According to ancient Chinese cosmology, the world was governed by a set of fundamental notions related to unity and multiplicity, space and time, and microcosm and macrocosm. The concepts of *tao* and *te* were not specific to Taoism but belonged to all currents of Chinese thought. Literally, *tao* means "road," or "way." *Tao* was also the efficacious power of kings and magicians who knew how to make the three spheres of the world—Heaven, Earth, and Man—communicate with one another. In cosmology the *t'ien-tao* ("way of Heaven") was the natural order as it manifests itself through the circulation of the sun and, more generally, through the movement of the celestial vault. The royal *tao (wang-tao)* existed solely for the sovereign in order that he might ritually restore the natural order of heavenly *tao,* which was constantly threatened by disorder. In case of catastrophe such as drought or flood, the sovereign was held responsible and had to expiate either his own sins or those of the world. In this way his virtue (*te* or *tao-te*) was manifested.

Yin-yang and Five Elements. The original meanings of *yin* and *yang* seem to refer to the shaded and sunny slopes of mountains, respectively. Eventually, the two terms came to describe the two antithetical and complementary aspects of the Tao as natural order: a shady aspect and a luminous aspect; a cold, passive aspect and a warm, active aspect; and finally, the feminine aspect and the masculine aspect. The terms are therefore relative classificatory headings only; any one thing can be either *yin* or *yang* in relation to another. These two notions played a fundamental role in all philosophical, scientific, and religious thought. The same applies to the "five elements," or "five phases" *(wu-hsing)* theory as it appeared in the *Hung-fan* (Great Norm), a treatise inserted in the *Shu ching* (Classic of History). Here the elements were presented as related to numbers: (1) water, (2) fire, (3) wood, (4) metal, and (5) earth. These were not merely substances or chemical phenomena but represented instead the principal cosmic forces or influences and classificatory headings. All phenomena—seasons, directions, flavors, foodstuffs, the viscera of the body, human activities, and so forth—could be classified under one or another of the Five Phases. Earth was central and neutral; the four other elements corresponded to the four directions and to the four seasons and were further classified as either *yin* or *yang*. In addition, the elements were symbolized by the five fundamental colors: water is equated with black, fire

LAO-TZU
The Author of Tao-te ching

LAO TAN, THE TEACHER OF CONFUCIUS. There is no textual evidence that the *Tao-te ching* itself existed prior to about 250 BCE. The source of inspiration for this hypothetical spokesman was a presumably historical figure known only as Lao Tan, "Old Tan." According to the *Li chi* (Book of Rites; c. 100 BCE), Lao Tan's reputation as an expert on mourning rituals was well established. On four occasions, Confucius is reported to have responded to inquiries about ritual procedure by quoting Lao Tan. It was knowledge he had apparently gained firsthand, for Confucius recalls how he had once assisted Lao Tan in a burial service. Lao Tan, on the other hand, is quoted as addressing Confucius by his given name, Ch'iu, a liberty only those with considerable seniority would have taken. Seven episodes supposedly document instances when Confucius sought advice from Lao Tan on various principles of the Tao. By the first century BCE, the legend that Lao-tzu was the author of the *Tao-te ching* had entered the annals of Chinese history as accepted fact.

Li Erh and the Journey West. Ssu-ma Ch'ien (145-86 BCE) is the first known to have attempted a biography of Lao-tzu. His *Shih chi* (Records of the Historian, c. 90 BCE) gives Lao-tzu's full name as Li Erh or Li Tan. It is said that after living in the domains under Chou rule for a considerable time, Lao-tzu took his leave when he perceived the imminent downfall of the regime. Heading west, he left the central plains of China, but at the Han-ku Pass he was detained by a gatekeeper named Yin Hsi and asked to compose a text on the concepts of *tao* and *te*.

The text Lao-tzu completed was reported to have contained altogether five thousand words filling two folios. That Ssu-ma Ch'ien incorporates this legend on the origins of the *Tao-te ching* into Lao-tzu's biography suggests that the text was fairly well established by his time. The earliest extant versions of a *Te ching* and a *Tao ching* appears to have been made sometime prior to 195 BCE and the other sometime between 180 and 168 BCE, both predating Ssu-ma's *Records* by a century or so. Apocryphal though the attribution to Lao-tzu may be, the *Tao-te ching* became a fundamental text not only for students of pre-Han thought but also for those who came to venerate Lao-tzu as a divine being.

The Divinization of Lao-tzu. An important shrine in the history of the veneration of Lao-tzu lies far to the northeast of Ch'eng-tu, at Lu-i, his putative birthplace. It is at this site, the T'ai-ch'ing Kung (Palace of Grand Clarity), that Emperor Huan (r. 147-167) of the Latter Han dynasty is known to have authorized sacrifices to Lao-tzu in the years 165-166. After a series of cosmic metamorphoses, Lao-tzu is said to have finally achieved an incarnate form and thus to have begun his descent as savior to the mortal realm. He then became a cosmic force capable of multiple reincarnations in the role of preceptor to the ruling elite.

Lao-tzu as Buddha. At the time that Emperor Huan ordered sacrifices at Lu-i, he also presided over an elaborate ritual at court held in honor of both Lao-tzu and the Buddha. An academician named Hsiang K'ai was moved to comment on this service in a memorial that he submitted to the throne in 166. Hsiang alludes in his address to a belief that Lao-tzu transformed himself into the Buddha after having ventured west of his homeland. Thus did the legend of Lao-tzu's disappearance at Han-ku Pass lead to the claim that the Buddha was none other than Lao-tzu, and that his journey was a mission to convert all mortals to the "way of the Tao."

Lao-tzu as a Messiah. The vision of Lao-tzu as a messiah, moving freely between the celestial and mundane realms, inspired a large body of sacred literature. Just as the motives of the authors of these texts varied, so too did their conceptions of what was meant by a deified Lao-tzu. One of the earliest and most enigmatic sources to take up the soteriological theme is the *Lao-tzu pien-hua ching* (Scripture on the Transformations of Lao-tzu).

Lao-tzu is seen as coeval with primordial chaos, circulating in advance of the creation of the universe. He is portrayed as the ultimate manifestation of spontaneity *(tzu-jan),* the source of the Tao itself.

During waves of spiritual innovation, many shrines to Lord Lao arose throughout the countryside, while others were restored or enlarged. Worshipers at these shrines were often rewarded by visions of their Lord, appearing in response to individual pleas for divine intervention. According to one inscription dated 1215, Lord Lao was expressly evoked by Taoist priests in an elaborate ritual to exorcise a victim of possessing spirits.

[*See also* Millenarianism.]

— JUDITH MAGEE BOLTZ

with red, wood with green, metal with white, and earth with yellow. Added to this symbolism were four animals, which often appeared in representations of sacred space: the dragon to the east, the red bird to the south, the white tiger to the west, and the tortoise, enlaced by a snake, to the north.

Symbols of I ching. The divinization of the *I ching* is founded on a series of symbols or diagrams formed by the combination of unbroken lines (representing *yang*) and broken lines (representing *yin*). When these lines are tiered three at a time, we obtain eight trigrams. The combination of any two of the trigrams yields one of the sixty-four possible hexagrams. Trigrams and hexagrams symbolized the totality of realities, the former in a more synthetic fashion and the latter in a more analytical fashion. By arranging them in a circle representing space and time, we readily see how *yin* and *yang* alternate, how one passes from a purely *yang* reality (Heaven, represented by the trigram or hexagram *ch'ien*) to a purely *yin* reality (earth, represented by the trigram or hexagram *k'un*).

老子

By permission of the Open Court Publishing Co.

LAO-TZE

The founder of the Chinese religion of Taoism, Lao-Tze, was born in 604 B.C., fifty-three years before the birth of Confucius. He taught humility, gentleness, and economy, "the three precious possessions." He also taught the doctrine of the transmigration of souls.

Lao-tzu is generally considered the patron, if not the founder, of Taoism. The legend that Lao-tzu was the author of the Tao-te ching has entered the annals of Chinese history as accepted fact.

CORBIS-BETTMANN

"He who loves the world as his body may be entrusted with the empire."

LAO-TZU
THE WAY OF LAO-TZU

Although the ancient Chinese availed themselves of many systems of correspondence and symbols to describe the universe, in general they conceived of the universe as a great hierarchical whole whose parts, spaces, and times corresponded to one another. The system of classification based on the Yin-yang Five Elements theory made it possible to describe the microcosm and its harmony or disharmony by means of the rhythms of the outside world. A correct hygiene and a proper cultivation of the vital principle naturally required a perfect adaptation of the vital rhythms to those of the universe. For example, the "five viscera," in close relation with the Five Elements and therefore with the seasons and directions, were "nourished" by the "five flavors"—whence the requirements of a diet in harmony with the seasons.

MYSTICISM. The two main works of Taoism during the Warring States period, called the "period of the philosophers," were the *Lao-tzu* and the *Chuang-tzu.* Both works are characterized by their emphasis on quietism and mysticism and by the metaphysical dimension they attribute to the Tao. As a primordial and eternal entity, the Tao exists before all visible things, including *ti,* the superior divinities of the official religion, such as Shang-ti ("lord on high") and T'ien-ti ("lord of heaven"). The Tao is beyond the grasp of the senses and is imperceptible. But from "nothingness" *(wu)* the visible world *(yu)* is born and particularized phenomena are produced. Tao is formless, limitless, and nameless: the term *tao* is not a name but a practical referent.

The Tao of the Taoist philosophers actually assumes many aspects. On the one hand, it is transcendent with respect to the world of phenomena, where diversity and change prevail; on the other hand, it becomes immanent as it manifests itself, penetrating the beings that it animates and orders. In the *Tao-te ching,* the Tao is a feminine principle, the mother of the world. It gives birth to all beings, and its *te,* or nourishing virtue, preserves them and brings them to maturity.

The Taoists in fact condemn all discursive knowledge, for, they maintain, it introduces multiplicity into the soul, which should, rather, "embrace Unity," that is, be unified in the Tao. This unity is preserved through the mastery of the senses and passions. The sense organs are conceived as apertures through which the vital principles escape if they are not controlled. The passions and emotions are a cause of depletion of vital and spiritual power. A certain amount of self-denial is advocated, but such aims at the harmonious use of the sense faculties, not at their suppression. The Taoist should be especially careful not to intervene in the course of things. This nonintervention is called *wu-wei* (nonaction), a term that suggests not absolute nonaction but an attitude of prudence and respect for the autonomy of other things.

Some passages of the *Tao-te ching* allude to longevity practices that were assuredly being used among quietist circles. If such techniques—gymnic, respiratory, and others—were of interest to wisdom and religion, it was because holiness was believed inseparable from the potent vitality that was acquired and nourished by regulating one's vital energy. By living in accordance with the principle of *wu-wei* one can preserve the suppleness and energy of an infant and, consequently, one may hope to live the longest possible life. Lao-tzu goes so far as to assert the invulnerability of the saint.

If a spiritual purification is necessary to attain illumination, it is because the Tao is veiled in our consciousness by the artificialities of civilization. Hence, a critical reflection on the relativity of commonly received ideas is the necessary first stage on the way to salvation. Under the silent direction of a master, the adept gradually sheds the constitutive elements of his social self. Thereafter, he loses awareness of his body, and his sense perceptions are no longer differentiated—he hears with his eyes and sees with his ears. Finally, the adept's entire being communes with the totality. According to Chuang-tzu, he has the internal impression of flying off and moving about freely in space but externally the individual in a state of ecstasy resembles a piece of dead wood. His vital essence seems to have left him: it has gone "to gambol at the beginning of things." Chuang-tzu uses the perennial theme of the spiritual voyage to illustrate the state of absolute freedom the saint attains when he lives in symbiosis with the cosmos. By identifying his vital rhythm with that of the natural forces he participates in the infinity and persistence of the universe. He thus attains a superior life that is no longer biological; he lives the very life of the Tao.

HISTORICAL SURVEY

Lao-tzu is generally considered the patron, if not the founder, of Taoism. From the first centuries of our era he became a popular divinity, and his text, the *Tao-te ching,* was used by the propagandists of sectarian movements. It was the latter who were at the origin of collective Taoism, which differed significantly from the small chapels of philosophers.

TAOISM AT THE BEGINNING OF THE IMPERIAL ERA: 221 BCE-220 CE. We know that as early as the end of the Warring States and the beginning of the imperial era *fang-shih* ("prescription-masters") were active in the eastern coastal regions of China. They specialized in the occult sciences and propagated the theory of history as set forth by the philosopher Tsou Yen (fourth century BCE). Some of these *fang-shih* peddled prophetic works and pseudo-Confucian writings (*wei-shu* or *ch'an-wei*), which exerted much influence on Taoism. These magicians offered formulas that would allow the sovereigns to establish communication with the immortals and to become immortals themselves. The *fang-shih* taught the Han emperor alchemical recipes that were supposed to enable him to become a *hsien-jen.* However, Wu-ti established Confucianism as the official doctrine of the imperial state and instituted the examination system to recruit candidates for public office. Such examinations dealt exclusively with the Confucian classics. This double attitude was typical of the ruling class and the lettered bureaucrats of all periods. Ostensibly Confucian in their public life, they were nevertheless Taoists in private.

In the first century CE Buddhism made its appearance in China. From historical sources we learn that the new religion had already been introduced in some provinces by the year 65 CE. At the court of Liu Ying, a brother of Emperor Ming (r. 58-75) who had a fief in present-day Kiangsu, there were Buddhist monks as in the capital. Our sources report that Liu Ying was surrounded by *fang-shih,* favored the Huang-Lao doctrine (i. e., the cult of Huang-ti and Lao-tzu, an expression referring to Taoism), and made common offerings to Huang-ti, Lao-tzu, and the Buddha. Later, the emperor Huan did the same in the imperial palace and in 165 ordered that rituals be performed at the birthplace of Lao-tzu. Here, Lao-tzu was presented as a cosmic man endowed with traits borrowed from the myth of Pan-ku, common to the religion of southern populations. In the developing legend, Lao-tzu became Lao-chün ("Lord Lao"), a sovereign god who in the course of successive reincarnations came down from Heaven to instruct past sovereigns and to reveal sacred scriptures.

As the cult and mythology of Lao-chün spread in popular circles they sporadically gave rise to messianic movements. An important movement occurred during the last decade of the Han dynasty, contributing to its decline. These movements seem to be more or less connected to a famous work, the *T'ai-ping ching.* This text was presented many times to the throne, once during the Former Han dynasty and then again during the reigns of the emperors Shun and Huan of the Latter Han, each time by *fang-shih* from Shantung. The work belonged to a genre of prophetic literature, and its authors clearly hoped to obtain reforms from the court. The text is utopian in outlook, aiming at establishing an era of *t'ai-p'ing* ("great peace") modeled on the golden age.

In order to retrieve *t'ai-p'ing,* one must find the Tao within oneself. There is much discussion of ethics and politics in the work, but it remains distinctly Taoist in the importance it gives to spiritual exercises and methods of longevity.

A certain version of the *T'ai-p'ing ching* was used by the leaders of a rebellion that exploded in 184 in eastern China and spread to many provinces. This so-called Rebellion of the Yellow Turbans, or T'ai-p'ing Tao ("way of great peace"), announced the end of the Han dynasty and the advent of a new era. In the same year, in northern Szechuan, another movement, called the T'ien-shih Tao ("way of the celestial masters") established a state organized like a church, with a *t'ien-shih* ("celestial master") at its head and local parishes under the authority of *chi-chiu* ("libationers"). The first

Taoist temple compounds are made up of halls dedicated to a variety of purposes. The majority are built for Taoist deities and usually house their images.

PAGE 661

and most famous Celestial Master was Chang Tao-ling, who is often considered the founder of the Taoist religion. This legendary figure began a religious movement using spells and talismans after having received a revelation from T'ai-shang Lao-chün (the divinized Lao-tzu). Converts had to offer a contribution of five pecks of rice, whence the other name of the sect, the Wu-tou-mi Tao ("way of the five pecks of rice"). One of the reasons for the success of the movement was that its religious leaders presented themselves as healers. The sick were considered sinners, or as those who inherited faults perpetrated by their forebears, and thus had to repent and confess themselves as part of the salvific process. The written confessions were conveyed to the gods of Heaven, earth, and water.

TAOISM OF THE SIX DYNASTIES: FOURTH TO SIXTH CENTURY. The division of the country into the Three Kingdoms following the fall of the Han dynasty fostered regionalism that was exacerbated by the fall of North China to the domination of non-Chinese invaders at the beginning of the fourth century. The South remained under the control of the Chinese emperors of the Wu dynasty (222-280), who withdrew south of the Yangtze in 317. Prior to that time, the Celestial Masters exerted no influence in the South.

Taoism of the southern dynasties. The fall of the Western Chin provoked an important migration southward, placing the Celestial Masters and their followers in the presence of the popular cults and Taoist circles of these regions. Inevitably, there ensued a syncretism between the Way of the Five Pecks and the religious traditions of the lower Yangtze, giving rise to a new Taoist sect, the Mao-shan school (also known as the Shang-ch'ing sect), named after a mountain in the region of Kou-jung in present day Kiangsu. This sect or school originated with an important series of sacred scriptures that were revealed through the mediation of the visionary Yang Hsi. A selection of these revelatory texts appears in the *Chen-kao* (Revelations of Immortals), compiled by T'ao Hung-ching (456-536), illustrious among the Taoists of this period. T'ao's broad knowledge won him the friendship of Emperor Wu of the Liang dynasty. Not only did he collect, edit, and annotate the Shang-ch'ing writings, but he was also known as a poet and calligrapher.

Taoism of the northern dynasties. During these centuries of division, the Taoism of the northern part of occupied China developed independently of the southern traditions. During the Wei dynasty (386-556), Taoism became the state religion owing to the activity of K'ou Ch'ien-chih, a member of the Celestial Masters. K'ou Ch'ien-chih received the title of "Celestial Master" from the emperor T'ai-wu (425) and thereby gained authority over all religious affairs in the territory. He conferred the Taoist insignia on the emperor, who considered himself the representative on

CHUANG-TZU
Master of Taoist Thought

CHUANG-TZU (369?-286? BCE), the most important exponent of Taoist thought in ancient China. His name was Chuang Chou; *tzu* is a suffix meaning "Master."

Chuang-tzu's thought, like that of Lao-tzu (reputed founder of Taoist philosophy), is strongly mystical in character. He confronts the same essential problem as that faced by the other early Chinese philosophers: how is one to live in a world beset by disorder, strife, and suffering? But whereas other philosophers customarily proposed some program of political, social, or ethical reform by which such evils might be ameliorated, Chuang-tzu approaches the problem in a radically different fashion. Rather than seeking to remake the world, he would free man from suffering by inducing him to shed the system of values that differentiates pleasure from pain, good from evil, and labels one desirable, the other undesirable. In effect, he would have the individual learn to achieve a kind of mystical identification with existence as a whole.

This totality of existence, which Chuang-tzu calls the Tao, or the Way, embraces all forms of being, all life, and is in a constant process of change.

The person who has attained the level of enlightenment that Chuang-tzu envisions will no longer be able to accept the values of ordinary human society. Its promises of pleasure and material gain will seem empty to him, and he will perceive only the perils that attend one who gains too much worldly prominence. His way of life will embody the Taoist ideal of *wu-wei,* or inaction, by which is meant not a forced quietude, but rather the renunciation of any action that is occasioned by conventional concepts of purpose or achievement, or aimed at the realization of conventional goals.

Naturally, it is a vision that can never appeal to more than a small group in society. A society made up entirely of Taoists would very quickly degenerate into chaos. But as a kind of antidote to the overwhelmingly political orientation of the other schools of Chinese philosophy and their emphasis upon conformity, the vision of Chuang-tzu and other Taoists has done much to broaden the Chinese character and nourish in it a respect for individualism and the life of the imagination.

— BURTON WATSON

earth of Lao-chün. In 446, K'ou finally succeeded in influencing the emperor to officially prohibit Buddhism. This was the first of many persecutions of Buddhism and the first serious manifestation of hostility between the two religions.

Buddhism was rehabilitated under the following reign. The quarrels, however, went on, centering on such issues as the "conversion of the barbarians" outlined in the *Hua-hu ching,* the mortality or immortality of the soul, and karmic retribution. But in fact, the two doctrines influenced each other. The Madhyamika notion that there is no difference between mundane existence and *nirvana,* and that the Buddha is present within oneself was perceived as congruent with the concept of the Tao dwelling in the heart, where one must find it through nonaction. The Taoist influence on Buddhism was particularly manifest in Ch'an (Jpn., Zen), the most Chinese of the Buddhist sects, in which one finds the distinctive flavor of Taoist mysticism.

TAOISM UNDER THE T'ANG: 618-907. Many of the T'ang emperors are noted for their lavish patronage of Taoism. Because the imperial family and Lao-tzu shared the surname Li, the former traced its genealogy back to Lao-tzu and proclaimed him the ancestor of the dynasty. The *Tao-te ching's* importance as a sacred work increased. Emperor Hsüan-tsung (Ming-huang, 712-756) wrote a famous commentary on it and included it among the required texts for the civil service examinations, which had hitherto been based on the Confucian classics. Furthermore, each family had now to keep a copy in its possession, and the birthday of Lao-tzu became a national holiday. Taoism spread throughout the vast empire and came into contact with other religions, such as Nestorianism and Manichaeism.

During the period between the end of the T'ang dynasty and the beginning of the Sung, China was once again divided. In the kingdom of Shu (in present-day Szechuan) Tu Kuang-t'ing (850-933) gained the support of the sovereign to undertake the search for Taoist scriptures. He wrote many important works, including some dealing solely with ritual. Another Taoist of the same period, Ch'en Tuan, devised the diagram that was to be a source of inspiration for Chou Tun-i's *T'ai-chi t'u* (Diagram of the Supreme Ultimate), an important factor in the formation of Sung Neo-Confucian metaphysics.

TAOISM UNDER THE SUNG AND YÜAN DYNASTIES. During the reign of Chen-tsung (r. 998-1022) of the Northern Sung dynasty (960-1126), Taoism once more became the official religion. The dynasty was given a prestigious ancestor in the figure of Huang-ti, who was assimilated to the Jade Sovereign (Yü-huang), considered the supreme divinity of Heaven in popular belief. It was also during this period that the lineage of the Celestial Masters was officially recognized at Lung-hu Shan (Dragon and Tiger Mountain), in the province of Kiangsi. Official temples and monasteries were established in all provinces and were administered by retired high officials. Under Chen-tsung's rule, the collection of Taoist works was reorganized and collated, and the very important Taoist encyclopedia, entitled *Yün-chi ch'i ch'ien* (Seven Bamboo Slips from the Book-pack of the Clouds), was compiled to preserve many texts predating the Sung.

The reign of Hui-tsung (1101-1125) was also an era of prosperity for Taoism. A devoted believer, the emperor installed a theocracy with himself as the supreme head of the Taoist pantheon and, like Hsüan-tsung of the T'ang dynasty, wrote a commentary on *Tao-te ching.* Also of note are the steps taken during Hui-tsung's reign for the first printing of the Taoist canon. His reign is marked by the appearance of new movements based on the entire corpora of revealed ritual texts, the most important being the Shen-hsiao ("divine empyrean") order. The order was founded by the emperor himself under the influence of the Taoist magician Lin Ling-su. It was also at the latter's instigation that Hui-tsung took measures against the Buddhists. However, the Chin invasions of North China in 1127 brought an end to the Northern Sung dynasty and, thus, to the recognition of Taoism as the official religion.

Many new Taoist sects appeared in the northern regions ravaged by war and occupied by foreign armies. The most important were the T'ai-i ("supreme unity"), Chen-ta-tao ("perfect and great Way" or "authentic great Way"), and Ch'üan-chen ("integral perfection") sects.

The Ch'üan-chen sect was to become one of the most significant and prevailing currents of Taoism. Its founder, Wang Ch'ung-yang (Wang Che; 1113-1170), supposedly met with Lü Tung-pin, the immortal whose cult had become widespread since the beginning of the Sung dynasty and to whom several important works were attributed. Following the meeting, Wang Ch'ung-yang decided to devote himself to religion: he recruited Ma Tan-yang (1123-1183), who was to become the sect's second patriarch, and six other disciples, all natives of Shantung. As seen in their required curriculum—the *Tao-te ching,* the *Hsiao ching* (Classic of Filial Piety), and the *Pan-jo hsin ching,* a summary of the famous *Pan-jo ching (Prajñaparamita Sutra)*—the Ch'üan-chen sect promoted a form of syncretism that reflected popular notions of the unity of the "three religions" (i. e., Taoism, Buddhism, and Confucianism). New adepts were invited to sever all links with the secular world and to steep themselves in meditation so that their hearts and minds might become as firm as T'ai Shan, that is, impervious to the lures of the outside

"All men know the utility of useful things; but they do not know the utility of futility."

CHUANG-TZU
THIS HUMAN WORLD

T

Taoism is fundamentally a religion of ch'i, the vital breath out of which nature, gods, and humans evolve.

PAGE 138

world. According to the Ch'üan-chen sect's synthesis of Ch'an Buddhism and mystical Taoism, man must retrieve his pure, original nature in order to enjoy an increased life span. The sect was characterized by its tendency toward asceticism and its rejection of magical practices. In many ways it represented a new form of Taoism.

Wang's most famous disciple, Ch'iu Ch'ang-ch'un (1148-1227), was invited to the court of Chinggis Khan, who hoped to obtain the drug of immortality from him. Although the Taoist master answered that he knew only about hygienic techniques to prolong life, Chinggis Khan proffered sentiments of friendship and promulgated an edict ordering tax exemptions for Taoist monks. The Taoists, availing themselves of the protection of Yüan emperors, took advantage of the situation to harass the Buddhists. Their polemics, based on the *Hua-hu ching,* backfired however, and the Taoists lost much prestige.

The other major current of the period was the Cheng-i ("orthodox unity") sect, which was none other than the sect of the Heavenly Masters, whose patriarchs were believed to be descendants of Chang Tao-ling. From the Sung dynasty to the present this school has continued to have a great impact on Taoism. Unlike the *tao-shih* of the Ch'üan-chen sect, who practice celibacy, the *tao-shih* of the Cheng-i marry and their charge is hereditary.

THE SEARCH FOR LONGEVITY

Longevity, or at least living out one's allotted life span, was considered proof of sainthood. For the most part, the methods used to attain longevity centered on avoiding the depletion of vital spirits.

The Taoists conceived of the body as a microcosm that incorporated the totality of the universe, that is, Heaven, earth, and the celestial bodies. Universe within the universe, the body was often depicted as a mountain or a gourd, the Taoist symbol of the cosmos. Taoist cosmology holds that before the beginning there existed a kind of cosmic energy, referred to as the *yüan-ch'i* ("primordial breath") and synonymous with the invisible and with the void. This primordial breath split into *yin* and *yang,* the gross and pure elements that, respectively, formed Heaven and earth. Each being hides within itself this primordial breath. Since its presence is needed to maintain life, and since its exhaustion brings about death, the goal of many Taoist practices was the preservation of the *yüan-ch'i.*

The most important elements in the body were considered the *ch'i* (breath, ether), *ching* (essence), and *shen* (spirit). The Taoists believed that *ch'i, ching,* and *shen* were present throughout the body but were especially concentrated in the *tan-t'ien* (three "cinnabar fields"), the psychic centers in the head, heart, and just below the navel. Although the Three Cinnabar Fields were centers of life, they were also inhabited by malevolent spirits called the "three corpses" or "three worms" *(san-shih),* whose main goal was to bring about death. Most Taoist practices and precepts aimed at both neutralizing the ruinous power of the "three worms" and preventing the three *hun* "souls" and the seven *p'o* "souls" from leaving the body. The *hun, yang* in nature, had a tendency to return to Heaven, whereas the *p'o,* which were *yin,* tried to return to earth. The departure of the souls from the body meant death. Thus, the *Huai-nan-tzu* describes the Taoist saint as one who preserves the *hun* and *p'o* souls through ataraxy and who avoids all agitation of the vital spirits.

METHODS OF INNER CONTEMPLATION. Perhaps the most important of the Taoist contemplative practices was that of *shou-i* ("preserving the One" or "meditating on the One"). Derived from the phrase *pao-i* ("to embrace the One") in Lao-tzu's *Tao-te ching, shou-i* came to represent many different methods of spiritual concentration. Although the One is identified with the Tao, *hsü* ("emptiness") and *wu* ("nonbeing"), it is at the same time understood as the cosmos, the mother, the matrix, the primordial breath, and the origin of all beings.

In practice, these abstract ideas were given concrete forms. The One was represented by the anthropomorphic images used in visualization exercises. The One is visualized in its dynamic aspect, that is, in the form of three divinities symbolizing the "three primordial breaths" and otherwise called the San I ("three ones"). It is believed that this triad, later called the San Yüan ("three primordials") dwells inside man in the Three Cinnabar Fields and inhabits the "three superior heavens." By visualization, the adept causes the triad to descend into his own body. According to T'ao Hung-ching, a famous Taoist of Mao-shan, these divinities inhabit the body of each individual, but they return permanently to Heaven if the individual does not practice visualization. The departure of the divinities brings about illness and even death. However, this visualization is possible only for initiates, since to visualize the divinities one must know their names, physical appearance, and complete attributes.

Visualization of the gods of the body. Each point and organ of the body possesses a subtle energy that the Taoists represented with a divinity. These divinities were arranged hierarchically into a celestial bureaucracy whose ranks, posts, and functions were as complex as those of the imperial bureaucracy on which it was modeled. The recitation of certain sacred texts and the simultaneous practice of visualization exercises served to actualize these divinities in the body. Famous works such as the *Huang-t'ing ching* (Book of the Yellow Court) and the *Ta-tung chen-ching* (Book of Great

Profundity) provide detailed information about the divinities, their personal names, their dress, their size, and so on. Besides the Three Ones, the most important divinities were those of the five viscera, who, according to the *T'ai-p'ing ching,* keep the registers of life and death.

Visualization of the heavenly bodies and the planets. Another of the Taoist contemplative techniques is the visualization of the heavenly bodies and planets. The adept visualizes either the light of the heavenly bodies as they descend into his body or the inner light that he "preserves" in, or directs to, a particular point in his body *(lien-hsing).* These exercises make the adept's body progressively luminous like the heavenly bodies. The *Pao-p'u-tzu* describes the technique whereby the *chen-jen* ("perfect man") preserves and purifies his body. The sun and moon rise up to the head where they unite; the elixir, sweet as honey, then descends into the mouth; the adept swallows the elixir and sends it to the *ming-men* ("door of destiny") located in the navel, where he preserves it.

Predominant among the exercises for the visualization of stars and constellations were those involving the Pei-tou. For the Taoists, the Pei-tou is made up of seven visible and two invisible stars. Owing to its circumpolar position as the central axis of Heaven it was always visible. Its handle indicated the progress of the year and determined the four seasons and the degrees of Heaven. Visualization of the Pei-tou was practiced in different ways, either in communal rituals or in individual exercises. The adept marked the place of the stars of the constellation in the holy enclosure and then proceeded to "pace the stars." Each time he stepped on one of them he visualized its divinity with all its attributes. The devotee accompanied this practice by holding his breath, swallowing, and reciting various invocations. The Pei-tou visualizations were believed to help the adept to ascend to paradise.

ALCHEMY. Among the Taoist techniques of immortality, alchemy is perhaps the most significant. Two types of alchemy may be distinguished: *wai-tan* ("external alchemy," also called laboratory alchemy) and *nei-tan* ("inner alchemy"), the concoction, in meditation, of internal elixirs of immortality.

During the Han dynasty the magician Li Shao-chün persuaded Emperor Wu to worship the "god of the stove." Through this sacrifice, Li Shao-chün hoped to be able to transmute cinnabar into gold in order to produce magical vessels that would bestow immortality on any person who ate or drank from them. Physical immortality was therefore the first goal of Chinese alchemy, although later its techniques were used to produce artificial gold and silver for profit.

It was primarily under the T'ang and Sung dynasties that the technique of *nei-tan* spread. During the Sung dynasty, *nei-tan* represented a syncretistic system whereby the ancient techniques of longevity were practiced under the guise of alchemical theories and language.

The development of *nei-tan* in the Sung dynasty was marked by the appearance of a series of prose texts distinctly influenced by Ch'an Buddhism. Both of these *nei-tan* traditions relied on two works, still influential today: the *Pi ch'uan cheng-yang chen-jen ling-pao pi-fa* (Secret Transmission of the Ultimate Methods of the Ling-pao of the Perfect Man of the True Yang; eleventh century) and the *Wu-chen p'ien* (Book of the Realization of Perfection) by Chang Po-tuan (d. 1082). The commentator of the *Wu-chen p'ien,* Weng Pao-kuang, was himself influenced by the Chung-Lü texts, using the terminology and notions found there to explain the *Wu-chen p'ien.* In his preface, dated 1173, he claims to divulge the secret teachings of Chang Po-tuan concerning the great medicine of the gold elixir. To refine the elixir one must first take the primordial breath as the basis, then establish the *yin* cauldron and *yang* store, and finally, gather into the cauldron the Primordial Breath, which will thereupon form a parcel the size of a grain of millet. It is this grain that is called *chin-tan* ("gold elixir"). One then swallows the *chin-tan* and guides it into the five viscera, where it will attract the breath *(ch'i)* and essence *(ching)* of the body and immobilize them, thereby preventing their escape. Afterward one induces the *chin-tan* to circulate, thereby nourishing the breath and essence, which then transform into a gold liqueur.

One day this liqueur will rise from the coccyx and reach the *ni-wan* (probably from an early transcription of the Sanskrit word *nirvana*) in the brain: this is the *chin-i huan-tan* ("gold liqueur returned cinnabar"). When the *chin-i huan-tan,* shaped like the egg of a sparrow, descends into the mouth, it is then swallowed and guided to the Lower Cinnabar Field where it coalesces to become the "holy embryo." After a ten-month gestation period, the Holy Embryo will be born in the form of an earthly immortal (a rank inferior to that of the celestial immortals).

— FARZEEN BALDRIAN
TRANSLATED FROM FRENCH BY
CHARLES LE BLANC

TEMPLE

HINDU TEMPLES

"The Indian temple, an exuberant growth of seemingly haphazard and numberless forms," wrote Stella Kramrisch in 1922, "never loses control over its extravagant

Some Taoist movements took up its practice after about 500 CE; it influenced both Buddhist and Taoist symbolism and liturgy.

PAGE 21

T

TEMPLE

Hindu Temples

"The householder, if he is anxious to be happy, should carefully preserve Brahman."

BRHAT SAMHITA 53.66

wealth. Their organic structure is neither derived from any example seen in nature, nor does it merely do justice to aesthetic consideration, but it visualizes the cosmic force which creates innumerable forms, and these are one whole, and without the least of them the universal harmony would lack completeness" ("The Expressiveness of Indian Art," *Journal of the Department of Letters,* University of Calcutta, 9, 1923, p. 67).

AXIS, ALTAR, AND ENCLOSURE. Hindu temples are built to shelter images that focus worship; they also shelter the worshiper and provide space for a controlled ritual. Between the fifth and the fifteenth century CE, Hindu worshipers constructed stone temples throughout India, but sacred enclosures of another sort had been built centuries before. Tree shrines and similar structures that enclose an object for worship (tree, snake, *linga,* pillar, standing *yaksa,* all marked by a vertical axis) within a square railing, or later within more complicated hypaethral structures, have been illustrated in narrative relief-sculptures from the first few centuries BCE and CE. Whatever the variations, these structures mark a nodal point of manifestation.

In creation myths and in the imagery of the lotus, as in the structure of Mauryan monolithic pillars (from the third century BCE), the cosmic axis separates heaven from the waters. Creation flows from this nodal point toward the cardinal directions, producing a universe that is square, marked by the railing-enclosure of these early shrines, by the *harmika* (upper platform) of the Buddhist stupa, and by the edges of the brick altar used for sacrifice.

DIAGRAM OF CONSTRUCTION. The Vastupurusa Mandala—the square diagram on which the altar, temples, houses, palaces, and cities are founded—also outlines creation. The myth of the *vastupurusa* portrays the first sacrifice, in which a demon is flayed and his skin held down by divinities who ring the diagram (*padadevatas;* lit., "feet deities"). In the center is the "place for *brahman*"—the formless, ultimate, "supreme reality."

ICONICITY OF ARCHITECTURAL FORM. In North India, the fifth century CE saw experimentation in the means by which architecture could supply shelter to images. Small cave shelters were excavated (Udayagiri), cavelike cells were constructed (Sañci), structures with towers were built in impermanent materials (Gangadhara), and stone "mountains" were built (as at Nachna) with cavelike sanctums. Some temples began to show multiple and variant images of the central divinity on the walls (Madhia), and others became complexes by adding subsidiary shrines to shelter other deities (Bhumara, Deogarh).

Only in the sixth century did such experiments lead to a North Indian temple form that was complete in its symbolism and architectural definition. On plan, the North Indian temple grows from the Vastupurusa Mandala; its corners are those of the square *vedi;* its walls are half the width of the sanctum in thickness (as prescribed in the *Brhat Samhita*); at its center is the *brahmasthana.* The outer walls begin to acquire projecting planes that measure the dimensions of the interior sanctum and the "place for *brahman*". In elevation, these planes continue up through the superstructure as bands that curve in to meet a square slab at the top of the temple, from which a circular necking projects. The necking supports a large, circular, ribbed stone *(amalaka)* that takes the form of an *amala* fruit and normally is crowned by a stone waterpot *(kalasa)* from which leaves sometimes sprout.

As North Indian architecture evolves between the sixth and the thirteenth centuries, the plan of the temple shows more and more offsets, the walls gain more images, and the central tower of the temple becomes clustered by other, miniature towers, increasingly giving the effect of a mountain peak through specifically architectural means. If this variety of constructional forms, buttresses, and images "body" forth reality in the manifest world, the ribbed *amala* stone at the top of the temple, much like the staff that sprouts in *Tannhäuser,* presents the ripening seed's potentiality for fruition.

PALACE, HUT, AND FORTRESS. The temple thus combines physically the pillar that marks the axis of cosmic parturition, the altar of sacrifice taking the shape of the created universe, and the need for shelter of the tender divinity and the human worshiper; it unites the cosmic mountain and potent cave. South Indian temples, built in stone from the seventh century CE, give emphasis to the temple's role as shelter for anthropomorphic divinities by retaining throughout their evolution a terraced, palatial form crowned by a domed *sikhara* that has the shape of the ascetic's hut.

The temple is called *prasada* ("palace") in North India, and the architectural veneer of its superstructure, in both north and south, allude to forms of palace architecture. In the north, these have been completely subordinated to the temple's vertical ascent, becoming body for the altar that still presents itself at the top of the temple, open to the sky.

If the temple is palace for divinity, it also is fortress, protecting the world from disorder and chaos. Corners are "attended with evils" according to the *Brhat Samhita* (53.84), and "the householder, if he is anxious to be happy, should carefully preserve Brahman, who is stationed in the center of the dwelling, from injury" (53.66).

THE TEMPLE IN THE HUMAN IMAGE. In such an architectural context, *yogin* and god are equal participants: the place of divine manifestation and the path of the aspirant have been given consubstantiality along the temple's longitudinal axis; sanctum and sacrificer's space both have become altars manifesting supreme reality in human form. In the Hindu temple, the axis of cosmic creation and the ritual path for release of the aspirant/worshiper/sacrificer *(yajamana)* meet; the temple shares in the image of the "Supernal Man" (Purusa).

[*See also* Iconography.]

— MICHAEL W. MEISTER

BUDDHIST TEMPLE COMPOUNDS

After Buddha's death, according to Buddhist tradition, his body was given royal cremation, and relics were distributed among eight city-states, which then established royal burial mounds (stupas) incorporating these relics in order to memorialize him. Two centuries later the Mauryan emperor Asoka (ruled 273-236 BCE) is said to have reopened these stupas to distribute the relics more widely in his attempt to spread the Buddha's teachings; Buddhist tradition relates that Asoka established eighty-four thousand stupas throughout his empire.

IN SOUTH AND SOUTHEAST ASIA. Though shelters for the monks and stupas as monuments to memorialize the Buddha and his teaching defined the physical requirements of Buddhist architecture for many centuries, symbolic and ritual requirements gradually transformed such elements into what properly can be called Buddhist temple compounds.

Stupas and stupa-shrines. A stupa originally was used to mark the relics of the Buddha or of one of his principal disciples, significant objects (such as his begging bowl), or places related to his life or sanctified by his presence. From these early enclosed stupas evolved a major type of Buddhist structure, the *caitya* hall, housing an object used as a focus for worship *(caitya)*. These *caitya* halls are typically apsidal structures with a central nave and side aisles; a stupa is placed prominently (and mysteriously) in the apse. The earliest of these, at Bhaja and Bedsa, date from the second or first centuries BCE. Located on trade routes and patronized by merchants and others from nearby urban centers, these large establishments also provided monastic cells for wandering monks and abbots and sheltered pilgrims and travelers. At Bhaja, the abbot's cave has a veranda guarded by large images of the sun and rain gods, Surya and Indra; the individual monastic cells at Kanheri, scattered across a hillside outside of Bombay, have stone beds and pillows, verandas and grilled windows, each carefully located to take advantage of views through the neighboring hills to the harbor beyond.

Monasteries and monastic shrines. For many centuries after the death of the Buddha, monastic retreats were principally provided for the assembly of monks during the rainy season, but such places took on other functions over time, becoming retreats for lay travelers and eventually centers for learning. Foundations at Taxila in the northwest and at the important Buddhist university of Nalanda in Bihar show monas-

The transformation of Buddhism into a civilizational religion also involved doctrinal and scholastic factors.

PAGE 92

INDIAN TEMPLE

This temple complex in Konorak, India is a good example of the Vastupurusa Mandala, the square diagram on which most Indian temples are founded.

ADAM WOOLFITT/CORBIS

T

TEMPLE

Buddhist Temple Compounds

During the eighth century Japanese religion reached an important stage of maturity under Chinese and Buddhist inspirations.

PAGE 380

tic complexes in the shape of rectilinear compounds with cells enclosing a central shared court.

Temples. Bodh Gaya, the site in Bihar at which the historical Buddha is said to have achieved enlightenment, clearly reflects successive changes in Buddhist belief and practice. Under the present Bodhi Tree rests a stone altar set up in the time of Asoka Maurya to mark the place of the Buddha's enlightenment. The tree and altar are surrounded by a modern railing, but railing pieces from the Sunga period (second to first centuries BCE) remain nearby. Such open enclosures set around objects of worship (trees, pillars, images of nature spirits, stupas) represent pre-Buddhist practices that were absorbed into the iconography of popular Buddhism. Set next to the tree shrine is a large brick temple, pyramidal in shape, its surface ornamented to suggest a multiterraced palatial structure. By the sixth century CE, a large image of the Buddha had been enshrined within it for worship. (The image on a second-century CE terracotta plaque from Kumrahar suggests that a shrine in the same form was already there by that period.)

Terraced "temples" of a different sort were built across North India. The most extensive representation of such terraced temple structures is found among the monuments scattered across the vast plains of Burma, particularly at Pagan. The Ananda Temple there has a cruciform plan, interior ambulatories, and a central templelike superstructure dating originally from the early eleventh century.

In China. Beginning in the third and especially the fourth centuries, the spread and acceptance of Buddhism in North and South China was so rapid that it was almost immediately necessary for craftsmen and builders to come to terms with the new religion's architecture. Two building types are most fundamental: the Buddha hall and the towerlike structure known in English as a pagoda.

For the hall dedicated to the Buddha himself, the Chinese would build a likeness of the imperial hall of state, in which the Buddha could be enshrined in the posture of an enthroned Chinese emperor. Texts and more recent archaeological confirmation tell us that these were four-sided buildings of timber frame, supported by columns on each side and sometimes on the interior, often with the roof form that was reserved for the most important Chinese halls, namely the simple hipped roof, consisting of a main roof ridge and two ridges projecting at angles from each of its sides.

The towerlike pagoda had its origins in the Indian stupa but evolved in northwest India and Central Asia as a higher and narrower structure; by the time it reached East Asia, it found its only semilikeness in the Chinese gate, or watchtower, which dates back to the Han dynasty (206 BCE-220 CE). By the sixth century, square-, octagonal-, and dodecagonal-plan pagodas with up to thirteen eaved tiers could be found in China.

Buddhist temple compounds built in China after the rule of the Mongols (known as the Yüan dynasty, 1279-1368) are similar in plan and building function to those from the Sung, Liao, or Chin. New in Buddhist temple construction at the time of the Mongols are buildings for Lamaist Buddhist worship, introduced to China from the region of Nepal and Tibet.

From the time of the Mongols on, the most impressive Buddhist structures and those exhibiting the most innovative features were built at Lamaist monasteries. Under the Ming dynasty (1368-1644) one innovation is the so-called five-pagoda cluster, composed of a central tower and four lower ones at its corners, all on a single platform, and representing a Lamaist *mandala.* An example of this construction is found at the Five-Pagoda Monastery at Ta-cheng-chüeh Monastery, Peking, built in 1573.

In Korea and Japan. Like much of Korean architecture, Buddhist monuments were transmitted directly from China, so that in the initial stages, before the year 668, Korean Buddhist buildings reflect the styles of the continent. Yet, owing to native taste and a harsher climate, Korean Buddhist architecture, while accommodating certain norms dictated by the faith, is never exactly identical to its Chinese sources.

Some of the earliest surviving Korean Buddhist monuments are seventh-century stone pagodas from the monasteries Miruksa and Chong-nim-sa in the Paekche kingdom. During this period of the Unified Silla (668-935), approximately contemporary with T'ang China, the most important Korean Buddhist architectural site is the capital, Kyongju. Within the walls of the T'ang-style capital, most of which was destroyed at the end of the sixteenth century, are the monasteries of Sokkulam and Pulgak-sa. Sokkulam, the best-preserved early Buddhist monument in Korea, more closely resembles a cave temple in the tradition of the rock-cut temples to Korea's west than any other type of temple compound construction. Yet it also includes a stone antechamber connected to a domed structure in the manner of earlier Korean tombs.

The most important surviving Buddhist temple compound of early Japan is Horyuji, located just south of modern-day Nara. In its initial building phase in the early sixth century it was huge. The nucleus of the late seventh-century monastery consists of pagoda and *kondo* (main hall) enclosed by a covered corridor, with the middle gate and lecture hall (a later building) adjoining the corridor to the south and north, respectively.

During the Tempyo period (711-781), about fifty years after the rebuilding of the Horyuji, an octagonal

Buddha hall known as Yumedono (Hall of Dreams) was built on the former site of the residence of Prince Shotoku (574-622), founder of the original monastery. This memorial hall to the prince is the focus of what is known as the Horyuji East Precinct, in contrast to the so-called West Precinct that predates it.

After the transfer of the Japanese capital north to Heian (modern-day Kyoto) at the end of the eighth century, a move due in part to the increased power of the Buddhist clergy within Nara, new forms of Buddhism necessitated new architectural spaces. The Esoteric sects, also introduced to Japan from China, were characterized architecturally by smaller, more modest temples, often built in isolated mountain settings. Among the buildings that survive at Daigoji and Jingoji in the Kyoto suburbs, and Muroji farther south, are those with cypress bark roofs and plank floors.

The final important phase of Buddhist architecture in Japan occurs in the Muromachi, or Ashikaga, period (1392-1572). Several building complexes stand out among the many surviving period structures. Two of these, the Gold and Silver Pavilions of the large villas of the ruling Ashikaga family, in the eastern and western suburbs of Kyoto respectively, were residential in style but functioned in part as Zen chapels. The abbot's quarters *(hojo)* of a Zen monastery in fact came to be a standard feature of residential, or *shoin,* architecture from this time onward. Indeed, since the Heian period the aesthetic taste of Japanese ruling families had been largely determined by current Buddhist practices and ideals.

[*See also* Iconography.]

— MICHAEL W. MEISTER AND NANCY SHATZMAN STEINHARDT

TAOIST TEMPLE COMPOUNDS

It is difficult to say what was the first Taoist structure in China or where or when it was built. It seems certain that large monasteries were not erected during the age of the philosophers Lao-tzu and Chuang-tzu in the Warring States period (403-221 BCE) nor, it appears, under the Han dynasty (206 BCE-220 CE), by which time small temples were built to popular gods. By the period of Chinese history known as the Six Dynasties (220-589), however, Taoism had evolved from a philosophical system with a focus on individuality or the attainment of immortality into an organized religion; with this new religion came a clergy, an increasing number of deities, and buildings to house and serve them.

Taoist temple compounds are made up of halls dedicated to a variety of purposes. The majority are built for Taoist deities and usually house their images. Taoist architecture also includes buildings located at potent sites, notably the five sacred peaks or other natural phenomena, which are themselves objects of worship.

Standard histories of Chinese architecture mention only a few Taoist temple compounds, none of which includes buildings earlier than the Sung dynasty (960-1279). Of the forty or so sites in China where Taoist temple compounds survive today, three are most noteworthy. First is T'ai Shan, the Eastern Peak, most popular of the five sacred peaks of Taoism. Located in Shantung province, it is considered the abode of life-giving forces as well as the site to which dead souls return. Inside the main shrine, the god of T'ai Shan is enthroned in the yellow robes of a Chinese emperor, and the emperor's journey from his capital to T'ai Shan is painted on the interior walls. Directly behind this main hall is the bedchamber of the wife of T'ai Shan, situated according to prescribed imperial palace layout.

The two other great repositories of Taoist temple architecture are located northeast of T'ai Shan, in Shansi province. More than thirty halls stand at the Chin shrines, but the focus of worship is the eleventh-century Holy Mother Hall, built to Prince T'ang's mother, who in the Sung dynasty was believed capable of giving rain and foretelling the future.

At the southern tip of Shansi is the Yung-le Kung (Monastery of Eternal Joy), where three halls and a gate from the thirteenth-century temple compound still stand.

[*See also* Iconography.]

— NANCY SHATZMAN STEINHARDT

CONFUCIAN TEMPLE COMPOUNDS

The architecture of Confucianism in China is built in honor of men. It is dedicated to Confucius (551-479 BCE), sage and secretary of justice of the ancient state of Lu, or his disciples and their teachings. Confucian monuments are distinct from other Chinese religious structures in their avoidance of images.

The temple or temple compound is the predominant form of Confucian architecture. The 3,500-year-old town of Ch'ü-fu, in Shantung province, birthplace of Confucius, has been the site of the most important Confucian temple in China since the time of the sage himself. However, a temple dedicated to Confucius was built in nearly every major city of traditional China. Several important Confucian temples survive in continental China and in Taiwan; the most active are located in Taiwan, in its capital city Taipei.

The number and arrangement of individual structures of a Confucian temple compound vary, but the architectural style of the buildings and the general plan always follow the standards set for an emperor's palace. The temple compound is isolated in its own precinct, enclosed at least partially by covered arcades. The

Another of the Taoist contemplative techniques is the visualization of the heavenly bodies and planets.

PAGE 657

The faithful assembled to celebrate the rites at the exterior alter (bomos), a square block of masonry.

PAGE 256

important halls of the temple stand in a line, all facing south. Generally three or four structures are situated on this prominent north-south axis: a gate serving as the main, central entryway to the temple grounds at the far south; a gate or hall adjoining the temple enclosure at the north; and at least one major, multi-eaved structure dominating the center. Other buildings radiate around the central structure or structures, sometimes built with bilateral symmetry in mind but always giving the impression of perfectly planned order and balance. This basic arrangement dates back at least one thousand years.

The function of the main temple building is in accordance with the human-oriented world of Confucianism: it houses tablets inscribed with the names of the sage, his disciples (the four best known are Meng-tzu [Mencius], Yen Hui, Tseng-tzu, and Tz'u-tzu), or the so-called twelve wise men (eleven of Confucius's disciples and the twelfth-century Confucian scholar Chu Hsi). The simplicity of a Chinese building interior contains only inscribed tablets. Only rarely can one find a statue of Confucius, and in such a case the making of the image represents the influence of popular religion.

[*See also* Iconography.]

— NANCY SHATZMAN STEINHARDT

ANCIENT NEAR EASTERN AND MEDITERRANEAN TEMPLES

Modern writers use the term *temple* in different ways. Applied to Egyptian religion, it refers to a complete architectural complex, integrated in a coherent axial arrangement, including an inner shrine or sanctuary. Applied to classical architecture, *temple* refers to the equivalent of this inner shrine, while the whole complex is termed *sanctuary.*

EGYPT. Essentially, Egyptian religion is based on the performance of ritual, and the temples are the location for that cult. The forms and practices of the religion first developed in the Old Kingdom of the third millennium BCE and had become definitive by the Middle Kingdom in the second millennium. Thereafter they are marked by a characteristic conservatism.

Architecturally, the basic characteristic of an Egyptian temple is its axial alignment from the entrance pylon—a gateway flanked by towers—in the outer wall to the innermost shrine room. Rooms and unroofed spaces are always rectangular. Their exact sequence corresponds to requirements of the daily ritual conducted in private by the priests, and the regular but less frequent ritual of the public festivals. Each temple was surrounded by a high outer wall, which served to exclude those not permitted to participate in the ritual. The pylon leads to the outer courts in which the populace gathered to watch sacred processions at the great festivals. Beyond the courts are colonnaded (hypostyle) halls, vestibules, and the inner shrines housing the statue of the god and the sacred boats which were carried in processions. In this inner area there were also storerooms for the treasures of the god and for the paraphernalia of ritual, and rooms serving administrative purposes. This inner part is set at a higher level, usually as the result of a gradual rise at each successive door passage.

The courts are unroofed, though often surrounded by a colonnade; the inner parts are completely roofed and increasingly in shadow. The roof level decreases as the floor level rises, thus enhancing a sense of mystery.

The precise arrangement of this plan varies from temple to temple, with some larger and more complex than others. The degree of complexity possible can be illustrated by the Temple of Amun at Karnak, one of the most important, which has been added to and altered over millennia.

CLASSICAL GREECE. The origin of the Classical temple is uncertain. The essential plan consists of a single rectangular room (*cella* or *naos*) with a porch at one end. All else is added decoration, but except in the poorest structures, the porch at least would be embellished with columns, while the more splendid have *cella* and porch surrounded by a colonnade. The columns are of distinctive regional types, Doric on the mainland and in the west, Ionic on the islands and in the east, though the geographical divisions are not rigid.

Similar temples are found in the Levant (Tell Taayanat, Hazor) with a continuous ancestry going back to the Bronze Age. Since Greek temples are first found in the eighth century BCE, when Greek traders were renewing direct contacts with this area, they may be a copy or adaptation of these Levantine prototypes. Certainly the details of at least the Ionic order are Eastern in inspiration. The purpose of the temples, the practice of religion and ritual, remains purely Greek.

Greek temples were not congregational buildings. The congregation (which at the chief festivals of major cults was very large, to be counted in tens of thousands) gathered round the altar. Like the crowds, the cult statue watched the sacrifices. Temples were normally oriented to face the point at which the sun rose on the day of the festival. Though some cult statues were large and valuable, the rooms in which they stood did not have to be particularly spacious. Even in the largest temples a surprising proportion of the total area was taken up by external embellishment. Otherwise, temples served as storerooms for objects, particularly those of value, offered to the gods. From inscriptions we learn that the quantity of these was often considerable.

The Parthenon on the Athenian Acropolis, dedicated to Athena, is probably the most famous, certainly the most lavishly decorated, but not the largest of Greek temples. A forerunner, it was started shortly after 490 BCE as an offering for the victory over the Persians at Marathon. The temple has seventeen Doric columns on each long side and eight at both short ends, and it measures overall some thirty-one by seventy meters. It has two rooms, the eastern *cella* and the western "rear room," which held the valuable offerings. Innumerable temples smaller than the Parthenon also exist, such as those in the sanctuary of Asklepios at Epidaurus.

ROME. Early Roman temples were built in the Etruscan manner, which had been influenced by early Greek temples of the seventh century BCE; the Etruscans (neighbors and, for a time, overlords of Rome) did not follow later Greek developments. They placed their temples on high bases, approachable by a flight of steps at the front only. Timber and mud brick, with tiles and embellishment in terracotta, were the normal building materials. Roman temples inherited the strictly frontal emphasis and high bases. Occasionally the Romans copied the full surrounding colonnades of Greek temples.

In essentials, a Roman temple functioned like the Greek as a house for a god and for offerings to the god. Burnt sacrifices were made at an altar, which was usually placed immediately in front of the temple at the bottom of the steps so that worshipers faced the altar (and the temple) rather than surrounding it. Where possible, the temple stood in a colonnaded precinct, which also emphasized the axial symmetry. Roman temples, however, showed greater concern than the Greek for the use of the *cella* as a room. The Roman *cella* often occupied a greater proportion of the total area, was wider, and was invariably freed from encumbering internal supports for the roof, a consequence of better carpentry techniques and the availability of better timber.

These developments culminated in the best-preserved of all Roman temples, the Pantheon in Rome, built by the emperor Hadrian (117-138) to replace an earlier building of Augustus's time. Dedicated to all the gods, it is circular rather than rectangular (a permissible plan for Roman but not Greek temples). It had a conventional precinct and porch, but the *cella,* 150 Roman feet in diameter, is roofed with a concrete dome. Light is admitted, for deliberate effect, through an opening in the center of the dome.

The most splendid of temples in the eastern Roman provinces is that dedicated to Jupiter at Heliopolis, the Roman military colony at Baalbek in Lebanon. A huge temple stands on a high podium in the Roman manner, but it was constructed in the local tradition. On the podium is a Greek-type stepped base. The surrounding Corinthian colonnade is arranged in the East Greek (Ionic) manner with a wider central spacing at each end. In the *cella* (now ruined) was a shrine structure with a cult crypt underneath (better preserved in the neighboring so-called Temple of Bacchus) serving local religious ritual. Outside was a tall tower altar of Eastern type. Finally, the temple was given a precinct (never completed) and forecourt with a gateway building flanked by towers which derives from local, not Roman, concepts.

[*See also* Iconography.]

— R. A. TOMLINSON

MESOAMERICAN TEMPLES

The most common form of sanctuary in Mesoamerica is the temple-pyramid-plaza, that is, the peculiar combination of an elevated foundation, almost always artificially built, with a temple on the upper platform. Usually adjoining this unit at the base of the access staircase is a series of open spaces (plaza, esplanade, altar platform).

The embryonic form of this temple combination can be found in the principal mounds built from compressed soil or from *adobe* (sun-dried brick) by the Olmec in areas around the Gulf of Mexico, such as San Lorenzo (in the present-day Mexican state of Veracruz) and La Venta (in Tabasco) between 1200 and 900 BCE. Associated with a thrust toward monumentality that reflected the cultural vigor in Mesoamerica at the end of the Preclassic period (600 BCE-200 CE), the temple-pyramid-plaza soon spread to other regions. In the northern part of Petén (Guatemala), in the heart of the Maya area, the massive pyramids of El Mirador, with their apexes emerging from the dense forest, foreshadow the great Maya temples of Tikal in the same region.

Together with this tendency toward monumental building there was a great preoccupation with architectural permanence. This concern was reflected in the emergence of large retaining walls for the compressed fill of earth and rubble. These walls constituted the solid nucleus of the pyramid, and their taluses tended to follow the natural sloping angle of the fill. The access staircase, generally the only one placed on the axis of the temple, was initially incorporated into the general mass of the pyramid itself. With the passing of time it tended to project outward, frequently bordered by two *alfardas,* or flat ramps, which in turn often projected slightly beyond the steps or, according to local or regional style, assumed more complex shapes. In the same manner, the sides of the pyramid could be decorated with large masks or other sculptures or ornamented rhythmically with moldings, notably variations on the talus panel (*tablero-talud* or *talud-tablero,* a panel, or *tablero,* usually framed with moldings, that projected from the slope).

"The Lord is in his holy temple: let all the earth keep silence before him."

HABAKKUK 2:20

Finally, the temple itself, which usually occupies the upper platform of the pyramid, evolved from a simple hut to a more elaborate building made of masonry. Depending on the region, it was covered with a flat roof supported by wooden timbers and surrounded by low parapets or, as can be observed among the Maya, with vaulting made up of different types of projecting (corbeled) arches. Various types of panels, moldings, and sculptures enrich the temple silhouettes, which could be crowned with more or less massive roof combs, as in the case of Classical Maya architecture, or with sculptured finials distributed at regular intervals on the outside perimeter of the parapet in the style of a battlement. Such finials can be observed in the architectural tradition of Mexico's central plateau from the period of Teotihuacán until the Spanish conquest.

[*See also* Iconography.]

— PAUL GENDROP

TRANSLATED FROM SPANISH BY GABRIELA MAHN

Every missionizing religion, thus, is by definition transcultural.

PAGE 444

THERAVADA

The term *Theravada Buddhism* refers, first, to a "school" and closely related "orientations" within the history of Buddhist monasticism and, second, to forms of Buddhist religious, political, and social life in various Buddhist countries. Although these two aspects of Theravada Buddhism must be distinguished, they overlap and interact in various ways at different points in Theravada history. In the present article, the specifically monastic aspects will receive priority, but reference will be made to the civilizational dimension as well.

ORIGINS AND EARLY DEVELOPMENT

Theravada Buddhism, like other forms of Buddhism, had its origin in the life of the early Buddhist community. However, during the earliest stages of Buddhist development schools had not yet crystallized in any formal sense. Although the claim to represent the earliest Buddhism is doctrinally important, none of the schools that developed later can be considered, on the basis of purely historical scholarship, to be the sole inheritor and preserver of the original form of Buddhist teaching and practice.

THE FIRST CENTURIES. We know that not longer than 110 years after the death of the Buddha the different emphases that existed within the earliest community culminated in a major schism. The school known as the Mahasamghika ("those of the great assembly") was more populist in its attitude toward doctrinal matters, disciplinary practices, and modes of communal organization. By contrast, the Sthaviravada school was more conservative in its approach.

It is impossible to identify "Buddhist civilization," much less its Theravada form, during the first centuries of Buddhist history. This is not to say that the Buddhist tradition generally, and the Theravadins in particular, did not have civilizational aspirations. From texts dating to this period, it seems clear that they did.

ASOKA AND AFTER. By the period of the reign of Asoka (third century BCE) the initial division of the Buddhist community into those of the "Great Assembly" and those of the "Way of the Elders" had subdivided further. But according to Theravada accounts dating from at least the fourth century CE, Asoka himself sponsored a council that clarified the major differences.

Further Theravada accounts record that Asoka sponsored Buddhist missions that traveled beyond the frontiers of his considerable empire. These accounts date the founding of the Theravada school in Southeast Asia and Sri Lanka to Asoka's missions to Suvannabhumi (i. e., Southeast Asia) and Tambapanni (i. e., Sri Lanka), respectively.

There is no substantial reason to doubt that by Asoka's time the Theravadins formed a distinctive group within the Buddhist *sangha.* They preserved the teachings of the Buddha in Pali through their oral tradition; by the Third Buddhist Council or shortly thereafter, the Theravadins held their own positions on specific points of doctrine and practice. They also actively contributed to the Buddhist missionary activity during the third and second centuries BCE.

SRI LANKA AND THE DHAMMADIPA TRADITION. Within this distinctive provincial area of Sri Lanka, Theravada traditions became firmly established and prospered. For example, the Theravada monks feared that the monastic community would be dispersed and the oral tradition broken and lost. In an effort to prevent this, they gathered together and committed to writing the Tipitaka (Skt., Tripitaka; "three baskets"), that is, the Buddhist canon. As a result, this aspect of the tradition was solidified in a basic form that has remained largely intact through Theravada history.

By this time, too, Theravada Buddhism in Sri Lanka had become a civilizational religion. Said to have been the son of Asoka, the monk named Mahinda (Skt., Mahendra) supposedly succeeded in his missionary goal of establishing the Theravada lineage in Sri Lanka and converting the Sinhala king, Devanampiyatissa. Shortly thereafter, according to the texts, Asoka's daughter, the nun Sanghamitta, brought to Sri Lanka the ordination lineage for women. King Devanampiyatissa is credited with founding the famous Mahavihara monastery, which not only encompassed the king's capital within its boundaries, but later housed the monks who authored the chronicles that we now possess.

Another possible point for the emergence of Theravada as a civilizational religion is the reign of the Sinhala hero, King Dutthagamani (r. 161-137 BCE). While still a prince he organized a campaign in which the struggle to establish centralized rule and the struggle to establish Theravada Buddhism as the "national" religion became closely identified. The civilizational character of Theravada found a powerful vehicle of expression. Certainly, by the end of the first century BCE, after the Pali scriptures had been committed to writing, the Theravada ideal of Sri Lanka as the Dhammadipa, the "Island of the Dhamma," seemed well-developed not only in Sri Lankan religious and political institutions, but in Sinhala identity as well.

THERAVADA BUDDHISM IN GREATER INDIA

In Southeast Asia, specifically among the Burmese of Lower Burma and the Mon peoples of Lower Burma and Thailand, the Theravada tradition became firmly rooted and exerted a significant civilizational influence. The first archaeological evidence of Buddhism's presence has been found along inland and coastal trade routes, and dates to early in the first millennium CE. In Lower Burma inscriptions have been found that confirm a preeminent Theravada presence in Pyu/Burmese royal centers beginning from the fifth century CE, and some sort of Theravada influence is attested in Pagan somewhat later. In Thailand, similar evidence indicates that the Theravada tradition was an important, perhaps central, religious element in the Mon civilization of Dvaravati that flourished over a wide area of central, northern, and northeastern Thailand from the sixth to the eleventh century.

In Sri Lanka, literary and archaeological remains provide many more details regarding local Theravada history. A famous monk named Mahatissa evidently built, with royal support, an impressive new monastery in Anuradhapura. Sometime thereafter, monks of the long-established Mahavihara fraternity (by whose account this story is preserved) accused Mahatissa of violating the monastic discipline and tried to expel him from the *sangha.* Monks loyal to Mahatissa then formed the fraternity of the Abhayagiri monastery, which became for some time the Mahavihara's archrival. The Abhayagiri lineage maintained independent institutional traditions that eventually gave rise to branch monastic communities as far distant as Java.

The willingness of the Abhayagiri Theravadins to welcome Mahayana adherents into their company generated, some three centuries after its founding, a schism within its own ranks. In the middle of the fourth century three hundred monks declared their aversion to the presence of Mahayana monks at the Abhayagiri, withdrew from that fraternity, and formed an independent group that came to be known as the Jetavana fraternity. The new Jetavana *nikaya* acquired affiliated monasteries and also considerable land and other wealth. But compared to the Mahavihara and Abhayagiri *nikayas,* the Jetavana remained relatively small. Certain tendencies remained common to all three *nikayas.* For example, the Theravada scholasticism that blossomed during the fifth century drew scholars from the Mahavihara and from other *nikayas* as well.

The most influential scholar associated with this efflorescence, if not Theravada scholasticism generally, was Bhadantacariya Buddhaghosa. Probably a native of northern India, Buddhaghosa traveled to Sri Lanka in order to translate the Sinhala commentarial tradition, preserved by the Mahaviharavasins, into Pali, which by this time was recognized as the lingua franca of the international Theravada community. Buddhaghosa's industriousness during his residence at the Mahavihara produced a rich and extensive corpus of Pali commentarial literature that became a fundamental resource for subsequent scholarship and practice throughout the Theravada world.

Another movement in Sri Lanka that drew interested monks from all Theravada *nikayas* was ascetic in character and led to the rise of at least two prominent groups. The first group, known as the Pamsukulikas ("those who wear robes made from rags"), began to play an important role during the seventh century. It is quite possible that at least some of the Pamsukulikas were strongly influenced by Tantric trends that were becoming increasingly prominent throughout the Buddhist world, including Sri Lanka.

The second group, which attracted many proponents, especially from among the Mahaviharavasins, first began to be mentioned in tenth-century records. Referred to as *araññikas* ("forest dwellers"), these monks declined to reside in the rich monasteries of the capital and established their own monastic centers in the countryside. They adopted a more stringent discipline than their urban contemporaries, and emphasized more rigorous modes of scholarship and meditation.

THE GREAT REVIVAL AND BEYOND

In Sri Lanka, the Theravada *sangha* had suffered serious setbacks as a result of Cola invasions from South India and the collapse of the hydraulic civilization of northern Sri Lanka. In Southeast Asia, the Pyu-Burmese and Mon civilizations in which the Theravadins had played a major role had lost much of their vitality. During this period, the kingdom of Pagan seemed to be more oriented toward Hinduism and

Here the accent is on the interpretation of certain basic elements of the doctrine of release, issues such as the nature of the arhat, the nonexistence of a permanent self, the process of causation, and so forth.

PAGE 105

T

THERAVADA

Theravada Buddhism since 1750

Between the thirteenth and fifteenth centuries, missionary monks established a Theravada Buddhist orthodoxy among the majority of peoples, both rural and urban, living in what are today Burma, Thailand, Laos, and Cambodia.

PAGE 628

Sanskritic forms of Buddhism than toward Theravada. And with hegemony over most of what is now Thailand, the powerful and expansive Khmer court at Angkor was strongly oriented toward Hinduism and Mahayana Buddhism.

Accounts of the beginnings of the Theravada resurgence that occurred in the latter half of the eleventh century vary according to the tradition that has preserved them. However, one primary fact stands clear both in Sri Lanka and in Burma: Theravada became the favored tradition at the major centers of political power.

SRI LANKA. In Sri Lanka, the revitalized Theravada tradition was given an important new direction in the twelfth century when, during the reign of Parakramabahu I, a major reform and reorganization of the *sangha* was implemented. Parakramabahu I requested the Mahavihara-oriented *araññikas,* who had begun to appear on the scene two to three centuries earlier, to preside over a council.

The council "purified" the *sangha,* which meant that the code of proper monastic conduct was ascertained and monks who refused to comply were expelled. The reforms then unified the *sangha* by bringing all the remaining factions (and it is clear there were many) together into a single communal order. In so doing, the reforms provided the basis for a new structure of ecclesiastical organization that was established either at that time or shortly thereafter.

This reformed tradition by and large remained preeminent and creative in Sri Lanka up to the coming of the Portuguese in the fifteenth century. However, during the period after 1500, when the authority of the indigenous Buddhist kingdom was increasingly confined to the inland highlands, the *sangha* suffered a serious erosion of standards. By the early eighteenth century, the level of monastic scholarship and discipline had reached a very low level indeed.

BURMA. In Southeast Asia, the resurgence of Theravada proceeded rather differently. Through the reforms initiated by Aniruddha and his monastic preceptor, Shin Arahan, and renewed by his successor, King Kyanzittha, a strong Theravada tradition was established in Upper Burma and given powerful royal support. In the twelfth century a further reformist element was introduced at Pagan by a monk named Chapata. Thus, by the end of the twelfth century, when the Pagan dynasty was still a very powerful force, the Theravada tradition had become firmly established as the preeminent religion in Burma.

Burmese monastic reforms took place when the fifteenth-century Mon king named Dhammaceti assumed the throne in Lower Burma. Formerly a monk, King Dhammaceti sponsored a delegation of eighteen monks to be reordained in Sri Lanka. When these monks returned, Dhammaceti insisted that all those within his realm who wished to remain in the *sangha* be reordained by the new fraternity. Following this "purification" and unification process, the king proceeded to establish a monastic hierarchy whose responsibility it was to maintain strict adherence to the Vinaya rules. King Dhammaceti's efforts served to emphasize the influence of Sinhala monastic traditions in Burma.

THAILAND, CAMBODIA, AND LAOS. Like their Mon predecessors, the Thais also venerated Theravada traditions. But during the mid-fourteenth century, Mon Theravada traditions had to make way for a Sinhala reformist movement that spread from a center at Martaban in Lower Burma to several Thai capitals including Ayutthaya, Sukhothai, and Chiangmai (Lanna).

Theravada monasteries continued to proliferate throughout the region. By the latter part of the fifteenth century the Lanna capital of Chiangmai had emerged as one of the major intellectual centers in the Theravada world. In central Thailand, where the locus of power gradually shifted from Sukhothai to Ayutthaya, the Theravada presence was consolidated. Farther east in Cambodia, Theravada gradually displaced the deeply entrenched traditions of Hinduism and Mahayana Buddhism, a transition facilitated by the abandonment of the old capital of Angkor in the mid-fifteenth century. According to chronicle accounts, Theravada became the preeminent tradition in Laos beginning with the conversion of a Laotian prince during his exile in the court of Angkor in the mid-fourteenth century. Indeed, by the beginning of the sixteenth century, reformist Sinhala fraternities dominated in all of the major royal centers and in many of the lesser ones as well.

THERAVADA BUDDHISM SINCE 1750

During the past two and a half centuries Theravada Buddhism has retained its basic structure, and the major regional traditions have maintained many of the particularities that had come to characterize them during premodern times.

In the monastic context the stage was set for the developments of the modern period by major reforms that were implemented in each of the three major Theravada regions. In Sri Lanka the relevant reform took place in the middle decades of the eighteenth century. Believing their ordination lineage to be defective, the reformers invited Thai monks to Sri Lanka to reintroduce an authentic Theravada lineage. Through their efforts a new Siyam (Thai) *nikaya* was established.

Later in the eighteenth century King Bodawpaya (r. 1781-1819) succeeded in uniting Burma under his rule

THERAVADA BUDDHISTS, LOTUS ROAD

Theravada Buddhism remains vital in today's Sri Lanka and Southeast Asia both as a monastic tradition and as a civilizational force. The Theravada Buddhists shown here are on Lotus Road in Colombo, Sri Lanka.

TIM PAGE/CORBIS

and in establishing a considerable degree of royally regulated discipline within the Burmese *sangha.* Having more or less unified the *sangha,* Bodawpaya's reforms established the basis for the Thudhamma segment of the Order that has continued to include the majority of Burmese monks.

In Indochina King Rama I claimed the throne and introduced a series of reforms that unified the *sangha* and strengthened discipline within its ranks. This more or less unified fraternity—later called the Mahanikaya—has never lost its majority position within the Thai *sangha.* In Cambodia and Laos closely related, although less reformed, Mahanikaya fraternities were dominant at the beginning of the modern period and have held that position ever since.

During the nineteenth century there emerged within the *sangha* in each area a major competing faction or factions. In Sri Lanka two competing fraternities appeared on the scene: The Amarapura *nikaya* was—and remains today—a rather loose confederation of several smaller groups from various other castes that are especially prominent in southwestern Sri Lanka.

The Ramañña *nikaya* has remained by far the smallest of the Sinhala fraternities, but has nevertheless exerted considerable influence on the Buddhist community in Sri Lanka.

In Burma, much more than in Sri Lanka, the nineteenth-century British conquest disrupted the fabric of social life. In response to a disrupted environment, numerous small, more tightly organized groups formed. These various groups both complemented one another and competed with each other for purity of monastic observance and its attendant lay support.

In western Indochina during the nineteenth century a single new *nikaya,* the Thammayut, emerged to complement and compete with the established Mahanikaya fraternity. The Thammayut's favored status and elite membership enabled it to play an important role in drawing provincial traditions into the central Thai *sangha,* and in extending central Thai influence into the *sanghas* of Cambodia and Laos as well.

Thus, by the beginning of the twentieth century the various fraternities that still constitute the Theravada *sanghas* in Sri Lanka and Southeast Asia had already come into being.

THERAVADA TODAY

Theravada Buddhism remains very much alive in Sri Lanka and Southeast Asia, both as a monastic tradition and as a civilizational force. The *sangha,* despite its many problems, carries on its traditions of Pali scholarship and meditational practice. It continues to produce persons with intellectual substance and spiritual prowess. And it continues to generate movements (often conflicting movements) aimed at monastic reform, spiritual development, and societal well-being.

In addition, Theravada Buddhism continues to exert its influence on the institutions and values of the societies in the traditionally Theravada areas. This influence takes quite different forms in Sri Lanka,

"Because the monk is free his state transcends all expression, predication, communication, and knowledge."

THE PALI CANON, SINGALAVADA SUTTA, DIGHA-NIKAYA 2:65

T

TIBETAN RELIGIONS

The Pre-Buddhist Religion

where ethnic differences often involve religious differences; in Burma, where the nation's leaders have sought to insulate the populace from many aspects of "modernity"; in Thailand, where the pace of "modernization" is rapid indeed; and in Cambodia and Laos, where Theravada Buddhism has been "disestablished" by recently installed Communist governments. But in each instance Theravada Buddhism continues to provide meaning in the everyday life of its adherents.

[*See also* Buddhism. *For a related discussion focusing on the interrelationships between Buddhism and local cultures, see* Southeast Asian Religions.]

— FRANK E. REYNOLDS AND REGINA T. CLIFFORD

The last wave of expansion is associated with the propagation of Buddhism in Tibet and Mongolia, where it eventually developed into the mainly Tantric creed known as Lamaism.

PAGE 449

TIBETAN RELIGIONS

To the Western mind, Tibet has traditionally appeared as a remote yet uniquely fascinating country. Profoundly Buddhist in all aspects of its social, cultural, and religious life, it was, until 1959, dominated by a monastic hierarchy. In the imagination of some, the so-called Land of Snow (as the Tibetans style their country) has also been regarded as the home of mysterious, superhuman beings, *mahatmas,* who, from their secret abodes in the Himalayas, give mystic guidance to the rest of humanity.

THE PRE-BUDDHIST RELIGION. The picture of pre-Buddhist religion that emerges on the basis of the ancient sources is, unfortunately, fragmentary. Certain rituals, beliefs, and parts of myths may be discerned, but the overall feeling of coherency is lacking. The welfare of the country depended on the welfare of the king. Accordingly, rites of divination and sacrifice were performed to protect his life, guarantee his victory in battle, and ensure his supremacy in all things. The king was regarded not only as a vitally important personage but above all as a sacred being. According to a frequently encountered myth, the first king of Tibet descended from heaven ("the sky").

A surviving early text outlines an eschatological cosmology that embodies a cyclical view of time. In a "golden age" plants and animals are transposed from their celestial home to the earth for the benefit of humanity. Virtue and "good religion" reign supreme.

Little is known of the pantheon of the pre-Buddhist religion. The universe was conceived of as having three levels: the world above (the sky), inhabited by gods *(lha);* the middle world (the earth), the abode of human beings; and the world below (the subterranean world, conceived of as aquatic), inhabited by a class of beings known as *klu* (and later assimilated to the Indian *nagas*).

It is difficult to establish which elements in the pre-Buddhist religion are truly indigenous. The later sources insist that many of the Bon-po priests came from countries bordering Tibet, in particular, areas to the west. Possible influences emanating from the Iranian world have also been the subject of speculation by Western scholars, so far without conclusive evidence. On the other hand, the importance of the Chinese influence, long ignored, has now been firmly established. The royal tombs have obvious Chinese prototypes, as does the sacredness of the king. It has been suggested that the pre-Buddhist religion was transformed into a coherent political ideology in the seventh century, modeled on the Chinese cult of the emperor.

BUDDHISM. Buddhism was established in Tibet under royal patronage in the eighth century. In the preceding century, Tibet had become a unified state and embarked upon a policy of military conquest resulting in the brief appearance of a powerful Central Asian empire. The introduction of Buddhism was certainly due to the need to provide this empire with a religion that enjoyed high prestige because of its well-established status in the mighty neighboring countries of India and China. The first Buddhist temple was built at Bsam yas (Samyé) in approximately 779; soon afterward the first monks were ordained. From the very start, the Buddhist monks were given economic and social privileges.

Buddhism rapidly became the dominant religion, suffering only a temporary setback after the collapse of the royal dynasty in 842. In several important respects, Buddhism in Tibet remained faithful to its Indian prototype. It must, of course, be kept in mind that this prototype was, by the seventh and eighth centuries, a form of Mahayana Buddhism that was, on the one hand, increasingly dependent on large monastic institutions, and on the other, permeated by Tantric rites and ideas. Both these features—vast monasteries and a pervasive Tantric influence—have remained characteristic of Buddhism in Tibet. A uniquely Tibetan feature of monastic rule was succession by incarnation—the head of an order, or of a monastery, being regarded as the reincarnation (motivated by compassion for all beings) of his predecessor.

POPULAR RELIGION. While the study of the Mahayana philosophical systems and the performance of elaborate Tantric rites take place within the confines of the monasteries, monks actively participate in a wide range of ritual activities outside the monasteries, and beliefs that do not derive from Buddhism are shared by monks and laypeople alike.

Turning, first of all, to elements inspired by Buddhism, the most important—and conspicuous—are undoubtedly the varied and ceaseless efforts to accumulate merit. The law of moral causality *(karman)* easily turns into a sort of balance in which the effect of evil deeds in this life or in former lives may be annulled by multiplying wholesome deeds. Ritual circumambulation of holy places, objects, and persons is also distinctly Buddhist.

Pilgrimages constitute an important religious activity: above all to the holy city of Lhasa—sanctified by its ancient temples and (since the seventeenth century) the presence of the Dalai Lama—but also to innumerable monasteries, shrines, and caves in which relics of holy men and women may be seen, honored, and worshiped.

Ritual practices, while generally having an overall Buddhist conceptual framework, often contain elements that point back to the pre-Buddhist religion. As in other Buddhist countries, regional and local deities have remained objects of worship, generally performed by laypeople. In particular, the deities connected with (or even identified with) sacred mountains, powerful gods of the land *(yul lha),* are worshiped during seasonal festivals with the burning of juniper branches. These gods have a martial nature and are accordingly known as enemy gods *(dgra bla);* they are also known as kings *(rgyal po).* Usually they are depicted as mounted warriors, dressed in archaic mail and armor and wearing plumed helmets.

The person, too, possesses a number of tutelary deities residing in different parts of the body. Every person is also accompanied, from the moment of birth, by a "white" god and a "black" demon whose task it is, after death, to place the white and the black pebbles—representing the good and evil deeds one has done in this life—on the scales of the judge of the dead.

An important aspect of popular religion (and, indeed, of the pre-Buddhist religion) is the emphasis on knowing the origins not only of the world but of all features of the landscape, as well as of elements of culture and society that are important to man. Tibetans have a vast number of myths centering on this theme of origins.

Rites of divination and of healing in which deities "descend" into a male or female medium (*lha pu,* "god-possessed," or *dpa' bo,* "hero") and speak through it are an important part of religious life, and such mediums are frequently consulted. Other, simpler means of divination are also extremely widespread.

TIBETAN RELIGION TODAY. An overview of Tibetan religion would be incomplete without an attempt to take stock of the situation in the present. The most significant single fact is the downfall of monastic religion. Starting in the 1950s and culminating in the period of the Cultural Revolution in the 1960s and 1970s, the Chinese unleashed a violent antireligious campaign in Tibet that resulted in the total destruction of monastic life. At the height of the campaign, even the most insignificant expression of religious faith would be severely punished by Chinese soldiers or Red Guards.

The new and more pragmatic policy in China began to take effect in Tibet around 1980. A number of buildings, officially regarded as historical monuments, have been carefully restored; a limited number of monks have been installed in a number of the largest monasteries; and hundreds of other monasteries are being reconstructed on a voluntary basis by the Tibetans themselves. On the whole, religious activity seems to be tolerated as long as it does not interfere with economic policies.

— PER KVAERNE

TORAH

Torah is a term that is used in many different ways. Of the etymologies suggested for the word, none has been proved, but most of them derive from the use of the word in the Hebrew scriptures. In *Genesis* and *Exodus* the plural of *torah*, *torot*, is usually coupled with other words, as in "mitsvotai huqqotai ve-torotai" ("my commandments, my laws, and my *torot*," *Gn.* 26:5), and "mitsvotai ve-torotai" (*Ex.* 16:28). Even when the word occurs in these books in the singular, it refers to specific commandments. In *Leviticus* and *Numbers* the word *torah* denotes specific groups of ceremonial rules for the priests; sometimes the word occurs when the rules are introduced, as in *Leviticus* 6:1 ("This is the torah of the burnt-offering") and *Numbers* 19:2 ("This is the law of the *torah*"), and sometimes it serves as a summary and conclusion, as in *Leviticus* 11:46-47 ("This is the torah of the beast and the bird . . . to distinguish between the ritually impure and the ritually pure"). In *Deuteronomy* the word *torah* is used with the emphatic he' ("the") as a general term including not only the laws and rules, but also the narrative, the speeches, and the blessings and the curses of the Pentateuch. All these are written in "this book of the torah" (Dt. 29:20, 30:10).

In the prophecies of Hosea, Amos, and Isaiah the word *torah* carries a broad meaning that includes cultic, ethical, and legal matters. The concept of *torah* in *Jeremiah* is likewise broad and all-inclusive, while in *Ezekiel* the use of the plural returns, referring to groupings of laws and rules (*Ez.* 44:24).

In the historical books one finds exhortations encouraging observance and study of the Torah, as in *1 Kings* 2:2-6, along with a clear allusion to the "book of the torah of Moses," in 2 Kings 14:6, citing *Deuteronomy* 24:16. In *Chronicles*, changes made by the kings in both the cult and the legal system are said to have been

For convenience of study, the material was written on five separate scrolls, but it was also written on a single scroll. It is solely in this form that it has played a role in the Jewish synagogal liturgy.

PAGE 70

carried out "according to all that is written in the *torah* of God" (*1 Chr.* 16:40, 22:11-12; *2 Chr.* 14:3, 17:9).

In *Ezra* and *Nehemiah* a number of citations from the Torah appear together with exegetical activity of the scribes and the Levites (*Ezr.* 9:11; *Neh.* 8:14, 10:35). Of Ezra himself it is said that "he prepared his heart to expound the torah of God and to do and to teach among the people of Israel law and justice" (*Ezr.* 7:10), while the Levites "read from the book, from the *torah* of the Lord, clearly, and gave the sense, so the people understood the reading" (*Neh.* 8:8).

In private and communal prayers and in the psalms, the word *torah* exhibits a broad range of meanings in accordance with the various literary types and historical circumstances represented in them. In *Proverbs* the word torah is used as a parallel for the terms *musar* ("instruction," *Prv.* 1:8), mitsvah ("commandment," *Prv.* 3:1, 6:20), and *leqah tov* ("a good doctrine," *Prv.* 4:2), and thus it is also used to refer to the person who draws upon the wisdom found in international wisdom literatures. Nevertheless, the word still preserves the primary religious connotation that characterizes its use in the rest of the books of the Hebrew scriptures, by referring to the totality of the commandments of the covenant between God and his people.

"Ezra read plainly from the book of the law of God."

NEHEMIAH 8:8

CONTENT OF THE PENTATEUCH. The collection of writings that we call "Torah" or "the Torah of Moses" comprises the first five books of the Bible (the Pentateuch) but in fact has been considered the one unified work, unlike the Prophets and the Hagiographa (or Writings), which together with it make up scripture. In content the Pentateuch is a continuous composition reporting history from the creation of the world until the death of Moses—when the people of Israel are arrayed in the plains of Moab—interspersed with groups of laws and rules. More precisely, in consideration of the central collection of several groups of laws and commandments that were given to the people of Israel, set in a framework of stories that explain the special status of the people before God.

The traditions about Moses are contained in the Pentateuch from Exodus to Deuteronomy.

PAGE 465

As is usual in Hebrew, the books of the Pentateuch are referred to by the first significant word in each book. The first book, *Bere'shit* (in the beginning")—opens with a description of the creation of the world—whence the designation *Genesis*—and the genealogy of mankind and continues with the genealogy of Noah and his descendants after the great flood.

The second book, *Shemot* ("names"), contains the description of the events from the time of the bondage in Egypt until the revelations at Mount Siaai, where God establishes his special covenant with Israel, gives the Torah, and prescribes the tabernacle and the ceremony in which it is to be consecrated.

The third book, *Vayiqra'* ("and he called"), is known in tannaitic literature as *Torat Kohanim* ("*torah* of the priests") and in Greek as *Leuitikon.* It includes laws relating to worship in the Temple and the laws of sacrifices; special commandments of sanctity applicable to the priests and commandments of sanctity incumbent on the entire people of Israel; laws of ritual purity and impurity and of incest and other forbidden sexual relations; laws about the sanctity of particular times, festivals, and holidays; and laws about the sanctity of the Land of Israel, the Sabbatical year, and the Jubilee year.

The fourth book of the Pentateuch is usually called *Bemidbar* ("in the wilderness"), after the first significant word. It records the history of the people of Israel in the desert from the second year after they left Egypt until the death of Aaron.

The last of the five books of the Pentateuch is *Elleh ha-devarim* ("These are the words"). In a series of speeches before his death, Moses summarizes the history of the people, intermixing his account with ethical teachings, warnings, and reproof.

LITERARY AND HISTORICAL CRITICISM. Comparison of Deuteronomy with parallels in the other books of the Pentateuch reveals numerous inconsistencies between both the narratives and the collections of laws as well as linguistic and stylistic differences. Modern biblical scholarship has attempted to uncover different sources upon which the five books of the Pentateuch are based.

A concerted effort to reconstruct the process that brought into being the books of the Torah as we have them was begun only in the middle of the eighteenth century. This effort resulted in the hypothesis that there are four sources or documents, given the designations J, E, P, and D. The distinction between J and E is based primarily on the different usages of the names of God (JHVH, or YHVH, and Elohim) and the names Jacob and Israel. Similar criteria were used to differentiate passages based on the priestly source, P, and the Deuteronomic source, D.

Besides the discernment and differentiation of these sources, there were also attempts to establish a chronology among them. A pioneer in this research, Wilhelm de Wette (1780-1849) proposed that *Deuteronomy,* which emphasizes the concentration of the cult in one place, reflects the situation that began to crystallize during the reign of Hezekiah, who concentrated the cult in Jerusalem (*2 Kgs.* 18:3-6), and that concluded in the time of Josiah, during whose reign Hilkiah discovered "the book" (*2 Kgs.* 22:8). This book, according to de Wette, was none other than the *Book of Deuteronomy,* which stands at the end of the development of the sources, as it is the only one in which there is any demand for the centralization of the cult.

Julius Wellhausen, in his studies during the second half of the nineteenth century, perfected and consolidated this type of historical criticism, according to which the Torah did not exist during the early part of the history of the people of Israel in their land, but rather reflects the historical circumstances of later generations. Objections to and criticism of this approach were voiced already in the time of Wellhausen, and they have increased in recent decades.

Even those who adopt the critical view, which sees the Pentateuch as a work compiled from different sources that reflect differing trends and styles, are nevertheless forced to admit its function and influence as a single, unified book. Every law and commandment in it is presented as the word of God to Moses, and taken together these laws form for Judaism an authoritative code whose authority infuses even the narrative sections with which they are intermixed. [*See also* Biblical Literature.]

WRITTEN TORAH AND ORAL TORAH. During the Hellenistic period, prior to the Hasmonean rebellion, the word *torah* had two distinct referents. On the one hand, it included not only the commandments but also the teachings of the prophets and the wisdom of the elders, while on the other hand, it meant the *torah* of Moses in its entirety. It would seem that for the Jews of Alexandria, torah was an institution that embodied the covenant between the nation and its Lord, reflecting a system of commandments, laws, customs, and traditions connected with the history of the people and the activities of their judges, kings, and prophets.

The term *oral torah* first appears in a story said to be from the time of Hillel and Shammai (fl. first century BCE–first century CE). In response to a prospective convert's question about how many *torot* exist, Shammai answered, "Two: the written *Torah* and the oral *torah*" (B. T., *Shab.* 31a).

'Aqiva' ben Yosef saw the oral *torah* as implicit in the written Torah, in its words and in its letters, whence it is recorded that he expounded: "'These are the laws and the rules and the *torot*' [Lv. 26:46]—from which we learn that two *torot* were given to Israel, one written and one oral. . . . 'On Mount Sinai by the hand of Moses' [ibid.]—from which we learn that *torah* was given complete with all its laws, details of interpretation, and explanations by the hand of Moses at Sinai" (*Sifra'*, Behuqqotai 8, p. 112c). In light of this, one can understand the term "*torah* from heaven"; the statement of 'Aqiva' was in response to those who said, "*torah* is not from heaven" (*Sifrei Dt.* 102, p. 161), meaning that they denied the revealed nature of the oral *torah.*

The third *Sibylline Oracle* (sec. 256), which dates from around 140 BCE, says that "Moses . . . [led] the people . . . to Mount Sinai, then God gave them the *torah* forth from heaven, writing all its ordinances on two tablets." For the school of 'Aqiva' and in the Mishnah, though, *torah* does not refer solely to the Ten Commandments. Furthermore, the revelation included not only the Torah and its interpretations, but also the assertion of the authority of the interpretation.

According to the method developed by 'Aqiva' and his school, the Torah scholar and exegete, by application of the principles used for the interpretation of the Torah and through his reasoning, can uncover within the Torah those same laws, details of interpretation, and explanations that were given together with it. In adopting this doctrine they follow Yehoshu'a ben Hananyah, teacher of 'Aqiva', who refused to admit the continued intervention of divine forces in the determination of halakhic matters. This contrasts with the position of Eli'ezer ben Hyrcanus and others, who refused to discount the possibility of further revelations, whether in the form of a heavenly voice or through prophecy. According to the understanding of Yehoshu'a and his disciples, "Torah is not in the heavens, so we do not listen to heavenly voices" (B. T., *B. M.* 59b). Those who adopted this position even denied that earlier prophets could have established innovations on the basis of their gift of prophecy. Rather, the exposition and expansion of the Torah were severed from any and all dependence on supernatural forces.

Many of the meanings of the word *torah* developed from polemics against different approaches and conceptions. One of the last amoraim, Yehudah bar Shalom, explained the prohibition of writing oral *torah* thus: "When the Holy One, blessed be he, told Moses to 'write yourself [this book of the Torah],' Moses wanted to write down the Mishnah also, but since God saw that the nations of the world would eventually translate the Torah and read it in Greek and claim 'I am Israel,' and up to this point the scales of judgment are balanced, he told the nations: 'You say you are my children, but I recognize only he who possesses my mystery; they are my children.' And to what does this refer? To the Mishnah" (*Tan.* Vayeira' 5, Tisa' 34). Clearly this saying defines the preference of the oral *torah* as a response to the claims of Pauline Christianity that the church is the true inheritor of Israel because it is the son of the free woman, while Israel is of the flesh, at best the progeny of the maidservant (*Gal.* 3:26, 4:21; *Rom.* 2:28). Following Paul, the church fathers from Justin through Augustine claimed scripture was no longer the property and heritage of the Jews (Justin, *Apologia* 1.53; Augustine, *Against the Jews,* 4.8). The oral *torah* supposedly refutes such claims.

Contradictions between various sayings about the relationship between Torah and the books of the prophets can be explained if one views these statements in a polemical context. Levi in the name of Hanina' said: "The eleven psalms which Moses composed are set down in the books of the prophets. And

The Bible makes no mention of oral law.

PAGE 395

The Hebrew term torah means "instruction, teaching."

PAGE 69

T

TORAH

Concept of Torah among the Medieval Philosophers

The Ten Commandments (or the Decalogue) appear twice in the Hebrew scriptures, at Exodus 20:1-17 and at Deuteronomy 5:6-21.

PAGE 372

why were they not included in the books of the law? Because the latter are words of torah and the former are words of prophecy" (*Midrash Tehillim* 90.4). According to this statement, even the words of prophecy by Moses himself are distinct from *torah.* In this saying and in others like it the revelation at Mount Sinai is restricted to a single, unique, all-inclusive event, thereby making impossible any additional revelation that could challenge the completeness of Torah. However, there were also sects that did not recognize the authority of the prophetic books at all.

Still, beyond all polemic, the books of the Prophets and Writings were sanctified as parts of the tripartite Torah (B. T., *Shab.* 88a; *Tan.* Yitro 10): the Pentateuch (Torah), Prophets (Nevi'im), and Writings (Ketuvim). Readings from the Prophets and some of the books of the Writings (*Esther, Lamentations,* and, according to some customs, the other three *megillot,* i. e., *Song of Songs, Ruth,* and *Ecclesiastes,* as well) are included in the synagogue service, preceded and followed by blessings. Nevertheless, the distinction between them and the Pentateuch is preserved, for the sanctity of the rest of the books is not equal to that of the Torah scroll: it was forbidden to join together the Torah and prophetic books in a single scroll (*Sofrim* 3.1) or to lay a prophetic book on top of the Pentateuch (B. T., *Meg.* 27a).

THE TEN COMMANDMENTS. There are also differing understandings of the relationship between the Ten Commandments and the rest of the Torah. Philo saw the Ten Commandments as the principles and sources, while the rest of the commandments of the Torah are only specific details. Thus he organized the specific commandments, grouping them according to their roots—that is, according to their agreement with the Ten Commandments. Yet Hananyah, nephew of Yehoshu'a, and others following him asserted that "the details of the Torah were written in the intervals between the commandments of the decalogue" (J. T., *Sheq.* 6.1, 49d; *Sg. Rab.* 5, 14). Thus these sages were interested in deemphasizing the Ten Commandments and denying them any special status, in order to prevent people from claiming that they alone were given from Sinai and not the rest of the commandments (J. T., *Ber.* 1.8, 3c).

CONCEPT OF TORAH AMONG THE MEDIEVAL PHILOSOPHERS. Jewish philosophy in the Middle Ages in the lands under Muslim dominance stood before two challenges: philosophical justification of Torah as a religion of divine revelation and rejection of the Muslim claim that the revelation to Israel was superseded by the revelation to Muhammad. For Sa'adyah Gaon (882-942), who is considered the father of medieval Jewish philosophy, the divine revelation is identified with the content of reason. Reason can recognize both the speculative and the ethical content of revelation, which is nevertheless necessary to reveal truth in a universally accessible form, making it available to the common man, who is incapable of thinking for himself, and also to the philosopher, who is thereby presented *a priori* with the truth that he could otherwise discover only through great effort. Still, it is a religious duty to come to truth also through the use of reason (Sa'adyah Gaon, *The Book of Beliefs and Opinions,* translated by S. Rosenblatt, New Haven, 1961). Out of this conception Sa'adyah developed the distinction between the commandments of reason, which revelation simply repeats, and the traditional commandments, which are known only through revelation. The latter category includes the sacrificial and ceremonial orders of the Torah (ibid., treatise 3, sections 1-3). Sa'adyah applied this conception in composing a liturgical poem in which he attempted to fit all 613 of the commandments into the framework of the Ten Commandments (*Azharot* in *Siddur Rav Sa'adyah Ga'on,* 1941, pp. 185ff.), which as in Philo can be considered general principles. This undertaking also answers those who claim that numerous divine revelations are possible: there was no such multiplicity of revelation to Israel, and the divine will is certainly not prone to change or to cancel the content of the true revelation (*The Book of Beliefs and Opinions,* treatise 3, sec. 7).

Maimonides (1135/8-1204) ascribed two purposes to *torah*: to order communal life and to enlighten the spirit of men by revealing to them the truth. The political laws, ethical commandments, and ceremonial and sacrificial laws of the Torah are all means toward the attainment of these two goals. All the laws that serve to educate the people ethically work toward the achievement of the first goal, while all the laws that strengthen certain specific beliefs advance the second goal. Maimonides attempted to demonstrate this point by developing an elaborate system of explanations of reasons for the commandments, some of them rationalistic and some historical, presenting certain commandments and prohibitions as protection against polytheistic ideas and customs of worship (Maimonides, *Guide of the Perplexed* 3.29-3.44). With great consistency Maimonides stressed in all of his works the uniqueness of the revelation of the Torah of Moses. For him the role of the prophets was not to create a religion: "As for the prophets from among us who came after Moses our master, you know the text of all their stories and the fact that their function was that of preachers who called upon the people to obey the Torah of Moses. . . . We likewise believe that things will always be this way, as it says, 'It is not in heaven'" (ibid. 2.39; translation by Shlomo Pines, Chicago, 1963).

VIEW OF THE QABBALISTS. Qabbalistic literature, which is mostly made up of commentaries on the

Torah, emphasizes the absolute virtues of the Torah over the rest of the books of the Bible. The conceptions of the qabbalists about the Torah are in part a radical development of ideas found in *midrashim* of the sages and in part bold innovation. A saying ascribed to the amora El'azar, which appears in *Midrash Tehillim* 3.2, explains a verse in *Job* (28:13) as follows: "The sections of the Torah were not given in order, for had they been given in order, anyone reading them would be able to resurrect the dead and to perform wonders. Therefore the order of the Torah was hidden, but it is revealed before the Holy One, blessed be he, as it says, 'And who is like unto me? Let him read and declare it and set it in order for me [*Is.* 44:7].'" The author of this saying hints at the possibility of use of the Torah for magic, but he rejects that possibility. Nevertheless, such magical use was described in the work *Shimushei Torah*, which apparently dates from the geonic period.

Nahmanides (Mosheh ben Nahman, c. 1194-1270) mentions reading the Torah "in the manner of the names," which was transmitted to Moses verbally, "for we possess a true tradition that the entire Torah is made up of the names of the Holy One, blessed be he" (Introduction to Nahmanides' commentary on the Torah). Similarly, the *Zohar* (Yitro 87.1) says, "The entire Torah is the holy name, for there is not a word in the Torah which is not included in the holy name." Based on this idea, Me'ir ibn Gabbai wrote in the beginning of the fourteenth century that Torah is called "the Torah of God" because it is in fact the name of God. This supposition relates to the preexistent reality of the Torah, in which it was used to create the world. The fact that the Torah is thought to have been made up by the interweaving of divine names implies that the Torah has multiple meanings. The different kinds of interpretations were summed up in the *Zohar* in the acronym *PaRDeS*, standing for *peshat*, *remez*, *derash*, and *sod*. *Peshat* includes the understanding of scripture evinced in the oral *torah*; *remez* includes allegory and philosophy; *derash* is the homiletic approach; while *sod* is made up of the qabbalistic explanations. In the qabbalistic exegesis, precisely those verses and words that seem unimportant are raised to the level of profound symbols.

The qabbalists propounded a distinction between the *torah* of the names of the messiah and the revealed Torah. In so doing they diverged from the saying of Yohanan that "the books of the Prophets and the Writings will in the future be canceled, but the Pentateuch will not be canceled in the future" (J. T., *Meg.* 3.7, 70d) as well as from the *midrashim* in which one may uncover hints of the possibility of changes, like: "The *torah* that a man learns in this world is empty in comparison with the *torah* of the Messiah" (*Eccl. Rab.* 11.8) or "'*Torah* will go out from me' (*Is.* 51:4)—a renewal of the Torah will go out from me" (*Lv. Rab.* 13.3). In these *midrashim* the innovative nature of the Torah is not specified, but the qabbalists explained the nature of the change in the light of their conceptions: the Torah will be understood in accordance with its spirituality, and its letters will join together to form a different reading.

Qabbalistic literature of the thirteenth century explained that in the dictum of Shim'on ben Laqish, "the Torah which the Holy One, blessed be he, gave to Moses was white fire engraved on black fire" (J. T., *Sheq.* 6.1); "white fire" refers to the Torah itself, while "black fire" refers to the oral *torah*. Thus the written Torah is hidden in the white parchment, but in the future the blank spaces in the Torah will reveal their letters.

The Hasidim of the eighteenth century essentially adopted the qabbalistic understanding that the elevated religious value of the Torah is found in its inner essence rather than in its exoteric manifestation. The simple meaning of the Torah is a symbolic expression of divine truths. In keeping with the individualistic tendency within Hasidism, achieving understanding of the secrets of Torah was considered to depend on the mending of the individual's specific personal soul and on his attempts to cleave to God in every aspect of his being.

An opponent of Hasidism, Eliyyahu ben Shelomoh Zalman (1720-1797), known as the Vilna Gaon, emphasized the all-encompassing, eternal nature of Torah. Everything that ever was, is, or will be existent is included in the Torah. The specific details of every person, animal, plant, and inanimate object are included in the Torah from the word *bere'shit* until the phrase *le-'einei kol Yisra'el* (the words that close *Deuteronomy*). He studied qabbalistic literature in the same way in which he studied the books of the Bible and halakhic works. Rather than expecting personal revelations as a result of occupying himself with Qabbalah, he anticipated that his devotion and absolute dedication to Torah study would aid him in understanding the Qabbalah.

TALMUD TORAH ("TORAH STUDY"). Alongside the demand that one must uphold the commandments written in the Torah, there is also in the Torah an explicit requirement to study, learn, and teach it (*Dt.* 6:6-7, 11:18-20; see also *Jos.* 1:8). This commandment from the start related to every part of the Torah. During the time of the First Temple, the priests were the main group encharged with teaching the Torah (*Jeremiah* 2:8 mentions together with them "those who handle the Torah"). In the time of the Second Temple, the *sofrim* ("scribes") were the teachers and explicators of *torah*, while the authority for halakhic instruction and legal determination was invested in the Great Court. The legislation and decrees, reports of the acts of the courts, and explanations of the words of the

"Let him read and declare it and set it in order for me."

ISAIAH 44:7

In the Talmud and Midrash, all of the rabbis are committed to the proposition that God is One.

PAGE 243

T

TORAH

Reading the Torah in the Synagogue

Many scriptures have primary or secondary schemes of division according to the needs of recitation or reading aloud in the community (e.g., the 154 divisions of the Torah for synagogal reading over a three-year span).

PAGE 593

Torah all become part of the oral *torah,* and the commandment of *talmud Torah* was considered to apply also to them.

The desire to know how to fulfill accurately the commandments of the Torah is only one of the justifications for *talmud Torah.* Also significant is the desire to gain understanding of the Torah, its intentions, and the way in which it develops and expands. The requirement to study torah is incumbent on every man, whatever his situation. The Babylonian amora Rav, describing God's daily schedule, declared that during the first three hours of the day he "sits and engages in *torah* study" (B. T., *'A. Z.* 3b).

The content of the studies, their breadth, and the method of study varied in different times and places. There were times when the study of the rest of the biblical books was not included together with the study of the Torah itself. Some students concentrated only on the study of *halakhah,* while others preferred the *aggadah.* There were those who included the study of philosophy and Qabbalah, while some stressed attention to *musar* ("ethical teachings"). Within the study of *halakhah* itself there were various methods of study: some emphasized casuistry and sharp-wittedness, while others stressed the importance of broad knowledge of the sources and drawing conclusions for practical application. Still, everyone recognized that the requirement to study *torah* is incumbent on the entire community in some form or another. Thus public homilies in the synagogues on Sabbaths and holidays were instituted.

READING THE TORAH IN THE SYNAGOGUE. Today the reading of the Torah occupies a central role in communal prayer. Public reading of the Torah is mentioned three times in the Bible, but always on special occasions. The first mention is in *Deuteronomy* 3:10-13: Moses commanded the reading of "this Torah before all Israel" in the Sabbatical year during the festival of Sukkot (Tabernacles). In the opinion of tannaim (*Sot* 3.8, *Sifrei Dt.* 160), the king was commanded to read *Deuteronomy* with certain abridgments during this ceremony. Another reading is mentioned in *2 Kings* (23:1-2), where King Josiah is said to have "read in their ears all the words of the book of the covenant which was found in the house of God." It seems reasonable to assume that this account served as a source for the aforementioned tannaitic description.

Nehemiah (8:1-8) tells how Ezra the scribe brought the scroll of the Torah before the congregation on the first day of the seventh month and read from it "in the ears of the entire people clearly, and he gave the sense." In this reading the people found "written in the Torah which God commanded by the hand of Moses that the people of Israel sat in tabernacles during the festival of the seventh month" (8:4). When they then celebrated this festival of Sukkot, they again read "in the book of the Torah of the Lord every day, from the first day until the last day" (8:18). This account can be viewed as the start of the custom of reading the Torah publicly on festivals.

Reading the Torah on the Sabbath is mentioned by Philo (*Moses* 2.216; see Eusebius's *Praeparatio evangelica* 8.2) and Josephus (*Against Apion* 2.175) and in the *Acts of the Apostles* (15:21) as an ancient custom. In the description of the ceremonial rite of Yom Kippur, the Mishnah (*Yoma'* 3.1) reports that the high priest read sections of the Torah appropriate to the day (*Lv.* 16:1-34, 23:26-32; *Nm.* 29:7-11). In addition to the readings on Sabbaths, festivals, and the holidays mentioned in the Torah, the Mishnah also fixes public readings for Hanukkah, Purim, New Moons, public fast days, Mondays and Thursdays (which were market days), and during the afternoon service on the Sabbath (*Meg.* 3.6, 4.1) as well as during *ma'amadot,* assemblies of the watches that gathered in the Temple and in their towns to pray and read from the Torah while the priests and Levites from their region performed the rites in the Temple (*Ta'an.* 3.4).

The Mishnah specifies only the portions to be read on festivals, on the four special Sabbaths between the beginning of the month of Adar and Passover, on public fast days, and during *maamadot* (*Meg.* 3.5-6). The Mishnah also fixes the number of people who go up to read from the Torah on each occasion. On Mondays, Thursdays, and Sabbath afternoons, three people read; on New Moons and the intermediate days of the festivals, four; on holidays, five; on Yom Kippur, six; and on the Sabbath, seven (*Meg.* 4.1-2). The first two people to go up to read are a *kohen* (one of priestly descent) and a Levite (*Git.* 8.8), if such are present. In Mishnaic times, the first person to go up pronounced the blessing before reading the Torah and the last person recited the afterblessing, while everyone who went up in between read without making a blessing (*Meg.* 4.1). Subsequently the custom was changed so that each reader recited a blessing before and after reading (B. T., *Meg.* 21b).

The Mishnah mentions the custom of translating each verse into the language spoken by the people—that is, Aramaic—at the same time as it was read in Hebrew (*Meg.* 4.4). This custom is apparently very ancient, perhaps as old as the custom of public Torah reading itself. In places where the vernacular was Greek, it was customary to begin and end the reading in Hebrew but to read the intermediate portions in Greek so that the congregation could understand the portion (Tosefta, *Meg.* 3.13).

The public Torah reading was supplemented with a reading from the prophetic books. This reading from the Prophets is called the *haftarah.* Generally the portion chosen to be read as the *haftarah* parallels in some way the content of the *seder* or *parashah* read from the Torah on the same occasion.

— E. E. URBACH

TRANSLATED FROM HEBREW BY AKIVA GARBER

TRICKSTERS

INTRODUCTION

TRICKSTER is the name given to a type of mythic figure distinguished by his skill at trickery and deceit as well as by his prodigious biological drives and exaggerated bodily parts. The myths of many cultures portray such a comic and amoral character, who is sometimes human but is more often animal in shape, typically an animal noted for agility and cunning: the wily coyote, the sly fox, the elusive rabbit, or the crafty spider. Sometimes the trickster is the agent who introduces fire, agriculture, tools, or even death to the human world. As such, he plays the part of another mythic archetype, the transformer, or culture hero, who in a mythic age at the beginning of the world helps shape human culture into its familiar form. However, the trickster's distinction lies not so much in his particular feats as in the peculiar quality of his exploits—a combination of guile and stupidity—and in the ludicrous dimensions of his bodily parts and biological drives. In those cultures where he stands independent of other mythic figures, his adventures are recounted in a separate cycle of myths and lore. The trickster represents a complicated combination of three modes of sacrality: the divine, the animal, and the human.

— LAWRENCE E. SULLIVAN

AFRICAN TRICKSTERS

Like their counterparts in Amerindian myth and folklore, African tricksters inject bawdiness, rebellion, and wild lying (one might aptly call it polymorphous perversity) into the mythic history and the common experience of divine-human relations wherever they appear. Unlike many tricksters elsewhere, however, these multiform world-shatterers and pathfinders in Africa are woven not only into the fabric of myth but also into the stuff of everyday life, playing a part in economics, rites of passage, and ordinary conversation.

African trickster figures are images of an ironic imagination that yokes together bodiliness and transcendence, society and individuality. The trickster in Africa shows by his witty juggling with meaning and absurdity that he is more accurately understood as a spectrum of commentaries on mythic commentary than as a "category." This epistemological playfulness seems to represent a sophisticated African form of religious thought. It is perhaps a commonplace to insist that in every system the order of the center and the wildness of the periphery are linked. It is a bold piece of spiritual logic to make this insistence a joke—or even more, a joking relationship.

The link between divination and the trickster represents a still deeper level of meaning that West Africans especially have found in him. The Yoruba, like the Fon (who have adopted much of the Yoruba system of divination, known as Ifa) and the Dogon, see their trickster god as the chief possessor of divination's language. Esu is a disruptive mediator, "the anger of the gods," who stirs up trouble to increase sacrifice, yet his quickness of eye and hand symbolizes a metaphysical slipperiness that makes him both sociotherapist and iconographer. At moments of conflict the meetings that create a world become collisions. Lines of connection break down, intersections turn into dead ends, and, as the myths say, all becomes as fluid as water, as destructive as fire. Divination seeks to transform these dead ends into thresholds of larger meaning; Yoruba divination particularly knows that to give answers to knotted social and spiritual questions is, finally, to redraw an *imago mundi,* to restore the shattered icon of the Yoruba cosmos. Esu is not the source of most divinatory responses, but he enables divination to run its course.

[*See also* African Religions.]

— ROBERT D. PELTON

NORTH AMERICAN TRICKSTERS

The most prominent and popular personage, generally speaking, in the varied oral traditions of the numerous Amerindian peoples living north of the Rio Grande is the figure known as the trickster. With rare exceptions, North American tricksters are beings of the mythic age only; they are not believed to be living gods or spirits, and they have no cult (other than the semiritualistic narration of their stories). Their relationship to shamanism, the definitive religious form in most of the region, is debated. Tricksters' activities in myths often resemble shamans' journeys to the spirit world, but tricksters ordinarily employ no "helpers," and shamans do not seek help from "trickster spirits."

The concept of the trickster as a type is based upon his most essential trait: his trickiness. Tricksters everywhere are deceitful, cunning, amoral, sexually hyperactive, taboo-breaking, voracious, thieving, adventurous, vainglorious—yet not truly evil or malicious—and always amusing and undaunted. Even though his activities are usually motivated by ungoverned desire, the trickster is capable of performing deeds that benefit

The Plains culture hero or trickster who figures importantly as the mediator between the supernaturals and humankind goes by a number of names.

PAGE 500

others: releasing imprisoned game, the sun, the tides, and such; vanquishing and/or transforming evil monsters; and, like the shaman, journeying to the land of the spirits or the dead to rescue a lost loved one. The significant element in all these deeds is trickery. Moreover, as a being of insatiable appetites (for food and sex), he cannot afford the luxury of scruples. Thus he breaks incest taboos (rapes or marries in disguise his daughter or mother-in-law) and hoodwinks small animals into dancing with eyes closed so he can kill them. Nothing is sacred in his eyes.

In addition to humorous trickster folk tales, which are remarkably similar all over North America, each region has its own set of traditions about the mythic age, and in a majority of instances the leading personage of that time was a trickster.

The central character in Mataco mythic narrative (pahlalís), Tokhwáh, is the one who imposes cosmic and ontological order on the present-day world.

PAGE 620

In the Plateau region of the northwestern United States, Coyote is usually regarded as the maker or procreator of the people, sometimes using the body of a river monster he kills, sometimes by cohabitation with trees after a flood. His principal cycle concerns his release of the salmon and his subsequent journey up the Columbia River, leading the salmon. He demands a "wife" at each village, and if his request is granted, he makes that place a good fishing spot.

In California and the Great Basin region, Coyote usually is involved in a dualistic relationship with a wise, benevolent creator (Eagle, Fox, Wolf, or an anthropomorphic figure). Set against the backdrop of a world flood (or fire), the earth is remade and repopulated by the two, with Coyote ordaining the "bad" things such as mountains, storms, and fruit growing out of reach. Coyote decrees death—and then his son is the first to die. So Coyote establishes mourning rites for people to "enjoy." He also decrees conception by sex and painful childbirth.

The Paiute and Shoshoni of the Great Basin consider Coyote the progenitor of the people (through intercourse with a mysterious woman following the flood). But among the Pueblo, whose mythology centers on an emergence from the underground, Coyote plays a rather minor role in most tribes. On the Great Plains, Coyote is known primarily as a trickster only. Some northern tribes credit him with the recreation of the earth after the deluge, and the Kiowa consider themselves the people of Sendah, a Coyote-like figure, who led them out of a hollow log in the beginning. The Oglala are one of the few groups in North America who consider the trickster genuinely evil, and almost the only tribe that believes the trickster to be a living spirit.

The Algonquins, inhabiting a large part of eastern and midwestern Canada, New England, and the area around the three western Great Lakes, have mythologies centered on anthropomorphic culture heroes who were also tricksters, though seldom foolish, plus several minor theriomorphic tricksters.

In some tribes humorous trickster tales are relegated to a category apart from the more serious "myths," but because all these narratives are set in "myth times," they are never confused with quasi-historical legends or accounts of shamanic experiences. Thus, to some degree, a quality of sacredness adheres to the person of the trickster everywhere, despite the seemingly profane nature of many of the narratives.

[*See also* North American Religions.]

— MAC LINSCOTT RICKETTS

MESOAMERICAN AND SOUTH AMERICAN TRICKSTERS

The peoples of Mesoamerica and South America maintain lively traditions concerning a cunning and deceitful mythic figure, the trickster. Although tricksters are ludicrous rather than solemn beings, they cannot be discounted as trivial because their activities and transformations touch on religious issues. For instance, they steal fire, which is deemed the center of social and physical life, and their clever bungling frequently introduces death.

Tricksters are usually animals that have bodies riddled with passages, or they may have excessively large orifices, any of which may be cut open or penetrated. The contemporary Huichol, who live in the Sierra Madre Occidental, in north-central Mexico, consider Káuyúumaari ("one who does not know himself" or "one who makes others crazy") one of their principal deities (Myerhoff, 1974). Káuyumarie is the animal sidekick of the supreme Huichol deity, Tatewari ("our grandfather fire"). Irreverent, clever, and amusing, Káuyumarie brought about the first sexual intercourse between man and woman.

Tricksters distort sight and sound purely to create illusion and noise. The Aztec divinity, Tezcatlipoca ("smoking mirror"), uses an obsidian mirror to distort images. He was able to trick Quetzalcoatl, for example, into looking into the mirror in which Quetzalcoatl saw a repulsive and misshapen being. Tezcatlipoca in one of his assumed shapes is Huehuecoyotl ("drum coyote"), the puckish patron of song and dance.

Extraordinary body designs or cross-sex dress, which the trickster sometimes manifests, is a way in which the contrary conditions of existence are mediated. In her study of Zinacantecan myth from the Chiapas Highlands of Mexico, Eva Hunt links contemporary female tricksters to the sixteenth-century goddess Cihuacoatl, a female deity with a tail, a fake baby, and a snake, which emerges from under her skirt and from between her legs.

Tricksters often opposed the dominant supernatural beings of their day and embarrassed or humiliated the divine patrons of priests, shamans, and other privileged religious specialists. In other myths tricksters steal various forms of life from the underworld. For example, the Sanumá (Yanoama) of the Venezuela-Brazil border region, tell of Hasimo, a mythic bird-man, who steals fire from a primordial alligator, which stores fire in its mouth, by shooting excrement into its face, forcing the alligator to laugh (Taylor, 1979).

Tricksters are sometimes wedged in the dangerous passages between two states of being, and through their efforts to rescue themselves—using perhaps a hole, or vine, as a passage—these states of being become altered forever.

In the Gran Chaco area of southern South America, the Mataco trickster Tokhwáh—also known as Tawkx-wax, Takwaj, Takjuaj, Tokhuah—is both good and bad, and, although he advances human capabilities, every step forward brings comic disaster (Simoneau and Wilbert, 1982). Tokhwáh acts bisexually, chasing women and often seduced by men. His exploits require an entire cycle of myths, and he is at once divine and earthly, creative and destructive.

The actions of Mesoamerican and South American tricksters reveal the contradictions at the heart of human experience: carnal and spiritual, living but mortal, ambitious but finite. With a blend of humor and tragedy, trickster myths describe the calamities that occur when contrary conditions of being collide and overlap in a single experience.

— LAWRENCE E. SULLIVAN

TRINITY

Trinitarian doctrine touches on virtually every aspect of Christian faith, theology, and piety, including Christology and pneumatology, theological epistemology (faith, revelation, theological methodology), spirituality and mystical theology, and ecclesial life (sacraments, community, ethics). This article summarizes the main lines of trinitarian doctrine without presenting detailed explanations of important ideas, persons, or terms.

The doctrine of the Trinity is the summary of Christian faith in God, who out of love creates humanity for union with God, who through Jesus Christ redeems the world, and in the power of the Holy Spirit transforms and divinizes (*2 Cor.* 3:18). The heart of trinitarian theology is the conviction that the God revealed in Jesus Christ is involved faithfully and unalterably in covenanted relationship with the world. Christianity is not unique in believing God is "someone" rather than "something," but it is unique in its belief that Christ is the personal Word of God, and that through Christ's death and resurrection into new life, "God was in Christ reconciling all things to God" (*2 Cor.* 5:19). Christ is not looked upon as an intermediary between God and world but as an essential agent of salvation. The Spirit poured out at Pentecost, by whom we live in Christ and are returned to God (Father), is also not a "lesser God" but one and the same God who creates and redeems us. The doctrine of the Trinity is the product of reflection on the events of redemptive history, especially the Incarnation and the sending of the Spirit.

DEVELOPMENT OF TRINITARIAN DOCTRINE. Exegetes and theologians today are in agreement that the Hebrew Bible does not contain a doctrine of the Trinity, even though it was customary in past dogmatic tracts on the Trinity to cite texts like *Genesis* 1:26, "Let us make humanity in our image, after our likeness" (see also *Gn.* 3:22, 11:7; *Is.* 6:2-3) as proof of plurality in God. Although the Hebrew Bible depicts God as the father of Israel and employs personifications of God such as Word *(davar)*, Spirit *(ruah)*, Wisdom *(hokhmah)*, and Presence *(shekhinah)*, it would go beyond the intention and spirit of the Old Testament to correlate these notions with later trinitarian doctrine.

Further, exegetes and theologians agree that the New Testament also does not contain an explicit doctrine of the Trinity. God the Father is source of all that is (Pantokrator) and also the father of Jesus Christ; "Father" is not a title for the first person of the Trinity but a synonym for God. Early liturgical and creedal formulas speak of God as "Father of our Lord Jesus Christ"; praise is to be rendered to God through Christ (see opening greetings in Paul and deutero-Paul). There are other binitarian texts (e.g., *Rom.* 4:24, 8:11; *2 Cor.* 4:14; *Col.* 2:12; *1 Tm.* 2:5-6, 6:13; *2 Tm.* 4:1), and a few triadic texts (the strongest are *2 Cor.* 13:14 and *Mt.* 28:19; others are *1 Cor.* 6:11, 12:4-6; *2 Cor.* 1:21-22; *1 Thes.* 5:18-19; *Gal.* 3:11-14). Christ is sent by God and the Spirit is sent by Christ so that all may be returned to God.

The language of the Bible, of early Christian creeds, and of Greek and Latin theology prior to the fourth century is "economic" (*oikonomia,* divine management of earthly affairs). It is oriented to the concrete history of creation and redemption: God initiates a covenant with Israel, God speaks through the prophets, God takes on flesh in Christ, God dwells within as Spirit. In the New Testament there is no reflective consciousness of the metaphysical nature of God ("immanent trinity"), nor does the New Testament contain the technical language of later doctrine *(hupostasis, ousia, substantia, subsistentia, prosopon, persona)*. Some theologians have concluded that all post-biblical trinitarian doctrine is therefore arbitrary.

The doctrine of the Trinity has from the beginning been one of the most productive–and one of the most problematic–points of contact between Christian theology and speculative philosophy.

PAGE 162

"Let us make humanity in our image after our likeness."

GENESIS 1:26

TRINITY COLUMN, BUDAPEST *The Father and Son seated beneath the Holy Ghost, represented by a dove, on the Trinity Column represent a universal doctrine of Christian faith.* ADAM WOOLFITT/CORBIS

While it is incontestable that the doctrine cannot be established on scriptural evidence alone, its origins may legitimately be sought in the Bible, not in the sense of "proof-texting" or of finding metaphysical principles, but because the Bible is the authoritative record of God's redemptive relationship with humanity. What the scriptures narrate as the activity of God among us, which is confessed in creeds and celebrated in liturgy, is the wellspring of later trinitarian doctrine.

Dogmatic development took place gradually, against the background of the emanationist philosophy of Stoicism and Neoplatonism (including the mystical theology of the latter), and within the context of strict Jewish monotheism. In the immediate post-New Testament period of the Apostolic Fathers no attempt was made to work out the God-Christ (Father-Son) relationship in ontological terms. By the end of the fourth century, and owing mainly to the challenge posed by various heresies, theologians went beyond the immediate testimony of the Bible and also beyond liturgical and creedal expressions of trinitarian faith to the ontological trinity of coequal persons "within" God. The shift is from function to ontology, from the "economic trinity" (Father, Son, and Spirit in relation to us) to the "immanent" or "essential Trinity" (Father, Son, and Spirit in relation to each other). It was prompted chiefly by belief in the divinity of Christ and later in the divinity of the Holy Spirit, but even earlier by the consistent worship of God in a trinitarian pattern and the practice of baptism into the threefold name of God. By the close of the fourth century the orthodox teaching was in place: God is one nature, three persons *(mia ousia, treis hupostaseis)*.

Questions of Christology and soteriology (salvation) occupied theologians of the early patristic period. What was Christ's relationship to God? What is Christ's role in our salvation? The Logos Christology of the apologists identified the preexistent Christ of Johannine and Pauline theology with the Logos ("word") of Greek philosophy. The Stoic distinction between the immanent word *(logos endiathetos)* and the expressed word *(logos prophorikos)* provided a way for Justin Martyr (d. 163/165) and others to explain how Christ had preexisted as the immanent word in the Father's mind and then became incarnate in time. Third-century monarchianism arose as a backlash against Logos theology, which was feared to jeopardize the unity of God; the modalism of Sabellius admitted the distinctions in history but denied their reality in God's being. Origen (died c. 254) contributed the idea of the eternal generation of the Son within the being of God; although other aspects of Origen's theology later were judged to be subordinationist, his teaching that the Son is a distinct hypostasis brought about subtle changes in conceptions of divine paternity and trinity. In the West, Tertullian (d. 225?) formulated an economic trinitarian theology that presents the three persons as a plurality in God. Largely because of the theology of Arius, who about 320 denied that Christ was fully divine, the Council of Nicaea (325) taught that Christ is *homoousios* (of the same substance) with God. The primary concern of Athanasius (d. 373), the great defender of Nicene orthodoxy, was salvation through Christ; if Christ is not divine, he cannot save. Like the bishops at Nicaea, Athanasius had a limited trinitarian vocabulary; *hupostasis* (person) and *ousia* (substance) could still be used interchangeably.

The fourth-century Cappadocian theologians (Basil of Caesarea, Gregory of Nyssa, and Gregory of Nazianzus) formulated orthodox trinitarian doctrine and made it possible for the Council of Constantinople (381) to affirm the divinity of the Holy Spirit. The speculatively gifted Cappadocians made a clear distinction between *hupostasis* and *ousia* (roughly equivalent to particular and universal), thereby establishing orthodox trinitarian vocabulary. At the close of the patristic period John of Damascus (d. 749) summarized Greek trinitarian doctrine with the doctrine of *perichoresis* (Lat., *circumincessio*), or the mutual indwelling of the divine persons.

Western trinitarian theology took a different course because of Augustine (d. 430). Instead of regarding the Father as source of divinity, Augustine's starting point was the one divine substance, which the three persons share. He sought the image of the Trinity within the rational soul and formulated psychological analogies (memory, intellect, will; lover, beloved, love) that conveyed unity more than plurality. The Augustinian approach served to effectively refute Arianism, but it also moved the doctrine of the Trinity to a transcendent realm, away from salvation history, from other areas of theology, and from liturgy. In the Latin West Boethius (died c. 525) formulated the classic definition of person, namely, "individual substance of a rational nature." Augustinian theology was given further elaboration in medieval theology, especially by Anselm (d. 1109) and in the Scholastic synthesis of Thomas Aquinas (d. 1274). Still Augustinian but focusing on person rather than nature, Richard of Saint-Victor (d. 1173) and Bonaventure (d. 1274) developed a psychology of love; charity is the essence of Trinity.

Although there are important exceptions to any typology, in general, Greek theology emphasizes the hypostases, the "trinity in unity," whereas Latin theology emphasizes the divine nature, or "unity in trinity." The Greek approach can be represented by a line: Godhood originates with the Father, emanates toward the Son, and passes into the Holy Spirit who is the bridge to the world. Greek theology (following the

"Now this Trinity of the mind is God's image, not because the mind resembles, understands, and loves itself [the superficial analogy], but because it has the power also to remember, understand, and love its Maker."

AUGUSTINE DE TRINITATE

T

TRINITY

Principles of Trinitarian Doctrine

"Thus you will be able to grasp fully, with all the holy ones the breadth, length, and depth of Christ's love."

EPHESIANS 3:18

New Testament and early Christian creeds) retains the "monarchy" of the Father who as sole principle of divinity imparts Godhood to Son and Spirit. The Greek approach tends toward subordinationism (though hardly of an ontological kind) or, in some versions, to tritheism since in Greek theology each divine person fully possesses the divine substance. The Latin approach can be represented by a circle or triangle. Because the emphasis is placed on what the divine persons share, Latin theology tends toward modalism (which obscures the distinctiveness of each person). Also the Trinity is presented as self-enclosed and not intrinsically open to the world.

PRINCIPLES OF TRINITARIAN DOCTRINE. Trinitarian theology is *par excellence* the theology of relationship. Its fundamental principle is that God, who is self-communicating and self-giving love for us, is from all eternity love perfectly given and received. The traditional formula "God is three persons in one nature" compactly expresses that there are permanent features of God's eternal being (the three persons) that are the ontological precondition for the three distinct manners of God's tripersonal activity in the world (as Father, Son, Spirit).

Technical terms, theological theories, and official (conciliar) statements function together as a "set of controls" over the correct way to conceive both of God's self-relatedness as Father, Son, and Spirit, and God's relatedness to creation as Father, Son, and Spirit. Although one must guard against reducing the mystery of God to a set of formal statements, precise distinctions are useful insofar as they refine theological vocabulary or protect against distortions ("heresy"). Still, doctrinal statements are inherently limited; they address specific points of controversy, leaving other questions unsettled and sometimes creating new problems. Conciliar statements and theological principles guard against egregious errors (for example, "the Holy Spirit is a creature") and serve as boundaries within which trinitarian discourse may take place.

First, God is ineffable and Absolute Mystery, whose reality cannot adequately be comprehended or expressed by means of human concepts. Trinitarian doctrine necessarily falls short of expressing the full "breadth and length and height and depth" of God's glory and wisdom and love. Even though God who "dwells in light inaccessible" is impenetrable mystery, the doctrine of the Trinity is not itself a mystery, nor is the doctrine revealed by God, nor is the doctrine a substitute for the knowledge of God gained in the union of love that surpasses all concepts (see *Eph.* 3:18-19). Trinitarian doctrine is a partial and fragmentary exegesis of what has been revealed, namely, that God is self-communicating love. Further, because God is a partner in love and not an object to be scrutinized or controlled by the intellect, speculative theology must be firmly rooted in spirituality, doxology, and a concrete community of faith so that trinitarian doctrine does not become "heavenly metaphysics" unrelated to the practice of faith.

Second, the revelation and self-communication of the incomprehensible God, attested in the concrete images and symbols of the Bible and celebrated in Christian liturgy, is the proper starting point of trinitarian theology. Theological thinking proceeds from "God with us" ("economic" Trinity) to the nature of God ("immanent" Trinity). The starting point "within" God led to an overly abstract doctrine in the West and to a virtual divorce of the "immanent" Trinity from the Trinity of history and experience. Friedrich Schleiermacher (d. 1834) reacted against the cleavage between "God" and "God for us" by relegating the idea of the essential Trinity to an appendix to his summary of Christian theology. Karl Rahner's (d. 1984) widely accepted axiom is pertinent: "the 'economic' Trinity is the 'immanent' Trinity and vice versa." God is who God reveals God to be. Concepts that describe the ontological intrarelatedness of God must be drawn from and are subject to control by the "facts" of redemptive history.

Third, because the three persons together and inseparably (though without mingling or confusion) bring about salvation and deification, and because the one God is worshiped as Father, Son, and Spirit, no divine person is inferior to any other person. Although undivided, God exists as the pure relationality of love given and received. The decree of the Council of Florence (1442) that "everything in God is one except where there is opposition of relation" was regarded as a final answer to tritheism (belief in three gods), Arian subordinationism (ontological hierarchy of persons), Sabellian modalism (no real distinctions "in" God), and Macedonianism (denial of the divinity of the Holy Spirit).

There are two divine processions: begetting and spiration ("breathing"). Each divine person exists by relation to the other two persons (Gr., "relation of origin"; Lat., "relation of oppositon"), and each fully possesses the divine substance. In Greek theology the three hypostases have the distinguishing characteristics *(sg., idiotes)* of "being unbegotten" *(agennesia),* "being begotten" *(gennesia),* and "proceeding" *(ekporeusis).* The Father is the fountainhead of Godhood *(fons divinitatis),* who imparts divinity to Son and Spirit. According to Latin theology there are four relations (begetting, being begotten, spirating, being spirated) but only three "subsistent" relations: paternity, filiation, spiration. Latin theology (following Augustine) understands divine unity to reside in the divine nature that is held in common by Father, Son, and Spirit; Greek theology (following the Cappadocians) understands the unity to reside in the "perichoretic" relatedness of the three persons.

A corollary of the inseparability of the three coequal divine persons is the axiom that "all works of the triune God *ad extra* are indivisibly one" ("opera trinitatis ad extra indivisa sunt"). According to Latin theology it is the three-personed substance of God that acts in history; according to Greek theology every action of God toward creation originates with the Father, passes through the Son, and is perfected in the Spirit (Gregory of Nyssa). In any case, the axiom must not be understood to obscure what is distinctive to each divine person.

Fourth, a false distinction must not be set up between what God is and what God does, between essence and existence, between unity and threefoldness, between nature and person (relation). There are no "accidents" in God; the statement of the Fourth Lateran Council (1215) that each divine person is the divine substance countered the claim of some theologians (Joachim of Fiore) that God is a quaternity (three persons + essence = four persons).

Fifth, since the nature of God is to love, and love naturally seeks an object, it might appear that God "needs" the world as a partner in love. This would make the world coeternal with God. Many Scholastic theologians speculated on this question. Thomas Aquinas admitted that while he saw no philosophical reason to deny the eternity of the world, the testimony of the *Book of Genesis* and his Christian faith constrained him to do so. In 1329 Meister Eckhart was condemned for asserting the eternity of the world. With respect to trinitarian theology, even though Rahner's axiom (see above) suggests that God's relations to us, including creation, are constitutive of God and vice versa, theologians traditionally speak of a perfect and reciprocal exchange of love "within" God, that is, among Father, Son, and Spirit independent of their relationship to creation, in order to preserve the absolute character of God's freedom.

CURRENT DIRECTIONS AND REMAINING PROBLEMS. After centuries of disinterest in trinitarian doctrine in the West, the riches of this vast tradition are once again being explored. Three basic directions may be observed. First, some theologians have revised analogies of the "immanent" Trinity according to contemporary philosophy (for example, process metaphysics), linguistics, or interpersonal psychology. While this approach overcomes some of the aporia of classical expositions, it perpetuates the metaphysical starting point "within" God apart from salvation history. A second approach focuses on soteriology and Christology and is circumspect about the "immanent" Trinity, though without denying that historical distinctions are grounded ontologically in God. A third approach uses trinitarian symbolism to describe God's deeds in redemptive history but resists positing real distinctions in God. Despite basic differences in method, these three approaches all move in a more personalist (relational) direction and, in the case of the latter two, a more "economic" direction.

Theologians who specialize in trinitarian doctrine suggest that several areas warrant further attention. First, most trinitarian doctrine is so abstract it is difficult to see its connection with praxis. The "summary of Christian faith" and the living out of that faith should be brought to bear more directly on each other. Creeds, doxologies, and liturgy are important loci of the trinitarian faith recapitulated in trinitarian doctrine.

Second, unlike the "mystical theology" of the Orthodox tradition, theology in the West has been separated from spirituality since the thirteenth century. Reintegrating theology and spirituality would help to overcome the rationalist tendencies of Western theology, to provide the field of spirituality with theological foundation, and also to strengthen the weakest component of Western theology, namely, pneumatology.

Third, the *filioque* ("and from the Son") clause, inserted into the Western creed in the sixth century but denounced by the Orthodox church, remains a serious obstacle to reunion between East and West. Theologians should work assiduously for ecumenical agreement.

Fourth, to speak of God as "three persons" always has been problematic and remains the same today. In the modern framework "person" means "individual center of consciousness." To avoid the tritheistic implications of positing three "persons" in God, the relational, or "toward-the-other" character of "person" should be reemphasized.

Fifth, the exclusively masculine imagery of trinitarian doctrine hinders full recovery of the trinitarian insight into the essential relatedness of God. The fatherhood of God should be rethought in light of the critique of feminist theologies and also in view of the nonpatriarchal understanding of divine paternity to be found in some biblical and early theological writings.

Sixth, revising trinitarian theology along soteriological lines raises the question of its place in the dogmatic schema, that is, whether it ought to be treated as a separate "tract," as prolegomenous to theology, as its apex and summary, or as an undergird that is presupposed throughout but never alluded to explicitly.

Seventh, trinitarian theology must be pursued within the context of the "God question" of every age, whether this question takes the form of existentialist atheism, secular humanism, or some other.

Eighth, the Christian doctrine of God must be developed also within the wider purview of other world religions. Trinitarian doctrine cannot be chris-

As the fragment of a traditional creedal formula cited by Paul in Romans 1:4 explicitly attests, that same Holy Spirit continued to be operative in the resurrection of Jesus.

PAGE 81

tomonistic, excluding persons of other faiths from salvation, nor can it surrender its conviction that God is fully present in Christ.

For trinitarian doctrine to be recovered as a vital expression of God's nearness in Christ, theologians must translate into a contemporary idiom the mystery of God's triune love in a way that does justice not only to the testimony of our predecessors but also to the ongoing and ever-new features of God's relationship with a people.

— CATHERINE MOWRY LACUGNA

The appearance of the Türk—the first Inner Asian people whose language is known and the first also to use with certainty a Turkic idiom—marks a turning point in the history of the steppe.

PAGE 330

TURKIC RELIGIONS

Throughout the course of their long history, the Turkic peoples have simultaneously or successively practiced all the universal religions (Christianity, especially Nestorian Christianity; Judaism; Manichaeism; Buddhism; and Mazdaism) before the majority of them were won over to Islam. However, before yielding to these religions, they held their own system of beliefs, their own personal representations. These are generally identified as "animism" or "shamanism," even though the last term cannot even begin to cover the whole of the religious phenomena.

Until recently, it had been considered impossible to understand the religion of the Turkic people in its ancient form. Studies, especially ethnographic ones, have been written on groups of people who continued to practice the religion in modern times (nineteenth to twentieth century). Only recently has it been observed that the inscribed Turkic stelae of the sixth to the tenth century, certain manuscripts (including the dictionary of Mahmud al-Kashghari, eleventh century), and foreign sources (especially Chinese but also Byzantine, Arabic, Latin, Armenian, and Syrian) present a considerable wealth of information. This information takes on full meaning when compared with ethnographic notes, medieval Mongolian sources, and pre-Islamic remnants in Turkic-Muslim plastic and literary works. Thus we begin to have, if not a complete knowledge of the ancient Turkic religion, at least a satisfactory view of the overall picture.

THE COMMON HERITAGE. With a few small exceptions, the Turkic religion has offered structures to all peoples of all social classes in all regions of the Turkic world throughout history. Admittedly, there was a less influential period during which the religion was developing, but it appears to have been firmly established as early as the first century CE.

Although the religion was fairly well established early on, certain innovations appeared over the course of time. Without doubt, the dualism already apparent in the Turkic religion has been accentuated through the influence of Manichaeism. From Buddhism has come a conception of hell as a cosmic zone situated under the earth in symmetry with the sky (a deity).

Ideas that have remained unchanged are those relative to death, the afterlife, and funerary rites (apart from the issue of burial versus incineration). Death, which one hopes will be violent and unnatural (in spite of the respect that is occasionally shown the elderly) is considered the Necessity, Kergek (perhaps a deity). However, it is deeply dreaded and has given rise to bitter regrets, supposedly issued from the mouths of the deceased. Death is eminently contagious and requires a sober approach toward the dying one (generally abandoned) or the deceased. The funerary ceremonies have survived the centuries without having been changed.

The universe is generally represented as composed of two parallel plains, the sky and the earth (ultimately extended to three with the addition of the underworld). At the same time, it is also seen as a square plateau (earth), covered by a circumscribed dome (sky), with the four corners of the earth being allowed to exist outside the shelter of the sky. The cosmic axis that links the sky, the earth, and the underworld can be a mountain or a tree with seven branches, each branch representing a level of the sky. The levels of the sky are in turn derived from the seven planets still known to have been popularly believed in during modern times but also attested to by prehistoric engravings and by every construction with symbolic value, for example, the pillar of the tent, the ensemble formed by the central hearth of the yurt, and its upper opening, through which the smoke escapes. This axis is at once the support for the sky and the path that permits access to it.

The observation of stars is an important occupation. The phases of the moon are considered lucky or unlucky. No projects are to be undertaken when the moon is in its last quarter, although a good time to launch a military campaign is when the moon is waxing or is full. The last days of the lunar month are favorable for obsequies because they mark an end and announce a rebirth. Similarly, human life closely parallels plant life.

In one way or another, all animals have had a numinous role, but certain animals are different from others: the bird of prey, the eagle or falcon, is a divine messenger that flies near Tengri and sits enthroned on the summit of the cosmic tree; the stag is often considered a saint, but is hunted nevertheless; the hare's position is as ambiguous as that of the camel, which is totemized or tabooed as impure; the bear is the quintessential lunar animal, whose hibernation stirs the imagination; geese or swans, which appear in the widespread legend of the swan maiden, may symbolize the celestial virgin; all birds are souls; and the horse, a member of the clan, is the epitome of the sacrificial animal and also often a solar or aquatic symbol.

Despite a strong family structure, accounts of adoption by animals or humans are numerous, and fraternity is not dependent upon birth alone. Fraternity can be pledged between two strangers through the exchange of significant gifts (osselets, arrows, horses) and particularly through the mixing of blood. The rite that establishes fraternity consists of the two postulants' joining their slashed wrists or drinking mixed drops of their blood from a cup that is often made from the dried skull top of a murdered enemy chief.

THE POPULAR RELIGION. Despite the pretensions of certain shamans to positions of tribal leadership, shamanism is essentially a religious phenomenon, a dominant one in the religious life of contemporary non-Muslim Turkic peoples and one that is at the heart of the popular religion. It speaks to the people of things that interest them most—the preservation of their life (magical healings), their future (divination), and their relations with the familiar gods and spirits (the shaman's sacerdotal role, his cosmic voyage). The institution of shamanism is surely quite ancient. Although poorly discernible in antiquity, it was in full bloom by the time of the Middle Ages, despite the total silence of the Türk inscriptions on the subject.

The totemic system, which can exist only in tribal societies that employ it to determine basic structures (families, clans), plays a role in the popular religion that is almost as important as that of shamanism. For a long time, totemism was unknown among the Altaic peoples in general; however, in the mid-twentieth century pioneering research by P. J. Strahlenberg, Chodzidlo, A. Billings, N. Shchukin, and others revealed a totemic system among both contemporary and extinct Turkic societies, such as the Bashkirs, the Oghuz, and the western Türk.

Out of a desire to maintain control over the earth's products, the people made "soul supports"; these represented the spirit protectors of animals and harvests. They were among the numerous idols placed in the yurts and were also transported in carts, which became veritable traveling altars. Constructed of felt, wood, and metal, these zoomorphic or anthropomorphic idols could also represent and contain the soul of ancestors and of all imaginable powers. One took care of them, fed them, and painted them with blood. Ethnographers eventually began to call these idols by the Mongol word *ongon* (Turkic equivalents: *töz, tyn, kürmes*), although *ongon* actually refers to totems.

THE IMPERIAL RELIGION. It is difficult to comprehend the significance and the success of the imperial religion without taking into account the tribal organization of society, with its attendant instability, internecine wars, anarchy, and misery. Despite the tribes' pronounced taste for independence and their attachment to tradition, the empire presented certain advantages that the tribes were prepared to accept, even if it meant losing part of their patrimony along with their autonomy. Certainly the sovereign, promoted through his own genius or through circumstances, was descended from the tribal regime and practiced the popular religion. This fact, together with his need to secure mass support, inclined him to tolerate the tribal religion; but he reorientated it, promoting elements that had been secondary, diluting or eliminating elements that were in essence antimonarchist. The two great victims were shamanism and totemism.

The popular gods suffered less from the imperial religion. Any major force that contributed to the power of the empire was welcomed, and the Turkic peoples, with their fundamental beliefs in the diffused divine, opposed the disappearance of these gods. (Popular sentiment also had to be respected.) Nevertheless, their fate was not always the same. Some were more or less forgotten, while others were promoted. Still others were obviously approached from a new perspective. The various *iduq yer sub,* the "forbidden places," the "master-possessors of the earth and waters," were apparently reduced to those originally belonging to the imperial family. On the other hand, everything that appeared to be universal, common to all man, grew disproportionately. The earth goddess was often associated with the sky god and partook of his indivisibility. The sky himself, principally Tengri, became the sky god and was "blue," "elevated," and "endowed with strength"; he clearly became, at least eventually, "eternal," the supreme god above all others because he was the god of the emperor and was as exceptional as the latter was.

The national god of the Turkic peoples, Tengri, was also the god of all men and demanded that all recognize him, that is, that they submit to the Turkic kaghan—a demand that caused him to take on the characteristics of a god of war. The worst transgression was to revolt against the prince, that is, against Tengri, and the god knew no other punishment for this than death.

If the popular religion has been passed over in silence by imperial Turkic texts, and often by others, there are nonetheless numerous deities that appear around the sky god without our knowing their connections to him: the earth goddess, the *iduq yer sub* and other master-possessors, the sacred springs and rivers, the trees, fire, and the mountain. The most powerful and stable of these deities that appear around the sky god is Umai (often still called this today but also known by other names, for example, Aiyysyt among the Siberian Yakuts), a placental goddess of whom al-Kashghari says, "If one worships her, a child will be born." Certain attempts seem to have been made to

"I call the gods to witness."

WILLIAM SHAKESPEARE
TIMON OF ATHENS

bring her closer to Tengri; she has been called "close to the khatun," that is, to the empress.

The *baba* are the funerary statues of deceased princes and, occasionally, princesses. They were not viewed as images of the departed but as images of the living, who, after their death, remained among the people. Not of great aesthetic value, these huge, crude statues, of which a good number of specimens are known, represent the individual standing or seated, always holding a cup in the right hand, which is drawn back over the stomach. These works were the original image of the "prince in majesty" of classical Islam.

It is impossible to know whether belief in an afterlife in the sky was of imperial or popular origin, although there is no lack of presumptions that favor imperial origins: having come from the sky and belonging to it, the prince can only return there. In so asserting, one says that he "flies away," later that he "becomes a gyrfalcon" or that he "climbs up to the sky" where he is "as among the living." But there are also attestations of a celestial beyond for those who did not attain sovereignty—a place for those close to the prince, his servants, horses, concubines, and all those who could serve him or be useful to him. However, even if the sky was easily accessible to all—something we do not know—there was nothing to prevent the various souls of the same man, even those of a kaghan, from finding other places to inhabit (the tomb, the banner, the *balbal,* the *baba*), from being reincarnated in a new body, or from roaming the universe as an unsatisfied phantom.

— JEAN-PAUL ROUX
TRANSLATED FROM FRENCH BY
SHERRI L. GRANKA

UNDERWORLD

The term *underworld* refers to the subterranean region inhabited by the dead. It is often the place of punishment of the wicked, the unrighteous, the unredeemed, the unbelieving, or the lost. The concept of an underworld is an ingredient in most belief systems in the history of religions, but there is no definite evidence indicating that the idea was present in the earliest stages of human culture. In the oldest strata of Egyptian and pre-Vedic Indian cultures, however, there exists a rich store of archaeological material suggesting that the aristocratic segments of society, at least, believed in some kind of an afterlife.

PRIMITIVE AND ARCHAIC RELIGIONS. Tales of heroic journeys to the underworld, often undertaken on behalf of the entire community, are extremely widespread among tribal peoples throughout the world. Particularly notable for such lore are the Maori of New Zealand; various Plains tribes of North America; the Zulu, the Ashanti, and the Dogon of Africa; and numerous other societies in North Asia.

Many tribal peoples situate the land of the dead in the west, on the western side of the world, or simply at some distance west of the village.

One important theme concerns the descent of a hero into the belly of a ferocious marine creature and his reemergence through the mouth or anus of the beast in an effort to conquer death and gain immortality. A second theme is of an arduous journey through wild and monster-infested areas in search of a precious object (magical ring, sacred fruit, golden vessel, elixir of immortality, etc.) that will benefit the hero or his people. In a third theme, a tribesman submits himself to a deadly ordeal in order to pass from a lower to a higher stage of existence and thereby achieves a superhuman or heroic state of being.

ANCIENT EGYPT. The afterlife of the Egyptian nobility is described in the Pyramid Texts. Royalty were believed to ascend at death to the Blessed Lands, or Fields of the Blessed, in the heavens. According to the Pyramid Texts, members of the aristocracy traveled to the celestial spheres to dwell there like gods, often traveling on the ship belonging to Re, the sun god. Highly elaborate and expensive mortuary rites, charms, and incantations were offered for the nobility to guarantee that the soul of the deceased would enjoy a blissful existence in the world beyond.

The dead traveled to many different realms, some to the east but most to the west. The west was the primary destination of the souls *(ka)* of the dead. Darkness and night were identified symbolically with death and postmortem existence. The realm of the dead was located sometimes in the sky and sometimes beneath the earth. This region was ruled by Osiris, the king of the dead.

ASSYRIA AND BABYLONIA. In the views of the ancient Akkadians and Babylonians, the underworld is a dreadful place. To get there one has to pass through seven gates and remove a piece of clothing at each. The realm is organized on the order of a political state under the tyrannical rule of a king and a queen, Nergal and Ereshkigal. Once in the underworld, the fate of the deceased is improved or worsened depending on whether the body is buried according to the prescribed funeral rites and is provided by the living with food, clothing, and other accoutrements required for the journey to the other realm.

Much more significant for our understanding of the religion of this period and of much that had been developing and evolving before it are the Pyramid Texts.

PAGE 213

WANDERING SOUL

This papyrus scroll from the Egyptian Book of the Dead describes the wanderings of the soul (ka) and its appraisal by the Gods of the Underworld.

CORBIS-BETTMANN

U

UNDERWORLD

Greece and Rome

There was another class of divinities associated with the waters beneath the earth's surface and with darkness.

PAGE 327

"Then death and the nether world were hurled into a pool of fire, which is the second death."

REVELATION 20:14

GREECE AND ROME. The earliest Greek accounts of the postmortem journey of the soul to the underworld are to be found in the *Iliad* (1.595, 3.279, 5.395-396, 15.187-188) and in the *Odyssey* (11). At the moment of death, the soul *(psuche)* is separated from the body, transformed into a ghostly double of the person *(eidolon)*, and transported down to Hades, an enormous cavern below the surface of the earth (*Odyssey* 11.204-222).

In ancient Greek cosmology, Hades lies within the ocean, perpetually shrouded in clouds and mist. Here there is no sunlight, only eternal darkness. The shades are depicted as being weak and extremely melancholy, always in search of escape from their sufferings and finding none. Especially painful are the sufferings of those who were either not properly buried on earth or not suitably nourished with sacrificial food offerings. The dire nature of the torments suffered by the inmates is graphically depicted in the story of Tantalos. Standing in water up to his chin, he found to his chagrin that the water mysteriously evaporated each time he sought to quench his thirst; surrounded by flowering fruit trees, he found that the wind blew the fruit away as he reached out to grasp it (*Odyssey* 11.582-592).

Not until the time of Plato do we encounter the notion that the righteous will be feted with sumptuous banquets "with garlands on their heads," or that the wicked will be plunged into a pit filled with mud, "where they will be forced to carry water in a sieve" (*Republic* 2.373c-d). Plato may have believed that the earthly experience of the fear of Hades is equivalent to being there already and that the suffering inflicted by a guilty conscience is sufficient punishment for the wicked act committed. This view coincides with the theory that Plato adopted many primitive beliefs about the fate of the soul and gave moral and psychological interpretations to allegorical tales (see *Gorgias* 493a-c).

JUDAISM. References to the underworld in the Hebrew scriptures are vague and derive largely from beliefs common throughout the ancient Near East (especially Egypt and Babylonia). Numerous terms are used to designate this shadowy realm, the two most popular names being *She'ol* (a word that seems peculiar to Hebrew) and *Gei' Hinnom* (Gr., *Geenna*; Eng., *Gehenna*).

The Hebrew scriptures place the domain of the dead at the center of the earth, below the floor of the sea (*Is.* 14:13-15, *Jb.* 26:5). Some passages locate the gates that mark the boundary of She'ol in the west. According to the Ethiopic *Apocalypse of Enoch* (22:9-13), She'ol is not an abode of all the dead, where the souls merely exist as vague shadowy figures devoid of individual characteristics, but is a spacious realm with three subdivisions. In time, She'ol came to be identified with Gehenna, the pit of torment, an idea that, in turn, informed the Christian concept of Hell (*Hb.* 2:5).

In the postbiblical Jewish apocalyptic tradition, among the seven heavens that extend above the earth, sinners are confined to the second heaven to await final judgment. North of Eden lies Gehenna, where dark fires perpetually smolder and a river of flames flows through a land of biting cold and ice. Here the wicked suffer numerous tortures (*2 En.* 3-9).

CHRISTIANITY. New Testament writers drew upon the postexilic Hebraic picture of Gehenna in formulating their understanding of the destination of the damned. Gehenna was imagined to be an enormous, deep pit that perpetually ejects clouds of putrid-smelling smoke from burning garbage, a pit where bodies of criminals and lepers are disposed of. Two significant alterations in the Hebraic concept of hell deserve mention: (1) there is a much sharper distinction between the realm of the blessed and the realm of the damned, and (2) the standard applied at the Last Judgment is defined by a person's attitude toward the person of Jesus and his teachings.

According to the eschatology of the *Book of Revelation*, a millennial reign is followed by the resurrection of the saints, and then by a period of universal conflict at the end of which Satan will be cast into a lake of fire and brimstone, preparatory to the resurrection of the remaining dead and the Last Judgment. Both Death and Hades are hypostatized as subterranean vaults that surrender the dead to be judged, after which Death and Hades themselves are thrown into the lake of fire, thus actualizing "the second death," that is, condemnation to the eternal fires of Hell (*Rv.* 20:11-15, 21:8).

Augustine (354-430 CE), the father of early medieval theology, perpetuated the concept of Hell as a bottomless pit containing a lake of fire and brimstone where both the bodies and the souls of men and the ethereal bodies of devils are tormented (*City of God* 21.10). For Thomas Aquinas, Hell never lacks space to accommodate the damned. it is a place where unhappiness infinitely exceeds all unhappiness of this world, a place of eternal damnation and torment.

The history of Christianity is dotted with periodic expressions of heretical dissent concerning the existence of Hell, notably by Origen, Erigena, Voltaire, and Nietzsche. But it was not until the seventeenth and eighteenth centuries, when rationalism began to find its voice, that a widespread decline of belief in Hell developed in Western culture.

ISLAM. According to the Qur'an, there are seven layers of heaven extending above the earth toward the celestial abode of God. Corresponding to the layers of heaven are seven descending depths of a vast funnel-shaped fire *(alnar)*. The topmost level of the netherworlds is Gehenna. This realm of death and torment is connected to the world of the living by a bridge that all the souls of the dead must traverse on the day of judgment. The varieties of punishment meted out to the damned become more painful and severe with each level of descent.

The Qur'an depicts Gehenna in highly pictorial and terrifying terms. It is referred to as the "Fire of Hell" (89:23) and is depicted as a kind of four-legged beast. Each leg is composed of seventy thousand demons; each demon has thirty thousand mouths. Each of the seven layers of the Fire is punctuated by a gate manned by a guardian who torments the damned.

The realms of the blessed and the damned are separated by a towering wall. Men who inhabit the heights of this partition can view the inhabitants of both worlds and recognize each group by their distinguishing marks. The blessed are recognizable by their smiling countenances; the damned, by their black faces and blue eyes (57:13).

In time, Muslim theologians began to emphasize God's grace and mercy and to downplay his anger and wrath.

HINDUISM. According to *Rgveda* 7.104 and *Atharvaveda* 8.4, the Vedic Hell is situated beneath the three earths, below the created order. It is characterized as a gigantic, bottomless chasm or abyss, a place of no return. In this infinitely deep pit, there is no light, only deep darkness (cf. *Rgveda* 2.29.6). In the very deepest realm lies the cosmic serpent, the archdemon Vrtra (*Rgveda* 1.32.10), who fell there after Indra slew him.

Some texts describe the Vedic Hell as insufferably hot or unbearably cold. It is a realm of absolute silence (*Rgveda* 7.104.5) and of total annihilation, a state that is depicted semi-anthropomorphically as lying in the lap of Nirrti, the destroyer. The inhabitants of Hell are those who live at cross-purposes with the universal law *(rta)*.

Later, in the Vedanta, hell came to be conceived in more strictly philosophical terms as the realm of pure nonbeing. Contrasted with this was the realm of being *(sat)*, the realm of living beings and of life itself that came to be referred to as *brahman*, the limitless and indefinable fulcrum of being.

In the Puranas (collections of classical Hindu mythologies), hells are depicted in terrifyingly graphic terms as places of extreme suffering and deprivation. In the *Ramayana* (7.21.10-20), Ravana, the ten-headed demon, witnesses a scene of indescribable wretchedness on entering Yama's abode. He hears the agonizing cries of the wicked being gnawed by dogs and devoured by worms. Pitiful screams shoot across the Vaitarani River from parched people on hot sand who are being sawed in half. The thirsty cry out for water; the hungry, for food.

SECULAR VISIONS. Among a growing number of religious intelligentsia the world over, both heaven and hell are gradually being sublimated or transmuted into psychological entities or realms, with the personal and collective unconscious serving as the source of both positive and negative feelings, images, and attitudes. Even the general mass of people in industrialized countries who claim to retain a belief in an underworld of some description have, in practice, largely transposed many of the ideas and themes previously associated with the underworld (e.g., divine judgment, suffering, torment, disease, death, and mental and physical anguish) into the arena of contemporary human affairs.

— J. BRUCE LONG

UNIATE CHURCHES

Uniate is the name given to former Eastern Christian or Orthodox churches that have been received under the jurisdiction of the church of Rome and retain their own ritual, practice, and canon law. The term carries a strong negative connotation in that it was first used by opponents to the union of Brest-Litovsk (1595) to indicate a betrayal of Orthodoxy. It is seldom used today by these churches to describe themselves.

MELCHITE CATHOLICS. The term *Melchite* refers to a Christian of the Byzantine rite—Catholic or Orthodox—from the patriarchates of Alexandria, Antioch, or Jerusalem. The Melchite faithful tried to preserve allegiance to both Rome and Constantinople. By 1724 renewed communication with Rome had resulted in the creation of a Catholic Melchite church alongside the Orthodox Melchite church, although no formal written agreement of union was ever drawn up. Many Melchite Catholics immigrated to North and South America at the beginning of the twentieth century and formed two eparchies (dioceses), in Newton, Massachusetts, and in Sao Paolo, Brazil.

MARONITE CHURCH. The Maronite church traces its origins to the fourth century and to the monk Maron, who received a Greek and Syrian literary education and went to Antioch to complete his studies. There he met and befriended John Chrysostom, who was soon to be the bishop of Constantinople. Centuries later, a community of Maronites grew up around the Monastery of Saint Maron on the banks of the Orontes River in northern Syria. Although the Maronite church never rejected the primacy of the Roman see, communication between the two churches was interrupted for centuries, and only after 1182 and the advent of the Crusaders was Roman recognition of the Maronite rite restored.

*The pages of the Hindu epics (*Mahabharata *and* Ramayana*) are littered with images of semidivine, angelic, and demonic creatures of a dizzying variety.*

PAGE 203

The Thomas Christians in Kerala and the Parava converts on the coast of Coromandel, on the other hand, declared and maintained their intention to be and to remain Indian Christians, a stance from which they have not departed in four centuries.

PAGE 452

The Maronite church is the only Uniate church that does not have a parallel Orthodox hierarchy. The church has undergone many influences tending to conform it to the Latin rite. The rite of the Maronite church belongs to a group of Antiochene rites, and its liturgical language is West Syriac or Aramaic.

RUTHENIANS. The most numerous Uniate church of the Byzantine rite is the Ruthenian. *Ruthenian* is derived from the Latin *Rutheni*, meaning "Russian" and is used by Western historians to designate Catholic Slavs of the Polish-Lithuanian state or of the Austro-Hungarian empire. The Ruthenians divided into two branches: to the north of the Carpathian Mountains under Polish or Russian control were the Galicians. The Subcarpathians lived on the southern side of the mountains and were influenced by Austro-Hungarian political and social conditions.

The subsequent political division of Galician territory subjected Byzantine Catholics there to persecution by their Orthodox brethern, who thought they had changed their traditions by allowing Latin rite deviations. In 1805 the see of Kiev was abolished and the Ruthenians placed under the protection of the Austro-Hungarian empire and the jurisdiction of the archbishop of Lvov (Lemberg), who was recognized as the primate of the Ruthenians of Galicia.

As nascent nationalism penetrated the Galician church, divisions began to arise. Ruthenians slowly developed a national consciousness in the Subcarpathian region and continued to refer to themselves as "Greek Catholics," an ethnic as well as a religious term. Those Ruthenians who assumed Hungarian culture called themselves Hungarians. The growth of Romanian nationalism created the same phenomenon among Byzantine rite Catholics in Romania.

After World War II the Soviet government actively persecuted Ruthenian Catholics to force them into the Russian Orthodox church. In a council of reunion held at Lvov (Lviv), the remaining faithful, whose families had been threatened with deportation, voted in March 1946 to abolish the union with Rome. The metropolitan see of Galicia was placed under the jurisdiction of the patriarchate of Moscow. In the case of the Subcarpathian Ruthenians, the territory of the diocese of Uzhgorod was ceded to the Soviet Union by Czechoslovakia after its occupation by the Soviet army. The Orthodox began to occupy Catholic churches under the protection of the civil administration. The abrogation of the union with Rome was signed in August 1949 in the Monastery of Saint Nicholas in Mukachevo.

The liturgy and ritual of the Ruthenian Catholics remained conservative for centuries and followed the main lines of the Orthodox tradition. The Synod of Zamosc (1720) did introduce a number of innovations as a result of pressure and persecution from the Polish government to conform the Ruthenian usage to the Latin rite.

Ruthenian emigration in large numbers began in the 1870s as a result of poor distribution of agricultural land, rising expectations from industrialization, and political and social pressures. The best statistics put the total emigration by 1919 at 220,000 to the United States; 180,000 to Canada; 128,000 to Brazil; 110,000 to Argentina; and 22,000 to Australia.

COPTIC UNIATE CHURCH. Despite attempts at union for centuries, the numbers of Uniate Copts remained small. Pope Leo XIII created a Coptic patriarchate of Alexandria, Egypt, in 1895, and a Catholic Coptic synod elected Cyril Makarios as patriarch in 1898. The see remained vacant from 1908 to 1947, when Mark II Khouzam was elected patriarch. Four dioceses were erected, and the number of the faithful began to increase dramatically.

MALABAR CHURCH OF INDIA. The Malabar church, according to tradition, was founded by the apostle Thomas. Hence the Malabarians refer to themselves as "Thomas Christians." Little is known about the Malabar church before the sixteenth century. Portuguese missionaries arrived in India in 1498. The Malabarians, who did not consider themselves to be separated from Rome, welcomed the Portuguese as brothers in the faith, but they refused to allow Latin practices into their church. The Portuguese archbishop of Goa, Alexis de Menezes, acted against what he thought were Nestorian errors in the Malabar church in 1597. He convoked and presided at the synod of Diamper in June 1599. At the synod the Malabar liturgy was changed. The anaphoras of Theodore of Mopsuestia and of Nestorius were suppressed; the formula "mother of God" was introduced wherever "mother of Christ" was discovered; the calendar of saints was rejected; and many Latin practices were introduced into the eucharistic liturgy and other sacramental rites. Further, the creed was inserted immediately after the reading of the gospel; unleavened bread and communion of the faithful under one species only was introduced; and a consecration prayer, translated from the Latin, was inserted at the fraction rite, instead of before the anamnesis and epiklesis. Currently a reform of the liturgy is taking place in the Malabar church that restores some of the pre-sixteenth-century ritual.

— THOMAS F. SABLE, S.J.

UNIFICATION CHURCH

The Unification Church was founded in Korea in 1954 by the Reverend Sun Myung Moon. Within a quarter of a century it had become one of the most widely known and controversial of the contemporary wave of new religious movements. In Korea it is known as the Tong Il movement. In the West it is referred to by a variety of names, such as the Holy Spirit Association for the Unification of World Christianity, the Unified Family, or the Moon Organization, but the movement's members are most popularly known as "Moonies." They believe in a messianic, millennial religion and dedicate their lives to the goal of restoring the kingdom of heaven on earth.

Moon was born in what is now North Korea in 1920. He has claimed that on Easter Day 1936 Jesus appeared to him and asked him to assume responsibility for the mission of establishing God's kingdom on earth. During the next two decades Moon is said to have communicated with various other religious leaders (such as Moses and the Buddha) and with God himself. Moon's teachings were written down by his followers and eventually published in English as the *Divine Principle.*

During the movement's early days in Korea it met with considerable opposition from both the established churches and government officials. Moon was imprisoned several times, and at one point spent two and a half years in a communist labor camp (from which he was released by United Nations forces during the Korean War).

In the late 1950s Unification missionaries went to Japan and the West. After a slow start the movement began to grow in Japan and in the United States, but it was not until the early seventies, when Moon himself moved to America, that the Unification Church became known to more than a handful of Westerners. Over the next ten years, however, Moon's name became a household word. He went on numerous lecture tours, always speaking through a Korean interpreter; large rallies were organized; leading academics were invited to international conferences and local and national dignitaries to lavish dinners and receptions, all sponsored by the Unification Church. The movement supported President Nixon during the Watergate crisis. Meanwhile, some valuable properties (including the New Yorker Hotel and the Tiffany building in Manhattan and several large estates elsewhere in New York State) were acquired by the organization. Businesses (such as fishing and ginseng products) run directly by or affiliated to the movement seemed to prosper; cultural activities (including the Little Angels dance troupe, the Go World Brass Band, and the New Hope Singers) flourished; a seminary for postgraduate studies was founded; daily newspapers in Tokyo, New York, and, later, Washington were launched; and, most visibly of all, clean-shaven, well-groomed, well-spoken young Moonies became a familiar sight, selling candles, candy, cut flowers, potted plants, Unification literature—and the Unification Church itself—on the streets of towns and cities throughout the free world.

Those who join the Unification Church tend to be disproportionately well-educated, middle-class youth in their early twenties. In Japan and the West full-time members usually live in communal centers and work for the movement. In Korea, membership is more likely to consist of families who live in their own homes and work for themselves or for Unification Church-related businesses. The number of fully committed members has been considerably lower than estimates in the media have suggested, partly because of a high drop-out rate; indeed, there have never been, at any one time, more than ten thousand full-time members in the whole of the West. (In the East, full-time membership has never exceeded about twice that number.) There is, however, a considerably larger category of membership, sometimes known as Home Church, which consists of those who are sympathetic toward the theology but continue to lead "normal" lives in the wider community.

The lifestyle of full-time Moonies is one of hard-working, sacrificial devotion to the task of "restoration." Frequently, long hours are spent raising funds or witnessing to potential converts. Members are expected to practice celibacy before marriage as well as for some time afterward. After they have been in the movement for two or three years, members can be "matched" with a partner suggested by Moon and, with hundreds or even thousands of other couples, take part in one of the movement's mass wedding ceremonies known as Blessings. The Blessing is the most important Unification rite, the members practicing relatively little else in the way of formal ritual, apart from a "pledge" which is taken on the first day of each week, month, and year and on the movement's holy days.

Unification theology is one of the most comprehensive to be produced by a contemporary new religion. *The Divine Principle* offers a reinterpretation of the Bible which, it is claimed, could unite all religions. God is portrayed as a personal being who created the world according to a few basic, universal principles. All creation consists of positive and negative (male and female) elements; these unite into larger units, which in turn unite through a give-and-take relationship to form a still larger whole. Adam and Eve were created in order that God might have a loving give-and-take relationship with them. The original plan was that they should mature to a stage of perfection at which they would be blessed in marriage and that, subsequently, their children and their children's children would populate a sinless world in complete harmony with God. This, however, was not to be. The Fall is interpreted not as the result of eating an apple, but as the conse-

World-accommodating movements, concentrate on providing religion for their followers' personal, interior lives.

PAGE 486

quence of a disobedience which involved the misuse of the most powerful of all forces: love. The special revelation claimed by Moon is that the archangel Lucifer, whom God had entrusted to look after Adam and Eve, became jealous of God's love for Adam and had a (spiritual) sexual relationship with Eve. Eve then persuaded Adam to have a (physical) sexual relationship with her. As a result of this premature union, which was Lucifer-centered rather than God-centered, the Fallen Nature, or original sin, of Adam and Eve has been transmitted to all subsequent generations. According to the *Divine Principle*, the whole of history can be seen as an attempt by God and man, and, in particular, by certain key figures of the Bible, to restore the world to the state originally intended by God.

Ultimately, restoration is only possible through the person of the Messiah, who with his wife will faithfully play the roles in which Adam and Eve failed—i. e., those of True Parents. They (and those whom they bless in marriage) will have children born without original sin. But for this to happen, man has to create a foundation ready to receive the Messiah. In practical terms this involves the concept of "indemnity," whereby a good, sacrificial deed can cancel "bad debts" accumulated in the past by a person or his ancestors. The role of the Messiah is seen as an office filled by a man born of human parents, but free of original sin. The *Divine Principle* teaches that Jesus was such a man, who could have restored the world, but, largely through the fault of John the Baptist, he was murdered before he had a chance to marry and he thus was able to offer the world only spiritual and not physical salvation through his death. Numerous parallels between the period before the time of Jesus and the last two thousand years are taken to indicate that the present time is the time of the Second Coming. Although it is not part of the official theology, members of the Unification Church believe that Moon and his wife are the True Parents, and it is apparent from the "internal" literature of the movement that Moon sees himself in the role of the Messiah and expects his followers to do likewise.

Throughout the world, the Unification Church has drawn considerable hostile attention from anticult movements and the media. Among the many accusations leveled at it are that it uses brainwashing or mind-control techniques to recruit and keep its members, that it breaks up families, that the leaders live in luxury while the rank-and-file membership is exploited and oppressed by its authoritarian organization, that it is strongly anticommunist and has (or has had) connections with the South Korean intelligence agency (the KCIA), that it produces armaments, that it is merely a front for a seditious organization which is attempting to take over the world and establish a theocracy with Moon at its head, and that it violates tax and immigration laws. (In 1982 a federal-court jury convicted Moon of conspiracy to evade taxes and sentenced him to eighteen months' imprisonment.) Needless to say, the movement has vehemently denied the criticisms leveled against it, expressing particular concern where such accusations have been used to justify the practice of "deprogramming," in which members of the movement are forcibly kidnapped and held until they are prepared to renounce their faith.

— EILEEN BARKER

U

UNITARIAN UNIVERSALIST ASSOCIATION

Unitarianism

A missionary is one who seizes or is seized by a universalistic vision and who feels a mandate, a commission, a vocation to bring the vision and its benefits to "all."

PAGE 444

UNITARIAN UNIVERSALIST ASSOCIATION

The Unitarian Universalist Association is a religious denomination that is the result of the 1961 merger of the American Unitarian Association and the Universalist Church of America.

UNITARIANISM

Unitarianism is a religious view that was organized in institutional form in Poland, Transylvania, England, and the United States. Its emergence is primarily the result of indigenous factors in each country. The separate movements had common characteristics: affirmations of the unity of God, the humanity of Jesus, and human religious responsibility, and rejections of the doctrines of the Trinity, the divinity of Jesus, and human corruption or total depravity. Formulations of these views differed in each country.

In Poland, disputes in the Polish Reformed Church in 1555 led to a schism and the formation of the Minor Reformed Church of Poland in 1565. A central community was founded at Racow in 1579. Fausto Sozzini (1539-1604), who came to Poland in that year, became the recognized leader of the Polish Brethren, who adopted his name by calling themselves Socinians. Sozzini's theology emphasized prayer to Christ, as the man whom God resurrected and to whom God gave all power in heaven and earth over the church. The Lithuanian Brethren, a sister group led by Simon Budny, were nonadorantist in theology, which meant they rejected prayer to Christ. The Polish and Lithuanian movements flourished primarily from 1580 to 1620. Roman Catholic opposition in 1632 required the Socinians to become Roman Catholics or go into exile or be executed. A few Socinian exiles found refuge with the Transylvanian Unitarians in Kolozsvár (present-day Cluj-Napoca).

In 1568 John Sigismund, the Unitarian king of Transylvania, granted them religious freedom. (The name Unitarian gradually came into use after debates at Gyulafehérvár in 1568 and at Nagyvárad in 1569.) The Transylvanian Unitarians still survive in Romania and Hungary.

In England, one group insisted on agreement with confessional statements, the other group required only the use of biblical terms and conformity with biblical views. Members of the latter group and their congregations gradually moved toward Unitarian views. Theophilus Lindsey (1723-1808) opposed the Anglican church's creedal restrictions, left that church's ministry, and founded Essex Street Chapel in London in 1774, the first English Unitarian congregation.

The British and Foreign Unitarian Association, founded in 1825, was aided by the repeal of laws against nonconformity and by parliamentary approval of the Dissenters' Chapels Act (1844), which assured Unitarians of their churches.

James Martineau (1805-1900), who exercised great influence among English Unitarians, challenged Priestley's theology with his emphasis on ethics and intuition. Martineau, who desired comprehension in a national liberal church, prefered the name Free Christian to Unitarian. In 1928, English Unitarian denominationalists and those who were influenced by Martineau's Free Christian views united to form the General Assembly of Unitarian and Free Christian Churches. The Non-Subscribing Presbyterian Church of Ireland, which derives from the influence of Thomas Emlyn (1663-1741), and some Welsh and Scottish churches, are different expressions of English Unitarianism.

American Unitarianism gradually emerged during the eighteenth century within Congregationalism, largely because of the influence of Arminian theology, which stressed the human capacity to respond to grace, and Arian Christology. This gradual development resulted in conflicts that culminated in the appointment of a liberal, Henry Ware, as Hollis Professor of Divinity at Harvard College in 1805. The liberals were accused of covertly agreeing with Belsham's humanitarian Christology. Boston minister William Ellery Channing (1780-1842) replied that, instead, most of the liberal ministers were Arians, for they believed that Christ's character included ethical, intellectual, and emotional perfection, and that he was subordinate to God.

Channing's famous Baltimore sermon "Unitarian Christianity" (1819) gave the liberals a coherent theological view that embraced assertions of the unity and moral perfection of God; of the unity of Jesus Christ, his inferiority to God, and his mediatorial mission; and of human moral responsibility. The American Unitarian Association (AUA), an association of individuals, not of churches, was organized in 1825. Ralph Waldo Emerson, in his Cambridge Divinity School address (1838), and Theodore Parker in his sermon "The Transient and Permanent in Christianity" (1841), challenged the prevailing Unitarian emphasis on the authority of rationally interpreted scripture. These addresses initiated a controversy over Transcendentalism within Unitarianism. Parker has influenced many Unitarians as an exemplar of public ministry, for he expressed his theology in outspoken sermons on social and economic issues, ceaseless efforts for social reform, and a willingness to disobey the Fugitive Slave Act of 1850, which he regarded as immoral, in obedience to a higher moral law.

In the early twentieth century, religious humanism appeared within Unitarianism under the leadership of John Dietrich and Curtis Reese, who were among those who signed the Humanist Manifesto (1933). A serious decline among the Unitarian churches during the depression led to the creation of a denominational Commission on Appraisal (1934-1936), whose chairman, Frederick May Eliot, reluctantly agreed to become president of the AUA. Eliot's leadership revived the movement.

UNIVERSALISM

Universalism is a religious view that affirms the ultimate salvation of all humans. In some formulations, that has meant the ultimate reconciliation of all, even Satan, with God. *Acts* 3:21 is one of the scriptural bases for the belief that some Universalists have in a universal restoration (Gr., *apokatastasis*). Modern Universalism derives from radical pietism and from dissenters from the Baptist and Congregational traditions.

In 1681, Jane Leade (1624-1704) became the recognized leader of a Philadelphian Society of pietists in London. The group's name came from the sixth church mentioned in *Revelation* 3:7-13. In Germany, Johann Wilhelm Petersen led a group of German Philadelphian pietists. He reinterpreted Leade's views, gave them scriptural foundations, and published his reinterpretation in *The Mystery of the Restoration of All Things*, 2 vols., 1700-1710. Groups of German Philadelphian pietists and people from other groups took copies of the treatise with them when they migrated to Pennsylvania in the eighteenth century. George de Benneville (1703-1793), who moved to Pennsylvania in 1741, maintained contacts with different groups in colonial Pennsylvania whose members affirmed Universalism and thus prepared the way for Universalism's later growth in America.

Individuals in several European countries affirmed Universalism, but they founded no effective organizations. In England, however, Universalism survived within Unitarianism which contained as members former General Baptists and other persons who held universalist views.

The institutional growth of Universalism, however,

Differences emerged at the turn of the century between the two wings of Congregationalism, those who continued to accept the modified Calvinism represented by Edwards and those who were moving toward Unitarianism.

PAGE 189

"With Jesus, we worship the Father, as the only living and true God."

WILLIAM ELLERY CHANNING
UNITARIAN CHRISTIANITY
1819

was to be in America. In 1803 at Winchester, New Hampshire, the General Convention of Universalists in the New England States embraced the varied Universalist views of the time. In 1870 the Universalist General Convention approved a resolution to affirm the authority of scripture and the lordship of Jesus Christ. This creedal period ended in 1899, when the restrictions were rescinded and a noncreedal statement was adopted in Boston. A revised noncreedal Bond of Fellowship, known as the Washington Profession, was adopted in 1935 and revised in 1953.

THE UNITARIAN UNIVERSALISTS

Sporadic contacts between the Unitarians and the Universalists in the nineteenth and early twentieth centuries were followed in 1953 by organization of the Council of Liberal Churches (Universalist-Unitarian). Cooperation in this council's departmental programs prepared the way for the churches' merger in 1961 into the Unitarian Universalist Association (UUA), of which Dana McLean Greeley became the first president.

The theological diversity that characterizes Unitarian Universalists is expressed in worship that varies greatly from congregation to congregation, ranging from structured liturgy to thematic or sermon-centered emphases. In 1980 the UUA's Commission on Common Worship continued the task of the preceding commissions, that of providing materials that will enable people holding widely differing theological views to worship together.

— JOHN C. GODBEY

VATICAN COUNCILS

VATICAN I

PRELIMINARY DISCUSSIONS. Pius IX was encouraged by prominent members of the episcopate to announce his intention of convoking a council; on 29 July 1868 he officially summoned all the bishops of Christendom to come to Rome by 8 December 1869, along with others who had the right to attend (especially the superiors general of the major religious orders).

The choice of the consultors who were to prepare the drafts of the conciliar decrees—the group included sixty Romans and thirty-six from abroad, almost all of them known for their ultramontane and antiliberal views—disturbed those who had been hoping that the council would provide an opportunity for bishops from the outer reaches of the church to open up the church somewhat to modern aspirations. A number of European governments did become apprehensive about possible conciliar decrees on civil marriage, the place of religion in public education, and the legitimacy of freedom of worship and the press. In the end, these governments chose to limit themselves to an attitude of distrustful expectation.

CONCILIAR DEBATES. The council opened on 8 December 1869, in the presence of about 700 bishops, about two-thirds of those with the right to attend. Among them were 70 prelates of the Eastern rite who were in union with Rome, most of these being from the Middle East, and almost 200 fathers from non-European countries: 121 from the Americas (49 from the United States), 41 from Southern Asia and the Far East, 11 from Oceania, and 9 from the African missions, which were then in their infancy

On 28 December the council began at last to examine the first drafted constitution, which was directed "against the numerous errors deriving from modern rationalism." This draft drew strong criticism because of its substance, which some found to be out of touch with contemporary forms of rationalism and too apodictic on points freely discussed among theologians. After six meetings for discussion, which had the advantage of showing that the council would be freer than some had feared, the presidents announced on 10 January that the draft would be sent back to the commission for recasting and that meanwhile the council would tackle the drafts on church discipline. In this area twenty-eight drafts had been prepared that were rather tame and showed hardly any pastoral openness to the future; to these were added eighteen others, much superior in character, on the adaptation of canon law to the new circumstances of the religious orders and congregations. In order to speed up the pace of the work (as the great majority of the fathers wanted), the pope, on 20 February 1870, amended the regulations that had been distributed at the opening of the council.

While the examination of texts that had little chance of proving explosive was advancing with prudent caution in the council hall, the attention of both the fathers and the public was increasingly focused on the question of infallibility. On the one side, many fathers who were very hostile to their contemporaries' infatuation with liberalism were not at all reluctant to have the council restate the principles according to which, in classical teaching, the relations between church and state should be ruled in an ideal Christian society. Many—often the same— wanted a solemn definition of the personal infallibility of the pope. Reasons of a nontheological kind strengthened many of these prelates in their conviction: their veneration of Pius IX; their belief that an increased emphasis on the monolithic character of the Roman church could only draw to this church various non-Catholics who were distressed by the hesitancies and lack of resoluteness of the churches separated from Rome; and their desire, in the face of the religious crisis they saw growing before their eyes, to give an increasingly centralized form to the defensive and offensive strategy of the church.

A comparable mixture of doctrinal considerations and nontheological motives inspired other prelates to think that such projects would overthrow the traditional constitution of the church and might well threaten the most legitimate aspirations of civil society. In addition, the way in which the question of infallibility was presented in the most prominent ultramontane newspapers could only confirm in their views those who were convinced that "the intention was to declare the pope infallible in matters of faith in order thereby to make people think him infallible in other matters as well" (Leroy-Beaulieu), that is, in matters more or less related to the political order.

The two groups had an opportunity to count heads

Pius's greatest triumph was the First Vatican Council. It produced two constitutions: Dei filius, *a reaffirmation of the centrality of revelation, and* Pastor aeternus, *a definition of papal primacy and infallibility.*

PAGE 548

Shamans are commonly thought to be elected directly by tutelary spirits, who in a visionary experience initiate the future shamans.

PAGE 537

Catholic ecclesiology in accord with the teaching of Vatican I recognizes an infallible teaching function that is exercised through ecumenical councils and the ex cathedra teaching of the pope.

PAGE 148

as early as January. The infallibilist pressure group, again acting independently (but in close contact with the Jesuits of *La civiltà cattolica*), circulated a petition asking the pope to put on the assembly's agenda a draft definition of papal infallibility, which the preparatory commission had preferred not to offer on its own initiative. The petition finally collected 450 signatures, and, despite a counterpetition signed by 140 bishops, Pius IX decided on 1 March to include the desired passage in the draft of the constitution.

CONCILIAR CONSTITUTIONS. The draft of the constitution against rationalism, which had been recast by bishops Martin, Deschamps, and Pie with the help of the Jesuit Joseph Kleutgen, came before the council again on 18 March. The new version was favorably received by the fathers. On 24 April the council unanimously gave its solemn approval to its first dogmatic document, the constitution *Dei filius*, which responded to pantheism, materialism, and modern rationalism with a substantial exposition of Catholic teaching on God, revelation, and faith; this exposition was to be for almost a century the basis of the treatises which made up fundamental theology.

Chapter 1 condemns pantheist views and briefly sets forth Catholic teaching on providence. Chapter 2 defines, against atheism and traditionalism, the possibility of knowing the existence of God with certainty by the natural light of reason and, against deism, the absolute necessity of revelation if man is to have knowledge of the supernatural order. Chapter 3 defines the reasonableness of the act of faith as against the illuminism of some Protestants and against those who deny the value of the external motives of credibility, such as miracles. Chapter 4 explains the relations that should exist between faith and reason, science and revelation: there are mysteries that cannot be demonstrated by reason, but reason can legitimately reflect on supernatural truths.

It quickly became clear that, given the pace at which work was proceeding, the constitution on the church, the text of which had been distributed to the fathers on 21 January, would not come up for discussion for several months; this was even more true of its eleventh chapter, which dealt with the special prerogatives of the pope. Consequently, as early as March, new petitions requested that this chapter, which made the council restive, be discussed out of its proper order as soon as the examination of the constitution against rationalism was concluded. Despite the reservations of three of the five presidents of the council, Pius IX, who was increasingly displeased at the opposition of the minority group, decided to alter the schedule. In order to avoid the anomaly of treating this chapter before the others, it was expanded into a short, independent constitution devoted entirely to the pope.

The general debate on the text as a whole began on 13 May. After some fifteen meetings, the fathers went on to examine the details of the texts; this discussion focused essentially on the chapter devoted to the definition of papal infallibility. The proposed text, although the commission had already improved it by comparison with the original draft, did not yet take sufficient account of the legitimate role that belonged to the episcopate, alongside and in collaboration with the pope, in the supreme teaching office of the church. Fifty-seven speakers took the floor, emphasizing theological arguments or historical difficulties, as well as the practical advantages or drawbacks of a definition in the circumstances of that time. When a final appeal of the minority to Pius IX had no result, some sixty bishops decided to leave Rome before the final vote in order not to have to cast a negative vote in the presence of the pope on a question that directly concerned him. The other members of the minority judged that the successive improvements of the text as well as Bishop Gasser's commentary had removed the principal substantive objections and they decided therefore to approve the final text. This text was solemnly accepted on 18 July by nearly everyone present.

Officially entitled First Constitution on the Church of Christ, the constitution *Pastor aeternus* expounds Catholic teaching on the privileges of the pope.

The fourth chapter declares that authority as supreme teacher is included in the primacy and then recalls how over the course of time the popes had always exercised this function by drawing upon the faith of the universal church as expressed in particular by the teaching of the bishops. The chapter then goes on to define solemnly that this supreme teaching office has attached to it the prerogative of infallibility, provided the pope is speaking *ex cathedra*, that is, provided that "in exercising his office as teacher and shepherd of all Christians he defines, in virtue of his supreme apostolic authority" (that is, with the intention of unequivocally putting an end to all discussion) "that a doctrine concerning faith or morals must be held by the universal Church; such definitions are irreformable of themselves and do not require ratification by the episcopate (*ex sese non autem ex consensu Ecclesiae*)."

After the vote taken on 18 July the council continued its work for two more months, but at a slower pace, since the majority of the fathers had left Rome for the summer. The occupation of Rome by the Italians on 20 September brought the work to a definitive end, and on 20 October the pope announced that the council was adjourned indefinitely.

When the immediate results of the council were compared with its ambitious program (fifty-one drafts had still to be voted on) and especially with the great hopes the convocation of the council had raised, the

First Vatican Council seemed to many to have been a failure, its principal outcome having been to aggravate the disunity among Christians. With the passage of time, however, people became aware of important results flowing from the intense intellectual ferment the convocation of the council had produced. The first dogmatic constitution that had been passed in April 1870 exercised a clarifying influence on subsequent theological teaching, especially in the burning question of the relations between reason and faith. On the other hand, it also strengthened the tendency to enlarge the role of authoritative doctrinal interventions in the development of Catholic thought; this tendency was strengthened even more by the definition of papal infallibility.

— ROGER AUBERT
TRANSLATED FROM FRENCH BY
MATTHEW J. O'CONNELL

VATICAN II

THE CHURCH BEFORE THE COUNCIL. The liturgical movement, whose roots go back to the time of the Reformation, reached a peak of activity in the twentieth century. The movement sought to revive liturgical forms in order to create the church anew by means of daily participation in the objective events of liturgy and the mysteries of the church. Connected with this was a new valuation of sacramentality and of the proclamation of the word.

Paralleling the liturgical movement was the biblical movement, which rediscovered the immediate religious meaning of holy scripture by means of new translations into vernacular languages and the formation of Catholic Bible associations.

The church's consciousness of itself changed. This was primarily a matter of the dissolution of the one-sided canonical understanding of the church as juridical, an understanding that had been set forth in the late Middle Ages and was firmly established once and for all by the Code of Canon Law (1917). The change culminated in ecclesiological projects during and after World War II that engendered an understanding of the church as people of faith subject to the Word.

The ecumenical movements, which since the beginning of the twentieth century had brought together and united the non-Catholic Christian church communities through world church conferences and the founding of the World Council of Churches, stood distanced for a long time from the Roman Catholic church. The opening of the Roman offices for ecumenism by John XXIII was made possible by contacts and conversations between Protestant and Catholic theologians and church leaders that took place for mutual defense against antiecclesiastical totalitarianism. The question of the reunification of all Christians appealed to parts of Catholic Christendom and exercised a great influence on theological reflection about the church's unity in diversity and its understanding of ministry, eucharist, and primacy.

Another important tendency in the Roman Catholic church before the calling of the council involved changes in theology itself. The most important stages were attempts to overcome through kerygmatic theology the objectivistic and unhistorical or superhistorical point of view of neoscholasticism; "nouvelle théologie," which emphasized open thinking and opposed scholasticism; transcendental theology, which reflected on the conditions of the possibilities of man; the acquisition of a genuinely theological understanding of history in hermeneutical theology; and finally the inclusion of the societal dimension in political theology. These positions gained more and more significance with regard to the church's self-understanding and its relationship to the world.

> *"Editions of sacred scriptures should be prepared for the use of non-Christians and adapted for their situation."*
>
> POPE PAUL I
> SECOND VATICAN COUNCIL'S DOGMATIC CONSTITUTION ON DIVINE REVELATION

HISTORY AND THEMES OF THE COUNCIL. The Second Vatican Council was the twenty-first ecumenical council (according to the official count of the Roman Catholic church), held from 1962 to 1965 at Saint Peter's Basilica in Rome. All bishops, the Curia Romana, and the theological and canonical faculties voted on topics for discussion. On 5 June 1960 the pope ordered ten specialized commissions to work on the schemata (protocols). There were also two permanent secretariats (one for the mass media, another for Christian unity). A central preparatory committee was responsible for organizing the work of the council. Of the 2,908 legitimate delegates, 2,540 participated in the opening. Of the invited non-Catholic Christian churches and communities, seventeen were present through thirty-five representatives. In the end, twenty-eight non-Roman churches, including the Russian Orthodox church, were represented by ninety-three observers. There were eighty-six governments and international bodies represented at the opening.

The council met in four sessions: 11 October to 8 December 1962; 29 September to 2 December 1963; 14 September to 21 November 1964; and 4 September to 8 December 1965. Ten public sessions and 168 general assembly meetings were held.

From the time of its proclamation, the council was intended to have a double goal: reform within the church and preparation for Christian and world unity. But already in the opening address this goal was expanded and deepened.

In the first session, which included the first thirty-six general assemblies, the commission members were not chosen according to the prepared list but rather, at the suggestion of Cardinal Achille Liénart (Lille), according to recommendations of the different groups of bishops. John XXIII died on 3 June 1963. His successor, Paul VI, continued the council. At the reopening of the second session (general assemblies 37-89) on 29 September 1963, Paul VI emphasized the pastoral orientation of the council. It was to deal with the nature of the church and the function of the bishops, to make efforts toward the unity of Christians, and to set in motion a dialogue with the contemporary world.

The Second Vatican Council was a council of the church about the church. In order to protect its freedom, John XXIII specifically avoided formulating a systematic plan of discussion.

The subjects treated in the documents produced by the council can be summarized briefly. The basic self-understanding of the church is addressed in the Dogmatic Constitution on the Church. The inner life of the church is discussed in various documents: the work of salvation through liturgy (the Constitution on the Sacred Liturgy); the church's function of oversight (the Decree on the Bishops' Pastoral Office in the Church and the Decree on Eastern Catholic Churches); the teaching office (the Dogmatic Constitution on Divine Revelation, including discussions of scripture, tradition, and teaching office, and the Declaration on Christian Education); and vocations (the Decree on the Ministry and Life of Priests, the Decree on Priestly Formation, the Decree on the Appropriate Renewal of the Religious Life, and the Decree on the Apostolate of the Laity). The mission of the church to the world is likewise elaborated on in several documents: the church's relationship to non-Catholic Christianity (the Decree on Ecumenism and the Decree on Eastern Catholic Churches); its relationship to non-Christians (the Declaration on the Relationship of the Church to non-Christian Religions, which makes special reference to the Jews, and the Decree on the Church's Missionary Activity); its relationship to the contemporary secular situation of the world in general (the Pastoral Constitution on the Church in the Modern World and the Decree on the Instruments of Social Communications); and its relationship to the philosophical pluralism of the present age (especially in the Declaration on Religious Freedom).

VATICAN COUNCIL II

This pen and ink drawing of the Second Vatican Council commemorates a turning point in the modern Catholic church in its understanding of the church and in its relationship with the world.

FRANKLIN MCMAHON/CORBIS

The council's understanding of the church. The Second Vatican Council, in contrast to Trent and to Vatican I, was oriented neither toward dogma nor toward theological controversy; rather it was pastorally oriented in that it set forth the meaning of the church, its message, and its missions for the world and for humanity.

In *Lumen gentium* the council set aside juridical and controversial questions and defined the church first as a mystery, as a sacrament of unity between God and human beings and among human beings themselves. The council, in full support of Vatican I, dealt extensively with the college of bishops. It accentuated the principles of collegiality and synod as structural elements of the church and the meaning of the local church as representative of the whole church. With reference to the priesthood of all believers, the council stressed the dignity, role, and responsibility of the laity as well as the presence of the church in the world, which is often possible only through the laity.

The council characterized the church's relationship to the other churches and Christian confessions not through the instrumental definition of union with Rome but through the living realities in these communities that are constitutive of church. The relationship of these churches to the Roman church is defined by the formula *"coniunctum esse"* ("to be joined together"). According to Vatican II, therefore, the unity of the church is not to be sought by imposing uniformity, that is, by an all-defining centralization, but in a legitimate plurality that strengthens unity and does not endanger it.

A council of the world church. The council seemed to be the first act in which the Catholic church began to realize itself as a truly worldwide community. This world church acted for the first time at the council with historical clarity concerning faith and morals. In spite of the undeniably powerful presence and influence of the European and North American regional churches, the members of this council, in contrast to all previous councils, were bishops from the whole world and not simply, as at Vatican I, European missionary bishops sent out to the whole world.

The council was also the cause of the abolition of Latin as the common cultic language. In the long run, the liturgy of the universal church will not be a mere translation of the liturgy of the Roman church but rather a liturgy formed from the unity in diversity of regional liturgies in which each has its own unique form that does not result from its language only but also from other cultural factors such as gesture and dance.

Relationship to the world. In several decrees, to which belong primarily the Pastoral Constitution on the Church in the World *(Gaudium et spes)* and the Decree on Religious Freedom, the council attempted to describe its fundamental relationship to the secular world on the basis of its nature and not simply by the force of external circumstances. The temptation for the church to reassert a false superiority over the world continues to exist, but since the decisions of Vatican II the church in principle can no longer yield to this temptation, because the council formulated an irrevocable norm. No longer, since the decrees of the council, can the limitation of freedom in the name of goodness and justice be so easily rationalized by the church.

Theology of the council. The theological situation in which the council found itself was transitional and difficult to define. On the one hand, neoscholastic theology was self-evident; it was the dominant theological position represented in the proposals that had been prepared for the council by Roman commissions. On the other hand, the theology of the council was more critically related to scripture than was neoscholasticism. It had opened itself to subject matter that did not originate in the repertory of neoscholasticism. It exercised a certain braking effect against theological excess (for example, in Mariology). It made an effort to be considerate of ecumenical needs. It also held that one could say something theologically important even if one did not proclaim it solemnly as dogma.

Change in ecumenical attitude. The council signified a break in the history of the relationship of the Catholic church both with other Christian churches and communities and with the non-Christian religions of the world. Naturally there were always contained in the faith consciousness of the church convictions that in principle legitimized the newly emerging relationship of the Catholic church with other Christian churches and communities and the non-Christian religions. The council initiated a point of view that it ratified as truly Christian, namely, that Catholic Christianity had assumed a different and new position relative to other Christians and their churches and relative to the non-Christian religions of the world.

Before the council the Catholic church considered the non-Roman Catholic churches and communities to be organizations and societies of people who differed with the old church only through errors and deficiencies and who ought to return to it in order to find in it the full truth and fullness of Christianity. From the point of view of the old attitude, the non-Christian religions were all forms of paganism, that is, religion that human beings, sinfully and without grace, produced on their own. Those views were changed by Vatican II, and since then a position of acceptance can no longer be excluded, because it is understood not as an aspect of the liberal modern mentality but rather as an integral element of Christian conviction.

[*See also* Roman Catholicism.]

— KARL RAHNER AND ADOLF DARLAP
TRANSLATED FROM GERMAN BY
CHARLOTTE PRATHER

VEDANTA

The word *vedanta* literally means "end [*anta*] of the Veda," that is to say, the concluding part of the *apauruseya*, or revealed Vedic literature, which is traditionally believed to comprise the Samhitas, the Brahmanas, the Aranyakas, and the Upanisads. Vedanta thus primarily denotes the Upanisads and their teachings. Metaphorically, Vedanta is also understood to represent the consummation or culmination *(anta)* of the entire Vedic speculation, or indeed of all knowledge *(veda)*.

UPANISADS. Over two hundred texts call themselves Upanisads, but they include even such recent works as the *Christopanisad* and the *Allopanisad*. The *Muktikopanisad* gives a traditional list of 108 *Upanisads*, but, even out of these, many texts seem to have been called Upanisads only by courtesy. Usually 13 Upanisads, namely, *Isa*, *Kena*, *Katha*, *Prasna*, *Mundaka*, *Mandu-kya*, *Taittiriya*, *Aitareya*, *Chandogya*, *Brhadaranyaka*, *Svetasvatara*, *Kausitaki*, and *Maitrayani*, are regarded as the principal Upanisads (eighth to fourth century BCE). They are traditionally connected with one Vedic school *(sakha)* or another, and several of them actually form part of a larger literary complex.

The Upanisads represent the fearless quest for truth by essentially uninhibited minds. They seek, among other things, to investigate the ultimate reality "from which, verily, these beings are born, by which, when born, they live, and into which, when departing, they enter" (*Taittiriya Upanisad* 3.1.1); to delve into the mystery of the *atman* "by whom one knows all this" but whom one cannot know by the usual means of knowledge (*Brhadaranyaka Upanisad* 4.5.15); and generally to promote "that instruction by which the unheard becomes heard, the unperceived becomes perceived, and the unknown becomes known" (*Chandogya Upanisad* 6.1.3).

Hinduism's fourth goal of life (moksa) was made the subject of efforts to develop distinctly Hindu philosophical "viewpoints" (darsanas) on the nature of reality.

PAGE 279

V

VEDANTA

Brahmasutras

An upanisad is literally a mystical—often "secret"—"connection," interpreted as the teaching of mystical homologies.

PAGE 274

The Upanisads presuppose a certain development of thought. The origin of some of their doctrines can be traced back to the *Rgveda*, or in certain cases, even to the pre-Vedic non-Aryan thought complex. It will also be seen that, from the methodological as well as from the conceptual point of view, the Upanisads owe not a little to the Brahmanas, as a reaction against which they were largely brought into existence. In a sense, the Upanisads represent an extension of the tendency of the Brahmanas toward *bandhuta*, that is, toward perpetually establishing equivalences between entities and powers apparently belonging to different levels and to different spheres.

The Upanisads clearly betray a trend toward inwardization and spiritualization, which presumably has its origin in their general aversion for the physical body and sensual experience (*Maitri Upanisad* 1.3). The Upanisadic teachers have consistently emphasized the view that the essential or real self *(atman)* has to be differentiated from the empirical or embodied self *(jiva)*. Indeed, true philosophical knowledge consists in not confusing the one for the other. The essential Self is of the nature of pure self-consciousness. It is neither the knower nor the known nor the act of knowing. The essential Self does exist. It is conscious, but not of any particular object, internal or external; it is pure *cit* (consciousness), that is to say, it is of the nature of consciousness *as such*.

Side by side with the analysis of the human personality, the Upanisadic thinker has attempted an analysis of the external world as well. He has thereby arrived at the conclusion that at the basis of this gross, manifold, changing phenomenal world—which ultimately is a conglomeration of mere names and forms—there lies one single, uniform, eternal, immutable, sentient reality (see, e.g., *Chandogya Upanisad* 6.1). The natural and logical next step is to identify the deepest level of the subjective person, namely, the essential Self *(atman)*, with the ultimate basis of the objective universe, namely, the cosmic reality (*brahman*, also called *sat*).

BRAHMASUTRAS. A vigorous and comprehensive cultural movement was set in motion that sought to resuscitate the Brahmanic way of life and thought by reorganizing, systematizing, simplifying, and popularizing it. The literary monuments of this movement were generally clothed in a practical literary form, namely, the *sutras*, or aphorisms, that were defined as being at once brief but unambiguous and to the point. By their very nature, the Upanisadic teachings, which were often sheer flashes of spiritual radiance rather than coherent philosophical formulations, were characterized by inherent ambiguities, inconsistencies, and contradictions. In order that they should prove reasonably meaningful, it was necessary to systematize and, more particularly, to harmonize them.

Apparently the *Brahma Sutra* was not the only work of this kind, for Badarayana mentions several predecessors as, for example, Atreya, Asmarathya, Kasakrtsna, and Jaimini. By themselves they could hardly be made to yield any cogent philosophical teaching. Yet it seems that the *Brahma Sutra* favors a kind of *bhedabheda*, or doctrine of distinction-*cum*-nondistinction. The world is represented as a transformation of the potency of God, God himself remaining unaffected and transcendent in the process. Hardly any of Badarayana's *sutras* can be shown to be unequivocally nondualistic in purport. It also seems that the *Brahma Sutra* is specifically disposed against Samkhya dualism and Mimamsa ritualism.

GAUDAPADA. The earliest complete extant commentary on the *Brahma Sutra* is that of Sankara (788-820 CE). But in his thinking Sankara is more vitally influenced by Gaudapada (fifth to sixth century) than by Badarayana.

Gaudapada lived at least three centuries before Sankara. True to the usual practice of Hindu thinkers, Gaudapada has set forth his philosophy in his commentary, in the form of *karikas* or memorial verses. The *Gaudapadakarika* constitutes the earliest treatise on absolute nondualism *(kevala advaita)*. The very names of the four books that make up the work—namely, *Agama* (Scripture), *Vaitathya* (Unreality of the World Experience), *Advaita* (Nondualism), and *Alata-santi* (Extinction of the Revolving Firebrand)—bring out the entire teaching of Gaudapada in a nutshell.

There can be hardly any doubt about the strong Buddhist influence on Gaudapada's thought. The *Gaudapadakarika* creates an irresistible impression that the Buddhist Sunyavada and the Vijñanavada schools present philosophical positions that are in no small measure consistent with those presented by the major classical Upanisads.

SANKARA. Sankara is by far the most outstanding and the most widely known exponent of Vedanta, particularly of the doctrine of absolute nonduality (Kevala Advaita). Many works pass as having been written by him, but among the philosophical works that can be ascribed to him with reasonable certainty are the commentaries on nine Upanisads; the commentaries on the *Brahma Sutra*, the *Bhagavadgita*, the *Gaudapadakarika*, the *Yogasutra-bhasya*, and the *Adhyatmapatala* of the *Apastamba Dharmasutra*; and the *Upadesasahasri* (with its nineteen verse tracts and three prose tracts).

Sankara's philosophy, like most Indian philosophy, is oriented toward the one practical aim of *moksa*, which implies liberation from suffering and regaining of the original state of bliss. Sankara takes for granted the validity of the Upanisads as an embodiment of the highest truth, and uses logic either to support his interpretation of the Upanisads or to refute other systems of thought. In his commentary on the *Brahma Sutra* he seeks to harmonize the apparently contradictory teachings of the Upanisads through the assumption of two points of view, the ultimate *(paramarthika)* and the contingent *(vyavaharika)*.

The main plank of Sankara's philosophy is the belief in the unity of all being and the denial of the reality of the many particular entities in the universe. Reality is that which is one without a second, which is not determined by anything else, which is not sublated at any point of time, which transcends all distinctions, to which the familiar categories of thought are inapplicable, and which can be only intuitively realized. Such is *brahman* of Sankara's Advaita. Sankara's most distinctive contribution is the philosophical and dialectical development of the concept of *brahman* as without qualities *(nirguna)*. *Nirguna brahman* is not to be understood as "void" or "blank"; it only signifies that nothing that the mind can think of can be attributed to it. *Sat* (pure, unqualified being), *cit* (pure consciousness), and *ananda* (pure bliss), which are often affirmed of *brahman*, are not qualifying attributes of *brahman* but rather together constitute the essential nature of *brahman*.

For Sankara the four prerequisites for *brahman* realization are discrimination between the eternal and the temporal, renunciation of nonspiritual desires, moral equipment, consisting of tranquility, self-control, and so forth, and an intense longing for *moksa*.

POST-SANKARA TEACHERS OF KEVALA ADVAITA. The school of Sankara's Kevala Advaita can boast of a long line of teachers and pupils who through their writings have brought tremendous popularity to that school.

Mandana Misra was a contemporary, perhaps a senior contemporary, of Sankara. His *Brahmasiddhi* shows that he is directly influenced by Sankara's philosophy. He emphasizes that it is the *jivas* who by their own individual *avidya* create for themselves the world appearance on the changeless *brahman*; he discountenances the theory that the world originates from the *maya* of *brahman*.

Padmapada is believed to have been the first pupil of Sankara, and was, according to a tradition, nominated by the master as the first pontiff of the *matha* at Puri. His only available work, called *Pañcapadika,* invests *maya* with a sort of substantiality and also assigns to it cognitive as well as vibratory activity. *Brahman* in association with *maya* as characterized by this twofold activity is, according to Padmapada, the root cause of *jagat*, while *avidya* manifests itself in *jiva*.

It is, however, Vacaspati (fl. 841) who may be said to have founded an independent subschool of Sankara's Vedanta. Vacaspati has sought to merge the teachings of Sankara and Mandana Misra into one system. He propounds the view that *avidya* has *brahman* as its object *(visaya)* and *jiva* as its support *(asraya)*. Like the Bhamati subschool of Advaita, Pra-kasatman (fl. 1200) inaugurated another independent subschool—the Vivarana subschool—through his *Vivarana* (exposition) of Padmapada's *Pañcapadika*. Prakasatman endorses the view of Sarvajñatman that *brahman* is both the support and the object of *avidya*. While in respect of *jiva* the Bhamati subschool puts forth the doctrine of limitation *(avaccheda)*, the Vivarana subschool puts forth the doctrine of reflection *(pratibimba)*.

SABDADVAITA. Although there is generally evident a tendency to equate Vedanta with Sankara's Kevala Advaita, one cannot afford to ignore the other schools of Vedanta that have been substantially influential. The doctrine of *sabdadvaita*, a monistic ontology presenting language as the basis of reality, was propounded by Bhartrhari (d. 651) in his *Vakyapadiya*; this doctrine cannot be said to belong to Vedanta proper, since it is not derived from any of the three *prasthanas*. Still, according to Bhartrhari the ideas that the ultimate reality, *brahman*, which is without beginning and end, is of the nature of the "word" and that the world proceeds from it can be traced back to the revelation of the Word *par excellence*, the Veda itself. This ultimate reality is one, but because of its many powers it manifests itself as many in the form of experiencer, the object of experience, and experience itself (the purpose of experience also being sometimes mentioned).

BHASKARA. The proper post-Sankara Vedanta begins with Bhaskara (fl. 850). Unlike the other post-Sankara schools of Vedanta, Bhaskara's Vedanta does not seem to have gained wide currency, presumably because it was not linked up with any theistic sect. According to Bhaskara, *brahman* has a dual form: *brahman* as pure being and intelligence, formless, the causal principle, which is the object of our highest knowledge; and *brahman* as the manifested effect or the world. Thus brahman represents unity *(abheda)* as well as distinction *(bheda)*, both of which are real. *Jiva* is *brahman* characterized by the limitations of the mind substance. Thus, unlike the material world, *jiva* is not the effect of *brahman*.

VISISTADVAITA. To Ramanuja (1017-1137) belongs the credit for successfully attempting to coordinate personal theism with absolutistic philosophy. Ramanuja's commentaries on two of the three *prasthanas*, namely, the *Brahma Sutra* (called *Sribhasya*) and the *Bhagavadgita*, have been preserved. According to Ramanuja, God, who possesses supremely good qualities, is the only absolute reality and therefore the only object worthy of love and devotion. Matter *(acit)* and souls *(cit)*, which are equally ultimate and real, are the qualities *(visesanas)* of God, but, as qualities, they are entirely dependent on God in the same way as the

Sankara established a monastic order and monasteries (mathas), *which, like the many hermitages* (asramas) *and the great shrines, became centers of religious activity and contributed to the realization of his ideal of Hindu unity.*

PAGE 325

body is dependent on the soul. They are directed and sustained by God and exist entirely for and within him. Ramanuja's doctrine is therefore known as Visista Advaita or the doctrine of one God qualified by *cit* (souls) and *acit* (matter). These three factors *(tattvatraya)* form a complex *(visista)* organic unity *(advaita)*. The omnipotent God creates the world of material objects out of himself, that is, out of acit (which is eternal in him), by an act of will. Ramanuja emphasizes that creation is a fact, a real act of God.

DVAITADVAITA. The philosophy of Nimbarka (fl. mid-fourteenth century?) is generally known as Svabhavika Bhedabheda or Dvaitadvaita. Nimbarka assumes the ultimate reality of the three entities, namely, Paramatman or Purusottama (God), Jiva, and Jagat. He does not accept *avidya* as a cosmic principle producing the world appearance. Rather, according to him, God actually transforms himself into the world of material objects and individual souls, but does not lose himself in these. He is simultaneously one with *(abheda)* and distinct from *(bheda)* the world of *jivas* and matter. This is so, not because of any imposition or supposition *(upadhi)*, but because of the specific peculiarity of God's spiritual nature *(svabhava)*. God alone has independent existence, while individual souls and matter, which are but derivative parts of God, are entirely dependent on and controlled by him.

The more prolific Madhva also wrote commentaries on the Rgveda and the epics.

PAGE 288

SUDDHADVAITA. Many works, large and small, are ascribed to Vallabha (1479-1531), the most important among them being the *Anubhasya*, a commentary on the *Brahma Sutra* (up to 3.2.34); the *Tattvarthadipanibandha*, an independent philosophical treatise; and the *Subodhini*, a commentary on a major part of the *Bhagavata*. *Suddha advaita* ("pure nondualism") and *pustimarga* are the two fundamental tenets of Vallabha's Vedanta. *Suddha advaita* implies that the one *brahman*, free from and untouched by *maya*, is the cause of the individual souls and the world of material objects. *Jivas* and the material world are, in reality, *brahman*, for they represent but partial manifestations of the essential attributes of *brahman*. *Brahman* (God) pervades the whole world. God manifests his qualities of *sat* and *cit* in the form of *jivas*, but the quality of bliss *(ananda)* remains unmanifested. Vallabha teaches that it is through *pusti* (literally, "nourishment, spiritual nourishment"), or the special grace of God, that *jivas* attain *goloka* ("the world of cows"), the world of bliss.

MADHVA. Among the Vedantins, Madhva (1238-1317) is reputed to be a confirmed dualist *(dvaitin)*. Madhva no doubt speaks of two mutually irreducible principles as constituting reality, but he regards only one of them, namely, God, as the one infinite independent principle, whereas the finite reality comprising matter, individual souls, and other entities is regarded as dependent. He emphasizes that Lord Sri Hari, who is omnipresent, omniscient, omnipotent, and without beginning and end, is the highest independent reality.

— R. N. DANDEKAR

VIETNAMESE RELIGION

Like the whole complex of Vietnamese culture, Vietnamese religion has long been presented as a pure copy of the Chinese model. Historically, the Red River delta, cradle of Vietnamese civilization, was occupied by the Han for more than a thousand years. Nonetheless, Dongsonian civilization, which flourished in this region before its destruction by the Han invasions, must have possessed a certain vigor, for despite the very long coercive occupation that followed it, the Vietnamese preserved their language and a part of their culture, finally succeeding in the tenth century of the common era after numerous revolts in liberating themselves from their deeply implanted Chinese occupants. Paradoxically, the consolidation for independence reinforced the prestige of the Chinese model among the literati. Their influence in this regard even resulted in the promulgation in 1812 by Emperor Gialong, who had recently reunified the country, of a new code that was nothing more than a translation of a Manchu dynasty treaty.

Yet, in a population that was more than 90 percent rural, ideology directly concerned only a relatively small number of people, those who wielded power and prestige. The ideals and beliefs they held touched but superficially the great masses, who remained bound to a set of rules transmitted orally and put to the test through daily observance. That the Vietnamese spoke a language belonging to a different family (Austroasiatic rather than Sino-Tibetan) was a considerable asset for the preservation of these rules.

In the religious sphere, this situation created a coexistence, on the one hand, of a Chinese model followed strictly by the most erudite men or those instructed in the faith, and on the other, of popular cults observed by the great mass of people.

The expansion southward along the entire length of the Vietnamese territory added further to this diversification of the religion by the absorption, on the small coastal plains, of the Chams, whose religious affiliation was divided between Brahmanism and Islam, and on the Mekong delta, of the Khmer adherents to Theravada Buddhism. These three religions, with that of the Proto-Indo-Chinese on which they were grafted, effected a syncretism.

I will not emphasize the Chinese model, already treated elsewhere, but will focus only on those aspects that touch directly on Vietnamese religion. On this

level of the individual, a fundamental concept is that of "souls" or "vital principles." This concept governs as many aspects of daily conduct as it does basic rituals such as funeral rites or ancestor worship.

Appropriate funeral rites are absolutely essential for the benefit of the departed. There is fear of two categories of malevolent spirits, the *ma* (Chin., *ma*) and the *gui* (Chin., *kuei*), souls of the dead without sepulchers. In contrast, one can benefit from the aid of the *thân* (Chin., *shen*), souls of ancestors, understood in a noble sense. These three entities, expressed in Sino-Vietnamese words, testify to the survival of the *hon*.

From words of the same family comes the Vietnamese *hoi*, with its Sino-Vietnamese doublet *khi* (Chin., *ch'i*), whose meaning ranges from breath, inhalation, emanations from living or dead bodies, to "supernatural influence" over man's life and destiny. This influence can emanate not only from a man but also from an animal, the ground, stones, plants, and so forth. The concept provides the essential basis of popular cults as well.

Prior to 1975, when asked his religion, an educated Vietnamese generally would have answered that he was a Buddhist.

On the civic or family level, however, he followed Confucian precepts; on the affective level or in the face of destiny, he turned to Taoist conceptions. His personal behavior would have remained impregnated with Taoism. This fact was evident in his concern to conform with cosmic harmony, to pay careful attention to sources and currents of energy traversing the universe, and to parallel equivalents between these and the human body. These concerns were manifested in his desire to withdraw into nature as well as in his recourse to geomancy and diverse divinatory procedures, even to magic. It was primarily Confucianism and Buddhism, however, that affected his moral conduct.

It is true that the observance of ancestor worship attested to the ascendancy of Confucianism, but the different Buddhas and *bodhisattvas* tended to join the ranks of the multiple divinities and deities of the Taoist pantheon. Taoism itself was immeasurably enriched with popular autochthonous beliefs and practices, to which it lent a certain respectability by a tint of sinicization; furthermore, magic played a proportionally more important role in activities of a religious type.

Ancestor worship occupied a central place in the family cult. It represented the ritual expression of a cardinal virtue, filial piety (*hiêu*; Chin., *hsiao*), the pivot of interpersonal relationships. The necessity of perfecting oneself morally and intellectually, loyalty to one's friends, respect for one's superiors, fidelity to the sovereign—all these were believed to arise from the domain of filial piety. [*See also* Ancestors.]

The extent of the economic impact of ancestor worship on a family depended on the wealth of that family. Reserved exclusively for the maintenance of such worship and for the performance of its ceremonies were revenues from property (rice fields, houses, etc.) that constituted the *huong-hoa* (Chin., *hsiang-huo*), the portion of "the incense and the fire" transmitted by inheritance from the father to his eldest son. It should be noted that Confucianism did not succeed in lowering the Vietnamese woman to the inferior rank occupied by her Chinese counterpart. Even in wealthy families the wife had the same status as her husband in family ceremonies, including those pertaining to ancestor worship in its strict sense.

The recourse to mediums and ritual decorative features representing the pantheon dominated by the Jade Emperor made possible the assimilation of Taoist elements into a certain number of Vietnamese popular cults. The one that came closest in form to a Taoist cult was that attributed to Trân Hung Dao, a spirit served by a male medium *(ông wông)*. Trân Hung Dao is a Vietnamese national hero from the thirteenth century. As well, the cult of the *chu vi*, "dignitaries" served by female mediums (*ba wông*), borrowed from Taoism some elements of the decor. Here the medium (a *ba wông* in this case) is "mounted" not by one god but successively, in the course of the same séance, by different spirits of both sexes and of different ages.

At the collective level, the cult of the tutelary deity (*thanh-hoang*; Chin., *sheng-huang*), the protector of the commune, held an eminent place in Vietnamese popular religion. Indeed, the most important public building in a village was the *winh*, both a communal house and a place of worship; it sheltered the altar of the tutelary deity and served as a meeting place of the notables for the settlement of questions of administration and internal justice.

The *thanh-hoang* could be a celestial deity, a deified legendary or historical personage, or even a disreputable person, such as a thief or a scavenger, whose violent death at a "sacred hour" endowed him with occult powers.

Certain trees, rocks, and natural boundaries were objects of cults that could lead to the construction of small altars. This veneration, very often fearful, could have varied origins. The tree, for example, could influence by the simple force of its being. It could also shelter a malevolent spirit, such as a *ma*, the soul of an unburied dead person, or of a *con tinh*, the soul of a young girl or woman who died before having experienced the joys of marriage.

[*See* Southeast Asian Religions *and* Chinese Religion.]

— GEORGES CONDOMINAS
TRANSLATED FROM FRENCH BY
MARIA PILAR LUNA-MAGANNON

The classical Southeast Asian religio-cultural synthesis, of which Theravada Buddhism has been a major component, has given the cultures of Burma, Thailand, Cambodia, Laos, and Vietnam a unique sense of identity

PAGE 97

VOODOO

African Influence

Voodoo, or Vodou (according to official Haitian Creole orthography), is a misleading but common term for the religious practices of 80 to 90 percent of the people of Haiti.

PAGE 123

VOODOO

Voodoo, or *Vodou* (according to official Haitian Creole orthography), is a misleading but common term for the religious practices of 80 to 90 percent of the people of Haiti. The term *voodoo* (or *hoodoo*, a derivative) is also used, mostly in a derogatory sense, to refer to systems of sorcery and magic. In contemporary Haiti, *vodou* refers to one ritual style or dance among many in the traditional religious system. Haitians prefer a verb to identify their religion: they speak of "serving the spirits."

AFRICAN INFLUENCE. Voodoo was born on the sugar plantations out of the interaction among slaves who brought with them a wide variety of African religious traditions. Three African groups appear to have had the strongest influence on Voodoo: the Yoruba of present-day Nigeria, the Fon of Dahomey (present-day Benin), and the Kongo of what are now Zaire and Angola. Many of the names of Voodoo spirits are easily traceable to their African counterparts; however, in the context of Haiti's social and economic history, these spirits have undergone change.

ROMAN CATHOLIC INFLUENCE. The French slaveholders were Catholic, and baptism was mandatory for slaves. While Catholicism may well have functioned in this utilitarian way for slaves on the plantations, it is also true that the religions of West Africa, from which Voodoo was derived, have a long tradition of syncretism. Whatever else Catholicism represented in the slave world, it was most likely also seen as a means to expand Voodoo's ritual vocabulary and iconography. Catholicism has had the greatest influence on the traditional religion of Haiti at the level of rite and image, rather than theology. This influence works in two ways. First, those who serve the spirits call themselves Catholic, attend Mass, go to confession, and undergo baptism and first communion, and, because these Catholic rituals are at times integral parts of certain larger Voodoo rites, they are often directed to follow them by the Voodoo spirits. Second, Catholic prayers, rites, images, and saints' names are integrated into the ritualizing in Voodoo temples and cult houses.

Currently there is an uneasy peace between Voodoo and the Catholic church. Until quite recently, the Catholic clergy routinely preached against serving the spirits. Since Catholicism is the official religion of Haiti and the church has been to some extent state-controlled, the degree to which Voodoo has been tolerated, or even encouraged, has been at least partly a function of politics.

VOODOO SPIRITS. Although no longer recognized as such by Haitians, the names of the Voodoo spirit nations *(nanchon)* almost all refer to places and peoples in Africa. For example, there are *nanchon* known as Rada (after the Dahomean principality Allada), Wangol (Angola), Mondon (Mandingo), Ibo, Nago (the Dahomean name for the Ketu Yoruba), and Kongo. In rural Voodoo, a person inherits responsibilities to one or more of these *nanchon* through maternal and paternal kin. Each spirit group has drum rhythms, dances, and food preferences that correspond to its identifying characteristics.

THE VOODOO VIEW OF THE PERSON. In Voodoo teachings the human being is composed of various parts: the body, that is, the gross physical part of the person, which perishes after death, and from two to four souls, of which the most widely acknowledged are the *gro bonanj* and the *ti bonanj*. The *gro bonanj* ("big guardian angel") is roughly equivalent to consciousness or personality. When a person dies the *gro bonanj* survives, and immediately after death it is most vulnerable to capture and misuse by sorcerers. The *ti bonanj* ("little guardian angel") may be thought of as the conscience or the spiritual energy reserve of a living person and, at times, as the ghost of a dead person. Each person is said to have one spirit who is the *mèt-tet* ("master of the head"). The *mèt-tet* is the major protector and central spirit served by that person, and it is that spirit that corresponds to the *gro bonanj*. Because the *gro bonanj* is the soul that endures after death and because it is connected to a particular *lwa*, a person who venerates the ancestors inherits the service of particular spirits.

VOODOO AND THE DEAD. In both urban and rural Haiti, cemeteries are major ritual centers. The first male buried in any cemetery is known as the Baron. Baron's wife is Gran Brijit, a name given to the first female buried in a cemetery. Every cemetery has a cross either in the center or at the gate. The cross is known as the *kwa Baron* ("Baron's cross"), and this is the ritualizing center of the cemetery.

Haitians make a distinction between *lemó* ("the dead") and *lemistè* ("the mysteries"). Within Voodoo, there are rituals and offerings for particular family dead; however, if these ancestral spirits are seen as strong and effective, they can, with time, become *mistè* (mysteries).

The *gèdè* are not only spirits of death but also patrons of human sexuality, protectors of children, and irrepressible social satirists. Dances for *gèdè* tend to be boisterous affairs, and new *gèdè* spirits appear every year.

VOODOO CEREMONIES. In rural Voodoo, the ideal is to serve the spirits as simply as possible because simplicity of ritual is said to reflect real power and the true African way of doing things (Larose, 1977).

Urban Voodoo, by contrast, has a more routine ritualizing calendar, and events tend to be larger and more elaborate. Ceremonies in honor of major spirits take place annually on or around the feast days of their

Catholic counterparts and usually include sacrifice of an appropriate animal—most frequently a chicken, a goat, or a cow. A wide variety of ceremonies meet specific individual and community needs: for example, healing rites, dedications of new temples and new ritual regalia, and spirit marriages in which a devotee "marries" a spirit of the opposite sex and pledges to exercise sexual restraint one night each week in order to receive that spirit in dreams. Death rituals include the *desounen*, in which the *gro bonanj* is removed from the corpse and sent under the waters, and the *rele mó nan dlo* ("calling the dead up from the waters") a ritual that can occur any time after a period of a year and a day from the date of death.

Annual pilgrimages draw thousands of urban and rural followers of Voodoo. The focal point of events, which are at once Catholic and Voodoo, is usually a Catholic church situated near some striking feature of the natural landscape that is believed to be sacred to the Voodoo spirits.

VOODOO AND MAGIC. Serge Larose (1977) has demonstrated that magic is not only a stereotypic label that outsiders have applied to Voodoo, but also a differential term internal to the religion. Thus an in-group among the followers of Voodoo identifies its own ritualizing as "African" while labeling the work of the outgroup as *maji* ("magic"). Generally speaking, this perspective provides a helpful means of grasping the concept of magic within Voodoo. There are, however, those individuals who, in their search for power and wealth, have self-consciously identified themselves with traditions of what Haitians would call the "work of the left hand." This includes people who deal in *pwen achte* ("purchased points"), which means spirits or powers that have been bought rather than inherited, and people who deal in *zombi.* A *zombi* may be either the disembodied soul of a dead person whose powers are used for magical purposes, or a soulless body that has been raised from the grave to do drone labor in the fields.

The "work of the left hand" should not be confused with more ordinary Voodoo ritualizing that treats problems of love, health, family, and work. Unless a problem is understood as coming from God, in which case the Voodoo priest can do nothing, the priest will treat it as one caused by a spirit or by a disruption in human relationships.

[*See* Yoruba Religion.]

— KAREN MCCARTHY BROWN

"'Tis true, there's magic in the web of it."

WILLIAM SHAKESPEARE
OTHELLO

WITCHCRAFT

The term *witchcraft* embraces a wide variety of phenomena. The word *witch* derives from the Old English noun *wicca*, "sorcerer," and the verb *wiccian*, "to cast a spell."

SIMPLE SORCERY

Simple sorcery, which can also be called low magic, is usually practiced by the uneducated and unsophisticated. It assumes a magical worldview, implicitly and preconsciously, in distinction to the sophisticated magical worldview of high magicians such as astrologers and alchemists, whose philosophy is often highly structured. The thought processes of sorcery are intuitive rather than analytical.

The Azande of the southern Sudan distinguished three types of sorcery. One was a benevolent magic involving oracles, diviners, and amulets; it was aimed at promoting fertility and good health and at averting evil spells. The second kind of sorcery was aimed at harming those whom one hated or resented, perhaps for no just cause. The third kind was peculiar to the Azande: possession of *mangu*, an internal spiritual power that a male Azande could inherit from his father and a female from her mother. Those possessing *mangu* held meetings at night at which they feasted and practiced magic; they used a special ointment to make themselves invisible; they sent out their spirits to seize and eat the souls of their victims.

Sorcery may have a variety of social functions: to relieve social tensions; to define and sustain social values; to explain or control terrifying phenomena; to give a sense of power over death. Private sorcery has the additional functions of providing the weak, powerless, and poor with a putative way of obtaining revenge.

Witch doctors, medicine men, or *curanderos* are sorcerers who by definition have a positive function in society, for their business is to cure victims of the effects of malevolent magic. Individuals consult witch doctors to obtain relief from disease or other misfortunes attributed to witchcraft; tribal and village authorities summon them to combat drought or other public calamities. Dances or other rituals, such as those performed by the *ndakó-gboyá* dancers of the Nupe tribe, serve to detect and repel witches and evil spirits.

Sorcery is less a well-defined body of beliefs and actions than a general term covering marked differences in perceptions among societies and within a given society over time. Among the Nyakyusa of Tanzania it was believed that malevolent sorcerers might be of either sex. They were often accused of eating the internal organs of their neighbors or drying up the milk of cattle. The Pondo of South Africa usually thought witches to be women whose chief crime was having sexual intercourse with malevolent spirits. One reason for the difference is that the Nyakyusa were sexually secure but nutritionally insecure and so expressed their insecurities in terms of food, whereas the Pondo were more insecure sexually and so expressed their fears in sexual terms. The function of witchcraft has changed over time among the Bakweri of Cameroon. Before the 1950s the Bakweri were threatened by poverty and a low fertility rate, and they translated these threats into widespread fear of sorcery. In the 1950s their economic status improved radically owing to a boom in the banana crop. The new prosperity occasioned first a cathartic purging of suspected sorcerers and then a decline in accusations and a relative period of calm. In the 1960s bad economic conditions returned, and fear of sorcery revived.

Patterns of sorcery exist in virtually all present societies and have existed in virtually all past societies. The classical Greco-Roman and Hebrew societies from which Western civilization sprang entertained a great variety of sorcery, from public rituals that melded with religion to the activities of the hideous hags described by the classical poet Horace.

The sorcery of most cultures involved incantations supposed to summon spirits to aid the sorcerer. In many societies the connection between sorcery and the spirits was not explicitly formulated. But in both Greco-Roman and Hebrew thought the connection was defined or elaborated. The Greeks believed that all sorcerers drew upon the aid of spirits called *daimones* or *daimonia*. A Greek "demon" could be either malevolent or benevolent. It could be almost a god *(theos)*, or it could be a petty spirit. In the thought of Plotinus (205-270 CE) and other Neoplatonists, the demons occupied an ontological rank between the gods and humanity. The Hebrews gradually developed the idea of the *mal'akh*, originally a manifestation of God's power, later an independent spirit sent down as a messenger by God. In Greek translations of Hebrew, *mal'akh*

In Cherokee myths witches are depicted as irredeemably evil people who can take on the appearance of any person, four-footed animal, or bird.

PAGE 497

The African concept of evil is that of perverse humanity: the human witch and sorcerer.

PAGE 5

became *angelos*, "messenger." Christians eventually identified "angels" with the Greek "demons" and defined them as beings ontologically between God and humanity. But a different element gained influence through the apocalyptic writings of the Hellenistic period (200 BCE–150 CE): the belief in evil spirits led by Satan, lord of all evil. The idea had limited precedents in earlier Jewish thought but gained prominence in the Hellenistic period under the influence of Iranian Mazdaism, or Zoroastrianism. Under such influence the Christians came to divide the Greek *daimones* into two groups, the good angels and the evil demons. The demons were supposed to be angels who, under Satan's leadership, had turned against God and thereby become evil spirits. Sorcerers sought to compel spirits to carry out their will, but angels under God's command could not be compelled; thus it was supposed that one practicing sorcery might well be drawing upon the aid of evil demons. This was the central idea of the second main variety of witchcraft, the alleged diabolism of the late medieval and Renaissance periods in Europe.

If there is one human experience ruled by myth, it is certainly that of evil.

PAGE 218

EUROPEAN WITCHCRAFT

Although simple sorcery had always existed, a new kind of diabolical witchcraft evolved in medieval and early modern Europe. The Christian concept of the devil transformed the idea of the sorcerer into that of the witch, consorter with demons and subject of Satan.

HISTORICAL DEVELOPMENT. The first element in diabolical witchcraft was simple sorcery, which existed in Europe as it did elsewhere. It persisted through the period of the witch craze and indeed has persisted to the present. Without this fundamental element, witchcraft would not have existed. The second, related aspect was the survival of pagan religion and folklore in Christian Europe, or rather the demonstrable survival and transmutation of certain elements *from* paganism.

Another element in the development of diabolical witchcraft in Europe was Christian heresy. The classical formulation of witchcraft had been established by the fifteenth century. Its chief elements were (1) pact with the Devil, (2) formal repudiation of Christ, (3) the secret, nocturnal meeting, (4) the ride by night, (5) the desecration of the Eucharist and the crucifix, (6) orgy, (7) sacrificial infanticide, and (8) cannibalism. At the first formal trial of heretics in the Middle Ages, at Orléans in 1022, the accused were said to hold orgies underground at night, to call up evil spirits and to pay homage to the Devil.

Scholastic theology was the next major element in the formation of the witch concept. In the twelfth through fourteenth centuries the Scholastics developed the tradition of the body of Satan, refined its details, and supplied it with a rational substructure. They extended the Devil's kingdom explicitly to include sorcerers, whom they considered a variety of heretic. Simple sorcerers had become, in the dominant scholastic thought of the later Middle Ages, servants of Satan.

The link between sorcerers, heretics, and Satan was the idea of pact. The notion of pact had been popularized in the eighth century by translations of the sixth-century legend of Theophilus who sold his soul to the Devil in exchange for ecclesiastical preferment. He met the Devil through a Jewish magician and signed a formal pact with "the evil one" in order to fulfill his desires. The Scholastics broadened the idea of pact to

WITCH BURNING

From 1450 to 1700, a hundred thousand people may have perished in what has been called the great witch craze. This wood engraving shows a suspected witch burning at a stake in Dernburg, 1555.

CHRISTEL GERSTENBERG/ CORBIS

include implicit as well as explicit consent. One did not actually have to sign a contract to be a member of Satan's army; anyone—heretic, sorcerer, Jew, Muslim—who knowingly opposed the Christian community, that is, the body of Christ, was deemed to have made an implicit pact with the Devil and to number among his servants.

Theology, then, made a logical connection between witchcraft and heresy.

The final element in the transformation of sorcery into diabolical witchcraft was the Inquisition. The connection of sorcery with heresy meant that sorcery could be prosecuted with much greater severity than before. Between 1227 and 1235 a series of decrees established the papal Inquisition. In 1233 Gregory IX accused the Waldensian heretics, who were in fact evangelical moralists, of Satan worship. In 1252 Innocent IV authorized the use of torture by the Inquisition, and Alexander IV (1254-1261) gave it jurisdiction over all cases of sorcery involving heresy. Gradually almost all sorcery came to be included under the rubric of heresy.

THE WITCH CRAZE. From 1450 to 1700—the period of the Renaissance and the origins of modern science—a hundred thousand may have perished in what has been called the great witch craze. In 1484 Pope Innocent VIII issued a bull confirming papal support for inquisitorial proceedings against the witches, and this bull was included as a preface to the *Malleus maleficarum* (The Hammer of Witches), a book by two Dominican inquisitors. The *Malleus* colorfully detailed the diabolical, orgiastic activities of the witches and helped persuade public opinion that a cosmic plot directed by Satan threatened all Christian society.

As the religious split between Catholicism and Protestantism widened during the sixteenth century and flared up into religious warfare, eschatological fears deepened. Catholics saw the Protestants as soldiers of Satan sent to destroy the Christian community; Protestants viewed the pope as the Antichrist. Terror of witchcraft and prosecution of witches grew in both Catholic and Protestant regions, reaching heights between 1560 and 1660, when religious wars were at their worst. The craze was restricted almost exclusively to western Europe and its colonies.

Skeptics such as Johann Weyer (fl. 1563) and Reginald Scot (fl. 1584), who wrote against belief in witchcraft, were rare and were often rewarded for their efforts by persecution; Weyer, for example, was accused of witchcraft himself. More typical of the period were the works of the learned King James I of England and VI of Scotland (d. 1625). Personally terrified of witches, James encouraged their prosecution. In 1681 Joseph Glanvill was still able to publish a popular second edition of a work supporting belief in diabolical witchcraft. But by that time the craze was beginning to fade. The date of the last execution for witchcraft in England was 1684, in America 1692, in Scotland 1727, in France 1745, and in Germany 1775.

CONCLUSIONS

Witchcraft will continue to be examined theologically, historically, mythologically, psychologically, anthropologically, and sociologically. No single approach can completely explain the phenomenon; even together they do not seem to provide full understanding of such a diverse subject. Witchcraft dwells in the shadowy land where the conscious and unconscious merge, where religion, magic, and technology touch dimly in darkness. Its forms are so varied that it cannot be said to represent any one kind of quasi-religious expression. Modern, neopagan witchcraft is a naive, genial, nature religion. Simple sorcery is usually located across the border into magic yet is frequently combined with religion in two important ways: it is often incorporated into the liturgy of public religion; its charms and spells are often amalgamated into prayers. The Anglo-Saxon clergy of the tenth and eleventh centuries, for example, christianized charms by taking over from wizards the right to say them and then introducing Christian elements into them. By incorporating the sign of the cross or an invocation of the Trinity into a pagan charm, the clergy legitimized the magic. They argued that everything that occurred resulted from God's power and will, and that the use of herbs and charms simply drew upon benevolent forces that God had appointed in nature. It was essential to use them reverently, with the understanding that they were God's and that whatever one accomplished through them was achieved only by appeal to him.

Simple sorcery could be malevolent as well as benevolent. Malevolent sorcery, practiced for private, unjust purposes, was universally condemned. But in late medieval and early modern Europe, evil sorcery merged with diabolism, the result being a different dimension in the religious meaning of witchcraft. This dimension is that of transcendent, transpersonal, or at least transconscious evil.

— JEFFREY BURTON RUSSELL

In the bull Ad extirpanda *(1252), Innocent ordered that heretics handed over to the secular arm should be executed within five days, and he ordained that torture could be used to elicit information for inquisitorial courts.*

PAGE 334

"The whole country's talkin' witchcraft! They'll be calling us witches, Abby!"

ARTHUR MILLER
THE CRUCIBLE

Y

YOGA

In Indian religion the term *yoga* serves, in general, to designate any ascetic technique and any method of meditation. The "classical" form of yoga is a *darsana* ("view, doctrine"; usually, although improperly, translated as "system of philosophy") expounded by Patañjali in his *Yoga Sutra*, and it is from this "system" that we must set out if we are to understand the position of yoga in the history of Indian thought. But side by side with classical Yoga there are countless forms of sectarian, popular (magical), and non-Brahmanic yogas such as Buddhist and Jain forms.

Patañjali is not the creator of the Yoga *darsana*. As he himself admits, he has merely edited and integrated the doctrinal and technical traditions of yoga (*Yoga Sutra* 1.1). Indeed, yogic practices were known in the esoteric circles of Indian ascetics and mystics long before Patañ-jali. Among these practices Patañjali retained those that the experiences of centuries had sufficiently tested. As to the theoretical framework and the metaphysical foundation that Patañjali provides for such techniques, his personal contribution is of the smallest. He merely rehandles the Samkhya philosophy in its broad outlines, adapting it to a rather superficial theism and exalting the practical value of meditation. The Yoga and Samkhya *darsanas* are so much alike that most of the assertions made by the one are valid for the other. The essential differences between them are two: (1) whereas Samkhya is atheistic, Yoga is theistic, since it postulates the existence of a "Lord" (Isvara); (2) whereas according to Samkhya the only path to final deliverance is that of metaphysical knowledge, Yoga accords marked importance to techniques of purification and meditation.

Thanks to Patañjali, Yoga, which had been an archaic ascetic and mystical tradition, became an organized "system of philosophy." Nothing is known of the author of the *Yoga Sutra*, not even whether he lived in the second or third century BCE or in the fifth century CE, although claims to both datings have been vigorously defended. The earliest commentary known to us is the *Yogabhasya* of Vyasa (seventh to eighth century CE), annotated by Vacaspatimisra (ninth century) in his *Tattvavaisaradi*. These two works, indispensable for understanding the *Yoga Sutra*, are complemented by two works of later centuries. At the beginning of the eleventh century King Bhoja wrote the commentary *Rajamartanda*, which is very useful for its insights into certain yogic practices, and in the sixteenth century Vijñanabhiksu annotated Vyasa's text in his remarkable treatise the *Yogavarttika*.

IGNORANCE AND SUFFERING. "All is suffering for the sage," writes Patañjali (*Yoga Sutra* 2.15), repeating a leitmotif of all post-Upansadic Indian speculation. The discovery of pain as the law of existence has a positive, stimulating value. It perpetually reminds the sage and the ascetic that the only way to attain freedom and bliss is withdrawal from the world, radical isolation. To liberate the self from suffering is the goal of all Indian philosophies and magico-mystical techniques. In India, metaphysical knowledge always has a soteriological purpose, for it is by knowledge of ultimate reality that man, casting off the illusions of the world of phenomena, awakens and discovers the true nature of spirit *(atman, purusa)*. For Samkhya and Yoga, suffering has its origin in ignorance of spirit, that is, in confusing spirit with psychomental states, which are the most refined products of nature *(prakrti)*. Consequently, liberation, absolute freedom, can be obtained only if this confusion is abolished. As the structure and unfolding of nature and the paradoxical mode of being of the self *(purusa)* are discussed elsewhere, here only the yogic practices themselves will be examined.

The point of departure of yogic meditation is concentration on a single object: a physical object (the space between the eyebrows, the tip of the nose, something luminous, etc.), a thought (a metaphysical truth), or God (Isvara). This determined and continuous concentration, called *ekagrata* ("on a single point"), is obtained by integrating the psychomental flux, *sarvarthata* ("variously directed, discontinued, diffused attention"; *Yoga Sutra* 3.11). This is the precise definition of yogic technique, and is called *cittavrtti-nirodha*, "the suppression of psychomental states" (*Yoga Sutra* 1.2). The practice of ekagrata tends to control the two generators of psychomental life: sense activity *(indriya)* and the activity of the unconscious *(samskara)*. A yogin is able to concentrate his attention on a single point and become insensible to any other sensory or mnemonic stimulus. It goes without saying that *ekagrata* can be obtained only through the practice of numerous exercises and techniques. One cannot obtain

Far more influential, however, were the pair Samkhya ("enumeration") and Yoga.

PAGE 280

"This is Enlightenment."

BHAGWAN SHREE PATANJALI, YOGA SUTRA

Y

YOGA

Restraints and Disciplines

NEUTRALIZED SENSES

A man practicing the yogic technique of asana (bodily attitudes and posture) on the Ganges River at Varanasi, India.

CHRIS RAINER/CORBIS

ekagrata if, for example, the body is in a tiring or even uncomfortable posture, or if the respiration is disorganized, unrhythmical. This is why yogic technique implies several categories of physiological practices and spiritual exercises, called *angas*, "members," or elements. The eight "members" of classical Yoga can be regarded both as forming a group of techniques and as being stages of the ascetic and spiritual itinerary whose end is final liberation. They are (1) restraints *(yama)*, (2) disciplines *(niyama)*, (3) bodily attitudes and postures *(asana)*, (4) rhythm of respiration *(pranayama)*, (5) emancipation of sensory activity from the domination of exterior objects *(pratyahara)*, (6) concentration *(dharana)*, (7) yogic meditation *(dhyana)*, and (8) enstasis (*samadhi*; *Yoga Sutra* 2.29).

In addition to this classical Yoga comprising eight *angas*, there exist a number of *sadangayogas*, that is, yogic regimens having only six members. Their main characteristic is the absence of the three first angas *(yama, niyama, asana)* and the introduction of a new "member," *tarka* ("reason, logic"). Attested already in the *Maitrayani Upanisad* (second century BCE–second century CE), the *sadangayoga* appears especially in certain sects of Hinduism and in the Buddhist Tantras (Grönbold, 1969, 1983).

RESTRAINTS AND DISCIPLINES. The first two groups of practices, *yama* and *niyama*, constitute the inevitable preliminaries for any asceticism. There are five "restraints," namely, *ahimsa* (restraint from violence), *satya* (restraint from falsehood), *asteya* (restraint from stealing), *brahmacarya* (restraint from sexual activity), and *aparigraha* (restraint from avarice). These restraints do not bring about a specifically yogic state but induce in the adept a purified state superior to that of the uninitiated. In conjunction with the *yamas*, the yogin must practice the *niyama*, that is, a series of bodily and psychic disciplines. "Cleanliness, serenity, asceticism [*tapas*], study of Yoga metaphysics, and an effort to make Isvara [God] the motive of all his actions constitute the disciplines," writes Patañjali (*Yoga Sutra* 2.32). Obviously, difficulties and obstacles arise during these exercises, most of them produced by the subconscious. The perplexity arising from doubt is the most dangerous. To overcome it, Patañjali recommends implanting the contrary thought (*Yoga Sutra* 2.33). To vanquish a temptation is to realize a genuine, positive gain. Not only does the yogin succeed in dominating the objects that he had renounced, but he also obtains a magic force infinitely more precious than all these objects. For example, he who successfully practices *asteya* "sees all jewels coming near to him" (*Yoga Sutra* 2.37).

ASANA AND PRANAYAMA. The specifically yogic techniques begin with *asana*, the well-known bodily posture of the Indian ascetics. *Asana* gives a rigid stability to the body while at the same time reducing physical effort to a minimum and finally eliminating it altogether. *Asana* is the first concrete step taken with a view to abolishing the modalities peculiar to the human condition. On the bodily plane, *asana* is an *ekagrata*; the body is "concentrated" in a single position. Thus, one arrives at a certain neutralization of the senses; consciousness is no longer troubled by the presence of the body. Furthermore, a tendency toward "unification" and "totalization" is typical of all yogic practices. Their goal is the transcendence (or the abolition) of the human condition, resulting from the refusal to obey one's natural inclinations.

The most important—and certainly the most specifically yogic—of these various "refusals" is the disciplining of respiration *(pranayama)*, the refusal to breathe like the majority of mankind, that is, unrhythmically. Patañjali defines this refusal as follows: "*Pranayama* is the arrest *[viccheda]* of the movements of inhalation and exhalation and it is obtained after *asana* has been realized (*Yoga Sutra* 2.49). He speaks of the "arrest," the suspension, of respiration; however, *pranayama* begins with making the respiratory rhythm as slow as possible; and this is its first objective.

A remark in Bhoja's commentary (on *Yoga Sutra* 1.34) reveals the deeper meaning of *pranayama*: "All the functions of the organs being preceded by that of respiration—there being always a connection between respiration and conciousness in their respective functions—respiration, when all the functions of the organs are suspended, realizes concentration of consciousness on a single object." The special relation of the rhythm of respiration to particular states of consciousness, which has undoubtedly been observed and experienced by yogins from the earliest times, has served them as an instrument for "unifying" consciousness. By making his respiration rhythmical and progressively slower the yogin can penetrate—that is experience in perfect lucidity—certain states of consciousness that are inaccessible in a waking condition, particularly the states of consciousness that are peculiar to sleep.

But the immediate goal of *pranayama* is more modest; it induces the respiratory rhythm by harmonizing the three "moments" of breathing: inhalation *(puraka)*, retention *(kumbhaka)*, and exhalation *(recaka)* of the inhaled air. These three moments must each fill an equal space of time. Practice enables the yogin to prolong them considerably. He begins by holding his breath for sixteen and a half seconds, then for thirty-three seconds, then for fifty seconds, three minutes, five minutes, and so on. (Similar respiratory technique were familiar to the Taoists, to Christian hesychasts, and to the Muslim contemplatives; see Eliade, 1969, pp. 59-65).

YOGIC CONCENTRATION AND MEDITATION. Making respiration rhythmical and, as far as possible, suspending it greatly promotes concentration (*dharana; Yoga Sutra* 2.52-53). The yogin can test the quality of his concentration by *pratyahara*, a term usually translated as "withdrawal of the senses" or "abstraction" but more accurately rendered as the "ability to free sense activity from the domination of external objects." According to the *Yoga Sutra* (2.54) and its commentators, the senses, instead of directing themselves toward an object, "abide within themselves" (Bhoja, on *Yoga Sutra* 2.54). When the intellect *(citta)* wishes to know an exterior object, it does not make use of sensory activity; it is able to know the object by its own powers. Being obtained directly, by contemplation, this knowledge is, from the yogic point of view, more effective than normal knowledge. "Then the wisdom [*prajña*] of the yogin knows all things as they are" (Vyasa, on *Yoga Sutra* 2.45). Thenceforth, the yogin will no longer be distracted or troubled by the activity of the senses, by the subconscious, and by the "thirst of life"; all activity is suspended. But this autonomy of the intellect does not result in the suppression of phenomena. Instead of knowing through forms *(rupa)* and mental states *(cittavrtti)* as formerly, the yogin now contemplates the essence *(tattva)* of all objects directly.

> *"Then the wisdom of the yogin knows all things as they are."*
>
> VYASA ON YOGA SUTRA 2.45

Such autonomy allows the yogin to practice a threefold technique that the texts call *samyama*. The term designates the last three "members" of yoga *(yoganga)*, namely concentration *(dharana)*, yogic meditation *(dhyana)*, and stasis *(samadhi)*. They do not imply new physiological practices. *Dharana*, from the root *dhr*, meaning "to hold fast," is in fact an *ekagrata*, undertaken for the purpose of comprehension. Patañjali's definition of *dharana* is "fixation of the thought on a single point" (*Yoga Sutra* 3.1). According to some authors (cf. Eliade, 1969, pp. 66-68), a *dharana* takes the time of twelve *pranayamas* (i. e., twelve controlled, equal, and delayed respirations). By prolonging this concentration on an object twelve times, one obtains yogic meditation, *dhyana*. Patañjali defines *dhyana* as "a current of unified thought" (*Yoga Sutra* 3.2) and Vyasa adds the following gloss to the definition: "continuum of mental effort to assimilate the object of meditation, free from any other effort to assimilate other objects." It is unnecessary to add that this yogic meditation is absolutely different from any secular meditation.

SAMADHI AND THE LORD OF THE YOGINS. Yogic enstasis, *samadhi*, is the final result and crown of all the ascetic's spiritual efforts and exercises. The term is first employed in a gnoseological sense: *samadhi* is the state in which thought grasps the object directly. Thus, there is a real coincidence between knowledge of the object and the object of knowledge. This kind of knowledge constitutes an enstatic modality of being that is peculiar to yoga. Patañjali and his commentators distinguish several sorts, or stages, of *samadhi*. When it is obtained with the help of an object or idea (that is, by fixing one's thought on a point in space or on an idea), it is called *samprajñata samadhi*, "enstasis with support." When, on the other hand, *samadhi* is obtained apart from any relation to externals, when it is simply a full comprehension of being, it is *asamprajñata samadhi*, "undifferentiated stasis."

Because it is perfectible and does not realize an absolute and irreducible state, the "differentiated enstasis" *(samprajñata samadhi)* comprises four stages, called *bija samadhi* ("*samadhi* with seed") or *salambana samadhi* ("*samadhi* with support"). By accomplishing these four stages, one after the other, one obtains the "faculty of absolute knowledge" *(rtambharaprajña)*. This is in itself an opening toward *samadhi* "without seed," pure *samadhi*, for absolute knowledge discovers the state of ontological plenitude in which being and knowing are no longer separated. According to Vijñanabhiksu, *asamprajñata samadhi* destroys the "impressions [*samskara*] of all antecedent mental functions" and even succeeds in arresting the karmic forces already set in motion by the yogin's past activities (Eliade, 1969, p. 84).

Indian ascetics practicing Yoga are well known for their miraculous powers.

PAGE 442

Fixed in *samadhi*, consciousness *(citta)* can now have direct revelation of the self *(purusa)*. For the devotional yogins, it is at this stage that the revelation of the Supreme Self, Isvara, the Lord, takes place. Unlike Samkhya, Yoga affirms the existence of a God, Isvara. He is not a creator god, for the cosmos, life, and man proceed from the primordial substance, *prakrti*. But in the case of certain men (i. e., the yogins), Isvara can hasten the process of deliverance. Isvara is a self *(purusa)* that has been eternally free. Patañjali says that the Isvara has been the guru of the sages of immemorial times (*Yoga Sutra* 1.26) and that he can bring about *samadhi* on condition that the yogin practice *isvara-pranidhana*, that is, devotion to Isvara (*Yoga Sutra* 2.45). But we have seen that *samadhi* can be obtained without such mystical exercises. In the classical Yoga of Patañjali, Isvara plays a rather minor role. It is only with the later commentators, such as Vijñanabhiksu and Nila-kantha, that Isvara gains the importance of a true God.

The "eight limbs" of Yoga represent the most important Hindu formulation of a step-by-step path to liberation.

PAGE 280

THE YOGIC POWERS; DELIVERANCE. By practicing *samyama*—that is, by means of concentration, meditation, and the realization of *samadhi*—the yogin acquires the "miraculous powers" *(siddhis)* to which book 3 of the *Yoga Sutra*, beginning with *sutra* 16, is devoted. The majority of these powers are related to different kinds of supranormal or mystical knowledge. Thus, by practicing *samyama* in regard to his own subconscious residues *(samskara)*, the yogin comes to know his previous existences (*Yoga Sutra* 3.105). Through *samyama* exercised in respect to "notions" *(pratyaya)*, he knows the mental states of other men (3.19). *Samyama* practiced on the umbilical plexus *(nabhicakra)* produces knowledge of the system of the body (3.28), on the heart, knowledge of the mind (3.33), and so forth." Whatever the yogin desires to know, he should perform *samyama* in respect to that object," writes Vacaspatimisra (on *Yoga Sutra* 3.30). According to Patañjali and the whole tradition of classical Yoga, the yogin uses the innumerable *siddhis* in order to attain the supreme freedom, *asamprajñata samadhi*, not in order to obtain a mastery over the elements (*Yoga Sutra* 3.37). We find a similar doctrine in Buddhism (Eliade, 1969, pp. 177-180; Pensa, 1969, pp. 23-24).

Through the illumination *(prajña)* spontaneously obtained when he reaches the last stage of his itinerary, the yogin realizes "absolute isolation" *(kaivalya)*, that is, liberation of the self *(purusa)* from the dominance of nature *(prakrti)*. But this mode of being of the spirit is not an "absolute emptiness"; it constitutes a paradoxical, because unconditioned, state. Indeed, the intellect *(buddhi)*, having accomplished its mission, withdraws, detaching itself from the *purusa* and returning into *prakrti*. The self remains free, autonomous; that is, the yogin attains deliverance. Like a dead man, he has no more real relation with life; he is a *jivanmukta*, one "liberated in life." He no longer lives in time and under the domination of time, but in an eternal present.

— MIRCEA ELIADE

YORUBA RELIGION

The twelve to fifteen million Yoruba people of southwestern Nigeria, the Republic of Benin (formerly Dahomey), and Togo are the heirs of one of the oldest cultural traditions in West Africa. Archaeological and linguistic evidence indicate that the Yoruba have lived in their present habitat since at least the fifth century BCE. The development of the regional dialects that distinguish the Yoruba subgroups and the process of urbanization, which developed into a social system unique among sub-Saharan African peoples, took place during the first millennium CE. By the ninth century the ancient city of Ile-Ife was thriving, and in the next five centuries Ife artists would create terracotta and bronze sculptures that are now among Africa's artistic treasures.

Both Yoruba myth and oral history refer to Oduduwa (also known as Odua) as the first king and founder of the Yoruba people. Some myths portray him as the creator god and assert that the place of creation was Ile-Ife, which subsequently became the site of Oduduwa's throne. Oral history, however, suggests that the story of Oduduwa's assumption of the throne at Ife refers to a conquest of the indigenes of the Ife area prior to the ninth century by persons from "the east." While it is increasingly apparent that the sociopolitical model of a town presided over by a paramount chief or king *(oba)*, was well established in Ife and present among other Yoruba subgroups, the followers of Oduduwa developed the urban tradition and enhanced the role of the king. In later years, groups of people who sought to establish their political legitimacy (even if they were immigrants) were required to trace their descent from Oduduwa. Such people were known as "the sons of Oduduwa," and they wore beaded crowns *(adenla)* given to them by Oduduwa as the symbol of their sacred authority *(ase)*.

Origin myths, festival rituals, and oral traditions associate the indigenous peoples with Obatala, the deity *(orisa)* who fashions the human body. And since he too was an *oba*, his priests wear white, conical, beaded crowns similar to those reserved for "the sons of Oduduwa." The myths and rituals also refer to a great struggle between Obatala and Oduduwa at the time of creation, following Oduduwa's theft of the privilege granted by Olorun (Olodumare), the high god, to Obatala to create the earth and its inhabitants. In the town of Itapa, the sequence of rituals that composes the annual festival of Obatala reenacts a battle between Oduduwa and Obatala, Oduduwa's victory over and the banishment of Obatala, and the rejoicing that took place among the gods and mankind with the return of Obatala at the invitation of Oduduwa. And there is the tradition among the Oyo Yoruba of the unwarranted imprisonment of Obatala by Sango and the thunder god's release of the wandering, ancient king after famine and barrenness threatened field and home.

In these myths and rituals there is a historical remembrance of a usurpation of power and the acknowledgment that a violent conflict and a tenuous reconciliation gave birth to modern Yoruba culture. The remembrance, however, has not only to do with a past time, with historical and cultural origins; it is also a statement about the nature and limits of the authority of kings in defining the moral basis of Yoruba society. It is also about the importance of Ile-Ife as the symbol of Yoruba cultural homogeneity, while acknowledging the distinctiveness and the independence of other Yoruba subgroups.

There are approximately twenty subgroups, each identifiable by its distinctive variation in linguistic, social, political, and religious patterns born of the history of the region. Among the principal groups are the Egba and Egbado in the southwest, the Ijebu in the southern and southeast, the Oyo in the central and northwest, the Ife and the Ijesa in the central, the Owo in the eastern, and the Igbomina and Ekiti in the northeast regions. Throughout Yorubaland, the social system is patrilineal and patrilocal, although among the Egba and Egbado there are elements of a dual descent system. The extended family *(idile)*, which dwells in the father's compound so long as space and circumstance permit, is the essential social unit and the primary context in which self-awareness and social awareness are forged. Thus, Odun Egungun, the annual festival for the patrilineal ancestors, is the most widespread and important festival in the Yoruba liturgical calendar. Elaborate masquerades *(egungun)*, are created of layers of cloths of dark colors with white serrated edges. The costume covers the dancer, who moves about the compound or town with stately pace, occasionally performing whirling movements, causing the cloths to splay out in constantly changing patterns. In movement and appearance the masquerade depicts the presence and power *(ase)* of the ancestors. The ancestors are those persons who established the "house" *(ile)* and the family and who continue to stand surety for its integrity and survival against threats of witchcraft and disease, so long as their heirs acknowledge the ancestral presence.

While masquerades for the patrilineal ancestors are found among all the Yoruba, there are other masked festivals that are distinctive to particular areas, reflecting the regional history that has shaped the Yoruba experience. The Yoruba peoples of the southwest (the Anago, Awori, Egbado, Ketu, and Egba) celebrate the Gelede festival at the time of the spring rains. The festival honors *awon iya wa* ("the mothers"), a collective term for the female power *(ase)* possessed by all women but especially manifest in certain elderly women and in female ancestors and deities. It is the awesome power of woman in its procreative and destructive capacities that is celebrated and acknowledged. Among the Ijebu peoples of the south the annual festival for Agemo, an *orisa* whose power is represented by the chameleon, brings sixteen priest-chiefs famed for their magical or manipulative powers from towns surrounding the capital city of Ijebu-Ode into ritual contests of curse and masked dance with one another and then into the city, where they petition and are received by the Awujale, the *oba* of Ijebu-Ode. The secret power of the priest-chiefs meets the sacred power of the crown. Each is required to acknowledge the role of the other in the complex balance of power that constitutes Ijebu political life. The Elefon and Epa festivals are masquerades performed in the towns of such Yoruba subgroups as the Igbomina and Ekiti in honor of persons and families whose lives embodied the social values by which Yoruba culture has been defined in the northeastern area. The helmet masks with their large sculptures are balanced on the dancers' heads and are the focus of ritual sacrifice *(ebo)* and songs of praise *(oriki)* throughout the festival. They are images of the sacred power of

Among the Igbomina Yoruba of southwestern Nigeria the costumes of the masquerades for the patrilineal ancestors, egungun paaka, *combine materials of the forest with those of human manufacture.*

PAGE 298

"Whoever obeys the gods, to him they particularly listen."

HOMER
THE ILIAD

those who founded the town or contributed to its life in important ways. Thus, while individual masks are associated with particular families, they also refer to the roles of hunter, warrior, king, herbalist-priest, and leader of women, roles that transcend lineage ties and express in their collectivity cultural achievement. Their powers are akin to those of the *orisa*, the gods of the Yoruba pantheon.

According to the Yoruba, there are 401 *orisa* who line the road to heaven. All of them are thought to have been humans who, because they led notable lives, became *orisa* at the time of their death. For example, Sango, the god of thunder, was a legendary king of Oyo before he became an *orisa*. The extraordinary number of *orisa* reflects the regional variation in their worship. Sango is the patron deity of the kings of Oyo, and his shrines are important in those towns that were once part of the old Oyo empire (c. 1600-1790). But in Ile-Ife, or in communities to the south and east, the role of Sango and the degree to which he is worshiped diminishes markedly. As one moves from one part of Yorubaland to another, it will be Osun, goddess of medicinal waters, or Oko, god of the farm, or Erinle, god of forest and stream, or Obatala or Agemo whose shrines and festivals shape the religious life of a people. Furthermore, the orisa have multiple names. Some call Sango Oba Koso ("king of Koso"); others greet him as Balogunnile Ado ("leader of warriors at Ado"). Sango is also addressed as Abinufarokotu ("one who violently uproots an *iroko* tree"), Oko Iyemonja ("husband of Iyemonja"), or Lagigaoogun ("he who is mighty in the use of magical powers"), names that reveal the varied and distinctive experiences of his devotees and their relationship to the *orisa*. The multiplicity (or fragmentation) of the *orisa* is also a consequence of the historical dislocation of peoples that occurred during the intertribal wars of the nineteenth century. When persons and groups were forced to move from one area to

ORISA SYMBOLS

These shrine figures made of iroko wood and found in Ede, Nigeria represent the orisa, the gods of the Yoruba pantheon.

© WERNER FORMAN/CORBIS

another, their *orisa* went with them, shaping and being shaped by the new world of their devotees' experience.

Of all the *orisa* it is Ogun, god of iron and of war, whose worship is most widespread. It is said that there are seven Ogun, including Ogun of the blacksmiths, Ogun of the hunters, Ogun of the warriors, and Ogun Onire. Ire is a town in northeast Yorubaland where Ogun was once the leader of warriors and where he "sank into the ground" after killing persons in a great rage, having misunderstood their vow of ritual silence as a personal affront. As with other *orisa*, Ogun expresses and shapes a people's experience with respect to a particular aspect of their lives. In the case of Ogun, it is the experience of violence and culture: his myths and rituals articulate for the Yoruba the irony that cultural existence entails destruction and death. One must kill in order to live. And such a situation carries with it the danger that the destruction will go beyond culturally legitimate need, destroying that which it should serve. Thus, to employ Ogun's power, one must be aware of Ogun's character *(iwa)* and be cognizant that the beneficent god can become the outraged *orisa* who bites himself.

As with Ogun, each of the *orisa*, in the diversity and individuality of their persons and attributes, may be understood as providing an explanatory system and a means of coping with human suffering. Rarely does only one orisa lay claim to a person. Ogun or Sango or Osun may dominate one's life and shape one's perception of self and world, but other *orisa* will have their artifacts on the shrine, as well as their claims and influence upon one's life. Just as the Yoruba dancer must respond to the multiple rhythms of the drums, so must the soul attentive to the powers of the *orisa* respond to their diverse claims. The complexity of the response may overwhelm one. But as in the ability of the dancer to be conscious of and respond to every instrument of the orchestra, so in sacrificing to all the *orisa* who call, the worshiper (*olusin*, "he who serves") can know the richness of life and its complexity and can achieve the superior poise, the equanimity of one who possesses *ase* amid the contradictions of life. Thus, when one considers the configuration of *orisa* symbols on a devotee's shrine or the cluster of shrines and festivals for the *orisa* in a particular town or the pantheon as a whole, as a total system, one discerns that the total assemblage of *orisa* expresses in it totality a worldview. And it is in the reality of this worldview that Yoruba experience, at the personal and social levels, is given coherence and meaning.

In addition to the *orisa* of the pantheon, there is one's personal *orisa*, known as *ori inun* ("inner head"), which refers to the destiny that one's ancestral guardian soul has chosen while kneeling before Olorun prior to entering the world. It is a personal destiny that can never be altered. Birth results in the loss of the memory of one's destiny. But one's "*ori*-in-heaven," which is also referred to as *ekejimi* ("my spiritual other"), stands surety for the possibilities and the limits of the destiny that one has received. Hence, one must make one's way in life, acknowledging one's *ori* as an *orisa* who can assist one in realizing the possibilities that are one's destiny. One can have an *ori buruku* ("a bad head"). In such a case a person must patiently seek to make the best of a foolish choice and seek the help of the other *orisa*.

In *orisa* worship it is the wisdom of Orunmila, the *orisa* of Ifa divination, and the work of Esu, the bearer of sacrifices, that stand for the meaningfulness of experience and the possibility of effective action. The vast corpus of Ifa poetry, organized into 256 collections called *odu* (also known as *orisa*) is a repository of Yoruba cultural values. It is the priest of Ifa, the *babalawo* ("father of ancient wisdom"), who knows Ifa and performs the rites of divination. Using the sixteen sacred palm nuts or the *opele* chain, the priest divines the *odu* whose verses he will chant in addressing the problem of the suppliant and determining the sacrifices that must be made. For the Yoruba, every ritual entails a sacrifice, whether it is the gift of prayer, the offering of a kola nut, or the slaughter of an animal. In the Ifa literature, sacrifice *(ebo)* has to do with death and the avoidance of such related experiences as loss, disease, famine, sterility, isolation, and poverty. It is an acknowledgment that human existence is ensnared in the interrelated contradictions of life and death. But sacrifice is also viewed as the reversal of the situation of death into life. Sacrifice is the food of the *orisa* and other spirits, and one sacrifices that which appropriately expresses the character *(iwa)* of the particular *orisa* or spirit of one's concern. Hence, Ogun receives a dog, the carnivorous animal that can be domesticated to assist the hunter and warrior. Sacrifice is the acknowledgement of the presence of powerful agents in the world, and the sacrificial act brings the creative power of the *orisa*, the ancestors, or the mothers to the worshiper; sacrifice can also temporarily stay the hand of Death and ward off other malevolent spirits *(ajogun)*. Such is the power of Esu, the bearer of sacrifices, the mediator and guardian of the ritual way, the "keeper of *ase*."

Those who have observed the ritual way and achieved the status of elders in the community may also become members of the secret Osugbo (Ogboni) society. Although Osugbo is found throughout Yorubaland, its role and rituals vary from one region to another. Osugbo members, who come from various lineage groups, worship Onile ("the owner of the house"). The "house" *(ile)* is the image of the universe in its totality, of which the Osugbo cult house is a microcosm. The *edan* of the Osugbo society, which are small, brass, linked staffs that depict male and female figures, are the sign of membership and the symbol of the Osugbo

The Gelede masks of the Yoruba honor the spiritual power of women, collectively known as "our mothers."

PAGE 6

For the Yoruba, every ritual entails a sacrifice, whether it is the gift of prayer, the offering of a kola nut, or the slaughter of an animal.

PAGE 398

understanding of reality. The secret of the Osugbo appears to be that its members know, and are in touch with, a primordial unity that transcends the oppositions characterizing human experience. Expressing the unity of male and female, the *edan* and their owners possess the power of adjudicating conflicts among persons or groups; when blood has been shed illicitly (as in a murder) it is the Osugbo members who must atone for this "violation of the house."

The worldview of the Yoruba is a monistic one. The universe of their experience is pervaded by *ase*, a divine energy in the process of generation and regeneration. *Ase* is without any particular signification and yet invests all things and all persons and, as the warrant for all creative activity, opposes chaos and the loss of meaning in human experience. Thus, for the Yoruba the universe is one, and it is amenable to articulation in terms of an elaborate cosmology, to critical reflection, and to innovative speculation.

— JOHN PEMBERTON III

Z

ZEN

THE PLANTING OF ZEN BUDDHISM IN JAPAN

The early history of Zen proper does not begin until the twelfth century, when Myoan Eisai attempted to transmit the Lin-chi teachings to Japan.

MYOAN EISAI. Myoan Eisai (1141-1215; also known as Myoan Yosai) encountered Ch'an Buddhists during a trip to China (1187-1191). He entered a Ch'an monastery where he practiced *tso-ch'an* (Jpn., *zazen*) and *kung-an* (Jpn., *koan*), achieved enlightenment, and was presented with the insignia of succession in the Huang-lung (Jpn., Oryo) line of the Lin-chi school. He did not, however, cut himself off entirely from the Tendai school to which he belonged and in whose doctrines and esoteric practices he was well versed.

Immediately upon his return to Japan, Eisai began to propagate the way of Zen in the southern island of Kyushu. His energetic labors stirred up the resentment of the Tendai monks, who succeeded in having a prohibition issued by the imperial palace against the "new sect" of the "Dharma school" (1194).

In his apologetic work of 1198, *Kozen gokokuron* (Treatise on the Spread of Zen for the Protection of the Country), Eisai stresses the value of the Tendai tradition, in which meditation and enlightenment hold a place of prominence. Meditation is set alongside the perfect doctrine *(engyo)*, secret rites *(mitsu)*, and disciplinary commandments *(kai)* as one of the four essential elements of Tendai. In his view, Rinzai Zen, as "the quintessence of all doctrines and the totality of the Buddha's Dharma," can contribute decisively to the renewal of Japanese Buddhism. Eisai felt that the time had not yet come for the organizational establishment of an independent Rinzai school. The Zen that he left to his disciples showed a strong mixture of Tendai, especially Tendai esotericism (Taimitsu), in its spirituality.

ENNI BEN'EN. The central figure during the following period was Enni Ben'en (best known by his posthumous title of Shoichi Kokushi, 1201-1280). The turning point in Enni's life came during the course of a seven-year stay in China (1235-1241). He entered the discipleship of the outstanding Lin-chi master Wu-chun Shih-fan (Jpn., Bushun Shihan), practiced pure Ch'an, and reached enlightenment. As abbot of Tofukuji, his daily visits to Kenninji allowed him to bring life to monastic discipline and to rekindle the zeal for meditation that had declined after the death of Eisai. All the same, he did not change Eisai's style of mixing Zen with received rites. The labors of Enni Ben'en mark a step forward in the long and drawn-out process of Zen's implantation in Japan. The "new sect" introduced from China gradually found acceptance in wide circles of the population.

CHINESE ZEN MASTERS IN JAPAN. During the second half of the Kamakura period Buddhism witnessed the establishment of Zen, in particular the Rinzai school. For these Chinese masters it was absolutely self-evident that their cloisters represented the Rinzai school in Japan independent of the older schools of Japanese Buddhism. Their highly successful labors contributed greatly to the rooting of Zen in Japan, and the cloisters they directed formed the core of a self-subsistent Japanese Rinzai school.

DOGEN KIGEN. The other school that flourished in China during the Sung period, Ts'ao-tung (Jpn., Soto), was brought to Japan by the Japanese monk Dogen Kigen (1200-1253).

In China Dogen encountered the "authentic teacher" in the person of the master Ju-ching (Jpn., Nyojo) of Mount T'ien-t'ung. In this master he placed his entire trust, and under his expert guidance achieved the great experience of the "dropping off of body and mind" *(shinjin datsuraku)*. By partaking in the perpetuation of the enlightenment experience through his master, Dogen entered a line of what he considered to be the essential transmission of the patriarchs reaching back to Sakyamuni Buddha.

What Dogen achieved for Japanese Zen Buddhism is significant. More than any other he is "the master of *zazen*." In his view, *zazen* embraced everything essential and valuable in Buddhism. In *zazen* practice and enlightenment come together. The seed of Buddhahood implanted in each individual at birth so that it might blossom to fulfillment—that is, the Buddha nature inherent in all reality—is disclosed in *zazen*. Dogen's impact as a master of *zazen* continues to the present day.

MAIN CURRENTS DURING THE MIDDLE AGES

Under the political leadership of the shoguns of the house of Ashikaga, the Muromachi period (1338-

By far the most influential religious sect during the Ashikaga period was Zen.

PAGE 382

Most typical of that final state of emptiness as Zen Buddhists conceive of it is that it results not in a withdrawal from the real but in an enhanced ability to see the real as it is.

PAGE 476

The abbot's quarters (hojo) *of a Zen monastery in fact came to be a standard feature of residential, or* shoin, *architecture*

PAGE 661

1573) witnessed the spread of Zen throughout the country and its opening out into art and culture.

THE FIVE MOUNTAINS OF THE RINZAI SCHOOL. The system of "five mountains" *(gozan)*, "ten temples" *(jissetsu)*, and affiliated temples *(shozan)* set up by the Japanese Rinzai school in imitation of the Chinese model helped the Zen movement to find its place in the order of Japanese society. Already in Kamakura the five main temples had formed a unit under the protection of the military government *(bakufu)*. With the transfer of power to Kyoto, the prominent temples of the capital city came to be referred to as the Five Mountains.

The leading personality in Rinzai Zen at the beginning of the Muromachi period was Muso Soseki (1275-1351), a monk of extraordinary intellectual power and high artistic gifts. His efforts to erect "temples for the pacification of the country" *(ankokuji)* and "pagodas for the use of the living" *(risshoto)* helped to disseminate Zen Buddhism further in Japan.

In the broad sense of the term, the Gozan movement included the way of life of the Zen temples of the Gozan system, with its Chinese influence and its wider cultural significance. In Gozan culture *(gozan bunka)* it was literature *(gozan bungaku)* that occupied first place, but other arts, such as calligraphy, painting, the creation of gardens, and so forth were also cultivated. The contribution of Gozan to the system of education remained as a positive contribution. The famous Ashikaga school *(Ashikaga-gakko)* founded by the Gozan monks passed on the higher levels of Chinese education while temple schools *(tera-koya)*, largely run by Zen monks, brought elementary knowledge to the common folk. The decline of the Rinzai school centered on the Five Mountains is signaled in the fact that none of the Gozan lines survived into the following era.

DAITOKUJI AND ITS LINE. The temple Daitokuji was one of the most significant centers of the Rinzai school in Kyoto. The main line of the monastery begins with Nampo Jomyo (1235-1309), the most important figure in the third stage of Zen's establishment in Japan. His disciple Shuho Myocho (1282-1338) founded Daitokuji under the patronage of the emperor Go-Daigo in 1327 and saw it through to full bloom.The influence of Daitokuji radiated far and wide into Japanese Zen culture and art in the Middle Ages. After a change in fortune during the civil war, the temple Daitokuji became the favorite center for the arts toward the end of the Middle Ages.

THE SOTO SCHOOL. The so-called "strife over succession in the third generation" did not end in an open break, but the longtime superior of Eiheiji, Tettsu Gikai (1219-1309), withdrew to Daitoji, a Shingon temple located in the Kaga district that had been taken over for use as a Zen cloister. There a second Soto center originated and came to wield great influence through Gikai's important disciple, Keizan Jokin (1268-1325).

Jokin, revered by adherents of the Soto school as the "great patriarch" *(taso)*, expanded Soto Zen into a popular movement. He founded the temples of Yokoji and Sojiji in the Noto area. Keizan's chief disciple, Gasan Joseki (1275-1365), succeeded him as abbot in Sojiji and there gathered a large flock of disciples. Twenty-five of them are spoken of as having spread Soto Zen throughout the entire country, so that from the end of the Middle Ages up to the present day it has remained numerically the second strongest Buddhist school.

THE MODERN PERIOD

The most significant figure in Rinzai Zen during the nineteenth century was Imakita Kosen (also known as Kosen Soon, 1816-1892). In 1875 he was entrusted with the superintendence of the ten great temple estates of the Rinzai and Obaku schools, while he himself was administering the temple of Engakuji (Kamakura) as abbot. Outstanding among his students was Shaku Soen (1856-1919), who had also found understanding and support for his open approach to modern times among the gifted dharmic successors of the following two generations. Soen was also a participant at the 1893 World's Parliament of Religions in Chicago, an interreligious congress that for many opened the door to new ways of looking at other religions.

[*See also* Buddhism.]

— HEINRICH DUMOULIN
TRANSLATED FROM GERMAN
BY JAMES W. HEISIG

ZIONISM

Although Jebusite in origin, the name *Zion* (Heb., *Tsiyyon*) was assimilated into the Israelite vocabulary and became associated with the Davidic monarchy and its capital in Jerusalem. In writings of such prophets as "First Isaiah" and Jeremiah and in *Psalms*, the name *Zion* is used as a synonym first for the Temple in Jerusalem, then for the kingdom of Judah, and finally, in postexilic literature, for the Land of Israel. In the Babylonian exile, the psalmist wrote: "By the waters of Babylon / There we sat down, yea, we wept / When we remembered Zion" (*Ps.* 137:1). Thus, what was first a specific place-name came to represent symbolically the whole Land of Israel whose people had been exiled. The particular associations between Zion and the Davidic monarchy gave the word a special resonance in later messianic literature that expressed longing not only for the return of the people to their land but also for the reestablishment of the kingdom of David.

MEDIEVAL PERIOD. The theme of Zion played an important role in the medieval liturgical poems *(piyyutim).*

The best examples of secular poetry devoted to longing for Zion can be found during the "classical age" of the Spanish Jews (900-1200).

Perhaps the most outstanding representative of this school of poets was Yehudah ha-Levi (c. 1075-1141) whose *Shirei Tsiyyon* (Songs of Zion) inspired many imitations later in the Middle Ages. In the sixteenth century, following the expulsion of the Jews from Spain, the community of Palestine increased and a number of "proto-Zionist" efforts were undertaken to establish Jewish agricultural colonies and reestablish the ancient Sanhedrin. This proto-Zionist sentiment cannot be dissociated from medieval Jewish messianism. All messianic thinkers in the Middle Ages considered the return to Zion to be among the primary tasks of the Messiah. Even as messianic expectations were embroidered with supernatural fantasies, such as the belief in the resurrection of the dead, the core of Jewish messianism remained political and nationalistic: the Messiah would return the Jews to Zion, reestablish the kingdom of David, and rebuild the Temple in Jerusalem.

On the other hand, another group of medieval thinkers deemphasized the importance of immigration to Zion. Maimonides (Mosheh ben Maimon, 1135/8-1204) said that the central event in Jewish history was at Mount Sinai, and the return to Zion in messianic times would be a means toward uninterrupted study of the law revealed at Sinai. Although Maimonides clearly believed in the coming of the Messiah (which he understood as a realistic and not solely supernatural process), he subordinated Zion to Sinai.

THE NINETEENTH CENTURY. Two important intellectual developments in the nineteenth century, among both modernizing and traditional Jews, prepared the ground for Zionism. The first was the movement of Jewish Enlightenment (Haskalah), which began in Germany in the late eighteenth century and spread to eastern Europe in the nineteenth. The Haskalah developed in two directions with respect to Zion. On the one hand, there was a general tendency to promote the emancipation of the Jews in Europe by glorifying the European nations. On the other hand, much of the new Hebrew literature written by Haskalah authors, especially in eastern Europe, harkened back to the land of the Bible.

The second important nineteenth-century development was among traditional Jews. Tsevi Hirsch Kalischer (1795-1874) advocated agricultural settlement in the Land of Israel. Kalischer never abandoned his messianic expectations, nor did he give up his hope that the sacrifices might be reinstituted by the new settlers.

A similar kind of religious "Zionism" can be found in the writings of Yehudah ben Shelomoh Alkalai (1798-1878), who argued in numerous pamphlets for Jewish settlement in the Holy Land as a means toward bringing the Messiah.

In 1878 a group of Orthodox Jews established the first agricultural colony, Petach Tikva. Scholars have come to appreciate the contribution that these religious Jews made in laying the groundwork for the later Zionist settlement.

MODERN SECULAR ZIONISM. Modern Zionism really began with Theodor Herzl (1860-1904). The term *Zionism* was coined in 1890 by Nathan Birnbaum in his journal *Selbstemanzipation* and was adopted by Herzl and his followers at the first Zionist Congress in 1897. Although some rabbis supported Herzl, most members of the movement, including Herzl himself, were secular and westernized. Nevertheless, Herzl was greeted by many eastern European Jews as a messianic figure. The first substantial Zionist emigration from eastern Europe to Palestine started after the pogroms of 1903 and 1905-1906 and was largely made up of young secular Russian Jews, many of whom were influenced by the Russian radicalism of the period.

*"Awake, awake!
Put on your strength
O, Zion."*

ISAIAH 52:1

The attitude toward religion among the early secular Zionist thinkers was frequently quite hostile. Traditional Judaism was viewed as the religion of the exile and the Zionists saw themselves as a movement to "negate the exile" *(shelilat ha-golah).* Nevertheless, there were other secular Zionists who tried to base the new Zionist culture on elements from the religious tradition.

The ambivalence toward the Jewish tradition that one finds in many of these early secular Zionists had much to do with their biographies. In most cases, they came from traditional homes and were educated in the *yeshivot* (rabbinic academies) of eastern Europe. Zionism was a radical revolution for them against the world of their childhood, but they never fully broke with their positive memories of this religious culture. Even if their way of life was secular, they wished to recreate an authentic Jewish culture on a new, national basis.

The Israeli political elite, in particular, have been strongly influenced by religious Zionists.

PAGE 540

RELIGIOUS ZIONISM. Among the first rabbis to join Herzl were Isaac Reines and Shemu'el Mohilever, who was perhaps the most prominent rabbi in the Hibbat Tsiyyon movement. In 1902, Reines formed Mizrahi, a religious faction within the World Zionist Organization (the name is a composite of some of the Hebrew letters from the words *merkaz ruhani*, "spiritual center"). Mizrahi consisted of two groups: one that opposed the introduction of any "cultural" issues into the Zionist movement, for fear that the secularists would set the tone in such endeavors, and another that saw that Zionism could not avoid confronting cultural issues and demanded that Mizrahi try to influence the Zionist movement in a religious direction.

"Prayer is the soul's sincere desire, uttered or unexpressed."

JAMES MONTGOMERY
WHAT IS PRAYER?

Mizrahi played a major role in mustering support for Zionism among Orthodox Jews in Europe and the United States. It created a network of schools in which Zionism was taught together with traditional religious subjects. At the same time, Mizrahi established schools in Palestine that formed the backbone of the religious educational system that is an important part of the general educational system in the state of Israel. The Mizrahi youth movements, Young Mizrahi and Benei Akiva, began establishing agricultural settlements in Palestine in the 1920s.

Since their inception the Mizrahi have sought to avoid the problem of the relationship of Zionism to Jewish messianism. Much opposition to Zionism in the religious world stemmed from the belief that human beings should not "force the end" (i. e., initiate messianic times by secular means). Instead of answering this position with a new messianic theory, the Mizrahi took a cautious stance, claiming that the Zionist movement constituted a "beginning of redemption."

There were, however, certain elements among the religious Zionists who took a bolder approach to the question of messianism. Primary among these was Avraham Yitshaq Kook, who was chief Ashkenazic rabbi of Palestine from 1921 until his death in 1935. Kook believed that the secular pioneers were a necessary force to prepare the material foundation for messianic times. He argued dialectically that the profane was necessary for subsequent emergence of the sacred.

The young religious Zionists, who grew up after the creation of the state in 1948, believed strongly in Zionism as the fulfillment of traditional Jewish messianism.

RELIGIOUS INSTITUTIONS IN THE STATE OF ISRAEL. Under both the Ottoman empire and the British Mandate, Jewish religious courts enjoyed official jurisdiction over matrimonial and inheritance law. The office of the *hakham basi* in the Ottoman empire was succeeded by the Ashkenazic and Sefardic chief rabbis under the British Mandate. These functions were carried over to the rabbinic courts and the chief rabbinate of the state of Israel, which were given jurisdiction over matters of personal law by a Knesset enactment of 1953. Rabbinical judges were given the same status as district court judges and their decisions were enforced by the civil authorities. Thus, in matters of marriage, divorce, and child custody, rabbinic courts—ruling according to Jewish law *(halakhah)*—have state sanction. Civil marriage and divorce do not exist, although civil marriages are recognized if contracted abroad. A Ministry of Religious Affairs deals with the needs of the various religious communities in Israel and funds the construction and maintenance of synagogues, *yeshivot*, and other religious facilities.

Although both the Conservative and Reform movements have followings in Israel, their rabbis are not authorized by the rabbinate to perform marriages and they do not benefit from the budgets available through the Ministry of Religious Affairs. Conversion to Judaism is supervised by the rabbinate, and thus Conservative and Reform conversions are not recognized as valid.

— DAVID BIALE

ZOROASTRIANISM

With a history of some three thousand years, Zoroastrianism is one of the most ancient living religions. Attempts have often been made to distinguish between various phases of Zoroastrianism and to endow each with a slightly different name. Thus it has been suggested that the religion contained in the *Gathas*, the texts attributed to Zarathushtra himself, be called "Zarathushtrianism," that the contents of the Younger Avesta be called "Zarathushtricism," and that the religion of the Sasanid period be called "Zoroastrianism" (Gershevitch, 1964). These definitions should be extended to include the religion of the Zoroastrian communities in Iran and India today.

ORIGINS. Zoroastrianism originated in the eastern and south-central regions of the Iranian world, between the great mountain ranges of the Hindu Kush and Seistan, an area that today is divided between Iran and Afghanistan. Current research on the religion's origin is based on geographical information contained in the Avesta, as well as on an evaluation of archaeological findings and on a reinterpretation of the few available sources.

Zoroastrianism grew out of a politically fragmented tribal society whose civilization centered upon oases rather than upon fixed urban settings. The society was ruled by a warrior aristocracy, that is, by one of the three classes—priests, warriors, and shepherds—that made up the original social structure of the Arya. Within this society, religion most likely revolved around young warrior *(mairya)* fraternities (the Aryan or Indo-Iranian *Männerbund*), with their bloody cults, violent gods, sacrificial rites, initiations, and ecstatic practices that climaxed in a state of "fury" called *aeshma*.

DISTINCTIVE CHARACTERISTICS. The primary innovation of Zoroastrianism, which sets it apart from the religions of other Indo-European peoples in the Near East and Central Asia, is its emphasis on monotheism.

The concept of Ahura Mazda as the creator of heaven and earth, day and night, and light and darkness (*Yasna* 44.3-5), as well as the ethical context in which Zarathushtra conceived his answer to the problem of evil, demonstrates that the prophet was an original thinker, a powerful religious figure who introduced radical changes to the spiritual and cultural world in which he was reared. He responded to a deeply formalistic and ritualistic religion by strongly and insistently praising human worth and dignity.

THEOLOGY AND PANTHEON. In Zarathushtra's conception, a dualistic vision is almost a natural consequence of monotheism, for dualism explains the evil that resides in the world and afflicts it. The problem of evil and suffering is basic to Zoroastrian thought, and the urgent human necessity of providing an answer to the problem is reconciled with an abiding faith in the dignity and freedom of humanity by means of belief in the so-called myth of choice.

It is not easy to understand the Zoroastrian concept of the beneficent immortals who form the retinue of the Wise Lord Ahura Mazda. For instance, Sraosha ("obedience'), the lord of prayer, is by his nature analogous to the entities in the *Gathas*. He is particularly important both in the *Gathas* and in later Zoroastrian tradition, where he protects against the evil of death and judges the soul after death.

Zoroastrianism did not integrate all of the ancient gods into its pantheon. Only those not thought to be in contrast with the main tenets of the prophet's new religion were absorbed into it. For the most part, the ancient *daivas* censured by Zarathushtra remained outside of the new pantheon, but a few deities, who had probably been widely and deeply venerated, reappeared in Zoroastrianism.

CUSTOMS, RITUALS, FESTIVALS. Despite its original antiritualistic character, Zoroastrianism soon became a religion in which ceremony played a leading role. It is not possible to know which religious rituals were recommended by the prophet to his disciples in addition to prayer. The importance of prayer was always fundamental, and some forms, particularly revered ones, have lasted through the centuries, for example, a type of traditional *manthra* (Skt., *mantra*) that is endowed with magical powers. The main prayers are Ahuna Vairya, Airyema Ishyo, Ashem Vohu, Yenhe Hatam. Even in modern times, the day of a pious Zoroastrian is divided into five prayer periods. Most likely, alongside the recitation of the *manthra*, Zarathushtra recommended meditating before the only basic symbol of the new religion—fire.

Although modified to fit the tenets of the Zoroastrian message, the old ritualism reemerged and asserted itself anew during the first centuries of the new faith. The reemergence most likely took place before the advent of the great Achaemenid empire. Animal sacrifice became accepted again, although only in forms that could be seen as compatible with the new ethical values, and even the *haoma* cult was reestablished.

The tendency to reject anthropomorphic representations of divine entities is typical of later Zoroastrianism. During the Sasanid period we find anthropomorphic representations of Ohrmazd, Mihr (Mithra), and Anahid (Anahita) in large rupestrian reliefs in Fars; during the Achaemenid period, in addition to the accounts of statues of the goddess Anahita, we find torsos of Ahura Mazda, emerging from a disk or a winged ring from which there emerge, as well, two paws and a bird tail. Other traditional symbols of Zoroastrianism are the fire altars and the *barsom* (Av., *baresman*), a ritual object consisting originally of a bunch of herbs and later of a bundle of consecrated twigs.

The complex Zoroastrian rituals involve many of the most significant moments in the lives of the faithful. Thus we find initiation rites, Naojot (a term deriving from an older one indicating a "new birth"), in which a child, at age seven or ten, is fitted with a shirt, *sadre*, and girded with a cord called *kusti*. Zoroastrians also celebrate marriage rituals. Funeral rites (for example, Zohr i atash, in which animal fat is poured onto the fire, obviously reminiscent of some ancient animal sacrifice) take place in the *dakhmas*, the "towers of silence," and are meant to free the soul of the dead man from the demon of corpses (Druj i Nasu) and to assist it along its heavenly journey.

A strongly ritualistic religion, Zoroastrianism marked the year with a series of fixed holidays, thus incorporating traditional ways and customs that were hard to eradicate.

The first month of the year was dedicated to the *fravashis*, the spirits of the just, who were originally thought to be transcendental doubles of the soul. Zoroastrians believed in the *fravashis* of the dead, of the living, and of the yet unborn. According to a most likely pre-Zoroastrian tradition, the *fravashis* returned to earth at the end of the year, before the vernal equinox, the No Ruz ("new day"), or the first month of the new year. Zoroastrians also celebrated six additional great feasts: Maidhyoizaremaya ("midspring"); Maidhyoi-shema ("midsummer"); Patishahya ("bringing in the corn"); Ayathrima ("the homecoming"); Maidhyairya ("midwinter").

— GHERARDO GNOLI

TRANSLATED FROM ITALIAN BY

UGHETTA FITZGERALD LUBIN

Vohu Manah ("good mind"), one of the Amesha Spentas ("holy immortals") in Zoroastrianism, appeared to Zarathushtra (Zoroaster) and revealed the true nature of God and his covenant with man.

PAGE 32

ZULU RELIGION

After nearly 150 years of missionary activity the majority of the some 5.5 million Zulu-speaking South Africans are Christians. For many, however, the *amadlozi* (ancestors or shades of dead kin) who once domi-

Z

ZULU RELIGION

Zulu Cosmology and the Natural Order

nated Zulu religion are still a force to be reckoned with and propitiated.

ZULU COSMOLOGY AND THE NATURAL ORDER. The Zulu say that in the beginning there was uMvelinqangi, literally the first "comer-out," who broke off from a reed bed followed by human beings, animals, and nature as a whole. In some tales uMvelinqangi is portrayed as the source of the known social order, for he gave human beings their ancestors and decided how the ancestors should be approached and placated. There is, however, little evidence that uMvelinqangi was worshiped directly. Distinct from uMvelinqangi is iNkosi yeZulu, the lord of the sky and personification of heaven. He is associated with thunder and lightning, which are greatly feared and against which specially trained herbalists offer protection.

Linked also with the sky or the "above" (*ezulwini*—a critical concept that contrasts with *phansi*, the "below," where the dead go before becoming ancestors) is iNkosazana yeZulu, or merely iNkosazana, the princess of heaven (uNomkhubulwana). She bestows fertility on crops, cattle, and human beings and is often actively placated in times of drought and searing heat. Before hoeing begins, women sometimes plant a small field for iNkosazana near a river, and a libation of beer is poured on the ground to the accompaniment of a prayer for a fruitful harvest. Because of its conceptual links with fertility and girls' puberty ceremonials, the cult of iNkosazana must be seen against the background of the widespread emphasis upon fertility in African cosmological systems.

The natural order impinges on life in other ways which affect health and well-being. In contrast to illnesses caused by sorcery or ancestral anger, there is an extremely wide range of diseases stretching from the common cold to more serious epidemics like smallpox

ZULU DANCERS

Traditionally dressed Zulu dancers performing on a hillside in South Africa, 1953.

PAUL ALMASY/© CORBIS

or measles, which are said to "just happen." Many are treated with medicines which are potent in themselves and do not necessarily require ritual or religious accompaniment, although protection against certain seasonal illnesses may be sought from iNkosazana. Another important class of natural illnesses are thought to result inevitably from imbalances in nature. Several categories of people are particularly at risk from environmental influences including newcomers to an area, infants who have only recently entered the world, and all those who are temporarily in a weakened state, known as *umnyama*. This last category includes the bereaved, newly delivered mothers, homicides, and menstruating women.

Women occupy a "marginal" position in Zulu cosmology and serve as a symbolic bridge between "this world" (the world of the living) and the "otherworld" (that of the spirits). Women, however, not only link this world and the otherworld, but in their roles as daughter in one kinship group and mother in another they form a bridge between two distinct patrilineages. Zulu society is strongly patrilineal, and marriage may occur only outside the clan. A bride is thus an outsider in her affinal home, yet it is only through her that her husband's group can reproduce itself.

ANCESTORS AND SOCIAL LIFE. When things are going well, the Zulu say that their ancestors are "with them," but when misfortune strikes, they say that the ancestors are "facing away."

A man's most important ancestors are his father, mother, father's father, and father's mother, as well as the father's brothers who act with and share sacrifices offered to deceased parents and grandparents. The living kin who gather for ancestral rituals largely include the patrilineal descendants of a grandfather, and the women who have married these men. At sacrifices, it is the genealogically senior male *(umnumzane)* who officiates. Among the Nyuswa-Zulu the married men of this cluster or segment *(umndeni)* of two or three generations often live close to each other and, under the headship of the *umnumzane*, act as a corporate group in the control and management of common resources (such as land) and in the settlement of internal disputes. The authority of the *umnumzane* is bolstered by his ritual position and the fact that younger agnates can approach the ancestors only through him.

The ancestor cult reflects a number of other important aspects of Zulu social life. The role of the chief wife who bears the heir is emphasized, for it is on the *umsamo* of her hut (the rear part of the dwelling associated with the spirits) that sacrificial meat is placed for the ancestors to share. Individual social identities are often fixed unambiguously by calling on the ancestors. Thus a baby is placed formally under the control of the ancestors to whose line it belongs by the sacrifice of a goat known as *imbeleko*, the skin of which is used to secure the baby on its mother's back. This ceremony is usually performed by the child's father or father's father, but in the case of an unmarried woman, the responsibility lies with her father and his *umndeni* to which the child belongs.

SPIRIT POSSESSION. Spirit possession is an important and dynamic aspect of Zulu life. The call to be a diviner takes the form of recognized mental and physical affliction, the cure for which are initiation and professional training. The traditional *isangoma* (and her counterpart in many Christian sects) is a pivotal force for order and rapprochement between man and the spirit world. There are, however, new forms of spirit possession. *Indiki* and *ufufunyane* (or *iziwe*) are the most prevalent types, resulting from possession by the deceased spirits of foreigners, which have not been integrated into the body of the ancestors. Treatment often involves replacing the alien spirit with an ancestral spirit, and the *indiki* may become a diviner. *Ufufunyane* is diagnosed as due to sorcery and is a particularly intractable form, for the alien spirit becomes violent when challenged. Treatment also involves dispelling the alien spirit—or often hordes of spirits of different race groups—and replacing them by spirits controlled by the doctor and referred to as a regiment *(amabutho)*.

TRADITIONAL BELIEF AND ZULU CHRISTIANITY. Zulu cosmological ideas have been incorporated into Zulu Christian thought in a number of subtle ways. The word for "breath" *(umoya)* is translated as "Holy Spirit," and people said to be filled with the Holy Spirit become leaders in African independent churches that have split off from orthodox congregations. Protection against sorcery and misfortune is given by prayer and also medicine. Healing, purification, and the search for fertility are major issues in African Christianity.

— ELEANOR M. PRESTON-WHYTE

"While you are not able to serve men, how can you serve spirits of dead?"

CONFUCIUS
CONFUCIAN ANALECTS

Appendixes

RELIGIOUS HOLIDAYS

Religious observations have long been a part of the lives of people around the world. They have provided opportunities to fight evil spirits and welcome the assistance of the compassionate ones. Religious festivals have provided the opportunity to mark the changing seasons and celebrate bountiful harvests and continued good health. Religious holidays have also served as times for honoring the accomplishments of prominent individuals of given religions and for commemorating significant religious events.

Different nations and religions use different calendars to divide up the solar year (365.242199 days) into meaningful periods. These calendars fall into three main types: lunar, solar, and lunisolar.

A lunar calendar is based on the length of the lunar month (29.5 days, the time from one new moon to the next) and disregards the length of the solar year. The Islamic calendar, which is a lunar calendar, contains the following twelve lunar months (some with 29 days and some with 30 days, supplying an average of 29.5 days):

Muharram (the sacred month)
Safar (the month that is void)
Rabi ʻal-Anwal
Rabi ʻal-Thani
Jumada al-Ula (the first month of dryness)
Jumada al-Akhirah (the second month of dryness)
Rajab (the revered month)
Sha ʻbān (the month of division)
Ramadān (the month of great heat)
Shawwāl (the month of hunting)
Dhūal-Qa ʻdah (the month of rest)
Dhūal-Hijja (the month of pilgrimage).

These twelve months, however, provide a lunar year of only 354.367056 days. Because the lunar year is 10.875143 days shorter than the solar year, the months regress (move backward) each solar year, causing the seasons to occur at earlier and earlier dates. In fact, any given month of the Islamic calendar will have regressed through an entire solar year in 33.585 solar years. Another complicating factor is that the decimal value of the length of a lunar year (which amounts to about 11.012 days in 30 lunar years) is unaccounted for in the Islamic calendar. Instead, 11 days are intercalated (inserted) once every thirty years to restore the accuracy with respect to the moon.

A solar calendar ignores the lunar cycle and adheres to the set length of the solar year, with this period divided into twelve set months. There are four critical periods in the solar cycle: two equinoxes and two solstices. The accuracy of a solar calendar can be judged based on the accuracy with which these four events occur on the same days each year. The two most relevant solar calendars are the Julian calendar and the Gregorian calendar. The Julian calendar was the result of an order by Julius Caesar to convert from the Roman lunar calendar to a solar calendar in 46 B.C.E. This conversion involved an intercalation of 90 days (23 days after February, and two months of 34 and 33 days added between November and December) to correct for a discrepancy that had been growing between the seasons and the calendar periods in which they had traditionally fallen. The intercalation meant that 46 B.C.E. had a total of 445 days, but thereafter, Caesar ordered that the normal length of the year would be 365 days, with one day added to February every four years to adjust for the true length of the solar year. However, this meant that a solar year would be calculated as 365.25 days, which exceeds the true solar year of 365.242199 days by 11 minutes and 14 seconds. This might seem to be a small discrepancy, but over time the calendar once again began to fall out of synchronization with the seasons. To correct for this discrepancy, Pope Gregory XIII instituted two alterations to the Julian calendar: (1) 10 days were dropped from the calendar of 1582, so the day after October 4 became October 15, a change that restored the vernal equinox date to March 21, and (2) century years were changed to common years (rather than leap years), unless the century year was divisible by 400. These modifications of the Julian calendar to create the Gregorian calendar restored the synchronization between the months and the seasons. Although the Gregorian calendar has become the most widely used of the two solar calendars, the Julian calendar is still used by Orthodox Christian churces.

A lunisolar calendar is generally a compromise between following a lunar calendar and the need to synchronize dates and the seasons. This type of calendar traditionally follows the lunar cycle but intercalates an additional month as necessary to maintain synchronization. Two examples of lunisolar calendars are the Jewish calendar and the Hindu calendar. The Jewish calendar contains the following twelve calendar months, which alternate between 30 and 29 days in length:

Tishri (September-October)
Heshvan (October-November)
Kislev (November-December)
Tevet (December-January)
Shevat (January-February)
Adar (February-March)
Nisan (March-April)
Iyyar (April-May)
Sivan (May-June)
Tammuz (June-July)
Av (July-August)
Elul (August-September).

A thirteenth month is intercalated into the Jewish calendar in the third, sixth, eighth, eleventh, fourteenth, seventeenth, and nineteenth years of a nineteen-year cycle. The standard months of the Hindu lunisolar calendar are as follows:

Asvina (September-October)
Karttika (October-November)
Margasirsa (November-December)
Pausa (December-January)
Magha (January-February)
Phalguna (February-March)
Caitra (March-April)
Vaisakha (April-May)
Jyaistha (May-June)
Asadha (June-July)
Sravana (July-August)
Bhadrapada (August-September).

A thirteenth month is intercalated in the Hindu calendar every sixty months.

BAHA'I HOLIDAYS

February 26

Ayyam-i-Ha: Marks the first of the four (five in leap years) intercalary days in the Baha'i calendar, a calendar made up of nineteen months of nineteen days each; Ayyam-i-Ha is followed by a nineteen-day fasting period (from March 2 through March 20), which in turn is followed by the Baha'i New Year's Day (Now Ruz) on March 21.

April 21

Feast of Ridvan: Marks the first day of the twelve-day celebration commemorating the 1863 declaration by Mirza Husain Ali Nuri (Baha Allah), the founder of the Baha'i religion, that he was God's messenger for the age.

May 23

Declaration of the Bab: Celebrates the announcement by Mirza Ali Muhammad Shirazi, that he was the "gate" (the Bab) to the coming of the promised one of all religions, a proclamation considered to be the beginning of the Baha'i religion.

May 29

Ascension of Baha Allah: Marks the anniversary of the 1892 death of Mirza Husain Ali Nuri, the founder of the Baha'i religion.

July 9

Martyrdom of the Bab: Commemorates the 1850 execution of Mirza Ali Muhammad Shirazi, the first prophet of the Baha'i religion.

October 20

Birth of the Bab: Celebrates the 1819 birth of Mirza Ali Muhammad Shirazi, who was the founder of the Babi faith and considered by those in the Baha'i religion to be the herald whose chief task was to announce the advent of the dispensation of Baha Allah (the founder of the Baha'i religion).

November 12

Birth of Baha Allah: Marks the anniversary of the 1817 birth of Mirza Husain Ali Nuri, the founder of the Baha'i religion.

November 26

Day of the Covenant: Commemorates the covenant that Baha Allah, the founder of the Baha'i religion, made with humanity and his followers, appointing his eldest son, Abd al-Baha, to be the head of the Baha'i religion and interpret Baha'i teachings.

November 28

Ascension of Abd al-Baha: Commemorates the 1921 death of Abbas Effendi, the eldest son of the founder of the Baha'i religion, Mirza Husain Ali Nuri.

BUDDHIST HOLIDAYS

Margasirsa (the nineteenth day)

Birthday of the Goddess of Mercy: Honors Kuan Yin, the goddess of infinite compassion and mercy.

Magha (full moon)

Magha Puja: Commemorates the occasion when 1,250 followers ordained by the Buddha arrived by coincidence at Veluvan Monastery in Rajagriha, India, to hear him lay down monastic regulations and predict his own death.

Phalguna (the sixth day)

Airing the Classics: Commemorates the time when the boat carrying the Buddhist scriptures from India to China was upset at a river crossing and all the books had to be spread to dry.

Vaisakha (full moon)

Vesak (Buddha Purnima): Commemorates the Buddha's birth, enlightenment, and attainment of Nirvana.

Jyaistha (full moon)

Poson: Commemorates the bringing of Buddhism to Sri Lanka in the third century B.C.E.

Asadha (the twenty-fifth day)

Ganden Ngamcho (Festival of Lights): Commemorates the birth and death of Tsongkhapa (1357-1419), a saintly scholar and teacher in Tibetan Buddhism, whose successors became the Dalai Lamas.

Asadha to Asvina

Waso (Buddhist Lent): Three-month period of abstinence and meditation, the day prior to which commemorates the Buddha's first sermon to his five disciples, forty-nine days after his enlightenment.

CHRISTIAN HOLIDAYS

January 1

St. Basil's Day: Celebrated in Greece to honor the fourth-century bishop of Caesarea.

January 5

Twelfth Night: Celebrated the evening before Epiphany as the traditional end to the Christmas season.

January 6

Feast of the Epiphany: Commemorates the worshipping of Jesus by the Three Kings (emphasized in Roman Catholic and Protestant churches) and the baptism of Jesus (emphasized in Eastern Orthodox churches), the first two occasions on which Christ was manifested. Epiphany is observed on January 19 by the Eastern Orthodox churches, which base religious observations on the Julian calendar.

January 8

St. Gudula's Day: Honors the patron saint of Brussels.

January 13

St. Knut's Day: Observed as the Swedish day for dismantling Christmas trees.

Tyvendedagen: Celebrates the official end of the Yuletide in Norway.

January 15

Feast of Christ of Esquipulas (The Black Christ Festival): Observed at Esquipulas in Guatemala and named after a figure of Christ that was carved out of dark brown balsam.

January 19

St. Henry of Uppsala's Day: Honoring the patron saint of Finland.

January 21

St. Altagracia's Day: Celebrated in the Dominican Republic with a pilgrimage to the St. Altagracia shrine.

January 26

St. Nino's Day: Honors St. Nino of Cappadocia, who introduced Christianity to Georgia in the fourth century.

January 27

St. Sava's Day: A Serbian children's festival in honor of St. Sava, a king's son who built schools and monasteries all over Serbia.

January 30

St. Charles's Day: Observed in commemoration of the 1649 execution of King Charles I for his defense of the Anglican Church.

February 1

St. Bridget's Day: Honors the patron saint of Ireland who established the first Irish convent, around which the city of Kildare eventually grew.

February 2

Candlemass (Feast of the Purification of the Blessed Virgin Mary): The blessing of candles is a great tradition of the Roman Catholic and Anglican observance that is particularly popular in Mexico and other Latin American countries.

February 2-March 8 (movable)

Shrove Monday: Observed the Monday before Ash Wednesday as a preparation day for Lent.

February 3

St. Anskar's Day: Honors the patron saint of Denmark, who was a missionary to Denmark, Sweden, Norway, and Northern Germany.

February 3-March 9 (movable)

Shrove Tuesday (Mardi Gras): Celebrated the day before Ash Wednesday as the last day of preparation for Lent.

February 4-March 10 (movable)

Ash Wednesday: Marks the first day of Lent, the forty-day period of abstinence before Palm Sunday, recalling the fasts of Moses, Elijah, and Jesus.

February 14

St. Cyril and St. Methodius's Day: Honors the two brothers from Thessalonica who became the "Apostles of the Slavs" and created the Glagolithic alphabet (from which the Cyrillic alphabet was later derived) to aid in their mission. (This feast day is observed on May 24 by Eastern Orthodox churches, which calculate religious dates according to the Julian calendar.)

March 1

St. David's Day: Honors the patron saint of Wales, who founded many churches in southern Wales in the sixth century and moved the seat of ecclesiastical government from Caerleon to Mynyw, the present cathedral city of Saint David's.

March 4

St. Casimir's Day: Honors the patron saint of Poland and Lithuania.

March 15-April 18 (movable)

Palm Sunday: Celebrated on the Sunday preceding Easter to commemorate the arrival of Jesus in Jerusalem, where palm branches, the symbol of victory, were spread before him by the people who viewed him as the leader who would deliver them from the domination of the Roman Empire.

March 17

St. Patrick's Day: Honors the patron saint of Ireland who, after becoming a bishop, returned to Ireland about 432 as a missionary to the pagans.

March 18-April 21 (movable)

Spy Wednesday: Observed on the Wednesday before Easter to commemorate the betrayal of Jesus by Judas Iscariot in the Garden of Gethsemane.

March 19

St. Joseph's Day: Honors the patron saint of Belgium and Colombia.

March 19-April 22 (movable)

Maundy Thursday: Celebrated the Thursday before Easter to commemorate Jesus Christ's institution of the Eucharist in the Last Supper.

March 20-April 23 (movable)

Good Friday: Observed the Friday before Easter to commemorate the crucifixion of Jesus.

March 21-April 24 (movable)

Holy Saturday: Celebrated on the day before Easter, bringing the season of Lent to a close.

March 22

St. Nicholas von Flüe's Day: Honors the patron saint of Switzerland.

March 22-April 25 (movable)

Easter: Celebrated the first Sunday after the first full moon on or following the vernal equinox to commemorate the anniversary of Jesus Christ's resurrection from the dead.

March 25

Feast of the Annunciation (Lady Day): Celebrates the appearance of the Archangel Gabriel to the Virgin Mary announcing that she was to become the mother of Jesus.

April 2

Martyrdom of Blessed Diego Luis de San Vitores: Commemorates the 1672 death of the priest who introduced Catholicism to Guam.

April 23

St. George's Day: Honors the patron saint of England, Canada, Portugal, Germany, Genoa, and Venice.

May 10-June 13 (movable)

Pentecost (Whitsunday, Pinkster Day): Celebrated on the seventh Sunday (fifty days) after Easter to commemorate the Holy Spirit's visit to the Apostles, giving them the gift of tongues that allowed them to preach about Jesus Christ to people from all over the world.

May 15

St. Isidore the Husbandman's Day: Honors the patron saint of Madrid.

May 18

St. Eric of Sweden's Day: Honors the patron saint of Sweden.

May 30

St. Joan's Day: Honors Joan of Arc, who helped save the French city of Orleans from the British in the fifteenth century.

May (movable)

Ascension Day (Holy Thursday): Celebrated forty days after Easter to commemorate Jesus Christ's ascension to heaven.

May (third week)

Carabao Festival: Honors San Isidro Labrador (St. Isidore the Farmer), the patron saint of the Filipino farmer.

June 5

St. Boniface's Day: Honors the patron saint of Germany. St. Euphrosynia of Polack's Day: Honors the patron saint of Belarus.

June 9

St. Columba's Day: Honors the patron saint of Ireland who went into self-imposed exile on the island of Iona, where he founded a monastery and school from which he and his disciples preached the Gospel.

June 13

St. Anthony of Padua's Day: Honors the patron saint of Portugal.

June 24

Feast of the Nativity of St. John the Baptist: Celebration, especially by the French in Canada, of the birth of the cousin of Jesus.

June 28

St. Vitus's Day: Commemorates the Serbian defeat by the Turks at Kosovo in 1389 and has come to symbolize a spiritual victory.

July 8

St. Elizabeth's Day: Honors the saint who was the mother of John the Baptist and a cousin of the Virgin Mary.

July 25

St. James the Great's Day: Honors the patron saint of Chile and Spain.

July 26

St. Anne's Day: Honors the patron saint of Canada.

July 28

St. Prince Vladimir of Kiev's Day: Honors (with celebrations of the Russian culture involving lectures, readings, and concerts) the saint who introduced Christianity to ancient Rus in 988.

July 29

St. Olav's Day: Commemorates the death of Olav Haraldsson (the second King Olav), who brought Christianity to Norway and was later killed in the Battle of Stiklestad in 1030.

August 15

Feast of the Assumption: Commemorates the belief that when Mary, the mother of Jesus, died, her body did not decay but was assumed into heaven and reunited there with her soul.

August 30

Rose of Lima Day: Honors the patron saint of South America and the Philippines.

SEPTEMBER 8

Feast of the Nativity of the Blessed Virgin Mary: Celebrates the birth of Mary, the mother of Jesus.

SEPTEMBER 14

Feast of the Exaltation of the Cross: Commemorates the finding of the cross on which Jesus was crucified, the dedication of a basilica built in 335 on the supposed site of Christ's crucifixion on Golgotha, and the recovery in 629 of the relic of the cross that had been stolen by the Persians.

SEPTEMBER 28

St. Vaclav's Day: Honors the patron saint, widely known as Good King Wenceslas, of the Czech Republic.

SEPTEMBER 29

Michaelmas: Honors St. Michael, traditionally viewed as the leader of the heavenly host of angels.

OCTOBER 4

St. Francis of Assisi's Day: Honors the patron saint of Italy.

OCTOBER 9

St. Denis's Day: Honors the patron saint of France.

OCTOBER 15

St. Teresa of Avila's Day: Honors the patron saint of Spain.

OCTOBER 18

El Señor de los Milagros Day: Honors the patron saint of Peru with special services and foods, as well as the wearing of purple, the symbolic color of the saint.

OCTOBER 26

St. Demetrius's Day: Honors the patron saint of Greece.

NOVEMBER 1

All Saints' Day: Celebration of all Christian saints, particularly those that do not have special feast days of their own.

NOVEMBER 2

All Souls' Day: Commemorates the souls of all the faithful departed.

NOVEMBER 8

Saints, Doctors, Missionaries, and Martyrs Day: Celebrated in England in memory and commemoration of the "unnamed saints of the nation."

NOVEMBER 11

Beggar's Day in the Netherlands: Honors St. Martin with children dressing as beggars and going from door to door.

NOVEMBER 30

St. Andrew's Day: Honors the patron saint of Scotland, Russia, and Greece.

NOVEMBER (MOVABLE; SUNDAY CLOSEST TO NOVEMBER 30)

Advent: Marks the beginning of the Christian year and consists of a period varying in length from twenty-two to twenty-eight days, beginning on the Sunday nearest to St. Andrew's Day and encompassing the next three Sundays, ending on Christmas Eve.

DECEMBER 4

St. Barbara's Day: Celebrated in parts of France, Germany, and Syria as the beginning of the Christmas season.

DECEMBER 6

St. Nicholas's Day: Honors the patron saint of Russia and children.

DECEMBER 12

Festival of Our Lady of Guadalupe: Religious ceremony commemorating the appearance of the Blessed Virgin to an Indian boy in Mexico in 1531.

DECEMBER 13

St. Lucia's Day: Swedish celebration of the festival of lights honoring St. Lucia, the "Queen of Light."

DECEMBER 16

Posadas: Marks the first day of a nine-day celebration in Mexico commemorating the journey Mary and Joseph took from Nazareth to Bethlehem, where Jesus was born.

DECEMBER 25

Christmas Day: Christian celebration of the birth of Jesus. Christmas is celebrated on January 7 by Eastern Orthodox churches, which base religious observations on the Julian calendar.

DECEMBER 26

St. Stephen's Day: Honors the patron saint of Hungary.

DECEMBER 28

Holy Innocents' Day: Commemorates the massacre of all male children under two years of age ordered by King Herod in an attempt to kill the baby Jesus.

DECEMBER 31

St. Sylvester's Day: Honors the saint who was pope in 325, the year Emperor Constantine declared the pagan religion of Rome abolished in favor of Christianity.

CONFUCIAN HOLIDAY

SEPTEMBER 28

Confucius's Birthday: Commemorates the birth in the sixth century B.C.E. of the Chinese philosopher and teacher.

HINDU HOLIDAYS

KARTTIKA (FIFTEENTH DAY OF THE WANING MOON)

Diwali (Deepavali, Festival of Lights): Commemorates Rama's rescue of Sita from Ravana, an important episode in the Mahabrahata, and marks the Hindu New Year.

PHALGUNA (FOURTEENTH DAY OF THE WAXING MOON)

Holi: A Hindu spring festival marking the triumph of Good over Evil with celebrants throwing red and yellow powder over one another and lighting bonfires to remember the burning of the demoness Holika.

PHALGUNA (FULL MOON)

Dol Purnima: Commemorates the birthday of Chaitanya Mahaprabhu (1486–1534), also known as Gauranga, the sixteenth-century Vishnavite saint and poet of Bengal who is regarded as an incarnation of Krishna.

PHALGUNA (FULL MOON)

Meenakshi Kalyanam: Honors the marriage of the goddess Meenakshi, an incarnation of Parvati, and the Lord Shiva.

PHALGUNA (THIRTEENTH DAY OF THE WANING MOON)

Shivaratri: Commemorates the night Lord Shiva, the god of destruction and the restorer, danced the Tandav, his celestial dance of creation, preservation, and destruction.

CAITRA

Hanuman Jayanti: Honors Hanuman, the Monkey-God and central figure in the Hindu epic Ramayana.

CAITRA (NINTH DAY OF THE WAXING MOON)

Ramanavami (Ram Navami): Honors the birth of Rama, the seventh incarnation of Lord Vishnu.

JYAISTHA

Ganga Dussehra: Honors the healing power of the Ganges River, which originally flowed only in heaven but was brought down to earth in the form of the goddess Ganga by King Bhagiratha to purify the ashes of his ancestors.

JYAISTHA (SIXTH DAY OF THE WAXING MOON)

Sithinakha: Honors the birthday of Kumara, the Hindu god of war and the first-born son of Lord Shiva.

SRAVANA (WAXING MOON)

Naag Panchami: Honors the sacred serpent Ananta, on whose coils Lord Vishnu rested while he created the universe.

SRAVANA (FOURTEENTH DAY OF THE WANING MOON)

Ghanta Karna: Commemorates the death of Ghanta Karna, who caused death and destruction wherever he went until a god in the form of a frog persuaded him to leap into a well, after which the people beat him to death and dragged his body to the river for cremation.

BHADRAPADA (WAXING MOON)

Ganesh Chathurthi: Honors Ganesh, the elephant-headed Hindu god of wisdom and success.

BHADRAPADA (WANING MOON)

Indra Jatra: Eight-day celebration to pay homage to the recently deceased and to honor the Hindu god Indra and his mother Dagini so they will bless the coming harvest.

BHADRAPADA (NEW MOON)

Janmashtami (Krishnastami; Krishna's Birthday): Celebrates the birthday of Lord Krishna, the eighth incarnation of Vishnu.

ASVINA (WAXING MOON)

Durga Puja: Honors Durga, one aspect of the Mother Goddess and the personification of energy, who rides a lion and destroys demons.

IGBO HOLIDAYS

APRIL

Awuru Odo Festival: Celebrated among the Igbo people of Nigeria in honor of the biannual visit of the Odo (the spirits of the dead).

AUGUST-SEPTEMBER

Agwunsi Festival: Honors the god of healing and divination among the Igbo people of Nigeria.

SEPTEMBER

Okpesi Festival: Ceremony of the Igbo people of Nigeria honoring their ancestors.

ISLAMIC HOLIDAYS

MUHARRAM (FIRST TEN DAYS)

'Ashura: Commemorates the death of Muhammad's grandson Husayn ibn 'Ali in the year 680 C.E. during a battle between Sunnis and the group of Shi'ah supporters with whom he was traveling.

RABI' AL-AWWAL (THE TWELFTH DAY)

Mawlid al-Nabi (Prophet's Birthday): Honors the birth of the Prophet Muhammad, the founder of Islam, who was born in Mecca in 570 C.E.

RAJAB (THE TWENTY-SEVENTH DAY)

Laylat al Mi'raj: Commemorates the ascent of the Prophet Muhammad into Heaven.

SHA'BĀN (NIGHT OF THE FIFTEENTH)

Shab-i Barat: A period of intense prayer in preparation for Ramadan during which individuals fast, pray and keep vigils. In Muslim folklore it is known as the night during which the fates for the coming year are fixed.

RAMADĀN

Ramadān: The holiest period of the Islamic year commemorates the time when the Qu'ran, the Islamic holy book, was revealed to the Prophet Muhammad. Devout Muslims abstain from food, drink, smoking, sex, and gambling from sunrise to sunset during this period.

RAMADĀN (LAST TEN DAYS)

Laylat al-Qadr (Night of Power): The night during which the first revelation of the Qur'an took place, generally considered the tweny-seventh night of Ramadan. Many people perform a long sequence of prayers after breaking the fast. Then they may enjoy entertainment. A second meal is taken before dawn.

'Id al-Fitr (Feast of Fast Breaking),

SHAWWĀL (FIRST DAY)

'Id al-Fitr (Feast of Fast-Breaking): Marks the end of the month-long fasting period of Ramadan at daylight. It is most eagerly awaited as a celebration of the return to normal life.

DHŪAL-HIJJAH (BETWEEN THE EIGHT AND THIRTEENTH DAYS)

Hajj (Pilgrimage to Mecca): A fundamental duty of each Muslim to be completed at least once in a lifetime.

DHŪAL-HIJJAH

'Id al-Adha (Feast of Sacrifice): Three-day feast serving as the concluding rite for those performing a pilgrimage to Mecca and, for those not performing a pilgrimage, as a commemoration of Ibrahim's (Abraham) near sacrifice of his son.

JAIN HOLIDAYS

CAITRA (THIRTEENTH DAY OF THE WAXING MOON)

Mahavir Jayanti: Honors Mahavira, who lived during the fifth century B.C.E. and is regarded by the Jains as the twenty-fourth and last in a series of Tirthankaras (Enlightened Teachers).

BHADRAPADA

Paryushana: A festival to focus on the cardinal virtues (i.e., forgiveness, charity, simplicity, contentment, truthfulness, self-restraint, fasting, detachment, humility, and continence) by individuals asking those whom they may have offended for forgiveness and restoring lapsed friendships.

JEWISH HOLIDAYS

TISHRI (THE FIRST DAY)

Ro'sh ha-Shanah: Marks the first day of the two-day observance of the Jewish New Year, which are also the first two days of the ten High Holy Days that conclude with Yom Kippur, the Day of Atonement.

Tishri (the third day)

Tsom Gedaliah (Fast of Gedaliah): Fast to commemorate the assassination of Gedaliah ben Ahikam, the Jewish governor left in charge by King Nebuchadnezzar to administer the affairs of Judah after the destruction of Jerusalem and the fall of the First Temple in 586 B.C.E.

TISHRI (THE TENTH DAY)

Yom Kippur (Day of Atonement): The holiest and most solemn day in the Jewish Calendar and the last of the ten High Holy Days (Days of Penitence) that begin with the Jewish New Year (Ro'sh ha-Shanah).

TISHRI (THE FIFTEENTH DAY)

Sukkot: Marks the first day of the eight-day commemoration of the forty years after the Exodus that Jews wandered in the desert under the leadership of Moses.

TISHRI (THE TWENTY-FIRST DAY)

Hoshana Rabbah: Considered to be the last possible day on which one can seek forgiveness for the sins of the preceding year.

TISHRI (THE TWENTY-SECOND DAY)

Shemini Atzeret (Eighth Day of Solemn Assembly): Marks the eighth day of the festival of Sukkot but is celebrated as a separate holiday dedicated to the love of God.

TISHRI (THE TWENTY-THIRD DAY)

Simhat Torah: Celebrates the annual completion of the public reading of the Torah, the first five books of the Bible.

KISLEV (THE TWENTY-FIFTH DAY)

Hanukkah: Marks the first day of an eight-day celebration to commemorate the successful rebellion of the Jews against the Syrians in the Maccabean War of 162 B.C.E. and the associated miracle of a small bottle of consecrated oil for the menorah (perpetual lamp) lasting eight days until more could be obtained.

Tevet (the tenth day)

Asarah be-Tevet (Tenth of Tevet): Fast day commemorating the beginning of the siege of Jerusalem by the Babylonians under King Nebuchadnezzar in 586 B.C.E. that was a prelude to the destruction of the First Temple.

Nisan

Hagodol: Observed on the Sabbath just prior to Passover to commemorate the Sabbath before the Exodus from Egypt that ended more than four hundred years of slavery.

Nisan (the fifteenth day)

Passover: Marks the first day of the eight-day celebration of the deliverance of the Jews from slavery in Egypt.

Nisan (the twenty-seventh day)

Yom Hasho'ah (Holocaust Day): Observed, as a memorial to the six million Jews killed by the Nazis between 1933 and 1945, on the anniversary of the date on which the Allied troops liberated the first Nazi concentration camp, Buchenwald, in Germany, in 1945.

Sivan (the sixth day)

Shavu 'ot: Observed fifty days after Passover to mark the end of the barley harvest and the beginning of the wheat harvest and to celebrate the return of Moses from the top of Mt. Sinai with the Ten Commandments, the fundamental laws of the Jewish faith.

Tammuz (the seventeenth day)

Shivah Asar be-Tammuz (Fast of the Seventeenth of Tammuz): Commemorates the breaching of the walls of Jerusalem in 586 B.C.E., when the Babylonians conquered Judah, destroyed the First Temple, and carried most the Jewish population off into slavery.

Av (the ninth day)

Tish'ah be-Av (Fast of Av): A twenty-four-hour period of fasting, lamentation, and prayer in memory of the destruction of both the First Temple (586 B.C.E.) and the Second Temple (70 C.E.) in Jerusalem.

ZOROASTRIAN HOLIDAYS

January 30

Joshne Sadeh: Celebration of the fire building festival with people saying prayers as they circle large bonfires.

March 16

Pange Porse Hamagoni: Observed on the first of the five days preceding New Year's day as the second of the two days of the year for commemoration of all deaths.

March 27

Tavalode Zartosht: Observed six days after Now Ruz (the Iranian New Year) to commemorate Zoroaster's birthday and the day he was named the prophet.

April 3

Sizda be Dar: Observed on the thirteenth day after the New Year with traditional picnics and the throwing out of the greens (from the New Year's table), which helps a young woman find a mate.

June 14

Ziarat Pir Sabz: A pilgrimage to Pir Sabz, a shrine (the most important of all shrines for most Zoroastrians) near Yazd in Iran.

June 19

Porse Hamagoni: The first of two celebrations commemorating all deaths together.

July 1

Tirgan: Celebration of the water (or rain) festival.

September 2

Joshne Mehregan: Celebration of the fall festival.

Index

B

D

F

G

H

I

J

K

L

M

N

O

P

R

S

U

X